W9-AYN-659

## ECONOMICS IN ACTION

**1:** A woman's work, 10 ■ Restoring equilibrium on the freeways, 16

**2:** ■■ *Rich nation, poor nation, 33* ■ Economists in government, 36

**3:** ■■ *Beating the traffic, 62* ■■ *Down (and up) on the farm, 67* ■ A fish story, 71 ■■ *Plain vanilla gets fancy, 76*

**4:** ■■ *Oil shortages in the 1970s, 90* ■■ *"Black labor" in Southern Europe, 94* ■ The clams of New Jersey, 100 ■ Who pays the FICA?, 104

**5:** Estimating elasticities, 113 ■■ *America's a nice place to live, but we can't afford to visit, 119* ■ Spending it, 122 ■■ *European farm surpluses, 125* ■ So who does pay the FICA?, 129

**6:** When money isn't enough, 142 ■ Gaining from disaster, 146 ■ eBay and efficiency, 151 ■ Missing the boats, 156

**7:** The mythical man-month, 167 ■ The cost of power, 176 ■ There's no business like snow business, 181

**8:** The pain of competition, 189 ■ California Screaming, 201 ■ A crushing reversal, 208

**9:** The factor distribution of income in the United States, 215 ■ Star power, 224 ■■ *The economics of apartheid, 229* ■ The decline of the summer job, 234

**10:** ■ A great leap—backward, 246 ■ Death and taxes, 250 ■ Spillovers in Silicon Valley, 257 ■ Old man river, 264

**11:** ■■ *Are diamond monopolies forever?, 276* ■ California power play?, 284 ■ Cable dilemmas, 290 ■ Sales, factory outlets, and ghost cities, 295

**12:** ■■ *The rise and fall and rise of OPEC, 308* ■ Air wars, 313 ■ Bagels from boom to bust, 319 ■ Any color, so long as it's black, 325

**13:** The comparative advantage of the United States, 334 ■■ *Trade, wages, and land prices in the nineteenth century, 341* ■ Trade protection in the United States, 344 ■ Declining tariffs, 347

**14:** ■■ *The Great Depression, 356* ■ Has the business cycle been tamed?, 361 ■ A fast (food) measure of inflation, 364

**15:** Creating the national accounts, 377 ■ Good decades, bad decades, 380 ■ Jobless recoveries, 384 ■ Indexing to the CPI, 388

**16:** Prices and output in the Great Depression, 403 ■ Moving along the aggregate demand curve, 1979–1980, 408 ■■ *Supply shocks versus demand shocks in practice, 419* ■ The end of the Great Depression, 422

**17:** ■■ *Expansionary fiscal policy in Japan, 432* ■ How much bang for the buck?, 437 ■■ *Stability pact—or stupidity pact?, 441* ■■ *Argentina's creditors take a haircut, 448*

**18:** The history of the dollar, 457 ■■ *It's a wonderful banking system, 461* ■■ *Building Europe's Fed, 465* ■ The Fed and the output gap, 1985–2004, 469

## FOR INQUIRING MINDS

**1:** Got a penny?, 8 ■ Pay for grades?, 10 ■■ *Choosing sides, 13*

**2:** ■■ *Models for money, 21* ■ When economists agree, 36

**3:** Supply, demand, and controlled substances, 76

**4:** The rent control aristocracy, 88 ■■ *Price floors and butter cookies, 92*

**5:** Where have all the farmers gone?, 121

**6:** I want a new drug ..., 141

**7:** Was Malthus right?, 165

**8:** ■■ *What's a standardized product?, 188*

**9:** ■■ *The factor distribution of income and social change in the Industrial Revolution, 215* ■ Why you can't find a cab when it's raining, 233

**10:** Defining economic efficiency, 240 ■ Theories of justice, 247 ■ Talking and driving, 253 ■ Voting as a public good, 263

**11:** Monopoly behavior and the price elasticity of demand, 283

**12:** ■■ *Prisoners of the arms race, 307* ■■ *The art of conspiracy, 312* ■ Hits and flops, 318 ■ Bucks for Starbucks, 321

**13:** ■■ *Does trade hurt poor countries?, 333* ■■ *Increasing returns and international trade, 334* ■■ *Bittersweet, 346*

**14:** ■■ *Defining recessions and expansions, 358*

**15:** Our imputed lives, 373 ■■ *Gross what?, 375* ■ Is the CPI biased?, 387

**16:** What's truly flexible, what's truly sticky, 397 ■ Keynes and the long run, 420

**17:** Investment tax credits, 430 ■ What happened to the debt from World War II?, 445

**18:** ■■ *What's with all the currency?, 457* ■ Is banking a con?, 460

# essentials of economics

## Paul Krugman
*Princeton University*

## Robin Wells
*Princeton University*

## Martha L. Olney
*University of California, Berkeley*

WORTH PUBLISHERS

**Publishers:** Catherine Woods and Craig Bleyer
**Senior Acquisitions Editor:** Sarah Dorger
**Executive Development Editor:** Sharon Balbos
**Associate Editor:** Marie McHale
**Director of Market Development:** Steven Rigolosi
**Marketing Manager:** Scott Guile
**Associate Managing Editor:** Tracey Kuehn
**Project Editor:** Mike Ederer, Graphic World Inc.
**Art Director, Cover Designer:** Babs Reingold
**Interior Designer:** Babs Reingold
**Layout Designer**: Lee Ann McKevitt
**Illustrations:** TSI Graphics and Lyndall Culbertson
**Photo Research Manager:** Patricia Marx
**Photo Researcher:** Elyse Rieder
**Production Manager:** Barbara Anne Seixas
**Composition:** TSI Graphics
**Printing and Binding:** RR Donnelley

ISBN-13: 978-0-7167-5879-2
ISBN-10: 0-7167-5879-2

Worth Publishers
41 Madison Avenue
New York, NY 10010

www.worthpublishers.com

*To beginning students everywhere, which we all were at one time.*

**Paul Krugman** is Professor of Economics at Princeton University, where he regularly teaches the principles course. He received his BA from Yale and his PhD from MIT. Prior to taking his current position, he taught at Yale, Stanford, and MIT. He also spent a year on the staff of the Council of Economic Advisers in 1982–1983. His research is mainly in the area of international trade, where he is one of the founders of the "new trade theory," which focuses on increasing returns and imperfect competition. He also works in international finance, with a concentration in currency crises. In 1991, Krugman received the American Economic Association's John Bates Clark medal. In addition to his teaching and academic research, Krugman writes extensively for nontechnical audiences. Krugman is a regular op-ed columnist for *The New York Times.* His latest trade book is a best-selling collection of his *Times* articles entitled *The Great Unraveling: Losing Our Way in the New Century.* His earlier books, *Peddling Prosperity* and *The Age of Diminished Expectations,* have become modern classics.

**Robin Wells** is Researcher in Economics at Princeton University, where she regularly teaches undergraduate courses. She received her BA from the University of Chicago and her PhD from the University of California, Berkeley; she then did postdoctoral work at MIT. She has taught at the University of Michigan, the University of Southampton (United Kingdom), Stanford, and MIT. Her teaching and research focus on the theory of organizations and incentives. She writes regularly for academic journals.

**Martha L. Olney** is Adjunct Professor of Economics at the University of California, Berkeley, where she teaches large-enrollment courses in principles, intermediate macro, and U.S. economic history, plus seminars in the economics of discrimination and in pedagogy. She received her BS from the University of Redlands and her PhD from UC Berkeley. Previously she taught at University of Massachusetts, Amherst, and at Stanford University. Honored several times for her excellence in teaching, Olney was chosen as a Great Teacher in Economics by the Stavros Center for Economic Education (2006), and is the recipient of Distinguished Teaching Awards from UMass Amherst (1991) and UC Berkeley (2003), and the Economic History Association's Hughes Prize for Excellence in Teaching (1997). Olney is the coauthor with J. Bradford DeLong of *Macroeconomics* and the author of *Economics as a Second Language.* Her research focuses on consumer spending and indebtedness in the early twentieth century. She is also the author of *Buy Now, Pay Later: Advertising, Credit, and Consumer Durables in the 1920s,* and several economic history articles.

# Preface

*"What is above all needed is to let the meaning choose the word, and not the other way about."*

George Orwell,
"Politics and the English Language," 1946

## FROM PAUL

Robin and I like to think that we wrote this book with Orwell's injunction in mind. We wanted to write a different sort of book, one that gives as much attention to the task of making sure the student understands how economic models apply to the real world as it gives to the models themselves. We wanted to adapt Orwell's principle to the writing of an economics textbook: to let the purpose of economics—to achieve a deeper understanding of the world—rather than the mechanics of economics—dictate the writing.

We believe that writing in this style reflects a commitment to the reader—a commitment to approach the material from a beginner's point of view, to make the material entertaining and accessible, to make discovery a joy. That's the fun part. But we also believe that there is another equally compelling obligation on the part of an author of a principles of economics text. Economics is an extremely powerful tool. Many of us who are economists originally started in other disciplines (I started in history; Robin, in chemistry). And we fell in love with economics because we believed it offers a coherent worldview that offers real guidelines to making the world a better place. (Yes, most economists are idealists at heart.) But like any powerful tool, economics should be treated with great care. For us, this obligation became a commitment that students would learn the appropriate use of the models— understand their assumptions and know their limitations as well as their positive uses. Why do we care about this? Because we don't live in a "one model of the economy fits all" world. To achieve deeper levels of understanding of the real world through economics, students must learn to appreciate the kinds of trade-offs and ambiguities that economists and policy makers face when applying their models to real-world problems. We hope this approach will make students more insightful and more effective participants in our common economic, social, and political lives.

To those familiar with my academic work, this perspective will probably look familiar. There I tried to make the problem to be solved the focus and to avoid unnecessary technique. I tried to simplify. And I tried to choose topics that had important real-world implications. Writing for a large, nontechnical audience has only reinforced and expanded these tendencies. I had to begin with the working assumption that readers initially have no reason to care about what I am writing about—that it is my responsibility to show them why they should care. So the beginning of each chapter of this book is written according to the dictum: "If you haven't hooked them by the third sentence, then you've lost them." I've also learned that about all you can take for granted in writing for a lay audience is basic numeracy—addition and subtraction, but no more than that. Concepts must be fully explained; likely confusions must be anticipated and headed off. And most of all, you must be judicious in choosing the content and pacing of the writing—don't overwhelm your reader.

## FROM ROBIN

Like Paul, I wanted to write a book that appeals to students without unduly sacrificing an instructor's obligation to teach economics well. I arrived at a similar perspective on how this book should be written, but by a different path. It came from my experiences teaching economics in a business school for a few years. Facing students who were typically impatient with abstraction and often altogether unhappy to be taking economics (and who would often exact bloody revenge in teaching evaluations), I learned how important it is to hook the students into the subject matter. Teaching with case studies, I found that concepts had been truly learned only when students could successfully apply them. And one of the most important lessons I learned was not to patronize. We—economists, that is—often assume that people who aren't familiar with conceptual thinking aren't smart and capable. Teaching in a business school showed me otherwise. The majority of my students were smart and capable, and many had shouldered a lot of responsibility in their working lives. Although adept at solving practical problems, they weren't trained to think conceptually. I had to learn to acknowledge the practical skills that they did have, but also show them the importance of the conceptual skills they didn't have. Although I eventually returned to an economics department, the lessons I learned about teaching economics in a business school stayed with me and, I believe, have been crucial ingredients in writing this textbook.

## FROM MARTHA

Paul and Robin wrote a terrific principles book. My task was to craft a one-semester version from their 35 chapters and nearly 900 pages that retained Paul and Robin's lively writing style. At Berkeley, I regularly teach a one-semester principles course in a large-enrollment 700-student setting. But we use a principles text and sprint through 30 or more chapters in 30 or fewer 50-minute lectures. I needed to draw on my experience at Berkeley, but also on experiences at UMass and years ago at a community college, the College of San Mateo. Students in a one-semester course need to be introduced to the essentials of economics, with enough real-world applications to help them see the applicability but not so much detail as to overwhelm them. And students in a one-semester course, where things move so rapidly, need to have worked examples that efficiently show numerical applications of the principles. Therefore, a new feature was added—the Work It Out boxes contain worked numerical examples. In creating the essentials text, some chapters for Krugman/Wells *Economics* were picked up almost unchanged, some were edited, some were omitted, and others were combined to form a text appropriate for the a one-semester course. The result of my efforts is *Essentials of Economics*.

## Advantages of This Book

Despite our fine words, why should any instructor use our text? We believe our book distinguishes itself in several ways that will make your introductory economics course an easier and more successful undertaking for the following reasons:

> **Chapters build intuition through real examples.** In every chapter, we use real-world examples, stories, applications, and case studies to teach concepts and motivate student learning. We believe that the best way to introduce concepts and reinforce them is through real-world examples; students simply relate more easily to them.

> **Pedagogical features reinforce learning.** We've worked hard to craft a set of features that will be genuinely helpful to students. We describe these features in the next section, "Tools for Learning."

> **Chapters have been written to be accessible and entertaining.** We have used a fluid and friendly writing style that makes the concepts accessible. And we have tried whenever possible to use examples that matter directly to students; for example, choosing what course to take or considering why decisions made by economic policy makers have important implications for what the job market will look like when they graduate.

> **Real-world data illustrate concepts.** Examples are often accompanied by real-world data so that students can see what real economic numbers look like and how they relate to the models.

> **Although easy to understand, the book also prepares students for further coursework.** Too often, instructors find that selecting a textbook means choosing between two unappealing alternatives: a textbook that is "easy to teach" but leaves major gaps in students' understanding, or a textbook that is "hard to teach" but adequately prepares students for future coursework. We have worked very hard to create an easy-to-understand textbook that offers the best of both worlds.

## Tools for Learning

We have structured each of the chapters around a common set of features. The following features are intended to help students learn better while also keeping them engaged.

### "What You Will Learn in This Chapter"

To help readers get oriented, the first page of each chapter contains a preview of the chapter's contents, in an easy-to-review bulleted list format, that alerts students to the critical concepts and details the objectives of the chapter.

### Opening Story

In contrast to other books in which each chapter begins with a recitation of some aspect of economics, we've adopted a unique approach: we open each chapter with a compelling story that often extends through the entire chapter. Stories were chosen to accomplish two things: to illustrate important concepts in the chapter and then to encourage students to want to read on to learn more.

As we've mentioned, one of our main goals is to build intuition with realistic examples. Because each chapter is introduced with a real-world story, students will relate more easily to the material. For example, Chapter 3 teaches supply and demand in the context of a market for scalped tickets to a sports event (our opening story on page 56 is "Gretzky's Last Game"). For a complete list of our opening stories, see the inside cover.

### "Economics in Action" Case Studies

In addition to introducing chapters with vivid stories, we conclude virtually every major text section with still more examples: a real-world case study called "Economics in Action." This feature provides a short but compelling application of the major concept just covered in that section. Students will experience an immediate payoff from being able to apply the concepts they've just read about. For example, in Chapter 6 we use the case of eBay, the online auctioneer, to communicate the concept of efficiency (see "eBay and Efficiency" on page 151). Our discussion of long-run fiscal issues (Chapter 17, "Fiscal Policy"), which includes the question of solvency, is followed by an account of Argentina's debt default (see "Argentina's Creditors Take a Haircut" on page 448). For a complete list of all the "Economics in Action" cases in the text, see the inside cover and the table of contents.

### "Work It Out" Boxes

Unique to *Essentials of Economics,* "Work It Out" boxes contain worked numerical examples. Our students often find it difficult to move from the text discussion to a hands-on example. We designed this feature to make that task easier. The "Work It Out" boxes set up a straightforward application of the principles just discussed and provide a full solution.

In Chapter 2, we illustrate the concepts of comparative advantage and the gains from trade with an example involving two countries, Alka and Baiwan, producing two goods, x-rays and yo-yos. In Chapter 17, we explore the role of the government spending multiplier. Nearly every chapter contains one "Work It Out" box.

### Unique End-of-Section Review: "Quick Review" and "Check Your Understanding" Questions

Economics contains a lot of jargon and abstract concepts that can quickly overwhelm the principles student. So we provide "Quick Reviews," short bulleted summaries of concepts at the end of each major section. This review helps ensure that students understand what they have just read.

The "Check Your Understanding" feature, which appears along with every "Quick Review," consists of a short set of review questions; solutions to these questions appear at the back of the book in the section set off with a burgundy tab at the edge of each page. These questions and solutions allow students to immediately test their understanding of the section just read. If they're not getting the questions right, it's a clear signal for them to go back and reread before moving on.

The "Economics in Action" cases, followed by the "Quick Reviews" and "Check Your Understanding" questions, comprise our unique end-of-section pedagogical set that encourages students to apply what they've learned (via the "Economics in Action") and then review it (with the "Quick Reviews" and "Check Your Understanding" questions). Our hope is that students will be more successful in the course if they use this carefully constructed set of study aids.

### "For Inquiring Minds" Boxes

To further our goal of helping students build intuition with real-world examples, almost every chapter contains one or more "For Inquiring Minds" boxes, in which con-

cepts are applied to real-world events in unexpected and sometimes surprising ways, generating a sense of the power and breadth of economics. These boxes help impress on students that economics can be fun despite being labeled "the dismal science."

In Chapter 18, "Money, the Federal Reserve System, and Monetary Policy," we point out the puzzling fact that there's $2,500 worth of currency in circulation for every man, woman, and child in the United States (how many people do you know who keep $2,500 in their wallets?). We then explain how currency in domestic cash registers and in the hands of foreigners resolves the puzzle (see "What's with All the Currency?" on page 457). For a list of all "For Inquiring Minds" boxes, see the inside cover and the table of contents.

### "Pitfalls" Boxes

Certain concepts are prone to be misunderstood when students begin their study of economics. We try to alert students to these mistakes in "Pitfalls" boxes, where common misunderstandings are spelled out and corrected. For example, the difference between increasing total cost and increasing marginal cost (see "Pitfalls" on page 170). For a list of all the "Pitfalls" boxes, see the table of contents.

### Student-Friendly Graphs

Comprehending graphs is often one of the biggest hurdles for principles students. To help alleviate that problem, this book has been designed so that figures are large, clear, and easy for students to follow. Many contain helpful annotations—in an easy-to-see balloon-label format—that link to concepts within the text. Figure captions have been written to complement the text discussion of figures and to help students more readily grasp what they're seeing.

We've worked hard to make these graphs student-friendly. For example, to help students navigate one of the stickier thickets—the distinction between a shifting curve and movement along a curve—we encourage students to see this difference by using two types of arrows: a shift arrow (——→) and what we call a "movement-along" arrow (——→). You can see these arrows in Figures 3-12 and 3-13 on pages 73 and 74.

In addition, several graphs in each chapter are accompanied by the icon **>web...,** which indicates that these graphs are available online as simulations (the graphs are animated in Flash format and can be manipulated). Every interactive graph is accompanied by a quiz on key concepts to further help students in their work with graphs.

Instructing students in the use of graphs is also enhanced by our use of real-world data (especially in the macroeconomics chapters), often presented in charts that can be compared directly to the analytical figures. For example, the aggregate supply curve can seem like a highly abstract concept, but in Chapter 16, "Aggregate Supply and Aggregate Demand," we make it less abstract by illustrating the concept with the actual behavior of aggregate output and the aggregate price level during the 1930s (see Figure 16-6 on page 403).

**Helpful Graphing Appendix** For students who would benefit from an explanation of how graphs are constructed, interpreted, and used in economics, we've included a detailed graphing appendix after Chapter 2 on page 41. This appendix is more comprehensive than most because we know that some students need this helpful background, and we didn't want to breeze through the material. Our hope is that this comprehensive graphing appendix will better prepare students to use and interpret the graphs in this textbook and then out in the real world (in newspapers, magazines, and elsewhere).

## Definitions of Key Terms

Every key term, in addition to being defined in the text, is also placed and defined in the margin to make it easier for students to study and review.

## "A Look Ahead"

The text of each chapter ends with "A Look Ahead," a short overview of what lies ahead in upcoming chapters. This concluding section provides students with a sense of continuity among chapters.

## End-of-Chapter Review

In addition to the "Quick Review" at the end of each major section, each chapter ends with a complete but brief **Summary** of the key terms and concepts. In addition, a list of the **Key Terms** is placed at the end of each chapter along with page references.

For each chapter we have a comprehensive set of **End-of-Chapter Problems** that test intuition and the ability to calculate important variables. Much care has been devoted to the creation of these problems. Instructors can be assured that they provide a true test of students' learning.

# The Organization of This Book and How to Use It

This book is organized as a series of building blocks in which conceptual material learned at one stage is clearly built upon and then integrated into the conceptual material covered in the next stage. These building blocks correspond to the eight parts into which the chapters are divided. We'll now walk through those building blocks, giving a brief overview of each part and chapter, followed by a look at the ways an instructor can tailor this book to meet his or her needs.

## Part 1: What Is Economics?

In the **Introduction, "The Ordinary Business of Life,"** students are initiated into the study of economics in the context of a shopping trip on any given Sunday in everyday America. It provides students with basic definitions of terms such as *economics,* the *invisible hand,* and *market structure.* In addition it serves as a "tour d'horizon" of economics, explaining the difference between microeconomics and macroeconomics.

In **Chapter 1, "First Principles,"** nine principles are presented and explained: four principles of individual choice, covering concepts such as opportunity cost, marginal analysis, and incentives; and five principles of interaction between individuals, covering concepts such as gains from trade, market efficiency, and market failure. In later chapters, we build intuition by frequently referring to these principles in the explanation of specific models. Students learn that these nine principles form a cohesive conceptual foundation for all of economics.

**Chapter 2, "Economic Models: Trade-offs and Trade,"** shows students how to think like economists by using three models—the production possibility frontier, comparative advantage and trade, and the circular-flow diagram—to analyze the world around them. It gives students an early introduction to gains from trade and to international comparisons. The **Chapter 2 Appendix** contains a comprehensive math and graphing review.

## Part 2: Supply and Demand

In this part we provide students with the basic analytical tools they need to understand how markets work, tools that are common to microeconomics and macroeconomics.

**Chapter 3, "Supply and Demand,"** covers the standard material in a fresh and compelling way: supply and demand, market equilibrium, and surplus and shortage are all illustrated using an example of the market for scalped tickets to a sports event. Students learn how the demand and supply curves of scalped tickets shift in response to the announcement of a star player's impending retirement.

**Chapter 4, "The Market Strikes Back,"** covers various types of market interventions and their consequences: price and quantity controls, inefficiency and deadweight loss, and excise taxes. Through tangible examples such as New York City rent control regulations and New York City taxi licenses, the costs generated by attempts to control markets are made real to students.

In **Chapter 5, "Elasticity,"** the actions of OPEC and their consequences for the world market for oil are the real-world motivating example in our discussion of the price elasticity of demand. In this chapter, we introduce the various elasticity measures and show how elasticities are used to evaluate the incidence of an excise tax.

Through examples such as a market for used textbooks and eBay, students learn how markets increase welfare in

**Chapter 6, "Consumer and Producer Surplus."** The concepts of market efficiency and deadweight loss are strongly emphasized.

## Part 3: The Producer

In **Chapter 7, "Behind the Supply Curve: Inputs and Costs,"** we develop the production function and the various cost measures of the firm. There is an extensive discussion of the difference between average cost and marginal cost, illustrated by examples such as a student's grade point average. **Chapter 8, "Perfect Competition and the Supply Curve,"** explains the output decision of the perfectly competitive firm, its entry/exit decision, the industry supply curve, and the equilibrium of a perfectly competitive market. We draw on examples such as generic pharmaceuticals and the California energy crisis of 2000–2001 to contrast the behavior of oligopolists and monopolists.

### What Comes Next: Markets and Efficiency or Market Structure?

Some instructors are likely to consider the next chapter—Chapter 9, "Factor Markets and the Distribution of Income,"—optional. Chapter 9 is likely to be used by instructors who want more in-depth coverage of microeconomics, as well as those who wish to emphasize labor markets. The desired placement of Chapter 10, "Efficiency, Inefficiency, and Equity"—is not universal. Some may wish to postpone Chapter 10 until after issues of market structure have been considered in Chapters 11 ("Monopoly") and 12 ("Oligopoly, Monopolistic Competition, and Product Differentiation"). We have written the chapters so that both sequences work equally well.

## Part 4: Markets and Efficiency

**Chapter 9, "Factor Markets and the Distribution of Income,"** covers the competitive factor market model and the factor distribution of income. In addition, the efficiency-wage model of the labor market is discussed, and the influences of education, discrimination, and market power are also addressed. It presents, we hope, a balanced and well-rounded view of the strengths and limitations of the competitive market model of labor markets and leads to a greater appreciation of the issues of efficiency and equity discussed in the next chapter.

**Chapter 10, "Efficiency, Inefficiency, and Equity,"** begins by considering what it means to have efficiency in a market economy as a whole. We then include the discussion of equity. Then two sections illustrate inefficiency in a market: the cases of externalities and public goods. Some instructors might be tempted to include the sections on externalities and public goods but skip the discussion of general equilibrium in the first section of this chapter. Why take time to delve into what can be a challenging topic—general equilibrium—in a one semester course? Doing so gives students a deeper understanding of the often-conflicting objectives of efficiency and equity—something that really can't be fully explored in a partial equilibrium setting. As a real-world example, we discuss the reunification of West and East Germany in terms of the trade-offs faced by German policy makers, who sacrificed some efficiency-enhancing measures in order to reduce the income differences between East and West Germans.

## Part 5: Market Structure: Beyond Perfect Competition

**Chapter 11, "Monopoly,"** is a full treatment of monopoly, including topics such as price discrimination and the welfare effects of monopoly. We provide an array of compelling examples, such as De Beers Diamonds, price manipulation by California power companies, and airline ticket pricing. In **Chapter 12, "Oligopoly, Monopolistic Competition, and Product Differentiation"** we provide students with an introduction to imperfect competition. We present basic game theory in both one-shot and repeated-game contexts. Students are brought face-to-face early on with an example of monopolistic competition that is a familiar feature of their lives: the food court at the local mall. We go on to cover entry and exit, efficiency considerations, and advertising.

## Part 6: Extending Market Boundaries

In Chapter 2, we presented a full exposition of gains from trade and the difference between comparative and absolute advantage, illustrated with an international example (trade between high-wage and low-wage countries). **Chapter 13, "International Trade,"** builds on that material. It traces the sources of comparative advantage, considers tariffs and quotas, and explores the politics of trade protection. In response to current events, we give in-depth coverage to the controversy over imports from low-wage countries.

## Part 7: Introduction to Macroeconomics

**Chapter 14, "Macroeconomics: The Big Picture,"** introduces the big ideas in macroeconomics. Starting with an example close to students' hearts—how the business cycle affects the job prospects of graduates—this chapter provides a quick overview of recessions and expansions, employment and unemployment, long-run growth, inflation versus deflation, and the open economy.

**Chapter 15, "Tracking the Macroeconomy,"** explains how the numbers macroeconomists use are calculated, and why. We start with a real-world example of how an estimate of real GDP helped save a country from policy mistakes, then turn to the basics of national income accounting, unemployment statistics, and price indexes.

### Part 8: Short-Run Economic Fluctuations

Part 8 begins with **Chapter 16, "Aggregate Supply and Aggregate Demand."** This chapter's opening story covers the economic slump of 1979–1982, which startled Americans with its combination of recession and inflation. This leads into an analysis of how both demand shocks and supply shocks affect the economy. In analyzing demand shocks, we offer a simple, intuitive explanation of the concept of the multiplier, using the idea of successive increases in spending after an initial shock to explain how the aggregate demand curve shifts. In analyzing supply shocks, we emphasize positive shocks, such as the productivity surge of the late 1990s, as well as negative shocks. The chapter concludes with the key insight that demand shocks affect only output in the short run.

**Chapter 17, "Fiscal Policy,"** starts in Japan, where discretionary fiscal policy has taken the form of huge public works projects, often of doubtful value. This leads into an analysis of the role of discretionary fiscal policy in shifting the aggregate demand curve, which makes use of the intuitive explanation of the multiplier from Chapter 16. We also cover automatic stabilizers—using the woes of Europe's "stability pact" to illustrate their importance—and long-run issues of debt and solvency.

**Chapter 18, "Money, the Federal Reserve System, and Monetary Policy,"** covers the roles of money, the ways in which banks create money, the structure and role of the Federal Reserve and other central banks, and the role of Federal Reserve policy in driving interest rates and aggregate demand. We use episodes from U.S. history together with the story of the creation of the euro to illustrate how money and monetary institutions have evolved. We also take full advantage of the dramatic developments in monetary policy since 2000, which make it easier than ever before to illustrate what the Federal Reserve does.

## Supplements and Media

Worth Publishers is pleased to offer an exciting and useful supplements and media package to accompany this textbook. The package has been crafted to help instructors teach their principles course and to help students grasp concepts more readily.

Since accuracy is so critically important, all the supplements have been scrutinized and double-checked by members of the supplements team, reviewers, and a team

of additional accuracy checkers. The time and care that have been put into the supplements and media ensure a seamless package.

## Companion Website for Students and Instructors
econ X change

### (www.worthpublishers.com/ krugmanwellsolney)

The companion website for the Krugman/Wells/Olney text offers valuable tools for both the instructor and students.

For instructors, this completely customized website offers many opportunities for quizzing and, most important, powerful grading tools. The site gives you the ability to track students' interaction with the Practice Quizzes and the Animated Graphs by accessing an online gradebook. Instructors have the option to have student results emailed directly to them.

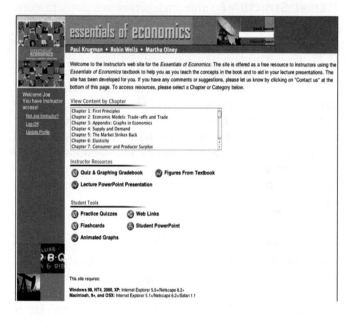

For students, the site offers many opportunities to practice. On the site, students can find animated graphs, practice quizzes, and links to many other resources designed to help them master economic concepts. In essence, this site provides students with a virtual study guide, 24 hours a day, 7 days a week by offering a pedagogically sound means of testing their understanding of text material.

This helpful, powerful site contains the following:

**Practice Quizzes**  This quizzing engine provides 20 multiple-choice questions per chapter with appropriate feedback and page references to the textbook. All student answers are saved in an online database that can be accessed by instructors.

**Animated Graphs** This includes selected graphs from the textbook that have been animated in Flash format. The key graphs from each chapter have been animated and are identified in the textbook by a web icon **>web...** within the appropriate figure. Working with these animated figures enhances student understanding of the effects of the shifts and movements of the curves. Every interactive graph is accompanied by questions that quiz students on key concepts from the textbook and provide instructors with feedback on student progress. Student responses and interactions are tracked and stored in an online database that can be accessed by the instructor.

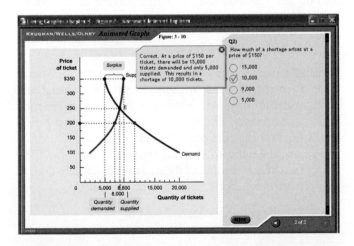

**Web Links** This allows students to easily and effectively locate outside resources and readings that relate to topics covered in the textbook. It lists web addresses that hotlink to relevant websites, allowing students to conduct research and explore related readings on specific topics with ease. Also hotlinked are relevant articles by Paul Krugman and other leading economists.

## ➤ Aplia

Aplia, founded by Paul Romer, Stanford University, is the first web-based company to integrate pedagogical features from a textbook with interactive media. Specifically designed for use with this text, the figures, end-of-chapter problems, boxes, text, and other pedagogical resources have been combined with Aplia's interactive media to save time for professors and encourage students to exert more effort in their learning.

The integrated online version of the Aplia media and the text includes:

➤ Extra problem sets suitable for homework and keyed to specific topics from each chapter

➤ Regularly updated news analyses

➤ Real-time online simulations of market interactions

➤ Interactive tutorials to assist with math

➤ Graphs and statistics

➤ Instant online reports that allow instructors to target student trouble areas more efficiently

With Aplia, you retain complete control and flexibility for your course. You choose the topics you want students to cover, and you decide how to organize it. You decide whether online activities are practice (ungraded or graded). You can even edit the Aplia content—making cuts or addtions as you see fit for your course.

For a preview of Aplia materials and to learn more, visit http://www.aplia.com.

## Additional Student Supplements

**Study Guide** The Study Guide reinforces the topics and key concepts covered in the text. For each chapter, the Study Guide provides:

➤ An introduction

➤ A fill-in-the-blank chapter review

➤ Learning tips with graphical analysis

➤ Four or five comprehensive problems and exercises

➤ Twenty multiple-choice questions

➤ Solutions to all fill-in-the-blank reviews, problems, exercises, and quizzes found in the Study Guide.

## Additional Instructor Supplements

**Instructor's Resource Manual** The Instructor's Resource Manual is an ideal resource for instructors teaching principles of economics. The manual includes:

➤ Chapter-by-chapter learning objectives

➤ Chapter outlines

- ➤ Teaching tips and ideas

- ➤ Hints on how to create student interest

- ➤ Common misunderstandings that are typical among students

- ➤ Activities that can be conducted in or out of the classroom

- ➤ Detailed solutions to every end-of-chapter problem from the textbook

**Printed Test Bank** The Test Bank provides a wide range of creative and versatile questions ranging in levels of difficulty. Selected questions are paired with original graphs and graphs from the textbook to reinforce comprehension. The Test Banks offers multiple-choice and true/false questions assessing comprehension, interpretation, analysis, and synthesis. Each question is conveniently cross-referenced to the page number in the text where the appropriate topic is discussed. Questions have been checked for continuity with the text content, reviewed extensively, and rechecked for accuracy.

**Diploma 6 Computerized Test Bank** The printed Test Bank is also available in CD-ROM format, powered by  Brownstone, for both Windows and Macintosh users. With Diploma, you can easily create and print tests and write and edit questions. The software's unique synthesis of flexible word-processing and database features creates a program that is extremely intuitive and capable.

- ➤ Post tests to Diploma's online testing site, TheTestingCenter.com.

This computerized Test Bank is accompanied by a gradebook that enables you to record students' grades throughout a course.

- ➤ Import and export student rosters.

**Lecture PowerPoint Presentation** The enhanced PowerPoint presentation slides are designed to assist you with lecture preparation and presentation by providing original animations, graphs from the textbook, data tables, and bulleted lists of key concepts suitable for large lecture presentation. Although the slides are organized by topic from the text's table of contents, you can customize these slides to suit your individual needs by adding your own data, questions, and lecture notes. You can access these files on the instructor's side of the website or on the Instructor's Resource CD-ROM.

**Instructor's Resource CD-ROM** Using the Instructor's Resource CD-ROM, you can easily build classroom presentations or enchance your online courses. This CD-ROM contains all text figures (in JPEG and PPT formats), animated graphs, and enhanced PowerPoint slides. You can choose from the various resources, edit, and save for use in your classroom.

**Overhead Transparencies** Worth is also happy to provide you with vivid color acetates of text figures designed for superior projection quality.

**Web-CT E-pack** The Krugman/Wells/Olney WebCT E-Packs enable you to create a thorough, interactive, and  pedagogically sound online course or course website. The E-Pack provides you with cutting-edge online materials that facilitate critical thinking and learning, including preprogrammed quizzes, links, animated graphs, and a whole array of other materials. Best of all, this material is preprogrammed and fully functional in the WebCT environment. Prebuilt materials eliminate hours of course-preparation work and offer significant support as you develop your online course. You can also obtain a WebCT-formatted version of the text's test bank.

**Blackboard** The Krugman/Wells/Olney Blackboard Course Cartridge allows you to combine Blackboard's popular tools and easy-to-use interface with the text-specific, rich web content, including preprogrammed quizzes, links, activities, interactive graphs, and a whole array of other materials. The result: an interactive, comprehensive online course that allow for effortless implementation, management, and use. The Worth electronic files are organized and prebuilt to work within the Blackboard software and can be easily downloaded from the Blackboard content showcases directly onto your department server. You can also obtain a Blackboard-formatted version of the book's test bank.

## Acknowledgments

Writing a textbook is a team effort and we could never have reached this point without all of the talented and thoughtful consultants, reviewers, focus-group participants, class testers, and others who have been so generous with their insights on our work.

We are indebted to the following reviewers for their comments and recommendations as we originally drafted this one-semester book, *Essentials of Economics*:

Irma T. Alonso, *Florida International University*

Clive Belfield, *Queens College*

Jose L. Esteban, *Palomar College*

Devra Golbe, *Hunter College*

Frances F. Lea, *Germanna Community College*

Noreen E. Lephardt, *Marquette University*

Chris N. McGrew, *Purdue University*

Abdulhamid Sukar, *Cameron University*

Jose J. Vazquez-Cognet, *University of Illinois at Urbana-Champaign*

We especially owe the following people for their guidance in creating *Essentials of Economics* and for their detailed feedback on each chapter:

Carlos Aguilar, *El Paso Community College*
Andreas Bentz, *Dartmouth College*
Norman R. Cloutier, *University of Wisconsin-Parkside*

We are indebted to the following reviewers and other consultants for their suggestions and advice on chapters of *Economics:*

Ashley Abramson, *Barstow College*
Ljubisa Adamovich, *Florida State University*
Lee Adkins, *Oklahoma State University*
Elena Alvarez, *State University of New York, Albany*
David A. Anderson, *Centre College*
Fahima Aziz, *Hamline University*
Sheryl Ball, *Virginia Polytechnic Institute and State University*
Charles L. Ballard, *Michigan State University*
Cynthia Bansak, *San Diego State University*
Richard Barrett, *University of Montana*
Daniel Barszcz, *College of DuPage*
Charles A. Bennett, *Gannon University*
Andreas Bentz, *Dartmouth College*
Ruben Berrios, *Clarion University*
Joydeep Bhattacharya, *Iowa State University*
Harmanna Bloemen, *Houston Community College*
Michael Bordo, *Rutgers University, NBER*
James Bradley, Jr., *University of South Carolina*
William Branch, *University of Oregon*
Michael Brandl, *University of Texas, Austin*
Greg Brock, *Georgia Southern University*
Raymonda L. Burgman, *DePauw University*
Charles Callahan III, *State University of New York, Brockport*
James Carden, *University of Mississippi*
Bill Carlisle, *University of Utah*
Leonard A. Carlson, *Emory University*
Andrew Cassey, *University of Minnesota*
Shirley Cassing, *University of Pittsburgh*
Yuna Chen, *South Georgia College*
Jim Cobbe, *Florida State University*
Eleanor D. Craig, *University of Delaware*
Rosemary Thomas Cunningham, *Agnes Scott College*
James Cypher, *California State University, Fresno*
Susan Dadres, *Southern Methodist University*
Ardeshir Dalal, *Northern Illinois University*
A. Edward Day, *University of Texas, Dallas*
Dennis Debrecht, *Carroll College*
Stephen J. DeCanio, *University of California, Santa Barbara*
J. Bradford DeLong, *University of California, Berkeley*
Julie Derrick, *Brevard Community College*

Carolyn Dimitri, *Montgomery College, Rockville*
Patrick Dolenc, *Keene State College*
Amitava Dutt, *University of Notre Dame*
Jim Eaton, *Bridgewater College*
Jim Eden, *Portland Community College*
Rex Edwards, *Moorpark College*
Can Erbil, *Brandeis University*
Sharon J. Erenburg, *Eastern Michigan University*
Joe Essuman, *University of Wisconsin, Waukesha*
David N. Figlio, *University of Florida*
David W. Findlay, *Colby College*
Eric Fisher, *Ohio State University/University of California, Santa Barbara*
Oliver Franke, *Athabasca University*
Rhona Free, *Eastern Connecticut State University*
K. C. Fung, *University of California, Santa Cruz*
Susan Gale, *New York University*
Neil Garston, *California State University, Los Angeles*
E. B. Gendel, *Woodbury University*
J. Robert Gillette, *University of Kentucky*
Lynn G. Gillette, *University of Kentucky*
James N. Giordano, *Villanova University*
Robert Godby, *University of Wyoming*
David Goodwin, *University of New Brunswick*
Lisa Grobar, *California State University, Long Beach*
Philip Grossman, *St. Cloud State University*
Wayne Grove, *Syracuse University*
Alan Gummerson, *Florida International University*
Jang-Ting Guo, *University of California, Riverside*
Jonathan Hamilton, *University of Florida*
Mehdi Haririan, *Bloomsburg University of Pennsylvania*
Hadley Hartman, *Santa Fe Community College*
Julie Heath, *University of Memphis*
John Heim, *Rensselaer Polytechnic Institute*
Jill M. Hendrickson, *University of the South*
Rob Holm, *Franklin University*
David Horlacher, *Middlebury College*
Robert Horn, *James Madison University*
Scott Houser, *California State University, Fresno*
Patrik T. Hultberg, *University of Wyoming*
Aaron Jackson, *Bentley College*
Nancy Jianakoplos, *Colorado State University*
Donn Johnson, *Quinnipiac University*
Bruce Johnson, *Centre College*
Philipp Jonas, *Western Michigan University*
Michael Jones, *Bridgewater State College*
James Jozefowicz, *Indiana University of Pennsylvania*
Kamran M. Kadkhah, *Northeastern University*
Matthew Kahn, *Columbia University*
Barry Keating, *University of Notre Dame*
Diane Keenan, *Cerritos College*

Bill Kerby, *California State University, Sacramento*

Kyoo Kim, *Bowling Green University*

Philip King, *San Francisco State University*

Sharmila King, *University of the Pacific*

Kala Krishna, *Penn State University, NBER*

Jean Kujawa, *Lourdes College*

Maria Kula, *Roger Williams University*

Michael Kuryla, *Broome Community College*

Tom Larson, *California State University, Los Angeles*

Susan K. Laury, *Georgia State University*

Jim Lee, *Texas A&M University, Corpus Christi*

Tony Lima, *California State University, Hayward*

Solina Lindahl, *California State Polytechnic University, Pomona*

Malte Loos, *Christian-Albrechts Universität Kiel*

Marty Ludlum, *Oklahoma City Community College*

Mark Maier, *Glendale Community College*

Rachel McCulloch, *Brandeis University*

Doug Meador, *William Jewell College*

Diego Mendez-Carbajo, *Illinois Wesleyan University*

Juan Mendoza, *State University of New York at Buffalo*

Jeffrey Michael, *Towson University*

Jenny Minier, *University of Miami*

Ida A. Mirzaie, *John Carroll University*

Kristen Monaco, *California State University, Long Beach*

Marie Mora, *University of Texas, Pan American*

W. Douglas Morgan, *University of California, Santa Barbara*

Peter B. Morgan, *University of Michigan*

Tony Myatt, *University of New Brunswick, Fredericton*

Kathryn Nantz, *Fairfield University*

John A. Neri, *University of Maryland*

Charles Newton, *Houston Community College*

Joe Nowakowski, *Muskingum College*

Seamus O'Cleireacain, *Columbia University/State University of New York, Purchase*

Martha Olney, *University of California, Berkeley*

Kerry Pannell, *DePauw University*

Chris Papageorgiou, *Louisiana State University*

Brian Peterson, *Central College*

John Pharr, *Dallas County Community College*

Clifford Poirot, *Shawnee State University*

Raymond E. Polchow, *Zane State College*

Adnan Qamar, *University of Texas, Dallas*

Jeffrey Racine, *University of South Florida*

Matthew Rafferty, *Quinnipiac University*

Dixie Watts Reaves, *Virginia Polytechnic Institute and State University*

Siobhán Reilly, *Mills College*

Thomas Rhoads, *Towson University*

Libby Rittenberg, *Colorado College*

Malcom Robinson, *Thomas More College*

Michael Rolleigh, *Williams College*

Christina Romer, *University of California, Berkeley*

Brian P. Rosario, *University of California, Davis*

Bernard Rose, *Rocky Mountain College*

Patricia Rottschaefer, *California State University, Fullerton*

Jeff Rubin, *Rutgers University*

Henry D. Ryder, *Gloucester Community College*

Allen Sanderson, *University of Chicago*

Rolando Santos, *Lakeland Community College*

Christine Sauer, *University of New Mexico*

Elizabeth Sawyer-Kelly, *University of Wisconsin, Madison*

Edward Sayre, *Agnes Scott College*

Robert Schwab, *University of Maryland*

Adina Schwartz, *Lakeland College*

Gerald Scott, *Florida Atlantic University*

Stanley Sedo, *University of Maryland*

William Shambora, *Ohio University*

Gail Shields, *Central Michigan University*

Amy Shrout, *West High School*

Eugene Silberberg, *University of Washington*

Bill Smith, *University of Memphis*

Ray Smith, *College of St. Scholastica*

Judy Smrha, *Baker University*

Marcia S. Snyder, *College of Charleston*

John Solow, *University of Iowa*

David E. Spencer, *Brigham Young University*

Denise Stanley, *California State University, Fullerton*

Martha A. Starr, *American University*

Richard Startz, *University of Washington*

Carol Ogden Stivender, *University of North Carolina, Charlotte*

Jill Stowe, *Texas A&M University, Austin*

William Stronge, *Florida Atlantic University*

Rodney Swanson, *University of California, Los Angeles*

Sarinda Taengnoi, *Western New England College*

Lazina Tarin, *Central Michigan University*

Jason Taylor, *University of Virginia*

Mark Thoma, *University of California, San Diego*

Mehmet Tosun, *West Virginia University*

Karen Travis, *Pacific Lutheran University*

Sandra Trejos, *Clarion University*

Arienne Turner, *Fullerton College*

Neven Valev, *Georgia State University*

Kristin Van Gaasbeck, *California State University*

Abu Wahid, *Tennessee State University*

Stephan Weiler, *Colorado State University*

James N. Wetzel, *Virginia Commonwealth University*

Robert Whaples, *Wake Forest University*

Roger White, *University of Georgia*

Jonathan B. Wight, *University of Richmond*

Mark Wohar, *University of Nebraska, Omaha*

William C. Wood, *James Madison University*

Ken Woodward, *Saddleback College*
Bill Yang, *Georgia Southern University*
Cemile Yavas, *Pennsylvania State University*
Andrea Zanter, *Hillsborough Community College*

We must also thank the following graduate student reviewers for their assistance: Kristy Piccinini, University of California, Berkeley; Lanwei Yang, University of California, Berkeley; Casey Rothschild, Massachusetts Institute of Technology; and Naomi E. Feldman, University of Michigan, Ann Arbor.

During the course of drafting the manuscript for *Economics*, we met with instructors of principles courses for face-to-face focus-group sessions that afforded us invaluable input. We appreciate the forthright advice and suggestions from these colleagues:

Michael Bordo, *Rutgers University*
Jim Cobbe, *Florida State University*
Tom Creahan, *Morehead State University*
Stephen DeCanio, *University of California, Santa Barbara*
Jim Eden, *Portland Community College, Sylvania*
David Flath, *North Carolina State University*
Rhona Free, *Eastern Connecticut State University*
Rick Godby, *University of Wyoming*
Wayne Grove, *Syracuse University*
Jonathan Hamilton, *University of Florida*
Robert Horn, *James Madison University*
Patrik Hultberg, *University of Wyoming*
Bruce Johnson, *Centre College*
Jim Jozefowicz, *Indiana University of Pennsylvania*
Jim Lee, *Texas A&M University, Corpus Christi*
Rachel McCulloch, *Brandeis University*
Ida Mirzaie, *John Carroll University*
Henry D. Ryder, *Gloucester Community College*
Marcia Snyder, *College of Charleston*
Brian Trinque, *University of Texas, Austin*
William C. Wood, *James Madison University*

Many thanks to the class testers who took the time to use early drafts of chapters for *Economics* in their classrooms. The following instructors should know that we made use of their helpful suggestions. We also extend special thanks to so many of your students who filled out user surveys about our chapters. This student input inspired us.

Ashley Abramson, *Barstow College*
Terry Alexander, *Iowa State University*
Fahima Aziz, *Hamline University*
Benjamin Balak, *Rollins College*
Leon Battista, *Bronx Community College*
Richard Beil, *Auburn University*

Charles Bennett, *Gannon University*
Scott Benson, *Idaho State University*
Andreas Bentz, *Dartmouth College*
John Bockino, *Suffolk County Community College*
Ellen Bowen, *Fisher College, New Bedford*
Anne Bresnock, *University of California, Los Angeles*
Bruce Brown, *California State Polytechnic University, Pomona*
John Buck, *Jacksonville University*
Raymonda Burgman, *University of Southern Florida*
William Carlisle, *University of Utah*
Kevin Carlson, *University of Massachusetts, Boston*
Fred Carstensen, *University of Connecticut*
Shirley Cassing, *University of Pittsburgh*
Ramon Castillo-Ponce, *California State University, Los Angeles*
Emily Chamlee-Wright, *Beloit College*
Anthony Chan, *Santa Monica College*
Mitch Charkiewiecz, *Central Connecticut State University*
Yuna Chen, *South Georgia College*
Maryanne Clifford, *Eastern Connecticut State University*
Julia Chismar, *St. Joseph's High School*
Gregory Colman, *Pace University*
Sarah Culver, *University of Alabama*
Rosa Lea Danielson, *College of DuPage*
Lew Dars, *University of Massachusetts/Dartmouth*
Stephen Davis, *Southwest Minnesota State University*
Tom DelGiudice, *Hofstra University*
Arna Desser, *United States Naval Academy*
Nikolay Dobrinov, *University of Colorado*
Patrick Dolenc, *Keene State College*
Stratford Douglas, *West Virginia University*
Julie Dvorak, *Warren Township High School*
Dorsey Dyer, *Davidson County Community College*
Mary Edwards, *St. Cloud State University*
Fritz Efaw, *University of Tennessee, Chattanooga*
Herb Elliot, *Alan Hancock College*
Can Erbil, *Brandeis University*
Yee Tien Fu, *Stanford University*
Yoram Gelman, *Lehman College, The City University of New York*
E.B. Gendel, *Woodbury College*
Doug Gentry, *St. Mary's College*
Tommy Georgiades, *DeVry University*
Satyajit Ghosh, *University of Scranton*
Richard Glendening, *Central College*
Patrick Gormely, *Kansas State University*
Richard Gosselin, *Houston Community College, Central*
Patricia Graham, *University of Northern Colorado*
Kathleen Greer Rossman, *Birmingham Southern College*
Wayne Grove, *Syracuse University*
Eleanor Gubins, *Rosemont College*
Alan Haight, *State University of New York, Cortland*

Gautam Hazarika, *University of Texas, Brownsville*

Tom Head, *George Fox University*

Susan Helper, *Case Western Reserve University*

Paul Hettler, *Duquesne University*

Roger Hewett, *Drake University*

Michael Hilmer, *San Diego State University*

Jill Holman, *University of Wisconsin, Milwaukee*

Scott Houser, *California State University, Fresno*

Ray Hubbard, *Central Georgia Technical College*

Murat Iyigun, *University of Colorado*

Habib Jam, *Rowan University*

Louis Johnston, *College of St. Benedict/St. John's University*

Jack Julian, *Indiana University of Pennsylvania*

Soheila Kahkashan, *Towson University*

Charles Kaplan, *St. Joseph's College*

Jay Kaplan, *University of Colorado, Boulder*

Bentzil Kasper, *Broome Community College*

Kurt Keiser, *Adams State College*

Ara Khanjian, *Ventura College*

Sinan Koont, *Dickinson College*

Emil Kreider, *Beloit College*

Kenneth Kriz, *University of Nebraska, Omaha*

Tom Larson, *California State University, Los Angeles*

Delores Linton, *Tarrant County College, Northwest*

Rolf Lokke, *Albuquerque Academy*

Ellen Magenheim, *Swarthmore College*

Diana McCoy, *Truckee Meadows Community College*

Garrett Milam, *Ryerson University*

Robert Miller, *Fisher College, New Bedford Campus*

Michael Milligan, *Front Range Community College*

Cathy Miners, *Fairfield University*

Larry Miners, *Fairfield University*

Kristen Monaco, *California State University, Long Beach*

Marie Mora, *University of Texas, Pan American*

James Mueller, *Alma College*

Ranganath Murthy, *Bucknell University*

Sylvia Nasar, *Columbia University*

Gerardo Nebbia, *Glendale Community College*

Anthony Negbenebor, *Gardner-Webb University*

Joseph Nowakowski, *Muskingum College*

Charles Okeke, *Community College of Southern Nevada*

Kimberley Ott, *Kent State University, Salem Campus*

Philip Packard, *St. Mary's College*

Jamie Pelley, *Mary Baldwin College*

Michael Perelman, *California State University*

Mary K. Perkins, *Howard University*

John Pharr, *Dallas Community College, Cedar Valley*

Jerome Picard, *Mount Saint Mary College*

Ray Polchow, *Muskingum Area Technical College*

Ernest Poole, *Fashion Institute of Technology*

Reza Ramazani, *St. Michael's College*

Charles Reichheld, *Cuyahoga Community College*

Siobhan Reilly, *Mills College*

Michael Righi, *Bellevue Community College*

Carl Riskin, *Queens College, The City University of New York*

Malcolm Robinson, *Thomas More College*

Charles Rock, *Rollins College*

Richard Romano, *Broome Community College*

Jeff Romine, *University of Colorado, Denver*

Bernie Rose, *Rocky Mountain College*

Dan Rubenson, *Southern Oregon University*

Jeff Rubin, *Rutgers University*

Lynda Rush, *California State Polytechnic University, Pomona*

Martin Sabo, *Community College of Denver*

Sara Saderion, *Houston Community College, Southwest*

George Sawdy, *Providence College*

Ted Scheinman, *Mt. Hood Community College*

Russell Settle, *University of Delaware*

Anna Shostya, *Pace University*

Amy Shrout, *West High School*

Millicent Sites, *Carson-Newman College*

Judy Smrha, *Baker University*

John Somers, *Portland Community College*

Jim Spellicy, *Lowell High School*

Tesa Stegner, *Idaho State University*

Kurt Stephenson, *Virginia Tech*

Charles Stull, *Kalamazoo College*

Laddie Sula, *Loras College*

David Switzer, *University of Northern Michigan*

Deborah Thorsen, *Palm Beach Community College*

Andrew Toole, *Cook College/Rutgers University*

Arienne Turner, *Fullerton College*

Anthony Uremovic, *Joliet Junior College*

Jane Wallace, *University of Pittsburgh*

Tom Watkins, *Eastern Kentucky University*

James Wetzel, *Virginia Commonwealth University*

Mark Witte, *Northwestern University*

Larry Wolfenbarger, *Macon State College*

James Woods, *Portland State University*

Mickey Wu, *Coe College*

David Yerger, *Indiana University of Pennsylvania*

Eric Young, *Bishop Amat Memorial High School*

Lou Zaera, *Fashion Institute of Technology*

Andrea Zanter, *Hillsborough Community College, Dale Mabry Campus*

Stephen Zill, *De Anza College*

We also appreciate the contributions of our Two-Year/Community College Advisory Panel:

Kathleen Bromley, *Monroe Community College*

Barbara Connolly, *Westchester Community College*

Will Cummings, *Grossmont College*

Richard Gosselin, *Houston Community College, Central*

Gus Herring, *Brookhaven College*

Charles Okeke, *Community College of Southern Nevada*

Charles Reichheld, *Cuyahoga Community College*

Sara Saderion, *Houston Community College, Southwest*

Ted Scheinman, *Mt. Hood Community College*

J. Ross Thomas, *Albuquerque Technical Vocational Institute*

Deborah Thorsen, *Palm Beach Community College*

Ranita Wyatt, *Dallas Community College*

We would also like to thank the hundreds of instructors who took the time to offer their useful feedback to online marketing surveys about our project. There are nearly 800 of you out there. We only wish we had enough room in this small space to thank each of you.

The following key people critically read every page in virtually every chapter from many of our drafts for *Economics,* and offered us so much: Andreas Bentz, Dartmouth College, oversaw accuracy checking, but his role turned into much more than that—a constant, tireless adviser who clarified our work at every step. It is extremely rare to find someone as faithful as Andreas has been to this project, and we are immensely grateful to him. Martha Olney, University of California, Berkeley, provided insightful input throughout the process of crafting *Economics*—we had a number of moments when we realized that her advice saved us from a serious pedagogical misstep. Our deepest thanks also go to Martha. Development editor Marilyn Freedman helped us in shaping a book that instructors can really use and injected much-needed doses of common sense at crucial moments. We've even relied on her to sort out pedagogical differences between the two of us. Several other people have played an invaluable role as close readers for *Economics:* Elizabeth Sawyer-Kelly, University of Wisconsin, Madison; David Findlay, Colby College; Sharon J. Ehrenburg, Eastern Michigan University; Malte Loos, Christian-Albrechts Universität Kiel; and Kristy Piccinni and Lanwei Yang, both graduate students at the University of California, Berkeley. The detailed and wise input from all of you has been enormously helpful to us! (Thanks, too, Kristy for your work on our glossary.) Special thanks go to Dave Figlio, University of Florida, for his invaluable help as a reviewer and for his contributions.

Thanks to Rhona Free for her contributions, particularly for the essential role she played in the development of our graphing appendix. We must also extend special thanks to Rosemary Cunningham, Agnes Scott College, for her assistance with end-of-chapter problems.

We'd like to thank the current and former Worth people who made this project possible. Paul Shensa and Bob Worth suggested that we write *Economics.* Craig Bleyer, publisher, kept the writing process moving, with just the right mix of patience and whip-cracking. Craig's able leadership and patience helped us realize our vision for this book and get all versions of it finished and out to the market.

Elizabeth Widdicombe, president of Freeman and Worth, and Catherine Woods, publisher at Worth, urged us on and kept faith with what must have been a very exasperating project at times.

We have had an incredible production and design team originally work on *Economics.* Tracey Kuehn, our associate managing editor, has worked tirelessly and with great skill to turn our rough manuscript into this beautiful textbook—and on a very tight schedule. And, thank you, Anthony Calcara, our project editor. Karen Osborne, our copyeditor, did a fine job helping us streamline and refine our writing. Babs Reingold created the spectacular cover for this book and came up with a book design that awed us each time we saw a new chapter in page proof. All we can say is "wow" and thanks. And we would not have been so awed with the look of each and every spread without the page-layout magic that Lee Mahler worked for us. Thanks, too, to Barbara Seixas for her work on the manufacturing end. We've heard about some of the miracles you've worked for us, Barbara, and we appreciate all you've done. The lovely photos you see in this book come to us courtesy of Elyse Rieder and Julie Tesser, our photo researchers. Thanks, too, to Patricia Marx and Ted Szczepanski for their assistance with photos.

Thanks to Steve Rigolosi, director of market development, and Scott Guile, marketing manager, for their energetic and creative work in marketing. Thanks to Tom Kling, national economics consultant, for his critical role in helping to seed business. And thank you, Bruce Kaplan, for all of your behind-the-scenes work supporting sales and marketing efforts. Thank you, Barbara Monteiro of Monteiro and Company as well as John Murphy and Dori Weintraub of St. Martin's Press, for your help with publicity.

And most of all, special thanks to Sharon Balbos, executive development editor on *Economics,* who must have been as stressed out as we were—but kept her cool throughout many years of tough slogging. We hope that this book lives up to the level of dedication and professionalism that she put into this project.

Paul Krugman            Robin Wells

I wish to thank Paul Krugman and Robin Wells for writing such a dynamic textbook. I started my project with a collection of gems and so if my result shines, it is to their credit.

Alan McClare and Craig Bleyer first invited me to join this project. I hope my work has lived up to their expectations. Charlie Van Wagner was terrific to work with, always full of energy and ideas and encouragement. Paul Shensa gets credit for bringing me into the publishing world, over two decades ago when Brad Schiller was looking for reviewers of his principles textbook and I was a graduate student. To have Paul join this project was a wonderful way of going full circle. Marie McHale's aid in almost every regard has been invaluable. Tracey Kuehn, Barbara Seixas, and Mike Ederer expertly oversaw production, forgave my delays when my mother took ill, and crafted solutions so that the page proofs still came in on time.

My partner, Esther Hargis, and our 8½-year-old son, Jimmy, are my world. Thank you for your love, support, and celebrations. We're going to Disneyland!

Martha L. Olney

# CONTENTS

**Preface** . . . . . . . . . . . . . . . . . . . . . . . . . . . . . . .IX

## Part 1  What Is Economics?

**Introduction  The Ordinary Business of Life** ..1
*Any Given Sunday  1*
**The Invisible Hand  2**
**My Benefit, Your Cost  3**
**Good Times, Bad Times  4**
**Onward and Upward  4**
**An Engine for Discovery  4**

**Chapter...1 • First Principles** . . . . . . . . . . . . . . . .5
*Common Ground  5*
**Individual Choice: The Core of Economics  6**
Resources are scarce  6
Opportunity cost: The real cost of something is what you must give up to get it  7
For Inquiring Minds: *Got a Penny?  8*
"How much?" is a decision at the margin  8
People usually exploit opportunities to make themselves better off  9
For Inquiring Minds: *Pay for Grades?  10*
Individual choice: Summing it up  10
Economics in Action: *A Woman's Work  10*
**Interaction: How Economies Work  11**
There are gains from trade  12
Markets move toward equilibrium  13
For Inquiring Minds: *Choosing Sides  13*
Resources should be used as efficiently as possible to achieve society's goals  14
Markets usually lead to efficiency  15
When markets don't achieve efficiency, government intervention can improve society's welfare  16
Economics in Action: *Restoring Equilibrium on the Freeways  16*
**A Look Ahead  17**

**Chapter...2 • Economic Models: Trade-offs and Trade** . . . . . . . . . . . . . . . . . . . . . . . . . . .20
*Tunnel Vision  20*
**Models in Economics: Some Important Examples  21**
For Inquiring Minds: *Models for Money  21*
Trade-offs: The production possibility frontier  22
Comparative advantage and gains from trade  25
Work It Out: *Gains from Trade  28*
Pitfalls: *Misunderstanding Comparative Advantage  29*

Comparative advantage and international trade  29
Transactions: The circular-flow diagram  30
Economics in Action: *Rich Nation, Poor Nation  33*
**Using Models  34**
Positive versus normative economics  34
When and why economists disagree  35
For Inquiring Minds: *When Economists Agree  36*
Economics in Action: *Economists in Government  36*
**A Look Ahead  37**

**Chapter 2 Appendix:  Graphs in Economics** . . . .41
**Getting the Picture  41**
**Graphs, Variables, and Economic Models  41**
**How Graphs Work  41**
Two-variable graphs  41
Pitfalls: *Why Y Is Not Always Y  42*
Curves on a graph  43
**A Key Concept: The Slope of a Curve  44**
The slope of a linear curve  44
Horizontal and vertical curves and their slopes  45
The slope of a nonlinear curve  46
Calculating the slope along a nonlinear curve  46
Maximum and minimum points  48
**Presenting Numerical Information  48**
Types of numerical graphs  49
Problems in interpreting numerical graphs  51

## Part 2  Supply and Demand

**Chapter...3 • Supply and Demand** . . . . . . . . . . .56
*Gretzky's Last Game  56*
**Supply and Demand: A Model of a Competitive Market  57**
**The Demand Curve  57**
The demand schedule and the demand curve  58
Shifts of the demand curve  59
Understanding shifts of the demand curve  60
Economics in Action: *Beating the Traffic  62*
**The Supply Curve  63**
The supply schedule and the supply curve  63
Shifts of the supply curve  64
Understanding shifts of the supply curve  66
Economics in Action: *Down (and Up) on the Farm  67*
**Supply, Demand, and Equilibrium  68**
Pitfalls: *Bought and Sold?  68*
Finding the equilibrium price and quantity  68

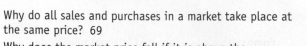

Why do all sales and purchases in a market take place at the same price? 69

Why does the market price fall if it is above the equilibrium price? 70

Why does the market price rise if it is below the equilibrium price? 70

Using equilibrium to describe markets 71

**Economics in Action:** *A Fish Story* 71

**Changes in Supply and Demand 72**

What happens when the demand curve shifts 72

What happens when the supply curve shifts 73

**Pitfalls:** *Which Curve Is It, Anyway?* 74

Simultaneous shifts in supply and demand 74

**For Inquiring Minds:** *Supply, Demand, and Controlled Substances* 76

**Economics in Action:** *Plain Vanilla Gets Fancy* 76

**Work It Out:** *Supply and Demand* 77

**Competitive Markets—and Others 78**

**A Look Ahead 79**

▶**Chapter...4 • The Market Strikes Back .......83**

*Big City, Not-So-Bright Ideas 83*

**Why Governments Control Prices 84**

**Price Ceilings 84**

Modeling a price ceiling 85

Why a price ceiling causes inefficiency 86

**For Inquiring Minds:** *The Rent Control Aristocracy* 88

So why are there price ceilings? 88

**Work It Out:** *Showing a Price Ceiling* 89

**Economics in Action:** *Oil Shortages in the 1970s* 90

**Price Floors 91**

**For Inquiring Minds:** *Price Floors and Butter Cookies* 92

Why a price floor causes inefficiency 93

So why are there price floors? 94

**Economics in Action:** *"Black Labor" in Southern Europe* 94

**Controlling Quantities 96**

The anatomy of quantity controls 96

The costs of quantity controls 99

**Economics in Action:** *The Clams of New Jersey* 100

**A Surprise Parallel: Taxes 100**

Why is a tax like a quota? 101

Who pays an excise tax? 102

The revenue from an excise tax 103

**Economics in Action:** *Who Pays the FICA?* 104

**A Look Ahead 105**

▶**Chapter...5 • Elasticity .......................109**

*Drive We Must 109*

**Defining and Measuring Elasticity 110**

The price elasticity of demand 110

Using the midpoint method to calculate elasticities 111

**Economics in Action:** *Estimating Elasticities* 113

**Interpreting the Price Elasticity of Demand 113**

How elastic is elastic? 114

What factors determine the price elasticity of demand? 116

Elasticity and total revenue 116

**Work It Out:** *Price Elasticity of Demand* 119

**Economics in Action:** *America's a Nice Place to Live, but We Can't Afford to Visit* 119

**Other Demand Elasticities 120**

The cross-price elasticity of demand 120

The income elasticity of demand 121

**For Inquiring Minds:** *Where Have All the Farmers Gone?* 121

**Economics in Action:** *Spending It* 122

**The Price Elasticity of Supply 123**

Measuring the price elasticity of supply 123

What factors determine the price elasticity of supply? 124

**Economics in Action:** *European Farm Surpluses* 125

**An Elasticity Menagerie 126**

**Using Elasticity: The Incidence of an Excise Tax 127**

When an excise tax is paid mainly by consumers 127

When an excise tax is paid mainly by producers 128

Putting it all together 129

**Economics in Action:** *So Who Does Pay the FICA?* 129

**A Look Ahead 130**

▶**Chapter...6 • Consumer and Producer Surplus .................................135**

*Making Gains by the Book 135*

**Consumer Surplus and the Demand Curve 136**

Willingness to pay and the demand curve 136

Willingness to pay and consumer surplus 137

How changing prices affect consumer surplus 139

**For Inquiring Minds:** *I Want a New Drug . . .* 141

**Economics in Action:** *When Money Isn't Enough* 142

**Producer Surplus and the Supply Curve 142**

Cost and producer surplus 142

Changes in producer surplus 145

**Economics in Action:** *Gaining from Disaster* 146

**Consumer Surplus, Producer Surplus, and the Gains from Trade 147**

The gains from trade 147

The efficiency of markets: A preliminary view 148

**Economics in Action:** *eBay and Efficiency* 151

**Applying Consumer and Producer Surplus: The Efficiency Costs of a Tax 151**

Deadweight loss and elasticities 153

**Work It Out:** *Calculating Deadweight Loss* 155
**Economics in Action:** *Missing the Boats* 156
**A Look Ahead** 156

# Part 3: The Producer

**▶Chapter...7 • Behind the Supply Curve: Inputs and Costs** .......................160

*The Farmer's Margin 160*
**The Production Function 161**
    Inputs and output 161
Pitfalls: *What's a Unit?* 164
**For Inquiring Minds:** *Was Malthus Right?* 165
    From the production function to cost curves 165
**Economics in Action:** *The Mythical Man-Month* 167
**Two Key Concepts: Marginal Cost and Average Cost 168**
    Marginal cost 169
Pitfalls: *Increasing Total Cost Versus Increasing Marginal Cost* 170
    Average cost 171
    Minimum average total cost 174
    Does the marginal cost curve always slope upward? 175
**Economics in Action:** *The Cost of Power* 176
**Short-Run Versus Long-Run Costs 177**
    Economies and diseconomies of scale 180
    Summing up costs: the short and long of it 180
**Economics in Action:** *There's No Business Like Snow Business* 181
**A Look Ahead** 182

**▶Chapter...8 • Perfect Competition and the Supply Curve** .........................186

*Doing What Comes Naturally 186*
**Perfect Competition 187**
    Defining perfect competition 187
    Two necessary conditions for perfect competition 187
**For Inquiring Minds:** *What's a Standardized Product?* 188
    Free entry and exit 189
**Economics in Action:** *The Pain of Competition* 189
**Production and Profits 190**
    Using marginal analysis to choose the profit-maximizing quantity of output 191
Pitfalls: *Muddled at the Margin* 191
Pitfalls: *What if Marginal Revenue and Marginal Cost Aren't Exactly Equal?* 192
    Accounting profit versus economic profit 193
    When is production profitable? 194
    The short-run production decision 197
Pitfalls: *Economic Profit, Again* 200

Changing fixed cost 200
    Summing up: The competitive firm's profitability and production conditions 201
**Economics in Action:** *California Screaming* 201
Work It Out: *Profit-Maximizing Quantity of Output* 202
**The Industry Supply Curve 202**
    The short-run industry supply curve 203
    The long-run industry supply curve 204
    The cost of production and efficiency in long-run equilibrium 207
**Economics in Action:** *A Crushing Reversal* 208
**A Look Ahead** 208

# Part 4 Markets and Efficiency

**▶Chapter...9 • Factor Markets and the Distribution of Income** ...................213

*The Value of a Degree 213*
**The Economy's Factors of Production 214**
    The factors of production 214
Pitfalls: *What Is a Factor, Anyway?* 214
    Why factor prices matter: The allocation of resources 214
    Factor incomes and the distribution of income 214
**For Inquiring Minds:** *The Factor Distribution of Income and Social Change in the Industrial Revolution* 215
**Economics in Action:** *The Factor Distribution of Income in the United States* 215
**Marginal Productivity and Factor Demand 216**
    Value of the marginal product 216
    Value of the marginal product and factor demand 218
    Shifts of the factor demand curve 220
    The marginal productivity theory of income distribution 222
Pitfalls: *Getting Marginal Productivity Right* 224
**Economics in Action:** *Star Power* 224
**Is the Marginal Productivity Theory of Income Distribution Really True? 225**
    Wage disparities in practice 225
    Marginal productivity and wage inequality 226
    Market power 227
    Efficiency wages 228
    Discrimination 228
    So does marginal productivity theory work? 229
**Economics in Action:** *The Economics of Apartheid* 229
**The Supply of Labor 230**
    Work versus leisure 230
    Wages and labor supply 231
**For Inquiring Minds:** *Why You Can't Find a Cab When It's Raining* 233
    Shifts of the labor supply curve 233

**Economics in Action:** *The Decline of the Summer Job* 234
**A Look Ahead** 234

▶ **Chapter...10 • Efficiency, Inefficiency, and Equity** ...............................238
*After the Fall 238*
**Efficiency 239**
  Efficiency, revisited 239
**For Inquiring Minds:** *Defining Economic Efficiency* 240
  Efficiency in consumption 240
  Efficiency in production 241
  Efficiency in output levels 242
**Economics in Action:** *A Great Leap—Backward* 246
**Efficiency and Equity 247**
  What's fair 247
**For Inquiring Minds:** *Theories of Justice* 247
  The utility possibility frontier 248
**Economics in Action:** *Death and Taxes* 250
**Market Failure: The Case of Externalities 250**
  Externalities 251
  Private versus social costs 251
**For Inquiring Minds:** *Talking and Driving* 253
  Environmental policy 253
  Private solutions to externalities 254
  Private versus social benefits 255
**Work It Out:** *Externality and Optimal Pigouvian Tax* 256
**Economics in Action:** *Spillovers in Silicon Valley* 257
**Market Failure: The Case of Public Goods 258**
  Private goods and public goods 259
  Providing public goods 259
  How much of a public good should be provided? 260
**Pitfalls:** *Marginal Cost of What, Exactly?* 261
**For Inquiring Minds:** *Voting as a Public Good* 263
  Cost-benefit analysis 263
**Economics in Action:** *Old Man River* 264
**A Look Ahead** 265

**Part 5 Market Structure: Beyond Perfect Competition**

▶ **Chapter...11 • Monopoly** ................271
*Everybody Must Get Stones 271*
**Types of Market Structure 272**
**The Meaning of Monopoly 273**
  Monopoly: Our first departure from perfect competition 273
  What monopolists do 273

Why do monopolies exist? 274
**Economics in Action:** *Are Diamond Monopolies Forever?* 276
**How a Monopolist Maximizes Profit 277**
  The monopolist's demand and marginal revenue curves 277
  The monopolist's profit-maximizing output and price 281
**Pitfalls:** *Finding the Monopoly Price* 282
  Monopoly versus perfect competition 282
**Pitfalls:** *Is There a Monopoly Supply Curve?* 282
**For Inquiring Minds:** *Monopoly Behavior and the Price Elasticity of Demand* 283
  Monopoly: The general picture 283
**Work It Out:** *Profit Maximization for a Monopolist* 284
**Economics in Action:** *California Power Play?* 284
**Monopoly and Public Policy 285**
  Welfare effects of monopoly 286
  Preventing monopoly 287
  Dealing with natural monopoly 287
**Economics in Action:** *Cable Dilemmas* 290
**Price Discrimination 291**
  The logic of price discrimination 291
  Price discrimination and elasticity 292
  Perfect price discrimination 293
**Economics in Action:** *Sales, Factory Outlets, and Ghost Cities* 295
**A Look Ahead** 297

▶ **Chapter...12 • Oligopoly, Monopolistic Competition, and Product Differentiation ..301**
*Caught in the Act 301*
**Oligopoly 302**
  Understanding oligopoly 303
  The prisoners' dilemma 303
**Pitfalls:** *Playing Fair in the Prisoners' Dilemma* 305
  Overcoming the prisoners' dilemma: Repeated interaction and tacit collusion 306
**For Inquiring Minds:** *Prisoners of the Arms Race* 307
**Economics in Action:** *The Rise and Fall and Rise of OPEC* 308
**Oligopoly in Practice 310**
  The legal framework 310
  Tacit collusion and price wars 311
**For Inquiring Minds:** *The Art of Conspiracy* 312
**Economics in Action:** *Air Wars* 313
**Monopolistic Competition 313**
  Monopolistic competition in the short run 315
  Monopolistic competition in the long run 316
**For Inquiring Minds:** *Hits and Flops* **318**

Work It Out: *Monopolistic Competition* 319
**Economics in Action:** *Bagels from Boom to Bust* 319
**Product Differentiation 320**
For Inquiring Minds: *Bucks for Starbucks* 321
   Controversies about product differentiation 322
**Economics in Action:** *Any Color, So Long as It's Black* 325
**A Look Ahead 325**

# Part 6 Extending Market Boundaries

▶ **Chapter...13 • International Trade** .........**330**

*A Rose by Any Other Nation* 330
**Comparative Advantage and International Trade 331**
Pitfalls: *The Pauper Labor Fallacy* 332
   Sources of comparative advantage 332
For Inquiring Minds: *Does Trade Hurt Poor Countries?* 333
For Inquiring Minds: *Increasing Returns and International Trade* 334
**Economics in Action:** *The Comparative Advantage of the United States* 334
**Supply, Demand, and International Trade 335**
   The effects of imports 335
   The effects of exports 338
   International trade and factor markets 339
Work It Out: *Imports and Total Surplus* 340
**Economics in Action:** *Trade, Wages, and Land Prices in the Nineteenth Century* 341
**The Effects of Trade Protection 341**
   The effects of a tariff 342
   The effects of an import quota 344
**Economics in Action:** *Trade Protection in the United States* 344
**The Political Economy of Trade Protection 345**
   Arguments for trade protection 345
For Inquiring Minds: *Bittersweet* 346
   The politics of trade protection 346
   International trade agreements and the World Trade Organization 346
**Economics in Action:** *Declining Tariffs* 347
**A Look Ahead 348**

# Part 7 Introduction to Macroeconomics

▶ **Chapter...14 • Macroeconomics: The Big Picture** ....................**352**

*Disappointed Graduates* 352
**Microeconomics Versus Macroeconomics 353**
   Macroeconomics: The whole is greater than the sum of its parts 354
   Macroeconomic policy 355
   Economic aggregates 355
**Economics in Action:** *The Great Depression* 356
**The Business Cycle 357**
For Inquiring Minds: *Defining Recessions and Expansions* 358
**Employment and Unemployment 358**
   Aggregate output 359
   Taming the business cycle 361
**Economics in Action:** *Has the Business Cycle Been Tamed?* 361
**Inflation and Deflation 362**
**Economics in Action:** *A Fast (Food) Measure of Inflation* 364
**A Look Ahead 364**

▶ **Chapter...15 • Tracking the Macroeconomy** ...............................**367**

*After the Revolution* 367
**The National Accounts 368**
   The circular-flow diagram, revisited and expanded 368
   Gross domestic product 371
   Calculating GDP 372
For Inquiring Minds: *Our Imputed Lives* 373
Pitfalls: GDP: *What's In and What's Out* 374
For Inquiring Minds: *Gross What?* 375
   What GDP tells us 376
**Economics in Action:** *Creating the National Accounts* 377
**Real GDP and Aggregate Output 378**
   Calculating real GDP 378
   A technical detail: "Chained" dollars 379
   What real GDP doesn't measure 379
**Economics in Action:** *Good Decades, Bad Decades* 380
**The Unemployment Rate 381**
   Understanding the unemployment rate 381
   Growth and unemployment 383
**Economics in Action:** *Jobless Recoveries* 384
**Price Indexes and the Aggregate Price Level 384**
   Market baskets and price indexes 385
   The consumer price index 386
   Other price measures 387
For Inquiring Minds: *Is the CPI Biased?* 387
**Economics in Action:** *Indexing to the CPI* 388
**A Look Ahead 389**

## Part 8 Short-Run Economic Fluctuations

▶ **Chapter...16 • Aggregate Supply and Aggregate Demand** . . . . . . . . . . . . . . . . . . . . .**394**

*Shocks to the System 394*

**Aggregate Supply 395**
   The short-run aggregate supply curve 395

**For Inquiring Minds:** *What's Truly Flexible, What's Truly Sticky 397*
   Shifts of the short-run aggregate supply curve 398
   The long-run aggregate supply curve 400
   From the short run to the long run 402

**Economics in Action:** *Prices and Output in the Great Depression 403*

**Aggregate Demand 404**
   Why is the aggregate demand curve downward-sloping? 405

**Pitfalls:** *Investment Versus Investment Spending 406*
   Shifts of the aggregate demand curve 406

**Pitfalls:** *Changes in Wealth: A Movement Along Versus a Shift of the Aggregate Demand Curve 407*
   Government policies and aggregate demand 407

**Economics in Action:** *Moving Along the Aggregate Demand Curve, 1979–1980 408*

**The Multiplier 409**

**Work It Out:** *The Multiplier 412*

**The AS–AD Model 413**
   Short-run macroeconomic equilibrium 413
   Shifts of the SRAS curve 414
   Shifts of aggregate demand: Short-run effects 415
   Long-run macroeconomic equilibrium 416

**Economics in Action:** *Supply Shocks Versus Demand Shocks in Practice 419*

**Macroeconomic Policy 420**

**For Inquiring Minds:** *Keynes and the Long Run 420*
   Policy in the face of demand shocks 421
   Responding to supply shocks 421

**Economics in Action:** *The End of the Great Depression 422*

**A Look Ahead 422**

▶ **Chapter...17 • Fiscal Policy** . . . . . . . . . . . . . . . .**427**

*A Bridge to Prosperity? 427*

**Fiscal Policy: The Basics 428**
   Taxes, purchases of goods and services, government transfers, and borrowing 428
   The government budget and total spending 429

**For Inquiring Minds:** *Investment Tax Credits 430*
   Expansionary and contractionary fiscal policy 430

A cautionary note: Lags in fiscal policy 432

**Economics in Action:** *Expansionary Fiscal Policy in Japan 432*

**Fiscal Policy and the Multiplier 433**
   Multiplier effects of an increase in government purchases of goods and services 433
   Multiplier effects of changes in government transfers and taxes 434

**Work It Out:** *Fiscal Policy Multiplier 435*
   How taxes affect the multiplier 435

**Economics in Action:** *How Much Bang for the Buck? 437*

**The Budget Balance 438**
   The budget balance as a measure of fiscal policy 438
   The business cycle and the cyclically adjusted budget balance 439
   Should the budget be balanced? 441

**Economics in Action:** *Stability Pact—or Stupidity Pact? 441*

**Long-Run Implications of Fiscal Policy 442**
   Deficits, surpluses, and debt 442

**Pitfalls:** *Deficits Versus Debt 443*
   Problems posed by rising government debt 443
   Deficits and debt in practice 444

**For Inquiring Minds:** *What Happened to the Debt from World War II? 445*
   Implicit liabilities 446

**Economics in Action:** *Argentina's Creditors Take a Haircut 448*

**A Look Ahead 449**

▶ **Chapter...18 • Money, the Federal Reserve System, and Monetary Policy** . . . . . . . . . . . . . . .**453**

*Eight Times a Year 453*

**The Meaning of Money 454**
   What is money? 454

**Pitfalls:** *Plastic and the Money Supply 454*
   Roles of money 455
   Types of money 455
   Measuring the money supply 456

**For Inquiring Minds:** *What's with All the Currency? 457*

**Economics in Action:** *The History of the Dollar 457*

**The Monetary Role of Banks 458**
   What banks do 458
   The problem of bank runs 459
   Bank regulation 460

**For Inquiring Minds:** *Is Banking a Con? 460*
   How banks create money 461

**Economics in Action:** *It's a Wonderful Banking System 461*

**The Federal Reserve system 462**
   The Fed: America's central bank 462
   What the Fed does: Reserve requirements and the discount rate 464
   Open-market operations 464

Economics in Action: *Building Europe's Fed* 465
**Monetary Policy and Aggregate Demand 466**
 Expansionary and contractionary monetary policy 466
 Monetary policy and the multiplier 468
Work It Out: *Monetary Policy* 468
Economics in Action: *The Fed and the Output Gap, 1985–2004* 469

**Solutions to "Check Your Understanding" Questions S-1**
**Glossary G-1**
**Index I-1**

# Credits

## Photo Credits

Grateful acknowledgment is given for permission to reprint the following cover photos:

**Front Cover**

**Row 1 (left to right)** Business man on cell phone in front of Petronas Towers, Kuala Lumpur, Malaysia, image100 Ltd.; Making cappuccino, Photodisc/Getty Images; Close-up of Euro/dollar, Corbis; **Row 2 (left to right)** Hip kids sharing headphones, image100 Ltd.; Empty shopping cart, Photodisc/Getty Images; Oil-pumping rig, EyeWire; New York stock exchange interior, Image Source; **Row 3 (left to right)** Gas pump, Trish Marx; Tractor hauling hay bales, Stockbyte; Nuclear plant cooling tower with steam, EyeWire; **Row 4 (left to right)** Depression-era man out of work, The Image Bank/Getty Images; Portrait of a young woman, Photodisc/Getty Images; Figures from Tokyo stock exchange, Media Bakery; Couple crossing street with sales signs in background, Image Source; **Row 5 (left to right)** Bar-b-q Sign, Photodisc/Getty Images; Buying shoes, SW Productions/Photodisc/Getty Images; Shoe repair window, Photodisc/Getty Images; **Row 6 (left to right)** St. Louis Arch at sunset, Photodisc/Getty Images; Man making pizza at a pizza stand, Photodisc/Getty Images; Plumber working, Photodisc; Barge with freight, Image State; **Row 7 (left to right)** Food stand, Photodisc/Getty Images; Fresh fish, Photodisc; Wood frame building under construction, EyeWire; **Row 8 (left to right)** Dark meeting with laptop and videoconference, Photodisc/Getty Images; Woman holding bicycle on assembly line, EyeWire; Chemical plant, EyeWire; International money, Lyndall Culbertson / Photodisc;

**Back Cover**

**Row 2:** Vancouver skyline, Photodisc; **Row 3:** Freight yard, Brand X Pictures; **Row 5:** Trishaw, Phnom Penh, Cambodia Photodisc/Getty Images; **Row 6 (left to right):** Meeting with laptop, Photodisc/Getty Images; Logging truck, EyeWire; **Row 7:** Bunches of asparagus, Photodisc/Getty Images;

Author photos of Paul Krugman and Robin Wells (p. vii):
Ted Szczepanski
Author photo of Martha L. Olney (p. vii): © Peg Skorpinski (p. vii)

## Text Credits

### Chapter 5

Source information for Table 5-1, page 113:

*Eggs, beef:* Kuo S. Huang and Biing-Hwan Lin, Estimation of Food Demand and Nutrient Elasticities from Household Survey Data, United States Department of Agriculture Economic Research Service Technical Bulletin, No. 1887 (Washington, DC: U.S. Department of Agriculture, 2000);

*Stationery, gasoline, airline travel, foreign travel:* H. S. Houthakker and Lester D. Taylor, *Consumer Demand in the United States, 1929-1970: Analyses and Projections* (Cambridge, MA: Harvard University Press, 1966);

*Housing, restaurant meals:* H. S. Houthakker and Lester D. Taylor, *Consumer Demand in the United States: Analyses and Projections,* 2nd ed. (Cambridge, MA: Harvard University Press, 1970).

### Chapter 9

Source article of "For Inquiring Minds" box on page 233:

C. Camerer et al., Labor Supply of New York City Cab Drivers: One Day at a Time. *Quarterly Journal of Economics, 112,* 407–471.

# >>Introduction: The Ordinary Business of Life

## ANY GIVEN SUNDAY

IT'S SUNDAY AFTERNOON IN THE SUMMER of 2003, and Route 1 in central New Jersey is a busy place. Thousands of people crowd the shopping malls that line the road for 20 miles, all the way from Trenton to New Brunswick. Most of the shoppers are cheerful—and why not? The stores in those malls offer an extraordinary range of choice; you can buy everything from sophisticated electronic equipment to fashionable clothes to organic carrots. There are probably 100,000 distinct items available

The scene along Route 1 that summer day was, of course, perfectly ordinary—very much like the scene along hundreds of other stretches of road, all across America, that same afternoon. But the discipline of economics is mainly concerned with ordinary things. As the great nineteenth-century economist Alfred Marshall put it, economics is "a study of mankind in the ordinary business of life."

What can economics say about this "ordinary business"? Quite a lot, it turns

Delivering the goods: the market economy in action

along that stretch of road. And most of these items are not luxury goods that only the rich can afford; they are products that millions of Americans can and do purchase every day.

out. What we'll see in this book is that even familiar scenes of economic life pose some very important questions—questions that economics can help answer. Among these questions are:

1

- How does our economic system work? That is, how does it manage to deliver the goods?

- When and why does our economic system go astray, leading people into counterproductive behavior?

- Why are there ups and downs in the economy? That is, why does the economy sometimes have a "bad year"?

- Finally, why is the long run mainly a story of ups rather than downs? That is, why has America, along with other advanced nations, become so much richer over time?

Let's take a look at these questions and offer a brief preview of what you will learn in this book.

## The Invisible Hand

That ordinary scene in central New Jersey would not have looked at all ordinary to an American from colonial times—say, one of the patriots who helped George Washington win the battle of Trenton in 1776. (At the time, Trenton was a small village with not a shopping mall in sight, and farms lined the unpaved road that would eventually become Route 1.)

Imagine that you could transport an American from the colonial period forward in time to our own era. (Isn't that the plot of a movie? Several, actually.) What would this time-traveler find amazing?

Surely the most amazing thing would be the sheer prosperity of modern America—the range of goods and services that ordinary families can afford. Looking at all that wealth, our transplanted colonial would wonder, "How can I get some of that?" Or perhaps he would ask himself, "How can my society get some of that?"

The answer is that to get this kind of prosperity, you need a well-functioning system for coordinating productive activities—the activities that create the goods and services people want and get them to the people who want them. That kind of system is what we mean when we talk about the **economy**. And **economics** is the study of economies, at the level both of individuals and of society as a whole.

An economy succeeds to the extent that it, literally, delivers the goods. A time-traveler from the eighteenth century—or even from 1950—would be amazed at how many goods and services the modern American economy delivers and at how many people can afford them. Compared with any past economy and with all but a few other countries today, America has an incredibly high standard of living.

So our economy must be doing something right, and the time-traveler might want to compliment the person in charge. But guess what? There isn't anyone in charge. The United States has a **market economy**, in which production and consumption are the result of decentralized decisions by many firms and individuals. There is no central authority telling people what to produce or where to ship it. Each individual producer makes what he or she thinks will be most profitable; each consumer buys what he or she chooses.

The alternative to a market economy is a *command economy*, in which there *is* a central authority making decisions about production and consumption. Command economies have been tried, most notably in the Soviet Union between 1917 and 1991. But they didn't work very well. Producers in the Soviet Union routinely found themselves unable to produce because they did not have crucial raw materials, or they succeeded in producing but then found that nobody wanted their products. Consumers were often unable to find necessary items—command economies are famous for long lines at shops.

Market economies, however, are able to coordinate even highly complex activities and to reliably provide consumers with the goods and services they want. Indeed, people quite casually trust their lives to the market system: residents of any major city

An **economy** is a system for coordinating society's productive activities.

**Economics** is the study of economies, at the level both of individuals and of society as a whole.

A **market economy** is an economy in which decisions about production and consumption are made by individual producers and consumers.

would starve in days if the unplanned yet somehow orderly actions of thousands of businesses did not deliver a steady supply of food. Surprisingly, the unplanned "chaos" of a market economy turns out to be far more orderly than the "planning" of a command economy.

In 1776, in a famous passage in his book *The Wealth of Nations*, the pioneering Scottish economist Adam Smith wrote about how individuals, in pursuing their own interests, often end up serving the interests of society as a whole. Of a businessman whose pursuit of profit makes the nation wealthier, Smith wrote: "[H]e intends only his own gain, and he is in this, as in many other cases, led by an invisible hand to promote an end which was no part of his intention." Ever since, economists have used the term **invisible hand** to refer to the way a market economy manages to harness the power of self-interest for the good of society.

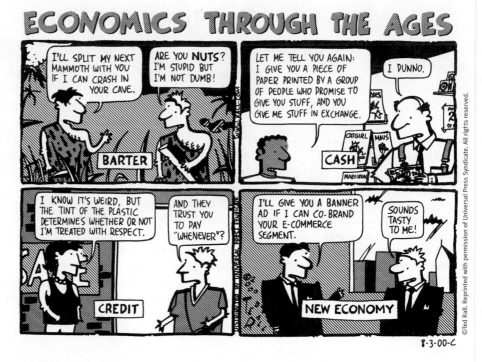

The study of how individuals make decisions and how these decisions interact is called **microeconomics**. One of the key themes in microeconomics is the validity of Adam Smith's insight: Individuals pursuing their own interests often do promote the interests of society as a whole.

So part of the answer to our time-traveler's question—"How can my society achieve the kind of prosperity you take for granted?"—is that his society should learn to appreciate the virtues of a market economy and the power of the invisible hand.

But the invisible hand isn't always our friend. It's also important to understand when and why the individual pursuit of self-interest can lead to counterproductive behavior.

> The **invisible hand** refers to the way in which the individual pursuit of self-interest can lead to good results for society as a whole.
>
> **Microeconomics** is the branch of economics that studies how people make decisions and how these decisions interact.

## My Benefit, Your Cost

One thing that our time-traveler would not admire about modern Route 1 is the traffic. In fact, although most things have gotten better in America over time, traffic congestion has gotten a lot worse.

When traffic is congested, each driver is imposing a cost on all the other drivers on the road—he is literally getting in their way (and they are getting in his way). This cost can be substantial: in major metropolitan areas, each time someone drives to work, as opposed to taking public transportation or working at home, he can easily impose $15 or more in hidden costs on other drivers. Yet when deciding whether or not to drive, commuters have no incentive to take the costs they impose on others into account.

Traffic congestion is a familiar example of a much broader problem: sometimes the individual pursuit of one's own interest, instead of promoting the interests of society as a whole, can actually make society worse off. When this happens, it is known as **market failure**. Other important examples of market failure involve air and water pollution as well as the overexploitation of natural resources such as fish and forests.

The good news, as you will learn as you use this book to study microeconomics, is that economic analysis can be used to diagnose cases of market failure. And often, economic analysis can also be used to devise solutions for the problem.

> When the individual pursuit of self-interest leads to bad results for society as a whole, there is **market failure**.

## Good Times, Bad Times

Route 1 was bustling on that summer day in 2003—but it wasn't bustling quite as much as merchants would have liked, because in mid-2003 the U.S. economy wasn't doing all that well. The main problem was jobs: in early 2001, businesses began laying off workers in large numbers, and as of June 2003, employment had not yet started to recover.

Such troubled periods are a regular feature of modern economies. The fact is that the economy does not always run smoothly: it experiences *fluctuations,* a series of ups and downs. By middle age, a typical American will have experienced three or four downs, known as **recessions**. (The U.S. economy experienced serious recessions beginning in 1973, 1980, 1981, 1990, and 2001.) During a severe recession, millions of workers may be laid off.

Like market failure, recessions are a fact of life; but also like market failure, they are a problem to which economic analysis offers some solutions. Recessions are one of the main concerns of the branch of economics known as **macroeconomics**, which is concerned with the overall ups and downs of the economy. In macroeconomics, you will learn how economists explain recessions and how government policies can be used to minimize the damage from economic fluctuations.

Despite the occasional recession, however, over the long run the story of the U.S. economy contains many more ups than downs. And that long-run ascent is the subject of our final question.

A **recession** is a downturn in the economy.

**Macroeconomics** is the branch of economics that is concerned with overall ups and downs in the economy.

## Onward and Upward

At the beginning of the twentieth century, most Americans lived under conditions that we would now think of as extreme poverty. Only 10 percent of homes had flush toilets, only 8 percent had central heating, only 2 percent had electricity, and almost nobody had a car, let alone a washing machine or air conditioning.

Such comparisons are a stark reminder of how much our lives have been changed by **economic growth**, the growing ability of the economy to produce goods and services.

Why does the economy grow over time? And why does economic growth occur faster in some times and places than in others? These are key questions for economics because economic growth is a good thing, as those shoppers on Route 1 can attest, and most of us want more of it.

**Economic growth** is the growing ability of the economy to produce goods and services.

## An Engine for Discovery

We hope we have convinced you that the "ordinary business of life" is really quite extraordinary, if you stop to think about it, and that it can lead us to ask some very interesting and important questions.

In this book, we will describe the answers economists have given to these questions. But this book, like economics as a whole, isn't a list of answers: it's an introduction to a discipline, a way to address questions like those we have just asked. Or as Alfred Marshall, who described economics as a study of the "ordinary business of life," put it: "Economics . . . is not a body of concrete truth, but an engine for the discovery of concrete truth."

So let's turn the key in the ignition.

## KEY TERMS

Economy, p. 2
Economics, p. 2
Market economy, p. 2

Invisible hand, p. 3
Microeconomics, p. 3
Market failure, p. 3

Recession, p. 4
Macroeconomics, p. 4
Economic growth, p. 4

# >>First Principles

## COMMON GROUND

THE ANNUAL MEETING OF THE AMERICAN Economic Association draws thousands of economists, young and old, famous and obscure. There are booksellers, business meetings, and quite a few job interviews. But mainly the economists gather to talk and listen. During the busiest times, 60 or more presentations may be taking place simultaneously, on questions that range from the future of the stock market to who does the cooking in two-earner families.

What do these people have in common? An expert on the stock market probably knows very little about the economics of housework, and vice versa. Yet an economist who wanders into the wrong seminar and ends up listening to presentations on some unfamiliar topic is nonetheless likely to hear much that is familiar. The reason is that all economic analysis is based on a set of common principles that apply to many different issues.

Some of these principles involve *individual choice*—for economics is, first of all, about the choices that individuals make. Do you choose to work over the summer or take a backpacking trip? Do you buy a new CD or go to a movie? These decisions involve *making a choice* among a limited number of alternatives—limited because no one can have everything that he or she wants. Every question in economics at its most basic level involves individuals making choices.

But to understand how an economy works, you need to understand more than how individuals make choices. None of us are Robinson Crusoe, alone on an island—we must make decisions in an environment that is shaped by the decisions of others. Indeed, in a modern economy even the simplest decisions you

One must choose.

Richard Hamilton Smith/Corbis

make—say, what to have for breakfast—are shaped by the decisions of thousands of other people, from the banana grower in Costa Rica who decided to grow the fruit you eat to the farmer in Iowa who provided the corn in your cornflakes. And because each of us in a market economy depends on

> ### What you will learn in this chapter:
>
> ➤ A set of principles for understanding the economics of how individuals make choices
>
> ➤ A set of principles for understanding how individual choices interact

so many others—and they, in turn, depend on us—our choices interact. So although all economics at a basic level is about individual choice, in order to understand how market economies behave we must also understand economy-wide *interaction*—how my choices affect your choices, and vice versa.

In this chapter, we will look at nine basic principles of economics—four principles involving individual choice and five involving the way individual choices interact.

## Individual Choice: The Core of Economics

**Individual choice** is the decision by an individual of what to do, which necessarily involves a decision of what *not* to do.

Every economic issue involves, at its most basic level, **individual choice**—decisions by an individual about what to do and what *not* to do. In fact, you might say that it isn't economics if it isn't about choice.

Step into a big store like a Wal-Mart or Home Depot. There are thousands of different products available, and it is extremely unlikely that you—or anyone else—could afford to buy everything you might want to have. And anyway, there's only so much space in your dorm room or apartment. So will you buy another bookcase or a mini-refrigerator? Given limitations on your budget and your living space, you must choose which products to buy and which to leave on the shelf.

The fact that those products are on the shelf in the first place involves choice—the store manager chose to put them there, and the manufacturers of the products chose to produce them. All economic activities involve individual choice.

Four economic principles underlie the economics of individual choice, as shown in Table 1-1. We'll now examine each of these principles in more detail.

### TABLE 1-1

**Principles That Underlie the Economics of Individual Choice**

1. Resources are scarce.

2. The real cost of something is what you must give up to get it.

3. "How much?" is a decision at the margin.

4. People usually exploit opportunities to make themselves better off.

### Resources Are Scarce

You can't always get what you want. Everyone would like to have a beautiful house in a great location (and help with the housecleaning), two or three luxury cars, and frequent vacations in fancy hotels. But even in a rich country like the United States, not many families can afford all that. So they must make choices—whether to go to Disney World this year or buy a better car, whether to make do with a small backyard or accept a longer commute in order to live where land is cheaper.

Limited income isn't the only thing that keeps people from having everything they want. Time is also in limited supply: there are only 24 hours in a day. And because the time we have is limited, choosing to spend time on one activity also means choosing not to spend time on a different activity—spending time studying for an exam means forgoing a night at the movies. Indeed, many people are so limited by the number of hours in the day that they are willing to trade money for time. For example, convenience stores normally charge higher prices than a regular supermarket. But they fulfill a valuable role by catering to time-pressured customers who would rather pay more than travel farther to the supermarket.

A **resource** is anything that can be used to produce something else.

Resources are **scarce**—the quantity available isn't large enough to satisfy all productive uses.

Why do individuals have to make choices? The ultimate reason is that *resources are scarce*. A **resource** is anything that can be used to produce something else. Lists of the economy's resources usually begin with land, labor (the available time of workers), capital (machinery, buildings, and other man-made productive assets), and human capital (the educational achievements and skills of workers). A resource is **scarce** when the quantity of the resource available isn't large enough to satisfy all productive uses. There are many scarce resources. These include natural resources—resources that come from the physical environment, such as minerals, lumber, and petroleum. There is also a limited quantity of human resources—labor, skill, and intelligence. And in a growing world economy with a rapidly increasing human population, even clean air and water have become scarce resources.

Just as individuals must make choices, the scarcity of resources means that society as a whole must make choices. One way for a society to make choices is simply to allow them to emerge as the result of many individual choices, which is what usually happens in a market economy. For example, Americans as a group have only so many hours in a week: how many of those hours will they spend going to supermarkets to get lower prices, rather than saving time by shopping at convenience stores? The answer is the sum of individual decisions: each of the millions of individuals in the economy makes his or her own choice about where to shop, and the overall choice is simply the sum of those individual decisions.

But for various reasons, there are some decisions that a society decides are best not left to individual choice. For example, across America, areas that until recently were mainly farmland are now being rapidly built up. Local residents often feel that the community would be a more pleasant place to live if some of the land were left undeveloped. But no individual has an incentive to keep his or her land as open space, rather than selling it to a developer. So a trend has emerged in many communities across the United States of local governments purchasing undeveloped land and preserving it as open space. We'll see in later chapters why decisions about how to use scarce resources are often best left to individuals but sometimes should be made at a higher, community-wide, level.

## Opportunity Cost: The Real Cost of Something Is What You Must Give Up to Get It

It is the last term before you graduate, and your class schedule allows you to take only one elective. There are two, however, that you would really like to take: History of Jazz and Beginning Tennis.

Suppose you decide to take the History of Jazz course. What's the cost of that decision? It is the fact that you can't take Beginning Tennis. Economists call that kind of cost—what you must forgo in order to get something you want—the **opportunity cost** of that item. So the opportunity cost of the History of Jazz class is the enjoyment you would have derived from the Beginning Tennis class.

The concept of opportunity cost is crucial to understanding individual choice because, in the end, all costs are opportunity costs. Sometimes critics claim that economists are concerned only with costs and benefits that can be measured in dollars and cents. But that is not true. Much economic analysis involves cases like our elective course example, where it costs no extra tuition to take one elective course—that is, there is no direct monetary cost. Nonetheless, the elective you choose has an opportunity cost—the other desirable elective course that you must forgo because your limited time permits taking only one.

You might think that opportunity cost is an add-on—that is, something *additional* to the monetary cost of an item. Suppose that an elective class costs additional tuition of $750; now there is a monetary cost to taking History of Jazz. Is the opportunity cost of taking that course something separate from that monetary cost?

Well, consider two cases. First, suppose that taking Beginning Tennis also costs $750. In this case, you would have to spend that $750 no matter which class you take. So what you give up to take the History of Jazz class is still the Beginning Tennis class, period—you would have to spend that $750 either way. But suppose there isn't any fee for the tennis class. In that case, what you give up to take the jazz class is the tennis class *plus* whatever you would have bought with the $750.

Either way, the cost of taking your preferred class is what you must give up to get it. *All* costs are ultimately opportunity costs.

Sometimes the money you have to pay for something is a good indication of its opportunity cost. But many times it is not. One very important example of how poorly monetary cost can indicate opportunity cost is the cost of attending college.

The real cost of an item is its **opportunity cost**: what you must give up in order to get it.

At many cash registers there is a little basket full of pennies. People are encouraged to use the basket to round their purchases up or down: if it costs $5.02, you give the cashier $5 and take two pennies from the basket; if it costs $4.99, you pay $5 and the cashier throws in a penny. It makes everyone's life a bit easier. Of course, it would be easier still if we just abolished the penny, a step that some economists have urged.

But then why do we have pennies in the first place? If it's too small a sum to worry about, why calculate prices that exactly?

The answer is that a penny wasn't always such a negligible sum: the purchasing power of a penny has been greatly reduced by inflation. Forty years ago, a penny had more purchasing power than a nickel does today.

Why does this matter? Well, remember the saying: "A penny saved is a penny earned." But there are other ways to earn money, so you must decide whether saving a penny is a productive use of your time. Could you earn more by devoting that time to other uses?

Forty years ago, the average wage was about $2 an hour. A penny was equivalent

to 18 seconds' worth of work—it was worth saving a penny if doing so took less than 18 seconds. But wages have risen along with overall prices, so that the average worker is now paid more than $17 per hour. A penny is therefore equivalent to just over 2 seconds of work—and so it's not worth the opportunity cost of the time it takes to worry about a penny more or less.

In short, the rising opportunity cost of time in terms of money has turned a penny from a useful coin into a nuisance.

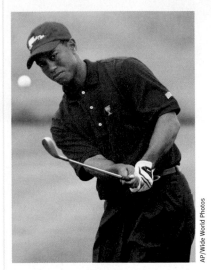

Tiger Woods understood the concept of opportunity cost. The rest is history.

AP/Wide World Photos

Tuition and housing are major monetary expenses for most students; but even if these things were free, attending college would still be an expensive proposition because most college students, if they were not in college, would have a job. That is, by going to college, students *forgo* the income they could have made if they had worked instead. This means that the opportunity cost of attending college is what you pay for tuition and housing *plus* the forgone income you would have earned in a job.

It's easy to see that the opportunity cost of going to college is especially high for people who could be earning a lot during what would otherwise have been their college years. That is why star athletes often skip college or, like Tiger Woods, leave before graduating.

## "How Much?" Is a Decision at the Margin

Some important decisions involve an "either-or" choice—for example, you decide either to go to college or to begin working; you decide either to take economics or to take something else. But other important decisions involve "how much" choices—for example, if you are taking both economics and chemistry this semester, you must decide how much time to spend studying for each. When it comes to understanding "how much" decisions, economics has an important insight to offer: "how much" is a decision made *at the margin*.

Suppose you are taking both economics and chemistry. And suppose you are a pre-med student, so that your grade in chemistry matters more to you than your grade in economics. Does that therefore imply that you should spend *all* your study time on chemistry and wing it on the economics exam? Probably not; even if you think your chemistry grade is more important, you should put some effort into studying for economics.

Spending more time studying for economics involves a benefit (a higher expected grade in that course) and a cost (you could have spent that time doing something else, such as studying to get a higher grade in chemistry). That is, your decision involves a **trade-off**—a comparison of costs and benefits.

How do you decide this kind of "how much" question? The typical answer is that you make the decision a bit at a time, by asking how you should spend the next hour.

You make a **trade-off** when you compare the costs with the benefits of doing something.

Say both exams are on the same day, and the night before you spend time reviewing your notes for both courses. At 6:00 P.M., you decide that it's a good idea to spend at least an hour on each course. At 8:00 P.M., you decide you'd better spend another hour on each course. At 10:00 P.M., you are getting tired and figure you have one more hour to study before bed—chemistry or economics? If you are pre-med, it's likely to be chemistry; if you are pre-MBA, it's likely to be economics.

Note how you've made the decision to allocate your time: at each point the question is whether or not to spend *one more hour* on either course. And in deciding whether to spend another hour studying for chemistry, you weigh the costs (an hour forgone of studying for economics or an hour forgone of sleeping) versus the benefits (a likely increase in your chemistry grade). As long as the benefit of studying one more hour for chemistry outweighs the cost, you should choose to study for that additional hour.

Decisions of this type—what to do with your next hour, what to do with your next dollar, and so on—are **marginal decisions**. They involve making trade-offs *at the margin*: comparing the costs and benefits of doing a little bit more of an activity versus doing a little bit less. The study of such decisions is known as **marginal analysis**.

Many of the questions that we face in economics—as well as in real life—involve marginal analysis: How many workers should I hire in my shop? At what mileage should I change the oil in my car? What is an acceptable rate of negative side effects from a new medicine? Marginal analysis plays a central role in economics because it is the key to deciding "how much" of an activity to do.

## People Usually Exploit Opportunities to Make Themselves Better Off

One day, the morning financial newscaster offered a great tip about how to park cheaply in Manhattan. Garages in the Wall Street area charge as much as $30 per day. But according to the newscaster, some people had found a better way: instead of parking in a garage, they had their oil changed at the Manhattan Jiffy Lube, where it costs $19.95 to change your oil—and they keep your car all day!

It's a great story, but unfortunately it turned out not to be true—in fact, there is no Jiffy Lube in Manhattan. But if there were, you can be sure there would be a lot of oil changes there. Why? Because when people are offered opportunities to make themselves better off, they normally take them—and if they could find a way to park their car all day for $19.95 rather than $30, they would.

When you try to predict how individuals will behave in an economic situation, it is a very good bet that they will exploit opportunities to make themselves better off. Furthermore, individuals will *continue* to exploit these opportunities until they have been fully exhausted—that is, people will exploit opportunities until those opportunities have been fully taken.

If there really were a Manhattan Jiffy Lube and an oil change really were a cheap way to park your car, we could safely predict that before long the waiting list for oil changes would be weeks, if not months.

In fact, the principle that people will exploit opportunities to make themselves better off is the basis of *all* predictions by economists about individual behavior. If the earnings of those who get MBAs soar while the earnings of those who get law degrees decline, we can expect more students to go to business school and fewer to go to law school. If the price of gasoline rises and stays high for an extended period of time, we can expect people to buy smaller cars with higher gas mileage—making themselves better off in the presence of higher gas prices by driving more fuel-efficient cars.

When changes in the available opportunities offer rewards to those who change their behavior, we say that people face new **incentives**. If the price of parking in Manhattan rises, those who can find alternative ways to get to their Manhattan jobs

Decisions about whether to do a bit more or a bit less of an activity are **marginal decisions**. The study of such decisions is known as **marginal analysis**.

An **incentive** is anything that offers rewards to people who change their behavior.

---

The true reward for learning is, of course, the learning itself. But teachers and schools often feel that it's worth throwing in a few extras. Elementary school students who do well get gold stars; at higher levels, students who score well on tests may receive trophies, plaques, or even gift certificates.

But what about cash?

A few years ago, some Florida schools stirred widespread debate by offering actual cash bonuses to students who scored high on the state's standardized exams. At Parrott Middle School, which offered the highest amounts, an eighth-grader with a top score on an exam received a $50 savings bond.

Many people questioned the monetary awards. In fact, the great majority of teachers feel that cash rewards for learning are a bad idea—the dollar amounts can't be made large enough to give students a real sense of how important their education is, and they make learning seem like work-for-pay. So why did the schools engage in the practice?

The answer, it turns out, is that the previous year the state government had introduced a pay-for-performance scheme for schools: schools whose students earned high marks on the state exams received extra state funds. The problem arose of how to motivate the students to take the exams as seriously as the school administrators

did. Parrott's principal defended the pay-for-grades practice by pointing out that good students would often "Christmas tree" their exams—ignore the questions and fill out the bubble sheets in the shape of Christmas trees. With large sums of money for the school at stake, he decided to set aside his misgivings and pay students to do well on the exams.

Does paying students for grades lead to higher grades? Interviews with students suggest that it does spur at least some students to try harder on state exams. And some Florida schools that have introduced rewards for good grades on state exams report substantial improvements in student performance.

---

will save money by doing so—and so we can expect fewer people to drive to work.

One last point: economists tend to be skeptical of any attempt to change people's behavior that *doesn't* change their incentives. For example, a plan that calls on manufacturers to reduce pollution voluntarily probably won't be effective; a plan that gives them a financial incentive to reduce pollution is a lot more likely to work.

## Individual Choice: Summing It Up

We have just seen that there are four basic principles of individual choice:

- *Resources are scarce.* It is always necessary to make choices.
- *The real cost of something is what you must give up to get it.* All costs are opportunity costs.
- *"How much?" is a decision at the margin.* Usually the question is not "whether," but "how much." And that is a question whose answer hinges on the costs and benefits of doing a bit more.
- *People usually exploit opportunities to make themselves better off.* As a result, people will respond to incentives.

So are we ready to do economics? Not yet—because most of the interesting things that happen in the economy are the result not merely of individual choices but of the way in which individual choices *interact.*

# *economics in action*

## A Woman's Work

One of the great social transformations of the twentieth century was the change in the nature of women's work. In 1900, only 6 percent of married women worked for pay outside the home. By the early twenty-first century, the number was about 60 percent.

What caused this transformation? Changing attitudes toward work outside the home certainly played a role: in the first half of the twentieth century, it was often considered improper for a married woman to work outside the home if she could afford not to, whereas today it is considered normal. But an important driving force was the invention and growing availability of home appliances, especially washing machines. Before these appliances became available, housework was an extremely laborious task—much more so than a full-time job. In 1945, government researchers clocked a farm wife as she did the weekly wash by hand; she spent 4 hours washing clothes and 4½ hours ironing, and she walked more than a mile. Then she was equipped with a washing machine; the same wash took 41 minutes, ironing was reduced to 1¾ hours, and the distance walked was reduced by 90 percent.

The point is that in pre-appliance days, the opportunity cost of working outside the home was very high: it was something women typically did only in the face of dire financial necessity. With modern appliances, the opportunities available to women changed—and the rest is history. ∎

> > > > > > > > > > > > > > > > > > > >

>>**CHECK YOUR UNDERSTANDING 1-1**

1. Explain how each of the following situations illustrates one of the four principles of individual choice.
   a. You are on your third trip to a restaurant's all-you-can-eat dessert buffet and are feeling very full. Although it would cost you no additional money, you forgo another slice of coconut cream pie but have a slice of chocolate cake.
   b. Even if there were more resources in the world, there would still be scarcity.
   c. Different teaching assistants teach several Economics 101 tutorials. Those taught by the teaching assistants with the best reputations fill up quickly, with spaces left unfilled in the ones taught by assistants with poor reputations.
   d. To decide how many hours per week to exercise, you compare the health benefits of one more hour of exercise to the effect on your grades of one less hour spent studying.

2. You make $45,000 per year at your current job with Whiz Kids Consultants. You are considering a job offer from Brainiacs, Inc., which will pay you $50,000 per year. Which of the following are elements of the opportunity cost of accepting the new job at Brainiacs, Inc.?
   a. The increased time spent commuting to your new job
   b. The $45,000 salary from your old job
   c. The more spacious office at your new job

*Solutions appear at back of book.*

# Interaction: How Economies Work

As we learned in the Introduction, an economy is a system for coordinating the productive activities of many people. In a market economy, such as the one we live in, that coordination takes place without any coordinator: each individual makes his or her own choices. Yet those choices are by no means independent of each other: each individual's opportunities, and hence choices, depend to a large extent on the choices made by other people. So to understand how a market economy behaves, we have to examine this **interaction** in which my choices affect your choices, and vice versa.

When studying economic interaction, we quickly learn that the end result of individual choices may be quite different from what any one individual intends.

For example, over the past century farmers in the United States have eagerly adopted new farming techniques and crop strains that have reduced their costs and increased their yields. Clearly, it's in the interest of each farmer to keep up with the latest farming techniques. But the end result of each farmer trying to increase his or her own income has actually been to drive many farmers out of business. Because American farmers have been so successful at producing larger yields, agricultural

**Interaction** of choices—my choices affect your choices, and vice versa—is a feature of most economic situations. The results of this interaction are often quite different from what the individuals intend.

## TABLE 1-2

### Principles That Underlie the Interaction of Individual Choices

1. There are gains from trade.

2. Markets move toward equilibrium.

3. Resources should be used as efficiently as possible to achieve society's goals.

4. Markets usually lead to efficiency.

5. When markets don't achieve efficiency, government intervention can improve society's welfare.

---

In a market economy, individuals engage in **trade**: They provide goods and services to others and receive goods and services in return.

There are **gains from trade**: people can get more of what they want through trade than they could if they tried to be self-sufficient. This increase in output is due to **specialization**: each person specializes in the task that he or she is good at performing.

---

prices have steadily fallen. These falling prices have reduced the incomes of many farmers, and as a result fewer and fewer people find farming worth doing. That is, an individual farmer who plants a better variety of corn is better off; but when many farmers plant a better variety of corn, the result may be to make farmers as a group worse off.

A farmer who plants a new, more productive corn variety doesn't just grow more corn. Such a farmer also affects the market for corn through the increased yields attained, with consequences that will be felt by other farmers, consumers, and beyond.

Just as there are four economic principles that fall under the theme of choice, there are five principles that fall under the theme of interaction. These five principles are summarized in Table 1-2. We will now examine each of these principles more closely.

## There Are Gains from Trade

Why do the choices I make interact with the choices you make? A family could try to take care of all its own needs—growing its own food, sewing its own clothing, providing itself with entertainment, writing its own economics textbooks. But trying to live that way would be very hard. The key to a much better standard of living for everyone is **trade**, in which people divide tasks among themselves and each person provides a good or service that other people want in return for different goods and services that he or she wants.

The reason we have an economy, not many self-sufficient individuals, is that there are **gains from trade**: by dividing tasks and trading, two people (or 6 billion people) can each get more of what they each want than they could get by being self-sufficient. Gains from trade arise, in particular, from this division of tasks, which economists call **specialization**—a situation in which different people each engage in a different task.

The advantages of specialization, and the resulting gains from trade, were the starting point for Adam Smith's 1776 book *The Wealth of Nations*, which many regard as the beginning of economics as a discipline. Smith's book begins with a description of an eighteenth-century pin factory where, rather than each of the 10 workers making a pin from start to finish, each worker specialized in one of the many steps in pin-making:

> One man draws out the wire, another straights it, a third cuts it, a fourth points it, a fifth grinds it at the top for receiving the head; to make the head requires two or three distinct operations; to put it on, is a particular business, to whiten the pins is another; it is even a trade by itself to put them into the paper; and the important business of making a pin is, in this manner, divided into about eighteen distinct operations . . . Those ten persons, therefore, could make among them upwards of forty-eight thousand pins in a day. But if they had all wrought separately and independently, and without any of them having been educated to this particular business, they certainly could not each of them have made twenty, perhaps not one pin a day. . . . (pp. 8–9)

The same principle applies when we look at how people divide tasks among themselves and trade in an economy. *The economy, as a whole, can produce more when each person specializes in a task and trades with others.*

The benefits of specialization are the reason a person typically chooses only one career. It takes many years of study and experience to become a doctor; it also takes many years of study and experience to become a commercial airline pilot. Many doctors might well have had the potential to become excellent pilots, and vice versa;

*"I hunt and she gathers—otherwise we couldn't make ends meet."*

but it is very unlikely that anyone who decided to pursue both careers would be as good a pilot or as good a doctor as someone who decided at the beginning to specialize in that field. So it is to everyone's advantage that individuals specialize in their career choices.

Markets are what allow a doctor and a pilot to specialize in their own fields. Because markets for commercial flights and for doctors' services exist, a doctor is assured that she can find a flight and a pilot is assured that he can find a doctor. As long as individuals know that they can find the goods and services that they want in the market, they are willing to forgo self-sufficiency and are willing to specialize. But what assures people that markets will deliver what they want? The answer to that question leads us to our second principle of economy-wide interaction.

## Markets Move Toward Equilibrium

It's a busy afternoon at the supermarket; there are long lines at the checkout counters. Then one of the previously closed cash registers opens. What happens?

The first thing that happens, of course, is a rush to that register. After a couple of minutes, however, things will have settled down; shoppers will have rearranged themselves so that the line at the newly opened register is about the same length as the lines at all the other registers.

How do we know that? We know from our fourth principle of individual choice that people will exploit opportunities to make themselves better off. This means that people will rush to the newly opened register in order to save time standing in line. And things will settle down when shoppers can no longer improve their position by switching lines— that is, when the opportunities to make themselves better off have all been exploited.

A story about supermarket checkout lines may seem to have little to do with economy-wide interactions, but in fact it illustrates an important principle. A situation in which individuals cannot make themselves better off by doing something different—the situation in which all the checkout lines are the same length—is what economists call an **equilibrium**. An economic situation is in equilibrium when no individual would be better off doing something different.

Recall the story about the mythical Jiffy Lube, where it was supposedly cheaper to leave your car for an oil change than to pay for parking. If that opportunity had

*Chuck Keeler/Stone/Getty Images*

Witness equilibrium in action at the checkout lines in your neighborhood supermarket.

---

An economic situation is in **equilibrium** when no individual would be better off doing something different.

---

**CHOOSING SIDES**

Why do people in America drive on the right side of the road? Of course, it's the law. But long before it was the law, it was an equilibrium.

Before there were formal traffic laws, there were informal "rules of the road," practices that everyone expected everyone else to follow. These rules included an understanding that people would normally keep to one side of the road. In some places, such as England, the rule was to keep to the left; in others, such as France, it was to keep to the right.

Why would some places choose the right and others, the left? That's not completely clear, although it may have depended on the dominant form of traffic. Men riding horses and carrying swords on their left hip preferred to ride on the left (think about getting on or off the horse, and you'll see why). On the other hand, right-handed people walking but leading horses apparently preferred to walk on the right.

In any case, once a rule of the road was established, there were strong incentives for each individual to stay on the "usual" side of the road: those who didn't would keep colliding with oncoming traffic. So once established, the rule of the road would be self-enforcing—that is, it would be an equilibrium. Nowadays, of course, which side you drive on is determined by law; some countries have even changed sides (Sweden went from left to right in 1967). But what about pedestrians? There are no laws—but there are informal rules. In the United States, urban pedestrians normally keep to the right. But if you should happen to visit Japan, watch out: the Japanese, who drive on the left, also typically walk on the left. So when in Japan, do as the Japanese do. You won't be arrested if you walk on the right, but you will be worse off than if you accept the equilibrium and walk on the left.

really existed and people were still paying $30 to park in garages, the situation would *not* have been an equilibrium.

And that should have been a giveaway that the story couldn't be true. In reality, people would have seized an opportunity to park cheaply, just as they seize opportunities to save time at the checkout line. And in so doing they would have eliminated the opportunity! Either it would have become very hard to get an appointment for an oil change or the price of a lube job would have increased to the point that it was no longer an attractive option (unless you really needed a lube job).

As we will see, markets usually reach equilibrium via changes in prices, which rise or fall until no opportunities for individuals to make themselves better off remain.

The concept of equilibrium is extremely helpful in understanding economic interactions because it provides a way of cutting through the sometimes complex details of those interactions. To understand what happens when a new line is opened at a supermarket, you don't need to worry about exactly how shoppers rearrange themselves, who moves ahead of whom, which register just opened, and so on. What you need to know is that any time there is a change, the situation will move to an equilibrium.

The fact that markets move toward equilibrium is why we can depend on them to work in a predictable way. In fact, we can trust markets to supply us with the essentials of life. For example, people who live in big cities can be sure that the supermarket shelves will always be fully stocked. Why? Because if some merchants who distribute food *didn't* make deliveries, a big profit opportunity would be created for any merchant who did—and there would be a rush to supply food, just like the rush to a newly opened cash register. So the market ensures that food will always be available for city dwellers. And, returning to our previous principle, this allows city dwellers to be city dwellers—to specialize in doing city jobs rather than living on farms and growing their own food.

A market economy also allows people to achieve gains from trade. But how do we know how well such an economy is doing? The next principle gives us a standard to use in evaluating an economy's performance.

## Resources Should Be Used as Efficiently as Possible to Achieve Society's Goals

Suppose you are taking a course in which the classroom is too small for the number of students—many people are forced to stand or sit on the floor—despite the fact that large, empty classrooms are available nearby. You would say, correctly, that this is no way to run a college. Economists would call this an *inefficient* use of resources.

But if an inefficient use of resources is undesirable, just what does it mean to use resources *efficiently*? You might imagine that the efficient use of resources has something to do with money, maybe that it is measured in dollars-and-cents terms. But in economics, as in life, money is only a means to other ends. The measure that economists really care about is not money but people's happiness or welfare. Economists say that *an economy's resources are used efficiently when they are used in a way that has fully exploited all opportunities to make everyone better off.* To put it another way, an economy is **efficient** if it takes all opportunities to make some people better off without making other people worse off.

In our classroom example, there clearly was a way to make everyone better off—moving the class to a larger room would make people in the class better off without hurting anyone else in the college. Assigning the course to the smaller classroom was an inefficient use of the college's resources, while assigning the course to the larger classroom would have been an efficient use of the college's resources.

When an economy is efficient, it is producing the maximum gains from trade possible given the resources available. Why? Because there is no way to rearrange how resources are used in a way that can make everyone better off. When an economy is efficient, one person can be made better off by rearranging how resources are used *only*

> An economy is **efficient** if it takes all opportunities to make some people better off without making other people worse off.

by making someone else worse off. In our classroom example, if all larger classrooms were already occupied, the college would have been run in an efficient way: your class could be made better off by moving to a larger classroom only by making people in the larger classroom worse off by making them move to a smaller classroom.

Should economic policy makers always strive to achieve economic efficiency? Well, not quite, because efficiency is not the only criterion by which to evaluate an economy. People also care about issues of fairness or **equity**. And there is typically a trade-off between equity and efficiency: policies that promote equity often come at a cost of decreased efficiency in the economy, and vice versa.

To see this, consider the case of disabled-designated parking spaces in public parking lots. Many people have great difficulty walking due to age or disability, so it seems only fair to assign closer parking spaces specifically for their use. You may have noticed, however, that a certain amount of inefficiency is involved. To make sure that there is always an appropriate space available should a disabled person want one, there are typically quite a number of disabled-designated spaces. So at any one time there are typically more such spaces available than there are disabled people who want one. As a result, desirable parking spaces are unused. (And the temptation for non-disabled people to use them is so great that we must be dissuaded by fear of getting a ticket.) So, short of hiring parking valets to allocate spaces, there is a conflict between *equity*, making life "fairer" for disabled people, and *efficiency*, making sure that all opportunities to make people better off have been fully exploited by never letting close-in parking spaces go unused.

Exactly how far policy makers should go in promoting equity over efficiency is a very difficult question that goes to the heart of the political process. As such, it is not a question that economists can answer. What is important for economists, however, is to always seek to use the economy's resources as efficiently as possible in the pursuit of society's goals, whatever those goals may be.

> **Equity** means that everyone gets his or her fair share. Since people can disagree about what's "fair," equity isn't as well-defined a concept as efficiency.

## Markets Usually Lead to Efficiency

No branch of the U.S. government is entrusted with ensuring the general economic efficiency of our market economy—we don't have agents who go around making sure that brain surgeons aren't plowing fields, that Minnesota farmers aren't trying to grow oranges, that prime beachfront property isn't taken up by used-car dealerships, that colleges aren't wasting valuable classroom space. The government doesn't need to enforce efficiency because in most cases the invisible hand does the job.

In other words, the incentives built into a market economy already ensure that resources are usually put to good use, that opportunities to make people better off are not wasted. If a college were known for its habit of crowding students into small classrooms while large classrooms go unused, it would soon find its enrollment dropping, putting the jobs of its administrators at risk. The "market" for college students would respond in a way that induces administrators to run the college efficiently.

A detailed explanation of why markets are usually very good at making sure that resources are used well will have to wait until we have studied how markets actually work. But the most basic reason is that in a market economy, in which individuals are free to choose what to consume and what to produce, opportunities for mutual gain are normally taken. If there is a way in which some people can be made better off, people will usually be able to take advantage of that opportunity. And that is exactly what defines efficiency: all the opportunities to make everyone better off have been exploited.

As we learned in the Introduction, however, there are exceptions to this principle that markets are generally efficient. In cases of *market failure*, the individual pursuit of self-interest found in markets makes society worse off—that is, the market outcome is inefficient. And, as we will see in examining the next principle, when markets fail, government intervention can help. But short of instances of market failure, the general rule is that markets are a remarkably good way of organizing an economy.

### When Markets Don't Achieve Efficiency, Government Intervention Can Improve Society's Welfare

Let's recall from the Introduction the nature of the market failure caused by traffic congestion—a commuter driving to work has no incentive to take into account the cost that his or her action inflicts on other drivers in the form of increased traffic congestion. There are several possible remedies to this situation; examples include charging road tolls, subsidizing the cost of public transportation, or taxing sales of gasoline to individual drivers. All these remedies work by changing the incentives of would-be drivers—motivating them to drive less and use alternative transportation. But they also share another feature: each relies on government intervention in the market.

This brings us to our fifth and last principle of interaction: *When markets don't achieve efficiency, government intervention can improve society's welfare.* That is, when markets go wrong, an appropriately designed government policy can sometimes move society closer to an efficient outcome by changing how society's resources are used.

A very important branch of economics is devoted to studying why markets fail and what policies should be adopted to improve social welfare. They fail for three principal reasons:

- Individual actions have *side effects* that are not properly taken into account by the market.
- One party prevents mutually beneficial trades from occurring in the attempt to capture a greater share of resources for itself.
- Some goods, by their very nature, are unsuited for efficient management by markets.

An important part of your education in economics is learning to identify not just when markets work but also when they don't work—and to judge what government policies are appropriate in each situation.

## *economics in action*

### Restoring Equilibrium on the Freeways

In 1994 a powerful earthquake struck the Los Angeles area, causing several freeway bridges to collapse and thereby disrupting the normal commuting routes of hundreds of thousands of drivers. The events that followed offer a particularly clear example of interdependent decision making—in this case, the decisions of commuters about how to get to work.

In the immediate aftermath of the earthquake, there was great concern about the impact on traffic, since motorists would now have to crowd onto alternative routes or detour around the blockages by using city streets. Public officials and news programs warned commuters to expect massive delays and urged them to avoid unnecessary travel, reschedule their work to commute before or after the rush, or use mass transit. These warnings were unexpectedly effective. In fact, so many people heeded them that in the first few days following the quake, those who maintained their regular commuting routine actually found the drive to and from work faster than before.

Of course, this situation could not last. As word spread that traffic was actually not bad at all, people abandoned their less convenient new commuting methods and reverted to their cars—and traffic got steadily worse. Within a few weeks after the quake, serious traffic jams had appeared. After a few more weeks, however, the situation stabilized: the reality of worse-than-usual congestion discouraged enough drivers to prevent the nightmare of citywide gridlock from materializing. Los Angeles traffic, in short, had settled into a new equilibrium, in which each commuter was making the best choice he or she could, given what everyone else was doing.

This was not, by the way, the end of the story: fears that the city would strangle on traffic led local authorities to repair the roads with record speed. Within only 18 months after the quake, all the freeways were back to normal, ready for the next one. ■

> > > > > > > > > > > > > > > > > > > >

## >>CHECK YOUR UNDERSTANDING 1-2

1. Explain how each of the following situations illustrates one of the five principles of interaction.
   a. Using the college website, any student who wants to sell a used textbook for at least $X is able to sell it to another who is willing to pay $X.
   b. At a college tutoring co-op, students can arrange to provide tutoring in subjects they are good in (like economics) in return for receiving tutoring in subjects they are poor in (like philosophy).
   c. The local municipality imposes a law that requires bars and nightclubs near residential areas to keep their noise levels below a certain threshold.
   d. To provide better care for low-income patients, the city of Tampa has decided to close some underutilized neighborhood clinics and shift funds to the main hospital.
   e. On the college website, books of a given title with approximately the same level of wear and tear sell for about the same price.

2. Which of the following describes an equilibrium situation? Which does not? Explain your answer.
   a. The restaurants across the street from the university dining hall serve better-tasting and cheaper meals than those served at the university dining hall. The vast majority of students continue to eat at the dining hall.
   b. You currently take the subway to work. Although taking the bus is cheaper, the ride takes longer. So you are willing to pay the higher subway fare in order to save time.

*Solutions appear at back of book.*

### • A LOOK AHEAD •

The nine basic principles we have described lie behind almost all economic analysis. Although they can be immediately helpful in understanding many situations, they are usually not enough. Applying the principles to real economic issues takes one more step.

That step is the creation of *models*—simplified representations of economic situations. Models must be realistic enough to provide real-world guidance but simple enough that they allow us to see clearly the implications of the principles described in this chapter. So our next step is to show how models are used to actually do economic analysis.

## SUMMARY

1. All economic analysis is based on a short list of basic principles. These principles apply to two levels of economic understanding. First, we must understand how individuals make choices; second, we must understand how these choices interact.

2. Everyone has to make choices about what to do and what *not* to do. **Individual choice** is the basis of economics—if it doesn't involve choice, it isn't economics.

3. The reason choices must be made is that **resources**—anything that can be used to produce something else—are **scarce.** Individuals are limited in their choices by money and time; economies are limited by their supplies of human and natural resources.

4. Because you must choose among limited alternatives, the true cost of anything is what you must give up to get it—all costs are **opportunity costs.**

5. Many economic decisions involve questions not of "whether" but of "how much"—how much to spend on some good, how much to produce, and so on. Such decisions must be taken by performing a **trade-off** *at the margin*—by comparing the costs and benefits of doing a bit more or a bit less. Decisions of this type are called **marginal decisions,** and the study of them, **marginal analysis,** plays a central role in economics.

6. The study of how people *should* make decisions is also a good way to understand actual behavior. Individuals usually exploit opportunities to make themselves better off. If opportunities change, so does behavior: people respond to **incentives.**

7. **Interaction**—my choices depend on your choices, and vice versa—adds another level to economic understanding.

When individuals interact, the end result may be different from what anyone intends.

8. The reason for interaction is that there are **gains from trade:** by engaging in the **trade** of goods and services with one another, the members of an economy can all be made better off. Underlying gains from trade are the advantages of **specialization,** of having individuals specialize in the tasks they are good at.

9. Economies normally move toward **equilibrium**—a situation in which no individual can make himself or herself better off by taking a different action.

10. An economy is **efficient** if all opportunities to make someone better off without making others worse off are taken. Resources should be used as efficiently as possible to achieve society's goals. But efficiency is not the sole way to evaluate an economy: **equity,** or fairness, is also desirable, and there is often a trade-off between equity and efficiency.

11. Markets usually lead to efficiency, with some well-defined exceptions.

12. When markets fail and do not achieve efficiency, government intervention can improve society's welfare.

## KEY TERMS

Individual choice, p. 6
Resource, p. 6
Scarce, p. 6
Opportunity cost, p. 7
Trade-off, p. 8

Marginal decisions, p. 9
Marginal analysis, p. 9
Incentive, p. 9
Interaction, p. 11
Trade, p. 12

Gains from trade, p. 12
Specialization, p. 12
Equilibrium, p. 13
Efficient, p. 14
Equity, p. 15

## PROBLEMS

1. In each of the following situations, identify which of the nine principles is at work.

   a. You choose to shop at the local discount store rather than paying a higher price for the same merchandise at the local department store.

   b. On your spring vacation trip, your budget is limited to $35 a day.

   c. The student union provides a website on which departing students can sell items such as used books, appliances, and furniture rather than giving them away to their roommates as they formerly did.

   d. You decide how many cups of coffee to have when studying the night before an exam by considering how much more work you can do by having another cup versus how jittery it will make you feel.

   e. There is limited lab space available to do the project required in Chemistry 101. The lab supervisor assigns lab time to each student based on when that student is able to come.

   f. You realize that you can graduate a semester early by forgoing a semester of study abroad.

   g. At the student union, there is a bulletin board on which people advertise used items for sale, such as bicycles. Once you have adjusted for differences in quality, all the bikes sell for about the same price.

   h. You are better at performing lab experiments, and your lab partner is better at writing lab reports. So the two of you agree that you will do all the experiments, and she will write up all the reports.

   i. State governments mandate that it is illegal to drive without passing a driving exam.

2. Describe some of the opportunity costs when you decide to do the following.

   a. Attend college instead of taking a job

   b. Watch a movie instead of studying for an exam

   c. Ride the bus instead of driving your car

3. Liza needs to buy a textbook for the next economics class. The price at the college bookstore is $65. One online site offers it for $55 and another site for $57. All prices include sales tax. The accompanying table indicates the typical shipping and handling charges for the textbook ordered online.

   a. What is the opportunity cost of buying online?

   b. Show the relevant choices for this student. What determines which of these options the student will choose?

| Shipping method | Delivery time | Charge |
|---|---|---|
| Standard shipping | 3–7 days | $3.99 |
| Second-day air | 2 business days | $8.98 |
| Next-day air | 1 business day | $13.98 |

4. Use the concept of opportunity cost to explain the following.

   a. More people choose to get graduate degrees when the job market is poor.

   b. More people choose to do their own home repairs when the economy is slow.

   c. There are more parks in suburban areas than in urban areas.

**d.** Convenience stores, which have higher prices than super-markets, cater to busy people.

**e.** Fewer students enroll in classes that meet before 10:00 A.M.

**5.** In the following examples, state how you would use the principle of marginal analysis to make a decision.

**a.** Deciding how many days to wait before doing your laundry

**b.** Deciding how much library research to do before writing your term paper

**c.** Deciding how many bags of chips to eat

**d.** Deciding how many lectures of a class to skip

**6.** This morning you made the following individual choices: you bought a bagel and coffee at the local café, you drove to school in your car during rush hour, and you typed your roommate's term paper because you are a fast typist—in return for which she will do your laundry for a month. In each of these actions, describe how your individual choices interacted with the individual choices made by others. Were other people left better off or worse off by your choices in each case?

**7.** On the east side of the Hatatoochie River lives the Hatfield family, while the McCoy family lives on the west side. Each family's diet consists of fried chicken and corn-on-the-cob, and each is self-sufficient, raising their own chickens and growing their own corn. Explain the conditions under which each of the following would be true.

**a.** The two families are made better off when the Hatfields specialize in raising chickens, the McCoys specialize in raising corn, and the two families trade.

**b.** The two families are made better off when the McCoys specialize in raising chickens, the Hatfields specialize in raising corn, and the two families trade.

**8.** Which of the following situations describes an equilibrium? Which does not? If the situation does not describe an equilibrium, what would an equilibrium look like?

**a.** Many people regularly commute from the suburbs to downtown Pleasantville. Due to traffic congestion, the trip takes 30 minutes when you travel by highway, but only 15 minutes when you go by side streets.

**b.** At the intersection of Main and Broadway are two gas stations. One station charges $3.00 per gallon for regular gas and the other charges $2.85 per gallon. Customers can get service immediately at the first station, but must wait in a long line at the second.

**c.** Every student enrolled in Economics 101 must also attend a weekly tutorial. This year there are two sections offered: section A and section B, which meet at the same time in adjoining classrooms and are taught by equally competent instructors. Section A is overcrowded, with people sitting on the floor and often unable to see the chalkboard. Section B has many empty seats.

**9.** In each of the following cases, explain whether you think the situation is efficient or not. If it is not efficient, why not? What actions would make the situation efficient?

**a.** Electricity is included in the rent at your dorm. Some residents in your dorm leave lights, computers, and appliances on when they are not in their rooms.

**b.** Although they cost the same amount to prepare, the cafeteria in your dorm consistently provides too many dishes that diners don't like, such as tofu casserole, and too few dishes that diners do like, such as roast turkey with dressing.

**c.** The enrollment for a particular course exceeds the spaces available. Some students who need to take this course to complete their major are unable to get a space while others who are taking it as an elective do get a space.

**10.** Discuss the efficiency and equity implications of each of the following policies. How would you go about balancing the concerns of equity and efficiency in these areas?

**a.** The government pays the full tuition for every college student to study whatever subject he or she wishes.

**b.** When people lose their jobs, the government provides unemployment benefits until they find new ones.

**11.** Governments often adopt certain policies in order to promote desired behavior among their citizens. For each of the following policies, determine what the incentive is and what behavior the government wishes to promote. In each case, why do you think that the government might wish to change people's behavior, rather than allow their actions to be solely determined by individual choice?

**a.** A tax of $5 per pack is imposed on cigarettes.

**b.** The government pays parents $100 when their child is vaccinated for measles.

**c.** The government pays college students to tutor children from low-income families.

**d.** The government imposes a tax on the amount of air pollution that a company discharges.

**12.** In each of the following situations, explain how government intervention could improve society's welfare by changing people's incentives. In what sense is the market going wrong?

**a.** Pollution from auto emissions has reached unhealthy levels.

**b.** Everyone in Woodville would be better off if streetlights were installed in the town. But no individual resident is willing to pay for installation of a streetlight in front of his or her house because it is impossible to recoup the cost by charging other residents for the benefit they receive from it.

---

**>web...** To continue your study and review of concepts in this chapter, please visit the Krugman/Wells/Olney website for quizzes, animated graph tutorials, web links to helpful resources, and more.

**www.worthpublishers.com/krugmanwellsolney**

# >>Economic Models: Trade-offs and Trade

## TUNNEL VISION

IN 1901 WILBUR AND ORVILLE WRIGHT built something that would change the world. No, not the airplane—their successful flight at Kitty Hawk would come two years later. What made the Wright brothers true visionaries was their wind tunnel, an apparatus that let them experiment with many different designs for wings and control surfaces. These experiments gave them the knowledge that would make heavier-than-air flight possible.

A miniature airplane sitting motionless in a wind tunnel isn't the same thing as an actual aircraft in flight. But it is a very useful model of a flying plane—a simplified representation of the real thing that can be used to answer crucial questions, such as how much lift a given wing shape will generate at a given airspeed.

Needless to say, testing an airplane design in a wind tunnel is cheaper and safer than building a full-scale version and hoping it will fly. More generally, models play a crucial role in almost all scientific research—economics very much included.

In fact, you could say that economic theory consists mainly of a collection of models, a series of simplified representations of economic reality that allow us to understand a variety of economic issues.

Clearly, the Wright brothers believed in their model.

In this chapter, we will look at three economic models that are crucially important in their own right and also illustrate why such models are so useful. We'll conclude with a look at how economists actually use models in their work.

## What you will learn in this chapter:

➤ Why **models**—simplified representations of reality—play a crucial role in economics

➤ Three simple but important models: the **production possibility frontier, comparative advantage,** and the **circular-flow diagram**

➤ The difference between **positive economics,** which tries to describe the economy and predict its behavior, and **normative economics,** which tries to prescribe economic policy

➤ When economists agree and why they sometimes disagree

# Models in Economics: Some Important Examples

A **model** is any simplified representation of reality that is used to better understand real-life situations. But how do we create a simplified representation of an economic situation?

One possibility—an economist's equivalent of a wind tunnel—is to find or create a real but simplified economy. For example, economists interested in the economic role of money have studied the system of exchange that developed in World War II prison camps, in which cigarettes became a universally accepted form of payment even among prisoners who didn't smoke.

Another possibility is to simulate the workings of the economy on a computer. For example, when changes in tax law are proposed, government officials use *tax models*—large computer programs—to assess how the proposed changes would affect different types of people.

The importance of models is that they allow economists to focus on the effects of only one change at a time. That is, they allow us to hold everything else constant and study how one change affects the overall economic outcome. So the **other things equal assumption,** which means that all other relevant factors remain unchanged, is an important assumption when building economic models.

But you can't always find or create a small-scale version of the whole economy, and a computer program is only as good as the data it uses. (Programmers have a saying: garbage in, garbage out.) For many purposes, the most effective form of economic modeling is the construction of "thought experiments": simplified, hypothetical versions of real-life situations.

In Chapter 1 we illustrated the concept of equilibrium with the example of how customers at a supermarket would rearrange themselves when a new cash register opens. Though we didn't say it, this was an example of a simple model—an imaginary supermarket, in which many details were ignored (what are the customers buying? never mind), that could be used to answer a "what if" question: what if another cash register were opened?

As the cash register story showed, it is often possible to describe and analyze a useful economic model in plain English. However, because much of economics involves changes in quantities—in the price of a product, the number of units produced, or the number of workers employed in its production—economists often find that using some mathematics helps clarify an issue. In particular, a numerical example, a simple equation, or—especially—a graph can be key to understanding an economic concept.

Whatever form it takes, a good economic model can be a tremendous aid to understanding. The best way to make this point is to consider some simple but important economic models and what they tell us. First, we will look at the *production possibility frontier*, a model that helps economists think about the trade-offs every economy faces. Then we will turn to *comparative advantage*, a model that clarifies the principle of gains from trade—trade both between individuals and between countries. Finally, we'll examine the *circular-flow model*, which helps economists analyze the monetary transactions taking place in the economy as a whole.

A **model** is a simplified representation of a real situation that is used to better understand real-life situations.

The **other things equal assumption** means that all other relevant factors remain unchanged.

## FOR INQUIRING MINDS

### MODELS FOR MONEY

What's an economic model worth, anyway? In some cases, quite a lot of money.

Although many economic models are developed for purely scientific purposes, others are developed to help governments make economic policies. And there is a growing business in developing economic models to help corporations make decisions.

Who models for money? There are dozens of consulting firms that use models to predict future trends, offer advice based on their models, or develop custom models for business and government clients. A notable example is Global Insight, the world's biggest economic consulting firm. It was created by a merger between Data Resources, Inc., founded by professors from Harvard and MIT, and Wharton Economic Forecasting Associates, founded by professors at the University of Pennsylvania.

In discussing these models, we make considerable use of graphs to represent mathematical relationships. Such graphs will play an important role throughout this book. If you are already familiar with the use of graphs, the material that follows should not present any problem. If you are not, this would be a good time to turn to the appendix of this chapter, which provides a brief introduction to the use of graphs in economics.

## Trade-offs: The Production Possibility Frontier

The hit movie *Cast Away*, starring Tom Hanks, was an update of the classic story of Robinson Crusoe, the hero of Daniel Defoe's eighteenth-century novel. Hanks played the sole survivor of a plane crash, stranded on a remote island. As in the original story of Robinson Crusoe, the character played by Hanks had limited resources: the natural resources of the island, a few items he managed to salvage from the plane, and, of course, his own time and effort. With only these resources, he had to make a life. In effect, he became a one-man economy.

The first principle of economics we introduced in Chapter 1 was that resources are scarce and that, as a result, any economy—whether it contains one person or millions of people—faces trade-offs. For example, if a castaway devotes resources to catching fish, he cannot use those same resources to gather coconuts.

To think about the trade-offs that face any economy, economists often use the model known as the **production possibility frontier.** The idea behind this model is to improve our understanding of trade-offs by considering a simplified economy that produces only two goods. This simplification enables us to show the trade-off graphically.

Figure 2-1 shows a hypothetical production possibility frontier for Tom, a castaway alone on an island, who must make a trade-off between production of fish and production of coconuts. The frontier—the curve in the diagram—shows the maximum number of fish Tom can catch during a week *given* the quantity of coconuts he gathers, and vice versa. That is, it answers questions of the form, "What is the maximum number of fish Tom can catch if he also gathers 20 (or 25, or 30) coconuts?" (We'll explain the bowed-out shape of the curve in Figure 2-1 shortly, after we've seen how to interpret the production possibility frontier.)

There is a crucial distinction between points *inside* or *on* the curve (the shaded area) and *outside* the curve. If a production point lies inside or on the frontier—like the point labeled C, at which Tom catches 20 fish and gathers 20 coconuts—it is feasible. After all, the frontier tells us that if Tom catches 20 fish, he could also gather a maximum of 25 coconuts, so he could certainly gather 20 coconuts. On the other hand, a production point that lies outside the frontier—such as the hypothetical production point shown in the figure as point D, where Tom catches 40 fish and gathers 30 coconuts—isn't feasible. (In this case, Tom could catch 40 fish and gather no coconuts *or* he could gather 30 coconuts and catch no fish, but he can't do both.)

In Figure 2-1 the production possibility frontier intersects the horizontal axis at 40 fish. This means that if Tom devoted all his resources to catching fish, he would catch 40 fish per week but would have no resources left over to gather coconuts. The production possibility frontier intersects the vertical axis at 30 coconuts; this means that if Tom devoted all his resources to gathering coconuts, he could gather 30 coconuts per week but would have no resources left over to catch fish.

The figure also shows less extreme trade-offs. For example, if Tom decides to catch 20 fish, he is able to gather 25 coconuts; this production choice is illustrated by point A. If Tom decides to catch 30 fish, he can gather at most only 20 coconuts, as shown by point B.

Thinking in terms of a production possibility frontier simplifies the complexities of reality. The real-world economy produces millions of different goods. Even a cast-

What to do? Even a castaway faces trade-offs.

The **production possibility frontier** illustrates the trade-offs facing an economy that produces only two goods. It shows the maximum quantity of one good that can be produced for any given quantity produced of the other.

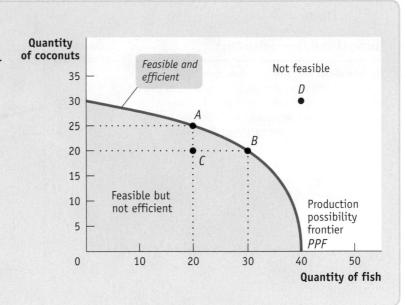

### Figure 2-1

**The Production Possibility Frontier**

The production possibility frontier illustrates the trade-offs facing an economy that produces two goods. It shows the maximum quantity of one good that can be produced given the quantity of the other good produced. Here, the maximum number of coconuts that Tom can gather depends on the number of fish he catches, and vice versa. His feasible production is shown by the area *inside or on* the curve. Production at point *C* is feasible but not efficient. Points *A* and *B* are feasible and efficient, but point *D* is not feasible.  **>web...**

**>web...**  Throughout our book, this icon will be used to indicate which graphs are available in an interactive format on our text's website. You can work with these interactive graph tutorials and find additional learning resources if you go to www.worthpublishers.com/krugmanwellsolney.

away on an island would produce more than two different items (for example, he would need clothing and housing as well as food). But in this model we imagine an economy that produces only two goods.

If we simplify reality, however, the production possibility frontier helps us understand some aspects of the real economy better than we could without the model.

First of all, the production possibility frontier is a good way to illustrate the general economic concept of *efficiency*. Recall from Chapter 1 that an economy is efficient if there are no missed opportunities—there is no way to make some people better off without making other people worse off. A key element of efficiency is that there are no missed opportunities in production—there is no way to produce more of one good without producing less of other goods.

As long as Tom is on the production possibility frontier, his production is efficient. At point *A*, the 25 coconuts he gathers are the maximum number he can get *given* that he has chosen to catch 20 fish; at point *B*, the 20 coconuts he gathers are the maximum he can get *given* his choice to catch 30 fish; and so on.

But suppose that for some reason Tom was at point *C*, producing 20 fish and 20 coconuts. Then this one-person economy would definitely be *inefficient*: it could be producing more of both goods.

The production possibility frontier is also useful as a reminder of the fundamental point that the true cost of any good is not just the amount of money it costs to buy, but everything else in addition to money that must be given up in order to get that good—the *opportunity cost*. If Tom were to catch 30 fish instead of 20, he would be able to gather only 20 coconuts instead of 25. So the opportunity cost of those 10 extra fish is the 5 coconuts not gathered. And if 10 extra fish have an opportunity cost of 5 coconuts, each 1 fish has an opportunity cost of $5/10 = 0.5$ coconuts.

We can now explain the bowed-out shape of the production possibility frontier we saw in Figure 2-1: it reflects an assumption about how opportunity costs change as the mix of output changes. Figure 2-2 on page 24 shows the same production possibility frontier as Figure 2-1. The arrows in Figure 2-2 illustrate the fact that with this bowed-out production possibility frontier, Tom faces *increasing opportunity cost*: the more fish he catches, the more coconuts he has to give up to catch an additional fish, and vice versa. For example, to go from producing zero fish to producing 20 fish, he has to give up 5 coconuts. That is, the opportunity cost of those 20 fish is 5 coconuts. But to increase his fish production to 40—that is, to produce an additional 20 fish— he must give up 25 more coconuts, a much higher opportunity cost.

## Figure 2-2

### Increasing Opportunity Cost

The bowed-out shape of the production possibility frontier reflects increasing opportunity cost. In this example, to produce the first 20 fish, Tom must give up 5 coconuts. But to produce an additional 20 fish, he must give up 25 more coconuts. **>web...**

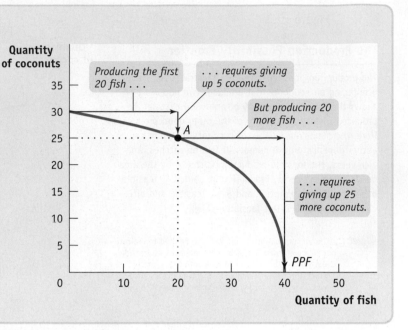

Economists believe that opportunity costs are usually increasing. The reason is that when only a small amount of a good is produced, the economy can use resources that are especially well suited for that production. For example, if an economy grows only a small amount of corn, that corn can be grown in places where the soil and climate are perfect for corn-growing but less suitable for growing anything else, like wheat. So growing that corn involves giving up only a small amount of potential wheat production. If the economy grows a lot of corn, however, land that isn't so great for corn and would have been well suited for wheat must be pressed into service, so the additional corn production will involve sacrificing considerably more wheat production.

Finally, the production possibility frontier helps us understand what it means to talk about *economic growth*. We introduced the concept of economic growth in the Introduction, defining it as *the growing ability of the economy to produce goods and services*. As we saw, economic growth is one of the fundamental features of the real economy. But are we really justified in saying that the economy has grown? After all, although the U.S. economy produces more of many things than it did a century ago, it produces less of other things—for example, horse-drawn carriages. Production of many goods, in other words, is actually down. So how can we say for sure that the economy as a whole has grown?

The answer, illustrated in Figure 2-3, is that economic growth means an *expansion of the economy's production possibilities*: the economy *can* produce more of everything. For example, if Tom's production is initially at point *A* (20 fish and 25 coconuts), economic growth means that he could move to point *E* (25 fish and 30 coconuts). *E* lies outside the original frontier; so in the production possibility frontier model, growth is shown as an outward shift of the frontier.

What the economy actually produces depends on the choices people make. After his production possibilities expand, Tom might not actually choose to produce both more fish and more coconuts—he might choose to increase production of only one good, or he might even choose to produce less of one good. But even if, for some reason, he chooses to produce either fewer coconuts or fewer fish than before, we would still say that his economy has grown—because he *could* have produced more of everything.

The production possibility frontier is a very simplified model of an economy. Yet it teaches us important lessons about real-life economies. It gives us our first clear sense of a key element of economic efficiency, it illustrates the concept of opportunity cost, and it makes clear what economic growth is all about.

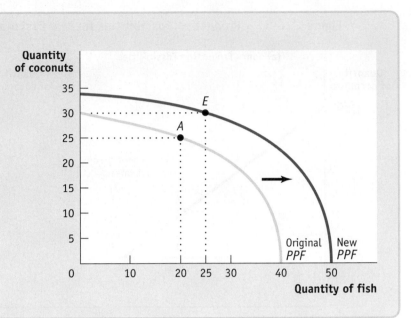

### Figure 2-3

#### Economic Growth

Economic growth results in an *outward shift* of the production possibility frontier because production possibilities are expanded. The economy can now produce more of everything. For example, if production is initially at point *A* (20 fish and 25 coconuts), it could move to point *E* (25 fish and 30 coconuts).

## Comparative Advantage and Gains from Trade

Among the nine principles of economics described in Chapter 1 was that of *gains from trade*—the mutual gains that individuals can achieve by specializing in doing different things and trading with one another. Our second illustration of an economic model is a particularly useful model of gains from trade—trade based on *comparative advantage*.

Let's stick with Tom stranded on his island, but now let's suppose that a second castaway, who just happens to be named Hank, is washed ashore. Can they benefit from trading with each other?

It's obvious that there will be potential gains from trade if the two castaways do different things particularly well. For example, if Tom is a skilled fisherman and Hank is very good at climbing trees, clearly it makes sense for Tom to catch fish and Hank to gather coconuts—and for the two men to trade the products of their efforts.

But one of the most important insights in all of economics is that there are gains from trade even if one of the trading parties isn't especially good at anything. Suppose, for example, that Hank is less well suited to primitive life than Tom; he's not nearly as good at catching fish, and compared to Tom even his coconut-gathering leaves something to be desired. Nonetheless, what we'll see is that both Tom and Hank can live better by trading with each other than either could alone.

For the purposes of this example, let's slightly redraw Tom's production possibilities represented by the production possibility frontier in panel (a) of Figure 2-4 on page 26. According to this diagram, Tom could catch at most 40 fish, but only if he gathered no coconuts, and could gather 30 coconuts, but only if he caught no fish, as before.

In Figure 2-4, we have replaced the curved production possibility frontier of Figure 2-1 with a straight line. Why do this, when we've already seen that economists regard a bowed-out production possibility frontier as normal? The answer is that it simplifies our discussion—and as we have explained, modeling is all about simplification. The principle of comparative advantage doesn't depend on the assumption of straight-line production possibility frontiers, but it is easier to explain with that assumption.

The straight-line production possibility frontier in panel (a) of Figure 2-4 has a *constant slope* of −¾. (The appendix to this chapter explains how to calculate the slope of a line.) That is, for every 4 additional fish that Tom chooses to catch, he gathers 3 fewer coconuts. So Tom's opportunity cost of a fish is ¾ of a coconut regardless of how many or how few fish he catches. In contrast, a production possibility frontier is curved when the opportunity cost of a good changes according to how much of

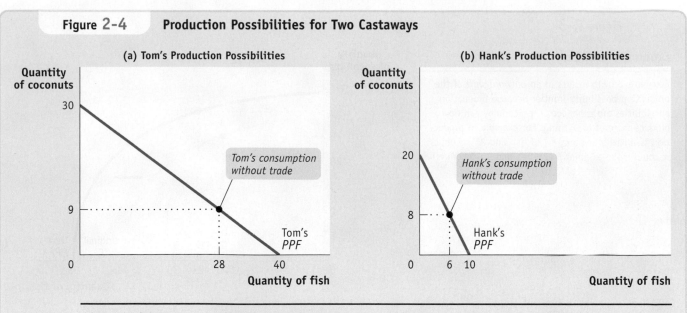

**Figure 2-4** **Production Possibilities for Two Castaways**

**(a) Tom's Production Possibilities**

**(b) Hank's Production Possibilities**

Here, each of the two castaways has a constant opportunity cost of fish and a straight-line production possibility frontier: In Tom's case, each fish always has an opportunity cost

of ¾ of a coconut. In Hank's case, each fish always has an opportunity cost of 2 coconuts. **>web...**

the good has already been produced. For example, you can see from Figure 2-2 that if Tom starts at the point of having caught zero fish and gathers 30 coconuts, his opportunity cost of catching 20 fish is 5 coconuts. But once he has already caught 20 fish, the opportunity cost of an additional 20 fish increases to 25 coconuts.

Panel (b) of Figure 2-4 shows Hank's production possibilities. Like Tom's, Hank's production possibility frontier is a straight line, implying a constant opportunity cost of fish in terms of coconuts. His production possibility frontier has a constant slope of −2. Hank is less productive all around: at most he can produce 10 fish or 20 coconuts. But he is particularly bad at fishing; whereas Tom sacrifices ¾ of a coconut per fish caught, for Hank the opportunity cost of a fish is 2 whole coconuts. Table 2-1 summarizes the two castaways' opportunity costs for fish and coconuts.

**TABLE 2-1**

**Tom's and Hank's Opportunity Costs of Fish and Coconuts**

|  | Tom's Opportunity Cost | Hank's Opportunity Cost |
|---|---|---|
| One fish | 3/4 coconut | 2 coconuts |
| One coconut | 4/3 fish | 1/2 fish |

Now Tom and Hank could go their separate ways, each living on his own side of the island, catching his own fish and gathering his own coconuts. Let's suppose that they start out that way and make the consumption choices shown in Figure 2-4: In the absence of trade, Tom consumes 28 fish and 9 coconuts per week, while Hank consumes 6 fish and 8 coconuts.

But is this the best they can do? No, it isn't. Given that the two castaways have different opportunity costs, they can strike a deal that makes both of them better off.

Table 2-2 shows how such a deal works: Tom specializes in the production of fish, catching 40 per week, and gives 10 to Hank. Meanwhile, Hank specializes in the production of coconuts, gathering 20 per week, and gives 10 to Tom. The result is shown in Figure 2-5. Tom now consumes more of both goods than before: Instead of 28 fish and 9 coconuts, he consumes 30 fish and 10 coconuts. And Hank also consumes more, going from 6 fish and 8 coconuts to 10 fish and 10 coconuts. As Table 2-2 also shows, both Tom and Hank experience gains from trade: Tom's consumption of fish increases by two, and his consumption of coconuts increases by one. Hank's consumption of fish increases by four, and his consumption of coconuts by two.

So both castaways are better off when they each specialize in what they are good at and trade. It's a good idea for Tom to catch the fish for both of them because his opportunity

**TABLE 2-2**

### How the Castaways Gain from Trade

|       |         | Without Trade | | With Trade | | Gains from Trade |
|-------|---------|------------|-------------|------------|-------------|----------|
|       |         | Production | Consumption | Production | Consumption |          |
| Tom   | Fish    | 28         | 28          | 40         | 30          | +2       |
|       | Coconuts | 9         | 9           | 0          | 10          | +1       |
| Hank  | Fish    | 6          | 6           | 0          | 10          | +4       |
|       | Coconuts | 8         | 8           | 20         | 10          | +2       |

cost of a fish is only ¾ of a coconut not gathered versus 2 coconuts for Hank. Correspondingly, it's a good idea for Hank to gather coconuts for the both of them.

Or we could put it the other way around: Because Tom is so good at catching fish, his opportunity cost of gathering coconuts is high: ⁴/₃ fish not caught for every coconut gathered. Because Hank is a pretty poor fisherman, his opportunity cost of gathering coconuts is much less, only ½ a fish per coconut.

What we would say in this case is that Tom has a **comparative advantage** in catching fish and Hank has a comparative advantage in gathering coconuts. An individual has a comparative advantage in producing something if the opportunity cost of that production is lower for that individual than for other people. In other words, Hank has a comparative advantage over Tom in producing a particular good or service if Hank's opportunity cost of producing that good or service is lower than Tom's.

The story of Tom and Hank clearly simplifies reality. Yet it teaches us some very important lessons that apply to the real economy, too.

First, the model provides a clear illustration of the gains from trade: by agreeing to specialize and provide goods to each other, Tom and Hank can produce more and therefore both be better off than if they tried to be self-sufficient.

> An individual has a **comparative advantage** in producing a good or service if the opportunity cost of producing the good is lower for that individual than for other people.

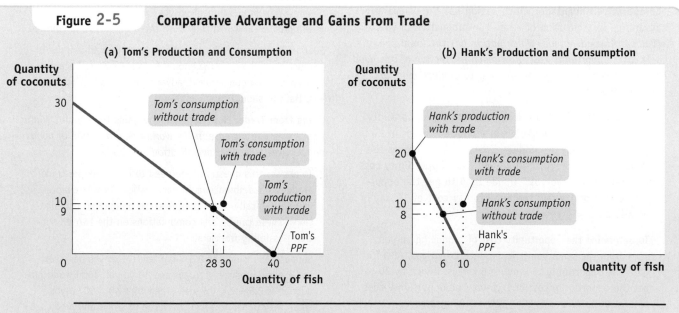

**Figure 2-5    Comparative Advantage and Gains From Trade**

By specializing and trading, the two castaways can produce and consume more of both goods. Tom specializes in catching fish, his comparative advantage, and Hank—who has an *absolute* disadvantage in both goods but a *comparative* advantage in coconuts—specializes in gathering coconuts. The result is that each castaway can consume more of both goods than either could without trade.

Second, the model demonstrates a very important point that is often overlooked in real-world arguments: As long as people have different opportunity costs, *everyone has a comparative advantage in something, and everyone has a comparative disadvantage in something.*

Notice that in our example Tom is actually better than Hank at producing both goods: Tom can catch more fish in a week, and he can also gather more coconuts. That is, Tom has an **absolute advantage** in both activities: he can produce more output with a given amount of input (in this case, his time) than Hank. You might therefore be tempted to think that Tom has nothing to gain from trading with the less competent Hank.

But we've just seen that Tom can indeed benefit from a deal with Hank because *comparative*, not *absolute*, advantage is the basis for mutual gain. It doesn't matter that it takes Hank more time to gather a coconut; what matters is that for him the oppor-

> An individual has an **absolute advantage** in an activity if he or she can do it better than other people. Having an absolute advantage is not the same thing as having a comparative advantage.

## WORK IT OUT

### GAINS FROM TRADE

The nations of Alka and Baiwan both produce only two goods: x-rays and yo-yos. With 100 workers, Alka can produce 5 x-rays or 20 yo-yos in 1 week, or any combination in between. And with 100 workers, Baiwan can produce 10 x-rays or 50 yo-yos, or any combination in between.

**Absolute Advantage:** Which nation has the absolute advantage in production of x-rays? In production of yo-yos? *(Absolute advantage: Which nation can produce more?)*

**SOLUTION:** Baiwan has the absolute advantage in the production of x-rays because it can produce 10 x-rays in a week and Alka can only produce 5 x-rays in a week. Baiwan has the absolute advantage in the production of yo-yos because it can produce more yo-yos in a week than Alka.

**Comparative Advantage:** Which nation has the comparative advantage in production of x-rays? In production of yo-yos? *(Comparative advantage: Which nation has the lower opportunity cost? Opportunity cost: How much production of one good must be given up—forgone—in order to produce more of another good?)*

To answer this question, first calculate the opportunity costs. In Alka, 100 workers can produce 5 x-rays or 20 yo-yos in a week. To produce 5 x-rays, Alka forgoes the opportunity to produce 20 yo-yos. The "opportunity cost of 5 x-rays is 20 yo-yos." Divide by 5 to get the opportunity cost of 1 x-ray: the opportunity cost of 1 x-ray in Alka is $20/5 = 4$ yo-yos.

To determine the opportunity cost of producing yo-yos, start from the same point: To produce 20 yo-yos, Alka forgoes the opportunity to produce 5 x-rays. Divide by 20 to get the opportunity cost of 1 yo-yo. The opportunity cost of 1 yo-yo in Alka is $5/20 = 1/4 = 0.25$ x-rays.

In Baiwan, 100 workers can produce 10 x-rays or 50 yo-yos in one week. To produce 10 x-rays, Baiwan forgoes the opportunity to produce 50 yo-yos. Divide by 10: the opportunity cost of 1 x-ray in Baiwan is $50/10 = 5$ yo-yos.

The opportunity cost of 50 yo-yos in Baiwan is 10 x-rays. Divide by 50: the opportunity cost of 1 yo-yo in Baiwan is $10/50 = 1/5 = 0.20$ x-rays.

| | Alka | Baiwan |
|---|---|---|
| One x-ray costs | 4 yo-yos | 5 yo-yos |
| One yo-yo costs | 0.25 x-rays | 0.20 x-rays |

**SOLUTION:** Alka has the comparative advantage in production of x-rays because it has the lower opportunity cost (just 4 yo-yos) of producing x-rays. Baiwan has the comparative advantage in production of yo-yos because it has the lower opportunity cost (just 0.20 x-rays) of producing yo-yos.

**Specialization:** Which nation should specialize in production of x-rays? In production of yo-yos? *(Nations should specialize in the product in which they have the comparative advantage.)*

**SOLUTION:** Because Alka has the comparative advantage in production of x-rays, Alka should produce x-rays. Because Baiwan has the comparative advantage in production of yo-yos, Baiwan should produce yo-yos.

**Gains from Trade:** How large are the gains from trade? *(Gains from trade: The increase in the worldwide production of goods and services following specialization and trade.)*

To answer this question, you need to know the pre-trade production combinations in each nation. In this chapter you are typically given the pre-trade production combinations. These can be any combinations on the two production possibility frontiers.

Suppose Alka produces 2.5 x-rays and 10 yo-yos per week, and Baiwan produces 2 x-rays and 40 yo-yos. Total world production is $2.5 + 2 = 4.5$ x-rays and $10 + 40 = 50$ yo-yos. When they trade, Alka will specialize in x-rays and produce 5 x-rays. Baiwan will specialize in yo-yos and will produce 50 yo-yos. Total world production will be 5 x-rays and 50 yo-yos.

**SOLUTION:** The gain from trade is $5 - 4.5 = 0.5$ x-ray. In this example, there is no increase in worldwide production of yo-yos.

tunity cost of that coconut in terms of fish is lower. So Hank, despite his absolute disadvantage, even in coconuts, has a comparative advantage in coconut-gathering. Meanwhile Tom, who can use his time better by catching fish, has a comparative *dis*advantage in coconut-gathering.

If comparative advantage were relevant only to castaways, it might not be that interesting. In fact, however, the idea of comparative advantage applies to many activities in the economy. Perhaps its most important application is to trade—not between individuals, but between countries. So let's look briefly at how the model of comparative advantage helps in understanding both the causes and the effects of international trade.

## Comparative Advantage and International Trade

Look at the label on a manufactured good sold in the United States, and there's a good chance you will find that it was produced in some other country—in China, or Japan, or even in Canada, eh? On the other side, many U.S. industries sell a large fraction of their output overseas (this is particularly true of agriculture, high technology, and entertainment).

Should all this international exchange of goods and services be celebrated, or is it cause for concern? Politicians and the public often question the desirability of international trade, arguing that the nation should produce goods for itself rather than buying them from foreigners. Industries around the world demand protection from foreign competition: Japanese farmers want to keep out American rice, American steelworkers want to keep out European steel. And these demands are often supported by public opinion.

Economists, however, have a very positive view of international trade. Why? Because they view it in terms of comparative advantage.

Figure 2-6 shows, with a simple example, how international trade can be interpreted in terms of comparative advantage. Although the example as constructed is

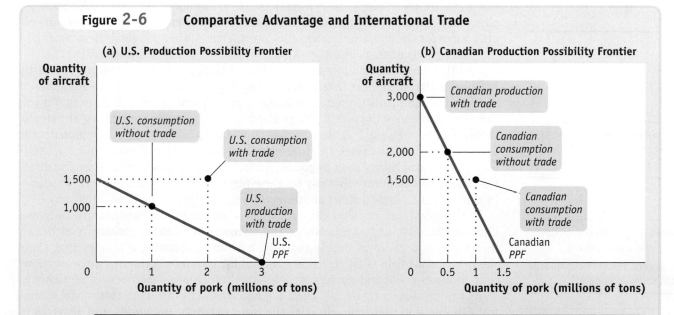

## Figure 2-6   Comparative Advantage and International Trade

In this hypothetical example, Canada and the United States produce only two goods: pork and aircraft. Aircraft are measured on the vertical axis and pork on the horizontal axis. Panel (a) shows the U.S. production possibility frontier. It is relatively flat, implying that the United States has a comparative advantage in pork production. Panel (b) shows the Canadian production possibility frontier. It is relatively steep, implying that Canada has a comparative advantage in aircraft production. Just like two individuals, both countries gain from specialization and trade. **>web...**

hypothetical, it is based on an actual pattern of international trade: American exports of pork to Canada and Canadian exports of aircraft to the United States. Panels (a) and (b) of Figure 2-6 illustrate hypothetical production possibility frontiers for the United States and Canada, with pork measured on the horizontal axis and aircraft measured on the vertical axis. The U.S. production possibility frontier is flatter than the Canadian frontier, implying that the United States has a comparative advantage in pork and Canada has a comparative advantage in aircraft.

Although the consumption points in Figure 2-6 are hypothetical, they illustrate a general principle: just like the example of Tom and Hank, the United States and Canada can both achieve mutual gains from trade. If the United States concentrates on producing pork and ships some of its output to Canada, while Canada concentrates on aircraft and ships some of its output to the United States, both countries can consume more than if they insisted on being self-sufficient.

Moreover, these mutual gains don't depend on each country being better at producing one kind of good. Even if one country has, say, higher output per person-hour in both industries—that is, even if one country has an absolute advantage in both industries—there are still mutual gains from trade.

But how does trade actually take place in market interactions? This brings us to our final model, the circular-flow diagram, which helps economists analyze the transactions that take place in a market economy.

## Transactions: The Circular-Flow Diagram

The little economy created by Tom and Hank on their island lacks many features of the economy modern Americans live in. For one thing, though millions of Americans are self-employed, most workers are employed by someone else, usually a company with hundreds or thousands of employees. Also, Tom and Hank engage only in the simplest of economic transactions, **barter,** in which an individual directly trades a good or service he or she has for a good or service he or she wants. In the modern economy, simple barter is rare: usually people trade goods or services for money—pieces of colored paper with no inherent value—and then trade those pieces of colored paper for the goods or services they want. That is, they sell goods or services and buy other goods or services.

And they both sell and buy a lot of different things. The U.S. economy is a vastly complex entity, with more than a hundred million workers employed by hundreds of thousands of companies, producing millions of different goods and services. Yet you can learn some very important things about the economy by considering the simple model shown in Figure 2-7, the **circular-flow diagram.** This diagram represents the transactions that take place in an economy by two kinds of flows around a circle: flows of physical things such as goods, services, labor, or raw materials in one direction, and flows of money that pay for these physical things in the opposite direction. In this case the physical flows are shown in yellow, the money flows in green.

The simplest circular-flow diagram models an economy that contains only two kinds of "inhabitants": **households** and **firms.** A household consists of either an individual or a group of people (usually, but not necessarily, a family) that share their income. A firm is an organization (usually, but not necessarily, a corporation) that produces goods and services for sale—and that employs members of households.

As you can see in Figure 2-7, there are two kinds of markets in this model economy. On one side (here the left side) there are **markets for goods and services** in which households buy the goods and services they want from firms. This produces a flow of goods and services to households and a return flow of money to firms.

On the other side, there are **factor markets.** A **factor of production** is a resource used to produce goods and services. Economists usually use the term *factor of production* to refer to a resource that is not used up in production. For example, workers use sewing machines to convert cloth into shirts; the workers and the sewing machines

---

Trade takes the form of **barter** when people directly exchange goods or services that they have for goods or services that they want.

The **circular-flow diagram** is a model that represents the transactions in an economy by flows around a circle.

A **household** is a person or a group of people that share their income.

A **firm** is an organization that produces goods and services for sale.

Firms sell goods and services that they produce to households in **markets for goods and services.**

Firms buy the resources they need to produce—**factors of production**—in **factor markets.**

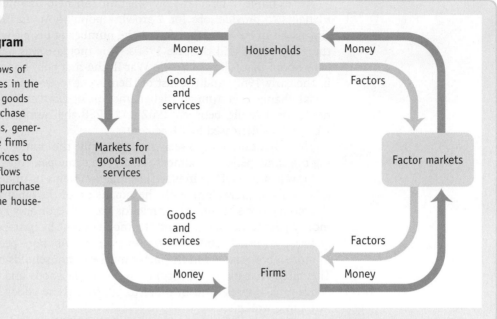

**Figure 2-7**

**The Circular-Flow Diagram**

This model represents the flows of money and goods and services in the economy. In the markets for goods and services, households purchase goods and services from firms, generating a flow of money to the firms and a flow of goods and services to the households. The money flows back to households as firms purchase factors of production from the households in factor markets.

are factors of production, but the cloth is not. Broadly speaking, the main factors of production are labor, land, capital, and human capital. Labor is the work of human beings; land is a resource supplied by nature; capital refers to "created" resources such as machines and buildings; and human capital refers to the educational achievements and skills of the labor force, which enhance its productivity. Of course, each of these is really a category rather than a single factor: land in North Dakota is quite different from land in Florida.

The factor market most of us know best is the *labor market*, in which workers are paid for their time. Besides labor, we can think of households as owning and selling the other factors of production to firms. For example, when a corporation pays dividends to its stockholders, who are members of households, it is in effect paying them for the use of the machines and buildings that ultimately belong to those investors.

In what sense is Figure 2-7 a model? That is, in what sense is it a *simplified* representation of reality? The answer is that this picture ignores a number of real-world complications. A few examples:

- In the real world, the distinction between firms and households isn't always that clear-cut. Consider a small, family-run business—a farm, a shop, a small hotel. Is this a firm or a household? A more complete picture would include a separate box for family businesses.

- Many of the sales firms make are not to households but to other firms; for example, steel companies sell mainly to other companies such as auto manufacturers, not to households. A more complete picture would include these flows of goods and money within the business sector.

- The figure doesn't show the government, which in the real world diverts quite a lot of money out of the circular flow in the form of taxes but also injects a lot of money back into the flow in the form of spending.

Figure 2-7, in other words, is by no means a complete picture either of all the types of "inhabitants" of the real economy or of all the flows of money and physical items that take place among these inhabitants.

Despite its simplicity, the circular-flow diagram, like any good economic model, is a very useful aid to thinking about the economy.

For example, a circular-flow diagram can help us understand how the economy manages to provide jobs for a growing population. To illustrate, consider the huge expansion in the U.S. labor force—the number of people who want to work—between the early 1960s and the late 1980s. This increase was partly caused by the 15-year baby boom that followed World War II; the first baby boomers began looking for jobs in the early 1960s and the last of them went to work in the late 1980s. In addition, social changes led a much higher fraction of women to seek paid work outside the home. As a result, between 1962 and 1988 the number of Americans employed or seeking jobs increased by 71 percent.

That's a lot of new job seekers. But luckily, the number of jobs also expanded during the same period, by almost exactly the same percentage.

Or was it luck? The circular-flow diagram helps us understand why the number of jobs available grew along with the expansion of the labor force. Figure 2-8 compares the money flows around the circle for the U.S. economy in 1962 and 1988. Both the money paid to households and the money spent by households increased enormously over the period—and that was no accident. As more people went to work—that is, as more labor was sold in the factor markets—households had more income to spend. They used that increased income to buy more goods and services in the market for goods and services. And in order to produce these goods and services, firms had to hire more workers!

So, despite being an extremely simple model of the economy, the circular-flow diagram helps us to understand some important facts about the real U.S. economy. The number of jobs isn't fixed, the model tells us, because it depends on how much households spend; and the amount households spend depends on how many people are working. It is, in other words, no accident that the economy somehow creates enough jobs even when the working population grows rapidly.

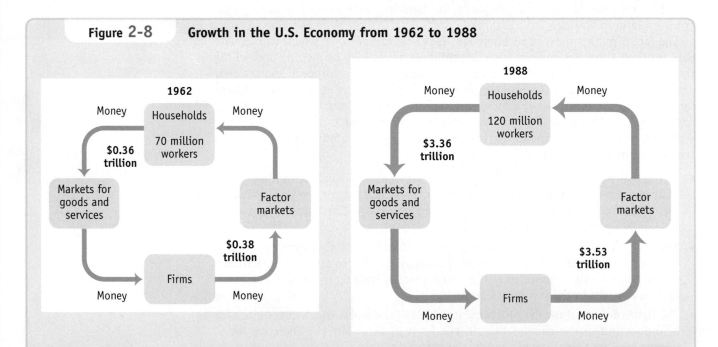

### Figure 2-8   Growth in the U.S. Economy from 1962 to 1988

These two circular-flow diagrams—one corresponding to 1962, the other corresponding to 1988—help us understand how the U.S. economy was able to produce enough jobs for its rapidly growing labor force. A roughly twofold increase in the number of workers from 1962 to 1988 was accompanied by a ninefold increase in money flows between households and firms. As the labor force grew, money going to households increased and their spending on goods and services increased. This led firms to hire more workers to meet the increased desire for goods and services and generated more jobs for households.

# *economics in action*

## Rich Nation, Poor Nation

Try taking off your clothes—at a suitable time and in a suitable place, of course—and take a look at the labels inside that say where they were made. It's a very good bet that much, if not most, of your clothing was manufactured overseas, in a country that is much poorer than the United States—say, in El Salvador, Sri Lanka, or Bangladesh.

Why are these countries so much poorer than we are? The immediate reason is that their economies are much less *productive*—firms in these countries are just not able to produce as much from a given quantity of resources as comparable firms in the United States or other wealthy countries. Why countries differ so much in productivity is a deep question—indeed, one of the main questions that preoccupy economists. But in any case, the difference in productivity is a fact.

But if the economies of these countries are so much less productive than ours, how is it that they make so much of our clothing? Why don't we do it for ourselves?

The answer is "comparative advantage." Just about every industry in Bangladesh is much less productive than the corresponding industry in the United States. But the productivity difference between rich and

Although less productive than American workers, Bengali workers have a comparative advantage in clothing production.

poor countries varies across goods; it is very large in the production of sophisticated goods like aircraft but not that large in the production of simpler goods like clothing. So Bangladesh's position with regard to clothing production is like Hank's position with respect to coconut gathering: he's not as good at it as his fellow castaway, but it's the thing he does comparatively well.

The point is that Bangladesh, though it is at an absolute disadvantage compared with the United States in almost everything, has a comparative advantage in clothing production. This means that both the United States and Bangladesh are able to consume more because they specialize in producing different things, with Bangladesh supplying our clothing and the United States supplying Bangladesh with more sophisticated goods. ■

> > > > > > > > > > > > > > > > > > > > >

## >> CHECK YOUR UNDERSTANDING 2-1

1. True or false? Explain your answer.
   a. An increase in the amount of resources available to Tom for use in producing coconuts and fish does not change his production possibility frontier.
   b. A technological change that allows Tom to catch more fish for any amount of coconuts gathered results in a change in his production possibility frontier.
   c. The production possibility frontier is useful because it illustrates how much of one good an economy must give up to get more of another good regardless of whether resources are being used efficiently.

2. In Italy, an automobile can be produced by 8 workers in one day and a washing machine by 3 workers in one day. In the United States, an automobile can be produced by 6 workers in one day, and a washing machine by 2 workers in one day.
   a. Which country has an absolute advantage in the production of automobiles? In washing machines?
   b. Which country has a comparative advantage in the production of washing machines? In automobiles?
   c. What pattern of specialization results in the greatest gains from trade between the two countries?

3. Use the circular-flow diagram to explain how an increase in the amount of money spent by households results in an increase in the number of jobs in the economy. Describe in words what the circular-flow model predicts.

*Solutions appear at back of book.*

# Using Models

Economics, we have now learned, is mainly a matter of creating models that draw on a set of basic principles but add some more specific assumptions that allow the modeler to apply those principles to a particular situation. But what do economists actually *do* with their models?

## Positive Versus Normative Economics

Imagine that you are an economic adviser to the governor of your state. What kinds of questions might the governor ask you to answer?

Well, here are three possible questions:

1. How much revenue will the tolls on the state turnpike yield next year?
2. How much would that revenue increase if the toll were raised from $1 to $1.50?
3. Should the toll be raised, bearing in mind that a toll increase will reduce traffic and air pollution near the road but will impose some financial hardship on frequent commuters?

There is a big difference between the first two questions and the third one. The first two are questions about facts. Your forecast of next year's toll collection will be proved right or wrong when the numbers actually come in. Your estimate of the impact of a change in the toll is a little harder to check—revenue depends on other factors besides the toll, and it may be hard to disentangle the causes of any change in revenue. Still, in principle there is only one right answer.

But the question of whether tolls should be raised may not have a "right" answer—two people who agree on the effects of a higher toll could still disagree about whether raising the toll is a good idea. For example, someone who lives near the turnpike but doesn't commute on it will care a lot about noise and air pollution but not so much about commuting costs. A regular commuter who doesn't live near the turnpike will have the opposite priorities.

This example highlights a key distinction between two roles of economic analysis. Analysis that tries to answer questions about the way the world works, which have definite right and wrong answers, is known as **positive economics.** In contrast, analysis that involves saying how the world *should* work is known as **normative economics.** To put it another way, positive economics is about description; normative economics is about prescription.

Positive economics occupies most of the time and effort of the economics profession. And models play a crucial role in almost all positive economics. As we mentioned earlier, the U.S. government uses a computer model to assess proposed changes in national tax policy, and many state governments have similar models to assess the effects of their own tax policy.

It's worth noting that there is a subtle but important difference between the first and second questions we imagined the governor asking. Question 1 asked for a simple prediction about next year's revenue—a **forecast.** Question 2 was a "what if" question, asking how revenue would change if the tax law were to change. Economists are often called upon to answer both types of questions, but models are especially useful for answering "what if" questions.

The answers to such questions often serve as a guide to policy, but they are still predictions, not prescriptions. That is, they tell you what will happen if a policy is changed; they don't tell you whether that result is good or not. Suppose that your economic model tells you that the governor's proposed increase in highway tolls will raise property values in communities near the road but will hurt those people who must use the turnpike to get to work. Does that make this proposed toll increase a good idea or a bad one? It depends on whom you ask. As we've just seen, someone who is very concerned with the communities near the road will support the increase, but someone who is very concerned with the welfare of drivers will feel differently. That's a value judgment—it's not a question of economic analysis.

**Positive economics** is the branch of economic analysis that describes the way the economy actually works. **Normative economics** makes prescriptions about the way the economy *should* work.

A **forecast** is a simple prediction of the future.

Still, economists often do end up giving policy advice. That is, they do engage in normative economics. How can they do this when there may be no "right" answer?

One answer is that economists are also citizens, and we all have our opinions. But economic analysis can often be used to show that some policies are clearly better than others, regardless of anyone's opinions.

Suppose that policy A makes everyone better off than policy B—or at least makes some people better off without making other people worse off. Then A is clearly more efficient than B. That's not a value judgment: we're talking about how best to achieve a goal, not about the goal itself.

For example, two different policies have been used to help low-income families obtain housing: rent control, which limits the rents landlords are allowed to charge, and rent subsidies, which provide families with additional money to pay rent. Almost all economists agree that subsidies are the more efficient policy. (In Chapter 4 we'll see why this is so.) And so the great majority of economists, whatever their personal politics, favor subsidies over rent control.

When policies can be clearly ranked in this way, then economists generally agree. But it is no secret that economists sometimes disagree. Why does this happen?

## When and Why Economists Disagree

Economists have a reputation for arguing with each other. Where does this reputation come from?

One important answer is that media coverage tends to exaggerate the real differences in views among economists. If nearly all economists agree on an issue—for example, the proposition that rent controls lead to housing shortages—reporters and editors are likely to conclude that there is no story worth covering, and so the professional consensus tends to go unreported. But when there is some issue on which prominent economists take opposing sides—for example, whether cutting taxes right now would help the economy—that does make a good news story. So you hear much more about the areas of disagreement within economics than you do about the large areas of agreement.

It is also worth remembering that economics is, unavoidably, often tied up in politics. On a number of issues powerful interest groups know what opinions they want to hear; they therefore have an incentive to find and promote economists who profess those opinions, giving these economists a prominence and visibility out of proportion to their support among their colleagues.

But although the appearance of disagreement among economists exceeds the reality, it remains true that economists often *do* disagree about important things. For example, some very respected economists argue vehemently that the U.S. government should replace the income tax with a *value-added tax* (a national sales tax, which is the main source of government revenue in many European countries). Other equally respected economists disagree. Why this difference of opinion?

One important source of differences is in values: as in any diverse group of individuals, reasonable people can differ. In comparison to an income tax, a value-added tax typically falls more heavily on people of modest means. So an economist who values a society with more social and income equality for its own sake will tend to oppose a value-added tax. An economist with different values will be less likely to oppose it.

A second important source of differences arises from economic modeling. Because economists base their conclusions on models, which are simplified representations of reality, two economists can legitimately disagree about which simplifications are appropriate—and therefore arrive at different conclusions.

"If all the economists in the world were laid end to end, they still couldn't reach a conclusion." So goes one popular economist joke. But do economists really disagree that much?

Not according to a classic survey of members of the American Economic Association, reported in the May 1992 issue of the *American Economic Review* and updated in the Fall 2003 issue of the *Journal of Economic Education*. The authors asked respondents to agree or disagree with a number of statements about the economy; what they found was a high level of agreement among professional economists on many of the statements. At the top, with more than 90 percent of the economists agreeing, were

"Tariffs and import quotas usually reduce general economic welfare" and "A ceiling on rents reduces the quantity and quality of housing available." What's striking about these two statements is that many noneconomists disagree: tariffs and import quotas to keep out foreign-produced goods are favored by many voters, and proposals to do away with rent control in cities like New York and San Francisco have met fierce political opposition.

So is the stereotype of quarreling economists a myth? Not entirely: economists do disagree quite a lot on some issues, especially in macroeconomics. But there is a large area of common ground.

Suppose that the U.S. government were considering introducing a value-added tax. Economist A may rely on a model that focuses on the administrative costs of tax systems—that is, the costs of monitoring, processing papers, collecting the tax, and so on. This economist might then point to the well-known high costs of administering a value-added tax and argue against the change. But Economist B may think that the right way to approach the question is to ignore the administrative costs and focus on how the proposed law would change savings behavior. This economist might point to studies suggesting that value-added taxes promote higher consumer saving, a desirable result.

Because the economists have used different models—that is, made different simplifying assumptions—they arrive at different conclusions. And so the two economists may find themselves on different sides of the issue.

Most such disputes are eventually resolved by the accumulation of evidence showing which of the various models proposed by economists does a better job of fitting the facts. However, in economics as in any science, it can take a long time before research settles important disputes—decades, in some cases. And since the economy is always changing, in ways that make old models invalid or raise new policy questions, there are always new issues on which economists disagree. The policy maker must then decide which economist to believe.

The important point is that economic analysis is a method, not a set of conclusions.

# *economics in action*

## Economists in Government

Many economists are mainly engaged in teaching and research. But quite a few economists have a more direct hand in events.

As described in For Inquiring Minds on page 21, economists play a significant role in the business world, especially in the financial industry. But the most striking involvement of economists in the "real" world is their extensive participation in government.

This shouldn't be surprising: One of the most important functions of government is to make economic policy, and almost every government policy decision must take economic effects into consideration. So governments around the world employ economists in a variety of roles.

In the U.S. government, a key role is played by the Council of Economic Advisers, a branch of the Executive Office (that is, the staff of the president) whose sole purpose is to advise the White House on economic matters and to prepare the annual Economic Report of the President. Unusually for a government agency, most of the economists at the Council are not long-term civil servants; instead, they are mainly professors on leave for one or two years from their universities. Many of the nation's best-known economists have served on the Council of Economic Advisers at some point during their careers.

Economists also play an important role in many other parts of the U.S. government. Indeed, as the Bureau of Labor Statistics *Occupational Outlook Handbook* says, "Some economists work in almost every area of government." Needless to say, the Bureau of Labor Statistics is itself a major employer of economists.

It's also worth noting that economists play an especially important role in two international organizations headquartered in Washington, D.C.: the International Monetary Fund, which provides advice and loans to countries experiencing economic difficulties, and the World Bank, which provides advice and loans to promote long-term economic development.

Do all these economists in government disagree with each other all the time? Are their positions largely dictated by political affiliation? The answer to both questions is no. Although there are important disputes over economic issues in government, and politics inevitably plays some role, there is broad agreement among economists on many issues, and most economists in government try very hard to assess issues as objectively as possible. ■

> > > > > > > > > > > > > > > > > > > >

## >>CHECK YOUR UNDERSTANDING 2-2

1. Which of the following statements is a positive statement? Which is a normative statement?
   a. Society should take measures to prevent people from engaging in dangerous personal behavior.
   b. People who engage in dangerous personal behavior impose higher costs on society through higher medical costs.

2. True or false? Explain your answer.
   a. Policy choice A and policy choice B attempt to achieve the same social goal. Policy choice A, however, results in a much less efficient use of resources than policy choice B. Therefore economists are more likely to agree on choosing policy choice B.
   b. When two economists disagree on the desirability of a policy, it's typically because one of them has made a mistake.
   c. Policy makers can always use economics to figure out which goals a society should try to achieve.

Solutions appear at back of book.

## • A LOOK AHEAD •

This chapter has given you a first view of what it means to do economics, starting with the general idea of models as a way to make sense of a complicated world and then moving on to three simple introductory models.

To get a real sense of how economic analysis works, however, and to show just how useful such analysis can be, we need to move on to a more powerful model. In the next two chapters we will study the quintessential economic model, one that has an amazing ability to make sense of many policy issues, predict the effects of many forces, and change the way you look at the world. That model is known as "supply and demand."

## SUMMARY

1. Almost all economics is based on **models,** "thought experiments" or simplified versions of reality, many of which use mathematical tools such as graphs. An important assumption in economic models is the **other things equal assumption,** which allows analysis of the effect of a change in one factor by holding all other relevant factors unchanged.

2. One important economic model is the **production possibility frontier.** It illustrates: opportunity cost (showing how much less of one good can be produced if more of the other good is produced); efficiency (an economy is efficient if it produces on the production possibility frontier); and economic growth (an expansion of thc production possibility frontier).

3. Another important model is **comparative advantage,** which explains the source of gains from trade between individuals and countries. Everyone has a comparative advantage in something—some good or service in which that person has a lower opportunity cost than everyone else. But it is often confused with **absolute advantage,** an ability to produce a particular good or service better than anyone else. This confusion leads some to erroneously conclude that there are no gains from trade between people or countries.

4. In the simplest economies people **barter**—trade goods and services for one another—rather than trade them for money, as in a modern economy. The **circular-flow diagram** is a model representing transactions within the economy as flows of goods, services, and income between **households** and **firms**. These transactions occur in **markets for goods and services** and **factor markets,** markets for **factors of production** such as labor. It is useful in understanding how spending, production, employment, income, and growth are related in the economy.

5. Economists use economic models for both **positive economics,** which describes how the economy works, and for **normative economics,** which prescribes how the economy should work. Positive economics often involves making **forecasts.** Economists can determine correct answers for positive questions, but typically not for normative questions, which involve value judgments. The exceptions are when policies designed to achieve a certain prescription can be clearly ranked in terms of efficiency.

6. There are two main reasons economists disagree. One, they may disagree about which simplifications to make in a model. Two, economists may disagree—like everyone else—about values.

## KEY TERMS

Model, p. 21
Other things equal assumption, p. 21
Production possibility frontier, p. 22
Comparative advantage, p. 27
Absolute advantage, p. 28

Barter, p. 30
Circular-flow diagram, p. 30
Household, p. 30
Firm, p. 30
Markets for goods and services, p. 30

Factors of production, p. 30
Factor markets, p. 30
Positive economics, p. 34
Normative economics, p. 34
Forecast, p. 34

## PROBLEMS

1. Atlantis is a small, isolated island in the South Atlantic. The inhabitants grow potatoes and catch fresh fish. The accompanying table shows the maximum annual output combinations of potatoes and fish that can be produced. Obviously, given their limited resources and available technology, as they use more of their resources for potato production, there are fewer resources available for catching fish.

| Maximum annual output options | Quantity of potatoes (pounds) | Quantity of fish (pounds) |
|:---:|:---:|:---:|
| A | 1,000 | 0 |
| B | 800 | 300 |
| C | 600 | 500 |
| D | 400 | 600 |
| E | 200 | 650 |
| F | 0 | 675 |

a. Draw a production possibility frontier with potatoes on the horizontal axis and fish on the vertical axis illustrating these options, showing points A–F.

b. Can Atlantis produce 500 pounds of fish and 800 pounds of potatoes? Explain. Where would this point lie relative to the production possibility frontier?

c. What is the opportunity cost of increasing the annual output of potatoes from 600 to 800 pounds?

d. What is the opportunity cost of increasing the annual output of potatoes from 200 to 400 pounds?

e. Can you explain why the answers to parts c and d are not the same? What does this imply about the slope of the production possibility frontier?

2. In the ancient country of Roma, only two goods, spaghetti and meatballs, are produced. There are two tribes in Roma, the Tivoli and the Frivoli. By themselves, the Tivoli each month can produce either 30 pounds of spaghetti and no meatballs,

or 50 pounds of meatballs and no spaghetti, or any combination in between. The Frivoli, by themselves, each month can produce 40 pounds of spaghetti and no meatballs, or 30 pounds of meatballs and no spaghetti, or any combination in between.

a. Assume that all production possibility frontiers are straight lines. Draw one diagram showing the monthly production possibility frontier for the Tivoli and another showing the monthly production possibility frontier for the Frivoli. Show how you calculated them.

b. Which tribe has the comparative advantage in spaghetti production? In meatball production?

In A.D. 100 the Frivoli discover a new technique for making meatballs that doubles the quantity of meatballs they can produce each month.

c. Draw the new monthly production possibility frontier for the Frivoli.

d. After the innovation, which tribe now has the absolute advantage in producing meatballs? In producing spaghetti? Which has the comparative advantage in meatball production? In spaghetti production?

3. Peter Pundit, an economics reporter, states that the European Union (EU) is increasing its productivity very rapidly in all industries. He claims that this productivity advance is so rapid that output from the EU in these industries will soon exceed that of the United States and, as a result, the United States will no longer benefit from trade with the EU.

a. Do you think Peter Pundit is correct or not? If not, what do you think is the source of his mistake?

b. If the EU and the United States continue to trade, what do you think will characterize the goods that the EU exports to the United States and the goods that the United States exports to the EU?

4. You are in charge of allocating residents to your dormitory's baseball and basketball teams. You are down to the last four people, two of whom must be allocated to baseball and two to basketball. The accompanying table gives each person's batting average and free-throw average. Explain how you would use the concept of comparative advantage to allocate the players. Begin by establishing each player's opportunity cost of free throws in terms of batting average.

| Name | Batting average | Free-throw average |
| --- | --- | --- |
| Kelley | 70% | 60% |
| Jackie | 50% | 50% |
| Curt | 10% | 30% |
| Gerry | 80% | 70% |

Why is it likely that the other basketball players will be unhappy about this arrangement but the other baseball players will be satisfied? Nonetheless, why would an economist say that this is an efficient way to allocate players for your dormitory's sports teams?

5. The economy of Atlantis has developed, and the inhabitants now use money in the form of cowry shells. Draw a circular-flow diagram showing households and firms. Firms produce potatoes and fish, and households buy potatoes and fish. Households also provide the land and labor to firms. Identify where in the flows of cowry shells or physical things (goods and services, or resources) each of the following impacts would occur. Describe how this impact spreads around the circle.

a. A devastating hurricane floods many of the potato fields.

b. A very productive fishing season yields a very large number of fish caught.

c. The inhabitants of Atlantis discover the Macarena and spend several days a month at dancing festivals.

6. An economist might say that colleges and universities "produce" education, using faculty members and students as inputs. According to this line of reasoning, education is then "consumed" by households. Construct a circular-flow diagram like the one found in this chapter to represent the sector of the economy devoted to college education: colleges and universities represent firms, and households both consume education and provide faculty and students to universities. What are the relevant markets in this model? What is being bought and sold in each direction? What would happen in the model if the government decided to subsidize 50 percent of all college students' tuition?

7. Your dormitory roommate plays loud music most of the time; you, however, would prefer more peace and quiet. You suggest that she buy some earphones. She responds that although she would be happy to use earphones, she has many other things that she would prefer to spend her money on right now. You discuss this situation with a friend who is an economics major. The following exchange takes place:

*He: How much would it cost to buy earphones?*
*You: $15.*

*He: How much do you value having some peace and quiet for the rest of the semester?*
*You: $30.*

*He: It is efficient for you to buy the earphones and give them to your roommate. You gain more than you lose; the benefit exceeds the cost. You should do that.*
*You: It just isn't fair that I have to pay for the earphones when I'm not the one making the noise.*

a. Which parts of this conversation contain positive statements and which parts contain normative statements?

b. Compose an argument supporting your viewpoint that your roommate should be the one to change her behavior. Similarly, compose an argument from the viewpoint of your roommate that you should be the one to buy the earphones. If your dormitory has a policy that gives residents the unlimited right to play music, whose argument is likely to win? If your dormitory has a rule that a person must stop playing music whenever a roommate complains, whose argument is likely to win?

8. A representative of the American clothing industry recently made the following statement: "Workers in Asia often work in sweatshop conditions earning only pennies an hour. American workers are more productive and as a result earn higher wages. In order to preserve the dignity of the American workplace, the government should enact legislation banning imports of low-wage Asian clothing."

   **a.** Which parts of this quote are positive statements? Which parts are normative statements?

   **b.** Is the policy that is being advocated consistent with the preceding statements about the wages and productivities of American and Asian workers?

   **c.** Would such a policy make some Americans better off without making any other Americans worse off? That is, would this policy be efficient from the viewpoint of all Americans?

   **d.** Would low-wage Asian workers benefit from or be hurt by such a policy?

9. Are the following statements true or false? Explain your answers.

   **a.** "When people must pay higher taxes on their wage earnings, it reduces their incentive to work" is a positive statement.

   **b.** "We should lower taxes to encourage more work" is a positive statement.

   **c.** Economics cannot always be used to completely decide what society ought to do.

   **d.** "The system of public education in this country generates greater benefits to society than the cost of running the system" is a normative statement.

   **e.** All disagreements among economists are generated by the media.

10. Evaluate the following statement: "It is easier to build an economic model that accurately reflects events that have already occurred than to build an economic model to forecast future events." Do you think that this is true or not? Why? What does this imply about the difficulties of building good economic models?

11. Economists who work for the government are often called on to make policy recommendations. Why do you think it is important for the public to be able to differentiate normative statements from positive statements in these recommendations?

12. The mayor of Gotham City, worried about a potential epidemic of deadly influenza this winter, asks an economic adviser the following series of questions. Does each question require the economic adviser to make a positive assessment or a normative assessment?

    **a.** How much vaccine will be in stock in the city by the end of November?

    **b.** If we offer to pay 10 percent more per dose to the pharmaceutical companies providing the vaccines, will they provide additional doses?

    **c.** If there is a shortage of vaccine in the city, whom should we vaccinate first—the elderly or the very young? (Assume that a person from one group has an equal likelihood of dying from influenza as a person from the other group.)

    **d.** If the city charges $25 per shot, how many people will pay?

    **e.** If the city charges $25 per shot, it will make a profit of $10 per shot, money that can go to pay for inoculating poor people. Should the city engage in such a scheme?

13. Assess the following statement: "If economists just had enough data, they could solve all policy questions in a way that maximizes the social good. There would be no need for divisive political debates, such as whether the government should provide free medical care for all."

---

**>web...** To continue your study and review of concepts in this chapter, please visit the Krugman/Wells/Olney website for quizzes, animated graph tutorials, web links to helpful resources, and more.

**www.worthpublishers.com/krugmanwellsolney**

## >> Chapter 2 Appendix: Graphs in Economics

## Getting the Picture

Whether you're reading about economics in the *Wall Street Journal* or in your economics textbook, you will see many graphs. Visual images can make it much easier to understand verbal descriptions, numerical information, or ideas. In economics, graphs are the type of visual image used to facilitate understanding. To fully understand the ideas and information being discussed, you need to be familiar with how to interpret these visual aids. This appendix explains how graphs are constructed and interpreted and how they are used in economics.

## Graphs, Variables, and Economic Models

One reason to attend college is that a bachelor's degree provides access to higher-paying jobs. Additional degrees, such as MBAs or law degrees, increase earnings even more. If you were to read an article about the relationship between educational attainment and income, you would probably see a graph showing the income levels for workers with different amounts of education. And this graph would depict the idea that, in general, more education increases income. This graph, like most of those in economics, would depict the relationship between two economic variables. A **variable** is a quantity that can take on more than one value, such as the number of years of education a person has, the price of a can of soda, or a household's income.

A quantity that can take on more than one value is called a **variable**.

As you learned in this chapter, economic analysis relies heavily on *models*, simplified descriptions of real situations. Most economic models describe the relationship between two variables, simplified by holding constant other variables that may affect the relationship. For example, an economic model might describe the relationship between the price of a can of soda and the number of cans of soda that consumers will buy, assuming that everything else that affects consumers' purchases of soda stays constant. This type of model can be described mathematically or verbally, but illustrating the relationship in a graph makes it easier to understand. Next we show how graphs that depict economic models are constructed and interpreted.

## How Graphs Work

Most graphs in economics are based on a grid built around two perpendicular lines that show the values of two variables, helping you visualize the relationship between them. So a first step in understanding the use of such graphs is to see how this system works.

### Two-Variable Graphs

Figure 2A-1 on page 42 shows a typical two-variable graph. It illustrates the data in the accompanying table on outside temperature and the number of sodas a typical vendor can expect to sell at a baseball stadium during one game. The first column shows the values of outside temperature (the first variable) and the second column shows the values of the number of sodas sold (the second variable). Five combinations or pairs of the two variables are shown, each denoted by *A* through *E* in the third column.

Now let's turn to graphing the data in this table. In any two-variable graph, one variable is called the *x*-variable and the other is called the *y*-variable. Here we have

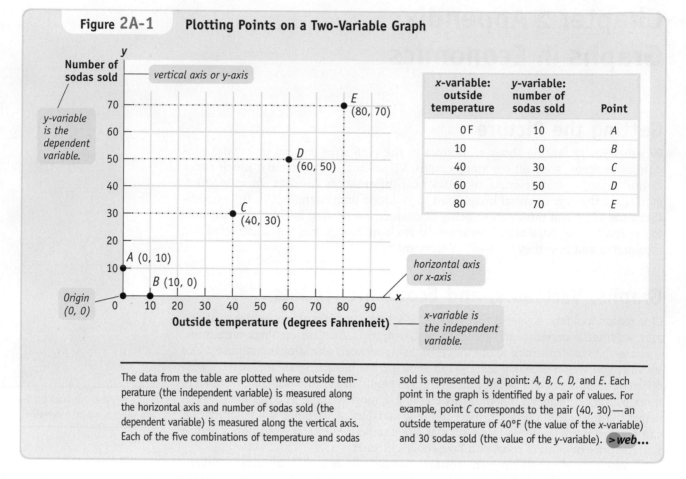

**Figure 2A-1    Plotting Points on a Two-Variable Graph**

| x-variable: outside temperature | y-variable: number of sodas sold | Point |
|---|---|---|
| 0 F | 10 | A |
| 10 | 0 | B |
| 40 | 30 | C |
| 60 | 50 | D |
| 80 | 70 | E |

The data from the table are plotted where outside temperature (the independent variable) is measured along the horizontal axis and number of sodas sold (the dependent variable) is measured along the vertical axis. Each of the five combinations of temperature and sodas sold is represented by a point: *A, B, C, D,* and *E*. Each point in the graph is identified by a pair of values. For example, point *C* corresponds to the pair (40, 30)—an outside temperature of 40°F (the value of the *x*-variable) and 30 sodas sold (the value of the *y*-variable). **>web...**

The line along which values of the *x*-variable are measured is called the **horizontal axis** or **x-axis**. The line along which values of the *y*-variable are measured is called the **vertical axis** or **y-axis**. The point where the axes of a two-variable graph meet is the **origin**.

## PITFALLS

### WHY Y IS NOT ALWAYS Y

In math class, you probably called the horizontal axis "the *x*-axis" and the vertical axis "the *y*-axis." Some economists do this too. But it can lead to confusion! When we study macroeconomics we will use the symbol *Y* to stand for income. When we graph the relationship between income and spending by households, we will put income *Y* on the horizontal axis.

Wait, you say! But that means we are putting *Y* on the *x*-axis and not on the *y*-axis. Yes, that's absolutely right. And that's why it is best to start thinking of them not as the *x*-axis and the *y*-axis, but as the horizontal and vertical axes.

made outside temperature the *x*-variable and number of sodas sold the *y*-variable. The solid horizontal line in the graph is called the **horizontal axis** or **x-axis,** and values of the *x*-variable—outside temperature—are measured along it. Similarly, the solid vertical line in the graph is called the **vertical axis** or **y-axis,** and values of the *y*-variable—number of sodas sold—are measured along it. At the **origin,** the point where the two axes meet, each variable is equal to zero. As you move rightward from the origin along the *x*-axis, values of the *x*-variable are positive and increasing. As you move up from the origin along the *y*-axis, values of the *y*-variable are positive and increasing.

You can plot each of the five points *A* through *E* on this graph by using a pair of numbers—the values that the *x*-variable and the *y*-variable take on for a given point. In Figure 2A-1, at point *C*, the *x*-variable takes on the value 40 and the *y*-variable takes on the value 30. You plot point *C* by drawing a line straight up from 40 on the *x*-axis and a horizontal line across from 30 on the *y*-axis. We write point *C* as (40, 30). We write the origin as (0, 0).

Looking at point *A* and point *B* in Figure 2A-1, you can see that when one of the variables for a point has a value of zero, it will lie on one of the axes. If the value of *x* is zero, the point will lie on the vertical axis, like point *A*. If the value of *y* is zero, the point will lie on the horizontal axis, like point *B*.

Most graphs that depict relationships between two economic variables represent a **causal relationship,** a relationship in which the value taken by one variable directly influences or determines the value taken by the other variable. In a causal relationship, the determining variable is called the **independent variable;** the variable it determines is called the **dependent variable.** In our example of soda sales, the outside temperature is the independent variable. It directly influences the number of sodas that are sold, the dependent variable in this case.

By convention, we put the independent variable on the horizontal axis and the dependent variable on the vertical axis. Figure 2A-1 is constructed consistent with this convention; the independent variable (outside temperature) is on the horizontal axis and the dependent variable (number of sodas sold) is on the vertical axis. An important exception to this convention is in graphs showing the economic relationship between the price of a product and quantity of the product: although price is generally the independent variable that determines quantity, it is always measured on the vertical axis.

> A **causal relationship** exists between two variables when the value taken by one variable directly influences or determines the value taken by the other variable. In a causal relationship, the determining variable is called the **independent variable;** the variable it determines is called the **dependent variable.**

## Curves on a Graph

Panel (a) of Figure 2A-2 contains some of the same information as Figure 2A-1, with a line drawn through the points *B*, *C*, *D*, and *E*. Such a line on a graph is called a **curve,** regardless of whether it is a straight line or a curved line. If the curve that shows the relationship between two variables is a straight line, or linear, the variables have a **linear relationship.** When the curve is not a straight line, or nonlinear, the variables have a **nonlinear relationship.**

> A **curve** is a line on a graph that depicts a relationship between two variables. It may be either a straight line or a curved line. If the curve is a straight line, the variables have a **linear relationship.** If the curve is not a straight line, the variables have a **nonlinear relationship.**

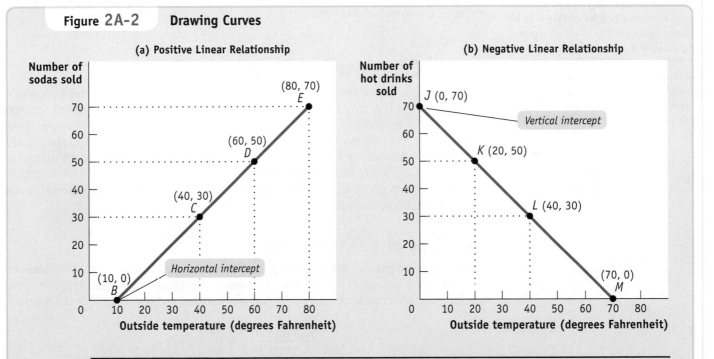

**Figure 2A-2   Drawing Curves**

**(a) Positive Linear Relationship**

**(b) Negative Linear Relationship**

The curve in panel (a) illustrates the relationship between the two variables, outside temperature and number of sodas sold. The two variables have a positive linear relationship: positive because the curve has an upward tilt, and linear because it is a straight line. It implies that an increase in *x* (outside temperature) leads to an increase in *y* (number of sodas sold). The curve in panel (b) is also a straight line, but it tilts downward. The two variables here, outside temperature and number of hot drinks sold, have a negative linear relationship: an increase in *x* (outside temperature) leads to a decrease in *y* (number of hot drinks sold). The curve in panel (a) has a horizontal intercept at point *B*, where it hits the horizontal axis. The curve in panel (b) has a vertical intercept at point *J*, where it hits the vertical axis and a horizontal intercept at point *M*, where it hits the horizontal axis. **>web...**

A point on a curve indicates the value of the *y*-variable for a specific value of the *x*-variable. For example, point *D* indicates that at a temperature of 60°F, a vendor can expect to sell 50 sodas. The shape and orientation of a curve reveal the general nature of the relationship between the two variables. The upward tilt of the curve in panel (a) of Figure 2A-2 suggests that vendors can expect to sell more sodas at higher outside temperatures.

When variables are related this way—that is, when an increase in one variable is associated with an increase in the other variable—the variables are said to have a **positive relationship.** It is illustrated by a curve that slopes upward from left to right. Because this curve is also linear, the relationship between outside temperature and number of sodas sold illustrated by the curve in panel (a) of Figure 2A-2 is a positive linear relationship.

When an increase in one variable is associated with a decrease in the other variable, the two variables are said to have a **negative relationship.** It is illustrated by a curve that slopes downward from left to right, like the curve in panel (b) of Figure 2A-2. Because this curve is also linear, the relationship it depicts is a negative linear relationship. Two variables that might have such a relationship are the outside temperature and the number of hot drinks a vendor can expect to sell at a baseball stadium.

Return for a moment to the curve in panel (a) of Figure 2A-2 and you can see that it hits the horizontal axis at point *B*. This point, known as the **horizontal intercept,** shows the value of the *x*-variable when the value of the *y*-variable is zero. In panel (b) of Figure 2A-2 the curve hits the vertical axis at point *J*. This point, called the **vertical intercept,** indicates the value of the *y*-variable when the value of the *x*-variable is zero.

> Two variables have a **positive relationship** when an increase in the value of one variable is associated with an increase in the value of the other variable. It is illustrated by a curve that slopes upward from left to right.
>
> Two variables have a **negative relationship** when an increase in the value of one variable is associated with a decrease in the value of the other variable. It is illustrated by a curve that slopes downward from left to right.
>
> The **horizontal intercept** of a curve is the point at which it hits the horizontal axis; it indicates the value of the *x*-variable when the value of the *y*-variable is zero.
>
> The **vertical intercept** of a curve is the point at which it hits the vertical axis; it shows the value of the *y*-variable when the value of the *x*-variable is zero.

## A Key Concept: The Slope of a Curve

The **slope** of a line or curve is a measure of how steep it is and indicates how sensitive the *y*-variable is to a change in the *x*-variable. In our example of outside temperature and the number of cans of soda a vendor can expect to sell, the slope of the curve would indicate how many more cans of soda the vendor could expect to sell with each 1° increase in temperature. Interpreted this way, the slope gives meaningful information. Even without numbers for *x* and *y*, it is possible to arrive at important conclusions about the relationship between the two variables by examining the slope of a curve at various points.

> The **slope** of a line or curve is a measure of how steep it is. The slope of a line is measured by "rise over run"—the change in the *y*-variable between two points on the line divided by the change in the *x*-variable between those same two points.

### The Slope of a Linear Curve

Along a linear curve the slope, or steepness, is measured by dividing the "rise" between two points on the curve by the "run" between those same two points. The rise is the amount that *y* changes, and the run is the amount that *x* changes. Here is the formula:

$$\frac{\text{Change in } y}{\text{Change in } x} = \frac{\Delta y}{\Delta x} = \text{Slope}$$

In the formula, the symbol $\Delta$ (the Greek uppercase delta) stands for "change in." When a variable increases, the change in that variable is positive; when a variable decreases, the change in that variable is negative.

The slope of a curve is positive when the rise (the change in the *y*-variable) has the same sign as the run (the change in the *x*-variable). That's because when two numbers have the same sign, the ratio of those two numbers is positive. The curve in panel (a) of Figure 2A-2 has a positive slope: along the curve, both the *y*-variable and the *x*-variable increase. The slope of a curve is negative when the rise and the run have

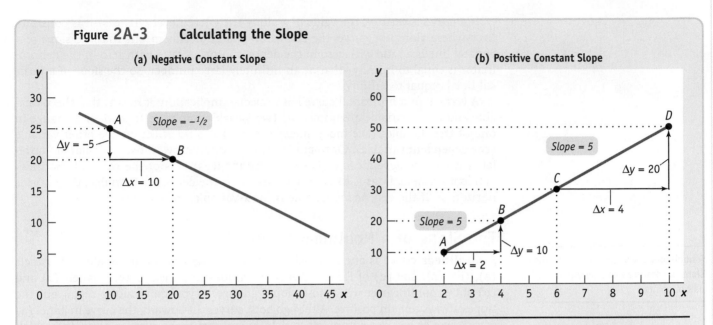

**Figure 2A-3    Calculating the Slope**

**(a) Negative Constant Slope**

**(b) Positive Constant Slope**

Panels (a) and (b) show two linear curves. Between points $A$ and $B$ on the curve in panel (a), the change in $y$ (the rise) is $-5$ and the change in $x$ (the run) is 10. So the slope from $A$ to $B$ is $\Delta y/\Delta x$ $= -5/10 = -1/2 = -0.5$, where the negative sign indicates that the curve is downward sloping. In panel (b), the curve has a slope from $A$ to $B$ of $\Delta y/\Delta x = 10/2 = 5$. The slope from $C$ to $D$ is $\Delta y/\Delta x =$

$20/4 = 5$. The slope is positive, indicating that the curve is upward sloping. Furthermore, the slope between $A$ and $B$ is the same as the slope between $C$ and $D$, making this a linear curve. The slope of a linear curve is constant: it is the same regardless of where it is calculated along the curve. **>web...**

different signs. That's because when two numbers have different signs, the ratio of those two numbers is negative. The curve in panel (b) of Figure 2A-2 has a negative slope: along the curve, an increase in the $x$-variable is associated with a decrease in the $y$-variable.

Figure 2A-3 illustrates how to calculate the slope of a linear curve. Let's focus first on panel (a). From point $A$ to point $B$ the value of $y$ changes from 25 to 20 and the value of $x$ changes from 10 to 20. So the slope of the line between these two points is:

$$\frac{\text{Change in } y}{\text{Change in } x} = \frac{\Delta y}{\Delta x} = \frac{-5}{10} = -\frac{1}{2} = -0.5$$

Because a straight line is equally steep at all points, the slope of a straight line is the same at all points. In other words, a straight line has a constant slope. You can check this by calculating the slope of the linear curve between points $A$ and $B$ and between points $C$ and $D$ in panel (b) of Figure 2A-3.

Between $A$ and $B$:         $$\frac{\Delta y}{\Delta x} = \frac{10}{2} = 5$$

Between $C$ and $D$:         $$\frac{\Delta y}{\Delta x} = \frac{20}{4} = 5$$

## Horizontal and Vertical Curves and Their Slopes

When a curve is horizontal, the value of $y$ along that curve never changes—it is constant. Everywhere along the curve, the change in $y$ is zero. Now, zero divided by any number is zero. So, regardless of the value of the change in $x$, the slope of a horizontal curve is always zero.

If a curve is vertical, the value of x along the curve never changes—it is constant. Everywhere along the curve, the change in x is zero. This means that the slope of a vertical line is a ratio with zero in the denominator. A ratio with zero in the denominator is equal to infinity—that is, an infinitely large number. So the slope of a vertical line is equal to infinity.

A vertical or a horizontal curve has a special implication: it means that the x-variable and the y-variable are unrelated. Two variables are unrelated when a change in one of the variables (the independent variable) has no effect on the other variable (the dependent variable). Or to put it a slightly different way, two variables are unrelated when the dependent variable is constant regardless of the value of the independent variable. If, as is usual, the y-variable is the dependent variable, the curve is horizontal. If the dependent variable is the x-variable, the curve is vertical.

## The Slope of a Nonlinear Curve

> A **nonlinear curve** is one in which the slope is not the same between every pair of points.

A **nonlinear curve** is one in which the slope changes as you move along it. Panels (a), (b), (c), and (d) of Figure 2A-4 show various nonlinear curves. Panels (a) and (b) show nonlinear curves whose slopes change as you move along them, but the slopes always remain positive. Although both curves tilt upward, the curve in panel (a) gets steeper as you move from left to right in contrast to the curve in panel (b), which gets flatter. A curve that is upward sloping and gets steeper, as in panel (a), is said to have *positive increasing* slope. A curve that is upward sloping but gets flatter, as in panel (b), is said to have *positive decreasing* slope.

When we calculate the slope along these nonlinear curves, we obtain different values for the slope at different points. How the slope changes along the curve determines the curve's shape. For example, in panel (a) of Figure 2A-4, the slope of the curve is a positive number that steadily increases as you move from left to right, whereas in panel (b), the slope is a positive number that steadily decreases.

> The **absolute value** of a negative number is the value of the negative number without the minus sign.

The slopes of the curves in panels (c) and (d) are negative numbers. Economists often prefer to express a negative number as its **absolute value,** which is the value of the negative number without the minus sign. In general, we denote the absolute value of a number by two parallel bars around the number; for example, the absolute value of −4 is written as $|-4| = 4$. In panel (c), the absolute value of the slope steadily increases as you move from left to right. The curve therefore has *negative increasing* slope. And in panel (d), the absolute value of the slope of the curve steadily decreases along the curve. This curve therefore has *negative decreasing* slope.

## Calculating the Slope Along a Nonlinear Curve

We've just seen that along a nonlinear curve, the value of the slope depends on where you are on that curve. So how do you calculate the slope of a nonlinear curve?

To calculate the slope along a nonlinear curve, you draw a straight line between two points of the curve. The slope of that straight line is a measure of the average slope of the curve between those two end-points. You can see from panel (a) of Figure 2A-4 that the straight line drawn between points A and B increases along the x-axis from 6 to 10 (so that $\Delta x = 4$) as it increases along the y-axis from 10 to 20 (so that $\Delta y = 10$). Therefore the slope of the straight line connecting points A and B is:

$$\frac{\Delta y}{\Delta x} = \frac{10}{4} = 2.5$$

This means that the average slope of the curve between points A and B is 2.5.

Now consider the same curve between points C and D. A straight line drawn through these two points increases along the x-axis from 11 to 12 ($\Delta x = 1$) as it

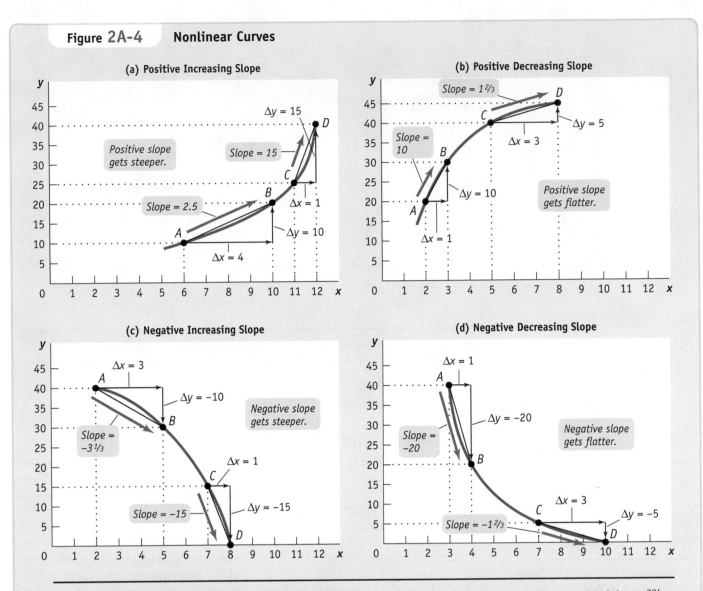

**Figure 2A-4    Nonlinear Curves**

In panel (a) the slope of the curve from A to B is $\Delta y/\Delta x = {}^{10}\!/_4$ = 2.5, and from C to D it is $\Delta y/\Delta x = {}^{15}\!/_1 = 15$. The slope is positive and increasing; it gets steeper as you move to the right. In panel (b) the slope of the curve slope from A to B is $\Delta y/\Delta x = {}^{10}\!/_1 = 10$, and from C to D it is $\Delta y/\Delta x = {}^5\!/_3 = 1^2\!/_3$. The slope is positive and decreasing; it gets flatter as you move to the right. In panel (c) the slope from A to B is $\Delta y/\Delta x = {}^{-10}\!/_3 = -3^1\!/_3$, and from C to D it is $\Delta y/\Delta x = {}^{-15}\!/_1 = -15$. The slope is negative and increasing; it gets steeper as you move to the

right. And in panel (d) the slope from A to B is $\Delta y/\Delta x = {}^{-20}\!/_1 = -20$, and from C to D it is $\Delta y/\Delta x = {}^{-5}\!/_3 = -1^2\!/_3$. The slope is negative and decreasing; it gets flatter as you move to the right. The slope in each case has been calculated by using the arc method—that is, by drawing a straight line connecting two points along a curve. The average slope between those two points is equal to the slope of the straight line between those two points. **>web...**

increases along the y-axis from 25 to 40 ($\Delta y = 15$). So the average slope between points C and D is:

$$\frac{\Delta y}{\Delta x} = \frac{15}{1} = 15$$

Therefore the average slope between points C and D is larger than the average slope between points A and B. These calculations verify what we have already observed—that this upward-tilted curve gets steeper as you move from left to right and therefore has positive increasing slope.

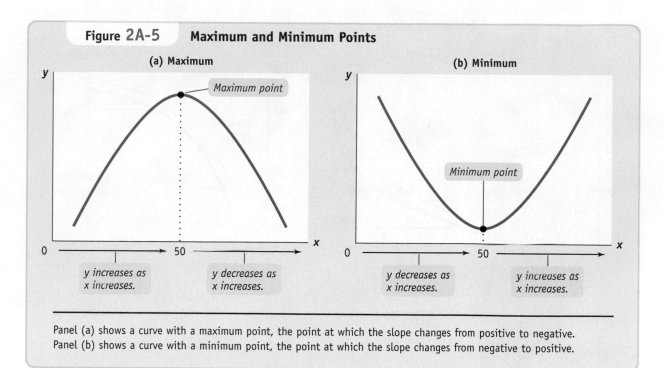

**Figure 2A-5** **Maximum and Minimum Points**

**(a) Maximum**

Maximum point

y increases as
x increases.

y decreases as
x increases.

**(b) Minimum**

Minimum point

y decreases as
x increases.

y increases as
x increases.

Panel (a) shows a curve with a maximum point, the point at which the slope changes from positive to negative.
Panel (b) shows a curve with a minimum point, the point at which the slope changes from negative to positive.

## Maximum and Minimum Points

The slope of a nonlinear curve can change from positive to negative or vice versa. When the slope of a curve changes from positive to negative, it creates what is called a *maximum* point of the curve. When the slope of a curve changes from negative to positive, it creates a *minimum* point.

Panel (a) of Figure 2A-5 illustrates a curve in which the slope changes from positive to negative as you move from left to right. When *x* is between 0 and 50, the slope of the curve is positive. At *x* equal to 50, the curve attains its highest point—the largest value of *y* along the curve. This point is called the **maximum** of the curve. When *x* exceeds 50, the slope becomes negative as the curve turns downward. Many important curves in economics, such as the curve that represents how the profit of a firm changes as it produces more output, are hill-shaped like this.

In contrast, the curve shown in panel (b) of Figure 2A-5 is U-shaped: it has a slope that changes from negative to positive. At *x* equal to 50, the curve reaches its lowest point—the smallest value of *y* along the curve. This point is called the **minimum** of the curve. Various important curves in economics, such as the curve that represents how the costs of some firms change as output increases, are U-shaped like this.

> A nonlinear curve may have a **maximum** point, the highest point along the curve. At the maximum, the slope of the curve changes from positive to negative.

> A nonlinear curve may have a **minimum** point, the lowest point along the curve. At the minimum, the slope of the curve changes from negative to positive.

## Presenting Numerical Information

Graphs, diagrams, and charts can also be used as a convenient way to summarize and display data without assuming some underlying causal relationship. Graphs that simply display numerical information are called *numerical graphs*. Here we will consider four types of numerical graphs: *time-series graphs*, *scatter diagrams*, *pie charts*, and *bar graphs*. These are widely used to display real, empirical data about different economic variables because they often help economists and policy makers identify patterns or trends in the economy. But as we will also see, you must be careful not to misinterpret or draw unwarranted conclusions from numerical graphs. That is, you must be aware of both the usefulness and the limitations of numerical graphs.

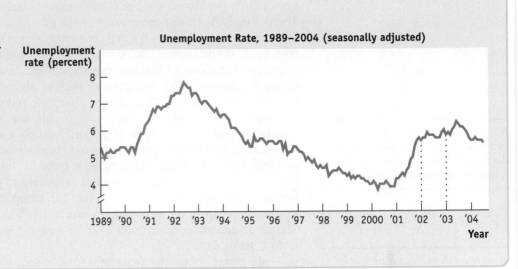

**Figure 2A-6**

### Time-Series Graph

Time-series graphs show successive dates on the *x*-axis and values for a variable on the *y*-axis. This time-series graph shows the seasonally adjusted unemployment rate in the United States from 1989 to mid-2004.

*Source*: Bureau of Labor Statistics.

**Unemployment rate (percent)**

**Unemployment Rate, 1989–2004 (seasonally adjusted)**

## Types of Numerical Graphs

You have probably seen graphs in newspapers that show what has happened over time to economic variables such as the unemployment rate or stock prices. A **time-series graph** has successive dates on the horizontal axis and the values of a variable that occurred on those dates on the vertical axis. For example, Figure 2A-6 shows the unemployment rate in the United States from 1989 to mid-2004. A line connecting the points that correspond to the unemployment rate for each year gives a clear idea of the overall trend in unemployment over these years.

Figure 2A-7 is an example of a different kind of numerical graph. It represents information from a sample of 158 countries on average life expectancy and gross national product (GNP) per capita—a rough measure of a country's standard of living. Each point here indicates an average resident's life expectancy and the log of

A **time-series graph** has dates on the horizontal axis and values of a variable that occurred on those dates on the vertical axis.

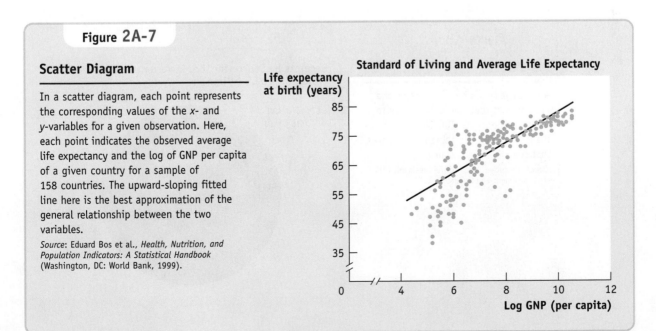

**Figure 2A-7**

### Scatter Diagram

In a scatter diagram, each point represents the corresponding values of the *x*- and *y*-variables for a given observation. Here, each point indicates the observed average life expectancy and the log of GNP per capita of a given country for a sample of 158 countries. The upward-sloping fitted line here is the best approximation of the general relationship between the two variables.

*Source*: Eduard Bos et al., *Health, Nutrition, and Population Indicators: A Statistical Handbook* (Washington, DC: World Bank, 1999).

**Life expectancy at birth (years)**

**Standard of Living and Average Life Expectancy**

**Log GNP (per capita)**

GNP per capita for a given country. (Economists have found that the log of GNP rather than the simple level of GNP is more closely tied to average life expectancy.) The points lying in the upper right of the graph, which show combinations of high life expectancy and high log GNP per capita, represent economically advanced countries such as the United States. Points lying in the bottom left of the graph, which show combinations of low life expectancy and low log GNP per capita, represent economically less advanced countries such as Afghanistan and Sierra Leone. The pattern of points indicates that there is a positive relationship between life expectancy and log GNP per capita: on the whole, people live longer in countries with a higher standard of living. This type of graph is called a **scatter diagram,** a diagram in which each point corresponds to an actual observation of the x-variable and the y-variable. In scatter diagrams, a curve is typically fitted to the scatter of points; that is, a curve is drawn that approximates as closely as possible the general relationship between the variables. As you can see, the fitted curve in Figure 2A-7 is upward sloping, indicating the underlying positive relationship between the two variables. Scatter diagrams are often used to show how a general relationship can be inferred from a set of data.

A **pie chart** shows the share of a total amount that is accounted for by various components, usually expressed in percentages. For example, Figure 2A-8 is a pie chart that depicts the various sources of revenue for the U.S. government budget in 2003, expressed in percentages of the total revenue amount, $1,782.3 billion. As you can see, social insurance receipts (the revenues collected to fund Social Security, Medicare, and unemployment insurance) accounted for 40% of total government revenue and individual income tax receipts accounted for 45%.

**Bar graphs** use bars of various heights or lengths to indicate values of a variable. In the bar graph in Figure 2A-9, the bars show the percent change in the number of unemployed workers in the United States from 2001 to 2002, separately for White, Black or African-American, and Asian workers. Exact values of the variable that is being measured may be written at the end of the bar as in this figure. For instance, the number of unemployed Asian workers in the United States increased by 35% between 2001 and 2002. But even without the precise values, comparing the heights or lengths of the bars can give useful insight into the relative magnitudes of the different values of the variable.

---

A **scatter diagram** shows points that correspond to actual observations of the x- and y-variables. A curve is usually fitted to the scatter of points.

---

A **pie chart** shows how some total is divided among its components, usually expressed in percentages.

---

A **bar graph** uses bars of varying height or length to show the comparative sizes of different observations of a variable.

---

### Figure 2A-8

**Pie Chart**

---

A pie chart shows the percentages of a total amount that can be attributed to various components. This pie chart shows the percentages of total federal revenues that come from each source.

*Source*: Executive Office of the President, Office of Management and Budget.

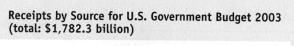

**Receipts by Source for U.S. Government Budget 2003 (total: $1,782.3 billion)**

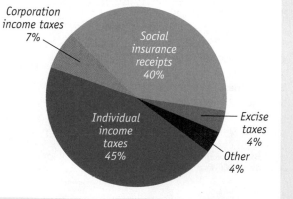

Corporation income taxes 7%

Social insurance receipts 40%

Individual income taxes 45%

Excise taxes 4%

Other 4%

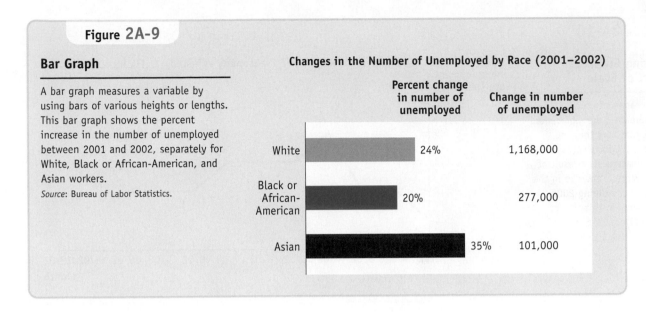

**Figure 2A-9**

**Bar Graph**

A bar graph measures a variable by using bars of various heights or lengths. This bar graph shows the percent increase in the number of unemployed between 2001 and 2002, separately for White, Black or African-American, and Asian workers.

*Source*: Bureau of Labor Statistics.

**Changes in the Number of Unemployed by Race (2001–2002)**

| | Percent change in number of unemployed | Change in number of unemployed |
|---|---|---|
| White | 24% | 1,168,000 |
| Black or African-American | 20% | 277,000 |
| Asian | 35% | 101,000 |

## Problems in Interpreting Numerical Graphs

Although the beginning of this appendix emphasized that graphs are visual images that make ideas or information easier to understand, graphs can be constructed (intentionally or unintentionally) in ways that are misleading and can lead to inaccurate conclusions. This section raises some issues that you should be aware of when you interpret graphs.

**Features of Construction**   Before drawing any conclusions about what a numerical graph implies, you should pay attention to the scale, or size of increments, shown on the axes. Small increments tend to visually exaggerate changes in the variables, whereas large increments tend to visually diminish them. So the scale used in construction of a graph can influence your interpretation of the significance of the changes it illustrates—perhaps in an unwarranted way.

Take, for example, Figure 2A-10 on page 52, which shows the unemployment rate in the United States in 2002 using a 0.1% scale. You can see that the unemployment rate rose from 5.6% at the beginning of 2002 to 6.0% by the end of the year. Here, the rise of 0.4% in the unemployment rate looks enormous and could lead a policy maker to conclude that it was a relatively significant event. But if you go back and reexamine Figure 2A-6, which shows the unemployment rate in the United States from 1989 to 2004, you can see that this would be a misguided conclusion. Figure 2A-6 includes the same data shown in Figure 2A-10, but it is constructed with a 1% scale rather than a 0.1% scale. From it you can see that the rise of 0.4% in the unemployment rate during 2002 was, in fact, a relatively insignificant event, at least compared to the rise in unemployment during 1990 or during 2001. This comparison shows that if you are not careful to factor in the choice of scale in interpreting a graph, you can arrive at very different, and possibly misguided, conclusions.

Related to the choice of scale is the use of *truncation* in constructing a graph. An axis is **truncated** when part of the range is omitted. This is indicated by two slashes (//) in the axis near the origin. You can see that the vertical axis of Figure 2A-10 has been truncated—the range of values from 0 to 5.6 has been omitted and a // appears in the axis. Truncation saves space in the presentation of a graph and allows larger increments to be used in constructing it. As a result, changes in the variable depicted

An axis is **truncated** when some of the values on the axis are omitted, usually to save space.

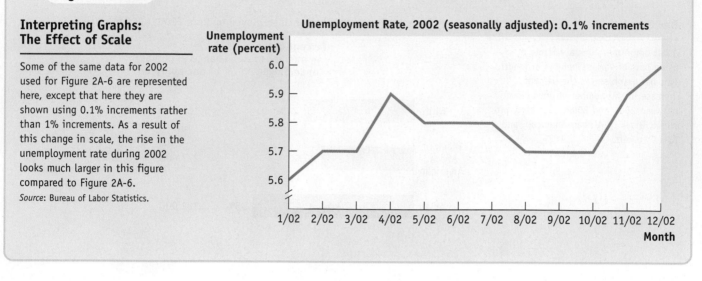

### Figure 2A-10

**Interpreting Graphs: The Effect of Scale**

Some of the same data for 2002 used for Figure 2A-6 are represented here, except that here they are shown using 0.1% increments rather than 1% increments. As a result of this change in scale, the rise in the unemployment rate during 2002 looks much larger in this figure compared to Figure 2A-6.

*Source:* Bureau of Labor Statistics.

on a graph that has been truncated appear larger compared to a graph that has not been truncated and that uses smaller increments.

You must also pay close attention to exactly what a graph is illustrating. For example, in Figure 2A-9, you should recognize that what is being shown here are percentage changes in the number of unemployed, not numerical changes. The unemployment rate for Asian workers increased by the highest percentage, 35% in this example. If you confused numerical changes with percentage changes, you would erroneously conclude that the greatest number of newly unemployed workers were Asian. But, in fact, a correct interpretation of Figure 2A-9 shows that the greatest number of newly unemployed workers were white: the total number of unemployed white workers grew by 1,168,000 workers, which is greater than the increase in the number of unemployed Asian workers, which is 101,000 in this example. Although there was a higher percentage increase in the number of unemployed Asian workers, the number of unemployed Asian workers in the United States in 2001 was much smaller than the number of unemployed white workers, leading to a smaller number of newly unemployed Asian workers than white workers.

**Omitted Variables** From a scatter diagram that shows two variables moving either positively or negatively in relation to each other, it is easy to conclude that there is a causal relationship. But relationships between two variables are not always due to direct cause and effect. Quite possibly an observed relationship between two variables is due to the *unobserved* effect of a third variable on each of the other two variables. An unobserved variable that, through its influence on other variables, creates the erroneous appearance of a direct causal relationship among those variables is called an **omitted variable.** For example, in New England, a greater amount of snowfall during a given week will typically cause people to buy more snow shovels. It will also cause people to buy more de-icer fluid. But if you omitted the influence of the snowfall and simply plotted the number of snow shovels sold versus the number of bottles of de-icer fluid, you would produce a scatter diagram that showed an upward tilt in the pattern of points, indicating a positive relationship between snow shovels sold and de-icer fluid sold. To attribute a causal relationship between these two variables, however, is misguided; more snow shovels sold do not cause more de-icer fluid to be sold, or vice versa. They move togeth-

An **omitted variable** is an unobserved variable that, through its influence on other variables, creates the erroneous appearance of a direct causal relationship among those variables.

er because they are both influenced by a third, determining, variable—the weekly snowfall—which is the omitted variable in this case. So before assuming that a pattern in a scatter diagram implies a cause-and-effect relationship, it is important to consider whether the pattern is instead the result of an omitted variable. Or to put it succinctly: Correlation is not causation.

**Reverse Causality**  Even when you are confident that there is no omitted variable and that there is a causal relationship between two variables shown in a numerical graph, you must also be careful that you don't make the mistake of **reverse causality**—coming to an erroneous conclusion about which is the dependent and which is the independent variable by reversing the true direction of causality between the two variables. For example, imagine a scatter diagram that depicts the grade point averages (GPAs) of 20 of your classmates on one axis and the number of hours that each of them spends studying on the other. A line fitted between the points will probably have a positive slope, showing a positive relationship between GPA and hours of studying. We could reasonably infer that hours spent studying is the independent variable and that GPA is the dependent variable. But you could make the error of reverse causality: you could infer that a high GPA causes a student to study more whereas a low GPA causes a student to study less.

The significance of understanding how graphs can mislead or be incorrectly interpreted is not purely academic. Policy decisions, business decisions, and political arguments are often based on interpretation of the types of numerical graphs that we've just discussed. Problems of misleading features of construction, omitted variables, and reverse causality can lead to very important and undesirable consequences.

The error of **reverse causality** is committed when the true direction of causality between two variables is reversed.

## PROBLEMS

**1.** Study the four accompanying diagrams. Consider the following statements and indicate which diagram matches each statement. Which variable would appear on the horizontal and which on the vertical axis? In each of these statements, is the slope positive, negative, zero, or infinity?

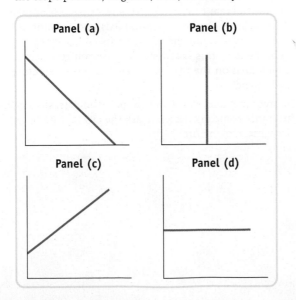

**a.** If the price of movies increases, fewer consumers go to see movies.

**b.** More experienced workers typically have higher incomes than less experienced workers.

**c.** Whatever the temperature outside, Americans consume the same number of hot dogs per day.

**d.** Consumers buy more frozen yogurt when the price of ice cream goes up.

**e.** Research finds no relationship between the number of diet books purchased and the number of pounds lost by the average dieter.

**f.** Regardless of its price, Americans buy the same quantity of salt.

**2.** During the Reagan administration, economist Arthur Laffer argued in favor of lowering income tax rates in order to increase tax revenues. Like most economists, he believed that at tax rates above a certain level, tax revenue would fall because high taxes would discourage some people from working and that people would refuse to work at all if they received no income after paying taxes. This relationship between tax rates and tax revenue is graphically summarized in what is widely known as the Laffer curve. Plot the Laffer curve relationship assuming that it has the shape of a non-linear curve. The following questions will help you construct the graph.

**a.** Which is the independent variable? Which is the dependent variable? On which axis do you therefore measure the income tax rate? On which axis do you measure income tax revenue?

**b.** What would tax revenue be at a 0% income tax rate?

**c.** The maximum possible income tax rate is 100%. What would tax revenue be at a 100% income tax rate?

**d.** Estimates now show that the maximum point on the Laffer curve is (approximately) at a tax rate of 80%. For tax rates less than 80%, how would you describe the relationship between the tax rate and tax revenue, and how is this relationship reflected in the slope? For tax rates higher than 80%, how would you describe the relationship between the tax rate and tax revenue, and how is this relationship reflected in the slope?

**3.** In the accompanying figures, the numbers on the axes have been lost. All you know is that the units shown on the vertical axis are the same as the units on the horizontal axis.

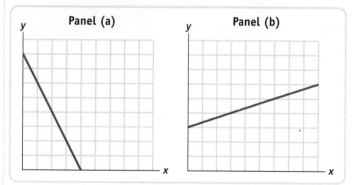

**a.** In panel (a), what is the slope of the line? Show that the slope is constant along the line.

**b.** In panel (b), what is the slope of the line? Show that the slope is constant along the line.

**4.** The accompanying table shows the relationship between workers' hours of work per week and their hourly wage rate. Apart from the fact that they receive a different hourly wage rate and work different hours, these five workers are otherwise identical.

| Name | Quantity of labor (hours per week) | Wage rate (per hour) |
|---|---|---|
| Athena | 30 | $15 |
| Boris | 35 | 30 |
| Curt | 37 | 45 |
| Diego | 36 | 60 |
| Emily | 32 | 75 |

**a.** Which variable is the independent variable? Which is the dependent variable?

**b.** Draw a scatter diagram illustrating this relationship. Draw a (nonlinear) curve that connects the points. Put the hourly wage rate on the vertical axis.

**c.** As the wage rate increases from $15 to $30, how does the number of hours worked respond according to the relationship depicted here? What is the average slope of the curve between Athena's and Boris's data points?

**d.** As the wage rate increases from $60 to $75, how does the number of hours worked respond according to the relationship depicted here? What is the average slope of the curve between Diego's and Emily's data points?

**5.** Studies have found a relationship between a country's yearly rate of economic growth and the yearly rate of increase in airborne pollutants. It is believed that a higher rate of economic growth allows a country's residents to have more cars and travel more, thereby releasing more airborne pollutants.

**a.** Which variable is the independent variable? Which is the dependent variable?

**b.** Suppose that in the country of Sudland, when the yearly rate of economic growth fell from 3.0% to 1.5%, the yearly rate of increase in airborne pollutants fell from 6% to 5%. What is the average slope of a nonlinear curve between these points?

**c.** Now suppose that when the yearly rate of economic growth rose from 3.5% to 4.5%, the yearly rate of increase in airborne pollutants rose from 5.5% to 7.5%. What is the average slope of a nonlinear curve between these two points?

**d.** How would you describe the relationship between the two variables here?

**6.** An insurance company has found that the severity of property damage in a fire is positively related to the number of firefighters arriving at the scene.

**a.** Draw a diagram that depicts this finding with number of firefighters on the horizontal axis and amount of property damage on the vertical axis. What is the argument made by this diagram? Suppose you reverse what is measured on the two axes. What is the argument made then?

**b.** In order to reduce its payouts to policyholders, should the insurance company therefore ask the city to send fewer firefighters to any fire?

**7.** The accompanying table illustrates annual salaries and income tax owed by five individuals. Apart from the fact that they receive different salaries and owe different amounts of income tax, these five individuals are otherwise identical.

| Name | Annual salary | Annual income tax owed |
|------|---------------|------------------------|
| Susan | $22,000 | $3,304 |
| Bill | 63,000 | 14,317 |
| John | 3,000 | 454 |
| Mary | 94,000 | 23,927 |
| Peter | 37,000 | 7,020 |

**a.** If you were to plot these points on a graph, what would be the average slope of the curve between the points for Bill's and Mary's salaries and taxes? How would you interpret this value for slope?

**b.** What is the average slope of the curve between the points for John's and Susan's salaries and taxes? How would you interpret that value for slope?

**c.** What happens to the slope as salary increases? What does this relationship imply about how the level of income taxes affects a person's incentive to earn a higher salary?

---

**>web...** To continue your study and review of concepts in this chapter, please visit the Krugman/Wells/Olney website for quizzes, animated graph tutorials, web links to helpful resources, and more.
**www.worthpublishers.com/krugmanwellsolney**

### chapter 3

## >>Supply and Demand

### GRETZKY'S LAST GAME

THERE ARE SEVERAL WAYS YOU CAN GET tickets for a sporting event. You might have a season pass that gives you a seat at every home game, you could buy a ticket for a single game from the box office, or you could buy a ticket from a *scalper*. Scalpers buy tickets in advance—either from the box office or from season ticket-holders who decide to forgo the game—and then resell them shortly before the event.

Scalping is not always legal, but it is often profitable. A scalper might buy tickets at the box office and then, after the box office has sold out, resell them at a higher price to fans who have decided at the last minute to attend the event. Of course, the profits are not guaranteed. Sometimes an event is unexpectedly "hot" and scalped tickets can be sold for high prices, but sometimes an event is unexpectedly "cold" and

scalpers end up selling at a loss. Over time, however, even with some unlucky nights, scalpers can make money from eager fans.

Ticket scalpers in the Canadian city of Ottawa had a good few days in April 1999. Why? Because Wayne Gretzky, the Canadian hockey star, unexpectedly announced that he would retire from the sport and that the April 15 match between the Ottawa Senators and his team, the New York Rangers, would be his last game on Canadian soil. Many Canadian fans wanted to see the great Gretzky play one last time—and would not give up just because the box office had long since sold out.

Clearly, scalpers who had already stocked up on tickets—or who could acquire more tickets—were in for a bonanza. After the announcement, scalped tickets began selling for four or five times their face value. It was just a matter of supply and demand.

## What you will learn in this chapter:

➤ What a **competitive market** is and how it is described by the **supply and demand model**

➤ What the **demand curve** is and what the **supply curve** is

➤ The difference between **movements along a curve** and **shifts of a curve**

➤ How the supply and demand curves determine a market's **equilibrium price** and **equilibrium quantity**

➤ In the case of a **shortage** or **surplus**, how price moves the market back to equilibrium

Shelly/Castellanos/Zuma — AFB/Corbis — Ronal Siemonet/Corbis

Fans paid hundreds, even thousands, of dollars to see Wayne Gretzky and Michael Jordan play their last games. How much would you pay to see a music star, such as Jennifer Lopez, one last time? What about your favorite athlete?

But what do we mean by that? Many people use *supply and demand* as a sort of catchphrase to mean "the laws of the marketplace at work." To economists, however, the concept of supply and demand has a precise meaning: it is a *model of how a market behaves* that is extremely useful for understanding many—but not all—markets.

In this chapter, we lay out the pieces that make up the supply and demand model, put them together, and show how this model can be used to understand how many—but not all—markets behave.

## Supply and Demand: A Model of a Competitive Market

Ticket scalpers and their customers constitute a market—a group of sellers and buyers. More than that, they constitute a particular type of market, known as a competitive market. Roughly, a **competitive market** is a market in which there are many buyers and sellers of the same good or service. More precisely, the key feature of a competitive market is that no individual's actions have a noticeable effect on the price at which the good or service is sold.

It's a little hard to explain why competitive markets are different from other markets until we've seen how a competitive market works. So let's take a rain check—we'll return to that issue at the end of this chapter. For now, let's just say that it's easier to model competitive markets than other markets. When taking an exam, it's always a good strategy to begin by answering the easier questions. In this book, we're going to do the same thing. So we will start with competitive markets.

When a market is competitive, its behavior is well described by a model known as the **supply and demand model**. And because many markets *are* competitive, the supply and demand model is a very useful one indeed.

There are five key elements in this model:

- The *demand curve*
- The *supply curve*
- The set of factors that cause the demand curve to shift, and the set of factors that cause the supply curve to shift
- The *equilibrium price*
- The way the equilibrium price changes when the supply or demand curves shift

To understand the supply and demand model, we will examine each of these elements.

> A **competitive market** is a market in which there are many buyers and sellers of the same good or service.

> The **supply and demand model** is a model of how a competitive market works.

## The Demand Curve

How many people wanted to buy scalped tickets to see the New York Rangers and the Ottawa Senators play that April night? You might at first think the answer was: every hockey fan in Ontario who didn't already have a ticket. But although every hockey fan wanted to see Wayne Gretzky play one last time, most fans weren't willing to pay four or five times the normal ticket price. In general, the number of people who want to buy a hockey ticket, or any other good, depends on the price. The higher the price, the fewer people who want to buy the good; the lower the price, the more people who want to buy the good.

So the answer to the question "How many people will want to buy a ticket to Gretzky's last game?" depends on the price of a ticket. If you don't yet know what the price will be, you can start by making a table of how many tickets people would want to buy at a number of different prices. Such a table is known as a *demand schedule*. This, in turn, can be used to draw a *demand curve*, which is one of the key elements of the supply and demand model.

## The Demand Schedule and the Demand Curve

A **demand schedule** is a table showing how much of a good or service consumers will want to buy at different prices. At the right of Figure 3-1, we show a hypothetical demand schedule for tickets to a hockey game.

A **demand schedule** shows how much of a good or service consumers will want to buy at different prices.

According to the table, if scalped tickets are available at $100 each (roughly their face value), 20,000 people are willing to buy them; at $150, some fans will decide this price is too high, and only 15,000 are willing to buy. At $200, even fewer people want tickets, and so on. So the higher the price, the fewer the tickets people want to purchase. In other words, as the price rises, the quantity of tickets demanded falls.

The graph in Figure 3-1 is a visual representation of the information in the table. (You might want to review the discussion of graphs in economics in the appendix to Chapter 2.) The vertical axis shows the price of a ticket, and the horizontal axis shows the quantity of tickets. Each point on the graph corresponds to one of the entries in the table. The curve that connects these points is a **demand curve.** A demand curve is a graphical representation of the demand schedule, another way of showing how much of a good or service consumers want to buy at any given price.

A **demand curve** is a graphical representation of the demand schedule. It shows how much of a good or service consumers want to buy at any given price.

The **quantity demanded** is the actual amount consumers are willing to buy at some specific price.

Suppose scalpers are charging $250 per ticket. We can see from Figure 3-1 that 8,000 fans are willing to pay that price; that is, 8,000 is the **quantity demanded** at a price of $250.

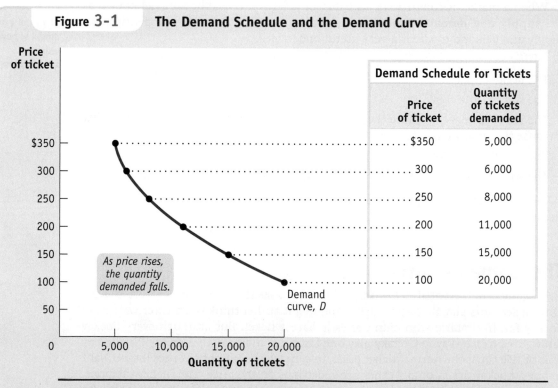

**Figure 3-1**    **The Demand Schedule and the Demand Curve**

As price rises, the quantity demanded falls.

Demand curve, *D*

**Demand Schedule for Tickets**

| Price of ticket | Quantity of tickets demanded |
|---|---|
| $350 | 5,000 |
| 300 | 6,000 |
| 250 | 8,000 |
| 200 | 11,000 |
| 150 | 15,000 |
| 100 | 20,000 |

The demand schedule for tickets is plotted to yield the corresponding demand curve, which shows how much of a good consumers want to buy at any given price. The demand curve and the demand schedule reflect the law of demand: As price rises, the quantity demanded falls. Similarly, a decrease in price raises the quantity demanded. As a result, the demand curve is downward sloping.

Note that the demand curve shown in Figure 3-1 slopes downward. This reflects the general proposition that a higher price reduces the number of people willing to buy a good. In this case, many people who would lay out $100 to see the great Gretzky aren't willing to pay $350. In the real world, demand curves almost always, with some very specific exceptions, *do* slope downward. The exceptions are goods called "Giffen goods," but economists think these are so rare that for practical purposes we can ignore them. Generally, the proposition that a higher price for a good, *other things equal*, leads people to demand a smaller quantity of that good is so reliable that economists are willing to call it a "law"—the **law of demand.**

> The **law of demand** says that a higher price for a good, other things equal, leads people to demand a smaller quantity of the good.

## Shifts of the Demand Curve

When Gretzky's retirement was announced, the immediate effect was that more people were willing to buy tickets for that April 15 game at any given price. That is, at every price the quantity demanded rose as a consequence of the announcement. Figure 3-2 illustrates this phenomenon in terms of the demand schedule and the demand curve for scalped tickets.

The table in Figure 3-2 shows two demand schedules. The second one shows the demand schedule after the announcement, the same one shown in Figure 3-1. But the first demand schedule shows the demand for scalped tickets *before* Gretzky announced his retirement. As you can see, after the announcement the number of people willing to pay $350 for a ticket increased, the number willing to pay $300 increased, and so on. So at each price, the second schedule—the schedule after the announcement—shows a larger quantity demanded. For example, at $200, the quantity of tickets fans were willing to buy increased from 5,500 to 11,000.

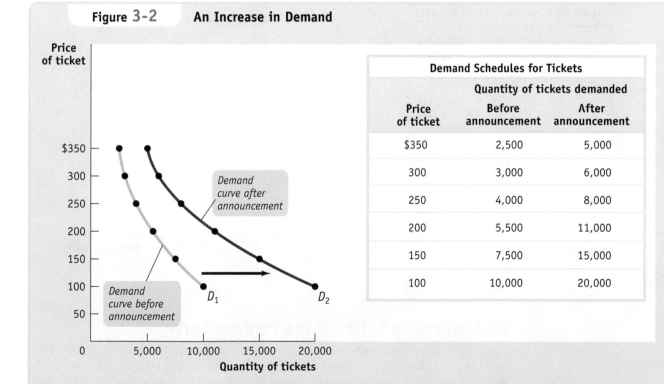

### Figure 3-2    An Increase in Demand

**Demand Schedules for Tickets**

| Price of ticket | Quantity of tickets demanded | |
| --- | --- | --- |
| | Before announcement | After announcement |
| $350 | 2,500 | 5,000 |
| 300 | 3,000 | 6,000 |
| 250 | 4,000 | 8,000 |
| 200 | 5,500 | 11,000 |
| 150 | 7,500 | 15,000 |
| 100 | 10,000 | 20,000 |

Announcement of Gretzky's retirement generates an increase in demand—a rise in the quantity demanded at any given price. This event is represented by the two demand schedules—one showing demand before the announcement, the other showing demand after the announcement—and their corresponding demand curves. The increase in demand shifts the demand curve to the right. **>web...**

The announcement of Gretzky's retirement generated a *new* demand schedule, one in which the quantity demanded is greater at any given price than in the original demand schedule. The two curves in Figure 3-2 show the same information graphically. As you can see, the new demand schedule after the announcement corresponds to a new demand curve, $D_2$, that is to the right of the demand curve before the announcement, $D_1$. This **shift of the demand curve** shows the change in the quantity demanded at any given price, represented by the change in position of the original demand curve $D_1$ to its new location at $D_2$.

It's crucial to make the distinction between such shifts of the demand curve and **movements along the demand curve**, changes in the quantity demanded of a good that result from a change in that good's price. Figure 3-3 illustrates the difference.

The movement from point $A$ to point $B$ is a movement along the demand curve: the quantity demanded rises due to a fall in price as you move down $D_1$. Here, a fall in price from $350 to $215 generates a rise in the quantity demanded from 2,500 to 5,000 tickets. But the quantity demanded can also rise when the price is unchanged if there is an increase in demand—a rightward shift of the demand curve. This is illustrated in Figure 3-3 by the shift of the demand curve from $D_1$ to $D_2$. Holding price constant at $350, the quantity demanded rises from 2,500 tickets at point $A$ on $D_1$ to 5,000 tickets at point $C$ on $D_2$.

When economists say "the demand for X increased" or "the demand for Y decreased," they mean that the demand curve for X or Y shifted—*not* that the quantity demanded rose or fell because of a change in the price.

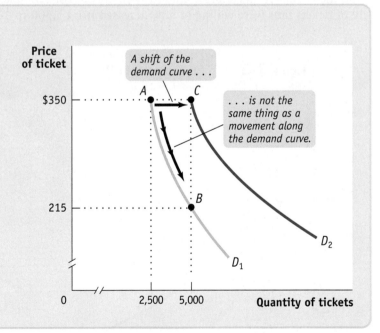

### Figure 3-3

**Movement Along the Demand Curve Versus Shift of the Demand Curve**

The rise in quantity demanded when going from point $A$ to point $B$ reflects a movement along the demand curve: it is the result of a fall in the price of the good. The rise in quantity demanded when going from point $A$ to point $C$ reflects a shift of the demand curve: it is the result of a rise in the quantity demanded at any given price.

*A shift of the demand curve . . .*

*. . . is not the same thing as a movement along the demand curve.*

## Understanding Shifts of the Demand Curve

Figure 3-4 illustrates the two basic ways in which demand curves can shift. When economists talk about an "increase in demand," they mean a *rightward* shift of the demand curve: at any given price, consumers demand a larger quantity of the good than before. This is shown in Figure 3-4 by the rightward shift of the original demand curve $D_1$ to $D_2$. And when economists talk about a "decrease in demand," they mean a *leftward* shift of the demand curve: at any given price, consumers demand a smaller quantity of the good than before. This is shown in Figure 3-4 by the leftward shift of the original demand curve $D_1$ to $D_3$.

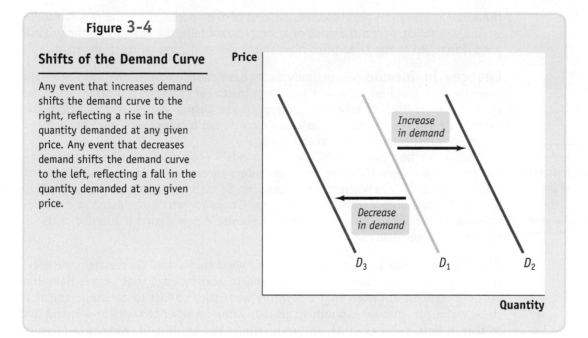

### Figure 3-4

**Shifts of the Demand Curve**

Any event that increases demand shifts the demand curve to the right, reflecting a rise in the quantity demanded at any given price. Any event that decreases demand shifts the demand curve to the left, reflecting a fall in the quantity demanded at any given price.

But what causes a demand curve to shift? In our example, the event that shifts the demand curve for tickets is the announcement of Gretzky's imminent retirement. But if you think about it, you can come up with other things that would be likely to shift the demand curve for those tickets. For example, suppose there is a music concert the same evening as the hockey game, and the band announces that it will sell tickets at half-price. This is likely to cause a decrease in demand for hockey tickets: hockey fans who also like music will prefer to purchase half-price concert tickets rather than hockey game tickets.

Economists believe that there are four principal factors that shift the demand curve for a good:

- Changes in the prices of related goods
- Changes in income
- Changes in tastes
- Changes in expectations

Although this is not an exhaustive list, it contains the four most important factors that can shift demand curves. When we said before that the quantity of a good demanded falls as its price rises, *other things equal,* we were referring to the factors that shift demand as remaining unchanged.

### Changes in the Prices of Related Goods

If you want to have a good night out but aren't too particular about what you do, a music concert is an alternative to the hockey game—it is what economists call a *substitute* for the hockey game. A pair of goods are **substitutes** if a fall in the price of one good (music concerts) makes consumers less willing to buy the other good (hockey games). Substitutes are usually goods that in some way serve a similar function: concerts and hockey games, muffins and doughnuts, trains and buses. A fall in the price of the alternative good induces some consumers to purchase it *instead of* the original good, shifting the demand for the original good to the left.

But sometimes a fall in the price of one good makes consumers *more* willing to buy another good. Such pairs of goods are known as **complements.** Complements are usually goods that in some sense are consumed together: sports tickets and parking at the stadium garage, hamburgers and buns, cars and gasoline. If the garage next to the hockey arena offered free parking, more people would be willing to buy tickets to see

> Two goods are **substitutes** if a fall in the price of one of the goods makes consumers less willing to buy the other good.

> Two goods are **complements** if a fall in the price of one good makes people more willing to buy the other good.

the game at any given price because the cost of the "package"—game plus parking—would have fallen. When the price of a complement falls, the quantity of the original good demanded at any given price rises; so the demand curve shifts to the right.

**Changes in Income** When individuals have more income, they are normally more likely to purchase a good at any given price. For example, if a family's income rises, it is more likely to take that summer trip to Disney World—and therefore also more likely to buy plane tickets. So a rise in consumer incomes will cause the demand curves for most goods to shift to the right.

Why do we say "most goods," not "all goods"? Most goods are **normal goods**—the demand for them increases when consumer income rises. However, the demand for some products falls when income rises—people with high incomes are less likely to take buses than people with lower incomes. Goods for which the demand decreases when income rises are known as **inferior goods**. When a good is inferior, a rise in income shifts the demand curve to the left.

> When a rise in income increases the demand for a good—the normal case—we say that the good is a **normal good.**
>
> When a rise in income decreases the demand for a good, it is an **inferior good.**

**Changes in Tastes** Why do people want what they want? Fortunately, we don't need to answer that question—we just need to acknowledge that people have certain preferences, or tastes, that determine what they choose to consume and that these tastes can change. Economists usually lump together changes in demand due to fads, beliefs, cultural shifts, and so on under the heading of changes in *tastes* or *preferences*.

For example, once upon a time men wore hats. Up until around World War II, a respectable man wasn't fully dressed unless he wore a dignified hat along with his suit. But the returning GIs adopted a more informal style, perhaps due to the rigors of the war. And, President Eisenhower, who had been supreme commander of Allied Forces, often went hatless. The demand curve for hats had shifted leftward, reflecting a decline in the demand for hats.

The main distinguishing feature of changes in tastes is that economists have little to say about them and usually take them as given. When tastes change in favor of a good, more people want to buy it at any given price, so the demand curve shifts to the right. When tastes change against a good, fewer people want to buy it at any given price, so the demand curve shifts to the left.

**Changes in Expectations** You could say that the increase in demand for tickets to the April 15 hockey game was the result of a change in expectations: fans no longer expected to have future opportunities to see Gretzky in action, so they became more eager to see him while they could.

Depending on the specifics of the case, changes in expectations can either decrease or increase the demand for a good. For example, savvy shoppers often wait for seasonal sales—say, buying holiday gifts during the post-holiday markdowns. In this case, expectations of a future drop in price lead to a decrease in demand today. Alternatively, expectations of a future rise in price are likely to cause an increase in demand today.

Expected changes in future income can also lead to changes in demand: if you expect your income to rise in the future, you will typically borrow today and increase your demand for certain goods; and if you expect your income to fall in the future, you are likely to save today and reduce your demand for some goods.

## *economics in action*

### Beating the Traffic

All big cities have traffic problems, and many local authorities try to discourage driving in the crowded city center. If we think of an auto trip to the city center as a good that people consume, we can use the economics of demand to analyze anti-traffic policies.

One common strategy of local governments is to reduce the demand for auto trips by lowering the prices of substitutes. Many metropolitan areas subsidize bus and rail service, hoping to lure commuters out of their cars.

An alternative strategy is raising the price of complements: several major U.S. cities impose high taxes on commercial parking garages, both to raise revenue and to discourage people from driving into the city. (Short time limits on parking meters, combined with vigilant parking enforcement, is a related tactic.)

However, few cities have been willing to adopt the politically controversial direct approach: reducing congestion by raising the price of driving. So it was a shock when, in 2003, London imposed a "congestion charge" of £5 (about $9) on all cars entering the city center during business hours.

Compliance is monitored with automatic cameras that photograph license plates. People can either pay the charge in advance or pay it by midnight of the day they have driven. If they don't pay and are caught, a fine of £100 (about $180) is imposed for each transgression. (A full description of the rules can be found at www.cclondon.com.)

Not surprisingly, the result of the new policy confirms the law of demand: according to an August 2003 news report, traffic into central London had fallen 32 percent and cars were traveling more than a third faster as a result of the congestion charge. ■

> > > > > > > > > > > > > > > > > > > >

**>>CHECK YOUR UNDERSTANDING 3-1**

**1.** Explain whether each of the following events represents (i) a *shift of* the demand curve or (ii) a *movement along* the demand curve.
   a. A store owner finds that customers are willing to pay more for umbrellas on rainy days.
   b. When XYZ Telecom, a long-distance telephone service provider, offered reduced rates on weekends, the volume of weekend calling increased sharply.
   c. People buy more long-stem roses the week of Valentine's Day, even though the prices are higher than at other times during the year.
   d. The sharp rise in the price of gasoline leads many commuters to join carpools in order to reduce their gasoline purchases.

Solutions appear at back of book.

# The Supply Curve

Ticket scalpers have to acquire the tickets they sell, and many of them do so from ticket-holders who decide to sell. The decision of whether to sell your own ticket to a scalper depends in part on the price offered: the higher the price offered, the more likely that you will be willing to sell.

So just as the quantity of tickets that people are willing to buy depends on the price they have to pay, the quantity that people are willing to sell—the **quantity supplied**—depends on the price they are offered. (Notice that this is the supply of tickets *to the market in scalped tickets*. The number of seats in the stadium is whatever it is, regardless of the price—but that's not the quantity we're concerned with here.)

The **quantity supplied** is the actual amount of a good or service people are willing to sell at some specific price.

## The Supply Schedule and the Supply Curve

The table in Figure 3-5 on page 64 shows how the quantity of tickets made available varies with the price—that is, it shows a hypothetical **supply schedule** for tickets to Gretzky's last game.

A supply schedule works the same way as the demand schedule shown in Figure 3-1: in this case, the table shows the quantity of tickets season subscribers are willing to sell at different prices. At a price of $100, only 2,000 people are willing to part with their tickets. At $150, some more people decide that it is worth passing up the game in order to have more money for something else, increasing the quantity of tickets available to 5,000. At $200, the quantity of tickets supplied rises to 7,000, and so on.

A **supply schedule** shows how much of a good or service would be supplied at different prices.

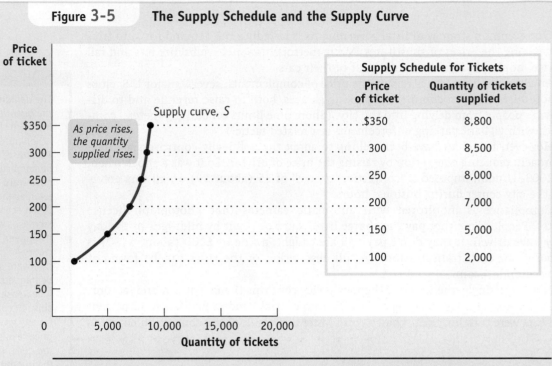

**Figure 3-5    The Supply Schedule and the Supply Curve**

Price of ticket

*As price rises, the quantity supplied rises.*

Supply curve, *S*

| Supply Schedule for Tickets | |
| --- | --- |
| Price of ticket | Quantity of tickets supplied |
| $350 | 8,800 |
| 300 | 8,500 |
| 250 | 8,000 |
| 200 | 7,000 |
| 150 | 5,000 |
| 100 | 2,000 |

Quantity of tickets

The supply schedule for tickets is plotted to yield the corresponding supply curve, which shows how much of a good people are willing to sell at any given price. The supply curve and the supply schedule reflect the fact that supply curves are usually upward sloping: the quantity supplied rises when the price rises.

---

A **supply curve** shows graphically how much of a good or service people are willing to sell at any given price.

In the same way that a demand schedule can be represented graphically by a demand curve, a supply schedule can be represented by a **supply curve,** as shown in Figure 3-5. Each point on the curve represents an entry from the table.

Suppose that the price scalpers offer rises from $200 to $250; we can see from Figure 3-5 that the quantity of tickets sold to them rises from 7,000 to 8,000. This is the normal situation for a supply curve, reflecting the general proposition that a higher price leads to a higher quantity supplied. So just as demand curves normally slope downward, supply curves normally slope upward: the higher the price being offered, the more hockey tickets people will be willing to part with—the more of any good they will be willing to sell.

## Shifts of the Supply Curve

When Gretzky's retirement was announced, the immediate effect was that people who already had tickets for the April 15 game became less willing to sell those tickets to scalpers at any given price. So the quantity of tickets supplied at any given price fell: the number of tickets people were willing to sell at $350 fell, the number they were willing to sell at $300 fell, and so on. Figure 3-6 shows us how to illustrate this event in terms of the supply schedule and the supply curve for tickets.

The table in Figure 3-6 shows two supply schedules; the schedule after the announcement is the same one as in Figure 3-5. The first supply schedule shows the supply of scalped tickets *before* Gretzky announced his retirement. And just as a change in demand schedules leads to a shift of the demand curve, a change in supply schedules leads to a **shift of the supply curve**—a change in the quantity supplied at any given price. This is shown in Figure 3-6 by the shift of the supply curve before the announcement, $S_1$, to its new position after the announcement, $S_2$. Notice that $S_2$ lies to the left of $S_1$, a reflection of the fact that quantity supplied decreased at any given price in the aftermath of Gretzky's announcement.

A **shift of the supply curve** is a change in the quantity supplied of a good or service at any given price. It is represented by the change of the original supply curve to a new position, denoted by a new supply curve.

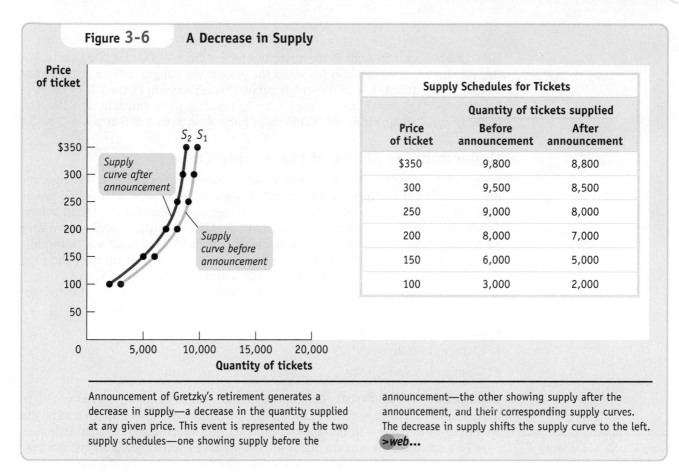

**Figure 3-6** **A Decrease in Supply**

| Supply Schedules for Tickets | | |
|---|---|---|
| | Quantity of tickets supplied | |
| Price of ticket | Before announcement | After announcement |
| $350 | 9,800 | 8,800 |
| 300 | 9,500 | 8,500 |
| 250 | 9,000 | 8,000 |
| 200 | 8,000 | 7,000 |
| 150 | 6,000 | 5,000 |
| 100 | 3,000 | 2,000 |

Announcement of Gretzky's retirement generates a decrease in supply—a decrease in the quantity supplied at any given price. This event is represented by the two supply schedules—one showing supply before the announcement—the other showing supply after the announcement, and their corresponding supply curves. The decrease in supply shifts the supply curve to the left. **>web...**

As in the analysis of demand, it's crucial to draw a distinction between such shifts of the supply curve and **movements along the supply curve**—changes in the quantity supplied that result from a change in price. We can see this difference in Figure 3-7. The movement from point *A* to point *B* is a movement along the supply curve: the quantity supplied falls along $S_1$ due to a fall in price. Here, a fall in price from

A **movement along the supply curve** is a change in the quantity supplied of a good that is the result of a change in that good's price.

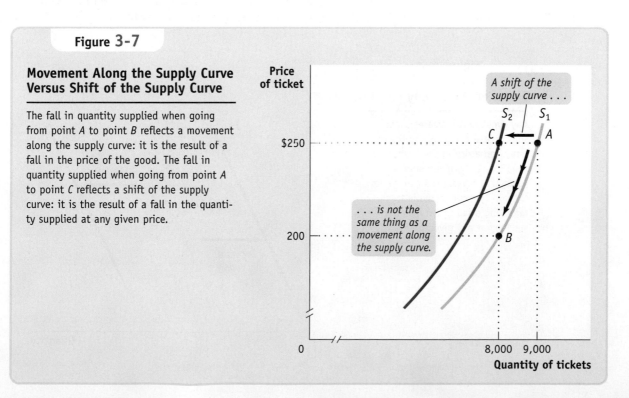

**Figure 3-7**

**Movement Along the Supply Curve Versus Shift of the Supply Curve**

The fall in quantity supplied when going from point *A* to point *B* reflects a movement along the supply curve: it is the result of a fall in the price of the good. The fall in quantity supplied when going from point *A* to point *C* reflects a shift of the supply curve: it is the result of a fall in the quantity supplied at any given price.

$250 to $200 leads to a fall in the quantity supplied from 9,000 to 8,000 tickets. But the quantity supplied can also fall when the price is unchanged if there is a decrease in supply—a leftward shift of the supply curve. This is shown in Figure 3-7 by the leftward shift of the supply curve from $S_1$ to $S_2$. Holding price constant at $250, the quantity supplied falls from 9,000 tickets at point *A* on $S_1$ to 8,000 at point *C* on $S_2$.

## Understanding Shifts of the Supply Curve

Figure 3-8 illustrates the two basic ways in which supply curves can shift. When economists talk about an "increase in supply," they mean a *rightward* shift of the supply curve: at any given price, sellers will supply a larger quantity of the good than before. This is shown in Figure 3-8 by the shift to the right of the original supply curve $S_1$ to $S_2$. And when economists talk about a "decrease in supply," they mean a *leftward* shift of the supply curve: At any given price, people supply a smaller quantity of the good than before. This is represented in Figure 3-8 by the leftward shift of $S_1$ to $S_3$.

Economists believe that shifts of supply curves are mainly the result of three factors (though, as in the case of demand, there are other possible causes):

- Changes in input prices
- Changes in technology
- Changes in expectations

**Changes in Input Prices**   To produce output, you need inputs—for example, to make vanilla ice cream, you need vanilla beans, cream, sugar, and so on. (Actually, you only need vanilla beans to make *good* vanilla ice cream; see Economics in Action on page 76.) An **input** is any good that is used to produce another good. Inputs, like output, have prices. And an increase in the price of an input makes the production of the final good more costly for those who produce and sell the good. So sellers are less willing to supply the good at any given price, and the supply curve shifts to the left. For example, newspaper publishers buy large quantities of newsprint (the paper on which newspapers are printed). When newsprint prices rose sharply in 1994–1995, the supply of newspapers fell: several newspapers went out of business and a number of new publishing ventures were canceled. Similarly, a fall in the price of an input makes the production of the final good less costly for sellers. They are more willing to supply the good at any given price, and the supply curve shifts to the right.

---

An **input** is a good that is used to produce another good.

---

### Figure 3-8

**Shifts of the Supply Curve**

Any event that increases supply shifts the supply curve to the right, reflecting a rise in the quantity supplied at any given price. Any event that decreases supply shifts the supply curve to the left, reflecting a fall in the quantity supplied at any given price.

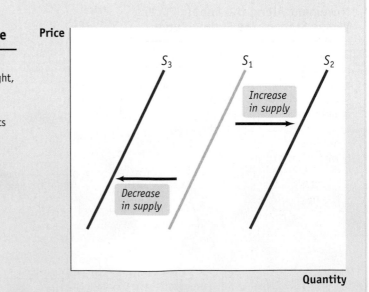

**Changes in Technology** When economists talk about "technology," they don't necessarily mean high technology—they mean all the ways in which people can turn inputs into useful goods. The whole complex set of activities that turn corn from an Iowa farm into cornflakes on your breakfast table is technology in this sense. And when a better technology becomes available, reducing the cost of production—that is, letting a producer spend less on inputs yet produce the same output—supply increases, and the supply curve shifts to the right. For example, an improved strain of corn that is more resistant to disease makes farmers willing to supply more corn at any given price.

**Changes in Expectations** Imagine that you had a ticket for the April 15 game but couldn't go. You'd want to sell the ticket to a scalper. But if you heard a credible rumor about Gretzky's imminent retirement, you would know that the ticket would soon skyrocket in value. So you'd hold off on selling the ticket until his decision to retire was made public. This illustrates how expectations can alter supply: an expectation that the price of a good will be higher in the future causes supply to decrease today, but an expectation that the price of a good will be lower in the future causes supply to increase today.

# *economics in action*

## Down (and Up) on the Farm

Many countries have designed farm policies based on the belief—or maybe the hope—that producers *won't* respond much to changes in the price of their product. But they have found out, to their dismay, that the price does indeed matter.

Advanced countries (including the United States) have historically tried to legislate farm prices *up*. (Chapter 4 describes how such price floors work in practice.) The point was to raise farmers' incomes, not to increase production—but production nonetheless did go up. Until the nations of the European Union began guaranteeing farmers high prices in the 1960s, they had limited agricultural production and imported much of their food. Once price supports were in place, production expanded rapidly, and European farmers began growing more grains and producing more dairy products than consumers wanted to buy.

In poorer countries, especially in Africa, governments have often sought to keep farm prices *down*. The typical strategy was to require farmers to sell their produce to a "marketing board," which then resold it to urban consumers or overseas buyers. A famous example is Ghana, once the world's main supplier of cocoa, the principal ingredient in chocolate. From 1965 until the 1980s, farmers were required to sell their cocoa beans to the government at prices that lagged steadily behind those chocolate manufacturers were paying elsewhere. The Ghanaian government hoped that cocoa production would be little affected by this policy and that it could profit by buying low and selling high. In fact, production fell sharply. By 1980, Ghana's share of the world market was down to 12 percent, while other cocoa-exporting countries that did not follow the same policy—including its African neighbors—were steadily increasing their sales.

Today Europe is trying to reform its agricultural policy, and most developing countries have abandoned their efforts to hold farm prices down. Governments seem finally to have learned that supply curves really do slope upward after all. ∎

> > > > > > > > > > > > > > > > > > > >

**>>CHECK YOUR UNDERSTANDING 3-2**

**1.** Explain whether each of the following events represents (i) a *shift of* the supply curve or (ii) a *movement along* the supply curve.
   a. More homeowners put their houses up for sale during a real estate boom that causes house prices to rise.
   b. Many strawberry farmers open temporary roadside stands during harvest season, even though prices are usually low at that time.

*continued*

**>> QUICK REVIEW**

> The *supply schedule* shows how the *quantity supplied* depends on the price. The relationship between the two is illustrated by the *supply curve.*

> Supply curves are normally upward sloping: at a higher price, people are willing to supply more of the good.

> A change in price results in a *movement along the supply curve* and a change in the quantity supplied.

> As with demand, when economists talk of increases or decreases in supply, they mean *shifts of the supply curve,* not changes in the quantity supplied. An increase in supply is a rightward shift: the quantity supplied rises for any given price. A decrease in supply is a leftward shift: the quantity supplied falls for any given price.

> The three main factors that can shift the supply curve are changes in (1) input prices, (2) technology, and (3) expectations.

*continued*

c. Immediately after the school year begins, fast-food chains must raise wages to attract workers.
d. Many construction workers temporarily move to areas that have suffered hurricane damage, lured by higher wages which represent the price of labor.
e. Since new technologies have made it possible to build larger cruise ships (which are cheaper to run per passenger), Caribbean cruise lines have offered more cabins, at lower prices, than before.

Solutions appear at back of book.

---

A competitive market is in equilibrium when price has moved to a level at which the quantity demanded of a good equals the quantity supplied of that good. The price at which this takes place is the **equilibrium price**, also referred to as the **market-clearing price**. The quantity of the good bought and sold at that price is the **equilibrium quantity**.

---

## PITFALLS

### BOUGHT *AND* SOLD?

We have been talking about the price at which a good is bought *and* sold, as if the two were the same. But shouldn't we make a distinction between the price received by sellers and that paid by buyers? In principle, yes; but it is helpful at this point to sacrifice a bit of realism in the interests of simplicity—by assuming away the difference between the prices received by sellers and those paid by buyers. In reality, people who sell hockey tickets to scalpers, although they sometimes receive high prices, generally receive less than those who eventually buy these tickets pay. No mystery there: that difference is how a scalper or any other "middleman"—someone who brings buyers and sellers together—makes a living. In many markets, however, the difference between the buying and selling price is quite small. It is therefore not a bad approximation to think of the price paid by buyers as being the *same* as the price received by sellers. And that is what we will assume in the remainder of this chapter.

# Supply, Demand, and Equilibrium

We have now covered the first three key elements in the supply and demand model: the supply curve, the demand curve, and the set of factors that shift each curve. The next step is to put these elements together to show how they can be used to predict the actual price at which a good will be bought and sold.

What determines the price at which a good is bought and sold? In Chapter 1 we learned the general principle that *markets move toward equilibrium*, a situation in which no individual would be better off taking a different action. In the case of a competitive market, we can be more specific: a competitive market is in equilibrium when the price has moved to a level at which the quantity demanded of a good equals the quantity supplied of that good. At that price, no individual seller could make herself better off by offering to sell either more or less of the good and no individual buyer could make himself better off by offering to buy more or less of the good.

The price that matches the quantity supplied and the quantity demanded is the **equilibrium price;** the quantity bought and sold at that price is the **equilibrium quantity.** The equilibrium price is also known as the **market-clearing price:** it is the price that "clears the market" by ensuring that every buyer willing to pay that price finds a seller willing to sell at that price, and vice versa.

You may notice from this point on that we will no longer focus on middlemen such as scalpers but focus directly on the market price and quantity. Why? Because the function of a middleman is to bring buyers and sellers together to trade. But what makes buyers and sellers willing to trade is in reality not the middleman, but the price they agree upon—the equilibrium price. By going deeper and examining how price functions within a market, we can safely assume that the middlemen are doing their job and leave them in the background.

So, how do we find the equilibrium price and quantity?

## Finding the Equilibrium Price and Quantity

The easiest way to determine the equilibrium price and quantity in a market is by putting the supply curve and the demand curve on the same diagram. Since the supply curve shows the quantity supplied at any given price and the demand curve shows the quantity demanded at any given price, the price at which the two curves cross is the equilibrium price: the price at which quantity supplied equals quantity demanded.

Figure 3-9 combines the demand curve from Figure 3-1 and the supply curve from Figure 3-5. They *intersect* at point *E*, which is the equilibrium of this market; that is, $250 is the equilibrium price and 8,000 tickets is the equilibrium quantity.

Let's confirm that point *E* fits our definition of equilibrium. At a price of $250 per ticket, 8,000 ticket-holders are willing to resell their tickets and 8,000 people who do not have tickets are willing to buy. So at the price of $250 the quantity of tickets supplied equals the quantity demanded. Notice that at any other price the market would not clear: every willing buyer would not be able to find a willing seller, or vice versa. In other words, if the price were more than $250, the quantity supplied would exceed the quantity demanded; if the price were less than $250, the quantity demanded would exceed the quantity supplied.

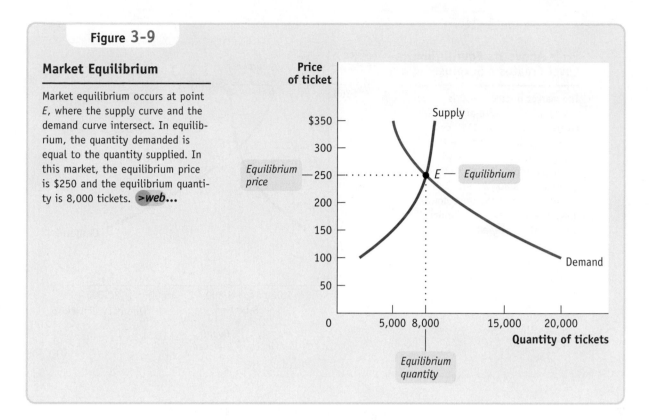

**Figure 3-9**

**Market Equilibrium**

Market equilibrium occurs at point *E*, where the supply curve and the demand curve intersect. In equilibrium, the quantity demanded is equal to the quantity supplied. In this market, the equilibrium price is $250 and the equilibrium quantity is 8,000 tickets. **>web...**

The model of supply and demand, then, predicts that given the demand and supply curves shown in Figure 3-9, 8,000 tickets would change hands at a price of $250 each.

But how can we be sure that the market will arrive at the equilibrium price? We begin by answering three simpler questions:

1. Why do all sales and purchases in a market take place at the same price?
2. Why does the market price fall if it is above the equilibrium price?
3. Why does the market price rise if it is below the equilibrium price?

## Why Do All Sales and Purchases in a Market Take Place at the Same Price?

There are some markets where the same good can sell for many different prices, depending on who is selling or who is buying. For example, have you ever bought a souvenir in a "tourist trap" and then seen the same item on sale somewhere else (perhaps even in the next store) for a lower price? Because tourists don't know which shops offer the best deals and don't have time for comparison shopping, sellers in tourist areas can charge different prices for the same good.

But in any market where the buyers and sellers have both been around for some time, sales and purchases tend to converge at a generally uniform price, so that we can safely talk about *the* market price. It's easy to see why. Suppose a seller offered a potential buyer a price noticeably above what the buyer knew other people to be paying. The buyer would clearly be better off shopping elsewhere—unless the seller was prepared to offer a better deal. Conversely, a seller would not be willing to sell for significantly less than the amount he knew most buyers were paying; he would be better off waiting to get a more reasonable customer. So in any well-established, ongoing market, all sellers receive and all buyers pay approximately the same price. This is what we call the *market price.*

The market price is the same for everyone.

### Figure 3-10

#### Price Above Its Equilibrium Level Creates a Surplus

The market price of $350 is above the equilibrium price of $250. This creates a surplus: at $350 per ticket, suppliers would like to sell 8,800 tickets but fans are willing to purchase only 5,000, so there is a surplus of 3,800 tickets. This surplus will push the price down until it reaches the equilibrium price of $250. **>web...**

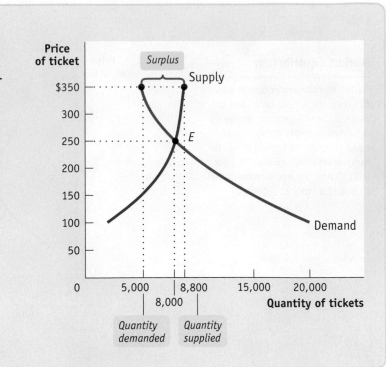

## Why Does the Market Price Fall If It Is Above the Equilibrium Price?

Suppose the supply and demand curves are as shown in Figure 3-9, but the market price is above the equilibrium level of $250—say, $350. This situation is illustrated in Figure 3-10. Why can't the price stay there?

As the figure shows, at a price of $350 there would be more tickets available than hockey fans wanted to buy: 8,800 versus 5,000. The difference of 3,800 is the **surplus**—also known as the *excess supply*—of tickets at $350.

This surplus means that some would-be sellers are being frustrated: they cannot find anyone to buy what they want to sell. So the surplus offers an incentive for those 3,800 would-be sellers to offer a lower price in order to poach business from other sellers. It also offers an incentive for would-be buyers to seek a bargain by offering a lower price. Sellers who reject the lower price will fail to find buyers, and the result of this price cutting will be to push the prevailing price down until it reaches the equilibrium price. So, the price of a good will fall whenever there is a surplus—that is, whenever the price is above its equilibrium level.

> There is a **surplus** of a good when the quantity supplied exceeds the quantity demanded. Surpluses occur when the price is above its equilibrium level.
>
> There is a **shortage** of a good when the quantity demanded exceeds the quantity supplied. Shortages occur when the price is below its equilibrium level.

## Why Does the Market Price Rise If It Is Below the Equilibrium Price?

Now suppose the price is below its equilibrium level—say, at $150 per ticket, as shown in Figure 3-11. In this case, the quantity demanded (15,000 tickets) exceeds the quantity supplied (5,000 tickets), implying that there are 10,000 would-be buyers who cannot find tickets: there is a **shortage**, also known as an *excess demand*, of 10,000 tickets.

When there is a shortage, there are frustrated would-be buyers—people who want to purchase tickets but cannot find willing sellers at the current price. In this situation, either buyers will offer more than the prevailing price or sellers will realize that they can charge higher prices. Either way, the result is to drive up the prevailing price. This bidding up of prices happens whenever there are shortages—and there will be shortages whenever the price is below its equilibrium level. So the price will always rise if it is below the equilibrium level.

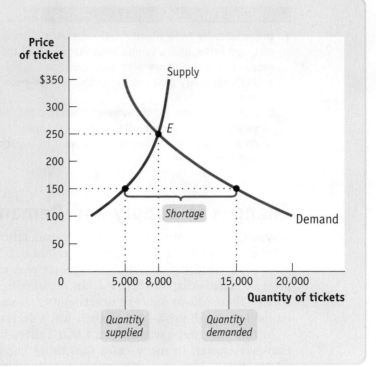

**Figure 3-11**

### Price Below Its Equilibrium Level Creates a Shortage

The market price of $150 is below the equilibrium price of $250. This creates a shortage: fans want to buy 15,000 tickets but only 5,000 are offered for sale, so there is a shortage of 10,000 tickets. This shortage will push the price up until it reaches the equilibrium price of $250. **web...**

## Using Equilibrium to Describe Markets

We have now seen that a market tends to have a single price; that the market price falls if it is above the equilibrium level but rises if it is below that level. So the market price always *moves toward* the equilibrium price, the price at which there is neither surplus nor shortage.

# *economics in action*

## A Fish Story

In market equilibrium, something remarkable supposedly happens: everyone who wants to sell a good finds a willing buyer, and everyone who wants to buy that good finds a willing seller. It's a beautiful theory—but is it realistic?

In New York City the answer can be seen every day, just before dawn, at the famous Fulton Fish Market, which has operated since 1835 (though it has moved from its original Fulton Street location). There, every morning, fishermen bring their catch and haggle over prices with restaurant owners, shopkeepers, and a variety of middlemen and brokers.

The stakes are high. Restaurant owners who can't provide their customers with the fresh fish they expect stand to lose a lot of business, so it's important that would-be buyers find willing sellers. It's even more important for fishermen to make a sale: unsold fish loses much, if not all, of its value. But the market does reach equilibrium: just about every would-be buyer finds a willing seller, and vice versa. The reason is that every day the price of each type of fish quickly converges to a level that matches the quantity supplied and the quantity demanded.

So the tendency of markets to reach equilibrium isn't just theoretical speculation. You can see (and smell) it happening, early every morning. ■

> > > > > > > > > > > > > > > > > > > > > > > > >

1. In the following three situations, the market is initially in equilibrium. After each event described below, does a surplus or shortage exist at the original equilibrium price? What will happen to the equilibrium price as a result?
   a. 1997 was a very good year for California wine-grape growers, who produced a bumper-size crop.
   b. After a hurricane, Florida hoteliers often find that many people cancel their upcoming vacations, leaving them with empty hotel rooms.
   c. After a heavy snowfall, many people want to buy secondhand snowblowers at the local tool shop.

*Solutions appear at back of book.*

# Changes in Supply and Demand

Wayne Gretzky's announcement that he was retiring may have come as a surprise, but the subsequent rise in the price of scalped tickets for that April game was no surprise at all. Suddenly the number of people who wanted to buy tickets at any given price increased—that is, there was an increase in demand. And at the same time, because those who already had tickets wanted to see Gretzky's last game, they became less willing to sell them—that is, there was a decrease in supply.

In this case, there was an event that shifted both the supply and the demand curves. However, in many cases something happens that shifts only one of the curves. For example, a freeze in Florida reduces the supply of oranges but doesn't change the demand. A medical report that eggs are bad for your health reduces the demand for eggs but does not affect the supply. That is, events often shift either the supply curve or the demand curve, but not both; it is therefore useful to ask what happens in each case.

We have seen that when a curve shifts, the equilibrium price and quantity change. We will now concentrate on exactly how the shift of a curve alters the equilibrium price and quantity.

## What Happens When the Demand Curve Shifts

Coffee and tea are substitutes: if the price of tea rises, the demand for coffee will increase, and if the price of tea falls, the demand for coffee will decrease. But how does the price of tea affect the *market* for coffee?

Figure 3-12 shows the effect of a rise in the price of tea on the market for coffee. The rise in the price of tea increases the demand for coffee. Point $E_1$ shows the equilibrium corresponding to the original demand curve, with $P_1$ the equilibrium price and $Q_1$ the equilibrium quantity bought and sold.

An increase in demand is indicated by a *rightward* shift of the demand curve from $D_1$ to $D_2$. At the original market price $P_1$, this market is no longer in equilibrium: a shortage occurs because the quantity demanded exceeds the quantity supplied. So the price of coffee rises and generates an increase in the quantity supplied, an upward *movement along the supply curve*. A new equilibrium is established at point $E_2$, with a higher equilibrium price $P_2$ and higher equilibrium quantity $Q_2$. This sequence of events reflects a general principle: *When demand for a good increases, the equilibrium price and the equilibrium quantity of the good both rise.*

And what would happen in the reverse case, a fall in the price of tea? A fall in the price of tea decreases the demand for coffee, shifting the demand curve to the *left*. At the original price, a surplus occurs as quantity supplied exceeds quantity demanded. The price falls and leads to a decrease in the quantity supplied, with a lower equilibrium price and a lower equilibrium quantity. This illustrates another general principle: *When demand for a good decreases, the equilibrium price of the good and the equilibrium quantity of the good both fall.*

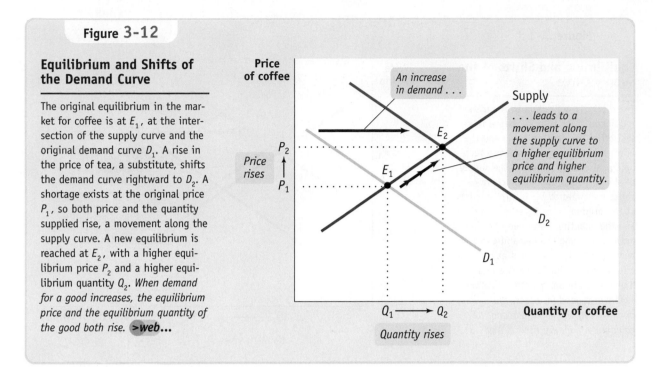

**Figure 3-12**

**Equilibrium and Shifts of the Demand Curve**

The original equilibrium in the market for coffee is at $E_1$, at the intersection of the supply curve and the original demand curve $D_1$. A rise in the price of tea, a substitute, shifts the demand curve rightward to $D_2$. A shortage exists at the original price $P_1$, so both price and the quantity supplied rise, a movement along the supply curve. A new equilibrium is reached at $E_2$, with a higher equilibrium price $P_2$ and a higher equilibrium quantity $Q_2$. When demand for a good increases, the equilibrium price and the equilibrium quantity of the good both rise. **>web...**

To summarize how a market responds to a change in demand: *An increase in demand leads to a rise in both the equilibrium price and the equilibrium quantity. A decrease in demand leads to a fall in both the equilibrium price and the equilibrium quantity.*

## What Happens When the Supply Curve Shifts

In the real world, it is a bit easier to predict changes in supply than changes in demand. Physical factors that affect supply, like the availability of inputs, are easier to get a handle on than the fickle tastes that affect demand. Still, with supply as with demand, what we really know are the *effects* of shifts of the supply curve.

A spectacular example of a change in technology increasing supply occurred in the manufacture of semiconductors—the silicon chips that are the core of computers, video games, and many other devices. In the early 1970s, engineers learned how to use a process known as photolithography to put microscopic electronic components onto a silicon chip; subsequent progress in the technique has allowed ever more components to be put on each chip. Figure 3-13 (page 74) shows the effect of such an innovation on the market for silicon chips. The demand curve does not change. The original equilibrium is at $E_1$, the point of intersection of the original supply curve $S_1$ and the demand curve, with equilibrium price $P_1$ and equilibrium quantity $Q_1$. As a result of the technological change, supply increases and $S_1$ shifts *rightward* to $S_2$. At the original price $P_1$, a surplus of chips now exists and the market is no longer in equilibrium. The surplus causes a fall in price and a rise in quantity demanded, a downward movement along the demand curve. The new equilibrium is at $E_2$, with an equilibrium price $P_2$ and an equilibrium quantity $Q_2$. In the new equilibrium $E_2$, the price is lower and the equilibrium quantity higher than before. This may be stated as a general principle: *An increase in supply leads to a fall in the equilibrium price and a rise in the equilibrium quantity.*

What happens to the market when supply decreases? A decrease in supply leads to a *leftward* shift of the supply curve. At the original price, a shortage now exists; as a result, the equilibrium price rises and the quantity demanded falls. This describes the sequence of events in the newspaper market in 1994–1995, which we

## Figure 3-13

### Equilibrium and Shifts of the Supply Curve

The original equilibrium in the market for silicon chips is at $E_1$, at the intersection of the demand curve and the original supply curve $S_1$. After a technological change increases the supply of silicon chips, the supply curve shifts rightward to $S_2$. A surplus exists at the original price $P_1$, so price falls and the quantity demanded rises, a movement along the demand curve. A new equilibrium is reached at $E_2$, with a lower equilibrium price $P_2$ and a higher equilibrium quantity $Q_2$. *When supply of a good increases, the equilibrium price of the good falls and the equilibrium quantity rises.* **>web...**

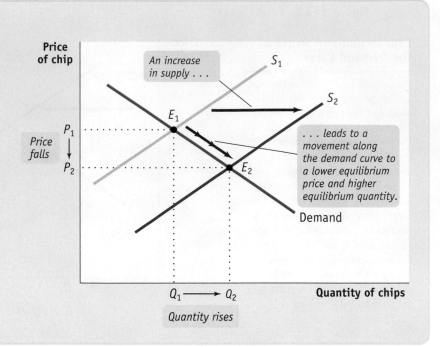

discussed earlier: a decrease in the supply of newsprint led to a rise in the price and the closure of many newspapers. We can formulate a general principle: *A decrease in supply leads to a rise in the equilibrium price and a fall in the equilibrium quantity.*

To summarize how a market responds to a change in supply: *An increase in supply leads to a fall in the equilibrium price and a rise in the equilibrium quantity. A decrease in supply leads to a rise in the equilibrium price and a fall in the equilibrium quantity.*

## Simultaneous Shifts in Supply and Demand

Finally, it sometimes happens that events shift *both* the demand and supply curves. In fact, this chapter began with an example of such a simultaneous shift. Wayne Gretzky's announcement that he was retiring increased the demand for scalped tickets because more people wanted to see him play one last time; but it also decreased the supply because those who already had tickets became less willing to part with them.

Figure 3-14 illustrates what happened. In both panels we show an increase in demand—that is, a rightward shift of the demand curve, from $D_1$ to $D_2$. Notice that the rightward shift in panel (a) is relatively larger than the one in panel (b). Both panels also show a decrease in supply—that is, a leftward shift of the supply curve, from $S_1$ to $S_2$. Notice that the leftward shift in panel (b) is relatively larger than the one in panel (a).

In both cases, the equilibrium price rises, from $P_1$ to $P_2$, as the equilibrium moves from $E_1$ to $E_2$. But what happens to the equilibrium quantity, the quantity of scalped tickets bought and sold? In panel (a) the increase in demand is large relative to the decrease in supply, and the equilibrium quantity rises as a result. In panel (b) the decrease in supply is large relative to the increase in demand, and the equilibrium quantity falls as a result. That is, when demand increases and

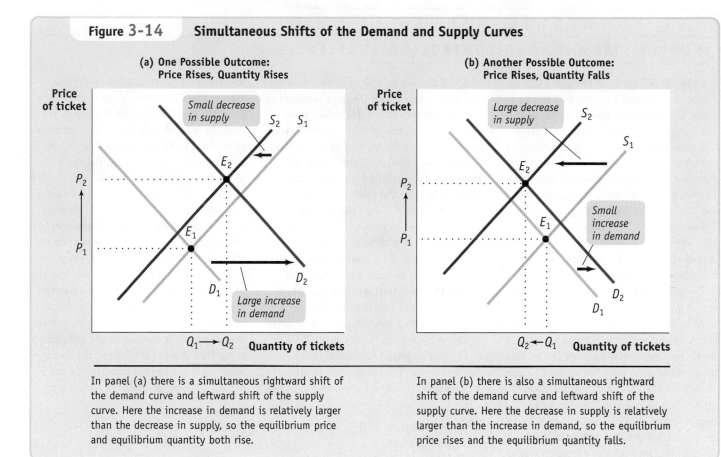

**Figure 3-14    Simultaneous Shifts of the Demand and Supply Curves**

**(a) One Possible Outcome:
Price Rises, Quantity Rises**

Price of ticket

Small decrease in supply

$S_2$    $S_1$

$E_2$

$P_2$

$E_1$

$P_1$

$D_1$

$D_2$

Large increase in demand

$Q_1 \rightarrow Q_2$    **Quantity of tickets**

**(b) Another Possible Outcome:
Price Rises, Quantity Falls**

Price of ticket

Large decrease in supply

$S_2$

$S_1$

$E_2$

$P_2$

Small increase in demand

$E_1$

$P_1$

$D_2$

$D_1$

$Q_2 \leftarrow Q_1$    **Quantity of tickets**

In panel (a) there is a simultaneous rightward shift of the demand curve and leftward shift of the supply curve. Here the increase in demand is relatively larger than the decrease in supply, so the equilibrium price and equilibrium quantity both rise.

In panel (b) there is also a simultaneous rightward shift of the demand curve and leftward shift of the supply curve. Here the decrease in supply is relatively larger than the increase in demand, so the equilibrium price rises and the equilibrium quantity falls.

supply decreases, the actual quantity bought and sold can go either way, depending on *how much* the demand and supply curves have shifted.

In general, when supply and demand shift in opposite directions, we can't predict what the ultimate effect will be on the quantity bought and sold. What we can say is that a curve that shifts a disproportionately greater distance than the other curve will have a disproportionately greater effect on the quantity bought and sold. That said, we can make the following prediction about the outcome when the supply and demand curves shift in opposite directions:

- When demand increases and supply decreases, the price rises but the change in the quantity is ambiguous.
- When demand decreases and supply increases, the price falls but the change in the quantity is ambiguous.

But suppose that the demand and supply curves shift in the same direction. Can we safely make any predictions about the changes in price and quantity? In this situation, the change in quantity bought and sold can be predicted but the change in price is ambiguous. The two possible outcomes when the supply and demand curves shift in the same direction (which you should check for yourself) are as follows:

- When both demand and supply increase, the quantity increases but the change in price is ambiguous.
- When both demand and supply decrease, the quantity decreases but the change in price is ambiguous.

## FOR INQUIRING MINDS

### SUPPLY, DEMAND, AND CONTROLLED SUBSTANCES

The big "issue" movie of the year 2000 was *Traffic*, a panoramic treatment of the drug trade. The movie was loosely based on the 1989 British TV miniseries *Traffik*. Despite the lapse of 11 years, the basic outlines of the situation—in which the drug trade flourishes despite laws that are supposed to prevent it—had not changed. Not only has the so-called war on drugs by law enforcement officials not succeeded in eliminating the trade in illegal drugs; according to most assessments, it has not even done much to reduce consumption.

The failure of the war on drugs has a historical precedent: during Prohibition, from 1920 to 1933, the sale and consumption of alcohol was illegal in the United States. But liquor, produced and distributed by "bootleggers," nonetheless remained widely available. In fact, by 1929 per capita consumption of alcohol was higher than it had been a decade earlier. As with illegal drugs today, the production and distribution of the banned substance became a large enterprise that flourished despite its illegality.

Why is it so hard to choke off markets in alcohol and drugs? Think of the war on drugs as a policy that shifts the supply curve but has not done much to shift the demand curve.

Although it is illegal to use drugs such as cocaine, just as it was once illegal to drink alcohol, in practice the war on drugs focuses mainly on the suppliers. As a result, the cost of supplying drugs includes the risk of being caught and sent to jail, perhaps even of being executed. This undoubtedly reduces the quantity of drugs supplied *at any given price*, in effect shifting the supply curve for drugs to the left. In Figure 3-15, this is shown as a shift in the supply curve from $S_1$

to $S_2$. If the war on drugs had no effect on the price of drugs, and the price remained at $P_1$, this leftward shift would reflect a reduction in the quantity of drugs supplied equal in magnitude to the leftward shift of supply.

But as we have seen, when the supply curve for a good shifts to the left, the effect is to raise the market price of that good. In Figure 3-15 the effect of the war on drugs would be to move the equilibrium from $E_1$ to $E_2$, and to raise the price of drugs from $P_1$ to $P_2$, a movement along the demand curve. Because the market price rises, the actual decline in the quantity of drugs supplied is less than the decline in the quantity that would have been supplied at the original price.

The crucial reason Prohibition was so ineffective was that as the market price of alcohol rose, consumers trimmed back only

slightly on their consumption—yet the higher prices were enough to induce many potential suppliers to take the risk of jail time. So while Prohibition raised the price of alcohol, it did not do much to reduce consumption. Unfortunately, the same seems to be true of current drug policy. The policy raises the price of drugs to those who use them, but this does not do much to discourage consumption. Meanwhile, the higher prices are enough to induce suppliers to provide drugs despite the penalties.

What is the answer? Some argue that the policy should be refocused on the demand side—more antidrug education, more counseling, and so on. If these policies worked, they would shift demand to the left. Others argue that drugs, like alcohol, should be made legal but heavily taxed. While the debate goes on, so does the war on drugs.

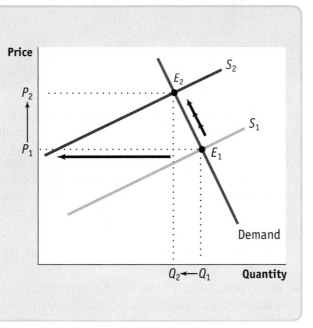

**Figure 3-15**

**Effects of the War on Drugs**

The war on drugs shifts the supply curve to the left. However, we can see by comparing the original equilibrium $E_1$ with the new equilibrium $E_2$ that the actual reduction in the quantity of drugs supplied is much smaller than the shift of the supply curve. The equilibrium price rises from $P_1$ to $P_2$—a movement along the demand curve. This leads suppliers to provide drugs despite the risks.

## *economics in action*

### Plain Vanilla Gets Fancy

Vanilla doesn't get any respect. It's such a common flavoring that "plain vanilla" has become a generic term for ordinary, unembellished products. But between 2000 and 2003, plain vanilla got quite fancy—at least if you looked at the price. At the supermarket, the price of a small bottle of vanilla extract rose from about $5 to about $15. The wholesale price of vanilla beans rose 400 percent.

The cause of the price spike was bad weather—not here, but in the Indian Ocean. Most of the world's vanilla comes from Madagascar, an island nation off Africa's southeast coast. A huge cyclone struck there in 2000, and a combination of colder-than-normal weather and excessive rain impeded recovery.

The higher price of vanilla led to a fall in the quantity demanded: worldwide consumption of vanilla fell about 35 percent from 2000 to 2003. Consumers didn't stop eating vanilla-flavored products; instead, they switched (often without realizing it) to ice cream and other products flavored with synthetic vanillin, which is a by-product of wood pulp and petroleum production.

Notice that there was never a shortage of vanilla: you could always find it in the store if you were willing to pay the price. That is, the vanilla market remained in equilibrium. ■

> > > > > > > > > > > > > > > > > > > >

## >>CHECK YOUR UNDERSTANDING 3-4

1. In each of the following examples, determine (i) the market in question; (ii) whether a shift in demand or supply occurred, the direction of the shift, and what induced the shift; and (iii) the effect of the shift on the equilibrium price and the equilibrium quantity.
   a. As the price of gasoline fell in the United States during the 1990s, more people bought large cars.
   b. As technological innovation has lowered the cost of recycling used paper, fresh paper made from recycled stock is used more frequently.
   c. As a local cable company offers cheaper pay-per-view films, local movie theaters have more unfilled seats.

2. Periodically, a computer chip maker like Intel introduces a new chip that is faster than the previous one. In response, demand for computers using the earlier chip decreases as customers put off purchases in anticipation of machines containing the new chip. Simultaneously, computer makers increase their production of computers containing the earlier chip in order to clear out their stocks of those chips.

   Draw two diagrams of the market for computers containing the earlier chip: (a) one in which the equilibrium quantity falls in response to these events and (b) one in which the equilibrium quantity rises. What happens to the equilibrium price in each diagram?

*Solutions appear at back of book.*

### >>QUICK REVIEW

➤ Changes in the equilibrium price and quantity in a market result from shifts in the supply curve, the demand curve, or both.

➤ An increase in demand—a rightward shift of the demand curve—increases both the equilibrium price and the equilibrium quantity. A decrease in demand—a leftward shift of the demand curve—pushes down both the equilibrium price and the equilibrium quantity.

➤ An increase in supply drives the equilibrium price down but increases the equilibrium quantity. A decrease in supply raises the equilibrium price but reduces the equilibrium quantity.

➤ Often the fluctuations in markets involve shifts of both the supply and demand curves. When they shift in the same direction, the change in quantity is predictable but the change in price is not. When they move in opposite directions, the change in price is predictable but the change in quantity is not. When there are simultaneous shifts of the demand and supply curves, the curve that shifts the greater distance has a greater effect on the change in price and quantity.

## WORK IT OUT

### SUPPLY AND DEMAND

Many shops in a large university town sell 12-ounce bottles of pink lemonade. A grad student surveyed the shops and learned they would be willing and able to sell more bottles of pink lemonade per week if the price of each bottle was higher. But her surveys of the town's residents revealed they would buy fewer bottles of pink lemonade per week if the price of each bottle was higher. The survey results are in the table.

| Price of 12-ounce bottle of pink lemonade | Bottles of pink lemonade shops would want to sell per week (quantity supplied) | Bottles of pink lemonade residents would want to buy per week (quantity demanded) |
|---|---|---|
| $0.50 | 1,000 | 5,000 |
| $1.00 | 2,000 | 4,000 |
| **$1.50** | **3,000** | **3,000** |
| $2.00 | 4,000 | 2,000 |
| $2.50 | 5,000 | 1,000 |

**Shortage:** If the price of a bottle of pink lemonade is $1.00, what is the weekly shortage of pink lemonade? (*Shortage: At a specific price, the amount by which quantity demanded exceeds quantity supplied.*)

SOLUTION: At a price of $1.00 per bottle, the shortage is 4,000 − 2,000 = 2,000 bottles of pink lemonade per week.

**Surplus:** If the price of a bottle of pink lemonade is $2.50, what is the weekly surplus of pink lemonade? (*Surplus: At a specific price, the amount by which quantity supplied exceeds quantity demanded.*)

SOLUTION: At a price of $2.50 per bottle, the surplus is 5,000 − 1,000 = 4,000 bottles of pink lemonade per week.

**Equilibrium price and quantity:** What is the equilibrium price of a bottle of pink lemonade? What is the equilibrium quantity of pink lemonade? (*Equilibrium price: The price at which quantity*

*continued*

supplied equals quantity demanded. Equilibrium quantity: The quantity supplied or demanded—they are the same—at the equilibrium price.)

**SOLUTION:** The equilibrium price is $1.50 because at this price quantity supplied and quantity demanded are equal. The equilibrium quantity is 3,000 bottles of pink lemonade per week because when the price is $1.50, quantity supplied is 3,000 bottles of pink lemonade per week and quantity demanded is also 3,000 bottles of pink lemonade per week.

**Graph:** Graph supply and demand. Show the equilibrium price and equilibrium quantity on your graph. (*Graphs of supply and demand **always** have price on the vertical axis and quantity on the horizontal axis.*)

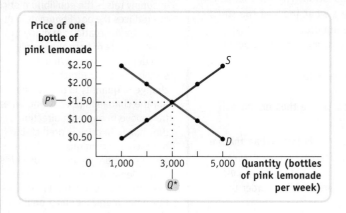

**SOLUTION:** Remember to label your axes ("price" and "quantity" are usually sufficient), label the equilibrium price and equilibrium quantity (here we used "P*" and "Q*"), and label your curves ("D" and "S" are usually sufficient).

**Shift versus Movement Along a Curve:** Widely published reports indicate that 2 bottles of pink lemonade per day will prevent students from gaining the dreaded "freshman fifteen." Which curve shifts? Which curve do we move along? What is the effect on the equilibrium price and equilibrium quantity? (*Shift: when the quantity changes at **any particular price**, we need an entirely new curve. Movement along: when the price changes, we move to a different point on an already existing curve.*)

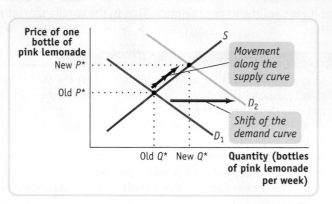

**SOLUTION:** If first-year students believe the reports and want to avoid gaining 15 pounds, they will buy more pink lemonade at any given price. The demand curve will shift to the right. At the previous price of $1.50, quantity demanded will now exceed quantity supplied. Equilibrium price will rise. As the price rises, sellers want to sell more bottles of pink lemonade; we move up along the old supply curve. The equilibrium price and equilibrium quantity both increase.

# Competitive Markets—And Others

Early in this chapter, we defined a competitive market and explained that the supply and demand framework is a model of competitive markets. But we took a rain check on the question of why it matters whether or not a market is competitive. Now that we've seen how the supply and demand model works, we can offer some explanation.

To understand why competitive markets are different from other markets, compare the problems facing two individuals: a wheat farmer who must decide whether to grow more wheat, and the president of a giant aluminum company—say, Alcoa—who must decide whether to produce more aluminum.

For the wheat farmer, the question is simply whether the extra wheat can be sold at a price high enough to justify the extra production cost. The farmer need not worry about whether producing more wheat will affect the price of the wheat he or she was already planning to grow. That's because the wheat market is competitive. There are thousands of wheat farmers, and no one farmer's decision will have much impact on the market price.

For the Alcoa executive, things are not that simple because the aluminum market is *not* competitive. There are only a few big players, including Alcoa, and each of them is well aware that its actions *do* have a noticeable impact on the market price. This adds a whole new level of complexity to the decisions producers have to make. Alcoa can't decide whether or not to produce more aluminum just by asking whether the additional product will sell for more than it costs to make. The company also has to ask whether producing more aluminum will drive down the market price and reduce its profit.

When a market is competitive, individuals can base decisions on less complicated analyses than those used in a noncompetitive market. This in turn means that it's easier for economists to build a model of a competitive market than of a noncompetitive market.

Don't take this to mean that economic analysis has nothing to say about noncompetitive markets. On the contrary, economists can offer some very important insights into how other kinds of markets work. But those insights require other models. In the next chapter, we will focus on what we can learn about competitive markets from the very useful model we have just developed: supply and demand.

### • A LOOK AHEAD •

We've now developed a model that explains how markets arrive at prices and why markets "work" in the sense that buyers can almost always find sellers, and vice versa. But this model could use a little more clarification.

But, nothing demonstrates a principle quite as well as what happens when people try to defy it. And governments do, fairly often, try to defy the principles of supply and demand. In the next chapter we consider what happens when they do—the revenge of the market.

## SUMMARY

1. The **supply and demand model** illustrates how a **competitive market**, one with many buyers and sellers, works.

2. The **demand schedule** shows the **quantity demanded** at each price and is represented graphically by a **demand curve.** The **law of demand** says that demand curves slope downward.

3. A **movement along the demand curve** occurs when the price changes and causes a change in the quantity demanded. When economists talk of increasing or decreasing demand, they mean **shifts of the demand curve**—a change in the quantity demanded at any given price. An increase in demand causes a rightward shift of the demand curve. A decrease in demand causes a leftward shift.

4. There are four main factors that shift the demand curve:
   - A change in the prices of related goods, such as **substitutes** or **complements**
   - A change in income: when income rises, the demand for **normal goods** increases and the demand for **inferior goods** decreases.
   - A change in tastes
   - A change in expectations

5. The **supply schedule** shows the **quantity supplied** at each price and is represented graphically by a **supply curve**. Supply curves usually slope upward.

6. A **movement along the supply curve** occurs when the price changes and causes a change in the quantity supplied. When economists talk of increasing or decreasing supply, they mean **shifts of the supply curve**—a change in the quantity supplied at any given price. An increase in supply causes a rightward shift of the supply curve. A decrease in supply causes a leftward shift.

7. There are three main factors that shift the supply curve:
   - A change in **input** prices
   - A change in technology
   - A change in expectations

8. The supply and demand model is based on the principle that the price in a market moves to its **equilibrium price,** or **market-clearing price,** the price at which the quantity demanded is equal to the quantity supplied. This quantity is the **equilibrium quantity**. When the price is above its market-clearing level, there is a **surplus** that pushes the price down. When the price is below its market-clearing level, there is a **shortage** that pushes the price up.

9. An increase in demand increases both the equilibrium price and the equilibrium quantity; a decrease in demand has the opposite effect. An increase in supply reduces the equilibrium price and increases the equilibrium quantity; a decrease in supply has the opposite effect.

10. Shifts of the demand curve and the supply curve can happen simultaneously. When they shift in opposite directions, the change in price is predictable but the change in quantity is not. When they shift in the same direction, the change in quantity is predictable but the change in price is not. In general, the curve that shifts the greater distance has a greater effect on the changes in price and quantity.

## KEY TERMS

Competitive market, p. 57
Supply and demand model, p. 57
Demand schedule, p. 58
Demand curve, p. 58
Quantity demanded, p. 58
Law of demand, p. 59
Shift of the demand curve, p. 60
Movement along the demand curve, p. 60

Substitutes, p. 61
Complements, p. 61
Normal good, p. 62
Inferior good, p. 62
Quantity supplied, p. 63
Supply schedule, p. 63
Supply curve, p. 64
Shift of the supply curve, p. 64

Movement along the supply curve, p. 65
Input, p. 66
Equilibrium price, p. 68
Equilibrium quantity, p. 68
Market-clearing price, p. 68
Surplus, p. 70
Shortage, p. 70

## PROBLEMS

1. A survey indicated that chocolate ice cream is America's favorite ice-cream flavor. For each of the following, indicate the possible effects on demand and/or supply and equilibrium price and quantity of chocolate ice cream.

   a. A severe drought in the Midwest causes dairy farmers to reduce the number of milk-producing cattle in their herds by a third. These dairy farmers supply cream that is used to manufacture chocolate ice cream.

   b. A new report by the American Medical Association reveals that chocolate does, in fact, have significant health benefits.

   c. The discovery of cheaper synthetic vanilla flavoring lowers the price of vanilla ice cream.

   d. New technology for mixing and freezing ice cream lowers manufacturers' costs of producing chocolate ice cream.

2. In a supply and demand diagram, draw the shift in demand for hamburgers in your hometown due to the following events. In each case show the effect on equilibrium price and quantity.

   a. The price of tacos increases.

   b. All hamburger sellers raise the price of their french fries.

   c. Income falls in town. Assume that hamburgers are a normal good for most people.

   d. Income falls in town. Assume that hamburgers are an inferior good for most people.

   e. Hot dog stands cut the price of hot dogs.

3. The market for many goods changes in predictable ways according to the time of year, in response to events such as holidays, vacation times, seasonal changes in production, and so on. Using supply and demand, explain the change in price in each of the following cases. Note that supply and demand may shift simultaneously.

   a. Lobster prices usually fall during the summer peak harvest season, despite the fact that people like to eat lobster during the summer months more than during any other time of year.

   b. The price of a Christmas tree is lower after Christmas than before and fewer trees are sold.

   c. The price of a round-trip ticket to Paris on Air France falls by more than $200 after the end of school vacation in September. This happens despite the fact that generally worsening weather increases the cost of operating flights to Paris, and Air France therefore reduces the number of flights to Paris at any given price.

4. Show in a diagram the effect on the demand curve, the supply curve, the equilibrium price, and the equilibrium quantity of each of the following events.

   a. The market for newspapers in your town.
      Case 1:  The salaries of journalists go up.
      Case 2:  There is a big news event in your town, which is reported in the newspapers.

   b. The market for St. Louis Rams cotton T-shirts.
      Case 1:  The Rams win the national championship.
      Case 2:  The price of cotton increases.

   c. The market for bagels.
      Case 1:  People realize how fattening bagels are.
      Case 2:  People have less time to make themselves a cooked breakfast.

   d. The market for the Krugman and Wells economics textbook.
      Case 1:  Your professor makes it required reading for all of his or her students.
      Case 2:  Printing costs for textbooks are lowered by the use of synthetic paper.

5. Suppose that the supply schedule of Maine lobsters is as follows:

| Price of lobster (per pound) | Quantity of lobster supplied (pounds) |
|---|---|
| $25 | 800 |
| 20 | 700 |
| 15 | 600 |
| 10 | 500 |
| 5 | 400 |

Suppose that Maine lobsters can be sold only in the United States. The U.S. demand schedule for Maine lobsters is as follows:

| Price of lobster (per pound) | Quantity of lobster demanded (pounds) |
|---|---|
| $25 | 200 |
| 20 | 400 |
| 15 | 600 |
| 10 | 800 |
| 5 | 1,000 |

**a.** Draw the demand curve and the supply curve for Maine lobsters. What is the equilibrium price and quantity of lobsters?

Now suppose that Maine lobsters can be sold in France. The French demand schedule for Maine lobsters is as follows:

| Price of lobster (per pound) | Quantity of lobster demanded (pounds) |
|---|---|
| $25 | 100 |
| 20 | 300 |
| 15 | 500 |
| 10 | 700 |
| 5 | 900 |

**b.** What is the demand schedule for Maine lobsters now that French consumers can also buy them? Draw a supply and demand diagram that illustrates the new equilibrium price and quantity of lobsters. What will happen to the price at which fishermen can sell lobster? What will happen to the price paid by U.S. consumers? What will happen to the quantity consumed by U.S. consumers?

**6.** Find the flaws in reasoning in the following statements, paying particular attention to the distinction between shifts of and movements along the supply and demand curves. Draw a diagram to illustrate what actually happens in each situation.

**a.** "A technological innovation that lowers the cost of producing a good might seem at first to result in a reduction in the price of the good to consumers. But a fall in price will increase demand for the good, and higher demand will send the price up again. It is not certain, therefore, that an innovation will really reduce price in the end."

**b.** "A study shows that eating a clove of garlic a day can help prevent heart disease, causing many consumers to demand more garlic. This increase in demand results in a rise in the price of garlic. Consumers, seeing that the price of garlic has gone up, reduce their demand for garlic. This causes the demand for garlic to decrease and the price of garlic to fall. Therefore, the ultimate effect of the study on the price of garlic is uncertain."

**7.** Some points on a demand curve for a normal good are given here:

| Price | Quantity demanded |
|---|---|
| $23 | 70 |
| 21 | 90 |
| 19 | 110 |
| 17 | 130 |

Do you think that the increase in quantity demanded (from 90 to 110 in the table) when price decreases (from 21 to 19) is due to a rise in consumers' income? Explain clearly (and briefly) why or why not.

**8.** Aaron Hank is a star hitter for the Bay City baseball team. He is close to breaking the major league record for home runs hit during one season, and it is widely anticipated that in the next game he will break that record. As a result, tickets for the team's next game have been a hot commodity. But today it is announced that, due to a knee injury, he will not in fact play in the team's next game. Assume that season ticket-holders are able to resell their tickets if they wish. Use supply and demand diagrams to explain the following.

**a.** Show the case in which this announcement results in a lower equilibrium price and a lower equilibrium quantity than before the announcement.

**b.** Show the case in which this announcement results in a lower equilibrium price and a higher equilibrium quantity than before the announcement.

**c.** What accounts for whether case a or case b occurs?

**d.** Suppose that a scalper had secretly learned before the announcement that Aaron Hank would not play in the next game. What actions do you think he would take?

**9.** In *Rolling Stone* magazine, several fans and rock stars, including Pearl Jam, were bemoaning the high price of concert tickets. One superstar argued, "It just isn't worth $75 to see me play. No one should have to pay that much to go to a concert." Assume this star sold out arenas around the country at an average ticket price of $75.

**a.** How would you evaluate the arguments that ticket prices are too high?

**b.** Suppose that due to this star's protests, ticket prices were lowered to $50. In what sense is this price too low? Draw a diagram using supply and demand curves to support your argument.

**c.** Suppose Pearl Jam really wanted to bring down ticket prices. Since the band controls the supply of its services, what do you recommend they do? Explain using a supply and demand diagram.

**d.** Suppose the band's next CD was a total dud. Do you think they would still have to worry about ticket prices being too high? Why or why not? Draw a supply and demand diagram to support your argument.

**e.** Suppose the group announced their next tour was going to be their last. What effect would this likely have on the demand for and price of tickets? Illustrate with a supply and demand diagram.

**10.** The accompanying table gives the annual U.S. demand and supply schedules for pickup trucks.

| Price of truck | Quantity of trucks demanded (millions) | Quantity of trucks supplied (millions) |
|---|---|---|
| $20,000 | 20 | 14 |
| 25,000 | 18 | 15 |
| 30,000 | 16 | 16 |
| 35,000 | 14 | 17 |
| 40,000 | 12 | 18 |

**a.** Plot the demand and supply curves using these schedules. Indicate the equilibrium price and quantity on your diagram.

**b.** Suppose the tires used on pickup trucks are found to be defective. What would you expect to happen in the market for pickup trucks? Show this on your diagram.

**c.** Suppose that the U.S. Department of Transportation imposes costly regulations on manufacturers that cause them to reduce supply by one-third at any given price. Calculate and plot the new supply schedule and indicate the new equilibrium price and quantity on your diagram.

11. After several years of decline, the market for handmade acoustic guitars is making a comeback. These guitars are usually made in small workshops employing relatively few highly skilled luthiers. Assess the impact on the equilibrium price and quantity of handmade acoustic guitars as a result of each of the following events. In your answers indicate which curve(s) shift(s) and in which direction.

**a.** Environmentalists succeed in having the use of Brazilian rosewood banned in the United States, forcing luthiers to seek out alternative, more costly woods.

**b.** A foreign producer reengineers the guitar-making process and floods the market with identical guitars.

**c.** Music featuring handmade acoustic guitars makes a comeback as audiences tire of heavy metal and grunge music.

**d.** The country goes into a deep recession and the income of the average American falls sharply.

12. *Demand twisters*: Sketch and explain the demand relationship in each of the following statements.

**a.** I would never buy a Britney Spears CD! You couldn't even give me one for nothing.

**b.** I generally buy a bit more coffee as the price falls. But once the price falls to $2 per pound, I'll buy out the entire stock of the supermarket.

**c.** I spend more on orange juice even as the price rises. (Does this mean that I must be violating the law of demand?)

**d.** Due to a tuition rise, most students at a college find themselves with lower disposable income. Almost all of them eat more frequently at the school cafeteria and less often at restaurants, even though prices at the cafeteria have risen too. (This one requires that you draw both the demand and the supply curves for dormitory cafeteria meals.)

13. Will Shakespeare is a struggling playwright in sixteenth-century London. As the price he receives for writing a play increases, he is willing to write more plays. For the following situations, use a diagram to illustrate how each event affects the equilibrium price and quantity in the market for Shakespeare's plays.

**a.** The playwright Christopher Marlowe, Shakespeare's chief rival, is killed in a bar brawl.

**b.** The bubonic plague, a deadly infectious disease, breaks out in London.

**c.** To celebrate the defeat of the Spanish Armada, Queen Elizabeth declares several weeks of festivities, which involves commissioning new plays.

14. The small town of Middling experiences a sudden doubling of the birth rate. After three years, the birth rate returns to normal. Use a diagram to illustrate the effect of these events on the following.

**a.** The market for an hour of babysitting services in Middling today

**b.** The market for an hour of babysitting services 14 years into the future, after the birth rate has returned to normal, by which time children born today are old enough to work as babysitters

**c.** The market for an hour of babysitting services 30 years into the future, when children born today are likely to be having children of their own

15. Use a diagram to illustrate how each of the following events affects the equilibrium price and quantity of pizza.

**a.** The price of mozzarella cheese rises.

**b.** The health hazards of hamburgers are widely publicized.

**c.** The price of tomato sauce falls.

**d.** The incomes of consumers rise and pizza is an inferior good.

**e.** Consumers expect the price of pizza to fall next week.

16. Although he was a prolific artist, Pablo Picasso painted only 1,000 canvases during his "Blue Period." Picasso is now dead, and all of his Blue Period works are currently on display in museums and private galleries throughout Europe and the United States.

**a.** Draw a supply curve for Picasso Blue Period works. Why is this supply curve different from ones you have seen?

**b.** Given the supply curve from part a, the price of a Picasso Blue Period work will be entirely dependent on what factor(s)? Draw a diagram showing how the equilibrium price of such a work is determined.

**c.** Suppose that rich art collectors decide that it is essential to acquire Picasso Blue Period art for their collections. Show the impact of this on the market for these paintings.

17. Draw the appropriate curve in each of the following cases. Is it like or unlike the curves you have seen so far? Explain.

**a.** The demand for cardiac bypass surgery, given that the government pays the full cost for any patient

**b.** The demand for elective cosmetic plastic surgery, given that the patient pays the full cost

**c.** The supply of Rembrandt paintings

**d.** The supply of reproductions of Rembrandt paintings

**>web...** To continue your study and review of concepts in this chapter, please visit the Krugman/Wells/Olney website for quizzes, animated graph tutorials, web links to helpful resources, and more.

**www.worthpublishers.com/krugmanwellsolney**

# >>The Market Strikes Back

## BIG CITY, NOT-SO-BRIGHT IDEAS

NEW YORK CITY IS A PLACE WHERE YOU can find almost anything—that is, almost anything, except a taxicab when you need one or a decent apartment at a rent you can afford. You might think that New York's notorious shortages of cabs and apartments are the inevitable price of big-city living. However, they are largely the product of government policies—specifically, of government policies that have, one way or another, tried to prevail over the market forces of supply and demand.

In the previous chapter, we learned the principle that a market moves to equilibrium—that the market price rises or falls to the level at which the quantity of a good that people are willing to supply is equal to the quantity that other people want to demand. But sometimes governments try to defy that principle. When they do, the market strikes back in predictable ways. And our ability to predict what will happen when governments try to defy supply and demand shows the power and usefulness of supply and demand analysis itself.

The shortages of apartments and taxicabs in New York are particular examples that illuminate what happens when the logic of the market is defied. New York's housing shortage is the result of *rent control,* a law that prevents landlords from raising rents except when specifically given permission. Rent control was introduced during World War II to protect the interests of tenants, and it still remains in force. Many other American cities have had rent control at one time or another, but with the notable exceptions of New York and San Francisco, these controls have largely been done away with. Similarly, New York's limited supply of taxis is the result of a licensing system introduced in the 1930s. New York taxi licenses are known as "medallions," and only taxis with medallions are allowed to pick up passengers. And although this

New York City: An empty taxi is hard to find.

system was originally intended to protect the interests of both drivers and customers, it has generated a shortage of taxis in the city. The number of medallions remained fixed from 1937 until 1995, and only a handful of additional licenses have been issued since then.

### What you will learn in this chapter:

➤ The meaning of **price controls** and **quantity controls,** two kinds of government intervention in markets

➤ How price and quantity controls create problems and make a market **inefficient**

➤ Why economists are often deeply skeptical of attempts to intervene in markets

➤ Who benefits and who loses from market interventions, and why they are used despite their well-known problems

➤ What an **excise tax** is and why its effect is similar to a quantity control

In this chapter, we begin by examining what happens when governments try to control prices in a competitive market, keeping the price in a market either below its equilibrium level—a *price ceiling* such as rent control—or above it—a *price floor*. We then turn to schemes such as taxi medallions that attempt to dictate the quantity of a good bought and sold. Finally, we consider the effects of taxes on sales or purchases.

## Why Governments Control Prices

You learned in Chapter 3 that a market moves to equilibrium—that is, the market price moves to the level at which the quantity supplied equals the quantity demanded. But this equilibrium price does not necessarily please either buyers or sellers.

After all, buyers would always like to pay less if they could, and sometimes they can make a strong moral or political case that they should pay lower prices. For example, what if the equilibrium between supply and demand for apartments in a major city leads to rental rates that an average working person can't afford? In that case, a government might well be under pressure to impose limits on the rents landlords can charge.

Sellers, however, would always like to get more money for what they sell, and sometimes they can make a strong moral or political case that they should receive higher prices. For example, consider the labor market: the price for an hour of a worker's time is the wage rate. What if the equilibrium between supply and demand for less-skilled workers leads to wage rates that are below the poverty level? In that case, a government might well find itself pressured to require employers to pay a rate no lower than some specified minimum wage.

> **Price controls** are legal restrictions on how high or low a market price may go. They can take two forms: a **price ceiling**, a maximum price sellers are allowed to charge for a good, or a **price floor**, a minimum price buyers are required to pay for a good.

In other words, there is often a strong political demand for governments to intervene in markets. When a government intervenes to regulate prices, we say that it imposes **price controls.** These controls typically take the form either of an upper limit, a **price ceiling,** or a lower limit, a **price floor.**

Unfortunately, it's not that easy to tell a market what to do. As we will now see, when a government tries to legislate prices—whether it legislates them *down* by imposing a price ceiling or *up* by imposing a price floor—there are certain predictable and unpleasant side effects.

We should note an important caveat here: our analysis in this chapter considers only what happens when price controls are imposed on *competitive markets*, which, as you should recall from Chapter 3, are markets with many buyers and sellers in which no buyer or seller can have any influence on the price. When markets are *not* competitive—as in a monopoly, where there is only one seller—price controls don't necessarily cause the same problems. In practice, however, price controls often *are* imposed on competitive markets—like the New York apartment market. And so the analysis in this chapter applies to many important real-world situations.

## Price Ceilings

Aside from rent control, there are not many price ceilings in the United States today. But at times they have been widespread. Price ceilings are typically imposed during crises—wars, harvest failures, natural disasters—because these events often lead to sudden price increases that hurt many people but produce big gains for a lucky few. The U.S. government imposed ceilings on many prices during World War II: the war sharply increased demand for raw materials, such as aluminum and steel, and price controls prevented those with access to these raw materials from earning huge profits. Price controls on oil were imposed in 1973, when an embargo by Arab oil-exporting countries seemed likely to generate huge profits for U.S. oil companies. (See

Economics in Action on page 90.) Price controls were imposed on California's whole-sale electricity market in 2001, when a shortage was creating big profits for a few power-generating companies but leading to higher bills for consumers.

Rent control in New York is, believe it or not, a legacy of World War II: it was imposed because the war produced an economic boom, which increased demand for apartments at a time when the labor and raw materials that might have been used to build them were being used to win the war instead. Although most price controls were removed soon after the war ended, New York's rent limits were retained and gradually extended to buildings not previously covered, leading to some very strange situations.

You can rent a one-bedroom apartment in Manhattan on fairly short notice—if you are able and willing to pay about $1,700 a month and live in a less-than-desirable area. Yet some people pay only a small fraction of this for comparable apartments and others pay hardly more for bigger apartments in better locations.

Aside from producing great deals for some renters, however, what are the broader consequences of New York's rent control system? To answer this question, we turn to the model we developed in Chapter 3: the supply and demand model.

## Modeling a Price Ceiling

To see what can go wrong when a government imposes a price ceiling on a competi-tive market, consider Figure 4-1, which shows a simplified model of the market for apartments in New York. For the sake of simplicity, we imagine that all apartments are exactly the same and would therefore rent for the same price in an uncontrolled market. The table in the figure shows the demand and supply schedules; the implied demand and supply curves are shown on the left of the figure. We show the quanti-ty of apartments on the horizontal axis and the monthly rent per apartment on the vertical axis. You can see that in an unregulated market the equilibrium would be at point E: 2 million apartments would be rented for $1,000 each per month.

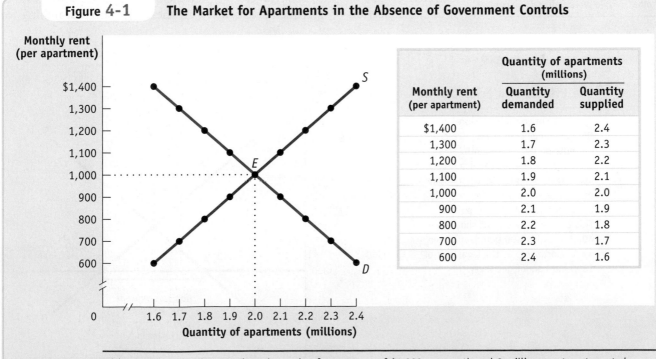

**Figure 4-1      The Market for Apartments in the Absence of Government Controls**

| Monthly rent (per apartment) | Quantity of apartments (millions) | |
|---|---|---|
| | Quantity demanded | Quantity supplied |
| $1,400 | 1.6 | 2.4 |
| 1,300 | 1.7 | 2.3 |
| 1,200 | 1.8 | 2.2 |
| 1,100 | 1.9 | 2.1 |
| 1,000 | 2.0 | 2.0 |
| 900 | 2.1 | 1.9 |
| 800 | 2.2 | 1.8 |
| 700 | 2.3 | 1.7 |
| 600 | 2.4 | 1.6 |

Without government intervention, the market for apart-ments reaches equilibrium at point E with a market rent **>web...** of $1,000 per month and 2 million apartments rented.

Now suppose that the government imposes a price ceiling, limiting rents to a price below the equilibrium price—say no more than $800.

Figure 4-2 shows the effect of the price ceiling, represented by the line at $800. At the enforced rental rate of $800, landlords will have less incentive to offer apartments, so they won't be willing to supply as many as they would at the equilibrium rate of $1,000. So they will choose point *A* on the supply curve, offering only 1.8 million apartments for rent, 200,000 fewer than in the free-market situation. At the same time, more people will want to rent apartments at a price of $800 than at the equilibrium price of $1,000; as shown at point *B* on the demand curve, at a monthly rent of $800 the quantity of apartments demanded rises to 2.2 million, 200,000 more than in the free-market situation and 400,000 more than are actually available at the price of $800. So there is now a persistent shortage of rental housing: at that price, 400,000 more people want to rent than are able to find apartments.

Do price ceilings always cause shortages? No. If a price ceiling is set above the equilibrium price, it won't have any effect. Suppose that the equilibrium rental rate on apartments is $1,000 per month and the city government sets a ceiling of $1,200. Who cares? In this case, the price ceiling won't be binding—it won't actually constrain market behavior—and it will have no effect.

## Why a Price Ceiling Causes Inefficiency

The housing shortage shown in Figure 4-2 is not merely annoying: Like any shortage induced by price controls, it can be seriously harmful because it leads to *inefficiency*. We introduced the concept of *efficiency* back in Chapter 1, where we learned that an economy is efficient if there is no way to make some people better off without making others worse off. We also learned the basic principle that a market economy, left to itself, is usually efficient.

A market or an economy becomes **inefficient** when there are missed opportunities—ways in which production or consumption could be rearranged that would make some people better off without making other people worse off.

Rent control, like all price ceilings, creates inefficiency in at least three distinct ways: in the allocation of apartments to renters, in the time wasted searching for

> A market or an economy is **inefficient** if there are missed opportunities: some people could be made better off without making other people worse off.

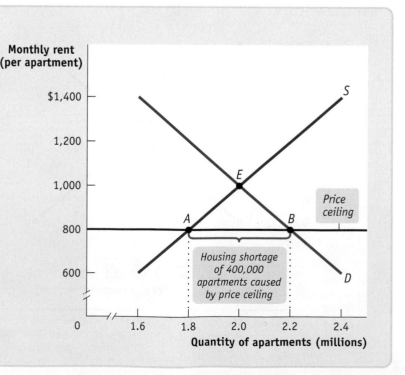

**Figure 4-2**

**The Effects of a Price Ceiling**

The dark horizontal line represents the government-imposed price ceiling on rents of $800 per month. This price ceiling reduces the quantity of apartments supplied to 1.8 million, point *A*, and increases the quantity demanded to 2.2 million, point *B*. This creates a persistent shortage of 400,000 units: 400,000 people who want apartments at the legal rent of $800 but cannot get them.

apartments, and in the inefficiently low quality or condition in which landlords maintain apartments. In addition to inefficiency, price ceilings give rise to illegal behavior as people try to circumvent them.

**Inefficient Allocation to Consumers** In the case shown in Figure 4-2, 2.2 million people would like to rent an apartment at $800 per month, but only 1.8 million apartments are available. Of those 2.2 million who are seeking an apartment, some want an apartment badly and are willing to pay a high price to get one. Others have a less urgent need and are only willing to pay a low price, perhaps because they have alternative housing. An efficient allocation of apartments would reflect these differences: people who really want an apartment will get one and people who aren't all that anxious to find an apartment won't. In an inefficient distribution of apartments, the opposite will happen: some people who are not especially anxious to find an apartment will get one but others who are very anxious to find an apartment won't. And because under rent control people usually get apartments through luck or personal connections, rent control generally results in an **inefficient allocation to consumers** of the few apartments available.

To see the inefficiency involved, consider the plight of the Lees, a family with young children who have no alternative housing and would be willing to pay up to $1,500 for an apartment—but are unable to find one. Also consider George, a retiree who lives most of the year in Florida but still has a lease on the New York apartment he moved into 40 years ago. George pays $800 per month for this apartment, but if the rent were even slightly more—say, $850—he would give it up and stay with his children when he is in New York.

This allocation of apartments—George has one and the Lees do not—is a missed opportunity: there is a way to make the Lees and George both better off at no additional cost. The Lees would be happy to pay George, say, $1,200 a month to sublet his apartment, which he would happily accept since the apartment is worth no more than $850 a month to him. George would prefer the money he gets from the Lees to keeping his apartment; the Lees would prefer to have the apartment rather than the money. So both would be made better off by this transaction—and nobody else would be hurt.

Generally, if people who really want apartments could sublet them from people who are less eager to stay in them, both those who gain apartments and those who trade their leases for more money would be better off. However, subletting is illegal under rent control because it would occur at prices above the price ceiling. But just because subletting is illegal doesn't mean it never happens; in fact, it does occur in New York, although not on a scale that would undo the effects of rent control. This illegal subletting is a kind of *black market activity*, which we will discuss shortly.

> Price ceilings often lead to inefficiency in the form of **inefficient allocation to consumers**: people who want the good badly and are willing to pay a high price don't get it, and those who care relatively little about the good and are only willing to pay a low price do get it.

**Wasted Resources** A second reason a price ceiling causes inefficiency is that it leads to **wasted resources.** The Economics in Action on page 90 describes the gasoline shortages of 1979, when millions of Americans spent hours each week waiting in lines at gas stations. The *opportunity cost* of the time spent in gas lines—the wages not earned, the leisure time not enjoyed—constituted wasted resources from the point of view of consumers and of the economy as a whole. Because of rent control, the Lees will spend all their spare time for several months searching for an apartment, time they would rather have spent working or in family activities. That is, there is an opportunity cost to the Lees' prolonged search for an apartment—the leisure or income they had to forgo. If the market for apartments worked freely, the Lees would quickly find an apartment at the equilibrium rent of $1,000 and have time to earn more or to enjoy themselves—an outcome that would make them better off without making anyone else worse off. Again, rent control creates missed opportunities.

> Price ceilings typically lead to inefficiency in the form of **wasted resources**: people spend money and expend effort in order to deal with the shortages caused by the price ceiling.

**Inefficiently Low Quality** A third way a price ceiling causes inefficiency is by causing goods to be of **inefficiently low quality.**

Again, consider rent control. Landlords have no incentive to provide better conditions because they cannot raise rents to cover their repair costs but are still able to find tenants easily. In many cases tenants would be willing to pay much more for improved

> Price ceilings often lead to inefficiency in that the goods being offered are of **inefficiently low quality**: sellers offer low-quality goods at a low price even though buyers would prefer a higher quality at a higher price.

## THE RENT CONTROL ARISTOCRACY

One of the ironies of New York's rent-control system is that some of the biggest beneficiaries are not the working-class families the system was intended to help but affluent tenants whose families have lived for many decades in choice apartments that would now command very high rents.

One well-known example: the 1986 movie *Hannah and Her Sisters* took place mainly in the real-life home of actress Mia Farrow, a spectacular 11-room apartment overlooking Central Park. Ms. Farrow "inherited" this apartment from her mother, the actress Maureen O'Sullivan. A few years after the movie came out, a study found that Ms. Farrow was paying less than $2,300 a month—about what a 2-bedroom apartment in a far less desirable location would have cost on the uncontrolled market.

conditions than it would cost for the landlord to provide them—for example, the upgrade of an antiquated electrical system that cannot safely run air conditioners or computers. But any additional payment for such improvements would be legally considered a rent increase, which is prohibited. Indeed, rent-controlled apartments are notoriously badly maintained, rarely painted, subject to frequent electrical and plumbing problems, sometimes even hazardous to inhabit. As one former manager of Manhattan buildings described his job: "At unregulated apartments we'd do most things that the tenants requested. But on the rent-regulated units, we did absolutely only what the law required. . . . We had a perverse incentive to make those tenants unhappy. With regulated apartments, the ultimate objective is to get people out of the building."

This whole situation is a missed opportunity—some tenants would be happy to pay for better conditions, and landlords would be happy to provide them for payment. But such an exchange would occur only if the market were allowed to operate freely.

**Black Markets** And that leads us to a last aspect of price ceilings: the incentive they provide for *illegal activities*, specifically the emergence of **black markets.** We have already described one kind of black market activity—illegal subletting by tenants. But it does not stop there. Clearly, there is a temptation for a landlord to say to a potential tenant, "Look, you can have the place if you slip me an extra few hundred in cash each month"—and for the tenant to agree, if he or she is one of those people who would be willing to pay much more than the maximum legal rent.

What's wrong with black markets? In general, it's a bad thing if people break *any* law, because it encourages disrespect for the law in general. Worse yet, in this case illegal activity worsens the position of those who try to be honest. If the Lees are scrupulous about not breaking the rent control law but others—who may need an apartment less than the Lees do—are willing to bribe landlords, the Lees may *never* find an apartment.

> A **black market** is a market in which goods or services are bought and sold illegally—either because it is illegal to sell them at all or because the prices charged are legally prohibited by a price ceiling.

## So Why Are There Price Ceilings?

We have seen three common results of price ceilings:

- A persistent shortage of the good
- Inefficiency arising from this persistent shortage in the form of inefficient allocation of the good to consumers, resources wasted in searching for the good, and the inefficiently low quality of the good offered for sale
- The emergence of illegal, black market activity

Given these unpleasant consequences, why do governments still sometimes impose price ceilings—and why does rent control, in particular, persist in New York?

One answer is that although price ceilings may have adverse effects, they do benefit some people. In practice, New York's rent control rules—which are more complex than our simple model—hurt most residents but give a small minority of renters much cheaper housing than they would get in an unregulated market. And those who benefit from the controls are typically better organized and more vocal than those who are harmed by them.

Also, when price ceilings have been in effect for a long time, buyers may not have a realistic idea of what would happen without them. In our previous example, the rental rate in an uncontrolled market (Figure 4-1) would be only 25 percent higher than in the controlled market (Figure 4-2)—$1,000 instead of $800. But how would renters know that? Indeed, they might have heard about black market transactions at much higher prices—the Lees or some other family paying George $1,200 or more—and would not realize that these black market prices are much higher than the price that would prevail in a fully free market.

A last answer is that government officials often do not understand supply and demand analysis! It is a great mistake to suppose that economic policies in the real world are always sensible or well informed.

## WORK IT OUT

## SHOWING A PRICE CEILING

Nearly every shop in Porttown sells 12-ounce bottles of water for $1 a bottle. About 1,000 bottles of water are sold on any given day. Unexpectedly a natural disaster contaminates the town's tap water, and demand for bottled water increases seven-fold so that at a price of $1 a bottle, 7,000 bottles can be sold in a day. Realizing they could run out of bottled water, sellers increase the price to $4 a bottle. They are able to sell 4,000 bottles of water each day. No one who wants to buy water at that price is turned away.

Residents of Porttown immediately complain that the stores are "gouging" customers. Government representatives, fielding calls from angry constituents, enact emergency legislation that sets a maximum price of $1 for a 12-ounce bottle of water.

**Graph:** Draw a graph that illustrates this scenario. *(Graph hint: In graphs of supply and demand, price always goes on the vertical axis and quantity is always on the horizontal axis.)*

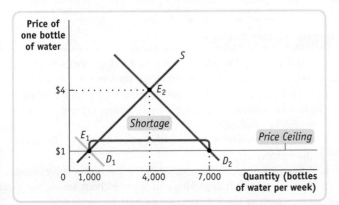

**SOLUTION:** The initial equilibrium is point $E_1$: the equilibrium price is $1 (first sentence) and the equilibrium quantity is 1,000 bottles (second sentence). After the natural disaster, the demand curve shifts to the right so that at a price of $1, quantity demanded is 7,000 (third sentence). The new equilibrium is

point $E_2$: the equilibrium price is $4 (fourth sentence) and the equilibrium quantity is 4,000 (fifth and sixth sentences). The supply curve must go through points $E_1$ and $E_2$. The first demand curve must go through point $E_1$; we don't know its slope. The second demand curve must go through point $E_2$ and the point (7,000, $1); those two points determine its slope.

**Price Ceiling and Price Floor:** Is the legislated price of $1 a "price ceiling" or a "price floor"? *(Price ceiling: The maximum value a price can take; prices cannot break through the ceiling. Price floor: The minimum value a price can take; prices cannot fall through the floor.)*

**SOLUTION:** The legislated price is a price ceiling; sellers are not permitted to sell at a price above $1 a bottle.

**Surplus or Shortage:** After the natural disaster, is there a shortage or a surplus at the legislated price? How large is the shortage or surplus? *(Shortage: The amount by which quantity demanded exceeds quantity supplied. Surplus: The amount by which quantity supplied exceeds quantity demanded.)*

**SOLUTION:** After the natural disaster, there is a shortage at the legislated price of $1. Quantity demanded exceeds quantity supplied. The shortage is 7,000 − 1,000 = 6,000 bottles of water per day.

**Efficiency:** Is the price ceiling efficient? Is the market price of $4 efficient? *(Efficient: when all potential trades are allowed to occur.)*

**SOLUTION:** The price ceiling is not efficient. There are buyers willing to pay $2 or $3 or $4 a bottle and sellers willing to sell at that price, but because of the emergency legislation these trades are not allowed. The market price of $4 is efficient. Everyone who wants to buy or sell water at that price is able to do so. (Note: We have not considered issues of fairness or equity, which usually prevail in instances of natural disaster. We take up the topic of equity in Chapter 10.)

# economics in action

## Oil Shortages in the 1970s

In 1979 a revolution overthrew the government of Iran, one of the world's major petroleum-exporting countries. The political chaos in Iran disrupted oil production there, and the sudden fall in world supply caused the price of crude oil to shoot up by 300 percent.

Hurry up and wait: filling your tank circa 1979.

In most of the world this price increase made gasoline more expensive at the pump but did not lead to shortages. In the United States, however, gasoline was subject to a price ceiling, imposed six years earlier during an oil crisis sparked by the Arab–Israeli war of 1973. The main purpose of those price controls was to prevent U.S. oil producers from reaping large profits as a result of temporary disruptions of supply.

As we learned in Chapter 3, a fall in supply generally raises prices. But here, because the price of gasoline at the pump couldn't rise, the reduction in supply showed up as shortages. As it turned out, these shortages became much worse because of panic: drivers who weren't sure when they would next be able to get gas rushed to fill up even if they still had plenty in their tanks. This produced a temporary surge in demand and long lines at gas stations.

For a few months the gasoline shortage dominated the national scene. Hours were wasted sitting in gasoline lines; families canceled vacations for fear of being stranded. Eventually, higher production began to work its way through the refineries, increasing supply. And the end of the summer driving season reduced demand. Both together led to a fall in price.

In 1981 price controls on gasoline, now discredited as a policy, were abolished. But the uncontrolled gasoline market faced a major test in the spring of 2000. Oil-producing nations restricted their output in order to drive up prices and achieved unexpected success, more than doubling world prices over a period of a few months. Prices at the pump rose sharply—many people altered their driving plans and some felt distinctly poorer as a result of the higher prices. But there were no shortages and life continued in the United States without nearly as much disruption as price controls had generated in the 1970s.

Interestingly, however, the oil price shock of 2000 *did* cause serious disruptions in some European countries—because truck drivers and farmers, protesting the high price of fuel, blocked deliveries. This protest was an extreme illustration of the reasons why governments sometimes try to control prices despite the known problems with price controls! ■

< < < < < < < < < < < < < < < < < <

## >>QUICK REVIEW

➤ *Price controls* take the form of either legal maximum prices—*price ceilings*—or legal minimum prices—*price floors*.
➤ A price ceiling below the equilibrium price benefits successful buyers but causes predictable adverse effects such as persistent *shortages*, which lead to three types of *inefficiencies: inefficient allocation to consumers, wasted resources,* and *inefficiently low quality.*
➤ Price ceilings also produce *black markets,* as buyers and sellers attempt to evade the price restriction.

## >>CHECK YOUR UNDERSTANDING 4-1

1. Homeowners near Middletown University's stadium used to rent parking spaces in their driveways to fans at a going rate of $11. A new town ordinance now sets a maximum parking fee of $7. Use the accompanying supply and demand diagram to explain how each of the following corresponds to a price-ceiling concept.
   a. Some homeowners now think it's not worth the hassle to rent out spaces.
   b. Some fans who used to carpool to the game now drive alone.
   c. Some fans can't find parking and leave without seeing the game.
   Explain how each of the following arises from the price ceiling.
   d. Some fans now arrive several hours early to find parking.
   e. Friends of homeowners near the stadium regularly attend games, even if they aren't big fans. But some serious fans have given up because of the parking situation.
   f. Some homeowners rent spaces for more than $7 but pretend that the buyers are non-paying friends or family.

Parking fee

$15 ············· S

11 ······· E

7

3 ············· D

0   3,200   3,600   4,000   4,400   4,800

**Quantity of parking spaces**

*continued*

**2.** True or false? Explain your answer. Compared to a free market, price ceilings at a price below the equilibrium price do the following:

a. Increase quantity supplied

b. Make some people who want to consume the good worse off

c. Make all producers worse off

*Solutions appear at back of book.*

# Price Floors

Sometimes governments intervene to push market prices up instead of down. *Price floors* have been widely legislated for agricultural products, such as wheat and milk, as a way to support the incomes of farmers. Historically, there were also price floors on such services as trucking and air travel, although these were phased out by the United States in the 1970s. If you have ever worked in a fast-food restaurant, you are likely to have encountered a price floor: the United States and many other countries maintain a lower limit on the hourly wage rate of a worker's labor—that is, a floor on the price of labor, called the **minimum wage.**

Just like price ceilings, price floors are intended to help some people but generate predictable and undesirable side effects. Figure 4-3 shows hypothetical supply and demand curves for butter. Left to itself, the market would move to equilibrium at point *E*, with 10 million pounds of butter bought and sold at a price of $1 per pound.

But now suppose that the government, in order to help dairy farmers, imposes a price floor on butter of $1.20 per pound. Its effects are shown in Figure 4-4 on page 92, where the line at $1.20 represents the price floor. At a price of $1.20 per pound, producers would want to supply 12 million pounds (point *B* on the supply curve) but consumers would want to buy only 9 million pounds (point *A* on the demand curve). There would therefore be a persistent surplus of 3 million pounds of butter.

> The **minimum wage** is a legal floor on the wage rate, which is the market price of labor.

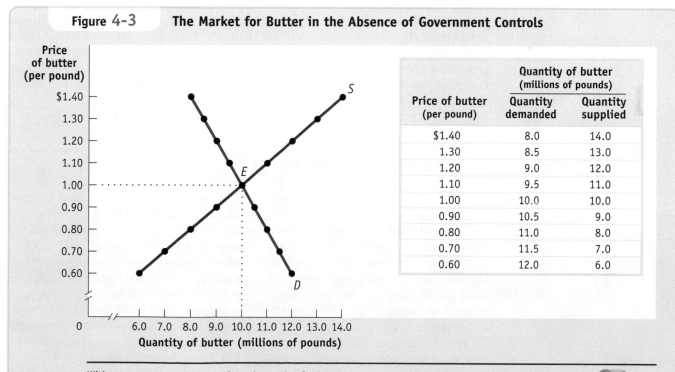

| Figure 4-3 | The Market for Butter in the Absence of Government Controls |

| Price of butter (per pound) | Quantity of butter (millions of pounds) | |
| --- | --- | --- |
| | Quantity demanded | Quantity supplied |
| $1.40 | 8.0 | 14.0 |
| 1.30 | 8.5 | 13.0 |
| 1.20 | 9.0 | 12.0 |
| 1.10 | 9.5 | 11.0 |
| 1.00 | 10.0 | 10.0 |
| 0.90 | 10.5 | 9.0 |
| 0.80 | 11.0 | 8.0 |
| 0.70 | 11.5 | 7.0 |
| 0.60 | 12.0 | 6.0 |

Without government intervention, the market for butter reaches equilibrium at a price of $1 per pound and with 10 million pounds of butter bought and sold. **>web...**

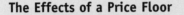

### Figure 4-4

**The Effects of a Price Floor**

The dark horizontal line represents the government-imposed price floor of $1.20 per pound of butter. The quantity of butter demanded falls to 9 million pounds while the quantity supplied rises to 12 million pounds, generating a persistent surplus of 3 million pounds of butter. **>web...**

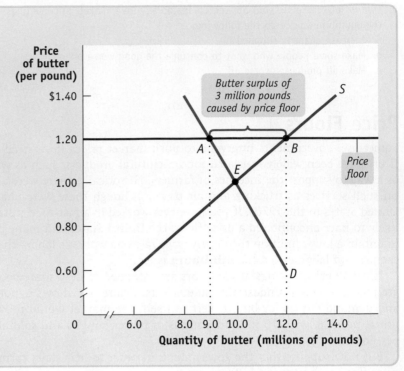

Does a price floor always lead to an unwanted surplus? No. Just as in the case of a price ceiling, the floor may not be binding—that is, it may be irrelevant. If the equilibrium price of butter is $1 per pound but the floor is set at only $0.80, the floor has no effect.

But suppose that a price floor is binding: what happens to the unwanted surplus? The answer depends on government policy. In the case of agricultural price floors, governments buy up unwanted surplus. Therefore the U.S. government has at times found itself warehousing thousands of tons of butter, cheese, and other farm products. (The European Commission, which administers price floors for a number of European countries, once found itself the owner of a so-called butter mountain,

---

## FOR INQUIRING MINDS

### PRICE FLOORS AND BUTTER COOKIES

Wander down the cookie aisle of your supermarket, and you will probably find a large section of imported cookies, especially "butter cookies"—cookies containing lots of butter—from Denmark and other countries. Why does the United States—with a pretty strong cookie-baking tradition of its own—import cookies from overseas? Part of the answer lies in European price floors.

Twenty-five European countries are currently members of the European Union, an organization that coordinates their policies on foreign trade, regulations, and other matters. The

European Union also sets price floors for agricultural goods, under the so-called Common Agricultural Policy, or CAP. These price floors have led to large surpluses, particularly of butter. To cope with these surpluses, the CAP pays a subsidy to companies that export goods such as butter—that is, sell them outside Europe.

And guess what: butter contained in a cookie sold in America counts as exported butter—and receives a subsidy. As a result, butter cookies from Europe are artificially cheap in America. So now you know why your supermarket stocks them. *Bon appetit!*

equal in weight to the entire population of Austria.) The government then has to find a way to dispose of these unwanted goods.

Some countries pay exporters to sell products at a loss overseas; this is standard procedure for the European Union. (See For Inquiring Minds on page 92.) At one point the United States tried giving away surplus cheese to the poor. In some cases, governments have actually destroyed the surplus production. To avoid the problem of dealing with the unwanted supplies, the U.S. government typically pays farmers not to produce the products at all.

When the government is not prepared to purchase the unwanted surplus, a price floor means that would-be sellers cannot find buyers. This is what happens when there is a price floor on the wage rate paid for an hour of labor, the *minimum wage*: when the minimum wage is above the equilibrium wage rate, some people who are willing to work—that is, sell labor—cannot find buyers—that is, employers willing to give them jobs.

## Why a Price Floor Causes Inefficiency

The persistent surplus that results from a price floor creates missed opportunities—inefficiencies—that resemble those created by the shortage that results from a price ceiling. These include:

- Inefficient allocation of sales among sellers
- Wasted resources
- Inefficiently high quality
- The temptation to break the law by selling below the legal price

**Inefficient Allocation of Sales Among Sellers** Like a price ceiling, a price floor can lead to *inefficient allocation*—but in this case **inefficient allocation of sales among sellers** rather than inefficient allocation to consumers.

> Price floors lead to **inefficient allocation of sales among sellers:** those who would be willing to sell the good at the lowest price are not always those who actually manage to sell it.

An episode from the Belgian movie *Rosetta*, a realistic fictional story, illustrates the problem of inefficient allocation of selling opportunities quite well. Like many European countries, Belgium has a high minimum wage, and jobs for young people are scarce. At one point Rosetta, a young woman who is very anxious to work, loses her job at a fast-food stand because the owner of the stand replaces her with his son—a very reluctant worker. Rosetta would be willing to work for less money, and with the money he would save, the owner could give his son an allowance and let him do something else. But to hire Rosetta for less than the minimum wage would be illegal.

**Wasted Resources** Also like a price ceiling, a price floor generates inefficiency by *wasting resources*. The most graphic examples involve agricultural products with price floors when the government buys up the unwanted surplus. The surplus production is sometimes destroyed, which is a pure waste; in other cases the stored produce goes, as officials euphemistically put it, "out of condition" and must be thrown away.

Price floors also lead to wasted time and effort. Consider the minimum wage. Would-be workers who spend many hours searching for jobs, or waiting in line in the hope of getting jobs, play the same role in the case of price floors as hapless families searching for apartments in the case of price ceilings.

**Inefficiently High Quality** Again like price ceilings, price floors lead to inefficiency in the quality of goods produced.

We saw that when there is a price ceiling, suppliers produce products that are of inefficiently low quality: buyers prefer higher-quality products and are willing to pay for them, but sellers refuse to improve the quality of their products because the price ceiling prevents their being compensated for doing so. This same logic applies to price floors, but in reverse: suppliers offer goods of **inefficiently high quality.**

> Price floors often lead to inefficiency in that goods of **inefficiently high quality** are offered: sellers offer high-quality goods at a high price, even though buyers would prefer a lower quality at a lower price.

How can this be? Isn't high quality a good thing? Yes, but only if it is worth the cost. Suppose that suppliers spend a lot to make goods of very high quality but that this quality is not worth all that much to consumers, who would rather receive the money spent on that quality in the form of a lower price. This represents a missed opportunity: suppliers and buyers could make a mutually beneficial deal in which buyers got goods of somewhat lower quality for a much lower price.

A good example of the inefficiency of excessive quality comes from the days when transatlantic airfares were set artificially high by international treaty. Forbidden to compete for customers by offering lower ticket prices, airlines instead offered expensive services, like lavish in-flight meals that went largely uneaten. At one point the regulators tried to restrict this practice by defining maximum service standards—for example, that snack service should consist of no more than a sandwich. One airline then introduced what it called a "Scandinavian Sandwich," a towering affair that forced the convening of another conference to define *sandwich*. All of this was wasteful, especially considering that what passengers really wanted was less food and lower airfares.

Since the deregulation of U.S. airlines in the 1970s, American passengers have experienced a large decrease in ticket prices accompanied by a decrease in the quality of in-flight service—smaller seats, lower-quality food, and so on. Everyone complains about the service—but thanks to lower fares, the number of people flying on U.S. carriers has grown several hundred percent since airline deregulation.

**Illegal Activity**    Finally, like price ceilings, price floors can provide an incentive for *illegal activity*. For example, in countries where the minimum wage is far above the equilibrium wage rate, workers desperate for jobs sometimes agree to work off the books for employers who conceal their employment from the government—or bribe the government inspectors. This practice, known in Europe as "black labor," is especially common in Southern European countries such as Italy and Spain (see Economics in Action below).

## So Why Are There Price Floors?

To sum up, a price floor creates various negative side effects:

- A persistent surplus of the good
- Inefficiency arising from the persistent surplus in the form of inefficient allocation of sales among sellers, wasted resources, and an inefficiently high level of quality offered by suppliers
- The temptation to engage in illegal activity, particularly bribery and corruption of government officials

So why do governments impose price floors when they have so many negative side effects? The reasons are similar to those for imposing price ceilings. Government officials often disregard warnings about the consequences of price floors either because they believe that the relevant market is poorly described by the supply and demand model or, more often, because they do not understand the model. Above all, just as price ceilings are often imposed because they benefit some influential buyers of a good, price floors are often imposed because they benefit some influential *sellers*.

# *economics in action*

## "Black Labor" in Southern Europe

The best-known example of a price floor is the minimum wage. Most economists believe, however, that the minimum wage has relatively little effect on the job market in the United States, mainly because the floor is set so low. (This effectively makes the U.S. minimum wage a *nonbinding* price floor—a political symbol more than a substantive policy.) In 1968, the U.S. minimum wage was 53 percent of the average wage of blue-collar workers; by 2003, it had fallen to about 34 percent.

The situation is different, however, in many European countries, where minimum wages have been set much higher than in the United States. This has happened despite the fact that European workers are somewhat less productive than their American counterparts, which means that the equilibrium wage in Europe—the wage that would clear the labor market—is probably lower in Europe than in the United States. Moreover, European countries often require employers to pay for health and retirement benefits, which are more extensive and therefore more costly than comparable American benefits. These mandated benefits make the actual cost of hiring a European worker considerably more than the worker's paycheck.

The result is that in Europe the price floor on labor is definitely binding: the minimum wage is well above the wage rate that would make the quantity of labor supplied by workers equal to the quantity of labor demanded by employers.

The persistent surplus that results from this price floor appears in the form of high unemployment—millions of workers, especially young workers, seek jobs but cannot find them. In countries where the enforcement of labor laws is lax, however, there is a second, entirely predictable result: widespread evasion of the law. In both Italy and Spain, officials believe there are hundreds of thousands, if not millions, of workers who are employed by companies that pay them less than the legal minimum, fail to provide the required health and retirement benefits, or both. In many cases the jobs are simply unreported: Spanish economists estimate that about a third of the country's reported unemployed are in the black labor market—working at unreported jobs. In fact, Spaniards waiting to collect checks from the unemployment office have been known to complain about the long lines that keep them from getting back to work!

Employers in these countries have also found legal ways to evade the wage floor. For example, Italy's labor regulations apply only to companies with 15 or more workers. This gives a big cost advantage to small Italian firms, many of which remain small in order to avoid having to pay higher wages and benefits. And sure enough, in some Italian industries there is an astonishing proliferation of tiny companies. For example, one of Italy's most successful industries is the manufacture of fine woolen cloth, centered in the Prato region. The average textile firm in that region employs only four workers! ■

> > > > > > > > > > > > > > > > > > >

**>> CHECK YOUR UNDERSTANDING 4-2**

1. The state legislature mandates a price floor for gasoline of $4 per gallon. Assess the following statements and illustrate your answer using the figure provided:

   a. Proponents of the law claim it will increase the income of gas station owners. Opponents claim it will hurt gas station owners because they will lose customers.

   b. Proponents claim consumers will be better off because gas stations will provide better service. Opponents claim consumers will be generally worse off because they prefer to buy gas at cheaper prices.

   c. Proponents claim that they are helping gas station owners without hurting anyone else. Opponents claim that consumers are hurt and will end up doing things like buying gas in a nearby state or on the black market.

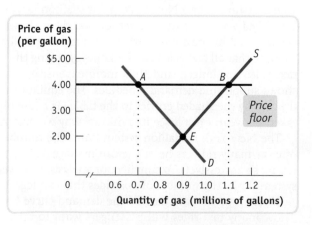

Solutions appear at back of book.

## Controlling Quantities

In the 1930s, New York City instituted a system of licensing for taxicabs: only taxis with a "medallion" were allowed to pick up passengers. Because this system was intended to ensure quality, medallion owners were supposed to maintain certain standards, including safety and cleanliness. A total of 11,787 medallions were issued, with taxi owners paying $10 for each medallion.

In 1995, there were still only 11,787 licensed taxicabs in New York, even though the city had meanwhile become the financial capital of the world, a place where hundreds of thousands of people in a hurry tried to hail a cab every day. (An additional 400 medallions were issued in 1995, and in 2003 plans were announced to issue 900 more over a period of three years.)

The result of this restriction on the number of taxis was that those medallions became very valuable: if you wanted to operate a New York taxi, you had to lease a medallion from someone else or buy one for a going price of about $250,000.

It turns out that the New York story is not unique; other cities introduced similar medallion systems in the 1930s and, like New York, have issued few new medallions since. In San Francisco and Boston, as in New York, taxi medallions trade for six-figure prices.

A **quantity control**, or **quota**, is an upper limit on the quantity of some good that can be bought or sold. The total amount of the good that can be legally transacted is the **quota limit**.

A **license** gives its owner the right to supply a good.

A taxi medallion system is a form of **quantity control,** or **quota,** by which the government regulates the quantity of a good that can be bought and sold rather than the price at which it is transacted. The total amount of the good that can be transacted under the quantity control is called the **quota limit.** Typically, the government limits quantity in a market by issuing **licenses;** only people with a license can legally supply the good. A taxi medallion is just such a license. The government of New York City limits the number of taxi rides that can be sold by limiting the number of taxis to only those who hold medallions. There are many other cases of quantity controls, ranging from limits on how much foreign currency (for instance, British pounds or Mexican pesos) people are allowed to buy to the quantity of clams New Jersey fishing boats are allowed to catch. Notice, by the way, that although there are price controls on both sides of the equilibrium price—price ceilings and price floors—in the real world, quantity controls always set an upper, not a lower, limit on quantities. After all, nobody can be forced to buy or sell more than they want to!

Some of these attempts to control quantities are undertaken for good economic reasons, some for bad ones. In many cases, as we will see, quantity controls introduced to address a temporary problem become politically hard to remove later because the beneficiaries don't want them abolished, even after the original reason for their existence is long gone. But whatever the reasons for such controls, they have certain predictable—and usually undesirable—economic consequences.

## The Anatomy of Quantity Controls

To understand why a New York taxi medallion is worth so much money, we consider a simplified version of the market for taxi rides, shown in Figure 4-5 on page 97. Just as we assumed in the analysis of rent controls that all apartments are the same, we now suppose that all taxi rides are the same—ignoring the real-world complication that some taxi rides are longer, and thus more expensive, than others. The table in the figure shows supply and demand schedules. The equilibrium—indicated by point *E* in the figure and by the shaded entries in the table—is a fare of $5 per ride, with 10 million rides taken per year. (You'll see in a minute why we present the equilibrium this way.)

The New York medallion system limits the number of taxis, but each taxi driver can offer as many rides as he or she can manage. (Now you know why New York taxi drivers are so aggressive!) To simplify our analysis, however, we will assume that a medallion system limits the number of taxi rides that can legally be given to 8 million per year.

Until now, we have derived the demand curve by answering questions of the form: "How many taxi rides will passengers want to take if the price is $5 per ride?" But it is possible to reverse the question and ask instead: "At what price will consumers want

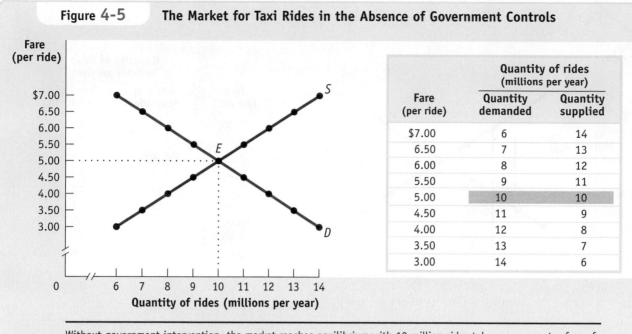

**Figure 4-5**   **The Market for Taxi Rides in the Absence of Government Controls**

| Fare (per ride) | Quantity of rides (millions per year) | |
| --- | --- | --- |
| | Quantity demanded | Quantity supplied |
| $7.00 | 6 | 14 |
| 6.50 | 7 | 13 |
| 6.00 | 8 | 12 |
| 5.50 | 9 | 11 |
| 5.00 | 10 | 10 |
| 4.50 | 11 | 9 |
| 4.00 | 12 | 8 |
| 3.50 | 13 | 7 |
| 3.00 | 14 | 6 |

Without government intervention, the market reaches equilibrium with 10 million rides taken per year at a fare of $5 per ride.

to buy 10 million rides per year?" The price at which consumers want to buy a given quantity—in this case, 10 million rides at $5 per ride—is the **demand price** of that quantity. You can see from the demand schedule in Figure 4-5 that the demand price of 6 million rides is $7, the demand price of 7 million rides is $6.50, and so on.

Similarly, the supply curve represents the answer to questions of the form: "How many taxi rides would taxi drivers supply at a price of $5 each?" But we can also reverse this question to ask: "At what price will suppliers be willing to supply 10 million rides per year?" The price at which suppliers will supply a given quantity—in this case, 10 million rides at $5 per ride—is the **supply price** of that quantity. We can see from the supply schedule in Figure 4-5 that the supply price of 6 million rides is $3, the supply price of 7 million rides is $3.50, and so on.

Now we are ready to analyze a quota. We have assumed that the city government limits the quantity of taxi rides to 8 million per year. Medallions, each of which carries the right to provide a certain number of taxi rides per year, are made available to selected people in such a way that a total of 8 million rides will be provided. Medallion holders may then either drive their own taxis or rent their medallions to others for a fee.

Figure 4-6 shows the resulting market for taxi rides, with the line at 8 million rides per year representing the quota limit. Because the quantity of rides is limited to 8 million, consumers must be at point A on the demand curve, corresponding to the shaded entry in the demand schedule: the demand price of 8 million rides is $6. Meanwhile, taxi drivers must be at point B on the supply curve, corresponding to the shaded entry in the supply schedule: the supply price of 8 million rides is $4.

But how can the price received by taxi drivers be $4 when the price paid by taxi riders is $6? The answer is that in addition to the market in taxi rides, there will also be a market in medallions. Medallion-holders may not always want to drive their own taxis: they may be ill or on vacation. So those who do not want to drive their own taxis will sell the right to use the medallion to someone else. So we need to consider two sets of transactions here, and hence two prices: (1) the transactions in taxi rides and the price at which these will occur, and (2) the transactions in medallions and

The **demand price** of a given quantity is the price at which consumers will demand that quantity.

The **supply price** of a given quantity is the price at which producers will supply that quantity.

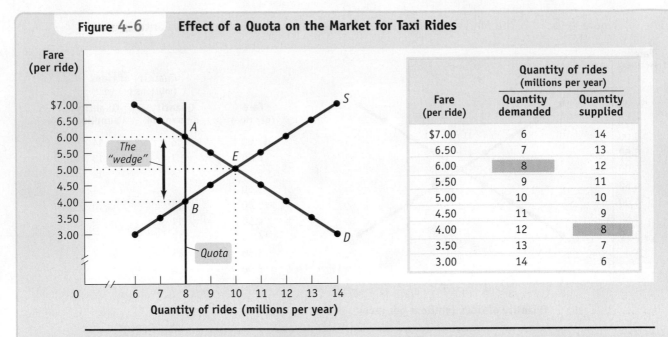

**Figure 4-6**     **Effect of a Quota on the Market for Taxi Rides**

| Fare (per ride) | Quantity of rides (millions per year) | |
| --- | --- | --- |
| | Quantity demanded | Quantity supplied |
| $7.00 | 6 | 14 |
| 6.50 | 7 | 13 |
| 6.00 | 8 | 12 |
| 5.50 | 9 | 11 |
| 5.00 | 10 | 10 |
| 4.50 | 11 | 9 |
| 4.00 | 12 | 8 |
| 3.50 | 13 | 7 |
| 3.00 | 14 | 6 |

The table shows the demand price and the supply price corresponding to each quantity: the price at which that quantity would be demanded and supplied, respectively. The city government imposes a quota of 8 million rides by selling licenses for only 8 million rides, represented by the dark vertical line. The price paid by consumers rises to $6 per ride, the demand price of 8 million rides, shown by point *A*. The supply price of 8 million rides is only $4 per ride, shown by point *B*. The difference between these two prices is the quota rent per ride, the earnings that accrue to the owner of a license. The quota rent drives a wedge between the demand price and the supply price. **>web...**

A quantity control, or quota, drives a **wedge** between the demand price and the supply price of a good; that is, the price paid by buyers ends up being higher than that received by sellers. The difference between the demand and supply price at the quota limit is the **quota rent,** the earnings that accrue to the license-holder from ownership of the right to sell the good. It is equal to the market price of the license when the licenses are traded.

the price at which these will occur. It turns out that since we are looking at two markets, the $4 and $6 prices will both be right.

To see how this all works, consider two imaginary New York taxi drivers, Sunil and Harriet. Sunil has a medallion but can't use it because he's recovering from a severely sprained wrist. So he's looking to rent his medallion out to someone else. Harriet doesn't have a medallion but would like to rent one. Furthermore, at any point in time there are many other people like Harriet who would like to rent a medallion as well as many others like Sunil who have a medallion to rent. Suppose Sunil agrees to rent his medallion to Harriet. To make things simple, assume that any driver can give only one ride per day and that Sunil is renting his medallion to Harriet for one day. What rental price will they agree on?

To answer this question, we need to look at the transactions from the viewpoints of both drivers. Once she has the medallion, Harriet knows she can make $6 per day—the demand price of a ride under the quota. And she is willing to rent the medallion only if she makes at least $4 per day—the supply price of a ride under the quota. So Sunil cannot demand a rent of more than $2—the difference between $6 and $4. And if Harriet offered Sunil less than $2—say, $1.50—there would be other eager drivers willing to offer him more, up to $2. Hence, in order to get the medallion, Harriet must offer Sunil at least $2. Therefore, since the rent can be no more than $2 and no less than $2, it must be exactly $2.

It is no coincidence that $2 is exactly the difference between $6, the demand price of 8 million rides, and $4, the supply price of 8 million rides. In every case in which the supply of a good is legally restricted, there is a **wedge** between the demand price of the quantity transacted and the supply price of the quantity transacted. This wedge, illustrated by the double-headed arrow in Figure 4-6, has a special name: the **quota rent.** It is the earnings that accrue to the license-holder from ownership of a valuable commodity, the license. In the case of Sunil and Harriet, the quota rent of $2 goes to Sunil because he owns the license, and the remaining $4 from the total fare of $6 goes to Harriet.

So Figure 4-6 also illustrates the quota rent in the market for New York taxi rides. The quota limits the quantity of rides to 8 million per year, a quantity at which the demand price of $6 exceeds the supply price of $4. The wedge between these two prices, $2, is the quota rent that results from the restrictions placed on the quantity of taxi rides in this market.

But wait a second. What if Sunil doesn't rent out his medallion? What if he uses it himself? Doesn't this mean that he gets a price of $6? No, not really. Even if Sunil doesn't rent out his medallion, he could have rented it out, which means that the medallion has an *opportunity cost* of $2: if Sunil decides to drive his own taxi rather than renting it to Harriet, the $2 represents his opportunity cost of not renting out his medallion. That is, the $2 quota rent is now the rental income he forgoes by driving his own taxi. In effect, Sunil is in two businesses—the taxi-driving business and the medallion-renting business. He makes $4 per ride from driving his taxi and $2 per ride from renting out his medallion. It doesn't make any difference that in this particular case he has rented his medallion to himself! So regardless of whether the medallion owner uses the medallion himself or herself, or rents it to others, it is a valuable asset. And this is represented in the going price for a New York City taxi medallion: in 2004, it was around $250,000.

Notice, by the way, that quotas—like price ceilings and price floors—don't always have a real effect. If the quota were set at 12 million rides—that is, above the equilibrium quantity in an unregulated market—it would have no effect because it would not be binding.

## The Costs of Quantity Controls

Like price controls, quantity controls can have some undesirable side effects. The first is the by-now-familiar problem of *inefficiency* due to missed opportunities: quantity controls prevent mutually beneficial transactions from occurring, transactions that would benefit both buyers and sellers. Looking back at Figure 4-6, you can see that starting at the quota limit of 8 million rides, New Yorkers would be willing to pay at least $5.50 per ride for an additional 1 million rides and that taxi drivers would be willing to provide those rides as long as they got at least $4.50 per ride. These are rides that would have taken place if there were no quota limit. The same is true for the next 1 million rides: New Yorkers would be willing to pay at least $5 per ride when the quantity of rides is increased from 9 to 10 million, and taxi drivers would be willing to provide those rides as long as they got at least $5 per ride. Again, these rides would have occurred without the quota limit. Only when the market has reached the free-market equilibrium quantity of 10 million rides are there no "missed-opportunity rides"—the quota limit of 8 million rides has caused 2 million "missed-opportunity rides." Generally, *as long as the demand price of a given quantity exceeds the supply price, there is a missed opportunity.* A buyer would be willing to buy the good at a price that the seller would be willing to accept, but such a transaction does not occur because it is forbidden by the quota.

And because there are transactions that people would like to make but are not allowed to, quantity controls generate an incentive to evade them or even to break the law. New York's taxi industry again provides clear examples. Taxi regulation applies only to those drivers who are hailed by passengers on the street. A car service that makes prearranged pickups does not need a medallion. As a result, such hired cars provide much of the service that might otherwise be provided by taxis, as in other cities. In addition, there are substantial numbers of unlicensed cabs that simply defy the law by picking up passengers without a medallion. Because these cabs are illegal, their drivers are completely unregulated, and they generate a disproportionately large share of traffic accidents in New York.

In fact, in 2004 the hardships caused by the limited number of New York taxis led city leaders to authorize an increase in the number of licensed taxis from 12,187 to a little over 13,000 by 2007—a move that certainly cheered New York riders. But those who already owned medallions were less happy with the increase; they understood that the nearly 900 new taxis would reduce or eliminate the shortage of taxis. As a result, taxi drivers might find their revenues decline as they would no longer always be assured of finding willing customers. And, in turn, the value of a medallion would fall. So to placate the medallion owners, city officials also agreed in 2004 to raise fares by 25 percent, a move that slightly diminished the newfound cheer of New York riders.

In sum, quantity controls typically create the following undesirable side effects:

- Inefficiencies, or missed opportunities, in the form of mutually beneficial transactions that don't occur
- Incentives for illegal activities

# economics in action

## The Clams of New Jersey

Forget the refineries along the Jersey Turnpike; one industry that New Jersey *really* dominates is clam fishing. The Garden State supplies 80 percent of the world's surf clams, whose tongues are used in fried-clam dinners, and 40 percent of the quahogs, which are used to make clam chowder.

In the 1980s, however, excessive fishing threatened to wipe out New Jersey's clam beds. To save the resource, the U.S. government introduced a clam quota, which sets an overall limit on the number of bushels of clams that may be caught and allocates licenses to owners of fishing boats based on their historical catches.

Notice, by the way, that this is an example of a quota that is probably justified by broader economic and environmental considerations—unlike the New York taxicab quota, which has long since lost any economic rationale. Still, whatever its rationale, the New Jersey clam quota works the same way as any other quota.

Once the quota system was established, many boat owners stopped fishing for clams. They realized that rather than operate a boat part time, it was more profitable to sell or rent their licenses to someone else, who could then assemble enough licenses to operate a boat full time. Today, there are about 50 boats fishing for clams; the license required to operate one is worth more than the boat itself. ∎

< < < < < < < < < < < < < < < < < <

>>**CHECK YOUR UNDERSTANDING 4-3**

1. Suppose that the supply and demand for taxi rides is given by Figure 4-5 but the quota is set at 6 million rides instead of 8 million. Find the following and indicate them on Figure 4-5.
   a. The price of a ride
   b. The quota rent
   c. Suppose the quota limit on taxi rides is increased to 9 million. What happens to the quota rent?
2. Assume that the quota limit is 8 million rides. Suppose demand decreases due to a decline in tourism. What is the smallest parallel leftward shift in demand that would result in the quota no longer having an effect on the market? Illustrate your answer using Figure 4-5.

Solutions appear at back of book.

# A Surprise Parallel: Taxes

To provide the services we want, from national defense to public parks, governments must collect taxes. But taxes impose costs on the economy. Among the most important roles of economics is tax analysis: figuring out the economic costs of taxation, determining who bears those costs, and suggesting ways to change the tax system that will reduce the costs it imposes. It turns out that the same analysis we have just used to understand quotas can be used, with hardly any modification, to make a preliminary analysis of taxes, too.

## Why Is a Tax Like a Quota?

Suppose that the supply and demand curves for New York taxis were exactly as shown in Figure 4-5. This means that in the absence of government action, the equilibrium price of a taxi ride will be $5 and 10 million rides will be bought and sold.

Now suppose that instead of imposing a quota on the quantity of rides, the city imposes an **excise tax**—a tax on sales. Specifically, it charges taxi drivers $2 for each ride they provide. What is the effect of the tax?

From the point of view of a taxi driver, the tax means that he or she doesn't get to keep all of the fare: if a passenger pays $5, $2 is collected as a tax, so the driver gets only $3. For any given quantity of rides supplied, the *post-tax supply price* is higher than the pre-tax supply price. For example, drivers will now require a price of $6 to supply as many rides as they would have been willing to supply at a price of $4 in the absence of the $2 tax.

So the tax on sales shifts the supply curve upward, by the amount of the tax. This is shown in Figure 4-7, where $S_1$ is the supply curve before the tax is imposed and $S_2$ is the supply curve after the tax is imposed. The market equilibrium moves from $E$, where the price is $5 per ride and 10 million rides are bought and sold, to $A$, where the price is $6 per ride and 8 million rides are bought and sold. $A$ is, of course, on both the demand curve $D$ and the new supply curve $S_2$.

But how do we know that 8 million rides will be supplied at a price of $6? Because the price *net of the tax* is $4 and the pre-tax supply price of 8 million rides is $4, as shown by point $B$ in Figure 4-7.

Does all this look familiar? It should. The equilibrium with a $2 tax on rides, which reduces the quantity bought and sold to 8 million rides, looks just like the equilibrium with a quota of 8 million rides, which leads to a quota rent of $2 per ride.

> An **excise tax** is a tax on sales of a good or service.

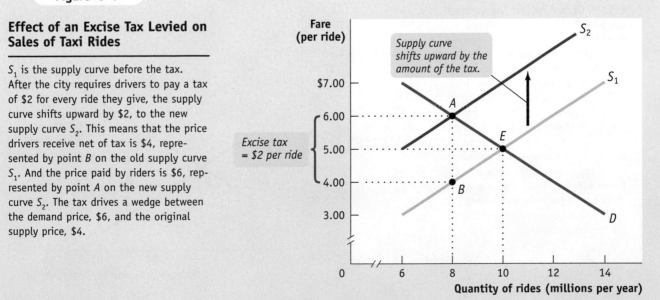

### Figure 4-7

**Effect of an Excise Tax Levied on Sales of Taxi Rides**

$S_1$ is the supply curve before the tax. After the city requires drivers to pay a tax of $2 for every ride they give, the supply curve shifts upward by $2, to the new supply curve $S_2$. This means that the price drivers receive net of tax is $4, represented by point $B$ on the old supply curve $S_1$. And the price paid by riders is $6, represented by point $A$ on the new supply curve $S_2$. The tax drives a wedge between the demand price, $6, and the original supply price, $4.

Just like a quota, the tax *drives a wedge* between the demand price and the original, pre-tax supply price.

The only difference is that instead of paying a $2 rent to the owner of a license, drivers pay a $2 tax to the city. In fact, there is a way to make an excise tax and a quota completely equivalent. Imagine that instead of issuing a limited number of licenses, the city simply sold licenses at $2 each. This $2 license fee would, for all practical purposes, be a $2 excise tax.

Finally, imagine that instead of selling licenses at a fixed price, the city were to issue 8 million licenses and auction them off—that is, sell them for whatever price the, um, traffic will bear. What would be the price of a license? Surely it would be $2—the quota rent. And so in this case the quota rent would act just like an excise tax.

## Who Pays an Excise Tax?

We have just imagined a tax that must be paid by the *sellers* of a good. But what would happen if the tax were instead paid by the *buyers*—say, if you had to pay a special $2 tax to ride in a taxicab?

The answer is shown in Figure 4-8. If a taxi rider must pay a $2 tax on each ride, then the price riders pay must be $2 less in order for the quantity of taxi rides demanded post-tax to be the same quantity as that demanded pre-tax. So the demand curve shifts *downward*, from $D_1$ to $D_2$, by the amount of the tax. This shifts the equilibrium from $E$ to $B$, where the market price is $4 per ride and 8 million rides are bought and sold. In this case, $4 is the supply price of 8 million rides and $6 is the demand price—but in effect riders do pay $6, when you include the tax. So it is just as if riders were on their original demand curve at point $A$.

If you compare Figures 4-7 and 4-8, you will immediately notice that they show the same price effect. In each case, buyers pay an effective price of $6, sellers receive an effective price of $4, and 8 million rides are bought and sold. *It doesn't seem to make any difference who officially pays the tax.*

### Figure 4-8

**Effect of an Excise Tax Levied on Purchases of Taxi Rides**

$D_1$ is the demand curve before the tax. After the city requires riders to pay the $2 tax per ride, the demand curve shifts down by $2 to the new demand curve $D_2$. Drivers again receive, net of tax, $4, represented by point $B$, while riders again pay a total price of $6, represented by point $A$. The incidence of the tax is exactly the same as in Figure 4-7. This shows that who officially pays a tax is irrelevant when answering the question of who bears the burden of the tax.

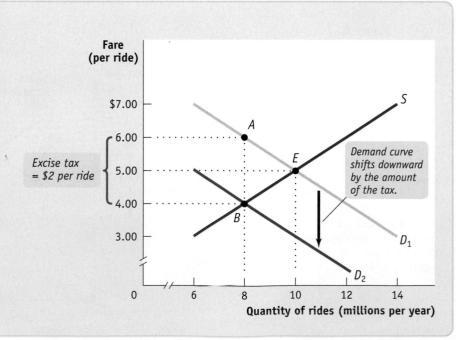

This insight is a general one in analyzing taxes: the **incidence** of a tax—who really bears the burden of the tax—is often not a question you can answer by asking who actually writes the check to the government. In this particular case, a $2 tax on taxi rides is reflected in a $1 increase in the price paid by buyers and a $1 decrease in the price received by sellers; so the incidence of the tax is actually evenly split between buyers and sellers. This incidence is the same regardless of whether the check to the city government is made out by buyers or by sellers.

The incidence of an excise tax isn't always split evenly between buyers and sellers as in this example. Depending on the shapes of supply and demand curves, the incidence of an excise tax may be divided differently.

> The **incidence** of a tax is a measure of who really pays it.

## The Revenue from an Excise Tax

Although both buyers and sellers lose from an excise tax, the government does collect revenue—which is the whole point of the tax. How much revenue does the government collect? The revenue is equal to the area of the shaded rectangle in Figure 4-9.

To see why this is the revenue collected by a $2 tax on taxi rides, notice that the *height* of the rectangle is $2. This is the amount of the tax per ride; it is also, as we have seen, the size of the wedge that the tax drives between the supply price and the demand price. Meanwhile, the *width* of the rectangle is 8 million rides, which is the equilibrium quantity of rides given that $2 tax.

The revenue collected by the tax is

*Revenue = $2 per ride × 8 million rides = $16 million*

But the area of the rectangle is

*Area = height × width = $2 per ride × 8 million rides = $16 million*

This is a general principle: *The revenue collected by an excise tax is equal to the area of the rectangle whose height is the wedge that the tax drives between the supply and demand curves, and whose width is the quantity bought and sold under the tax.*

### Figure 4-9

**The Revenue from an Excise Tax**

The government revenue collected by this excise tax is equal to the area of the shaded rectangle. In this case it is $2 per ride × 8 million rides = $16 million.

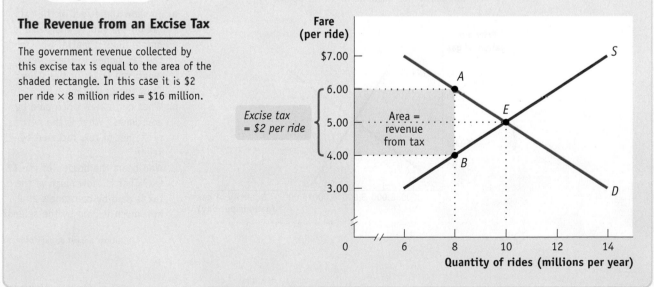

# *economics in action*

## Who Pays the FICA?

Anyone who works for an employer receives a paycheck that itemizes not only the money received but also the money deducted for various taxes. One of the big items for most people is *FICA*, which stands for Federal Insurance Contributions Act. This is the money taken out of your paycheck for the Social Security and Medicare systems, which provide income and medical care to retired and disabled Americans.

As of the time of writing, most American workers paid 7.65 percent of their earnings in FICA. But this is literally only the half of it: employers are required to pay an equal amount.

So how should we think about FICA? Well, it's like an excise tax—a tax on the sale and purchase of labor. Half of it is a tax on the sellers—that is, workers. The other half is a tax on the buyers—that is, employers.

But we already know that the incidence of a tax does not really depend on who actually makes out the check. So the fact that employers nominally pay half the FICA tells us nothing about who really bears the burden.

In fact, most economists believe that the real effect of the FICA is, to a very good approximation, to reduce wages by the full amount of the combined employee and employer payments. That is, you not only pay your own share; your employer's share is reflected in a lower wage, so that you really pay that share, too. Your employer, though she pays the tax, is fully compensated by the lower wage rate. So workers, not employers, bear the burden of both halves of the tax.

The reason economists think that workers, not employers, really pay the FICA is that the supply of labor (the number of workers willing to take jobs) is much less responsive to the wage rate than is the demand for labor (the number of jobs employers are willing to offer). According to this reasoning, since workers are relatively unresponsive to decreases in the wage rate, employers can easily pass the burden of the tax on to them through lower wages. ∎

< < < < < < < < < < < < < < < < <

## >>CHECK YOUR UNDERSTANDING 4-4

1. To help pay for road repairs, the government places a $1 per gallon tax on gasoline. The pre-tax market for gasoline is shown below.

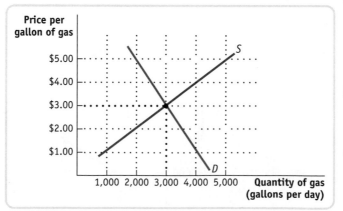

a. To show the effect of the excise tax on the supply and demand graph, does it matter who sends the tax money to the government: the buyer or the seller? Draw the new graph.

b. What is the new price paid by consumers? What is the new price, net of tax, received by sellers?

c. Who bears the burden of the $1 tax? That is, how much of the tax is paid by consumers and how much is paid by the sellers?

Solutions appear at back of book.

## • A LOOK AHEAD •

In the last two chapters we have gotten a first taste of how economic models help us understand the real world. As we've seen, supply and demand—a simple model of how competitive markets work—can be used to understand and predict the effects of everything from bad weather to misconceived government policies.

In the chapters to come, we'll see how models—including supply and demand, but also going beyond it—can shed light on a wide variety of economic phenomena and issues.

## SUMMARY

1. Governments often intervene in markets in attempts to "defy" supply and demand. Interventions can take the form of **price controls** or **quantity controls.** But they generate predictable and undesirable side effects, consisting of various forms of inefficiency and illegal activity.

2. A **price ceiling,** a maximum market price below the equilibrium price, benefits successful buyers but creates persistent shortages: Because the price is maintained below the equilibrium price, the quantity demanded is increased and the quantity supplied is decreased compared to the equilibrium quantity. This leads to predictable problems: **inefficiencies** in the form of **inefficient allocation to consumers**, **wasted resources,** and **inefficiently low quality.** It also encourages illegal activity as people turn to **black markets** to get the good. Because of these problems, price ceilings have generally lost favor as an economic policy tool. But some governments continue to impose them either because they don't understand the effects or because the price ceilings benefit some influential group.

3. A **price floor,** a minimum market price above the equilibrium price, benefits successful sellers but creates persistent surplus: because the price is maintained above the equilibrium price, the quantity demanded is decreased and the quantity supplied is increased compared to the equilibrium quantity. This leads to predictable problems: inefficiencies in the form of **inefficient allocation of sales among sellers, wasted resources,** and

**inefficiently high quality.** It also encourages illegal activity and black markets. The most well-known kind of price floor is the **minimum wage,** but price floors are also commonly applied to agricultural products.

4. **Quantity controls,** or **quotas,** limit the quantity of a good that can be bought or sold. The amount allowed for sale is the **quota limit.** The government issues **licenses** to individuals, the right to sell a given quantity of the good. The owner of a license earns a **quota rent,** earnings that accrue from ownership of the right to sell the good. It is equal to the difference between the **demand price** at the quota limit, what consumers are willing to pay for that amount, and the **supply price** at the quota limit, what suppliers are willing to accept for that amount. Economists say that a quota drives a **wedge** between the demand price and the supply price; this wedge is equal to the quota rent. Quantity controls generate inefficiency in the form of mutually beneficial transactions that don't occur in addition to encouraging illegal activity.

5. **Excise taxes**—taxes on the purchase or sale of a good—have effects similar to quotas. They raise the price paid by buyers and reduce the price received by sellers, driving a wedge between the two. The **incidence** of the tax—the division of higher prices to consumers and lower prices to sellers—does not depend on who officially pays the tax.

## KEY TERMS

Price controls,  p. 84
Price ceiling,  p. 84
Price floor,  p. 84
Inefficient,  p. 86
Inefficient allocation to consumers,  p. 87
Wasted resources,  p. 87
Inefficiently low quality,  p. 87
Black markets,  p. 88

Minimum wage,  p. 91
Inefficient allocation of sales among sellers,  p. 93
Inefficiently high quality,  p. 93
Quantity control,  p. 96
Quota,  p. 96
Quota limit,  p. 96
License,  p. 96

Demand price,  p. 97
Supply price,  p. 97
Wedge,  p. 98
Quota rent,  p. 98
Excise tax,  p. 101
Incidence,  p. 103

## PROBLEMS

1. Suppose it is decided that rent control in New York City will be abolished and that market rents will now prevail. Assume that all rental units are identical and are therefore offered at the same rent. To address the plight of residents who may be unable to pay the market rent, an income supplement will be paid to all low-income households equal to the difference between the old controlled rent and the new market rent.

   a. Use a diagram to show the effect on the rental market of the elimination of rent control. What will happen to the quality and quantity of rental housing supplied?

   b. Now use a second diagram to show the additional effect of the income-supplement policy on the market. What effect does it have on the market rent and quantity of rental housing supplied in comparison to your answers to part a?

   c. Are tenants better or worse off as a result of these policies? Are landlords better or worse off?

   d. From a political standpoint, why do you think cities have been more likely to resort to rent control rather than a policy of income supplements to help low-income people pay for housing?

2. In order to ingratiate himself with voters, the mayor of Gotham City decides to lower the price of taxi rides. Assume, for simplicity, that all taxi rides are the same distance and therefore cost the same. The accompanying table shows the demand and supply schedules for taxi rides.

| Fare (per ride) | Quantity of rides (millions per year) | |
|---|---|---|
| | Quantity demanded | Quantity supplied |
| $7.00 | 10 | 12 |
| 6.50 | 11 | 11 |
| 6.00 | 12 | 10 |
| 5.50 | 13 | 9 |
| 5.00 | 14 | 8 |
| 4.50 | 15 | 7 |

   a. Assume that there are no restrictions on the number of taxi rides that can be supplied in the city (i.e., there is no medallion system). Find the equilibrium price and quantity.

   b. Suppose that the mayor sets a price ceiling at $5.50. How large is the shortage of rides? Illustrate with a diagram. Who loses and who benefits from this policy?

   c. Suppose that the stock market crashes and, as a result, people in Gotham City are poorer. This reduces the quantity of taxi rides demanded by 6 million rides per year at any given price. What effect will the mayor's new policy have now? Illustrate with a diagram.

   d. Suppose that the stock market rises and the demand for taxi rides returns to normal (that is, returns to the demand schedule given in the table). The mayor now

decides to ingratiate himself with taxi drivers. He announces a policy in which operating licenses are given to existing taxi drivers; the number of licenses is restricted such that only 10 million rides per year can be given. Illustrate the effect of this policy on the market and indicate the resulting price and quantity transacted. What is the quota rent per ride?

3. In the late eighteenth century, the price of bread in New York City was controlled, set at a predetermined price above the market price.

   a. Draw a diagram showing the effect of the policy. Did the policy act as a price ceiling or a price floor?

   b. What kinds of inefficiencies were likely to have arisen when the controlled price of bread was above the market price? Explain in detail.

   One year during this period, a poor wheat harvest caused a leftward shift in the supply of bread and therefore an increase in its market price. New York bakers found that the controlled price of bread in New York was below the market price.

   c. Draw a diagram showing the effect of the price control on the market for bread during this one-year period. Did the policy act as a price ceiling or a price floor?

   d. What kinds of inefficiencies do you think occurred during this period? Explain in detail.

4. The accompanying table shows the demand and supply schedules for milk per year. The U.S. government decides that the incomes of dairy farmers should be maintained at a level that allows the traditional family dairy farm to survive. It therefore implements a price floor of $1 per pint by buying surplus milk until the market price is $1 per pint.

| Price of milk (per pint) | Quantity of milk (millions of pints per year) | |
|---|---|---|
| | Quantity demanded | Quantity supplied |
| $1.20 | 550 | 850 |
| 1.10 | 600 | 800 |
| 1.00 | 650 | 750 |
| 0.90 | 700 | 700 |
| 0.80 | 750 | 650 |

   a. How much surplus milk will be produced as a result of this policy?

   b. What will be the cost to the government of this policy?

   c. Since milk is an important source of protein and calcium, the government decides to provide the surplus milk it purchases to elementary schools at a price of only $0.60 per pint. Assume that schools will buy any amount of milk available at this low price. But parents now reduce their purchases of milk at any price by 50 million pints per year because they know their children are getting milk at school. How much will the dairy program now cost the government?

**d.** Give two examples of inefficiencies arising from wasted resources that are likely to result from this policy. What is the missed opportunity in each case?

**5.** As noted in the text, European governments tend to make greater use of price controls than does the American government. For example, the French government sets minimum starting yearly wages for new hires who have completed *le bac,* certification roughly equivalent to a high school diploma. The demand schedule for new hires with *le bac* and the supply schedule for similarly credentialed new job seekers are given in the accompanying table. The price here—given in euros, the currency used in France—is the same as the yearly wage.

| Wage (per year) | Quantity demanded (new job offers per year) | Quantity supplied (new job seekers per year) |
|---|---|---|
| €45,000 | 200,000 | 325,000 |
| 40,000 | 220,000 | 320,000 |
| 35,000 | 250,000 | 310,000 |
| 30,000 | 290,000 | 290,000 |
| 25,000 | 370,000 | 200,000 |

**a.** In the absence of government interference, what is the equilibrium wage and number of graduates hired per year? Illustrate with a diagram. Will there be anyone seeking a job at the equilibrium wage who is unable to find one—that is, will there be anyone who is involuntarily unemployed?

**b.** Suppose the French government sets a minimum yearly wage of €35,000. Is there any involuntary unemployment at this wage? If so, how much? Illustrate with a diagram. What if the minimum wage is set at €40,000? Also illustrate with a diagram.

**c.** Given your answer to part b and the information in the table, what do you think is the relationship between the level of involuntary unemployment and the level of the minimum wage? Who benefits from such a policy? Who loses? What is the missed opportunity here?

**6.** Until recently, the standard number of hours worked per week for a full-time job in France was 39 hours, just as in the United States. But in response to social unrest over high levels of involuntary unemployment, the French government instituted a 35-hour workweek—a worker could not work more than 35 hours per week even if both the worker and employer wanted it. The motivation behind this policy was that if current employees worked fewer hours, employers would be forced to hire more new workers. Assume that it is costly for employers to train new workers. French employers were greatly opposed to this policy and threatened to move their operations to neighboring countries that did not have such employment restrictions. Can you explain their attitude? Give an example of both an inefficiency and an illegal activity that are likely to arise from this policy.

**7.** For the last 70 years the U.S. government has used price supports to provide income assistance to American farmers. At times the government has used price floors, which it maintains by buying up the surplus farm products. At other times, it has used target prices, a policy by which the government gives the farmer an amount equal to the difference between the market price and the target price for each unit sold. Consider the market for corn depicted in the accompanying figure.

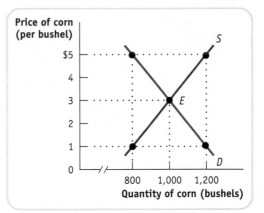

**a.** If the government sets a price floor of $5 per bushel, how many bushels of corn are produced? How many are purchased by consumers? By the government? How much does the program cost the government? How much revenue do corn farmers receive?

**b.** Suppose the government sets a target price of $5 per bushel for any quantity supplied up to 1,000 bushels. How many bushels of corn are purchased by consumers and at what price? By the government? How much does the program cost the government? How much revenue do corn farmers receive?

**c.** Which of these programs (in parts a and b) costs corn consumers more? Which program costs the government more? Explain.

**d.** What are the inefficiencies that arise in each of these cases (parts a and b)?

**8.** The waters off the North Atlantic coast were once teeming with fish. Now, due to overfishing by the commercial fishing industry, the stocks of fish are seriously depleted. In 1991, the National Marine Fishery Service of the U.S. government implemented a quota to allow fish stocks to recover. The quota limited the amount of swordfish caught per year by all U.S.-licensed fishing boats to 7 million pounds. As soon as the U.S. fishing fleet had met the quota limit, the swordfish catch was closed down for the rest of the year. The accompanying table gives the hypothetical demand and supply schedules for swordfish caught in the United States per year.

| Price of swordfish (per pound) | Quantity of swordfish (millions of pounds per year) | |
|---|---|---|
| | Quantity demanded | Quantity supplied |
| $20 | 6 | 15 |
| 18 | 7 | 13 |
| 16 | 8 | 11 |
| 14 | 9 | 9 |
| 12 | 10 | 7 |

**a.** Use a diagram to show the effect of the quota on the market for swordfish in 1991.

**b.** How do you think fishermen will change how they fish in response to this policy?

**c.** Use your diagram from part a to show an excise tax that achieves the same reduction in the amount of pounds of swordfish caught as the quota. What is the amount of the tax per pound?

**d.** What kinds of activities do you think an excise tax will tempt people to engage in?

**e.** The excise tax is collected from the fishermen, who protest that they alone are bearing the burden of this policy. Why might this protest be misguided?

**9.** The U.S. government would like to help the American auto industry compete against foreign automakers that sell trucks in the United States. It can do this either by imposing a quota on the number of foreign trucks imported or by imposing an excise tax on each foreign truck sold in the United States. The hypothetical demand and supply schedules for imported trucks are given in the accompanying table.

| Price of imported truck | Quantity of imported trucks (thousands) | |
|---|---|---|
| | Quantity demanded | Quantity supplied |
| $32,000 | 100 | 400 |
| 31,000 | 200 | 350 |
| 30,000 | 300 | 300 |
| 29,000 | 400 | 250 |
| 28,000 | 500 | 200 |
| 27,000 | 600 | 150 |

**a.** In the absence of government interference, what is the price of an imported truck? How many are sold in the United States? Illustrate with a diagram.

**b.** Suppose the government adopts a quota, allowing no more than 200,000 foreign trucks to be imported. What is the effect on the market for these trucks? Illustrate using your diagram from part a and explain.

**c.** Now suppose that, instead of a quota, the government imposes an excise tax of $3,000 per truck. Illustrate the effect of this excise tax in your diagram from part a. How many trucks will now be purchased and at what price? What will the foreign automaker receive per truck?

**d.** Calculate the government revenue raised by the excise tax in part c. Then illustrate it on your diagram from that part. Do you think the government, from a revenue standpoint, prefers an excise tax or a quota?

**10.** In Maine, you must have a license to harvest lobster commercially; these licenses are issued yearly. The state of Maine is concerned about the dwindling supplies of lobsters found off its coast. The state fishery department has decided to place a yearly quota of 80,000 pounds of lobsters harvested in all Maine waters. It has also decided to give licenses this year only to those fishermen who had licenses last year. The accompanying figure shows the demand and supply curves for Maine lobsters.

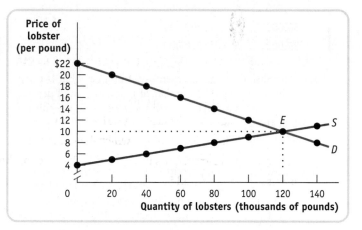

**a.** In the absence of government restrictions, what are the equilibrium price and quantity?

**b.** What is the *demand price* at which consumers wish to purchase 80,000 pounds of lobsters?

**c.** What is the *supply price* at which suppliers are willing to supply 80,000 pounds of lobsters?

**d.** What is the *quota rent* per pound of lobster when 80,000 pounds are sold?

**e.** Find an excise tax that achieves the same reduction in the harvest of lobsters. Show it on the figure. What is the government revenue collected from this tax?

**f.** Explain a transaction that benefits both buyer and seller but is prevented by the quota restriction. Explain a transaction that benefits both buyer and seller but is prevented by the excise tax.

---

**>web...** To continue your study and review of concepts in this chapter, please visit the Krugman/Wells/Olney website for quizzes, animated graph tutorials, web links to helpful resources, and more.

**www.worthpublishers.com/krugmanwellsolney**

# >>Elasticity

## DRIVE WE MUST

IN EARLY 1998, LUIS TELLEZ HELD A SECRET meeting with his Saudi Arabian counterpart. Tellez was Mexico's oil minister, the government official who decided how many barrels of oil Mexico would produce and sell to other countries. The purpose of the secret meeting? To increase their earnings, or revenues, from selling oil by raising the world price of oil, which had fallen 50 percent over the previous two years. This low world price was creating serious problems for both governments, which depended on revenue from oil sales. But a plan to raise oil prices would not succeed unless other oil-exporting countries were also willing to commit to reductions in oil production.

Why was it necessary to reduce production? Why not just raise prices? Because by the *law of demand*, a price increase leads to a fall in the quantity demanded. So if output didn't also fall, there would soon be a surplus of oil on the market, pushing the price right back down again. To make the plan work, Tellez had to persuade his fellow oil ministers to produce less. But how much less?

If consumers responded to the price increase by using a lot less oil, output would have to fall by a large amount. And if output fell by a large enough amount in response to the price increase, revenue would decline, not increase. The crucial question for Tellez, then, was how responsive the quantity of oil demanded was to changes in the price of oil.

But how do we define *responsiveness?* The answer, and what Tellez needed to know in this case, is a particular number: the *price elasticity of demand*. In this chapter, we will show how the price elasticity of demand is measured and why it is the best measure of how the quantity demanded

Gassing up: A hard habit to break.

responds to changes in price. We will then see that the price elasticity of demand is only one of a family of related concepts, including the *income elasticity of demand* and the *price elasticity of supply*. Finally, we will see how elasticities are used to determine who bears the greater share of the burden of a tax—producers or consumers.

---

### What you will learn in this chapter:

➤ The definition of **elasticity,** a measure of responsiveness to changes in prices or incomes

➤ The importance of the **price elasticity of demand,** which measures the responsiveness of the quantity demanded to price

➤ The meaning and importance of the **income elasticity of demand,** a measure of the responsiveness of demand to income

➤ The significance of the **price elasticity of supply,** which measures the responsiveness of the quantity supplied to price

➤ What factors influence the size of these various elasticities

➤ How elasticity affects the incidence of a tax, the measure of who bears its burden

# Defining and Measuring Elasticity

Luis Tellez, who is a trained economist, knew that to calculate the cut in oil output needed to achieve his price target, he would have to know the *price elasticity of demand* for oil.

## The Price Elasticity of Demand

Figure 5-1 shows a hypothetical world demand curve for oil. At a price of $20 per barrel, world consumers would demand 10 million barrels of oil per day (point *A*); at a price of $21 per barrel, the quantity demanded would fall to 9.9 million barrels (point *B*).

Figure 5-1, then, tells us the response of the quantity demanded to a particular change in the price. But how can we turn this into a measure of price responsiveness? The answer is to calculate the *price elasticity of demand*.

The price elasticity of demand compares the *percent change in quantity demanded* to the *percent change in price* as we move along the demand curve. As we'll see later in this chapter, the reason economists use percent changes is to get a measure that doesn't depend on the units in which a good is measured (say, gallons versus barrels of oil). But before we get to that, let's look at how elasticity is calculated.

To calculate the price elasticity of demand, we first calculate the *percent change in the quantity demanded* and the corresponding *percent change in the price* as we move along the demand curve. These are defined as follows:

$$(5\text{-}1) \quad \% \text{ change in quantity demanded} = \frac{\text{Change in quantity demanded}}{\text{Initial quantity demanded}} \times 100$$

and

$$(5\text{-}2) \quad \% \text{ change in price} = \frac{\text{Change in price}}{\text{Initial price}} \times 100$$

In Figure 5-1, we see that when the price rises from $20 to $21, the quantity demanded falls from 10 million to 9.9 million barrels, yielding a change in the

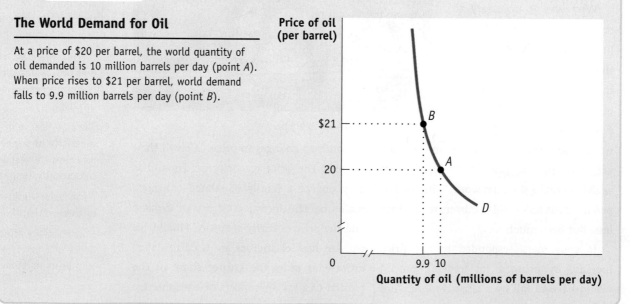

**Figure 5-1**

**The World Demand for Oil**

At a price of $20 per barrel, the world quantity of oil demanded is 10 million barrels per day (point *A*). When price rises to $21 per barrel, world demand falls to 9.9 million barrels per day (point *B*).

Price of oil (per barrel)

Quantity of oil (millions of barrels per day)

quantity demanded of 0.1 million barrels. So the percent change in the quantity demanded is

$$\text{\% change in quantity demanded} = \frac{0.1 \text{ million barrels}}{10 \text{ million barrels}} \times 100 = 1\%$$

The initial price is $20 and the change in the price is $1, so the percent change in price is

$$\text{\% change in price} = \frac{\$1}{\$20} \times 100 = 5\%$$

To calculate the price elasticity of demand, we find the ratio of the percent change in the quantity demanded to the percent change in the price:

**(5-3)   Price elasticity of demand** = $\dfrac{\text{\% change in quantity demanded}}{\text{\% change in price}}$

In Figure 5-1, the price elasticity of demand is therefore

$$\frac{1\%}{5\%} = 0.2$$

> The **price elasticity of demand** is the ratio of the percent change in the quantity demanded to the percent change in the price as we move along the demand curve.

The *law of demand* says that demand curves slope downward. This means that the price elasticity of demand is, in strictly mathematical terms, a negative number (if the price rises, which is a positive percent change, the quantity demanded falls, which is strictly speaking a *negative* percent change). However, it is a nuisance to keep writing that minus sign. So when economists talk about the price elasticity of demand, they usually drop the minus sign and report the absolute value of the elasticity. In this case, for example, economists would usually say "the price elasticity of demand is 0.2," taking it for granted that you understand they mean *minus* 0.2. We follow this convention and drop the minus sign when referring to the price elasticity of demand.

The larger the price elasticity of demand, the more responsive the quantity demanded is to the price. When the price elasticity of demand is large—when consumers change their quantity demanded by a large percentage compared with the percent change in the price—economists say that demand is highly elastic.

A price elasticity of 0.2 indicates a small response of quantity demanded to price. That is, the quantity demanded will fall by a relatively small amount when price rises. This is what economists call *inelastic* demand. And inelastic demand was exactly what Tellez needed for his strategy to increase revenue by raising oil prices.

## Using the Midpoint Method to Calculate Elasticities

Price elasticity of demand compares the *percent change in quantity demanded* with the *percent change in price*. When we look at some other elasticities, which we will do shortly, we'll see why it is important to focus on percent changes. But at this point we need to discuss a technical issue that arises when you calculate percent changes in variables and how economists deal with it.

The best way to understand the issue is with a real example. Suppose you were trying to estimate the price elasticity of demand for gasoline by comparing gasoline prices and consumption in different countries. Because of high taxes, gasoline usually costs about three times as much per gallon in Europe as it does in the United States. So what is the percent difference between American and European gas prices?

Well, it depends on which way you measure it. The price of gasoline in Europe is three times higher than in the United States, so it is 200 percent higher. The price of gasoline in the United States is one-third as high as in Europe, so it is 66.7 percent lower.

This is a nuisance: we'd like to have a percent measure of the difference in prices that doesn't depend on which way you measure it. A good way to avoid computing different elasticities for rising and falling prices is to use the *midpoint method*.

The **midpoint method** replaces the usual definition of the percent change in a variable, X, with a slightly different definition:

**The midpoint method** is a technique for calculating the percent change. In this approach, we calculate changes in a variable compared with the average, or midpoint, of the starting and final values.

$$\textbf{(5-4)} \quad \% \text{ change in } X = \frac{\text{Change in } X}{\text{Average value of } X} \times 100$$

where the average value of X is defined as

$$\text{Average value of } X = \frac{\text{Starting value of } X + \text{final value of } X}{2}$$

When calculating the price elasticity of demand using the midpoint method, both the percent change in the price and the percent change in the quantity demanded are found using this method.

To see how this method works, suppose you have the following data for some good:

|  | **Price** | **Quantity demanded** |
| --- | --- | --- |
| **Situation A** | $0.90 | 1,100 |
| **Situation B** | $1.10 | 900 |

To calculate the percent change in quantity going from situation A to situation B, we compare the change in the quantity demanded—200 units—with the *average* of the quantity demanded in the two situations. So we calculate

$$\% \text{ change in quantity demanded} = \frac{200}{(1,100 + 900)/2} \times 100 = \frac{200}{1,000} \times 100$$

$$= 20\%$$

In the same way, we calculate

$$\% \text{ change in price} = \frac{\$0.20}{(\$0.90 + \$1.10)/2} \times 100 = \frac{\$0.20}{\$1.00} \times 100$$

$$= 20\%$$

So in this case we would calculate the price elasticity of demand to be

$$\text{Price elasticity of demand} = \frac{\% \text{ change in quantity demanded}}{\% \text{ change in price}} = \frac{20\%}{20\%} = 1$$

The important point is that we would get the same result, a price elasticity of demand of 1, whether we go up the demand curve from situation A to situation B or down from situation B to situation A.

To arrive at a more general formula for price elasticity of demand, suppose that we have data for two points on a demand curve. At point 1 the quantity demanded and price are $(Q_1, P_1)$; at point 2 they are $(Q_2, P_2)$. Then the formula for calculating the price elasticity of demand is:

$$\text{(5-5)} \quad \text{Price elasticity of demand} = \frac{\dfrac{Q_2 - Q_1}{(Q_1 + Q_2)/2}}{\dfrac{P_2 - P_1}{(P_1 + P_2)/2}}$$

As before, when reporting a price elasticity of demand calculated by the midpoint method, we usually drop the negative sign and report the absolute value.

## *economics in action*

### Estimating Elasticities

You might think it's easy to estimate price elasticities of demand from real-world data: just compare percent changes in prices with percent changes in quantities demanded. Unfortunately, it's rarely that simple because changes in price aren't the only thing affecting changes in the quantity demanded: other factors—such as changes in income, changes in population, and changes in the prices of other goods—shift the demand curve, thereby changing the quantity demanded for any given price. To estimate price elasticities of demand, economists must use careful statistical analysis to separate the influence of these different factors, holding other things equal.

The most comprehensive effort to estimate price elasticities of demand was a mammoth study by the economists Hendrik S. Houthakker and Lester D. Taylor. Some of their results are summarized in Table 5-1. These estimates show a wide range of price elasticities. There are some goods, like eggs, for which demand hardly responds at all to changes in the price; there are other goods, most notably foreign travel, where the quantity demanded is very sensitive to the price.

Notice that Table 5-1 is divided into two parts: inelastic and elastic demand. We'll explain in the next section the significance of that division. ∎

> > > > > > > > > > > > > > > > > > >

### >>CHECK YOUR UNDERSTANDING 5-1

1. The price of strawberries falls from $1.50 to $1.00 per carton and the quantity demanded goes from 100,000 to 200,000 cartons. Use the midpoint method to find the price elasticity of demand.

2. At the present level of consumption, 4,000 movie tickets, and at the current price, $5 per ticket, the price elasticity of demand for movie tickets is 1. Using the midpoint method, calculate the percentage by which the owners of movie theaters must reduce price in order to sell 5,000 tickets.

3. The price elasticity of demand for ice-cream sandwiches is 1.2 at the current price of $0.50 per sandwich and the current consumption level of 100,000 sandwiches. Calculate the change in the quantity demanded when price rises by $0.05. Use Equations 5-1 and 5-2 to calculate percent changes, and Equation 5-3 to relate price elasticity of demand to the percent changes.

Solutions appear at back of book.

## Interpreting the Price Elasticity of Demand

Mexico and other oil-producing countries believed they could succeed in driving up oil prices with only a small decrease in the quantity sold because the price elasticity of oil demand was low. But what does that mean? How low does a price elasticity have to be for us to classify it as low? How high does it have to be for us to consider it high? And what determines whether the price elasticity of demand is high or low, anyway?

To answer these questions, we need to look more deeply at the price elasticity of demand.

### TABLE 5-1

**Some Estimated Price Elasticities of Demand**

| Good | Price elasticity of demand |
|---|---|
| **Inelastic demand** | |
| Eggs | 0.1 |
| Beef | 0.4 |
| Stationery | 0.5 |
| Gasoline | 0.5 |
| **Elastic demand** | |
| Housing | 1.2 |
| Restaurant meals | 2.3 |
| Airline travel | 2.4 |
| Foreign travel | 4.1 |

Please find source information on the copyright page.

### >> QUICK REVIEW

- The *price elasticity of demand* is equal to the percent change in the quantity demanded divided by the percent change in the price as you move along the demand curve.
- Percent changes are best measured using the *midpoint method*, in which the percent change in each variable is calculated using the average of starting and final values.

## How Elastic Is Elastic?

As a first step toward classifying price elasticities of demand, let's look at the extreme cases.

First, consider the demand for a good when people pay no attention to the price—say, shoelaces. Suppose that U.S. consumers will buy 1 billion pairs of shoelaces per year regardless of the price. In this case, the demand curve for shoelaces would look like the curve shown in panel (a) of Figure 5-2: it would be a vertical line at 1 billion pairs of shoelaces. Since the percent change in the quantity demanded is zero for *any* change in the price, the price elasticity of demand in this case is zero. The case of a zero price elasticity of demand is known as **perfectly inelastic demand.**

The opposite extreme occurs when even a tiny rise in the price will cause the quantity demanded to drop to zero or even a tiny fall in the price will cause the quantity demanded to get extremely large. Panel (b) of Figure 5-2 shows the case of pink tennis balls; we suppose that tennis players really don't care what color their balls are and that other colors, such as neon green and vivid yellow, are available at $5 per dozen balls. In this case, consumers will buy no pink balls if they cost more than $5 per dozen but will buy only pink balls if they cost less than $5. The demand curve will therefore be a horizontal line at a price of $5 per dozen balls. As you move back and forth along this line, there is a change in the quantity demanded but no change in the price. Roughly speaking, when you divide a number by zero, you get infinity, so a horizontal demand curve implies an infinite price elasticity of demand. When the price elasticity of demand is infinite, economists say that demand is **perfectly elastic.**

The price elasticity of demand for the vast majority of goods is somewhere between these two extreme cases. Economists use one main criterion for classifying these intermediate cases: they ask whether the price elasticity of demand is higher or lower than 1. When the price elasticity of demand is greater than 1, economists say that demand is **elastic.** When the price elasticity of demand is less than 1, they say that demand is **inelastic.** The borderline case is **unit-elastic demand,** where the price elasticity of demand is—surprise—exactly 1.

> Demand is **perfectly inelastic** when the quantity demanded does not respond at all to changes in the price. When demand is perfectly inelastic, the demand curve is a vertical line.

> Demand is **perfectly elastic** when any price increase will cause the quantity demanded to drop to zero. When demand is perfectly elastic, the demand curve is a horizontal line.

> Demand is **elastic** if the price elasticity of demand is greater than 1, **inelastic** if the price elasticity of demand is less than 1, and **unit-elastic** if the price elasticity of demand is exactly 1.

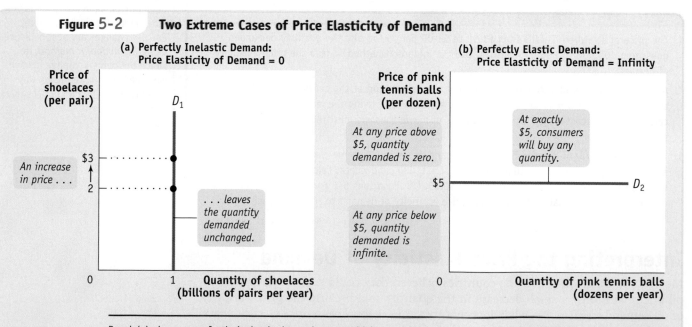

### Figure 5-2    Two Extreme Cases of Price Elasticity of Demand

Panel (a) shows a perfectly inelastic demand curve, which is a vertical line. The quantity of shoelaces demanded is always 1 billion pairs, regardless of price. As a result, the price elasticity of demand is zero—the quantity demanded is unaffected by the price. Panel (b) shows a perfectly elastic demand curve, which is a horizontal line. At a price of $5, consumers will buy any quantity of pink tennis balls, but will buy none at a price above $5. If price falls below $5, they will buy an extremely large number of pink tennis balls and none of any other color.

To see why a price elasticity of demand equal to 1 is a useful dividing line, let's consider a hypothetical example: a toll bridge operated by the state highway department. Other things equal, the number of drivers who use the bridge depends on the toll, the price the highway department charges for crossing the bridge: the higher the toll, the fewer the drivers who use the bridge.

Figure 5-3 shows three hypothetical demand curves—one in which demand is unit-elastic, one in which it is inelastic, and one in which it is elastic. In each case, point *A* shows the quantity demanded if the toll is $0.90 and point *B* shows the quantity demanded if the toll is $1.10. An increase in the toll from $0.90 to $1.10 is an increase of 20% if we use the midpoint method to calculate percent changes.

Panel (a) shows what happens when the toll is raised from $0.90 to $1.10 and the demand curve is unit-elastic. Here the 20% price rise leads to a fall in the quantity of cars using the bridge each day from 1,100 to 900, which is a 20% decline (again using the midpoint method). So the price elasticity of demand is 20%/20% = 1.

Panel (b) shows a case of inelastic demand when the toll is raised from $0.90 to $1.10. The same 20% price rise reduces the quantity demanded from 1,050 to 950. That's only a 10% decline, so in this case the price elasticity of demand is 10%/20% = 0.5.

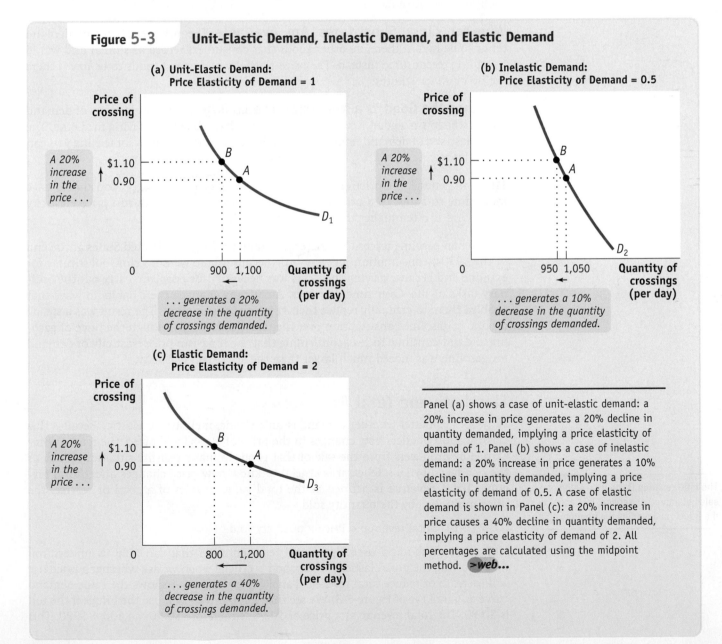

**Figure 5-3   Unit-Elastic Demand, Inelastic Demand, and Elastic Demand**

Panel (a) shows a case of unit-elastic demand: a 20% increase in price generates a 20% decline in quantity demanded, implying a price elasticity of demand of 1. Panel (b) shows a case of inelastic demand: a 20% increase in price generates a 10% decline in quantity demanded, implying a price elasticity of demand of 0.5. A case of elastic demand is shown in Panel (c): a 20% increase in price causes a 40% decline in quantity demanded, implying a price elasticity of demand of 2. All percentages are calculated using the midpoint method. **>web...**

Panel (c) shows a case of elastic demand when the toll is raised from $0.90 to $1.10. The 20% price increase causes the quantity demanded to fall from 1,200 to 800—a 40% decline, so the price elasticity of demand is 40%/20% = 2.

## What Factors Determine the Price Elasticity of Demand?

1998 was not the first time Americans had been subject to an attempt by oil-exporting countries to increase revenue by raising oil prices. In the 1970s, gasoline prices in the United States jumped significantly after oil exporters reduced output and raised oil prices. Americans initially reacted by changing their consumption of gasoline very little. Over time, however, they gradually adapted to the higher prices. After a few years, drivers had cut their consumption of gasoline in various ways: increased carpooling, greater use of public transportation, and, most importantly, replacement of large, gas-guzzling cars with smaller, more fuel-efficient models.

The experience of the 1970s illustrates the three main factors that determine elasticity: whether close substitutes are available, whether the good is a necessity or a luxury, and how much time has elapsed since the price change. We'll briefly examine each of these three factors.

**Whether Close Substitutes Are Available** The price elasticity of demand tends to be high if there are other goods that consumers regard as similar and would be willing to consume instead. The price elasticity of demand tends to be low if there are no close substitutes.

**Whether the Good Is a Necessity or a Luxury** The price elasticity of demand tends to be low if a good is something you must have, like a life-saving medicine. The price elasticity of demand tends to be high if the good is a luxury—something you can easily live without.

**Time** In general, the price elasticity of demand tends to increase as consumers have more time to adjust to a price change. This means that the long-run price elasticity of demand is often higher than the short-run elasticity.

So when gasoline prices first increased dramatically in the United States at the end of the 1970s, consumption fell very little because there were no close substitutes for gasoline and because driving their cars was necessary for people to carry out the ordinary tasks of life. Over time, however, Americans changed their habits in ways that enabled them to gradually reduce their gasoline consumption. The result was a steady decline in gasoline consumption over the next decade, even though the price of gasoline did not continue to rise, confirming that the long-run price elasticity of demand for gasoline was indeed much larger than the short-run elasticity.

## Elasticity and Total Revenue

Why does it matter whether demand is unit-elastic, inelastic, or elastic? Because this classification predicts how changes in the price of a good will affect the *total revenue* earned by producers from the sale of that good. In many real-life situations, such as the one faced by Luis Tellez, it is crucial to know how price changes affect total revenue. **Total revenue** is defined as the total value of sales of a good or service: the price multiplied by the quantity sold.

> The **total revenue** is the total value of sales of a good or service. It is equal to the price multiplied by the quantity sold.

(5-6) Total revenue = Price × quantity sold

Total revenue has a useful graphical representation that can help us understand why knowing the price elasticity of demand is crucial when we ask whether a price rise will increase or reduce total revenue. Panel (a) of Figure 5-4 shows the same demand curve as panel (a) of Figure 5-3. We see that 1,100 drivers will use the bridge if the toll is $0.90. The total revenue at a price of $0.90 is therefore $0.90 × 1,100 = $990. This

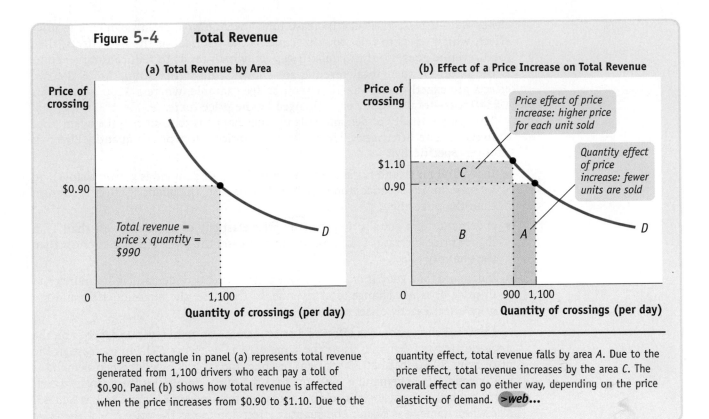

**Figure 5-4    Total Revenue**

**(a) Total Revenue by Area**

Price of crossing

$0.90

Total revenue = price x quantity = $990

D

0                    1,100

Quantity of crossings (per day)

**(b) Effect of a Price Increase on Total Revenue**

Price of crossing

*Price effect of price increase: higher price for each unit sold*

*Quantity effect of price increase: fewer units are sold*

$1.10

0.90

C

B        A

D

0                    900  1,100

Quantity of crossings (per day)

The green rectangle in panel (a) represents total revenue generated from 1,100 drivers who each pay a toll of $0.90. Panel (b) shows how total revenue is affected when the price increases from $0.90 to $1.10. Due to the quantity effect, total revenue falls by area *A*. Due to the price effect, total revenue increases by the area *C*. The overall effect can go either way, depending on the price elasticity of demand. **>web...**

value is equal to the area of the green rectangle, which is drawn with the bottom left corner at the point (0, 0) and the top right corner at (1,100, 0.90). In general, the total revenue at any given price is equal to the area of a rectangle whose height is the price and whose width is the quantity demanded at that price.

To get an idea of why total revenue is important, consider the following scenario. Suppose that the toll on the bridge is currently $0.90 but that the highway department must raise extra money for road repairs. One way to do this is to raise the toll on the bridge. But this plan might backfire, since a higher toll will reduce the number of drivers who use the bridge. And if traffic on the bridge dropped a lot, a higher toll would actually reduce total revenue instead of increasing it. So it's important for the highway department to know how drivers will respond to a toll increase.

We can see graphically how the toll increase affects total bridge revenue by examining panel (b) of Figure 5-4. At a toll of $0.90, total revenue is given by the sum of the areas *A* and *B*. After the toll is raised to $1.10, total revenue is given by the sum of areas *B* and *C*. So when the toll is raised, revenue represented by area *A* is lost but revenue represented by area *C* is gained. These two areas have important interpretations. Area *C* represents the revenue gain that comes from the additional $0.20 paid by drivers who continue to use the bridge. That is, the 900 who continue to use the bridge contribute an additional $0.20 × 900 = $180 per day to total revenue, represented by area *C*. On the other hand, 200 drivers who would have used the bridge at a price of $0.90 no longer do so, generating a loss to total revenue of $0.90 × 200 = $180 per day, represented by area *A*.

Except in the rare case of a good with perfectly elastic or perfectly inelastic demand, when a seller raises the price of a good, two countervailing effects are present:

■ *A price effect*. After a price increase, each unit sold sells at a higher price, which tends to raise revenue.

■ *A quantity effect*. After a price increase, fewer units are sold, which tends to lower revenue.

But then, you may ask, what is the ultimate effect on total revenue: does it go up or down? The answer is that, in general, the effect on total revenue can go either way—a price rise may increase total revenue or may lower it. If the price effect, which tends to raise total revenue, is the stronger of the two effects, then total revenue goes up. If the quantity effect, which tends to reduce total revenue, is the stronger, then total revenue goes down. And if the strengths of the two effects are exactly equal—as in our toll bridge example, where a $180 gain offsets a $180 loss—total revenue is unchanged by the price increase.

The price elasticity of demand tells us what happens to total revenue when price changes: its size determines which effect—the price effect or the quantity effect—is stronger. Specifically:

- If demand for a good is *elastic* (the price elasticity of demand is greater than 1), an increase in price reduces total revenue. In this case, the quantity effect is stronger than the price effect.

- If demand for a good is *inelastic* (the price elasticity of demand is less than 1), a higher price increases total revenue. In this case, the price effect is stronger than the quantity effect.

- If demand for a good is *unit-elastic* (the price elasticity of demand is 1), an increase in price does not change total revenue. In this case, the quantity effect and the price effect exactly offset each other.

Table 5-2 shows how the effect of a price increase on total revenue depends on the price elasticity of demand, using the same data as in Figure 5-3. An increase in the price from $0.90 to $1.10 leaves total revenue unchanged at $990 when demand is unit-elastic. When demand is inelastic, the price effect dominates the quantity effect; the same price increase leads to an increase in total revenue from $945 to $1,045. And when demand is elastic, the quantity effect dominates the price effect; the price increase leads to a decline in total revenue from $1,080 to $880.

The price elasticity of demand also predicts the effect of a *fall* in price on total revenue. When the price falls, the same two countervailing effects are present, but they work in the opposite directions as in the case of a price rise. There is the price effect of a lower price per unit sold, which tends to lower revenue. This is countered by the quantity effect of more units sold, which tends to raise revenue. Which effect dominates depends on the price elasticity. Here is a quick summary:

- When demand is *elastic*, the quantity effect dominates the price effect; so a fall in price increases total revenue.

- When demand is *inelastic*, the price effect dominates the quantity effect; so a fall in price reduces total revenue.

- When demand is *unit-elastic*, the two effects exactly balance; so a fall in price has no effect on total revenue.

## TABLE 5-2

**Price Elasticity of Demand and Total Revenue**

| | Price of crossing = $0.90 | Price of crossing = $1.10 | Effect of price increase | Effect of price decrease |
|---|---|---|---|---|
| **Unit-elastic demand** (price elasticity of demand = 1) | | | | |
| Quantity demanded | 1,100 | 900 | Total revenue unchanged | Total revenue unchanged |
| Total revenue | $990 | $990 | | |
| **Inelastic demand** (price elasticity of demand = 0.5) | | | | |
| Quantity demanded | 1,050 | 950 | Total revenue increases | Total revenue decreases |
| Total revenue | $945 | $1,045 | | |
| **Elastic demand** (price elasticity of demand = 2) | | | | |
| Quantity demanded | 1,200 | 800 | Total revenue decreases | Total revenue increases |
| Total revenue | $1,080 | $880 | | |

## WORK IT OUT

### PRICE ELASTICITY OF DEMAND

Why do grocery stores put some items—such as one particular variety of apple—on sale much more often than they put other items—such as milk—on sale? Because of differences in the price elasticity of demand. Suppose that when the grocery store cuts the price of gala apples by 10%, quantity demanded rises by 20%. But when they cut the price of milk by 10%, quantity demanded rises by just 1%.

**Price Elasticity:** Which good has elastic demand? Which good has inelastic demand? *(Price elasticity of demand: the responsiveness of quantity demanded to a change in price. Elastic: very responsive. Inelastic: not very responsive.)*

To answer this question, first calculate the price elasticity of demand. To do this, divide the percent change in quantity demanded by the percent change in price. Ignore the sign. Elasticity of demand for gala apples is 20%/10% = 2. Elasticity of demand for milk is 1%/10% = 0.1 *(There are no units on measures of elasticity.)*

Demand is elastic if the percent change in quantity demanded is greater than the percent change in price. In this case, the price elasticity of demand is greater than 1. It is inelastic if the percent change in quantity demanded is smaller than the percent change in price. In this case, the price elasticity of demand is less than 1.

**SOLUTION:** Demand for gala apples is elastic; the price elasticity of demand for gala apples is 2. Demand for milk is inelastic; the price elasticity of demand for milk is 0.1.

**Total Revenue:** Will total revenue from sales of gala apples increase when their price is cut 10%? Will total revenue from sales of milk increase when its price is cut 10%? *(Total revenue: price × quantity.)*

Total revenue rises when price is cut if the percent change in quantity demanded is greater than the percent change in price (both measured in absolute value). So total revenue rises when price is cut and demand is elastic. A small drop in price results in such a relatively large increase in quantity that price × quantity rises. The small price effect is dominated by the large quantity effect.

Total revenue falls when price is cut if the percent change in quantity demanded is smaller than the percent change in price (both measured in absolute value). So total revenue falls when price is cut when demand is price-inelastic. Even a big drop in price results in such a relatively small increase in quantity that price × quantity falls. The large price effect swamps the small quantity effect.

**SOLUTION:** Total revenue from sales of gala apples will rise when their price is cut 10% because demand for gala apples is elastic. Total revenue from sales of milk will fall when its price is cut 10% because demand for milk is inelastic.

# *economics in action*

## America's a Nice Place to Live, but We Can't Afford to Visit

In 1992, 18.6 million Canadians visited the United States, but only 11.8 million U.S. residents visited Canada. By 2002, however, roles had been reversed: more U.S. residents visited Canada than vice versa.

Why did the tourist traffic reverse direction? Canada didn't get any warmer from 1992 to 2002—but it did get cheaper for Americans. The reason was a large change in the exchange rate between the two nations' currencies: in 1992 a Canadian dollar was worth $0.80, but by 2002 it had fallen in value by nearly 20 percent to about $0.65. This meant that Canadian goods and services, particularly hotel rooms and meals, were about 20 percent cheaper for Americans in 2002 compared to 1992. So Canada had become a cheap vacation destination for Americans by 2002. Things were not so rosy, however, when viewed from the other side of the border: American vacations had become 20 percent more expensive for Canadians. Canadians responded by vacationing in their own country or in other parts of the world besides the United States.

Foreign travel is an example of a good that has a high price elasticity of demand: as we saw in Table 5-1, it has been estimated at about 4.1. One reason is that foreign travel is a luxury good for most people—you may regret not going to Paris this year, but you can live without it. A second reason is that a good substitute for foreign travel typically exists—domestic travel. A Canadian who finds it too expensive to vacation in San Francisco this year is likely to find that Vancouver is a pretty good alternative. ∎

< < < < < < < < < < < < < < < < < < <

**>> CHECK YOUR UNDERSTANDING 5-2**

1. For each case, choose the condition that characterizes demand: elastic demand, inelastic demand, or unit-elastic demand.
   a. Total revenue decreases when price increases.
   b. The additional revenue generated by an increase in quantity sold is exactly offset by revenue lost from the fall in price received per unit.
   c. Total revenue falls when output increases.
   d. Producers in an industry find they can increase their total revenues by working together to reduce industry output.
2. For the following goods, what is the elasticity of demand? Explain. What is the shape of the demand curve?
   a. Demand by a snake-bite victim for an antidote
   b. Demand by students for green erasers

*Solutions appear at back of book.*

# Other Demand Elasticities

The quantity of a good demanded depends not only on the price of that good but on other variables. In particular, demand curves shift because of changes in the prices of related goods and changes in consumers' incomes. It is often important to have a measure of these other effects, and the best measures are—you guessed it—elasticities. Specifically, we can best measure how the demand for a good is affected by prices of other goods using a measure called the *cross-price elasticity of demand*, and we can best measure how demand is affected by changes in income using the *income elasticity of demand*.

## The Cross-Price Elasticity of Demand

In Chapter 3 you learned that the demand for a good is often affected by the prices of other, related goods—goods that are substitutes or complements. There you saw that a change in the price of a related good shifts the demand curve of the original good, reflecting a change in the quantity demanded at any given price. The strength of such a "cross" effect on demand can be measured by the **cross-price elasticity of demand,** defined as the ratio of the percent change in the quantity demanded of one good to the percent change in the price of the other.

The **cross-price elasticity of demand** between two goods measures the effect of the change in one good's price on the quantity demanded of the other good. It is equal to the percent change in the quantity demanded of one good divided by the percent change in the other good's price.

(5-7) Cross-price elasticity of demand between goods A and B

$$= \frac{\% \text{ change in quantity of A demanded}}{\% \text{ change in price of B}}$$

When two goods are substitutes, like hot dogs and hamburgers, the cross-price elasticity of demand is positive: a rise in the price of hot dogs increases the demand for hamburgers—that is, it causes a rightward shift of the demand curve for hamburgers. If the goods are close substitutes, the cross-price elasticity will be positive and large; if they are not close substitutes, the cross-price elasticity will be positive and small. So when the cross-price elasticity of demand is positive, it is a measure of how closely substitutable for each other two goods are.

When two goods are complements, like hot dogs and hot dog buns, the cross-price elasticity is negative: a rise in the price of hot dogs decreases the demand for hot dog buns—that is, it causes a leftward shift of the demand curve for hot dog buns. As with substitutes, the size of the cross-price elasticity of demand between two complements tells us how strongly complementary they are: if the cross-price elasticity is only slightly below zero, they are weak complements; if it is very negative, they are strong complements.

Note that in the case of the cross-price elasticity of demand, the sign (plus or minus) is very important: it tells us whether the two goods are complements or substitutes. So we cannot drop the minus sign as we did for the price elasticity of demand.

Our discussion of the cross-price elasticity of demand is a useful place to return to a point we made earlier: elasticity is a *unit-free* measure—that is, it doesn't depend on the units in which goods are measured.

To see the potential problem, suppose someone told you that "if the price of hot dog buns rises by $0.30, Americans will buy 10 million fewer hot dogs this year." If you've ever bought hot dog buns, you'll immediately wonder: is that a $0.30 increase in the price *per bun*, or is it a $0.30 increase in the price *per package* (buns are usually sold by the dozen)? It makes a big difference what units we are talking about! However, if someone says that the cross-price elasticity of demand between buns and hot dogs is –0.3, it doesn't matter whether buns are sold individually or by the package. So elasticity is defined as a ratio of percent changes, as a way of making sure that confusion over units doesn't arise.

## The Income Elasticity of Demand

The **income elasticity of demand** is a measure of how much the demand for a good is affected by changes in consumers' incomes. It allows us to determine whether a good is a normal or inferior good as well as measure how intensely the demand for the good responds to changes in income.

$$(5\text{-}8) \quad \text{Income elasticity of demand} = \frac{\%\ \text{change in quantity demanded}}{\%\ \text{change in income}}$$

> The **income elasticity of demand** is the percent change in the quantity of a good demanded when a consumer's income changes divided by the percent change in the consumer's income.

Just as the cross-price elasticity of demand between two goods can be either positive or negative, depending on whether the goods are substitutes or complements, the income elasticity of demand for a good can also be either positive or negative. Recall from Chapter 3 that goods can be either *normal goods*, for

---

### FOR INQUIRING MINDS

### WHERE HAVE ALL THE FARMERS GONE?

What percentage of Americans live on farms? Sad to say, the U.S. government no longer publishes that number. In 1991 the official percentage was 1.9, but in that year the government decided it was no longer a meaningful indicator of the size of the agricultural sector because a large proportion of those who live on farms actually make their living doing something else. But in the days of the Founding Fathers, the great majority of Americans lived on farms. As recently as the 1940s, one American in six—or approximately 17%—still did.

Why do so few people now live and work on farms in the United States? There are two main reasons, both involving elasticities.

First, the income elasticity of demand for food is much less than 1—it is income-inelastic. As consumers grow richer, other things equal, spending on food rises less than income. As a result, as the U.S. economy has grown, the share of income it spends on food—and therefore the share of total income earned by farmers—has fallen.

Second, agriculture has been a technologically progressive sector for approximately 150 years in the United States, with steadily increasing yields over time. You might think that technological progress would be good for farmers. But competition among farmers means that technological progress leads to lower food prices. Meanwhile, the demand for food is price-inelastic, so falling prices of agricultural goods, other things equal, reduce the total revenue of farmers. That's right: progress in farming is good for consumers but bad for farmers.

The combination of these effects explains the relative decline of farming. Even if farming weren't such a technologically progressive sector, the low income elasticity of demand for food would ensure that the income of farmers grows more slowly than the economy as a whole. The combination of rapid technological progress in farming with price-inelastic demand for farm products reinforces this effect, further reducing the growth of farm income. In short, the U.S. farm sector has been a victim of success—the U.S. economy's success as a whole (which reduces the importance of spending on food) and its own success in increasing yields.

which demand increases when income rises, or *inferior goods*, for which demand decreases when income rises. These definitions relate directly to the sign of the income elasticity of demand:

- When the income elasticity of demand is positive, the good is a normal good—that is, the quantity demanded at any given price increases as income increases.
- When the income elasticity of demand is negative, the good is an inferior good—that is, the quantity demanded at any given price decreases as income increases.

Economists often use estimates of the income elasticity of demand to predict which industries will grow most rapidly as the incomes of consumers grow over time. In doing this, they often find it useful to make a further distinction among normal goods, identifying which are *income-elastic* and which are *income-inelastic*.

The demand for a good is **income-elastic** if the income elasticity of demand for that good is greater than 1. When income rises, the demand for income-elastic goods rises *faster* than income. Luxury goods such as second homes and international travel tend to be income-elastic. The demand for a good is **income-inelastic** if the income elasticity of demand for that good is positive but less than 1. When income rises, the demand for income-inelastic goods rises, but more slowly than income. Necessities such as food and clothing tend to be income-inelastic.

> The demand for a good is **income-elastic** if the income elasticity of demand for that good is greater than 1.
>
> The demand for a good is **income-inelastic** if the income elasticity of demand for that good is positive but less than 1.

# *economics in action*

## Spending It

The U.S. Bureau of Labor Statistics carries out extensive surveys of how families spend their incomes. This is not just a matter of intellectual curiosity. Quite a few government programs involve some adjustment for changes in the cost of living; to estimate those changes, the government must know how people spend their money. But an additional payoff to these surveys is evidence on the income elasticity of demand for various goods.

What stands out from these studies? The classic result is that the income elasticity of demand for "food eaten at home" is considerably less than 1: as a family's income rises, the share of its income spent on food consumed at home falls. Correspondingly, the lower a family's income, the higher the share of income spent on food consumed at home. In poor countries, many families spend more than half their income on food consumed at home. While the income elasticity of "food eaten at home" is estimated at less than 0.5 in the United States, "food eaten away from home" (restaurant meals) is estimated to be much higher—close to 1. Families with higher incomes eat out more often and at fancier places.

Judging from the activity at this busy McDonald's, incomes are rising in Jakarta, Indonesia.

In 1950, about 19 percent of U.S. income was spent on food consumed at home, a number which has dropped to 7 percent today. But over the same time period, the share of U.S. income spent on food away from home has stayed constant at 5 percent. In fact, a sure sign of rising income levels in developing countries is the arrival of fast-food restaurants that cater to newly affluent customers. For example, McDonald's can now be found in Jakarta, Shanghai, and Bombay.

There is one clear example of an inferior good found in the surveys: rental housing. Families with higher income actually spend less on rent than families with lower income, because they are much more likely to own their own homes. And the category identified as "other housing"—which basically means second homes—is highly income-elastic. Only higher-income families can afford a vacation home at all, so "other housing" has an income elasticity of demand greater than 1. ∎

> > > > > > > > > > > > > > > > > > >

## >>CHECK YOUR UNDERSTANDING 5-3

1. After Chelsea's income increased from $12,000 to $18,000 a year, her purchases of CDs increased from 10 to 40 CDs a year. Calculate Chelsea's income elasticity of demand for CDs using the midpoint method.

2. Expensive restaurant meals are income-elastic goods for most people, including Sanjay. Suppose his income falls by 10% this year. What can you predict about the change in Sanjay's consumption of expensive restaurant meals?

3. As the price of margarine rises by 20%, a manufacturer of baked goods increases its quantity of butter demanded by 5%. Calculate the cross-price elasticity of demand between butter and margarine. Are butter and margarine substitutes or complements for this manufacturer?

*Solutions appear at back of book.*

# The Price Elasticity of Supply

The Tellez plan to drive up the price of oil would have been much less effective if a higher price had induced large increases in output by countries that were not party to the agreement. For example, if American oil producers had responded to the higher price by significantly increasing their production, they could have pushed the price of oil back down. But they didn't—in fact, producers of oil who were not members of OPEC (Organization of Petroleum Exporting Countries) did not respond much to the higher price. This was another critical element in the success of the Tellez plan: a low responsiveness in output to a higher price of oil from other oil producers. To measure the response of producers to price changes, we need a measure parallel to the price elasticity of demand—the *price elasticity of supply*.

## Measuring the Price Elasticity of Supply

The **price elasticity of supply** is defined the same way as the price elasticity of demand:

$$(5-9) \quad \text{Price elasticity of supply} = \frac{\text{\% change in quantity supplied}}{\text{\% change in price}}$$

The **price elasticity of supply** is a measure of the responsiveness of the quantity of a good supplied to the price of that good. It is the ratio of the percent change in the quantity supplied to the percent change in the price as we move along the supply curve.

The only difference is that this time we consider movements along the supply curve rather than movements along the demand curve.

Suppose that the price of tomatoes rises by 10%. If the quantity of tomatoes supplied also increases by 10% in response, the price elasticity of supply of tomatoes is 1 (10%/10%), and supply is unit-elastic. If the quantity supplied increases by 5%, the price elasticity of supply is 0.5 and supply is inelastic; if the quantity increases by 20%, the price elasticity of supply is 2 and supply is elastic.

As in the case of demand, the extreme values of the price elasticity of supply have a simple graphical representation.

Panel (a) of Figure 5-5 on page 124 shows the supply of cell phone frequencies, the portion of the radio spectrum which is suitable for sending and receiving cell phone signals. Governments own the right to sell the use of this part of the radio spectrum to cell phone operators inside their borders. But governments can't increase or decrease the number of cell phone frequencies that they have to offer—for technical reasons, the quantity of frequencies suitable for cell phone operation is a fixed quantity. So the supply curve for cell phone frequencies is a vertical line, which we have assumed is set at the quantity of 100 frequencies. As you move up and down that curve, the change in the quantity supplied by the government is zero, whatever the

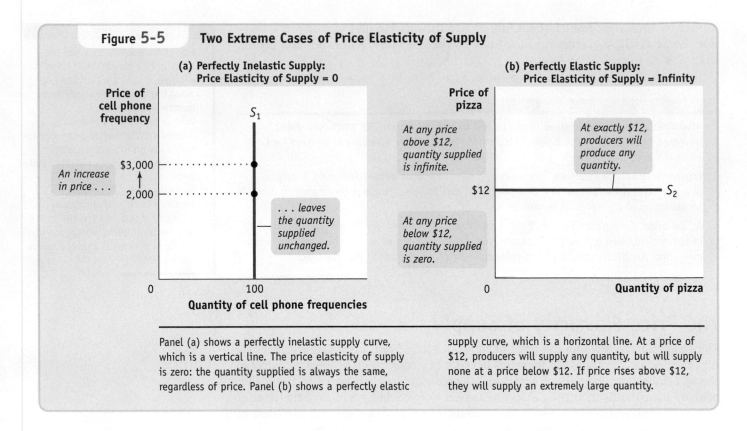

**Figure 5-5**    **Two Extreme Cases of Price Elasticity of Supply**

**(a) Perfectly Inelastic Supply:**
**Price Elasticity of Supply = 0**

Price of cell phone frequency

$S_1$

$3,000

*An increase in price . . .*

2,000

*. . . leaves the quantity supplied unchanged.*

0    100

**Quantity of cell phone frequencies**

**(b) Perfectly Elastic Supply:**
**Price Elasticity of Supply = Infinity**

Price of pizza

*At any price above $12, quantity supplied is infinite.*

*At exactly $12, producers will produce any quantity.*

$12    $S_2$

*At any price below $12, quantity supplied is zero.*

0    **Quantity of pizza**

Panel (a) shows a perfectly inelastic supply curve, which is a vertical line. The price elasticity of supply is zero: the quantity supplied is always the same, regardless of price. Panel (b) shows a perfectly elastic supply curve, which is a horizontal line. At a price of $12, producers will supply any quantity, but will supply none at a price below $12. If price rises above $12, they will supply an extremely large quantity.

There is **perfectly inelastic supply** when the price elasticity of supply is zero, so that changes in the price of the good have no effect on the quantity supplied. A perfectly inelastic supply curve is a vertical line.

There is **perfectly elastic supply** when even a tiny increase or reduction in the price will lead to very large changes in the quantity supplied, so that the price elasticity of supply is infinite. A perfectly elastic supply curve is a horizontal line.

change in price. So panel (a) illustrates a case in which the price elasticity of supply is zero. This is a case of **perfectly inelastic supply.**

Panel (b) shows the supply curve for pizza. We suppose that it costs $12 to produce a pizza, including all opportunity costs such as the implicit cost of capital invested in pizza parlors. At any price below $12, it would be unprofitable to produce pizza and all the pizza parlors in America would go out of business. Alternatively, there are many producers who could operate pizza parlors if they were profitable. The ingredients—dough, tomatoes, cheese—are plentiful. And if necessary, more tomatoes could be grown, more milk could be produced to make mozzarella, and so on. So any price above $12 would elicit an extremely large quantity of pizzas supplied. The implied supply curve is therefore a horizontal line at $12. Since even a tiny increase in the price would lead to a huge increase in the quantity supplied, the price elasticity of supply would be more or less infinite. This is a case of **perfectly elastic supply.**

As our cell phone frequencies and pizza examples suggest, real-world instances of both perfectly inelastic and perfectly elastic supply are easy to find—much easier than their counterparts in demand.

## What Factors Determine the Price Elasticity of Supply?

Our examples tell us the main determinant of the price elasticity of supply: the availability of inputs. In addition, as with the price elasticity of demand, time may also play a role in the price elasticity of supply. Here we briefly summarize the two factors.

**The Availability of Inputs** The price elasticity of supply tends to be large when inputs are easily available. It tends to be small when inputs are difficult to obtain.

**Time** The price elasticity of supply tends to become larger as producers have more time to respond to a price change. This means that the long-run price elasticity of supply is often higher than the short-run elasticity.

The price elasticity of pizza supply is very high because the inputs needed to expand the industry are readily available. The price elasticity of cell phone frequencies is zero because an essential input—the radio spectrum—cannot be increased at all.

Many industries are like pizza and have large price elasticities of supply: they can be readily expanded because they don't require any special or unique resources. On the other hand, the price elasticity of supply is usually substantially less than perfectly elastic for goods that involve limited natural resources: minerals like gold or copper, agricultural products like coffee that flourish only on certain types of land, renewable resources like ocean fish that can only be exploited up to a point without destroying the resource.

But given enough time, producers are often able to significantly change the amount they produce in response to a price change, even when production involves a limited natural resource. For example, consider again the effects of a surge in oil prices, but this time focus on the supply response. If oil prices were to rise to $50 per barrel and stay there for a number of years, there would almost certainly be a substantial increase in oil production. Oil companies would search for and exploit oil in inaccessible places, such as deep-sea waters; costly equipment would be put in place to squeeze still more oil out of already-exploited reservoirs; and so on. But Rome wasn't built in a day, and all these oil-production efforts can't take place in a month or even a year.

For this reason, economists often make a distinction between the short-run elasticity of supply, usually referring to a few weeks or months, and the long-run elasticity of supply, usually referring to several years. In most industries, the long-run elasticity of supply is larger than the short-run elasticity.

# *economics in action*

## European Farm Surpluses

One of the policies we analyzed in Chapter 4 was the imposition of a *price floor*, a lower limit on the price of a good. We saw that price floors are often used by governments to support the incomes of farmers but create large unwanted surpluses of farm produce. The most dramatic example of this is found in the European Union, where price floors have created a "butter mountain," a "wine lake," and so on.

Were European politicians unaware that their price floors would create huge surpluses? They probably knew that surpluses would arise, but underestimated the price elasticity of agricultural supply. In fact, when the agricultural price supports were put in place, many analysts thought they were unlikely to lead to big increases in production. After all, European countries are densely populated and there was little new land available for cultivation.

What the analysts failed to realize, however, was how much farm production could expand by adding other resources, especially fertilizer and pesticides. So although farm acreage didn't increase much, farm production did! ∎

> > > > > > > > > > > > > > > > > > >

### >>CHECK YOUR UNDERSTANDING 5-4

1. Using the midpoint method, calculate the price elasticity of supply for web-design services when the price per hour rises from $100 to $150 and the number of hours transacted increases from 300,000 hours to 500,000. Is supply elastic, inelastic, or unit-elastic?

2. True or false? If the demand for milk were to rise, then, in the long run, milk-drinkers would be better off if supply were elastic rather than inelastic.

3. True or false? Long-run price elasticities of supply are generally larger than short-run price elasticities of supply. Therefore the short-run supply curves are generally flatter than the long-run supply curves.

4. True or false? When supply is perfectly elastic, changes in demand have no effect on price.

Solutions appear at back of book.

# An Elasticity Menagerie

We've just run through quite a few different elasticities. Keeping them all straight can be a problem. So in Table 5-3 we provide a summary of all the elasticities we have discussed and their implications.

**TABLE 5-3**

**An Elasticity Menagerie**

| Name | Possible values | Significance |
|------|-----------------|--------------|
| **Price elasticity of demand** $= \dfrac{\% \text{ change in quantity demanded}}{\% \text{ change in price}}$ (use absolute value) | | |
| Perfectly inelastic demand | 0 | Price has no effect on quantity demanded (vertical demand curve). |
| Inelastic demand | Between 0 and 1 | A rise in price increases total revenue. |
| Unit-elastic demand | Exactly 1 | Changes in price have no effect on total revenue. |
| Elastic demand | Greater than 1, less than ∞ | A rise in price reduces total revenue. |
| Perfectly elastic demand | ∞ | A rise in price causes quantity demanded to fall to 0. A fall in price leads to an infinite quantity demanded (horizontal demand curve). |
| **Cross-price elasticity of demand** $= \dfrac{\% \text{ change in quantity } of\ one\ good \text{ demanded}}{\% \text{ change in price } of\ another\ good}$ | | |
| Complements | Negative | Quantity demanded of one good falls when the price of another rises. |
| Substitutes | Positive | Quantity demanded of one good rises when the price of another rises. |
| **Income elasticity of demand** $= \dfrac{\% \text{ change in quantity demanded}}{\% \text{ change in income}}$ | | |
| Inferior good | Negative | Quantity demanded falls when income rises. |
| Normal good, income-inelastic | Positive, less than 1 | Quantity demanded rises when income rises, but not as rapidly as income. |
| Normal good, income-elastic | Greater than 1 | Quantity demanded rises when income rises, and more rapidly than income. |
| **Price elasticity of supply** $= \dfrac{\% \text{ change in quantity supplied}}{\% \text{ change in price}}$ | | |
| Perfectly inelastic supply | 0 | Price has no effect on quantity supplied (vertical supply curve). |
| | Greater than 0, less than ∞ | Ordinary upward-sloping supply curve. |
| Perfectly elastic supply | ∞ | Any fall in price causes quantity supplied to fall to 0. Any rise in price elicits an infinite quantity supplied (horizontal supply curve). |

# Using Elasticity: The Incidence of an Excise Tax

In Chapter 4 we introduced the concept of the *incidence* of a tax—the measure of who really bears the burden of the tax. We saw in the case of an excise tax—a tax on sales or purchases of a product—that the incidence does not depend on who literally pays the money to the government. It doesn't matter, in other words, whether the tax is assessed on the sellers or the buyers. But we also noted that to determine who really pays the tax, we need the concept of elasticity.

We are now ready to see how the price elasticity of demand and the price elasticity of supply determine the incidence of an excise tax.

## When an Excise Tax Is Paid Mainly by Consumers

Figure 5-6 shows an excise tax that falls mainly on consumers: an excise tax on gasoline, which we set at $1 per gallon. (There really is a federal excise tax on gasoline, though it is actually only about $0.18 per gallon in the United States. In addition, states impose excise taxes between $0.08 and $0.30 per gallon.) According to Figure 5-6, in the absence of the tax, gasoline would sell for $1 per gallon.

Two key assumptions are reflected in the supply and demand curves. First, the price elasticity of demand for gasoline is very low, so the demand curve is relatively steep. Second, the price elasticity of supply is very high, so the supply curve is relatively flat.

We know from Chapter 4 that an excise tax drives a wedge, equal to the size of the tax, between the price paid by consumers and the price received by producers. This wedge drives the price paid by consumers up, and the price received by producers down. But as we can see from the figure, in this case those two effects are very unequal in size. The price received by producers falls only slightly, from $1.00 to $0.95, while the price paid by consumers rises by a lot, from $1.00 to $1.95.

This example illustrates a general principle: When the price elasticity of demand is low and the price elasticity of supply is high, the burden of an excise tax falls mainly on consumers. This is probably a good description of the main excise taxes actually collected in the United States today, such as taxes on cigarettes and alcoholic beverages.

---

### Figure 5-6

**An Excise Tax Paid Mainly by Consumers**

The relatively steep demand curve here reflects a low price elasticity of demand for gasoline. The relatively flat supply curve reflects a high price elasticity of supply. The pre-tax price of a gallon of gas is $1.00, and a tax of $1.00 per gallon is imposed. The cost to consumers rises by $0.95 to $1.95, reflecting the fact that most of the burden of the tax falls on consumers. Only a small portion of the tax is borne by producers: the price they receive falls by only $0.05 to $0.95.

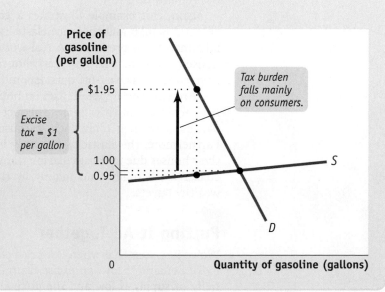

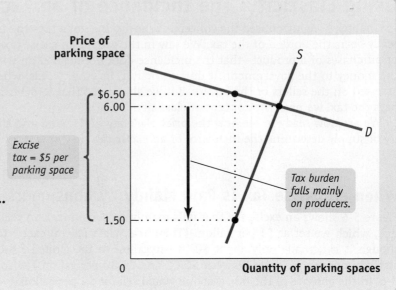

### Figure 5-7

**An Excise Tax Paid Mainly by Producers**

The relatively flat demand curve here reflects a high price elasticity of demand for downtown parking, and a relatively steep supply curve results from a low price elasticity of supply. The pre-tax price of a daily parking space is $6.00 and a tax of $5.00 is imposed. The price received by producers falls a lot, to $1.50, reflecting the fact that they bear most of the burden of the tax. The price paid by consumers rises a small amount, $0.50, to $6.50, as they bear very little of the burden. **>web...**

## When an Excise Tax Is Paid Mainly by Producers

Figure 5-7 shows an excise tax paid mainly by producers. In this case, we consider a $5.00 per day tax on downtown parking in a small city. In the market equilibrium, parking would cost $6.00 per day in the absence of the tax.

The price elasticity of supply is assumed to be very low because the lots used for parking have very few alternative uses. So the supply curve is relatively steep. The price elasticity of demand, however, is high: consumers can easily switch to other parking spaces a few minutes' walk from downtown. So the demand curve is relatively flat.

The tax drives a wedge between the price paid by consumers and the price received by producers. This time, however, the price to consumers rises only slightly, from $6.00 to $6.50, but the price received by producers falls a lot, from $6.00 to $1.50. So a consumer bears only $0.50 of the $5 tax, with a producer bearing the remaining $4.50.

Again, this example illustrates a general principle: When the price elasticity of demand is high and the price elasticity of supply is low, the burden of an excise tax falls mainly on producers. A real-world example is the tax on purchases of existing houses. Over the past few years, house prices in many towns in desirable locations have gone up as well-off outsiders move in, a process called gentrification. Some of these towns have imposed taxes on house sales in an effort to extract money from the new arrivals. But this ignores the fact that the elasticity of demand for houses in a particular town is often high, because buyers can choose to move to other towns. Furthermore, the elasticity of supply is probably low, because most sellers must sell their houses due to things like job transfers to other locations. So taxes on home purchases are actually paid mainly by the sellers—not, as town officials imagine, by wealthy buyers.

## Putting It All Together

We've just seen that when the price elasticity of supply is high and the price elasticity of demand is low, an excise tax falls mainly on consumers; when the price elasticity of supply is low and the price elasticity of demand is high, an excise tax falls mainly on producers. This leads us to the general rule: When the price elasticity of demand is higher than the price elasticity of supply, an excise tax falls mainly on the producers. When the price elasticity of supply is higher than the price elasticity of demand, an excise tax falls mainly on consumers. So elasticity—not who literally pays the tax—determines the incidence of an excise tax.

## *economics in action*

### So Who Does Pay the FICA?

As we explained in Chapter 4, one of the main taxes levied by the federal government is the FICA, or payroll tax. Half of this tax is paid by workers, half by their employers. But we have learned that this tells us nothing about who *really* pays the tax, that is, about the incidence of the FICA.

So who does pay the FICA? Almost all economists who have studied the issue agree that the answer is that the FICA is a tax on workers, not on their employers.

The reason for this conclusion lies in a comparison of the price elasticities of the supply of labor by households and the demand for labor by firms. The evidence suggests that the price elasticity of demand for labor is quite high, at least 3. That is, an increase in average wages of 1 percent would lead to at least a 3 percent decline in the number of hours of work demanded. The price elasticity of supply of labor, however, is generally believed to be very low. The reason is that although a rise in the wage rate increases the incentive to work, it also makes people richer and more able to afford leisure. So the number of hours people are willing to work increases very little—if at all—when the wage per hour goes up.

Our analysis already tells us that when the price elasticity of demand is much higher than the price elasticity of supply, the burden of an excise tax falls mainly on the suppliers. So the FICA falls mainly on the suppliers of labor, that is, workers—even though on paper half the tax is paid by employers.

This conclusion tells us something important about our tax system: that the FICA, rather than the much-hated income tax, is the main tax on most families. The FICA is 15.3 percent of all wages and salaries up to more than $90,000 per year; that is, the great majority of workers in the United States pay 15.3 percent of their wages in FICA. But only a minority of American families pay more than 15 percent of their income in income tax. According to estimates by the Congressional Budget Office, the FICA is Uncle Sam's main bite out of the income of more than 70 percent of families. ∎

> > > > > > > > > > > > > > > > > > > >

> The price elasticity of demand and the price elasticity of supply determine the incidence of a tax.
> In general, the higher the price elasticity of supply and the lower the price elasticity of demand, the more heavily the burden of an excise tax falls on consumers. The lower the price elasticity of supply and the higher the price elasticity of demand, the more heavily the burden falls on producers.

>> CHECK YOUR UNDERSTANDING 5-5

1. The demand for economics textbooks is very inelastic, but the supply is somewhat elastic. What does this imply about the incidence of a tax? Illustrate with a diagram.

2. True or false? When a substitute for a good is readily available to consumers, but it is difficult for producers to adjust the quantity of the good produced, then the burden of a tax on the good falls more heavily on producers.

3. The supply of bottled spring water is very inelastic, but the demand for it is somewhat elastic. What does this imply about the incidence of a tax? Illustrate with a diagram.

4. True or false? Other things equal, consumers would prefer to face a less elastic supply curve when a tax is imposed.

Solutions appear at back of book.

**• A LOOK AHEAD •**

The concept of elasticity deepens our understanding of supply and demand, among other things, helping us predict not only in which direction prices will move but also by how much. For example, we now know that supply and demand elasticities determine how the burden of a tax will be divided between producers and consumers. And, to come back to an example from very early on in this chapter, the concept of elasticity was just what Luis Tellez needed to be able to engineer a reduction in output by oil-exporting countries that led to an increase in oil prices and an increase in their total oil revenues.

But we don't yet have a way to translate the changes in prices that result from a tax, or from any other change in the situation, into a measure of gains or losses to individuals. In the next chapter, we show how to make that translation—how to use the supply and demand curves to calculate gains and losses to producers and consumers.

## SUMMARY

1. Many economic questions depend on the size of consumer or producer response to changes in prices or other variables. *Elasticity* is a general measure of responsiveness that can be used to answer such questions.

2. The **price elasticity of demand**—the percent change in the quantity demanded divided by the percent change in the price (dropping the minus sign)—is a measure of the responsiveness of the quantity demanded to changes in the price. In practical calculations, it is usually best to use the **midpoint method**, which calculates percent changes in prices and quantities based on the average of starting and final values.

3. The responsiveness of the quantity demanded to price can range from **perfectly inelastic demand**, where the quantity demanded is unaffected by the price, to **perfectly elastic demand**, where there is a unique price at which consumers will buy as much or as little as they are offered. When demand is perfectly inelastic, the demand curve is a vertical line; when it is perfectly elastic, the demand curve is a horizontal line.

4. The price elasticity of demand depends on whether there are close substitutes for the good in question, whether the good is a necessity or a luxury, and the length of time that has elapsed since the price change.

5. The price elasticity of demand is classified according to whether it is more or less than 1. If it is greater than 1, demand is **elastic**; if it is less than 1, demand is **inelastic**; if it is exactly 1, demand is **unit-elastic**. This classification determines how **total revenue**, the total value of sales, changes when the price changes. If demand is elastic, total revenue falls when the price increases and rises when the price decreases. If demand is inelastic, total revenue rises when the price increases and falls when the price decreases.

6. The **cross-price elasticity of demand** measures the effect of a change in one good's price on the quantity of another good demanded. The cross-price elasticity of demand can be positive, in which case the goods are substitutes, or negative, in which case they are complements.

7. The **income elasticity of demand** is the percent change in the quantity of a good demanded when a consumer's income changes divided by the percent change in income. The income elasticity of demand indicates how intensely the demand for a good responds to changes in income. It can be negative; in that case the good is an inferior good. Goods with positive income elasticities of demand are normal goods. If the income elasticity is greater than 1, a good is **income-elastic**; if it is positive and less than 1, the good is **income-inelastic**.

8. The **price elasticity of supply** is the percent change in the quantity of a good supplied divided by the percent change in the price. If the quantity supplied does not change at all, we have an instance of **perfectly inelastic supply**; the supply curve is a vertical line. If the quantity supplied is zero below some price but infinite above that price, we have an instance of **perfectly elastic supply**; the supply curve is a horizontal line.

9. The price elasticity of supply depends on the availability of resources to expand production and on time. It is higher when inputs are easily available and the longer the time elapsed since the price change.

10. The incidence of an excise tax depends on the price elasticities of supply and demand. If the price elasticity of demand is higher than the price elasticity of supply, the tax falls mainly on producers; if the price elasticity of supply is higher than the price elasticity of demand, the tax falls mainly on consumers.

## KEY TERMS

Price elasticity of demand, p. 111
Midpoint method, p. 112
Perfectly inelastic demand, p. 114
Perfectly elastic demand, p. 114
Elastic demand, p. 114

Inelastic demand, p. 114
Unit-elastic demand, p. 114
Total revenue, p. 116
Cross-price elasticity of demand, p. 120
Income elasticity of demand, p. 121

Income-elastic demand, p. 122
Income-inelastic demand, p. 122
Price elasticity of supply, p. 123
Perfectly inelastic supply, p. 124
Perfectly elastic supply, p. 124

## PROBLEMS

1. TheNile.com, the online bookseller, wants to increase its total revenue. Currently, every book it sells is priced at $10.50. One suggested strategy is to offer a discount that lowers the price of a book to $9.50, a 10% reduction in price using the midpoint method. TheNile.com knows that its customers can be divided into two distinct groups according to their likely responses to the discount. The accompanying table shows how the two groups respond to the discount.

| | Group A (sales per week) | Group B (sales per week) |
|---|---|---|
| Volume of sales before the 10% discount | 1.55 million | 1.50 million |
| Volume of sales after the 10% discount | 1.65 million | 1.70 million |

   a. Calculate the price elasticities of demand for Group A and Group B.

   b. Explain how the discount will affect total revenue from each group.

   c. Suppose TheNile.com knows which group each customer belongs to when he or she logs on and can choose whether or not to offer the 10% discount. If TheNile.com wants to increase its total revenue, should discounts be offered to Group A or to Group B, to neither group, or to both groups?

2. Do you think the price elasticity of demand for Ford sport-utility vehicles (SUVs) will increase, decrease, or remain the same when each of the following events occurs? Explain your answer.

   a. Other car manufacturers, such as General Motors, decide to make and sell SUVs.

   b. SUVs produced in foreign countries are banned from the American market.

   c. Due to ad campaigns, Americans believe that SUVs are much safer than ordinary passenger cars.

   d. The time period over which you measure the elasticity lengthens. During that longer time, new models such as four-wheel-drive cargo vans appear.

3. U.S. winter wheat production increased dramatically in 1999 after a bumper harvest. The supply curve shifted rightward; as a result, the price decreased and the quantity demanded increased (a movement along the demand curve). The accompanying table describes what happened to prices and the quantity demanded of wheat.

| | 1998 | 1999 |
|---|---|---|
| Quantity demanded (bushels) | 1.74 billion | 1.9 billion |
| Average price (per bushel) | $3.70 | $2.72 |

   a. Calculate the price elasticity of demand for winter wheat.

   b. What is the total revenue for U.S. wheat farmers in 1998 and 1999?

   c. Did the bumper harvest increase or decrease the total revenue of American wheat farmers? How could you have predicted this from your answer to part a?

4. The accompanying table gives part of the supply schedule for personal computers in the United States.

| Price of computer | Quantity of computers supplied |
|---|---|
| $1,100 | 12,000 |
| 900 | 8,000 |

   a. Calculate the price elasticity of supply when the price increases from $900 to $1,100.

   b. Suppose firms produce 1,000 more computers at any given price due to improved technology. As price increases from $900 to $1,100, is the price elasticity of supply now greater than, less than, or the same as it was in part a?

   c. Suppose a longer time period under consideration means that the quantity supplied at any given price is 20% higher than the figures given in the table. As price increases from $900 to $1,100, is the price elasticity of supply now greater than, less than, or the same as it was in part a?

5. The accompanying table lists the cross-price elasticities of demand for several goods, where the percent price change is measured for the first good of the pair, and the percent quantity change is measured for the second good.

| Good | Cross-price elasticities of demand |
|---|---|
| Air-conditioning units and kilowatts of electricity | −0.34 |
| Coke and Pepsi | +0.63 |
| High-fuel-consuming sport-utility vehicles (SUVs) and gasoline | −0.28 |
| McDonald's burgers and Burger King burgers | +0.82 |
| Butter and margarine | +1.54 |

a. Explain the sign of each of the cross-price elasticities. What does it imply about the relationship between the two goods in question?

b. Compare the absolute values of the cross-price elasticities and explain their magnitudes. For example, why is the cross-price elasticity of McDonald's and Burger King less than the cross-elasticity of butter and margarine?

c. Use the information in the table to calculate how a 5% increase in the price of Pepsi affects the quantity of Coke demanded.

d. Use the information in the table to calculate how a 10% decrease in the price of gasoline affects the quantity of SUVs demanded.

6. What can you conclude about the price elasticity of demand in each of the following statements?

a. "The pizza delivery business in this town is very competitive. I'd lose half my customers if I raised the price by as little as 10%."

b. "I owned both of the two Jerry Garcia autographed lithographs in existence. I sold one on eBay for a high price. But when I sold the second one, the price dropped a lot."

c. "My economics professor has chosen to use the Krugman/Wells/Olney textbook for this class. I have no choice but to buy this book."

d. "I always spend a total of exactly $10 per week on coffee."

7. The accompanying table shows the price and yearly quantity sold of souvenir T-shirts in the town of Crystal Lake according to the average income of the tourists visiting.

| Price of T-shirt | Quantity of T-shirts demanded when average tourist income is $20,000 | Quantity of T-shirts demanded when average tourist income is $30,000 |
|---|---|---|
| $4 | 3,000 | 5,000 |
| 5 | 2,400 | 4,200 |
| 6 | 1,600 | 3,000 |
| 7 | 800 | 1,800 |

a. Calculate the price elasticity of demand when the price of a T-shirt rises from $5 to $6 when the average tourist income is $20,000. Also calculate it when the average tourist income is $30,000.

b. Calculate the income elasticity of demand when the average tourist income increases from $20,000 to $30,000 when the price of a T-shirt is $4. Also calculate it when the price is $7.

8. A recent study determined the following elasticities for Volkswagen Beetles:

Price elasticity of demand = 2
Income elasticity of demand = 1.5

The supply of Beetles is elastic. Based on this information, are the following statements true or false? Explain your reasoning.

a. A 10% increase in the price of a Beetle will reduce the quantity demanded by 20%.

b. An increase in consumer income will increase the price and quantity sold of Beetles. Since price elasticity of demand is greater than 1, total revenue will go down.

9. In each of the following cases, do you think the price elasticity of supply is (i) perfectly elastic; (ii) perfectly inelastic; (iii) elastic, but not perfectly elastic; or (iv) inelastic, but not perfectly inelastic? Explain using a diagram.

a. An increase in demand this summer for luxury cruises leads to a huge jump in the sales price of a cabin on the Queen Mary.

b. The price of a kilowatt of electricity is the same during periods of high electricity demand as during periods of low electricity demand.

c. Fewer people want to fly during February than during any other month. The airlines cancel about 10% of their flights as ticket prices fall about 20% during this month.

d. Owners of vacation homes in Maine rent them out during the summer. Due to the soft economy this year, a 30% decline in the price of a vacation rental leads more than half of homeowners to occupy their vacation homes themselves during the summer.

10. Use an elasticity concept to explain each of the following observations.

a. During economic boom times, the number of new personal care businesses, such as gyms and tanning salons, is proportionately greater than the number of other new businesses, such as grocery stores.

b. Cement is the primary building material in Mexico. After new technology makes cement cheaper to produce, the supply curve for the Mexican cement industry becomes relatively flatter.

**c.** Some goods that were once considered luxuries, like a telephone, are now considered virtual necessities. As a result, the demand curve for telephone services has become steeper over time.

**d.** Consumers in a less developed country like Guatemala spend proportionately more of their income on equipment for producing things at home, like sewing machines, than consumers in a more developed country like Canada.

**11.** Taiwan is a major world supplier of semiconductor chips. A recent earthquake severely damaged the production facilities of Taiwanese chip-producing companies, sharply reducing the amount of chips they could produce.

**a.** Assume that the total revenue of a typical non-Taiwanese chip manufacturer rises due to these events. In terms of an elasticity, what must be true for this to happen? Illustrate the change in total revenue with a diagram, indicating the price effect and the quantity effect of the Taiwan earthquake on this company's total revenue.

**b.** Now assume that the total revenue of a typical non-Taiwanese chip manufacturer falls due to these events. In terms of an elasticity, what must be true for this to happen? Illustrate the change in total revenue with a diagram, indicating the price effect and the quantity effect of the Taiwan earthquake on this company's total revenue.

**12.** There is a debate about whether sterile hypodermic needles should be passed out free of charge in cities with high drug use. Proponents argue that doing so will reduce the incidence of diseases, such as HIV/AIDS, that are often spread by needle sharing among drug users. Opponents believe that doing so will encourage more drug use by reducing the risks of this behavior. As an economist asked to assess the policy, you must know the following: (i) how responsive the spread of diseases like HIV/AIDS is to the price of sterile needles; and (ii) how responsive drug use is to the price of sterile needles. Assuming that you know these two things, use the concepts of price elasticity of demand for sterile needles and the cross-price elasticity between drugs and sterile needles to answer the following questions.

**a.** In what circumstances do you believe this is a beneficial policy?

**b.** In what circumstances do you believe this is a bad policy?

**13.** Suppose the government imposes an excise tax of $1 for every gallon of gas sold. Before the tax, the price of a gallon of gas is $2. Consider the following four after-tax scenarios. In each case, (i) use an elasticity concept to explain what must be true for this scenario to arise; (ii) determine who bears relatively more of the burden of the tax, producers or consumers; and (iii) illustrate your answer with a diagram.

**a.** The price of gasoline paid by consumers rises to $3 per gallon. Assume that the demand curve is downward sloping.

**b.** The price paid by consumers remains at $2 per gallon after the tax is imposed. Assume that the supply curve is upward sloping.

**c.** The price of gasoline paid by consumers rises to $2.75.

**d.** The price of gasoline paid by consumers rises to $2.25.

**14.** Describe how the following events will affect the incidence of taxation—that is, after the event, will the tax fall more heavily on consumers or producers in comparison to before the event? Use the concept of elasticity to explain your answer.

**a.** Sales of gasoline are taxed. Ethanol, a substitute for gasoline, becomes widely available.

**b.** Sales of electricity to California residents are taxed. Regulations are introduced that make it much more difficult for California utility companies to divert supplies of electricity from the California market to markets in neighboring states like Nevada.

**c.** Sales of electricity to California residents are taxed. Regulations are introduced that make it much easier for California utility companies to divert supplies of electricity from the California market to markets in neighboring states like Nevada.

**d.** The sale of municipally provided water is taxed. Legislation is introduced that forbids the use of private sources of water such as wells and the diversion of rivers.

**15.** In devising taxes, there is often a debate about (i) who bears the burden of the tax and (ii) whether the tax achieves some desirable social goal, such as discouraging undesirable behavior by making it more expensive. In the case of cigarettes, smokers tend to be highly addicted and have lower income than the average nonsmoker. Taxes on cigarettes have historically had the effect of raising the price to consumers almost one for one with the size of the tax.

**a.** Why might such a tax be undesirable when considering issues of tax equity—that is, whether or not the tax burden falls more heavily on lower-income people? How do the price elasticities of supply and demand for cigarettes affect the equity of cigarette taxation?

**b.** How do the price elasticities of supply and demand for cigarettes affect the effectiveness of the tax in discouraging smoking?

**c.** In light of your answers to parts a and b and the historical response of price to the tax, what trade-offs must policy makers make when considering a cigarette tax?

**16.** Worldwide, the average coffee grower has increased the amount of acreage under cultivation over the past few years. The result has been that the average coffee plantation produces significantly more coffee than it did 10 to 20 years ago. Unfortunately for the growers, however, this has also been a period in which their total revenues have plunged. In terms of an elasticity, what must be true for these events to have occurred? Illustrate these events with a diagram, indicating the quantity effect and the price effect that gave rise to these events.

> **web...** To continue your study and review of concepts in this chapter, please visit the Krugman/Wells/Olney website for quizzes, animated graph tutorials, web links to helpful resources, and more.
>
> **www.worthpublishers.com/krugmanwellsolney**

# >>Consumer and Producer Surplus

## MAKING GAINS BY THE BOOK

THERE IS A LIVELY MARKET IN SECOND-hand college textbooks. At the end of each term, some students who took a course decide that the money they can get by selling their used books is worth more to them than keeping the books. And some students who are taking the course next term prefer to buy a somewhat battered but inexpensive used textbook rather than pay the full price for a new one.

Textbook publishers and authors are not happy about these transactions, because they cut into sales of new books. But both the students who sell used books and those who buy them clearly benefit from the existence of the market. That is why many college bookstores facilitate their trade, buying used textbooks and selling them alongside the new books.

But can we put a number on what used textbook buyers and sellers gain from these transactions? Can we answer the question, "*How much* do the buyers and sellers of textbooks gain from the existence of the used-book market?"

Yes, we can. In this chapter we will see how to measure benefits, such as those to buyers of used textbooks, from being able to purchase a good—known as *consumer surplus*. And we will see that there is a corresponding measure, *producer surplus*, of the benefits sellers receive from being able to sell a good.

The concepts of consumer surplus and producer surplus are extremely useful for analyzing a wide variety of economic issues.

How much am I willing to pay for that used textbook?

They let us calculate how much benefit producers and consumers receive from the existence of a market. They also allow us to calculate how the welfare of consumers and producers is affected by changes in market

## What you will learn in this chapter:

➤ The meaning of **consumer surplus** and its relationship to the demand curve

➤ The meaning of **producer surplus** and its relationship to the supply curve

➤ The meaning and importance of **total surplus** and how it can be used both to measure the gains from trade and to evaluate the efficiency of a market

➤ Why the **deadweight loss** of a tax means that its true cost is more than the amount of tax revenue collected

➤ How to use changes in total surplus to measure the deadweight loss of taxes

prices. Such calculations play a crucial role in evaluating many economic policies.

What information do we need to calculate consumer and producer surplus? The answer, surprisingly, is that all we need are the demand and supply curves for a good. That is, the supply and demand model isn't just a model of how a competitive market works—it's also a model of how much consumers and producers gain from participating in that market. So our first step will be to learn how consumer and producer surplus can be derived from the demand and supply curves. We will then see how these concepts can be applied to actual economic issues.

# Consumer Surplus and the Demand Curve

The market in used textbooks is not a big business in terms of dollars and cents. But it is a convenient starting point for developing the concepts of consumer and producer surplus.

So let's look at the market for used textbooks, starting with the buyers. The key point, as we'll see in a minute, is that the demand curve is derived from their tastes or preferences—and that those same preferences also determine how much they gain from the opportunity to buy used books.

## Willingness to Pay and the Demand Curve

A used book is not as good as a new book—it will be battered and coffee-stained, may include someone else's highlighting, and may not be completely up to date. How much this bothers you depends on your own preferences. Some potential buyers would prefer to buy the used book if it is only slightly cheaper than a new book, while others would buy the used book only if it is considerably cheaper. Let's define a potential buyer's **willingness to pay** as the maximum price at which he or she would buy a good, in this case a used textbook. An individual won't buy the book if it costs more than this amount but is eager to do so if it costs less. If the price is just equal to an individual's willingness to pay, he or she is indifferent between buying and not buying.

The table in Figure 6-1 shows five potential buyers of a used book that costs $100 new, listed in order of their willingness to pay. At one extreme is Aleisha, who will buy a second-hand book even if the price is as high as $59. Brad is less willing to have a used book and will buy one only if the price is $45 or less. Claudia is willing to pay only $35, Darren only $25. And Edwina, who really doesn't like the idea of a used book, will buy one only if it costs no more than $10.

How many of these five students will actually buy a used book? It depends on the price. If the price of a used book is $55, only Aleisha buys one; if the price is $40, Aleisha and Brad both buy used books, and so on. So the information in the table on willingness to pay also defines the *demand schedule* for used textbooks.

As we saw in Chapter 3, we can use this demand schedule to derive the market demand curve shown in Figure 6-1. Because we are considering only a small number of consumers, this curve doesn't look like the smooth demand curves of earlier chapters, where markets contained hundreds or thousands of consumers. This demand curve is step-shaped, with alternating horizontal and vertical segments. Each horizontal segment—each step—corresponds to one potential buyer's willingness to pay. However, we'll see shortly that for the analysis of consumer surplus it doesn't matter whether the demand curve is stepped, as in this figure, or whether there are many consumers, making the curve smooth.

A consumer's **willingness to pay** for a good is the maximum price at which he or she would buy that good.

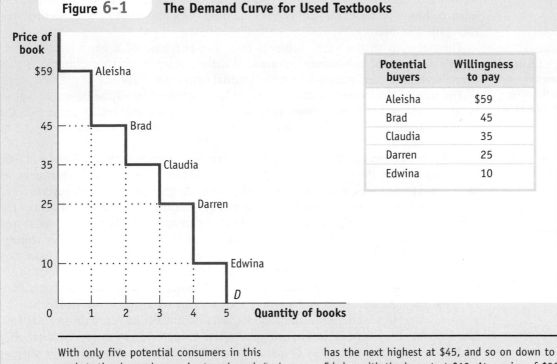

**Figure 6-1**    **The Demand Curve for Used Textbooks**

| Potential buyers | Willingness to pay |
|---|---|
| Aleisha | $59 |
| Brad | 45 |
| Claudia | 35 |
| Darren | 25 |
| Edwina | 10 |

With only five potential consumers in this market, the demand curve is step-shaped. Each step represents one consumer, and its height indicates that consumer's willingness to pay, the maximum price at which each student will buy a used textbook, as indicated in the table. Aleisha has the highest willingness to pay at $59, Brad has the next highest at $45, and so on down to Edwina with the lowest at $10. At a price of $59 the quantity demanded is one (Aleisha); at a price of $45 the quantity demanded is two (Aleisha and Brad), and so on until you reach a price of $10 at which all five students are willing to purchase a book.

## Willingness to Pay and Consumer Surplus

Suppose that the campus bookstore makes used textbooks available at a price of $30. In that case Aleisha, Brad, and Claudia will buy books. Do they gain from their purchases, and if so, how much?

The answer, shown in Table 6-1, is that each student who purchases a book does achieve a net gain but that the amount of the gain differs among students.

Aleisha would have been willing to pay $59, so her net gain is $59 − $30 = $29. Brad would have been willing to pay $45, so his net gain is $45 − $30 = $15. Claudia

**TABLE 6-1**

**Consumer Surplus When the Price of a Used Textbook Is $30**

| Potential buyer | Willingness to pay | Price paid | Individual consumer surplus = willingness to pay − price paid |
|---|---|---|---|
| Aleisha | $59 | $30 | $29 |
| Brad | 45 | 30 | 15 |
| Claudia | 35 | 30 | 5 |
| Darren | 25 | — | — |
| Edwina | 10 | — | — |
| | | | **Total consumer surplus: $49** |

**Individual consumer surplus** is the net gain to an individual buyer from the purchase of a good. It is equal to the difference between the buyer's willingness to pay and the price paid.

**Total consumer surplus** is the sum of the individual consumer surpluses of all the buyers of a good.

The term **consumer surplus** is often used to refer to both individual and to total consumer surplus.

would have been willing to pay $35, so her net gain is $35 − $30 = $5. Darren and Edwina, however, won't be willing to buy a used book at a price of $30, so they neither gain nor lose.

The net gain that a buyer achieves from the purchase of a good is called that buyer's **individual consumer surplus.** What we learn from this example is that every buyer of a good achieves some individual consumer surplus.

The sum of the individual consumer surpluses achieved by all the buyers of a good is known as the **total consumer surplus** achieved in the market. In Table 6-1, the total consumer surplus is the sum of the individual consumer surpluses achieved by Aleisha, Brad, and Claudia: $29 + $15 + $5 = $49.

Economists often use the term **consumer surplus** to refer to both individual and total consumer surplus. We will follow this practice; it will always be clear in context whether we are referring to the consumer surplus achieved by an individual or by all buyers.

Total consumer surplus can be represented graphically. Figure 6-2 reproduces the demand curve from Figure 6-1. Each step in that demand curve is one book wide and represents one consumer. For example, the height of Aleisha's step is $59, her willingness to pay. This step forms the top of a rectangle, with $30—the price she actually pays for a book—forming the bottom. The area of Aleisha's rectangle, ($59 − $30) × 1 = $29, is her consumer surplus from purchasing a book at $30. So the individual consumer surplus Aleisha gains is the *area of the dark blue rectangle* shown in Figure 6-2.

In addition to Aleisha, Brad and Claudia will also buy books when the price is $30. Like Aleisha, they benefit from their purchases, though not as much, because they each have a lower willingness to pay. Figure 6-2 also shows the consumer surplus gained by Brad and Claudia; again, this can be measured by the areas of the appropriate rectangles. Darren and Edwina, because they do not buy books at a price of $30, receive no consumer surplus.

The total consumer surplus achieved in this market is just the sum of the individual consumer surpluses received by Aleisha, Brad, and Claudia. So total consumer surplus is equal to the combined area of the three rectangles—the entire shaded area in Figure 6-2. Another way to say this is that total consumer surplus is equal to the area that is under the demand curve but above the price.

### Figure 6-2

**Consumer Surplus in the Used-Textbook Market**

At a price of $30, Aleisha, Brad, and Claudia each buy a book but Darren and Edwina do not. Aleisha, Brad, and Claudia get individual consumer surpluses equal to the difference between their willingness to pay and the price, illustrated by the areas of the shaded rectangles. Both Darren and Edwina have a willingness to pay less than $30, so they are unwilling to buy a book in this market; they receive zero consumer surplus. The total consumer surplus is given by the entire shaded area—the sum of the individual consumer surpluses of Aleisha, Brad, and Claudia—equal to $29 + $15 + $5 = $49.

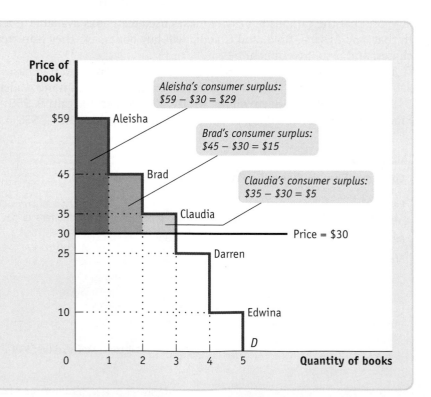

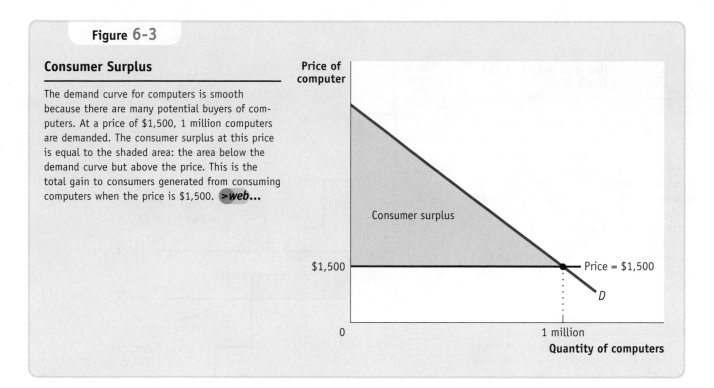

**Figure 6-3**

**Consumer Surplus**

The demand curve for computers is smooth because there are many potential buyers of computers. At a price of $1,500, 1 million computers are demanded. The consumer surplus at this price is equal to the shaded area: the area below the demand curve but above the price. This is the total gain to consumers generated from consuming computers when the price is $1,500. **>web...**

This illustrates the following general principle: *The total consumer surplus generated by purchases of a good at a given price is equal to the area below the demand curve but above that price.* The same principle applies regardless of the number of consumers.

When we consider large markets, this graphical representation becomes extremely helpful. Consider, for example, the sales of personal computers to millions of potential buyers. Each potential buyer has a maximum price that he or she is willing to pay. With so many potential buyers, the demand curve will be smooth, like the one shown in Figure 6-3.

Suppose that at a price of $1,500, a total of 1 million computers are purchased. How much do consumers gain from being able to buy those 1 million computers? We could answer that question by calculating the consumer surplus of each individual buyer and then adding these numbers up to arrive at a total. But it is much easier just to look at Figure 6-3 and use the fact that the total consumer surplus is equal to the shaded area. As in our original example, consumer surplus is equal to the area below the demand curve but above the price.

## How Changing Prices Affect Consumer Surplus

It is often important to know how much consumer surplus *changes* when the price changes. For example, we may want to know how much consumers are hurt if a frost in Florida drives up orange prices or how much consumers gain if the introduction of fish farming makes salmon less expensive. The same approach we have used to derive consumer surplus can be used to answer questions about how changes in prices affect consumers.

Let's return to the example of the market for used textbooks. Suppose that the bookstore decided to sell used textbooks for $20 instead of $30. How much would this increase consumer surplus?

The answer is illustrated in Figure 6-4 on page 140. As shown in the figure, there are two parts to the increase in consumer surplus. The first part, shaded dark blue, is the gain of those who would have bought books even at the higher price. Each of the students who would have bought books at $30—Aleisha, Brad, and Claudia—pays $10 less, and therefore each gains $10 in consumer surplus from the fall in price to

### Figure 6-4

#### Consumer Surplus and a Fall in the Price of Used Textbooks

There are two parts to the increase in consumer surplus generated by a fall in price from $30 to $20. The first is given by the dark blue rectangle: each person who would have bought at the original price of $30—Aleisha, Brad, and Claudia—receives an increase in consumer surplus equal to the total fall in price, $10. So the area of the dark blue rectangle corresponds to an amount equal to 3 × $10 = $30. The second part is given by the light blue rectangle: the increase in consumer surplus for those who would *not* have bought at the original price of $30 but who buy at the new price of $20—namely, Darren. Darren's willingness to pay is $25, so he now receives consumer surplus of $5. The total increase in consumer surplus is 3 × $10 + $5 = $35, represented by the sum of the shaded areas. Likewise, a rise in price from $20 to $30 would decrease consumer surplus by an amount equal to the sum of the shaded areas.

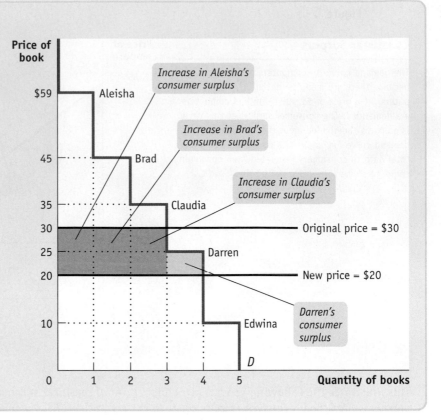

$20. So the dark blue area represents the $30 increase in consumer surplus to those three buyers. The second part, shaded light blue, is the gain to those who would not have bought a book at $30 but are willing to pay more than $20. In this case that means Darren, who would not have bought a book at $30 but does buy one at $20. He gains $5—the difference between his willingness to pay $25 and the new price of $20. So the light blue area represents a further $5 gain in consumer surplus. The total increase in consumer surplus is the sum of the shaded areas, $35. Likewise, a rise in price from $20 to $30 would decrease consumer surplus by an amount equal to the sum of the shaded areas.

Figure 6-4 illustrates that when the price of a good falls, the area under the demand curve but above the price—which we have seen is equal to the total consumer surplus—increases. Figure 6-5 shows the same result for the case of a smooth demand curve, the demand for personal computers. Here we assume that the price of computers falls from $5,000 to $1,500, leading to an increase in the quantity demanded from 200,000 to 1 million units. As in the used-textbook example, we divide the gain in consumer surplus into two parts. The dark blue rectangle in Figure 6-5 corresponds to the dark blue area in Figure 6-4: it is the gain to the 200,000 people who would have bought computers even at the higher price of $5,000. As a result of the price fall, each receives additional surplus of $3,500. The light blue triangle in Figure 6-5 corresponds to the light blue area in Figure 6-4: it is the gain to people who would not have bought the good at the higher price but are willing to do so at a price of $1,500. For example, the light blue triangle includes the gain to someone who would have been willing to pay $2,000 for a computer and therefore gains $500 in consumer surplus when he or she is able to buy a computer for only $1,500. As before, the total gain in consumer surplus is the sum of the shaded areas, the increase in the area under the demand curve but above the price.

What would happen if the price of a good were to rise instead of fall? We would do the same analysis in reverse. Suppose, for example, that for some reason the price

## Figure 6-5

### A Fall in the Price Increases Consumer Surplus

A fall in the price of a computer from $5,000 to $1,500 leads to an increase in the quantity demanded and an increase in consumer surplus. The change in total consumer surplus is given by the sum of the shaded areas: the total area below the demand curve but between the old and new prices. Here, the dark blue area represents the increase in consumer surplus for the 200,000 consumers who would have bought a computer at the original price of $5,000; they each receive an increase in consumer surplus of $3,500. The light blue area represents the increase in consumer surplus for those willing to buy at a price equal to or greater than $1,500 but less than $5,000. Similarly, a rise in the price of a computer from $1,500 to $5,000 generates a decrease in consumer surplus equal to the sum of the two shaded areas. **>web...**

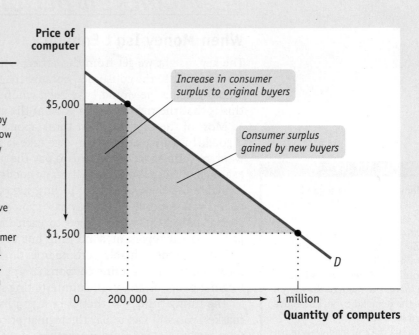

of computers rises from $1,500 to $5,000. This would lead to a fall in consumer surplus, equal to the shaded area in Figure 6-5. This loss consists of two parts. The dark blue rectangle represents the loss to consumers who would still buy a computer, even at a price of $5,000. The light blue triangle represents the loss to consumers who decide not to buy a computer at the higher price.

## FOR INQUIRING MINDS

### I WANT A NEW DRUG . . .

The pharmaceutical industry is constantly introducing new prescription drugs. Some of these drugs do the same thing as other, existing drugs, but a bit better—for example, pretty good allergy medicines have been around for years, but newer versions that are somewhat more effective or have fewer side effects keep emerging. Other drugs do something that was previously considered impossible—a famous example from the late 1990s was Propecia, the pill that slows and in some cases reverses hair loss.

Such innovations raise a difficult question for the people who are supposed to measure economic growth: how do you calculate the contribution of a new product to the economy?

You might at first say that it's just a matter of dollars and cents. But that could be wrong, in either direction. A new painkiller that is just slightly better than aspirin might have huge sales, because it would take over the painkiller market—but it wouldn't really add much to

consumer welfare. On the other hand, the benefits of a drug that cures the previously incurable might be much larger than the money actually spent on it—after all, people *would have been willing* to pay much more.

Consider, for example, the benefits of antibiotics. When penicillin was introduced in 1941, it transformed the treatment of infectious disease; illnesses that had previously crippled or killed millions of people were suddenly easy to treat. Presumably most people would be willing to pay a lot not to go back to the days before penicillin. Yet the average American spends only a few dollars per year on antibiotics.

The right way to measure the gains from a new drug—or any new product—is therefore to try to figure out what people would have been willing to pay for the good, and subtract what they actually pay. In other words, the gains from a new drug should be measured by calculating consumer surplus!

# economics in action

## When Money Isn't Enough

The key insight we get from the concept of consumer surplus is that purchases yield a net benefit to the consumer, because the consumer pays a price that is less than the amount he or she would have been willing to pay for the good. Another way to say this is that the right to buy a good at the going price is a valuable thing in itself.

Most of the time we don't think about the value associated with the right to buy a good. In a market economy, we take it for granted that we can buy whatever we want, as long as we are willing to pay the price. But that hasn't always been true. For example, during World War II many goods were rationed in order to make resources available for the war effort. To buy sugar, meat, coffee, gasoline, and many other goods, you not only had to pay cash; you also had to present stamps or coupons from special books that were issued to each family by the government. These pieces of paper, which represented nothing but the right to buy goods at the market price, quickly became valuable commodities in themselves. As a result, black markets in meat stamps and gasoline coupons sprang into existence. Moreover, criminals began stealing coupons and even counterfeiting stamps.

The funny thing was that even if you had bought a gasoline coupon on the black market, you still had to pay the regular price of gasoline to fill your tank. So what you were buying on the black market was not the good but *the right to buy the good*—that is, people who bought ration coupons on the black market were paying for the right to get some consumer surplus. ■

‹ ‹ ‹ ‹ ‹ ‹ ‹ ‹ ‹ ‹ ‹ ‹ ‹ ‹ ‹ ‹ ‹ ‹ ‹ ‹

>>CHECK YOUR UNDERSTANDING 6-1

1. Consider the market for cheese-stuffed jalapeno peppers. There are two consumers, Casey and Josie, and their willingness to pay for each pepper is given in the accompanying table. Use the table (i) to construct the demand schedule for peppers for prices of $0.00, $0.10, and so on, up to $0.90; and (ii) to calculate the total consumer surplus when the price of a pepper is $0.40.

| Quantity of peppers | Casey's willingness to pay | Josie's willingness to pay |
| --- | --- | --- |
| 1st pepper | $0.90 | $0.80 |
| 2nd pepper | 0.70 | 0.60 |
| 3rd pepper | 0.50 | 0.40 |
| 4th pepper | 0.30 | 0.30 |

Solutions appear at back of book.

## >>QUICK REVIEW

- The demand curve for a good is determined by the *willingness to pay* of each potential consumer.
- *Individual consumer surplus* is the net gain an individual consumer gets from buying a good.
- The *total consumer surplus* in a given market is equal to the area under the demand curve but above the price.
- A fall in the price of a good increases consumer surplus through two channels: a gain to consumers who would have bought at the original price and a gain to consumers who are persuaded to buy by the lower price. A rise in the price of a good reduces consumer surplus in a similar fashion.

# Producer Surplus and the Supply Curve

Just as buyers of a good would have been willing to pay more for their purchase than the price they actually pay, sellers of a good would have been willing to sell it for less than the price they actually receive. We can therefore carry out an analysis of producer surplus and the supply curve that is almost exactly parallel to that of consumer surplus and the demand curve.

## Cost and Producer Surplus

Consider a group of students who are potential sellers of used textbooks. Because they have different preferences, the various potential sellers differ in the price at which they are willing to sell their books. The table in Figure 6-6 shows the prices at which several different students would be willing to sell. Andrew is willing to sell the book as long as he can get anything more than $5; Betty won't sell unless she can get at least $15; Carlos, unless he can get $25; Donna, unless she can get $35; Engelbert, unless he can get $45.

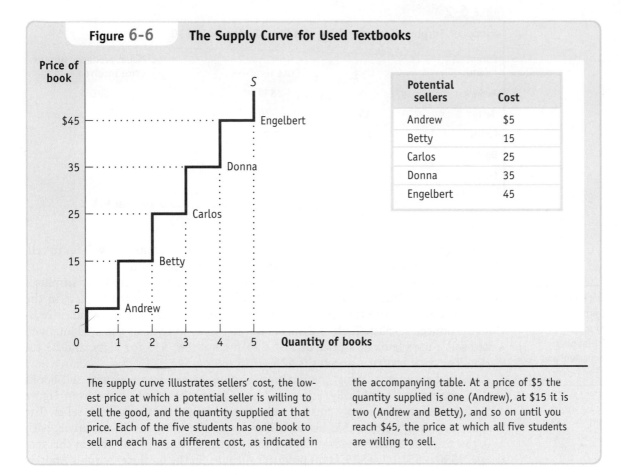

**Figure 6-6  The Supply Curve for Used Textbooks**

| Potential sellers | Cost |
|---|---|
| Andrew | $5 |
| Betty | 15 |
| Carlos | 25 |
| Donna | 35 |
| Engelbert | 45 |

The supply curve illustrates sellers' cost, the lowest price at which a potential seller is willing to sell the good, and the quantity supplied at that price. Each of the five students has one book to sell and each has a different cost, as indicated in the accompanying table. At a price of $5 the quantity supplied is one (Andrew), at $15 it is two (Andrew and Betty), and so on until you reach $45, the price at which all five students are willing to sell.

The lowest price at which a potential seller is willing to sell has a special name in economics: it is called the seller's **cost.** So Andrew's cost is $5, Betty's is $15, and so on.

Using the term *cost*, which people normally associate with the monetary cost of producing a good, may sound a little strange when applied to sellers of used textbooks. The students don't have to manufacture the books, so it doesn't cost the student who sells a book anything to make that book available for sale, does it?

Yes, it does. A student who sells a book won't have it later, as part of a personal collection. So there is an *opportunity cost* to selling a textbook, even if the owner has completed the course for which it was required. And remember that one of the basic principles of economics is that the true measure of the cost of doing anything is always its opportunity cost—the real cost of something is what you must give up to get it.

So it is good economics to talk of the minimum price at which someone will sell a good as the "cost" of selling that good, even if he or she doesn't spend any money to make the good available for sale. Of course, in most real-world markets the sellers are also those who produce the good—and therefore *do* spend money to make the good available for sale. In this case the cost of making the good available for sale *includes* monetary costs—but it may also include other opportunity costs.

Getting back to the example, suppose that Andrew sells his book for $30. Clearly he has gained from the transaction: he would have been willing to sell for only $5, so he has gained $25. This gain, the difference between the price he actually gets and his cost—the minimum price at which he would have been willing to sell—is known as his **individual producer surplus.**

Just as we derived the demand curve from the willingness to pay of different consumers, we can derive the supply curve from the cost of different producers. The step-shaped curve in Figure 6-6 shows the supply curve implied by the costs shown in the

A potential seller's **cost** is the lowest price at which he or she is willing to sell a good.

**Individual producer surplus** is the net gain to a seller from selling a good. It is equal to the difference between the price received and the seller's cost.

## TABLE 6-2

### Producer Surplus When the Price of a Used Textbook Is $30

| Potential seller | Cost | Price received | Individual producer surplus = price received − cost |
|---|---|---|---|
| Andrew | $5 | $30 | $25 |
| Betty | 15 | 30 | 15 |
| Carlos | 25 | 30 | 5 |
| Donna | 35 | — | — |
| Engelbert | 45 | — | — |
| | | | **Total producer surplus: $45** |

accompanying table. At a price less than $5, none of the students are willing to sell; at a price between $5 and $15, only Andrew is willing to sell, and so on.

As in the case of consumer surplus, we can add the individual producer surpluses of sellers to calculate the **total producer surplus,** the total gains to sellers in the market. Economists use the term **producer surplus** to refer to either total or individual producer surplus. Table 6-2 shows the net gain to each of the students who would sell a used book at a price of $30: $25 for Andrew, $15 for Betty, and $5 for Carlos. The total producer surplus is $25 + $15 + $5 = $45.

As with consumer surplus, the producer surplus gained by those who sell books can be represented graphically. Figure 6-7 reproduces the supply curve from Figure 6-6. Each step in that supply curve is one book wide and represents one seller. The height of Andrew's step is $5, his cost. This forms the bottom of a rectangle, with $30, the price he actually receives for his book, forming the top. The area of this rectangle, ($30 − $5) × 1 = $25, is his producer surplus. So the producer surplus Andrew gains from selling his book is the *area of the dark red rectangle* shown in the figure.

Let's assume that the campus bookstore is willing to buy all the used copies of this book that students are willing to sell at a price of $30. Then, in addition to Andrew, Betty and Carlos will also sell their books. They will also benefit from their sales, though not as much as Andrew, because they have higher costs. Andrew, as we have

> **Total producer surplus** in a market is the sum of the individual producer surpluses of all the sellers of a good. Economists use the term **producer surplus** to refer both to individual and to total producer surplus.

---

### Figure 6-7

**Producer Surplus in the Used-Textbook Market**

At a price of $30, Andrew, Betty, and Carlos each sell a book but Donna and Engelbert do not. Andrew, Betty, and Carlos get individual producer surpluses equal to the difference between the price and their cost, illustrated here by the shaded rectangles. Donna and Engelbert each have a cost that is greater than the price of $30, so they are unwilling to sell a book and therefore receive zero producer surplus. The total producer surplus is given by the entire shaded area, the sum of the individual producer surpluses of Andrew, Betty, and Carlos, equal to $25 + $15 + $5 = $45.

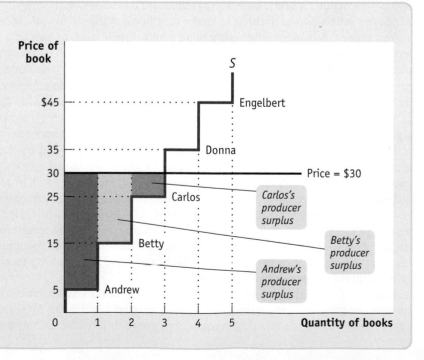

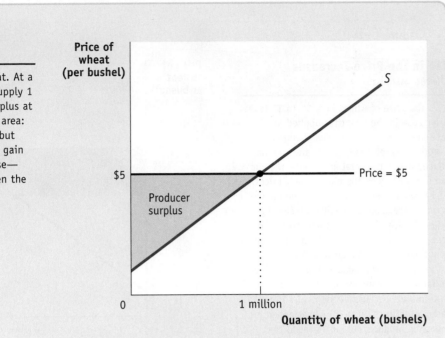

**Figure 6-8**

**Producer Surplus**

Here is the supply curve for wheat. At a price of $5 per bushel, farmers supply 1 million bushels. The producer surplus at this price is equal to the shaded area: the area above the supply curve but below the price. This is the total gain to producers—farmers in this case—from supplying their product when the price is $5. **>web...**

*Price of wheat (per bushel)*

*S*

$5 ————————————————— Price = $5

Producer surplus

0     1 million

**Quantity of wheat (bushels)**

---

seen, gains $25. Betty gains a smaller amount: since her cost is $15, she gains only $15. Carlos gains even less, only $5.

Again, as with consumer surplus, we have a general rule for determining the total producer surplus from sales of a good: *The total producer surplus from sales of a good at a given price is the area above the supply curve but below that price.*

This rule applies both to examples like the one shown in Figure 6-7, where there are a small number of producers and a step-shaped supply curve, and to more realistic examples where there are many producers and the supply curve is more or less smooth.

Consider, for example, the supply of wheat. Figure 6-8 shows how producer surplus depends on the price per bushel. Suppose that, as shown in the figure, the price is $5 per bushel and farmers supply 1 million bushels. What is the benefit to the farmers from selling their wheat at a price of $5? Their producer surplus is equal to the shaded area in the figure—the area above the supply curve but below the price of $5 per bushel.

## Changes in Producer Surplus

If the price of a good rises, producers of the good will experience an increase in producer surplus, though not all producers gain the same amount. Some producers would have produced the good even at the original price; they will gain the entire price increase on every unit they produce. Other producers will enter the market because of the higher price; they will gain only the difference between the new price and their cost.

Figure 6-9 on page 146 is the supply counterpart of Figure 6-5. It shows the effect on producer surplus of a rise in the price of wheat from $5 to $7 per bushel. The increase in producer surplus is the entire shaded area, which consists of two parts. First, there is a red rectangle corresponding to the gains to those farmers who would have supplied wheat even at the original $5 price. Second, there is an additional pink triangle that corresponds to the gains to those farmers who would not have supplied wheat at the original price but are drawn into the market by the higher price.

If the price were to fall from $7 to $5 per bushel, the story would run in reverse. The whole shaded area would now be the decline in producer surplus, the fall in the area above the supply curve but below the price. The loss would consist of two parts, the loss to farmers who would still grow wheat at a price of $5 (the red rectangle) and the loss to farmers who decide not to grow wheat because of the lower price (the pink triangle).

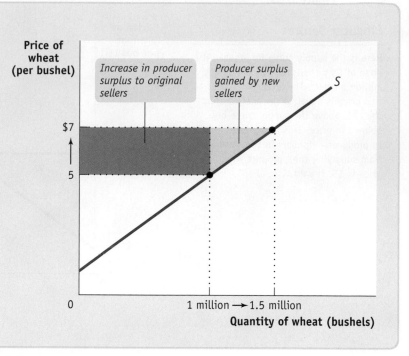

### Figure 6-9

#### A Rise in the Price Increases Producer Surplus

A rise in the price of wheat from $5 to $7 leads to an increase in the quantity supplied and an increase in producer surplus. The change in total producer surplus is given by the sum of the shaded areas: the total area above the supply curve but between the old and new prices. The red area represents the gain to the farmers who would have supplied 1 million bushels at the original price of $5; they each receive an increase in producer surplus of $2 for each of those bushels. The triangular pink area represents the increase in producer surplus achieved by the farmers who supply the additional 500,000 bushels because of the higher price. Similarly, a fall in the price of wheat generates a decrease in producer surplus equal to the shaded areas. **>web...**

## economics in action

### Gaining from Disaster

In 1992 Hurricane Andrew swept through Florida, destroying thousands of homes and businesses. The state quickly began rebuilding, with the help of thousands of construction workers who moved temporarily to Florida to help out.

These construction workers were not motivated mainly by sympathy for Florida residents. They were lured by the high wages available there—and took home billions of dollars.

But how much did the temporary workers actually gain? Certainly we should not count all the money they earned in Florida as a net benefit. For one thing, most of these workers would have earned something—though not as much—if they had stayed home. In addition to this opportunity cost, the temporary move to Florida had other costs: the expense of motel rooms and of transportation, the wear and tear of being away from families and friends.

Clearly the workers viewed the benefits as being larger than the costs—otherwise they wouldn't have gone down to Florida in the first place. But the producer surplus earned by those temporary workers was much less than the money they earned. ∎

< < < < < < < < < < < < < < < < < <

#### >>CHECK YOUR UNDERSTANDING 6-2

1. Consider the market for cheese-stuffed jalapeno peppers. There are two producers, Cara and Jamie, and their costs of producing each pepper are given in the accompanying table. Use the table (i) to construct the supply schedule for peppers for prices of $0.00, $0.10, and so on, up to $0.90; and (ii) to calculate the total producer surplus when the price of a pepper is $0.70.

| Quantity of peppers | Cara's cost | Jamie's cost |
|---|---|---|
| 1st pepper | $0.10 | $0.30 |
| 2nd pepper | 0.10 | 0.50 |
| 3rd pepper | 0.40 | 0.70 |
| 4th pepper | 0.60 | 0.90 |

Solutions appear at back of book.

# Consumer Surplus, Producer Surplus, and the Gains from Trade

One of the nine core principles of economics we introduced in Chapter 1 is that markets are a remarkably effective way to organize economic activity: they generally make society as well off as possible given the available resources. The concepts of consumer surplus and producer surplus can help us deepen our understanding of why this is so.

## The Gains from Trade

Let's go back to the market in used textbooks but now consider a much bigger market—say, one at a large state university—where there are many potential buyers and sellers. Let's line up incoming students—who are potential buyers of the book—in order of their willingness to pay, so that the entering student with the highest willingness to pay is potential buyer number 1, the student with the next highest willingness to pay is number 2, and so on. Then we can use their willingness to pay to derive a demand curve like the one in Figure 6-10. Similarly, we can line up outgoing students, who are potential sellers of the book, in order of their cost, starting with the student with the lowest cost, then the student with the next lowest cost, and so on, to derive a supply curve like the one shown in the same figure.

As we have drawn the curves, the market reaches equilibrium at a price of $30 per book, and 1,000 books are bought and sold at that price. The two shaded triangles show the consumer surplus (blue) and the producer surplus (red) generated by this market. The sum of consumer and producer surplus is known as the **total surplus** generated in a market.

The striking thing about this picture is that both consumers and producers gain—that is, both consumers and producers are better off because there is a market in this good. But this should come as no surprise—it illustrates another core principle of economics: there are *gains from trade*. These gains from trade are the reason everyone is better off participating in a market economy than they would be if each individual tried to be self-sufficient.

But are we as well off as we could be? This brings us to the question of the efficiency of markets.

> The **total surplus** generated in a market is the total net gain to consumers and producers from trading in the market. It is the sum of the producer and the consumer surplus.

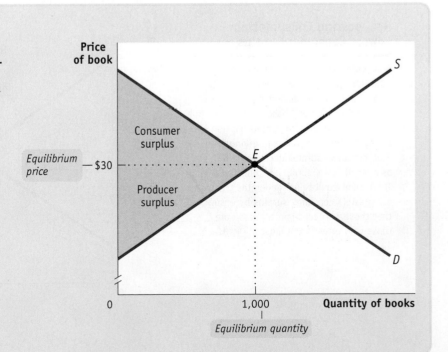

### Figure 6-10

**Total Surplus**

In the market for used textbooks, the equilibrium price is $30 and the equilibrium quantity is 1,000 books. Consumer surplus is given by the blue area, the area below the demand curve but above the price. Producer surplus is given by the red area, the area above the supply curve but below the price. The sum of the blue and the red areas is total surplus, the total benefit to society from the production and consumption of the good. **>web...**

## The Efficiency of Markets: A Preliminary View

Markets produce gains from trade, but in Chapter 1 we made a bigger claim: that markets are usually *efficient*. That is, we claimed that once the market has produced its gains from trade, there is usually no way to make some people better off without making others worse off (with some well-defined exceptions).

We can get an intuitive sense of the efficiency of markets by noticing a key feature of the market equilibrium shown in Figure 6-10: the maximum possible total surplus is achieved at market equilibrium. That is, the market equilibrium allocates the consumption of the good among potential consumers and sales of the good among potential sellers in a way that achieves the highest possible gain to society.

How do we know this? By comparing the total surplus generated by the consumption and production choices in the market equilibrium to the surplus generated by a different set of production and consumption choices. We can show that any change from the market equilibrium reduces total surplus.

Let's consider three ways in which you might try to increase the total surplus:

1. *Reallocate consumption among consumers*—take the good away from buyers who would have purchased the good in the market equilibrium, and instead give it to potential consumers who would not have bought it in equilibrium.

2. *Reallocate sales among sellers*—take sales away from sellers who would have sold the good in the market equilibrium, and instead compel potential sellers who would not have sold the good in equilibrium to sell it.

3. *Change the quantity traded*—compel consumers and producers to transact either more or less than the equilibrium quantity.

It turns out that each of these actions will not only fail to increase the total surplus; in fact, each will reduce the total surplus.

Figure 6-11 shows why reallocating consumption of the good among consumers will reduce the total surplus. Points *A* and *B* show the positions on the demand curve of two potential buyers of a used book, Ana and Bob. As we can see from the figure, Ana is willing to pay $35 for a book, but Bob is willing to pay only $25. Since the equilibrium price is $30, Ana buys a book and Bob does not.

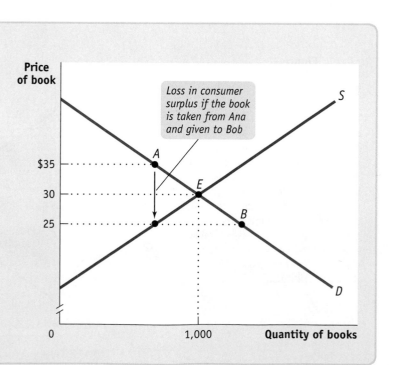

### Figure 6-11

**Reallocating Consumption Lowers Consumer Surplus**

Ana (point *A*) has a willingness to pay of $35. Bob (point *B*) has a willingness to pay of only $25. At the market equilibrium price of $30, Ana purchases a book but Bob does not. If we rearrange consumption by taking a book from Ana and giving it to Bob, consumer surplus declines by $10 and, as a result, total surplus declines by $10. The market equilibrium generates the highest possible consumer surplus by ensuring that those who consume the good are those who value it the most. **>web...**

*Loss in consumer surplus if the book is taken from Ana and given to Bob*

Now suppose that we try to reallocate consumption. This would mean taking a book away from somebody who *would* have bought one at the equilibrium price of $30, like Ana, and giving that book to someone who would *not* have bought at that price, like Bob. But since the book is worth $35 to Ana, but only $25 to Bob, this would *reduce total consumer surplus* by $35 − $25 = $10.

This result doesn't depend on which two students we pick. Every student who buys a book in equilibrium has a willingness to pay that is *more* than $30, and every student who doesn't buy a book has a willingness to pay that is *less* than $30. So reallocating the good among consumers always means taking a book away from a student who values it more and giving it to a student who values it less, which necessarily reduces consumer surplus.

A similar argument, illustrated by Figure 6-12, holds for producer surplus. Here points *X* and *Y* show the positions on the supply curve of Xavier, who has a cost of $25, and Yvonne, who has a cost of $35. At the equilibrium price of $30, Xavier would sell his book but Yvonne would not. If we reallocated sales, forcing Xavier to keep his book and forcing Yvonne to give up hers, total producer surplus would be reduced by $35 − $25 = $10. Again, it doesn't matter which two students we choose. Any student who sells a book in equilibrium has a lower cost than any student who does not, so reallocating sales among sellers necessarily increases total cost and reduces producer surplus. In this way the market equilibrium generates the highest possible producer surplus: it ensures that those who sell their books are those who most value the right to sell them.

Finally, changing the quantity bought and sold reduces the sum of producer and consumer surplus. Figure 6-13 on page 150 shows all four students: potential buyers Ana and Bob, and potential sellers Xavier and Yvonne. To reduce sales, we would have to prevent someone like Xavier, who would have sold the book in equilibrium, from making the sale; and the book would then not be made available to someone like Ana who would have bought it in equilibrium. As we've seen, however, Ana would be willing to pay $35, but Xavier's cost is only $25. So preventing this sale would reduce total surplus by $35 − $25 = $10. Once again, this result doesn't depend on which two students we pick: any student who would have sold the book in equilibrium has a cost of *less* than $30, and any student who would have purchased the book in equi-

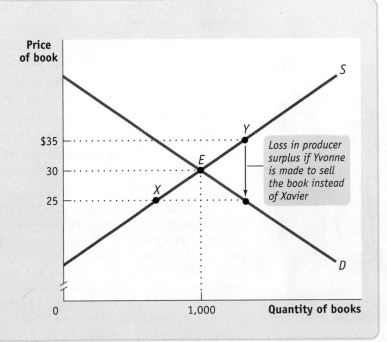

### Figure 6-12

**Reallocating Sales Lowers Producer Surplus**

Yvonne (point *Y*) has a cost of $35, $10 more than Xavier (point *X*) who has a cost of $25. At the market equilibrium price of $30, Xavier sells a book, but Yvonne does not. If we rearrange sales by preventing Xavier from selling his book and compelling Yvonne to sell hers, producer surplus declines by $10 and, as a result, total surplus declines by $10. The market equilibrium generates the highest possible producer surplus by assuring that those who sell the good are those who value the right to sell it the most. **>web...**

Price of book

Loss in producer surplus if Yvonne is made to sell the book instead of Xavier

Quantity of books

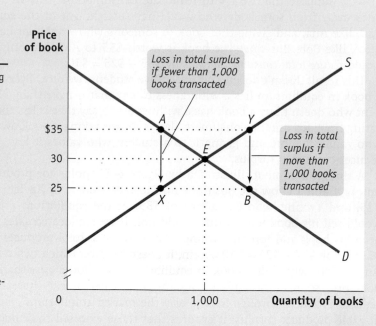

**Figure 6-13**

**Changing the Quantity Lowers Total Surplus**

If Xavier (point *X*) were prevented from selling his book to someone like Ana (point *A*), total surplus would fall by $10, the difference between Ana's willingness to pay ($35) and Xavier's cost ($25). This means that total surplus falls whenever fewer than 1,000 books—the equilibrium quantity—are transacted. Likewise, if Yvonne (point *Y*) were compelled to sell her book to someone like Bob (point *B*), total surplus would also fall by $10, the difference between Yvonne's cost ($35) and Bob's willingness to pay ($25). This means that total surplus falls whenever more than 1,000 books are transacted. These two examples show that at market equilibrium, all beneficial transactions—and only beneficial transactions—occur.

librium would be willing to pay *more* than $30, so preventing any sale that would have taken place in equilibrium reduces total surplus.

Finally, to increase sales would mean forcing someone like Yvonne, who would not have sold her book in equilibrium, to sell it, and giving it to someone like Bob, who would not have bought a book in equilibrium. Because Yvonne's cost is $35 but Bob is only willing to pay $25, this reduces total surplus by $10. And once again it doesn't matter which two students we pick—anyone who wouldn't have bought the book is willing to pay less than $30, and anyone who wouldn't have sold has a cost of more than $30.

What we have shown is that the market equilibrium maximizes total surplus—the sum of producer and consumer surplus. It does this because the market performs four important functions:

1. It allocates consumption of the good to the potential buyers who value it the most, as indicated by the fact that they have the highest willingness to pay.

2. It allocates sales to the potential sellers who most value the right to sell the good, as indicated by the fact that they have the lowest cost.

3. It ensures that every consumer who makes a purchase values the good more than every seller who makes a sale, so that all transactions are mutually beneficial.

4. It ensures that every potential buyer who doesn't make a purchase values the good less than every potential seller who doesn't make a sale, so that no mutually beneficial transactions are missed.

A caveat: it's important to realize that although the market equilibrium maximizes the total surplus, this does not mean that it is the best outcome for every individual consumer and producer. Other things being equal, each buyer would like to pay less and each seller would like to receive more. So some people would benefit from the price controls discussed in Chapter 4. A price ceiling that held down the market price would leave some consumers—those who managed to make a purchase—better off than they would be at equilibrium. A price floor that kept the price up would benefit some sellers—those who managed to make a sale.

But in the market equilibrium there is no way to make some people better off without making others worse off—and that's the definition of efficiency.

Maximizing total surplus at your local hardware store.

Photodisc/Getty Images

# economics in action

## eBay and Efficiency

Garage sales are an old American tradition: they are a way for families to sell items they don't want to other families that have some use for them, to the benefit of both parties. But many potentially beneficial trades were missed. For all Mr. Smith knew, there was someone 1,000 miles away who would really have loved that 1930s gramophone he had in the basement; for all Ms. Jones knew, there was someone 1,000 miles away who had that 1930s gramophone she had always wanted. But there was no way for Mr. Smith and Ms. Jones to find each other.

Enter eBay, the online auction service. eBay was founded in 1995 by Pierre Omidyar, a programmer whose fiancée was a collector of Pez candy dispensers and wanted a way to find potential sellers. The company, which says that its mission is "to help practically anyone trade practically anything on earth," provides a way for would-be buyers and would-be sellers of unique or used items to find each other, even if they don't live in the same neighborhood or even the same city.

The potential gains from trade were evidently large: in 2004, 135 million people were registered by eBay, and in the same year $34 billion in goods were bought and sold using the service. The Omidyars now possess a large collection of Pez dispensers. They are also billionaires. ■

*"I got it from eBay"*

> **QUICK REVIEW**
> - *Total surplus* measures the gains from trade in a market.
> - Markets are usually efficient. We can demonstrate this by considering what happens to total surplus if we start from the equilibrium and rearrange consumption, rearrange sales, or change the quantity traded. Any outcome other than the market equilibrium reduces total surplus, which means that the market equilibrium is efficient.

> > > > > > > > > > > > > > > > > >

## >>CHECK YOUR UNDERSTANDING 6-3

1. Using the tables in Check Your Understanding 6-1 and 6-2, find the equilibrium price and quantity in the market for cheese-stuffed jalapeno peppers. What is total surplus in the equilibrium in this market, and who receives it?

2. Show how each of the following three actions reduces total surplus:
   a. Having Josie consume one less pepper, and Casey one more pepper, than in the market equilibrium
   b. Having Cara produce one less pepper, and Jamie one more pepper, than in the market equilibrium
   c. Having Josie consume one less pepper, and Cara produce one less pepper, than in the market equilibrium

*Solutions appear at back of book.*

# Applying Consumer and Producer Surplus: The Efficiency Costs of a Tax

The concepts of consumer and producer surplus are extremely useful in many economic applications. Among the most important of these is assessing the efficiency cost of taxation.

In Chapter 4 we introduced the concept of an *excise tax*, a tax on the purchase or sale of a good. We saw that such a tax drives a *wedge* between the price paid by consumers and that received by producers: the price paid by consumers rises, and the price received by producers falls, with the difference equal to the tax per unit. The *incidence* of the tax—how much of the burden falls on consumers, how much on producers—does not depend on who actually writes the check to the government. Instead, as we saw in Chapter 5, the burden of the tax depends on the price elasticities of supply and demand: the higher the price elasticity of demand, the greater the burden on producers; the higher the price elasticity of supply, the greater the burden on consumers.

There is an additional cost of a tax, over and above the money actually paid to the government. A tax causes an **excess burden** or **deadweight loss** to society, because

The **excess burden**, or **deadweight loss**, from a tax is the extra cost in the form of inefficiency that results because the tax discourages mutually beneficial transactions.

less of the good is produced and consumed than in the absence of the tax. As a result, some mutually beneficial trades between producers and consumers do not take place. The concepts of consumer and producer surplus are what we need to pin down precisely the deadweight loss that an excise tax imposes.

Figure 6-14 shows the effects of an excise tax on consumer and producer surplus. In the absence of the tax, the equilibrium is at $E$, and the equilibrium price and quantity are $P_E$ and $Q_E$, respectively. An excise tax drives a wedge equal to the amount of the tax between the price received by producers and the price paid by consumers, reducing the quantity bought and sold. In this case, where the tax is $T$ dollars per unit, the quantity bought and sold falls to $Q_T$. The price paid by consumers rises to $P_C$, the demand price of the reduced quantity, $Q_T$, and the price received by producers falls to $P_P$, the supply price of that quantity. The difference between these prices, $P_C - P_P$, is equal to the excise tax, $T$.

We can now use the concepts of producer and consumer surplus to show exactly how much surplus producers and consumers lose as a result of the tax. We saw earlier, in Figure 6-5, that a fall in the price of a good generates a gain in consumer surplus that is equal to the sum of the areas of a rectangle and a triangle. A price increase causes a loss to consumers that looks exactly the same. In the case of an excise tax, the rise in the price paid by consumers causes a loss equal to the sum of the area of the dark blue rectangle labeled $A$ and the area of the light blue triangle labeled $B$ in Figure 6-14.

Meanwhile, the fall in the price received by producers causes a fall in producer surplus. This, too, is the sum of the areas of a rectangle and a triangle. The loss in producer surplus is the sum of the areas of the red rectangle labeled $C$ and the pink triangle labeled $F$ in Figure 6-14.

Of course, although consumers and producers are hurt by the tax, the government gains revenue. The revenue the government collects is equal to the tax per unit sold, $T$, multiplied by the quantity sold, $Q_T$. This revenue is equal to the area of a rectangle $Q_T$ wide and $T$ high. And we already have that rectangle in the figure: it is the sum of rectangles $A$ and $C$. So the government gains part of what consumers and producers lose from an excise tax.

But there is a part of the loss to producers and consumers from the tax that is not offset by a gain to the government—specifically, the two triangles $B$ and $F$. The deadweight loss caused by the tax is equal to the combined area of these triangles. It rep-

### Figure 6-14

**A Tax Reduces Consumer and Producer Surplus**

Before the tax, the equilibrium price and quantity are $P_E$ and $Q_E$, respectively. After an excise tax of $T$ per unit is imposed, the price to consumers rises to $P_C$ and consumer surplus falls by the sum of the dark blue rectangle, labeled $A$, and the light blue triangle, labeled $B$. The tax also causes the price to producers to fall to $P_P$; producer surplus falls by the sum of the red rectangle, labeled $C$, and the pink triangle, labeled $F$. The government receives revenue from the tax, $Q_T \times T$, which is given by the sum of the areas $A$ and $C$. Areas $B$ and $F$ represent the losses to consumer and producer surplus that are not collected by the government as revenue; they are the deadweight loss to society of the tax. **>web...**

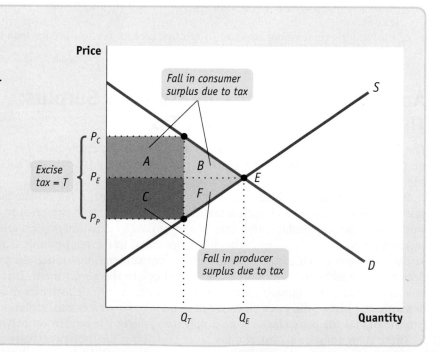

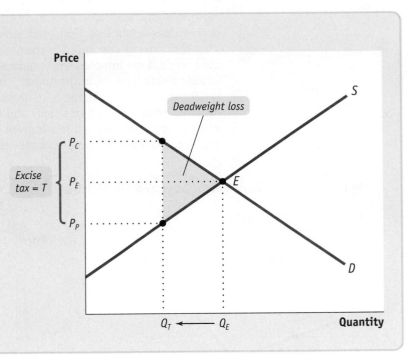

**Figure 6-15**

**The Deadweight Loss of a Tax**

A tax leads to a deadweight loss because it creates inefficiency: some mutually beneficial transactions never take place because of the tax, namely the transactions $Q_E - Q_T$. The yellow area here represents the value of the deadweight loss: it is the total surplus that would have been gained from the $Q_E - Q_T$ transactions. If the tax had not discouraged transactions—had the number of transactions remained at $Q_E$—no deadweight loss would have been incurred.

**>web...**

resents the total surplus that would have been generated by transactions that do not take place because of the tax.

Figure 6-15 is a version of the same picture, leaving out the shaded rectangles—which represent money shifted from consumers and producers to the government—and showing only the deadweight loss, this time as a triangle shaded yellow. The base of that triangle is the tax wedge, $T$; the height of the triangle is the reduction the tax causes in the quantity sold, $Q_E - Q_T$. Notice that if the excise tax *didn't* reduce the quantity bought and sold in this market—if $Q_T$ weren't less than $Q_E$—the deadweight loss represented by the yellow triangle would disappear. An excise tax generates a deadweight loss to society because it discourages mutually beneficial transactions between buyers and sellers.

The idea that deadweight loss can be measured by the area of a triangle recurs in many economic applications. Deadweight-loss triangles are produced not only by excise taxes but also by other types of taxation. They are also produced by other kinds of distortions of markets, such as monopoly. And triangles are often used to evaluate other public policies besides taxation—for example, decisions about whether to build new highways.

The general rule for economic policy is that other things equal, you want to choose the policy that produces the smallest deadweight loss. This principle gives valuable guidance on everything from the design of the tax system to environmental policy. But how can we predict the size of the deadweight loss associated with a given policy? For the answer to that question, we return to a familiar concept: elasticity.

## Deadweight Loss and Elasticities

The deadweight loss from an excise tax arises because it prevents some mutually beneficial transactions from occurring. In particular, the producer and consumer surplus that is forgone from these missing transactions is equal to the size of the deadweight loss itself. This means that the larger the number of transactions that are impeded by the tax, the larger the deadweight loss.

This gives us an important clue in understanding the relationship between elasticity and the size of the deadweight loss from a tax. Recall that when demand or supply is elastic, it means that the quantity demanded or the quantity supplied is relatively responsive to price. So a tax imposed on a good for which either demand or supply, or both, is elastic will cause a relatively large decrease in the quantity bought and sold and a large deadweight loss. And when we say that demand or supply is inelastic, we mean that the quantity demanded or the quantity supplied is relatively unresponsive to price. As a result, a tax imposed when demand or supply, or both, is inelastic will cause a relatively small decrease in the quantity bought and sold and a small deadweight loss.

The four panels of Figure 6-16 illustrate the positive relationship between price elasticity of either demand or supply and the deadweight loss of taxation. In each panel, the size of the deadweight loss is given by the area of the shaded triangle. In panel (a), the deadweight-loss triangle is large because demand is relatively elastic—a large num-

### Figure 6-16 Deadweight Loss and Elasticities

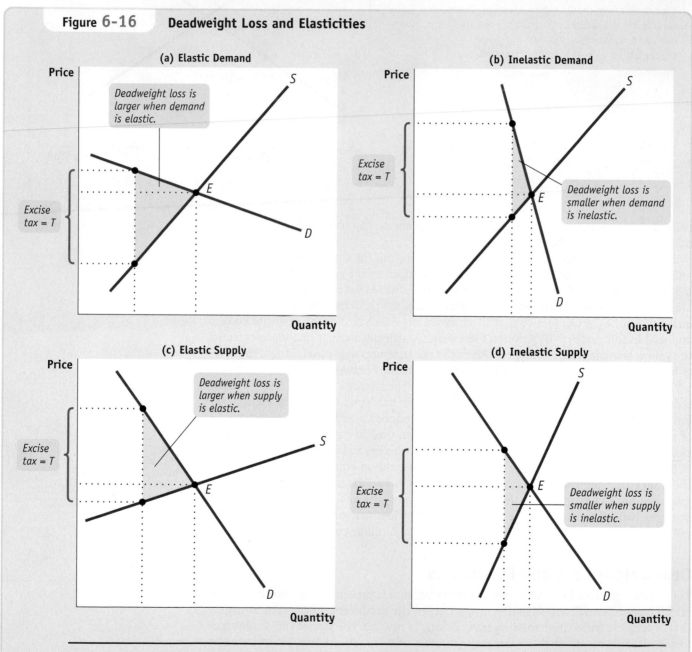

Demand is elastic in panel (a) and inelastic in panel (b), but the supply curves are the same. Supply is elastic in panel (c) and inelastic in panel (d), but the demand curves are the same. The deadweight losses are larger in panels (a) and (c) than in panels (b) and (d) because the greater the elasticity of demand or supply, the greater the tax-induced fall in the quantity bought and sold. In contrast, when demand or supply is inelastic, the smaller the tax-induced fall in the quantity bought and sold, and the smaller the deadweight loss.

ber of transactions fail to occur because of the tax. In panel (b), the same supply curve is drawn as in panel (a), but demand is now relatively inelastic; as a result, the triangle is small because only a small number of transactions are forgone. Likewise, panels (c) and (d) contain the same demand curve but different supply curves. In panel (c), an elastic supply curve gives rise to a large deadweight-loss triangle, but in panel (d) an inelastic supply curve gives rise to a small deadweight-loss triangle.

As Economics in Action on page 156 illustrates, the implication of this result is clear: if you want to lessen the efficiency costs of taxation, you should devise taxes to fall on goods for which either demand or supply, or both, is relatively inelastic. And this lesson carries a flip-side: using a tax to purposely decrease the amount of a harmful activity, such as underage drinking, will have the most impact when that activity is elastically demanded or supplied. In the extreme case in which demand is perfectly inelastic (a vertical demand curve), the quantity demanded is unchanged by the imposition of the tax. As a result, the tax imposes no deadweight loss. Similarly, if supply is perfectly inelastic (a vertical supply curve), the quantity supplied is unchanged by the tax and there is also no deadweight loss.

## WORK IT OUT

### CALCULATING DEADWEIGHT LOSS

Consider the market shown below. The original equilibrium is at a price $P_E$ of $6 with a quantity bought and sold $Q_E$ of 4,000 units.

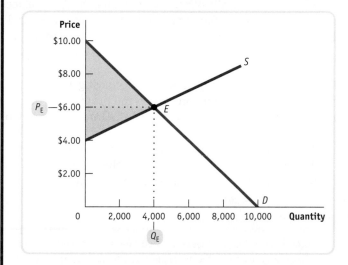

**Total Surplus:** What is the total surplus in the market at the original equilibrium? (*Total surplus: The sum of consumer surplus and producer surplus. Consumer surplus: The excess of willingness to pay over price actually paid. Producer surplus: The excess of price received over lowest price willing to accept.*)

To answer this question, we first need to calculate the consumer and producer surpluses. The consumer surplus is the area below the demand curve and above the price. It is the area of the blue triangle in the figure above. The area of a triangle is ½ × base × height. So the consumer surplus is ½ × 4,000 × $4 = $8,000.

The producer surplus is the area above the supply curve and below the price. It is the area of the red triangle in the figure above. The producer surplus is ½ × 4,000 × $2 = $4,000.

**SOLUTION:** Total surplus is $12,000, the sum of the consumer surplus of $8,000 and the producer surplus of $4,000.

**Deadweight Loss:** The government is considering imposing a $3 excise tax, which would increase the price paid by consumers to $8 and decrease the quantity bought and sold to 2,000 units. What is the deadweight loss imposed by the tax? (*Deadweight loss: The decline in total surplus, less any tax revenue.*)

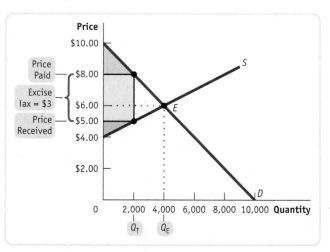

The deadweight loss is the surplus that is lost to society. In calculating deadweight loss, it does not matter how the surplus is shifted between consumers, producers, and the government. It is the area of the yellow triangle in the figure above.

To calculate the deadweight loss, we can calculate the area of the yellow triangle. The area of the yellow triangle is ½ × base × height, or ½ × 2,000 × $3 = $3,000.

Or, we can subtract the sum of the new consumer surplus, the new producer surplus, and the tax revenue received by the government from the original total surplus. The new consumer surplus is the area of the blue

continued

triangle: ½ × 2,000 × $2 = $2,000. The new producer surplus is the area of the red triangle: ½ × 2,000 × $1 = $1,000. The tax revenue is the area of the green rectangle: 2,000 × $3 = $6,000. The deadweight loss is computed by subtracting the sum of these three items

($2,000 + $1,000 + $6,000 = $9,000) from the original total surplus: $12,000 − $9,000 = $3,000.

**SOLUTION:** The deadweight loss to society as a result of the excise tax is $3,000.

# *economics in action*

## Missing the Boats

Because of deadweight losses, the costs of a tax to consumers and producers can sometimes be much larger than the actual value of taxes paid. In fact, if demand or supply, or both, is sufficiently elastic, a tax can inflict considerable losses even though it raises hardly any revenue.

A case in point was the infamous "yacht tax" of 1990, a special sales tax imposed by the U.S. government on yachts whose price exceeded $100,000. The purpose was to raise taxes on the wealthy, the only people who could afford such boats. But the tax generated much less revenue than expected, only $7 million. The reason for the low yield was that sales of $100,000-plus yachts in the United States fell sharply, by 71 percent. The number of jobs in the yacht industry, in both manufacturing and sales, also fell, by about 25 percent.

What happened? Basically, potential yacht buyers changed their behavior to avoid the tax. Some decided not to buy yachts at all; others bought their boats in places where the sales tax did not apply, such as the Bahamas; and still others scaled back, buying boats costing less than $100,000 and thereby avoiding the tax. In other words, the demand for yachts was very elastic. And the size of the job losses in the industry indicates that supply was relatively elastic as well.

Despite the fact that few potential yacht buyers ended up paying the tax, you would not want to say that it imposed no costs on consumers and producers. For consumers, avoiding the tax had its own costs, such as the expense and inconvenience of buying a boat overseas or the loss in satisfaction from buying a $99,000 boat when you really wanted something fancier. Moreover, the sales force and boat builders suffered a loss in producer surplus. Policy makers eventually concluded that pain had been inflicted for little gain in tax revenue, and the tax was repealed in 1993. ■

< < < < < < < < < < < < < < < < < < < <

**>>CHECK YOUR UNDERSTANDING 6-4**

1. Suppose that an excise tax of $0.40 is imposed on cheese-stuffed jalapeno peppers, raising the price paid by consumers to $0.70 and lowering the price received by producers to $0.30. Compared to the market equilibrium without the tax from Check Your Understanding 6-3, calculate the following:
   a. The loss in consumer surplus and who loses consumer surplus
   b. The loss in producer surplus and who loses producer surplus
   c. The government revenue from this tax
   d. The deadweight loss of the tax

2. In each of the following cases, focus on the elasticity of demand and use a diagram to illustrate the likely size—small or large—of the deadweight loss resulting from a tax. Explain your reasoning.
   a. Gasoline
   b. Milk chocolate bars

Solutions appear at back of book.

## • A LOOK AHEAD •

We have now completed our tour of the supply and demand model. But now we need to know something more about the decisions that producers must make. In the next two chapters we will see how profit-maximizing producers determine how much output to produce.

## SUMMARY

1. The **willingness to pay** of each individual consumer determines the demand curve. When price is less than or equal to the willingness to pay, the potential consumer purchases the good. The difference between price and willingness to pay is the net gain to the consumer, the **individual consumer surplus.**

2. The **total consumer surplus** in a market, the sum of all individual consumer surpluses in a market, is equal to the area below the demand curve but above the price. A rise in the price of a good reduces consumer surplus; a fall in the price increases consumer surplus. The term **consumer surplus** is often used to refer both to individual and to total consumer surplus.

3. The **cost** of each potential producer, the lowest price at which he or she is willing to supply a unit of that good, determines the supply curve. If the price of a good is above a producer's cost, a sale generates a net gain to the producer, known as the **individual producer surplus.**

4. The **total producer surplus,** the sum of the individual producer surpluses, is equal to the area above the supply curve but below the price. A rise in the price of a good increases producer surplus; a fall in the price reduces producer surplus. The term **producer surplus** is often used to refer both to the individual and to the total producer surplus.

5. **Total surplus,** the total gain to society from the production and consumption of a good, is the sum of consumer and producer surplus.

6. Usually, markets are efficient and achieve the maximum total surplus. Any possible rearrangement of consumption or sales, or change in the quantity bought and sold, reduces total surplus.

7. Economic policies can be evaluated by their effect on total surplus. For example, an excise tax generates revenue for the government but lowers total surplus. The loss in total surplus exceeds the tax revenue, resulting in an **excess burden** or **deadweight loss** to society. The value of this deadweight loss is shown by the triangle that represents the value of the transactions discouraged by the tax. The greater the elasticity of demand or supply, or both, the larger the deadweight loss of a tax.

## KEY TERMS

Willingness to pay, p. 136
Individual consumer surplus, p. 138
Total consumer surplus, p. 138
Consumer surplus, p. 138

Cost, p. 143
Individual producer surplus, p. 143
Total producer surplus, p. 144
Producer surplus, p. 144

Total surplus, p. 147
Excess burden, p. 151
Deadweight loss, p. 151

## PROBLEMS

1. Determine the amount of consumer surplus generated in each of the following situations.

   a. Paul goes to the clothing store to buy a new T-shirt, for which he is willing to pay up to $10. He picks out one he likes with a price tag of exactly $10. At the cash register, he is told that his T-shirt is on sale for half the posted price.

   b. Robin goes to the CD store hoping to find a used copy of the *Eagles Greatest Hits* for up to $10. The store has one copy selling for $10.

   c. After soccer practice, Phil is willing to pay $2 for a bottle of mineral water. The 7-Eleven sells mineral water for $2.25 per bottle.

2. Determine the amount of producer surplus generated in each of the following situations.

   a. Bob lists his old Lionel electric trains on eBay. He sets a minimum acceptable price, known as his *reserve price*, of $75. After five days of bidding, the final high bid is exactly $75.

   b. Jenny advertises her car for sale in the used-car section of the student newspaper for $2,000, but she is willing to sell the car for any price higher than $1,500. The best offer she gets is $1,200.

   c. Sanjay likes his job so much that he would be willing to do it for free. However, his annual salary is $80,000.

3. Hollywood writers negotiate a new agreement with movie producers that they will receive 10 percent of the revenue from every video rental of a movie they worked on. They have no such agreement for movies shown on pay-per-view television.

   a. When the new writers' agreement comes into effect, what will happen in the market for video rentals—that is, will supply or demand shift, and how? As a result, how will consumer surplus in the market for video rentals change? Illustrate with a diagram. Do you think the writers' agreement will be popular with consumers who rent videos?

   b. Consumers consider video rentals and pay-per-view movies substitutable to some extent. When the new writers' agreement comes into effect, what will happen in the market for pay-per-view movies—that is, will supply or demand shift, and how? As a result, how will producer surplus in the market for pay-per-view movies change? Illustrate with a diagram. Do you think the writers' agreement will be popular with cable television companies that show pay-per-view movies?

**4.** There are six potential consumers of computer games, each willing to buy only one game. Consumer 1 is willing to pay $40 for a computer game, consumer 2 is willing to pay $35, consumer 3 is willing to pay $30, consumer 4 is willing pay $25, consumer 5 is willing to pay $20, and consumer 6 is willing to pay $15.

**a.** Suppose the market price is $29. What is the total consumer surplus?

**b.** Now the market price decreases to $19. What is the total consumer surplus now?

**c.** When the price fell from $29 to $19, how much did each consumer's individual consumer surplus change?

**5.** In an effort to provide more affordable rental housing for low-income families, the city council of Collegetown decides to impose a rent ceiling well below the current market equilibrium rent.

**a.** Illustrate the effect of this policy in a diagram. Indicate consumer and producer surplus before and after the introduction of the rent ceiling.

**b.** Will this policy be popular with renters? With landlords?

**c.** An economist explains to the city council that this policy is creating a deadweight loss. Illustrate the deadweight loss in your diagram.

**6.** On Thursday nights, a local restaurant has a pasta special. Ari likes the restaurant's pasta, and his willingness to pay for each serving is shown in the accompanying table.

| Quantity of pasta (servings) | Willingness to pay for pasta (per serving) |
|---|---|
| 1 | $10 |
| 2 | 8 |
| 3 | 6 |
| 4 | 4 |
| 5 | 2 |
| 6 | 0 |

**a.** If the price of a serving of pasta is $4, how many servings will Ari buy? How much consumer surplus does he receive?

**b.** The following week, Ari is back at the restaurant again, but now the price of a serving of pasta is $6. By how much does his consumer surplus decrease compared to the previous week?

**c.** One week later, he goes to the restaurant again. He discovers that the restaurant is offering an "all you can eat" special for $25. How much pasta will Ari eat, and how much consumer surplus does he receive now?

**d.** Suppose you own the restaurant and Ari is a "typical" customer. What is the highest price you can charge for the "all you can eat" special and still attract customers?

**7.** The accompanying diagram shows the market for cigarettes. The current equilibrium price per pack is $4, and every day 40 million packs of cigarettes are sold. In order to recover some of the health care costs associated with smoking, the government imposes a tax of $2 per pack. This will raise the equilibrium price to $5 per pack and reduce the equilibrium quantity to 30 million packs.

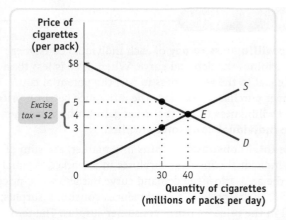

The economist working for the tobacco lobby claims that this tax will reduce consumer surplus for smokers by $40 million per day, since 40 million packs now cost $1 more per pack. The economist working for the lobby for sufferers of second-hand smoke argues that this is an enormous overestimate and that the reduction in consumer surplus will be only $30 million per day, since after the imposition of the tax only 30 million packs of cigarettes will be bought and each of these packs will now cost $1 more. They are both wrong. Why?

**8.** Consider the original market for pizza in Collegetown, illustrated in the accompanying table. Collegetown officials decide to impose an excise tax on pizza of $4 per pizza.

| Price of pizza | Quantity of pizza demanded | Quantity of pizza supplied |
|---|---|---|
| $10 | 0 | 6 |
| 9 | 1 | 5 |
| 8 | 2 | 4 |
| 7 | 3 | 3 |
| 6 | 4 | 2 |
| 5 | 5 | 1 |
| 4 | 6 | 0 |
| 3 | 7 | 0 |
| 2 | 8 | 0 |
| 1 | 9 | 0 |

**a.** What is the quantity of pizza bought and sold after the imposition of the tax? What is the price paid by consumers? What is the price received by producers?

**b.** Calculate the consumer surplus and the producer surplus after the imposition of the tax. By how much has the imposition of the tax reduced consumer surplus? By how much has it reduced producer surplus?

**c.** How much tax revenue does Collegetown earn from this tax?

**d.** Calculate the deadweight loss from this tax.

**9.** Consider once more the original market for pizza in Collegetown, illustrated in the table in Problem 8. Now Collegetown officials impose a price floor on pizza of $8.

**a.** What is the quantity of pizza bought and sold after the imposition of the price floor?

**b.** Calculate the consumer surplus and the producer surplus after the imposition of the price floor.

**10.** You are the manager of Fun World, a small amusement park. The accompanying diagram shows the demand curve of a typical customer at Fun World.

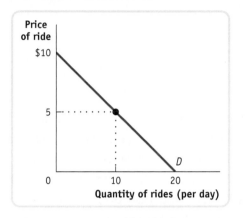

**a.** Suppose that the price of each ride is $5. At that price, how much consumer surplus does an individual consumer get? (Recall that the area of a triangle is ½ × the base of the triangle × the height of the triangle.)

**b.** Suppose that Fun World considers charging an admission fee, even though it maintains the price of each ride at $5. What is the maximum admission fee it could charge? (Assume that all potential customers have enough money to pay the fee.)

**c.** Suppose that Fun World lowered the price of each ride to zero. How much consumer surplus does an individual consumer get? What is the maximum admission fee Fun World could therefore charge?

**11.** The accompanying diagram illustrates a taxi driver's individual supply curve (assume that each taxi ride is the same distance).

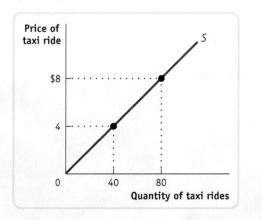

**a.** Suppose the city sets the price of taxi rides at $4 per ride. What is this taxi driver's producer surplus? (Recall that the area of a triangle is ½ × the base of the triangle × the height of the triangle.)

**b.** Suppose now that the city keeps the price of a taxi ride set at $4, but it decides to charge taxi drivers a "licensing fee." What is the maximum licensing fee the city could extract from this taxi driver?

**c.** Suppose that the city allowed the price of taxi rides to increase to $8 per ride. How much producer surplus does an individual taxi driver now get? What is the maximum licensing fee the city could charge this taxi driver?

**12.** The state needs to raise money, and the governor has a choice of imposing an excise tax of the same amount on one of two previously untaxed goods: the state can tax either sales of restaurant meals or sales of gasoline. Both the demand for and the supply of restaurant meals are more elastic than the demand for and the supply of gasoline. If the governor wants to minimize the deadweight loss caused by the tax, which good should be taxed? For each good, draw a diagram that illustrates the deadweight loss from taxation.

**13.** In each of the following cases involving taxes, explain: (i) whether the incidence of the tax falls more heavily on consumers or producers, (ii) why government revenue raised from the tax is not a good indicator of the true cost of the tax, and (iii) what missed opportunity, or inefficiency, arises.

**a.** The government imposes an excise tax on the sale of all college textbooks. Before the tax was imposed, 1 million textbooks were sold every year at a price of $50. After the tax is imposed, 600,000 books are sold yearly; students pay $55 per book, $30 of which publishers receive.

**b.** The government imposes an excise tax on the sale of all airplane tickets. Before the tax was imposed, 3 million airline tickets were sold every year at a price of $500. After the tax is imposed, 1.5 million tickets are sold yearly; travelers pay $550 per ticket, $450 of which the airlines receive.

**c.** The government imposes an excise tax on the sale of all toothbrushes. Before the tax, 2 million toothbrushes were sold every year at a price of $1.50. After the tax is imposed, 800,000 toothbrushes are sold every year; consumers pay $2 per toothbrush, $1.25 of which producers receive.

---

**>web...** To continue your study and review of concepts in this chapter, please visit the Krugman/Wells/Olney website for quizzes, animated graph tutorials, web links to helpful resources, and more.

**www.worthpublishers.com/krugmanwellsolney**

# >>Behind the Supply Curve: Inputs and Costs

## What you will learn in this chapter:

➤ The importance of the firm's **production function,** the relationship between quantity of inputs and quantity of output

➤ Why production is often subject to **diminishing returns to inputs**

➤ What the various forms of a firm's costs are and how they generate the firm's **marginal** and **average cost curves**

➤ Why a firm's costs may differ in the **short run** versus the **long run**

➤ How the firm's technology of production can generate **economies of scale**

## THE FARMER'S MARGIN

O BEAUTIFUL FOR SPACIOUS SKIES, FOR amber waves of grain." So begins the song "America the Beautiful." And those amber waves of grain are for real: though farmers are now only a small minority of America's population, our agricultural industry is immensely productive and feeds much of the world.

If you look at agricultural statistics, however, something may seem a bit surprising: when it comes to yield per acre, U.S. farmers are often nowhere near the top. For example, farmers in western European countries grow about three times as much wheat per acre as their U.S. counterparts. Are the Europeans better at growing wheat than we are?

No: European farmers are very skillful, but no more so than Americans. They pro-duce more wheat per acre because they employ more inputs—more fertilizer and, especially, more labor—per acre. Of course, this means that European farmers have higher costs than their American counterparts. But because of government policies, European farmers receive a much higher price for their wheat than American farmers. This gives them an incentive to use more inputs and to expend more effort at the margin to increase the crop yield per acre.

Notice our use of the phrase "at the margin." Like most decisions that involve a comparison of benefits and costs, decisions about inputs and production involve a comparison of marginal (or, additional) quantities—the marginal cost versus the marginal benefit of producing a bit more from each acre.

American farming practices (at left) or European farming practices (at right)? How intensively an acre of land is worked—a decision at the margin—depends on the price of wheat a farmer faces.

In this chapter and in Chapter 8, we will show how marginal analysis can be used to understand the output decisions that lie behind the supply curve. The first step in this analysis is to show how the relationship between a firm's inputs and its output—its *production function*—determines its *cost curves*, the relationship between cost and quantity of output produced. In Chapter 8, we will see how to go from the firm's cost curves to the supply curve.

# The Production Function

A *firm* is an organization that produces goods or services for sale. To do this, it must transform inputs into output. The quantity of output a firm produces depends on the quantity of inputs; this relationship is known as the firm's **production function.** As we'll see, a firm's production function underlies its *cost curves*. But as a first step, let's look at the characteristics of a hypothetical production function.

> A **production function** is the relationship between the quantity of inputs a firm uses and the quantity of output it produces.

## Inputs and Output

To understand the concept of a production function, let's consider a farm that we assume, for the sake of simplicity, produces only one output, wheat, and uses only two inputs, land and labor. This particular farm is owned by a couple named George and Martha. They hire workers to do the actual physical labor on the farm. Moreover, we will assume that all potential workers are of the same quality—they are all equally knowledgeable and capable of performing farmwork.

George and Martha's farm sits on 10 acres of land; no more acres are available to them, and they are currently unable to either increase or decrease the size of their farm by selling, buying, or leasing acreage. Land here is what economists call a **fixed input**—an input whose quantity is fixed and cannot be varied. On the other hand, George and Martha are free to decide how many workers to hire. The labor provided by these workers is called a **variable input**—an input whose quantity the firm can vary.

> A **fixed input** is an input whose quantity is fixed and cannot be varied.
>
> A **variable input** is an input whose quantity the firm can vary.

In reality, whether or not the quantity of an input is really fixed depends on the time horizon. In the **long run**—that is, given that a long enough period of time has elapsed—firms can adjust the quantity of any input. So there are no fixed inputs in the long run, only in the **short run.** Later in this chapter we'll look more carefully at the distinction between the short run and the long run. But for now, we will restrict our attention to the short run and assume that at least one input is fixed.

> The **long run** is the time period in which all inputs can be varied.
>
> The **short run** is the time period in which at least one input is fixed.

George and Martha know that the quantity of wheat they produce depends on the number of workers they hire. Given modern farming techniques, one worker can cultivate the 10-acre farm, albeit not very intensively. When an additional worker is added, the land is divided equally among all the workers: each worker has 5 acres to cultivate when 2 workers are employed, each cultivates 3⅓ acres when 3 are employed, and so on. So as additional workers are employed, the 10 acres of land are cultivated more intensively and more bushels of wheat are produced. The relationship between the quantity of labor and the quantity of output, for a given amount of the fixed input, constitutes the farm's production function. The production function for George and Martha's farm is given in the first two columns of the table in Figure 7-1 on page 162; the diagram there shows the same information graphically. The curve in Figure 7-1 shows how the quantity of output depends on the quantity of the variable input, for a given quantity of the fixed input; it is called the farm's **total product curve.** The physical quantity of output, bushels of wheat, is measured on the vertical axis, while the quantity of the variable input, labor, that is, the number of workers

> The **total product curve** shows how the quantity of output depends on the quantity of the variable input, for a given quantity of the fixed input.

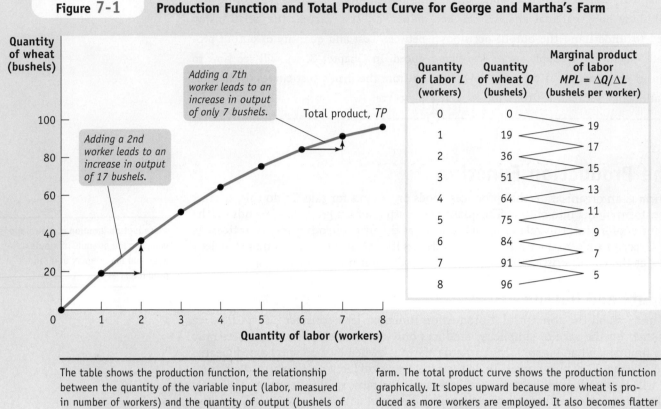

**Figure 7-1    Production Function and Total Product Curve for George and Martha's Farm**

| Quantity of labor L (workers) | Quantity of wheat Q (bushels) | Marginal product of labor MPL = ΔQ/ΔL (bushels per worker) |
|---|---|---|
| 0 | 0 | |
| | | 19 |
| 1 | 19 | |
| | | 17 |
| 2 | 36 | |
| | | 15 |
| 3 | 51 | |
| | | 13 |
| 4 | 64 | |
| | | 11 |
| 5 | 75 | |
| | | 9 |
| 6 | 84 | |
| | | 7 |
| 7 | 91 | |
| | | 5 |
| 8 | 96 | |

The table shows the production function, the relationship between the quantity of the variable input (labor, measured in number of workers) and the quantity of output (bushels of wheat) for a given quantity of the fixed input. It also calculates the marginal product of labor on George and Martha's farm. The total product curve shows the production function graphically. It slopes upward because more wheat is produced as more workers are employed. It also becomes flatter because the marginal product of labor declines as more and more workers are employed.

The **marginal product** of an input is the additional quantity of output that is produced by using one more unit of that input.

employed, is measured on the horizontal axis. The total product curve here is upward sloping, reflecting the fact that more bushels of wheat are produced as more workers are employed.

Although the total product curve in Figure 7-1 slopes upward along its entire length, the slope isn't constant: as you move up the curve to the right, it flattens out. To understand this changing slope, look at the third column of the table in Figure 7-1, which shows the *change in the quantity of output* that is generated by adding one more worker. That is, it shows the **marginal product** of labor: the additional quantity of output from using one more unit of labor (that is, one more worker).

In this case, we have data at intervals of 1 worker—that is, we have information on the quantity of output when there are 3 workers, 4 workers, and so on. Sometimes data aren't available in increments of 1 unit—for example, you might have information only on the quantity of output when there are 40 workers and when there are 50 workers. In this case, you can use the following equation to figure out the marginal product of labor:

$$(7\text{-}1) \quad \begin{array}{c} \text{Marginal} \\ \text{product} \\ \text{of labor} \end{array} = \frac{\text{Change in quantity of output}}{\text{Change in quantity of labor}} = \begin{array}{c} \text{Change in quantity of} \\ \text{output generated by one} \\ \text{additional unit of labor} \end{array}$$

or

$$MPL = \Delta Q/\Delta L$$

In this equation, Δ, the Greek uppercase delta, represents the change in a variable.

Now we can explain the significance of the slope of the total product curve: it is equal to the marginal product of labor. Remember from the Chapter 2 Appendix that the slope of a line is equal to "rise" over "run" (see page 44). This implies that the slope of the total product curve is the change in the quantity of output (the "rise") divided by the change in the quantity of labor (the "run"). And this, as we can see from Equation 7-1, is simply the marginal product of labor. So the fact that the marginal product of the first worker is 19 also means that the slope of the total product curve in going from 0 to 1 worker is 19. Similarly, the slope of the total product curve in going from 1 to 2 workers is the same as the marginal product of the second worker, 17, and so on.

In this example, the marginal product of labor steadily declines as more workers are hired—that is, each successive worker adds less to output than the previous worker. So as employment increases, the total product curve gets flatter.

Figure 7-2 shows how the marginal product of labor depends on the number of workers employed on the farm. The marginal product of labor, *MPL*, is measured on the vertical axis in units of physical output—bushels of wheat—produced per additional worker, and the number of workers employed is measured on the horizontal axis. You can see from the table in Figure 7-1 that if 5 workers are employed instead of 4, output rises from 64 to 75 bushels; so in this case the marginal product of labor is 11 bushels—the same number found in Figure 7-2. To indicate that 11 bushels is the marginal product when employment rises from 4 to 5, we place the point corresponding to that information halfway between 4 and 5 workers.

In this example the marginal product of labor falls as the number of workers increases. That is, there are *diminishing returns to labor* on George and Martha's farm. In general, there are **diminishing returns to an input** when an increase in the quantity of that input, holding the quantity of all other inputs fixed, reduces that input's marginal product.

To grasp why diminishing returns can occur, think about what happens as George and Martha add more and more workers, without increasing the number of acres. As the number of workers increases, the land is farmed more intensively and the number of bushels increases. But each additional worker is working with a smaller share of the 10 acres—the fixed input—than the previous worker. As a result, the additional

> There are **diminishing returns to an input** when an increase in the quantity of that input, holding the levels of all other inputs fixed, leads to a decline in the marginal product of that input.

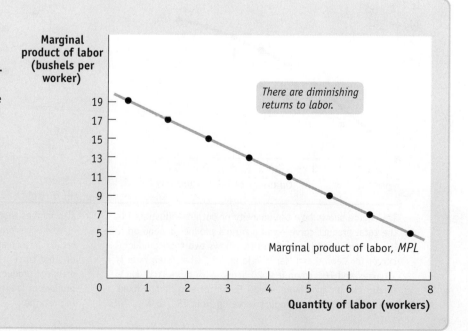

### Figure 7-2

**Marginal Product of Labor Curve for George and Martha's Farm**

The marginal product of labor curve plots each worker's marginal product, the increase in the quantity of output generated by each additional worker. The change in the quantity of output is measured on the vertical axis and the number of workers employed on the horizontal axis. The first worker employed generates an increase in output of 19 bushels, the second worker generates an increase of 17 bushels, and so on. The curve slopes downward due to diminishing returns. **>web...**

*There are diminishing returns to labor.*

Marginal product of labor, *MPL*

### WHAT'S A UNIT?

The marginal product of labor (or any other input) is defined as the increase in the quantity of output when you increase the quantity of that input by one unit. But what do we mean by a "unit" of labor? Is it an additional hour of labor, an additional week, or a person-year?

The answer is that it doesn't matter, *as long as you are consistent*. One common source of error in economics is getting units confused— say, comparing the output added by an additional *hour* of labor with the cost of employing a worker for a *week*. Whatever units you use, always be careful that you use the same units throughout your analysis of any problem.

worker cannot produce as much output as the previous worker. So it's not surprising that the marginal product of the additional worker falls.

The crucial thing to emphasize about diminishing returns is that, like many propositions in economics, it is an "other things equal" proposition: each successive unit of an input will raise production by less than the last *if the quantity of all other inputs is held fixed*.

What would happen if the levels of other inputs were allowed to change? You can see the answer in Figure 7-3. Panel (a) shows two total product curves, $TP_{10}$ and $TP_{20}$. $TP_{10}$ is the farm's total product curve when its total area is 10 acres (the same curve as in Figure 7-1). $TP_{20}$ is the total product curve when the farm has increased to 20 acres. Except when 0 workers are employed, $TP_{20}$ lies everywhere above $TP_{10}$ because with more acres available, any given number of workers produces more output. Panel (b) shows the corresponding marginal product of labor curves. $MPL_{10}$ is the marginal product of labor curve given 10 acres to cultivate (the same curve as in Figure 7-2) and $MPL_{20}$ is the marginal product of labor curve given 20 acres. Both curves slope downward because, in each case, the amount of land is fixed, albeit at different levels. But $MPL_{20}$ lies everywhere above $MPL_{10}$, reflecting the fact that the marginal product of the same worker is higher when he or she has more of the fixed input to work with.

Figure 7-3 demonstrates a general result: the position of the total product curve depends on the quantities of other inputs. If you change the quantity of the other inputs, both the total product curve and the marginal product curve of the remaining input will shift. The importance of the "other things equal" assumption in discussing diminishing returns is illustrated in the following For Inquiring Minds.

### Figure 7-3 — Total Product, Marginal Product, and the Fixed Input

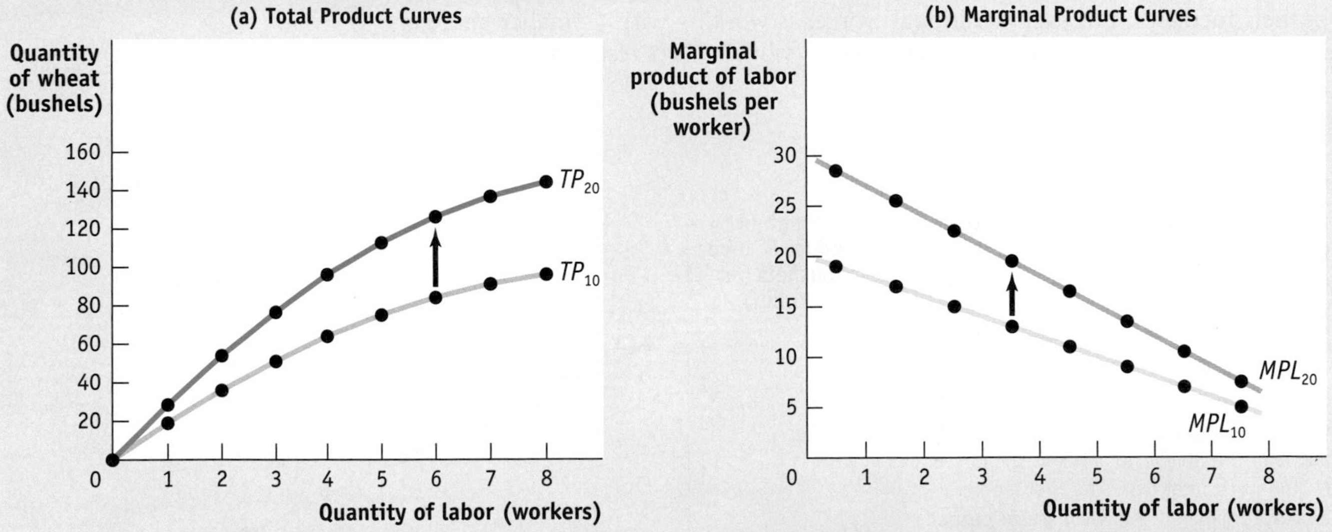

**(a) Total Product Curves**

**(b) Marginal Product Curves**

This figure shows how the quantity of output—illustrated by the total product curve—and marginal product depend on the level of the fixed input. Panel (a) shows two total product curves for George and Martha's farm, $TP_{10}$ when their farm is 10 acres and $TP_{20}$ when it is 20 acres. With more land, each worker can produce more wheat. So an increase in the fixed input shifts the total product curve up from $TP_{10}$ to $TP_{20}$. This also implies that the marginal product of each worker is higher when the farm is 20 acres than when it is 10 acres. As a result, an increase in acreage also shifts the marginal product of labor curve up from $MPL_{10}$ to $MPL_{20}$. Panel (b) shows the marginal product of labor curves. Note that both marginal product of labor curves still slope downward due to diminishing returns.

## WAS MALTHUS RIGHT?

The idea of diminishing returns first became influential with the writings of Thomas Malthus, an English pastor whose 1798 book *An Essay on the Principle of Population* was deeply influential in its own time and continues to provoke heated argument to this day.

Malthus argued that as its population grew (while its land area remained fixed), a country would find it increasingly difficult to grow enough food. Though more intensive cultivation of the land could increase yields, each successive farmer would add less to the total than the last as the marginal product of labor declined. Eventually, food production per capita (the average output of an existing worker) would decline as the population exceeded some level.

He drew a powerful conclusion from this argument—namely, that misery was the normal condition of humankind. Imagine a country in which land was abundant and population low, so that everyone had plenty

to eat. Then families would, he argued, be large (as they were at the time in the United States, where land was abundant), and the population would grow rapidly—until the pressure of population on the land had reduced the condition of most people to a level where starvation and disease held the population in check. (It was arguments like these that led the historian Thomas Carlyle to dub economics the "dismal science").

Happily, Malthus's prediction has turned out to be quite wrong. The world's population has increased from about 1 billion people when Malthus wrote to more than 6 billion today, but in most of the world people eat better now than ever before. In England, in particular, a fivefold increase in population was accompanied by a dramatic rise in the standard of living.

So was Malthus completely wrong? And does the wrongness of his prediction refute the whole idea of diminishing returns? No, on both counts.

First of all, the Malthusian story actually works pretty well as a description of 57 out of the last 59 centuries: peasants in eighteenth-century France probably did not live much better than Egyptian peasants in the age of the pyramids. It just so happens that scientific and technological progress since the eighteenth century has been so rapid that it has far outpaced any problems caused by diminishing returns.

The concept of diminishing returns does not mean that using more labor to grow food, even on a given amount of land, will lead to a decline in the marginal product of labor—*if* there is also a radical improvement in farming technology. It does mean that the marginal product declines when *all* other things—land, farming technology, and a host of other factors—remain the same. And so the happy fact that Malthus's predictions were wrong does not invalidate the concept of diminishing returns.

## From the Production Function to Cost Curves

Once George and Martha know their production function, they know the relationship between inputs of labor and land and output of wheat. How can they translate this knowledge into information about the relationship between the quantity of output and cost?

To translate information about a firm's production function into information about its cost, we need to know how much the firm must pay for its inputs. Any cost can be broken into two parts: the *explicit cost* and the *implicit cost*. An **explicit cost** is a cost that requires an outlay of money. For example, if George and Martha must rent the land for $400 from someone else, the explicit cost of the land would be $400. An **implicit cost,** on the other hand, does not involve an outlay of money; instead it is measured by the value, in dollar terms, of all the benefits that are forgone. For example, if George and Martha own the land themselves and forgo earning $400 by renting it to someone else, the implicit cost of the land would be $400. So whether George and Martha rent the land from someone else or own it themselves, they pay an opportunity cost of $400 by using the land to grow wheat.

Moreover, since the land is a fixed input, the $400 George and Martha pay for it is a **fixed cost,** denoted by *FC*—a cost that does not depend on the quantity of output produced. In business, fixed cost is often referred to as "overhead cost."

We also assume that George and Martha must pay each worker $200. Using their production function, George and Martha know that the number of workers they must hire depends on the amount of wheat they intend to produce. So the cost of labor, which is equal to the number of workers multiplied by $200, is a **variable cost,** denoted by *VC*—a cost that depends on the quantity of output produced. Adding the

An **explicit cost** is a cost that involves actually laying out money. An **implicit cost** does not require an outlay of money; it is measured by the value, in dollar terms, of the benefits that are forgone.

A **fixed cost** is a cost that does not depend on the quantity of output produced. It is the cost of the fixed input.

A **variable cost** is a cost that depends on the quantity of output produced. It is the cost of the variable input.

The **total cost** of producing a given quantity of output is the sum of the fixed cost and the variable cost of producing that quantity of output.

fixed cost and the variable cost of a given quantity of output gives the **total cost,** or *TC*, of that quantity of output. We can express the relationship among fixed cost, variable cost, and total cost as an equation:

**(7-2)** Total cost = Fixed cost + Variable cost

or

$$TC = FC + VC$$

The table in Figure 7-4 shows how total cost is calculated for George and Martha's farm. The second column shows the number of workers employed. The third column shows the corresponding level of output, taken from the table in Figure 7-1. The fourth column shows the variable cost, equal to the number of workers multiplied by $200. The fifth column shows the fixed cost, which is $400 regardless of how many workers are employed. The sixth column shows the total cost of output, which is the variable cost plus the fixed cost.

The first column labels each row of the table with a letter, from *A* to *I*. These labels will be helpful in understanding our next step: drawing the **total cost curve,** a curve that shows how total cost depends on the quantity of output.

The **total cost curve** shows how total cost depends on the quantity of output.

## Figure 7-4

### Total Cost Curve for George and Martha's Farm

The table shows the variable cost, fixed cost, and total cost for various output quantities on George and Martha's 10-acre farm. The total cost curve shows how total cost (measured on the vertical axis) depends on the quantity of output (measured on the horizontal axis). The labeled points on the curve correspond to the rows of the table. The total cost curve slopes upward because the number of workers employed, and hence total cost, increases as the quantity of output increases. The curve gets steeper as output increases due to diminishing returns to labor.

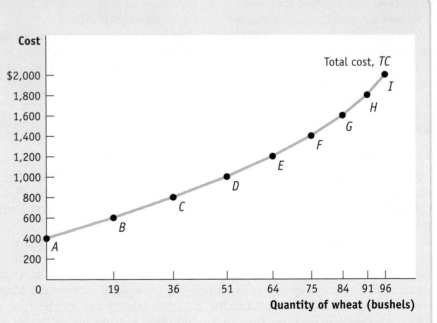

| Point on graph | Quantity of labor *L* (workers) | Quantity of wheat *Q* (bushels) | Variable cost *VC* | Fixed cost *FC* | Total cost *TC = FC + VC* |
|---|---|---|---|---|---|
| *A* | 0 | 0 | $0 | $400 | $400 |
| *B* | 1 | 19 | 200 | 400 | 600 |
| *C* | 2 | 36 | 400 | 400 | 800 |
| *D* | 3 | 51 | 600 | 400 | 1,000 |
| *E* | 4 | 64 | 800 | 400 | 1,200 |
| *F* | 5 | 75 | 1,000 | 400 | 1,400 |
| *G* | 6 | 84 | 1,200 | 400 | 1,600 |
| *H* | 7 | 91 | 1,400 | 400 | 1,800 |
| *I* | 8 | 96 | 1,600 | 400 | 2,000 |

George and Martha's total cost curve is shown in the diagram in Figure 7-4, where the horizontal axis measures the quantity of output in bushels of wheat and the vertical axis measures total cost in dollars. Each point on the curve corresponds to one row of the table in Figure 7-4. For example, point A shows the situation when 0 workers are employed: output is zero, and total cost is equal to fixed cost, $400. Similarly, point B shows the situation when 1 worker is employed: output is 19 bushels, and total cost is $600, equal to the sum of $400 in fixed cost and $200 in variable cost.

Like the total product curve, the total cost curve is upward sloping: due to the variable cost, the more output produced, the higher the farm's total cost. But unlike the total product curve, which gets flatter as employment rises, the total cost curve gets *steeper*. That is, the slope of the total cost curve is greater as the amount of output produced increases. And as we will soon see, the steepening of the total cost curve is also due to diminishing returns to the variable input. Before we can understand this, we must first look at the relationships among several useful measures of cost.

# *economics in action*

## The Mythical Man-Month

The concept of diminishing returns to an input was first formulated by economists during the late eighteenth century. These economists, notably including Thomas Malthus, drew their inspiration from agricultural examples; they noticed, in particular, that as an individual tried to employ more workers in agriculture, he or she was forced to cultivate poorer quality land. Although still valid, such examples can seem somewhat musty and old-fashioned in our modern information economy.

However, the idea of diminishing returns to an input applies with equal force to the most modern of economic activities—such as, say, the design of software. In 1975 Frederick P. Brooks, Jr., a project manager at IBM during the days when it dominated the computer business, published a book titled *The Mythical Man-Month* that soon became a classic—so much so that a special anniversary edition was published 20 years later.

The chapter that gave its title to the book is basically about diminishing returns in the writing of software. Brooks observed that multiplying the number of programmers assigned to a project did not produce a proportionate reduction in the time it took to get the program written. A project that could be done by 1 programmer in 12 months could *not* be done by 12 programmers in 1 month—hence the "mythical man-month," the false notion that the number of lines of programming code produced was proportional to the number of code writers employed. In fact, above a certain number, adding another programmer on a project actually *increased* the time to completion.

The argument of *The Mythical Man-Month* is summarized in Figure 7-5. The upper part of the figure shows how the quantity of the project's output, as measured by the number of lines of code produced per month, varies with the number of programmers. Each additional programmer accomplishes less than the previous one, and beyond a certain point an additional programmer is actually counterproductive. The lower part of the figure shows the marginal product of each successive programmer, which falls

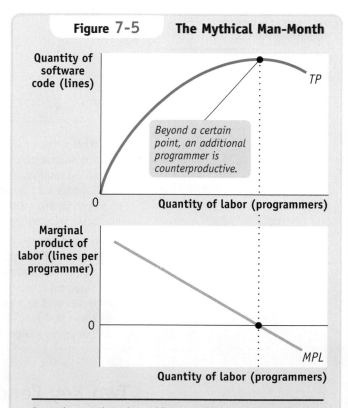

**Figure 7-5    The Mythical Man-Month**

Quantity of software code (lines)

*Beyond a certain point, an additional programmer is counterproductive.*

TP

0    Quantity of labor (programmers)

Marginal product of labor (lines per programmer)

0

MPL

Quantity of labor (programmers)

Beyond a certain point, adding an additional programmer is counterproductive—output falls and the slope of the total product curve becomes negative. At this point the marginal product of labor curve crosses the horizontal axis—and the marginal product of labor becomes negative.

as more programmers are employed and eventually becomes negative. In other words, programming is subject to diminishing returns so severe that at some point more programmers actually have negative marginal product. The source of the diminishing returns lies in the nature of the production function for a programming project: each programmer must coordinate his or her work with that of all the other programmers on the project, leading to each person spending more and more time communicating with others as the number of programmers increases. In other words, other things equal, there are diminishing returns to labor. It is likely, however, that if fixed inputs devoted to programming projects are increased—say, installing a faster e-mail system—the problem of diminishing returns for additional programmers can be mitigated.

A reviewer of the reissued edition of *The Mythical Man-Month* summarized the reasons for these diminishing returns: "There is an inescapable overhead to yoking up programmers in parallel. The members of the team must 'waste time' attending meetings, drafting project plans, exchanging e-mail, negotiating interfaces, enduring performance reviews, and so on . . . At Microsoft, there will be at least one team member that just designs T-shirts for the rest of the team to wear." (from www.ercb.com, Dr. Dobb's Electronic Review of Computer Books.) ∎

< < < < < < < < < < < < < < < < < < <

**>> CHECK YOUR UNDERSTANDING 7-1**

1. Bernie's ice-making company produces ice cubes using a 10-ton machine and electricity. The quantity of output, measured in terms of pounds of ice, is given in this table:

| Quantity of electricity (kilowatts) | Quantity of ice (pounds) |
|---|---|
| 0 | 0 |
| 1 | 1,000 |
| 2 | 1,800 |
| 3 | 2,400 |
| 4 | 2,800 |

a. What is the fixed input? What is the variable input?
b. Construct a table showing the marginal product of the variable input. Does it show diminishing returns?
c. Suppose a 50 percent increase in the size of the fixed input increases output by 100 percent for any given amount of the variable input. What is the fixed input now? Construct a table showing the quantity of output and marginal product in this case.

2. Karma and Don run a furniture-refinishing business from their home. Which of the following represent explicit costs of the business and which represent implicit costs?
a. Supplies such as paint stripper, varnish, polish, and sandpaper
b. Basement space that has been converted into a workroom
c. Wages paid to a part-time helper
d. A van that they inherited and use only for transporting furniture
e. The job at a larger furniture restorer that Karma gave up in order to run the business

Solutions appear at back of book.

# Two Key Concepts: Marginal Cost and Average Cost

We've just seen how to derive a firm's total cost curve from its production function. Our next step is to take a deeper look at total cost by deriving two extremely useful measures: *marginal cost* and *average cost*. As we'll see, these two measures of the cost of production have a somewhat surprising relationship to each other. Moreover, they will prove to be vitally important in Chapter 8, where we will use them to analyze the firm's output decision and the market supply curve.

## Marginal Cost

**Marginal cost** is the change in total cost generated by producing one more unit of output. We've already seen that marginal product is easiest to calculate if data on output are available in increments of one unit of input. Similarly, marginal cost is easiest to calculate if data on total cost are available in increments of one unit of output. When the data come in less convenient increments, it's still possible to calculate marginal cost over each interval. But for the sake of simplicity, let's work with an example in which the data come in convenient increments.

Ben's Boots produces leather footwear; Table 7-1 shows how its costs per day depend on the number of boots it produces per day. The firm has fixed cost of $108 per day, shown in the second column, which represents the daily cost of its boot-making machine. The third column shows the variable cost, and the fourth column shows the total cost. Panel (a) of Figure 7-6 on page 170 plots the total cost curve. Like the total cost curve for George and Martha's farm in Figure 7-4, this curve is upward sloping, getting steeper as you move up it to the right.

The significance of the slope of the total cost curve is shown by the fifth column of Table 7-1, which calculates *marginal cost*: the cost of each additional unit produced. The general formula for marginal cost is

> The **marginal cost** of an activity is the additional cost incurred by doing one more unit of that activity.

$$(7\text{-}3) \quad \text{Marginal cost} = \frac{\text{Change in total cost}}{\text{Change in quantity of output}} = \frac{\text{Change in total cost generated by one additional unit of output}}{}$$

or

$$MC = \Delta TC / \Delta Q$$

## TABLE 7-1

### Costs at Ben's Boots

| Quantity of boots Q (pairs) | Fixed cost FC | Variable cost VC | Total cost TC = FC + VC | Marginal cost of pair MC = $\Delta TC/\Delta Q$ |
|---|---|---|---|---|
| 0 | $108 | $0 | $108 | |
| | | | | $12 |
| 1 | 108 | 12 | 120 | |
| | | | | 36 |
| 2 | 108 | 48 | 156 | |
| | | | | 60 |
| 3 | 108 | 108 | 216 | |
| | | | | 84 |
| 4 | 108 | 192 | 300 | |
| | | | | 108 |
| 5 | 108 | 300 | 408 | |
| | | | | 132 |
| 6 | 108 | 432 | 540 | |
| | | | | 156 |
| 7 | 108 | 588 | 696 | |
| | | | | 180 |
| 8 | 108 | 768 | 876 | |
| | | | | 204 |
| 9 | 108 | 972 | 1,080 | |
| | | | | 228 |
| 10 | 108 | 1,200 | 1,308 | |

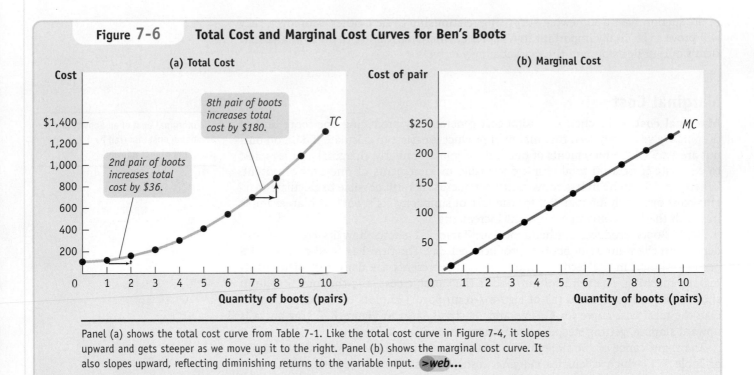

**Figure 7-6**   **Total Cost and Marginal Cost Curves for Ben's Boots**

**(a) Total Cost**

*8th pair of boots increases total cost by $180.*

*2nd pair of boots increases total cost by $36.*

**(b) Marginal Cost**

Panel (a) shows the total cost curve from Table 7-1. Like the total cost curve in Figure 7-4, it slopes upward and gets steeper as we move up it to the right. Panel (b) shows the marginal cost curve. It also slopes upward, reflecting diminishing returns to the variable input. **>web...**

---

### PITFALLS

#### INCREASING TOTAL COST VERSUS INCREASING MARGINAL COST

The concept of *increasing marginal cost* plays an important role in economic analysis, but students sometimes get confused about what it means. That's because it is easy to wrongly conclude that whenever total cost is increasing, marginal cost must also be increasing. But the following example shows that this conclusion is misguided.

Suppose that we change the numbers of our example: the marginal cost of producing the 6th pair of boots is now $130, and the marginal cost of producing the 7th pair is $100. In both instances total cost increases as Ben's Boots produces an additional pair of boots: it increases by $130 for the 6th pair and by $100 for the 7th pair. But in this example marginal cost is *decreasing*: the marginal cost of the 7th pair of boots is less than the marginal cost of the 6th pair. So we have a case of increasing total cost and decreasing marginal cost. What this shows us is that, in fact, totals and marginals can sometimes move in opposite directions.

There is **increasing marginal cost** from an activity when each additional unit of the activity costs more than the previous unit.

The **marginal cost curve** shows how the cost of undertaking one more unit of an activity depends on the quantity of that activity that has already been done.

Marginal cost is equal to "rise" (the increase in total cost) divided by "run" (the increase in the quantity of output). Just as marginal product is equal to the slope of the total product curve, marginal cost is equal to the slope of the total cost curve.

Now we can understand why the total cost curve gets steeper as we move up it to the right: as you can see in Table 7-1, Ben's Boots has what economists call **increasing marginal cost:** each additional pair of boots costs more to produce than the previous one. Or, to put it slightly differently, with increasing marginal cost, the marginal cost of an activity rises as the quantity already done rises.

Panel (b) of Figure 7-6 shows the **marginal cost curve** corresponding to the data in Table 7-1. Notice that, as in Figure 7-2, we plot the marginal cost for increasing output from 0 to 1 pair of boots halfway between 0 and 1, the marginal cost for increasing output from 1 to 2 pairs of boots halfway between 1 and 2, and so on.

Why is the marginal cost curve upward sloping? Because there are diminishing returns to inputs in this example. As output increases, the marginal product of the variable input declines. This implies that more and more of the variable input must be used to produce each additional unit of output as the amount of output already produced rises. And since each unit of the variable input must be paid for, the cost per additional unit of output also rises.

In addition, recall that the flattening of the total product curve is also due to diminishing returns to inputs in production: the marginal product of an input falls as more of that input is used if the quantities of other inputs are fixed. The flattening of the total product curve as output increases and the steepening of the total cost curve as output increases are just flip-sides of the same phenomenon. That is, as output increases, the marginal cost of output also increases because the marginal product of the variable input is falling.

We will return to marginal cost in Chapter 8, when we consider the firm's profit-maximizing output decision. But our next step is to introduce another measure of cost: *average cost*.

## Average Cost

In addition to total cost and marginal cost, it's useful to calculate one more measure, **average total cost,** often simply called **average cost.** The average total cost is total cost divided by the quantity of output produced; that is, it is equal to total cost per unit of output. If we let *ATC* denote average total cost, the equation looks like this:

$$\text{(7-4)} \quad ATC = \frac{\text{Total cost}}{\text{Quantity of output}} = TC/Q$$

Average total cost is important because it tells the producer how much the *average* or *typical* unit of output costs to produce. Marginal cost, meanwhile, tells the producer how much *one more* unit of output costs to produce. Although they may look very similar, these two measures of cost typically differ. And confusion between them is a major source of error in economics, both in the classroom and in real life, as illustrated by Economics in Action on page 176.

Table 7-2 uses the data from Ben's Boots to calculate average total cost. For example, the total cost of producing 4 pairs of boots is $300, consisting of $108 in fixed cost and $192 in variable cost (see Table 7-1). You can see from Table 7-2 that as quantity of output increases, average total cost first falls, then rises.

Figure 7-7 on page 172 plots that data to yield the *average total cost curve,* which shows how average total cost depends on output. As before, cost in dollars is measured on the vertical axis and quantity of output is measured on the horizontal axis. The average total cost curve has a distinctive U shape that corresponds to how average total cost first falls and then rises as output increases. Economists believe that such **U-shaped average total cost curves** are the norm for producers in many industries.

> **Average total cost,** often referred to simply as **average cost,** is total cost divided by quantity of output produced.

> A **U-shaped average total cost curve** falls at low levels of output, then rises at higher levels.

## TABLE 7-2

**Average Costs for Ben's Boots**

| Quantity of boots Q (pairs) | Fixed Cost FC | Variable Cost VC | Total cost TC = FC + VC | Average total cost of pair ATC = TC/Q | Average fixed cost of pair AFC = FC/Q | Average variable cost of pair AVC = VC/Q |
|---|---|---|---|---|---|---|
| 1 | $108 | $12 | $120 | $120.00 | $108.00 | $12.00 |
| 2 | 108 | 48 | 156 | 78.00 | 54.00 | 24.00 |
| 3 | 108 | 108 | 216 | 72.00 | 36.00 | 36.00 |
| 4 | 108 | 192 | 300 | 75.00 | 27.00 | 48.00 |
| 5 | 108 | 300 | 408 | 81.60 | 21.60 | 60.00 |
| 6 | 108 | 432 | 540 | 90.00 | 18.00 | 72.00 |
| 7 | 108 | 588 | 696 | 99.43 | 15.43 | 84.00 |
| 8 | 108 | 768 | 876 | 109.50 | 13.50 | 96.00 |
| 9 | 108 | 972 | 1,080 | 120.00 | 12.00 | 108.00 |
| 10 | 108 | 1,200 | 1,308 | 130.80 | 10.80 | 120.00 |

## Figure 7-7

### Average Total Cost Curve for Ben's Boots

The average total cost curve at Ben's Boots is U-shaped. At low levels of output, average total cost falls because the "spreading effect" of falling average fixed cost dominates the "diminishing returns effect" of rising average variable cost. At higher levels of output, the opposite is true and average total cost rises. At point *M*, corresponding to an output of three pairs of boots per day, average total cost is at its minimum level, the minimum average total cost. **>web...**

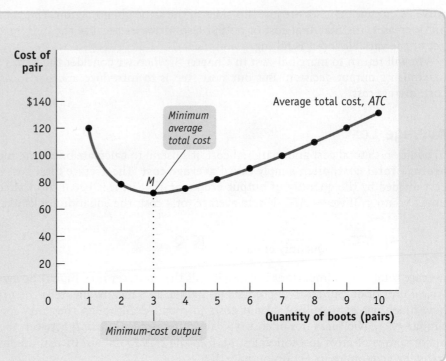

---

**Average fixed cost** is the fixed cost per unit of output.

**Average variable cost** is the variable cost per unit of output.

---

To help our understanding of why the average total cost curve is U-shaped, Table 7-2 breaks average total cost into its two underlying components, *average fixed cost* and *average variable cost*. **Average fixed cost,** or *AFC*, is fixed cost divided by the quantity of output, also known as the fixed cost per unit of output. For example, if Ben's Boots produces 4 pairs of boots, average fixed cost is $108/4 = $27 per pair of boots. **Average variable cost,** or *AVC*, is variable cost divided by the quantity of output, also known as variable cost per unit of output. At an output of 4 pairs of boots, average variable cost is $192/4 = $48 per pair. Writing these in the form of equations,

$$(7\text{-}5) \quad AFC = \frac{\text{Fixed cost}}{\text{Quantity of output}} = FC/Q$$

$$AVC = \frac{\text{Variable cost}}{\text{Quantity of output}} = VC/Q$$

Average total cost is the sum of average fixed cost and average variable cost; it has a U shape because these components move in opposite directions as output rises.

Average fixed cost falls as more output is produced because the numerator (the fixed cost) is a fixed number but the denominator (the quantity of output) increases as more is produced. Another way to think about this relationship is that, as more output is produced, the fixed cost is spread over more units of output; the end result is that the fixed cost *per unit of output*—the average fixed cost—falls. You can see this effect in the fourth column of Table 7-2: average fixed cost drops continuously as output increases.

Average variable cost, however, rises as output increases. As we've seen, this reflects diminishing returns to the variable input: each additional unit of output incurs more variable cost to produce than the previous unit. So variable cost rises at a faster rate than the quantity of output increases.

Increasing output, therefore, has two opposing effects on average total cost—the "spreading effect" and the "diminishing returns effect":

- The spreading effect: the larger the output, the more production that can "share" the fixed cost, and therefore the lower the average fixed cost.

- The diminishing returns effect: the more output produced, the more variable input it requires to produce additional units, and therefore the higher the average variable cost.

At low levels of output, the spreading effect is very powerful because even small increases in output cause large reductions in average fixed cost. So at low levels of output, the spreading effect dominates the diminishing returns effect and causes the average total cost curve to slope downward. But when output is large, average fixed cost is already quite small, so increasing output further has only a very small spreading effect. Diminishing returns, on the other hand, usually grow increasingly important as output rises. As a result, when output is large, the diminishing returns effect dominates the spreading effect, causing the average total cost curve to slope upward. At the bottom of the U-shaped average total cost curve, point M in Figure 7-7, the two effects exactly balance each other. At this point average total cost is at its minimum level, the minimum average total cost.

Figure 7-8 brings together in a single picture four members of the family of cost curves that we have derived from the total cost curve: the marginal cost curve (MC), the average total cost curve (ATC), the average variable cost curve (AVC), and the average fixed cost curve (AFC). All are based on the information in Tables 7-1 and 7-2. As before, cost is measured on the vertical axis and the quantity of output is measured on the horizontal axis.

Let's take a moment to note some features of the various cost curves. First of all, marginal cost is upward sloping—the result of diminishing returns that make an additional unit of output more costly to produce than the one before. Average variable cost also is upward sloping—again, due to diminishing returns—but is flatter than the marginal cost curve. This is because the higher cost of an additional unit of output is averaged across all units, not just the additional units, in the average variable cost measure. Meanwhile, average fixed cost is downward sloping because of the spreading effect.

Finally, notice that the marginal cost curve intersects the average total cost curve from below, crossing it at its lowest point, point M in Figure 7-8. This last feature is our next subject of study.

## Figure 7-8

**Marginal Cost and Average Cost Curves for Ben's Boots**

Here we have the family of cost curves for Ben's Boots: the marginal cost curve (MC), the average total cost curve (ATC), the average variable cost curve (AVC), and the average fixed cost curve (AFC). Note that the average total cost curve is U-shaped and the marginal cost curve crosses the average total cost curve at the bottom of the U, point M, corresponding to the minimum average total cost from Table 7-2 and Figure 7-7. **>web...**

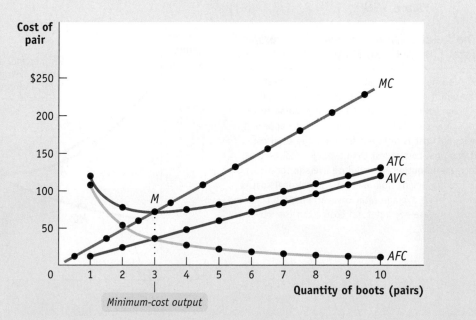

## Minimum Average Total Cost

The **minimum-cost output** is the quantity of output at which average total cost is lowest—the bottom of the U-shaped average total cost curve.

For a U-shaped average total cost curve, average total cost is at its minimum level at the bottom of the U. Economists call the quantity that corresponds to the minimum average total cost the **minimum-cost output.** In the case of Ben's Boots, the minimum-cost output is three pairs of boots per day.

In Figure 7-8, the bottom of the U is at the level of output at which the marginal cost curve crosses the average total cost curve from below. Is this an accident? No—it reflects general principles that are always true about a firm's marginal cost and average total cost curves:

- At the minimum-cost output, average total cost *is equal to* marginal cost.
- At output less than the minimum-cost output, marginal cost *is less than* average total cost and average total cost is falling.
- And at output greater than the minimum-cost output, marginal cost *is greater than* average total cost and average total cost is rising.

To understand this principle, think about how your grade in one course—say, a 3.0 in physics—affects your overall grade point average. If your GPA before receiving that grade was more than 3.0, the new grade lowers your average.

Similarly, if marginal cost—the cost of producing one more unit—is less than average total cost, producing that extra unit lowers average total cost. This is shown in Figure 7-9 by the movement from $A_1$ to $A_2$. In this case, the marginal cost of producing an additional unit of output is low, as indicated by the point $MC_L$ on the marginal cost curve. And when the cost of producing the next unit of output is less than average total cost, increasing production reduces average total cost. So any quantity of output at which marginal cost is less than average total cost must be on the downward-sloping segment of the U.

But if your grade in physics is more than the average of your previous grades, this new grade raises your GPA. Similarly, if marginal cost is greater than average total cost, producing that extra unit raises average total cost. This is illustrated by the move from $B_1$ to $B_2$ in Figure 7-9, where the marginal cost, $MC_H$, is higher than average

### Figure 7-9

**The Relationship Between the Average Total Cost and the Marginal Cost Curves**

To see why the marginal cost curve (*MC*) must cut through the average total cost curve at the minimum average total cost (point *M*), corresponding to the minimum-cost output, we look at what happens if marginal cost is different from average total cost. If marginal cost is *less* than average total cost, an increase in output must reduce average total cost, as in the movement from $A_1$ to $A_2$. If marginal cost is *greater* than average total cost, an increase in output must increase average total cost, as in the movement from $B_1$ to $B_2$.

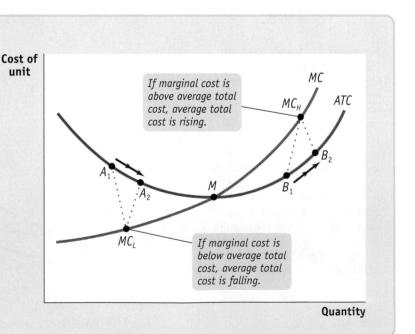

total cost. So any quantity of output at which marginal cost is greater than average total cost must be on the upward-sloping segment of the U.

Finally, if a new grade is exactly equal to your previous GPA, the additional grade neither raises nor lowers that average—it stays the same. This corresponds to point *M* in Figure 7-9: when marginal cost equals average total cost, we must be at the bottom of the U, because only at that point is average total cost neither falling nor rising.

## Does the Marginal Cost Curve Always Slope Upward?

Up to this point, we have emphasized the importance of diminishing returns, which lead to a marginal product curve that is always downward sloping and a marginal cost curve that is always upward sloping. In practice, however, economists believe that marginal cost curves often slope *downward* as a firm increases its production from zero up to some low level, sloping upward only at higher levels of production: they look like the curve *MC* in Figure 7-10.

This initial downward slope occurs because a firm that employs only a few workers often cannot reap the benefits of specialization of labor. For example, one individual producing boots would have to perform all the tasks involved: making soles, shaping the upper part, sewing the pieces together, and so on. As more workers are employed, they can divide the tasks, with each worker specializing in one or a few aspects of boot-making. This specialization can lead to *increasing* returns at first, and so to a downward-sloping marginal cost curve. Once there are enough workers to permit specialization, however, diminishing returns set in. So typical marginal cost curves actually have the "swoosh" shape shown by *MC* in Figure 7-10. For the same reason, average variable cost curves typically look like *AVC* in Figure 7-10: they are U-shaped rather than strictly upward sloping.

However, as Figure 7-10 also shows, the key features we saw from the example of Ben's Boots remain true: the average total cost curve is U-shaped, and the marginal cost curve passes through the point of minimum average total cost as well as through the point of minimum average variable cost.

### Figure 7-10

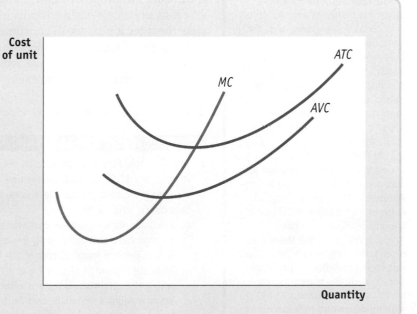

**More Realistic Cost Curves**

In practice, the marginal cost curve often begins with a section that slopes downward. As output rises from a low level, a firm is capable of engaging in specialization and division of labor, which leads to increasing returns. At higher levels of output, however, diminishing returns lead to upward-sloping marginal cost. When marginal cost has a downward-sloping section, average variable cost is U-shaped. However, the basic results—U-shaped average total cost, and marginal cost that cuts through the minimum average total cost—remain the same. **>web...**

# economics in action

## The Cost of Power

One of the great resources of the western United States is the availability of suitable sites for producing hydroelectric power: electricity generated by the force of water penned up behind a dam. When conditions are right—basically, when a large river runs through a deep but narrow valley—hydroelectric power can be much cheaper than electricity generated using fossil fuels, such as coal, or nuclear power. The western states, although they contain less than one-sixth of America's population, have more than half of the country's hydroelectric generating capacity. This advantage in cheap power has helped them attract industries, such as aluminum smelting, that are heavy users of electricity.

Is it a good idea for the governments of these western states to encourage more industries that make heavy use of electricity to move into their jurisdictions? Until the 1980s, most politicians and business leaders thought so, and many energy-intensive industries did in fact move into the region. But then, to the surprise and anger of consumers, western power companies began demanding higher prices, saying that they were no longer able to cover their costs at the old rates. What went wrong?

The answer is that officials had confused the *average total cost* of producing electricity with its *marginal cost*. Because of this confusion, they underestimated the cost of providing electricity to the new industries moving into their states.

The average total cost of producing power using existing facilities in the West is low, because much of it comes from hydroelectric power. But the marginal cost of providing additional power capacity is high, because it has become increasingly difficult to add new dams—most of the good sites have already been taken, and environmental considerations rule out many of the remaining sites. So when new energy-using businesses move to the West, to satisfy the new demand power companies must build expensive new power plants that run on fossil fuels or nuclear energy. So the marginal cost of electricity is much higher than the average total cost.

But electricity is a regulated industry and the rates electricity companies charge consumers are generally set to reflect average total cost. This gives rise to a seemingly paradoxical effect: when a factory moves into a western state, it pays less for the electricity it consumes than the extra, or marginal, cost incurred by the utility company to provide that electricity—so to cover its higher average total cost, the power company must raise the rates it charges all consumers.

If public officials had understood the difference between average total cost and marginal cost, they might have avoided this trap—either by charging new electricity users higher rates or by discouraging new electricity-using businesses from moving to their states. ∎

< < < < < < < < < < < < < < < < < <

Confusing marginal cost and average total cost proved a very costly mistake for the company that built this dam and its customers.

Corbis

## ▶▶ QUICK REVIEW

➤ *Marginal cost* is equal to the slope of the total cost curve. Diminishing returns result in *increasing marginal cost* and cause the *marginal cost curve* to be upward sloping.

➤ *Average total cost* (or *average cost*) is equal to the sum of *average fixed cost* and *average variable cost*. When the *U-shaped average total cost curve* slopes downward, the spreading effect dominates: fixed cost is spread over more units of output. When it slopes upward, the diminishing returns effect dominates: an additional unit of output requires more variable inputs.

➤ Marginal cost is equal to average total cost at the *minimum-cost output*. At higher output levels, marginal cost is greater than average total cost and average total cost is rising. At lower output levels, marginal cost is lower than average total cost and average total cost is falling.

➤ At low levels of output there are often increasing returns to an input due to the benefits of specialization, making the marginal cost curve "swoosh"-shaped: initially sloping downward before sloping upward.

## ▶▶ CHECK YOUR UNDERSTANDING 7-2

1. Alicia's Apple Pies is a roadside business. Alicia must pay $9.00 in rent each day. In addition, it costs her $1.00 to produce the first pie of the day, and each subsequent pie costs 50% more to produce than the one before. For example, the second pie costs $1.00 × 1.5 = $1.50 to produce, and so on.
   a. Calculate Alicia's marginal cost, variable cost, average total cost, average variable cost, and average fixed cost as her daily pie output rises from 0 to 6. (*Hint:* The variable cost of two pies is just the marginal cost of the first, plus the marginal cost of the second pie, and so on.)
   b. Indicate the range of pies for which the spreading effect dominates and the range for which the diminishing returns effect dominates.
   c. What is Alicia's minimum-cost output? Explain why making one more pie lowers Alicia's average total cost when output is lower than the minimum-cost output. Similarly, explain why making one more pie raises Alicia's average total cost when output is greater than the minimum-cost output.

Solutions appear at back of book.

# Short-Run Versus Long-Run Costs

Up to this point, we have treated fixed cost as completely outside the control of a firm because we have focused on the short run. But as we noted earlier, all inputs are variable in the long run: this means that in the long run fixed cost may also be varied. In the long run, in other words, a firm's fixed cost becomes a variable it can choose. For example, given time, Ben's Boots can acquire additional boot-making machinery or dispose of some of its existing machinery. In this section, we will examine how a firm's costs behave in the short run and in the long run. We will also see that the firm will choose its fixed cost in the long run based on the level of output it expects to produce.

Let's begin by supposing that Ben's Boots is considering whether to acquire additional boot-making machines. Acquiring additional machinery will affect its total cost in two ways. First, the firm will have to either rent or buy the additional machinery; either way, that will mean higher fixed cost in the short run. Second, if the workers have more equipment, they will be more productive: fewer workers will be needed to produce any given output, so variable cost for any given output level will be reduced.

The table in Figure 7-11 shows how acquiring an additional machine affects costs. In our original example, we assumed that Ben's Boots had a fixed cost of $108. The

## Figure 7-11

### Choosing the Level of Fixed Cost for Ben's Boots

There is a trade-off between higher fixed cost and lower variable cost for any given output level, and vice versa. $ATC_1$ is the average total cost curve corresponding to a fixed cost of $108; it leads to high variable cost. $ATC_2$ is the average total cost curve corresponding to a higher fixed cost of $216 but lower variable cost. At low output levels, fewer than 4 pairs of boots per day, $ATC_1$ lies below $ATC_2$: average total cost is lower with only $108 in fixed cost. But as output goes up, average total cost is lower with the higher amount of fixed cost, $216: at more than 4 pairs of boots per day, $ATC_2$ lies below $ATC_1$.

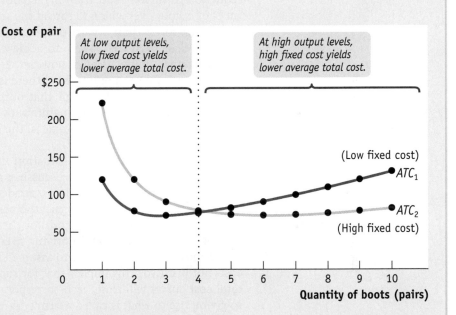

|  | Low fixed cost (FC = $108) | | | High fixed cost (FC = $216) | | |
|---|---|---|---|---|---|---|
| Quantity of boots (pairs) | High variable cost | Total cost | Average total cost of pair $ATC_1$ | Low variable cost | Total cost | Average total cost of pair $ATC_2$ |
| 1 | $12 | $120 | $120.00 | $6 | $222 | $222.00 |
| 2 | 48 | 156 | 78.00 | 24 | 240 | 120.00 |
| 3 | 108 | 216 | 72.00 | 54 | 270 | 90.00 |
| 4 | 192 | 300 | 75.00 | 96 | 312 | 78.00 |
| 5 | 300 | 408 | 81.60 | 150 | 366 | 73.20 |
| 6 | 432 | 540 | 90.00 | 216 | 432 | 72.00 |
| 7 | 588 | 696 | 99.40 | 294 | 510 | 72.90 |
| 8 | 768 | 876 | 109.50 | 384 | 600 | 75.00 |
| 9 | 972 | 1,080 | 120.00 | 486 | 702 | 78.00 |
| 10 | 1,200 | 1,308 | 130.80 | 600 | 816 | 81.60 |

left half of the table shows variable cost as well as total cost and average total cost assuming a fixed cost of $108. The average total cost curve for this level of fixed cost is given by $ATC_1$ in Figure 7-11. Let's compare that to a situation in which the firm buys an additional boot-making machine, doubling its fixed cost to $216 but reducing its variable cost at any given level of output. The right half of the table shows the firm's variable cost, total cost, and average total cost with this higher level of fixed cost. The average total cost curve corresponding to $216 in fixed cost is given by $ATC_2$ in Figure 7-11.

From the figure you can see that when output is small, 4 pairs of boots per day or fewer, average total cost is smaller when Ben's Boots forgoes the additional machinery and maintains the lower fixed cost of $108: $ATC_1$ lies below $ATC_2$. For example, at 3 pairs of boots per day, average total cost is $72 without the additional machinery and $90 with the additional machinery. But as output increases beyond 4 pairs per day, the firm's average total cost is lower if it acquires the additional machinery, raising its fixed cost to $216. For example, at 9 pairs of boots per day, average total cost is $120 when fixed cost is $108, but only $78 when fixed cost is $216.

Why does average total cost change like this when fixed cost increases? When output is low, the increase in fixed cost from the additional machinery outweighs the reduction in variable cost from higher worker productivity—that is, there are too few units of output over which to spread the additional fixed cost. So if Ben's Boots plans to produce fewer than 4 pairs of boots per day, it would be better off to choose the lower level of fixed cost, $108, to achieve a lower average total cost of production. When planned output is high, however, it should acquire the additional machinery.

In general, for each output level there is some choice of fixed cost that minimizes the firm's average total cost for that output level. So when the firm has a desired output level that it expects to maintain over time, it should choose the level of fixed cost appropriate to that level—that is, the level of fixed cost that minimizes its average total cost.

Now that we are studying a situation in which fixed cost can change, we need to take time into account when discussing average total cost. All of the average cost curves we have considered until now are defined for a given level of fixed cost—that is, they are defined for the short run, the period of time over which fixed cost doesn't vary. To reinforce that distinction, for the rest of this chapter we will refer to these average total cost curves as "short-run average total cost curves."

For most firms, it is realistic to assume that there are many possible choices of fixed cost, not just two. This implies that for such a firm, many possible short-run average total cost curves will exist, each corresponding to a different choice of fixed cost and so giving rise to what is called a firm's "family" of short-run average total cost curves.

At any given time, a firm will find itself on one of its short-run cost curves, the one corresponding to its current level of fixed cost; a change in output will cause it to move along that curve. If the firm expects that change in output level to be long-standing, then it is likely that the firm's current level of fixed cost is no longer appropriate. Given sufficient time, it will want to adjust its fixed cost to a new level that minimizes average total cost for its new output level. For example, if Ben's Boots had been producing 2 pairs of boots per day with a fixed cost of $108 but found itself increasing its output to 8 pairs per day for the foreseeable future, then in the long run it should increase its fixed cost to a level that minimizes average total cost at the 8-pairs-per-day output level.

Suppose we do a thought experiment and calculate the lowest possible average total cost that can be achieved for each output level if the firm were to choose its fixed cost for each output level. Economists have given this thought experiment a name: the *long-run average total cost curve*. Specifically, the **long-run average total cost curve,** or *LRATC*, is the relationship between output and average total cost when fixed cost has been chosen to minimize average total cost *for each level*

The **long-run average total cost curve** shows the relationship between output and average total cost when fixed cost has been chosen to minimize average total cost for each level of output.

| Figure 7-12 | |

### Short-Run and Long-Run Average Total Cost Curves

If Ben's Boots has chosen the level of fixed cost that minimizes short-run average total cost at an output of six pairs of boots per day and actually ends up producing six pairs per day, it will be on *LRATC* at point *C*. But if it produces more or less, in the short run it will be on the short-run average total cost curve *ATC₆* and not on *LRATC*. So if it produces only three pairs per day, its average total cost is shown by point *B*, not point *A*. If it produces nine pairs per day, its average total cost is shown by point *Y*, not point *X*. There are economies of scale when long-run average total cost declines as output increases, and there are diseconomies of scale when long-run average total cost increases as output increases.

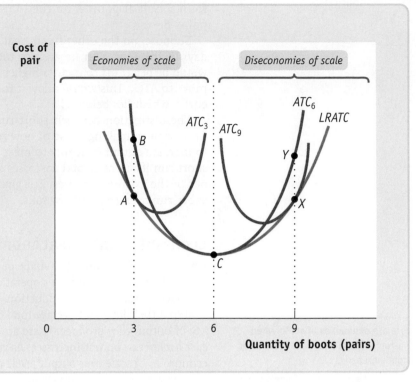

*of output.* If there are many possible choices of fixed cost, the long-run average total cost curve will have the familiar, smooth U shape, as shown by *LRATC* in Figure 7-12.

We can now draw the distinction between the short run and the long run more fully. In the long run, when a producer has had time to choose the fixed cost appropriate for its desired level of output, that producer will be on some point on the long-run average total cost curve. But if the output level is altered, the firm will no longer be on its long-run average total cost curve and will instead be moving along its current short-run average total cost curve. It will not be on its long-run average total cost curve again until it readjusts its fixed cost for its new output level.

Figure 7-12 illustrates this point. The curve *ATC₃* shows short-run average total cost if a boot producer has chosen the level of fixed cost that minimizes average total cost at an output of 3 pairs of boots per day. This is confirmed by the fact that at 3 pairs per day, *ATC₃* touches *LRATC*, the long-run average total cost curve. Similarly, *ATC₆* shows short-run average total cost if a boot producer has chosen the level of fixed cost that would minimize average total cost if its output is 6 pairs of boots per day. It touches *LRATC* at 6 pairs per day. And *ATC₉* shows short-run average total cost if a boot producer has chosen the level of fixed cost that would minimize average total cost if its output is 9 pairs of boots per day. It touches *LRATC* at 9 pairs per day.

Suppose that the firm has initially chosen to be on *ATC₆*. If the firm actually produces 6 pairs of boots per day, it will be at point *C* on both its short-run and long-run average total cost curves. Suppose, however, that the firm ends up producing only 3 pairs of boots per day. In the short run, its average total cost is indicated by point *B* on *ATC₆*; it is no longer on *LRATC*. If the firm had known that it would be producing only 3 pairs per day, it would have been better off to reduce its fixed cost and achieve lower average total cost. That is, it would have been better off to choose the level of fixed cost corresponding to *ATC₃*. Then it would have found itself at point *A* on the long-run average total cost curve, which lies below point *B*.

Suppose, on the other hand, that the firm ends up producing 9 pairs of boots per day. In the short run its average total cost is indicated by point *Y* on $ATC_6$. But it would be better off to incur a higher fixed cost in order to reduce its variable cost and move to $ATC_9$. This would allow it to reach point *X* on the long-run average total cost curve, which lies below *Y*.

The distinction between short-run and long-run average total costs is extremely important in making sense of how real firms operate over time. A company that has to increase output suddenly to meet a surge in demand will typically find that in the short run its average total cost rises sharply because it is hard to get extra production out of the existing facilities. But given time to build new factories or add machinery, short-run average total cost falls.

## Economies and Diseconomies of Scale

Finally, what determines the shape of the long-run average total cost curve? The answer is that *scale*, the size of a firm's operations, is often an important determinant of its long-run average total cost of production. Firms that experience scale effects in production find that their long-run average total cost changes substantially depending on the quantity of output they produce. There are **economies of scale** when long-run average total cost declines as output increases. As you can see in Figure 7-12, Ben's Boots experiences economies of scale over output levels ranging from 0 to 6 pairs of boots—the output levels over which the long-run average total cost curve is declining. There are **diseconomies of scale** when long-run average total cost increases as output increases. For Ben's Boots, diseconomies of scale occur at output levels of 6 pairs of boots or more, the output levels over which its long-run average total cost curve is rising.

Although it is not shown in Figure 7-12, there is a third possible relationship between long-run average total cost and scale: firms experience **constant returns to scale** when long-run average total cost is constant as output increases. In this case, the firm's long-run average total cost curve is horizontal over the output levels for which there are constant returns to scale.

What explains these scale effects in production? The answer ultimately lies in the firm's technology of production. Economies of scale often arise from the increased *specialization* that larger output levels allow—a larger scale of operation means that individual workers can limit themselves to more specialized tasks, becoming more skilled and efficient at doing them. Another source of economies of scale is very large initial set-up cost; in some industries—such as auto manufacturing, electricity generating, or petroleum refining—a very large initial cost in the form of plant and equipment is necessary to produce any output. As we'll see in Chapter 11, where we study monopoly, economies of scale have very important implications for how firms and industries interact and behave.

Diseconomies of scale, on the other hand, typically arise in large firms due to problems of coordination and communication: as the firm grows in size, it becomes ever more difficult and therefore costly to communicate and organize its activities. While economies of scale induce firms to get larger, diseconomies of scale tend to limit their size. And when constant returns to scale exist, scale has no effect on a firm's long-run average total cost: it is the same regardless of whether the firm produces 1 unit or 100,000 units.

## Summing Up Costs: The Short and Long of It

If a firm is to make the best decisions about how much to produce, it has to understand how its costs relate to the quantity of output it chooses to produce. Table 7-3 provides a quick summary of the concepts and measures of cost you have learned about.

There are **economies of scale** when long-run average total cost declines as output increases.

There are **diseconomies of scale** when long-run average total cost increases as output increases.

There are **constant returns to scale** when long-run average total cost is constant as output increases.

## TABLE 7-3

### Concepts and Measures of Cost

| | Measurement | Definition | Mathematical term |
|---|---|---|---|
| **Short run** | Fixed cost | Cost that does not depend on the quantity of output produced | $FC$ |
| | Average fixed cost | Fixed cost per unit of output | $AFC = FC/Q$ |
| **Short run and long run** | Variable cost | Cost that depends on the quantity of output produced | $VC$ |
| | Average variable cost | Variable cost per unit of output | $AVC = VC/Q$ |
| | Total cost | The sum of fixed cost (short-run) and variable cost | $TC = FC$ (short-run) $+ VC$ |
| | Average total cost (average cost) | Total cost per unit of output | $ATC = TC/Q$ |
| | Marginal cost | The change in total cost generated by producing one more unit of output | $MC = \Delta TC/\Delta Q$ |
| **Long run** | Long-run average total cost | Average cost when fixed cost has been chosen to minimize total cost for each level of output | $LRATC$ |

A lesson in economies of scale: cities with higher average annual snowfall maintain larger snowplow fleets.

# *economics in action*

## There's No Business Like Snow Business

Anyone who has lived both in a snowy city, like Chicago, and in a city that only occasionally experiences significant snowfall, like Washington, D.C., is aware of the differences in total cost that arise from making different choices about fixed cost.

In Washington, even a minor snowfall—say, an inch or two overnight—is enough to create chaos during the next morning's commute. The same snowfall in Chicago has hardly any effect at all. The reason is not that Washingtonians are wimps and Chicagoans are made of sterner stuff; it is that Washington, where it rarely snows, has only a fraction as many snowplows and other snow-clearing equipment as cities where heavy snow is a fact of life.

In this sense Washington and Chicago are like two producers who expect to produce different levels of output, where the "output" is snow removal. Washington, which rarely has significant snow, has chosen a low level of fixed cost in the form of snow-clearing equipment. This makes sense under normal circumstances but leaves the city unprepared when major snow does fall. Chicago, which knows that it will face lots of snow, chooses to accept the higher fixed cost that leaves it in a position to respond effectively. ■

> > > > > > > > > > > > > > > > > > > >

## >>CHECK YOUR UNDERSTANDING 7-3

1. The accompanying table shows three possible combinations of fixed cost and average variable cost.

   a. For each of the three choices, calculate the average total cost of producing 12,000, 22,000, and 30,000 units. For each of these quantities, which choice results in the lowest average total cost?

| Choice | Fixed cost | Average variable cost |
|---|---|---|
| 1 | $8,000 | $1.00 |
| 2 | 12,000 | 0.75 |
| 3 | 24,000 | 0.25 |

**>>QUICK REVIEW**

➤ In the long run, firms choose fixed cost according to expected output. Higher fixed cost reduces average total cost when output is high. Lower fixed cost reduces average total cost when output is low.

➤ There are many possible short-run average total cost curves, each corresponding to a different level of fixed cost. The *long-run average total cost curve, LRATC,* shows average total cost over the long run, when the firm has chosen fixed cost to minimize average total cost for each level of output.

➤ A firm that has fully adjusted its fixed cost for its output level will operate at a point that lies on both its current short-run and long-run average total cost curves. A change in output moves the firm along its current short-run average total cost curve. Once it has readjusted its fixed cost, the firm will operate on a new short-run average total cost curve and on the long-run average total cost curve.

➤ Scale effects arise from the technology of production. *Economies of scale* tend to make firms larger. *Diseconomies of scale* tend to limit their size. With *constant returns to scale,* scale has no effect.

b. Suppose that the firm, which has historically produced 12,000 units, experiences a sharp, permanent increase in demand that leads it to produce 22,000 units. Explain how its average total cost will change in the short run and in the long run.

c. Explain what the firm should do instead if it believes the change in demand is temporary.

2. In each of the following cases, explain what kind of scale effects you think the firm will experience and why.

a. A telemarketing firm in which employees make sales calls using computers and telephones

b. An interior design firm in which design projects are based on the expertise of the firm's owner

c. A diamond-mining company

Solutions appear at back of book.

## • A LOOK AHEAD •

We've now seen how to use information about how a firm produces to analyze that firm's costs. Our next step is to go from our analysis of costs to an analysis of the supply curve. To understand the supply curve for a particular good, we will need to look both at how a profit-maximizing firm chooses its quantity of output and at how it decides whether to enter or exit the industry producing that good.

## SUMMARY

1. The relationship between inputs and output is a producer's **production function.** In the **short run,** the quantity of a **fixed input** cannot be varied but the quantity of a **variable input** can. In the **long run,** the quantities of all inputs can be varied. For a given amount of fixed input, the **total product curve** shows how the quantity of output changes as the quantity of the variable input changes. We may also calculate the **marginal product** of an input, the increase in output from using one more unit of that input.

2. There are **diminishing returns to an input** when its marginal product declines as more of the input is used, holding the quantity of all other inputs fixed.

3. Some costs are **explicit costs;** they involve a direct payment of cash. Other costs, however, are **implicit costs;** they involve no outlay of money but represent the inflows of cash that are forgone. Both explicit and implicit costs should be taken into account in determining the costs of production.

4. **Total cost,** represented by the **total cost curve,** is equal to the sum of **fixed cost,** which does not depend on output, and **variable cost,** which does depend on output. Due to diminishing returns, **marginal cost,** the increase in total cost generated by producing one more unit of output, normally increases as output increases. These **increasing marginal costs** result in an upward-sloping **marginal cost curve.**

5. **Average total cost** (also known as **average cost**), total cost divided by quantity of output, is the cost of the average unit of output while marginal cost is the cost of one more unit produced. Economists believe that

U-shaped average total cost curves are typical, because average total cost consists of two parts: **average fixed cost,** which falls when output increases (the spreading effect) and **average variable cost,** which rises with output (the diminishing returns effect).

6. When average total cost is U-shaped, the bottom of the U is the level of output at which average total cost is minimized, the point of **minimum-cost output.** This is also the point at which the marginal cost curve crosses the average total cost curve from below. Due to gains from specialization, the marginal cost curve may slope downward initially before sloping upward, giving it a "swoosh" shape.

7. In the long run, a producer can change its fixed input and its level of fixed cost. By accepting higher fixed cost, a firm can lower its variable cost for any given output level, and vice versa. The **long-run average total cost curve** shows the relationship between output and average total cost when fixed cost has been chosen to minimize average total cost at each level of output. A firm moves along its short-run average total cost curve as it increases output, and returns to a point on both its short-run and long-run average total cost curves once it has adjusted fixed cost to its new output level.

8. As output increases, there are **economies of scale** if long-run average total cost declines; **diseconomies of scale** if it increases; and **constant returns to scale** if it remains constant. Scale effects depend on the technology of production.

## KEY TERMS

Production function, p. 161
Fixed input, p. 161
Variable input, p. 161
Long run, p. 161
Short run, p. 161
Total product curve, p. 161
Marginal product, p. 162
Diminishing returns to an input, p. 163
Explicit cost, p. 165

Implicit cost, p. 165
Fixed cost, p. 165
Variable cost, p. 165
Total cost, p. 166
Total cost curve, p. 166
Marginal cost, p. 169
Increasing marginal cost, p. 170
Marginal cost curve, p. 170
Average total cost, p. 171

Average cost, p. 171
U-shaped average total cost curve, p. 171
Average fixed cost, p. 172
Average variable cost, p. 172
Minimum-cost output, p. 174
Long-run average total cost curve, p. 178
Economies of scale, p. 180
Diseconomies of scale, p. 180
Constant returns to scale, p. 180

## PROBLEMS

1. Marty's Frozen Yogurt is a small shop that sells cups of frozen yogurt in a university town. Marty owns three frozen-yogurt machines. His other inputs are refrigerators, frozen-yogurt mix, cups, sprinkle toppings, and, of course, workers. He estimates that his daily production function when he varies the number of workers employed (and at the same time, of course, yogurt mix, cups, and so on) is as shown in the accompanying table.

| Quantity of labor (workers) | Quantity of frozen yogurt (cups) |
|---|---|
| 0 | 0 |
| 1 | 110 |
| 2 | 200 |
| 3 | 270 |
| 4 | 300 |
| 5 | 320 |
| 6 | 330 |

   a. What are the fixed inputs and variable inputs in the production of cups of frozen yogurt?

   b. Draw the total product curve. Put the quantity of labor on the horizontal axis and the quantity of frozen yogurt on the vertical axis.

   c. What is the marginal product of the first worker? The second worker? The third worker? Why does marginal product decline as the number of workers increases?

2. The production function for Marty's Frozen Yogurt is given in Problem 1. Marty pays each of his workers $80 per day. The cost of his other variable inputs is $0.50 per cup of yogurt. His fixed cost is $100 per day.

   a. What is Marty's variable cost and total cost when he produces 110 cups of yogurt? 200 cups? Calculate variable and total cost for every level of output given in Problem 1.

   b. Draw Marty's variable cost curve. On the same diagram, draw his total cost curve.

   c. What is the marginal cost per cup for the first 110 cups of yogurt? For the next 90 cups? Calculate the marginal cost for all remaining levels of output.

3. The production function for Marty's Frozen Yogurt is given in Problem 1. The costs are given in Problem 2.

   a. For each of the given levels of output, calculate the average fixed cost (AFC), average variable cost (AVC), and average total cost (ATC) per cup of frozen yogurt.

   b. On one diagram, draw the AFC, AVC, and ATC curves.

   c. What principle explains why the AFC declines as output increases? What principle explains why the AVC increases as output increases? Explain your answers.

   d. How many cups of frozen yogurt are produced when average total cost is minimized?

4. The accompanying table shows a car manufacturer's total cost of producing cars.

| Quantity of cars | TC |
|---|---|
| 0 | $500,000 |
| 1 | 540,000 |
| 2 | 560,000 |
| 3 | 570,000 |
| 4 | 590,000 |
| 5 | 620,000 |
| 6 | 660,000 |
| 7 | 720,000 |
| 8 | 800,000 |
| 9 | 920,000 |
| 10 | 1,100,000 |

   a. What is this manufacturer's fixed cost?

   b. For each level of output, calculate the variable cost (VC). For each level of output except zero output, calculate the average variable cost (AVC), average total cost (ATC), and average fixed cost (AFC). What is the minimum-cost output?

**c.** For each level of output, calculate this manufacturer's marginal cost (*MC*).

**d.** On one diagram, draw the manufacturer's *AVC*, *ATC*, and *MC* curves.

5. Amy, Bill, and Carla all mow lawns for money. Each of them operates a different lawn mower. The accompanying table shows the total cost to Amy, Bill, and Carla of mowing lawns.

| Quantity of lawns mowed | Amy's total cost | Bill's total cost | Carla's total cost |
|---|---|---|---|
| 0 | $0 | $0 | $0 |
| 1 | 20 | 10 | 2 |
| 2 | 35 | 20 | 7 |
| 3 | 45 | 30 | 17 |
| 4 | 50 | 40 | 32 |
| 5 | 52 | 50 | 52 |
| 6 | 53 | 60 | 82 |

**a.** Calculate Amy's, Bill's, and Carla's marginal costs, and draw each of their marginal cost curves.

**b.** Who has increasing marginal cost, who has decreasing marginal cost, and who has constant marginal cost?

6. Magnificent Blooms is a florist specializing in floral arrangements for weddings, graduations, and other events. Magnificent Blooms has a fixed cost associated with space and equipment of $100 per day. Each worker is paid $50 per day. The daily production function for Magnificent Blooms is shown in the accompanying table.

| Quantity of labor (workers) | Quantity of floral arrangements |
|---|---|
| 0 | 0 |
| 1 | 5 |
| 2 | 9 |
| 3 | 12 |
| 4 | 14 |
| 5 | 15 |

**a.** What is the marginal product, *MPL*, of the first, second, third, fourth, and fifth workers? What principle explains why the marginal product per worker declines as the number of workers employed increases?

**b.** What is the marginal cost (*MC*) of producing each of the first 5 floral arrangements? The sixth through ninth floral arrangements? The remaining levels of output? What principle explains why the marginal cost per floral arrangement increases as the number of arrangements increases?

7. You have the information shown in the accompanying table about a firm's costs. Complete the missing data.

| Quantity | TC | MC | ATC | AVC |
|---|---|---|---|---|
| 0 | $20 | | | |
| | | $20 | | |
| 1 | ? | | ? | ? |
| | | 10 | | |
| 2 | ? | | ? | ? |
| | | 16 | | |
| 3 | ? | | ? | ? |
| | | 20 | | |
| 4 | ? | | ? | ? |
| | | 24 | | |
| 5 | ? | | ? | ? |

8. Evaluate each of the following statements: If a statement is true, explain why; if it is false, identify the mistake and try to correct it.

**a.** A decreasing marginal product tells us that marginal cost must be rising.

**b.** An increase in fixed cost increases the minimum-cost output.

**c.** An increase in fixed cost increases marginal cost.

**d.** When marginal cost is above average total cost, average total cost must be falling.

9. Mark and Jeff operate a small company that produces souvenir footballs. Their fixed cost is $2,000 per month. They can hire workers for $1,000 per worker per month. Their monthly production function for footballs is as given in the accompanying table.

| Quantity of labor (workers) | Quantity of footballs |
|---|---|
| 0 | 0 |
| 1 | 300 |
| 2 | 800 |
| 3 | 1,200 |
| 4 | 1,400 |
| 5 | 1,500 |

**a.** For each quantity of labor, calculate average variable cost (*AVC*), average fixed cost (*AFC*), average total cost (*ATC*), and marginal cost (MC).

**b.** On one diagram, draw in the *AVC*, *ATC*, and *MC* curves.

**c.** At what level of output is Mark and Jeff's average total cost minimized?

10. You produce widgets. Currently you produce 4 widgets at a total cost of $40.

**a.** What is your average total cost?

**b.** Suppose you could produce one more (the fifth) widget at a marginal cost of $5. If you do produce that fifth widget, what will your average total cost be? Has your average total cost increased or decreased? Why?

**c.** Suppose instead that you could produce one more (the fifth) widget at a marginal cost of $20. If you do produce that fifth widget, what will your average total cost be? Has your average total cost increased or decreased? Why?

**11.** In your economics class, each homework problem set is graded on the basis of a maximum score of 100. You have completed 9 out of 10 of the problem sets for the term, and your current average grade is 88. What range of grades for your 10th problem set will raise your overall average? What range will lower your overall average? Explain.

**12.** Don owns a small concrete-mixing company. His fixed cost is the cost of the concrete-batching machinery and his mixer trucks. His variable cost is the cost of the sand, gravel, and other inputs for producing concrete; the gas and maintenance for the machinery and trucks; and his workers. He is trying to decide how many mixer trucks to purchase. He has estimated the costs shown in the accompanying table based on estimates of the number of orders his company will receive per week.

| Quantity of trucks | FC | VC 20 orders | VC 40 orders | VC 60 orders |
|---|---|---|---|---|
| 2 | $6,000 | $2,000 | $5,000 | $12,000 |
| 3 | 7,000 | 1,800 | 3,800 | 10,800 |
| 4 | 8,000 | 1,200 | 3,600 | 8,400 |

**a.** For each level of fixed cost, calculate Don's total cost for producing 20, 40, and 60 orders per week.

**b.** If Don is producing 20 orders per week, how many trucks should he purchase and what will his average total cost be? Answer the same questions for 40 and 60 orders per week.

**13.** Consider Don's concrete-mixing business described in Problem 12. Suppose Don purchased 3 trucks, expecting to produce 40 orders per week.

**a.** Suppose that, in the short run, business declines to 20 orders per week. What is Don's average total cost per order in the short run? What will his average total cost per order in the short run be if his business booms to 60 orders per week?

**b.** What is Don's long-run average total cost for 20 orders per week? Explain why his short-run average total cost of producing 20 orders per week when the number of trucks is fixed at 3 is greater than his long-run average total cost of producing 20 orders per week.

**c.** Sketch Don's long-run average total cost curve. Sketch his short-run average total cost curve if he owns 3 trucks.

**14.** True or False? Explain your reasoning.

**a.** The short-run average total cost can never be less than the long-run average total cost.

**b.** The short-run average variable cost can never be less than the long-run average total cost.

**c.** In the long run, choosing a higher level of fixed cost shifts the long-run average total cost curve upward.

**15.** Wolfsburg Wagon (WW) is a small automaker. The accompanying table shows WW's long-run average total cost.

| Quantity of cars | LRATC of car |
|---|---|
| 1 | $30,000 |
| 2 | 20,000 |
| 3 | 15,000 |
| 4 | 12,000 |
| 5 | 12,000 |
| 6 | 12,000 |
| 7 | 14,000 |
| 8 | 18,000 |

**a.** For which levels of output does WW experience economies of scale?

**b.** For which levels of output does WW experience diseconomies of scale?

**c.** For which levels of output does WW experience constant returns to scale?

>**web**... To continue your study and review of concepts in this chapter, please visit the Krugman/Wells/Olney website for quizzes, animated graph tutorials, web links to helpful resources, and more.

**www.worthpublishers.com/krugmanwellsolney**

# >>Perfect Competition and the Supply Curve

## DOING WHAT COMES NATURALLY

FOOD CONSUMERS IN THE UNITED States are concerned about health issues. Demand for "natural" foods and beverages, such as bottled water and organically grown fruits and vegetables, increased rapidly over the past decade. The small group of farmers who had pioneered organic farming techniques prospered thanks to higher prices.

But everyone knew that the high prices of organic produce were unlikely to persist even if the new, higher demand for naturally grown food continued: the supply of organic food, while not that price-elastic in the short run, was surely much more price-elastic in the long run. Over time, farms already producing organically would increase their capacity, and conventional farmers would enter the organic food business. So the increase in the quantity supplied in response to the increase in price would be much larger in the long run than in the short run.

Where does the supply curve come from? Why is there a difference between the short-run and the long-run supply curve? In this chapter we will use our understanding of costs, developed in Chapter 7, as the basis for an analysis of the supply curve. As we'll see, this will require that we understand the behavior both of individual firms and of an entire industry, composed of these many individual firms.

Our analysis in this chapter assumes that the industry in question is characterized by

*perfect competition*. We begin by explaining the concept of perfect competition, providing a brief introduction to the conditions that give rise to a perfectly competitive industry. We then show how a producer under perfect competition decides how much to produce. Finally, we use the cost curves of the individual producers to derive the *industry supply curve* under perfect competition. By analyzing the way a competitive industry evolves over time, we will come to understand the distinction between the short-run and long-run effects of changes in demand on a competitive industry—such as, for example, the effect of America's new taste for organic food on the organic farming industry. We will conclude with a deeper discussion of the conditions necessary for perfect competition.

Whether it's organic strawberries or satellites, how a good is produced determines its cost of production.

## What you will learn in this chapter:

➤ The meaning of **perfect competition** and the characteristics of a **perfectly competitive industry**

➤ The difference between **accounting profit** and **economic profit**, and why economic profit is the correct basis for decisions

➤ How a **price-taking producer** determines its profit-maximizing quantity of output

➤ How to assess whether or not a producer is profitable and why an unprofitable producer may continue to operate in the short run

➤ Why industries behave differently in the short run and the long run

➤ What determines the **industry supply curve** in both the short run and the long run

Peter Dean/Agriculture//Grant Heilman Photography

# Perfect Competition

Suppose that Yves and Zoe are neighboring farmers, both of whom grow organic tomatoes. Both sell their output to the same grocery store chains that carry organic foods; so, in a real sense, Yves and Zoe compete with each other.

Does this mean that Yves should try to stop Zoe from growing tomatoes or that Yves and Zoe should form an agreement to grow less? Almost certainly not: there are hundreds or thousands of organic tomato farmers, and Yves and Zoe are competing with all those other growers as well as with each other. Because so many farmers sell organic tomatoes, if any one of them produced more or less, there would be no measureable effect on market prices.

When people talk about business competition, the image they often have in mind is a situation in which two or three rival firms are intensely struggling for advantage. But economists know that when a business focuses on a few main competitors, it's actually a sign that competition is fairly limited. As the example of organic tomatoes suggests, when there is enough competition it doesn't even make sense to identify your opponents: there are so many competitors that you cannot single out any one of them as a rival.

We can put it another way: Yves and Zoe are **price-taking producers.** A producer is a price-taker when its actions cannot affect the market price of the good it sells. As a result, a price-taking producer considers the market price as given. When there is enough competition—when competition is what economists call "perfect"—then every producer is a price-taker. And there is a similar definition for consumers: a **price-taking consumer** is a consumer who cannot influence the market price of the good by his or her actions. That is, the market price is unaffected by how much or how little of the good the consumer buys.

> A **price-taking producer** is a producer whose actions have no effect on the market price of the good it sells.
>
> A **price-taking consumer** is a consumer whose actions have no effect on the market price of the good he or she buys.

## Defining Perfect Competition

In a **perfectly competitive market,** all market participants, both consumers and producers, are price-takers. That is, neither consumption decisions by individual consumers nor production decisions by individual producers affect the market price of the good.

> A **perfectly competitive market** is a market in which all market participants are price-takers.

The supply and demand model, which we introduced in Chapter 3 and have used repeatedly since then, is a model of a perfectly competitive market. It depends fundamentally on the assumption that no individual buyer or seller of a good, such as scalped tickets to a hockey game or organic tomatoes, believes that he or she can affect the price at which he or she can sell or buy the good.

As a general rule, consumers are indeed price-takers. Instances in which consumers are able to affect the prices they pay are rare. It is, however, quite common for producers to have a significant ability to affect the prices they receive, a phenomenon we'll address in Chapter 11. So the model of perfect competition is appropriate for some but not all markets. An industry in which producers are price-takers is called a **perfectly competitive industry.** Clearly, some industries aren't perfectly competitive; in later chapters we'll see how to analyze industries that don't fit the perfectly competitive model.

> A **perfectly competitive industry** is an industry in which producers are price-takers.

Under what circumstances will all producers be price-takers? In the next section we will see that there are two necessary conditions for a perfectly competitive industry and that a third condition is often present as well.

## Two Necessary Conditions for Perfect Competition

The markets for major grains, like wheat and corn, are perfectly competitive: individual wheat and corn farmers, as well as individual buyers of wheat and corn, take market prices as given. In contrast, the markets for some of the food items made from these grains—in particular, breakfast cereals—are by no means perfectly competitive. There is intense competition among cereal brands, but not *perfect* competition. To understand the difference between the market for wheat and the market for shredded wheat cereal is to understand the two necessary conditions for perfect competition.

First, for an industry to be perfectly competitive, it must contain many producers, none of whom have a large **market share.** A producer's market share is the fraction of the total industry output represented by that producer's output. The distribution of market share constitutes a major difference between the grain industry and the breakfast cereal industry. There are thousands of wheat farmers, none of whom account for more than a small fraction of 1 percent of total wheat sales. The breakfast cereal industry, however, is dominated by four producers: Kellogg's, General Mills, Post, and Quaker Foods. Kellogg's alone accounts for about one-third of all cereal sales. Kellogg's executives know that if they try to sell more corn flakes, they are likely to drive down the market price of corn flakes. That is, they know that their actions influence market prices, simply because they are so large a part of the market that changes in their production will significantly affect the overall quantity supplied. It makes sense to assume that producers are price-takers only when an industry does *not* contain any large players like Kellogg's.

Second, an industry can be perfectly competitive only if consumers regard the products of all producers as equivalent. This clearly isn't true in the breakfast cereal market: consumers don't consider Cap'n Crunch to be a good substitute for Wheaties. As a result, the maker of Wheaties has some ability to increase its price without fear that it will lose all its customers to the maker of Cap'n Crunch. Contrast this with the case of a **standardized product,** sometimes known as a **commodity.** Consumers regard the output of one wheat producer as a perfect substitute for that of another producer. Consequently, one farmer cannot increase the price for his or her wheat without losing all his or her sales to other wheat farmers. So the second necessary condition for a competitive industry is that the industry output is a standardized product.

> A producer's **market share** is the fraction of the total industry output represented by that producer's output.

> A good is a **standardized product,** also known as a **commodity,** when consumers regard the products of different producers as the same good.

## FOR INQUIRING MINDS

### WHAT'S A STANDARDIZED PRODUCT?

A perfectly competitive industry must produce a standardized product. But is it enough for the products of different firms actually to be the same? No: people must also *think* that they are the same. And producers often go to great lengths to convince consumers that they have a distinctive, or *differentiated*, product, even when they don't.

Consider, for example, champagne—not the superexpensive premium champagnes but the more ordinary stuff. Most people cannot tell the difference between champagne actually produced in the Champagne region of France, where the product originated, and similar products from Spain or California. But the French government has sought and obtained legal protection for the firms of Champagne, ensuring that around the world only bubbly wine from that region

In the end, only kimchi eaters can tell you if there is truly a difference between Korean-produced kimchi and the Japanese-produced variety.

AP/Wide World Photos

can be called champagne. If it's from someplace else, all the seller can do is say that it was produced by the *méthode Champenoise*. This creates a differentiation in the minds of consumers and lets the champagne producers of Champagne charge higher prices.

In a less Eurocentric example, Korean producers of *kimchi*, the spicy fermented cabbage that is the national side dish, are doing their best to convince consumers that the same product packaged by Japanese firms is just not the real thing. The purpose is, of course, to ensure higher prices for Korean *kimchi*.

So is an industry perfectly competitive if it sells products that are indistinguishable except in name but that consumers, for whatever reason, don't think are standardized? No. When it comes to defining the nature of competition, the consumer is always right.

## Free Entry and Exit

All perfectly competitive industries have many producers with small market shares, producing a standardized product. Most perfectly competitive industries are also characterized by one more feature: it is easy for new firms to enter the industry or for firms that are currently in the industry to leave. That is, no obstacles in the form of government regulations or limited access to key resources prevent new producers from entering the market. And no additional costs are associated with shutting down a company and leaving the industry. Economists refer to the arrival of new firms into an industry as *entry*; they refer to the departure of firms from an industry as *exit*. When there are no obstacles to entry into or exit from an industry, we say that the industry has **free entry and exit.**

Free entry and exit is not strictly necessary for perfect competition. In Chapter 4 we described the case of New Jersey clam fishing, where regulations have the effect of limiting the number of fishing boats. Despite this, there are enough boats operating that the fishermen are price-takers. But free entry and exit is a key factor in most competitive industries. It ensures that the number of producers in an industry can adjust to changing market conditions. And, in particular, it ensures that producers in an industry cannot artificially keep other firms out.

> There is **free entry and exit** into and from an industry when new producers can easily enter into or leave that industry.

To sum up, then, perfect competition depends on two necessary conditions. First, the industry must contain many producers, each having a small market share. Second, the industry must produce a standardized product. In addition, perfectly competitive industries are normally characterized by free entry and exit.

How does an industry that meets these three criteria behave? As a first step toward answering that question, let's look at how an individual producer in a perfectly competitive industry maximizes profit.

# economics in action

## The Pain of Competition

Sometimes it is possible to see an industry become perfectly competitive. In fact, it happens on a regular basis in the case of pharmaceuticals: the conditions for perfect competition are often met as soon as the patent on a popular drug expires.

When a company develops a new drug, it is usually able to receive a patent—a legal monopoly that gives it the exclusive right to sell that drug for 20 years from the date of filing. When the patent expires, the field is open for other companies to sell their own versions of the drug—marketed as "generics" and sold under the medical name of the drug rather than the brand name used by the original producer. Generics are standardized products, much like aspirin, and are often sold by many producers.

A good example came in 1984, when Upjohn's patent on ibuprofen—a painkiller that the company still markets under the brand name Motrin—expired. Most people who use ibuprofen, like most people who use aspirin, now purchase a generic version made by one of many producers.

The shift to perfect competition, not coincidentally, is accompanied by a sharp fall in market price. When its patent expired, Upjohn immediately cut the price of Motrin by 35 percent, but as more companies started selling the generic drug, the price of ibuprofen eventually fell by another two-thirds.

Ten years later the patent on the painkiller naproxen—sold under the brand name Naprosyn—expired. The generic version of naproxen was soon selling at only one-tenth of the original price of Naprosyn. ∎

> **>> QUICK REVIEW**
>
> - ➤ Neither the actions of a *price-taking producer* nor those of a *price-taking consumer* can influence the market price of a good.
> - ➤ In a *perfectly competitive market* all producers and consumers are price-takers. Consumers are almost always price-takers, but this is often not true of producers. An industry in which producers are price-takers is a *perfectly competitive industry.*
> - ➤ A perfectly competitive industry contains many producers, each of which produces a *standardized product* (also known as a *commodity*) but none of which has a large *market share.*
> - ➤ Most perfectly competitive industries are also characterized by *free entry and exit.*

> > > > > > CHAPTER > > > > > PERFECT > > COMPETITION > > > > —

1. In each of the following situations, do you think the industry described will be perfectly competitive or not? Explain your answer.
   a. There are two producers of aluminum in the world, a good sold in many places.
   b. Only a handful of companies produce natural gas from the North Sea. The price of natural gas is determined by global supply and demand, of which North Sea production represents a small share.
   c. Dozens of designers sell high-fashion clothes. Each designer has a distinctive style and a loyal clientele.
   d. There are many baseball teams in the United States, one or two in each major city, and each selling tickets to its events.

Solutions appear at back of book.

# Production and Profits

Consider Jennifer and Jason, who run an organic tomato farm. Suppose that the market price of organic tomatoes is $18 per bushel and that Jennifer and Jason are price-takers—they can sell as much as they like at that price. Then we can use the data in Table 8-1 to find their profit-maximizing level of output by direct calculation.

### TABLE 8-1

#### Profit for Jennifer and Jason's Farm When Market Price Is $18

| Quantity of tomatoes $Q$ (bushels) | Total revenue $TR = P \times Q$ | Total cost $TC$ | Profit $TR - TC$ |
|---|---|---|---|
| 0 | $0 | $14 | $−14 |
| 1 | 18 | 30 | −12 |
| 2 | 36 | 36 | 0 |
| 3 | 54 | 44 | 10 |
| 4 | 72 | 56 | 16 |
| 5 | 90 | 72 | 18 |
| 6 | 108 | 92 | 16 |
| 7 | 126 | 116 | 10 |

The first column shows the quantity of output in bushels, and the second column shows Jennifer and Jason's total revenue from their output: the market value of their output. Total revenue, $TR$, is equal to the market price multiplied by the quantity of output:

$$(8\text{-}1) \quad TR = P \times Q$$

In this example, total revenue is equal to $18 per bushel times the quantity of output in bushels.

The third column of Table 8-1 shows Jennifer and Jason's total cost. The fourth column of Table 8-1 shows their **profit,** equal to total revenue minus total cost:

$$(8\text{-}2) \quad \text{Profit} = TR - TC$$

As indicated by the numbers in the table, profit is maximized at an output of 5 bushels, where profit is equal to $18. But we can gain more insight into the profit-maximizing choice of output by viewing it as a problem of marginal analysis, a task we'll do next.

---

**Profit** is the difference between total revenue and total cost.

## Using Marginal Analysis to Choose the Profit-Maximizing Quantity of Output

Recall from Chapter 1 one of our four principles of individual choice: "How much?" is a decision at the margin. We call this the **principle of marginal analysis:** the optimal amount of an activity is the level at which marginal benefit is equal to marginal cost. To apply this principle, consider the effect on a producer's profit of increasing output by 1 unit. The marginal benefit of that unit is the additional revenue generated by selling it; this measure has a name—it is called the **marginal revenue** of that output. The general formula for marginal revenue is:

> The **principle of marginal analysis** says that the optimal quantity of an activity is the quantity at which marginal benefit is equal to marginal cost.

> **Marginal revenue** is the change in total revenue generated by an additional unit of output.

$$\text{(8-3)} \quad \text{Marginal revenue} = \frac{\text{Change in total revenue}}{\text{Change in output}} = \begin{array}{c}\text{Change in total revenue}\\ \text{generated by one}\\ \text{additional unit of output}\end{array}$$

or

$$MR = \Delta TR/\Delta Q$$

So Jennifer and Jason would maximize their profit by producing bushels up to the point at which the marginal revenue is equal to marginal cost. We can summarize this as the producer's **optimal output rule:** profit is maximized by producing the quantity at which the marginal revenue of the last unit produced is equal to its marginal cost. That is, $MR = MC$ at the optimal quantity of output.

We can learn how to apply the optimal output rule with the help of Table 8-2, which provides various short-run cost measures for Jennifer and Jason's farm. The second column contains the farm's variable cost, and the third column shows its total cost of output based on the assumption that the farm incurs a fixed cost of $14. The fourth column shows their marginal cost. Notice that, in this example, the marginal cost falls as output increases from a low level before rising, so that the marginal cost curve has the "swoosh" shape described in Chapter 7. (Shortly it will become clear that this shape has important implications for short-run production decisions.)

> The **optimal output rule** says that profit is maximized by producing the quantity of output at which the marginal revenue of the last unit produced is equal to its marginal cost.

### TABLE 8-2

**Short-Run Costs for Jennifer and Jason's Farm**

| Quantity of tomatoes Q (bushels) | Variable cost VC | Total cost TC | Marginal cost of bushel MC = ΔTC/ΔQ | Marginal revenue of bushel | Net gain of bushel = MR − MC |
|---|---|---|---|---|---|
| 0 | $0 | $14 | | | |
| | | | $16 | $18 | $2 |
| 1 | 16 | 30 | | | |
| | | | 6 | 18 | 12 |
| 2 | 22 | 36 | | | |
| | | | 8 | 18 | 10 |
| 3 | 30 | 44 | | | |
| | | | 12 | 18 | 6 |
| 4 | 42 | 56 | | | |
| | | | 16 | 18 | 2 |
| 5 | 58 | 72 | | | |
| | | | 20 | 18 | −2 |
| 6 | 78 | 92 | | | |
| | | | 24 | 18 | −6 |
| 7 | 102 | 116 | | | |

The fifth column contains the farm's marginal revenue, which has an important feature: Jennifer and Jason's marginal revenue is constant at $18 for every output level. The sixth and final column of Table 8-2 shows the calculation of the net gain per bushel of tomatoes, which is equal to marginal revenue minus marginal cost—or, equivalently, market price minus marginal cost. As you can see, it is positive for the 1st through 5th bushels; producing each of these bushels raises Jennifer and Jason's profit. For the 6th and 7th bushels, however, net gain is negative: producing

### PITFALLS

**MUDDLED AT THE MARGIN**
The idea of setting marginal revenue *equal* to marginal cost sometimes confuses people. Aren't we trying to maximize the *difference* between revenue and costs? And don't we wipe out our gains by setting revenue and costs equal to each other? Yes and yes. But we aren't setting revenue and costs equal to each other—what we are doing is setting *marginal,* not *total,* revenue and cost equal to each other.

Once again, the point is to maximize the total net gain—the profit—from an activity. If the marginal revenue is greater than the marginal cost, producing a bit more will increase profit. If the marginal revenue is less than the marginal cost, producing a bit less will increase the total profit. So only when the *marginal* revenue and cost are equal is the difference between *total* revenue and cost at a maximum.

## PITFALLS

### WHAT IF MARGINAL REVENUE AND MARGINAL COST AREN'T EXACTLY EQUAL?

The optimal output rule says that to maximize profit, you should produce the quantity at which marginal revenue is equal to marginal cost. But what do you do if there is no output level at which marginal revenue equals marginal cost? In that case, you produce the largest quantity for which marginal revenue exceeds marginal cost. This is the case in Table 8-2 at an output of 5 bushels. The simpler version of the optimal output rule applies when production involves large numbers, such as hundreds or thousands of units. In such cases marginal cost comes in small increments, and there is always a level of output at which marginal cost almost exactly equals marginal revenue.

The **price-taking firm's optimal output rule** says that a price-taking firm's profit is maximized by producing the quantity of output at which the market price is equal to the marginal cost of the last unit produced.

The **marginal revenue curve** shows how marginal revenue varies as output varies.

them would decrease, not increase, profit. (You can verify this by examining Table 8-1.) So 5 bushels are Jennifer and Jason's profit-maximizing output; it is the level of output at which marginal cost is equal to the market price, $18.

This example, in fact, illustrates another general rule derived from marginal analysis—the **price-taking firm's optimal output rule,** which says that a price-taking firm's profit is maximized by producing the quantity of output at which the market price is equal to the marginal cost of the last unit produced. That is, $P = MC$ at the *price-taking firm's* optimal quantity of output. In fact, the price-taking firm's optimal output rule is just an application of the optimal output rule to the particular case of a price-taking firm. Why? Because in the case of a price-taking firm, *marginal revenue is equal to price.* A price-taking firm cannot influence the market price by its actions. It always takes the market price as given because it cannot lower the market price by selling more or raise the market price by selling less. So, for a price-taking firm, the additional revenue generated by producing one more unit is always the market price. We will need to keep this fact in mind in future chapters, where we will learn that marginal revenue is not equal to the market price if the industry is not perfectly competitive and, as a result, firms are not price-takers.

For the remainder of this chapter, we will assume that the firms in question are, like Jennifer and Jason's farm, perfectly competitive. Figure 8-1 shows that Jennifer and Jason's profit-maximizing quantity of output is, indeed, the number of bushels at which the marginal cost of production is equal to price. The figure shows the marginal cost curve, *MC,* drawn from the data in the last column of Table 8-1. As in Chapter 7, we plot the marginal cost of increasing output from 1 to 2 bushels halfway between 1 and 2, and so on. The horizontal line at $18 is Jennifer and Jason's **marginal revenue curve, MR.** Note that whenever a firm is a price-taker, its marginal revenue curve is a horizontal line at the market price: it can sell as much as it likes at the market price. Regardless of whether it sells more or less, the market price is unaffected. In effect, the individual firm faces a horizontal, perfectly elastic demand curve for its output—an individual demand curve for its output that is equivalent to

### Figure 8-1

#### The Price-Taking Firm's Profit-Maximizing Quantity of Output

At the profit-maximizing quantity of output, the market price is equal to marginal cost. It is located at the point where the marginal cost curve crosses the marginal revenue curve, which is a horizontal line at the market price. Here, the profit-maximizing point is at an output of 5 bushels of tomatoes, the output quantity at point *E*.

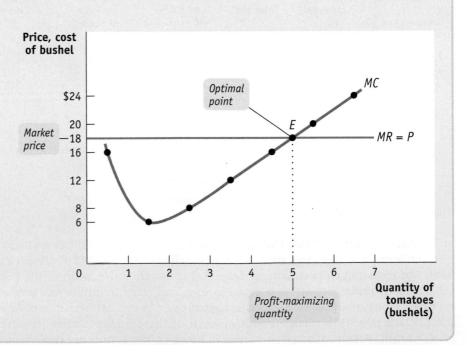

its marginal revenue curve. The marginal cost curve crosses the marginal revenue curve at point *E*. Sure enough, the quantity of output at *E* is 5 bushels.

Does this mean that the firm's production decision can be entirely summed up as "produce up to the point where the marginal cost of production is equal to the price"? No, not quite. Before applying the principle of marginal analysis to determine how much to produce, a potential producer must as a first step answer an "either–or" question: should it produce at all? If the answer to that question is yes, it then proceeds to the second step—a "how much" decision: maximizing profit by choosing the quantity of output at which marginal cost is equal to price.

To understand why the first step in the production decision involves an "either–or" question, we need to ask how we determine whether it is profitable or unprofitable to produce at all.

## Accounting Profit Versus Economic Profit

First we need to distinguish between two definitions of profit: *accounting profit* and *economic profit*. To do so, recall our definitions from Chapter 7 of explicit and implicit costs. Explicit costs require an outlay of money, such as paying wages to workers. Implicit costs are measured by the dollar value of forgone benefits, such as the income Jennifer and Jason could have made working for someone else instead of running their own organic tomato farm.

So let's consider again Jennifer and Jason's farm. We suppose that Jennifer and Jason own the farm and its buildings themselves. Last year Jennifer and Jason had $150,000 in revenue and $80,000 in expenses. Was their business profitable?

At first it might seem that the answer is obviously yes: they received $150,000 from their customers and had expenses of only $80,000. Doesn't this mean that they had a profit of $70,000? Not according to their accountant, who reduced the number by $5,000 for the yearly depreciation (reduction in value) of the farm buildings. Depreciation occurs because buildings wear out over time. The yearly depreciation amount reflects what an accountant estimates to be the reduction in the value of the buildings due to wear and tear that year. This leaves $65,000, which is the business's **accounting profit.** Basically, the accounting profit of a company is its revenue minus its explicit cost and depreciation. The accounting profit is the number that Jennifer and Jason have to report on their income tax forms and that they would be obliged to report to anyone thinking of investing in their business.

> The **accounting profit** of a business is the business's revenue minus the explicit cost and depreciation.

Accounting profit is a very useful number, but it doesn't answer Jennifer and Jason's question of whether it is profitable or unprofitable to produce at all. Jennifer and Jason need to calculate their **economic profit**—the revenue they receive minus their opportunity cost, which may include implicit as well as explicit costs. In general, when economists use the simple term *profit*, they are referring to economic profit. (We will adopt this simplification in this book.)

> The **economic profit** of a business is the business's revenue minus the opportunity cost of its resources. It is usually less than the accounting profit.

Why does Jennifer and Jason's economic profit differ from their accounting profit? Because they may have implicit costs over and above the explicit cost their accountant has calculated. Businesses can face implicit costs for two reasons. First, a business's **capital**—its equipment, buildings, tools, inventory, and financial assets—could have been put to use in some other way. If the business owns its capital, it does not pay any money for its use, but it pays an implicit cost because it does not use the capital in some other way. Second, the owner devotes time and energy to the business that could have been used elsewhere—a particularly important factor in small businesses, whose owners tend to put in many long hours.

> The **capital** of a business is the value of its assets—equipment, buildings, tools, inventory, and financial assets.

If Jennifer and Jason had rented their farm from its owner, their rent would have been an explicit cost. But because they own the farm buildings, they do not pay rent and their accountant deducts an estimate of their depreciation in the profit statement. However, this does not account for the opportunity cost of the farm buildings—what Jennifer and Jason forgo by owning them. Suppose that instead of using the farm for their own business, the best alternative Jennifer and

The **implicit cost of capital** is the opportunity cost of the capital used by a business—the income the owner could have realized from that capital if it had been used in its next best alternative way.

Jason have is to sell the farm for $200,000 and put the money into a bank account where it would earn yearly interest of $10,000. This $10,000 is an implicit cost of running the business.

It is generally known as the **implicit cost of capital,** the opportunity cost of the capital used by a business; it reflects the income that could have been realized if the capital had been used in its next best alternative way. It is just as much a true cost as if Jennifer and Jason had rented the farm instead of owning it.

Finally, Jennifer and Jason should take into account the opportunity cost of their own time. Suppose that instead of running the farm, they could earn $49,000 managing a farm. That $49,000 is also an implicit cost of their business.

So Jennifer and Jason face $144,000 in total costs—$80,000 in expenses plus $5,000 depreciation plus $10,000 implicit cost of capital plus $49,000 opportunity cost of their time. Their economic profit was the difference between their revenue of $150,000 and total costs of $144,000, $6,000 for the year or just over $16 a day.

## When Is Production Profitable?

That was last year. Is Jennifer and Jason's farm profitable this year? Let's look at their daily costs. We will assume that all costs, implicit as well as explicit, are included in the cost numbers given in Table 8-1; as a result, the profit numbers in Table 8-2 are economic profit. So what determines whether Jennifer and Jason's farm earns a profit or generates a loss? The answer is that, given the farm's cost curves, whether or not it is profitable depends on the market price of tomatoes—specifically, *whether the market price is more or less than the farm's minimum average total cost.*

Table 8-3 calculates short-run average variable cost and short-run average total cost for Jennifer and Jason's farm. These are short-run values, because we take fixed cost as given. (We'll turn to the effects of changing fixed cost shortly.) The short-run average total cost curve, ATC, is shown in Figure 8-2, along with the marginal cost curve, MC, from Figure 8-1. As you can see, average total cost is minimized at point C, corresponding to an output of 4 bushels—the *minimum-cost output*—and an average total cost of $14 per bushel.

To see how these curves can be used to decide whether production is profitable or unprofitable, recall that profit is equal to total revenue minus total cost, $TR - TC$. This means:

- If $TR > TC$, the firm is profitable.
- If $TR = TC$, the firm breaks even.
- If $TR < TC$, the firm incurs a loss.

## TABLE 8-3

### Average Costs for Jennifer and Jason's Farm

| Quantity of tomatoes Q (bushels) | Variable cost VC | Total cost TC | Average variable cost of bushel AVC = VC/Q | Average total cost of bushel ATC = TC/Q |
|---|---|---|---|---|
| 1 | $16.00 | $30.00 | $16.00 | $30.00 |
| 2 | 22.00 | 36.00 | 11.00 | 18.00 |
| 3 | 30.00 | 44.00 | 10.00 | 14.67 |
| 4 | 42.00 | 56.00 | 10.50 | 14.00 |
| 5 | 58.00 | 72.00 | 11.60 | 14.40 |
| 6 | 78.00 | 92.00 | 13.00 | 15.33 |
| 7 | 102.00 | 116.00 | 14.57 | 16.57 |

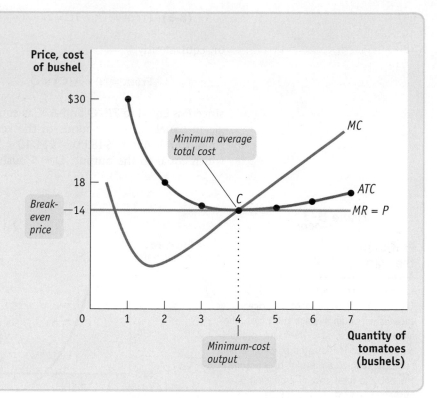

**Figure 8-2**

**Costs and Production in the Short Run**

This figure shows the marginal cost curve, *MC*, and the short-run average total cost curve, *ATC*. When the market price is $14, output will be 4 bushels of tomatoes (the minimum-cost output), represented by point *C*. The price of $14, equal to the firm's minimum average total cost, is the firm's *break-even price.* **>web...**

We can also express this idea in terms of revenue and cost per unit of output. If we divide profit by the number of units of output, *Q*, we obtain the following expression for profit per unit of output:

**(8-4)** $\text{Profit}/Q = TR/Q - TC/Q$

*TR/Q* is average revenue—that is, the market price. *TC/Q* is average total cost. So a firm is profitable if the market price for its product exceeds the average total cost of the quantity the firm produces; a firm loses money if the market price is less than average total cost of the quantity the firm produces. This means:

- If *P* > *ATC*, the firm is profitable.
- If *P* = *ATC*, the firm breaks even.
- If *P* < *ATC*, the firm incurs a loss.

Figure 8-3 on page 196 illustrates this result, showing how the market price determines whether a firm is profitable. It also shows how profits are depicted graphically. Each panel shows the marginal cost curve, *MC*, and the short-run average total cost curve, *ATC*. Average total cost is minimized at point *C*. Panel (a) shows the case we have already analyzed, in which the market price of tomatoes is $18 per bushel. Panel (b) shows the case in which the market price of tomatoes is lower, $10 per bushel.

In panel (a), we see that at a price of $18 per bushel the profit-maximizing quantity of output is 5 bushels, indicated by point *E* where the marginal cost curve, *MC*, intersects the marginal revenue curve—which for a price-taking firm is a horizontal line at the market price. At that quantity of output, average total cost is $14.40 per bushel, indicated by point *Z*. Since the price per bushel exceeds average total cost per bushel, Jennifer and Jason's farm is profitable.

Jennifer and Jason's total profits when the market price is $18 are represented by the area of the shaded rectangle in panel (a). To see why, notice that total profit can be expressed in terms of profit per unit:

**(8-5)** Profit = $TR - TC = (TR/Q - TC/Q) \times Q$

or, equivalently,

Profit = $(P - ATC) \times Q$

since $P$ is equal to $TR/Q$ and $ATC$ is equal to $TC/Q$. The height of the shaded rectangle in panel (a) corresponds to the vertical distance between points $E$ and $Z$. It is equal to $P - ATC = \$18.00 - \$14.40 = \$3.60$ per bushel. The shaded rectangle has a width equal to the output: $Q = 5$ bushels. So the area of that rectangle is equal to

## Figure 8-3

### Profitability and the Market Price

In panel (a) the market price is $18. The farm is profitable because price exceeds minimum average total cost, the break-even price, $14. The farm's optimal output choice is indicated by point $E$, corresponding to an output of 5 bushels. The average total cost of producing 5 bushels is indicated by point $Z$ on the $ATC$ curve, corresponding to an amount of $14.40. The vertical distance between $E$ and $Z$ corresponds to the farm's per-unit profit, $18.00 − $14.40 = $3.60. Total profit is given by the area of the shaded rectangle, 5 × $3.60 = $18.00.

In panel (b) the market price is $10; the farm is unprofitable because the price falls below the minimum average total cost, $14. The farm's optimal output choice when producing is indicated by point $A$, corresponding to an output of three bushels. The farm's per-unit loss, $14.67 − $10.00 = $4.67, is represented by the vertical distance between $A$ and $Y$. The farm's total loss is represented by the shaded rectangle, 3 × $4.67 = $14.00 (adjusted for rounding error). **>web...**

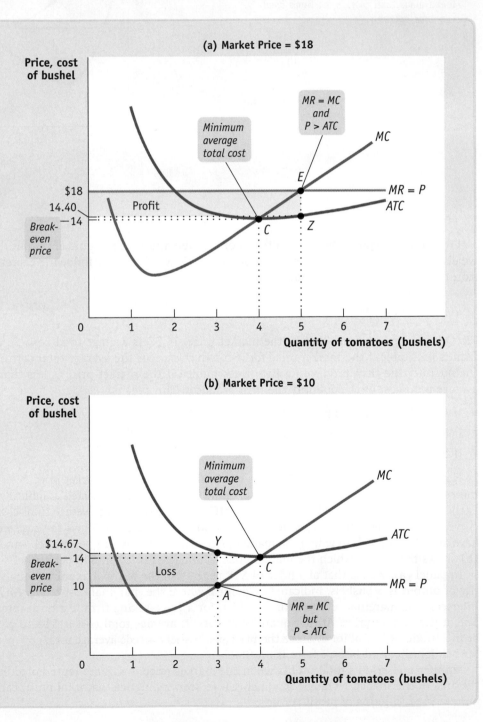

Jennifer and Jason's profit: 5 bushels × $3.60 profit per bushel = $18—the same number we calculated in Table 8-2.

What about the situation illustrated in panel (b)? Here the market price of tomatoes is $10 per bushel. Setting price equal to marginal cost leads to a profit-maximizing output of 3 bushels, indicated by point A. At this output, Jennifer and Jason have an average total cost of $14.67 per bushel, indicated by point Y. At their profit-maximizing output quantity—3 bushels—average total cost exceeds the market price. This means that Jennifer and Jason's farm generates losses, not profits.

How much do they lose by producing when the market price is $10? On each bushel they lose $ATC - P = \$14.67 - \$10.00 = \$4.67$, an amount corresponding to the vertical distance between points A and Y. And, they would produce 3 bushels, which corresponds to the width of the shaded rectangle. So, the total value of the losses is $\$4.67 \times 3 = \$14.00$ (adjusted for rounding error), an amount that corresponds to the area of the shaded rectangle in panel (b).

But how does a producer know, in general, whether or not its business will be profitable? It turns out that the crucial test lies in a comparison of the market price to the producer's *minimum average total cost*. On Jennifer and Jason's farm, minimum average total cost, which is equal to $14, occurs at an output quantity of 4 bushels. Whenever the market price exceeds minimum average total cost, the producer can find some output level for which the average total cost is less than the market price. That means that the producer can find a level of output at which the firm makes a profit. Jennifer and Jason's farm will be profitable whenever the market price exceeds $14. And they will achieve the highest profit by producing the quantity at which marginal cost equals the market price.

On the other hand, if the market price is less than minimum average total cost, there is no output level at which price exceeds average total cost. As a result, the firm will be unprofitable at any quantity of output. As we saw, at a price of $10—an amount less than minimum average total cost—Jennifer and Jason did indeed lose money. By producing the quantity at which marginal cost equals the market price, Jennifer and Jason did the best they could, but the best that they could do was a loss of $14. Any other quantity would have increased the size of their loss.

The minimum average total cost of a price-taking firm is called its **break-even price,** the price at which it earns zero profits. A firm will earn positive profits when the market price is above the break-even price, and it will suffer losses when the market price is below the break-even price. Jennifer and Jason's break-even price of $14 is the price at point C in Figures 8-2 and 8-3.

The **break-even price** of a price-taking firm is the market price at which it earns zero profits.

So the rule for determining whether a producer of a good is profitable depends on a comparison of the market price of the good to the producer's break-even price—its minimum average total cost:

- Whenever the market price exceeds minimum average total cost, the producer is profitable.

- Whenever the market price equals minimum average total cost, the producer breaks even.

- Whenever the market price is less than minimum average total cost, the producer is unprofitable.

## The Short-Run Production Decision

You might be tempted to say that if a firm is unprofitable because the market price is below its minimum average total cost, it shouldn't produce any output. In the short run, however, this conclusion is not correct. In the short run, sometimes the firm should produce even if price falls below minimum average total cost. The reason is that total cost includes *fixed cost*—cost that does not depend on the amount of output produced. In the short run, fixed cost must still be paid, regardless of whether or not a firm produces. For example, if Jennifer and Jason have rented a tractor for the year, they have to pay that rent regardless of whether they produce any tomatoes. Since it cannot be changed in the short run, their fixed cost is irrelevant to their decision about whether to produce or shut down in the short run. Although fixed cost should play no role in the decision about whether to produce at all in the short run, other costs—variable costs—do matter. An example of variable costs is the wages of workers who must be hired to help with planting and harvesting. Variable costs can be saved by *not* producing; so they should play a role in determining whether or not to produce in the short run.

Let's turn to Figure 8-4: it shows both the short-run average total cost curve, *ATC*, and the short-run average *variable* cost curve, *AVC*, drawn from the information in Table 8-3. Recall that the difference between the two curves—the vertical distance between them—represents average fixed cost, the fixed cost per unit of output, *FC/Q*. Because the marginal cost curve has a "swoosh" shape—falling at first before rising— the short-run average variable cost curve is U-shaped: the initial fall in marginal cost causes average variable cost to fall as well, before rising marginal cost eventually pulls it up again. The short-run average variable cost curve reaches its minimum value of $10 at point *A*, at an output of 3 bushels.

We are now prepared to fully analyze the optimal production decision in the short run. We need to consider two cases:

■ When the market price is below minimum average *variable* cost

■ When the market price is greater than or equal to minimum average *variable* cost

When the market price is below minimum average variable cost, the price the firm receives is not covering its variable cost per unit. A firm in this situation should cease production immediately. Why? Because there is no level of output at which the firm's total revenue covers its variable costs—the costs it can avoid by not operating. In this case the firm maximizes its profits by not producing at all—by, in effect, minimizing its losses. It will still incur a fixed cost in the short run, but it

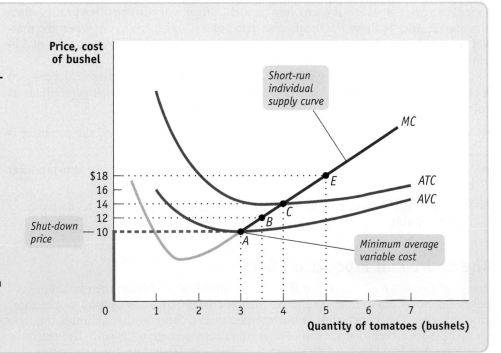

### Figure 8-4

### The Short-Run Individual Supply Curve

When the market price exceeds Jennifer and Jason's *shut-down price* of $10, the minimum average variable cost indicated by point *A*, they will produce the output quantity at which marginal cost is equal to price. So at any price above minimum average *variable* cost, the short-run individual supply curve is the firm's marginal cost curve; this corresponds to the upward-sloping segment of the individual supply curve. When market price falls below minimum average variable cost, the firm ceases operation in the short run. This corresponds to the vertical segment of the individual supply curve along the vertical axis.

will no longer incur any variable cost. This means that the minimum average variable cost is equal to the **shut-down price,** the price at which the firm ceases production in the short run.

When price is greater than minimum average variable cost, however, the firm should produce in the short run. In this case, the firm maximizes profit—or minimizes its loss—by choosing the output quantity at which its marginal cost is equal to the market price. For example, if the market price of tomatoes is $18 per bushel, Jennifer and Jason should produce at point E in Figure 8-4, corresponding to an output of 5 bushels. Note that point C in Figure 8-4 corresponds to the farm's break-even price of $14 per bushel. Since E lies above C, Jennifer and Jason's farm will be profitable; they will generate a per-bushel profit of $18.00 − $14.40 = $3.60 when the market price is $18.

But what if the market price lies between the shut-down price and the break-even price—that is, between minimum average *variable* cost and minimum average *total* cost? In the case of Jennifer and Jason's farm, this corresponds to prices anywhere between $10 and $14—say, a market price of $12. At $12, Jennifer and Jason's farm is not profitable; since the market price is below minimum average total cost, the farm is losing the difference between price and average total cost per unit produced. Yet, even if it isn't covering its total cost per unit, it is covering its variable cost per unit and some—but not all—of the fixed cost per unit. If a firm in this situation shuts down, it would incur no variable cost but would incur the *full* fixed cost. As a result, shutting down generates an even greater loss than continuing to operate.

This means that whenever price falls between minimum average total cost and minimum average variable cost, the firm is better off producing some output in the short run. The reason is that by producing, it can cover its variable cost per unit and at least some of its fixed cost, even though it is incurring a loss. In this case, the firm maximizes profit—that is, minimizes its loss—by choosing the quantity of output at which its marginal cost is equal to the market price. So if Jennifer and Jason face a market price of $12 per bushel, their profit-maximizing output is given by point B in Figure 8-4, corresponding to an output of 3.5 bushels.

It's worth noting that the decision to produce when the firm is covering its variable costs but not all of its fixed cost is similar to the decision to ignore sunk costs. A **sunk cost** is a cost that has already been incurred and cannot be recouped; and because it cannot be changed, it should have no effect on any current decision. In the short-run production decision, fixed cost is, in effect, like a sunk cost—it has been spent, and it can't be recovered in the short run. This comparison also illustrates why variable cost does indeed matter in the short run: it can be avoided by not producing.

And what happens if market price is exactly equal to the shut-down price, minimum average variable cost? In this instance, the firm is indifferent between producing 3 units or 0 units. As we'll see shortly, this is an important point when looking at the behavior of an industry as a whole.

Putting everything together, we can now draw the **short-run individual supply curve** of Jennifer and Jason's farm; it shows how the profit-maximizing quantity of output in the short run depends on the price, the red line in Figure 8-4. As you can see, the curve is in two segments. The upward-sloping red segment starting at point A shows the short-run profit-maximizing output when market price is above the shut-down price of $10 per bushel. As long as the market price is above the shut-down price, Jennifer and Jason produce the quantity of output at which marginal cost is equal to the market price. That is, at market prices above the shut-down price, the firm's short-run supply curve corresponds to its marginal cost curve. But at any market price below minimum average variable cost—in this case, $10 per bushel—the firm shuts down and output drops to zero in the

A firm will cease production in the short run if the market price falls below the **shut-down price**, which is equal to minimum average variable cost.

A **sunk cost** is a cost that has already been incurred and is nonrecoverable. A sunk cost should be ignored in decisions about future actions.

The **short-run individual supply curve** shows how an individual producer's profit-maximizing output quantity depends on the market price, taking fixed cost as given.

**ECONOMIC PROFIT, AGAIN**

Some readers may wonder why firms would enter an industry when they will do little more than break even. Wouldn't people prefer to go into other businesses that yield a better profit?

The answer is that here, as always, when we calculate cost, we mean *opportunity cost*—that is, cost that includes the return a business owner could get by using his or her resources elsewhere. And so the profit that we calculate is *economic profit*; if the market price is above the break-even level, potential business owners can earn more in this industry than they could elsewhere.

short run. This corresponds to the vertical segment of the curve that lies on top of the vertical axis.

Do firms really shut down temporarily without going out of business? Yes. In fact, in some businesses temporary shut-downs are routine. The most common examples are industries in which demand is highly seasonal, like outdoor amusement parks in climates with cold winters. Such parks would have to offer very low prices to entice customers during the colder months—prices so low that the owners would not cover their variable costs (principally wages and electricity). The wiser choice economically is to shut down until warm weather brings enough customers who are willing to pay a higher price.

## Changing Fixed Cost

Although fixed cost cannot be altered in the short run, in the long run firms can acquire or get rid of machines, buildings, and so on. As we learned in Chapter 7, in the long run the level of fixed cost is a matter of choice. We saw that a firm will choose the level of fixed cost that minimizes the average total cost for its desired output quantity. Now we will focus on an even bigger question facing a firm when choosing its fixed cost: whether to incur *any* fixed cost at all by remaining in its current business.

In the long run, a producer can always eliminate fixed cost by selling off its plant and equipment. If it does so, of course, it can't ever produce—it has exited the industry. In contrast, a potential producer can take on some fixed cost by acquiring machines and other resources, which puts it in a position to produce—it can enter the industry. In most perfectly competitive industries the set of producers, although fixed in the short run, changes in the long run as firms enter or leave the industry.

Consider Jennifer and Jason's farm once again. In order to simplify our analysis, we will sidestep the problem of choosing among several possible levels of fixed cost. Instead, we will assume from now on that Jennifer and Jason have only one possible choice of fixed cost if they operate, the amount of $14 that was the basis for the calculations in Tables 8-1, 8-2, and 8-3. Alternatively, they can choose a fixed cost of zero if they exit the industry. (With this assumption, Jennifer and Jason's short-run average total cost curve and long-run average total cost curve are one and the same.)

Suppose that the market price of organic tomatoes is consistently less than $14 over an extended period of time. In that case, Jennifer and Jason never fully cover their fixed cost: their business runs at a loss. In the long run, then, they can do better by closing their business and leaving the industry. In other words, *in the long run* firms will exit an industry if the market price is consistently less than their break-even price—their minimum average total cost.

On the other hand, suppose that the price of organic tomatoes is consistently above the break-even price, $14, for an extended period of time. Because their farm is profitable, Jennifer and Jason will remain in the industry and continue producing. But things won't stop there. The organic tomato industry meets the criterion of *free entry*: there are many potential organic tomato producers because the necessary inputs are easy to obtain. And the cost curves of those potential producers are likely to be similar to those of Jennifer and Jason, since the technology used by other producers is likely to be very similar to that used by Jennifer and Jason. If the price is high enough to generate profits for existing producers, it will also attract some of these potential producers into the industry. So *in the long run* a price in excess of $14 should lead to entry: new producers will come into the organic tomato industry.

As we will see in the next section, exit and entry lead to an important distinction between the *short-run industry supply curve* and the *long-run industry supply curve*.

## Summing Up: The Perfectly Competitive Firm's Profitability and Production Conditions

In this chapter, we've studied where the supply curve for a perfectly competitive firm comes from. Every perfectly competitive firm makes its production decisions by maximizing profit, and these decisions determine the supply curve. Table 8-4 summarizes the competitive firm's profitability and production conditions. It also relates them to entry and exit from the industry.

**TABLE 8-4**

### Summary of the Perfectly Competitive Firm's Profitability and Production Conditions

| Profitability Condition (minimum *ATC* = break-even price) | Result |
|---|---|
| $P$ > minimum $ATC$ | Firm profitable. Entry into industry in the long run. |
| $P$ = minimum $ATC$ | Firm breaks even. No entry into or exit from industry in the long run. |
| $P$ < minimum $ATC$ | Firm unprofitable. Exit from industry in the long run. |

| Production Condition (minimum *AVC* = shut-down price) | Result |
|---|---|
| $P$ > minimum $AVC$ | Firm produces in the short run. If $P$ < minimum $ATC$, firm covers variable cost and some but not all of fixed cost. If $P$ > minimum $ATC$, firm covers all variable cost and fixed cost. |
| $P$ = minimum $AVC$ | Firm indifferent between producing in the short run or not. Just covers variable cost. |
| $P$ < minimum $AVC$ | Firm shuts down in the short run. Does not cover variable cost. |

# *economics in action*

## California Screaming

Between November 2000 and May 2001, the state of California went through an electricity crisis. Supplies of power were limited, and the wholesale price of electricity—the price at which generators sell power to the local utilities, which then provide it to customers—ran consistently at more than 10 times its normal level.

During the crisis, some economists accused the power generators of deliberately withholding electricity from the market in order to drive up prices. That is, they argued that competition wasn't perfect, that producers weren't taking prices as given.

How could you tell whether or not producers were acting as price-takers? Economists used data on electricity generating costs to estimate marginal cost curves for producers. They could then ask whether the producers were actually generating as much power as they should have if they were setting price equal to marginal cost. The conclusion of several influential studies, including a federal investigation by the Justice Department, was that they were not.

Eventually, power companies were caught red-handed: tape recordings revealed they purposely shut down plants in order to drive up prices. Economists applying marginal analysis had gotten it right. ∎

> > > > > > > > > > > > > > > > > > > >

>> **QUICK REVIEW**

➤ The optimal quantity of an activity is found by applying the *principle of marginal analysis*. It says that the optimal quantity of an activity is the quantity at which marginal benefit is equal to marginal cost.

➤ A producer chooses output according to the *optimal output rule*. For a price-taking firm, *marginal revenue* is equal to price and it chooses output according to the *price-taking firm's optimal output rule*.

➤ Companies report their *accounting profit*, which is not necessarily equal to their *economic profit*. Due to the *implicit cost of capital*, the opportunity cost of a company's *capital*, and the opportunity cost of the owner's time, economic profit is often substantially less than accounting profit.

➤ A firm is profitable whenever market price exceeds its *break-even price*, equal to its minimum average total cost. A firm is unprofitable whenever price falls below its break-even price. And a firm breaks even when price is equal to its break-even price.

➤ Fixed cost, like *sunk cost*, is irrelevant to the firm's optimal short-run production decision. When price exceeds its *shut-down price*—minimum average variable cost—the price-taking firm produces the quantity of output at which marginal cost equals price. When price is lower than its shut-down price, it ceases production in the short run. This defines the firm's *short-run individual supply curve*.

➤ In the long run, fixed cost matters. If price falls below minimum average total cost for an extended period of time, a firm will exit the industry. If price exceeds minimum average total cost, the firm is profitable and will remain in the industry; in addition, other firms will enter the industry.

## PROFIT-MAXIMIZING QUANTITY OF OUTPUT

Ada's Donut Shop is one of dozens of donut shops in town, all of which sell crumb donuts that look and taste the same. The cost curves for Ada's Donut Shop are shown below.

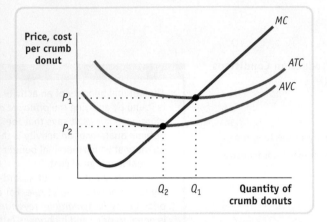

**Profit Max:** If crumb donuts are selling at the price $P_1$, what quantity of output will maximize Ada's profit? *(Profit: The difference between revenue and total costs, which include opportunity cost of time and implicit cost of capital.)* How much profit will Ada's Donut Shop earn?

Profit is maximized when Ada chooses to produce the quantity of output where marginal cost equals marginal revenue. *(Marginal cost: The additional cost of producing one more unit of output. Marginal revenue: The additional revenue from selling one more unit of output.)* Because Ada is a perfect competitor, a price-taker, her marginal revenue

is simply the price. Her total profit is the difference between price and average total cost, times the quantity.

**SOLUTION:** Profit is maximized when Ada produces $Q_1$ donuts, the amount of output where marginal cost equals price $P_1$. At that output, $P_1$ equals the average total cost so profit is zero.

**Economic Profit:** Why would Ada continue to operate Ada's Donut Shop if she earned no profit?

**SOLUTION:** Ada has zero **economic** profit, which means that her revenue covers her operating costs **and** the opportunity cost of her time and the implicit cost of her capital. Her accounting profit thus equals the opportunity cost of her time plus the implicit cost of her capital. Ada is doing as well running the donut shop as she could doing anything else.

**Economic Loss:** Over what range of prices will Ada incur an economic loss but continue to operate in the short run? *(Economic loss: When profit is negative; when revenue is less than total costs.)*

There is an economic loss—profit is negative—whenever price is less than the minimum average total cost (the break-even price). Even if Ada's Donut Shop is incurring losses, it will continue to operate so long as revenues cover the fixed cost of production. That is, Ada's will continue to sell donuts in the short run whenever price is above the minimum average variable cost (the shut-down price).

**SOLUTION:** Ada's Donut Shop will incur an economic loss but continue to operate in the short run when the price is between the break-even price $P_1$ and the shut-down price $P_2$.

---

1. Draw a short-run diagram showing a U-shaped average total cost curve, a U-shaped average variable cost curve, and a "swoosh"-shaped marginal cost curve. On it, indicate the range of output and the range of price for which the following actions are optimal.
   a. The firm shuts down immediately.
   b. The firm operates in the short run despite sustaining a loss.
   c. The firm operates while making a profit.

2. The state of Maine has a very active lobster industry, which harvests lobsters during the summer months. During the rest of the year, lobsters can be obtained from other parts of the world but at a much higher price. Maine is also full of "lobster shacks," roadside restaurants serving lobster dishes that are open only during the summer. Explain why it is optimal for lobster shacks to operate only during the summer.

*Solutions appear at back of book.*

---

> The **industry supply curve** shows the relationship between the price of a good and the total output of the industry as a whole.

# The Industry Supply Curve

Why will an increase in the demand for organic tomatoes lead to a large price increase at first but a much smaller increase in the long run? The answer lies in the behavior of the **industry supply curve**—the relationship between the price and the total output of an industry as a whole. The industry supply curve is what we referred to in earlier chapters as the *supply curve* or the *market supply curve*. But here we take some extra care to distinguish between the *individual supply curve* of a single firm and the supply curve of the industry as a whole.

As you might guess from the previous section, the industry supply curve must be analyzed in somewhat different ways for the short run and the long run. Let's start with the short run.

## The Short-Run Industry Supply Curve

Recall that in the short run the number of producers in an industry is fixed—there is no entry or exit. We can best understand how the industry supply curve emerges from individual producer supply curves by imagining that all the producers are alike. So let's assume that there are 100 organic tomato farms, each with the same costs as Jennifer and Jason's farm.

Each of these 100 farms will have an individual short-run supply curve like the one in Figure 8-4 on page 198. At a price below $10, no farms will produce. At a price of more than $10, each farm will produce the quantity of output at which its marginal cost is equal to the market price. As you can see from Figure 8-4, this will lead them to produce 4 bushels if the price is $14 per bushel, 5 bushels if the price is $18, and so on. So if there are 100 organic tomato farmers and the price of organic tomatoes is $18 per bushel, the industry as a whole will produce 500 bushels, corresponding to 100 farmers × 5 bushels per farmer, and so on. The result is the **short-run industry supply curve**, shown as S in Figure 8-5. This curve shows the quantity that producers will supply at each price, *taking the number of producers as given*.

The demand curve D in Figure 8-5 crosses the short-run industry supply curve at $E_{MKT}$, corresponding to a price of $18 and a quantity of 500 bushels. Point $E_{MKT}$ is a **short-run market equilibrium:** the quantity supplied equals the quantity demanded, taking the number of producers as given. But the long run may look quite different, because in the long run farms may enter or exit the industry.

> The **short-run industry supply curve** shows how the quantity supplied by an industry depends on the market price given a fixed number of producers.
>
> There is a **short-run market equilibrium** when the quantity supplied equals the quantity demanded, taking the number of producers as given.

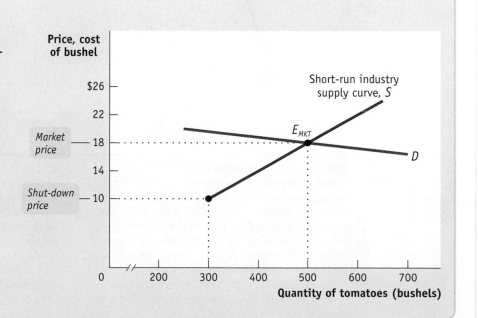

### Figure 8-5

**The Short-Run Market Equilibrium**

The short-run industry supply curve, *S*, is the industry supply curve taking the number of producers—here, 100—as given. It is generated by adding together the individual supply curves of the 100 producers. Below the shut-down price of $10, no producer wants to produce in the short run. Above $10, the short-run industry supply curve slopes upward, as each producer increases output as price increases. It intersects the demand curve, *D*, at point $E_{MKT}$, the point of short-run market equilibrium, corresponding to a market price of $18 and a quantity of 500 bushels. **>web...**

## The Long-Run Industry Supply Curve

Suppose that in addition to the 100 farmers currently in the organic tomato business, there are many other potential producers. Suppose also that each of these potential producers would have the same cost curves as existing producers like Jennifer and Jason if it entered the industry

When will additional producers enter the industry? Whenever existing producers are making a profit—that is, whenever the market price is above the break-even price of $14 per bushel, the minimum average total cost of production. For example, at a price of $18 per bushel, new firms will enter the industry.

What will happen as additional producers enter the industry? Clearly, the quantity supplied at any given price will increase. The short-run industry supply curve will shift to the right. This will, in turn, alter the market equilibrium and result in a lower market price. Existing firms will respond to the lower market price by reducing their output, but the total industry output will increase because of the larger number of firms in the industry.

Figure 8-6 illustrates the effects of this chain of events on an existing firm and on the market; panel (a) shows how an individual existing firm responds to entry, and panel (b) shows how the market responds to entry. (Note that these two graphs have been rescaled in comparison to Figure 8-4 to better illustrate how profit changes in response to price.) In panel (b), $S_1$ is the initial short-run industry supply curve, based on the existence of 100 producers. The initial short-run market equilibrium is at $E_{MKT}$, with an equilibrium market price of $18 and a quantity of 500 bushels. At this price existing producers are profitable, which is reflected in panel (a): an existing firm makes a total profit represented by the shaded rectangle labeled $A$ when market price is $18.

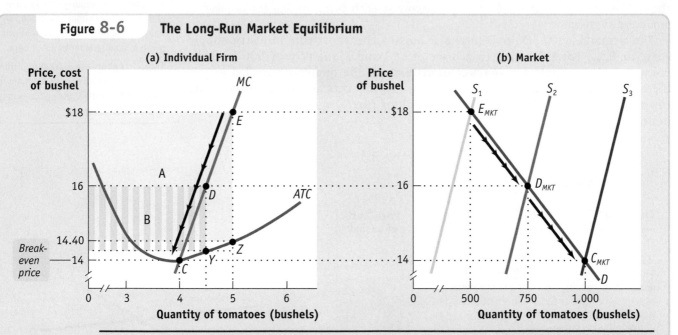

### Figure 8-6    The Long-Run Market Equilibrium

Point $E_{MKT}$ of panel (b) shows the initial short-run market equilibrium, at the intersection of the demand curve, $D$, and the initial short-run industry supply curve, $S_1$. Because the market price ($18) is above the break-even price ($14), each of the 100 existing producers makes an economic profit; this is illustrated in panel (a), where the rectangle labeled $A$ shows the profit of an existing firm. These profits induce entry by additional producers, shifting the short-run industry supply curve outward from $S_1$ to $S_2$ in panel (b). This results in a new short-run equilibrium at point $D_{MKT}$ with a lower market

price of $16 and higher industry output. The output and profits of existing firms are reduced; but some profit remains, as shown by the rectangle labeled $B$ in panel (a). Entry continues shifting out the short-run industry supply curve, as price falls and industry output increases yet again. Entry finally ceases once an equilibrium, at point $C_{MKT}$ on supply curve $S_3$, is reached. Here market price is equal to the break-even price; existing producers make zero economic profits and there is no incentive for entry or exit. Therefore $C_{MKT}$ is also a long-run market equilibrium.

These profits will induce new producers to enter the industry, shifting the short-run industry supply curve to the right. For example, the short-run industry supply curve when the number of producers has increased to 167 is $S_2$. Corresponding to this supply curve is a new short-run market equilibrium labeled $D_{MKT}$, with a market price of $16 and a quantity of 750 bushels. At $16, each firm produces 4.5 bushels, so that industry output is $167 \times 4.5 = 750$ bushels (rounded). From panel (a) you can see the effect of the entry of 67 new producers on an existing firm: the fall in price causes it to reduce its output, and its profit falls to the area represented by the shaded rectangle labeled B.

Although diminished, the profit of existing firms at $D_{MKT}$ means that entry will continue and the number of firms will continue to rise. If the number of producers rises to 250, the short-run industry supply curve shifts out again to $S_3$, and the market equilibrium is at $C_{MKT}$, with a quantity supplied and demanded of 1,000 bushels and a market price of $14 per bushel.

Like $E_{MKT}$ and $D_{MKT}$, $C_{MKT}$ is a short-run equilibrium. But it is also something more. Because the price of $14 is each firm's break-even price, an existing producer makes zero economic profits—neither a profit nor a loss—when producing its profit-maximizing output of 4 bushels. At this price there is no incentive either for potential producers to enter or for existing producers to exit the industry. So $C_{MKT}$ corresponds to a **long-run market equilibrium**—a situation in which quantity supplied equals the quantity demanded given that sufficient time has elapsed for producers to either enter or exit the industry. In a long-run market equilibrium, all existing and potential producers have fully adjusted to their optimal long-run choices; as a result, no producer has an incentive to either enter or exit the industry.

To explore further the significance of the difference between short-run and long-run equilibrium, consider the effect of an increase in demand on an industry with free entry that is initially in long-run equilibrium. Panel (b) in Figure 8-7 on page 206 shows the market adjustment; panels (a) and (c) show how an existing individual firm behaves during the process.

In panel (b) of Figure 8-7, $D_1$ is the initial demand curve and $S_1$ is the initial short-run industry supply curve. Their intersection at point $X_{MKT}$ is both a short-run and a long-run market equilibrium, because the equilibrium price of $14 leads to zero economic profits—and therefore neither entry nor exit. It corresponds to point X in panel (a), where an individual existing firm is operating at the minimum of its average total cost curve.

Now suppose that the demand curve shifts out for some reason to $D_2$. As shown in panel (b), in the short run, industry output moves along the short-run industry supply curve $S_1$ to the new short-run market equilibrium at $Y_{MKT}$, the intersection of $S_1$ and $D_2$. The market price rises to $18 per bushel and industry output increases from $Q_X$ to $Q_Y$. This corresponds to the movement from X to Y in panel (a), as an existing firm increases its output in response to the rise in the market price.

But we know that $Y_{MKT}$ is not a long-run equilibrium, because $18 is higher than minimum average total cost, so existing producers are making economic profits. This will lead additional firms to enter the industry. Over time entry will cause the short-run industry supply curve to shift to the right. In the long run, the short-run industry supply curve will have shifted out to $S_2$, and the equilibrium will be at $Z_{MKT}$—with the price falling back to $14 per bushel and industry output increasing yet again, from $Q_Y$ to $Q_Z$. Like $X_{MKT}$ before the increase in demand, $Z_{MKT}$ is both a short-run and a long-run market equilibrium.

The effect of entry on an existing firm is illustrated in panel (c), in the movement from Y to Z along the firm's individual supply curve. The firm reduces its output in response to the fall in price, ultimately arriving back at its original output quantity, corresponding to the minimum of its average total cost curve. In fact, every firm that is now in the industry—the initial set of firms and the new entrants—will operate at the minimum of its average total cost curves, at point Z. This means that the entire increase in industry output, from $Q_X$ to $Q_Z$, comes from production by new entrants.

A market is in **long-run market equilibrium** when the quantity supplied equals the quantity demanded, given that sufficient time has elapsed for entry into and exit from the industry to occur.

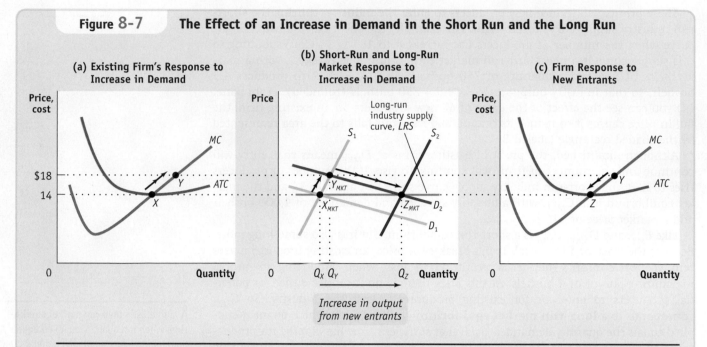

### Figure 8-7 · The Effect of an Increase in Demand in the Short Run and the Long Run

**(a) Existing Firm's Response to Increase in Demand**

**(b) Short-Run and Long-Run Market Response to Increase in Demand**

**(c) Firm Response to New Entrants**

*Increase in output from new entrants*

Panel (b) shows how an industry adjusts in the short and long run to an increase in demand; panels (a) and (c) show the corresponding adjustments by an existing firm. Initially the market is at point $X_{MKT}$ in panel (b), a short-run and long-run equilibrium at a price of $14 and industry output of $Q_X$. An existing firm makes zero profit, operating at point $X$ in panel (a) at minimum average total cost. Demand increases as $D_1$ shifts rightward to $D_2$, and raises the market price to $18. Existing firms increase their output and industry output moves along the short-run industry supply curve $S_1$ to a short-run equilibrium at $Y_{MKT}$. Correspondingly, the existing firm in panel (a) moves from point $X$ to point $Y$. But at a price of $18 existing firms are profitable. As shown in panel (b), in the long run new entrants arrive and the short-run industry suppply curve shifts rightward, from $S_1$ to $S_2$. There is a new equilibrium at point $Z_{MKT}$, at a lower price of $14 and higher industry output of $Q_Z$. An existing firm responds by moving from $Y$ to $Z$ in panel (c), returning to its initial output level and zero profit. Production by new entrants accounts for the total increase in industsy output, $Q_Z - Q_X$. Like $X_{MKT}$, $Z_{MKT}$ is also a short-run and long-run equilibrium: with existing firms earning zero economic profits, there is no incentive for any firms to enter or exit the industry. The horizontal line passing through $X_{MKT}$ and $Z_{MKT}$, $LRS$, is the *long-run industry supply curve*: at the break-even price of $14, producers will produce any amount that consumers demand in the long run.

---

**The long-run industry supply curve** shows how the quantity supplied responds to the price once producers have had time to enter or exit the industry.

The line $LRS$ that passes through $X_{MKT}$ and $Z_{MKT}$ in panel (b) is the **long-run industry supply curve.** It shows how the quantity supplied by an industry responds to the price given that producers have had time to enter or exit the industry.

In this particular case, the long-run industry supply curve is horizontal at $14. In other words, in this industry supply is *perfectly elastic* in the long run—given time to enter or exit, producers will supply any quantity consumers demand at a price of $14. Perfectly elastic long-run supply is actually a good assumption for many industries. However, in other industries even the long-run industry supply curve is upward sloping. The usual reason even the long-run industry supply curve is upward sloping is that producers must use some input that is in limited supply and as the industry expands, the price of that input is driven up. For example, beach-resort hotels must compete for a limited quantity of prime beachfront property.

Whether the long-run industry supply curve is horizontal or upward sloping, however, the long-run price elasticity of supply is *higher* than the short-run price elasticity whenever there is free entry and exit. As shown in Figure 8-8, the long-run industry supply curve is always flatter than the short-run industry supply curve. The reason is entry and exit: a high price attracts entry by new producers, resulting in a

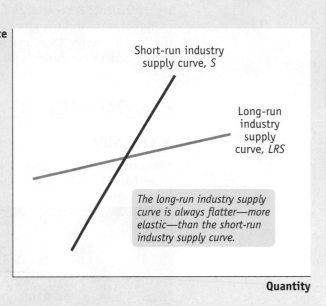

**Figure 8-8**

**Comparing the Short-Run and Long-Run Industry Supply Curves**

The long-run industry supply curve may slope upward, but it is always flatter—more elastic—than the short-run industry supply curve. This is because of entry and exit: a higher price attracts new entrants in the long run, resulting in a rise in industry output and a fall in price; a fall in price induces existing producers to exit in the long run, generating a fall in industry output and a rise in price. >web...

*Price*

Short-run industry supply curve, *S*

Long-run industry supply curve, *LRS*

*The long-run industry supply curve is always flatter—more elastic—than the short-run industry supply curve.*

*Quantity*

rise in industry output and a fall in price; a low price induces existing firms to exit, leading to a fall in industry output and an increase in price.

The distinction between the short-run industry supply curve and the long-run industry supply curve is very important in practice. We often see a sequence of events like that shown in Figure 8-7: an increase in demand initially leads to a large price increase, but prices return to their initial level once new firms have entered the industry. Or we see the sequence in reverse: a fall in demand reduces prices in the short run, but they return to their initial level as producers exit the industry.

## The Cost of Production and Efficiency in Long-Run Equilibrium

Our analysis leads us to three conclusions about the cost of production and efficiency in the long-run equilibrium of a perfectly competitive industry. These results will be important in our discussion in Chapter 11 of how monopoly gives rise to inefficiency.

First, in a perfectly competitive industry in equilibrium, the value of marginal cost is the same for all firms. That's because all firms produce the quantity of output at which marginal cost equals the market price, and as price-takers they all face the same market price.

Second, in a perfectly competitive industry with free entry and exit, each firm will have zero economic profit in long-run equilibrium. Each firm produces the quantity of output that minimizes its average total cost—corresponding to point *Z* in panel (c) of Figure 8-7. So the total cost of production of the industry's output is minimized in a perfectly competitive industry.

The third and final conclusion is that the long-run market equilibrium of a perfectly competitive industry is efficient: no mutually beneficial transactions go unexploited. To understand this we need to recall a fundamental requirement for efficiency from Chapter 6: all consumers who have a willingness to pay greater than or equal to sellers' costs actually get the good. And we also learned that a market is efficient (except under certain, well-defined conditions)—the market price matches all consumers with a willingness to pay greater than or equal to the market price to all sellers who have a cost of producing the good less than or equal to the market price.

How do we know that the long-run equilibrium of a perfectly competitive industry is efficient? Because each firm produces the output level at which price is equal to marginal cost. And marginal cost is in fact the same as seller's cost—the lowest price the firm is willing to accept for the good. So the long-run equilibrium of a market with a perfectly competitive industry is indeed efficient.

# *economics in action*

## A Crushing Reversal

For some reason, starting in the mid-1990s, Americans began drinking a lot more wine. Part of this increase in demand may have reflected a booming economy, but the surge in wine consumption continued even after the economy stumbled in 2001. By 2002, Americans were consuming 35 percent more wine than they did in 1993.

At first, the increase in wine demand led to sharply higher prices; between 1993 and 2000, the price of red wine grapes rose approximately 50 percent, and California grape growers earned high profits. As a result, there was a rapid expansion of the industry, both because existing grape growers expanded their capacity and because new growers entered the market. Between 1994 and 2002, production of red wine grapes almost doubled.

The result was predictable: the price of grapes fell as the supply curve shifted out. As demand growth slowed in 2002, prices plunged by 17 percent. The effect was to end the California wine industry's expansion. In fact, some grape producers began to exit the industry. ∎

Kate Kline/Foodpix/Getty Images

As production expanded and prices fell, profits in the California wine industry shriveled.

< < < < < < < < < < < < < < < < < <

>>**CHECK YOUR UNDERSTANDING 8-3**

1. Which of the following events will induce firms to enter an industry? Which will induce firms to exit? When will entry or exit cease? Explain your answer.
   a. A technological advance lowers the fixed cost of production of every firm in the industry.
   b. The wages paid to workers in the industry go up.
   c. A change in consumer tastes increases demand for the good.
   d. The price of a key input rises due to a shortage of that input.

2. Assume that the egg industry is perfectly competitive and is in long-run equilibrium with a perfectly elastic long-run industry supply curve. Health concerns about cholesterol then lead to a decrease in demand. Construct a figure similar to Figure 8-7, showing the short-run behavior of the industry and how long-run equilibrium is reestablished.

Solutions appear at back of book.

● **A LOOK AHEAD** ●

In this chapter, we have seen how the rational decisions of producers in a perfectly competitive industry give rise to that industry's supply curve. Next we turn to the study of factor markets, which allocate factors of production such as physical capital and labor to various producers.

## SUMMARY

1. In a **perfectly competitive market** all producers are **price-taking producers** and all consumers are **price-taking consumers**—no one's actions can influence the market price. Consumers are normally price-takers, but producers often are not. In a **perfectly competitive industry,** all producers are price-takers.

2. There are two necessary conditions for a perfectly competitive industry: there are many producers, none of whom have a large **market share,** and the industry produces a **standardized product** or **commodity**—goods that consumers regard as equivalent. A third condition is often satisfied as well: **free entry and exit** into and from the industry.

3. An example of the **principle of marginal analysis** is the **optimal output rule:** producers choose to produce the quantity of output at which **marginal revenue** equals marginal cost. For a price-taking firm, marginal revenue is equal to price and its **marginal revenue curve** is a horizontal line at the market price. It chooses output according to the **price-taking firm's optimal output rule:** produce the quantity at which price equals marginal cost. However, a firm that produces the optimal quantity may not be profitable.

4. Companies use **capital** and their owners' time. So companies should base decisions on **economic profit,** which takes into account implicit costs such as the opportunity cost of the owners' time and the **implicit cost of capital.** The **accounting profit,** which companies calculate for the purposes of taxes and public reporting, is often considerably larger than the economic profit because accounting profit considers only explicit costs and depreciation, not implicit costs.

5. A firm is profitable if total revenue exceeds total cost or, equivalently, if the market price exceeds its **break-even price**—minimum average total cost. If market price exceeds the break-even price, the firm is profitable; if it is less, the firm is unprofitable; if it is equal, the firm breaks even. When profitable, the firm's per-unit profit is $P - ATC$; when unprofitable, its per-unit loss is $ATC - P$.

6. Fixed cost, like **sunk cost,** is irrelevant to the firm's optimal short-run production decision, which depends on its **shut-down price**—its minimum average variable cost—and the market price. When the market price exceeds the shut-down price, the firm produces the output quantity where marginal cost equals the market price. When the market price falls below the shut-down price, the firm ceases production in the short run. This generates the firm's **short-run individual supply curve.**

7. Fixed cost matters in the long run. If the market price is below minimum average total cost for an extended period of time, firms will exit the industry. If above, existing firms are profitable and new firms will enter the industry.

8. The **industry supply curve** depends on the time period. The **short-run industry supply curve** is the industry supply curve given that the number of firms is fixed. The **short-run market equilibrium** is given by the intersection of the short-run industry supply curve and the demand curve.

9. The **long-run industry supply curve** is the industry supply curve given sufficient time for entry into and exit from the industry. In the **long-run market equilibrium**—given by the intersection of the long-run industry supply curve and the demand curve—no producer has an incentive to enter or exit. The long-run industry supply curve is often horizontal. It may slope upward if there is limited supply of an input; but it is always flatter than the short-run industry supply curve.

10. In the long-run market equilibrium of a competitive industry, profit maximization leads each firm to produce at the same marginal cost, which is equal to market price. Free entry and exit means that each firm earns zero economic profit—producing the output corresponding to its minimum average total cost. So the total cost of production of an industry's output is minimized. The outcome is efficient because every consumer with a willingness to pay greater or equal to marginal cost gets the good.

## KEY TERMS

Price-taking producer, p. 187
Price-taking consumer, p. 187
Perfectly competitive market, p. 187
Perfectly competitive industry, p. 187
Market share, p. 188
Standardized product, p. 188
Commodity, p. 188
Free entry and exit, p. 189
Profit, p. 190
Principle of marginal analysis, p. 191

Marginal revenue, p. 191
Optimal output rule, p. 191
Price-taking firm's optimal output rule, p. 192
Marginal revenue curve, p. 192
Accounting profit, p. 193
Economic profit, p. 193
Capital, p. 193
Implicit cost of capital, p. 194

Break-even price, p. 197
Shut-down price, p. 199
Sunk costs, p. 199
Short-run individual supply curve, p. 199
Industry supply curve, p. 202
Short-run industry supply curve, p. 203
Short-run market equilibrium, p. 203
Long-run market equilibrium, p. 205
Long-run industry supply curve, p. 206

## PROBLEMS

1. For each of the following, is the business a price-taking producer? Explain your answers.

   a. A cappuccino café in a university town where there are dozens of very similar cappuccino cafés

   b. The makers of Pepsi-Cola

   c. One of many sellers of zucchini at a local farmers' market

2. For each of the following, is the industry perfectly competitive? Referring to market share, standardization of the product, and/or free entry and exit, explain your answers.

   a. Aspirin

   b. Shania Twain concerts

   c. SUVs

3. Hiro owns and operates a small business that provides economic consulting services. During the year he spends $55,000 on travel to clients and other expenses, and the computer that he owns depreciates by $2,000. If he didn't use the computer, he could sell it and earn yearly interest of $100 on the money created through this sale. Hiro's total revenue for the year is $100,000. Instead of working as a consultant for the year, he could teach economics at a small local college and make a salary of $50,000.

   a. What is Hiro's accounting profit?

   b. What is Hiro's economic profit?

   c. Should Hiro continue working as a consultant, or should he teach economics instead?

4. You own and operate a bike store. Each year, you receive revenue of $200,000 from your bike sales, and it costs you $100,000 to obtain the bikes. In addition, you pay $20,000 for electricity, taxes, and other expenses per year. Instead of running the bike store, you could become an accountant and receive a yearly salary of $40,000. A large clothing retail chain wants to expand and offers to rent the store from you for $50,000 per year. How do you explain to your friends that despite making a profit, it is too costly for you to continue running your store?

5. Kate's Katering provides catered meals, and the catered meals industry is perfectly competitive. Kate's machinery costs $100 per day and is the only fixed input. Her variable cost is comprised of the wages paid to the cooks and the food ingredients. The variable cost associated with each level of output is given in the accompanying table.

| Quantity of meals | VC |
|---|---|
| 0 | $0 |
| 10 | 200 |
| 20 | 300 |
| 30 | 480 |
| 40 | 700 |
| 50 | 1,000 |

   a. Calculate the total cost, the average variable cost, the average total cost, and the marginal cost for each quantity of output.

   b. What is the break-even price? What is the shut-down price?

   c. Suppose that the price at which Kate can sell catered meals is $21 per meal. In the short run, will Kate earn a profit? In the short run, should she produce or shut down?

   d. Suppose that the price at which Kate can sell catered meals is $17 per meal. In the short run, will Kate earn a profit? In the short run, should she produce or shut down?

   e. Suppose that the price at which Kate can sell catered meals is $13 per meal. In the short run, will Kate earn a profit? In the short run, should she produce or shut down?

6. You are the manager of a gym, and you have to decide how many customers to admit each hour. Assume that each customer stays exactly one hour. Customers are costly to admit because they inflict wear and tear on the exercise equipment. Moreover, each additional customer generates more wear and tear than the customer before. As a result, the gym faces increasing marginal cost. The accompanying table shows the marginal costs associated with each number of customers per hour.

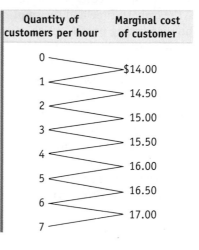

| Quantity of customers per hour | Marginal cost of customer |
|---|---|
| 0 | |
| | $14.00 |
| 1 | |
| | 14.50 |
| 2 | |
| | 15.00 |
| 3 | |
| | 15.50 |
| 4 | |
| | 16.00 |
| 5 | |
| | 16.50 |
| 6 | |
| | 17.00 |
| 7 | |

   a. Suppose that each customer pays $15.25 for a one-hour workout. Use the principle of marginal analysis to find the optimal number of customers that you should admit per hour.

   b. You increase the price of a one-hour workout to $16.25. What is the optimal number of customers per hour that you should admit now?

**7.** Bob produces DVD movies for sale, which requires only a building and a machine that copies the original movie onto a DVD. Bob rents a building for $30,000 per month and rents a machine for $20,000 a month. Those are his fixed costs. His variable cost is given in the accompanying table.

| Quantity of DVDs | VC |
|---|---|
| 0 | $0 |
| 1,000 | 5,000 |
| 2,000 | 8,000 |
| 3,000 | 9,000 |
| 4,000 | 14,000 |
| 5,000 | 20,000 |
| 6,000 | 33,000 |
| 7,000 | 49,000 |
| 8,000 | 72,000 |
| 9,000 | 99,000 |
| 10,000 | 150,000 |

**a.** Calculate Bob's average variable cost, average total cost, and marginal cost for each quantity of output.

**b.** There is free entry into the industry: anyone who enters will face the same costs as Bob. Suppose that currently the price of a DVD is $23. What will Bob's profit be? Is this a long-run equilibrium? If not, what will the price of DVD movies be in the long run?

**8.** Consider Bob's DVD company described in Problem 7. Assume that DVD production is a perfectly competitive industry. In each case, explain your answers.

**a.** What is Bob's break-even price? What is his shut-down price?

**b.** Suppose the price of a DVD is $2. What should Bob do in the short run?

**c.** Suppose the price of a DVD is $7. What is the profit-maximizing quantity of DVDs that Bob should produce? What will his total profit be? Will he produce or shut down in the short run? Will he stay in the industry or exit in the long run?

**d.** Suppose instead that the price of DVDs is $20. Now what is the profit-maximizing quantity of DVDs that Bob should produce? What will his total profit be now? Will he produce or shut down in the short run? Will he stay in the industry or exit in the long run?

**9.** Consider again Bob's DVD company described in Problem 7.

**a.** Draw Bob's marginal cost curve.

**b.** Over what range of prices will Bob produce no DVDs in the short run?

**c.** Draw Bob's individual supply curve.

**10. a.** A profit-maximizing business incurs an economic loss of $10,000 per year. Its fixed cost is $15,000 per year. Should it produce or shut down in the short run? Should it stay in the industry or exit in the long run?

**b.** Suppose instead this business has a fixed cost of $6,000 per year. Should it produce or shut down in the short run? Should it stay in the industry or exit in the long run?

**11.** Four students have each started companies selling late-night snack deliveries to dorms and student apartment complexes. Each student has estimated her or his individual supply schedule as given in the accompanying table.

| Delivery charge | Quantity supplied by: | | | |
|---|---|---|---|---|
| | Aleesha | Brent | Christine | Dominic |
| $1 | 1 | 5 | 3 | 7 |
| 2 | 3 | 8 | 6 | 12 |
| 3 | 5 | 11 | 9 | 17 |
| 4 | 7 | 15 | 12 | 21 |
| 5 | 9 | 21 | 15 | 23 |

**a.** Draw the four individual supply curves.

**b.** Determine the short-run industry supply schedule. Draw the short-run industry supply curve.

**12.** The first sushi restaurant opens in town. Initially people are very cautious about eating tiny portions of raw fish, as this is a town where large portions of grilled meat have always been popular. Soon, however, an influential health report warns consumers against grilled meat and suggests that they increase their consumption of fish, especially raw fish. The sushi restaurant becomes very popular and its profit increases.

**a.** What will happen to the short-run profit of the sushi restaurant? What will happen to the number of sushi restaurants in town in the long run? Will the first sushi restaurant be able to sustain its short-run profit over the long run? Explain your answers.

**b.** Local steakhouses suffer from the popularity of sushi and start incurring losses. What will happen to the number of steakhouses in town in the long run? Explain your answer.

**13.** A perfectly competitive firm has the following short-run total cost:

| Quantity | TC |
|---|---|
| 0 | $5 |
| 1 | 10 |
| 2 | 13 |
| 3 | 18 |
| 4 | 25 |
| 5 | 34 |
| 6 | 45 |

Market demand for the firm's product is given by the following market demand schedule:

| Price | Quantity demanded |
|-------|-------------------|
| $12 | 300 |
| 10 | 500 |
| 8 | 800 |
| 6 | 1,200 |
| 4 | 1,800 |

a. Calculate this firm's marginal cost and, for all output levels except zero, the firm's average variable cost and average total cost.

b. There are 100 firms in this industry that all have identical costs to those of this firm. Draw the short-run industry supply curve. In the same diagram, draw the market demand curve.

c. What is the market price, and how much profit will each firm make?

14. A new vaccine against a deadly disease has just been discovered. Presently, 55 people die from the disease each year. The new vaccine will save lives, but it is not completely safe. Some recipients of the shots will die from adverse reactions. The projected effects of the inoculation are given in the accompanying table:

| Percent of population inoculated | Total deaths due to disease | Total deaths due to inoculation | Marginal benefit of inoculation | Marginal cost of inoculation | "Profit" of inoculation |
|---|---|---|---|---|---|
| 0 | 55 | 0 | — | — | — |
| 10 | 45 | 0 | — | — | — |
| 20 | 36 | 1 | — | — | — |
| 30 | 28 | 3 | — | — | — |
| 40 | 21 | 6 | — | — | — |
| 50 | 15 | 10 | — | — | — |
| 60 | 10 | 15 | — | — | — |
| 70 | 6 | 20 | — | — | — |
| 80 | 3 | 25 | — | — | — |
| 90 | 1 | 30 | — | — | — |
| 100 | 0 | 35 | — | — | — |

a. What are the interpretations of "marginal benefit" and "marginal cost" here? Calculate marginal benefit and marginal cost per each 10 percent increase in the rate of inoculation. Write your answers in the table.

b. What proportion of the population should optimally be inoculated?

c. What is the interpretation of "profit" here? Calculate the profit for all levels of inoculation.

15. Evaluate each of the following statements. If a statement is true, explain why; if it is false, identify the mistake and try to correct it.

a. A profit-maximizing firm should select the output level at which the difference between the market price and marginal cost is greatest.

b. An increase in fixed cost lowers the profit-maximizing quantity of output produced in the short run.

>web...  To continue your study and review of concepts in this chapter, please visit the Krugman/Wells/Olney website for quizzes, animated graph tutorials, web links to helpful resources, and more.

**www.worthpublishers.com/krugmanwellsolney**

# >>Factor Markets and the Distribution of Income

## THE VALUE OF A DEGREE

DOES HIGHER EDUCATION PAY? YES, IT does: in the modern economy, employers are willing to pay a premium for workers with more education. And the size of that premium has increased a lot over the last few decades. Back in 1973 workers with advanced degrees, such as law degrees or MBAs, earned only 76 percent more than those who had only graduated from high school. By 2003 the premium for an advanced degree had risen to 120 percent.

Who decided that the wages of workers with advanced degrees would rise so much compared with those of high school grads? The answer, of course, is that nobody decided it. Wage rates are prices, the prices of different kinds of labor; and they are decided, like other prices, by supply and demand.

Still, there is a difference between the wage rate of high school grads and the price of used textbooks: the wage rate isn't the price of a *good*, it's the price of a *factor of production*. And although markets for factors of pro-

duction are in many ways similar to those for goods, there are also some important differences.

In this chapter, we examine *factor markets,* the markets in which factors of production such as labor are traded. Factor markets play a crucial role in the economy: they allocate productive resources to producers and help ensure that those resources are used efficiently.

This chapter begins by describing the major factors of production. Then we consider the demand for factors of production, which leads us to a crucial insight: the *marginal productivity theory of income distribution.*

If you've ever had doubts about attending college, consider this: factory workers with only high school degrees will make much less than college grads. The difference in earnings is as much as $30,000 annually.

We then consider some challenges to the marginal productivity theory. The final section of the chapter looks at the supply of the most important factor, labor.

### What you will learn in this chapter:

➤ How factors of production— resources like land, labor, and both **physical capital** and **human capital**—are traded in factor markets, determining the **factor distribution of income**

➤ How the demand for factors leads to the **marginal productivity theory of income distribution**

➤ An understanding of the sources of wage disparities and the role of discrimination

➤ The way in which a worker's decision about **time allocation** gives rise to labor supply

# The Economy's Factors of Production

You may recall that we defined a *factor of production* in Chapter 2 in the context of the circular-flow model; it is any resource that is used by firms to produce *goods* and *services*, items that are consumed by households. Factors of production are bought and sold in *factor markets,* and the prices in factor markets are known as *factor prices*.

What are these factors of production, and why do factor prices matter?

## The Factors of Production

As we learned in Chapter 2, economists divide factors of production into four principal classes: land, labor, physical capital, and human capital. *Land* is a resource provided by nature; *labor* is the work done by human beings.

In Chapter 8 we defined *capital*; it is the assets that are used by a firm in producing its output. There are two broad types of capital. **Physical capital**—often referred to simply as "capital"—consists of manufactured resources such as buildings and machines.

In the modern economy, **human capital,** the improvement in labor created by education and knowledge, and embodied in the workforce, is at least equally significant. The importance of human capital has been greatly increased by the progress of technology, which has made a high level of technical sophistication essential to many jobs—one cause of the increased premium paid for workers with advanced degrees.

## Why Factor Prices Matter: The Allocation of Resources

Factor markets and factor prices play a key role in one of the most important processes that must take place in any economy: the allocation of resources among producers.

Consider the example of Florida in 1992, in the aftermath of Hurricane Andrew, which was the costliest hurricane to hit the U.S. mainland to date. The state had an urgent need for workers in the building trades—carpenters, plumbers, and so on—to repair or replace damaged homes and businesses. What ensured that those needed workers actually came? The high demand for construction workers in Florida drove up their wages, which led large numbers of workers with the right skills to move temporarily to the state to do the work. In other words, the market for a factor of production—construction workers—allocated that factor of production to where it was needed.

In this sense factor markets are similar to markets for goods and services, which allocate goods and services among consumers. But there are two features that make factor markets somewhat special. Unlike in a market for a good or service, demand in a factor market is what we call *derived demand*. That is, demand for the factor is derived from the firm's output choice. The second feature is that factor markets are where most of us get the largest shares of our income (government transfers being the next largest source of income in the economy).

## Factor Incomes and the Distribution of Income

Most American families get most of their income in the form of wages and salaries—that is, they get their income by selling labor. Some people, however, get most of their income from physical capital: when you own stock in a company, what you really own is a share of that company's physical capital. And some people get much of their income from the rents on land they own.

Obviously, then, the prices of factors of production have a major impact on how the economic "pie" is sliced among different groups. For example, a higher wage rate, other things equal, means that more of the income in the economy goes to people who derive their income from labor, as opposed to capital. Economists refer to how the economic pie is sliced as the "distribution of income."

Specifically, factor prices determine the **factor distribution of income**—how the total income of the economy is divided among labor, land, and capital.

---

**Physical capital**—often referred to simply as "capital"—consists of manufactured resources such as buildings and machines.

**Human capital** is the improvement in labor created by education and knowledge that is embodied in the workforce.

---

### PITFALLS

#### WHAT IS A FACTOR, ANYWAY?

Imagine a business that produces shirts. The business will make use of workers and machines—that is, of labor and capital. But it will also use other inputs, such as electricity and cloth. Are all of these inputs factors of production? No: labor and capital are factors of production, but cloth and electricity are not.

The key distinction is that a factor of production earns income from the selling of its services over and over again but an input cannot. For example, a worker earns income over time from repeatedly selling his or her efforts; the owner of a machine earns income over time from repeatedly selling the use of that machine. So a factor of production, such as labor and capital, represents an enduring source of income. An input like electricity or cloth, however, is used up in the production process. Once exhausted, it cannot be a source of future income for its owner.

---

The **factor distribution of income** is the division of total income among labor, land, and capital.

## THE FACTOR DISTRIBUTION OF INCOME AND SOCIAL CHANGE IN THE INDUSTRIAL REVOLUTION

Have you read any novels by Jane Austen? How about Charles Dickens? If you've read both, you probably noticed that they seem to be describing quite different societies. Austen's novels, set around 1800, describe a world in which the leaders of society are land-owning aristocrats. Dickens, writing about 50 years later, describes a world in which businessmen, especially factory owners, seem to be in control.

This literary shift reflects a dramatic transformation in the factor distribution of income. The Industrial Revolution, which took place between the late

By altering how people lived and worked, the Industrial Revolution led to huge economic and social changes.

eighteenth century and the middle of the nineteenth century, changed England from a mainly agricultural country, in which land earned a fairly substantial share of income, to an urbanized and industrial one, in which land rents were dwarfed by capital income. Recent estimates by the economist Nancy Stokey show that between 1780 and 1850 the share of land represented in national income fell from 20 to 9 percent, while the share represented by capital rose from 35 to 44 percent. That shift changed everything—even literature.

As the following Economics in Action explains, the factor distribution of income in the United States has been quite stable over the past few decades. In other times and places, however, large changes have taken place in the factor distribution. One notable example: during the Industrial Revolution, the share of total income earned by land owners fell sharply, while that earned by capital owners rose. As explained in For Inquiring Minds, this shift had a profound effect on society.

# *economics in action*

## The Factor Distribution of Income in the United States

When we talk about the factor distribution of income, what are we talking about in practice?

In the United States, as in all advanced economies, payments to labor account for most of the economy's total income. Figure 9-1 shows the factor distribution of income in the United States in 2004: in that year, 71 percent of total income in the economy took the form of "compensation of employees"—a number that includes both wages

### Figure 9-1

**Factor Distribution of Income in the United States in 2004**

In 2004, compensation of employees accounted for most income earned in the United States—71 percent of the total. Most of the remainder—consisting of earnings paid in the form of interest, corporate profits, and rent—went to owners of physical capital. Finally, proprietors' income—9 percent of the total—went to individual owners of businesses as compensation for their labor and capital expended in their businesses.

*Source:* Bureau of Economic Analysis.

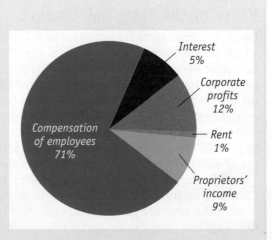

Interest
5%

Corporate profits
12%

Compensation of employees
71%

Rent
1%

Proprietors' income
9%

and benefits such as health insurance. This number has been quite stable over the long run; roughly 30 years earlier, in 1971, compensation of employees was very similar, at 73 percent of total income.

However, measured wages and benefits don't capture the full income of "labor" because a significant fraction of total income in the United States (usually between 8 and 9 percent) is "proprietors' income"—the earnings of people who own their own businesses. Part of that income should be considered wages these business owners pay themselves. So the true share of labor in the economy is probably a few percentage points higher than the "compensation of employees" share.

But much of what we call compensation of employees is really a return on human capital. A surgeon isn't just supplying the services of a pair of ordinary hands (at least the patient hopes not!): that individual is also supplying the result of many years and hundreds of thousands of dollars invested in training and experience. We can't directly measure what fraction of wages is really a payment for education and training, but many economists believe that human capital has become *the* most important factor of production in modern economies. ∎

< < < < < < < < < < < < < < < < <

### >>CHECK YOUR UNDERSTANDING 9-1

1. Suppose that the government places price controls on the market for college professors, imposing a wage that is lower than the market wage. Describe the effect of this policy on the production of college degrees. What sectors of the economy do you think will be adversely affected by this policy? What sectors of the economy might benefit?

*Solutions appear at back of book.*

# Marginal Productivity and Factor Demand

All economic decisions are about comparing costs and benefits—and usually about comparing marginal costs and *marginal benefits.* This goes both for a consumer, deciding whether to buy another pound of fried clams, and for a producer, deciding whether to hire an additional worker.

Although there are some important exceptions, most factor markets in the modern American economy are perfectly competitive, meaning that buyers and sellers of a given factor are price-takers. And in a competitive labor market, it's clear how to define an employer's marginal cost of a worker: it is simply the worker's wage rate. But what is the marginal benefit of that worker? To answer that question, we return to a concept first introduced in Chapter 7: the *production function,* which relates inputs to output. And as in Chapter 8, we will assume throughout this chapter that all producers are price-takers—they operate in a perfectly competitive industry.

## Value of the Marginal Product

Figure 9-2 reproduces Figures 7-1 and 7-2, which showed the production function for wheat on George and Martha's farm. Panel (a) uses the total product curve to show how total wheat production depends on the number of workers employed on the farm; panel (b) shows how the *marginal product* of labor, the increase in output from employing one more worker, depends on the number of workers employed. Table 9-1, which reproduces the table in Figure 7-1, shows the numbers behind the figure.

Assume that George and Martha want to maximize their profit, that workers must be paid $200 each, and that wheat sells for $20 per bushel. What is their optimal number of workers? That is, how many workers should they employ to maximize profit?

In Chapters 7 and 8 we showed how to answer this question in several steps. In Chapter 7 we used information from the producer's production function to derive the firm's total cost and its marginal cost. And in Chapter 8 we derived the *price-taking firm's optimal output rule:* a price-taking firm's profit is maximized by producing the

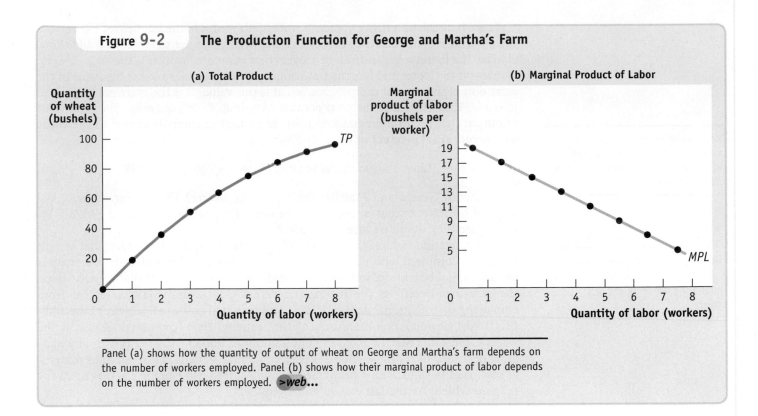

**Figure 9-2**    **The Production Function for George and Martha's Farm**

**(a) Total Product**

**(b) Marginal Product of Labor**

Panel (a) shows how the quantity of output of wheat on George and Martha's farm depends on the number of workers employed. Panel (b) shows how their marginal product of labor depends on the number of workers employed.  **>web...**

quantity of output at which the marginal cost of the last unit produced is equal to the market price. Having determined the optimal quantity of output, we can go back to the production function and find the optimal number of workers—it is simply the number of workers needed to produce the optimal quantity of output.

There is, however, another way to find the number of workers that maximizes a producer's profit. We can go directly to the question of what level of employment maximizes profit. This alternative approach is equivalent to the approach we outlined in the preceding paragraph—it's just a different way of looking at the same thing, which gives us more insight into the demand for factors as opposed to the supply of goods.

**TABLE 9-1**

**Employment and Output for George and Martha's Farm**

| Quantity of labor $L$ (workers) | Quantity of wheat $Q$ (bushels) | Marginal product of labor $MPL = \dfrac{\Delta Q}{\Delta L}$ (bushels per worker) |
|:---:|:---:|:---:|
| 0 | 0 | |
| | | 19 |
| 1 | 19 | |
| | | 17 |
| 2 | 36 | |
| | | 15 |
| 3 | 51 | |
| | | 13 |
| 4 | 64 | |
| | | 11 |
| 5 | 75 | |
| | | 9 |
| 6 | 84 | |
| | | 7 |
| 7 | 91 | |
| | | 5 |
| 8 | 96 | |

To see how this alternative approach works, let's return to the example of George and Martha and suppose that they are considering whether or not to employ an additional worker. The increase in *cost* from employing that additional worker is the wage rate, *W*. The *benefit* to George and Martha from employing that extra worker is the value of the extra output that worker can produce. What is this value? It is the marginal product of labor, *MPL*, multiplied by the price per unit of output, *P*. This quantity—the extra value of output that comes from employing one more unit of labor—is known as the **value of the marginal product** of labor, or *VMPL*:

> The **value of the marginal product** of a factor is the value of the additional output generated by employing one more unit of that factor.

**(9-1)**   Value of the marginal product of labor = $VMPL = P \times MPL$

So should George and Martha hire that extra worker? The answer is yes, if the value of the extra output is more than the cost of the worker—that is, if $VMPL > W$. Otherwise they shouldn't hire that worker.

So the decision to hire labor is a marginal decision, in which the marginal benefit should be compared with the marginal cost. The **marginal benefit** of an activity is the additional benefit derived from undertaking one more unit of that activity. Here, the marginal benefit is the increased revenue George and Martha receive from employing one additional worker, *VMPL*. The marginal cost of an activity is the additional cost of doing one more unit of that activity. Here, the marginal cost is the wages George and Martha must pay one additional worker, *W*. And as with any marginal decision, the optimal choice is where marginal benefit is just equal to marginal cost. That is, to maximize profit George and Martha will employ workers up to the point at which, for the last worker employed,

> The **marginal benefit** from an activity is the additional benefit derived from undertaking one more unit of that activity.

**(9-2)**   $VMPL = W$

This rule doesn't apply only to labor; it applies to any factor of production. The value of the marginal product of any factor is its marginal product times the price of the good it produces. The general rule is that *a profit-maximizing price-taking producer employs each factor of production up to the point at which the value of the marginal product of the last unit of the factor employed is equal to that factor's price.*

It's important to realize that this rule doesn't conflict with our analysis in Chapters 7 and 8. There we saw that a profit-maximizing producer of a good chooses the level of output at which the price of that good is equal to the marginal cost of production. It's just a different way of looking at the same rule. If the level of output is chosen so that price equals marginal cost, then it is also true that at that output level the value of the marginal product of labor will equal the wage rate.

Now let's look more closely at why choosing the level of employment at which the value of the marginal product of the last worker employed is equal to the wage rate works—and at how it helps us understand factor demand.

## Value of the Marginal Product and Factor Demand

Table 9-2 calculates the value of the marginal product of labor on George and Martha's farm, on the assumption that the price of wheat is $20 per bushel. In Figure 9-3 the horizontal axis shows the number of workers employed; the vertical axis measures the value of the marginal product of the last worker employed *and* the wage rate. The curve shown is the **value of the marginal product curve** of labor. This curve, like the marginal product of labor curve, is downward sloping due to diminishing returns to labor in production. That is, the value of the marginal product of each worker is less than that of the preceding worker, because the marginal product of each worker is less than that of the preceding worker.

> The **value of the marginal product curve** of a factor shows how the value of the marginal product of that factor depends on the quantity of the factor employed.

We have just seen that to maximize profit, George and Martha must hire workers up to the point at which the wage rate is equal to the value of the marginal product of the last worker employed. Let's use the example to see that this principle really works.

## TABLE 9-2

### Value of the Marginal Product of Labor for George and Martha's Farm

| Quantity of labor L (workers) | Marginal product of labor MPL (bushels per worker) | Value of the marginal product of labor VMPL = P × MPL |
|---|---|---|
| 0 | | |
| | 19 | $380 |
| 1 | | |
| | 17 | 340 |
| 2 | | |
| | 15 | 300 |
| 3 | | |
| | 13 | 260 |
| 4 | | |
| | 11 | 220 |
| 5 | | |
| | 9 | 180 |
| 6 | | |
| | 7 | 140 |
| 7 | | |
| | 5 | 100 |
| 8 | | |

Assume that George and Martha currently employ 3 workers and that workers must be paid the market wage rate of $200. Should they employ an additional worker?

Looking at Table 9-2, we see that if George and Martha currently employ 3 workers, the value of the marginal product of an additional worker is $260. So if they employ an additional worker, they will increase the value of their production by $260 but increase their cost by only $200, yielding an increase of $60 in the farm's profit. In fact, a producer can always increase profit by employing one more unit of a factor of production as long as the value of the marginal product produced by that unit exceeds the factor price.

### Figure 9-3

**The Value of the Marginal Product Curve**

This curve shows how the value of the marginal product of labor depends on the number of workers employed. It is downward sloping due to diminishing returns to labor in production. To maximize profit, George and Martha choose the level of employment at which the value of the marginal product of labor is equal to the market wage rate. For example, at a wage rate of $200 the profit-maximizing level of employment is 5 workers, shown by point A. The value of the marginal product curve for a factor is the producer's individual demand curve for that factor. >web...

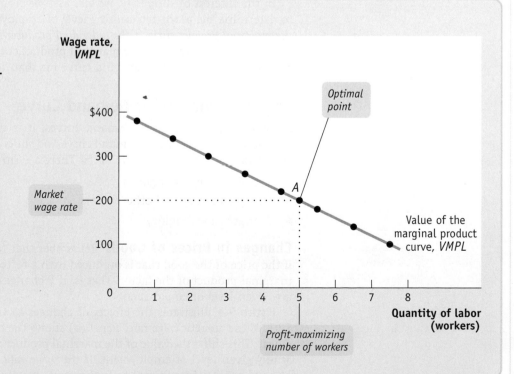

Alternatively, suppose that George and Martha employ 8 workers. By reducing the number of workers to 7, they can save $200 in wages. Meanwhile, the value of the marginal product of that last worker was only $100. So, by reducing employment by one worker they can increase profit by $100. A producer can always increase profit by employing one less unit of a factor of production as long as the value of the marginal product produced by that unit is less than the factor price.

Using this method, we can see from Table 9-2 that the profit-maximizing employment level is 5 workers given a wage rate of $200. The value of the marginal product of the 5th worker is $220, so adding that worker results in $20 of additional profit. But George and Martha should not hire more than 5 workers: the value of the marginal product of the 6th worker is only $180, which is $20 less than the cost of that worker. So, to maximize profit, George and Martha should employ workers up to but not beyond the point at which the value of the marginal product of the last worker employed is equal to the wage rate.

Now look again at the value of the marginal product curve in Figure 9-3. To determine the profit-maximizing level of employment, we set the price of labor—$200 per worker—equal to the value of the marginal product of labor. This means that the profit-maximizing level of employment is at point A, corresponding to an employment level of 5 workers. If the price of labor were higher or lower, we would simply move up or down the curve.

In this example, George and Martha have a small farm in which the potential employment level varies from 0 to 8 workers, and they hire workers up to the point where the value of the marginal product of the last worker is no less than the wage rate. Suppose, however, that the firm in question is large and has the potential of hiring many workers. When there are many employees, the value of the marginal product of labor falls only slightly when an additional worker is employed. As a result, there will be some worker whose value of the marginal product almost exactly equals the wage rate. (In keeping with the George and Martha example, this means that some worker has a value of the marginal product of approximately $200.) In this case, the firm maximizes profit by choosing a level of employment at which the value of the marginal product of the last worker hired *equals* (to a very good approximation) the wage rate.

In the interest of simplicity, we will assume from now on that firms use this rule to determine the profit-maximizing level of employment. *This means that the value of the marginal product curve is the individual producer's labor demand curve.* And in general, a producer's value of the marginal product curve for any factor of production is that producer's individual demand curve for that factor of production.

## Shifts of the Factor Demand Curve

As in the case of ordinary demand curves, it is important to distinguish between *movements along* the factor demand curve and *shifts of* the factor demand curve. What causes factor demand curves to shift? There are three main causes:

- Changes in prices of goods
- Changes in supply of other factors
- Changes in technology

**Changes in Prices of Goods** Remember that factor demand is derived demand: if the price of the good that is produced with a factor changes, so will the value of the marginal product of the factor. That is, if $P$ changes, $VMPL = P \times MPL$ will change at any given level of employment.

Figure 9-4 illustrates the effects of changes in the price of wheat, assuming that $200 is the current wage rate. Panel (a) shows the effect of an *increase* in the price of wheat. This shifts the value of the marginal product curve upward, because $VMPL$ rises at any given level of employment. If the wage rate remains unchanged at $200, the optimal point moves from A to B: the profit-maximizing level of employment rises.

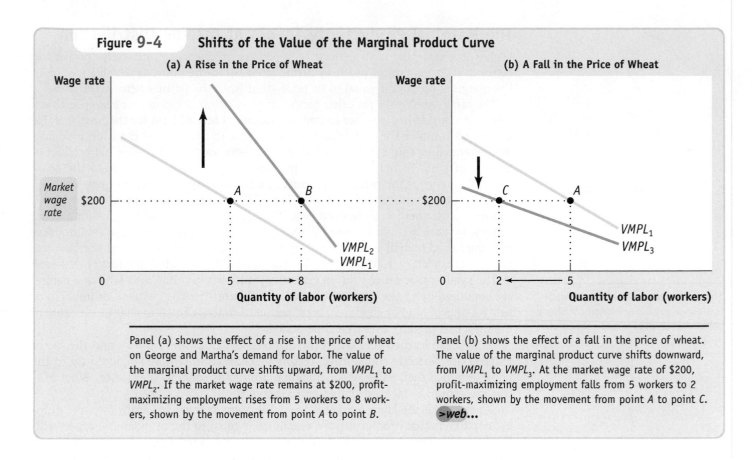

### Figure 9-4    Shifts of the Value of the Marginal Product Curve

**(a) A Rise in the Price of Wheat**

**(b) A Fall in the Price of Wheat**

Panel (a) shows the effect of a rise in the price of wheat on George and Martha's demand for labor. The value of the marginal product curve shifts upward, from $VMPL_1$ to $VMPL_2$. If the market wage rate remains at $200, profit-maximizing employment rises from 5 workers to 8 workers, shown by the movement from point A to point B.

Panel (b) shows the effect of a fall in the price of wheat. The value of the marginal product curve shifts downward, from $VMPL_1$ to $VMPL_3$. At the market wage rate of $200, profit-maximizing employment falls from 5 workers to 2 workers, shown by the movement from point A to point C. **>web...**

Panel (b) shows the effect of a *decrease* in the price of wheat. This shifts the value of the marginal product curve downward. If the wage rate remains unchanged at $200, the optimal point moves from A to C: the profit-maximizing level of employment falls.

**Changes in Supply of Other Factors** Suppose that George and Martha acquire more land to cultivate—say, by clearing a woodland on their property. Each worker could then produce more wheat because each one would have more land to work with. So the marginal product of labor on the farm would rise at any given level of employment. This would have the same effect as an increase in the price of wheat, which we have already seen in panel (a) of Figure 9-4: the value of the marginal product curve would shift upward, and at any given wage rate the profit-maximizing level of employment would increase. Similarly, if George and Martha cultivate less land, the marginal product of labor at any given employment level would fall—each worker would produce less wheat because of having less land to work with. As a result, the value of the marginal product curve would shift downward—as in panel (b) of Figure 9-4—and the profit-maximizing level of employment would decrease.

**Changes in Technology** In general, the effect of technological progress on the demand for any given factor can go either way: improved technology can either increase or decrease the demand for a given factor of production.

How can technological progress decrease factor demand? Consider horses, which were once an important factor of production. The development of substitutes for horse power, such as automobiles and tractors, greatly reduced the demand for horses.

The usual effect of technological progress, however, is to increase factor demand. In particular, although there have been persistent fears that machinery would reduce the demand for labor, over the long run the U.S. economy has seen both large wage increases and large increases in employment, suggesting that technological progress has greatly increased labor demand.

## The Marginal Productivity Theory of Income Distribution

We've now seen that each perfectly competitive producer in a perfectly competitive factor market maximizes profit by hiring labor up to the point at which its value of the marginal product is equal to its price—that is, to the point where $VMPL = W$.

The same logic works for other factors of production. Suppose, for example, that a farmer is considering whether to rent an additional acre of land for the next year. He or she will compare the cost of renting that acre with the value of the additional output generated by employing an additional acre—the value of the marginal product of an acre of land. To maximize profit, the farmer must employ land up to the point where the value of the marginal product of an acre is equal to the rent per acre.

What if the farmer already owns the land? We saw the answer in Chapter 8: even if you own land, there is an implicit cost—the opportunity cost—of using it for a given activity, because it could be used for something else. So a profit-maximizing producer will employ additional acres of land up to the point where the cost of the last acre employed, explicit or implicit, is equal to the value of the marginal product of that acre.

The same is true for capital. In general, economists say that both land and capital are employed up to the point where the **rental rate**—the cost, explicit or implicit, of using a unit of land or capital for a set period of time—is equal to that unit's value of the marginal product over that time period.

So we have learned that when the markets for goods and services and the factor markets are perfectly competitive, factors of production will be employed up to the point at which their value of the marginal product is equal to their price. What does this say about the factor distribution of income?

Suppose that the labor market is in equilibrium: at the going wage rate, the number of workers that producers want to employ is equal to the number of workers willing to work. Then all employers will pay the *same* wage rate, and *each* employer, whatever he or she is producing, will employ labor up to the point where the value of the marginal product of one more worker is equal to that wage rate.

This situation is illustrated in Figure 9-5, which shows the value of the marginal product curves of two producers—Farmer Jones, who produces wheat, and Farmer

> The **rental rate** of either land or capital is the cost, explicit or implicit, of using a unit of that asset for a given period of time.

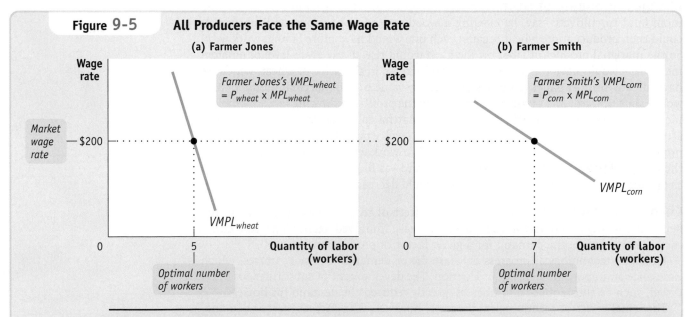

**Figure 9-5     All Producers Face the Same Wage Rate**

Although Farmer Jones grows wheat and Farmer Smith grows corn, they both compete in the same market for labor and must therefore pay the same wage rate, $200.

Each producer hires labor up to the point at which *VMPL* = $200: 5 workers for Jones, 7 workers for Smith.

Smith, who produces corn. Despite the fact that they produce different products, they compete for the same workers, and so must pay the same wage rate, $200. So when both farmers maximize profit, both hire labor up to the point where its value of the marginal product is equal to the wage rate. In the figure, this corresponds to employment of 5 workers by Jones and 7 by Smith.

Figure 9-6 illustrates the general situation in the labor market as a whole. The *market labor demand curve* is the horizontal sum of all the individual labor demand curves—which is the same as each producer's value of the marginal product curve. For now, let's simply assume an upward-sloping supply curve for labor; we'll discuss labor supply later in this chapter. Then the equilibrium wage rate is the wage rate at which the quantity of labor supplied is equal to the quantity of labor demanded. In Figure 9-6, this equilibrium wage rate is $W^*$ and the corresponding equilibrium employment level is $L^*$.

And as we showed in the examples of the farms of George and Martha and of Farmer Jones and Farmer Smith (where the equilibrium wage rate corresponds to $200), each firm will hire labor up to the point at which the value of the marginal product of labor is equal to the equilibrium wage rate. This means that, in equilibrium, the marginal product of labor will be the same for all employers. So the equilibrium (or market) wage rate is equal to the **equilibrium value of the marginal product** of labor—the additional value produced by the last unit of labor employed in the labor market as a whole. It doesn't matter where that additional unit is employed, since VMPL is the same for all producers.

What we have just learned, then, is that the market wage rate is equal to the equilibrium value of the marginal product of labor. And the same is true of each factor of production: in a perfectly competitive market economy, the market price of each factor is equal to its equilibrium value of the marginal product.

The theory that each factor is paid the value of the output generated by the last unit employed in the factor market as a whole is known as the **marginal productivity theory of income distribution.**

The **equilibrium value of the marginal product** of a factor is the additional value produced by the last unit of that factor employed in the factor market as a whole.

According to the **marginal productivity theory of income distribution**, every factor of production is paid its equilibrium value of the marginal product.

---

### Figure 9-6

### Equilibrium in the Labor Market

The market labor demand curve is the horizontal sum of the individual labor demand curves of all producers. Here the equilibrium wage rate is $W^*$, the equilibrium employment level is $L^*$, and every producer hires labor up to the point at which VMPL = $W^*$. So labor is paid its equilibrium value of the marginal product, the value of the marginal product of the last worker hired in the labor market as a whole. **>web...**

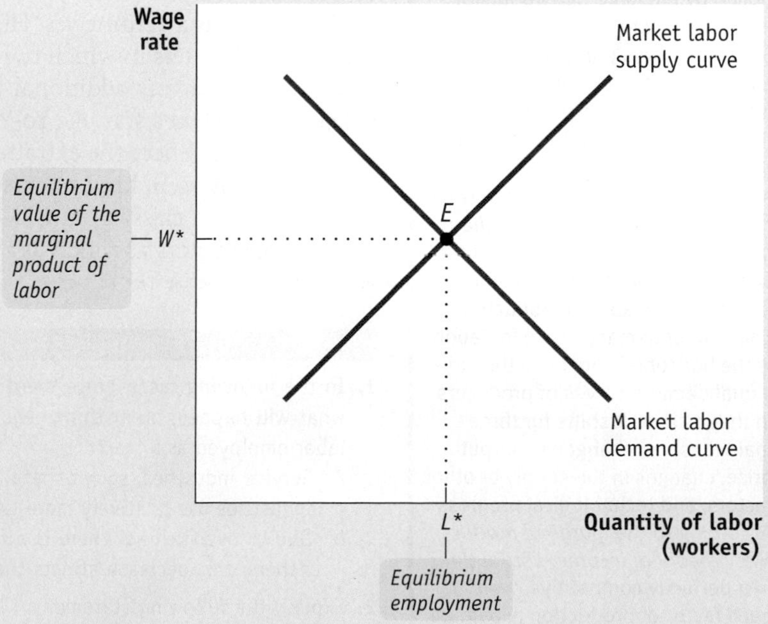

**GETTING MARGINAL PRODUCTIVITY RIGHT**

It's important to be careful about what the marginal productivity theory of income distribution says: it says that *all* units of a factor get paid the factor's equilibrium value of the marginal product—the additional value produced by the *last* unit of the factor employed.

The most common source of error is to forget that the relevant value of the marginal product is the equilibrium value, not the value of the marginal products you calculate on the way to equilibrium. In looking at Table 9-2, you might be tempted to think that because the first worker has a value of the marginal product of $380 that worker is paid $380 in equilibrium. Not so: if the equilibrium value of the marginal product in the labor market is equal to $200, then *all* workers receive $200.

- In a perfectly competitive market economy, the price of the good multiplied by the marginal product of labor is equal to the *value of the marginal product of labor: VMPL = P × MPL*. A profit-maximizing producer hires labor up to the point at which the *marginal benefit*, the value of the marginal product of labor, is equal to the marginal cost, the wage rate: *VMPL = W*. The *value of the marginal product of labor curve* slopes downward due to diminishing returns to labor in production.
- The market demand curve for labor is the horizontal sum of all the individual demand curves of producers in that market. It shifts for three main reasons: changes in output price, changes in the supply of other factors, and technological progress.
- According to the *marginal productivity theory of income distribution*, in a perfectly competitive economy each factor of production is paid its *equilibrium value of the marginal product*.

To understand why the marginal productivity theory of income distribution is an important theory, take a look back at Figure 9-1, which showed the factor distribution of income in the United States, and ask yourself this question: who or what decided that labor would get 71 percent of total U.S. income? Why not 90 percent or 50 percent?

The answer, according to the marginal productivity theory of income distribution, is that the division of income among the economy's factors of production isn't arbitrary: it is determined by each factor's marginal productivity at the economy's equilibrium. The wage rate earned by *all* workers in the economy is equal to the increase in the value of output generated by the last worker employed in the economy-wide labor market.

Here we have assumed that all workers are of the same ability. But in reality workers may differ considerably in ability. Rather than thinking of one labor market for all workers in the economy, we can instead think of different markets for different types of workers, where workers are of equivalent ability within each market. For example, the market for computer programmers is different from the market for pastry chefs. And in the market for computer programmers, all participants are assumed to have equal ability; likewise for the market for pastry chefs. In this scenario, the marginal productivity theory of income distribution still holds. That is, when the labor market for computer programmers is in equilibrium, the wage rate earned by all computer programmers is equal to the market's equilibrium value of the marginal product—the value of the marginal product of the last computer programmer hired in that market.

## economics in action

### Star Power

If you want to be rich, don't become a classical musician or an opera singer. Most musical artists earn quite little considering the many years of training required.

There are, however, a handful of performers who command very large fees, in the vicinity of $30,000 for a single performance. Can the fees paid to stars be explained by the marginal productivity theory of income distribution?

The answer is a definite yes. High fees for stars reflect a careful calculation by managers of the theaters in which they perform. These managers know—with considerable precision—how many additional tickets they will sell, and how much they can raise ticket prices, when a star like Yo-Yo Ma is performing. The high fees paid to these classical superstars reflect the extra revenues they will generate from ticket sales.

All this may seem kind of crass—aren't we talking about art and beauty here? Yes, but music—even classical music—is also a business, and the principles of economics apply to opera stars as much as they do to fast-food workers. ∎

< < < < < < < < < < < < < < < < <

1. In the following cases, state the direction of the shift of the demand curve for labor and what will happen, other things equal, to the market equilibrium wage rate and quantity of labor employed as a result.
   a. Service industries, such as retailing and banking, experience an increase in demand. These industries use relatively more labor than nonservice industries.
   b. Due to over-fishing, there is a fall in the amount of fish caught per day by commercial fishers; this decrease affects their demand for workers.
2. Explain the following statement: "When firms in different industries all compete for the same workers, then the value of the marginal product of the last worker hired will be equal across all firms regardless of whether they are in different industries."

Solutions appear at back of book.

# Is the Marginal Productivity Theory of Income Distribution Really True?

Although the marginal productivity theory of income distribution is a well-established part of economic theory, closely linked to the analysis of markets in general, it is a source of some controversy. There are two main objections to it.

First, in the real world we see large disparities in income between factors of production that, in the eyes of some observers, should receive the same payment. Perhaps the most conspicuous examples in the United States are the large differences in the average wages between women and men and among various racial and ethnic groups. Do these wage differences really reflect differences in marginal productivity, or is something else going on?

Second, many people wrongly believe that the marginal productivity theory of income distribution gives a *moral* justification for the distribution of income, implying that the existing distribution is fair and appropriate. (We'll explain in Chapter 10 why this is a misconception.) This misconception sometimes leads people who believe that the current distribution of income is unfair to reject marginal productivity theory.

To address these controversies, we'll start by looking at income disparities across gender and ethnic groups. Then we'll ask what factors might account for these disparities and whether these explanations are consistent with the marginal productivity theory of income distribution.

## Wage Disparities in Practice

Wage rates in the United States cover a very wide range. In 2004, hundreds of thousands of workers received the legal federal minimum of $5.15 per hour. At the other extreme, the chief executives of several companies were paid more than $100 million, which is $20,000 per hour even if they worked 100-hour weeks. Even leaving out these extremes, there is a huge range of wage rates. Are people really that different in their marginal productivities?

A particular source of concern is the existence of systematic wage differences across gender and ethnicity. Figure 9-7 compares annual median earnings in 2004 of workers 25 years old and over classified by gender and ethnicity. As a group, white males

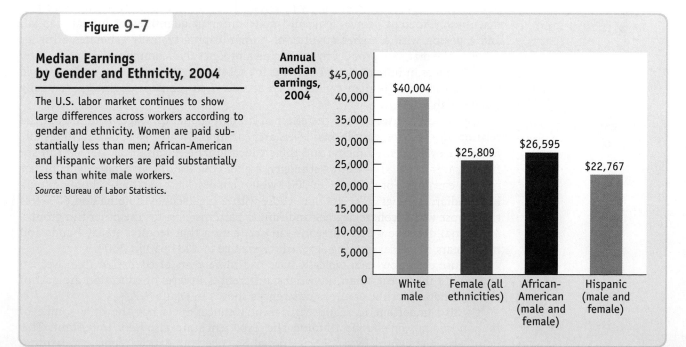

**Figure 9-7**

**Median Earnings by Gender and Ethnicity, 2004**

The U.S. labor market continues to show large differences across workers according to gender and ethnicity. Women are paid substantially less than men; African-American and Hispanic workers are paid substantially less than white male workers.

*Source:* Bureau of Labor Statistics.

had the highest earnings. The data show that women (averaging across all ethnicities) earned only about 65% as much; African-American workers (male and female combined) only 66% as much; Hispanic workers only 57 percent as much.

We are a nation founded on the belief that all men are created equal—and if the Constitution were rewritten today, we would say that *all people* are created equal. So why do they receive such unequal pay? Let's start with the marginal productivity explanations, then look at other influences.

## Marginal Productivity and Wage Inequality

A large part of the observed inequality in wages can be explained by considerations that are consistent with the marginal productivity theory of income distribution. In particular, there are three well-understood sources of wage differences across occupations and individuals: compensating differentials, differences in talent, and differences in the quantity of human capital.

First is the existence of **compensating differentials:** across different types of jobs, wages are often higher or lower depending on how attractive or unattractive the job is. Workers with unpleasant or dangerous jobs demand a higher wage in comparison to workers with jobs that require the same skill and effort but lack the unpleasant or dangerous qualities. For example, truckers who haul hazardous loads are paid more than truckers who haul normal loads. But for any *given* job, the marginal productivity theory of income distribution generally holds true. For example, hazardous-load truckers are paid a wage equal to the equilibrium value of the marginal product of the last person employed in the market for hazardous-load truckers.

A second reason for wage inequality that is clearly consistent with marginal productivity theory is differences in talent. People differ in their abilities: a high-ability person, by producing a better product that commands a higher price compared to a lower-ability person, generates a higher value of the marginal product. And these differences in the value of the marginal product translate into differences in earning potential. We all know that this is true in sports: practice is important, but 99.99 percent (at least) of the population just doesn't have what it takes to hit golf balls like Tiger Woods or skate like Michelle Kwan. The same is true, though less obvious, in other fields of endeavor.

A third, very important reason for wage differences is differences in the quantity of *human capital*. Recall that human capital—education and training—is at least as important in the modern economy as physical capital in the form of buildings and machines. Different people "embody" quite different quantities of human capital, and a person with a higher quantity of human capital typically generates a higher value of the marginal product by producing a product that commands a higher price. So differences in human capital account for substantial differences in wages. People with high levels of human capital, such as skilled surgeons or engineers, generally receive high wages.

The most direct way to see the effect of human capital on wages is to look at the relationship between educational levels and earnings. Figure 9-8 shows earnings differentials by gender, ethnicity, and three educational levels in 2004. As you can see from it, regardless of gender or ethnicity, higher education is associated with higher median earnings. For example, in 2004 white females without a high school diploma had median earnings 33% less than those with a high school diploma and 60% less than those with a college degree—and similar patterns exist for the other five groups. Additional data show that surgeons—an occupation that requires steady hands and many years of formal training—earned an average of $181,610 in 2004.

Because even now men typically have had more years of education than women and whites more years than nonwhites, differences in level of education are part of the explanation for the earnings differences shown in Figure 9-7.

It's also important to realize that formal education is not the only source of human capital; on-the-job training and experience are also very important. This point was highlighted by a 1999 National Science Foundation report on earnings

**Compensating differentials** are wage differences across jobs that reflect the fact that some jobs are less pleasant than others.

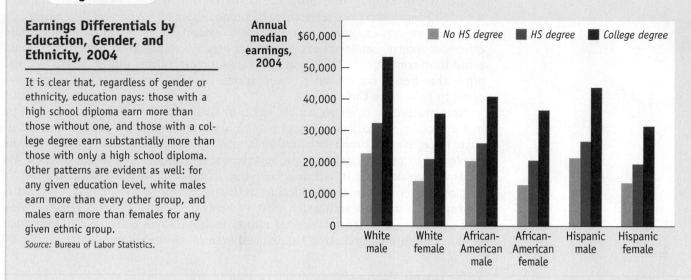

**Figure 9-8**

**Earnings Differentials by Education, Gender, and Ethnicity, 2004**

It is clear that, regardless of gender or ethnicity, education pays: those with a high school diploma earn more than those without one, and those with a college degree earn substantially more than those with only a high school diploma. Other patterns are evident as well: for any given education level, white males earn more than every other group, and males earn more than females for any given ethnic group.

*Source:* Bureau of Labor Statistics.

differences between male and female engineers. The study was motivated by concerns over the male–female earnings gap: on average, men with engineering degrees earn about 25 percent more than women with equivalent degrees. The study found that women in engineering are, on average, younger than men and have considerably less experience than their male counterparts. This difference in age and experience, according to the study, explained most of the earnings differential. Differences in job tenure and experience can partly explain one notable aspect of Figure 9-8: that, across all ethnicities, women's median earnings are less than men's median earnings for any given education level.

But it's also important to emphasize that earnings differences that arise from differences in human capital are not necessarily "fair." A society in which nonwhite children typically receive a poor education because they live in underfunded school districts, then go on to earn low wages because they are poorly educated, may have labor markets that are well described by marginal productivity theory (and would be consistent with the earnings differentials across ethnic groups shown in Figure 9-7). Yet many people would still consider the resulting distribution of income unfair.

Still, many observers think that actual wage differentials cannot be entirely explained by compensating differentials, differences in talent, and human capital. They believe that market power, *efficiency wages,* and discrimination also play an important role. We will examine these forces next.

## Market Power

The marginal productivity theory of income distribution is based on the assumption that factor markets are perfectly competitive. In such markets we can expect workers to be paid the equilibrium value of their marginal product, regardless of who they are. But how valid is this assumption?

We haven't yet studied markets that are *not* perfectly competitive (we'll get there in Chapter 11), but let's touch briefly on the ways in which labor markets may deviate from the competitive assumption.

One undoubted source of differences in wages between otherwise similar workers is the role of **unions**—organizations that try to raise wages and improve working conditions for their members. Labor unions, when they are successful, replace one-on-one wage deals between workers and employers with "collective bargaining," in which the employer must negotiate wages with union representatives. Without question, this

**Unions** are organizations of workers that try to raise wages and improve working conditions for their members.

leads to higher wages for those workers who are represented by unions. In 2004 the median weekly earnings of union members in the United States were $781, compared with $612 for workers not represented by unions—about a 22 percent difference.

Just as workers can sometimes organize to extract higher wages than they would otherwise receive, employers can sometimes organize to pay *lower* wages than would result from competition. Health care workers—doctors, nurses, and so on—sometimes argue that health maintenance organizations (HMOs) are engaged in a collective effort to hold down their wages.

How much does collective action, either by workers or by employers, affect wages in the modern United States? Most economists think that it is a fairly minor influence. To begin with, union membership is relatively limited: less than 9 percent of the employees of private businesses are represented by unions. And although there are fields like health care in which a few large firms account for a sizeable share of employment in certain geographical areas, the sheer size of the U.S. labor market is enormous and the ease with which most workers can move in search of higher-paying jobs probably means that concerted efforts to hold wages below the unrestrained market equilibrium level rarely happen and even more rarely succeed.

## Efficiency Wages

A second source of wage inequality is the phenomenon of *efficiency wages*—a type of incentive scheme to motivate workers to work hard and reduce worker turnover used by employers. Suppose that a worker performs a job that is extremely important but in which the employer can observe only at infrequent intervals how well the job is being performed—say, serving as a caregiver for the employer's child. Then it often makes sense for the employer to pay more than the worker could earn in an alternative job—that is, more than the equilibrium wage. Why? Because earning a premium makes losing this job and having to take the alternative job quite costly for the worker. So a worker who happens to be observed performing poorly and is therefore fired is now worse off for having to accept a lower-paying job. The threat of losing a job that pays a premium motivates the worker to perform well and avoid being fired. Likewise, paying a premium also reduces worker turnover—the frequency with which an employee leaves a job voluntarily. Despite the fact that it may take no more effort and skill to be a child's caregiver than to be an office worker, efficiency wages show why it often makes economic sense for a parent to pay a caregiver more than the equilibrium wage of an office worker.

According to the **efficiency-wage model**, some employers pay an above-equilibrium wage as an incentive for better performance.

The **efficiency-wage model** explains why we may observe wages offered above their equilibrium level. Like the price floors that we studied in Chapter 4—and, in particular, much like the minimum wage—this phenomenon leads to a surplus of labor supplied in the markets for labor that are characterized by the efficiency wage model. This surplus of labor translates into unemployment—some workers are actively searching for a high-paying efficiency-wage job but are unable to get one, and other more fortunate but no more deserving workers are able to acquire one. As a result, two workers with exactly the same profile—the same skills and same job history—may earn unequal wages: the worker who is lucky enough to get an efficiency-wage job earns more than the worker who gets a standard job (or who remains unemployed while searching for a higher-paying job). Efficiency wages are a type of market failure that arises from the fact that some employees don't always perform as well as they should and are able to hide that fact. As a result, employers use nonequilibrium wages in order to motivate their employees, leading to an inefficient outcome.

## Discrimination

It is a real and ugly fact that throughout history there has been discrimination against workers who are considered to be the wrong race, ethnicity, or gender. How does this fit into our economic models?

The main insight economic analysis offers is that discrimination is *not* a natural consequence of market competition. On the contrary, market forces tend to work against discrimination. To see why, consider the incentives that would exist if social convention dictated that women be paid, say, 30 percent less than men with equivalent qualifications and experience. A company whose management was itself unbiased would then be able to reduce its costs by hiring women rather than men—and such companies would have an advantage over other companies that hired men despite their higher cost. The result would be to create an excess demand for female workers, which would tend to drive up their wages.

But if market competition works against discrimination, how is it that so much discrimination has taken place? The answer is twofold. First, when labor markets don't work well, employers may have the ability to discriminate without hurting their profits. For example, market interferences (such as unions or minimum-wage laws) or market failures (such as efficiency wages) can lead to wages that are above their equilibrium levels. In these cases, there are more job applicants than there are jobs—leaving employers free to discriminate among applicants. In research published in 2003, two economists, Marianne Bertrand and Sendhil Mullainathan, documented discrimination in hiring by sending fictitious résumés to prospective employers on a random basis. Applicants with "white-sounding" names such as Emily Walsh were 50 percent more likely to be contacted than applicants with "African-American-sounding" names such as Lakisha Washington. Also, applicants with white-sounding names and good credentials were much more likely to be contacted than those without such credentials. By contrast, potential employers seemed to ignore the credentials of applicants with African-American-sounding names.

Second, discrimination has sometimes been institutionalized in government policy. This institutionalization of discrimination has made it easier to maintain it against market pressure, and historically it is the form that discrimination has typically taken. For example, at one time in the United States, African-Americans were barred from attending "whites-only" public schools and universities in many parts of the country and forced to attend inferior schools. So although market competition tends to work against *current* discrimination, it is not a remedy for past discrimination, which typically has had an impact on the education and experience of its victims and thereby reduces their income. Economics in Action below illustrates the way in which government policy enforced discrimination in the world's most famous racist regime, that of South Africa.

## So Does Marginal Productivity Theory Work?

The main conclusion you should draw from this discussion is that marginal productivity theory is not a perfect description of how factor incomes are determined but that it works pretty well. The deviations are important. But, by and large, in a modern economy with well-functioning labor markets, factors of production are paid the equilibrium value of the marginal product—the value of the marginal product of the last unit employed in the market as a whole.

It's important to emphasize, once again, that this does not mean that the factor distribution of income is morally justified. We'll turn to issues of fairness and equity in the next chapter.

## *economics in action*

### The Economics of Apartheid

The Republic of South Africa is the richest nation in Africa, but it also has a harsh political history. Until the peaceful transition to majority rule in 1994, the country was controlled by its white minority, Afrikaners, the descendants of European (mainly Dutch) immigrants. This minority imposed an economic system known as apartheid, which overwhelmingly favored white interests over those of native Africans and other groups considered "nonwhite," such as Asians.

South Africa is a democracy now, but the human legacy of apartheid persists.

The origins of apartheid go back to the early years of the twentieth century, when large numbers of white farmers began moving into South Africa's growing cities. There they discovered, to their horror, that they did not automatically earn higher wages than other races. But they had the right to vote—and nonwhites did not. And so the South African government instituted "job-reservation" laws designed to ensure that only whites got jobs that paid well. The government also set about creating jobs for whites in government-owned industries. As Allister Sparks notes in *The Mind of South Africa* (1990), in its efforts to provide high-paying jobs for whites, the country "eventually acquired the largest amount of nationalized industry of any country outside the Communist bloc."

In other words, racial discrimination was possible because it was backed by the power of the government, which prevented markets from following their natural course.

A postscript: in 1994, in one of the political miracles of modern times, the white regime ceded power and South Africa became a full-fledged democracy. Apartheid was abolished. Unfortunately, large racial differences in earnings remain. The main reason is that apartheid created huge disparities in human capital, which will persist for many years to come. ∎

< < < < < < < < < < < < < < < < < < <

**>> CHECK YOUR UNDERSTANDING 9-3**

1. Assess each of the following statements. Do you think they are true, false, or ambiguous? Explain.
   a. The marginal productivity theory of income distribution is inconsistent with the presence of income disparities associated with gender, race, or ethnicity.
   b. Companies that engage in workplace discrimination but whose competitors do not are likely to have lower profits as a result of their actions.
   c. Workers who are paid less because they have less experience are not the victims of discrimination.

Solutions appear at back of book.

# The Supply of Labor

Up to this point we have focused on the demand for factors, which determines the quantities demanded of labor, capital or land by producers as a function of their factor prices. What about the supply of factors?

In this section we focus exclusively on the supply of labor. We do this for two reasons. First, in the modern U.S. economy, labor is the most important factor of production, accounting for most of factor income. Second, as we'll see, labor supply is the area in which factor markets look most different from markets for goods and services.

## Work Versus Leisure

In the labor market, the roles of firms and households are the reverse of what they are in markets for goods and services. On the one hand, a good such as wheat is supplied by firms and demanded by households; on the other hand, labor is demanded by firms and supplied by households. How do people decide how much labor to supply?

As a practical matter, most people have limited control over their work hours: either you take a job that involves working a set number of hours per week, or you don't get the job at all. To understand the logic of labor supply, however, it helps to put realism to one side for a bit and imagine an individual who can choose to work as many or as few hours as he or she likes.

Why wouldn't such an individual work as many hours as possible? Because workers are human beings, too, and have other uses for their time. An hour spent on the job is an hour not spent on other, presumably more pleasant, activities. So the decision about how much labor to supply involves making a decision about **time allocation**—how many hours to spend on different activities.

Decisions about labor supply result from decisions about **time allocation:** how many hours to spend on different activities.

By working, people earn income that they can use to buy goods. The more hours an individual works, the more goods he or she can afford to buy. But this increased purchasing power comes at the expense of a reduction in **leisure,** the time spent not working. (Leisure doesn't necessarily mean time goofing off. It could mean time spent with one's family, pursuing hobbies, exercising, and so on). And though purchased goods yield the benefit of **utility,** or satisfaction, so does leisure. Indeed, we can think of leisure itself as a normal good, which most people would like to consume more of as their incomes increase.

How does a rational individual decide how much leisure to consume? By making a marginal comparison, of course. In analyzing labor supply, we ask how an individual uses a marginal *hour*. The individual compares the marginal benefit of devoting one more hour to leisure with the marginal cost of doing so. The marginal benefit is the additional utility derived from one more unit (hour) of leisure time. The marginal cost of more leisure is an opportunity cost. It is forgone utility: an additional hour of leisure is one hour less to earn income, and that income could have been used to purchase goods and services, which yield utility.

Consider Clive, an individual who likes both leisure and the goods money can buy. And suppose that his wage rate is $10 per hour. In deciding how many hours he wants to work, he must compare the additional utility of an additional hour of leisure with the additional utility he gets from $10 worth of goods. If $10 worth of goods adds more to his total utility than an additional hour of leisure, he can increase his total utility by giving up an hour of leisure in order to work an additional hour. If an extra hour of leisure adds more to his total utility than $10 in income, he can increase his total utility by working one fewer hour in order to gain an hour of leisure.

At Clive's optimal labor supply choice, then, his marginal benefit—the additional utility of one hour of leisure—is equal to the marginal cost—the forgone utility he would have gotten from the goods that his hourly wage could have purchased.

Our next step is to ask how Clive's decision about time allocation is affected when his wage rate changes.

## Wages and Labor Supply

Suppose that Clive's wage rate doubles, from $10 to $20 per hour. How will he change his time allocation?

You could argue that Clive will work longer hours, because his incentive to work has increased: by giving up an hour of leisure, he can now gain twice as much money as before. But you could equally well argue that he will work less, because he doesn't need to work as many hours to generate the income to pay for the goods he wants.

As these opposing arguments suggest, the quantity of labor Clive supplies can either rise or fall when his wage rate rises. To understand why, we recognize that a price change affects consumer choice in two ways. When the price of a good increases, an individual will normally consume less of that good and more of other goods. We call this the **substitution effect**—the change in the quantity consumed as the consumer substitutes the good that has become relatively cheaper in place of the good that has become relatively more expensive.

But there's a second effect. When the price of a good increases, an individual's purchasing power is reduced. The individual's income will buy less than before. This change in the quantity consumed of a good that results from a change in the overall purchasing power of the consumer due to the change in the price of a good is known as the **income effect.**

We need to apply these definitions to one particular price—the wage rate. Wages measure the benefit of working but also the opportunity cost of leisure. The hourly wage rate is Clive's price of one hour of leisure.

Now think about how a rise in Clive's wage rate affects his demand for leisure. On the one hand, the opportunity cost of leisure—the amount of money he gives up by taking an hour off instead of working—rises. That substitution effect gives him an incentive, other

**Leisure** is time available for purposes other than earning money to buy marketed goods.

**Utility** is a measure of the satisfaction a consumer derives from the consumption of goods, services, and leisure.

The **substitution effect** of a change in the price of a good is the change in the quantity consumed of that good as the consumer substitutes the good that has become relatively cheaper in place of the good that has become relatively more expensive.

The **income effect** of a change in the price of a good is the change in the quantity consumed of that good that results from a change in the consumer's purchasing power due to the change in the price of the good.

things equal, to consume less leisure and work longer hours. But on the other hand, a higher wage rate makes Clive richer—and this income effect leads him, other things equal, to want to consume *more* leisure and supply less labor, because leisure is a normal good.

So in the case of labor supply, the substitution effect and the income effect work in opposite directions. If the substitution effect is so powerful that it dominates the income effect, an increase in Clive's wage rate leads him to supply more hours of labor. If the income effect is so powerful that it dominates the substitution effect, an increase in the wage rate leads him to supply *fewer* hours of labor.

We see, then, that the **individual labor supply curve**—the relationship between the wage rate and the number of hours of labor supplied by an individual worker—is not necessarily upward sloping. If the income effect dominates, a higher wage rate will reduce the quantity of labor supplied.

Figure 9-9 illustrates the two possibilities for labor supply. If the substitution effect dominates the income effect, the individual labor supply curve slopes upward; panel (a) shows an increase in the wage rate from $10 to $20 per hour leading to a rise in the number of hours worked from 40 to 50. However, if the income effect dominates, the quantity of labor supplied goes down when the wage rate increases. Panel (b) shows the same rise in the wage rate leading to a *fall* in the number of hours worked from 40 to 30. (Economists refer to an individual labor supply curve that contains both upward-sloping and downward-sloping segments as a "backward-bending labor supply curve."

Is a negative response of the quantity of labor supplied to the wage rate a real possibility? Yes: many labor economists believe that income effects on the supply of labor may be somewhat stronger than substitution effects. The most compelling piece of evidence for this belief comes from Americans' increasing consumption of leisure over the past century. At the end of the nineteenth century, wages adjusted for inflation were only about one-eighth what they are today; the typical work week was 70 hours, and very few workers retired at 65. Today the typical work week is less than 40 hours, and most people retire at 65 or earlier. So it seems that Americans have chosen to take advantage of higher wages in part by consuming more leisure.

The **individual labor supply curve** shows how the quantity of labor supplied by an individual depends on that individual's wage rate.

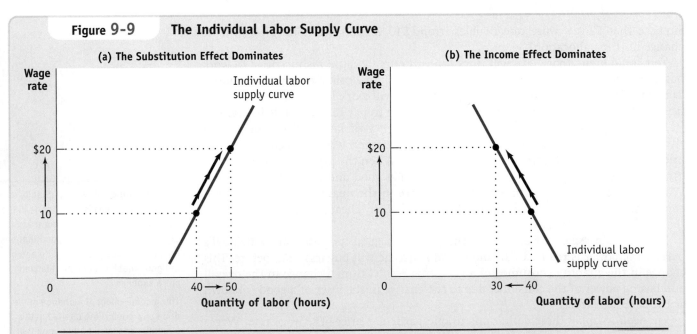

**Figure 9-9    The Individual Labor Supply Curve**

**(a) The Substitution Effect Dominates**

**(b) The Income Effect Dominates**

When the substitution effect of a wage increase dominates the income effect, the individual labor supply curve is upward sloping as in panel (a). Here a rise in the wage rate from $10 to $20 per hour increases the number of hours worked from 40 to 50.

But when the income effect of a wage increase dominates the substitution effect, the individual labor supply curve is downward sloping as in panel (b). Here the same rise in the wage rate reduces the number of hours worked from 40 to 30. **>web...**

## Shifts of the Labor Supply Curve

Now that we have examined how income and substitution effects shape the individual labor supply curve, we can turn to the market labor supply curve. In any labor market, the market supply curve is the horizontal sum of the individual labor supply curves of all workers in that market. A change in any factor *other than the wage* that alters workers' willingness to supply labor causes a shift of the labor supply curve. A variety of factors can lead to such shifts, including changes in preferences and social norms, changes in population, changes in opportunities, and changes in wealth.

**Changes in Preferences and Social Norms**   Changes in preferences and social norms can lead workers to increase or decrease their willingness to work at any given wage. A striking example of this phenomenon is the large increase in the number of employed women—particularly married employed women—that has occurred in the United States since the 1960s. Until that time, women who could afford to largely avoided working outside the home. Changes in preferences and norms in post–World War II America (helped along by the invention of labor-saving home appliances such as washing machines, increasing urbanization of the population, and higher female education levels) have induced large numbers of American women to join the workforce—a phenomenon often repeated in other countries that experience similar social and technological forces.

**Changes in Population**   Changes in the population size generally lead to shifts of the labor supply curve. A larger population tends to shift the labor supply rightward as more workers are available at any given wage; a smaller population tends to shift the labor supply curve leftward. Currently the size of the U.S. labor force grows by approximately 1 percent per year, a result of immigration from other countries and, in comparison to other developed countries, a relatively high U.S. birth rate. As a result, many labor markets in the United States are experiencing rightward shifts of their labor supply curves.

**Changes in Opportunities**   At one time, teaching was the only occupation considered suitable for well-educated women. However, as opportunities in other professions opened up to women starting in the 1960s, many women left teaching and potential female teachers chose other careers. This generated a leftward shift of the supply curve for teachers, reflecting a fall in the willingness to work at any given wage and forcing school districts to pay more to maintain an adequate teaching staff. These events illustrate a general result: when superior alternatives arise for workers in another labor market, the supply curve in the original labor market shifts leftward as workers move to the new opportunities. Similarly, when opportunities diminish in one labor market—say, layoffs in the manufacturing industry occur because of increased foreign competition—the supply in alternative labor markets increases as workers move to these other markets.

**Changes in Wealth** A person whose wealth increases will buy more normal goods, including leisure. So when a class of workers experiences a general rise in their wealth levels—say, due to a stock market boom—the income effect from the wealth increase will shift the labor supply curve associated with those workers leftward as workers consume more leisure and work less. Note that *the income effect caused by a change in wealth shifts the labor supply curve,* but *the income effect from a wage increase—*as we discussed in the case of the individual labor supply curve—*is a movement along the labor supply curve.* The following Economics in Action illustrates how such a change in the wealth levels of many families during the late 1990s led to a shift of the market labor supply curve associated with their employable children.

## *economics in action*

### The Decline of the Summer Job

In the summer of 2000, according to the *New York Times,* the New Jersey resort town of Ocean City found itself facing a serious shortage of lifeguards. Traditionally lifeguard positions, together with many other seasonal jobs, have been filled mainly by high school and college students. But in recent years a growing number of young Americans have chosen not to take summer jobs. In 1979, 71 percent of Americans between the ages of 16 and 19 were in the summer workforce. Twenty years later that number had fallen to 63 percent; and by 2005, it was 55 percent. Data show that it was young men in particular who became much less willing to take summer jobs during the 1990s.

One explanation for the decline in summer labor supply is that more students feel that they should devote their summers to additional study. But an important factor in the decline, according to the article, was that an economic and stock market boom in the late 1990s had made many more American families affluent—affluent enough that their children no longer felt pressure to make a financial contribution by working all summer.

In short, the income effect led to a reduced labor supply. ∎

< < < < < < < < < < < < < < < < < <

>>CHECK YOUR UNDERSTANDING 9-4

1. Formerly, Clive was free to work as many or as few hours per week as he wanted. But a new law limits the maximum number of hours he can work per week to 35. Explain under what circumstances, if at all, he is made:
   a. Worse off
   b. Equally as well off
   c. Better off

2. Explain in terms of the income and substitution effects how a fall in Clive's wage can induce him to work more hours than before.

Solutions appear at back of book.

• A LOOK AHEAD •

We have now put together all the pieces for understanding how a perfectly competitive market economy works. We've seen how supply and demand determine market prices, and how profit maximization gives rise to the supply curve for each good. We've also just seen how factor markets determine the prices of factors of production and therefore the factor incomes of individuals.

But the ultimate purpose of an economy is to provide people with what they want. How well does a market economy do that job? In the next chapter we finally examine the *efficiency* of a market economy, two examples of inefficiency, and the question of *equity.*

SUMMARY

1. Just as there are markets for goods and services, there are markets for factors of production, including labor, land, and both **physical capital** and **human capital.** These markets determine the **factor distribution of income.**

2. Profit-maximizing price-taking producers will employ a factor up to the point at which its price is equal to its **value of the marginal product**—the marginal product of the factor multiplied by the price of the good. The **value of the marginal product curve** is therefore the individual price-taking producer's demand curve for a factor.

3. The market demand curve for labor is the sum of the individual demand curves of producers in that market. It shifts for three main reasons: changes in output price, changes in the supply of other factors, and technological changes.

4. When a competitive labor market is in equilibrium, the market wage is equal to the **equilibrium value of the marginal product** of labor, the additional value produced by the last worker hired in the labor market as a whole. The same principle applies to other factors of production: the **rental rate** of land or capital is equal to the equilibrium value of the marginal products. This insight leads to the **marginal productivity theory of income distribution,** according to which each factor is paid the value of the marginal product of the last unit of that factor employed in the factor market as a whole.

5. Large disparities in wages raise questions about the validity of the marginal productivity theory of income distribution. Many disparities can be explained by **compensating dif-**

**ferentials** and by differences in talent, job experience, and human capital across workers. Market interference in the forms of **unions** and collective action by employers also creates wage disparities. The **efficiency-wage model,** which arises from a type of market failure, shows how wage disparities can arise from employers' attempts to increase worker performance. Free markets tend to diminish discrimination, but discrimination remains a real source of wage disparity. Discrimination is typically maintained either through problems in labor markets or (historically) through institutionalization in government policies.

6. Labor supply is the result of **marginal benefit** versus marginal cost decisions about **time allocation,** where each worker faces a **utility** trade-off between **leisure** and work. An increase in the hourly wage rate tends to increase work hours by the **substitution effect** but to reduce work hours by the **income effect.** If the net result is that a worker increases the quantity of labor supplied in response to a higher wage, the **individual labor supply curve** slopes upward. If the net result is that a worker reduces their work hours, the individual labor supply curve—unlike supply curves for goods and services—slopes downward.

7. The market labor supply curve is the sum of the individual labor supply curves of all workers in that market. It shifts for four main reasons: changes in preferences and social norms, changes in population, changes in opportunities, and changes in wealth.

KEY TERMS

Physical capital, p. 214
Human capital, p. 214
Factor distribution of income, p. 214
Value of the marginal product, p. 218
Marginal benefit, p. 218
Value of the marginal product curve, p. 218
Rental rate, p. 222

Equilibrium value of the marginal product, p. 223
Marginal productivity theory of income distribution, p. 223
Compensating differentials, p. 226
Unions, p. 227
Efficiency-wage model, p. 228

Time allocation, p. 230
Leisure, p. 231
Utility, p. 231
Substitution effect, p. 231
Income effect, p. 231
Individual labor supply curve, p. 232

PROBLEMS

1. In 2001, national income in the United States was $8,122.0 billion. In the same year, 135 million workers were employed, at an average wage of $43,518 per worker per year.

   a. How much compensation of employees was paid in the United States in 2001?

   b. Analyze the factor distribution of income. What percentage of national income was received in terms of compensation of employees in 2001?

   c. Suppose that a huge wave of corporate downsizing leads many terminated employees to open their own businesses. What is the effect on the factor distribution of income?

   d. Suppose the supply of labor rises due to an increase in the retirement age. What happens to the percentage of national income received in terms of compensation of employees?

**2.** Marty's Frozen Yogurt has the production function per day shown in the accompanying table. The equilibrium wage rate for a worker is $80 per day. Each cup of frozen yogurt sells for $2.

| Quantity of labor (workers) | Quantity of frozen yogurt (cups) |
|---|---|
| 0 | 0 |
| 1 | 110 |
| 2 | 200 |
| 3 | 270 |
| 4 | 300 |
| 5 | 320 |
| 6 | 330 |

**a.** Calculate the marginal product of labor for each worker and the value of the marginal product per worker.

**b.** How many workers should Marty employ?

**3.** Patty's Pizza Parlor has the production function per hour shown in the accompanying table. The hourly wage rate for each worker is $10. Each pizza sells for $2.

| Quantity of labor (workers) | Quantity of pizza |
|---|---|
| 0 | 0 |
| 1 | 9 |
| 2 | 15 |
| 3 | 19 |
| 4 | 22 |
| 5 | 24 |

**a.** Calculate the marginal product of labor for each worker and the value of the marginal product per worker.

**b.** Draw the value of the marginal product curve. Use your diagram to determine how many workers Patty should employ.

**c.** Now the price of pizza increases to $4. Calculate the value of the marginal product per worker, and draw the new value of the marginal product curve into your diagram. Use your diagram to determine how many workers Patty should employ now.

**4.** The production function for Patty's Pizza Parlor is given in the table in Problem 3. The price of pizza is $2, but the hourly wage rate rises from $10 to $15. Use a diagram to determine how Patty's demand for workers responds as a result of this wage rate increase.

**5.** Patty's Pizza Parlor initially had the production function given in the table in Problem 3. A worker's hourly wage rate was $10, and pizza sold for $2. Now Patty buys a new high-tech pizza oven that allows her workers to become twice as productive as before. That is, the first worker now produces 18 pizzas per hour instead of 9, and so on.

**a.** Calculate the new marginal product of labor and the new value of the marginal product of labor.

**b.** Use a diagram to determine how Patty's hiring decision responds to this increase in the productivity of her workforce.

**6.** Jameel runs a driver education school. The more driving instructors he hires, the more driving lessons he can sell. But because he owns a limited number of training automobiles, each additional driving instructor adds less to Jameel's output of driving lessons. The accompanying table shows Jameel's production function per day. Each driving lesson can be sold at $35 per hour.

| Quantity of labor (driving instructors) | Quantity of driving lessons (hours) |
|---|---|
| 0 | 0 |
| 1 | 8 |
| 2 | 15 |
| 3 | 21 |
| 4 | 26 |
| 5 | 30 |
| 6 | 33 |

Determine Jameel's labor demand schedule (his demand schedule for driving instructors) for each of the following daily wage rates for driving instructors: $160, $180, $200, $220, $240, and $260.

**7.** Dale and Dana work at a self-service gas station and convenience store. Dale opens up everyday and Dana arrives later to help stock the store. They are both paid the current market wage of $9.50 per hour. But Dale feels he should be paid much more because the revenue generated from the gas pumps he turns on every morning is much higher than the revenue generated by the items that Dana stocks. Assess this argument.

**8.** In the Shire, farmers can rent land for $100 per acre per year. All the acres are identical. Merry Brandybuck rents 30 acres on which he grows carrots. Pippin Took rents 20 acres on which he grows corn. They sell their produce in a perfectly competitive market. Merry boasts that his value of the marginal product of land is twice as large as Pippin's. Pippin replies that, if this is true and if Merry wants to maximize his profit, Merry is renting too much land. Is Pippin right? Explain your answer.

**9.** For each of the following situations in which similar workers are paid different wages, give the most likely explanation for these wage differences.

**a.** Test pilots for new jet aircraft earn higher wages than airline pilots.

**b.** College graduates usually have higher earnings in their first year on the job than workers without college degrees have in their first year on the job.

**c.** Full professors command higher salaries than assistant professors for teaching the same class.

**d.** Unionized workers are generally better paid than non-unionized workers.

10. Research consistently finds that despite nondiscrimination policies, African-American workers on average receive lower wages than white workers do. What are the possible reasons for this? Are these reasons consistent with marginal productivity theory?

11. Greta is an enthusiastic amateur gardener and spends a lot of her free time working in her yard. She also has a demanding and well-paid job as a freelance advertising consultant. The advertising business is going through a difficult time and the hourly consulting fee Greta can charge falls. Greta decides to spend more time gardening and less time consulting. Explain her decision in terms of income and substitution effects.

12. Wendy works at a fast-food restaurant. When her wage rate was $5 per hour, she worked 30 hours per week. When her wage rate rose to $6 per hour, she decided to work 40 hours. But when her wage rate rose further to $7, she decided to work only 35 hours.

**a.** Draw Wendy's individual labor supply curve.

**b.** Is Wendy's behavior irrational, or can you find a rational explanation? Explain your answer.

13. You are the governor's economic policy adviser. The governor wants to put in place policies that encourage employed people to work more hours at their jobs and that encourage unemployed people to find and take jobs. Assess each of the following policies in terms of reaching that goal. Explain your reasoning in terms of income and substitution effects, and indicate when the impact of the policy may be ambiguous.

**a.** The state income tax rate is lowered, which has the effect of increasing workers' after-tax wage rate.

**b.** The state income tax rate is increased, which has the effect of decreasing workers' after-tax wage rate.

**c.** The state property tax rate is increased, which reduces workers' after-tax income.

---

>*web*... To continue your study and review of concepts in this chapter, please visit the Krugman/Wells/Olney website for quizzes, animated graph tutorials, web links to helpful resources, and more.

**www.worthpublishers.com/krugmanwellsolney**

## >>Efficiency, Inefficiency, and Equity

### What you will learn in this chapter:

➤ How the overall concept of efficiency can be broken down into three components—**efficiency in consumption, efficiency in production,** and **efficiency in output levels**

➤ Why an economy consisting of many perfectly competitive markets is typically, but not always, efficient

➤ Why it is easier to determine if an economy is efficient than to determine if it is fair or equitable

➤ What **externalities** are and why they can lead to inefficiency in a market economy and support for government intervention

➤ What **public goods** are and why markets fail to supply them efficiently

### AFTER THE FALL

WHEN THE BERLIN WALL CAME down in 1989, Western observers got their first good look at the centrally planned economy of East Germany. What they found was a stunningly inefficient system. Although investment had been lavished on politically favored industries such as energy production, producers of consumer goods and services were starved for capital. And the consumer goods that were produced were often not what consumers wanted to buy.

The revelation of East German inefficiency showed how badly such a planned economy worked compared with a market economy, like that of West Germany.

But even after the wall had come down, the government of the newly unified Federal Republic of Germany was not willing to let the free market run its course. Instead, both industry and individuals in East Germany received huge amounts of financial aid. The goal was to prevent the emergence of a politically unacceptable level of inequality between the former East Germans, many of whom lost their jobs in the aftermath of reunification, and West Germans.

Over time, many economists have come to believe that this aid actually delayed the reconstruction of the East German economy. They argue that the aid reduced incentives for workers to relocate to areas where more jobs were available or to learn new skills. But German officials insist that the price was well worth paying: sometimes a sense of fairness, they argue, is more important than efficiency.

Germany's experience reminds us that although we want our economy to be efficient, we also want it to be fair. In this chapter we will address both concerns. We begin by discussing the *efficiency* of a

Goods produced in centrally planned economies (consider the East German–produced Trabant at left) are notorious for their poor quality compared to stylish, high-quality goods produced in market economies (consider the West German–produced Mercedes at right).

competitive market economy—the effectiveness of a competitive market economy at producing the goods and services that people want to consume. We then turn to the less well-defined but equally important issue of *equity*—is the distribution of consumption among individuals "fair"? As we'll see, there is no generally accepted definition of *fairness*; nonetheless, societies often choose to sacrifice some efficiency in the pursuit of equity. Finally, we will look at two examples of inefficiency or market failure: externalities and public goods.

# Efficiency

The economy as a whole consists of many, many markets, all interrelated in two ways:

- On the consumption side, the demand for each good is affected by the prices of other goods.
- On the production side, producers of different goods compete for the same factors of production.

To think about the economy as a whole, then, we have to think of many markets, for both goods and factors. A **competitive market economy** is an economy in which all of these markets are perfectly competitive, with equilibrium prices determined by supply and demand. In each market both the supply and demand curves are likely to be affected by events in other markets.

A **competitive market economy** is an economy in which all markets, for goods and for factors, are perfectly competitive.

When all markets have reached equilibrium—when the quantity of each good and factor demanded is equal to the quantity of each good and factor supplied at the going market prices—we say that the economy is in **general equilibrium.** To put it another way, general equilibrium is the economy-wide counterpart of ordinary equilibrium in a single market.

An economy is in **general equilibrium** when the quantity supplied is equal to the quantity demanded in all markets.

Our next task is to show that a competitive market economy in general equilibrium is usually *efficient*—that is, it is efficient except in certain well-defined cases. What do we mean by saying that the economy as a whole is efficient? Actually, we defined efficiency way back in Chapter 1. We will start by revisiting that definition to see why it is the right approach to analyzing the economy as a whole. Then we will describe the three criteria that an economy as a whole must satisfy in order to be efficient.

## Efficiency, Revisited

When economists discuss efficiency in an individual market as we did in Chapter 6, they usually use the concepts of consumer and producer surplus, which measure costs and benefits in monetary terms. This makes sense when you are talking about the market for just one good, because you can take the prices of other goods—and therefore the value of a dollar—as given. When we are analyzing the economy as a whole, however, measuring costs and benefits in dollar terms no longer makes sense, because all prices are "to be determined."

Instead, economists focus on the basic definition of efficiency. Recall from Chapter 1: an economy is efficient if it does not pass up any opportunities to make some people better off without making other people worse off.

To achieve efficiency, an economy must meet three criteria. The economy must be *efficient in consumption, efficient in production,* and *efficient in output levels*. Let's look at these criteria and see how a competitive market economy satisfies them.

## DEFINING ECONOMIC EFFICIENCY

The economist's definition of *efficiency*—that an economy is efficient if nobody can be made better off without making others worse off—may seem to be oddly indirect. Why can't we define efficiency in terms of a positive achievement rather than the absence of something?

Many other definitions of efficiency have been proposed, but none of them have survived careful scrutiny—all of them turn out either to be incomplete or to involve unacceptable implications. A good example is the fate of the principle known as utilitarianism, proposed by the nineteenth-century English philosopher Jeremy Bentham.

Bentham offered a simple principle: "the greatest good for the greatest number." In effect, he argued that society should try to maximize the total utility of its members. This sounded persuasive but eventually ran into two problems. First, how do we add up the utility of different people? We may loosely say that Ms. Martineau is happier than Mr. Ricardo, but is she twice as happy or three

Whose happiness counts more? Efficiency has been difficult to define because we can't compare utility across people.

times as happy? You may argue that it makes no sense even to ask that question—but in that case Bentham's principle becomes meaningless because we have no way to add up the total utility of all members of society.

Second, even if we imagine that it is somehow possible to add up the utility of different people, critics of Bentham point out that his doctrine has the disturbing

implication that we should cater to the tastes of "utility monsters"—people who derive especially high pleasure from excessive consumption. Bentham's criterion implies that if Martineau really likes owning luxury automobiles and going to fancy restaurants but Ricardo is a modest sort who can make do with a bicycle and macaroni-and-cheese dinners, we should take money from Ricardo and give it to Martineau—even if Ricardo is a hard worker and Martineau notably lazy. This doesn't seem right.

Because of these difficulties, Bentham's principle has pretty much vanished from economic thought. The same is true of other ideas, such as the Marxist slogan "from each according to his ability, to each according to his needs." The only definition of efficiency that has managed to survive practical and logical criticism is the negative one: an economy is inefficient if there is a way to make at least one person better off without making others worse off, and it is efficient if it is not inefficient.

## Efficiency in Consumption

An economy is **efficient in consumption** if there is no way to redistribute goods among consumers that makes some consumers better off without making others worse off.

> An economy is **efficient in consumption** if there is no way to redistribute goods among consumers that makes some consumers better off without making others worse off.

> An **economic signal** is any piece of information that helps people make better economic decisions.

To see what efficiency in consumption involves, it helps to imagine scenarios for inefficiency. Imagine, for example, an economy that produces both cornflakes and shredded wheat but that provides those who prefer shredded wheat with cornflakes, and vice versa. Then it would be possible to make at least one person better off without making anyone else worse off by redistributing the goods, giving people the breakfast cereal they prefer.

The first piece of good news is that as long as prices perform properly as **economic signals**—that is, as pieces of information that help people make economic decisions—this kind of inefficiency won't occur in a competitive market economy. We've seen this already in the case of market equilibrium in one individual market: the consumers who actually receive a good at the market equilibrium are those with the greatest willingness to pay—thanks to the role prices play in helping people make the right economic decisions. Consumers who prefer an additional box of cornflakes will be willing to pay more for that box than consumers who would rather have an additional box of shredded wheat. So if the markets for cornflakes and shredded wheat are both in equilibrium, there won't be any way to make at least one consumer better off without making others worse off by redistributing the available quantities of breakfast cereals.

In other words, prices in goods markets ensure that you can't increase total surplus in a single market by taking a good away from one person and giving it to another. Similarly, prices also ensure that when all markets in an economy are in perfectly competitive general equilibrium, there is no way to redistribute goods that makes some consumers better off without making others worse off.

It's important, however, to realize the limitations of that statement: even though an economy is efficient, you can always make *some* consumers better off if you are willing to make others worse off. We'll come back to that point shortly.

## Efficiency in Production

Economists say that an economy is **efficient in production** if it is not possible to produce more of some goods without producing less of others.

We can use the *production possibility frontier* model from Chapter 2 to understand this. This model uses a diagram like Figure 10-1 to illustrate the economy's trade-offs: the more wheat it produces, the less corn it can produce, and vice versa. If the economy produces the quantities at either point *A* or point *B* on the production possibility frontier, it is efficient in production: it is possible to produce more corn than the economy produces at *A*, but only by producing less wheat; it is possible to produce more wheat than the economy produces at *B*, but only by producing less corn. The economy is not efficient in production, however, if it produces at point *C:* it is possible to produce more wheat *and* more corn than the economy does at that point.

An economy will be efficient in production if it has an **efficient allocation of resources**—if there is no way to reallocate factors of production among producers to produce more of some goods without producing less of others. This is an important result: *An economy that is efficient in allocation of resources is efficient in production, and vice versa.*

Here is another way to think about Figure 10-1: at point *A* the economy can produce more corn only by taking resources away from wheat production. Similarly, at point *B* the economy can produce more wheat only by taking resources away from corn production.

Just as in the case of efficiency in consumption, it helps to imagine scenarios for inefficiency. In the United States, land in Iowa is ideally suited for growing corn, land in Minnesota is much better suited for growing wheat, and most land in Maine isn't suitable for growing either. It would clearly be inefficient if good land in the Midwest

> An economy is **efficient in production** if there is no way to produce more of some goods without producing less of other goods.

> An economy has an **efficient allocation of resources** if there is no way to reallocate factors of production among producers to produce more of some goods without producing less of others.

### Figure 10-1

**The Production Possibility Frontier and Efficiency in Production**

An economy is efficient in production if it cannot produce more of one good without producing less of other goods. Equivalently, an economy is efficient in production if it is on its production possibility frontier. Here *A* and *B* are efficient production points—at each point the economy can produce more of one good only by producing less of the other. *C* is not an efficient production point because more corn *and* more wheat can be produced. **>web...**

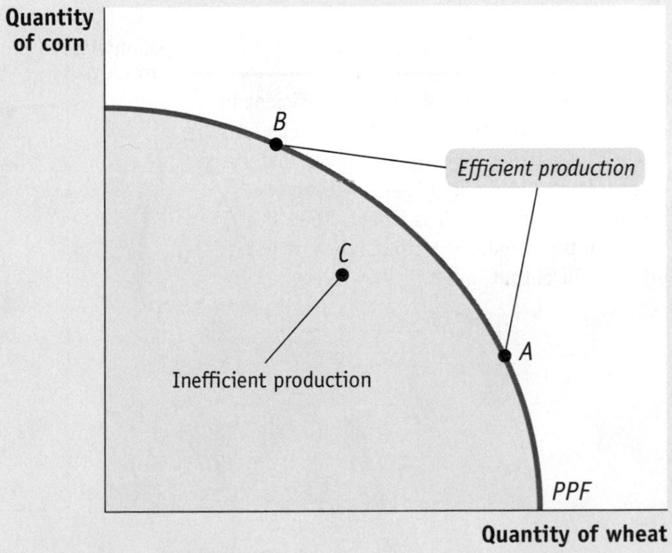

were left idle but farmers struggled with the stony soil of Maine; it would also be inefficient if Iowa farms grew wheat and Minnesota farms grew corn.

The second piece of good news is that, just as in the case of consumption, the role of prices as economic signals ensures that a competitive market economy in general equilibrium achieves efficiency in production. The logic is similar, but this time it applies to prices in factor markets rather than prices in goods markets. Corn farmers are willing to pay more for Iowa land than wheat farmers; wheat farmers are willing to pay more for Minnesota land than are corn farmers. And much of New England is no longer farmed but has returned to forest, because labor and capital can be more productively employed on richer lands elsewhere. In short, when factor markets are competitive, resources are allocated to the producers that can make the best use of them, and the economy is indeed efficient in production.

Notice, however, that this does not say *what* the economy produces. Both A and B in Figure 10-1 represent efficient production. We still need to ask whether the economy produces at the "right" place on the production possibility frontier—or, rather, *a* right place, because there may be many efficient outcomes. But let's hold off on that for a moment and finish our description of efficiency in the competitive market economy as a whole.

## Efficiency in Output Levels

Suppose that a competitive market economy is efficient in production—it cannot produce more of some goods without producing less of others. Suppose also that it is efficient in consumption—there is no way to redistribute the goods produced that will make some consumers better off without making others worse off. There is still the question of whether the competitive market economy is producing the *right mix* of goods to start with. For example, suppose that point A in Figure 10-2 corresponds to producing enough wheat to let everyone have shredded wheat five times a week and cornflakes two times a week. This will still be inefficient if everyone prefers to have shredded wheat only three times a week but cornflakes four times a week—*and if* point B would allow them to do so. In that case, moving from A to B—that is, shifting resources into corn production—would make everyone better off. Our third criterion for efficiency, then, is that the economy be **efficient in output levels:** there

> An economy is **efficient in output levels** if there isn't a different mix of output that would make some people better off without making others worse off.

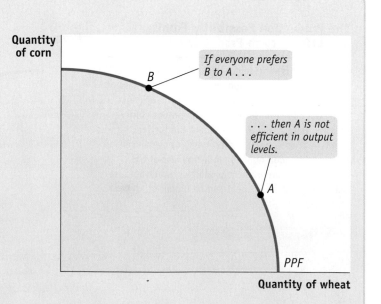

### Figure 10-2

#### Efficiency in Output Levels

The output levels A and B are both efficient in production. However, suppose that B represents a mix of quantities of corn and wheat that everyone prefers to the mix at A—at A everyone prefers more corn and less wheat. Then the economy that produces output mix A is not efficient in output levels.

must not be a different mix of output that would make some people better off without making others worse off.

The third and final piece of good news about the general equilibrium of a competitive market economy is that it will be efficient in output levels when prices perform properly as economic signals.

How do we know this? We already saw that in an individual competitive market producers produce the quantity of output that maximizes total surplus. The reason is that consumers and producers face the same price—the market price is an economic signal telling producers what one more unit of output is worth to consumers. This signal induces producers to produce that extra unit of output if the cost of the resources they would need to produce it is less than the market price.

In the economy as a whole, producers learn how much consumers are willing to pay for a bit more of one good versus a bit more of another when market prices operate as economic signals. This process ensures that a competitive market economy in general equilibrium produces the right mix of goods.

To see how this happens, imagine an economy in which the only resource that can be shifted between industries is labor, and all producers are hiring from the same labor market. (We'll also assume there are no complications like compensating differentials that make wages differ.) Imagine that right now consumers would prefer more corn and less wheat than the economy is currently producing. The economy can provide what consumers want by transferring labor from wheat production to corn production—by forgoing some wheat output in order to produce more corn. But will this adjustment take place?

Yes, it will, because consumers are willing to pay more for the additional corn that one more worker employed in corn production can produce than they are willing to pay for the wheat forgone by employing one fewer worker in wheat production. We can express this algebraically. The extra corn that a unit of labor can produce is $MPL_{corn}$, the marginal product of labor in corn. The wheat that unit of labor would have produced is $MPL_{wheat}$, the marginal product of labor in wheat. When we say that consumers are willing to pay more for the extra corn than for the wheat, we are saying that at the current employment and output levels in the corn and wheat sectors

**(10-1)**  $P_{corn} \times MPL_{corn} > P_{wheat} \times MPL_{wheat}$

where $P_{corn}$ and $P_{wheat}$ are the prices of corn and wheat, respectively.

We've already seen the expressions in Equation 10-1 in Chapter 9. $P_{corn} \times MPL_{corn}$ is the *value of the marginal product* of labor in corn production, and $P_{wheat} \times MPL_{wheat}$ is the value of the marginal product of labor in wheat production. So we can restate Equation 10-1 as

**(10-2)**  $VMPL_{corn} > VMPL_{wheat}$

This expression says that the value produced by an additional unit of labor employed in corn production is greater than that of an additional unit of labor employed in wheat production when consumers prefer more corn and less wheat than is being produced.

Can this be an equilibrium? No; we learned in Chapter 9 that producers maximize profits by hiring labor up until the point that $VMPL = W$, where $W$ is the wage rate. That is, a producer hires labor until the value of the output produced by the last worker employed is equal to the current market wage rate. In this example, corn producers and wheat producers hire workers from the same labor market. So the direct implication of $VMPL_{corn} > VMPL_{wheat}$ is that, at current employment levels, corn producers are willing to pay a higher wage rate than wheat producers. Corn producers will hire workers away from wheat producers.

When will this process stop? When the wage rate that corn producers are willing to pay is equal to the wage rate that wheat producers are willing to pay; that is, when

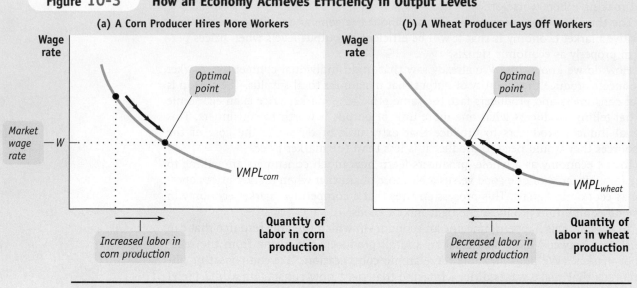

**Figure 10-3**   **How an Economy Achieves Efficiency in Output Levels**

If at current employment levels $VMPL_{corn} > VMPL_{wheat}$, then corn producers will increase their profits by hiring workers away from wheat producers, who will, in turn, increase their profits by laying off workers. This process is illustrated for a corn producer in panel (a). As a corn producer hires workers, she increases her corn production and moves down her $VMPL$ curve until she reaches her optimal employment level, the number of workers at which $VMPL_{corn} = W$, the market wage rate. Panel (b) shows the corresponding changes for a wheat producer: he decreases his wheat production and moves up his $VMPL$ curve as he lays off workers. He also reaches his optimal employment level at $VMPL_{wheat} = W$. Workers cease moving between sectors once $VMPL_{corn} = VMPL_{wheat}$. It is an equilibrium because at that point the value of the additional output produced by a worker in the corn sector no longer exceeds the value of the additional output produced by a worker in the wheat sector and corn producers are no longer willing to pay a higher wage than wheat producers. **>web...**

$VMPL_{corn} = VMPL_{wheat}$. The evolution of this process is illustrated in Figure 10-3. In panel (a), a corn producer starts at a $VMPL_{corn}$ greater than the current market wage rate. She increases her profits by hiring more workers and moves down her $VMPL$ curve until she reaches her optimal employment level, at which $VMPL_{corn} = W$.

Where are these new workers in the corn sector coming from? They are coming from the wheat sector. This is illustrated in panel (b), where a wheat producer is losing workers and in the process is moving up his $VMPL$ curve. He increases his profits by laying off workers, letting them go until he reaches his optimal employment level, at which $VMPL_{wheat} = W$.

So as labor in the economy is reallocated from wheat production to corn production, the output of corn rises and the output of wheat falls. Eventually, workers cease moving from the wheat sector to the corn sector when $VMPL_{corn} = VMPL_{wheat}$. At this point the value of the additional output produced by a worker in the corn sector no longer exceeds the value of the additional output produced by a worker in the wheat sector. That is, we have finally reached an equilibrium.

This example helps us understand that, in a market economy, markets for goods and services are linked via the factor markets. Or to put it a slightly different way, any change in the amount of one good or service produced will ultimately affect the amounts of other goods and services as factors of production shift from one sector to another. Figure 10-4 helps us make sense of the interconnectedness of markets for goods and services and factor markets in a market economy. To appreciate its significance, it may help recalling the circular-flow diagram of Chapter 2. There we saw how firms and households are linked via the factor markets and the markets for goods and services through flows of money. That is, in the factor markets, firms pay households

**Figure 10-4** **Efficiency in Output Levels in a Circular-Flow Framework**

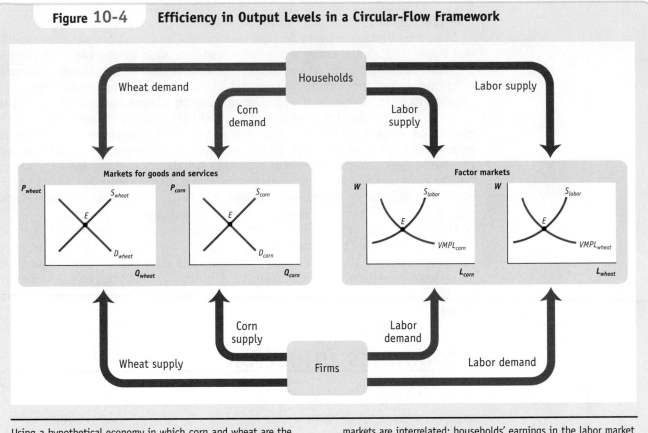

Using a hypothetical economy in which corn and wheat are the only goods and labor is the only factor of production, we can see how the markets for goods and services are linked via the factor markets. The factor markets bring the supply of labor from households and the demand for labor by firms into equilibrium, and the markets for goods and services bring the supply of goods and services from firms and the demand for goods and services by households into equilibrium. But supply and demand in all these markets are interrelated: households' earnings in the labor market determine their demand for goods and services, and vice versa; firms' profits from hiring labor in the labor market and producing output determine their supply of goods and services, and vice versa. Any change in one market will ultimately generate corresponding changes in all the other markets. When every market for goods and services and every factor market in the economy is in equilibrium, the economy as a whole is in general equilibrium.

for factors of production; in the markets for goods and services, households pay firms for goods and services.

Figure 10-4 presents an alternative and richer version of the same phenomenon, this time expressed in terms of the forces of supply and demand for resources that underlie the money flows of the circular-flow diagram. Here, we imagine that the only goods in the economy are corn and wheat and that labor is the only factor of production. The right portion of the figure represents how the supply of labor from households and the demand for labor from firms meet and are brought into equilibrium in the factor markets. But supply and demand in the labor market are themselves affected by supply and demand in the markets for goods and services: firms' demand for labor is derived from the demand for their goods and services, and households' supply of labor is determined by the earnings required for purchases in the markets for goods and services.

Similarly, the left portion of Figure 10-4 represents how the supply of goods and services from firms and the demand for goods and services from households meet and are brought into equilibrium in the markets for goods and services. Again, there is an interrelationship between the market for goods and services and factor markets: households' demand for goods and services is determined by the wages they earn in the labor market, and firms' supply of goods and services is determined by the returns they generate from hiring labor in the labor market.

Moreover, any change in the demand for a good will initiate a cascade of events that will ripple through the entire economy as resources shift among various sectors in response. So, for example, an increase in demand for corn relative to wheat causes a rightward shift of the demand for corn and a leftward shift in the demand for wheat. This results in an increase in the equilibrium quantity of corn supplied and a decrease in the equilibrium quantity of wheat supplied, which in turn causes an increase in the equilibrium employment level in the corn sector and a decrease in the equilibrium employment in the wheat sector. So the incentives in a competitive market economy in which prices perform properly as economic signals will lead the economy to produce the mix of goods that consumers prefer—that is, the economy will indeed be efficient in output levels. When each market for goods and services and each factor market is in equilibrium, the economy as a whole is in general equilibrium.

How does a competitive market economy achieve this amazing result? It comes down to the point we have emphasized throughout this discussion: the role of prices as *economic signals*. The fact that everyone faces the same prices ensures that goods and services are efficiently allocated among consumers, that factors of production are efficiently allocated among producers, and that the mix of goods and services produced reflects what people want.

# economics in action

## A Great Leap—Backward

We began this chapter with the observation that the planned economy of East Germany did not, as its founders had hoped, surpass the market economies of the West. But possibly the most compelling example of inefficiency in a planned economy comes from China.

In the late 1950s, China's leader Mao Zedong put into effect an ambitious plan, the so-called Great Leap Forward, to speed up the nation's industrialization. Key to this plan was a shift from urban to rural manufacturing: farming villages were supposed to start producing such heavy industrial goods as steel.

Unfortunately, this plan backfired. Diverting farmers from their usual work led to a sharp fall in food production. Meanwhile, because raw materials like coal and iron ore were sent to ill-equipped and inexperienced rural producers rather than to urban factories, industrial output declined as well. The plan, in short, led to a fall in the production of everything.

Because China was a very poor nation to start with, the results were catastrophic. The famine that followed is estimated to have reduced China's population by as much as 30 million. ■

< < < < < < < < < < < < < < < < < < <

1. In the small country of Bountiful, labor is the only factor of production, all workers are paid the same wage, all food is produced domestically, and all markets are perfectly competitive. Imagine that, due to health concerns, each Bountifullian experiences a greater demand for breakfast cereals and a lower demand for sausage.
   a. Explain how the change in preferences will lead to a reallocation of labor between the sausage and breakfast cereal industries. Use the concepts of $VMPL_S$, $VMPL_C$, and wage rate in your answer (the subscript $S$ refers to sausage and $C$ to cereal).
   b. How will you know that the Bountiful economy has fully adjusted to the change in preferences? Use the three conditions of efficiency in your answer.

Solutions appear at back of book.

> **QUICK REVIEW**
> - To achieve efficiency, an economy must be *efficient in consumption*, *efficient in production*, and *efficient in output levels*.
> - When prices perform properly as *economic signals*, a *competitive market economy* in *general equilibrium* is efficient. It is efficient in consumption because goods and services are allocated to consumers according to their prices, which are signals of consumers' willingnesses to pay. Second, it is efficient in production because factors of production are allocated to producers according to their prices, signals of producers' valuation of those factors. Finally, it is efficient in output levels: because everyone faces the same prices, the mix of goods and services will be the mix that people prefer.

# Efficiency and Equity

We have now shown why a perfectly competitive market economy is typically efficient: there is no way to make some people better off without making others worse off.

This conclusion refutes the claims of would-be economic planners, who insist that markets are disorganized free-for-alls and that centralized decision making would be more efficient. But we need to be careful: it is easy to get carried away with the idea that markets get it right and to then draw inappropriate conclusions about economic policy.

It's important to remember that efficiency is about *how to achieve goals;* it does not say anything about what your goals should be. Saying that the market outcome is efficient doesn't mean that that outcome is necessarily desirable. In fact, in some circumstances a well-thought-out economic policy may deliberately choose an outcome that is *not* efficient.

When can an outcome be efficient without being desirable? When it's not fair.

## What's Fair?

Imagine an economy in which a dictator controls everything, keeping almost everything the economy produces for himself and allowing his subjects only the bare minimum they need to survive. Could such an economy be efficient?

Yes, it could. If there is no way to make one of the suffering citizens better off without making the dictator worse off, then the economy is efficient. But that doesn't mean we have to approve of it. The situation is clearly unjust; the contrast between the dictator's wealth and his subjects' poverty isn't fair.

This extreme example shows that we want something more than efficiency from an economy. We also want *equity:* we want the distribution of utility among individuals to be reasonably fair.

But what exactly is "fair"? That turns out to be a very hard question to answer. To see why it's such a tricky question, let's consider how plausible ideas about fairness become problematic when you start to think about them carefully.

First, you sometimes hear that people should be given an equal chance at the starting line—that is, at birth, or maybe at the age of 18, everyone should have the same opportunities to be successful in life. That sounds fair—but what about the natural

## FOR INQUIRING MINDS
### THEORIES OF JUSTICE

In 1971 the philosopher John Rawls published *A Theory of Justice,* which represents the most famous attempt to date to develop a theory of economic fairness. He asked readers to imagine deciding economic and social policies behind a "veil of ignorance" about their identity. That is, suppose that you knew you would be a human being but you did not know whether you would be rich or poor, healthy or sick, and so on. What kind of policies would you want?

Rawls answered that you would probably choose policies that placed a high weight on the utility of the worst-off members of society: after all, you might end up being one of them. And because of diminishing marginal utility, having a few dollars more would do you a lot of good if you find yourself poor, but having a few dollars less wouldn't do you much harm if you find yourself well-off.

Although no nation has ever made this theory the basis for its economic policy, Rawls-type arguments do play an important role in the debate over economic and social policy. For example, when Congress debated a plan to cut tax rates on large estates— those valued at over $1.3 million—from their 2000 rate of 55 percent, Bill Gates, Sr., father of the Microsoft billionaire, offered a defense of the existing tax based on a Rawlsian view of fairness. He made his case by asking people to imagine traveling back to the moment of their birth. At that point, you get to decide, for a price, where you are going to be born—the hugely rich United States or impoverished Ethiopia. The price for choosing Ethiopia is zero; the price for choosing the United States is 55 percent of the value of your estate should it exceed $1.3 million when you die. Or to put it another way, imagine that the price of being born in the United States instead of Ethiopia is your commitment to pay the current level of the U.S. estate tax. What would you choose?

*"FAIR IS FAIR... IF IT'S TURN-OFF-YOUR-TV WEEK FOR ME, THEN IT'S UNPLUG-YOUR-E-MAIL WEEK FOR YOU."*

desire of parents to do well by their children? Shouldn't parents who own their own businesses have the right to appoint their children to executive positions in those businesses? Shouldn't parents who can afford to do so have the right to send their children to expensive private schools? It seems unfair that children of successful parents should have an advantage over children whose parents don't have the same resources. Yet it would also seem unfair to prevent successful parents from helping their children. How do you resolve this contradiction?

Another familiar concept is that people should be rewarded for the work they do. And that, too seems reasonable: if you are a skilled worker, with twice my marginal product, it seems only fair that you should receive twice my wage. But what about someone who suffers an injury and cannot work? To say that that person should go without any income seems unfair.

The attempt to define fairness has led to some fascinating debates among philosophers; we describe the views of one influential thinker, John Rawls, in For Inquiring Minds on page 247. However, those debates have not led to any generally accepted definition.

Do we need a definition of *fairness*? Not necessarily—virtually everyone agrees that some outcomes, like our hypothetical dictator-dominated economy, are unfair, and in other cases we can agree to differ. But sometimes the lack of agreement on fairness means that economic analysis alone cannot be used to decide between alternative policies. To see why, let's introduce a new concept, the *utility possibility frontier*.

## The Utility Possibility Frontier

Let's think of an economy that contains only two kinds of people, Easterners and Westerners. In Figure 10-5, the horizontal axis measures the total utility of the typical Westerner and the vertical axis measures the total utility of the typical Easterner.

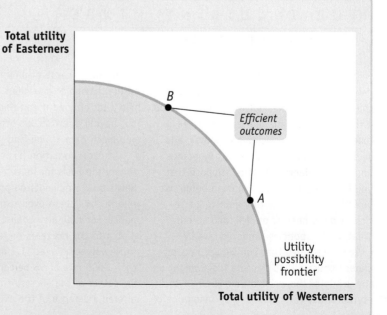

### Figure 10-5

**The Utility Possibility Frontier**

The utility possibility frontier reminds us that there may be many efficient outcomes for an economy. The utility possibility frontier shows the maximum level of total utility of a typical Easterner, given the level of total utility of a typical Westerner. Any point on the curve is efficient because at such a point there is no way to make a typical Easterner better off without making a typical Westerner worse off, and vice versa. But this means that we cannot decide on economic grounds alone whether point A or B is better. **>web...**

Total utility of Easterners

*Efficient outcomes*

B

A

Utility possibility frontier

**Total utility of Westerners**

An efficient outcome in this economy would be one in which there was no way to make either Easterners or Westerners better off without making members of the other group worse off. But there may be many such possible outcomes. In the figure we show what the possibilities might look like by drawing a **utility possibility frontier,** which shows how well-off each group *could* be given the economy's resources and the total utility of the other. Any point on the utility possibility frontier is efficient—that is, once you are on the frontier, the only way to make some people better off is to make others worse off. Any point inside the frontier is inefficient.

So suppose that you were asked to choose between two sets of economic policies— one that would bring the economy to point A and one that would bring it to point B. For example, suppose there is a question of who should receive ownership of some disputed land. As long as the property rights are clearly defined, the economy will be efficient, but Westerners would prefer that they get the rights, and Easterners would prefer the reverse. So which outcome is better?

The answer is that it's a matter of taste. Westerners would, of course, prefer A; Easterners would prefer B. For government officials trying to decide how to assign the property rights, the answer would depend on what relative weight they give to the welfare of the two groups. The question of whether A or B is better is, in other words, a question of values that economics cannot answer.

Notice, by the way, that A and B don't differ just in how goods and services are distributed to individuals; they might well involve producing a different mix of goods and services. If Westerners like cornflakes but Easterners prefer shredded wheat, the economy probably produces more corn and less wheat at B than at A. Is it more efficient to produce corn or wheat? There is no answer to this question, because both can be efficient, depending on our goals.

The point that efficiency is a means to achieve goals, not a goal in itself, can be further illustrated by considering what is wrong with *inefficient* policies. Figure 10-6 shows the same utility possibility frontier as Figure 10-5 but now also shows point C—an inefficient outcome, one that lies inside the frontier. You might think of C as the result of a policy that favors Easterners in an inefficient way. In fact, many economists believe that the actual policies the newly reunited Germany followed to help the former East Germans were poorly designed, providing them with few incentives

> A **utility possibility frontier** shows how well-off one individual or group could be for each given total utility level of another individual or group.

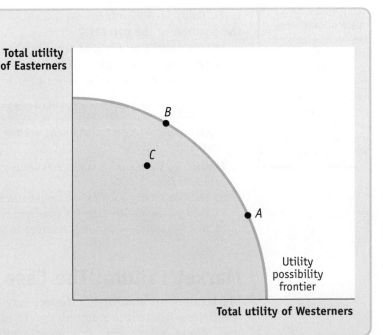

### Figure 10-6

### Efficiency Versus Equity

Suppose that for some reason the policy choices that are available are restricted: you can choose only between the efficient outcome A and the inefficient outcome C. Does this mean that A is preferable? Not necessarily. If you place a high enough weight on the utility of Easterners, you may be willing to trade *efficiency* for *equity*: even though the economy is not efficient at C, the utility of Easterners is higher at C than at A.

Total utility of Easterners

Utility possibility frontier

Total utility of Westerners

to take new jobs or acquire new skills. That is, many economists believe that Germany as a whole ended up at a point like *C*.

Is there any reason why you might want to choose an inefficient point such as *C*? Not if better choices are genuinely available: there are points on the utility possibility frontier that are better than *C* whatever relative weight you give to the welfare of the two groups. For example, *B* is better than *C* by any standard.

But what if the real choices are limited to *A* or *C*? Should you as a voter prefer the efficient policies proposed by the Western party?

Not necessarily. *A* is efficient, and *C* is not; but it is still true that Easterners are better off at *C* than they are at *A*. So if the utility of Easterners matters enough to you, you might well prefer *C* to *A* even though you would prefer *B* to either. As economists say, it is often—but by no means always—worth trading less efficiency for more equity.

So it's important to remember what efficiency is *not*. Efficiency is not a goal in itself, to be pursued at the expense of other goals. It is only a way to achieve our goals more effectively—whatever those goals may be.

## *economics in action*

### Death and Taxes

Earlier, we used the example of parents giving their children a head start by paying for expensive private schooling to show how simple questions of fairness can give conflicting answers. In fact, inheritance is one of those areas in which differing notions of fairness translate directly into different policy conclusions.

One notion of fairness focuses on individual positions at the starting line: it says that it is unfair that some children should inherit large sums but others get nothing. The natural conclusion from this notion is that inheritances should be heavily taxed. This has, in fact, been the policy of many countries, including to some extent the United States.

The alternative notion of fairness focuses on the right of people to choose what to do with their money: it says that it is unfair to deny parents the right to pass on their savings to their children.

These competing notions are reflected in different names for the "estate tax," the tax levied on the assets individuals leave behind them at death. Politicians who focus on the starting line call it the "inheritance tax," emphasizing the position of the heirs. Politicians who focus on individual choice call it the "death tax," emphasizing the position of the parents.

Who's right? Economic analysis can't say. However, legislation passed in 2001 will eliminate the estate tax by 2010. ∎

< < < < < < < < < < < < < < < < < < < <

>> CHECK YOUR UNDERSTANDING 10-2

1. Explain why it is easier to determine whether an economy is efficient than to determine whether it is fair.

2. Explain why the following statements are problematic to use in determining whether or not a society is fair.
   a. In a fair society, each person contributes to society according to his or her means, and each person receives benefits according to his or her needs.
   b. In a fair society, a person is rewarded in proportion to how hard he or she works.

Solutions appear at back of book.

## Market Failure: The Case of Externalities

Markets are an amazingly effective way to organize economic activity. A market is efficient—there is literally no way to make some people better off without making others worse off. But how secure is this result? Are markets really that good?

The answer is "not always." As we discussed briefly in Chapter 1 in our ninth and final principle of economics (*when markets don't achieve efficiency, government intervention can improve society's welfare*), markets can fail to be efficient for a number of reasons. When a market is not efficient, we have what is known as a case of **market failure.** In this section and the next, we will look at two examples of market failure: *externalities* and *public goods.*

**Market failure** occurs when a market fails to be efficient.

## Externalities

Pollution is a bad thing. Yet most pollution is a side effect of activities that provide us with good things: our air is polluted by power plants generating the electricity that lights our cities, and our rivers are damaged by fertilizer runoff from farms that grow our food. Why don't we accept a certain amount of pollution as the cost of a good life?

Actually, we do. Even highly committed environmentalists don't think that we can or should completely eliminate pollution—even an environmentally conscious society would accept *some* pollution as the cost of producing useful goods and services. What environmentalists argue is that unless there is a strong and effective environmental policy, our society will generate *too much* pollution—too much of a bad thing. And the majority of economists agree.

The environmental costs of pollution are the best-known and most important example of an **external cost**—an uncompensated cost that an individual or firm imposes on others. There are also important examples of **external benefits,** benefits that individuals or firms confer on others without receiving compensation. External costs and benefits are jointly known as **externalities,** with external costs called **negative externalities** and external benefits called **positive externalities.**

Nobody imposes external costs like pollution out of malice. Pollution, traffic congestion, and other harmful externalities are side effects of activities, like electricity generation or driving, that are otherwise desirable. Government policies in these situations must be geared to changing the quantity of the original activity, which in turn changes the quantity of the side effect produced.

An **external cost** is an uncompensated cost that an individual or firm imposes on others.

An **external benefit** is a benefit that an individual or firm confers on others without receiving compensation.

External costs and benefits are known as **externalities;** external costs are **negative externalities,** and external benefits are **positive externalities.**

## Private Versus Social Costs

Given current technology, there is no affordable way to breed and raise livestock on a commercial scale without hurting the environment. Whatever it is—cows, pigs, chicken, sheep, or salmon—livestock farming produces prodigious amounts of what is euphemistically known as "muck." But that's not all: scientists estimate that the amount of methane gas produced by livestock (the same gas produced when a person—heaven forbid!—belches) currently rivals the pollution caused by the burning of fossil fuels in the creation of greenhouses gases. From the point of view of society as a whole, then, the cost of livestock farming includes both direct production costs to the farmer (payments for factors of production and inputs such as animal feed) and the external environmental costs imposed as a by-product. In the absence of government intervention, however, livestock farmers have no incentive to take into account the environmental costs of their production decisions. As a result, in the absence of government intervention, livestock farmers will produce too much output.

Panel (a) of Figure 10-7 on page 252 illustrates this point. The market demand curve for livestock by consumers is represented by the curve $D$; the market, or industry, supply curve is given by the curve $S$. In the absence of government intervention, market equilibrium will be at point $E_{MKT}$, yielding the amount produced and consumed $Q_{MKT}$ and the market price $P_{MKT}$. At that point, the marginal benefit to society of another unit of livestock (measured by the market price) is equal to the marginal cost *incurred by the industry* for producing that unit.

Let's look a little more closely at the supply curve. Assuming that the livestock industry is competitive, we know from Chapter 8 that the industry supply

Muck and methane gas: the costly side effects of producing a side of bacon.

### Figure 10-7 Negative Externalities and Production

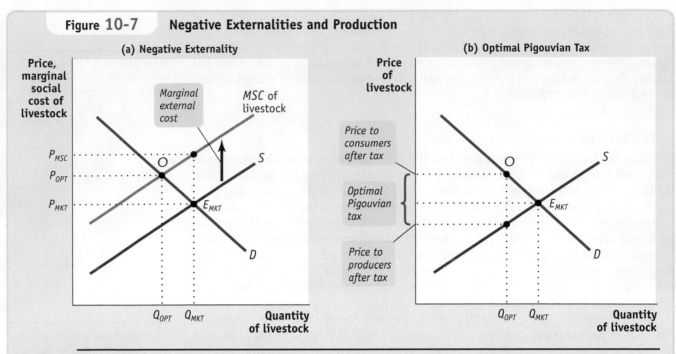

Livestock production generates external costs, so the marginal social cost curve of livestock, *MSC*, corresponds to the supply curve, *S*, shifted upward by the marginal external cost. Panel (a) shows that without government action, the market produces the quantity $Q_{MKT}$. It is greater than the socially optimal quantity of livestock production, $Q_{OPT}$, the quantity at which *MSC* crosses the demand curve, *D*. At $Q_{MKT}$, the market price, $P_{MKT}$, is less than $P_{MSC}$, the true marginal cost to society of livestock production. Panel (b) shows how an optimal Pigouvian tax on livestock production, equal to its marginal external cost, moves the production to $Q_{OPT}$, resulting in lower output and a higher price to consumers.  **>web...**

---

curve corresponds to the horizontal sum of all the individual supply curves of producers in the industry. In addition, we know that each individual producer's supply curve corresponds to its marginal cost curve. These two facts taken together imply that the industry supply curve is the horizontal sum of the individual producers' marginal cost curves: a given point on *S* corresponds to the total industry-wide marginal cost at the corresponding output level. But this estimation of marginal cost does not include the external cost that production imposes on others. In other words, when external costs are present, the industry supply curve does not reflect the true cost to society of production of the good.

In order to account for the true cost to society of an additional unit of the good, we must define the **marginal social cost of a good or activity,** which is equal to the marginal cost of production plus the marginal external cost generated by an additional unit of the good or activity. It captures the increase in production cost to the industry *and* the increase in external cost to the rest of society caused by producing one more unit. Panel (a) of Figure 10-7 shows the marginal social cost of livestock curve, *MSC*; it corresponds to the industry supply curve *shifted upward* by the amount of the marginal external cost. With the marginal social cost curve and the demand curve, we can find the socially optimal quantity of a good or activity that creates external costs: it is the quantity $Q_{OPT}$, the quantity corresponding to *O*, the point at which *MSC* and *D* cross. Reflecting the proper accounting for external cost, $Q_{OPT}$ is less than $Q_{MKT}$. So left to its own, a market will result in too much of a good that carries external costs being produced and consumed. Correspondingly, without government action, the price to consumers of such a good is too low: at the output level $Q_{MKT}$, the unregulated market price $P_{MKT}$ is lower than $P_{MSC}$, the true marginal cost to society of a unit of livestock.

The **marginal social cost of a good or activity** is equal to the marginal cost of production plus its marginal external cost.

## FOR INQUIRING MINDS

### TALKING AND DRIVING

Why is that woman in the car in front of us driving so erratically? Is she drunk? No, she's talking on her cell phone.

Traffic safety experts take the risks posed by driving while talking very seriously. Using hands-free, voice-activated phones doesn't seem to help much because the main danger is distraction. As one traffic safety consultant put it, "It's not where your eyes are; it's where your head is." And we're not talking about a trivial problem. One estimate suggests that people who talk on their cell phones while driving may be responsible for 600 or more traffic deaths each year.

The National Safety Council urges people not to use phones while driving. But a growing

"It's not where your eyes are, it's where your head is."

Bob Daemmrich/The Image Works

number of people say that voluntary standards aren't enough; they want the use of cell phones while driving made illegal, as it already is in Japan, Israel, and several other countries.

Why not leave the decision up to the driver? Because the risk posed by driving while talking isn't just a risk to the driver; it's also a safety risk to others—especially people in other cars. Even if you decide that the benefit to you of taking that call is worth the cost, you aren't taking into account the cost to other people. Driving while talking, in other words, generates a serious—sometimes fatal—negative externality.

## Environmental Policy

Are there methods that lead to an efficient quantity of pollution when regulators can target only the original activity or good, such as livestock production? Yes, there are. They take the form of a tax on livestock sales or a license to produce a unit of livestock. These methods will move the market to the efficient quantity by compelling producers to take externalities into account when making decisions.

In general, taxes designed to reduce external costs are known as **Pigouvian taxes,** after the economist A. C. Pigou, who emphasized their usefulness in a classic 1920 book, *The Economics of Welfare.* Consider first the case of a Pigouvian tax on livestock transactions. Once such a tax is in effect, the cost to a livestock farmer of producing an additional unit of livestock includes both the marginal cost of production and the tax. If the tax is set at the right amount, it is exactly equal to the marginal external cost. As shown in panel (b) of Figure 10-7, the optimal Pigouvian tax will move the market outcome to the optimal point O.

A system of tradable production permits that restricts the industry-wide quantity of livestock produced to the optimal level has the same effect. Suppose that in order to produce an additional unit of livestock, a farmer must purchase a permit. The cost of this permit behaves like a Pigouvian tax, and once again external costs are completely internalized in the private decisions of producers. Even if the farmer already possesses the permit, its opportunity cost—the price it could command in the market for permits—acts like a Pigouvian tax.

So $Q_{OPT}$, the efficient quantity of livestock produced and consumed, corresponds to the efficient quantity of pollution generated by livestock production. Note that in

> Taxes designed to reduce external costs are known as **Pigouvian taxes.**

panel (b) of Figure 10-7, consumers consume less livestock (in the form of meat purchased at supermarkets and restaurants) and pay a higher market price at the socially optimal quantity. (We know from Chapter 5 that exactly how the burden of the tax is allocated between producers and consumers depends on the price elasticities of demand and supply.)

## Private Solutions to Externalities

Our livestock example relied on government intervention to achieve the socially optimal outcome. Can the private sector solve the problem of externalities without government intervention? Bear in mind that when an outcome is inefficient, there is potentially a deal that makes people better off. Why don't individuals find a way to make that deal?

In an influential 1960 article, the economist and Nobel laureate Ronald Coase pointed out that in an ideal world the private sector could indeed deal with all externalities. According to the **Coase theorem,** even in the presence of externalities an economy can always reach an efficient solution provided that the costs of making a deal are sufficiently low. The costs of making a deal are known as **transaction costs.**

To get a sense of Coase's argument, imagine two neighbors, Mick and Britney, who both like to barbecue in their backyards on summer afternoons. Mick likes to play golden oldies on his boombox while barbecuing; but this annoys Britney, who can't stand that kind of music.

Who prevails? You might think that it depends on the legal rights involved in the case: if the law says that Mick has the right to play whatever music he wants, Britney just has to suffer; if the law says that Mick needs Britney's consent to play music in his backyard, Mick has to live without his favorite music while barbecuing.

But as Coase pointed out, the outcome need not be determined by legal rights, because Britney and Mick can make a private deal. Even if Mick has the right to play his music, Britney could pay him not to. Even if Mick can't play the music without an OK from Britney, he can offer to pay her to give that OK. These payments allow them to reach an efficient solution, regardless of who has the legal upper hand. If the benefit of the music to Mick exceeds its cost to Britney, the music will go on; if the benefit to Mick is less than the cost to Britney, there will be silence.

The implication of Coase's analysis is that externalities need not lead to inefficiency because individuals have an incentive to make mutually beneficial deals—deals that lead them to take externalities into account when making decisions. When individuals *do* take externalities into account when making decisions, economists say that they **internalize the externality.** If externalities are fully internalized, the outcome is efficient even without government intervention.

Why can't individuals always internalize externalities? Our barbecue example implicitly assumes the transaction costs are low enough for Mick and Britney to be able to make a deal. In many situations involving externalities, however, transaction costs prevent individuals from making efficient deals. Examples of transaction costs include the following:

- The costs of communication among the interested parties—costs that may be very high if many people are involved
- The costs of making legally binding agreements—costs that may be high if the employment of expensive lawyers is required
- Costly delays involved in bargaining—even if there is a potentially beneficial deal, both sides may hold out in an effort to extract more favorable terms, leading to increased effort and forgone utility

In some cases, people do find ways to reduce transaction costs, allowing them to internalize externalities. For example, many people live in private communities that set rules for home maintenance and behavior, making bargaining between neighbors unnecessary. But in many other cases, transaction costs are too high to make it possible to deal

---

According to the **Coase theorem,** even in the presence of externalities an economy can always reach an efficient solution as long as **transaction costs**—the costs to individuals of making a deal—are sufficiently low.

---

When individuals take external costs or benefits into account, they **internalize the externality.**

with externalities through private action. For example, tens of millions of people are adversely affected by acid rain. It would be prohibitively expensive to try to make a deal among all those people and all those power companies.

## Private Versus Social Benefits

Not all externalities are negative. In some important cases, an economic activity creates external benefits—that is, individual actions provide benefits to other people for which the producers are not compensated.

The most important source of external benefits in the modern economy probably involves creation of knowledge. In high-tech industries like semiconductors, innovations by one firm are quickly emulated and improved upon both by rival firms in the same industry and by firms in other industries. Such spreading of knowledge among individuals and firms is known as a **technology spillover.** Such spillovers often take place through face-to-face contact. As Economics in Action on page 257 explains, bars and restaurants in California's Silicon Valley are famed for their technical gossip, and the need to keep tabs on the latest innovations is a major reason so many high-tech firms are clustered near each other.

A **technology spillover** is an external benefit that results when knowledge spreads among individuals and firms.

What are the implications of external benefits in general for economic efficiency and economic policy? Suppose that the production of some good—say, semiconductor chips—yields positive externalities. How does this affect our analysis of the chip market, and does it create a justification for government intervention?

Just as external costs cause the marginal social *cost* of producing a good to exceed the industry's marginal cost, when there are external benefits from a good, the marginal social *benefit* exceeds consumers' marginal benefit. This is illustrated in panel (a) of Figure 10-8, which shows the market for semiconductor chips. Since there are

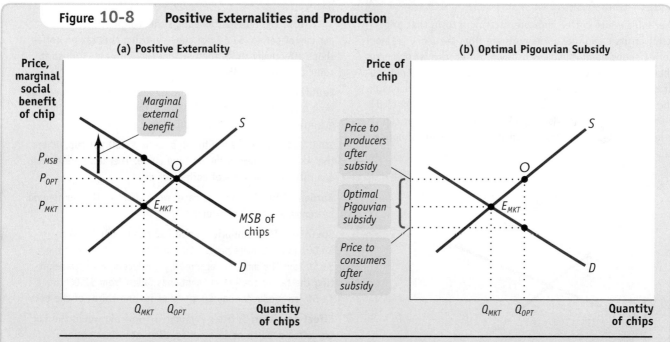

**Figure 10-8     Positive Externalities and Production**

Semiconductor chip production generates external benefits, so the marginal social benefit curve of chips, *MSB*, corresponds to the demand curve, *D*, shifted upward by the marginal external benefit. Panel (a) shows that without government action, the market produces $Q_{MKT}$. It is lower than the socially optimal quantity of production, $Q_{OPT}$, the quantity at which *MSB* crosses the supply curve, *S*. At $Q_{MKT}$, the market price, $P_{MKT}$, is less than $P_{MSB}$, the true marginal benefit to society of semiconductor chip production. Panel (b) shows how an optimal Pigouvian subsidy to chip producers, equal to its marginal external benefit, moves the production to $Q_{OPT}$, resulting in higher output and a higher price to producers. **>web...**

no external costs in this case, the industry supply curve, S, represents the true marginal social cost to society of production. The demand curve, D, represents the marginal benefit that accrues to *consumers of the good:* each point on the demand curve corresponds to the willingness to pay of the last consumer to purchase the good at the corresponding price. But it does not incorporate the benefits to society as a whole from production of the good—the technological spillover an additional unit provides to the economy as a whole.

To explore this phenomenon we need a new concept, the **marginal social benefit of a good or activity**—the marginal benefit that accrues to consumers from an additional unit of the good or activity, plus the marginal external benefit to society from an additional unit. As you can see from panel (a) of Figure 10-8, the marginal social benefit curve, MSB, corresponds to the demand curve D *shifted upward* by the amount of the marginal external benefit.

The analysis in this case is very similar to that of external costs. Left to itself, the market will reach an equilibrium at $E_{MKT}$, the point at which the demand curve D crosses the supply curve S at a market price $P_{MKT}$. But the quantity of output at this equilibrium, $Q_{MKT}$, is inefficiently low: at that output level, the marginal social benefit of an additional unit, $P_{MSB}$, exceeds the industry's marginal cost of producing that unit, $P_{MKT}$. The optimal quantity of production and consumption is $Q_{OPT}$, the quantity at which marginal cost is equal to marginal social benefit.

How can the economy be induced to produce $Q_{OPT}$ chips? The answer is a **Pigouvian subsidy:** a payment designed to encourage activities that yield external benefits. The optimal Pigouvian subsidy, shown in panel (b) of Figure 10-8, is equal

> The **marginal social benefit of a good or activity** is equal to the marginal benefit that accrues to consumers plus its marginal external benefit.

> A **Pigouvian subsidy** is a payment designed to encourage activities that yield external benefits.

## WORK IT OUT

### EXTERNALITY AND OPTIMAL PIGOUVIAN TAX

Discarded white coffee cups are littering a town that prides itself on its cleanliness. The cups are from the many take-out coffee shops doing business in town. An economist estimates that the marginal external cost of the litter is $1.50 per cup of coffee sold. Residents implore the City Council to clean up the mess. The market for cups of coffee per day is depicted below. The original market equilibrium price is $2 per cup. The original market equilibrium quantity is 2,000 cups of coffee per day.

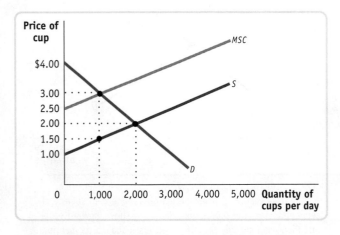

**Optimal Pigouvian Tax:** What is the optimal tax the City Council should impose on the coffee shops?

**SOLUTION:** The optimal tax equals the marginal external cost per cup of coffee: $1.50 per cup. Imposing this tax on coffee shops effectively shifts their supply curve up by $1.50 so it coincides with the MSC curve.

**Equilibrium:** Once the tax is imposed, what is the new equilibrium price per cup of coffee? What is the new equilibrium quantity of cups of coffee sold per day?

**SOLUTION:** The new equilibrium price is $3.00 per cup, where the MSC curve crosses the demand curve. The new equilibrium quantity is 1,000 cups of coffee per day.

**Burden of the Tax:** In this case, what share of the tax is paid by consumers? By producers?

**SOLUTION:** The equilibrium price has risen from $2.00 to $3.00, so consumers pay $1.00 (that is, two-thirds) of the $1.50 tax. The amount retained by producers, after transmitting the tax to the government, has fallen from $2.00 to $1.50, so producers pay $0.50 (that is, one-third) of the tax.

**Effect on Litter:** Is litter eliminated? How big would the tax on coffee need to be in order to eliminate litter entirely?

**SOLUTION:** Litter is not eliminated so long as coffee is being sold. To eliminate litter with a tax on cups sold, the tax would need to be $3.00 per cup. A tax of $3.00 per cup would shift the supply curve up so it meets the demand curve at a quantity of 0 cups of coffee.

to the marginal external benefit of producing an additional unit. Producers receive the price paid by consumers plus the per-unit subsidy, inducing them to produce more output. Such a subsidy is an example of an **industrial policy**, a general term for a policy of supporting industries believed to yield positive externalities.

Although the strict economic logic supporting such efforts is impeccable, economists are generally less enthusiastic about industrial policies to promote positive externalities than they are about taxes and permit schemes to discourage negative externalities. This lack of enthusiasm reflects a mixture of practical and political judgments. First, positive externalities—which most often involve the creation of knowledge and new technologies—are typically much harder to identify and measure than negative externalities. (A simple sensor can keep track of how many tons of sulfur dioxide come out of a smokestack. But how do you tell whether and when a new product embodies a technology that will benefit other producers and consumers?) In addition, producers gain monetarily from subsidies: they receive a higher price than they otherwise would. So many economists also fear, with some historical justification, that a program intended to promote industries that yield positive externalities will degenerate into a program that promotes industries with political pull.

However, there is one activity that is widely believed to generate positive externalities and is provided with considerable subsidies: education!

> An **industrial policy** is a policy that supports industries believed to yield positive externalities.

## *economics in action*

### Spillovers in Silicon Valley

The author Tom Wolfe is best known for his social essays, like "Radical Chic," and his novels, like *Bonfire of the Vanities*. But his article "The Tinkerings of Robert Noyce: How the Sun Rose on the Silicon Valley," published in *Esquire* in 1983, is one of the best descriptions ever written of technological spillovers at work.

Wolfe emphasized the role of informal contact in spreading useful knowledge: "Every year there was some place, the Wagon Wheel, Chez Yvonne, Rickey's, the Roundhouse, where members of this esoteric fraternity, the young men and women of the semiconductor industry, would head after work to have a drink and gossip and brag and trade war stories about contacts, burst modes, bubble memories, pulse trains, bounceless modes, slow-death episodes, RAMs, NAKs, MOSes, PCMs, PROMs, PROM blowers, PROM blasters, and teramagnitudes, meaning multiples of a million millions." If you don't know what he's talking about, that's the point: the way to find out what all this was about, and keep in touch with the latest technologies, was to hang around in the right places. The informal spread of knowledge Wolfe described was and is the key to Silicon Valley's success.

> > > > > > > > > > > > > > > > > > > > >

>>CHECK YOUR UNDERSTANDING 10-3

1. Explain how the London congestion charge described in Chapter 3 (pages 62-63), in which cars entering central London during business hours must pay a fee of £5, can be an optimal policy to manage inner-city pollution and congestion.

2. In each of the following cases, determine whether an external cost or an external benefit is imposed and what an appropriate policy response would be.
   a. Trees planted in urban areas improve air quality and lower summer temperatures.
   b. Water-saving toilets reduce the need to pump water from rivers and aquifers. The cost of a gallon of water to homeowners is virtually zero.
   c. Old computer monitors contain toxic materials that pollute the environment when improperly disposed of.

Solutions appear at back of book.

>> QUICK REVIEW

- *Market failure* occurs when a market fails to be efficient.
- Pollution is an example of an *external cost,* or *negative externality*; in contrast, some activities can give rise to *external benefits,* or *positive externalities*. External costs and benefits are known as *externalities*.
- When there are external costs, the *marginal social cost of a good or activity* exceeds the industry's marginal cost of producing the good. In the absence of government intervention, the industry typically produces too much of the good.
- The socially optimal quantity can be achieved by an optimal *Pigouvian tax,* equal to the marginal external cost, or by a system of tradable production permits.
- According to the *Coase theorem,* the private sector can sometimes resolve externalities on its own: if *transaction costs* aren't too high, individuals can reach a deal to *internalize the externality*.
- The most common examples of external benefits are *technology spillovers*. When these occur, the *marginal social benefit of a good or activity* exceeds the marginal benefit to consumers, and too little of the good is produced in the absence of government intervention. The socially optimal quantity can be achieved by an optimal *Pigouvian subsidy*—a type of *industrial policy*—equal to the marginal external benefit.

# Market Failure: The Case of Public Goods

By the middle of the nineteenth century, London had become the world's largest city, with close to 2.5 million inhabitants. Unfortunately, all those people produced a lot of waste—and there was no place for the stuff to go except the Thames, the river flowing through the city. Nobody with a working nose could ignore the results. And the river didn't just smell bad—it carried waterborne diseases like cholera and typhoid. London neighborhoods close to the Thames had death rates from cholera more than six times greater than the neighborhoods farthest away. And the great majority of Londoners drew their drinking water from the Thames.

What the city needed, said reformers, was a sewage system that would carry waste away from the river. Yet no private individual was willing to build such a system, and influential people were opposed to the idea that the government should take responsibility for the problem. For example, the magazine *The Economist* weighed in against proposals for a government-built sewage system, declaring that "suffering and evil are nature's admonitions—they cannot be got rid of."

But the hot summer of 1858 brought what came to be known as the Great Stink, which was so bad that one health journal reported "men struck down with the stench." Even the privileged and powerful suffered: Parliament met in a building next to the river. After unsuccessful efforts to stop the smell by covering the windows with chemical-soaked curtains, Parliament finally approved a plan for an immense system of sewers and pumping stations to direct sewage away from the city. The system, opened in 1865, brought dramatic improvement in the city's quality of life; cholera and typhoid epidemics, which had been regular occurrences, completely disappeared. The Thames was turned from the filthiest to the cleanest metropolitan river in the world, and the sewage system's principal engineer, Sir Joseph Bazalgette, was lauded as having "saved more lives than any single Victorian public official." It was estimated at the time that Bazalgette's sewer system added 20 years to the life span of the average Londoner.

The story of the Great Stink and the policy response that followed illustrate two important reasons for government intervention in the economy. London's new sewage system was a clear example of a *public good*—a good that benefits many people, whether or not they have paid for it, and whose benefits to any one individual do not depend on how many others also benefit. As we will see shortly, public goods differ in important ways from the private goods we have studied so far—and these differences mean that public goods cannot be efficiently supplied by the market.

London's River Thames then . . .

. . . and the same river now, thanks to government intervention.

## Private Goods and Public Goods

What's the difference between installing a new bathroom in a house and building a municipal sewage system? What's the difference between growing wheat and fishing in the open ocean? Bathroom appliances and wheat—but not sewage systems and fish in the sea—have the two characteristics needed to allow markets to work efficiently.

- They are **excludable:** suppliers of the good can prevent people who don't pay from consuming it.

- They are **rival in consumption:** the same unit of the good cannot be consumed by more than one person at the same time.

When a good is both excludable and rival in consumption, it is called a **private good.** Wheat is an example of a private good. It is *excludable:* the farmer can sell a bushel to one consumer without having to provide wheat to everyone in the county. And it is *rival in consumption:* if I bake bread with a farmer's wheat, that wheat can no longer be used by someone else.

A **public good** is the exact opposite of a private good: it is a good that is both *nonexcludable* and *nonrival in consumption.* Goods are **nonexcludable** if the supplier cannot prevent consumption of the good by people who do not pay for it. An improved environment is one example: the city of London couldn't have ended the Great Stink for some residents while leaving the River Thames foul for others.

Goods are **nonrival in consumption** if more than one person can consume the same unit of the good at the same time. TV programs are nonrival in consumption: your decision to watch a show does not prevent other people from watching the same show.

Here are some other examples of public goods:

- *Disease prevention.* When doctors act to stamp out the beginnings of an epidemic before it can spread, they protect people around the world.

- *National defense.* A strong military protects all citizens.

- *Scientific research.* More knowledge benefits everyone.

Because these goods are nonexcludable, rational consumers won't be willing to pay for them—they will take a "free ride" on anyone who *does* pay. Nonexcludable goods are thus said to suffer from the **free-rider problem,** so no private firm would be willing to produce them. And because they are nonrival in consumption, it would be inefficient to charge people for consuming them. As a result, society must find nonmarket methods for providing these goods.

## Providing Public Goods

Public goods are provided through a variety of means. The government doesn't always get involved—in many cases a nongovernmental solution has been found for the free-rider problem. But these solutions are usually imperfect in some way.

Some public goods are supplied through voluntary contributions. For example, private donations support a considerable amount of scientific research. But private donations are insufficient to finance huge, socially important projects like basic medical research.

Some public goods are supplied by self-interested individuals or firms because those who produce them are able to make money in an indirect way. The classic example is broadcast television, which in the United States is supported entirely by advertising. The downside of such indirect funding is that it skews the nature and quantity of the public goods that are supplied, as well as imposing additional costs

A good is **excludable** if the supplier of that good can prevent people who do not pay from consuming it.

A good is **rival in consumption** if the same unit of the good cannot be consumed by more than one person at the same time.

A good that is both excludable and rival in consumption is a **private good.**

A **public good** is both nonexcludable and nonrival in consumption.

When a good is **nonexcludable,** the supplier cannot prevent consumption by people who do not pay for it.

A good is **nonrival in consumption** if more than one person can consume the same unit of the good at the same time.

Goods that are nonexcludable suffer from the **free-rider problem:** individuals have no incentive to pay for their own consumption and instead will take a "free ride" on anyone who does pay.

On the prowl: a British TV detection van at work.

on consumers. TV stations show the programs that yield the most advertising revenue (that is, programs best suited for selling antacids, hair-loss remedies, antihistamines, and the like to the segment of the population that buys them), which are not necessarily the programs people most want to see. And viewers must also endure many commercials.

Some potentially public goods are deliberately made excludable and therefore subject to charge, like pay-per-view movies. In the U.K., where most television programming is paid for by a yearly license fee assessed on every television owner, television viewing is made artificially excludable by the use of "television detection vans": vans that roam neighborhoods in an attempt to detect televisions in nonlicensed households and fine them. However, when suppliers charge a price greater than zero for a nonrival good, consumers will consume an inefficiently low quantity of that good.

In small communities, a high level of social encouragement or pressure can be brought to bear on people to contribute money or time to provide the efficient level of a public good. Volunteer fire departments, which depend both on the volunteered services of the firefighters themselves and on contributions from local residents, are a good example. But as communities grow larger and more anonymous, social pressure is increasingly difficult to apply, so that larger towns and cities must depend on salaried firefighters.

As this last example suggests, when these other solutions fail, it is up to the government to provide public goods. Indeed, the most important public goods—national defense, the legal system, disease control, fire protection in large cities, and so on—are provided by government and paid for by taxes. Economic theory tells us that the provision of public goods is one of the crucial roles of government.

## How Much of a Public Good Should Be Provided?

In some cases, provision of a public good is an "either–or" decision: London would either have a sewage system—or not. But in most cases, governments must decide not only whether to provide a public good but also *how much* of that public good to provide. For example, street cleaning is a public good—but how often should the streets be cleaned? Once a month? Twice a month? Every other day?

Imagine a city in which there are only two residents, Ted and Alice. Assume that the public good in question is street cleaning and that Ted and Alice truthfully tell the government how much they value a unit of the public good, where a unit is equal to one street cleaning per month. Specifically, each of them tells the government *his or her willingness to pay for another unit of the public good supplied*—an amount that corresponds to that *individual's marginal benefit* of another unit of the public good.

Using this information plus information on the cost of providing the good, the government can use marginal analysis to find the efficient level of providing the public good: the level at which the *marginal social benefit* of the public good is equal to the marginal cost of producing it.

But what is the marginal social benefit of another unit of a public good—a unit that generates utility for *all* consumers, not just one consumer, because it is nonexcludable and nonrival in consumption? This question leads us to an important principle: *in the special case of a public good, the marginal social benefit of a unit of the good is equal to the sum of the individual marginal benefits that are enjoyed by all consumers of that unit.* Or to consider it from a slightly different angle, if a consumer could be compelled to pay for a unit before consuming it (the good is made excludable), then the marginal social benefit of a unit is equal to the *sum of*

We all benefit when someone does the cleaning up.

each consumer's willingness to pay for that unit. Using this principle, the marginal social benefit of an additional street cleaning per month is equal to Ted's individual marginal benefit from that additional cleaning *plus* Alice's individual marginal benefit.

Why? Because a public good is nonrival in consumption—Ted's benefit from a cleaner street does not diminish Alice's benefit from that same clean street, and vice versa. Because people can all simultaneously consume the same unit of a public good, the marginal social benefit of an additional unit of that good is the *sum* of the individual marginal benefits of all who enjoy the public good. And the efficient quantity of a public good is the quantity at which the marginal social benefit is equal to the marginal cost of providing it.

Figure 10-9 on page 262 illustrates the efficient provision of a public good, showing three marginal benefit curves. Panel (a) shows Ted's individual marginal benefit curve from street cleanings, $MB_T$: he would be willing to pay \$25 for the city to clean its streets once per month, an additional \$18 to have it done a second time, and so on. Panel (b) shows Alice's individual marginal benefit curve from street cleanings, $MB_A$. Panel (c) shows the marginal social benefit curve from street cleanings, $MSB$: it is the vertical sum of Ted's and Alice's individual marginal benefit curves, $MB_T$ and $MB_A$.

To maximize society's welfare, the government should clean the street up to the level at which the marginal social benefit of an additional cleaning is no longer greater than the marginal cost. Suppose that the marginal cost of street cleaning is \$6 per cleaning. Then the city should clean its streets 5 times per month, because the marginal social benefit of going from 4 to 5 cleanings is \$8, but going from 5 to 6 cleanings would yield a marginal social benefit of only \$2.

Figure 10-9 can help reinforce our understanding of why we cannot rely on individual self-interest to yield provision of an efficient quantity of public goods. Suppose that the city did one fewer street cleaning than the efficient quantity and that either Ted or Alice was asked to pay for the last cleaning. Neither one would be willing to pay for it! Ted would personally gain only the equivalent of \$3 in utility from adding one more street cleaning—so he wouldn't be willing to pay the \$6 marginal cost of another cleaning. Alice would personally gain the equivalent of \$5 in utility—so she wouldn't be willing to pay either. The point is that the marginal social benefit of one more unit of a public good is always greater than the individual marginal benefit to any one individual. That is why no individual is willing to pay for the efficient quantity of the good.

Does this description of the public good problem, in which the marginal social benefit of an additional unit of the public good is greater than any individual's marginal benefit, sound a bit familiar? It should: we encountered a somewhat similar situation in our discussion of *positive externalities*. Remember that in the case of a positive externality, the marginal social benefit accruing to all consumers of another unit of the good is greater than the producer's marginal benefit of producing that unit and the market alone produces too little of the good. In the case of a public good, the individual marginal benefit of a consumer plays the same role that the producer's marginal benefit plays in the case of positive externalities. So the problem of providing public goods is very similar to the problem of dealing with positive externalities; in both cases there is a market failure that calls for government intervention. One basic rationale for the existence of government is

## PITFALLS

### MARGINAL COST OF WHAT, EXACTLY?

In the case of a good that is nonrival in consumption, it's easy to confuse the marginal cost of *producing* a unit of the good with the marginal cost of *allowing* a unit of the good *to be consumed*. For example, your local cable company incurs a marginal cost in making a movie available to its subscribers that is equal to the cost of the resources it uses to produce and broadcast that movie. However, *once that movie is being broadcast,* no marginal cost is incurred by letting an additional family watch it. In other words, no costly resources are "used up" when one more family consumes a movie that has already been produced and is being broadcast.

This complication does not arise, however, when a good is rival in consumption. In that case, the resources used to produce a unit of the good are "used up" by a person's consumption of it—they are no longer available to satisfy someone else's consumption. So when a good is rival in consumption the marginal cost to society of allowing an individual to consume a unit is equal to the resource cost of producing that unit—that is, equal to the marginal cost of producing it.

### Figure 10-9    A Public Good

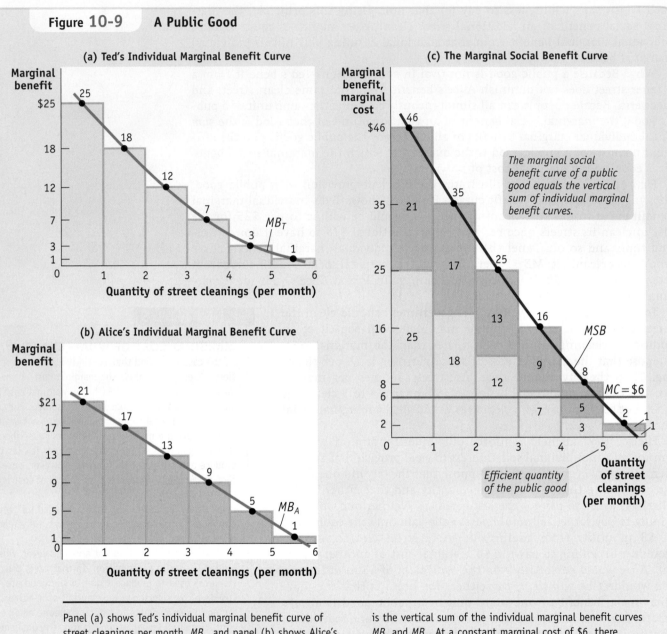

Panel (a) shows Ted's individual marginal benefit curve of street cleanings per month, $MB_T$, and panel (b) shows Alice's individual marginal benefit curve, $MB_A$. Panel (c) shows the marginal social benefit of the public good, equal to the *sum* of the individual marginal benefits to all consumers (in this case, Ted and Alice). The marginal social benefit curve, *MSB*, is the vertical sum of the individual marginal benefit curves $MB_T$ and $MB_A$. At a constant marginal cost of $6, there should be 5 street cleanings per month, because the marginal social benefit of going from 4 to 5 cleanings is $8 ($3 for Ted plus $5 for Alice), but the marginal social benefit of going from 5 to 6 cleanings is only $2. **>web...**

that it provides a way for citizens to tax themselves in order to provide public goods—particularly a vital public good like national defense.

Of course, if society really consisted of only two individuals, they would probably manage to strike a deal to provide the good. But imagine a city with a million residents, each of whose individual marginal benefit from provision of the good is only a tiny fraction of the marginal social benefit. It would be impossible for people to reach a voluntary agreement to pay for the efficient level of street cleaning—the

---

> ## FOR INQUIRING MINDS
> ### VOTING AS A PUBLIC GOOD
>
> It's a sad fact that many Americans who are eligible to vote don't bother to. As a result their interests tend to be ignored by politicians. But what's even sadder is that this self-defeating behavior may be completely rational.
>
> As the economist Mancur Olson pointed out in a famous book titled *The Logic of Collective Action*, voting is a public good, one that suffers from severe free-rider problems.
>
> Imagine that you are one of a million people who would stand to gain the equivalent of $100 each if some plan is passed in a statewide referendum—say, a plan to improve public schools. And sup-
>
> pose that the opportunity cost of the time it would take you to vote is $10. Will you be sure to go to the polls and vote for the referendum? If you are rational, the answer is no! The reason is that it is very unlikely that your vote will decide the issue, either way. If the measure passes, you benefit, even if you don't bother to vote—the benefits are nonexcludable. If the measure doesn't pass, your vote would not have changed the outcome. Either way, by not voting—by free-riding on those who do vote—you save $10.
>
> Of course, many people do vote out of a sense of civic duty. But because political action is a public good, in general people
>
> devote too little effort to defending their own interests.
>
> The result, Olson pointed out, is that when a large group of people share a common political interest, they are likely to exert too little effort promoting their cause and so will be ignored. Conversely, small, well-organized interest groups that act on issues narrowly targeted in their favor tend to have disproportionate power.
>
> Is this a reason to distrust democracy? Winston Churchill said it best: "Democracy is the worst form of government, except for all the other forms that have been tried."

potential for free-riding makes it too difficult to make and enforce an agreement among so many people. But they could and would vote to tax themselves to pay for a citywide sanitation department.

## Cost-Benefit Analysis

How do governments decide in practice how much of a public good to provide? Sometimes policy makers just guess—or do whatever they think will get them reelected. However, responsible governments try to estimate both the social benefits and the social costs of providing a public good, a process known as **cost-benefit analysis.**

It's straightforward to estimate the cost of supplying a public good. Estimating the benefit is harder. In fact, it is a very difficult problem.

Now you might wonder why governments can't figure out the marginal social benefit of a public good just by asking people their willingness to pay for it (their individual marginal benefit). But it turns out that it's hard to get an honest answer.

This is not a problem with private goods: we can determine how much an individual is willing to pay for one more unit of a private good by looking at his or her actual choices. But because people don't actually pay for public goods, the question of willingness to pay is always hypothetical.

Worse yet, it's a question that people have an incentive not to answer truthfully. People naturally want more rather than less. Because they cannot be made to pay for whatever quantity of the public good they use, when asked how much they desire a public good people are apt to overstate their true feelings. For example, if street cleaning were scheduled according to the stated wishes of homeowners alone, the streets would be cleaned every day—an inefficient level of provision. So governments must be aware that they cannot simply rely on the public's statements when deciding how much of a public good to provide—if they do, they are likely to provide too much. In contrast, as the For Inquiring Minds explains above, relying on the public to indicate how much of the public good they want through voting has problems as well—and is likely to lead to too little of the public good being provided.

> Governments engage in **cost-benefit analysis** when they estimate the social costs and social benefits of providing a public good.

# *economics in action*

## Old Man River

It just keeps rolling along—but now and then it decides to roll in a different direction. In fact, the Mississippi River changes its course every few hundred years. Sediment carried downstream gradually clogs the river's route to the sea, and eventually the river breaches its banks and opens a new channel. Over the millennia the mouth of the Mississippi has swung back and forth along an arc some 200 miles wide.

So when is the Mississippi due to change course again? Oh, about 35 years ago. The Mississippi currently runs to the sea past New Orleans; but by 1950 it was apparent that the river was about to shift course, taking a new route to the sea. If the Army Corps of Engineers hadn't gotten involved, the shift would probably have happened by 1970.

A shift in the Mississippi would have severely damaged the Louisiana economy. A major industrial area would have lost good access to the ocean, and salt water would have contaminated much of its water supply. So the Army Corps of Engineers has kept the Mississippi in its place with a huge complex of dams, walls, and gates known as the Old River Control Structure. At times the amount of water released by this control structure is five times the flow at Niagara Falls.

The Old River Control Structure is a dramatic example of a public good. No individual would have had an incentive to build it, yet it protects many billions of dollars' worth of private property. The history of the Army Corps of Engineers, which handles water-control projects across the United States, illustrates the problems with government provision of public goods. Everyone wants a project that benefits his or her own property—if other people are going to pay for it. So there is a systematic tendency for potential beneficiaries of Corps projects to overstate the benefits. And the Corps has become notorious for undertaking expensive projects that cannot be justified with any reasonable cost-benefit analysis.

In other countries the counterparts of the Army Corps of Engineers are even more prone to overspending. In Japan, almost every river now runs through a concrete channel, and an amazing 60 percent of the coastline is now "armored" with concrete barriers. ■

< < < < < < < < < < < < < < < < <

1. The town of Centreville, population 16, has two types of residents, Homebodies and Revelers. Using the accompanying table, the town must decide how much to spend on its New Year's Eve party. No individual resident expects to directly bear the cost of the party.

   a. Suppose there are 10 Homebodies and 6 Revelers. Determine the marginal social benefit schedule of money spent on the party. What is the efficient level of spending?

   b. Suppose there are 6 Homebodies and 10 Revelers. How do your answers to part a change? Explain.

   c. Suppose that the individual marginal benefit schedules are known but no one knows

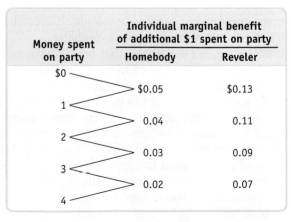

| Money spent on party | Individual marginal benefit of additional $1 spent on party | |
|---|---|---|
| | Homebody | Reveler |
| $0 | | |
| | $0.05 | $0.13 |
| 1 | | |
| | 0.04 | 0.11 |
| 2 | | |
| | 0.03 | 0.09 |
| 3 | | |
| | 0.02 | 0.07 |
| 4 | | |

the true numbers of Homebodies and Revelers. Individuals are asked their preferences. What is the likely outcome? Why is it likely to result in an inefficiently high level of spending? Explain.

*Solutions appear at back of book.*

### • A LOOK AHEAD •

We have now answered the first of the big questions we raised in the Introduction: *Why does a competitive market economy generally work so well?* Part of the answer involved defining what it means to work "well": an economy works badly if it misses opportunities to make at least one person better off without making others worse off, and it works well if it does not miss those opportunities.

What we've now seen is that in a well-functioning competitive market economy in general equilibrium, consumers can buy as much or as little as they choose at the same price, and producers can sell as much or as little as they choose, also at the same price. And this means that all the opportunities to make at least one person better off without making others worse off—whether by redistributing goods among consumers, rearranging output among producers, or changing what the economy produces—will *already have been taken.*

But things sometimes go wrong. Market economies sometimes work badly. We have looked at two cases that arise when prices don't work well as economic signals: externalities and public goods. Now we need to look at two more cases. The next two chapters examine what happens when markets are not competitive—when there are just one or very few sellers, or when sellers are able to differentiate their products. Here again, as we will see, markets fail to be efficient.

## SUMMARY

1. When we assess the performance of the economy as a whole, we use the economic definition of efficiency: the **general equilibrium** of a **competitive market economy** is efficient if there is no way to make some people better off without making others worse off.

2. Economic efficiency requires **efficiency in consumption**—there is no way to redistribute goods and services that makes some consumers better off without making others worse off. It requires **efficiency in production**, which arises from an **efficient allocation of resources**—there is no way to reallocate resources that allows the economy to produce more of some goods and services without producing less of others. And it requires **efficiency in output levels**—there is no other choice of output mix that makes some people better off without making others worse off. In the same way in which a competitive market maximizes total surplus, the general equilibrium of a

competitive market economy as a whole is efficient—in consumption, in production, and in output levels—when prices perform properly as **economic signals.** In cases of market failure, however, prices fail to lead people to exploit all mutually beneficial transactions; as a result, when markets fail, the economy as a whole is inefficient.

3. It is not enough for an economy to be efficient. We also want it to deliver an outcome that is "fair" in terms of the distribution of utility among individuals. Economic fairness is known as equity. Unfortunately, there is no generally accepted definition of *fairness.* The ambiguity this sometimes creates for evaluating economic policy can be illustrated with the **utility possibility frontier,** which shows the trade-offs between the utility achieved by one individual or group and that achieved by other individuals or groups.

4. Under certain conditions, **market failure** occurs and markets fail to be efficient. Externalities and public goods are two examples.

5. The costs to society of pollution are an example of an **external cost;** in some cases, however, economic activities yield **external benefits.** External costs and benefits are jointly known as **externalities,** with external costs called **negative externalities** and external benefits called **positive externalities.**

6. When only the original good or activity can be controlled, government policies are geared to influencing how much of it is produced. When there are external costs from production, the **marginal social cost of a good or activity** exceeds its marginal cost to producers, the difference being the marginal external cost. Without government action, the market produces too much of the good or activity. The optimal **Pigouvian tax** on production of the good or activity is equal to its marginal external cost, yielding lower output and a higher price to consumers. A system of tradable production permits for the right to produce the good or activity can also achieve efficiency at minimum cost.

7. According to the **Coase theorem,** individuals can find a way to **internalize the externality,** making government intervention unnecessary, as long as **transaction costs**—the costs of making a deal—are sufficiently low. However, in many cases transaction costs are too high to permit such deals.

8. When a good or activity yields external benefits, such as **technology spillovers,** the **marginal social benefit of the good or activity** is equal to the marginal benefit accruing to consumers plus its marginal external benefit. Without government intervention, the market produces too little of the good or activity. An optimal **Pigouvian**

**subsidy** to producers, equal to the marginal external benefit, moves the market to the socially optimal quantity of production. This yields higher output and a higher price to producers. It is a form of **industrial policy,** a policy to support industries that are believed to generate positive externalities. Economists are often skeptical of industrial policies because external benefits are hard to measure and they motivate producers to lobby for lucrative benefits.

9. Free markets can deliver efficient levels of production and consumption for private goods, which are both **excludable** and **rival in consumption.** When goods are **nonexcludable** and **nonrival in consumption,** as in the case of **public goods,** free markets cannot achieve efficient outcomes. When goods are nonexcludable, there is a **free-rider problem:** consumers will not pay for the good, leading to inefficiently low production.

10. In most cases a public good must be supplied by the government. The marginal social benefit of a public good is equal to the sum of the individual marginal benefits to each consumer. The efficient quantity of a public good is the quantity at which marginal social benefit equals marginal cost. Like a positive externality, marginal social benefit is greater than any one individual's marginal benefit, so no individual is willing to provide the efficient quantity.

11. One rationale for the presence of government is that it allows citizens to tax themselves in order to provide public goods. Governments use **cost-benefit analysis** to determine the efficient provision of a public good. Such analysis is difficult, however, because individuals have an incentive to overstate the good's value to them.

## KEY TERMS

Competitive market economy, p. 239
General equilibrium, p. 239
Efficient in consumption, p. 240
Economic signal, p. 240
Efficient in production, p. 241
Efficient allocation of resources, p. 241
Efficient in output levels, p. 242
Utility possibility frontier, p. 249
Market failure, p. 251
External cost, p. 251
External benefit, p. 251

Externalities, p. 251
Negative externalities, p. 251
Positive externalities, p. 251
Marginal social cost of a good or activity, p. 252
Pigouvian taxes, p. 253
Coase theorem, p. 254
Transaction costs, p. 254
Internalize the externality, p. 254
Technology spillover, p. 255
Marginal social benefit of a good or activity, p. 256

Pigouvian subsidy, p. 256
Industrial policy, p. 256
Excludable, p. 259
Rival in consumption, p. 259
Private good, p. 259
Public good, p. 259
Nonexcludable, p. 259
Nonrival in consumption, p. 259
Free-rider problem, p. 259
Cost-benefit analysis, p. 263

# PROBLEMS

1. Lakshmi and Sam have a cake that they want to divide in an efficient way, and the cake is the only good in their little economy. Both Lakshmi and Sam like cake and would always prefer to have more of it. Using the standard of efficiency in consumption, determine whether the following ways of dividing the cake are efficient.

   a. Lakshmi and Sam each get half of the cake.

   b. Lakshmi and Sam each get one-third of the cake and one-third is thrown away.

   c. Lakshmi gets the whole cake and Sam gets nothing.

2. In the town of Rockport, only two goods are produced: left shoes and right shoes. And this economy produces on the production possibility frontier. That is, there is no way of producing more left shoes without producing fewer right shoes, and vice versa. What else would you need to know, if anything, to determine whether the economy of Rockport as a whole is efficient? That is, does it satisfy efficiency in production, efficiency in consumption, and efficiency in output levels? Explain your answer.

3. The economy of Dunk, IN, produces only two goods, bagels and doughnuts, using labor as the only factor of production. There are 8 workers in Dunk and all are paid the same wage. The accompanying table shows the amount of output that can be produced with a certain number of workers.

| Quantity of labor in doughnut production (workers) | Quantity of doughnuts | Quantity of labor in bagel production (workers) | Quantity of bagels |
|---|---|---|---|
| 0 | 0 | 0 | 0 |
| 1 | 34 | 1 | 50 |
| 2 | 40 | 2 | 86 |
| 3 | 46 | 3 | 92 |
| 4 | 49 | 4 | 98 |
| 5 | 52 | 5 | 104 |
| 6 | 53 | 6 | 106 |

   a. Suppose that the price of a doughnut is $0.50 and the price of a bagel is also $0.50. There are 2 workers producing doughnuts and 3 workers producing bagels. The other 3 workers are unemployed. Given what you know about the relationship between the value of the marginal products and efficiency, determine whether this economy is efficient in the production of doughnuts versus the production of bagels—that is, is the economy efficient in output levels? Also determine whether the economy is efficient in production—that is, is it producing on the production possibility frontier?

   b. Suppose that the price of doughnuts is $0.20, and the price of bagels is $0.10. There are 4 workers producing doughnuts and 4 workers producing bagels, and nobody is unemployed. Is this economy efficient in production? Is it efficient in output levels?

   c. Initially, the price of doughnuts is $0.20, the price of bagels is $0.10, and there are 4 workers producing doughnuts and 4 workers producing bagels, just as in part b. Now consumers' tastes change: due to health concerns, consumers are now willing to pay $0.75 per bagel but only $0.10 per doughnut. These new prices act as signals of consumers' preferences. In response to this change, will the allocation of workers to bagel or doughnut production change?

4. Land in the Shire can be used for growing carrots or potatoes, and the only variable input into production is labor (land is fixed). All workers are paid the same wage. There are two farmers: Sam grows carrots, and the marginal product of labor on his farm is 30 pounds of carrots per month. Merry grows potatoes, and the marginal product of labor on his farm is 44 pounds of potatoes per month. Each experiences diminishing returns to labor. The price of carrots is $3 per pound, and the price of potatoes is $2 per pound.

   a. Calculate the value of the marginal product of labor in carrots and in potatoes to assess whether the economy of the Shire is efficient in output levels. Is the economy in general equilibrium?

   b. Do the prices of carrots and potatoes signal that farmers should produce more or less of their crops? In which direction will employment levels adjust in response to the market prices for the two crops? Describe how the economy reaches general equilibrium.

5. The economy of Leisureville, CO, produces only two goods: skis and bikes. Labor is the only variable input into production, there are diminishing returns to labor, and all workers are paid the same wage. All markets are competitive, and initially the economy is in general equilibrium. Now, due to a change in tastes, consumers' preferences change away from skis and toward bikes.

   a. What will happen to consumers' willingness to pay for bikes and for skis? What will therefore happen to the market prices for bikes and skis?

   b. As the prices adjust, what will happen to the value of the marginal product of labor in bikes and in skis? What will happen to bike producers' and ski producers' willingness to pay for workers?

   c. As adjustments are made in employment, what happens to the output of bikes and of skis? How does the marginal product of labor in bikes and in skis respond? What therefore happens to the value of the marginal product of labor in bikes and in skis?

   d. At what point does this process stop?

6. Consider the utility possibility frontier in the accompanying diagram.

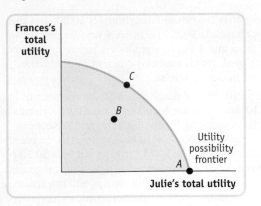

a. Is point A efficient? Would you describe point A as fair? Why or why not?

b. Is point B efficient?

c. Is point C better than point B? Why or why not?

d. Is point A better than point B? Why or why not?

7. The table shows how much total utility Jeremy and John Stuart experience from various amounts of income. (Utility is measured in units of utils.)

| Jeremy's income | Jeremy's total utility (utils) | John Stuart's income | John Stuart's total utility (utils) |
|---|---|---|---|
| $0 | 0 | $0 | 0 |
| 1 | 12 | 1 | 12 |
| 2 | 22 | 2 | 22 |
| 3 | 30 | 3 | 30 |
| 4 | 36 | 4 | 36 |
| 5 | 40 | 5 | 40 |
| 6 | 42 | 6 | 42 |

a. There are $6 that we can distribute between Jeremy and John Stuart. Suppose that Jeremy and John Stuart live in a utilitarian society that tries to distribute income in such a way as to create the greatest sum of the total utility of each member. How can we distribute $6 between Jeremy and John Stuart so that the sum of their total utilities is the greatest?

b. Now Jeremy falls ill, and his illness requires expensive treatment. As a result, the utility he gets from each dollar of income is now only half of what the table above shows. If our aim is to distribute income in such a way as to create the greatest sum of the total utility of both Jeremy and John Stuart, how should we distribute the $6 now? Does this seem fair to you?

8. What type of externality (positive or negative) is described in each of the following examples? Is the marginal social benefit of the activity greater than or equal to the marginal benefit to the individual? Is the marginal social cost of the activity greater than or equal to the marginal cost to the individual? Consequently, without intervention, will there be too little or too much (relative to what would be socially optimal) of this activity?

a. Mrs. Chau plants lots of colorful flowers in her front yard.

b. Anna Crombie and Fritz, a popular clothing store, opens in a mall, attracting more shoppers who also visit other stores.

c. The fraternity next to your dorm plays loud music, keeping you from studying.

d. Maija, who lives next to an apple orchard, decides to keep bees to produce honey.

e. Justine buys a large SUV that consumes a lot of gasoline.

9. The accompanying table shows the total social benefit from steel production and the total cost to steel producers of producing steel. Producing a ton of steel imposes a marginal external cost of $60 per ton.

| Quantity of steel (tons) | Total social benefit | Total cost to producers |
|---|---|---|
| 1 | $115 | $10 |
| 2 | 210 | 30 |
| 3 | 285 | 60 |
| 4 | 340 | 100 |
| 5 | 375 | 150 |

a. Calculate the marginal social benefit per ton of steel and the marginal cost per ton of steel to steel producers. Then calculate the marginal social cost per ton of steel.

b. What is the market equilibrium quantity of steel production?

c. What is the socially optimal quantity of steel production?

d. If you wanted to impose a Pigouvian tax to remedy the problem created by the negative externality, how high would the Pigouvian tax have to be per ton of steel?

10. Education is an example of a positive externality: acquiring more education benefits the individual student and having a more highly educated work force is good for the economy as a whole. The accompanying table illustrates the marginal benefit to Sian per year of education and the marginal cost per year of education. Each year of education has a marginal external benefit to society equal to $8,000. Assume that the marginal

social cost is the same as the marginal cost paid by an individual student.

| Quantity of education (years) | Sian's marginal benefit per year | Sian's marginal cost per year |
|---|---|---|
| 9 | | |
| | $20,000 | $15,000 |
| 10 | | |
| | 19,000 | 16,000 |
| 11 | | |
| | 18,000 | 17,000 |
| 12 | | |
| | 17,000 | 18,000 |
| 13 | | |
| | 16,000 | 19,000 |
| 14 | | |
| | 15,000 | 20,000 |
| 15 | | |
| | 14,000 | 21,000 |
| 16 | | |
| | 13,000 | 22,000 |
| 17 | | |

**a.** Find Sian's market equilibrium number of years of education.

**b.** Calculate the marginal social benefit schedule. What is the socially optimal number of years of education?

**c.** You are in charge of education funding. Would you use a Pigouvian tax or a Pigouvian subsidy to induce Sian to choose the socially optimal amount of education? How high would you set this tax or subsidy per year of education?

**11.** Getting a flu shot reduces not only your chance of getting the flu but also the chance that you will pass it on to someone else.

**a.** Draw a diagram showing the supply and demand curves of inoculating different proportions of the population. Assume that the marginal cost of each flu shot is constant and is equal to the marginal social cost, and that the demand curve is downward sloping.

**b.** Will the marginal social benefit curve be higher, lower, or the same as the demand curve? Why? Draw the marginal social benefit curve into your diagram.

**c.** In your diagram, show the market equilibrium quantity and the socially optimal quantity of flu shots. Is the market equilibrium quantity of flu shots socially efficient? Why or why not?

**d.** Many university health centers offer free flu shots to students and employees. Does this solution necessarily achieve efficiency? Explain, using your diagram.

**12.** Ronald owns a cattle farm at the source of a long river. His cattle's waste flows into the river, and down many miles to where Carla lives. Carla gets her drinking water from the river. By allowing his cattle's waste to flow into the river, Ronald imposes a negative externality on Carla. In each of the two following cases, do you think that through negotiation, Ronald and Carla can find an efficient solution? What might this solution look like?

**a.** There are no telephones, and for Carla to talk to Ronald, she has to travel for two days on a rocky road.

**b.** Carla and Ronald both have e-mail access, making it costless for them to communicate.

**13.** In many planned communities, various aspects of community living are subject to regulation by a homeowners' association. These rules can regulate house architecture; require snow removal from sidewalks; exclude outdoor equipment, such as backyard swimming pools; and so on. There has been some conflict, as some homeowners feel that some of the regulations are overly intrusive. You have been called in to mediate. Using economics, how would you decide what types of regulations are warranted and what types are not?

**14.** A residential community has 100 residents who are concerned about security. The accompanying table gives the total cost of hiring a 24-hour security service as well as each individual resident's total benefit.

| Quantity of security guards | Total cost | Total individual benefit to each resident |
|---|---|---|
| 0 | $0 | $0 |
| 1 | 150 | 10 |
| 2 | 300 | 16 |
| 3 | 450 | 18 |
| 4 | 600 | 19 |

**a.** Explain why the security service is a public good for the residents of the community.

**b.** Calculate the marginal cost, the individual marginal benefit for each resident, and the marginal social benefit.

**c.** If an individual resident were to decide about hiring and paying for security guards on his or her own, how many guards would that resident hire?

**d.** If the residents act together, how many security guards will they hire?

270 **PART 4** MARKETS AND EFFICIENCY

**15.** The accompanying table shows Tanisha's and Ari's individual marginal benefit of different amounts of street cleanings per month. Suppose that the marginal cost of street cleanings is constant at $9 each.

| Quantity of street cleanings per month | Tanisha's individual marginal benefit | Ari's individual marginal benefit |
|---|---|---|
| 0 | | |
| | $10 | $8 |
| 1 | | |
| | 6 | 4 |
| 2 | | |
| | 2 | 1 |
| 3 | | |

**a.** If Tanisha had to pay for street cleaning on her own, how many street cleanings would there be?

**b.** Calculate the marginal social benefit of street cleaning. What is the optimal number of street cleanings?

**c.** Consider the optimal number of street cleanings. The last street cleaning of that number costs $9. Is Tanisha willing to pay for that last cleaning on her own? Is Ari willing to pay for that last cleaning on his own?

**16.** Anyone with a radio receiver can listen to public radio, which is funded largely by donations.

**a.** Is public radio excludable or nonexcludable? Is it rival in consumption or nonrival? What type of good is it?

**b.** Should the government support public radio? Explain your reasoning.

**>web...** To continue your study and review of concepts in this chapter, please visit the Krugman/Wells/Olney website for quizzes, animated graph tutorials, web links to helpful resources, and more.

**www.worthpublishers.com/krugmanwellsolney**

# 11

## >> Monopoly

### EVERYBODY MUST GET STONES

A FEW YEARS AGO DE BEERS, THE world's main supplier of diamonds, ran an ad urging men to buy their wives diamond jewelry. "She married you for richer, for poorer," read the ad. "Let her know how it's going."

Crass? Yes. Effective? No question. For generations diamonds have been a symbol of luxury, valued not only for their appearance but also for their rarity.

But geologists will tell you that diamonds aren't all that rare. In fact, according to the *Dow Jones-Irwin Guide to Fine Gems and Jewelry*, diamonds are "more common than any other gem-quality colored stone. They only seem rarer . . ."

Why do diamonds seem rarer than other gems? Part of the answer is a brilliant marketing campaign (We'll talk more about marketing and product differentiation in Chapter 12.) But mainly diamonds seem rare because De Beers *makes* them rare: the company controls most of the world's diamond mines and limits the quantity of diamonds supplied to the market.

Got stones?

Up to now we have concentrated exclusively on perfectly competitive markets—markets in which the producers are perfect competitors. But De Beers isn't like the producers we've studied so far: it is a *monopolist*, the sole (or almost sole) producer of a good. Monopolists behave differently from producers in perfectly competitive industries: whereas perfect competitors take the price at which they can sell their output as given, monopolists know that their actions affect market prices and take that effect into account when deciding how much to produce. Before we begin our analysis, let's step back and look at monopoly and perfect competition as parts of a broader system for classifying markets.

Perfect competition and monopoly are particular types of *market structure*. They are particular categories in a system economists use to classify markets and industries according to two main dimensions. This chapter begins with a brief overview of types of market structure. It will help us here and in the next chapter to understand on a deeper level why markets differ and why producers in those markets behave quite differently.

### What you will learn in this chapter:

➤ The significance of **monopoly**, where a single **monopolist** is the only producer of a good

➤ How a monopolist determines its profit-maximizing output and price

➤ The difference between monopoly and perfect competition, and the effects of that difference on society's welfare

➤ How policy makers address the problems posed by monopoly

➤ What **price discrimination** is, and why it is so prevalent when producers have **market power**

# Types of Market Structure

In the real world, there is a mind-boggling array of different markets. We observe widely different behavior patterns by producers across markets: in some markets producers are extremely competitive; in others, they seem somehow to coordinate their actions to avoid competing with one another; and, as we have just described, some markets are monopolies in which there is no competition at all. In order to develop principles and make predictions about markets and how producers will behave in them, economists have developed four principal models of market structure: *perfect competition, monopoly, oligopoly,* and *monopolistic competition.*

This system of market structures is based on two dimensions:

- The number of producers in the market (one, few, or many)
- Whether the goods offered are identical or *differentiated*

Differentiated goods are goods that are different but considered somewhat substitutable by consumers (think Coke versus Pepsi).

Figure 11-1 provides a simple visual summary of the types of market structure classified according to the two dimensions. In *monopoly,* a single producer sells a single, undifferentiated product. In *oligopoly,* a few producers—more than one but not a large number—sell products that may be either identical or differentiated. In *monopolistic competition,* many producers each sell a differentiated product (think of producers of economics textbooks). And finally, as we know, in *perfect competition* many producers each sell an identical product.

You might wonder what determines the number of firms in a market: whether there is one (monopoly), few (oligopoly), or many (perfect competition and monopolistic competition). We won't answer that question here, because it will be covered in detail later in this chapter and in Chapter 12, which analyzes oligopoly and monopolistic competition. We will just briefly note that in the long run it depends on whether there are conditions that make it difficult for new firms to enter the market, such as government regulations that discourage entry, economies of scale in production, technological superiority, or control of necessary resources or inputs. When these conditions are present, industries tend to be monopolies or oligopolies; when they are not present, industries tend to be perfectly competitive or monopolistically competitive.

You might also wonder why some markets have differentiated products but others have identical ones. The answer is that it depends on the nature of the good and consumers' preferences. Some goods—soft drinks, economics textbooks, breakfast cereals—

## Figure 11-1

### Types of Market Structure

The behavior of any given firm and the market it occupies are analyzed using one of four models of market structure—monopoly, oligopoly, perfect competition, or monopolistic competition. This system for categorizing market structure is based on two dimensions: (1) whether products are differentiated or identical and (2) the number of producers in the industry—one, few, or many.

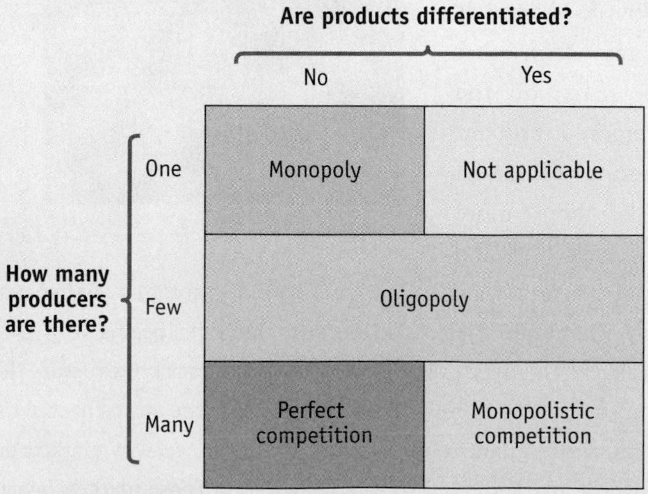

| How many producers are there? | Are products differentiated? | |
|---|---|---|
| | **No** | **Yes** |
| One | Monopoly | Not applicable |
| Few | Oligopoly | Oligopoly |
| Many | Perfect competition | Monopolistic competition |

can readily be made into different varieties in the eyes and tastes of consumers. Other goods—hammers, for example—are much less easy to differentiate.

Although this chapter is devoted to monopoly, important aspects of monopoly carry over to other market structures—to oligopoly and monopolistic competition. In the next section, we will define monopoly and review the conditions that make it possible. These same conditions, in less extreme form, also give rise to oligopoly. We then show how a monopolist can increase profit by limiting the quantity supplied to a market—behavior that also occurs in oligopoly and monopolistic competition. As we'll see, this kind of behavior is good for the producer but bad for consumers; it also causes inefficiency. An important topic of study will be the ways in which public policy tries to limit the damage. Finally, we turn to one of the surprising effects of monopoly—one that is very often present in oligopoly and monopolistic competition as well: the fact that different consumers often pay different prices for the same good.

# The Meaning of Monopoly

The De Beers monopoly of South Africa was created in the 1880s by Cecil Rhodes, a British businessman. By 1880 mines in South Africa already dominated the world's supply of diamonds. There were, however, many mining companies, all competing with each other. During the 1880s Rhodes bought the great majority of those mines and consolidated them into a single company, De Beers. By 1889 De Beers controlled almost all of the world's diamond production.

De Beers, in other words, became a **monopolist.** A producer is a monopolist if it is the sole supplier of a good that has no close substitutes. When a firm is a monopolist, the industry is a **monopoly.**

> A **monopolist** is a firm that is the only producer of a good that has no close substitutes. An industry controlled by a monopolist is known as a **monopoly.**

## Monopoly: Our First Departure from Perfect Competition

As we saw in the Chapter 8 section "Defining Perfect Competition," the supply and demand model of a market is not universally valid. Instead, it's a model of perfect competition, which is only one of several different types of market structure.

Back in Chapter 8 we learned that a market will be perfectly competitive only if there are many producers, all of whom produce the same standardized product. Monopoly is the most extreme departure from perfect competition.

In practice, true monopolies are hard to find in the modern American economy, partly because of legal obstacles. A contemporary entrepreneur who tried to consolidate all the firms in an industry the way that Rhodes did would soon find himself in court, accused of breaking *antitrust* laws, which are intended to prevent monopolies from emerging. Oligopoly, a market structure in which there is a small number of large producers, is much more common. In fact, most of the goods and services you buy, from autos to airline tickets, are supplied by oligopolies, which we will examine in Chapter 12.

Monopolies do, however, play an important role in some sectors of the economy, such as pharmaceuticals. Furthermore, our analysis of monopoly will provide a foundation for our later analysis of other departures from perfect competition, such as oligopoly and monopolistic competition.

## What Monopolists Do

Why did Rhodes want to consolidate South African diamond producers into a single company? What difference did it make to the world diamond market?

Figure 11-2 on page 274 offers a preliminary view of the effects of monopoly. It shows an industry in which the supply curve under perfect competition intersects the demand curve at C, leading to the price $P_C$ and the output $Q_C$.

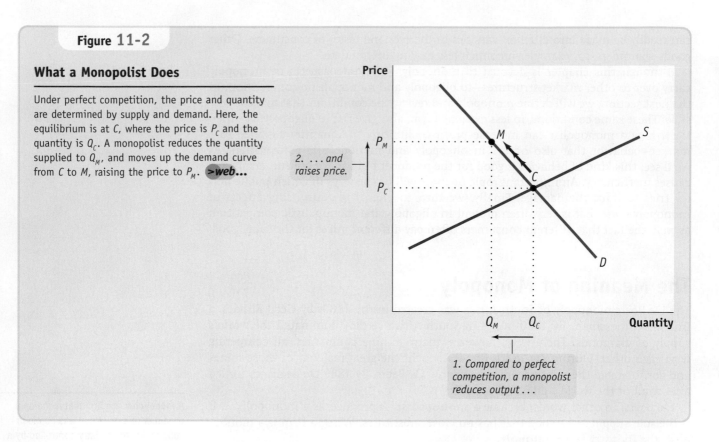

**Figure 11-2**

### What a Monopolist Does

Under perfect competition, the price and quantity are determined by supply and demand. Here, the equilibrium is at $C$, where the price is $P_C$ and the quantity is $Q_C$. A monopolist reduces the quantity supplied to $Q_M$, and moves up the demand curve from $C$ to $M$, raising the price to $P_M$. **>web...**

2. ...and raises price.

1. Compared to perfect competition, a monopolist reduces output...

Suppose that this industry is consolidated into a monopoly. The monopolist *moves up the demand curve* by reducing quantity supplied to a point like $M$, at which the quantity produced, $Q_M$, is lower and the price $P_M$, is higher than under perfect competition.

The ability of a monopolist to raise its price above the competitive level by reducing output is known as **market power.** And market power is what monopoly is all about. A wheat farmer who is one of 100,000 wheat farmers has no market power: he or she must sell wheat at the going market price. Your local cable TV company, though, does have market power: it can raise prices and still keep many (though not all) of its customers, because they have nowhere else to go. In short, it's a monopolist.

The reason a monopolist reduces output and raises price compared to the perfectly competitive industry levels is to increase profit. Cecil Rhodes consolidated the diamond producers into De Beers because he realized that the whole would be worth more than the sum of its parts—the monopoly would generate more profit than the sum of the profits of the individual competitive firms. In fact, we saw in Chapter 8 that under perfect competition economic profits normally vanish in the long run. Under monopoly the profits don't go away—a monopolist is able to continue earning profits in the long run.

In fact, monopolists are not the only types of firms that possess market power. In the next chapter we will study *oligopolists,* firms that can have market power as well. Under certain conditions, oligopolists can earn positive economic profits in the long run by restricting output like monopolists do.

But why don't profits get competed away? What allows monopolists to be monopolists?

### Why Do Monopolies Exist?

A monopolist making profits will not go unnoticed by others. But won't other firms crash the party, grab a piece of the action, and drive down prices and profits in the long run? For a profitable monopoly to persist, something must keep others from

---

**Market power** is the ability of a producer to raise prices.

going into the same business; that "something" is known as a **barrier to entry.** There are four principal types of barriers to entry: control of a scarce resource or input, economies of scale, technological superiority, and government-created barriers.

### Control of a Scarce Resource or Input

A monopolist that controls a resource or input crucial to an industry can prevent other firms from entering its market. Cecil Rhodes created the De Beers monopoly by establishing control over the mines that produced the great bulk of the world's diamonds.

### Economies of Scale

Many Americans have natural gas piped into their homes, for cooking and heating. Invariably, the local gas company is a monopolist. But why don't rival companies compete to provide gas?

In the early nineteenth century, when the gas industry was just starting up, companies did compete for local customers. But this competition didn't last long; soon local gas supply became a monopoly in almost every town because of the large fixed costs involved in providing a town with gas lines. Since the cost of laying gas lines didn't depend on how much gas a company sold, firms with a larger volume of sales had a cost advantage: because they were able to spread the fixed costs over a larger volume, they had lower average total costs than smaller firms.

Local gas supply is an industry in which average total cost always falls as output increases. As we learned in Chapter 7, this phenomenon is called *economies of scale.* There we learned that when average total cost falls as output increases, firms tend to grow larger. In an industry characterized by economies of scale, larger companies are more profitable and drive out smaller ones. For the same reason, established companies have a cost advantage over any potential entrant—a potent barrier to entry. So economies of scale can both give rise to and sustain monopoly.

A monopoly created and sustained by economies of scale is called a **natural monopoly.** The defining characteristic of a natural monopoly is that it possesses economies of scale over the range of output that is relevant for the industry. This is illustrated in Figure 11-3, showing the firm's average total cost curve and the market demand curve. Here we can see that the natural monopolist's *ATC* curve declines over the output levels at which price is greater than or equal to average total cost. So

> To earn profits, a monopolist must be protected by a **barrier to entry**—something that prevents other firms from entering the industry.

> A **natural monopoly** exists when economies of scale provide a large cost advantage to having all of an industry's output produced by a single firm.

### Figure 11-3

#### Economies of Scale Create Natural Monopoly

A natural monopoly can arise when fixed costs required to operate are very high. When this occurs, the firm's *ATC* curve declines over the range of output at which price is greater than or equal to average total cost. This gives the firm economies of scale over the entire range of output at which the firm would at least break even in the long run. As a result, a given quantity of output is produced more cheaply by one large firm than by two or more smaller firms. **>web...**

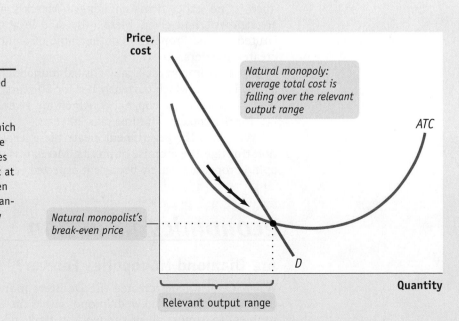

the natural monopolist has economies of scale over the entire range of output for which any firm would want to remain in the industry—the range of output at which the firm would at least break even in the long run. The source of this condition is large fixed costs: when large fixed costs are required to operate, a given quantity of output is produced at lower average total cost by one large firm than by two or more smaller firms.

The most visible natural monopolies in the modern economy are local utilities—water, gas, electricity, local phone service, and cable television. As we'll see later in this chapter, natural monopolies pose a special challenge to public policy.

**Technological Superiority** A firm that maintains a consistent technological advantage over potential competitors can establish itself as a monopolist. For example, from the 1970s through the 1990s the chip manufacturer Intel was able to maintain a consistent advantage over potential competitors in both the design and the production of microprocessors, the chips that run computers. But technological superiority is typically a short-run, not a long-run, barrier to entry: over time competitors will invest in upgrading their technology to match that of the technology leader. In fact, in the last few years Intel found its technological superiority eroded by a competitor, Advanced Micro Devices (also known as AMD), which now produces chips approximately as fast and as powerful as Intel chips.

We should note, however, that in certain high-tech industries, technological superiority is not a guarantee of success against competitors. Some high-tech industries are characterized by network externalities, a condition that arises when the value to the consumer of a good rises as the number of people who also use the good rises. In these industries, the firm possessing the largest network—the largest number of consumers currently using its product—has an advantage over its competitors in attracting new customers, an advantage that may allow it to become a monopolist. Microsoft is often cited as an example of a company with a technologically inferior product—its computer operating system—that grew into a monopolist through the phenomenon of network externalities.

**Government-Created Barriers** In 1998 the pharmaceutical company Merck introduced Propecia, a drug effective against baldness. Despite the fact that Propecia was very profitable and other drug companies had the know-how to produce it, no other firms challenged Merck's monopoly. That's because the U.S. government had given Merck the sole legal right to produce the drug in the United States. Propecia is an example of a monopoly protected by government-created barriers.

The most important legally created monopolies today arise from *patents* and *copyrights*. Patents, which currently last for 20 years, are given to inventors of new products, such as drugs; copyrights, which are given to authors and composers, usually last for the creator's lifetime plus 70 years.

Why does the government create these legal monopolies? To encourage innovation through the promise of profits. Merck was willing to invest large sums in developing Propecia precisely because it expected to profit from the resulting monopoly.

# *economics in action*

## Are Diamond Monopolies Forever?

When Cecil Rhodes created the De Beers monopoly, it was a particularly opportune moment. The new diamond mines in South Africa dwarfed all previous sources, so almost all of the world's diamond production was concentrated in a few square miles.

Since that time, however, diamond deposits similar to those in South Africa have been found in a number of places—other African countries, Russia, and Australia, which is now the largest producer. So how does De Beers remain a monopolist?

Until quite recently De Beers was able to extend its control of resources even as new mines were opened. De Beers either bought out new producers or entered into agreements with local governments which controlled some of the new mines, effectively making them part of the De Beers monopoly. The most remarkable of these was an agreement with the former Soviet Union, which ensured that Russian diamonds would be marketed through De Beers, preserving its ability to control world supplies.

In recent years, however, the spread of diamond production—together with competition from synthetic diamonds, which are becoming better substitutes for natural stones—has led to some erosion of De Beers's control, and prices have even dropped somewhat. De Beers is arguably the most successful monopolist in history—but even diamond monopolies may not be forever. ∎

> > > > > > > > > > > > > > > > > > > > > >

>>CHECK YOUR UNDERSTANDING 11-1

1. Currently, Texas Tea Oil Co. is the only local supplier of home heating oil in Frigid, Alaska. This winter residents were shocked that the cost of a gallon of heating oil had doubled and believed that they were the victims of market power. Explain which of the following pieces of evidence support or undermine that conclusion.
   a. There is a national shortage of heating oil, and Texas Tea could procure only a limited amount.
   b. Last year, Texas Tea and several other competing local oil-supply firms merged into a single firm.
   c. The cost to Texas Tea of purchasing heating oil from refineries has gone up significantly.
   d. Recently, some nonlocal firms have begun to offer heating oil to Texas Tea's regular customers at a price much lower than Texas Tea's.
   e. Texas Tea has acquired an exclusive government license to draw oil from the only heating oil pipeline in the state.

Solutions appear at back of book.

# How a Monopolist Maximizes Profit

As we've suggested, once Cecil Rhodes consolidated the competing diamond producers of South Africa into a single company, the industry's behavior changed: the quantity supplied fell and the market price rose. In this section we will learn how a monopolist increases its profits by reducing output. And we will see the crucial role that market demand plays in leading a monopolist to behave differently from a perfectly competitive industry.

## The Monopolist's Demand and Marginal Revenue Curves

In Chapter 8 we derived the producer's optimal output rule: a profit-maximizing producer produces the quantity of output at which the marginal cost of producing the last unit of output equals marginal revenue—the change in total revenue generated by that last unit of output. That is, $MR = MC$ at the profit-maximizing quantity of output. Although the optimal output rule holds for *all* producers, we will see shortly that its application leads to different profit-maximizing output levels for a monopolist compared to a perfectly competitive producer—that is, a price-taking producer. The source of that difference lies in the comparison of the demand curve faced by a monopolist to the demand curve faced by an individual, perfectly competitive producer.

In addition to the optimal output rule, we also learned in Chapter 8 that even though the *market* demand curve is always downward sloping, each of the producers that make up a perfectly competitive industry faces a horizontal, *perfectly elastic* demand curve, like $D_C$ in panel (a) of Figure 11-4 on page 278. Any attempt by an individual producer in a perfectly competitive industry to charge more than the going market price will cause it to lose all its sales. It can, however, sell as much as it likes at the market price. As we saw

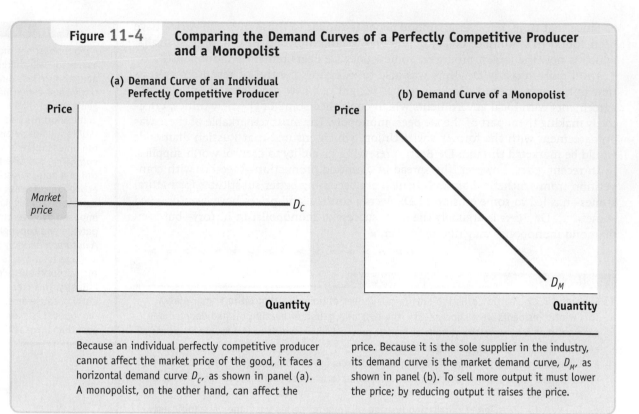

**Figure 11-4    Comparing the Demand Curves of a Perfectly Competitive Producer and a Monopolist**

**(a) Demand Curve of an Individual Perfectly Competitive Producer**

Price

Market price — $D_C$

Quantity

**(b) Demand Curve of a Monopolist**

Price

$D_M$

Quantity

Because an individual perfectly competitive producer cannot affect the market price of the good, it faces a horizontal demand curve $D_C$, as shown in panel (a). A monopolist, on the other hand, can affect the price. Because it is the sole supplier in the industry, its demand curve is the market demand curve, $D_M$, as shown in panel (b). To sell more output it must lower the price; by reducing output it raises the price.

in Chapter 8, the marginal revenue of a perfectly competitive producer is simply the market price. As a result, the price-taking firm's optimal output rule is to produce the output level at which the marginal cost of the last unit produced is equal to the market price.

A monopolist, in contrast, is the sole supplier of its good. So its demand curve is simply the market demand curve, which is downward sloping, like $D_M$ in panel (b). This downward slope creates a "wedge" between the price of the good and the marginal revenue of the good—the change in revenue generated by producing one more unit.

Table 11-1 shows this wedge between price and marginal revenue for a monopolist, by calculating the monopolist's total revenue and marginal revenue schedules from its demand schedule.

The first two columns of Table 11-1 show a hypothetical demand schedule for De Beers diamonds. For the sake of simplicity, we assume that all diamonds are exactly alike. And to make the arithmetic easy, we suppose that the number of diamonds sold is far smaller than is actually the case. For instance, at a price of $500 per diamond, we assume that only 10 diamonds are sold. The demand curve implied by this schedule is shown in panel (a) of Figure 11-5 on page 280.

The third column of Table 11-1 shows De Beers's total revenue from selling each quantity of diamonds—the price per diamond multiplied by the number of diamonds sold. The last column calculates marginal revenue, the change in total revenue from producing and selling one more diamond.

Clearly, after the 1st diamond, the marginal revenue a monopolist receives from selling one more unit is less than the price at which that unit is sold. For example, if De Beers sells 10 diamonds, the price at which the 10th diamond is sold is $500. But the marginal revenue—the change in total revenue in going from 9 to 10 diamonds—is only $50.

Why is the marginal revenue from that 10th diamond less than the price? An increase in production by a monopolist has two opposing effects on revenue:

■ *A quantity effect.* One more unit is sold, increasing total revenue by the price at which the unit is sold (in this case, $500).

■ *A price effect*. In order to sell that last unit, the monopolist must cut the market price on *all* units sold. This decreases total revenue (in this case, by $9 \times (-\$50) = -\$450$).

The quantity effect and the price effect are illustrated by the two shaded areas in panel (a) of Figure 11-5 on page 280. Increasing diamond sales from 9 to 10 means moving down the demand curve from *A* to *B*, reducing the price per diamond from $550 to $500. The green-shaded area represents the quantity effect: De Beers sells the 10th diamond at a price of $500. This is offset, however, by the price effect, represented by the orange-shaded area. In order to sell that 10th diamond, De Beers must reduce the price on all its diamonds from $550 to $500. So it loses $9 \times \$50 = \$450$ in revenue, the orange-shaded area. So, as point *C* indicates, the total effect on revenue of selling one more diamond—the marginal revenue—derived from an increase in diamond sales from 9 to 10 is only $50.

Point *C* lies on the monopolist's marginal revenue curve, labeled *MR* in panel (a) of Figure 11-5 and taken from the last column of Table 11-1. The crucial point about the monopolist's marginal revenue curve is that it is always *below* the demand curve.

## TABLE 11-1

### Demand, Total Revenue, and Marginal Revenue for the De Beers Monopoly

| Price of diamond $P$ | Quantity of diamonds $Q$ | Total revenue $TR = P \times Q$ | Marginal revenue $MR = \Delta TR/\Delta Q$ |
|---|---|---|---|
| $1,000 | 0 | $0 | |
| | | | $950 |
| 950 | 1 | 950 | |
| | | | 850 |
| 900 | 2 | 1,800 | |
| | | | 750 |
| 850 | 3 | 2,550 | |
| | | | 650 |
| 800 | 4 | 3,200 | |
| | | | 550 |
| 750 | 5 | 3,750 | |
| | | | 450 |
| 700 | 6 | 4,200 | |
| | | | 350 |
| 650 | 7 | 4,550 | |
| | | | 250 |
| 600 | 8 | 4,800 | |
| | | | 150 |
| 550 | 9 | 4,950 | |
| | | | 50 |
| 500 | 10 | 5,000 | |
| | | | −50 |
| 450 | 11 | 4,950 | |
| | | | −150 |
| 400 | 12 | 4,800 | |
| | | | −250 |
| 350 | 13 | 4,550 | |
| | | | −350 |
| 300 | 14 | 4,200 | |
| | | | −450 |
| 250 | 15 | 3,750 | |
| | | | −550 |
| 200 | 16 | 3,200 | |
| | | | −650 |
| 150 | 17 | 2,550 | |
| | | | −750 |
| 100 | 18 | 1,800 | |
| | | | −850 |
| 50 | 19 | 950 | |
| | | | −950 |
| 0 | 20 | 0 | |

## Figure 11-5

### A Monopolist's Demand, Total Revenue, and Marginal Revenue Curves

Panel (a) shows the monopolist's demand and marginal revenue curves for diamonds from Table 11-1. The marginal revenue curve lies below the demand curve. To see why, consider point *A* on the demand curve, where 9 diamonds are sold at $550 each, generating total revenue of $4,950. To sell a 10th diamond, the price on all 10 diamonds must be cut to $500, as shown by point *B*. As a result, total revenue increases by the green area (the quantity effect: $500) but decreases by the orange area (the price effect: –$450). So the marginal revenue from the 10th diamond is $50 (the difference between the green and orange areas) which is much lower than its price, $500.

Panel (b) shows the monopolist's total revenue curve for diamonds. As output goes from 0 to 10 diamonds, total revenue increases. It reaches its maximum at 10 diamonds—the level at which marginal revenue is equal to 0—and declines thereafter. The quantity effect dominates the price effect when total revenue is rising; the price effect dominates the quantity effect when total revenue is falling. **>web...**

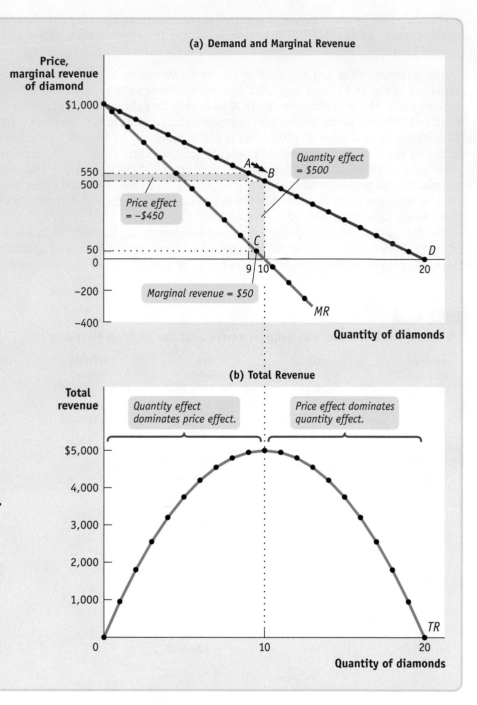

**(a) Demand and Marginal Revenue**

Price, marginal revenue of diamond

Quantity effect = $500

Price effect = –$450

Marginal revenue = $50

MR

Quantity of diamonds

**(b) Total Revenue**

Total revenue

Quantity effect dominates price effect.

Price effect dominates quantity effect.

TR

Quantity of diamonds

That's because of the price effect, which means that a monopolist's marginal revenue from selling an additional unit is always less than the price the monopolist receives for that unit. It is the price effect that creates the wedge between the monopolist's marginal revenue curve and the demand curve: in order to sell an additional diamond, De Beers must cut the market price on all units sold.

In fact, this wedge exists for any firm that possesses market power, such as oligopolists. Having market power means that the firm faces a downward-sloping demand curve. As a result, there will always be a price effect from an increase in its output. So for a firm with market power, the marginal revenue curve always lies below its demand curve.

Take a moment to compare the monopolist's marginal revenue curve with the marginal revenue curve for a perfectly competitive producer, one without market power. For such a producer there is no price effect from an increase in output: its marginal revenue curve is simply its horizontal demand curve. So for a perfectly competitive producer, market price and marginal revenue are always equal.

To emphasize how the quantity and price effects offset each other for a producer with market power, De Beers's total revenue curve is shown in panel (b) of Figure 11-5. Notice that it is hill-shaped: as output rises from 0 to 10 diamonds, total revenue increases. This reflects the fact that *at low levels of output, the quantity effect is stronger than the price effect:* as the monopolist sells more, it has to lower the price on only very few units, so the price effect is small. As output rises beyond 10 diamonds, total revenue actually falls. This reflects the fact that *at high levels of output, the price effect is stronger than the quantity effect:* as the monopolist sells more, it now has to lower the price on many units of output, making the price effect very large. Correspondingly, the marginal revenue curve lies below zero at output levels above 10 diamonds. For example, an increase in diamond production from 11 to 12 yields only $400 for the 12th diamond, simultaneously reducing the revenue from diamonds 1 through 11 by $550. As a result, the marginal revenue of the 12th diamond is –$150.

## The Monopolist's Profit-Maximizing Output and Price

To complete the story of how a monopolist maximizes profit, we now bring in the monopolist's marginal cost. Let's assume that there is no fixed cost of production, and we'll also assume that the marginal cost of producing an additional diamond is constant at $200, no matter how many diamonds De Beers produces. Then marginal cost will always equal average total cost and the marginal cost curve (and the average total cost curve) is a horizontal line at $200, as shown in Figure 11-6.

---

### Figure 11-6

**The Monopolist's Profit-Maximizing Output and Price**

This figure shows the demand, marginal revenue, and marginal cost curves. Marginal cost per diamond is $200, so the marginal cost curve is horizontal at $200. According to the optimal output rule, the profit-maximizing quantity of output for the monopolist is at $MR = MC$, shown by point $A$, where the marginal cost and marginal revenue curves cross at an output of 8 diamonds. The price De Beers can charge per diamond is found by going to the point on the demand curve directly above point $A$, which is point $B$ here—a price of $600 per diamond. It makes a profit of $400 \times 8 = $3,200. A perfectly competitive industry produces the output level at which $P = MC$, given by point $C$, where the demand curve and marginal cost curves cross. So a competitive industry produces 16 diamonds, sells at a price of $200, and makes zero profit.

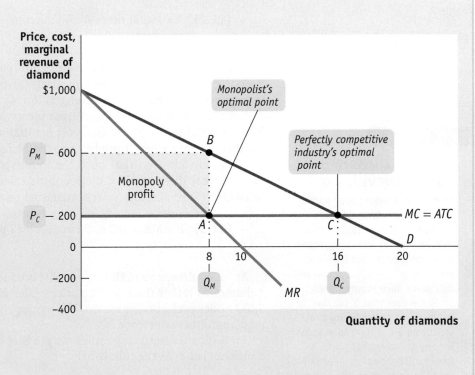

**FINDING THE MONOPOLY PRICE**

In order to find the *profit-maximizing quantity of output* for a monopolist, you look for the point where the marginal revenue curve crosses the marginal cost curve. Point *A* in Figure 11-6 is an example.

However, it's important not to fall into a common error: imagining that point *A* also shows the *price* at which the monopolist sells its output. It doesn't: it shows the *marginal revenue* received by the monopolist, which we know is less than the price.

To find the monopoly price, you have to go up vertically from *A* to the demand curve. There you find the price at which consumers demand the profit-maximizing quantity. So the profit-maximizing price–quantity combination is always a point on the demand curve, like *B* in Figure 11-6.

To maximize profit, the monopolist compares marginal cost with marginal revenue. If marginal revenue exceeds marginal cost, De Beers increases profit by producing more; if marginal revenue is less than marginal cost, De Beers increases profit by producing less. So the monopolist maximizes its profit by using the optimal output rule:

**(11-1)** *MR = MC at the monopolist's profit-maximizing quantity of output*

The monopolist's optimal point is shown in Figure 11-6. At *A*, the marginal cost curve, *MC*, crosses the marginal revenue curve, *MR*. The corresponding output level, 8 diamonds, is the monopolist's profit-maximizing quantity of output, $Q_M$. The price at which consumers demand 8 diamonds is $600, so the monopolist's price, $P_M$, is $600—corresponding to point *B*. The cost of producing each diamond is $200, so the monopolist earns a profit of $600 – $200 = $400 per diamond, and total profit is 8 × $400 = $3,200, as indicated by the shaded area.

## Monopoly versus Perfect Competition

When Cecil Rhodes consolidated many independent diamond producers into De Beers, he converted a perfectly competitive industry into a monopoly. We can now use our analysis to see the effects of such a consolidation.

Let's look again at Figure 11-6 and ask how this same market would work if, instead of being a monopoly, the industry were perfectly competitive. We will continue to assume that there is no fixed cost, and that marginal cost is constant, so average total cost and marginal cost are equal.

If the diamond industry consists of many perfectly competitive firms, each of those producers takes the market price as given. That is, each producer acts as if its marginal revenue is equal to the market price. So each firm within the industry uses the price-taking firm's optimal output rule:

**(11-2)** *P = MC at the perfectly competitive firm's profit-maximizing quantity of output*

In Figure 11-6, this would correspond to producing at *C*, where the price per diamond, $P_C$, is $200, equal to the marginal cost of production. Profit-maximizing industry output under perfect competition, $Q_C$, is therefore 16 diamonds.

But does the perfectly competitive industry earn any profits at *C*? No: the price of $200 is equal to the production cost per diamond. So there are no economic profits for this industry when it produces at the perfectly competitive output level.

We've already seen that once the industry is consolidated into a monopoly, the result is very different. The monopolist's calculation of marginal revenue takes the price effect into account, so that marginal revenue is less than the price. That is,

**(11-3)** *P > MR = MC at the monopolist's profit-maximizing quantity of output*

As we've already seen, the monopolist produces less than the competitive industry—8 diamonds rather than 16. The price under monopoly is $600, compared with only $200 under perfect competition. The monopolist earns a positive profit, but the competitive industry does not.

So, just as we suggested earlier, we see that compared with a competitive industry, a monopolist does the following:

- Produces a smaller quantity: $Q_M < Q_C$
- Charges a higher price: $P_M > P_C$
- Earns a profit

**IS THERE A MONOPOLY SUPPLY CURVE?**

Given how a monopolist applies the optimal output rule, you might be tempted to ask what this implies for the supply curve of a monopolist. But this is a meaningless question: *monopolists don't have supply curves.*

Remember that a supply curve shows the quantity that producers are willing to supply for any given market price. A monopolist, however, does not take the price as given; it chooses a profit-maximizing quantity, taking into account its own ability to influence the price.

## MONOPOLY BEHAVIOR AND THE PRICE ELASTICITY OF DEMAND

A monopolist faces marginal revenue that is less than the market price. But how much lower? The answer depends on the *price elasticity of demand*.

Remember from Chapter 5 that the price elasticity of demand determines how *total revenue* from sales changes when the price falls. If the price elasticity is greater than 1, a fall in the price increases total revenue, because the rise in the quantity demanded outweighs the lower price of each unit sold. If the elasticity is less than 1, a lower price reduces total revenue.

When a monopolist increases output by one unit, it must reduce the market price in order to sell that unit. If the price elasticity of demand is less than 1, this will actually reduce revenue—that is, marginal revenue will be negative. The monopolist can only increase revenue by producing more if the price elastic-

ity of demand is greater than 1; the higher the elasticity, the closer the additional revenue is to the initial market price.

What this tells us is that the difference between monopoly behavior and perfect competition depends on the price elasticity of demand. A monopolist that faces highly elastic demand will behave almost like a firm in a perfectly competitive industry.

For example, Amtrak has a monopoly of intercity passenger service in the Northeast Corridor, but it has very little ability to raise prices: potential train travelers will switch to cars and planes. In contrast, a monopolist that faces less elastic demand—like most cable TV companies—will behave very differently from a perfect competitor: it will charge much higher prices and restrict output more.

## Monopoly: The General Picture

Figure 11-6 involved specific numbers and assumed that the marginal cost curve was a horizontal line. Figure 11-7 shows a more general picture of monopoly in action: *D* is the market demand curve; *MR*, the marginal revenue curve; *MC*, the marginal cost curve; and *ATC*, the average total cost curve. Here we return to the usual assumption that the marginal cost curve has a "swoosh" shape and the average total cost curve is U-shaped.

Applying the optimal output rule, we see that the profit-maximizing level of output is the output at which marginal revenue equals marginal cost, indicated by point

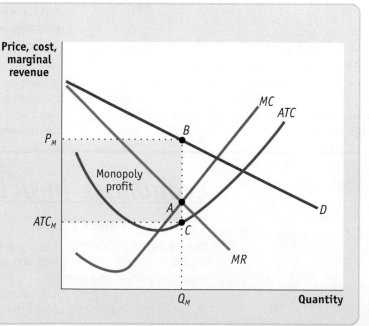

### Figure 11-7

**The Monopolist's Profit**

In this case, the marginal cost curve has a "swoosh" shape and the average total cost curve is U-shaped. The monopolist maximizes profit by producing the level of output at which $MR = MC$, given by point *A*, generating quantity $Q_M$. It finds its monopoly price, $P_M$, from the point on the demand curve directly above point *A*, point *B* here. The average total cost of $Q_M$ is shown by point *C*. Profit is given by the area of the shaded rectangle. **>web...**

A. The profit-maximizing quantity of output is $Q_M$, and the price charged by the monopolist is $P_M$. At the profit-maximizing level of output, the monopolist's average total cost is $ATC_M$, shown by point C.

Recalling how we calculated profit in Equation 8-5 on page 196, profit is equal to the difference between total revenue and total cost. So we have

$$
\begin{aligned}
\textbf{(11-4)} \quad \text{Profit} &= TR - TC \\
&= (P_M \times Q_M) - (ATC_M \times Q_M) \\
&= (P_M - ATC_M) \times Q_M
\end{aligned}
$$

Profit is equal to the area of the shaded rectangle in Figure 14-7, with a height of $P_M - ATC_M$ and a width of $Q_M$.

In Chapter 8 we learned that a perfectly competitive industry can have profits *in the short run but not in the long run*. In the short run price can exceed average total cost, allowing a perfectly competitive firm to make a profit. But we also know that this cannot persist. In the long run, any profit in a perfectly competitive industry will be competed away as new firms enter the market. In contrast, a monopolist can make profits in both the short run and the long run.

## WORK IT OUT

### PROFIT MAXIMIZATION FOR A MONOPOLIST

Suppose a monopolist faces the demand curve depicted below. The monopolist's marginal cost curve is also shown.

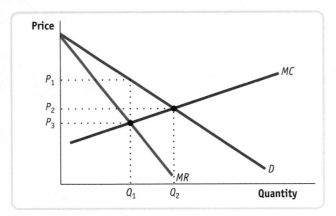

**Profit-Maximizing Quantity:** What quantity should the monopolist produce in order to maximize profit?

SOLUTION: As always, the profit-maximizing quantity is the quantity where MR equals MC. In this case, the monopolist should produce quantity $Q_1$ because this is the quantity where MR equals MC.

**Profit-Maximizing Price:** What price should the monopolist charge?

SOLUTION: The monopolist should charge the maximum price the market will bear at the profit-maximizing quantity, $Q_1$. That price is read off the demand curve. The monopolist should charge price $P_1$.

**Monopolist's Profit:** Can we determine how much profit the monopolist will receive?

SOLUTION: No, we can't. We need an average total cost (ATC) curve in order to answer the question. With the information given in the graph, the question is unanswerable.

**Comparison with Perfect Competition:** Suppose that this industry was instead characterized by perfect competition, and that the monopolist's marginal cost curve was instead the market supply curve, S. In this case, what would be the equilibrium market price and equilibrium market quantity?

SOLUTION: If instead this market was characterized by perfect competition, and the individual marginal cost curves summed to the monopolist's marginal cost curve, the equilibrium market price would be $P_2$, lower than the monopolist's price. The equilibrium quantity would be $Q_2$, greater than the monopolist's quantity.

# economics in action

## California Power Play?

The winter of 2000–2001 was a grim time for California, as power shortages gripped the state. One factor involved was the soaring price of natural gas, especially in the southern part of the state.

The strange thing was that natural gas prices in California were much higher than in Texas, the source of most of the state's natural gas. That is, the marginal cost of supplying natural gas to California—the cost of buying it in Texas, plus the small expense of shipping it across state lines—was much less than the price of California gas. So why wasn't more gas supplied?

The answer appears to have been that natural gas is transported via interstate pipelines and that the El Paso Corporation, which held a near-monopoly of pipelines supplying southern California, deliberately restricted the quantity of gas available in order to drive up market prices.

Because pipelines tend to be monopolies, they are subject to *price regulation*, discussed later in this chapter. As a result, the price a pipeline company can charge for shipping natural gas is limited. However, El Paso, in addition to running the pipelines, also has an unregulated subsidiary that sells natural gas in California. A judge at the Federal Energy Regulatory Commission concluded that the company used its control of the pipeline to drive up the prices received by its marketing subsidiary. It did this by reducing output—by running pipelines at low pressure and by scheduling nonessential maintenance during periods of peak demand. This conclusion was partly based on internal memos at El Paso, which seemed to say that the company was "idling large blocks of transport" to widen price spreads between natural gas delivered to Texas and to California.

El Paso denied the charges and has never admitted exercising market power. In 2003, however, the company agreed to a settlement in which it paid the state of California $1.7 billion. Many analysts—including the staff at the Federal Energy Regulatory Commission—believe that El Paso's exercise of market power in the natural gas market was part of a broad pattern of market manipulation that played a key role in California's energy crisis during 2000–2001. ■

> > > > > > > > > > > > > > > > > > > >

## >>CHECK YOUR UNDERSTANDING 11-2

1. Use the accompanying total revenue schedule of Emerald, Inc., a monopoly producer of 10-carat emeralds, to calculate the answers to parts a–d. Then answer part e.
   a. The demand schedule
   b. The marginal revenue schedule
   c. The quantity effect component of marginal revenue per output level
   d. The price effect component of marginal revenue per output level
   e. What additional information is needed to determine Emerald, Inc.'s profit-maximizing output?

| Quantity of emeralds demanded | Total revenue |
|---|---|
| 1 | $100 |
| 2 | 186 |
| 3 | 252 |
| 4 | 280 |
| 5 | 250 |

2. Use Figure 11-6 to show what happens to the following when the marginal cost of diamond production rises from $200 to $400.
   a. Marginal cost curve
   b. Profit-maximizing quantity
   c. Profit of the monopolist
   d. Perfectly competitive industry profits

Solutions appear at back of book.

## >>QUICK REVIEW

➤ The crucial difference between a producer with market power, such as a monopolist, and a producer in a perfectly competitive industry is that perfectly competitive producers are price-takers that face horizontal demand curves, but a producer with market power faces a downward-sloping demand curve.

➤ Due to the price effect of an increase in output, the marginal revenue curve of a producer with market power always lies below its demand curve. So a profit-maximizing monopolist chooses the output level at which marginal cost is equal to marginal revenue—*not* to price.

➤ As a result, the monopolist produces less and sells its output at a higher price than a perfectly competitive industry would. It earns a profit in the short run and the long run.

# Monopoly and Public Policy

It's good to be a monopolist, but it's not so good to be a monopolist's customer. A monopolist, by reducing output and raising prices, benefits at the expense of consumers. But buyers and sellers always have conflicting interests. Is the conflict of interest under monopoly any different than it is under perfect competition?

The answer is yes, because monopoly is a source of inefficiency: the losses to consumers from monopoly behavior are larger than the gains to the monopolist. Because monopoly leads to net losses for the economy, governments often try either to prevent the emergence of monopolies or to limit their effects. In this section we will see why monopoly leads to inefficiency and examine the policies governments adopt in an attempt to prevent this inefficiency.

## Welfare Effects of Monopoly

By restricting output below the level at which marginal cost is equal to the market price, a monopolist increases its profit but hurts consumers. To assess whether this is a net benefit or loss to society, we must compare the monopolist's gain in profit to the consumer loss. And what we learn is that the consumer loss is larger than the monopolist's gain. Monopoly causes a net loss for the economy.

To see why, let's return to the case where the marginal cost curve is horizontal and there is no fixed cost, as shown in the two panels of Figure 11-8. Here the marginal cost curve is $MC$, the demand curve is $D$, and, in panel (b), the marginal revenue curve is $MR$.

Panel (a) shows what happens if this industry is perfectly competitive. Equilibrium output is $Q_C$; the price of the good, $P_C$, is equal to marginal cost, and marginal cost is also equal to average total cost because there is no fixed cost and marginal cost is constant. Each firm is earning exactly its cost per unit of output, so there is no producer surplus in this equilibrium. The consumer surplus generated by the market is equal to the area of the blue-shaded triangle $CS_C$ shown in panel (a). Since there is no producer surplus when the industry is perfectly competitive, $CS_C$ also represents the total surplus.

Panel (b) shows the results for the same market, but this time assuming that the industry is a monopoly. The monopolist produces the level of output, $Q_M$, at which

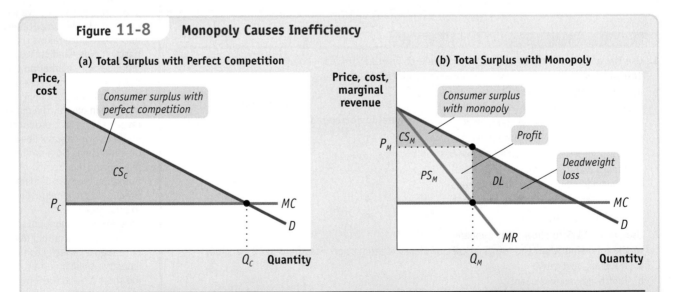

**Figure 11-8** **Monopoly Causes Inefficiency**

**(a) Total Surplus with Perfect Competition**

**(b) Total Surplus with Monopoly**

Panel (a) depicts a perfectly competitive industry: output is $Q_C$ and market price, $P_C$, is equal is to $MC$. Since price is exactly equal to each producer's cost of production per unit, there is no producer surplus. Total surplus is therefore equal to consumer surplus, the entire shaded area. Panel (b) depicts the industry under monopoly: the monopolist decreases output to $Q_M$ and charges $P_M$.

Consumer surplus (blue area) has shrunk because a portion of it is has been captured as profit (green area). Total surplus falls: the deadweight loss (orange area) represents the value of mutually beneficial transactions that do not occur because of monopoly behavior. **>web...**

marginal cost is equal to marginal revenue, and it charges the price $P_M$. The monopolist now earns profit—which is also the producer surplus—equal to the area of the green rectangle, $PS_M$. Note that this profit is surplus that has been captured from consumers as consumer surplus shrinks to the area of the blue triangle, $CS_M$.

By comparing panels (a) and (b), we see that in addition to the redistribution of surplus from consumers to the monopolist, another important change has occurred: the sum of profit and consumer surplus—total surplus—is *smaller* under monopoly than under perfect competition. That is, the sum of $CS_M$ and $PS_M$ is less than the area $CS_C$ in panel (a). In Chapter 6, we analyzed the concept of *deadweight loss*, the net loss caused by government policies such as taxes. Here we show that monopoly creates a deadweight loss to society equal to the area of the orange triangle, $DL$. So monopoly produces a net loss for the economy.

This net loss exists because some mutually beneficial transactions do not occur. There are people for whom an additional unit of the good is worth more than the marginal cost of producing it, but who don't consume it because they are not willing to pay $P_M$.

Those who recall our discussion of the deadweight loss from taxes in Chapter 6 will notice that the deadweight loss from monopoly looks quite similar. Indeed, by driving a wedge between price and marginal cost, monopoly acts much like a tax on consumers and produces the same kind of inefficiency.

So monopoly hurts the welfare of society as a whole and is a source of market failure. Is there anything government policy can do about it?

## Preventing Monopoly

Policy toward monopoly depends crucially on whether or not the industry in question is a natural monopoly, one in which economies of scale ensure that bigger producers have lower average total cost. If the industry is *not* a natural monopoly, the best policy is to prevent monopoly from arising or break it up if it already exists. Let's focus on that case first, then turn to the more difficult problem of dealing with natural monopoly.

The De Beers monopoly on diamonds didn't have to happen. Diamond production is not a natural monopoly: the industry's costs would be no higher if it consisted of a number of independent, competing producers (as is the case, for example, in gold production).

So if the South African government had been worried about how a monopoly would have affected consumers, it could have blocked Cecil Rhodes in his drive to dominate the industry or broken up his monopoly after the fact. Today, governments often try to prevent monopolies from forming and break up existing ones.

De Beers is a rather unique case: for complicated historical reasons, it was allowed to remain a monopoly. But over the last century, most similar monopolies have been broken up. The most celebrated example in the United States is Standard Oil, founded by John D. Rockefeller in 1870. By 1878 Standard Oil controlled almost all U.S. oil refining; but in 1911 a court order broke the company into a number of smaller units, including the companies that later became Exxon and Mobil (and more recently merged to become ExxonMobil).

The government policies used to prevent or eliminate monopolies are known as *antitrust policy*, which we will discuss in the next chapter.

## Dealing with Natural Monopoly

Breaking up a monopoly that isn't natural is clearly a good idea: the gains to consumers outweigh the loss to the producer. But it's not so clear whether a natural monopoly, one in which large producers have lower average total costs than small producers, should be broken up, because this would raise average total cost. For example, a town government that tried to prevent a single company from dominating local gas supply—which, as we've discussed, is almost surely a natural monopoly—would raise the cost of providing gas to its residents.

Yet even in the case of a natural monopoly, a profit-maximizing monopolist acts in a way that causes inefficiency—it charges consumers a price that is higher than marginal cost, and therefore prevents some potentially beneficial transactions. Also, it can seem unfair that a firm that has managed to establish a monopoly position earns large profits at the expense of consumers.

What can public policy do about this? There are two common answers.

### Public Ownership

In many countries, the preferred answer to the problem of natural monopoly has been **public ownership.** Instead of allowing a private monopolist to control an industry, the government establishes a public agency to provide the good and protect consumers' interests. For example, before 1984 in Britain, telephone service was provided by the state-owned British Telecom, and before 1987 airline travel was provided by the state-owned British Airways. (These companies still exist, but they have been privatized, competing with other firms in their respective industries.)

> In **public ownership** of a monopoly, the good is supplied by the government or by a firm owned by the government.

There are some examples of public ownership in the United States. Passenger rail service is provided by the public company Amtrak; regular mail delivery is provided by the U.S. Postal Service; some cities, including Los Angeles, have publicly owned electric power companies.

The advantage of public ownership, in principle, is that a publicly owned natural monopoly can set prices based on the criterion of efficiency rather than profit maximization. In a perfectly competitive industry, profit-maximizing behavior *is* efficient, because producers set prices equal to marginal cost; that is why there is no economic argument for public ownership of, say, wheat farms.

Experience suggests, however, that public ownership as a solution to the problem of natural monopoly often works badly in practice. One reason is that publicly owned firms are often less eager than private companies to keep costs down or offer high-quality products. Another is that publicly owned companies all too often end up serving political interests—providing contracts or jobs to people with the right connections. For example, Amtrak has notoriously provided train service at a loss to destinations that attract few passengers—but that are located in the districts of influential members of Congress.

### Regulation

In the United States, the more common answer has been to leave the industry in private hands but subject it to regulation. In particular, most local utilities like electricity, telephone service, natural gas, and so on are covered by **price regulation** that limits the prices they can charge.

> **Price regulation** limits the price that a monopolist is allowed to charge.

We saw in Chapter 4 that imposing a *price ceiling* on a competitive industry is a recipe for shortages, black markets, and other nasty side effects. Doesn't imposing a limit on the price that, say, a local gas company can charge have the same effects?

Not necessarily: a price ceiling on a monopolist need not create a shortage—in the absence of a price ceiling, a monopolist would charge a price that is higher than its marginal cost of production. So even if forced to charge a lower price—as long as that price is above *MC* and the monopolist at least breaks even on total output—the monopolist still has an incentive to produce the quantity demanded at that price.

Figure 11-9 shows an example of price regulation of a natural monopoly—a highly simplified version of a local gas company. The company faces a demand curve *D*, with an associated marginal revenue curve *MR*. For simplicity, we assume that the firm's total cost consists of two parts: a fixed cost and a variable cost that is incurred at a constant proportion to output. So marginal cost is constant in this case, and the marginal cost curve (which here is also the average variable cost curve) is a horizontal line at *MC*. The average total cost curve is the downward-sloping curve *ATC*; it is downward sloping because the higher the output, the lower the average fixed cost (the fixed cost per unit of output). Because average total cost is downward sloping over the range of output relevant for market demand, this is a natural monopoly.

Panel (a) illustrates a case of natural monopoly without regulation. The unregulated natural monopolist chooses the monopoly output $Q_M$ and charges the price $P_M$. Since the monopolist receives a price greater than its average total cost, it earns a profit. This profit is exactly equal to the producer surplus in this market,

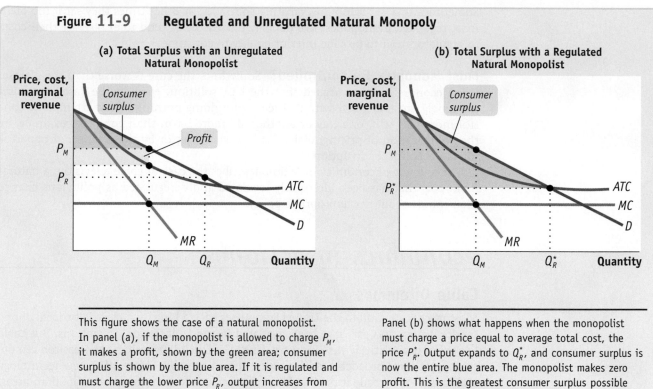

### Figure 11-9   Regulated and Unregulated Natural Monopoly

**(a) Total Surplus with an Unregulated Natural Monopolist**

Price, cost, marginal revenue

Consumer surplus

Profit

$P_M$

$P_R$

ATC

MC

D

MR

$Q_M$   $Q_R$   Quantity

**(b) Total Surplus with a Regulated Natural Monopolist**

Price, cost, marginal revenue

Consumer surplus

$P_M$

$P_R^*$

ATC

MC

D

MR

$Q_M$   $Q_R^*$   Quantity

This figure shows the case of a natural monopolist. In panel (a), if the monopolist is allowed to charge $P_M$, it makes a profit, shown by the green area; consumer surplus is shown by the blue area. If it is regulated and must charge the lower price $P_R$, output increases from $Q_M$ to $Q_R$, and consumer surplus increases.

Panel (b) shows what happens when the monopolist must charge a price equal to average total cost, the price $P_R^*$. Output expands to $Q_R^*$, and consumer surplus is now the entire blue area. The monopolist makes zero profit. This is the greatest consumer surplus possible when the monopolist is allowed to at least break even, making $P_R^*$ the best regulated price.

represented by the green-shaded rectangle. Consumer surplus is given by the blue-shaded triangle.

Now suppose that regulators impose a price ceiling on local gas deliveries—one that falls below the monopoly price $P_M$ but above ATC, say, at $P_R$ in panel (a). At that price the quantity demanded is $Q_R$.

Does the company have an incentive to produce that quantity? Yes. If the price at which the monopolist can sell its product is fixed by regulators, the firm's output no longer affects the market price—so it ignores the MR curve and is willing to expand output to meet the quantity demanded as long as the price it receives for the next unit is greater than marginal cost and the monopolist at least breaks even on total output. So with price regulation, the monopolist produces more, at a lower price.

Of course, the monopolist will not be willing to produce at all if the imposed price means producing at a loss. That is, the price ceiling has to be set high enough to allow the firm to cover its average total cost. Panel (b) shows a situation in which regulators have pushed the price down as far as possible, at the level where the average total cost curve crosses the demand curve. At any lower price the firm loses money. The price here, $P_R^*$, is the best regulated price: the monopolist is just willing to operate and produces $Q_R^*$, the quantity demanded at that price. Consumers and society gain as a result.

The welfare effects of this regulation can be seen by comparing the shaded areas in the two panels of Figure 11-9. Consumer surplus is increased by the regulation, with the gains coming from two sources. First, profits are eliminated and added instead to consumer surplus. Second, the larger output and lower price leads to an overall welfare gain—an increase in total surplus.

This all looks terrific: consumers are better off, profits are eliminated, and overall welfare increases. Unfortunately, things are rarely that easy in practice. The main problem is that regulators don't have the information required to set the price exactly at the level at which the demand curve crosses the average total cost curve.

Sometimes they set it too low, creating shortages; at other times they set it too high. Also, regulated monopolies, like publicly owned firms, tend to exaggerate their costs to regulators and to provide inferior quality to consumers.

**Must Monopoly Be Controlled?** Sometimes the cure is worse than the disease. Some economists have argued that the best solution, even in the case of natural monopoly, may be to live with it. The case for doing nothing is that attempts to control monopoly will, one way or another, do more harm than good—for example, by the politicization of pricing, which leads to shortages or by the creation of opportunities for political corruption.

The following Economics in Action describes the case of cable television, a natural monopoly that has been alternately regulated and deregulated as politicians change their minds about the appropriate policy.

# economics in action

## Cable Dilemmas

Most price regulation in the United States goes back a long way: electricity, local phone service, water, and gas have been regulated in most places for generations. But cable television is a relatively new industry. Until the late 1970s only rural areas too remote to support local broadcast stations were served by cable. After 1972 new technology and looser rules made it profitable to offer cable service to major metropolitan areas; new networks like HBO and CNN emerged to take advantage of the possibilities.

But local cable TV is clearly a natural monopoly: there are large fixed costs to running cable through a town that don't depend on how many people actually subscribe, so that having more than one cable company would involve a lot of wasteful duplication. But if the local cable company is a monopoly, should its prices be regulated?

At first most local governments thought so, and cable TV was subject to price regulation. In 1984, however, Congress passed a law prohibiting most local governments from regulating cable prices. (The law was the result both of widespread skepticism about whether price regulation was actually a good idea and of intensive lobbying by the cable companies.)

After the law went into effect, however, cable television rates increased sharply. The resulting consumer backlash led to a new law, in 1992, which once again allowed local governments to set limits on cable prices.

Was the new regulation a success? As measured by the prices of "basic" cable service, it was: after rising rapidly during the period of deregulation, the cost of basic service leveled off.

However, price regulation in cable applies only to "basic" service. Cable operators can try to evade the restrictions by charging more for premium channels like HBO or by offering fewer channels in the "basic" package. So some skeptics have questioned whether the regulation has actually been effective.

The story of cable television shows that making policy for natural monopolies is harder than the simplified model suggests. It also shows that sometimes governments have a hard time making up their minds! ■

< < < < < < < < < < < < < < < < < < < <

## >>CHECK YOUR UNDERSTANDING 11-3

1. What policy should the government adopt in the following cases? Explain.
   a. Internet service in Anytown, OH, is provided by cable. Customers feel they are being overcharged, but the cable company claims it must charge prices that let it recover the costs of laying cable.
   b. The only two airlines that currently fly to Alaska need government approval to merge. Other airlines wish to fly to Alaska but need government-allocated landing slots to do so.

continued

2. True or false? Explain your answer.
   a. Society's welfare is lower under monopoly because some consumer surplus is transformed into profit for the monopolist.
   b. A monopolist causes inefficiency because there are consumers who are willing to pay a price greater than or equal to marginal cost but less than the monopoly price.

3. Suppose a monopolist mistakenly believes that its marginal revenue is always equal to the market price. Assuming constant marginal cost and no fixed cost, draw a diagram comparing the level of profit, consumer surplus, total surplus, and deadweight loss for this misguided monopolist compared to a smart monopolist.

*Solutions appear at back of book.*

# Price Discrimination

Up to this point we have considered only the case of a **single-price monopolist,** one who charges all consumers the same price. As the term suggests, not all monopolists do this. In fact, many if not most monopolists find that they can increase their profits by charging different customers different prices for the same good: they engage in **price discrimination.**

The most striking example of price discrimination most of us encounter regularly involves airline tickets. Although there are a number of airlines, most routes in the United States are serviced by only one or two carriers, which, as a result, have market power and can set prices. So any regular airline passenger quickly becomes aware that the question "How much will it cost me to fly there?" rarely has a simple answer. If you are willing to buy a nonrefundable ticket a month in advance and stay over a Saturday night, the round trip may cost only $150—or less if you are a senior citizen or a student. But if you have to go on a business trip tomorrow, which happens to be Tuesday, and come back on Wednesday, the round trip might cost $550. Yet the business traveler and the visiting grandparent receive the same product—the same cramped seat, the same awful food.

You might object that airlines are not usually monopolists—that the airline industry is an oligopoly. In fact, price discrimination takes place under oligopoly and monopolistic competition as well as monopoly. But it doesn't happen under perfect competition. And once we've seen why monopolists sometimes price discriminate, we'll be in a good position to understand why it happens in other cases, too.

## The Logic of Price Discrimination

To get a preliminary view of why price discrimination might be more profitable than charging all consumers the same price, imagine that Air Sunshine offers the only nonstop flights between Bismarck, North Dakota, and Ft. Lauderdale, Florida. Assume that there are no capacity problems—the airline can fly as many planes as the number of passengers warrants. Also assume that there is no fixed cost. The marginal cost to the airline of providing a seat is $125, however many passengers it carries.

Further assume that the airline knows there are two kinds of potential passengers. First, there are business travelers, 2,000 of whom want to travel between the destinations each week. Second, there are students, 2,000 of whom also want to travel each week.

Will potential passengers take the flight? It depends on the price. The business travelers, it turns out, really want to fly; they will take the plane as long as the price is no more than $550. The students, however, have less money and more time; if the price goes above $150, they will take the bus.

So what should the airline do? If it has to charge everyone the same price, its options are limited. It could charge $550; that way it would get as much as possible out of the business travelers but lose the student market. Or it could charge only $150; that way it would get both types of travelers but would not make as much money on the business travelers as it might have.

We can quickly calculate the profits from each of these alternatives. If the airline charged $550, it would sell 2,000 tickets to the business travelers, getting total revenues

**A single-price monopolist** offers its product to all consumers at the same price.

Sellers engage in **price discrimination** when they charge different prices to different consumers for the same good.

### Figure 11-10

#### Two Types of Airline Customers

Air Sunshine has two types of customers, business travelers willing to pay $550 per ticket and students willing to pay $150 per ticket. There are 2,000 of each kind of customer. Air Sunshine has constant marginal cost of $125 per seat. If Air Sunshine could charge these two types of customers different prices, it would maximize its profit by charging business travelers $550 and students $150 per ticket. It would capture all of the consumer surplus as profit.

**>web...**

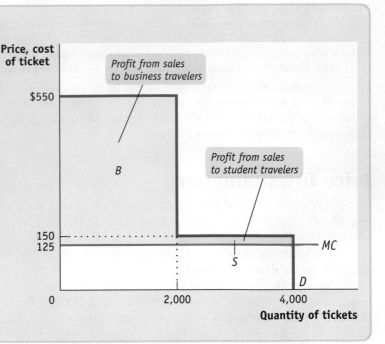

of 550 × 2,000 = $1.1 million and incurring costs of 125 × 2,000 = $250,000; so its profit would be $850,000. If the airline charged only $150, it would sell 4,000 tickets, receiving revenue of 4,000 × 150 = $600,000 and incurring costs of 4,000 × 125 = $500,000; so its profit would be $100,000. If the airline must charge everyone the same price, charging the higher price is clearly more profitable.

What the airline would really like to do, however, is charge the business travelers the full $550 but offer $150 tickets to the students. That's a lot less than the price paid by business travelers, but it's still above marginal cost; so if the airline could sell those extra 2,000 tickets to students, it would make an additional $50,000 in profit.

In this example we assume that cutting the price below $550 will not lead to *any* additional business travel and that at a price above $150 *no* students will fly. The implied demand curve is shown in Figure 11-10.

It would be more realistic to suppose that there is some "give" in the demand of each group. But this, it turns out, does not do away with the argument for price discrimination. The important point is that the two groups of consumers differ in their *sensitivity to price*—that a high price has a larger effect in discouraging purchases by students than by business travelers. As long as different groups of customers respond differently to the price, a monopolist will find that it can capture more consumer surplus and increase its profit by charging them different prices.

## Price Discrimination and Elasticity

A more realistic description of the demand that airlines face would not specify particular prices at which different types of travelers would choose to fly. Instead, it would distinguish between the groups on the basis of their sensitivity to the price—their price elasticity of demand.

Suppose that a company sells its product to two easily identifiable groups of people—business travelers and students. It just so happens that business travelers are very insensitive to the price: there is a certain amount of the product they just have to have whatever the price, but they cannot be persuaded to buy much more than that no matter how cheap it is. Students, though, are more flexible: offer a good enough price and they will buy quite a lot, but raise the price too high and they will switch to something else. What should the company do?

The answer is the one already suggested by our simplified example: the company should charge business travelers, with their low price elasticity of demand, a higher price than it charges students, with their high price elasticity of demand.

The actual situation of the airlines is very much like this hypothetical example. Business travelers typically place a high priority on being at the right place at the right time and are not too sensitive to the price. But nonbusiness travelers faced with a high price might take the bus, drive to another airport to get a lower fare, or skip the trip altogether.

So why doesn't an airline simply announce different prices for business and nonbusiness customers? First, this would probably be illegal (U.S. law places severe limits on the ability of companies to practice open price discrimination). Second, even if it were legal, it would be a hard policy to enforce: business travelers might be willing to wear casual clothing and claim they were visiting family in Ft. Lauderdale in order to save $400.

On many airline routes, the fare you pay depends on the type of traveler you are.

So what the airlines do—quite successfully—is impose rules that indirectly have the effect of charging business and nonbusiness travelers different fares. Business travelers usually travel during the week and want to be home on the weekend; so the round-trip fare is much higher if you don't stay over a Saturday night. The requirement of a weekend stay for a cheap ticket effectively separates business from nonbusiness travelers. Similarly, business travelers often visit several cities in succession rather than make a simple round trip; so round-trip fares are much lower than twice the one-way fare. Many business trips are scheduled on short notice; so fares are much lower if you book far in advance. Fares are also lower if you travel standby, taking your chances on whether you actually get a seat—business travelers have to make it to that meeting; people visiting their relatives don't. And by requiring customers to show their ID upon check-in, airlines make sure there are no resales of tickets between the two groups that would undermine their ability to price-discriminate—students can't buy cheap tickets and resell them to business travelers. Look at the rules that govern ticket-pricing, and you will see an ingenious implementation of profit-maximizing price discrimination.

## Perfect Price Discrimination

Let's return to the example of business travelers and students traveling between Bismarck and Ft. Lauderdale, illustrated in Figure 11-10, and ask what would happen if the airline could distinguish between the two groups of customers in order to charge each a different price.

Clearly, the airline would charge each group its willingness to pay—that is, as we learned in Chapter 6, the maximum that each group is willing to pay. For business travelers, the willingness to pay is $550, and it is $150 for students. As we have assumed, the marginal cost is $125 and does not depend on output, so that the marginal cost curve is a horizontal line. We can easily read off the airline's profit: it is the sum of the areas of the rectangle *B* and the rectangle *S*.

In this case, the consumers do not get any consumer surplus! The entire surplus is captured by the monopolist in the form of profit. When a monopolist is able to capture the entire surplus in this way, we say that it achieves **perfect price discrimination.**

In general, the greater the number of different prices a monopolist is able to charge, the closer it can get to perfect price discrimination. Figure 11-11 on page 294 shows a monopolist facing a downward-sloping demand curve; we suppose that this monopolist is able to charge different prices to different groups of consumers, with the consumers who are willing to pay the most being charged the most. In panel (a)

**Perfect price discrimination** takes place when a monopolist charges each consumer his or her willingness to pay—the maximum that consumer is willing to pay.

**Figure 11-11** **Price Discrimination**

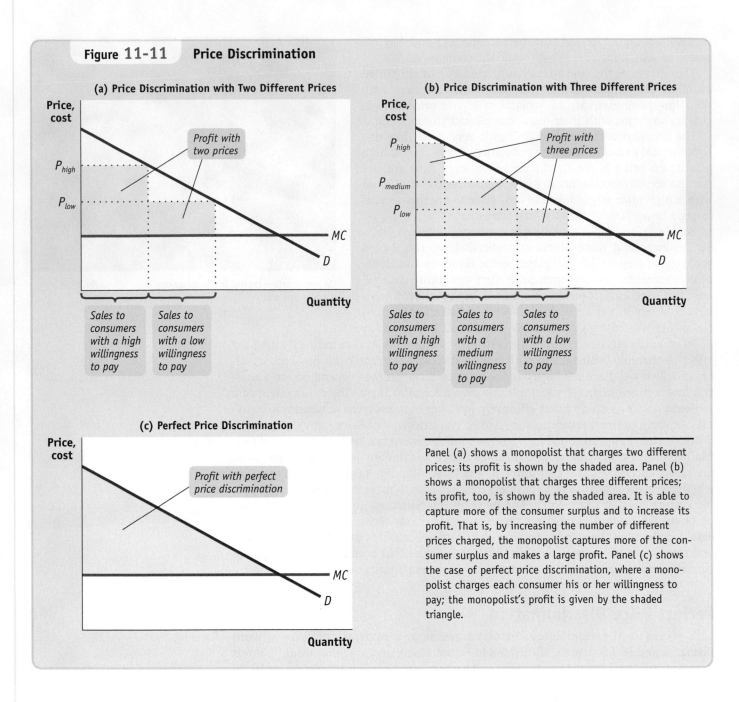

Panel (a) shows a monopolist that charges two different prices; its profit is shown by the shaded area. Panel (b) shows a monopolist that charges three different prices; its profit, too, is shown by the shaded area. It is able to capture more of the consumer surplus and to increase its profit. That is, by increasing the number of different prices charged, the monopolist captures more of the consumer surplus and makes a large profit. Panel (c) shows the case of perfect price discrimination, where a monopolist charges each consumer his or her willingness to pay; the monopolist's profit is given by the shaded triangle.

the monopolist charges two different prices; in panel (b) the monopolist charges three different prices. Two things are apparent:

- The greater the number of prices the monopolist charges, the lower the lowest price—that is, some consumers will pay prices that approach marginal cost.

- The greater the number of prices the monopolist charges, the more money it extracts from consumers.

With a very large number of different prices, the picture would look like panel (c), a case of perfect price discrimination. Here, consumers least willing to buy the good pay marginal cost, and the entire consumer surplus is extracted as profit.

Both our airline example and the example in Figure 11-11 can be used to make another point: a monopolist that can engage in perfect price discrimination doesn't cause any inefficiency! The reason is that the source of inefficiency is eliminated:

there are no potential consumers who would be willing to purchase the good at a price equal to or above marginal cost but do not get the chance to do so. Instead, the monopolist manages to "scoop up" these consumers by offering them lower prices than it charges others.

Perfect price discrimination is probably never possible in practice. At a fundamental level, the inability to achieve perfect price discrimination is a problem of prices as economic signals, a phenomenon we noted in Chapter 10. When prices work as economic signals, they convey the information needed to ensure that all mutually beneficial transactions will indeed occur: the market price signals the seller's cost, and a consumer signals willingness to pay by purchasing the good whenever that willingness to pay is at least as high as the market price. The problem in reality, however, is that prices are often not perfect signals: a consumer's true willingness to pay can be disguised, as by a business traveler who claims to be a student when buying a ticket in order to obtain a lower fare. When such disguises work, a monopolist cannot achieve perfect price discrimination. However, monopolists do try to move in the direction of perfect price discrimination through a variety of pricing strategies. Common techniques for price discrimination include the following:

- *Advance purchase restrictions.* Prices are lower for those who purchase well in advance (or in some cases for those who purchase at the last minute). This separates those who are likely to shop for better prices from those who won't.

- *Volume discounts.* Often the price is lower if you buy a large quantity. For a consumer who plans to consume a lot of a good, the cost of the last unit—the marginal cost to the consumer—is considerably less than the average price. This separates those who plan to buy a lot and are therefore likely to be more sensitive to price from those who don't.

- *Two-part tariffs.* In a discount club like Sam's Club (which is not a monopolist but a monopolistic competitor), you pay an annual fee in addition to the cost of the items you purchase. So the cost of the first item you buy is in effect much higher than that of subsequent items, thereby making the two-part tariff behave like a volume discount.

Our discussion also helps explain why government policies on monopoly typically focus on preventing deadweight losses, not preventing price discrimination—unless it causes serious issues of equity. Compared to a single-price monopolist, price discrimination—even when it is not perfect—can increase the efficiency of the market. If sales to consumers formerly priced out of the market but now able to purchase the good at a lower price generate enough surplus to offset the loss in surplus to those now facing a higher price and no longer buying the good, then total surplus increases when price discrimination is introduced. An example of this might be a drug that is disproportionately prescribed to senior citizens, who are often on fixed incomes and so are very sensitive to price. A policy that allows a drug company to charge senior citizens a low price and everyone else a high price may indeed increase total surplus compared to a situation in which everyone is charged the same price. But price discrimination that creates serious concerns about equity is likely to be prohibited—for example, an ambulance service that charges patients based on the severity of their emergency.

# *economics in action*

## Sales, Factory Outlets, and Ghost Cities

Have you ever wondered why department stores occasionally hold sales, offering their merchandise for considerably less than the usual prices? Or why, driving along America's highways, you sometimes encounter clusters of "factory outlet" stores, often a couple of hours' drive from the nearest city? These familiar features of the economic landscape are actually rather peculiar if you think about them: why should sheets and towels be suddenly cheaper for a week each winter, or raincoats be offered for less in Freeport, Maine, than in Boston? In each case the answer is that the sellers—who are often oligopolists or monopolistic competitors—are engaged in a subtle form of price discrimination.

Why hold regular sales of sheets and towels? Stores are aware that some consumers buy these goods only when they discover that they need them; they are not likely to put a lot of effort into searching for the best price and so have a relatively low price elasticity of demand. So the store wants to charge high prices for customers who come in on an ordinary day. But shoppers who plan ahead, looking for the lowest price, will wait until there is a sale. So by scheduling such sales only now and then, the store is in effect able to discriminate between high-elasticity and low-elasticity customers.

An outlet store serves the same purpose: by offering merchandise for low prices, but only a considerable distance away from downtown, a seller is able to establish a separate market for those customers who are willing to make a significant effort to search out lower prices—and who therefore have a relatively high price elasticity of demand.

Finally, let's return to airline tickets to mention one of the truly odd features of their prices. Often a flight from one major destination to another—say, from Chicago to Los Angeles—is cheaper than a much shorter flight to a smaller city—say, from Chicago to Salt Lake City. Again, the reason is a difference in the price elasticity of demand: customers have a choice of many airlines between Chicago and Los Angeles, so the demand for any one flight is quite elastic; customers have very little choice in flights to a small city, so the demand is much less elastic.

But often there is a flight between two major destinations that makes a stop along the way—say, a flight from Chicago to Los Angeles with a stop in Salt Lake. In these cases, it is sometimes cheaper to fly to the more distant city than to the city that is a stop along the way. For example, it may be cheaper to purchase a ticket to Los Angeles and get off in Salt Lake City than to purchase a ticket to Salt Lake City! It sounds ridiculous but makes perfect sense given the logic of monopoly pricing.

So why don't passengers simply buy a ticket from Chicago to Los Angeles, but get off at Salt Lake? Well, some do—but the airlines, understandably, make it difficult for customers to find out about such "ghost cities." In addition, the airline will not allow you to check baggage only part of the way if you have a ticket for the final destination. (And airlines refuse to honor tickets for return flights when a passenger has not completed all the legs of the outbound flight.) All these restrictions are meant to enforce the separation of markets necessary to allow price discrimination. ∎

< < < < < < < < < < < < < < < < < <

## >>CHECK YOUR UNDERSTANDING 11-4

1. True or false? Explain your answer.
   a. A single-price monopolist sells to some customers that a price-discriminating monopolist refuses to.
   b. A price-discriminating monopolist creates more inefficiency than a single-price monopolist because it captures more of the consumer surplus.
   c. Under price discrimination, a customer with highly elastic demand will pay a lower price than a customer with inelastic demand.

2. Which of the following are cases of price discrimination and which are not? In the cases of price discrimination, identify the consumers with high and those with low price elasticity of demand.
   a. Damaged merchandise is marked down.
   b. Restaurants have senior citizen discounts.
   c. Food manufacturers place discount coupons for their merchandise in newspapers.
   d. Airline tickets cost more during the summer peak flying season.

Solutions appear at back of book.

**>> QUICK REVIEW**

➤ Not every monopolist is a *single-price monopolist*. Many monopolists, as well as oligopolists and monopolistic competitors, engage in *price discrimination*.

➤ Price discrimination is profitable when consumers differ in their sensitivity to the price. A monopolist would like to charge high prices to consumers willing to pay them without driving away others who are willing to pay less.

➤ It is profit-maximizing to charge higher prices to consumers with a low price elasticity of demand and lower prices to those with a high price elasticity of demand.

➤ A monopolist able to charge each consumer his or her willingness to pay for the good achieves *perfect price discrimination* and does not cause inefficiency because all mutually beneficial transactions are exploited.

## • A LOOK AHEAD •

We've now taken one large step away from the world of perfect competition. As we have seen, a monopoly behaves quite differently from a perfectly competitive industry.

But pure monopoly is actually quite rare in the modern economy. More typical are industries in which there is some competition, but not perfect competition—that is, where there is *imperfect competition*. In the next chapter we examine two types of imperfect competition: oligopoly and monopolistic competition.

You might expect an oligopoly to act something like a cross between a monopoly and a perfectly competitive industry, but it turns out that oligopoly raises issues that arise neither in perfect competition nor in monopoly, issues of *strategic interaction* and *collusion* between firms. Likewise, monopolistic competition creates yet another set of issues, such as tastes, product differentiation, and advertising.

## SUMMARY

1. There are four main types of market structure based on number of firms in the industry and product differentiation: perfect competition, monopoly, oligopoly, and monopolistic competition.

2. A **monopolist** is a producer who is the sole supplier of a good without close substitutes. An industry controlled by a monopolist is a **monopoly.**

3. The key difference between a monopoly and a perfectly competitive industry is that an individual, perfectly competitive firm faces a horizontal demand curve but a monopolist faces a downward-sloping demand curve. This gives the monopolist **market power,** the ability to raise the market price by reducing output compared to a perfectly competitive industry.

4. To persist, a monopoly must be protected by a **barrier to entry.** This can take the form of control of natural resources or inputs, economies of scale that give rise to **natural monopoly,** technological advantage, or government rules that prevent entry by other firms.

5. The marginal revenue of a monopolist is composed of a quantity effect (the price received from the additional unit) and a price effect (the reduction in the price at which all units are sold). Because of the price effect, a monopolist's marginal revenue is always less than the market price, and the marginal revenue curve lies below the demand curve.

6. At the monopolist's profit-maximizing quantity of output, marginal cost equals marginal revenue, which is less than market price. At the perfectly competitive firm's profit-maximizing quantity of output, marginal cost equals the market price. So in comparison to perfectly competitive industries, monopolies produce less, charge higher prices, and earn higher profits in both the short run and the long run.

7. A monopoly creates deadweight loss by charging a price above marginal cost: the loss in consumer surplus exceeds the monopolist's profit. Thus monopolies are a source of market failure and should be prevented or broken up, except in the case of natural monopolies.

8. Natural monopolies can still cause deadweight losses. To limit these losses, governments sometimes impose **public ownership** and at other times impose **price regulation.** A price ceiling on a monopolist, as opposed to a perfectly competitive industry, need not cause shortages and can increase total surplus.

9. Not all monopolists are **single-price monopolists.** Monopolists, as well as oligopolists and monopolistic competitors, often engage in **price discrimination** to make higher profits, using various techniques to differentiate consumers based on their sensitivity to price and charging those with less elastic demand higher prices. A monopolist that achieves **perfect price discrimination** charges each consumer a price equal to his or her willingness to pay and captures the total surplus in the market. Although perfect price discrimination creates no inefficiency, it is practically impossible to implement.

## KEY TERMS

Monopolist, p. 273
Monopoly, p. 273
Market power, p. 274
Barrier to entry, p. 275

Natural monopoly, p. 275
Public ownership, p. 288
Price regulation, p. 288
Single-price monopolist, p. 291

Price discrimination, p. 291
Perfect price discrimination, p. 293

## PROBLEMS

1. Each of the following firms possesses market power. Explain its source.

   a. Merck, the producer of the patented cholesterol-lowering drug Zetia

   b. Verizon, a provider of local telephone service

   c. Chiquita, a supplier of bananas and owner of most banana plantations

2. Skyscraper City has a subway system, for which a one-way fare is $1.50. There is pressure on the mayor to reduce the fare by one-third, to $1.00. The mayor is dismayed, thinking that this will mean Skyscraper City is losing one-third of its revenue from sales of subway tickets. The mayor's economic adviser reminds her that she is focusing only on the price effect and ignoring the quantity effect. Explain why the mayor's estimate of a one-third loss of revenue is likely to be an overestimate. Illustrate with a diagram.

3. Consider an industry with the demand curve and marginal cost (MC) curve shown in the accompanying diagram. There is no fixed cost. If the industry is a single-price monopoly, the monopolist's marginal revenue curve would be MR. Answer the following questions by naming the appropriate points or areas.

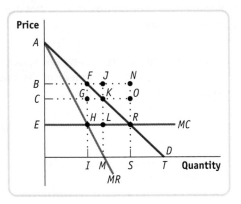

   a. If the industry is perfectly competitive, what will be the total quantity produced? At what price?

   b. Which area reflects consumer surplus under perfect competition?

   c. If the industry is a single-price monopoly, what quantity will the monopolist produce? Which price will it charge?

   d. Which area reflects the single-price monopolist's profit?

   e. Which area reflects consumer surplus under single-price monopoly?

   f. Which area reflects the deadweight loss to society from single-price monopoly?

   g. If the monopolist can price-discriminate perfectly, what quantity will the perfectly price-discriminating monopolist produce?

4. Bob, Bill, Ben, and Brad Baxter have just made a documentary movie about their basketball team. They are thinking about making the movie available for download on the Internet, and they can act as a single-price monopolist if they choose to. Each time the movie is downloaded, their Internet service provider charges them a fee of $4. The Baxter brothers are arguing about which price to charge customers per download. The accompanying table shows the demand schedule for their film.

| Price of download | Quantity of downloads demanded |
|---|---|
| $10 | 0 |
| 8 | 1 |
| 6 | 3 |
| 4 | 6 |
| 2 | 10 |
| 0 | 15 |

   a. Calculate the total revenue and the marginal revenue per download.

   b. Bob is proud of the film and wants as many people as possible to download it. Which price would he choose? How many downloads would be sold?

   c. Bill wants as much total revenue as possible. Which price would he choose? How many downloads would be sold?

   d. Ben wants to maximize profit. Which price would he choose? How many downloads would be sold?

   e. Brad wants to charge the efficient price. Which price would he choose? How many downloads would be sold?

5. Jimmy has a room that overlooks, from some distance, a major league baseball stadium. He decides to rent a telescope for $50.00 a week and charge his friends and classmates to use it to peep at the game for 30 seconds. He can act as a single-price monopolist for renting out "peeps." For each person who takes a 30-second peep, it costs Jimmy $0.20 to clean the eyepiece. The accompanying table shows the information Jimmy has gathered about the demand for the service.

| Price of peep | Quantity of peeps demanded |
|---|---|
| $1.20 | 0 |
| 1.00 | 100 |
| 0.90 | 150 |
| 0.80 | 200 |
| 0.70 | 250 |
| 0.60 | 300 |
| 0.50 | 350 |
| 0.40 | 400 |
| 0.30 | 450 |
| 0.20 | 500 |
| 0.10 | 550 |

**a.** For each price in the table, calculate the total revenue from selling peeps and the marginal revenue per peep.

**b.** At what quantity will Jimmy's profit be maximized? What price will he charge? What will his total profit be?

**c.** Jimmy's landlady complains about all the visitors coming into the building and tells Jimmy to stop selling peeps. Jimmy discovers, however, that if he gives the landlady $0.20 for every peep he sells, she will stop complaining. What effect does the $0.20-per-peep bribe have on Jimmy's marginal cost per peep? What is the new profit-maximizing quantity of peeps? What effect does the $0.20-per-peep bribe have on Jimmy's total profit?

6. Suppose that De Beers is a single-price monopolist in the market for diamonds. De Beers has five potential customers: Raquel, Jackie, Joan, Mia, and Sophia. Each of these customers will buy at most one diamond—and only if the price is just equal to, or lower than, her willingness to pay. Raquel's willingness to pay is $400; Jackie's, $300; Joan's, $200; Mia's, $100; and Sophia's, $0. De Beers's marginal cost per diamond is $100. This leads to the demand schedule for diamonds shown in the accompanying table.

| Price of diamond | Quantity of diamonds demanded |
|---|---|
| $500 | 0 |
| 400 | 1 |
| 300 | 2 |
| 200 | 3 |
| 100 | 4 |
| 0 | 5 |

**a.** Calculate De Beers's total revenue and its marginal revenue. From your calculation, draw the demand curve and the marginal revenue curve.

**b.** Explain why De Beers faces a downward-sloping demand curve.

**c.** Explain why the marginal revenue from an additional diamond sale is less than the price of the diamond.

**d.** Suppose De Beers currently charges $200 for its diamonds. If it lowered the price to $100, how large is the price effect? How large is the quantity effect?

**e.** Draw the marginal cost curve into your diagram and determine which quantity maximizes De Beers's profit and which price De Beers will charge.

7. Use the demand schedule for diamonds given in Problem 6. The marginal cost of producing diamonds is constant at $100. There is no fixed cost.

**a.** If De Beers charges the monopoly price, how large is the individual consumer surplus that each buyer experiences? Calculate total consumer surplus by summing the individual consumer surpluses. How large is producer surplus?

Suppose that upstart Russian and Asian producers enter the market and the market becomes perfectly competitive.

**b.** What is the perfectly competitive price? What quantity will be sold in this perfectly competitive market?

**c.** At the competitive price and quantity, how large is the consumer surplus that each buyer experiences? How large is total consumer surplus? How large is producer surplus?

**d.** Compare your answer to part c to your answer to part a. How large is the deadweight loss associated with monopoly in this case?

8. Use the demand schedule for diamonds given in Problem 6. De Beers is a monopolist, but it can now price-discriminate perfectly among all five of its potential customers. De Beers's marginal cost is constant at $100. There is no fixed cost.

**a.** If De Beers can price-discriminate perfectly, to which customers will it sell diamonds and at what prices?

**b.** How large is each individual consumer surplus? How large is total consumer surplus? Calculate producer surplus by summing the producer surplus generated by each sale.

9. Download Records decides to release an album by the group Mary and the Little Lamb. It produces the album with no fixed cost, but the total cost of downloading an album to a CD and paying Mary her royalty is $6 per album. Download Records can act as a single-price monopolist. Its marketing division finds that the demand schedule for the album is as shown in the accompanying table.

| Price of album | Quantity of albums demanded |
|---|---|
| $22 | 0 |
| 20 | 1,000 |
| 18 | 2,000 |
| 16 | 3,000 |
| 14 | 4,000 |
| 12 | 5,000 |
| 10 | 6,000 |
| 8 | 7,000 |

**a.** Calculate the total revenue and the marginal revenue per album.

**b.** The marginal cost of producing each album is constant at $6. To maximize profit, what level of output should Download Records choose, and which price should it therefore charge?

**c.** Mary renegotiates her contract and now needs to be paid a royalty of $14 per album. So the marginal cost rises to be constant at $14. To maximize profit, what level of output should Download Records now choose, and which price should it charge for each album?

10. The accompanying diagram illustrates your local electricity company's natural monopoly. The diagram shows the demand curve for kilowatt-hours (kWh) of electricity, the company's

marginal revenue (*MR*) curve, the marginal cost (*MC*) curve, and its average total cost (*ATC*) curve. The government wants to regulate the monopolist by imposing a price ceiling.

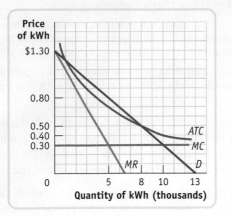

**a.** If the government does not regulate this monopolist, which price will it charge? Illustrate the inefficiency this creates by shading the deadweight loss from monopoly.

**b.** If the government imposes a price ceiling equal to the marginal cost, $0.30, will the monopolist make profits or lose money? Shade the area of profit (or losses) for the monopolist. If the government does impose this price ceiling, do you think the firm will continue to produce in the long run?

**c.** If the government imposes a price ceiling of $0.50, will the monopolist make a profit or lose money?

11. The movie theater in Collegetown serves two kinds of customers: students and professors. There are 900 students and 100 professors in Collegetown. Each student's willingness to pay for a movie ticket is $5. Each professor's willingness to pay for a movie ticket is $10. Each will buy at most one ticket. The movie theater's marginal cost per ticket is constant at $3, and there is no fixed cost.

   **a.** Suppose the movie theater cannot price-discriminate and needs to charge both students and professors the same price per ticket. If the movie theater charges $5, who will buy tickets and what will the movie theater's profit be? How large is consumer surplus?

   **b.** If the movie theater charges $10, who will buy movie tickets and what will the movie theater's profit be? How large is consumer surplus?

   **c.** Now suppose that, if it chooses to, the movie theater can price-discriminate between students and professors by requiring students to show their student ID. If the movie theater charges students $5 and professors $10, how much profit will the movie theater make? How large is consumer surplus?

12. A monopolist knows that if it expands the quantity of output it produces from 8 to 9 units, that will lower the price of its output from $2 to $1. Calculate the quantity effect and the price effect. Use these results to calculate the monopolist's marginal revenue of producing the 9th unit. The marginal cost of producing the 9th unit is positive. Is is a good idea for the monopolist to produce the 9th unit?

---

**>web...** To continue your study and review of concepts in this chapter, please visit the Krugman/Wells/Olney website for quizzes, animated graph tutorials, web links to helpful resources, and more.

**www.worthpublishers.com/krugmanwellsolney**

# >>Oligopoly, Monopolistic Competition, and Product Differentiation

## CAUGHT IN THE ACT

THE AGRICULTURAL PRODUCTS COMPANY Archer Daniels Midland (also known as ADM) likes to describe itself as "supermarket to the world." Its name is familiar to many Americans not only because of its important role in the economy but also because of its advertising and sponsorship of public television programs. But on October 25, 1993, ADM itself was on camera.

On that day executives from ADM and its Japanese competitor Ajinomoto met at the Marriott Hotel in Irvine, California, to discuss the market for lysine, an additive used in animal feed. (How is lysine produced? It's excreted by genetically engineered bacteria.) In this and subsequent meetings, the two companies joined with several other competitors to set targets for the market price of lysine. Each company agreed to limit its production in order to achieve those targets. Agreeing on specific limits would be their biggest challenge—or so they thought.

What the participants in the meeting didn't know was that they had a bigger problem: the FBI had bugged the room and was filming them with a camera hidden in a lamp.

What the companies were doing was illegal. To understand why it was illegal and why the companies were doing it anyway, we need to examine the issues posed by industries that are neither perfectly competitive nor pure monopolies. In this chapter we focus on *oligopoly*, an industry in which there are only a few producers. As we'll see, oligopoly is a very important reality—much more important, in fact, than monopoly and arguably more typical of modern economies than perfect competition.

Although much that we have learned about both perfect competition and monopoly is relevant to oligopoly, oligopoly

The law catches up with a colluding oligopolist.

AP/Wide World Photos

also raises some entirely new issues. Among other things, firms in an oligopoly are often tempted to engage in the kind of behavior that got ADM, Ajinomoto, and other lysine producers into trouble with the

## What you will learn in this chapter:

➤ The meaning of **oligopoly**, and why it occurs

➤ How our understanding of oligopoly can be enhanced by using **game theory**, especially the concept of the **prisoners' dilemma**

➤ How repeated interactions among oligopolists can help them achieve **tacit collusion**

➤ How oligopoly works in practice, under the legal constraints of **antitrust policy**

➤ How prices and profits are determined in **monopolistic competition** in the short run and the long run

➤ Why oligopolists and monopolistically competitive firms differentiate their products

➤ The economic significance of advertising and **brand names**

law. For example, in 2002 five of the largest music companies and three of the largest music retailers in the United States settled government charges that they worked together to keep the prices of CDs artificially high during the 1990s.

We will begin by examining what oligopoly is and how oligopolistic industries behave. Then we'll look at *antitrust policy*, which is primarily concerned with trying to keep oligopolies "well behaved."

Next we'll turn to a different market structure, *monopolistic competition*, and examine its characteristic features. Finally, we'll explore how oligopolistic and monopolistically competitive firms differentiate their products, in particular, the role of advertising.

# Oligopoly

---

An **oligopoly** is an industry with only a small number of producers. A producer in such an industry is known as an **oligopolist.**

---

At the time of that elaborately bugged meeting, no one company controlled the world lysine industry, but there were only a few major producers. An industry with only a few sellers is known as an **oligopoly;** a firm in such an industry is known as an **oligopolist.**

Oligopolists obviously compete with each other for sales. But ADM and Ajinomoto weren't like firms in a perfectly competitive industry, which take the price at which they can sell their product as given. Each of these firms knew that its decision about how much to produce would affect the market price. That is, like monopolists, each of the firms had some *market power*. So the competition in this industry wasn't "perfect."

---

When no one firm has a monopoly, but producers nonetheless realize that they can affect market prices, an industry is characterized by **imperfect competition.**

---

Economists refer to a situation in which firms compete but also possess market power—which enables them to affect market prices—as **imperfect competition.** As we saw in Chapter 11, there are actually two important forms of imperfect competition: oligopoly and *monopolistic competition*. Of these, oligopoly is probably the more important in practice.

Although lysine is a multibillion-dollar business, it is not exactly a product familiar to most consumers. However, many familiar goods and services are supplied by only a few competing sellers, which means the industries in question are oligopolies.

For example, most air routes are served by only two or three airlines: in recent years, regularly scheduled shuttle service between New York and either Boston or Washington, D.C. has been provided only by Delta and US Airways. Similarly, most long-distance telephone service is supplied by one of three carriers: AT&T, MCI, or Sprint. Most cola beverages are sold by Coca-Cola and Pepsi. This list could go on for many pages.

It's important to realize that an oligopoly isn't necessarily made up of large firms. What matters isn't size per se; the question is how many competitors there are. When a small town has only two grocery stores, grocery service there is just as much an oligopoly as air shuttle service between New York and Washington.

Why are oligopolies so prevalent? Essentially, oligopoly is the result of the same factors that sometimes produce monopoly, but in somewhat weaker form. Probably the most important source of oligopoly is the existence of *economies of scale*, which give bigger producers a cost advantage over smaller ones. When these economies of scale are very strong, they lead to monopoly, but when they are not that strong they lead to competition among a small number of firms. For example, larger grocery stores typically have lower costs than smaller stores. But the advantages of large scale taper off once gro-

Rhonda Sidney/The Image Works

Froot Loops or Wheaties? Four firms control nearly 83 percent of the breakfast cereal market.

cery stores are reasonably large, which is why two or three stores often survive in small towns.

If oligopoly is so common, why has most of this book focused on competition in industries where the number of sellers is very large? And why did we study monopoly, which is relatively uncommon, first? The answer has two parts. First, much of what we learn from the study of perfectly competitive markets—about costs, entry and exit, and efficiency—remains valid despite the fact that many industries are not perfectly competitive. Second, the analysis of oligopoly turns out to present some puzzles for which there is no easy solution. It is almost always a good idea—in exams and in life—first to deal with the questions you can answer, then to puzzle over the harder ones. We have simply followed the same strategy, developing the relatively clear-cut theories of perfect competition and monopoly first, and only then turning to the puzzles presented by oligopoly.

## Understanding Oligopoly

How much will a firm produce? Up to this point we have always answered: the quantity that maximizes its profit. The assumption that firms maximize profit is enough to determine their output when they are perfect competitors or when the industry is a monopoly.

When it comes to oligopoly, however, we run into some difficulties. Indeed, economists often describe the behavior of oligopolistic firms as a "puzzle."

Let's begin looking at the puzzle of oligopoly with the simplest version, an industry in which there are only two producing firms—a **duopoly**—and each is known as a **duopolist.** With only two firms in the industry, each would realize that by producing more it would drive down the market price. So each firm would, like a monopolist, realize that profits would be higher if it limited its production.

One way for the two companies to increase their profits is to engage in **collusion**— they will cooperate to raise each other's profits. The strongest form of collusion is a **cartel,** an arrangement—illegal in the United States—that determines how much each firm is allowed to produce. But even if the two firms agreed on a deal, they might have a problem: each of the firms would have an incentive to break its word and produce more than the agreed-upon quantity.

And if one firm in a duopoly increases its production, prices will fall, lowering the other firm's profit. Each oligopolist realizes both that its profit depends on what its competitor does and that its competitor's profit depends on what it does. That is, the two firms are in a situation of **interdependence.**

In effect, the two firms are playing a "game" in which the profit of each player depends not only on its own actions but on those of the other player. The area of study of such games, known as **game theory,** has many applications, not just to economics but also to military strategy, politics, and other social sciences.

Let's see how game theory helps us understand oligopoly.

## The Prisoners' Dilemma

Game theory deals with any situation in which the reward to any one player—the **payoff**—depends not only on his or her own actions but also on those of other players in the game. In the case of oligopolists, the payoff is simply each firm's profit.

When there are only two players, as in a duopoly, the interdependence between the players can be represented with a **payoff matrix** like that shown in Figure 12-1 on page 304. Each row corresponds to an action by one player (in this case, ADM); each column corresponds to an action by the other (in this case, Ajinomoto). For simplicity, let's assume that ADM can pick only one of two alternatives: produce 30 million pounds of lysine or produce 40 million pounds. Ajinomoto has the same pair of choices.

The matrix contains four boxes, each divided by a diagonal line. Each box shows the payoff to the two firms that results from a pair of choices; the number

An oligopoly consisting of only two firms is a **duopoly.** Each firm is known as a **duopolist.**

Sellers engage in **collusion** when they cooperate to raise each others' profits. A **cartel** is an agreement by several producers that increases their combined profits by telling each one how much to produce.

When the decisions of two or more firms significantly affect each others' profits, they are in a situation of **interdependence.**

The study of behavior in situations of interdependence is known as **game theory.**

The reward received by a player in a game, such as the profit earned by an oligopolist, is that player's **payoff.**

A **payoff matrix** shows how the payoff to each of the participants in a two-player game depends on the actions of both. Such a matrix helps us analyze interdependence.

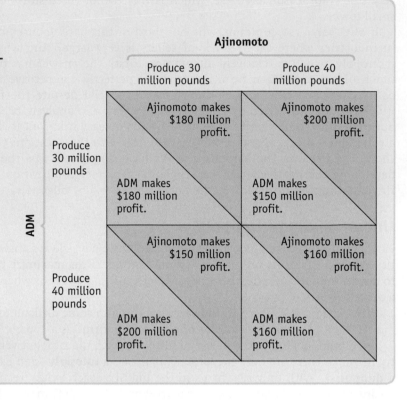

### Figure 12-1

### A Payoff Matrix

Two firms, ADM and Ajinomoto, must decide how much lysine to produce. The profits of the two firms are *interdependent*: each firm's profit depends not only on its own decision but also on the other's decision. Each row represents an action by ADM, each column one by Ajinomoto. Both firms will be better off if they both choose the lower output; but it is in each firm's individual interest to choose higher output.

below the diagonal shows ADM's profits; the number above the diagonal shows Ajinomoto's profits.

These payoffs show the benefits of collusion: the combined profit of the two firms is maximized if they each produce only 30 million pounds. Either firm can, however, increase its own profits by producing 40 million pounds while the other produces only 30 million pounds. But if both produce the larger quantity, both will have lower profits than if they had both held their output down.

The particular situation shown here is a version of a famous—and seemingly paradoxical—case of interdependence that appears in many contexts. Known as the **prisoners' dilemma,** it is a type of game in which the payoff matrix implies the following:

- Each player has an incentive, regardless of what the other player does, to cheat—to take an action that benefits him or her at the other's expense.

- When both players cheat, both are worse off than they would have been if neither had cheated.

**Prisoners' dilemma** is a game based on two premises: (1) Each player has an incentive to choose an action that benefits himself or herself at the other player's expense. (2) When both players act in this way, both are worse off than if they had chosen different actions.

The original illustration of the prisoners' dilemma occurred in a fictional story about two accomplices in crime—let's call them Thelma and Louise—who have been caught by the police. The police have enough evidence to put them behind bars for 5 years. They also know that the pair have committed a more serious crime, one that carries a 20-year sentence; unfortunately, they don't have enough evidence to convict the women on that charge. To do so, they would need each of the prisoners to implicate the other in the second crime.

So the police put the miscreants in separate cells and say the following to each: "Here's the deal: If neither of you confesses, you know that we'll send you to jail for 5 years. If you confess and implicate your partner, and she doesn't do the same, we'll reduce your sentence from 5 years to 2. But if your partner confesses and you don't, you'll get the maximum 20 years. And if both of you confess, we'll give you both 15 years."

Figure 12-2 shows the payoffs that face the prisoners, depending on the decision of each to remain silent or to confess. (Usually the payoff matrix reflects the players' payoffs, and higher payoffs are better than lower payoffs. This case is an exception: a higher number of years in prison is bad, not good!) Let's assume that the prisoners have no way to communicate and that they have not sworn an oath not to harm each other or anything of that sort. So each acts in her own self-interest. What will they do?

The answer is clear: both will confess. Look at it first from Thelma's point of view: she is better off confessing, regardless of what Louise does. If Louise doesn't confess, Thelma's confession reduces her own sentence from 5 years to 2. If Louise *does* confess, Thelma's confession reduces her sentence from 20 to 15 years. Either way, it's clearly in Thelma's interest to confess. And because she faces the same incentives, it's clearly in Louise's interest to confess, too. To confess in this situation is a type of action that economists call a *dominant strategy*. An action is a **dominant strategy** when it is the player's best action regardless of what action the other player takes. It's important to note that not all games have a dominant strategy—it depends on the structure of payoffs in the game. But in the case of Thelma and Louise, it is clearly in the interest of the police to structure the payoffs so that confessing is a dominant strategy for each person. So as long as the two prisoners have no way to make an enforceable agreement that neither will confess (something they can't do if they can't communicate, and the police certainly won't allow them to do because the police want to compel each one to confess), Thelma and Louise will each act in a way that hurts the other.

So if each prisoner acts rationally in her own interest, both will confess. Yet if neither of them had confessed, both would have received a much lighter sentence! In a prisoners' dilemma, each player has a clear incentive to act in a way that hurts the other player—but when both make that choice, it leaves both of them worse off.

An action is a **dominant strategy** when it is a player's best action regardless of the action taken by the other player.

---

### Figure 12-2

**The Prisoners' Dilemma**

Each of two prisoners, held in separate cells, is offered a deal by the police—a light sentence if she confesses and implicates her accomplice but her accomplice does not do the same, a heavy sentence if she does not confess but her accomplice does, and so on. It is in the joint interest of both prisoners not to confess; it is in each one's individual interest to confess.

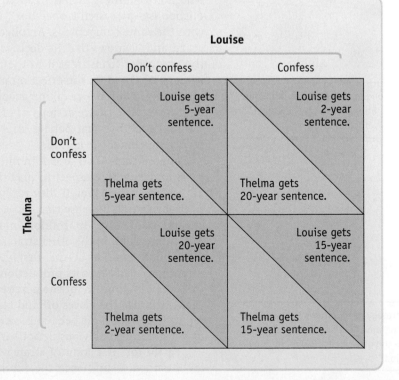

Louise

|  | Don't confess | Confess |
|---|---|---|
| **Thelma — Don't confess** | Louise gets 5-year sentence. / Thelma gets 5-year sentence. | Louise gets 2-year sentence. / Thelma gets 20-year sentence. |
| **Thelma — Confess** | Louise gets 20-year sentence. / Thelma gets 2-year sentence. | Louise gets 15-year sentence. / Thelma gets 15-year sentence. |

A **Nash equilibrium,** also known as a **noncooperative equilibrium,** is the result when each player in a game chooses the action that maximizes his or her payoff given the actions of other players, ignoring the effects of his or her action on the payoffs received by those other players.

When Thelma and Louise both confess, they reach an *equilibrium* of the game. We have used the concept of equilibrium many times in this book; it is an outcome in which no individual or firm has any incentive to change his or her action. In game theory, this kind of equilibrium, in which each player takes the action that is best for her given the actions taken by other players, and vice versa, is known as a **Nash equilibrium,** after the mathematician and Nobel Laureate John Nash. (Nash's life was chronicled in the best-selling biography *A Beautiful Mind,* which was made into a movie.) Because the players in a Nash equilibrium do not take into account the effect of their actions on others, this is also known as a **noncooperative equilibrium.**

Now look back at Figure 12-1; ADM and Ajinomoto are in the same situation as Thelma and Louise. Each firm is better off producing the higher output, regardless of what the other firm does. Yet if both produce 40 million pounds, both are worse off than if they had followed their agreement and produced only 30 million pounds. In both cases, then, the pursuit of individual self-interest—the effort to maximize profits or to minimize jail time—has the perverse effect of hurting both players.

Prisoners' dilemmas appear in many situations. The For Inquiring Minds on page 307 describes an example from the days of the Cold War. Clearly, the players in any prisoners' dilemma would be better off if they had some way of enforcing cooperative behavior—if Thelma and Louise had both sworn to a code of silence, or if ADM and Ajinomoto had signed an enforceable agreement not to produce more than 30 million pounds of lysine.

But in the United States an agreement setting the output levels of two oligopolists isn't just unenforceable, it's illegal. So it seems that the undesirable noncooperative equilibrium is the only possible outcome. Or is it?

## Overcoming the Prisoners' Dilemma: Repeated Interaction and Tacit Collusion

Thelma and Louise in their cells are playing what is known as a *one-shot* game—that is, they play the game with each other only once. They get to choose once and for all whether to confess or hang tough, and that's it. However, most of the games that oligopolists play aren't one-shot; instead, they expect to play the game repeatedly with the same competitors. An oligopolist usually expects to be in business for many years, and it knows that its decision today about whether to cheat is likely to affect the way other firms treat it in the future. So a smart oligopolist doesn't just decide what to do based on the effect on profit in the short run. Instead, he or she engages in **strategic behavior,** taking account of the effects of the action he or she chooses today on the future actions of other players in the game. And under some conditions oligopolists that behave strategically can manage to behave as if they had a formal agreement to collude.

A firm engages in **strategic behavior** when it attempts to influence the future behavior of other firms.

Suppose that ADM and Ajinomoto expect to be in the lysine business for many years and therefore expect to play the game of cheat versus collude shown in Figure 12-1 many times. Would they really betray each other time and again?

Probably not. Suppose that ADM considers two strategies. In one strategy it always cheats, producing 40 million pounds of lysine each year, regardless of what Ajinomoto does. In the other strategy, it starts off with good behavior, producing only 30 million pounds in the first year, and watches to see what its rival does. If Ajinomoto also keeps its production down, ADM will stay cooperative, producing 30 million pounds again for the next year. But if Ajinomoto produces 40 million pounds, ADM will take the gloves off and also produce 40 million pounds next year. This latter strategy—start off behaving cooperatively, but thereafter do whatever the other player did in the previous period—is generally known as **tit for tat.**

A strategy of **tit for tat** involves playing cooperatively at first, then doing whatever the other player did in the previous period.

"Tit for tat" is a form of strategic behavior, which we have just defined as behavior intended to influence the future actions of other players. "Tit for tat" offers a

# FOR INQUIRING MINDS

## PRISONERS OF THE ARMS RACE

Between World War II and the late 1980s, the United States and the Soviet Union were locked in a seemingly endless struggle that never broke out into open war. During this Cold War, both countries spent huge sums on arms, sums that were a significant drain on the U.S. economy and eventually proved a crippling burden for the Soviet Union, whose underlying economic base was much weaker. Yet neither country was ever able to achieve a decisive military advantage.

As many people pointed out, both nations would have been better off if they had both spent less on arms. Yet the arms race continued for 40 years.

Why? As political scientists were quick to notice, one way to explain the arms race was to suppose that the two countries were locked in a classic prisoners' dilemma. Each government would have

TASS/Soufoto

Caught in the prisoners' dilemma: heavy military spending hastened the collapse of the Soviet Union.

liked to achieve decisive military superiority, and each feared military inferiority. But both would have preferred a stalemate with low military spending to one with high spending. However, each government rationally chose to engage in high spending. If its rival did not spend heavily, this would lead to military superiority; *not* spending heavily would lead to inferiority if the other government continued its arms buildup. So the countries were trapped.

The answer to this trap could have been an agreement not to spend as much; indeed, the two sides tried repeatedly to negotiate limits on some kinds of weapons. But these agreements weren't very effective. In the end the issue was resolved as heavy military spending hastened the collapse of the Soviet Union in 1991.

reward to the other player for cooperative behavior—if you behave cooperatively, so will I. It also provides a punishment for cheating—if you cheat, don't expect me to be nice in the future.

The payoff to ADM of each of these strategies would depend on which strategy Ajinomoto chooses. Consider the four possibilities, shown in Figure 12-3 on page 308:

1. If ADM plays "tit for tat" and so does Ajinomoto, both firms will make a profit of $180 million each year.

2. If ADM plays "always cheat" but Ajinomoto plays "tit for tat," ADM makes a profit of $200 million the first year but only $160 million per year thereafter.

3. If ADM plays "tit for tat" but Ajinomoto plays "always cheat," ADM makes a profit of only $150 million in the first year but $160 million per year thereafter.

4. If ADM plays "always cheat" and Ajinomoto does the same, both firms will make a profit of $160 million each year.

Which strategy is better? In the first year, ADM does better playing "always cheat," whatever its rival's strategy: it assures itself that it will get either $200 million or $160 million (which of the two payoffs it actually receives depends upon whether Ajinomoto plays "always cheat" or "tit for tat"). This is better than what it would get in the first year if it played "tit for tat": either $180 million or $150 million. But by the second year, a strategy of "always cheat" gains ADM only $160 million per year for the second and all subsequent years, regardless of Ajinomoto's actions. This amount is inferior to the amount ADM would gain by playing "tit for tat": for the second and all subsequent years, it would never get any less than $160 million and would get as much as $180 million if Ajinomoto played "tit for tat" as well. So which strategy is more profitable depends on two things: how many years ADM expects to play the game and what strategy its rival follows.

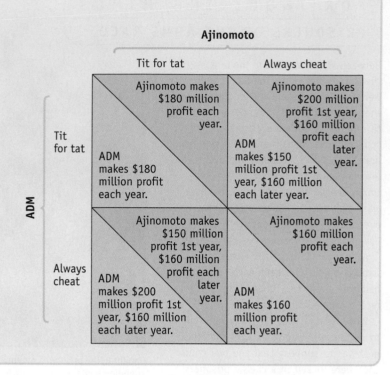

**Figure 12-3**

**How Repeated Interaction Can Support Collusion**

A strategy of "tit for tat" involves playing cooperatively at first, then following the other player's move. This rewards good behavior and punishes bad behavior. If the other player cheats, playing "tit for tat" will lead to only a short-term loss in comparison to playing "always cheat." But if the other player plays "tit for tat," also playing "tit for tat" leads to a long-term gain. So a firm that expects other firms to play "tit for tat" may well choose to do the same, leading to successful tacit collusion.

If ADM expects the lysine business to end in the near future, it is in effect playing a one-shot game. So it might as well grab what it can. Even if ADM expects to remain in the lysine business for many years (therefore to find itself repeatedly playing this game with Ajinomoto) and expects, for some reason, Ajinomoto always to cheat, it should also always cheat. That is, ADM should follow the old rule "Do unto others before they do unto you."

But if ADM expects to be in the business for a long time and thinks Ajinomoto is likely to play "tit for tat," it will make more profits over the long run by playing "tit for tat," too. It could have made some extra short-term profits by cheating at the beginning, but this would provoke Ajinomoto into cheating too, and would, in the end, mean lower profits.

The lesson of this story is that when oligopolists expect to compete with each other over an extended period of time, each individual firm will often conclude that it is in its own best interest to be helpful to the other firms in the industry. So it will restrict its output in a way that raises the profits of the other firms, expecting them to return the favor. Even though the firms have no way of making an enforceable agreement to limit output and raise prices, they manage to act "as if" they had such an agreement. When this happens, we say that firms engage in **tacit collusion**.

> When firms limit production and raise prices in a way that raises each others' profits, even though they have not made any formal agreement, they are engaged in **tacit collusion**.

# *economics in action*

## The Rise and Fall and Rise of OPEC

Call it the cartel that does not need to meet in secret. The Organization of Petroleum Exporting Countries, usually referred to as OPEC, includes 11 national governments (Algeria, Indonesia, Iran, Iraq, Kuwait, Libya, Nigeria, Qatar, Saudi Arabia, United Arab Emirates, and Venezuela). Two other oil-exporting countries, Norway and Mexico, are not formally part of the cartel but act as if they were. (Russia, also an important oil exporter, has not yet become part of the club.) Unlike corporations, which are often legally prohibited by governments from reaching agreements about production and prices, national governments can talk about whatever they feel like. OPEC members routinely meet to try to set targets for production.

These nations are not particularly friendly with one another. Indeed, OPEC members Iraq and Iran fought a spectacularly bloody war with each other in the 1980s. And, in 1990, Iraq invaded another member, Kuwait. (A mainly American force based in yet another OPEC member, Saudi Arabia, drove the Iraqis out of Kuwait.)

Yet the members of OPEC, like one another or not, are effectively players in a game with repeated interactions. In any given year it is in their combined interest to keep output low and prices high. But it is also in the interest of any one producer to cheat and produce more than the agreed-upon quota—unless that producer believes that this action will bring future retaliation.

So how successful is the cartel? Well, it's had its ups and downs.

Figure 12-4 shows the price of oil in constant dollars (that is, the value of a barrel of oil in terms of other goods) since 1947. OPEC first demonstrated its muscle in 1974: in the aftermath of a war in the Middle East, several OPEC producers limited their output—and they liked the results so much that they decided to continue the practice. Following a second wave of turmoil in the aftermath of Iran's 1979 revolution, prices shot still higher.

By the mid-1980s, however, there was a growing glut of oil on world markets, and cheating by cash-short OPEC members became widespread. The result, in 1985, was that producers who had tried to play by the rules—especially Saudi Arabia, the largest producer—got fed up, and collusion collapsed.

The cartel began to act effectively again at the end of the 1990s, thanks largely to the efforts of Mexico's oil minister to orchestrate output reductions. To assure greater adherence to production targets, OPEC meets very frequently—seven times in 2003 alone—seeking to keep the price of a barrel of oil in the range of $22 to $28. And this discipline appears to be paying off; a decrease of 900,000 barrels per day in late 2003 coupled with rising demand from China and production difficulties in Iraq resulted in oil prices above $50 a barrel in 2004. ■

> > > > > > > > > > > > > > > > > > > >

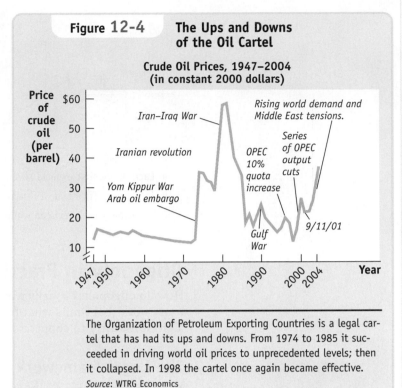

**Figure 12-4    The Ups and Downs of the Oil Cartel**

**Crude Oil Prices, 1947–2004 (in constant 2000 dollars)**

The Organization of Petroleum Exporting Countries is a legal cartel that has had its ups and downs. From 1974 to 1985 it succeeded in driving world oil prices to unprecedented levels; then it collapsed. In 1998 the cartel once again became effective.

*Source*: WTRG Economics

>>**CHECK YOUR UNDERSTANDING 12-1**

1. Explain why each of the following industries is an oligopoly, not a perfectly competitive industry.
   a. The world oil industry, where a few countries near the Persian Gulf control much of the world's oil reserves
   b. The microprocessor industry, where two firms, Intel and its bitter rival AMD, dominate the technology
   c. The wide-bodied passenger jet industry, composed of the American firm Boeing and the European firm Airbus, where production is characterized by extremely large fixed cost

*continued*

>>**QUICK REVIEW**

➤ *Oligopoly* is a common market structure and is a form of *imperfect competition*. Some of the key issues in oligopoly can be understood by looking at the simplest case, a *duopoly*.

➤ *Duopolists* recognize that their profit depends on the other firm's behavior. So there is an incentive to collude. An extreme form of *collusion* is a *cartel*.

➤ Economists use *game theory* to study firms' behavior when there is *interdependence* between their *payoffs*. The game can be represented with a *payoff matrix*. Depending on the payoffs, a player may or may not have a *dominant strategy*.

➤ When each firm has an incentive to cheat, but both are worse off if both cheat, the situation is known as a *prisoners' dilemma*.

➤ Players who don't take their interdependence into account arrive at a *Nash*, or *noncooperative*, *equilibrium*. But if a game is played repeatedly, players may engage in *strategic behavior*, sacrificing short-run profit to influence future behavior.

➤ In repeated prisoners' dilemma games, *tit for tat* is often a good strategy, leading to successful *tacit collusion*.

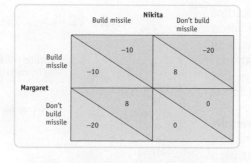

2. Find the Nash (noncooperative) equilibrium actions for the accompanying payoff matrix. Which actions maximize the total payoff of Nikita and Margaret? Why is it unlikely that they will choose those actions without some communication?

3. Which factors make it more likely that oligopolists will play noncooperatively? Which make it more likely that they will engage in tacit collusion? Explain.

   a. Each oligopolist expects several new firms to enter the market in the future.

   b. It is very difficult for a firm to detect whether another firm has raised output.

   c. The firms have coexisted while maintaining high prices for a long time.

*Solutions appear at back of book.*

# Oligopoly in Practice

How do oligopolies usually work in practice? The answer depends both on the legal framework that limits what firms can do and on the underlying ability of firms in a given industry to cooperate without formal agreements.

## The Legal Framework

To understand oligopoly pricing in practice, we must be familiar with the legal constraints under which oligopolistic firms operate. In the United States, oligopoly first became an issue during the second half of the nineteenth century, when the growth of railroads—themselves an oligopolistic industry—created a national market for many goods. Large firms producing oil, steel, and many other products soon emerged. The industrialists quickly realized that profits would be higher if they could limit price competition. So many industries formed cartels—that is, they signed formal agreements to limit production and raise prices. Until 1890, when the first federal legislation against such cartels was passed, this was perfectly legal.

However, although these cartels were legal, they weren't legally *enforceable*—members of a cartel couldn't ask the courts to force a firm that was violating its agreement to reduce its production. And firms often did violate their agreements, for the reason already suggested by our duopoly example: there is always a temptation for each firm in a cartel to produce more than it is supposed to.

In 1881 clever lawyers at John D. Rockefeller's Standard Oil Company came up with a solution—the so-called *trust*. In a trust, shareholders of all the major companies in an industry placed their shares in the hands of a board of trustees who controlled the companies. This, in effect, merged the companies into a single firm that could then engage in monopoly pricing. In this way, the Standard Oil Trust established what was essentially a monopoly of the oil industry, and it was soon followed by trusts in sugar, whiskey, lead, cottonseed oil, and linseed oil.

Eventually there was a public backlash, driven partly by concern about the economic effects of the trust movement, partly by fear that the owners of the trusts were simply becoming too powerful. The result was the Sherman Antitrust Act of 1890, which was intended both to prevent the creation of more monopolies and to break up existing ones. At first this law went largely unenforced. But over the decades that followed, the federal government became increasingly committed to making it difficult for oligopolistic industries either to become monopolies or to behave like them. Such efforts are known to this day as **antitrust policy.**

One of the most striking early actions of antitrust policy was the breakup of Standard Oil in 1911. (Its components formed the nuclei of many of today's large oil companies—Standard Oil of New Jersey became Exxon, Standard Oil of New York became Mobil, and so on.) In the 1980s a long-running case led to the breakup of

**Antitrust policy** refers to the efforts of the government to prevent oligopolistic industries from becoming or behaving like monopolies.

Bell Telephone, which once had a monopoly of both local and long-distance phone service in the United States.

The details of antitrust policy can be exceedingly complex, especially because corporations can and do fight costly legal battles against decisions they dislike. The core of what antitrust means in practice can, however, be understood by turning, once again, to our lysine example. In that example, there are two obvious ways for the companies to avoid getting trapped in the prisoners' dilemma. One is the solution they actually tried: for the companies to meet with each other to agree to produce less and get higher prices. The other is to eliminate conflict by combining the two companies into one—let one company buy the other, or let them exchange their shares and merge.

Antitrust law makes both of these solutions illegal. If the executives meet to collude on prices, they can be sent to jail and their companies fined. If the companies try to merge, the Justice Department or the Federal Trade Commission will tell them that they cannot.

So what's an oligopolist to do?

## Tacit Collusion and Price Wars

If a real industry were as simple as our lysine example, it probably wouldn't be necessary for the company presidents to meet or do anything that could land them in jail. Both firms would realize that it was in their mutual interest to restrict output to 30 million pounds each and that any short-term gains to either firm from producing more would be much less than the later losses as the other firm retaliated. So even without any explicit agreement, the firms would probably achieve the tacit collusion needed to maximize their combined profits.

Real industries are nowhere near that simple; nonetheless, in most oligopolistic industries, most of the time, the sellers do appear to succeed in keeping prices above their noncooperative level. Tacit collusion, in other words, is the normal state of oligopoly.

Although tacit collusion is common, it rarely allows an industry to push prices all the way up to their monopoly level; collusion is usually far from perfect. A variety of factors make it hard for an industry to coordinate on high prices.

**Large Numbers**   Suppose that there were three instead of two firms in the lysine industry and that each was currently producing only 20 million pounds. You can confirm for yourself that in that case any one firm that decided to produce an extra 10 million pounds would gain more in short-term profits—and lose less once another firm responded in kind—than in our original example. The general point is that the more firms there are in an oligopoly, the less is the incentive of any one firm to behave cooperatively, taking into account the impact of its actions on the profits of the other firms. Large numbers of firms in an industry typically are an indication that there are low barriers to entry.

**Complex Products and Pricing Schemes**   In our lysine example the two firms produce only one product. In reality, however, oligopolists often sell thousands or even tens of thousands of different products. Under these circumstances, keeping track of what other firms are producing and what prices they are charging is difficult. This makes it hard to determine whether a firm is cheating on the tacit agreement.

**Differences in Interests**   In the lysine example, a tacit agreement for the firms to split the market equally is a natural outcome, probably acceptable to both firms. In real industries, however, firms often differ both in their perceptions about what is fair and in their real interests.

For example, suppose that Ajinomoto was a long-established lysine producer and ADM a more recent entrant to the industry. Ajinomoto might feel that it deserved to continue producing more than ADM, but ADM might feel that it was entitled to 50 percent of the business. (A disagreement along these lines was one of the contentious issues in those meetings the FBI was filming.)

Alternatively, suppose that ADM's marginal costs were lower than Ajinomoto's. Even if they could agree on market shares, they would then disagree about the profit-maximizing level of output.

**Bargaining Power of Buyers** Often oligopolists sell not to individual consumers but to large buyers—other industrial enterprises, nationwide chains of stores, and so on. These large buyers are in a position to bargain for lower prices from the oligopolists: they can ask for a discount from an oligopolist, and warn that they will go to a competitor if they don't get it. An important reason why large retailers like Wal-Mart are able to offer lower prices to customers than small retailers is precisely their ability to use their size to extract lower prices from their suppliers.

These difficulties in enforcing tacit collusion have sometimes led companies to defy the law and create illegal cartels. We've already examined the cases of the lysine industry and the bulk vitamin industry. An older, classic example was the U.S. electrical equipment conspiracy of the 1950s, which led to the indictment of and jail sentences for some executives. The industry was one in which tacit collusion was especially difficult because of all the reasons just mentioned. There were many firms—40 companies were indicted. They produced a very complex array of products, often more or less custom-built for particular clients. They differed greatly in size, from giants like General Electric to family firms with only a few dozen employees. And the customers in many cases were large buyers like electrical utilities, which would normally try to force suppliers to compete for their business. Tacit collusion just didn't seem practical—so executives met secretly and illegally to decide who would bid what price for which contract.

The following For Inquiring Minds describes yet another price-fixing conspiracy: the one between the very posh auction houses Sotheby's and Christie's.

## FOR INQUIRING MINDS

### THE ART OF CONSPIRACY

If you want to sell a valuable work of art, there are really only two places to go: Christie's, the London-based auction house, or Sotheby's, its New York counterpart and competitor. Both are classy operations— literally: many of the employees of Christie's come from Britain's aristocracy, and many of Sotheby's come from blue-blooded American families that might as well have titles. They're not the sort of people you would expect to be seeking plea bargains from prosecutors.

But on October 6, 2000, Diana D. Brooks, the very upper-class former president of Sotheby's, pleaded guilty to a conspiracy. With her counterpart at Christie's, she had engaged in the illegal practice of price-fixing—agreeing on the fees they would charge people who sold artwork through either house. As part of her guilty plea, and in an effort to avoid going to jail, she agreed to help in the investigation of her boss, the former chairman of Sotheby's.

Why would such upper-crust types engage in illegal practices? For the same reasons that respectable electrical equipment industry executives did. By definition, no two works of art are alike; it wasn't easy for the two houses to collude tacitly, because it was too hard to determine what commissions they were charging on any given transaction. To increase profits, then, the companies felt that they needed to reach a detailed agreement. They did, and they got caught.

---

A **price war** occurs when tacit collusion breaks down and prices collapse.

Because tacit collusion is often hard to achieve, most oligopolies charge prices that are well below what the same industry would charge if it were controlled by a single firm—or what they would charge if they were able to collude explicitly. In addition, sometimes collusion breaks down and there is a **price war.** A price war sometimes involves simply a collapse of prices to their noncooperative level. Sometimes they even go *below* that level, as sellers try to put each other out of business or at least punish what they regard as cheating.

# *economics in action*

## Air Wars

The first time Robert Crandall, then CEO of American Airlines, tried to collude on prices, he was blunt: in 1983 he called the head of rival Braniff (now defunct) and proposed in so many words (many of them unprintable) that the two airlines both raise fares 20 percent. Alas for Crandall, the conversation was being taped.

Eight years later, Crandall tried a more legal approach: declaring himself a "statesman," he raised American's fares in the hopes that rivals would follow suit. But they didn't, and the airline lost many passengers.

On both occasions the airline industry was in the midst of a price war. Indeed, price wars—in which fares fall 50 percent or more for a time, then soar again—are something of an industry specialty.

Why are airlines so prone to price wars? There are at least three reasons, all bearing on the problems of tacit collusion we have just discussed. First, although each airline tries to differentiate its product, creating a perception among consumers that it offers better service, most fliers choose airlines on the basis of schedule and price—period. So competition is intense. Second, airline pricing is complex: as discussed in Chapter 11, airlines engage in complex price-discrimination schemes that make it hard to figure out when tacit collusion is being broken. Third, airlines often differ in their interests: many of the most severe price wars have been set off by attempts of a new competitor to break into established markets. And this indicates yet another source of airline price wars: low barriers to entry. ■

> > > > > > > > > > > > > > > > > > > >

>> **CHECK YOUR UNDERSTANDING 12-2**

1. Which of the following factors are likely to support the conclusion that there is tacit collusion in this industry? Which are not? Explain.
   a. For many years the price in the industry has changed infrequently, and all the firms in the industry charge the same price. The largest firm publishes a catalog containing a "suggested" retail price. Changes in price coincide with changes in the catalog.
   b. There has been considerable variation in the market shares of the firms in the industry over time.
   c. Firms in the industry build into their products unnecessary features that make it hard for consumers to switch from one company's products to another's.
   d. Firms meet yearly to discuss their annual sales forecasts.
   e. Firms tend to adjust their prices upward at the same times.

Solutions appear at back of book.

# Monopolistic Competition

Joe manages the Wonderful Wok stand in the food court of a big shopping mall. He offers the only Chinese food there, but there are more than a dozen alternatives, from Bodacious Burgers to Pizza Paradise. When deciding what to charge for a meal, Joe knows that he must take those alternatives into account: even people who normally prefer stir-fry won't order a $15 lunch from Joe when they can get a burger, fries, and drink for $4.

But Joe also knows that he won't lose all his business even if his lunches cost a bit more than the alternatives. Chinese food isn't the same thing as burgers or pizza. Some people will really be in the mood for Chinese that day, and they will buy from Joe even if they could have dined more cheaply on burgers. Of course, the reverse is also true: even if Chinese is a bit cheaper, some people will choose burgers instead. In other words, Joe does have some market power: he has *some* ability to set his own price.

So how would you describe Joe's situation? He definitely isn't a price-taker, so he isn't in a situation of perfect competition. But you wouldn't exactly call him a monopolist, either. Although he's the only seller of Chinese food in that food court, he does face competition from other food vendors.

Yet it would also be wrong to call him an oligopolist. Oligopoly, remember, involves competition among a small number of firms in an industry protected by some—albeit limited—barriers to entry and whose profits are highly interdependent. This interdependence provides an incentive for oligopolists to try to find a way to collude, if only tacitly. But in Joe's case there are *lots* of vendors in the shopping mall, too many to make tacit collusion feasible.

Economists describe Joe's situation as one of **monopolistic competition.** Monopolistic competition is particularly common in service industries like restaurants and gas stations, but it also exists in some manufacturing industries. In a monopolistically competitive industry, each producer has some ability to set the price of her differentiated good. But exactly how high she can set it is limited by the competition she faces from other existing and potential producers that produce close, but not identical, products. Monopolistic competition involves three conditions:

> **Monopolistic competition** is a market structure in which there are many competing producers in an industry, each producer sells a differentiated product, and there is free entry into and exit from the industry in the long run.

- Large numbers of competing producers
- Differentiated products
- Free entry into and exit from the industry in the long run

**Large Numbers of Competing Producers** In a monopolistically competitive industry there are many producers. Such an industry does not look either like a monopoly, where the firm faces no competition, or an oligopoly, where each firm has only a few rivals. Instead, each seller has many competitors. There are many vendors in a big food court, many gas stations along a major highway, and many hotels in a popular beach resort.

Differentiating one burger from another.

**Differentiated Products** In a monopolistically competitive industry, each producer has a product that consumers view as differentiated—as somewhat distinct from the products of competing firms—but at the same time are considered close substitutes. If Joe's food court contained 15 vendors selling exactly the same kind and quality of food, there would be perfect competition: any seller who tried to charge a higher price would have no customers. But suppose that Wonderful Wok is the only Chinese food vendor, Bodacious Burgers is the only hamburger stand, and so on. The result of this differentiation is that each seller has some ability to set his own price: each producer has some—albeit limited—market power.

**Free Entry Into and Exit From the Industry in the Long Run** In monopolistically competitive industries, new producers, with their own distinct products, can enter the industry freely in the long run. For example, other food vendors would open outlets in the shopping mall if they thought it would be profitable to do so. In addition, firms will exit the industry if they find they are not covering their costs in the long run.

Monopolistic competition, then, differs from the three market structures we have examined so far. As the term *monopolistic competition* suggests, this market structure combines some features typical of monopoly with others typical of perfect competition. Because each firm is offering a distinct product, it is in a way like a monopolist: it faces a downward-sloping demand curve and has some market power—the ability within limits to determine the price of its product. However, unlike a pure monopolist, a monopolistically competitive firm does face competition: the amount of its product it can sell depends on the prices and products offered by other firms in the industry.

The same, of course, is true of an oligopoly. In a monopolistically competitive industry, however, there are *many* producers, as opposed to the small number that defines an oligopoly. If all the gas stations or all the restaurants in a town could agree—explicitly or tacitly—to raise prices, it would be in their mutual interest to do so. But such collusion is virtually impossible when the number of firms is large and, by implication, there are no barriers to entry.

## Monopolistic Competition in the Short Run

We introduced the distinction between short-run and long-run equilibrium back in Chapter 8. The short-run equilibrium of an industry takes the number of firms as given. The long-run equilibrium, by contrast, is reached only after enough time has elapsed for firms to enter or exit the industry. To analyze monopolistic competition, we focus first on the short run and then on how an industry moves from the short run to the long run.

Panels (a) and (b) of Figure 12-5 show two possible situations that a typical firm in a monopolistically competitive industry might face in the short run. In each case the firm looks like any monopolist: it faces a downward-sloping demand curve, which implies a downward-sloping marginal revenue curve.

We assume that every firm has an upward-sloping marginal cost curve but that it also faces some fixed costs, so that its average total cost curve is U-shaped. This

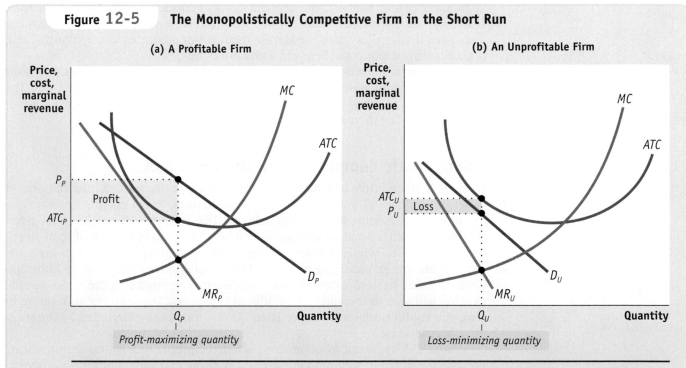

**Figure 12-5   The Monopolistically Competitive Firm in the Short Run**

**(a) A Profitable Firm**

**(b) An Unprofitable Firm**

The firm in panel (a) can be profitable for some output quantity: the quantity at which its average total cost curve, *ATC*, lies below its demand curve, $D_P$. The profit-maximizing output quantity is $Q_P$, the output at which marginal revenue, $MR_P$, is equal to marginal cost, *MC*. The firm charges price $P_P$ and earns a profit, represented by the area of the shaded rectangle. The firm in panel (b), however, can never be profitable because its average total cost curve lies above its demand curve, $D_U$, for every output quantity. The best that it can do if it produces at all is to produce quantity $Q_U$ and charge price $P_U$. This generates a loss, indicated by the area of the shaded rectangle. Any other output quantity results in a greater loss. **>web...**

assumption doesn't matter in the short run, but, as we'll see shortly, it is crucial to understanding the long-run equilibrium.

In each case the firm, in order to maximize profit, sets marginal revenue equal to marginal cost. So how do these two figures differ? In panel (a) the firm is profitable; in panel (b) it is unprofitable.

In panel (a) the firm faces the demand curve $D_P$ and the marginal revenue curve $MR_P$. It produces the profit-maximizing output $Q_P$, the quantity at which marginal revenue is equal to marginal cost, and sells it at the price $P_P$. This price is above the average total cost at this output, $ATC_P$. The firm's profit is indicated by the area of the shaded rectangle.

In panel (b) the firm faces the demand curve $D_U$ and the marginal revenue curve $MR_U$. It chooses the quantity $Q_U$ at which marginal revenue is equal to marginal cost. However, in this case the price $P_U$ is *below* the average total cost $ATC_U$; so at this quantity the firm loses money. Its loss is equal to the area of the shaded rectangle. Since $Q_U$ is the profit-maximizing quantity—which means, in this case, the loss-minimizing quantity—there is no way for a firm in this situation to make a profit. We can confirm this by noting that at *any* quantity of output, the average total cost curve in panel (b) lies above the demand curve $D_U$. Because $ATC > P$ at all quantities of output, this firm always suffers a loss.

As this comparison suggests, the key to whether a firm with market power is profitable or unprofitable in the short run lies in the relationship between its demand curve and its average total cost curve. In panel (a) the demand curve $D_P$ crosses the average total cost curve, meaning that some of the demand curve lies above the average total cost curve. So there are some price–quantity combinations available at which price is higher than average total cost, indicating that the firm can choose a quantity at which it makes positive profit.

In panel (b), by contrast, the demand curve $D_U$ does not cross the average total cost curve—it always lies below it. So the price corresponding to each quantity demanded is always less than the average total cost of producing that quantity. There is no quantity at which the firm can avoid losing money.

These figures, showing firms facing downward-sloping demand curves and their associated marginal revenue curves, look just like ordinary monopoly analysis. The "competition" aspect of monopolistic competition comes into play, however, when we move from the short run to the long run.

## Monopolistic Competition in the Long Run

Obviously, an industry in which existing firms are losing money, like the one in panel (b) of Figure 12-5, is not in long-run equilibrium. When existing firms are losing money, some firms will *exit* the industry. The industry will not be in long-run equilibrium until the persistent losses have been eliminated by the exit of some firms.

It may be less obvious that an industry in which existing firms are earning profits, like the one in panel (a) of Figure 12-5, is also not in long-run equilibrium. Given there is *free entry* into the industry, persistent profits by the firms already existing will lead to the entry of additional producers. The industry will not be in long-run equilibrium until the persistent profits have been eliminated by the entry of new producers.

How will entry or exit by other firms affect the profits of a typical existing firm? Because the differentiated products offered by firms in a monopolistically competitive industry compete for the same set of customers, entry or exit by other firms will affect the demand curve facing every existing producer. If new gas stations open along a highway, each of the existing gas stations will sell less gas at any given price. So, as illustrated in panel (a) of Figure 12-6, entry of additional producers into a monopolistically competitive industry will lead to a *leftward* shift of the demand curve and the marginal revenue curve facing a typical existing producer.

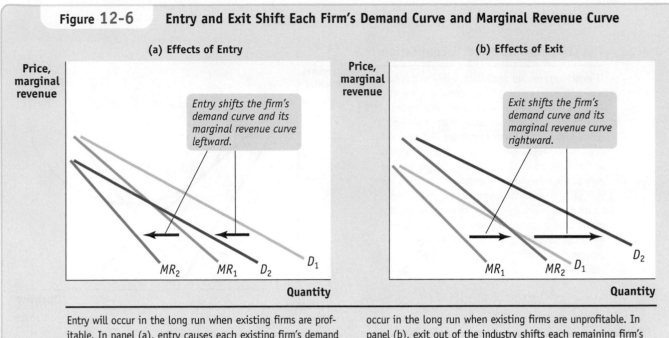

**Figure 12-6**   **Entry and Exit Shift Each Firm's Demand Curve and Marginal Revenue Curve**

**(a) Effects of Entry**

Price, marginal revenue

*Entry shifts the firm's demand curve and its marginal revenue curve leftward.*

$MR_2$   $MR_1$   $D_2$   $D_1$

Quantity

**(b) Effects of Exit**

Price, marginal revenue

*Exit shifts the firm's demand curve and its marginal revenue curve rightward.*

$MR_1$   $MR_2$   $D_1$   $D_2$

Quantity

Entry will occur in the long run when existing firms are profitable. In panel (a), entry causes each existing firm's demand curve and marginal revenue curve to shift to the left. The firm receives a lower price for every unit it sells, and its profit falls. Entry will cease when firms make zero profit. Exit will occur in the long run when existing firms are unprofitable. In panel (b), exit out of the industry shifts each remaining firm's demand curve and marginal revenue curve to the right. The firm receives a higher price for every unit it sells, and profit rises. Exit will cease when the remaining firms make zero profit.

Conversely, suppose that some of the gas stations along the highway close. Then each of the remaining stations will sell more gasoline at any given price. So as illustrated in panel (b), exit of firms from an industry leads to a *rightward* shift of the demand curve and marginal revenue curve facing a typical remaining producer.

The industry will be in long-run equilibrium when there is neither entry nor exit. This will occur only when every firm earns zero profit. So in the long run, a monopolistically competitive industry will end up in **zero-profit equilibrium,** in which firms just manage to cover their costs at their profit-maximizing output quantities.

We have seen that a firm facing a downward-sloping demand curve will earn positive profits if any part of that demand curve lies above its average total cost curve; it will incur a loss if its demand curve lies everywhere below its average total cost curve. So in zero-profit equilibrium, the firm must be in a borderline position between these two cases; its demand curve must just touch its average total cost curve. That is, it must be just *tangent* to it at the firm's profit-maximizing output quantity—the output quantity at which marginal revenue equals marginal cost.

If this is not the case, the firm operating at its profit-maximizing quantity will find itself making either a profit or loss, as illustrated in the panels of Figure 12-5. But we also know that free entry and exit means that this cannot be a long-run equilibrium. Why? In the case of a profit, new firms will enter the industry, shifting the demand curve of every existing firm leftward until all profits are extinguished. In the case of a loss, some existing firms exit and so shift the demand curve of every remaining firm to the right until all losses are extinguished. All entry and exit ceases only when every existing firm makes zero profit at its profit-maximizing quantity of output.

Figure 12-7 on page 318 shows a typical monopolistically competitive firm in such a zero-profit equilibrium. The firm produces $Q_{MC}$, the output at which $MR = MC$, and charges price $P_{MC}$. At this price and quantity, represented by point Z, the demand

In the long run, a monopolistically competitive industry ends up in **zero-profit equilibrium:** each firm makes zero profit at its profit-maximizing quantity.

**Figure 12-7**

### The Long-Run Zero-Profit Equilibrium

If existing firms are profitable, entry will occur and shift each existing firm's demand curve leftward. If existing firms are unprofitable, each remaining firm's demand curve shifts rightward as some firms exit the industry. Entry and exit will cease when every existing firm makes zero profit at its profit-maximizing quantity. So, in long-run zero-profit equilibrium, the demand curve of each firm is tangent to its average total cost curve at its profit-maximizing quantity: at the profit-maximizing quantity, $Q_{MC}$, price, $P_{MC}$, equals average total cost, $ATC_{MC}$. A monopolistically competitive firm is like a monopolist without monopoly profits. **>web...**

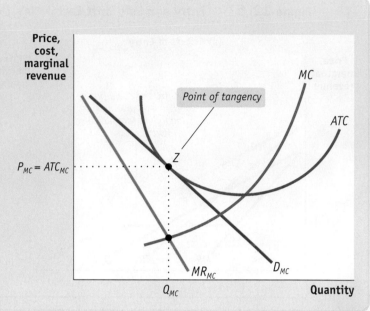

curve is just tangent to its average total cost curve. The firm earns zero profit because price, $P_{MC}$, is equal to average total cost, $ATC_{MC}$.

The normal long-run condition of a monopolistically competitive industry, then, is that each producer is in the situation shown in Figure 12-7. Each producer acts like a monopolist, setting marginal cost equal to marginal revenue so as to maximize profits. But this is just enough to achieve zero economic profit. The producers in the industry are like monopolists without monopoly profits.

---

## FOR INQUIRING MINDS

### HITS AND FLOPS

On the face of it, the movie business seems to meet the criteria for monopolistic competition. Movies compete for the same consumers; each movie is different from the others; new companies can and do enter the business. But where's the zero-profit equilibrium? After all, some movies are enormously profitable.

The key is to realize that for every successful blockbuster, there are several flops—and that the movie studios don't know in advance which will be which. (One observer of Hollywood summed up his conclusions as follows: "Nobody knows anything.") And by the time it becomes clear that a movie will be a flop, it's too late to cancel it.

The difference between movie-making and the type of monopolistic competition we model in this chapter is that the fixed costs of

making a movie are also *sunk costs*—once they've been incurred, they can't be recovered.

Yet there is still, in a way, a zero-profit equilibrium. If movies on average were highly profitable, more studios would enter the industry and more movies would be made. If movies on average lost money, fewer movies would be made. In fact, as you might expect, the movie industry on average earns just about enough to cover the cost of production—that is, it earns roughly zero economic profit.

This kind of situation—in which firms earn zero profit on average but have a mixture of highly profitable hits and money-losing flops—can be found in other industries, characterized by high, up-front sunk costs. A notable example is the pharmaceutical industry, where many research projects lead nowhere, but a few lead to highly profitable drugs.

## WORK IT OUT

### MONOPOLISTIC COMPETITION

In Collegetown there are many Chinese restaurants. Each restaurant distinguishes itself slightly from the others. Some have linen tablecloths, others do not. Some serve Ching-Tao beer, others serve only domestic beer. Some have traditional Chinese music in the background, others play American pop. Some provide orange slices with the bill, others just fortune cookies. Their menus are all similar. There is free entry into the industry. Renee's Chinese Restaurant is depicted in the accompanying graph.

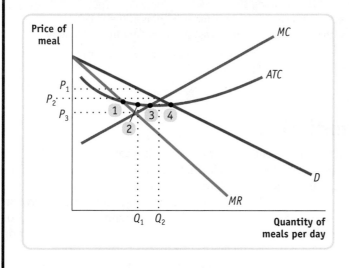

**Profit Maximization in the Short Run:** What quantity of meals should Renee's restaurant produce in order to maximize profit? What price should it charge per meal?

**SOLUTION:** As always, to maximize profit the firm should produce the quantity where marginal revenue MR equals marginal cost MC. In this case, the restaurant should sell $Q_1$ meals per day and should charge $P_1$ per meal.

**How Much Profit?** When determining how much profit Renee's restaurant is earning per day, what point labeled on the ATC should we use: point 1, 2, 3, or 4? Is this restaurant earning positive, zero, or negative profit in the short run?

**SOLUTION:** Profit is equal to the quantity $Q_1$ multiplied by the difference between the price $P_1$ and the average total cost of producing quantity $Q_1$ which is point 2 on the graph. Price is above ATC, so the restaurant is earning positive profit.

**What Changes in the Long Run?** If you were to draw another graph that shows the long-run equilibrium position for Renee's restaurant, which curve(s) would shift?

**SOLUTION:** Because of free entry into the industry, Renee's restaurant cannot continue to earn positive profits in the long run. Other restaurants will be established in town. When other restaurants open, the demand curve D and the marginal revenue curve MR for Renee's restaurant shift to the left. Entry will continue and Renee's demand and marginal revenue curves will continue to shift to the left until the demand curve just touches the average total cost curve ATC at the profit-maximizing quantity as is depicted in Figure 12-7.

# *economics in action*

## Bagels from Boom to Bust

Bagels have always been big in New York City, but in the mid-1990s they suddenly became popular across the entire country. Nobody was quite sure why. One factor may have been health consciousness (bagels are low in fat and cholesterol—until you smother them in cream cheese). Another may have been the popularity of New York–based TV shows, like *Seinfeld*. In any case, bagel consumption surged. Those who already owned bagel shops suddenly found their businesses highly profitable.

The fresh-bagel sector fits the definition of monopolistic competition quite well: there are many shops, all competing with one another, but the shops are differentiated by location as well as by style (some shops offer traditional bagels; others offer new items like bagels with blueberries or jalapenos). Each has some market power—it will not lose all its business if it charges slightly higher prices than other shops. And the industry is also characterized by free entry. Sure enough, once bagel shops became highly profitable, many new competitors entered the business. This, in turn, reduced the profitability of every bagel shop. By the end of the 1990s bagels were no longer a

- In *monopolistic competition* there are many competing producers, each with a differentiated product, and free entry and exit in the long run.

- Like a monopolist, each firm in a monopolistically competitive industry faces a downward-sloping demand curve and marginal revenue curve. In the short run, it may earn a profit or incur a loss at its profit-maximizing quantity.

- If the typical firm earns positive profit, new firms will enter the industry in the long run, shifting each existing firm's demand curve to the left. If the typical firm incurs a loss, some existing firms will exit the industry in the long run, shifting the demand curve of each remaining firm to the right.

- In the long-run equilibrium of a monopolistically competitive industry, the *zero-profit equilibrium*, firms just break even. The typical firm's demand curve is tangent to its average total cost curve at its profit-maximizing quantity.

Firms engage in **product differentiation** when they try to convince buyers that their product is different from the products of other firms in the industry.

highly profitable business. Indeed, quite a few companies dropped out of the business or went bankrupt.

< < < < < < < < < < < < < < < < <

>> CHECK YOUR UNDERSTANDING 12-3

1. You must determine which of two types of market structure best describes an industry, but you are allowed to ask only one question about the industry. What question should you ask to determine if an industry is:
   a. Perfectly competitive or monopolistically competitive?
   b. Monopoly or monopolistically competitive?

2. Currently a monopolistically competitive industry, composed of firms with U-shaped average total cost curves, is in long-run equilibrium. Describe how the industry adjusts, in both the short and long run, in each of the following situations.
   a. A technological change that increases fixed cost for every firm in the industry
   b. A technological change that decreases marginal cost for every firm in the industry

3. Why, in the long run, is it impossible for firms in a monopolistically competitive industry to create a monopoly by joining together to form a single firm?

Solutions appear at back of book.

# Product Differentiation

In many oligopolies, firms produce products that consumers regard as similar but not identical. A $10 difference in the price won't make many customers switch from a Ford to a Chrysler, or vice versa. Sometimes the differences between products are real, like differences between Froot Loops and Wheaties; sometimes, like differences between brands of vodka (which is supposed to be tasteless), they exist mainly in the minds of consumers. Either way, the effect is to reduce the intensity of the competition among the firms: consumers will not all rush to buy whichever product is cheapest.

As you might imagine, oligopolists welcome the extra market power that comes when consumers think that their product is different from that of competitors. So in many oligopolistic industries, firms make considerable efforts to create the perception that their product is different—that is, they engage in **product differentiation.**

Product differentiation plays an even more crucial role in monopolistically competitive industries. Because tacit collusion is virtually impossible when there are many producers, product differentiation is the only way monopolistically competitive firms can acquire some market power.

How do firms in the same industry—such as fast-food vendors, gas stations, or chocolate companies—differentiate their products? Sometimes the difference is mainly in the minds of consumers rather than in the products themselves. We'll discuss the role of advertising and the importance of brand names in achieving this kind of product differentiation in a moment. But, in general, firms differentiate their products by—surprise!—actually making them different.

The key to product differentiation is that consumers have different preferences and that each producer can carve out a market niche by producing something that caters to the particular preferences of some group of consumers better than the products of other firms. There are three important forms of product differentiation:

- Differentiation by style or type
- Differentiation by location
- Differentiation by quality

**Differentiation by Style or Type** The sellers in Joe's food court offer different types of fast food: hamburgers, pizza, Chinese food, Mexican food, and so on. Each consumer arrives at the food court with some preference for one or another of these offerings. This

### BUCKS FOR STARBUCKS

The coffee shop industry has always been monopolistically competitive, with each local shop selling a somewhat differentiated product. Until the middle of the 1980s, however, products were mainly differentiated by location: customers chose a coffee shop because it was near their workplace or on the way to work. There was also a bit of differentiation by quality—some places made better coffee than others—but that was it. After all, coffee was coffee.

That is, coffee was coffee until it started becoming cappuccino, latte, frappuccino, and other more or less Italian-style beverages. Call it the Starbucks revolution: the Seattle-based chain led the transformation of America's caffeine intake, growing from 15 stores in Seattle in 1987 to more than 9,000 around the world by 2005.

Is this a true expansion of the choices available to consumers? Are the coffee varieties now available really different? Yes, they are. The authors are old enough to remember what typical coffee shop coffee tasted like in the dark ages: things really have improved. Is the

Mocha lattes served here—the Starbucks revolution comes to Beijing.

improvement worth the price of a Starbucks latte? Well, people are willing to pay those prices, and the customer is always right.

preference may depend on the consumer's mood, her diet, or what she has already eaten that day. These preferences will not make consumers indifferent to price: If Wonderful Wok were to charge $15 for an egg roll, everybody would go to Bodacious Burgers or Pizza Paradise instead. But, some people will choose a more expensive meal if that type of food is closer to their preference. So the products of the different vendors are substitutes, but they aren't *perfect* substitutes—they are *imperfect substitutes*.

Vendors in a food court aren't the only sellers who differentiate their offerings by type. Clothing stores concentrate on women's or men's clothes, on business attire or sportswear, on trendy or classic styles, and so on. Auto manufacturers offer sedans, minivans, sport-utility vehicles, and sports cars, each type aimed at drivers with different needs and tastes.

Books offer yet another example of differentiation by type and style. Mysteries are differentiated from romances; among mysteries, we can differentiate among hard-boiled detective stories, whodunits, and police procedurals. And no two writers of hard-boiled detective stories are exactly alike: Raymond Chandler and Sue Grafton each have their devoted fans.

In fact, product differentiation is characteristic of most consumer goods. As long as people differ in their tastes, producers find it possible and profitable to produce a range of varieties.

**Differentiation by Location**   Gas stations along a road offer differentiated products. True, the gas may be exactly the same. But the location of the stations is different, and location matters to consumers: it's more convenient to stop for gas near your home, near your workplace, or near wherever you are when the gas gauge gets low.

In fact, many monopolistically competitive industries supply goods differentiated by location. This is especially true in service industries, from dry cleaners to hairdressers, where customers often choose the seller who is closest rather than cheapest.

**Differentiation by Quality** Do you have a craving for chocolate? How much are you willing to spend on it? You see, there's chocolate and then there's chocolate: although ordinary chocolate may not be very expensive, gourmet chocolate can cost dollars for every bite.

With chocolate, as with many goods, there is a range of possible qualities. You can get a usable bicycle for less than $100; you can get a much fancier bicycle for 10 times as much. It all depends on how much the additional quality matters to you and how much you will miss the other things you could have purchased with that money.

Because consumers vary in what they are willing to pay for higher quality, producers can differentiate their products by quality—some offering lower-quality, inexpensive products, and others offering higher-quality products at a higher price.

Product differentiation, then, can take several forms. Whatever form it takes, however, there are two important features of industries with differentiated products: *competition among sellers* and *value in diversity*.

Competition among sellers means that even though sellers of differentiated products are not offering identical goods, they are to some extent competing for a limited market. If more businesses enter the market, each will find that it sells less quantity at any given price. For example, if a new gas station opens along a road, each of the existing gas stations will sell a bit less.

Value in diversity refers to the gain to consumers from the proliferation of differentiated products. A food court with eight vendors makes consumers happier than one with only six vendors, even if the prices are the same, because some customers will get a meal that is closer to what they had in mind. A road on which there is a gas station every two miles is more convenient for motorists than a road where gas stations are five miles apart. When a product is available in many different qualities, fewer people are forced to pay for more quality than they need or to settle for lower quality than they want. There are, in other words, benefits to consumers from a greater diversity of available products.

## Controversies About Product Differentiation

Up to this point, we have assumed that products are differentiated in a way that corresponds to some real desire of consumers. There is real convenience in having a gas station in your neighborhood; Chinese food and Mexican food are really different from each other.

In the real world, however, some instances of product differentiation can seem puzzling if you think about them. What is the real difference between the long-distance phone service of AT&T and MCI? Between Energizer and Duracell batteries? Or a Marriot and a Ramada hotel room? Most people would be hard-pressed to answer any of these questions. Yet the producers of these goods make considerable efforts to convince consumers that their products are different from and better than those of their competitors.

A classic case of how products may be perceived as different even when they are really pretty much the same is over-the-counter medication. For many years there were only three widely sold pain relievers—aspirin, ibuprofen, and acetaminophen. Yet these generic pain relievers were marketed under a number of brand names, each brand using a marketing campaign implying some special superiority (one classic slogan was "contains the pain reliever doctors recommend most"—that is, aspirin).

No discussion of product differentiation is complete without spending at least a bit of time on the two related issues—and puzzles—of *advertising* and *brand names*.

**The Role of Advertising** Wheat farmers don't advertise their wares on TV; car dealers do. That's not because farmers are shy and car dealers are outgoing; it's because advertising is worthwhile only in industries in which firms have at least some market power. The purpose of advertisements is to get people to buy more of a seller's product at the going price. A perfectly competitive firm, which can sell as much as it likes at the going market price, would have no incentive to spend money convincing consumers to buy more. Only a firm that has some market power, and which therefore charges a price that is above marginal cost, can gain from advertising. (Industries that are more or less perfectly competitive, like the milk industry, do advertise—but these ads are sponsored by an association on behalf of the industry as a whole, not on behalf of the milk that comes from the cows on a particular farm.)

Given that advertising "works," it's not hard to see why firms with market power would spend money on it. But the big question about advertising is *why* it works. A related question is whether advertising is, from society's point of view, a waste of resources.

Not all advertising poses a puzzle. Much of it is straightforward: it's a way for sellers to inform potential buyers about what they have to offer (or, occasionally, for buyers to inform potential sellers about what they want). Nor is there much controversy about the economic usefulness of ads that provide information: the real estate ad that declares "sunny, charming, 2 br, 1 ba, a/c" tells you things you need to know (even if a few euphemisms are involved—"charming," of course, means "small").

But what information is being conveyed when a TV actress proclaims the virtues of one or another long-distance telephone service or a sports hero declares that some company's batteries are better than those inside that pink mechanical rabbit? Surely nobody believes that the sports star is an expert on batteries—or that he chose the company that he personally believes makes the best batteries, as opposed to the company that offered to pay him the most. Yet companies believe, with good reason, that money spent on such promotions increases their sales—and that they would be in big trouble if they stopped advertising but their competitors continued to do so.

Why are consumers influenced by ads that do not really provide any information about the product? One answer is that consumers are not as rational as economists typically assume. Perhaps consumers' judgments, or even their tastes, can be influenced by things that economists think ought to be irrelevant, such as which company has hired the most charismatic celebrity to endorse its product. And there is surely some truth to this. Consumer rationality is a useful working assumption; it is not an absolute truth.

However, another answer is that consumer response to advertising is not entirely irrational, because ads can serve as indirect "signals" in a world where consumers don't have good information about products. Suppose, to take a common example, that you need to avail yourself of some local service that you don't use regularly—body work on your car, say, or furniture moving. You turn to the Yellow Pages, where you see a number of small listings and several large display ads. You know that those display ads are large because the firms paid extra for them; still, it may be quite rational to call one of the firms with a big display ad. After all, the big ad probably means that it's a relatively large, successful company—otherwise, the company wouldn't have found it worth spending the money for the larger ad.

The same principle may partly explain why ads feature celebrities. You don't really believe that the supermodel prefers that watch; but the fact that the watch manufacturer is willing and able to pay her fee tells you that it is a major company that is likely to stand behind its product. According to this reasoning, an expensive advertisement serves to establish the quality of a firm's products in the eyes of consumers.

The possibility that it is rational for consumers to respond to advertising also has some bearing on the question of whether advertising is a waste of resources. If ads only work by manipulating the weak-minded, the $128 billion U.S. businesses spent on advertising in 2003 would have been an economic waste—except to the extent that ads sometimes provide entertainment. To the extent that advertising conveys important information, however, it is an economically productive activity after all.

**Brand Names** You've been driving all day, and you decide that it's time to find a place to sleep. On your right, you see a sign for the Bates Motel; on your left, you see a sign for a Motel 6, or a Best Western, or some other national chain. Which one do you choose?

Unless they were familiar with the area, most people would head for the chain. In fact, most motels in the United States are members of major chains; the same is true of most fast-food restaurants and many, if not most, stores in shopping malls.

Motel chains and fast-food restaurants are only one aspect of a broader phenomenon: the role of **brand names,** names owned by particular companies that differentiate their products in the minds of consumers. In many cases, a company's brand name is the most important asset it has: clearly, McDonald's is worth far more than the sum of the deep-fat fryers and hamburger grills the company owns.

In fact, companies often go to considerable lengths to defend their brand names, suing anyone else who uses them without permission. You may talk about blowing your nose on a kleenex or xeroxing a term paper, but unless the product in question comes from Kleenex or Xerox, the seller must describe it as a facial tissue or a photocopier.

As with advertising, with which they are closely linked, the social usefulness of brand names is a source of dispute. Does the preference of consumers for known brands reflect consumer irrationality? Or do brand names convey real information? That is, do brand names create unnecessary market power, or do they serve a real purpose?

As in the case of advertising, the answer is probably some of both. On the one hand, brand names often do create unjustified market power. Consumers often pay more for brand-name goods in the supermarket even though consumer experts assure us that the cheaper store brands are equally good. Similarly, many common medicines, like aspirin, are cheaper—with no loss of quality—in their generic form.

On the other hand, for many products the brand name does convey information. A traveler arriving in a strange town can be sure of what awaits in a Holiday Inn or a McDonald's; a tired and hungry traveler may find this preferable to trying an independent hotel or restaurant that might be better—but might be worse.

In addition, brand names offer some assurance that the seller is engaged in repeated interaction with its customers and so has a reputation to protect. If a trav-

---

A **brand name** is a name owned by a particular firm that distinguishes its products from those of other firms.

eler eats a bad meal at a restaurant in a tourist trap and vows never to eat there again, the restaurant owner may not care, since the chance is small that the traveler will be in the same area again in the future. But if that traveler eats a bad meal at McDonald's and vows never to eat at a McDonald's again, that matters to the company. This gives McDonald's an incentive to provide consistent quality and so gives travelers some assurance that quality controls are in place.

# *economics in action*

## Any Color, So Long as It's Black

The early history of the auto industry offers a classic illustration of the power of product differentiation.

The modern automobile industry was created by Henry Ford, who first introduced assembly-line production. This technique made it possible for him to offer the famous Model T at a far lower price than anyone else was charging for a car; by 1920, Ford dominated the automobile business.

Ford's strategy was to offer just one style of car, which maximized his economies of scale but made no concessions to differences in taste. He supposedly declared that customers could get the Model T in "any color, so long as it's black."

This strategy was challenged by Alfred P. Sloan, who had merged a number of smaller automobile companies into General Motors. Sloan's strategy was to offer a range of car types, differentiated by quality and price. Chevrolets were basic cars that directly challenged the Model T, Buicks were bigger and more expensive, and so on up to Cadillacs. And you could get each model in several different colors.

By the 1930s the verdict was clear: customers preferred a range of styles, and General Motors, not Ford, became the dominant auto manufacturer for the rest of the twentieth century. ∎

> > > > > > > > > > > > > > > > > > >

## >>CHECK YOUR UNDERSTANDING 12-4

1. In which of the following cases is advertisement likely to be economically useful? Economically wasteful? Explain.
   a. Advertisements on the benefits of aspirin
   b. Advertisements for Bayer aspirin
   c. Advertisements on the benefits of drinking orange juice
   d. Advertisements for Tropicana orange juice
   e. Advertisements that state how long a plumber or an electrician has been in business

2. Some industry analysts have stated that a successful brand name is like a barrier to entry. Explain.

Solutions appear at back of book.

### >> QUICK REVIEW

- *Product differentiation* can occur in oligopolies that fail to achieve tacit collusion as well as in monopolistic competition. It takes three main forms: by style or type, by location, or by quality.
- In industries with product differentiation, firms advertise in order to increase the demand for their products.
- Advertising is not a waste of resources when it gives consumers useful information about products.
- Advertising that simply touts a product is harder to explain. Either consumers are irrational, or expensive advertising communicates that the firm's products are of high quality.
- Some firms create *brand names*. As with advertising, the economic value of brand names can be ambiguous. They convey real information when they assure consumers of the quality of a product.

## • A LOOK AHEAD •

Over the last two chapters we have taken the basic analysis of a perfectly competitive market and extended it in one important direction: to include other kinds of *market structures*. Next we turn to a different kind of extension: to different kinds of *markets*. How does economic analysis change when a national economy can exchange goods and services with other national economies? Next stop: international trade.

## SUMMARY

1. Many industries are **oligopolies:** there are only a few sellers. In particular, a **duopoly** has only two sellers. Oligopolies exist for more or less the same reasons that monopolies exist, but in weaker form. They are characterized by **imperfect competition:** firms compete but possess market power.

2. Predicting the behavior of **oligopolists** poses something of a puzzle. Firms in an oligopoly have an incentive to engage in **collusion** by acting as a **cartel.**

3. The situation of **interdependence,** in which each firm's profit depends noticeably on what other firms do, is the subject of **game theory.** In the case of a game with two players, the **payoff** of each player depends both on its own actions and on the actions of the other; this interdependence can be represented as a **payoff matrix.** Depending upon the structure of payoffs in the payoff matrix, a player may have a **dominant strategy**—an action that is always the best regardless of the other player's actions.

4. **Duopolists** face a particular type of game known as a **prisoners' dilemma;** if each acts independently in its own interest, the resulting **Nash equilibrium** or **noncooperative equilibrium** will be bad for both. However, firms that expect to play a game repeatedly tend to engage in **strategic behavior,** trying to influence each other's future actions. A particular strategy that seems to work well in such situations is **tit for tat,** which often leads to **tacit collusion.**

5. In order to limit the ability of oligopolists to collude and act like monopolists, most governments pursue an **antitrust policy** designed to make collusion more difficult. In practice, however, tacit collusion is widespread. A variety of factors make tacit collusion difficult: large numbers of firms, complex products and pricing, differences in interests, and bargaining power of buyers. When tacit collusion breaks down, there is a **price war.**

6. **Monopolistic competition** is a market structure in which there are many competing producers, each producing a differentiated product, and there is free entry and exit in the long run. Product differentiation takes three main forms: by style or type, by location, or by quality. Products of competing sellers are considered imperfect substitutes, and each firm has its own downward-sloping demand curve and marginal revenue curve.

7. Short-run profits will attract entry of new firms. This reduces the quantity each existing producer sells at any given price and shifts its demand curve to the left. Short-run losses will induce exit by some firms. This shifts the demand curve of each remaining firm to the right.

8. In the long run, a monopolistically competitive industry is in **zero-profit equilibrium:** at its profit-maximizing quantity, the demand curve for each existing firm is tangent to its average total cost curve. There are zero profits in the industry and no entry or exit.

9. A monopolistically competitive firm will always prefer to make an additional sale at the going price, so it will engage in advertising to increase demand for its product and enhance its market power. Advertising and **brand names** that provide useful information to consumers are economically valuable. But they are economically wasteful when their only purpose is to create market power. In reality, advertising and brand names are likely to be some of both: economically valuable and economically wasteful.

## KEY TERMS

Oligopoly, p. 302
Oligopolist, p. 302
Imperfect competition, p. 302
Duopoly, p. 303
Duopolist, p. 303
Collusion, p. 303
Cartel, p. 303
Interdependence, p. 303
Game theory, p. 303
Payoff, p. 303
Payoff matrix, p. 303
Prisoners' dilemma, p. 304
Dominant strategy, p. 305
Nash equilibrium, p. 306
Noncooperative equilibrium, p. 306
Strategic behavior, p. 306
Tit for tat, p. 306
Tacit collusion, p. 308
Antitrust policy, p. 310
Price war, p. 312
Monopolistic competition, p. 314
Zero-profit equilibrium, p. 317
Product differentiation, p. 320
Brand name, p. 324

## PROBLEMS

1. To preserve the North Atlantic fish stocks, it is initially decided that only two fishing fleets, one from the United States and one from the European Union (EU) can fish in those waters. But soon the fisheries agreement breaks down, so that the fleets behave noncooperatively. Assume that the U.S. and the EU each can send out either one or two fleets. Also assume that the more fleets in the area, the more fish they catch in total but the lower the catch of each fleet. The accompanying matrix shows the profit (in dollars) per week earned by the two sides.

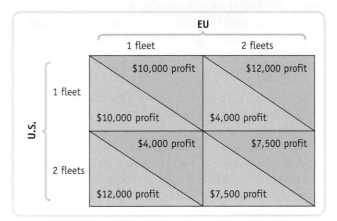

a. What is the noncooperative Nash equilibrium? Will each side choose to send out one or two fleets?

b. Suppose that the fish stocks are being depleted. Each region considers the future and comes to a "tit-for-tat" agreement whereby each side will send only one fleet out as long as the other does the same. If either of them breaks the agreement and sends out a second fleet, the other will also send out two and will continue to do so until its competitor sends out only one fleet. If both play this "tit for tat" strategy, how much profit will each make every week?

2. Untied and Air 'R' Us are the only two airlines operating flights between Collegeville and Bigtown. That is, they operate in a duopoly. Each airline can charge either a high price or a low price for a ticket. The accompanying matrix shows their payoffs, in profits per seat (in dollars), for any choice that the two airlines can make.

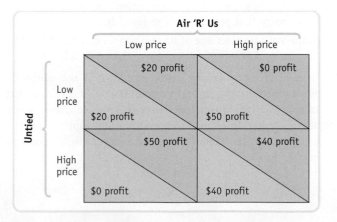

a. Suppose the two airlines play a one-shot game—that is, they interact only once and never again. What will be the Nash (noncooperative) equilibrium in this one-shot game?

b. Now suppose the two airlines play this game twice. And suppose each airline can play one of two strategies: it can play either "always charge the low price" or "tit for tat"—that is, it starts off charging the high price in the first period, and then in the second period it does whatever the other airline did in the previous period. Write down the payoffs to Untied from the following four possibilities:

   i. Untied plays "always charge the low price" when Air 'R' Us also plays "always charge the low price."

   ii. Untied plays "always charge the low price" when Air 'R' Us plays "tit for tat."

   iii. Untied plays "tit for tat" when Air 'R' Us plays "always charge the low price."

   iv. Untied plays "tit for tat" when Air 'R' Us also plays "tit for tat."

3. Philip Morris and R.J. Reynolds spend huge sums of money each year to advertise their tobacco products in an attempt to steal customers from each other. Suppose each year Philip Morris and R.J. Reynolds have to decide whether or not they want to spend money on advertising. If neither firm advertises, each will earn a profit of $2 million. If they both advertise, each will earn a profit of $1.5 million. If one firm advertises and the other does not, the firm that advertises will earn a profit of $2.8 million and the other firm will earn $1 million.

a. Use a payoff matrix to depict this problem.

b. Suppose Philip Morris and R.J. Reynolds can write an enforceable contract about what they will do. What is the cooperative solution to this game?

c. What is the Nash equilibrium without an enforceable contract? Explain why this is the likely outcome.

4. Over the last 30 years the Organization of Petroleum Exporting Countries (OPEC) has had varied success in forming and maintaining its cartel agreements. Explain how the following factors may contribute to the difficulty of forming and/or maintaining its price and output agreements.

a. New oil fields are discovered and increased drilling is undertaken in the Gulf of Mexico and the North Sea by nonmembers of OPEC.

b. Crude oil is a product that is differentiated by sulfur content: it costs less to refine low-sulfur crude oil into gasoline. Different OPEC countries possess oil reserves of different sulfur content.

c. Cars powered by hydrogen are developed.

5. Suppose you are an economist working for the Antitrust Division of the Department of Justice. In each of the following cases you are given the task of determining whether the behavior warrants an antitrust investigation for possible illegal acts, or is just an example of undesirable, but not illegal, tacit collusion. Explain your reasoning.

   a. Two companies dominate the industry for industrial lasers. Several people sit on the boards of directors of both companies.

   b. Three banks dominate the market for banking in a given state. Their profits have been going up recently as they add new fees for customer transactions. Advertising among the banks is fierce, and new branches are springing up in many locations.

   c. The two oil companies that produce most of the petroleum for the western half of the United States have decided to forgo building their own pipelines and to share a common pipeline, the only means of transporting petroleum products to that market.

   d. The two major companies that dominate the market for herbal supplements have each created a subsidiary that sells the same product as the parent company in large quantities but with a generic name.

   e. The two largest credit card companies, Passport and OmniCard, have required all banks and retailers who accept their cards to agree to limit their use of rival credit cards.

6. Use the three conditions for monopolistic competition discussed in the chapter to decide which of the following firms are likely to be operating as monopolistic competitors. If they are not monopolistically competitive firms, are they monopolists, oligopolists, or perfectly competitive firms?

   a. A local band that plays for weddings, parties, and so on

   b. Minute Maid, a producer of individual-serving juice boxes

   c. Your local dry cleaner

   d. A farmer who produces soybeans

7. You are thinking of setting up a coffee shop. The market structure for coffee shops is monopolistic competition. There are three Starbucks shops and two other coffee shops very much like Starbucks in your town already. In order for you to have some degree of market power, you may want to differentiate your coffee shop. Thinking about the three different ways in which products can be differentiated, explain how you would decide whether you should copy Starbucks or whether you should sell coffee in a completely different way.

8. The restaurant business in town is a monopolistically competitive industry in long-run equilibrium. One restaurant owner asks for your advice. She tells you that, each night, not all tables in her restaurant are full. She also tells you that if she lowered the prices on her menu, she would attract more customers and that doing so would lower her average total cost. Should she lower her prices? Draw a diagram showing the demand curve, marginal revenue curve, marginal cost curve, and average total cost curve for this restaurant to explain your advice. Show in your diagram what would happen to the restaurant owner's profit if she were to lower the price so that she sells the minimum-cost output.

9. The local hairdresser industry has the structure of monopolistic competition. Your hairdresser boasts that he is making a profit and that if he continues to do so, he will be able to retire in five years. Use a diagram to illustrate your hairdresser's current situation. Do you expect this to last? In a separate diagram, draw what you expect to happen in the long run. Explain your reasoning.

10. Magnificent Blooms is a florist in a monopolistically competitive industry. It is a successful operation, producing the quantity that minimizes its average total cost and making a profit. The owner also boasts that at its current level of output, its marginal cost is above marginal revenue. Illustrate the current situation of Magnificent Blooms in a diagram. Answer the following questions by illustrating with a diagram.

    a. In the short run, could Magnificent Blooms increase its profit?

    b. In the long run, could Magnificent Blooms increase its profit?

11. "In both the short run and in the long run, the typical firm in monopolistic competition and a monopolist each make a profit." Do you agree with this statement? Explain your reasoning.

12. For each of the following situations, decide whether advertising is directly informative about the product or simply an indirect signal of its quality. Explain your reasoning.

    a. Golf champion Tiger Woods drives a Buick in a TV commercial and claims that he prefers it to any other car.

    b. A newspaper ad states "For sale: 1989 Honda Civic, 160,000 miles, new transmission."

    c. McDonald's spends millions of dollars on an advertising campaign that proclaims: "I'm lovin' it."

    d. Subway advertises one of its sandwiches claiming that it contains 6 grams of fat and fewer than 300 calories.

13. In each of the following cases, explain how the advertisement functions as a signal to a potential buyer. Explain what information the buyer lacks that is being supplied by the advertisement and how the information supplied by the advertisement is likely to affect the buyer's willingness to buy the good.

a. "Looking for work. Excellent references from previous employers available."

b. "Electronic equipment for sale. All merchandise carries a one-year, no-questions-asked warranty."

c. "Car for sale by original owner. All repair and maintenance records available."

14. McDonald's spends millions of dollars each year on legal protection of its brand name, thereby preventing any unauthorized use of it. Explain what information this conveys to you as a consumer about the quality of McDonald's products.

**>web...** To continue your study and review of concepts in this chapter, please visit the Krugman/Wells/Olney website for quizzes, animated graph tutorials, web links to helpful resources, and more.

**www.worthpublishers.com/krugmanwellsolney**

chapter

# >>International Trade

## A ROSE BY ANY OTHER NATION

**What you will learn in this chapter:**

➤ The sources of international comparative advantage

➤ Who gains and who loses from international trade, and why the gains exceed the losses

➤ How **tariffs** and **import quotas** cause inefficiency and reduce total surplus

➤ Why governments often engage in **trade protection** to shelter domestic industries from imports and how **international trade agreements** counteract this

IVING YOUR BELOVED ROSES ON Valentine's Day is a well-established tradition in the United States. But in the past it was a very expensive gesture: in the northern hemisphere, Valentine's Day falls not in summer, when roses are in bloom, but in the depths of winter. Until recently, that meant that the roses in the florist's shop were grown at great cost in heated greenhouses. Nowadays, however, most of the Valentine's Day roses sold in this country are flown in from South America, mainly from Colombia, where growing a rose in February is no trouble at all.

Is it a good thing that we now buy our winter roses from abroad? The vast majority of economists say yes: international trade, in which countries specialize in producing different goods and trade those goods with each other, is a source of mutual benefit to the countries involved. In Chapter 2 we laid out the basic principle that there are *gains from trade*; it's a principle that applies to countries as well as individuals.

But politicians and the public arc oftcn not convinced. In fact, during the 1996 presidential cam-

paign one contender used the occasion of Valentine's Day to visit a flower-growing greenhouse in New Hampshire, where he denounced imports of South American roses as a threat to U.S. jobs.

Up to now this book has analyzed the economy as if it were self-sufficient, as if the economy produced all the goods and

What do these sweethearts and this rose farmer have in common? They are enjoying the mutual benefits of international trade.

Rolf Bruderer/Masterfile

Pablo Corral V/Corbis

services it consumes, and vice versa. This is, of course, true of the world economy as a whole. But it is not true of any individual country. It's true that 40 years ago the United States exported only a small fraction of what it produced and imported only a small fraction of what it consumed. Since then, however, both U.S. imports and U.S. exports have grown much faster than the U.S. economy as a whole. And other countries engage in far more foreign trade, relative to the size of their economies, than does the United States.

does the United States. To have a full picture of how national economies work, we must understand international trade.

This chapter examines the economics of international trade. Comparative advantage, as we saw in Chapter 2, explains why there are gains from international trade. But what creates differences in comparative advantage? And how is it that some individuals can be hurt by international trade? We also look at the effects of trade policies that countries use to limit imports or promote exports.

## Comparative Advantage and International Trade

The United States buys roses—and many other goods and services—from other countries. At the same time, it sells many goods and services to other countries. Goods and services purchased from abroad are **imports;** goods and services sold abroad are **exports.**

As illustrated by the opening story, imports and exports have taken on an increasingly important role in the U.S. economy. Over the last 40 years, both imports into the United States and exports from the United States have grown faster than the U.S. economy; panel (a) of Figure 13-1 shows how the values of imports and exports have

Goods and services purchased from other countries are **imports;** goods and services sold to other countries are **exports.**

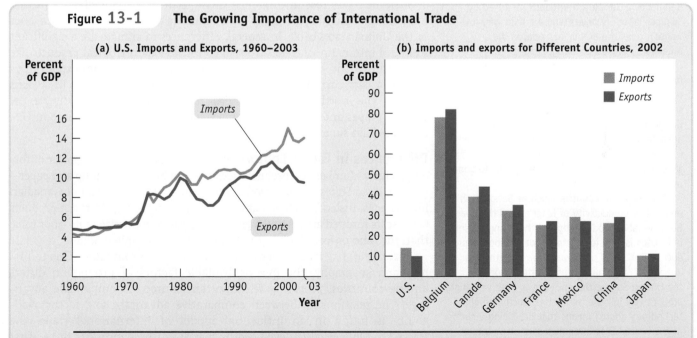

**Figure 13-1    The Growing Importance of International Trade**

Panel (a) illustrates the fact that over the past 40 years, the United States has exported a steadily growing share of its output (that is, its gross domestic product) to other countries and imported a growing share of what it consumes from abroad. Panel (b) demonstrates that international trade is even more important to many other countries than it is to the United States.

*Source:* U.S. Department of Commerce, National Income and Product Accounts [for panel (a)] and United Nations Human Development Report 2004 [for panel (b)].

grown as a percentage of gross domestic product. As panel (b) demonstrates, foreign trade is even more important for many other countries than for the United States.

Why does international trade occur? Recall from Chapter 2 our discussion of comparative advantage and the gains from trade. *A country has a comparative advantage in producing a good if the opportunity cost of producing the good is lower for that country than for other countries.* For example, suppose the United States has low opportunity cost of producing computers and high opportunity cost of producing roses. And suppose that Colombia has the opposite: high opportunity cost of producing computers and low opportunity cost of producing roses. Then the United States has the comparative advantage in producing computers and Colombia has the comparative advantage in producing roses.

*When countries specialize in producing the goods in which they have a comparative advantage and trade for other goods, worldwide output of all goods will increase.* The United States could specialize in producing computers. Colombia could specialize in producing roses. And then the United States and Colombia could trade. The United States can sell computers and buy Colombian roses. Colombians can sell roses and buy U.S. computers. With trade, the world will have more computers and more roses than without trade. Specialization and trade generate gains from trade.

## PITFALLS

**THE PAUPER LABOR FALLACY**

One common argument about international trade goes as follows: it's true that Bangladesh (to pick an example) can produce some goods, such as clothing, more cheaply than we can—but that cost advantage is based only on lower wages. In fact, it takes *fewer* hours of labor to produce a shirt in the United States than in Bangladesh. So importing goods produced by "pauper labor" (workers who are paid very low wages), goes the argument, reduces the American standard of living.

Why is this a misconception? Because it confuses *comparative advantage* with *absolute advantage*. Yes, it takes less labor to produce a shirt in the United States than it does in Bangladesh. But what determines comparative advantage is not the amount of resources used to produce a good but the opportunity cost of that good—the quantity of other goods forgone in order to produce a shirt.

Low wages in countries such as Bangladesh reflect low productivity of labor across the board. Because labor productivity in other Bangladeshi industries is very low, using a lot of labor to produce a shirt does not require forgoing the production of large quantities of other goods. But in the United States, the opposite is true: very high productivity in other industries (such as high-technology goods) means that producing a shirt in the United States requires sacrificing lots of other goods. So the opportunity cost of producing a shirt is less in Bangladesh than in the United States. Despite its lower labor productivity, Bangladesh has a comparative advantage in clothing production, although the United States has an absolute advantage. As a result, importing clothing from Bangladesh actually raises the standard of living in the United States.

## Sources of Comparative Advantage

International trade is driven by comparative advantage, but where does comparative advantage come from? Economists who study international trade have found three main sources of comparative advantage: international differences in *climate*, international differences in *factor endowments*, and international differences in *technology*.

**Differences in Climate** A key reason the opportunity cost of producing a Valentine's Day rose in Colombia is less than in the United States is that nurseries in Colombia can grow roses outdoors all year round but nurseries in the United States can't. In general, differences in climate are a significant source of international trade. Tropical countries export tropical products like coffee, sugar, and bananas. Countries in the temperate zones export crops like wheat and corn. Some trade is even driven by the difference in seasons between the northern and southern hemispheres: winter deliveries of Chilean grapes and New Zealand apples have become commonplace in U.S. and European supermarkets.

**Differences in Factor Endowments** Canada is a major exporter of forest products—lumber and products derived from lumber, like pulp and paper—to the United States. These exports don't reflect the special skill of Canadian lumberjacks. Instead, Canada has a comparative advantage in forest products because its forested area is much greater compared to the size of its labor force than the ratio of forestland to the labor force in the United States.

Forestland, like labor and capital, is a factor of production. Due to history and geography, the mix of available factors of production differs among countries, providing an important source of comparative advantage. The relationship between comparative advantage and factor availability is found in an influential model of international trade, the *Heckscher–Ohlin model* (developed by two Swedish economists in the first half of the twentieth century).

A key concept in the model is *factor intensity*. Producers use different ratios of factors of production in the production of different goods. For example, at any given wage rate and rental rate of capital, oil refineries will use much more capital per worker than clothing factories. Economists use the term **factor intensity** to describe this difference among goods: oil refining is capital-intensive, because it tends to use a high ratio of capital

F O R   I N Q U I R I N G   M I N D S

DOES TRADE HURT POOR COUNTRIES?

It's a good bet that the clothes you are wearing right now were produced in a labor-abundant country such as Bangladesh or Sri Lanka. If so, the workers who produced those clothes were paid very low wages by Western standards: in 2002 (the most recent data available) workers in Sri Lankan factories were paid an average of $0.33 an hour. Doesn't this mean that Sri Lankan workers are getting a bad deal?

The answer of most economists is that it doesn't. The wages paid to export workers in poor countries should be compared not to what workers get in rich countries but to what they would get if those export jobs weren't available. The reason Sri Lankans are willing to work for so little is that in an underdeveloped economy, with lots of labor but very little of other factors of production like capital, the opportunities available to workers are very limited. It's almost certain that international trade makes Sri Lanka and other low-wage countries *less* poor than they would be otherwise and raises workers' wages relative to what they would be without international trade.

Nonetheless, many people in advanced countries—students in particular—are disturbed by the thought that their consumer goods are produced by such poorly paid workers and want to see those workers receive higher pay and better working conditions. The dilemma is whether it is possible to insist on higher wages and better working conditions without eliminating the job altogether, thereby choking off the benefits of international trade.

---

to labor, but clothing manufacture is labor-intensive, because it tends to use a high ratio of labor to capital.

According to the **Heckscher–Ohlin model,** a country will have a comparative advantage in a good whose production is intensive in the factors that are abundantly available in that country. So a country that has an abundance of capital will have a comparative advantage in capital-intensive industries such as oil refining, but a country that has an abundance of labor will have a comparative advantage in labor-intensive industries such as clothing production. The basic intuition behind this result is simple and based on opportunity cost. The opportunity cost of a given factor—the value that the factor would generate in alternative uses—is low for a country when it possesses an abundance of that factor. (For example, in rainy parts of the United States, the opportunity cost of water for residences is low because there is a plentiful supply for other uses, such as agriculture.) So the opportunity cost of producing goods that are intensive in the use of an abundantly available factor is also low.

The most dramatic example of the validity of the Heckscher–Ohlin model is world trade in clothing. Clothing production is a labor-intensive activity: it doesn't take much physical capital, nor does it require a lot of human capital in the form of highly educated workers. So you would expect labor-abundant countries such as China and Bangladesh to have a comparative advantage in clothing production. And they do.

That much international trade is the result of differences in factor endowments helps explain another fact: international specialization of production is often *incomplete*. That is, a country often maintains some domestic production of a good that it imports. A good example of this is the United States and oil. Saudi Arabia exports oil to the United States because Saudi Arabia has an abundant supply of oil relative to its other factors of production; the United States exports medical devices to Saudi Arabia because it has an abundant supply of medical technical expertise relative to its other factors of production. But the United States also produces some oil domestically because the size of its domestic oil reserves make it economical to do so. In our demand and supply analysis in the next section, we'll consider incomplete specialization by a country to be the norm. We should emphasize, however, that the fact that countries often incompletely specialize does not in any way change the conclusion that there are gains from trade.

**Differences in Technology**  In the 1970s and 1980s, Japan became by far the world's largest exporter of automobiles, selling large numbers to the United States and the rest of the world. Japan's comparative advantage in automobiles wasn't the result of climate. Nor can it easily be attributed to differences in factor endowments:

The **factor intensity** of production of a good is a measure of which factor is used in relatively greater quantities than other factors in production.

According to the **Heckscher–Ohlin model,** a country has a comparative advantage in a good whose production is intensive in the factors that are abundantly available in that country.

## INCREASING RETURNS AND INTERNATIONAL TRADE

Most analysis of international trade focuses on how differences between countries—differences in climate, factor endowments, and technology—create national comparative advantage. However, economists have also pointed out another reason for international trade: the role of *increasing returns*.

Production of a good is characterized by increasing returns if the productivity of labor and other resources rises with the quantity of output. For example, in an industry characterized by increasing returns, increasing output by 10 percent might require only 8 percent more labor and 9 percent more raw materials. Increasing returns (sometimes also called economies of scale) can give rise to monopoly, because they give large firms an advantage over small firms.

But increasing returns can also give rise to international trade. The logic runs as follows: if production of a good is characterized by increasing returns, it makes sense to concentrate production in only a few locations, so as to achieve a high level of production in each location. But that also means that the good is produced in only a few countries, which export that good to other countries. A commonly cited example is the North American auto industry: although both the United States and Canada produce automobiles and their components, each particular model or component tends to be produced in only one of the two countries and exported to the other. Increasing returns probably play a large role in the trade in manufactured goods between advanced countries, which is about 25 percent of the total value of world trade.

aside from a scarcity of land, Japan's mix of available factors is quite similar to that in other advanced countries. Instead, Japan's comparative advantage in automobiles was based on the superior production techniques developed by that country's manufacturers, which allowed them to produce more cars with a given amount of labor and capital than their American or European counterparts.

Japan's comparative advantage in automobiles was a case of comparative advantage caused by differences in technology—the techniques used in production.

The causes of differences in technology are somewhat mysterious. Sometimes they seem to be based on knowledge accumulated through experience—for example, Switzerland's comparative advantage in watches reflects a long tradition of watchmaking. Sometimes they are the result of a set of innovations that for some reason occur in one country but not in others. Technological advantage is also often transitory. American auto manufacturers have now closed much of the gap in productivity with their Japanese competitors; Europe's aircraft industry has closed a similar gap with the U.S. aircraft industry. At any given point in time, however, differences in technology are a major source of comparative advantage.

In the United States, an abundance of engineering know-how has led to a comparative advantage in aircraft.

AP/Wide World Photos

## *economics in action*

### The Comparative Advantage of the United States

The United States is a country of superlatives: a nation richly endowed with many resources, human and natural, it has an *absolute* advantage in almost everything—that is, it is better at producing almost everything than anyone else. But what is its *comparative* advantage?

In 1953 the economist Wassily Leontief made a surprising discovery. Until his work, many economists had assumed that because U.S. workers were clearly better-equipped with machinery than their counterparts in other countries, the production of U.S. exports was more capital-intensive than the production of U.S. imports. That is, they expected that U.S. exports were more capital-intensive than U.S. imports. But Leontief's work showed that this wasn't true: in fact, goods that the United States exported were slightly less capital-intensive than goods the country imported. The "Leontief paradox" led to a sustained effort to make sense of U.S. trade patterns.

The main resolution of this paradox, it turns out, depends on the definition of capital. U.S. exports aren't intensive in *physical* capital—machines and buildings. Instead, they are intensive in *human* capital. U.S. exporting industries use a substantially higher ratio of highly educated workers to other workers than is found in U.S. industries that compete against imports. For example, one of America's biggest export sectors is aircraft; the aircraft industry employs large numbers of engineers and other people with graduate degrees relative to the number of manual laborers. Conversely, we import a lot of clothing, which is often produced by workers with little formal education. ■

> > > > > > > > > > > > > > > > > > > > >

>>**CHECK YOUR UNDERSTANDING 13-1**

1. Explain the following patterns of trade using the Heckscher–Ohlin model:
   a. France exports wine to the United States, and the United States exports movies to France.
   b. Brazil exports shoes to the United States, and the United States exports shoe-making machinery to Brazil.

   *Solutions appear at back of book.*

# Supply, Demand, and International Trade

Simple models of comparative advantage are helpful for understanding the fundamental causes of international trade. However, to analyze the effects of international trade at a more detailed level and to understand trade policy, it helps to return to the supply and demand model. We'll start by looking at the effects of imports on domestic producers and consumers, then turn to the effect of exports.

## The Effects of Imports

Figure 13-2 shows the U.S. market for roses, ignoring international trade for a moment. It introduces a few new concepts: the *domestic demand curve,* the *domestic supply curve,* and the domestic or *autarky* price.

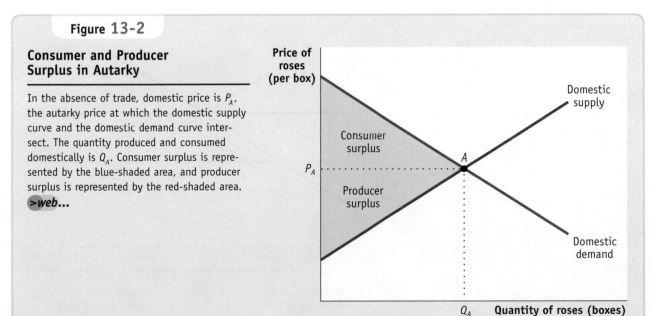

**Figure 13-2**

**Consumer and Producer Surplus in Autarky**

In the absence of trade, domestic price is $P_A$, the autarky price at which the domestic supply curve and the domestic demand curve intersect. The quantity produced and consumed domestically is $Q_A$. Consumer surplus is represented by the blue-shaded area, and producer surplus is represented by the red-shaded area.

**>web...**

The **domestic demand curve** shows how the quantity of a good demanded by domestic consumers depends on the price of that good.

The **domestic supply curve** shows how the quantity of a good supplied by domestic producers depends on the price of that good.

**Autarky** is a situation in which a country cannot trade with other countries.

The **world price** of a good is the price at which that good can be bought or sold abroad.

The **domestic demand curve** shows how the quantity of a good demanded by residents of a country depends on the price of that good. Why "domestic"? Because people living in other countries may demand the good, too. Once we introduce international trade, we need to distinguish between purchases of a good by domestic consumers and purchases by foreign consumers. So the domestic demand curve reflects only the demand of residents of our own country. Similarly, the **domestic supply curve** shows how the quantity of a good supplied by producers inside a country depends on the price of that good. Once we introduce international trade, we need to distinguish between the supply of domestic producers and foreign supply—supply brought in from abroad.

Economists use the term **autarky** to describe a situation in which a country cannot trade with other countries. In autarky, with no international trade in roses, the equilibrium in this market would be determined by the intersection of the domestic demand and domestic supply curves, point A. The equilibrium price of roses would be $P_A$, and the equilibrium quantity of roses produced and consumed would be $Q_A$. As always, both consumers and producers would gain from the existence of the domestic market. Consumer surplus would be equal to the area of the upper shaded triangle in Figure 13-2. Producer surplus would be equal to the area of the lower shaded triangle. And total surplus would be equal to the sum of these two shaded triangles.

Now let's imagine opening up this market to imports. To do this, we must make some assumption about the supply of imports. The simplest assumption, which we will adopt here, is that unlimited quantities of roses can be purchased from abroad at a fixed price, known as the **world price** of roses. Figure 13-3 shows a situation in which the world price of roses, $P_W$, is lower than the price of roses that would prevail in the domestic market in autarky, $P_A$.

Given the world price of roses is below the domestic price of roses, it is profitable for importers to buy roses abroad and resell them domestically. The imported roses increase the supply of roses to the domestic market, driving down the domestic market price.

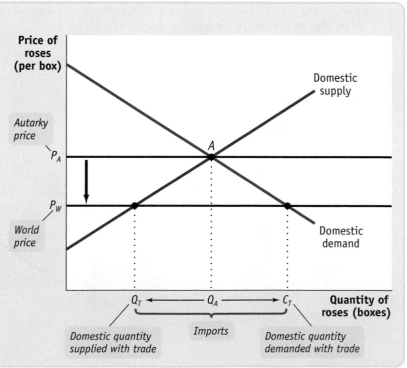

### Figure 13-3

**The Domestic Market with Imports**

Here the world price of roses, $P_W$, is below the autarky price, $P_A$. When the economy is opened to international trade, imports enter the domestic market, and the domestic price falls from the autarky price, $P_A$, to the world price, $P_W$. As the price falls, the domestic quantity demanded rises from $Q_A$ to $C_T$ and domestic production falls from $Q_A$ to $Q_T$. The difference between domestic quantity demanded and domestic quantity supplied at $P_W$, the quantity $C_T - Q_T$, is filled by imports.

**>web...**

Roses will continue to be imported until the domestic price falls to a level equal to the world price.

The result is shown in Figure 13-3. Because of imports, the domestic price of roses falls from $P_A$ to $P_W$. The quantity of roses demanded by domestic consumers rises from $Q_A$ to $C_T$, and the quantity supplied by domestic producers falls from $Q_A$ to $Q_T$. The difference between the domestic quantity demanded and the domestic quantity supplied, $C_T - Q_T$, is filled by imports.

Now let's turn to the effects of imports on consumer surplus and producer surplus. Because imports of roses lead to a fall in their domestic price, consumer surplus rises and producer surplus falls. Figure 13-4 shows how this works. We label four areas: $W$, $X$, $Y$, and $Z$. The autarky consumer surplus we identified in Figure 13-2 corresponds to $W$, and the autarky producer surplus corresponds to the sum of $X$ and $Y$. The fall in the domestic price to the world price leads to an increase in consumer surplus; it increases by the areas $X$ and $Z$, so that it now equals the sum of $W$, $X$, and $Z$. At the same time, producers lose the area $X$ in surplus, so that producer surplus now equals only $Y$.

The table in Figure 13-4 summarizes the changes in consumer and producer surplus when the rose market is opened to imports. Consumers gain surplus equal to the area $X + Z$. Producers lose surplus equal to the area $X$. So the sum of producer and consumer surplus—the total surplus generated in the rose market—increases by the area $Z$. As a result of trade, consumers gain and producers lose, but the gain to consumers exceeds the loss to producers.

This is an important result. We have just shown that opening up a market to imports leads to a net gain in total surplus, which is what we should have expected given the proposition that there are gains from international trade. However, we have also learned that although the country as a whole gains, some groups—in this case,

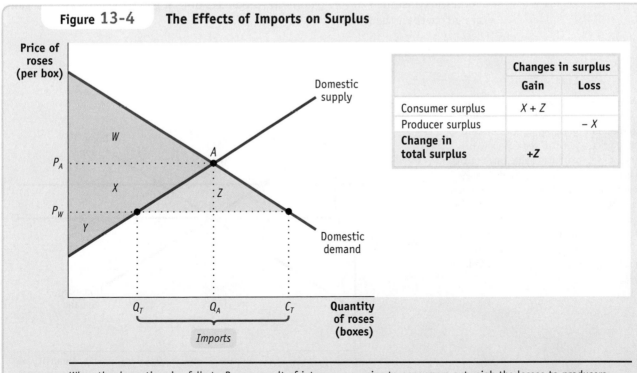

**Figure 13-4** **The Effects of Imports on Surplus**

| | Changes in surplus | |
|---|---|---|
| | Gain | Loss |
| Consumer surplus | $X + Z$ | |
| Producer surplus | | $- X$ |
| **Change in total surplus** | $+Z$ | |

When the domestic price falls to $P_W$ as a result of international trade, consumers gain additional surplus (areas $X + Z$) and producers lose surplus (area $X$). Because the gains to consumers outweigh the losses to producers, there is an increase in the total surplus in the economy as a whole (area $Z$).

domestic producers of roses—lose as a result of international trade. As we'll see shortly, the fact that international trade typically creates losers as well as winners is crucial for understanding the politics of trade policy.

We turn next to the case in which a country exports a good.

## The Effects of Exports

Figure 13-5 shows the effects on a country when it exports a good, in this case computers. For this example, we assume that unlimited quantities of computers can be sold abroad at a given world price, $P_W$, which is higher than the price that would prevail in the domestic market in autarky, $P_A$.

The higher world price makes it profitable for exporters to buy computers domestically and sell them overseas. The purchases of domestic computers drives the domestic price up until the domestic price is equal to the world price. As a result, the quantity demanded by domestic consumers falls from $Q_A$ to $C_T$, and the quantity supplied by domestic producers rises from $Q_A$ to $Q_T$. This difference between domestic production and domestic consumption, $Q_T - C_T$, is exported.

Like imports, exports lead to an overall gain in total surplus for the exporting country, but also create losers as well as winners. Figure 13-6 shows the effects of computer exports on producer and consumer surplus. In the absence of trade, the price of computers would be $P_A$. Consumer surplus in the absence of trade is the sum of the areas $W$ and $X$, and producer surplus would be the area $Y$. As a result of trade, price rises from $P_A$ to $P_W$, consumer surplus falls to $W$, and producer surplus rises to $Y + X + Z$. So producers gain $X + Z$, consumers lose $X$, and, as shown in the table accompanying the figure, the economy as a whole gains total surplus in the amount of $Z$.

We have learned, then, that imports of a particular good hurt domestic producers of that good but help domestic consumers, whereas exports of a particular good hurt domestic consumers but help domestic producers of that good. In each case, the gains are larger than the losses.

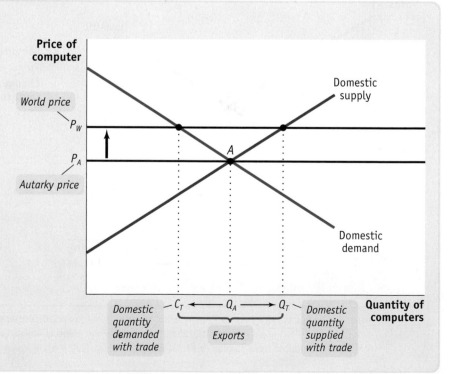

### Figure 13-5

#### The Domestic Market with Exports

Here the world price, $P_W$, is greater than the autarky price, $P_A$. When the economy is opened to international trade, some of the domestic supply is now exported. The domestic price rises from the autarky price, $P_A$, to the world price, $P_W$. As the price rises, the domestic quantity demanded falls from $Q_A$ to $C_T$ and domestic production rises from $Q_A$ to $Q_T$. The remainder of the domestic quantity supplied, $Q_T - C_T$, is exported.

**>web...**

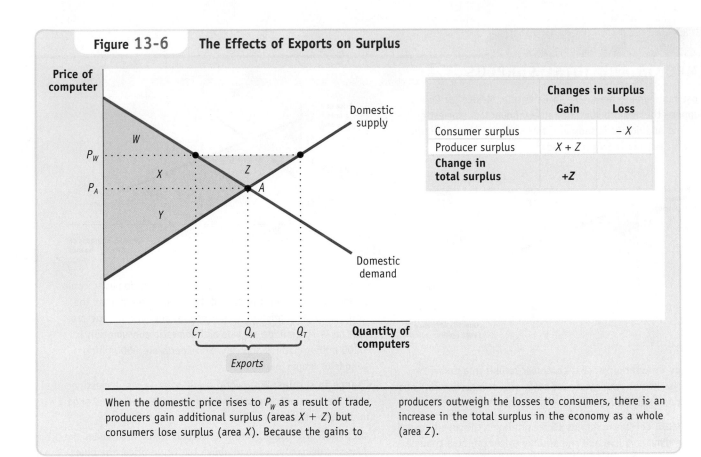

**Figure 13-6**     **The Effects of Exports on Surplus**

| | Changes in surplus | |
| --- | --- | --- |
| | Gain | Loss |
| Consumer surplus | | – X |
| Producer surplus | X + Z | |
| **Change in total surplus** | **+Z** | |

When the domestic price rises to $P_W$ as a result of trade, producers gain additional surplus (areas $X + Z$) but consumers lose surplus (area $X$). Because the gains to producers outweigh the losses to consumers, there is an increase in the total surplus in the economy as a whole (area $Z$).

## International Trade and Factor Markets

So far we have focused on the effects of international trade on producers and consumers in a particular industry. For many purposes this is a very helpful approach. But to understand the long-run effects of international trade on income distribution, this approach can be inadequate, because factors of production move between industries.

To see the problem, consider the position of Maria, a trained accountant who currently works for a U.S. company that grows flowers. If the economy is opened up to imports of roses from South America, the domestic rose-growing industry will contract, and it will hire fewer accountants. But accounting is a profession with employment opportunities in many industries, and Maria might well find a better job in the computer industry, which expands as a result of international trade. So it may not be appropriate to think of her as a producer of flowers who is hurt by competition from imported roses. Rather, what matters to her is the effect of international trade on the salaries of accountants, wherever they are employed. In other words, sometimes it is important to analyze the effect of trade on *factor prices*.

Earlier in this chapter we described the Heckscher–Ohlin model of trade, which states that comparative advantage is determined by a country's factor endowment. This model also suggests how international trade affects factor prices in a country: compared to autarky, international trade tends to raise the prices of factors that are abundantly available and reduce the prices of factors that are scarce.

We won't work this out in detail, but the idea is intuitively simple. Think of a country's industries as consisting of two kinds: **exporting industries,** which produce goods and services that are sold abroad, and **import-competing industries,** which produce goods and services that are also imported. Compared with autarky, interna-

**Exporting industries** produce goods and services that are sold abroad.

**Import-competing industries** produce goods and services that are also imported.

# WORK IT OUT

## IMPORTS AND TOTAL SURPLUS

Most table grapes are grown in California, Mexico, or Chile. Suppose the graph below shows the annual U.S. domestic demand and domestic supply of table grapes. The equilibrium price in autarky is $4 per pound.

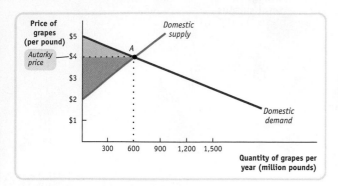

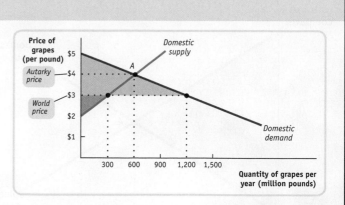

**Surplus in Autarky:** What is consumer surplus in autarky? (*Autarky: When a country cannot trade with other countries.*) What is producer surplus in autarky? What is total surplus in autarky?

SOLUTION: Consumer surplus *CS* in autarky is the area bounded by the demand curve and the autarky price, the blue triangle. *CS* = ($1 × 600 million) / 2 = $300 million. Producer surplus *PS* in autarky is the area bounded by the supply curve and the autarky price, the red triangle. *PS* = ($2 × 600 million) / 2 = $600 million. Total surplus *TS* is the sum of consumer and producer surplus. *TS* = $300 + $600 million = $900 million.

**Imports:** The world price is $3 per pound. How many million pounds of grapes are imported per year?

SOLUTION: Imports are the difference between domestic consumption at the world price and domestic production at the world price. At a price of $3 per pound, annual domestic production is 300 million pounds and domestic consumption is 1,200 million pounds annually. So imports are 900 million pounds of grapes per year.

**Change in surplus:** With world trade, what is the domestic consumer surplus, domestic producer surplus, and the change in domestic total surplus?

SOLUTION: With trade, consumer surplus is the area under the domestic demand curve and above the world price, the blue triangle. *CS* = ($2 × 1,200 million) / 2 = $1,200 million. Producer surplus with trade is the area above the domestic supply curve and below the world price, the red triangle. *PS* = ($1 × 300 million) / 2 = $150 million. Total surplus with trade is the sum of consumer and producer surplus. *TS* = $1,200 + 150 million = $1,350 million. Total domestic surplus increased by $450 million as a result of trade.

tional trade leads to higher production in exporting industries and lower production in import-competing industries. This indirectly increases the demand for the factors used by exporting industries and decreases the demand for factors used by import-competing industries. In addition, the Heckscher–Ohlin model says that a country tends to export goods that are intensive in its abundant factors and to import goods that are intensive in its scarce factors. *So international trade tends to increase the demand for factors that are abundant in our country compared with other countries, and to decrease the demand for factors that are scarce in our country compared with other countries. As a result, the prices of abundant factors tend to rise, and the prices of scarce factors tend to fall.*

Economics in Action on page 334 pointed out that U.S. exports tend to be human-capital-intensive and U.S. imports tend to be unskilled-labor-intensive. This suggests that the effect of international trade on U.S. factor markets is to raise the wage rate of highly educated workers and to reduce the wage rate of unskilled workers.

This effect has been a source of some concern in recent years. Wage inequality—the gap between the wages of highly paid and low-paid workers—has increased substantially over the last 25 years. Some economists believe that growing international trade is an important factor in that trend. If international trade has the effects predicted by the Heckscher–Ohlin model, it raises the wages of highly educated workers, who already have relatively high wages, and lowers the wages of less educated workers, who already have relatively low wages.

How important are these effects? In some historical episodes, the impacts of international trade on factor prices have been very large. As we explain in the Economics in Action that follows, the opening of transatlantic trade in the late nineteenth century had a large negative impact on land rents in Europe, hurting landowners but helping workers and owners of capital. The effects of trade on wages in the United States have generated considerable controversy in recent years. Most economists who have studied the issue agree that growing imports of labor-intensive products from newly industrializing economies, and the export of high-technology goods in return, have helped cause a widening wage differential between highly educated and less educated workers in this country. However, other forces, especially technological change, are probably more important in explaining growing wage inequality.

## *economics in action*

### Trade, Wages, and Land Prices in the Nineteenth Century

Beginning around 1870, there was an explosive growth of world trade in agricultural products, based largely on the steam engine. Steam-powered ships could cross the ocean much more quickly and reliably than sailing ships. Until about 1860, steamships had higher costs than sailing ships, but after that rates dropped sharply. At the same time, steam-powered rail transport made it possible to bring grain and other bulk goods cheaply from the interior to ports. The result was that land-abundant countries—the United States, Canada, Argentina, Australia—began shipping large quantities of agricultural goods to the densely populated, land-scarce countries of Europe.

This opening up of international trade led to higher prices of agricultural products, such as wheat, in exporting countries and a decline in their prices in importing countries. Notably, the difference between wheat prices in the midwestern United States and England plunged.

The change in agricultural prices created both winners and losers on both sides of the Atlantic as factor prices adjusted. In England, land prices fell by half compared with average wages; landowners found their purchasing power sharply reduced, but workers benefited from cheaper food. In the United States, the reverse happened: land prices doubled compared with wages. Landowners did very well, but workers found the purchasing power of their wages dented by rising food prices. ∎

> > > > > > > > > > > > > > > > > > > > >

**>>CHECK YOUR UNDERSTANDING 13-2**

1. Due to a strike by truckers, trade in food between the United States and Mexico is halted. In autarky, the price of Mexican grapes is lower than that of U.S grapes. Using a diagram of the U.S. domestic demand curve and the U.S domestic supply curve for grapes, explain the effect of these events on the following:
   a. U.S grape consumers' surplus
   b. U.S grape producers' surplus
   c. U.S total surplus

2. What effect do you think these events have on Mexican grape producers? Mexican grape pickers? Mexican grape consumers? U.S. grape pickers?

Solutions appear at back of book.

## The Effects of Trade Protection

David Ricardo laid out the principle of comparative advantage in the early nineteenth century. Ever since most economists have advocated **free trade**. That is, they have argued that government policy should not attempt either to reduce or to

>>**QUICK REVIEW**

➤ The intersection of the *domestic demand curve* and the *domestic supply curve* determines the *autarky* price of a good. When a market is opened to international trade, the domestic price is driven to equal the *world price*.

➤ If the world price is lower than the autarky price, trade leads to imports, and the domestic price falls to the world price. There are overall gains from trade because the gain in consumer surplus exceeds the loss in producer surplus.

➤ If the world price is higher than the autarky price, trade leads to exports, and the domestic price rises to the world price. There are overall gains from trade because the gain in producer surplus exceeds the loss in consumer surplus.

➤ Trade leads to an expansion of *exporting industries*, which increases demand for a country's abundant factors, and a contraction of *import-competing industries*, which decreases demand for its scarce factors.

An economy has **free trade** when the government does not attempt either to reduce or to increase the levels of exports and imports that occur naturally as a result of supply and demand.

Policies that limit imports are known as **trade protection** or simply as **protection**.

increase the levels of exports and imports that occur naturally as a result of supply and demand. Despite the free-trade arguments of economists, however, many governments use taxes and other restrictions to limit imports. Much less frequently, governments offer subsidies to encourage exports. Policies that limit imports, usually with the goal of protecting domestic producers in import-competing industries from foreign competition, are known as **trade protection** or simply as **protection.**

Let's look at the two most common protectionist policies, tariffs and import quotas, then turn to the reasons governments follow these policies.

## The Effects of a Tariff

A **tariff** is a tax levied on imports.

A **tariff** is a form of excise tax, one that is levied only on sales of imported goods. For example, the U.S. government could declare that anyone bringing in roses from Colombia must pay a tariff of $2 per rose, or $200 per box of 100 roses. In the distant past, tariffs were an important source of government revenue because they were relatively easy to collect. But in the modern world, tariffs are usually intended to discourage imports and protect import-competing domestic producers rather than as a source of government revenue.

The effect of a tariff is to raise both the price received by domestic producers and the price paid by domestic consumers. Suppose, for example, that our country imports roses, and a box of 100 roses is available on the world market at $400. As we saw earlier, under free trade the domestic price would also be $400. But if a tariff of $200 per box is imposed, the domestic price will rise to $600, and it won't be profitable to import roses unless the price in the domestic market is high enough to compensate importers for the cost of paying the tariff.

Figure 13-7 illustrates the effects of a tariff on rose imports. As before, we assume that $P_W$ is the world price of roses. Before the tariff is imposed, imports have driven

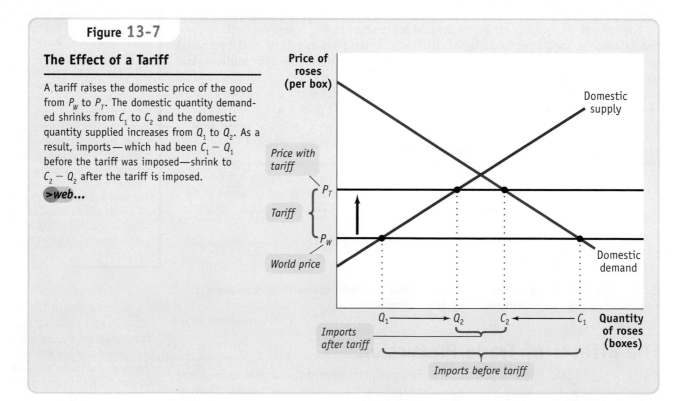

### Figure 13-7

### The Effect of a Tariff

A tariff raises the domestic price of the good from $P_W$ to $P_T$. The domestic quantity demanded shrinks from $C_1$ to $C_2$ and the domestic quantity supplied increases from $Q_1$ to $Q_2$. As a result, imports—which had been $C_1 - Q_1$ before the tariff was imposed—shrink to $C_2 - Q_2$ after the tariff is imposed.

**>web...**

the domestic price down to $P_W$, so that pre-tariff domestic production is $Q_1$, pre-tariff domestic consumption is $C_1$, and pre-tariff imports are $C_1 - Q_1$.

Now suppose that the government imposes a tariff on each box of roses imported. As a consequence, it is no longer profitable to import roses unless the domestic price received by the importer is greater than or equal to the world price *plus* the tariff. So the domestic price rises to $P_T$, which is equal to the world price, $P_W$, plus the tariff. Domestic production rises to $Q_2$, domestic consumption falls to $C_2$, and imports fall to $C_2 - Q_2$.

A tariff, then, raises domestic prices, and leads to increased domestic production and reduced domestic consumption compared to the situation under free trade. Figure 13-8 shows the effects on surplus. There are three effects. First, the higher domestic price increases producer surplus, a gain equal to area $A$. Second, the higher domestic price reduces consumer surplus, a reduction equal to the sum of areas $A$, $B$, $C$, and $D$. Finally, the tariff yields revenue to the government. How much revenue? The government collects the tariff—which, remember, is equal to the difference between $P_T$ and $P_W$ on each of the $C_2 - Q_2$ roses imported. So total revenue is $(P_T - P_W) \times (C_2 - Q_2)$. This is equal to area $C$.

The welfare effects of a tariff are summarized in the table in Figure 13-8. Producers gain, consumers lose, the government gains. But consumer losses are greater than the sum of producer and government gains, leading to a net reduction in total surplus equal to areas $B + D$.

Recall that in Chapter 6 we analyzed the effect of an excise tax—a tax on buyers or sellers of a good. We saw that an excise tax creates inefficiency, or deadweight loss, because it prevents mutually beneficial trades from occurring. The same is true of a tariff, where its deadweight loss on society is equal to the loss in total surplus represented by areas $B + D$. Tariffs generate deadweight losses because they create

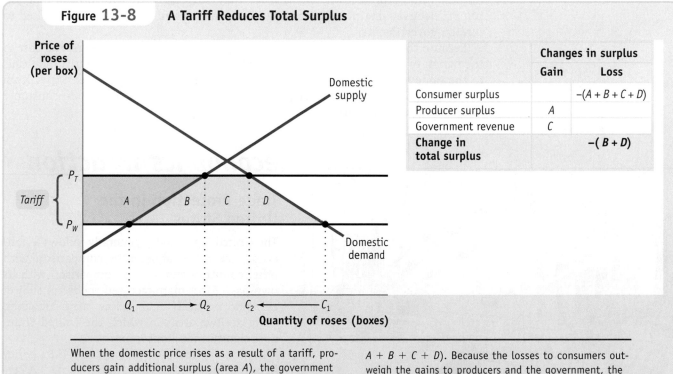

**Figure 13-8      A Tariff Reduces Total Surplus**

| | Changes in surplus | |
|---|---|---|
| | **Gain** | **Loss** |
| Consumer surplus | | $-(A + B + C + D)$ |
| Producer surplus | $A$ | |
| Government revenue | $C$ | |
| **Change in total surplus** | | $-(B + D)$ |

When the domestic price rises as a result of a tariff, producers gain additional surplus (area $C$), and consumers lose surplus (areas $A + B + C + D$). Because the losses to consumers outweigh the gains to producers and the government, the economy as a whole loses surplus (areas $B + D$).  **>web...**

inefficiencies in two ways. First, some mutually beneficial trades go unexploited: some consumers who are willing to pay more than the world price, $P_W$, do not purchase the good, even though $P_W$ is the true cost of a unit of the good to the economy. The cost of this inefficiency is represented in Figure 13-8 by area $D$. Second, the economy's resources are wasted on inefficient production: some producers whose cost exceeds $P_W$ produce the good, even though an additional unit of the good can be purchased abroad for $P_W$. The cost of this inefficiency is represented in Figure 13-8 by area $B$.

## The Effects of an Import Quota

An **import quota** is a legal limit on the quantity of a good that can be imported.

An **import quota,** another form of trade protection, is a legal limit on the quantity of a good that can be imported. For example, a U.S. import quota on Colombian roses might limit the number imported each year to 50 million. Import quotas are usually administered through licenses: a number of licenses are issued, each giving the license-holder the right to import a limited quantity of the good each year.

We discussed quotas in Chapter 4, where we saw that a quota on sales has the same effect as an excise tax, with one difference: the money that would otherwise have accrued to the government as tax revenue under an excise tax becomes quota rents to license-holders under a quota. Similarly, an import quota has the same effect as a tariff, with one difference: the money that would otherwise have been government revenue becomes quota rents to license-holders. Look again at Figure 13-8. An import quota that limits imports to $C_2 - Q_2$ will raise the domestic price of roses by the same amount as the tariff we considered previously. That is, it will raise the domestic price from $P_W$ to $P_T$. However, area $C$ will now represent quota rents rather than government revenue.

Who receives import licenses and so collects the quota rents? In the case of U.S. import protection, the answer may surprise you: the most important import licenses—mainly for clothing, to a lesser extent for sugar—are granted to foreign governments.

Because the quota rents for most U.S. import quotas go to foreigners, the cost to the nation of such quotas is larger than that of a comparable tariff (a tariff that leads to the same level of imports). In Figure 13-8 the net loss to the United States from such an import quota would be equal to $B + C + D$, the difference between consumer losses and producer gains.

KAL, Cartoonists & Writers Syndicate http://CartoonWeb.com

# economics in action

## Trade Protection in the United States

The United States today generally follows a policy of free trade, at least in comparison with other countries and also in comparison with its own past. Most manufactured goods are subject either to no tariff or to a low tariff. However, there are two areas in which the United States does significantly limit imports.

One is agriculture. The typical U.S. policy here is something called a "tariff quota." A certain amount of the imports are subject to a low tariff rate; this acts like an import quota because an importer is allowed to pay the low rate only if she has a license. Any additional imports are subject to a much higher tariff rate. We have tariff quotas on beef, dairy products, sugar, peanuts, and other things. For Inquiring Minds on page 346 discusses the sugar quota in the context of worldwide sugar policy.

The other area in which the United States significantly limits imports is clothing and textiles, where the government applies an elaborate system of import quotas.

The peculiar thing about U.S. trade protection is that in most cases quota licenses are assigned to foreigners, often foreign governments. For example, rights to sell clothing in the United States are allotted to various exporting countries, which can then hand those rights out as they see fit. This means that the quota rents go overseas, greatly increasing the cost to the United States of the import limitations. In fact, according to some estimates, about 70 percent of the total cost of U.S. import restrictions comes not from deadweight loss but from the transfer of quota rents to foreigners. ∎

> > > > > > > > > > > > > > > > > > > > >

## >>CHECK YOUR UNDERSTANDING 13-3

1. Suppose that the world price of butter is $0.50 per pound and the domestic price in autarky is $1.00 per pound. Use a diagram similar to Figure 13-7 to show the following:
   a. If there is free trade, domestic butter producers want the government to impose a tariff of no less than $0.50 per pound.
   b. What happens if a tariff greater than $0.50 per pound is imposed.

2. Suppose the government imposes an import quota rather than a tariff on butter. What quota limit would generate the same quantity of imports as a tariff of $0.50 per pound?

Solutions appear at back of book.

# The Political Economy of Trade Protection

We have seen that international trade produces mutual benefits to the countries that engage in it. We have also seen that tariffs and import quotas, although they produce winners as well as losers, reduce total surplus. Yet many countries continue to impose tariffs and import quotas, and to enact other protectionist measures.

To understand why trade protection takes place, we will first look at some common justifications for protection. Then we will look at the politics of trade protection. Finally, we will look at an important feature of trade protection in today's world: tariffs and import quotas are the subject of international negotiation and are policed by international organizations.

## Arguments for Trade Protection

Advocates of tariffs and import quotas offer a variety of arguments. Three common arguments are *national security*, *job creation*, and the *infant industry argument*.

The national security argument is based on the proposition that overseas sources of goods are vulnerable to disruption in times of international conflict; therefore a country should protect domestic suppliers of crucial goods with the aim to be self-sufficient in those goods. In the 1960s, the United States—which had begun to import oil as domestic oil reserves ran low—had an import quota on oil, justified on national security grounds. Some people have argued that we should again have policies to discourage imports of oil, especially from the Middle East.

The job creation argument points to the additional jobs created in import-competing industries as a result of trade protection. Economists argue that these jobs are offset by the jobs lost elsewhere, such as industries that use imported inputs and now face higher input costs. But noneconomists don't always find this argument persuasive.

Finally, the infant industry argument, often raised in newly industrializing countries, holds that new industries require a temporary period of trade protection to get

If there's one good in which we can be absolutely sure that neither the European Union nor the United States has a comparative advantage, it's sugar. The cheapest way to produce sugar is by growing sugar cane, a crop that requires a tropical climate. A few places in the United States can grow cane sugar (basically along the Gulf of Mexico and in Hawaii), but they are no match for the sugar-growing capacity of genuinely tropical countries. And it's almost impossible to grow sugar cane in Western Europe.

Yet Europe is a net *exporter* of sugar, and the United States imports only a fraction of its consumption. How is this possible, and why does it happen?

It's possible because there is another less efficient way to produce sugar: sugar beets can survive even in cold climates. On both sides of the Atlantic, sugar producers receive huge amounts of government support. In the United States, an import quota keeps prices on average at twice world levels. In Europe, import restrictions are supplemented by huge government subsidies to farmers.

What's the rationale for this trade protection? Governments hardly even bother to make excuses: on both sides of the Atlantic, there's a powerful farm lobby. In fact, agriculture in industrial countries is heavily subsidized, at the expense of both consumers and taxpayers.

The really sad thing is that some of the protected goods—sugar in particular— would be major exports of poor countries (and major sources of income for their poor farmers) if it weren't for the import quotas and subsidies in advanced countries.

established. For example, in the 1950s many countries in Latin America imposed tariffs and import quotas on manufactured goods, in an effort to switch from their traditional role as exporters of raw materials to a new status as industrial countries.

## The Politics of Trade Protection

In reality, much trade protection has little to do with the arguments just described. Instead, it reflects the political influence of import-competing producers.

We've seen that a tariff or import quota leads to gains for import-competing producers and losses for consumers. Producers, however, usually have much more influence over trade policy decisions. The producers who compete with imports of a particular good are usually a smaller, more cohesive group than the consumers of that good.

An example is trade protection for sugar, discussed in For Inquiring Minds above. The United States has an import quota on sugar, which on average leads to a domestic price about twice the world price. This quota is difficult to rationalize in terms of any economic argument. However, consumers rarely complain about the quota because they are unaware that it exists: Because no individual consumer buys large amounts of sugar, the cost of the quota is only a few dollars per family each year, not enough to attract notice. But there are only a few thousand sugar growers in the United States. They are very aware of the benefits they receive from the quota and make sure that their representatives in Congress are aware of their interest in the matter.

Given these political realities, it may seem surprising that trade is as free as it is. The United States has low tariffs, and its import quotas are mainly confined to clothing and a few agricultural products. It would be nice to say that the main reason trade protection is so limited is that economists have convinced governments of the virtues of free trade. A more important reason, however, is the role of *international trade agreements*.

## International Trade Agreements and the World Trade Organization

When a country engages in trade protection, it hurts two groups. We've already emphasized the adverse effect on domestic consumers, but protection also hurts foreign export industries. This means that countries care about each others' trade policies: the Canadian lumber industry has a strong interest in keeping U.S. tariffs on forest products low.

Because countries care about each others' trade policies, they engage in **international trade agreements:** treaties in which a country promises to engage in less trade protection against the exports of another country in return for a promise by the other country to do the same for its exports. Most world trade is now governed by such agreements.

Some international trade agreements involve just two countries or a small group of countries. In 1993, the U.S. Congress approved the North American Free Trade Agreement (NAFTA) between the United States, Canada, and Mexico. Once fully implemented, this agreement will remove all barriers to trade among the three nations. Free trade has already been implemented among the 25 nations of the European Union.

There are also global trade agreements, covering most of the world. Such global agreements are overseen by the **World Trade Organization,** or WTO, which plays two roles. First, it provides the framework for the massively complex negotiations involved in a major international trade agreement (the full text of the last major agreement, approved in 1994, was 24,000 pages long). Second, the WTO resolves disputes between members. These disputes typically arise when one country claims that another country's policies violate its previous agreements.

Here are two examples that illustrate the WTO's role. First, in 1999 the WTO ruled that the European Union's import restrictions on bananas, which discriminate in favor of producers in former European colonies and against Central American producers, are in violation of international trade rules. The banana dispute had threatened to become a major source of conflict between the European Union and the United States because the United States has taken the side of the Central American countries. Europe is currently in the process of revising its system. In 2002 the United States was on the losing side of a WTO decision: the European Union complained that a provision in U.S. tax law, intended to help exporting companies, is in effect an export subsidy—which is not allowed according to international agreements. The WTO ruled in Europe's favor and the United States is now obliged to revise its tax law.

The WTO is sometimes, with great exaggeration, described as a world government. In fact, it has no army, no police, and no direct enforcement power. The grain of truth in that description is that when a country joins the WTO, it agrees to accept the organization's judgments—and these judgments apply not only to tariffs and import quotas but also to domestic policies that, according to the organization, are in effect trade protection under another name. So in joining the WTO a country does give up a bit of its sovereignty.

> **International trade agreements** are treaties in which a country promises to engage in less trade protection against the exports of other countries in return for a promise by other countries to do the same for its own exports.

> The **World Trade Organization** oversees international trade agreements and rules on disputes between countries over those agreements.

# *economics in action*

## Declining Tariffs

The United States began basing its trade policy on international agreements in the 1930s, and global trade negotiations began soon after World War II. The success of these agreements in reducing trade protection is illustrated by Figure 13-9 on page 348, which shows the average U.S. tariff rate on imports subject to tariffs since the 1920s.

Tariffs reached a peak in the early 1930s after the passage of a very protectionist bill, known as the Smoot-Hawley tariff, in 1930. (Some people blame Smoot-Hawley for causing the Great Depression of the 1930s, though few economists think it was *that* bad.) From then on, tariff rates have steadily ratcheted down, with U.S. moves matched in other advanced countries, and later in many poorer countries as well.

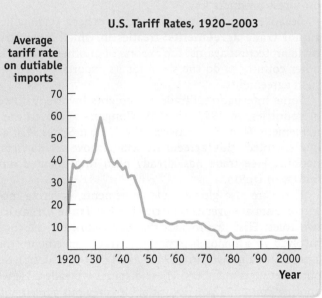

**Figure 13-9**

**Declining Tariff Rates**

U.S. tariff rates were very high in the early 1930s but have steadily fallen since then. This move toward relatively free trade has been achieved in large part through international trade agreements.

*Source:* U.S. International Trade Commission.

**U.S. Tariff Rates, 1920–2003**

At this point world trade in manufactured goods is subject to low tariffs and relatively few import quotas, with clothing the main exception. Agricultural products are subject to many more restrictions, reflecting the political power of farmers in advanced countries. ∎

< < < < < < < < < < < < < < < < <

**>>CHECK YOUR UNDERSTANDING 13-4**

1. In 2002 the U.S. imposed tariffs on steel imports, which are an input in a large number and variety of U.S. industries. Explain why political lobbying to eliminate these tariffs is more likely to be effective than political lobbying to eliminate tariffs on consumer goods such as sugar or clothing.

2. Over the years, the WTO has increasingly found itself adjudicating trade disputes that involve not just tariffs or quota restrictions but also restrictions based on quality, health, and environmental considerations. Why do you think this has occurred? What method would you, as a WTO official, use to decide whether a quality, health, or environmental restriction is in violation of a free-trade agreement?

Solutions appear at back of book.

**● A LOOK AHEAD ●**

We have now completed our survey of microeconomics—the study of economic decision-making by individuals. We have encountered some important principles. Prices of products are determined in markets by the forces of supply and demand. Marginal analysis helps us to answer many of the important questions in microeconomics. Markets usually work well but in some cases fail, creating a role for government intervention. Specialization and trade can increase worldwide output and total surplus.

Now we turn to the survey of macroeconomics—the study of the economy as a whole. What determines not the price of a product, but the overall trend of prices? What determines not labor demand in a market, but the overall level of employment? What role can the government take in improving the macroeconomy? These are the questions we address in the last third of the book.

## SUMMARY

1. International trade is of growing importance to the United States and of even greater importance to most other countries. International trade, like trade among individuals, arises from comparative advantage: the opportunity cost of producing an additional unit of a good is lower in some countries than in others. Goods and services purchased abroad are **imports;** those sold abroad are **exports.**

2. In practice, comparative advantage reflects differences between countries in climate, factor endowments, and technology. The **Heckscher–Ohlin model** shows how differences in factor endowments determine comparative advantage: goods differ in **factor intensity,** and countries tend to export goods that are intensive in the factors they have in abundance.

3. The **domestic demand curve** and the **domestic supply curve** determine the price of a good in **autarky.** When international trade occurs, the domestic price is driven to equality with the **world price,** the price at which the good may be bought or sold abroad.

4. If the world price is below the autarky price, a good is imported. This leads to an increase in consumer surplus, a fall in producer surplus, and a gain in total surplus. If the world price is above the autarky price, a good is exported. This leads to an increase in producer surplus, a fall in consumer surplus, and a gain in total surplus.

5. International trade leads to expansion in **exporting industries** and contraction in **import-competing**

industries. This raises the domestic demand for abundant factors of production, reduces the demand for scarce factors, and so affects factor prices.

6. Most economists advocate **free trade,** but in practice many governments engage in **trade protection.** The two most common forms of **protection** are tariffs and quotas; in rare occasions, export industries are subsidized.

7. A **tariff** is a tax levied on imports. It raises the domestic price above the world price, hurting consumers, benefiting domestic producers, and generating government revenue. As a result, total surplus falls. An **import quota** is a legal limit on the quantity of a good that can be imported. It has the same effects as a tariff, except that the revenue goes not to the government but to those who receive import licenses.

8. Although several popular arguments have been made in favor of trade protection, in practice the main reason for protection is probably political: import-competing industries are well organized and well informed about how they gain from trade protection, while consumers are unaware of the costs they pay. Still, U.S. trade is fairly free, mainly because of the role of **international trade agreements,** in which countries agree to reduce trade protection against each others' exports. Trade negotiations are overseen, and the resulting agreements are enforced, by the **World Trade Organization.**

## KEY TERMS

Imports, p. 331
Exports, p. 331
Factor intensity, p. 333
Heckscher–Ohlin model, p. 333
Domestic demand curve, p. 336
Domestic supply curve, p. 336

Autarky, p. 336
World price, p. 336
Exporting industries, p. 339
Import-competing industries, p. 339
Free trade, p. 341
Trade protection, p. 342

Protection, p. 342
Tariff, p. 342
Import quota, p. 344
International trade agreements, p. 347
World Trade Organization, p. 347

## PROBLEMS

1. For each of the following trade relationships, explain the likely source of the comparative advantage of each of the exporting countries.

   a. The United States exports software to Venezuela, and Venezuela exports oil to the United States.

   b. The United States exports airplanes to China, and China exports clothing to the United States.

   c. The United States exports wheat to Colombia, and Colombia exports coffee to the United States.

2. Shoes are labor-intensive and satellites are capital-intensive to produce. The United States has abundant capital. China has abundant labor. According to the Heckscher–Ohlin model, which good will China export? Which good will the United

States export? In the United States, what will happen to the price of labor (the wage) and to the price of capital?

3. Before the North American Free Trade Agreement (NAFTA) gradually eliminated import tariffs on goods, the autarky price of tomatoes in Mexico was below the world price and in the United States was above the world price. Similarly, the autarky price of poultry in Mexico was above the world price and in the United States was below the world price. Draw diagrams with domestic supply and demand curves for each country and each of the two goods. As a result of NAFTA, the United States now imports tomatoes from Mexico and the United States now exports poultry to Mexico. How would you expect the following groups to be affected?

a. Mexican and U.S. consumers of tomatoes. Illustrate the effect on consumer surplus in your diagram.

b. Mexican and U.S. producers of tomatoes. Illustrate the effect on producer surplus in your diagram.

c. Mexican and U.S. tomato workers.

d. Mexican and U.S. consumers of poultry. Illustrate the effect on consumer surplus in your diagram.

e. Mexican and U.S. producers of poultry. Illustrate the effect on producer surplus in your diagram.

f. Mexican and U.S. poultry workers.

4. The accompanying table indicates the U.S. domestic demand schedule and domestic supply schedule for commercial jet airplanes. Suppose that the world price of a commercial jet airplane is $100 million.

| Price of jet (millions) | Quantity of jets demanded | Quantity of jets supplied |
| --- | --- | --- |
| $120 | 100 | 1,000 |
| 110 | 150 | 900 |
| 100 | 200 | 800 |
| 90 | 250 | 700 |
| 80 | 300 | 600 |
| 70 | 350 | 500 |
| 60 | 400 | 400 |
| 50 | 450 | 300 |
| 40 | 500 | 200 |

a. In autarky, how many commercial jet airplanes does the United States produce, and at what price are they bought and sold?

b. With trade, what will the price for commercial jet airplanes be? Will the United States import or export airplanes? How many?

5. The accompanying table shows the U.S. domestic demand schedule and domestic supply schedule for oranges. Suppose that the world price of oranges is $0.30 per orange.

| Price of orange | Quantity of oranges demanded (thousands) | Quantity of oranges supplied (thousands) |
| --- | --- | --- |
| $1.00 | 2 | 11 |
| 0.90 | 4 | 10 |
| 0.80 | 6 | 9 |
| 0.70 | 8 | 8 |
| 0.60 | 10 | 7 |
| 0.50 | 12 | 6 |
| 0.40 | 14 | 5 |
| 0.30 | 16 | 4 |
| 0.20 | 18 | 3 |

a. Draw the U.S. domestic supply curve and domestic demand curve.

b. With free trade, how many oranges will the United States import or export?

Suppose that the U.S. government imposes a tariff on oranges of $0.20 per orange.

c. How many oranges will the United States import or export after introduction of the tariff?

d. In your diagram, shade the gain or loss to the economy as a whole from the introduction of this tariff.

6. The U.S. domestic demand schedule and domestic supply schedule for oranges was given in Problem 8. Suppose that the world price of oranges is $0.30. The United States introduces an import quota of 3,000 oranges. Draw the domestic demand and supply curves and answer the following questions.

a. What will the domestic price of oranges be after introduction of the quota?

b. What is the value of the quota rents that importers of oranges receive?

7. The accompanying diagram illustrates the U.S. domestic demand curve and domestic supply curve for beef.

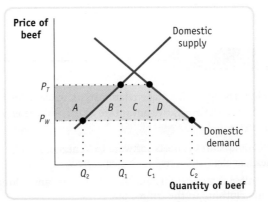

The world price of beef is $P_W$. The United States currently imposes an import tariff on beef, so the price of beef is $P_T$. Congress decides to eliminate the tariff. In terms of the areas marked in the diagram, answer the following questions.

**a.** What is the gain/loss in consumer surplus?

**b.** What is the gain/loss in producer surplus?

**c.** What is the gain/loss to the government?

**d.** What is the gain/loss to the economy as a whole?

**8.** As the United States has opened up to trade, it has lost many of its low-skill manufacturing jobs, but it has gained jobs in high-skill industries, such as the software industry. Explain whether the United States as a whole has been made better off by trade.

**9.** The United States is highly protective of its agricultural industry, imposing import tariffs, and sometimes quotas, on imports of agricultural goods. The chapter has presented three arguments for trade protection. For each argument, discuss whether it is a valid justification for trade protection of U.S. agricultural products.

**10.** In World Trade Organization (WTO) negotiations, if a country agrees to reduce trade barriers (tariffs or quotas), it usually refers to this as a *concession* to other countries. Do you think that this terminology is appropriate?

**11.** Producers in import-competing industries often make the following argument: "Other countries have an advantage in production of certain goods purely because workers abroad are paid lower wages. In fact, American workers are much more productive than foreign workers. So import-competing industries need to be protected." Is this a valid argument? Explain your answer.

> **web...** To continue your study and review of concepts in this chapter, please visit the Krugman/Wells/Olney website for quizzes, animated graph tutorials, web links to helpful resources, and more.
>
> **www.worthpublishers.com/krugmanwellsolney**

# 14

## >> Macroeconomics: The Big Picture

**What you will learn in this chapter:**

➤ An overview of macroeconomics, the study of the economy as a whole, and how it differs from microeconomics

➤ The importance of the **business cycle** and why policy makers seek to diminish the severity of business cycles

➤ The meaning of **inflation** and **deflation** and why **price stability** is preferred

### DISAPPOINTED GRADUATES

2000 WAS A VERY GOOD YEAR TO BE a new graduate of an American university or college. As one newspaper put it, companies were "tripping over themselves to entice graduating seniors with fat salaries and other perks." 2000 was a particularly good year for students graduating with an MBA degree. But events were not nearly as kind to those who graduated just two years later. For many members of the class of 2002 at American business schools, graduation was not the happy occasion they had expected—a golden ticket to a well-paying job and success. Even at top business schools, such as Harvard, the University of Pennsylvania, and Stanford, students and faculty watched in disbelief as recruiters reneged on job offers that had already been extended to hundreds of newly graduated MBAs. Months after commencement, many graduates still had not landed jobs. As shown in Table 14-1,

Even the best students had a tough time finding a job in 2002.

Jose Luis Pelaez/Corbis

graduates who did find jobs typically received lower salaries than those of graduates just two years earlier. (If you rank salaries from high to low, the median salary is the salary right at the middle.)

There was nothing wrong with the new MBAs in 2002; they were every bit as talented and motivated as the graduates two years earlier. And the phenomenon wasn't limited to business school graduates. The difference was that in the spring of 2000 the economy was booming, and employers were anxious to hire more people. In the spring of 2002 the economy was weak. Many firms were laying off employees and were in no hurry to hire more. As you can see from Table 14-1, by 2004 job prospects had improved somewhat; however, starting salaries still lagged behind the levels MBA graduates enjoyed in the spring of 2000.

The alternation between boom and bust—between years in which jobs are plentiful and years in

## TABLE 14-1

**Median Starting Salaries of New MBAs from Selected Schools in 2000, 2002, and 2004**

| School | 2000 starting salary | 2002 starting salary | 2004 starting salary |
|--------|---------------------|---------------------|---------------------|
| Stanford | $165,500 | $138,100 | $150,000 |
| Harvard | 160,000 | 134,600 | 147,500 |
| Pennsylvania | 156,000 | 124,500 | 144,000 |
| Columbia | 142,500 | 123,600 | 142,500 |
| Dartmouth | 149,500 | 122,100 | 135,000 |

*Source: Business Week* Graduate Survey, October 18, 2004.

which jobs are hard to find—is known as the *business cycle.* But why is there a business cycle, and can anything be done to smooth it out? That's one question addressed by *macroeconomics,* the area of economics that focuses on the behavior of the economy as a whole.

In contrast, *microeconomics* is concerned with the production and consumption decisions of consumers and producers and with the allocation of scarce resources among industries. Returning to our example of business school graduates, a typical question for microeconomics would be why different industries—say, investment banking versus marketing—pay different salaries to new graduates. Macroeconomics is concerned with developments in the national economy, such as the total output level, the overall level of prices, and the total level of employment.

Earlier chapters have given you a grasp of some fundamental microeconomic concepts and principles. To understand the scope and sweep of macroeconomics, let's begin by looking more carefully at the difference between microeconomics and macroeconomics. Following that, we'll present an overview of the three main areas of macroeconomic study.

# Microeconomics Versus Macroeconomics

Table 14-2 on page 354 lists some questions that are often asked in economics. A microeconomic version of the question appears on the left paired with a similar macroeconomic question on the right. By comparing the questions, you can begin to get a sense of the difference between microeconomics and macroeconomics.

As you can see, microeconomics focuses on how decisions are made by individuals and firms and the consequences of those decisions. For example, we use microeconomics to determine how much it would cost a university or college to offer a new course—a cost that includes the instructor's salary, the cost of class materials, and so on. The school can then decide whether or not to offer the course by weighing the costs and benefits. Macroeconomics, in contrast, examines the *aggregate* behavior of the economy—how the actions of all the individuals and firms in the economy interact to produce a particular economy-wide level of economic performance. For example, macroeconomics is concerned with the overall level of prices in the economy and how high or how low they are relative to prices last year, rather than focusing on the price of one particular good or service.

You might imagine that macroeconomic questions can be answered simply by adding up microeconomic answers. For example, the model of supply and demand

**TABLE 14-2**

**Microeconomic versus Macroeconomic Questions**

| Microeconomic Questions | Macroeconomic Questions |
| --- | --- |
| Should I go to business school or take a job right now? | How many people are employed in the economy as a whole this year? |
| What determines the salary offered by Citibank to Cherie Camajo, a new Columbia MBA? | What determines the overall salary levels paid to workers in a given year? |
| What determines the cost to a university or college of offering a new course? | What determines the overall level of prices in the economy as a whole? |
| What government policies should be adopted to make it easier for low-income students to attend college? | What government policies should be adopted to promote employment in the economy as a whole? |

we introduced in Chapter 3 tells us how the equilibrium price of an individual good or service is determined in a competitive market. So you might think that applying supply and demand analysis to every good and service in the economy, then summing the results, is the way to understand the overall level of prices in the economy as a whole.

But that turns out not to be the case: although basic concepts such as supply and demand are as essential to macroeconomics as they are to microeconomics, answering macroeconomic questions requires an additional set of tools and an expanded frame of reference. We'll start by considering three principal ways in which macroeconomics differs from microeconomics.

## Macroeconomics: The Whole Is Greater Than the Sum of Its Parts

If you occasionally drive on a highway, you probably know what a "rubber-necking" traffic jam is and why it is so annoying. Someone pulls over to the side of the road for something minor, such as changing a flat tire, and, pretty soon, a long traffic jam occurs as drivers slow down to take a look. What makes it so annoying is that the length of the traffic jam is greatly out of proportion to the minor event that precipitated it. Because some drivers hit their brakes in order to "rubber-neck," the drivers behind them must also hit their brakes, those behind them must do the same, and so on. The accumulation of all the individual tappings of brakes eventually leads to a long, wasteful traffic jam as each driver slows down a little bit more than the driver in front of him or her.

Understanding a rubber-necking traffic jam gives us some insight into one very important way in which macroeconomics is different from microeconomics: many thousands or millions of individual actions accumulate to produce an outcome that is larger than the simple sum of those individual actions. Consider, for example, what macroeconomists call the "Paradox of Thrift": when families and businesses are worried about the possibility of economic hard times, they prepare by cutting their spending. This reduction in spending depresses the economy as consumers spend less and businesses react by laying off workers. As a result, families and businesses may end up worse off than if they hadn't tried to act responsibly by cutting their spending. This is called a paradox because seemingly virtuous behavior—cautiously preparing for hard times by saving more—ends up harming everyone. And there is a flip-side to this story: when families and businesses are feeling optimistic about the future, they spend more today. This stimulates the economy, leading businesses to hire more workers, which further expands the economy. Seemingly profligate behavior leads to good times for all.

A key insight into macroeconomics is that in the short run—a time period consisting of several years but typically less than a decade—the combined effect of individual decisions can have effects that are very different from what any one individual intended, effects that are sometimes perverse. The behavior of the macroeconomy is, indeed, greater than the sum of individual actions and market outcomes.

## Macroeconomic Policy

The fact that the sum of individual decisions can sometimes lead to bad results for the macroeconomy leads us to another critical difference between microeconomics and macroeconomics: the role of government policy. Careful study of how markets work has led microeconomists to the conclusion that government should typically leave markets alone. Except in certain well-defined cases, government intervention in markets usually leaves society as a whole worse off. There are, to be sure, important tasks for microeconomic policy—ensuring that markets perform well and intervening appropriately in the well-defined cases in which markets don't work well. But the area of microeconomics, in general, suggests a limited role for government intervention.

In contrast, economists generally believe there is a much wider role for government to play in macroeconomics—most importantly, to manage short-term fluctuations and adverse events in the economy. Like the highway police who work to prevent or reduce the effects of rubber-necking traffic jams, government policy makers work to prevent or reduce the effects of adverse events on the macroeconomy.

The widely held view that the government should take an active role in the management of the macroeconomy dates back to the Great Depression of the 1930s, a pivotal event in world economic history. A global event in which output plunged, banks failed, companies went bust, and workers were laid off en masse, it was as if the world economic engine had been thrown sharply into reverse. Lasting more than a decade, from 1929 through the end of the 1930s, it caused a thorough rethinking of the principles and aims of macroeconomics. During and after the Great Depression, economists developed the modern macroeconomic toolkit—*fiscal policy*, control of government spending and taxation, and *monetary policy*, control over interest rates and the quantity of money in circulation—now used to manage the performance of the macroeconomy.

## Economic Aggregates

A distinctive feature of modern macroeconomics is that both its theory and policy implementation focus on **economic aggregates**—economic measures that summarize data across many different markets for goods, services, workers, and *assets*. (Assets are items that serve as a store of value, like cash or real estate.) For example, macroeconomics analyzes the performance of the economy by studying *aggregate output*, the total output of the economy over a given time period, and the *aggregate price level*, a measure of the overall level of prices in the economy. Using these aggregate measures, we will study the business cycle and how fiscal policy and monetary policy can be used to manage the business cycle. As the lucky and unlucky business school grads discovered, these fluctuations affect *unemployment*, a measure of the total number of unemployed workers in the economy. We'll also see how the business cycle is affected by *investment spending*, additions to the economy's supply of productive *physical capital*, including machines, buildings, and inventories.

In the remainder of this chapter and in Chapter 15, we'll focus on how many of these economic aggregates are calculated and measured.

Now that we have an idea of how macroeconomics and microeconomics differ, we're ready to begin learning about some of the key features of the business cycle. Before we do that, however, let's take a moment to look at the episode that created macroeconomics as we know it—and almost destroyed civilization as we know it.

> **Economic aggregates** are economic measures that summarize data across different markets for goods, services, workers, and assets.

# economics in action

## The Great Depression

Historians agree that the Great Depression, which began in 1929 and lasted through the 1930s, was one of the great defining moments in American history. And its effect wasn't just limited to the United States; the catastrophe was felt in virtually all the world's market economies—in Europe, Latin America, Japan, Canada, and Australia. Germany had one of the hardest-hit economies. Historians agree that this was a major reason for the rise of Nazism, which ultimately led to World War II.

The Great Depression was also *the* defining moment for modern macroeconomics: if we had to express in a few words the central mission of modern macroeconomics, it is to prevent anything like the Great Depression from ever happening again.

The Depression began in August 1929 with a mild fall in aggregate output. This, in turn, contributed to the single event most associated with the Great Depression—the famous stock market crash of October 1929. If the economic effects had been limited to the fallout from the stock market crash, then the economy would probably have experienced a short-term downturn. But what made the Depression a long-term disaster was the catastrophic rise in unemployment and huge decline in aggregate output that occurred after the market crash. In 1929, the *unemployment rate*—loosely speaking, the percentage of the working population unable to find jobs—was only 3.2%, as shown in panel (a) of Figure 14-1. By 1933 it was 24.9%: one American worker in four was out of work, with many people forced to rely on soup kitchens and other forms of charity simply to eat. Families were evicted from their homes, and shantytowns—enclaves with dwellings made from cast-off materials—arose across the country. Labor strife was pervasive because workers

Much of modern macroeconomics arose as a way to understand the economic devastation caused by the Great Depression. Shown here is the family of an unemployed Appalachian coal miner in 1938.

*Marion Post Wolcott/Corbis*

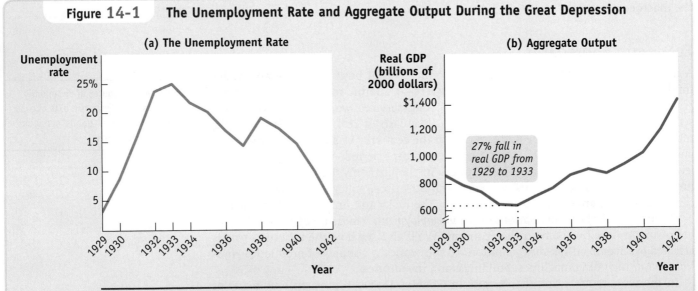

**Figure 14-1** **The Unemployment Rate and Aggregate Output During the Great Depression**

**(a) The Unemployment Rate**

**(b) Aggregate Output**

*27% fall in real GDP from 1929 to 1933*

The economic slump that began in 1929 led to a drastic rise in the unemployment rate, shown in panel (a), and a drastic fall in aggregate output, shown in panel (b). Aggregate output, as measured by real GDP in 2000 dollars (we'll explain what "2000 dollars" are in Chapter 15), didn't rise above its 1929 level until 1937. The unemployment rate didn't return to single digits until 1941.

*Source: U.S. Census Bureau.* **>web...**

felt abandoned by the market economy. (In one famous example, World War I veterans, called "Bonus Marchers," erected a shantytown on the Mall in Washington, D.C. They were driven off by the U.S. Army after they made large and vocal demands for a government-paid bonus.) Along with the collapse in employment came an extraordinary collapse in *real gross domestic product* (or *real GDP*)—a measure of aggregate output. Real GDP fell 27% from 1929 to 1933, as panel (b) of Figure 14-1 shows. It was a time of incredible, unexpected misery, all the more shocking because the previous decade, the "Roaring Twenties," had been a time of unprecedented growth and prosperity. By the 1930s, many people felt that even democracy in America was at risk.

Although the economy eventually recovered, it took a very long time. In 1939, after a full decade of policy attempts to reverse the downturn, the unemployment rate was 17%—far higher than anything seen since. Real GDP did not get above its 1929 level until 1936, and it took until 1941 for the unemployment rate to drop back into single digits. Only with the coming of World War II did economic prosperity return.

The Great Depression led to a feverish effort by economists to understand what had happened and what could be done about it. This led to a breakthrough in economic measurement, and many of the statistics we now rely on to track the economy's performance first began to be collected during the 1930s. Economic theory changed dramatically with the 1936 publication of *The General Theory of Employment, Interest, and Money* by the British economist John Maynard Keynes—a book that ranks in influence with Adam Smith's *The Wealth of Nations*. Keynes's work, and the interpretations and critiques of his work by other economists, gave rise to both the field of macroeconomics and macroeconomic policy-making as we know it. ∎

> > > > > > > > > > > > > > > > > > > > >

**>> CHECK YOUR UNDERSTANDING 14 -1**

1. Which of the following questions is appropriate to the study of microeconomics? Of macroeconomics? Explain your answers.
   a. How much profit is gained by installing a new piece of equipment in the Otis Furniture Factory?
   b. How does the overall level of sales of manufactured goods change as the state of the economy changes?
   c. Should Melanie buy a new car or not?

2. Explain why there is typically less scope for government intervention in microeconomics than in macroeconomics.

Solutions appear at back of book.

# The Business Cycle

As we mentioned in our opening story, the poor job market of 2002 created a difficult time for all job-seekers, regardless of their skills. And it was particularly disappointing given that just two years earlier America had enjoyed a very strong job market.

The short-run alternation between economic downturns and upturns is known as the **business cycle.** A **depression** is a very deep and prolonged downturn; fortunately, the United States hasn't had one since the 1930s. But what we have had are less prolonged economic downturns known as **recessions,** periods in which output and *employment* are falling. In contrast, economic upturns, periods in which output and employment are rising, are known as **expansions** (sometimes called *recoveries*). According to the National Bureau of Economic Research there have been 10 recessions in the United States since World War II. Over that period the average recession has lasted 10 months and the average expansion has lasted 57 months. The average length of a business cycle, from the beginning of a recession to the beginning of the next recession, has been 5 years and 7 months. The shortest business cycle was 18 months and the longest was 10 years and 8 months. The recession felt by the 2002 job-seekers began in March 2001. Figure 14-2 on page 358 shows the history of the U.S. unemployment rate since 1948 and the timing of

The **business cycle** is the short-run alternation between economic downturns, known as recessions, and economic upturns, known as expansions.

A **depression** is a very deep and prolonged downturn.

**Recessions** are periods of economic downturns when output and employment are falling.

**Expansions,** or recoveries, are periods of economic upturns when output and employment are rising.

## FOR INQUIRING MINDS

### DEFINING RECESSIONS AND EXPANSIONS

Some readers may be wondering exactly how recessions and expansions are defined. The answer is that there is no exact definition!

In many countries, economists adopt the rule that a recession is a period of at least two consecutive quarters (a quarter is 3 months), during which aggregate output falls. The two-consecutive-quarter requirement is designed to avoid classifying brief hiccups in the economy's performance, with no lasting significance, as recessions. Sometimes, however, this definition seems too strict. For example, an economy that has three months of sharply declining output,

then three months of slightly positive growth, then another three months of rapid decline, should surely be considered to have endured a nine-month recession.

In the United States, we try to avoid such misclassifications by assigning the task of determining when a recession begins and ends to an independent panel of experts at the National Bureau of Economic Research (NBER). This panel looks at a variety of economic indicators, with the main focus on employment and production. But, ultimately, the panel makes a judgment call.

Sometimes this judgment is controversial. In fact, there is lingering controversy over the 2001 recession. According to the NBER, that recession began in March 2001 and ended in November 2001 when output began rising. Some critics argue, however, that the recession really began several months earlier, when industrial production began falling. Other critics argue that the recession didn't really end in 2001 because employment continued to fall and the job market remained weak for another year and a half.

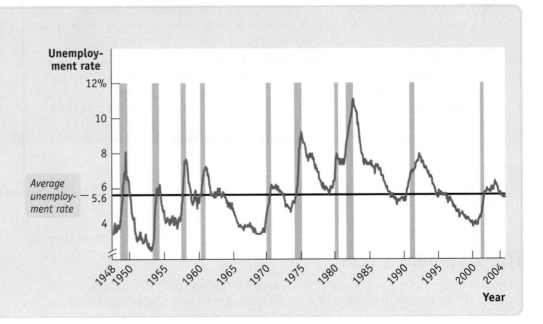

### Figure 14-2

**The Unemployment Rate and Recessions Since 1948**

The unemployment rate normally rises during recessions and falls during expansions. As shown here, there were large fluctuations in the U.S. unemployment rate during the period after World War II. Shaded areas show periods of recession; unshaded areas are periods of expansion. Over the entire period from 1948 to 2004, the unemployment rate averaged 5.6%.

*Source:* Bureau of Labor Statistics; National Bureau of Economic Research.

post–World War II business cycles. The average unemployment rate over that period was 5.6%, and recessions are indicated in the figure by the shaded areas.

What happens during a business cycle, and what can be done about it? Let's look at three issues: the effects of recessions and expansions on unemployment; the effects on aggregate output; and the possible role of government policy.

## Employment and Unemployment

Although not as severe as a depression, a recession is clearly an undesirable event. Like a depression, a recession leads to higher unemployment, reduced output, reduced incomes, and lower living standards.

To understand unemployment and how it relates to the adverse effects of recessions, we need to understand something about how the labor force is structured. **Employment** is the total number of people currently employed, and **unemployment** is the total number of people who are actively looking for work but aren't currently employed. A country's **labor force** is the sum of employment and unemployment. The official labor force doesn't include **discouraged workers,** people who are capable of working but have given up looking for jobs because they don't think they will find them. Labor statistics don't include information on **underemployment,** the number of people who work during a recession but receive lower wages than they would during an expansion due to a smaller number of hours worked, lower-paying jobs, or both.

The **unemployment rate** is the percentage of the total number of people in the labor force who are unemployed. It is calculated as follows:

**(14-1)** $\dfrac{\text{Unemployment}}{\text{rate}} = \dfrac{\text{Number of unemployed workers}}{\text{Number of unemployed workers} + \text{Number of employed workers}} \times 100$

The unemployment rate is usually a good indicator of what conditions are like in the job market: a high unemployment rate signals a poor job market in which jobs are hard to find; a low unemployment rate indicates a good job market in which jobs are relatively easy to find. In general, during recessions the unemployment rate is rising; during expansions it is falling.

Look again at Figure 14-2, which shows the monthly unemployment rate from 1948 through 2004. The average unemployment rate for the whole period was 5.6%, but there were large fluctuations around that average. A booming economy, like that of the late 1960s or late 1990s, can push the unemployment rate down to 4% or even lower. But a severe recession, like that of 1981–1982, can push the unemployment rate into double digits (unemployment in that recession peaked in November 1982, at 10.8%).

These abstract numbers translate into enormous differences in personal experiences. For example, the 10.8% unemployment rate of late 1982 meant nearly 12 million people in the United States were actively seeking work but couldn't find jobs. More recently, as unemployment rose in the early 1990s, hundreds of thousands of workers were laid off, and many of those who did find jobs were severely underemployed. As a result, the nation was gripped by malaise and doubt. (One influential book at the time was titled *America: What Went Wrong?*) But at the end of the 1990s, as unemployment fell to 30-year lows, businesses scrambled to find workers and even students with mediocre grades and minimal experience got very good job offers. Alas, as is the nature of the business cycle, this happy era ended when the economy hit a rough patch in early 2001 and the unemployment rate rose again.

"WOULD YOU LIKE A COPY OF MY MASTERS THESIS WITH THAT?"

Jim Borgman

> **Employment** is the number of people currently employed in the economy.
>
> **Unemployment** is the number of people who are actively looking for work but aren't currently employed.
>
> The **labor force** is equal to the sum of employment and unemployment.
>
> **Discouraged workers** are nonworking people who are capable of working but have given up looking for a job.
>
> **Underemployment** is the number of people who work during a recession but receive lower wages than they would during an expansion due to fewer number of hours worked, lower-paying jobs, or both.
>
> The **unemployment rate** is the percentage of the total number of people in the labor force who are unemployed.

## Aggregate Output

Rising unemployment is the most painful consequence of a recession, and falling unemployment the most urgently desired feature of an expansion. But the business cycle isn't just about jobs—it's also about output. Over the business cycle, the economy's level of output and its unemployment rate move in opposite directions.

Formally, **aggregate output** is the economy's total production of *final goods and services* for a given time period—usually a year. It excludes goods and services that are produced as inputs for the production of other goods (inputs are often called

> **Aggregate output** is the economy's total production of final goods and services for a given time period.

*intermediate goods*). Steel manufactured for the purpose of producing a car is not counted in aggregate output, but the car is. Real GDP is the actual numerical measure of aggregate output typically used by economists. We'll see how real GDP is calculated in Chapter 15. For now, the important point is that aggregate output normally falls in recessions but rises during expansions.

Panel (a) of Figure 14-3 shows the annual growth rate of U.S. real GDP from 1948 to 2004. That is, it plots the percent change in aggregate output from 1947 to 1948, from 1948 to 1949, and so on. On average, aggregate output grew 3.5% per year. As you can see, however, the actual growth rate fluctuated widely around that average, going as high as 8.7% in 1950 and as low as −1.9% in 1982. Comparison of panel (a) of Figure 14-3 to Figure 14-2 shows that the year in which aggregate output had its steepest post–World War II decline, 1982, was also the year in which the unemployment rate hit its post–World War II peak.

Panel (b) of Figure 14-3 shows the growth of U.S. real GDP over the same period, from 1948 to 2004. As you can see from the sustained upward trend line, de-

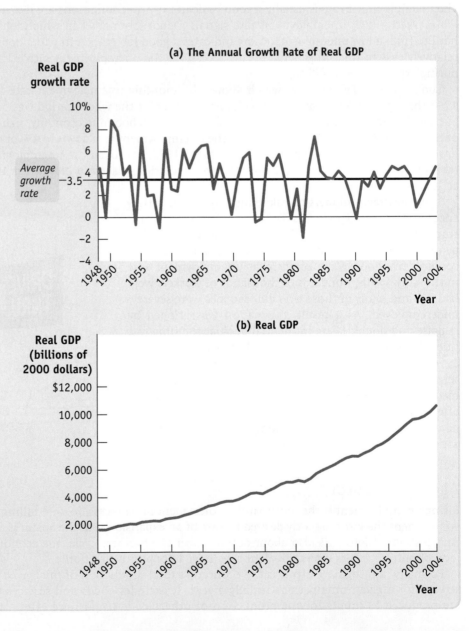

### Figure 14-3

#### Growth in Aggregate Output, 1948–2004

Real GDP is a numerical measure of aggregate output, the output of the economy as a whole. Panel (a) shows the annual rate of growth of U.S. real GDP from 1948 to 2004, which averaged 3.5% over that period. Although real GDP rose in most years, the actual growth rate fluctuated with the business cycle, with real GDP actually falling in some years. Panel (b) shows the same data presented in a different form: it shows real GDP from 1948 to 2004. From it we see that when viewed from a period of time long enough to be independent of the business cycle, real GDP has grown substantially.

*Source:* Bureau of Economic Analysis.

clines in real GDP that occurred during recessions have been temporary events. Over the post–World War II period, real GDP has grown by more than 500% in the United States.

## Taming the Business Cycle

As we've explained, one of the key missions of macroeconomics is to understand why recessions happen and what, if anything, can be done about them. Another major macroeconomic concern is inflation, a rise in the overall price level that often results from an excessively strong expansion.

Policy efforts undertaken to reduce the severity of recessions or to rein in excessively strong expansions are called **stabilization policy.** Stabilization policy is based on two main tools—monetary policy and fiscal policy. **Monetary policy** attempts to stabilize the economy through changes in the quantity of money in circulation or in interest rates, or both. **Fiscal policy** attempts to stabilize the economy through changes in taxation or in government spending, or both. We'll examine these tools in Chapters 17 and 18, where we'll see how they can diminish the length and severity of recessions as well as dampen overly robust expansions. But we'll also see in those chapters why they don't work perfectly—that is, fiscal policy and monetary policy can't eliminate fluctuations in the economy altogether. So, in the end, the business cycle is still with us.

Although the business cycle is one of the main concerns of macroeconomics and historically played a crucial role in fostering the development of the field, macroeconomists are also concerned with other issues. We turn next to the question of inflation.

> Policy efforts undertaken to reduce the severity of recessions and to rein in excessively strong expansions are called **stabilization policy.**
>
> **Monetary policy** is a type of stabilization policy that involves changes in the quantity of money in circulation or in interest rates, or both.
>
> **Fiscal policy** is a type of stabilization policy that involves changes in taxation or in government spending, or both.

# economics in action

## Has the Business Cycle Been Tamed?

Macroeconomics as we know it came into existence during the Great Depression, created by economists determined to prevent anything like that from happening again. From the evidence, it appears that U.S. policy makers and economists have been successful: the United States has not suffered any downturn severe enough to be considered a depression since then. But have we succeeded in the related task of taming the business cycle?

Sort of. Figure 14-4 shows the average annual U.S. unemployment rate going all the way back to 1900. The figure is dominated by the huge rise in unemployment during the 1930s; since World War II the United States has managed to avoid anything comparably severe. Macroeconomists believe that part of the reason is that since World War II macroeconomic policies have been smarter because they are based on better macroeconomic theory.

Economists have learned, however, to be wary of pronouncements that the business cycle has been brought under control and that recessions are a thing of the past. Such pronouncements were common during the long expansion of the 1960s, but two severe recessions that drove unemployment to post–World War II highs followed. Claims that the business cycle was no more

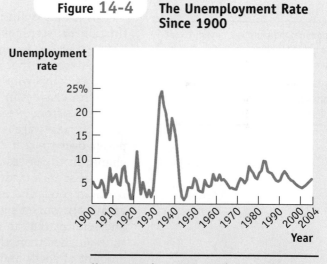

**Figure 14-4    The Unemployment Rate Since 1900**

Has progress in macroeconomics made the economy more stable? This figure shows average annual U.S. unemployment rates since 1900. Clearly, nothing like the Great Depression—the huge surge in unemployment that dominates the figure—has happened since. But economists who argued during the 1960s that the business cycle had been tamed were proven wrong by severe recessions in the 1970s and early 1980s.

*Source:* U.S. Census Bureau; Bureau of Labor Statistics.

arose again during the long expansion of the 1990s, only to be belied by the recession of 2001.

In recent times other countries have suffered economic downturns almost as severe as the Great Depression. For example, between 1998 and 2002 Argentina suffered an 18% fall in its aggregate output. The unemployment rate rose to 24%, and many middle-class families were plunged into poverty. These downturns inspired some humility in macroeconomists. Although they believe they know enough to prevent another Great Depression, the task of economic stabilization remains far from complete. ■

< < < < < < < < < < < < < < < < <

>> CHECK YOUR UNDERSTANDING 14-2

1. Why do the unemployment rate and aggregate output move in opposite directions over the business cycle?

2. Describe some of the costs to society of having a high unemployment rate.

3. What are likely signs that a stabilization policy has been successful over a period of time?

Solutions appear at back of book.

# Inflation and Deflation

Although 2002 was a difficult year for all new graduates seeking jobs, the jobs actually on offer paid extremely well by historical standards. The pay package of an average U.S. worker in 2002, even after correcting for higher prices of goods and services, was worth almost three times as much as the pay of an average worker in 1948. *After correcting for higher prices of goods and services:* That's an important qualification. If we don't correct for the higher prices of goods and services, the rise in wages from 1948 to 2002 appears much larger—increasing by a factor of 20 rather than by a factor of only 3.

This example illustrates an important distinction in macroeconomics: the distinction between *nominal* versus *real*. A **nominal** measure of something, such as nominal wages, is a measure that has not been adjusted for changes in prices over time. So we say that *nominal wages* have increased by a factor of 20 from 1948 to 2002. By comparison, a **real** measure of something is a measure that has been adjusted for changes in prices over time. So we say that *real wages* have increased by a factor of 3 from 1948 to 2002. Economists typically express wages in real terms because the real wage is a better indicator of the actual change in workers' purchasing power over time: it captures how much wages have changed over and above the change in the prices of goods and services that workers buy. So although nominal wages rose by a factor of 20 in those 55 years, workers could buy only 3 times as much in goods and services rather than 20 times as much. To say this another way, an average worker's wage in 2002, expressed in *2002 dollars*—the amount of goods and services that an average worker's wage from 2002 would buy in 2002—was 3 times higher than the wage in 1948 when it is expressed in *2002 dollars*—the amount of goods and services that an average worker's wage from 1948 would buy in 2002.

We refer to the overall price level of all final goods and services in the economy—that is, the price level of aggregate output—as the **aggregate price level.** When this price level rises, we say that the economy is experiencing **inflation.** When it falls, the economy is experiencing **deflation.**

As we'll explain in Chapter 15, there are two widely used measures of the aggregate price level—the *GDP deflator* and the *consumer price index*, or *CPI*. Figure 14-5 shows the consumer price index from 1913 to 2004.

You can see from the figure that the aggregate price level, like aggregate output (see Figure 14-3(b)), has risen substantially over time. Overall prices were almost 20

---

A **nominal** measure is a measure that has not been adjusted for changes in prices over time.

A **real** measure is a measure that has been adjusted for changes in prices over time.

---

The **aggregate price level** is the overall price level for final goods and services in the economy.

A rising aggregate price level is **inflation.**

A falling aggregate price level is **deflation.**

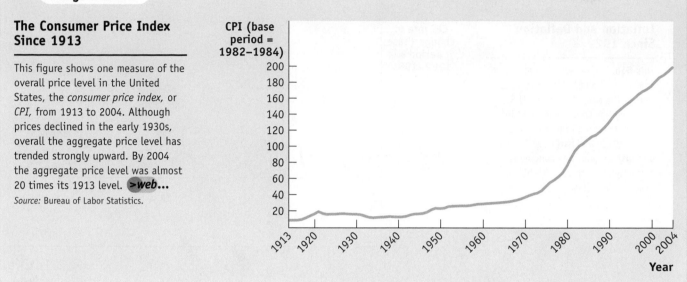

### Figure 14-5

**The Consumer Price Index Since 1913**

This figure shows one measure of the overall price level in the United States, the *consumer price index,* or *CPI,* from 1913 to 2004. Although prices declined in the early 1930s, overall the aggregate price level has trended strongly upward. By 2004 the aggregate price level was almost 20 times its 1913 level. **>web...**

*Source:* Bureau of Labor Statistics.

times higher in 2004 than they were in 1913. An upward trend in aggregate output is a good thing. It is a sign of a well-functioning economy. However, the upward trend in prices is not a necessary feature of a well-performing economy. Nor is it necessarily a good thing.

Both inflation and deflation can pose problems for the economy, although these problems are subtler than those associated with recession. Here are two examples: Inflation discourages people from holding on to cash, because cash loses value over time if the aggregate price level is rising. This raises the cost of making purchases and sales for which cash is required. In extreme cases, people stop holding cash altogether and turn to barter. Deflation can cause the reverse problem. If the price level is falling, holding on to cash, which gains value over time, can become more attractive than investing in new factories and other productive assets. This can deepen a recession. In general economists regard **price stability**—in which the aggregate price level is changing, if at all, only slowly—as a desirable goal. (We say "changing slowly" instead of "not changing" because many macroeconomists believe that an inflation rate of 2 or 3% per year does little harm and may even do some good.) Price stability is a goal that seemed far out of reach for much of the post–World War II period but has been achieved to most macroeconomists' satisfaction in recent years.

The annual percent change in the aggregate price level is known as the **inflation rate** (which is negative in the case of deflation). Figure 14-6 on page 364 shows the annual inflation rate in the United States from 1929 to 2004, measured as percent changes in the CPI. There were two brief bursts of inflation associated with World War II—one at the beginning, before the government imposed price controls, and one at the end, when the controls came off. Aside from those events, three main things stand out. First, there was sharp deflation in the early 1930s, associated with the onset of the Great Depression. Second, there was a prolonged period of high inflation in the 1970s and early 1980s. Finally, in the 1990s the aggregate price level returned to near-stability.

Macroeconomists have devoted a lot of effort to understanding the causes of inflation and deflation and to providing advice to governments on how to steer a path between the two undesirable extremes.

The economy has **price stability** when the aggregate price level is changing only slowly.

The **inflation rate** is the annual percent change in the aggregate price level.

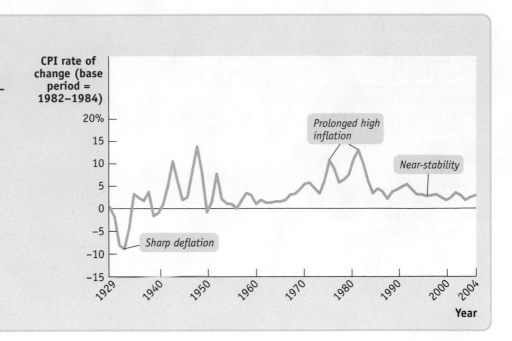

**Figure 14-6**

**Inflation and Deflation Since 1929**

This figure shows the annual rate of change of the CPI. After the deflation of the early 1930s, the U.S. economy has consistently had inflation. But the high inflation rates of the 1970s and early 1980s have diminished, and the economy is currently close to price stability.

*Source:* Bureau of Labor Statistics.

## *economics in action*

### A Fast (Food) Measure of Inflation

The original McDonald's opened in 1954. It offered fast service—it was, indeed, the original fast-food restaurant—and it was also very inexpensive. Hamburgers cost only $0.15; $0.25 with fries. Today a hamburger at a typical McDonald's costs five times as much—between $0.70 and $0.80. Has McDonald's lost touch with its fast-food roots? Have burgers become luxury cuisine?

No—in fact, a burger is, compared with other consumer goods, a better bargain today than it was in 1954. Burger prices have risen about 400%, from $0.15 to about $0.75, over the last half century. But the overall CPI has increased more than 600%. If McDonald's had matched the overall price-level increase, a hamburger would now cost between $0.90 and $1.00.

Inflation subsided in the 1990s—that is, the rate of increase in the aggregate price level slowed. And the same was true of burger prices—in fact, in 1997 McDonald's actually cut the price of many of its items, including the signature Big Mac. ∎

< < < < < < < < < < < < < < < < <

>> **CHECK YOUR UNDERSTANDING 14-3**

1. Suppose your wages rose by 10% over the past year. In each of the following cases, determine whether you are better or worse off in comparison to the year before. Explain your answers.
   a. The yearly inflation rate was 5%.
   b. The yearly inflation rate was 15%.
   c. The economy experienced deflation, with prices falling at a rate of 2% per year.

Solutions appear at back of book.

• **A LOOK AHEAD** •

In the chapters ahead we will examine the issues described briefly here. We'll start our discussion of macroeconomic models with an analysis of the business cycle. There we learn how business cycles happen. In subsequent chapters, we learn how monetary policy and fiscal policy can be used to stabilize the economy.

Before we begin analyzing macroeconomic models, however, we need to know something about the numbers we are analyzing. How do we actually estimate aggregate output, the aggregate price level, and other key measures of macroeconomic performance?

## SUMMARY

1. Macroeconomics is the study of the behavior of the economy as a whole—the total output level, the overall level of prices, total employment, and so on.

2. There are three principal ways in which macroeconomics differs from microeconomics: it focuses on how the accumulated effects of individual actions can lead to unintended macroeconomic outcomes; it allows greater scope for government intervention; and it uses **economic aggregates,** measures that summarize data across various markets for goods, services, workers, and assets. Modern macroeconomics arose from efforts to understand the Great Depression.

3. One key concern of macroeconomics is the **business cycle,** the short-run alternation between **recessions,** periods of falling employment and output, and **expansions,** periods of rising employment and output. Modern macroeconomics arose largely in order to prevent the occurrence of another **depression,** a deep and prolonged economic downturn. The **labor force,** the sum of **employment** and **unemployment,** does not include **discouraged workers,** non-working people capable of working but who have given up looking for a job. Labor statistics also do not contain data on **underemployment,** employed workers who earn less than they would in an expansion due to lower-paying jobs or fewer hours worked. The **unemployment rate,** which is usually a good measure of conditions in the labor market, has risen and fallen repeatedly over time. **Aggregate output,** the total level of output of final goods and services in the economy, moves in the opposite direction of unemployment over the business cycle.

4. **Stabilization policy,** the effort by governments to smooth out the business cycle, has two main tools: **monetary policy,** changes in the quantity of money in circulation or in interest rates, or both; and **fiscal policy,** changes in taxation or in government spending, or both.

5. Economists distinguish between **nominal** measures, measures that haven't been adjusted for changing prices, and **real** measures, measures that have been adjusted for changing prices. Changes in real wages are a better measure of changes in workers' purchasing power. The **aggregate price level** is the overall price level for all final goods and services in the economy. The **inflation rate,** the annual percent change in the aggregate price level, is positive when the aggregate price level is rising (**inflation**) and negative when the aggregate price level is falling (**deflation**). Because inflation and deflation can cause problems, **price stability** is generally preferred. Currently, the U.S. economy is close to price stability.

## KEY TERMS

Economic aggregates, p. 355
Business cycle, p. 357
Depression, p. 357
Recessions, p. 357
Expansions, p. 357
Employment, p. 359
Unemployment, p. 359
Labor force, p. 359

Discouraged workers, p. 359
Underemployment, p. 359
Unemployment rate, p. 359
Aggregate output, p. 359
Stabilization policy, p. 361
Monetary policy, p. 361
Fiscal policy, p. 361
Nominal, p. 362

Real, p. 362
Aggregate price level, p. 362
Inflation, p. 362
Deflation, p. 362
Price stability, p. 363
Inflation rate, p. 363

## PROBLEMS

1. Which of the following questions are relevant for the study of macroeconomics and which for microeconomics?

   a. How will Ms. Martin's tips change when a large manufacturing plant near the restaurant where she works closes?

   b. What will happen to spending by consumers when the economy enters a downturn?

   c. How will the price of oranges change when a late frost damages Florida's orange groves?

**d.** How will wages at a manufacturing plant change when its workforce is unionized?

**e.** What is the relationship between a nation's unemployment rate and its inflation rate?

**2.** When one person saves, that person's wealth is increased, meaning that he or she can consume more in the future. But when everyone saves, everyone's income falls, meaning that everyone must consume less today. Explain this seeming contradiction.

**3.** What was the Great Depression? How did it affect the role of government in the economy and the macroeconomic toolkit?

**4.** There are 100,000 inhabitants in Macronesia. Among those 100,000 inhabitants, 25,000 are too old to work and 15,000 inhabitants are too young to work. Among the remaining 60,000 inhabitants, 10,000 are not working and have given up looking for work, 45,000 are currently employed, and the remaining 5,000 are looking for work but do not currently have a job.

**a.** What is the number of people in the labor force in Macronesia?

**b.** What is the unemployment rate in Macronesia?

**c.** How many people in Macronesia are discouraged workers?

**5.** College tuition has risen significantly in the last few decades. From the 1971–1972 academic year to the 2001–2002 academic year, total tuition, room, and board paid by full-time undergraduate students went from $1,357 to $8,022 at public institutions and from $2,917 to $21,413 at private institutions. This is an average annual tuition increase of 6.1% at public institutions and 6.9% at private institutions. Over the same time, average personal income after taxes rose from $3,860 to $26,156 per year, which is an average annual rate of growth of personal income of 6.6%. Have these tuition increases made it more difficult for the average student to afford college tuition?

---

**>web...** To continue your study and review of concepts in this chapter, please visit the Krugman/Wells/Olney website for quizzes, animated graph tutorials, web links to helpful resources, and more.

**www.worthpublishers.com/krugmanwellsolney**

# >>Tracking the Macroeconomy

## AFTER THE REVOLUTION

IN DECEMBER 1975 THE GOVERNMENT of Portugal—a provisional government in the process of establishing a democracy—feared that it was facing an economic crisis. Business owners, alarmed by the rise of leftist political parties, were issuing dire warnings about plunging production. Newspapers speculated that the economy had shrunk 10 or even 15% since the 1974 revolution that had overthrown the country's long-standing dictatorship.

In the face of this supposed economic collapse, some Portuguese were pronouncing democracy itself a failure. Others declared that capitalism was the culprit and demanded that the government seize control of the nation's factories to force them to produce more. But how bad was the situation, really?

To answer this question, Portugal's top monetary official invited his old friend Richard Eckaus, an economist at the Massachusetts Institute of Technology, and two other MIT economists to look at the country's national accounts, the set of data collected on the country's economic activity. The visiting experts had to engage in a lot of educated guesswork: Portugal's economic data collection had always been somewhat incomplete, and it had been further disrupted by political upheavals. For example, the country's statisticians normally tracked construction with data on the sales of structural steel and concrete. But in the somewhat chaotic situation of 1975, these indicators were moving in

With accurate economic data, Portugal was able to make the transition from revolution in 1975 to a prosperous democracy today.

## What you will learn in this chapter:

➤ How economists use aggregate measures to track the performance of the economy

➤ What **gross domestic product,** or **GDP,** is and the three ways of calculating it

➤ The difference between **real GDP** and **nominal GDP** and why real GDP is the appropriate measure of real economic activity

➤ The significance of the **unemployment rate** and how it moves over the business cycle

➤ What a **price index** is and how it is used to calculate the **inflation rate**

opposite directions because many builders were ignoring the construction regulations and using very little steel. (Travel tip: if you find yourself visiting Portugal, try to avoid being in a 1975-vintage building during an earthquake.)

Still, they went to work with the available data, and within a week they were able to make a rough estimate: aggregate output had declined only 3% from 1974 to 1975. The economy had suffered a serious setback, but its decline was much less drastic than the calamity being portrayed in the newspapers. (Later revisions pushed the decline up to 4.5%, but that was still much less than feared.) The Portuguese government certainly had work to do, but there was no need to abandon either democracy or a market economy. In fact, the economy soon began to re-

cover. Over the past three decades, Portugal—though it has had its problems—has, on the whole, been a success story. A once-backward dictatorship is now a fairly prosperous, solidly democratic member of the European Union.

What's the lesson of this story? It is that economic measurement matters. If the government of Portugal had believed the scare stories some were telling at the time, it might have made major policy mistakes. Good macroeconomic policy depends on good measurement of what is happening in the economy as a whole.

In this chapter, we explain how macroeconomists measure key aspects of the economy—the level of income and aggregate output, the level of employment and unemployment, and the level and rate of change of prices.

# The National Accounts

Almost all countries calculate a set of numbers known as the *national income and product accounts*. In fact, the accuracy of a country's accounts is a remarkably reliable indicator of its state of economic development—in general, the more reliable the accounts, the more economically advanced the country. When international economic agencies seek to help a less developed country, typically the first order of business is to send a team of experts to audit and improve the country's accounts.

In the United States, these numbers are calculated by the Bureau of Economic Analysis, a division of the U.S. government's Commerce Department. The **national income and product accounts,** often referred to simply as the **national accounts,** keep track of the spending of consumers, sales of producers, business investment spending, government purchases, and a variety of other flows of money between different sectors of the economy. Let's see how they work.

## The Circular-Flow Diagram, Revisited and Expanded

To understand the principles behind the national accounts, it helps to look at Figure 15-1, a revised and expanded *circular-flow diagram* similar to the one we introduced in Chapter 2. Recall that in Figure 2-7 we showed the flows of money, goods and services, and factors of production through the economy. Here we restrict ourselves to flows of money but add extra elements that allow us to show the key concepts behind the national accounts. As in our original version of the circular-flow diagram, the underlying principle is that the flow of money into each market or sector is equal to the flow of money coming out of that market or sector.

Figure 2-7 showed a simplified world containing only two kinds of "inhabitants," households and firms. And it illustrated the circular flow of money between households and firms, which remains visible in Figure 15-1. In the markets for goods and services, households engage in **consumer spending,** buying goods and services from

---

The **national income and product accounts,** or **national accounts,** keep track of the flows of money between different sectors of the economy.

---

**Consumer spending** is household spending on goods and services.

### Figure 15-1 An Expanded Circular-Flow Diagram: The Flows of Money Through the Economy

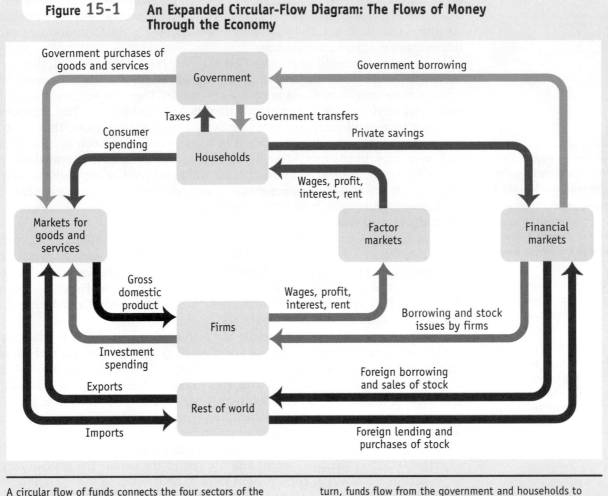

A circular flow of funds connects the four sectors of the economy—households, firms, government, and the rest of the world—via three types of markets: the factor markets, the markets for goods and services, and the financial markets. Funds flow from firms to households in the form of wages, profit, interest, and rent through the factor markets. After paying taxes to the government and receiving government transfers, households allocate the remaining income—disposable income—to private savings and consumer spending. Via the financial markets, private savings and funds from the rest of the world are channeled into investment spending by firms, government borrowing, foreign borrowing and lending, and foreign transactions of stocks. In turn, funds flow from the government and households to firms to pay for purchases of goods and services. Finally, exports to the rest of the world generate a flow of funds into the economy and imports lead to a flow of funds out of the economy. If we add up consumer spending on goods and services, investment spending by firms, government purchases of goods and services, and exports, then subtract the value of imports, the total flow of funds represented by this calculation is total spending on final goods and services produced in the United States. Equivalently, it's the value of all the final goods and services produced in the United States—that is, the gross domestic product of the economy.

domestic firms and from firms in the rest of the world. Households also own factors of production—labor, land, physical capital, and financial capital. They sell the use of these factors of production to firms, receiving wages, profit, interest payments, and rent in return. Firms buy and pay households for the use of those factors of production in the factor markets. Most households derive the bulk of their income from wages earned by selling labor. But households derive additional income from their indirect ownership of the physical capital used by firms, mainly in the form of **stocks,** shares in the ownership of a company, and **bonds,** borrowing in the form of an IOU that pays interest. So the income households receive from the factor markets includes

A **stock** is a share in the ownership of a company held by a shareholder.

A **bond** is borrowing in the form of an IOU that pays interest.

profit distributed to shareholders, and the interest payments on bonds held by households. Finally, households receive rent in return for allowing firms to use land or structures that they own. So households receive income in the form of wages, profit, interest, and rent via factor markets.

In our original, simplified circular-flow diagram, households spent all the income they received via factor markets on goods and services. Figure 15-1, however, illustrates a more complicated and more realistic model. There we see two reasons why goods and services don't in fact absorb all of households' income. First, households don't get to keep all the income they receive via the factor markets. They must pay part of their income to the government in the form of taxes, such as income taxes and sales taxes. In addition, some households receive **government transfers**—payments by the government to individuals for which no good or service is provided in return, such as Social Security benefits and unemployment insurance payments. The total income households have left after paying taxes and receiving government transfers is **disposable income.**

In addition, households normally don't spend all their disposable income on goods and services. Instead, part of their income is typically set aside as **private savings,** which goes into **financial markets** where individuals, banks, and other institutions buy and sell stocks and bonds as well as make loans. As Figure 15-1 shows, the financial markets also receive funds from the rest of the world and provide funds to the government, to firms, and to the rest of the world.

Before going further, we can use the box representing households to illustrate an important general feature of the circular-flow diagram: the total sum of flows of money out of a given box is equal to the total sum of flows of money into that box. It's simply a matter of accounting: what goes in must come out. So, for example, the total flow of money out of households—the sum of taxes paid, consumer spending, and private savings—must equal the total flow of money into households—the sum of wages, profit, interest, rent, and government transfers.

Now let's look at the other types of inhabitants we've added to the circular-flow diagram, including the government and the rest of the world. The government returns part of the money it collects from taxes to households in the form of government transfers. However, it uses much of its tax revenue, plus additional funds borrowed in the financial markets through **government borrowing,** to buy goods and services. **Government purchases of goods and services,** the total purchases by federal, state, and local governments, include everything from the military spending on ammunition to your local public school's spending on chalk, erasers, and teacher salaries.

The rest of the world participates in the U.S. economy in three ways. First, some of the goods and services produced in the United States are sold to residents of other countries. For example, more than half of America's annual wheat and cotton crops are sold abroad. Goods and services sold to other countries are known as **exports.** Export sales lead to a flow of funds from the rest of the world into the United States to pay for them. Second, some of the goods and services purchased by residents of the United States are produced abroad. For example, many consumer goods are made in China. Goods and services purchased from residents of other countries are known as **imports.** Import purchases lead to a flow of funds out of the United States to pay for them. Third, foreigners can participate in U.S. financial markets by making transactions. Foreign lending—lending by foreigners to parties in the United States, and purchases by foreigners of shares of stock in American companies—generates a flow of funds into the United States from the rest of the world. Conversely, foreign borrowing—borrowing by foreigners from U.S. parties and purchases by Americans of stock in foreign companies—leads to a flow of funds out of the United States to the rest of the world.

Finally, let's go back to the markets for goods and services. In Chapter 2 we focused only on purchases of goods and services by households. We now see that there

---

**Government transfers** are payments by the government to individuals for which no good or service is provided in return.

**Disposable income,** equal to income plus government transfers minus taxes, is the total amount of household income available to spend on consumption and to save.

**Private savings,** equal to disposable income minus consumer spending, is disposable income that is not spent on consumption.

The banking, stock, and bond markets, which channel private savings and foreign lending into investment spending, government borrowing, and foreign borrowing are known as the **financial markets.**

**Government borrowing** is the amount of funds borrowed by the government in the financial markets.

**Government purchases of goods and services** are government expenditures on goods and services.

Goods and services sold to residents of other countries are **exports;** goods and services purchased from residents of other countries are **imports.**

are other types of spending on goods and services, including government purchases, imports, and exports. Notice that firms also buy goods and services in our expanded economy. For example, an automobile company that is building a new factory will buy investment goods, stamping presses, welding robots, and other machines from companies that specialize in producing these items. It will also accumulate an inventory of finished cars in preparation for shipping them to dealers. The national income accounts count this **investment spending**—spending on productive physical capital, such as machinery and construction of structures, and on changes to *inventories*—as part of total spending on goods and services.

You might ask why changes to inventories are included in investment spending—finished cars aren't, after all, used to produce more cars. Additional inventories of finished goods are counted as investment spending because, like machinery, they contribute to greater future sales for a firm. So spending on additions to inventories is a form of investment spending by a firm. Conversely, a drawing-down of inventories is counted as a fall in investment spending because it leads to lower future sales. It's also important to understand that investment spending includes spending on construction of any structure, regardless of whether it is an assembly plant or a new house. Why include construction of homes? Because, like a plant, a new house produces a future stream of services—housing services for its occupants.

Suppose that we add up consumer spending on goods and services, investment spending, government purchases of goods and services, and the value of exports, then subtract the value of imports. That measure has a name: it's a country's *gross domestic product*. But before we can formally define gross domestic product, or GDP, we have to examine an important distinction between classes of goods and services: the difference between *final goods and services* versus *intermediate goods and services*.

## Gross Domestic Product

A consumer's purchase of a new car from a dealer is one example of a sale of **final goods and services:** goods and services sold to the final, or end, user. But an automobile manufacturer's purchase of steel from a steel foundry or glass from a glassmaker is an example of purchasing **intermediate goods and services:** goods and services that are inputs for production of final goods and services. In the case of intermediate goods and services, the purchaser—another firm—is *not* the final user.

**Gross domestic product,** or **GDP,** is the total value of all *final* goods and services produced in an economy during a given period, usually a year. In 2004 the GDP of the United States was $11,734 billion, or about $40,000 per person. So if you are an economist trying to construct a country's national accounts, *one way to calculate GDP is to calculate it directly: survey firms and find out the value of their production of final goods and services.* We'll explain in detail in the next section why intermediate goods, and some other types of goods as well, are not included in the calculation of GDP.

But adding up the total value of final goods and services produced isn't the only way of calculating GDP. Since GDP is equal to the total value of final goods and services produced in the economy, it must also equal the flow of funds received by firms from sales in the goods and services market. If you look again at the circular-flow diagram in Figure 15-1, you will see that the arrow going from markets for goods and services to firms is indeed labeled "Gross domestic product." By our basic rule of accounting, which says that flows out of any box are equal to flows into the box, the flow of funds out of the markets for goods and services to firms is equal to the total flow of funds into the markets for goods and services from other sectors. And as you can see from Figure 15-1, the total flow of funds into the markets for goods and services is total or **aggregate spending** on domestically produced final goods and

**Investment spending** is spending on productive physical capital, such as machinery and construction of structures, and on changes to inventories.

**Final goods and services** are goods and services sold to the final, or end, user.

**Intermediate goods and services** are goods and services—bought from one firm by another firm—that are inputs for production of final goods and services.

**Gross domestic product,** or **GDP,** is the total value of all final goods and services produced in the economy during a given year.

**Aggregate spending,** the sum of consumer spending, investment spending, government purchases, and exports minus imports, is the total spending on domestically produced final goods and services in the economy.

*"You wouldn't think there'd be much money in potatoes, chickens, and woodchopping, but it all adds up."*

services—the sum of consumer spending, investment spending, government purchases of goods and services, and exports minus imports. *So a second way of calculating GDP is to add up aggregate spending on domestically produced final goods and services in the economy.*

And there is yet another way of calculating GDP. The flow from firms to the factor markets is the factor income paid out by firms to households in the form of wages, profit, interest, and rent. Again, by accounting rules, the value of the flow of factor income from firms to households must be equal to the flow of money into firms from the markets for goods and services. And this last value, we know, is the total value of production in the economy—GDP. An intuitive explanation of why GDP is equal to the total value of factor income paid by firms in the economy to households is the fact that the value of each sale in the economy must accrue to someone as income—either as wages, profit, interest, or rent. *So a third way of calculating GDP is to sum the total factor income earned by households from firms in the economy.*

## Calculating GDP

We've just explained that there are in fact three methods for calculating GDP. Government statisticians use all three methods. To explain how these three methods work, we will consider a hypothetical economy, shown in Figure 15-2. This economy consists of three firms—American Motors, Inc., which produces one car per year; American Steel, Inc., which produces the steel that goes into the car; and American Ore, Inc., which mines the iron ore that goes into the steel. This economy produces one car, worth $21,500. So GDP is $21,500. Let's look at how the three different methods of calculating GDP yield the same result.

**Measuring GDP as the Value of Production of Final Goods and Services**   The first method for calculating GDP is to add up the value of all the final goods and services produced in the economy—a calculation that excludes the value

---

### Figure 15-2

**Calculating GDP**

In this hypothetical economy consisting of three firms, GDP can be calculated in three different ways: measuring GDP as the value of production of final goods and services, by summing each firm's value added; measuring GDP as aggregate spending on domestically produced final goods and services; and measuring GDP as factor income earned from firms in the economy.

*Aggregate spending on domestically produced final goods and services = $21,500*

| | American Ore, Inc. | American Steel, Inc. | American Motors, Inc. | Total factor income |
|---|---|---|---|---|
| **Value of sales** | $4,200 (ore) | $9,000 (steel) | $21,500 (car) | |
| **Intermediate goods** | 0 | 4,200 (iron ore) | 9,000 (steel) | |
| **Wages** | 2,000 | 3,700 | 10,000 | $15,700 |
| **Interest payments** | 1,000 | 600 | 1,000 | 2,600 |
| **Rent** | 200 | 300 | 500 | 1,000 |
| **Profit** | 1,000 | 200 | 1,000 | 2,200 |
| **Total expenditure by firm** | 4,200 | 9,000 | 21,500 | |
| **Value added per firm** **=** **Value of sales − cost of intermediate goods** | 4,200 | 4,800 | 12,500 | |

*Total payments to factors = $21,500*

*Sum of value added = $21,500*

---

An old line says that when a person marries his or her housekeeper or chef, GDP falls. And it's true: when someone provides services for pay, those services are counted as a part of GDP. But the services family members provide to each other are not. Some economists have produced alternative measures that try to "impute" the value of household work—that is, assign an estimate of what the market value of that work would have been if it had been paid for. But the standard measure of GDP doesn't contain that imputation.

GDP estimates do, however, include an imputation for the value of "owner-occupied housing." That is, if you buy the home you were formerly renting, GDP does not go down. It's true that because you no longer pay rent to your landlord, the landlord no longer sells a service to you—namely, use of the house or apartment. But the statisticians make an estimate of what you would have paid if you rented whatever you live in, whether it's an apartment or a house. For the purposes of the statistics,

it's as if you were renting your dwelling from yourself.

If you think about it, this makes a lot of sense. In a homeowning country like the United States, the pleasure we derive from our houses is an important part of the standard of living. So to be accurate, estimates of GDP must take into account the value of housing that is occupied by owners as well as the value of rental housing.

---

of intermediate goods and services. Why are intermediate goods and services excluded? After all, don't they represent a very large and valuable portion of the economy?

To understand why only final goods and services are included in GDP, look at the simplified economy described in Figure 15-2. Should we measure the GDP of this economy by adding up the total sales of the iron ore producer, the steel producer, and the auto producer? If we did, we would in effect be counting the value of the steel twice—once when it is sold by the steel plant to the auto plant, and again when the steel auto body is sold to a consumer as a finished car. And we would be counting the value of the iron ore *three* times—once when it is mined and sold to the steel company, a second time when it is made into steel and sold to the auto producer, and a third time when the steel is made into a car and sold to the consumer. So counting the full value of each producer's sales would cause us to count the same items several times and artificially inflate the calculation of GDP. For example, in Figure 15-2, the total value of all sales, intermediate and final, is $34,700: $21,500 from the sale of the car, plus $9,000 from the sale of the steel, plus $4,200 from the sale of the iron ore. Yet we know that GDP is only $21,500.

The way we avoid double-counting is to count only each producer's **value added** in the calculation of GDP: the difference between the value of its sales and the value of the inputs it purchases from other businesses. In this case, the value added of the auto producer is the dollar value of the cars it manufactures *minus* the cost of the steel it buys, or $12,500. The value added of the steel producer is the dollar value of the steel it produces *minus* the cost of the ore it buys, or $4,800. Only the ore producer, which we have assumed doesn't buy any intermediate inputs, has value added equal to its total sales, $4,200. The sum of the three producers' value added is $21,500, equal to GDP.

> The **value added** of a producer is the value of its sales minus the value of its purchases of inputs.

### Measuring GDP as Spending on Domestically Produced Final Goods and Services

Another way to calculate GDP is by adding up aggregate spending on domestically produced final goods and services. That is, GDP can be measured by the flow of funds into firms. Like the method that estimates GDP as the value of production, this measurement must be carried out in a way that avoids double-counting. In terms of our steel and auto example, we don't want to count both consumer spending on a car (represented in Figure 15-2 by the sales price of the car) and the auto producer's spending on steel (represented in Figure 15-2 by the price of a car's worth of steel). If we counted both, we would be counting the steel embodied in the car twice. We solve this problem by counting only the value of sales to *final*

### GDP: WHAT'S IN AND WHAT'S OUT

It's easy to confuse what is included and what isn't included in GDP. So let's stop here for a moment and make sure the distinction is clear. Probably the biggest source of confusion is the difference between investment spending and spending on inputs. Investment spending—spending on investment goods, construction of structures (residential as well as commercial), and changes to inventories—is included in GDP. But spending on inputs is not. Why the difference? Recall from Chapter 2 that we made a distinction between resources that are *used up* and those that are *not used up* in production. An input, like steel, is used up in production. A metal-stamping machine, an investment good, is not; it will last for many years and will be used repeat-

edly to make many cars. Since spending on investment goods and construction of structures is not directly tied to current output, economists consider such spending to be spending on final goods. And spending on changes to inventories, considered a part of investment spending, is also included in GDP. Why? Because, like a machine, additional inventory is an investment in future sales. And when a good is released for sale from inventories, its value is subtracted from the value of inventories and so from GDP. Used goods are not included in GDP because, as with inputs, to include them would be to double-count: counting them once when sold as new and again when re-sold as used. Finally, financial assets such as stocks and bonds are not included in GDP because they don't represent either the pro-

duction or the sale of final goods and services. Rather, a bond represents a promise to repay with interest, and a stock represents a proof of ownership.

Here is a summary of what's included and not included in GDP.

*Included*
- Domestically produced final goods and services, including capital goods, new construction of structures, and changes to inventories

*Not Included*
- Intermediate goods and services
- Inputs
- Used goods
- Financial assets like stocks and bonds
- Foreign-produced goods and services

*buyers,* such as consumers, firms that purchase investment goods, the government, or foreign buyers. In other words, in order to avoid double-counting of spending, we omit sales of inputs from one business to another when estimating GDP using spending data.

As we've already pointed out, however, the national accounts *do* include investment spending by firms as a part of final spending. That is, an auto company's purchase of steel to make a car isn't considered a part of final spending, but the company's purchase of new machinery for its factory *is* considered a part of final spending. What's the difference? Steel is an input that is used up in production; machinery, although it is used to make cars, will last for a number of years. Since purchases of capital goods, like machinery, that will last for a considerable time aren't closely tied to current production, the national accounts consider such purchases a form of final sales.

It is useful at this point to look at a breakdown of the types of spending that make up GDP. Look again at the markets for goods and services in Figure 15-1, and you will see that one component of sales by firms is consumer spending. Let's denote consumer spending with the symbol C. Figure 15-1 also shows three other components of sales: sales of investment spending goods to other businesses, which we will denote by I; government purchases of goods and services, which we will denote by G; and sales to foreigners—that is, exports—which we will denote by X.

But not all of this final spending goes toward domestically produced goods and services: spending on imports, which we will denote by IM, "leaks" across national borders. Putting this all together gives us the following equation that breaks GDP down by the four sources of aggregate spending:

**(15-1)** $GDP = C + I + G + X - IM$

We'll be seeing a lot of Equation 15-1 in later chapters.

### Measuring GDP as Factor Income Earned from Firms in the Economy

A final way to calculate GDP is to add up all the income earned by factors of production from firms in the economy—the wages earned by labor; the interest earned by those who lend their savings to firms and the government; the rent earned by those who lease their land or structures to firms; and the profit earned by the shareholders, the owners of the firms' physical capital. This is a valid measure because the money firms earn by selling goods and services must go somewhere; whatever isn't paid as wages, interest, or rent is profit. And part of profit is paid out to shareholders as *dividends*.

Figure 15-2 shows how this calculation works for our simplified economy. The shaded column at far right shows the total wages, interest, and rent paid by all these firms as well as their total profit. Summing up all of these yields total factor income of $21,500—again, equal to GDP.

We won't emphasize factor income as much as the other two methods of calculating GDP. It's important to keep in mind, however, that all the money spent on domestically produced goods and services generates factor income to households—that is, there really is a circular flow.

**The Components of GDP** Now that we know how GDP is calculated in principle, let's see what it looks like in practice.

Figure 15-3 on page 376 shows the first two methods of calculating GDP side by side. The height of each bar above the horizontal axis represents the GDP of the U.S. economy in 2004: $11,734 billion. Each bar is divided to show the breakdown of that total in terms of where the value was added and how the money was spent.

In the left bar in Figure 15-3, we see the breakdown of GDP by value added according to sector, the first method of calculating GDP. Of the $11,734 billion, $2,300 billion—less than 20%—consisted of the value added by producers of physical goods. Another $7,977 billion, or 68%, consisted of value added by private producers of services. The rest consisted of value added by government, in the form of military, education, and other government services. As commentators often emphasize, the United States is now largely a service economy.

The right bar in Figure 15-3 corresponds to the second method of calculating GDP, showing the breakdown by the four types of aggregate spending. The total length of the right bar is longer than the total length of the left bar, a difference of $607 billion (which, as you can see, extends below the horizontal axis). That's because the total length of the right bar represents total spending in the economy, spending on both domestically produced and foreign produced final goods and services. Within the bar, consumer spending (C), which is 70.1% of GDP, dominates

## FOR INQUIRING MINDS

### GROSS WHAT?

Occasionally you may see references not to gross domestic product but to gross *national* product, or GNP. Is this just another name for the same thing? Not quite.

If you look at Figure 15-1 carefully, you may realize that there's a possibility that is missing from the figure. According to the figure, all factor income goes to domestic households. But what happens when profits are paid to foreigners who own stock in General Motors or Microsoft? And where do the profits earned by American companies operating overseas fit in?

The answer is that they go into GNP but not GDP. GNP is defined as the total factor income earned by residents of a country. It *excludes* factor income earned by foreigners, like profits

paid to Japanese investors who own American stocks and payments to Mexican farm workers temporarily in the United States. But it *includes* factor income earned abroad by Americans, like the profits of IBM's European operations that accrue to IBM's American shareholders and the wages of American consultants who work temporarily in Asia.

In the early days of national income accounting, economists usually used GNP rather than GDP as a measure of the economy's size—although the measures were generally very close to each other. They switched to GDP mainly because it's considered a better indicator of short-run movements in production and because data on international flows of factor income are considered somewhat unreliable.

In practice, it doesn't make much difference which measure is used for large economies like that of the United States, where the flows of net factor income to other countries are small. In 2004, America's GNP was about 0.4% larger than its GDP, mainly because of the overseas profit of U.S. companies. For smaller countries, however, GDP and GNP can diverge significantly. For example, much of Ireland's industry is owned by American corporations, whose profit must be deducted from Ireland's GNP. In addition, Ireland has become a host to many temporary workers from poorer regions of Europe, whose wages must also be deducted from Ireland's GNP. As a result, in 2004 Ireland's GNP was only 84% of its GDP.

**Figure 15-3**

**U.S. GDP in 2004: Two Methods of Calculating GDP**

The two bars show two equivalent ways of calculating GDP. The height of each bar above the horizontal axis represents $11,734 billion, U.S. GDP in 2004. The left bar shows the breakdown of GDP according to the value added of each sector of the economy. From it we see that slightly less than 20% of GDP in 2004 came from the value added in the production of goods. The rest came from the value added in the production of services. The right bar shows the breakdown of GDP according to the four types of spending: C, I, G, and X − IM. The right bar has a total length of $11,734 billion + $607 billion = $12,341 billion. The $607 billion, shown as the area extending below the horizontal axis, is the amount of total spending absorbed by net imports (negative net exports) in 2004.

*Source:* Bureau of Economic Analysis.

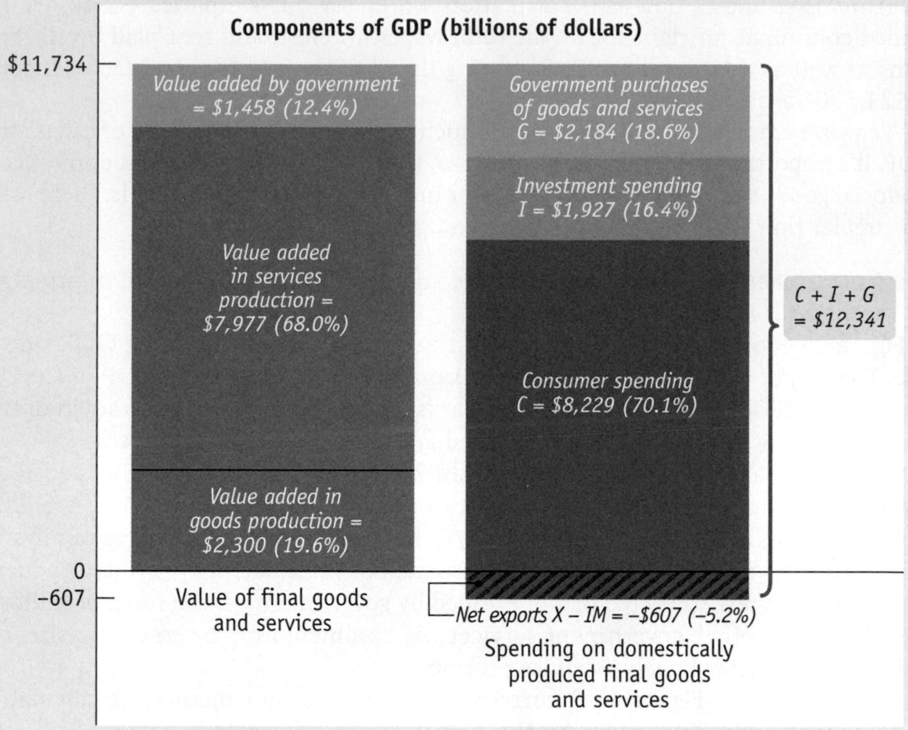

**Components of GDP (billions of dollars)**

Value added by government = $1,458 (12.4%)

Value added in services production = $7,977 (68.0%)

Value added in goods production = $2,300 (19.6%)

$11,734

0

−607

Value of final goods and services

Government purchases of goods and services G = $2,184 (18.6%)

Investment spending I = $1,927 (16.4%)

Consumer spending C = $8,229 (70.1%)

Net exports X − IM = −$607 (−5.2%)

C + I + G = $12,341

Spending on domestically produced final goods and services

---

**Net exports** are the difference between the value of exports and the value of imports.

the picture. But some of that spending was absorbed by foreign-produced goods and services. In 2004, **net exports,** the difference between the value of exports and the value of imports (X − IM in Equation 15-1) was negative—the United States was a net importer of foreign goods and services. The 2004 value of X − IM was −$607 billion, or −5.2% of GDP. Thus a portion of the right bar extends below the horizontal axis by $607 billion to represent the amount of total spending that was absorbed by net imports and therefore did not lead to higher U.S. GDP. Investment spending (I) constituted 16.4% of GDP, while government purchases of goods and services (G) constituted 18.6% of GDP.

## What GDP Tells Us

Now we've seen the various ways that gross domestic product is calculated. But what does the measurement of GDP tell us?

The most important use of GDP is as a measure of the size of the economy, providing us a scale against which to measure the economic performance of other years, or compare the economic performance of other countries. For example, suppose you want to compare the economies of different nations. A natural approach is to compare their GDPs. In 2004, as we've seen, U.S. GDP was $11,734 billion; Japan's GDP was $4,665 billion; and the combined GDP of the 25 countries that make up the European Union was $12,758 billion. This comparison tells us that Japan, although it has the world's second-largest national economy, carries considerably less economic weight than does the United States. When taken in aggregate, Europe is America's equal.

Still, one must be careful when using GDP numbers, especially when making comparisons over time. That's because part of the increase in the value of GDP over time represents increases in the *prices* of goods and services rather than an increase in output. For example, U.S. GDP was $5,803 billion in 1990 and had roughly doubled to

$11,734 billion by 2004. But the U.S. economy didn't actually double in size over that period. To measure actual changes in aggregate output, we need a modified version of GDP that is adjusted for price changes, known as *real GDP*. We'll see next how real GDP is calculated.

# *economics in action*

## Creating the National Accounts

The national accounts, like modern macroeconomics, owe their creation to the Great Depression. As the economy plunged into depression, government officials found their ability to respond crippled not only by the lack of adequate economic theories but also by the lack of adequate information. All they had were scattered statistics: railroad freight car loadings, stock prices, and incomplete indexes of industrial production. They could only guess at what was happening to the economy as a whole.

In response to this perceived lack of information, the Department of Commerce commissioned Simon Kuznets, a young Russian-born economist, to develop a set of national income accounts. (Kuznets later won the Nobel Prize in economics for his work.) The first version of these accounts was presented to Congress in 1937 and in a research report titled *National Income, 1929-35*.

There was, at first, some skepticism about the usefulness of such accounts. In 1936 the British economist John Maynard Keynes published *The General Theory of Employment, Interest, and Money,* the book that created modern macroeconomic theory. Keynes argued against trying to use the concepts of aggregate output or the aggregate price level: "To say that net output to-day is greater, but the price-level lower, than ten years ago or one year ago, is a proposition of a similar character to the statement that Queen Victoria was a better queen but not a happier woman than Queen Elizabeth—a proposition not without meaning and not without interest, but unsuitable as material for the differential calculus." But macroeconomists soon found that the concepts of aggregate output and the aggregate price level, tied to actual measurements of these quantities, were powerful aids to understanding economic developments.

Kuznets's initial estimates fell short of the full modern set of accounts because they focused on income, not production. The push to fill out the national accounts came during World War II, when policy makers were in even more need of comprehensive measures of the economy's performance. The federal government began issuing estimates of gross domestic product and gross national product in 1942.

In January 2000, in its publication *Survey of Current Business,* the Department of Commerce ran an article titled "GDP: One of the Great Inventions of the 20th Century." This may seem a bit over the top, but national income accounting, invented in the United States, has since become a tool of economic analysis and policy making around the world. ∎

> > > > > > > > > > > > > > > > > > > > > >

>>CHECK YOUR UNDERSTANDING 15-1

1. Explain why the three methods of calculating GDP produce the same estimate of GDP.

2. What are the various sectors to which firms make sales? What are the various ways in which households are linked with other sectors of the economy?

3. Consider Figure 15-2 and suppose you mistakenly believed that total value added was $30,500, the sum of the sales price of a car and a car's worth of steel. What items would you be counting twice?

Solutions appear at back of book.

# Real GDP and Aggregate Output

Although the commonly cited GDP number is an interesting and useful statistic, it is not a useful measure for tracking changes in aggregate output over time. For example, GDP can rise either because the economy is producing more or simply because the prices of the goods and services it produces have increased. Likewise, GDP can fall either because the economy is producing less or because prices have fallen. In order to separate these possibilities, we must calculate how much the economy has changed in *real* terms over any given period. That is, we need to calculate how much of the change in GDP is due to a change in aggregate output separate from a change in prices. The measure that is used for this purpose is known as *real GDP*. Let's look first at how real GDP is calculated, then at what it means.

## Calculating Real GDP

To understand how real GDP is calculated, imagine an economy in which only two goods, apples and oranges, are produced and in which both goods are sold only to final consumers. The outputs and prices of the two fruits for two consecutive years are shown in Table 15-1.

The first thing we can say about these data is that the value of sales increased from year 1 to year 2. In the first year, the total value of sales was (2,000 billion × $0.25) + (1,000 billion × $0.50) = $1,000 billion; in the second it was (2,200 billion × $0.30) + (1,200 billion × $0.70) = $1,500 billion, which is 50% larger. But it is also clear from the table that this increase in the dollar value of GDP overstates the real growth in the economy. Although the quantities of both apples and oranges increased, the prices of both apples and oranges also rose. So part of the 50% increase in the dollar value of GDP simply reflects higher prices, not higher production of output.

To estimate the true increase in aggregate output produced, we have to ask the following question: How much would GDP have gone up if prices had *not* changed? To answer this question, we need to find the value of output in year 2 expressed in year 1 prices. In year 1 the price of apples was $0.25 each and the price of oranges $0.50 each. So year 2 output *at year 1 prices* is (2,200 billion × $0.25) + (1,200 billion × $0.50) = $1,150 billion. And output in year 1 at year 1 prices was $1,000 billion. So in this example GDP measured in year 1 prices rose 15%—from $1,000 billion to $1,150 billion.

Now we can define **real GDP:** it is the total value of final goods and services produced in the economy during a year, calculated as if prices had stayed constant at the level of some given base year. A real GDP number always comes with information about what the base year is. A GDP number that has not been adjusted for changes in prices is calculated using the prices in the year in which the output is produced. Economists call this measure **nominal GDP,** GDP at current prices. If we had used nominal GDP to measure the true change in output from year 1 to year 2 in our apples and oranges example, we would have overstated the true growth in output: we would have claimed it to be 50%, when in fact it was only 15%. By comparing output in the two years using a common set of prices—the year 1 prices in this example—we are able to focus solely on changes in the quantity of output by eliminating the influence of changes in prices.

Table 15-2 shows a real-life version of our apples and oranges example. The second column shows nominal GDP in 1996, 2000, and 2004. The third column shows real GDP for each year in 2000 dollars. For 2000 the two numbers are the same. But real GDP in 1996 expressed in 2000 dollars was higher than nominal GDP in 1996, reflecting the fact

**TABLE 15-1**

### Calculating GDP and Real GDP in a Simple Economy

|  | Year 1 | Year 2 |
|---|---|---|
| Quantity of apples (billions) | 2,000 | 2,200 |
| Price of apple | $0.25 | $0.30 |
| Quantity of oranges (billions) | 1,000 | 1,200 |
| Price of orange | $0.50 | $0.70 |
| GDP (billions of dollars) | $1,000 | $1,500 |
| Real GDP (billions of year 1 dollars) | $1,000 | $1,150 |

**Real GDP** is the total value of all final goods and services produced in the economy during a given year, calculated using the prices of a selected base year.

**Nominal GDP** is the value of all final goods and services produced in the economy during a given year, calculated using the prices current in the year in which the output is produced.

**TABLE 15-2**

### Nominal versus Real GDP in 1996, 2000, and 2004

|  | Nominal GDP (billions of current dollars) | Real GDP (billions of 2000 dollars) |
|---|---|---|
| 1996 | $7,817 | $8,329 |
| 2000 | 9,817 | 9,817 |
| 2004 | 11,734 | 10,842 |

*Source:* Bureau of Economic Analysis.

that prices were in general higher in 2000 than in 1996. Real GDP in 2004 expressed in 2000 dollars, however, was less than nominal GDP in 2004 because prices in 2000 were lower than in 2004.

## A Technical Detail: "Chained" Dollars

Until the 1990s, the government's real GDP estimates were calculated exactly as we did in Table 15-1: real GDP was calculated in a base year's prices. But the U.S. national accounts now report real GDP in "billions of chained 2000 dollars." What does "chained" mean?

What if we had measured real GDP in Table 15-1 using the prices of year 2 rather than year 1 as the base-year prices? Real GDP in year 1 at year 2 prices is (2,000 billion × $0.30) + (1,000 billion × $0.70) = $1,300 billion; real GDP in year 2 in year 2 prices is $1,500 billion, the same as nominal GDP in year 2. So using year 2 prices as the base year, the growth in real GDP is ($1,500 billion–$1,300 billion)/$1,300 billion = 0.154, or 15.4%. When we used year 1 prices, we found that real GDP increased by 15%. Neither answer, 15.4% or 15%, is more "correct" than the other.

15.4% and 15% are pretty close to each other, so in this example it doesn't matter much which base year you choose. But economists estimating 1980s and 1990s growth in U.S. real GDP found that the results differed significantly depending on which base year they used. The main reason was the rapid pace of technological progress in computers, which led both to rapid growth in computer output and to falling prices of computers relative to those of other goods and services. When economists used an early base year, a year when computers were still expensive, they calculated a higher rate of real GDP growth than if they used a later base year, a year when computers were cheap. Because there was such a huge increase in output of computers, the two calculations produced very different estimates for real GDP.

As a result, the government economists now calculate real GDP using "chained" dollars, which splits the difference between using early base years and late base years. We won't go into the details; for our purposes, we can think of calculating real GDP in the prices of a single base year.

## What Real GDP Doesn't Measure

GDP is a measure of a country's aggregate output. Other things equal, a country with a larger population will have higher GDP simply because there are more people working. So if we want to compare GDP across countries but want to eliminate the effect of differences in population size, we use the measure **GDP per capita**—GDP divided by the size of the population, equivalent to the average GDP per person. Correspondingly, real GDP per capita is the average real GDP per person.

> **GDP per capita** is GDP divided by the size of the population; it is equivalent to the average GDP per person.

Although real GDP per capita can be a useful measure in some circumstances, it has well-known limitations as a measure of a country's living standards. Every once in a while economists are accused of believing that growth in real GDP per capita is the only thing that matters—that increasing real GDP per capita is a goal in itself. In fact, economists rarely make that mistake; the idea that economists care only about real GDP per capita is a sort of urban legend. Let's be clear about why a country's real GDP per capita is not a sufficient measure of human welfare in that country and why growth in real GDP per capita is not an appropriate policy goal in itself.

One way to think about this issue is to say that an increase in real GDP means an expansion in the economy's production possibility frontier. Because the economy has increased its productive capacity, there are more things that society can achieve. But whether society actually makes good use of that increased potential to improve living standards is another matter. To put it in a slightly different way, your income may be higher this year than last year, but whether you use that higher income to actually improve your quality of life is your choice.

The United Nations produces an annual document, the *Human Development Report*, that tries to rank countries by measures other than real GDP per capita. These measures include data on infant mortality, life expectancy, and literacy. It compiles these measures into the Human Development Index, which is an effort to determine how well societies are doing, aside from how much they produce. The index suggests that real GDP per capita is one of many important determinants of human welfare—but by no means the only one. Countries with high real GDP per capita—like the United States, European nations, and Japan—also score very well on just about every other indicator of human welfare. But some relatively poor countries—like Costa Rica—have remarkably high literacy and life expectancy along with low infant mortality. And some relatively rich countries—especially countries with valuable natural resources—score quite low on these criteria.

So let's say it again: real GDP per capita is a measure of an economy's average aggregate output per person—and so of what it *can* do. It is not a sufficient goal in itself because it doesn't address how a country uses that output to affect living standards. A country with a high GDP can afford to be healthy, to be well-educated, and in general to have a good quality of life. But there is not a one-to-one match between GDP and the quality of life.

# *economics in action*

## Good Decades, Bad Decades

How important is the distinction between nominal GDP and real GDP? If you are trying to interpret U.S. economic history, the answer is that it is very important indeed. Figure 15-4 tells the tale.

Figure 15-4 shows the cumulative percent change in both U.S. nominal GDP and U.S. real GDP over successive decades since national income accounting

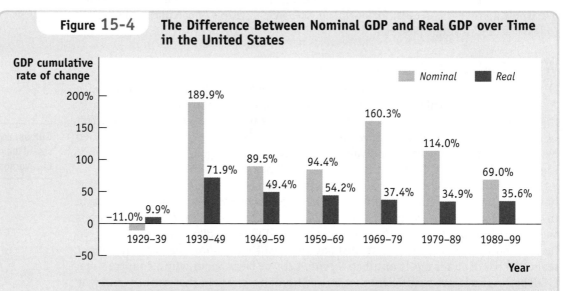

**Figure 15-4** **The Difference Between Nominal GDP and Real GDP over Time in the United States**

GDP cumulative rate of change

Nominal / Real

- 1929–39: −11.0% / 9.9%
- 1939–49: 189.9% / 71.9%
- 1949–59: 89.5% / 49.4%
- 1959–69: 94.4% / 54.2%
- 1969–79: 160.3% / 37.4%
- 1979–89: 114.0% / 34.9%
- 1989–99: 69.0% / 35.6%

Year

To illustrate the difference between nominal GDP and real GDP, this figure shows the percent change in both measures over successive decades within the United States. (Real GDP was calculated using chained 2000 dollars.) The years 1929–1939 show the effect of deflation on the difference between nominal and real GDP: U.S. nominal GDP in 1939 was 11% lower than in 1929, but U.S. aggregate output as measured by real GDP was nearly 10% higher. The remaining years show the effect of inflation on the difference between the two measures: relatively high growth of U.S. nominal GDP in the years 1969–1979 and 1979–1989 contrast with relatively low growth of U.S. real GDP during those same periods. Those years experienced high levels of inflation and a simultaneous slowdown in real GDP growth. **>web...**

*Source:* Bureau of Economic Analysis.

began. That is, we show percent changes from 1929 to 1939, 1939 to 1949, and so on. In each pair, the bar on the left shows the percent change in U.S. nominal GDP over the time period, and the bar on the right shows the percent change in U.S. real GDP over the same period. (Real GDP was calculated using chained 2000 dollars.)

What we see right away is the effect of deflation during the 1930s: nominal GDP and real GDP actually moved in opposite directions during the Great Depression. Due to a falling price level, U.S. nominal GDP in 1939 was 11% lower than in 1929, but U.S. aggregate output as measured by real GDP was nearly 10% higher. After that, both nominal and real GDP rose every decade, but at different rates due to the influence of a changing price level. For example, U.S. nominal GDP grew much faster than U.S. real GDP for the years 1969–1979 and 1979–1989. The explanation is that those years saw high levels of inflation. ∎

> > > > > > > > > > > > > > > > > > > > > > >

## >>CHECK YOUR UNDERSTANDING 15-2

1. Assume there are only two goods in the economy, french fries and onion rings. In 2004, 1,000,000 servings of french fries were sold at $0.40 each and 800,000 servings of onion rings at $0.60 each. From 2004 to 2005, the price of french fries rose by 25% and the servings sold fell by 10%; the price of onion rings fell by 15% and the servings sold rose by 5%.
   a. Calculate the nominal GDP in 2004 and 2005. Calculate real GDP in 2005 using 2004 as the base year.
   b. Why would an assessment of growth using nominal GDP be misguided?

2. From 1990 to 2000, the price of electronic equipment fell dramatically and the price of housing rose dramatically. What are the implications of this in deciding whether to use 1990 or 2000 as the base year in calculating 2005 real GDP?

*Solutions appear at back of book.*

# The Unemployment Rate

In addition to measures of GDP, a number of other measures help us track the performance of the economy. As we learned in Chapter 14, one extremely important statistic for economic policy is the unemployment rate because unemployment leads to lost output and lower social welfare. Cases of very high unemployment, such as in a depression, often lead to political unrest. What exactly does the unemployment rate tell us about the economy?

## Understanding the Unemployment Rate

Every month, the U.S. Census Bureau carries out the Current Population Survey, which involves interviewing a random sample of 60,000 American families. People are asked whether they are currently employed. If they are not employed, they are asked whether they have been looking for a job during the past four weeks. As you may recall from Chapter 14, the labor force is equal to the total of those who are either working or have recently been seeking employment; it does not include discouraged workers, those who have given up actively looking for a job. Those who are actively looking for work but have not, or at least not yet, found a job are classified as unemployed. The unemployment rate, which we showed how to calculate in Chapter 14, is the percent of the labor force that is unemployed.

What does the unemployment rate tell us? It indicates how easy or difficult it is to find a job given the current state of the economy. When the unemployment rate is low, nearly everyone who wants a job can find one. When the unemployment rate is high, jobs are hard to find. As an illustration, recall the story that we told at the beginning of Chapter 14: in the spring of 2000, when the U.S. unemployment rate was only about 4%, potential employers were anxiously wooing potential employees.

Two years later, when the unemployment rate had risen to 6%, new graduates found their job search much more difficult.

Although the unemployment rate is a good indicator of current conditions in the job market, it should not be taken literally as a measure of the percentage of people who want to work but can't find jobs. In some ways the unemployment rate exaggerates the difficulty people have in finding work. In other ways, the opposite is true: low measured unemployment can conceal deep frustration felt by discouraged workers.

Let's start with the argument that the measured unemployment rate is an overstatement of the percentage of people who want to work but can't find jobs. It's normal for someone searching for work to take at least a few weeks to find a suitable job. Yet a worker who is quite confident of getting a job, but has not yet accepted a position, is counted as unemployed. This means that even in boom times, when jobs are very easy to find, the unemployment rate does not fall to zero.

Meanwhile, an individual who has given up looking for a job for the time being—say, a laid-off steelworker in a deeply depressed steel town—isn't counted as unemployed because he or she has not been searching for work during the previous four weeks. Because it does not count discouraged workers, the measured unemployment rate may understate the percentage of people who want to work but are unable to find jobs.

Finally, it's important to realize that the unemployment rate varies greatly among demographic groups. Figure 15-5 shows unemployment rates for different groups in January 2005, when the overall unemployment rate of 5.2% was low by historical standards. As you can see, in January 2005 the unemployment rate for African-American workers was more than twice the national average, the unemployment rate for white teenagers was more than three times the national average, and the unemployment rate for African-American teenagers, at more than 30%, was almost seven times the national average. So even at a time when the overall unemployment rate was relatively low, jobs were hard to find for some groups.

So you should interpret the unemployment rate as an indicator of labor market conditions, not as a literal measure of the percentage of people unable to find jobs.

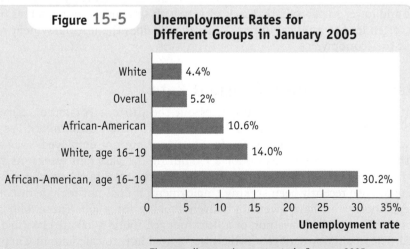

**Figure 15-5**   **Unemployment Rates for Different Groups in January 2005**

The overall unemployment rate in January 2005 was 5.2%. But underlying this average were wide variations in unemployment rates for different demographic groups: African-Americans had a much higher unemployment rate than whites, and young workers had much higher unemployment rates than older workers.

*Source:* Bureau of Labor Statistics.

Still, the ups and downs of the unemployment rate have a significant impact on people's lives. What causes these fluctuations? We already saw, in Chapter 14, that the unemployment rate rises and falls with the business cycle. Now we can be more specific: there is a close relationship between the unemployment rate and the growth rate of real GDP.

## Growth and Unemployment

Figure 15-6 is a scatter diagram showing observations of the growth rate of real GDP and changes in the unemployment rate over time in the United States. Each dot represents one year over the period 1949–2004. The horizontal axis measures the annual rate of growth in real GDP—the percent by which each year's real GDP changed compared to the previous year's real GDP. The vertical axis measures the *change* in the unemployment rate over the previous year in percentage points. For example, the average unemployment rate fell from 4.2% in 1999 to 4.0% in 2000; this is shown as a value of −0.2 along the vertical axis for the year 2000. Over the same period, real GDP grew by 3.7%; this is the value shown along the horizontal axis for the year 2000.

From the downward trend of the scatter points in Figure 15-6, it's clear that, in general, there is a negative relationship between growth in the economy and the rate of unemployment. Years of high growth in real GDP were years in which the unemployment rate fell, and years of low or negative growth in real GDP were years in

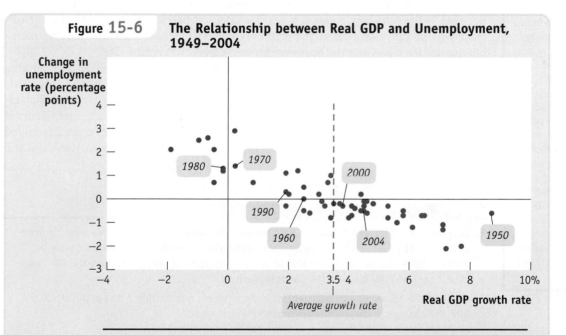

**Figure 15-6    The Relationship between Real GDP and Unemployment, 1949–2004**

The horizontal axis measures the annual growth rate of real GDP, the vertical axis measures the *change* in the unemployment rate over the previous year, and each dot represents one year over the period 1949–2004. The data show that there is typically a negative relationship between growth in the economy and the change in the rate of unemployment. The vertical dashed line is drawn at a value of 3.5%, the average growth rate of real GDP from 1949 to 2004. Points lying to the right of the vertical dashed line indicate that years of above-average growth were typically years of a falling unemployment rate. Points lying to the left show that years of below-average growth were typically years of a rising unemployment rate. The downward trend of the scatter points shows that there is, in general, a negative relationship between the real GDP growth rate and the change in the unemployment rate. **>web...**

*Source:* Bureau of Economic Analysis; Bureau of Labor Statistics.

which the unemployment rate rose. The average growth rate of real GDP over the period from 1949 to 2004 was 3.5%, and for reference we've included a dashed vertical line indicating that value. You can see from examining the points lying to the right of the dashed vertical line that, with few exceptions, years when the economy grew faster than average were also years of a falling unemployment rate. For those years, the value on the vertical axis is negative. Points lying to the left of the dashed vertical line show that years when the economy grew more slowly than average were typically years with a rising unemployment rate. This relationship helps us understand why recessions, periods when real GDP falls, are so painful. As illustrated by the points to the left of the vertical axis in Figure 15-6, falling real GDP is always associated with a rising rate of unemployment, causing a great deal of hardship to families.

Our next and final subject in this chapter will be *price indexes,* which are measures of the aggregate price level.

## *economics in action*

### Jobless Recoveries

During recessions real GDP falls and the unemployment rate always rises. During expansions real GDP rises. Does the unemployment rate automatically fall?

Not necessarily. Look again at Figure 15-6. The data suggest that unemployment falls when growth in real GDP is *above average* (the points lying to the right of the dashed vertical line), where the average growth rate of real GDP has been about 3.5% per year. If the economy grows at a positive rate, but below 3.5% per year, can the unemployment rate rise even as the economy grows? Put another way, can the unemployment rate rise when the economy grows at a below-average rate?

Yes, it can. The combination of slow but positive growth in real GDP with a rising unemployment rate is sometimes called a jobless recovery. It's not a usual occurrence. Normally, once an expansion gets going, growth picks up to a level that reduces unemployment. But jobless recoveries have happened. In fact, one occurred during the most recent economic expansion: the recession of 2001 officially ended in November of that year, but the unemployment rate continued to rise until the summer of 2003. ∎

< < < < < < < < < < < < < < < < < <

**>>CHECK YOUR UNDERSTANDING 15-3**

1. Suppose the advent of employment websites enables job-seekers to find a suitable job more quickly. What effect will this have on the unemployment rate over time? Also suppose that these websites encourage job-seekers who had given up their search to begin looking again. What effect will this have on the unemployment rate?

2. Which of the following are consistent with the observed relationship between growth in real GDP and changes in the unemployment rate? Which are not?
   a. A rise in the unemployment rate accompanies a fall in real GDP.
   b. A business recovery is associated with a greater percentage of the labor force being employed.
   c. Negative real GDP growth is associated with a fall in the unemployment rate.

Solutions appear at back of book.

## Price Indexes and the Aggregate Price Level

Both inflation and deflation can pose problems for the economy. For that reason, we must have a way of measuring changes in the economy's overall price level over time. The aggregate price level, a single number, is supposed to be a measure of the overall price level of final goods and services. But a huge variety of goods and services are produced and consumed within the economy. How can we summarize the prices of all these goods and services with a single number? The answer lies in the concept of a *price index*—a concept best introduced with an example.

## Market Baskets and Price Indexes

Suppose that a frost in Florida destroys most of the citrus harvest. As a result, the price of oranges rises from $0.20 each to $0.40 each, the price of grapefruit rises from $0.60 to $1.00, and the price of lemons rises from $0.25 to $0.45. How much has the price of citrus fruit increased?

One way to answer that question is to state three numbers, the changes in prices for oranges, grapefruit, and lemons. But this is a very cumbersome method. Rather than having to recite three numbers every time someone asks what has happened to the prices of citrus fruit, we would prefer to have some kind of overall measure of the *average* price increase.

Economists measure average price changes for consumer goods and services by asking how much more or less a typical consumer would have to spend to buy his or her previous *consumption bundle*—the typical basket of goods and services purchased before the price changes. Suppose that before the frost a typical consumer bought 200 oranges, 50 grapefruit, and 100 lemons over the course of a year. The average individual might change that pattern of consumption after the price changes caused by the frost. But we can still ask how much it would cost if he or she were to buy the same mix of fruit. A hypothetical consumption bundle, used to measure changes in the overall price level, is known as a **market basket.**

Table 15-3 shows the pre-frost and post-frost cost of the market basket. Before the frost, it cost $95. After the frost, the same bundle of goods cost $175. Since $175/$95 = 1.842, the post-frost basket costs 1.842 times the cost of the pre-frost basket, an increase in cost of 84.2%. So in this case we would say that the average price of citrus fruit increased 84.2% since the base year as a result of the frost.

> A **market basket** is a hypothetical set of consumer purchases of goods and services.

## TABLE **15-3**

### Calculating the Cost of a Market Basket

| | Pre-frost | Post-frost |
|---|---|---|
| Price of orange | $0.20 | $0.40 |
| Price of grapefruit | $0.60 | $1.00 |
| Price of lemon | $0.25 | $0.45 |
| Cost of market basket (200 oranges, 50 grapefruit, 100 lemons) | (200 × $0.20) + (50 × $0.60) + (100 × $0.25) = $95.00 | (200 × $0.40) + (50 × $1.00) + (100 × $0.45) = $175.00 |

Economists use the same method to measure changes in the overall price level: they track changes in the cost of buying a given market basket. In addition, economists perform another simplification in order to avoid having to keep track of the information that the market basket cost, for example, $95 in such-and-such a year. They *normalize* the measure of the aggregate price level so that it is equal to 100 in some given base year. A normalized measure of the overall price level is known as a **price index,** and it is always cited along with the year for which the aggregate price level is being measured and the base year. A price index can be calculated using the following formula:

> A **price index** measures the cost of purchasing a given market basket in a given year, where that cost is normalized so that it is equal to 100 in the selected base year.

$$\textbf{(15-2)} \quad \text{Price index in a given year} = \frac{\text{Cost of market basket in a given year}}{\text{Cost of market basket in base year}} \times 100$$

For example, our citrus fruit market basket cost $95 before the frost; so we would define the price index for citrus fruit as (current cost of market basket/$95) × 100. This yields an index of 100 for the period before the frost and 184.2 for the period afterward. You should note that applying Equation 15-2 to calculate the price index for the base year always results in a price index equal to 100. That is, the price index in the base year is equal to: (cost of market basket in base year/cost of market basket in base year) × 100 = 100.

The price index makes it clear that the average price of citrus has risen 84.2% as a consequence of the frost. Because of its simplicity and intuitive appeal, this method is used to calculate a variety of price indexes to track the average price change among different groups of goods and services. For example, the *consumer price index* is the most widely used measure of the aggregate price level, the overall price level of final consumer goods and services across the economy. Price indexes are also the basis for measuring inflation. The **inflation rate** is the annual percent change in a price index. The inflation rate from year 1 to year 2 is calculated using the following formula:

> The **inflation rate** is the percent change per year in a price index—typically the consumer price index.

$$(15\text{-}3) \quad \text{Inflation rate} = \frac{\text{Price index in year 2} - \text{Price index in year 1}}{\text{Price index in year 1}} \times 100$$

Typically, a news report that cites "the inflation rate" is referring to the annual percent change in the consumer price index.

## The Consumer Price Index

> The **consumer price index**, or **CPI**, measures the cost of the market basket of a typical urban American family.

The most widely used measure of prices in the United States is the **consumer price index** (often referred to simply as the **CPI**), which is intended to show how the cost of all purchases by a typical urban family has changed over time. It is calculated by surveying market prices for a market basket that is constructed to represent the consumption of a typical family of four living in a typical American city. The base period for the index is currently 1982–1984; that is, the index is calculated so that the average of consumer prices in 1982–1984 is 100.

The market basket used to calculate the CPI is far more complex than the three-fruit market basket we described above. In fact, to calculate the CPI, the Bureau of Labor Statistics sends its employees out to survey supermarkets, gas stations, hardware stores, and so on—some 21,000 retail outlets in 85 cities. Every month it tabulates about 90,000 prices, on everything from Romaine lettuce to video rentals. Figure 15-7 shows the makeup of the market basket underlying the current consumer price index by broad categories. The largest component, housing, includes all the costs of owning or renting a residence, including heating and electricity.

Figure 15-8 shows how the CPI has changed over the past 90 years. Since 1940 the CPI has risen steadily, although its annual percent increases in recent years have been much smaller than those of the 1970s and early 1980s. A proportional scale is used so that equal percent changes in the CPI appear the same.

The United States is not the only country that calculates a consumer price index. In fact, nearly every country has one. As you might expect, the market baskets that make up these indexes differ quite a lot from country to country. In poor countries, where people must spend a high proportion of their income just to feed themselves, food makes up a large share of the price index. Among high-income countries, differences in consumption patterns lead to differences in the price indexes: the Japanese price index puts a larger weight on raw fish and a smaller weight on beef than ours does, and the French price index puts a larger weight on wine.

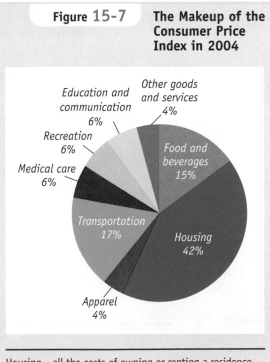

**Figure 15-7** | **The Makeup of the Consumer Price Index in 2004**

Education and communication 6%
Other goods and services 4%
Recreation 6%
Medical care 6%
Transportation 17%
Apparel 4%
Food and beverages 15%
Housing 42%

Housing—all the costs of owning or renting a residence—is the largest component of the market basket underlying the 2004 CPI, followed by transportation and food.
*Source:* Bureau of Labor Statistics.

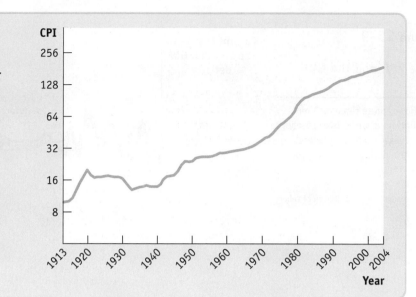

### Figure 15-8

### The CPI, 1913–2004

Since 1940 the CPI has risen steadily. But the annual percent increases in recent years have been much smaller than those of the 1970s and early 1980s. (The vertical axis is measured in log scale so that equal percent changes in the CPI appear the same.) **>web...**

*Source:* Bureau of Labor Statistics.

## Other Price Measures

There are two other price measures that are also widely used to track economy-wide price changes. One is the **producer price index** (or **PPI**, which used to be known as the *wholesale price index*). As its name suggests, the producer price index measures the cost of a typical basket of goods and services—containing raw commodities such as steel, electricity, coal, and so on—purchased by producers. Because commodity producers are relatively quick to raise prices when they perceive a change in overall demand for their goods, the PPI often responds to inflationary or deflationary pressures more quickly than the CPI. As a result, the PPI is often regarded as an "early warning signal" of changes in the inflation rate.

The **producer price index**, or **PPI**, measures changes in the prices of goods purchased by producers.

---

## FOR INQUIRING MINDS

### IS THE CPI BIASED?

The U.S. government takes considerable care in measuring consumer prices. Nonetheless, many—but not all—economists believe that the consumer price index systematically overstates the actual rate of inflation. Because many government payments are tied to the CPI, this is an important fact if true.

What do we mean by saying that the CPI overstates inflation? Imagine comparing two families: one in 1983, with an after-tax income of $20,000, and another in 2004, with an after-tax income of $40,000. According to the CPI, prices in 2004 were about twice as high as in 1983, so those two families should have about the same standard of living. Many economists argue, however, that the 2004 family would have a higher standard of living for two reasons.

One reason is the fact that the CPI measures the cost of buying a given market basket, when in fact consumers typically alter the mix of goods and services they buy away from products that have become relatively more expensive and toward products that have become relatively cheaper. For example, suppose that the price of hamburgers were to double suddenly. Americans currently eat a lot of burgers, but in the face of such a price rise many of them would switch to other foods—and a price index based on a market basket with a lot of hamburgers in it would overstate the true rise in the cost of living.

Actual changes in prices and in the mix of goods and services Americans consume are usually less dramatic than our hypothetical example. But the changing mix of consumption probably leads to some overstatement of inflation by the CPI.

The second reason arises from innovation. In 1983 many goods we now take for granted, especially those using information technology, didn't exist: there was no Internet and there were no iPods. By widening the range of consumer choice, innovation makes a given amount of money worth more. That is, innovation is like a fall in consumer prices.

For both these reasons, many economists believe that the CPI somewhat overstates inflation when we think of inflation as measuring the actual change in the cost of living of a typical urban American family. But there is no consensus on how large the bias is, and for the time being the official CPI remains the basis for most estimates of inflation.

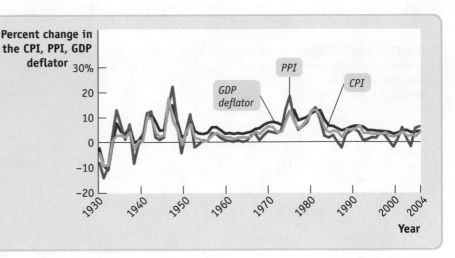

**Figure 15-9**

**The CPI, the PPI, and the GDP Deflator**

As the figure shows, these three different measures of inflation usually move closely together. Each reveals a drastic acceleration in the inflation rate during the 1940s and the 1970s and a return to relative price stability in the 1990s.

*Source:* Bureau of Economic Analysis; Bureau of Labor Statistics.

---

The **GDP deflator** for a given year is 100 times the ratio of nominal GDP to real GDP in that year.

---

The other widely used price measure is the *GDP deflator*; it isn't exactly a price index, although it serves the same purpose. Recall how we distinguished between nominal GDP (GDP in current prices), and real GDP (GDP calculated using the prices of a base year). The **GDP deflator** for a given year is equal to 100 times the ratio of nominal GDP for that year to real GDP for that year expressed in prices of a selected base year. Since real GDP is currently expressed in 2000 dollars, the GDP deflator for 2000 is equal to 100. If nominal GDP doubles but real GDP does not change, the GDP deflator indicates that the aggregate price level doubled.

Perhaps the most important point about the different inflation rates generated by these three measures of prices is that they usually move closely together (although the producer price index tends to fluctuate more than either of the other two measures). Figure 15-9 shows the annual percent changes in the three indexes since 1930. By all three measures, the U.S. economy experienced deflation during the early years of the Great Depression, wartime inflation, accelerating inflation during the 1970s, and a return to relative price stability in the 1990s.

## economics in action

### Indexing to the CPI

Although GDP is a very important number for shaping economic policy, official statistics on GDP don't have a direct effect on people's lives. The CPI, by contrast, has a

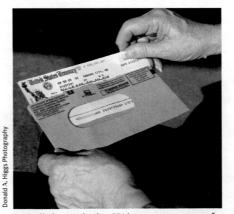

A small change in the CPI has consequences for those dependent on Social Security payments.

direct and immediate impact on millions of Americans. The reason is that many payments are tied or "indexed" to the CPI—the amount paid rises or falls when the CPI rises or falls.

The practice of indexing payments to consumer prices goes back to the dawn of the United States as a nation. In 1780 the Massachusetts state legislature recognized that the pay of its soldiers fighting the British needed to be increased because of inflation that occurred during the Revolutionary War. The legislature adopted a formula that made a soldier's pay proportional to the cost of a market basket, consisting of

5 bushels of corn, 68⁴/₇ pounds of beef, 10 pounds of sheep's wool, and 16 pounds of sole leather.

Today, 48 million people, most of them old or disabled, receive checks from Social Security, a national retirement program that accounts for almost a quarter of current total federal spending—more than the defense budget. The amount of an individual's check is determined by a formula that reflects his or her previous payments into the system as well as other factors. In addition, all Social Security payments are adjusted each year to offset any increase in consumer prices over the previous year. The CPI is used to calculate the official estimate of the inflation rate used to adjust these payments yearly. So every percentage point added to the official estimate of the rate of inflation adds 1% to the checks received by tens of millions of individuals.

Other government payments are also indexed to the CPI. In addition, income tax brackets, the bands of income levels that determine a taxpayer's income tax rate, are also indexed to the CPI. (An individual in a higher income bracket pays a higher income tax rate in a progressive tax system like ours.) Indexing also extends to the private sector, where many private contracts, including some wage settlements, contain cost-of-living allowances (called COLAs) that adjust payments in proportion to changes in the CPI.

Because the CPI plays such an important and direct role in people's lives, it's a politically sensitive number. The Bureau of Labor Statistics, which calculates the CPI, takes great care in collecting and interpreting price and consumption data. They use a complex method in which households are surveyed to determine what they buy and where they shop and a carefully selected sample of stores are surveyed to get representative prices.

As explained in For Inquiring Minds on p. 387, however, there is still considerable controversy about whether the CPI accurately measures inflation. ■

> > > > > > > > > > > > > > > > > > > > > > >

## >>CHECK YOUR UNDERSTANDING 15-4

1. Consider Table 15-3 but suppose that the market basket is composed of 100 oranges, 50 grapefruit, and 200 lemons. How does this change the pre-frost and post-frost price indexes? Explain. Generalize your explanation to how the construction of the market basket affects the price index.

2. Using what you have learned from Question 1, explain the effect of each of the following events on how well a CPI based on a market basket determined 10 years ago functions in measuring the change in prices today.
   a. A typical family owns more cars than it would have a decade ago. Over that time, the average price of a car has increased more than the average prices of other goods.
   b. Virtually no households had broadband Internet access a decade ago. Now, many households have it, and the price has regularly fallen each year.

3. The consumer price index in the United States (base period 1982–1984) was 184.0 in 2003 and 188.9 in 2004. Calculate the inflation rate from 2003 to 2004.

Solutions appear at back of book.

### • A LOOK AHEAD •

We have now seen how economists put actual numbers to key macroeconomic variables such as aggregate output, the unemployment rate, and the aggregate price level.

Now it's time for us to turn to the business cycle—that is, to understand the short-run fluctuations of aggregate output. Our next step, then, is to develop the Aggregate Supply–Aggregate Demand model, which we will use to analyze how the behavior of producers, consumers, and the government influences the economy's short-run performance.

1. Economists keep track of the flows of money between sectors with the **national income and product accounts,** or **national accounts.** Households earn income via the factor markets from wages, interest on **bonds,** profit accruing to owners of **stocks,** and rent on land. In addition, they receive **government transfers** from the government. **Disposable income,** total household income minus taxes plus government transfers, is allocated to **consumer spending** (C) and **private savings.** Via the **financial markets,** private savings and foreign lending are channeled to **investment spending** (I), government borrowing, and foreign borrowing. **Government purchases of goods and services** (G) are paid for by tax revenues and any **government borrowing. Exports** (X) generate an inflow of funds into the country from the rest of the world, but **imports** (IM) lead to an outflow of funds to the rest of the world. Foreigners can also buy stocks and bonds in the U.S. financial markets.

2. **Gross domestic product,** or **GDP,** measures the value of all **final goods and services** produced in the economy. It does not include the value of **intermediate goods and services.** It can be calculated in three ways: add up the **value added** by all producers; add up all spending on domestically produced final goods and services, leading to the equation $GDP = C + I + G + X - IM$; or add up all the income paid by domestic firms to factors of production. These three methods are equivalent because in the economy as a whole, total income paid by domestic firms to factors of production must equal total spending on domestically produced final goods and services. $(X - IM)$, exports minus imports, is often called **net exports.**

3. **Real GDP** is the value of the final goods and services produced calculated using the prices of a selected base year. Except in the base year, real GDP is not the same as **nominal GDP,** aggregate output calculated using current prices. Analysis of the growth rate of aggregate output must use real GDP because doing so eliminates any change in the value of aggregate output due solely to price changes. Real **GDP per capita** is a measure of average aggregate output per person, but is not in itself an appropriate policy goal.

4. The unemployment rate is an indicator of the state of the labor market, but it should not be taken literally as a measure of the percentage of people who want to work but can't find jobs. It may overstate the true level of unemployment because a person typically spends time unemployed while searching for a job. It may also understate the true level of unemployment because it does not include discouraged workers.

5. There is a strong negative relationship between growth in real GDP and changes in the unemployment rate: when growth is above average, the unemployment rate falls; when it is below average, the unemployment rate rises.

6. To measure the aggregate price level, economists calculate the cost of purchasing a **market basket.** A **price index** is the ratio of the current cost of that market basket to the cost in a selected base year, multiplied by 100.

7. The **inflation rate** is the yearly percent change in a price index, typically based on the **consumer price index,** or **CPI,** the most common measure of the aggregate price level. A similar index for goods and services purchased by firms is the **producer price index.** Finally, economists also use the **GDP deflator,** which measures the price level by calculating the ratio of nominal to real GDP times 100.

National income and product accounts (national accounts), p. 368
Consumer spending, p. 368
Stock, p. 369
Bond, p. 369
Government transfers, p. 370
Disposable income, p. 370
Private savings, p. 370
Financial markets, p. 370
Government borrowing, p. 370

Government purchases of goods and services, p. 370
Exports, p. 370
Imports, p. 370
Investment spending, p. 371
Final goods and services, p. 371
Intermediate goods and services, p. 371
Gross domestic product (GDP), p. 371
Aggregate spending, p. 371
Value added, p. 373

Net exports, p. 376
Real GDP, p. 378
Nominal GDP, p. 378
GDP per capita, p. 379
Market basket, p. 385
Price index, p. 385
Inflation rate, p. 386
Consumer price index (CPI), p. 386
Producer price index (PPI), p. 387
GDP deflator, p. 388

## PROBLEMS

**1.** At right is a simplified circular-flow diagram for the economy of Micronia.

   **a.** What is the value of GDP in Micronia?

   **b.** What is the value of net exports?

   **c.** What is the value of disposable income?

   **d.** Does the total flow of money out of households—the sum of taxes paid, consumer spending, and private savings—equal the total flow of money into households?

   **e.** How does the government of Micronia finance its purchases of goods and services?

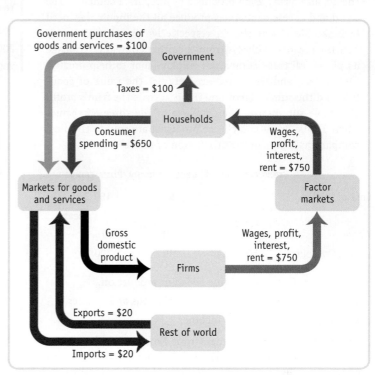

**2.** A more complex circular-flow diagram for the economy of Macronia is shown at right.

   **a.** What is the value of GDP in Macronia?

   **b.** What is the value of net exports?

   **c.** What is the value of disposable income?

   **d.** Does the total flow of money out of households—the sum of taxes paid, consumer spending, and private savings—equal the total flow of money into households?

   **e.** How does the government finance its spending?

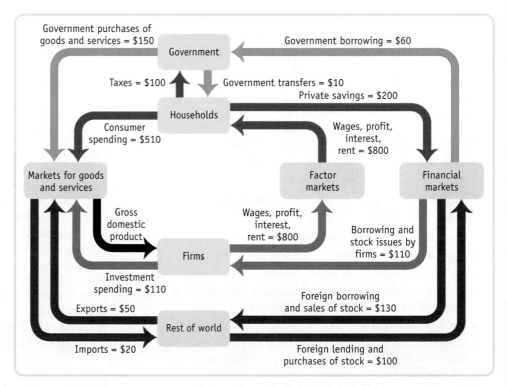

3. The small economy of Pizzania produces three goods (bread, cheese, and pizza), each produced by a separate company. The bread and cheese companies produce all the inputs they need to make bread and cheese, respectively; the pizza company uses the bread and cheese from the other companies to make its pizzas. All three companies employ labor to help produce their goods, and the difference between the value of goods sold and the sum of labor and input costs is the firm's profit. This table summarizes the activities of the three companies when all the bread and cheese produced are sold to the pizza company as inputs in the production of pizzas.

| | Bread company | Cheese company | Pizza company |
|---|---|---|---|
| Cost of inputs | $0 | $0 | $50 Bread |
| | | | 35 Cheese |
| Wages | 15 | 20 | 75 |
| Value of output | 50 | 35 | 200 |

a. Calculate GDP as the value added in production.

b. Calculate GDP as spending on final goods and services.

c. Calculate GDP as factor income.

4. In the economy of Pizzania (from Problem 3), bread and cheese produced are sold both to the pizza company for inputs in the production of pizzas and to consumers as final goods. The accompanying table summarizes the activities of the three companies.

| | Bread company | Cheese company | Pizza company |
|---|---|---|---|
| Cost of inputs | $0 | $0 | $50 Bread |
| | | | 35 Cheese |
| Wages | 25 | 30 | 75 |
| Value of output | 100 | 60 | 200 |

a. Calculate GDP as the value added in production.

b. Calculate GDP as spending on final goods and services.

c. Calculate GDP as factor income.

5. Which of the following transactions will be included in GDP for the United States?

a. Coca-Cola builds a new bottling plant in the United States.

b. Delta sells one of its existing airplanes to Korean Air.

c. Ms. Moneybags buys an existing share of Disney stock.

d. A California winery produces a bottle of Chardonnay and sells it to a customer in Montreal, Canada.

e. An American buys a bottle of French perfume.

f. A book publisher produces too many copies of a new book; the books don't sell this year, so the publisher adds the surplus books to inventories.

6. The economy of Britannica produces three goods: computers, DVDs, and pizza. The accompanying table shows the prices and output of the three goods for the years 2002, 2003, and 2004.

| | Computers | | DVDs | | Pizza | |
|---|---|---|---|---|---|---|
| Year | Price | Quantity | Price | Quantity | Price | Quantity |
| 2002 | $900 | 10 | $10 | 100 | $15 | 2 |
| 2003 | 1,000 | 10.5 | 12 | 105 | 16 | 2 |
| 2004 | 1,050 | 12 | 14 | 110 | 17 | 3 |

a. What is the percent change in production of each of the goods from 2002 to 2003 and from 2003 to 2004?

b. What is the percent change in prices of each of the goods from 2002 to 2003 and from 2003 to 2004?

c. Calculate nominal GDP in Britannica for each of the three years. What is the percent change in nominal GDP from 2002 to 2003 and from 2003 to 2004?

d. Calculate real GDP in Britannica using 2002 prices for each of the three years. What is the percent change in real GDP from 2002 to 2003 and from 2003 to 2004?

7. The accompanying table shows data on nominal GDP (in billions of dollars), real GDP (in billions of dollars) using 2000 as the base year, and population (in thousands) of the U.S. in 1960, 1970, 1980, 1990, 2000, and 2004, years in which the U.S. price level consistently rose.

| Year | Nominal GDP (billions of dollars) | Real GDP (billions of 2000 dollars) | Population (thousands) |
|---|---|---|---|
| 1960 | $526.4 | $2,501.8 | 180,671 |
| 1970 | 1,038.5 | 3,771.9 | 205,052 |
| 1980 | 2,789.5 | 5,161.7 | 227,726 |
| 1990 | 5,803.1 | 7,112.5 | 250,132 |
| 2000 | 9,817.0 | 9,817.0 | 282,388 |
| 2004 | 11,734.0 | 10,841.9 | 293,907 |

a. Why is real GDP greater than nominal GDP for all years before 2000 and lower for 2004? Does nominal GDP have to equal real GDP in 2000?

b. Calculate the percent change in real GDP from 1960 to 1970, 1970 to 1980, 1980 to 1990, and 1990 to 2000. Which period had the highest growth rate?

c. Calculate real GDP per capita for each of the years in the table.

d. Calculate the percent change in real GDP per capita from 1960 to 1970, 1970 to 1980, 1980 to 1990, and 1990 to 2000. Which period had the highest growth rate?

e. How do the percent change in real GDP and the percent change in real GDP per capita compare? Which is larger? Do we expect them to have this relationship?

8. This table shows the Human Development Index (HDI) and real GDP per capita in U.S. dollars for six nations in 2002.

| | HDI | Real GDP per capita |
|---|---|---|
| Brazil | 0.775 | $7,770 |
| Canada | 0.943 | 29,480 |
| Japan | 0.938 | 26,940 |
| Mexico | 0.802 | 8,970 |
| Saudi Arabia | 0.768 | 12,650 |
| United States | 0.939 | 35,750 |

Rank the nations according to HDI and according to real GDP per capita. Why do the two vary?

9. In general, how do changes in the unemployment rate vary with changes in real GDP? After several quarters of a severe recession, explain why we might observe a decrease in the official unemployment rate. Could we see an increase in the official unemployment rate after several quarters of a strong expansion?

10. Each month, usually on the first Friday of the month, the Bureau of Labor Statistics releases the Employment Situation Summary for the previous month. Go to www.bls.gov and find the latest report. (On the Bureau of Labor Statistics home page, click on "National unemployment rate" and then choose "Employment Situation Summary.") How does the unemployment rate compare to the rate one year earlier? What percentage of unemployed workers are long-term unemployed workers?

11. Eastland College is concerned about the rising price of textbooks that students must purchase. To better identify the increase in the price of textbooks, the dean asks you, the Economics Department's star student, to create an index of textbook prices. The average student purchases three English, two math, and four economics textbooks. The prices of these books are given in the accompanying table.

   a. Create the price index for these books for all years with a base year of 2002.

| | 2002 | 2003 | 2004 |
|---|---|---|---|
| English textbook | $50 | $55 | $57 |
| Math textbook | 70 | 72 | 74 |
| Economics textbook | 80 | 90 | 100 |

   b. What is the percent change in the price of an English textbook from 2002 to 2004?

   c. What is the percent change in the price of a math textbook from 2002 to 2004?

   d. What is the percent change in the price of an economics textbook from 2002 to 2004?

   e. What is the percent change in the market index from 2002 to 2004?

12. The consumer price index, or CPI, measures the cost of living for the average consumer by multiplying the price for each category of expenditure (housing, food, and so on) times a measure of the importance of that expenditure in the average consumer's market basket and summing over all categories. However, using data from the consumer price index, we can see that changes in the cost of living for different types of consumers can vary a great deal. Let's compare the cost of living for a hypothetical retired person and a hypothetical college student. Let's assume that the market basket of a retired person is allocated in the following way: 10% on housing, 15% on food, 5% on transportation, 60% on medical care, 0% on education, and 10% on recreation. The college student's market basket is allocated as follows: 5% on housing, 15% on food, 20% on transportation, 0% on medical care, 40% on education, and 20% on recreation. The accompanying table shows the December 2004 CPI for each of the relevant categories.

| | CPI, December 2004 |
|---|---|
| Housing | 190.7 |
| Food | 188.9 |
| Transportation | 164.8 |
| Medical care | 314.9 |
| Education | 112.6 |
| Recreation | 108.5 |

Calculate the overall CPI for the retired person and for the college student by multiplying the CPI for each of the categories by the relative importance of that category to the individual and then summing each of the categories. The CPI for all items in December 2004 was 190.3. How do your calculations for a CPI for the retired person and the college student compare to the overall CPI?

13. Each month the Bureau of Labor Statistics releases the Consumer Price Index Summary for the previous month. Go to www.bls.gov and find the latest report. (On the Bureau of Labor Statistics home page, click on "CPI" under "Latest Numbers" and then choose "Consumer Price Index Summary.") What was the CPI for the previous month? How did it change from the previous month? How does the CPI compare to the same month one year ago?

14. The accompanying table contains two price indexes for the years 2002, 2003, and 2004: the GDP deflator and the CPI. For each price index, calculate the inflation rate from 2002 to 2003 and from 2003 to 2004.

| Year | GDP deflator | CPI |
|---|---|---|
| 2002 | 104.1 | 179.9 |
| 2003 | 106.0 | 184.0 |
| 2004 | 108.3 | 188.9 |

> web... To continue your study and review of concepts in this chapter, please visit the Krugman/Wells/Olney website for quizzes, animated graph tutorials, web links to helpful resources, and more.

**www.worthpublishers.com/krugmanwellsolney**

# 16

## >>Aggregate Supply and Aggregate Demand

### SHOCKS TO THE SYSTEM

### What you will learn in this chapter:

➤ How the **aggregate supply curve** illustrates the relationship between the aggregate price level and the quantity of aggregate output supplied in the economy

➤ Why the aggregate supply curve is different in the short run compared to the long run

➤ How the **aggregate demand curve** illustrates the relationship between the aggregate price level and the quantity of aggregate output demanded in the economy

➤ The importance of the **multiplier,** which determines the total change in aggregate output arising from a shift of the aggregate demand curve

➤ How the *AS–AD* **model** is used to analyze economic fluctuations

➤ How monetary policy and fiscal policy can stabilize the economy

ON NOVEMBER 4, 1979, MILITANT Iranian students seized the U.S. embassy in Tehran, taking 66 Americans hostage. For the next 444 days the news was dominated by the plight of the hostages, the threat of U.S. military action, and the resulting political instability. The home front was further shaken by a quadrupling of the price of oil, another repercussion of the hostage crisis in the Persian Gulf. Price controls on gasoline, which limited its price at the pump and had been imposed in response to an earlier jump in the price of oil, led to gasoline shortages and long lines. Next came a severe recession, the worst since the Great Depression. The industrial Midwest, experiencing a catastrophic loss in the number of jobs, became

known as the Rust Belt. In Michigan, ground zero of the hard-hit auto industry, the unemployment rate rose to over 16%.

But if the economic slump that followed the Persian Gulf crisis looked in many ways like a small-scale repeat of the Great Depression, it was very different in one important respect. During the Great Depression, from 1929 to 1933, the U.S. economy experienced severe *deflation*—a falling aggregate price level. During the slump from 1979 to 1982, the economy experienced severe *inflation*—a rising aggregate price level—reaching a peak rate of more than 13%. Many people were as upset by the high inflation as by the job losses because they saw the purchasing power of their incomes shrinking. And the emergence of *stagflation,*

In the late 1970s and early 1980s, energy price increases arising from events in the Middle East led to recession and inflation here at home.

the combination of inflation and rising unemployment, also shook the confidence of economists and policy makers in their ability to manage the economy.

Why did the recession of 1979–1982 look different from the slump at the beginning of the Great Depression? Because it had a different cause. Indeed, the lesson of the 1970s was that recessions can have different causes and that the appropriate policy response depends on the cause. The Great Depression was caused by a crisis of confidence that led businesses and consumers to spend less, exacerbated by a banking crisis. This led to a combination of recession and deflation, which policy makers at that time didn't know how to respond to. But today we think we know what they should have done: pump cash into the economy, fighting the slump and stabilizing prices.

But the recession of 1979–1982, like the earlier recession of 1973–1975, was largely caused by events in the Middle East that led to sudden cuts in world oil production and soaring prices for oil and other fuels. These energy price increases led to a combination of recession and inflation. They also led to a dilemma: should economic policy fight the slump by pumping cash *into* the economy, or should it fight inflation by pulling cash *out* of the economy?

In this chapter, we'll develop a model that shows us how to distinguish between different types of short-run economic fluctuations—*demand shocks*, like the Great Depression, and *supply shocks*, like those of the 1970s. This model helps us understand short-run macroeconomics and macroeconomic policy.

To develop this model, we'll proceed in three steps. First, we'll develop the concept of *aggregate supply*. Then we'll turn to the parallel concept of *aggregate demand*. Finally, we'll put them together in the *AS–AD model*.

# Aggregate Supply

Between 1929 and 1933, the demand curve for almost every good produced in the United States shifted to the left—the quantity demanded at any given price fell. We'll turn to the reasons for that decline in the next section, but let's focus first on the effects on producers.

One consequence of the economy-wide decline in demand was a fall in the prices of most goods and services. By 1933 the GDP deflator, one of the price indexes we defined in Chapter 15, was 26% below its 1929 level, and other indexes were down by similar amounts. A second consequence was a decline in the output of most goods and services: by 1933 real GDP was 27% below its 1929 level. A third consequence, closely tied to the fall in real GDP, was a surge in the unemployment rate from 3% to 25%.

The association between the plunge in real GDP and the plunge in prices wasn't an accident. Between 1929 and 1933, the U.S. economy was moving down its **aggregate supply curve,** which shows the relationship between the economy's aggregate price level (the overall price level of final goods and services in the economy) and the total quantity of final goods and services, or aggregate output, producers are willing to supply. (As we learned in Chapter 15, we use real GDP to measure aggregate output. So we'll often use the two terms interchangeably.) More specifically, between 1929 and 1933 the U.S. economy moved down its *short-run aggregate supply curve.*

The **aggregate supply curve** shows the relationship between the aggregate price level and the quantity of aggregate output supplied.

## The Short-Run Aggregate Supply Curve

The period from 1929 to 1933 demonstrated that there is a positive relationship in the short run between the aggregate price level and the quantity of aggregate output supplied. That is, a rise in the aggregate price level leads to a rise in the quantity of aggregate output supplied, other things equal; a fall in the aggregate price level leads to a fall in the quantity of aggregate output supplied, other things equal. To understand why this positive relationship exists, let's think about the most basic question facing a producer: is producing a unit of output profitable or not? The answer depends on whether the price the producer receives for a unit of output, such as a bushel of corn, is greater or less than the cost of producing that unit of output. That is,

**(16-1)** Profit per unit output =
Price per unit output − Production cost per unit output

At any given point in time, many of the costs producers face are fixed and can't be changed for an extended period of time. Typically, the largest source of inflexible production cost is the wages paid to workers. *Wages* here refers to all forms of worker compensation, such as employer-paid health care and retirement benefits in addition to earnings. Wages are typically an inflexible production cost because the dollar amount of any given wage paid, called the **nominal wage,** is often determined by contracts that were signed several years earlier. And even when there are no formal contracts, there are often informal agreements between management and workers, reflecting reluctance by companies to change wages in response to economic conditions. For example, companies usually will not reduce wages during poor economic times—unless the downturn has been particularly long and severe—for fear of generating worker resentment. Correspondingly, they typically won't raise wages during better economic times—until they are at risk of losing workers to competitors—because they don't want to encourage workers to routinely demand higher wages. So as a result of both formal and informal agreements, nominal wages are "sticky": slow to fall even in the face of high unemployment, and slow to rise even in the face of labor shortages. Nominal wages cannot be sticky forever: ultimately, formal contracts and informal agreements will be renegotiated to take into account changed economic circumstances. How long it takes for nominal wages to become flexible is an integral component of what distinguishes the short run from the long run.

Let's return to the question of the positive relationship between the aggregate price level and the quantity of aggregate output supplied in the short run. Imagine that, for some reason, the aggregate price level falls, which means that the price received by the typical producer of a final good or service falls. Because many production costs are fixed in the short run, production cost per unit of output doesn't fall by the same proportion as the fall in the price of output. So the profit per unit of output declines, leading producers to reduce the quantity supplied in the short run. In the economy as a whole, when the aggregate price level falls, aggregate output falls in the short run.

Now consider what would happen if, for some reason, the aggregate price level rises. As a result, the typical producer receives a higher price for his or her final good or service. Because many production costs are fixed in the short run, production cost per unit of output doesn't rise by the same proportion as the rise in the price of a unit. So profit per unit of output rises, the producer increases output, and aggregate output increases in the short run.

The positive relationship between the aggregate price level and the quantity of aggregate output producers are willing to supply during the time period when many production costs, particularly nominal wages, can be taken as fixed is illustrated by the **short-run aggregate supply curve.** The positive relationship between the aggregate price level and aggregate output in the short run gives the short-run aggregate supply curve its upward slope. Figure 16-1 shows a hypothetical short-run aggregate supply curve, *SRAS*, which matches actual U.S. data for 1929 and 1933. On the horizontal axis is aggregate output (or, equivalently, real

The **nominal wage** is the dollar amount of the wage paid.

The **short-run aggregate supply curve** shows the relationship between the aggregate price level and the quantity of aggregate output supplied that exists in the short run, the time period when many production costs can be taken as fixed.

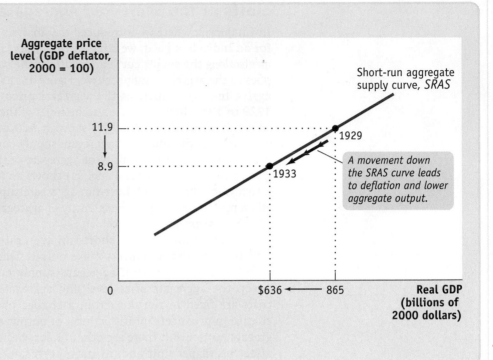

### Figure 16-1

**The Short-Run Aggregate Supply Curve**

The short-run aggregate supply curve shows the relationship between the aggregate price level and the quantity of aggregate output supplied in the short run, the period in which many production costs such as nominal wages are fixed. It is upward-sloping because a higher aggregate price level leads to higher profit per unit of output and higher aggregate output given fixed nominal wages. Here we show numbers corresponding to the Great Depression, from 1929 to 1933: when deflation occurred and the aggregate price level fell from 11.9 (in 1929) to 8.9 (in 1933), firms responded by reducing the quantity of aggregate output supplied from $865 billion to $636 billion measured in 2000 dollars.

GDP)—the total quantity of final goods and services supplied in the economy—measured in 2000 dollars. On the vertical axis is the aggregate price level as measured by the GDP deflator, with the value for year 2000 equal to 100. In 1929, the aggregate price level was 11.9 and real GDP was $865 billion. In 1933, the aggregate price level was 8.9 and real GDP was only $636 billion. The movement down the SRAS curve corresponds to the deflation and fall in aggregate output experienced over those years.

---

## FOR INQUIRING MINDS

### WHAT'S TRULY FLEXIBLE, WHAT'S TRULY STICKY

Most macroeconomists agree that the basic picture shown in Figure 16-1 is correct: there is, other things equal, a positive short-run relationship between the aggregate price level and aggregate output. But many would argue that the details are a bit more complicated.

So far we've stressed a difference in the behavior of the aggregate price level and the behavior of nominal wages. That is, we've said that the aggregate price level is flexible but nominal wages are sticky in the short run. Although this assumption is a good way to explain why the short-run aggregate supply curve is upward-sloping, empirical data on wages and prices don't wholly support a sharp distinction between flexible

prices of final goods and services and sticky nominal wages. On one side, some nominal wages are in fact flexible even in the short run because some workers are not covered by a contract or informal agreement with their employers. Since some nominal wages are sticky but others are flexible, we observe that the *average nominal wage*—the nominal wage averaged over all workers in the economy—falls when there is a steep rise in unemployment. For example, nominal wages fell substantially in the early years of the Great Depression. On the other side, some prices of final goods and services are sticky rather than flexible. For example, some firms, particularly the makers of luxury or

name-brand goods, are reluctant to cut prices even when demand falls. Instead they prefer to cut output even if their profit per unit hasn't declined.

These complications, as we've said, don't change the basic picture. When the aggregate price level falls, some producers cut output because the nominal wages they pay are sticky. And some producers don't cut their prices in the face of a falling aggregate price level, preferring instead to reduce their output. In both cases the positive relationship between the aggregate price level and aggregate output is maintained. So, in the end, the short-run aggregate supply curve is still upward-sloping.

## Shifts of the Short-Run Aggregate Supply Curve

In Chapter 3, where we introduced the analysis of supply and demand in the market for an individual good, we stressed the importance of the distinction between *movements along* the supply curve and *shifts of* the supply curve. The same distinction applies to the aggregate supply curve. Figure 16-1 shows a *movement along* the short-run aggregate supply curve, as the aggregate price level and aggregate output fell from 1929 to 1933. But there can also be *shifts of* the short-run aggregate supply curve, as shown in Figure 16-2. Panel (a) shows a *decrease in short-run aggregate supply*—a leftward shift of the short-run aggregate supply curve. Aggregate supply decreases when producers reduce the quantity of aggregate output they are willing to supply at any given aggregate price level. Panel (b) shows an *increase in short-run aggregate supply*—a rightward shift of the short-run aggregate supply curve. Aggregate supply increases when producers increase the quantity of aggregate output they are willing to supply at any given aggregate price level.

To understand why the short-run aggregate supply curve can shift, it's important to recall that producers make output decisions based on their profit per unit of output. The short-run aggregate supply curve illustrates the relationship between the aggregate price level and aggregate output: because some production costs are fixed in the short run, a change in the aggregate price level leads to a change in producers' profit per unit of output and, in turn, leads to a change in aggregate output. But there are other factors besides the aggregate price level that can affect profit per unit and, in turn, aggregate output. It is changes in these other factors that will shift the short-run aggregate supply curve.

To develop some intuition, suppose that something happens that raises production costs—say an increase in the price of oil. At any given price of output, a producer now earns a smaller profit per unit of output. As a result, producers reduce the quantity supplied at any given aggregate price level, and the short-run aggregate supply curve shifts to the left. If, in contrast, something happens that lowers production costs—say a fall in the nominal wage—a producer now earns a higher profit per unit of output at any given price of output. This leads producers to increase the quantity

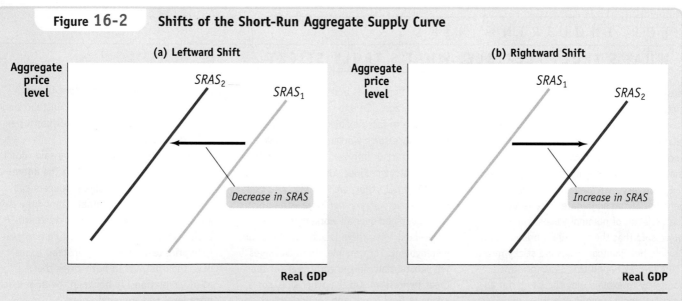

**Figure 16-2** **Shifts of the Short-Run Aggregate Supply Curve**

**(a) Leftward Shift**

Aggregate price level

$SRAS_2$   $SRAS_1$

Decrease in SRAS

Real GDP

**(b) Rightward Shift**

Aggregate price level

$SRAS_1$   $SRAS_2$

Increase in SRAS

Real GDP

Panel (a) shows a decrease in short-run aggregate supply: the short-run aggregate supply curve shifts leftward from $SRAS_1$ to $SRAS_2$, and the quantity of aggregate output supplied at any given aggregate price level falls. Panel (b) shows an increase in short-run aggregate supply: the short-run aggregate supply curve shifts rightward from $SRAS_1$ to $SRAS_2$, and the quantity of aggregate output supplied at any given aggregate price level rises.

of aggregate output supplied at any given aggregate price level, and the short-run aggregate supply curve shifts to the right.

Now we'll discuss some of the other important factors that affect producers' profit per unit and so can lead to shifts of the short-run aggregate supply curve.

### Changes in Commodity Prices

In this chapter's opening story, we described how a surge in the price of oil caused problems for the U.S. economy in 1979. Oil is a commodity, a standardized input bought and sold in bulk quantities. An increase in the price of a commodity—oil—raised production costs across the economy and reduced the quantity of aggregate output supplied at any given aggregate price level, shifting the short-run aggregate supply curve to the left. Conversely, a decline in commodity prices will reduce production costs, leading to an increase in the quantity supplied at any given aggregate price level and a rightward shift of the short-run aggregate supply curve.

Why isn't the influence of commodity prices already captured by the short-run aggregate supply curve? Because commodities—unlike, say, soft drinks—are not a final good, their prices are not included in the calculation of the aggregate price level. Further, commodities represent a significant cost of production to most suppliers, just like nominal wages do. So changes in commodity prices have large impacts on production costs. And in contrast to non-commodities, the prices of commodities can sometimes change drastically due to industry-specific shocks to supply—such as wars in the Middle East.

### Changes in Nominal Wages

At any given point in time, the dollar wages of many workers are fixed because they are set by contracts or informal agreements made in the past. Nominal wages can change, however, once enough time has passed for contracts and informal agreements to be renegotiated. Suppose, for example, that there is an economy-wide rise in the cost of health care insurance premiums paid by employers as part of employees' wages. From the employers' perspective, this is equivalent to a rise in nominal wages because it is an increase in employer-paid compensation. So this rise in nominal wages increases production costs and shifts the short-run aggregate supply curve to the left. Conversely, suppose there is an economy-wide fall in the cost of such premiums. This is equivalent to a fall in nominal wages from the point of view of employers; it reduces production costs and shifts the short-run aggregate supply curve to the right.

An important historical fact is that during the 1970s the surge in the price of oil had the indirect effect of also raising nominal wages. This "knock-on" effect occurred because many wage contracts included *cost-of-living allowances* that automatically raised the nominal wage when consumer prices increased. Through this channel, the surge in the price of oil—which led to an increase in overall consumer prices—ultimately caused a rise in nominal wages. So the economy, in the end, experienced two leftward shifts of the aggregate supply curve: the first generated by the initial surge in the price of oil, the second generated by the induced increase in nominal wages. The negative effect on the economy of rising oil prices was greatly magnified through the cost-of-living allowances in wage contracts. Today, cost-of-living allowances in wage contracts are rare.

### Changes in Productivity

An increase in productivity means that a worker can produce more units of output with the same quantity of inputs. For example, the introduction of bar-code scanners in retail stores greatly increased the ability of a single worker to stock, inventory, and resupply store shelves. As a result, the cost to a store of "producing" a dollar of sales fell and profit rose. And, correspondingly, the quantity supplied increased. (Think of Wal-Mart and the increase in the number of its stores as an increase in aggregate supply.) So a rise in productivity, whatever the source, increases producers' profits and shifts the short-run aggregate supply curve to the right. Conversely, a fall in productivity—say, due to new regulations that require workers to spend more time filling out forms—reduces the number of units of output a worker can produce with the same quantity of inputs. Consequently, the cost per unit of output rises, profit falls, and quantity supplied falls. This shifts the short-run aggregate supply curve to the left.

## The Long-Run Aggregate Supply Curve

We've just seen that in the short run a fall in the aggregate price level leads to a decline in the quantity of aggregate output supplied because nominal wages are sticky in the short run. But, as we mentioned earlier, contracts and informal agreements are renegotiated in the long run. So in the long run, nominal wages—like the aggregate price level—are flexible, not sticky. This fact greatly alters the long-run relationship between the aggregate price level and aggregate supply. In fact, in the long run the aggregate price level has *no* effect on the quantity of aggregate output supplied.

To see why, let's conduct a thought experiment. Imagine that you could wave a magic wand—or maybe a magic bar-code scanner—and cut *all prices* in the economy in half at the same time. By "all prices" we mean the prices of all inputs, including nominal wages, as well as the prices of final goods and services. What would happen to aggregate output, given that the aggregate price level has been halved and all input prices, including nominal wages, have been halved?

The answer is: nothing. Consider Equation 16-1 again: each producer would receive a lower price for his or her product, but costs would fall by the same proportion. As a result, every unit of output profitable to produce before the change in prices would still be profitable to produce after the change in prices. So a halving of *all* prices in the economy has no effect on the economy's aggregate output. In other words, changes in the aggregate price level now have no effect on the quantity of aggregate output supplied.

In reality, of course, no one can change all prices by the same proportion at the same time. But in the long run, when all prices are fully flexible, inflation or deflation has the same effect as someone changing all prices by the same proportion. *As a result, changes in the aggregate price level do not change the quantity of aggregate output supplied in the long run.* That's because changes in the aggregate price level will, in the long run, be accompanied by equal proportional changes in *all* input prices, including nominal wages.

The **long-run aggregate supply curve,** illustrated in Figure 16-3 by the curve *LRAS*, shows the relationship between the aggregate price level and the quantity of aggregate output supplied that would exist if all prices, including nominal wages, were fully flexible. The long-run aggregate supply curve is vertical because changes in the aggregate price level have *no* effect on aggregate output in the long run. At an aggregate price level of 15.0, the quantity of aggregate output supplied is $800 billion in

> The **long-run aggregate supply curve** shows the relationship between the aggregate price level and the quantity of aggregate output supplied that would exist if all prices, including nominal wages, were fully flexible.

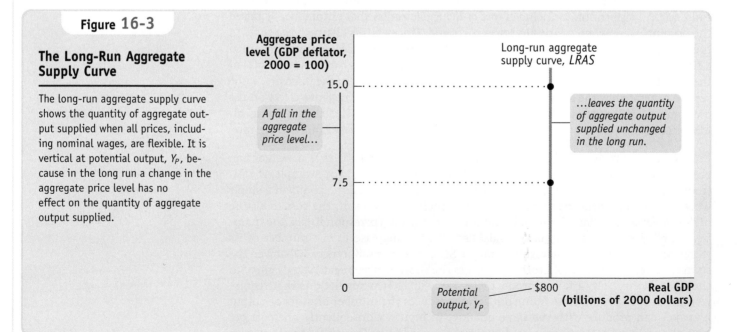

### Figure 16-3

### The Long-Run Aggregate Supply Curve

The long-run aggregate supply curve shows the quantity of aggregate output supplied when all prices, including nominal wages, are flexible. It is vertical at potential output, $Y_P$, because in the long run a change in the aggregate price level has no effect on the quantity of aggregate output supplied.

Aggregate price level (GDP deflator, 2000 = 100)

Long-run aggregate supply curve, *LRAS*

15.0

*A fall in the aggregate price level...*

*...leaves the quantity of aggregate output supplied unchanged in the long run.*

7.5

0

*Potential output, $Y_P$*

$800

**Real GDP (billions of 2000 dollars)**

2000 dollars. If the aggregate price level falls by 50% to 7.5, the quantity of aggregate output supplied is unchanged in the long run at $800 billion in 2000 dollars.

It's important to understand not only that the *LRAS* curve is vertical but also that its position along the horizontal axis represents a significant measure. The horizontal intercept in Figure 16-3, where *LRAS* touches the horizontal axis ($800 billion in 2000 dollars), is the economy's **potential output,** $Y_P$: the level of real GDP the economy would produce if all prices, including nominal wages, were fully flexible.

In reality, the actual level of real GDP is almost always either above or below potential output. We'll see why later in this chapter, when we discuss the *AS-AD* model. Still, an economy's potential output is an important number because it defines the trend around which actual aggregate output fluctuates from year to year.

In the United States, the Congressional Budget Office (CBO) estimates annual potential output for the purpose of federal budget analysis. Panel (a) of Figure 16-4 shows the CBO's estimates of U.S. potential output from 1989 to 2004 and the actual values of U.S. real GDP over the same period. Purple-shaded years correspond to periods in which potential output exceeded actual aggregate output; green-shaded years to periods in which actual aggregate output exceeded potential output.

As you can see in panel (a), U.S. potential output has risen steadily over time—implying a series of rightward shifts of the *LRAS* curve. What has caused these rightward shifts? Increases in physical capital and human capital as well as technological progress. Over the long run, as the size of the labor force and the productivity of labor

> **Potential output** is the level of real GDP the economy would produce if all prices, including nominal wages, were fully flexible.

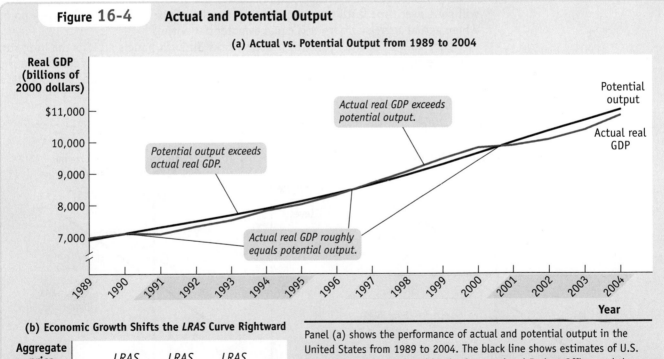

**Figure 16-4   Actual and Potential Output**

**(a) Actual vs. Potential Output from 1989 to 2004**

Panel (a) shows the performance of actual and potential output in the United States from 1989 to 2004. The black line shows estimates of U.S. potential output, produced by the Congressional Budget Office, and the blue line shows actual aggregate output. The purple-shaded years are periods in which actual aggregate output fell below potential output, and the green-shaded years are periods in which actual aggregate output exceeded potential output. As shown, significant shortfalls occurred in the recessions of the early 1990s and after 2000. Actual aggregate output was significantly above potential output in the boom of the late 1990s. Panel (b) shows how the long-run aggregate supply curve, *LRAS,* has shifted rightward over time.

both rise, the level of real GDP that the economy is capable of producing also rises. As illustrated in panel (b) of Figure 16-4, we generally think of the long-run aggregate supply curve as shifting to the right over time.

## From the Short Run to the Long Run

As you can see in panel (a) of Figure 16-4, the economy almost always produces more or less than potential output: in only three periods during the years from 1989 to 2004 did actual aggregate output roughly equal potential output (the three years at which the two lines cross). The economy is almost always on its short-run aggregate supply curve—producing an aggregate output level more than or less than potential output—not on its long-run aggregate supply curve. So why is the long-run curve relevant? Does the economy ever move from the short run to the long run? And if so, how?

The first step to answering these questions is to understand that the economy is always in one of only two states with respect to the short-run and long-run aggregate supply curves. It can be on both curves simultaneously by being at a point where the curves cross (as in the three periods in panel (a) of Figure 16-4 in which actual aggregate output and potential output roughly coincide). Or it can be on the short-run aggregate supply curve but not the long-run aggregate supply curve (as in the years in panel (a) of Figure 16-4 in which actual aggregate output and potential output *did not* coincide). But that is not the end of the story. If the economy is on the short-run but not the long-run aggregate supply curve, the short-run aggregate supply curve will shift over time until the economy is at a point where both curves cross—a point where actual aggregate output is equal to potential output.

Figure 16-5 illustrates how this process works. In both panels *LRAS* is the long-run aggregate supply curve, *SRAS*$_1$ is the initial short-run aggregate supply curve, and the aggregate price level is at $P_1$. In panel (a) the economy starts at the initial production

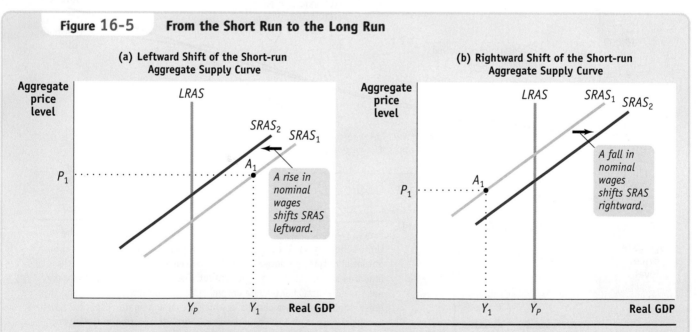

**Figure 16-5** **From the Short Run to the Long Run**

**(a) Leftward Shift of the Short-run Aggregate Supply Curve**

**(b) Rightward Shift of the Short-run Aggregate Supply Curve**

In panel (a), the initial short-run aggregate supply curve is *SRAS*$_1$. At the aggregate price level, $P_1$, the quantity of aggregate output supplied, $Y_1$, exceeds potential output, $Y_P$. Eventually, low unemployment will cause nominal wages to rise, leading to a leftward shift of the short-run aggregate supply curve from *SRAS*$_1$ to *SRAS*$_2$. In panel (b), the reverse happens: at the aggregate price level, $P_1$, the quantity of aggregate output supplied is less than potential output. High unemployment eventually leads to a fall in nominal wages over time and a rightward shift of the short-run aggregate supply curve.

point, $A_1$, which corresponds to a quantity of aggregate output supplied, $Y_1$, that is higher than potential output, $Y_P$. Producing an aggregate output level (such as $Y_1$) that is higher than potential output ($Y_P$) is possible only because nominal wages haven't yet fully adjusted upward. Until this upward adjustment in nominal wages occurs, producers are earning high profits and producing a high level of output. But a level of aggregate output higher than potential output means a low level of unemployment. Because jobs are abundant and workers are scarce, nominal wages will rise over time, gradually shifting the short-run aggregate supply curve leftward. Eventually it will be in a new position, such as $SRAS_2$. (Later in this chapter we'll show where the short-run aggregate supply curve ends up. As we'll see, that depends on the aggregate demand curve as well.)

In panel (b) of Figure 16-5, the initial production point, $A_1$, corresponds to the aggregate output level, $Y_1$, that is lower than potential output, $Y_P$. Producing an aggregate output level (such as $Y_1$) that is lower than potential output ($Y_P$) is possible only because nominal wages haven't yet fully adjusted downward. Until this downward adjustment occurs, producers are earning low (or negative) profits and producing a low level of output. An aggregate output level lower than potential output means high unemployment. Because workers are abundant and jobs are scarce, nominal wages will fall over time, shifting the short-run aggregate supply curve gradually to the right. Eventually it will be in a new position, such as $SRAS_2$.

We'll see shortly that these shifts of the short-run aggregate supply curve will return the economy to potential output in the long run. To explain why, however, we first need to introduce the concept of the *aggregate demand curve*.

# economics in action

## Prices and Output During the Great Depression

Figure 16-6 shows the actual track of the aggregate price level, as measured by the GDP deflator, and real GDP, from 1929 to 1942. As you can see, aggregate output and the aggregate price level fell together from 1929 to 1933 and rose together during 1933 to 1937. This is what we'd expect to see if the economy were moving down the

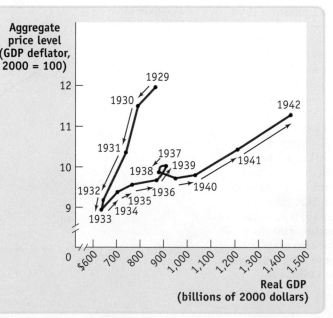

### Figure 16-6

**Prices and Output During the Great Depression**

From 1929 to 1933, prices and aggregate output fell together. And from 1933 to 1937, prices and aggregate output rose together. That is, during the period of 1929 to 1937, the economy behaved as if it were first moving down and then up the short-run aggregate supply curve. By the late 1930s, however, aggregate output was above 1929 levels even though the aggregate price level was still lower than it was in 1929. This reflects the fact that the short-run aggregate supply curve had shifted to the right during this period, due to both the short-run adjustment process in the economy and to a rightward shift of the long-run aggregate supply curve.

short-run aggregate supply curve from 1929 to 1933 and moving up it (with a brief reversal in 1937–1938) thereafter.

But even in 1942 the aggregate price level was still lower than it was in 1929; yet real GDP was much higher. What happened?

The answer is that the short-run aggregate supply curve shifted to the right over time. This shift partly reflected rising productivity—a rightward shift of the underlying long-run aggregate supply curve. But since the U.S. economy was producing below potential output and had high unemployment during this period, the rightward shift of the short-run aggregate supply curve also reflected the adjustment process shown in panel (b) of Figure 16-5. So the movement of aggregate output from 1929 to 1942 reflected both movements along and shifts of the short-run aggregate supply curve. ∎

< < < < < < < < < < < < < < < < < <

>>CHECK YOUR UNDERSTANDING 16-1

1. Determine the effect on short-run aggregate supply of each of the following events. Explain whether it represents a movement along the *SRAS* curve or a shift of the *SRAS* curve.
   a. A rise in the consumer price index (CPI) leads producers to increase output.
   b. A fall in the price of oil leads producers to increase output.
   c. A rise in legally mandated retirement benefits paid to workers leads producers to reduce output.

2. Suppose the economy is initially at potential output and the quantity of aggregate output supplied increases. What information would you need to determine whether this was due to a movement along the *SRAS* curve or a shift of the *LRAS* curve?

Solutions appear at back of book.

The **aggregate demand curve** shows the relationship between the aggregate price level and the quantity of aggregate output demanded by households, businesses, the government, and the rest of the world.

# Aggregate Demand

Just as the aggregate supply curve shows the relationship between the aggregate price level and the quantity of aggregate output supplied by producers, the **aggregate demand curve** shows the relationship between the aggregate price level and the quantity of aggregate output demanded by households, firms, the government, and the rest of the world. Figure 16-7 shows an aggregate demand curve, *AD*. One point on

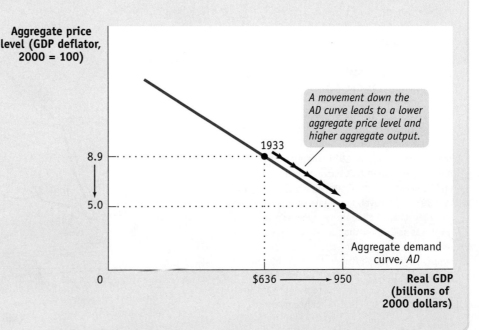

**Figure 16-7**

### The Aggregate Demand Curve

The aggregate demand curve shows the relationship between the aggregate price level and the quantity of aggregate output demanded. The curve is downward-sloping due to the wealth effect of a change in the aggregate price level and the interest rate effect of a change in the aggregate price level. Corresponding to the actual 1933 data, here the total quantity of goods and services demanded at an aggregate price level of 8.9 is $636 billion in 2000 dollars. According to our hypothetical curve, however, if the aggregate price level had been only 5.0, the quantity of aggregate output demanded would have risen to $950 billion.

*A movement down the AD curve leads to a lower aggregate price level and higher aggregate output.*

Aggregate price level (GDP deflator, 2000 = 100)

1933

8.9

5.0

Aggregate demand curve, *AD*

0          $636 ——→ 950          **Real GDP (billions of 2000 dollars)**

the curve corresponds to actual data for 1933, when the aggregate price level was 8.9 and the total quantity of domestic final goods and services purchased was $636 billion in 2000 dollars. *AD* is downward-sloping, indicating a negative relationship between the aggregate price level and the quantity of aggregate output demanded. A higher aggregate price level, other things equal, reduces the quantity of aggregate output demanded; a lower aggregate price level, other things equal, increases the quantity of aggregate output demanded. According to Figure 16-7, if the price level in 1933 had been 5.0 instead of 8.9, the total quantity of domestic final goods and services demanded would have been $950 billion in 2000 dollars instead of $636 billion.

## Why Is the Aggregate Demand Curve Downward-Sloping?

In Figure 16-7, the curve *AD* is downward-sloping. Why? Recall the basic equation of national income accounting:

**(16-2)**   $GDP = C + I + G + X - IM$

where *C* is consumer spending, *I* is investment spending, *G* is government purchases of goods and services, *X* is exports to other countries, and *IM* is imports. If we measure these variables in constant dollars—that is, in prices of a base year—then $C + I + G + X - IM$ is the quantity of domestically produced final goods and services demanded during a given period. *G* is decided by the government, but the other variables are private-sector decisions. To understand why the aggregate demand curve slopes downward, we need to understand why a rise in the aggregate price level reduces *C, I,* and *X – IM.*

You might think that the downward slope of the aggregate demand curve is a natural consequence of the *law of demand* we defined back in Chapter 3. That is, since the demand curve for any one good is downward-sloping, isn't it natural that the demand curve for aggregate output is downward-sloping? This turns out to be a misleading parallel. The demand curve for any individual good shows how the quantity demanded depends on the price of that good, *holding the prices of other goods and services constant.* The main reason the quantity of a good demanded falls when the price of that good rises is that people switch their consumption to other goods and services.

But when we consider movements up or down the aggregate demand curve, we're considering *a simultaneous change in the prices of all final goods and services.* Furthermore, changes in the composition of goods and services in consumer spending aren't relevant to the aggregate demand curve: if consumers decide to buy fewer clothes but more cars, this doesn't necessarily change the total quantity of final goods and services they demand.

Why, then, does a rise in the aggregate price level lead to a fall in the quantity of all domestically produced final goods and services demanded? There are two main reasons: the *wealth effect* and the *interest rate effect* of a change in the aggregate price level.

**The Wealth Effect** An increase in the aggregate price level, other things equal, reduces the purchasing power of many assets. Consider, for example, someone who has $5,000 in a bank account. If the aggregate price level were to rise by 25%, that $5,000 would buy only as much as $4,000 would have bought previously. With the loss in purchasing power, the owner of that bank account would probably scale back his or her consumption plans, leading to a fall in spending on final goods and services. The **wealth effect of a change in the aggregate price level** is the effect on consumer spending caused by the effect of a change in the aggregate price level on the purchasing power of consumers' assets. Because of it, consumer spending, *C*, falls when the aggregate price level rises, leading to a downward-sloping aggregate demand curve.

The **wealth effect of a change in the aggregate price level** is the effect on consumer spending caused by the effect of a change in the aggregate price level on the purchasing power of consumers' assets.

PITFALLS ---------------------○

## INVESTMENT VERSUS INVESTMENT SPENDING

When macroeconomists use the term *investment spending,* they almost always mean "spending on new physical capital." This can be confusing, because in ordinary life we often say that someone who buys stocks or purchases an existing building is "investing." The important point to keep in mind is that only spending that adds to the economy's stock of physical capital (buildings, machinery, and equipment) is "investment spending." In contrast, the act of purchasing an asset such as stocks, bonds, or existing real estate is "making an investment."

The **interest rate** is the price, calculated as a percentage of the amount borrowed, charged by the lender to a borrower for the use of their savings for one year.

The **interest rate effect of a change in the aggregate price level** is the effect on consumer spending and investment spending caused by the effect of a change in the aggregate price level on the purchasing power of consumers' and firms' money holdings.

**The Interest Rate Effect** Economists use the term *money* in its narrowest sense to refer to cash and bank deposits on which people can write checks. People and firms hold money because it reduces the cost and inconvenience of making transactions. An increase in the aggregate price level, other things equal, reduces the purchasing power of a given amount of money holdings. To purchase the same basket of goods and services as before, people and firms now need to hold more money. So, in response to an increase in the aggregate price level, the public tries to increase its money holdings, either by borrowing more or by selling other assets such as bonds. This reduces the funds available for lending to other borrowers and has the effect of driving interest rates up. A rise in the **interest rate** reduces investment spending because it makes the cost of borrowing higher. It also reduces consumer spending as households save more of their disposable income. So a rise in the aggregate price level depresses investment spending, *I,* and consumer spending, *C,* through its effect on the purchasing power of money holdings, an effect known as the **interest rate effect of a change in the aggregate price level.** This also leads to a downward-sloping aggregate demand curve.

## Shifts of the Aggregate Demand Curve

When we talk about an increase in aggregate demand, we mean a shift of the aggregate demand curve to the right, as shown in panel (a) of Figure 16-8 by the shift from $AD_1$ to $AD_2$. A rightward shift occurs when the quantity of aggregate output demanded increases at any given aggregate price level. A decrease in aggregate demand means that *AD* shifts to the left, as in panel (b). A leftward shift implies that the quantity of aggregate output demanded falls at any given aggregate price level.

A number of factors can shift the aggregate demand curve. Among the most important factors are changes in expectations, changes in wealth, and changes in the

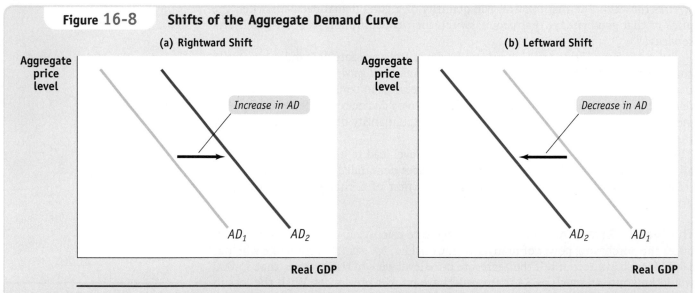

### Figure 16-8    Shifts of the Aggregate Demand Curve

**(a) Rightward Shift**

Aggregate price level

*Increase in AD*

$AD_1$    $AD_2$

Real GDP

**(b) Leftward Shift**

Aggregate price level

*Decrease in AD*

$AD_2$    $AD_1$

Real GDP

Panel (a) shows the effect of events that increase the quantity of aggregate output demanded at any given aggregate price level, such as improvements in business and consumer expectations or increased government spending. Such changes shift the aggregate demand curve to the right, from $AD_1$ to $AD_2$. Panel (b) shows the effect of events that decrease the quantity of aggregate output demanded at any given price level, such as a fall in wealth caused by a stock market decline. This shifts the aggregate demand curve leftward from $AD_1$ to $AD_2$.

stock of physical capital. In addition, both fiscal and monetary policy can shift the aggregate
demand curve.

### Changes in Expectations

Both consumer
spending and investment spending depend in
part on people's expectations about the future. Consumers base their spending not only
on the income they have now but also on the
income they expect to have in the future.
Firms base their investment spending not
only on current conditions but also on the
sales they expect to make in the future. As a
result, changes in expectations can push consumer spending and investment spending up
or down. If consumers and firms become
more optimistic, spending rises; if they become more
pessimistic, spending falls. In fact, short-run economic
forecasters pay careful attention to surveys of consumer
and business sentiment. In particular, forecasters watch the Consumer Confidence Index, a monthly measure calculated by the Conference Board, and the
Michigan Consumer Sentiment Index, a similar measure calculated by the University of Michigan.

"CONSUMER CONFIDENCE CRISIS IN AISLE THREE!"

### Changes in Wealth

Consumer spending depends in part on
the value of household assets. When the real value of these assets
rises, the purchasing power they embody also rises, leading to an
increase in aggregate demand. For example, in the 1990s there
was a significant rise in the stock market that shifted aggregate
demand. And when the real value of household assets falls—for
example, because of a stock market crash—the purchasing power
they embody is reduced and aggregate demand also falls. The
stock market crash of 1929 was one factor in the Great Depression. Similarly, a sharp decline in the stock market in the United
States after 2000 was an important factor in the 2001 recession.

### Changes in the Stock of Physical Capital

Firms engage in
investment spending to add to their stock of physical capital.
Their incentive to spend depends in part on how much physical
capital they already have: the more they have, the less they will
feel a need to add more, other things equal. Investment spending
fell in 2000–2001 partly because high investment spending over
the previous few years had left companies with more of certain
kinds of capital, such as computers and fiber-optic cable, than
they needed at that time.

## Government Policies and Aggregate Demand

One of the key insights of macroeconomics is that the government can have a powerful influence on aggregate demand and
that, in some circumstances, this influence can be used to improve economic performance.

The two main ways the government can influence the aggregate demand curve are through fiscal policy and monetary policy.
We'll briefly discuss their influence on aggregate demand, pend-
ing full-length discussions in Chapters 17 and 18.

### PITFALLS

#### CHANGES IN WEALTH: A MOVEMENT ALONG VERSUS A SHIFT OF THE AGGREGATE DEMAND CURVE

In the last section we explained that one reason that the
AD curve was downward-sloping was due to the wealth effect of a change in the aggregate price level: a higher aggregate price level reduces the purchasing power of
households' assets and leads to a fall in consumer spending, C. But in this section we've just explained that
changes in wealth lead to a shift of the AD curve. Aren't
those two explanations contradictory? Which one is it—
does a change in wealth move the economy along the AD
curve or does it shift the AD curve? The answer is both: it
depends on the *source* of the change in wealth. A movement along the AD curve occurs when a change in the aggregate price level changes the purchasing power of
consumers' existing wealth (the real value of their assets).
This is the *wealth effect of a change in the aggregate price
level*—a change in the aggregate price level is the source
of the change in wealth. For example, a fall in the aggregate price level increases the purchasing power of consumers' assets and leads to a movement down the AD
curve. In contrast, a change in wealth *independent of a
change in the aggregate price level* shifts the AD curve. For
example, a rise in the stock market or a rise in real estate
values leads to an increase in the real value of consumers'
assets at any given aggregate price level. In this case, the
source of the change in wealth is a change in the values
of assets without any change in the aggregate price
level—that is, a change in asset values holding the prices
of all final goods and services constant.

**Fiscal Policy** Fiscal policy is the use of either government spending—government purchases of final goods and services and government transfers—or tax policy to stabilize the economy. In practice, governments often respond to recessions by increasing spending, cutting taxes, or both. They often respond to inflation by reducing spending or increasing taxes.

The effect of government purchases of final goods and services, G, on the aggregate demand curve is *direct* because government purchases are themselves a component of aggregate demand. So an increase in government purchases shifts the aggregate demand curve to the right and a decrease shifts it to the left. History's most dramatic example of how increased government purchases affect aggregate demand was the effect of wartime government spending during World War II. Because of the war, U.S. federal purchases surged 400%. This increase in purchases is usually given the credit for ending the Great Depression. In the 1990s Japan used large public works projects—such as government-financed construction of roads, bridges, and dams—in an effort to increase aggregate demand in the face of a slumping economy.

In contrast, government transfers affect aggregate demand *indirectly*: by changing disposable income, they change consumer spending. Likewise, changes in tax rates also influence the economy indirectly through their effect on disposable income. A lower tax rate means that consumers get to keep more of what they earn, increasing their disposable income. This increases consumer spending and shifts the aggregate demand curve to the right. A higher tax rate or lower transfer payments reduce the amount of disposable income received by consumers. This reduces consumer spending and shifts the aggregate demand curve to the left.

**Monetary Policy** Monetary policy is the use of changes in the quantity of money or the interest rate to stabilize the economy. We've just discussed how a rise in the aggregate price level, by reducing the purchasing power of money holdings, causes a rise in the interest rate. That, in turn, reduces both investment spending and consumer spending.

But what happens if the quantity of money in the hands of households and firms changes? In modern economies, the quantity of money in circulation is largely determined by the decisions of a *central bank* created by the government. (As we'll learn in Chapter 18, the Federal Reserve, the U.S. central bank, is a special institution that is neither exactly part of the government nor exactly a private institution.) When the central bank increases the quantity of money in circulation, people have more money, which they are willing to lend out. The effect is to drive the interest rate down at any given aggregate price level and to increase investment spending and consumer spending. That is, increasing the quantity of money shifts the aggregate demand curve to the right. Reducing the quantity of money has the opposite effect: people have less money than before, leading them to borrow more and lend less. This raises the interest rate, reduces investment spending and consumer spending, and shifts the aggregate demand curve to the left.

## *economics in action*

### Moving Along the Aggregate Demand Curve, 1979–1980

When looking at data, it's often hard to distinguish between changes in spending that represent *movements along* the aggregate demand curve and *shifts of* the aggregate demand curve. One telling exception, however, is what happened right after the oil crisis of 1979, which we described in this chapter's opening story. Faced with a sharp increase in the aggregate price level—the rate of consumer price inflation reached 14.8% in March of 1980—the Federal Reserve stuck to a policy of increasing the quantity of money slowly. The aggregate price level was rising steeply, but the quantity of money going into the economy was growing slowly. The net result was that the purchasing power of the quantity of money in circulation in the economy fell.

This led to an increase in the demand for borrowing and a surge in interest rates. The *prime rate,* which is the interest rate banks charge their best customers, went above 20%. High interest rates, in turn, caused both consumer spending and investment spending to fall: in 1980 purchases of durable consumer goods like cars fell by 5.3% and real investment spending fell by 8.9%.

In other words, in 1979–1980 the economy responded just as we'd expect if it were moving along the aggregate demand curve: due to the wealth effect and the interest rate effect of a change in the aggregate price level, the quantity of aggregate output demanded fell as the aggregate price level rose. In the section "The *AS–AD* Model" we'll see that although this interpretation of the events in 1979–1980 is correct, the facts are a bit more complicated. There was indeed a movement along the aggregate demand curve. And the cause of this shift of the aggregate demand curve was a shift of the short-run aggregate supply curve. ■

> > > > > > > > > > > > > > > > > > > > > >

## >>CHECK YOUR UNDERSTANDING 16-2

1. Determine the effect on aggregate demand of each of the following events. Explain whether it represents a movement along the aggregate demand curve (up or down) or a shift of the curve (leftward or rightward).
   a. A rise in the interest rate caused by a change in monetary policy
   b. A fall in the real value of money in the economy due to a higher aggregate price level
   c. Expectations of a poor job market next year
   d. A fall in tax rates
   e. A rise in the real value of assets in the economy due to a lower aggregate price level
   f. A rise in the real value of assets in the economy due to a surge in real estate values

*Solutions appear at back of book.*

# The Multiplier

Suppose that businesses become more optimistic about future sales and increase investment spending by $50 billion. This shifts the aggregate demand curve rightward—increasing the quantity of aggregate output demanded at any given aggregate price level. But suppose that we want to know *how much* the aggregate demand curve will shift to the right. To answer that question we use the concept of the *multiplier,* which plays an important role in the analysis of economic policy.

When we ask how far to the right a $50 billion autonomous increase in investment spending shifts the aggregate demand curve, what we really want to know is the magnitude of the shift shown in Figure 16-9 on page 410: the increase in the quantity of aggregate output demanded at a *given* aggregate price level, $P^*$. So we will hold the aggregate price level constant. (This means, among other things, that there is no difference between changes in *nominal* GDP and changes in *real* GDP.) We'll also make some additional simplifying assumptions: we'll hold the interest rate constant, and we'll ignore the roles of taxes and foreign trade.

Assuming a constant aggregate price level and a fixed interest rate, you might be tempted to say that a $50 billion increase in investment spending will shift the aggregate demand curve to the right by $50 billion. That, however, is an underestimate. It's true that an increase in investment spending leads firms that produce investment goods to increase output. If the process stopped there, then the rightward shift of the *AD* curve would indeed be $50 billion.

But the process doesn't stop there. The increase in output leads to an increase in disposable income that flows to households in the form of profits and wages. The increase in households' disposable income leads to a rise in consumer spending, which, in turn, induces firms to increase output yet again. This generates another rise in disposable income, which leads to another round of consumer spending increases, and so on. So there are multiple rounds of increases in aggregate output.

How large is the total effect on aggregate output if we sum the effect from all these rounds of spending increases? To answer this question, we need to introduce the concept of the **marginal propensity to consume,** or *MPC:* the increase in consumer

The **marginal propensity to consume,** or *MPC,* is the increase in consumer spending when disposable income rises by $1.

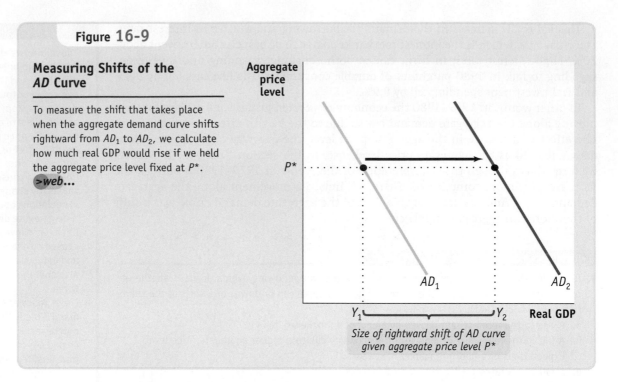

**Figure 16-9**

**Measuring Shifts of the AD Curve**

To measure the shift that takes place when the aggregate demand curve shifts rightward from $AD_1$ to $AD_2$, we calculate how much real GDP would rise if we held the aggregate price level fixed at $P^*$.
**>web...**

*Size of rightward shift of AD curve given aggregate price level $P^*$*

spending when disposable income rises by $1. When consumer spending changes because of a rise or fall in disposable income, $MPC$ is the change in consumer spending divided by the change in disposable income:

**(16-3)** $MPC = \dfrac{\Delta \text{ Consumer spending}}{\Delta \text{ Disposable income}}$

For example, if consumer spending goes up by $6 billion when disposable income goes up by $10 billion, $MPC$ is $6 billion/$10 billion = 0.6.

Because consumers normally spend part but not all of an additional dollar of disposable income, $MPC$ is a number between 0 and 1. The additional disposable income that consumers don't spend is saved; the **marginal propensity to save,** or **MPS** is the fraction of an additional dollar of disposable income that is saved, and it is equal to $1 - MPC$.

Since we're ignoring taxes for now, we can assume that each $1 increase in real GDP raises real disposable income by $1. So the $50 billion increase in investment spending initially raises real GDP by $50 billion. This leads to a second-round increase in consumer spending, which raises real GDP by a further $MPC \times \$50$ billion. It is followed by a third-round increase in consumer spending of $MPC \times MPC \times \$50$ billion, and so on for several more rounds. The total effect on real GDP is:

> The **marginal propensity to save,** or **MPS**, is the increase in household savings when disposable income rises by $1.

|  |  |  |
|---|---|---|
| Increase in investment spending | = | $50 billion |
| + Second-round increase in consumer spending | $= MPC$ | $\times \$50$ billion |
| + Third-round increase in consumer spending | $= MPC^2$ | $\times \$50$ billion |
| + Fourth-round increase in consumer spending | $= MPC^3$ | $\times \$50$ billion |

$\cdots$

Total increase in real GDP $= (1 + MPC + MPC^2 + MPC^3 + \ldots) \times \$50$ billion

So the initial $50 billion increase in investment spending arising from more optimistic expectations sets off a chain reaction in the economy. The net result of this chain reaction is that a $50 billion increase in investment spending leads to a change in real GDP that is a *multiple* of the size of that initial change in spending.

How large is this multiple? It's a mathematical fact that a series of the form $1 + x + x^2 + x^3 + \ldots$, where $x$ is between 0 and 1, is equal to $1/(1 - x)$. So the total effect of a $50 billion increase in investment spending, taking into account all the subsequent increases in consumer spending (and assuming no taxes and no trade), is given by:

**(16-4)**   Total increase in real GDP from $50 billion rise in $I$

$$= \$50 \text{ billion} \times \frac{1}{1 - MPC}$$

Let's consider a numerical example in which $MPC = 0.6$: each $1 in additional disposable income causes a $0.60 rise in consumer spending. In that case, a $50 billion increase in investment spending raises real GDP by $50 billion in the first round. The second-round increase in consumer spending raises real GDP by another $0.6 \times \$50$ billion, or $30 billion. The third-round increase in consumer spending raises real GDP by another $0.6 \times \$30$ billion, or $18 billion. Table 16-1 shows the successive stages of increases, where "..." means the process goes on an infinite number of times. In the end, real GDP rises by $125 billion as a consequence of the initial $50 billion rise in investment spending. We know that is true by Equation 16-4:

$$\$50 \text{ billion} \times \frac{1}{1 - 0.6} = \$50 \text{ billion} \times 2.5 = \$125 \text{ billion}$$

Notice that even though there are an infinite number of rounds of expansion of real GDP, the total rise in real GDP is limited to $125 billion. The reason is that at each stage some of the rise in disposable income "leaks out" because it is saved. How much of an additional dollar of disposable income is saved depends on $MPS$, the marginal propensity to save.

Figure 16-10 illustrates the effect of the increase in investment spending on the aggregate demand curve. Panel (a) shows the successive rounds of increasing real

**TABLE 16-1**

**Rounds of Increases of Real GDP**

| | Increase in real GDP (billions of dollars) | Total increase in real GDP (billions of dollars) |
|---|---|---|
| First round | $50 | $50 |
| Second round | 30 | 80 |
| Third round | 18 | 98 |
| Fourth round | 10.8 | 108.8 |
| ... | ... | ... |
| Final round | 0 | 125 |

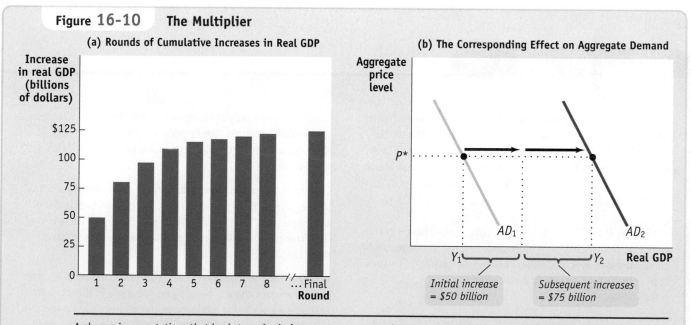

**Figure 16-10   The Multiplier**

**(a) Rounds of Cumulative Increases in Real GDP**

**(b) The Corresponding Effect on Aggregate Demand**

A change in expectations that leads to a rise in investment spending shifts the aggregate demand curve rightward for two reasons. Holding the aggregate price level constant, there is an initial increase in real GDP from the rise in $I$. Then there are subsequent increases in real GDP as rising disposable income leads to higher consumer spending. Panel (a) shows how the rise in real GDP at a given aggregate price level takes place. Panel (b) shows how this shifts the aggregate demand curve.

GDP from Table 16-1. Panel (b) shows the corresponding effect on aggregate demand: the total amount of the rightward shift of the AD curve, from $AD_1$ to $AD_2$, is $125 billion, the sum of the initial increase in investment spending, $50 billion, plus the subsequent rise in consumer spending, $75 billion.

We've described the effects of a change in investment spending arising from a change in expectations, but the same analysis can be applied to other causes of a shift in the aggregate demand curve. Shifts in the aggregate demand curve can arise from autonomous changes in any of the components of aggregate spending. The important thing is to distinguish between the initial change in aggregate spending, before real GDP rises, and the additional change in aggregate spending caused by the change in real GDP as the chain reaction unfolds. For example, suppose that total wealth in the economy increases for some reason. This will lead to an initial rise in consumer spending, before real GDP rises. But it will also lead to second and later rounds of higher consumer spending as real GDP rises.

> An **autonomous change in aggregate spending** is an initial change in the desired level of spending by firms, households, and government at a given level of real GDP.
>
> The **multiplier** is the ratio of the total change in real GDP caused by an autonomous change in aggregate spending to the size of that autonomous change.

An initial rise or fall in aggregate spending at a given level of real GDP is called an **autonomous change in aggregate spending.** It's autonomous—which means "self-governing"—because it's the cause, not the result, of the chain reaction we've just described. The **multiplier** is the ratio of the total change in real GDP caused by an autonomous change in aggregate spending to the size of that autonomous change. If we let $\Delta AAS$ stand for autonomous change in aggregate spending and $\Delta Y$ stand for the change in real GDP, then the multiplier is equal to $\Delta Y / \Delta AAS$. And we've already seen from Equation 16-4 how to find the value of the multiplier. Assuming no taxes and no trade, it's

$$\textbf{(16-5)} \quad \text{Multiplier} = \frac{1}{1 - MPC} = \frac{\Delta Y}{\Delta AAS}$$

Accordingly, the multiplier lets us calculate the change in real GDP that arises from an autonomous change in aggregate spending. Re-arranging Equation 16-5 we get:

$$\textbf{(16-6)} \quad \Delta Y = \frac{1}{1 - MPC} \times \Delta AAS$$

Notice that the size of the multiplier—and so the size of the shift in the aggregate demand curve resulting from any given initial change in aggregate spending—depends on MPC. If the marginal propensity to consume is high, so is the multiplier. This is

---

## WORK IT OUT

## THE MULTIPLIER

**MPC:** Suppose that economists estimate that consumers spend 80 percent of any increase in disposable income. What is the size of the MPC? *(MPC: marginal propensity to consume.)* If disposable income is $1,000 billion in January and $1,100 billion in February, what's the increase in consumption between January and February?

**SOLUTION:** The MPC is 0.8. The MPC tells us the change in consumption from a change in disposable income. If disposable income increases by $100 billion between January and February, then consumption spending must increase by 0.8 × $100 billion = $80 billion.

**Multiplier:** With an MPC of 0.8, what is the size of the multiplier? *(Multiplier: The ratio of the total change in real GDP to the change in autonomous spending.)*

**SOLUTION:** When only consumption and nothing else changes when income changes, the formula for the multiplier is 1/ (1 − MPC). So with an MPC of 0.8, the multiplier equals 1 / (1 − 0.8) = 1 / 0.2 = 5.

**Change in Aggregate Demand:** Suppose government spending increases from $2 trillion to $3 trillion per year. Suppose the aggregate price level is fixed. With an MPC of 0.8, what is the total change in real GDP as a result of the increase in government spending?

**SOLUTION:** The change in real GDP, $\Delta Y$, equals the multiplier times the autonomous change in aggregate spending. In this case, the multiplier equals 5. The autonomous change in aggregate spending is $1 trillion per year ($3 trillion − $2 trillion). So the change in real GDP, which is the size of the shift to the right of the aggregate demand curve, is 5 × $1 trillion per year = $5 trillion per year.

true because the size of *MPC* determines how large each round of expansion is compared with the previous round. To put it another way, the higher *MPC* is, the less disposable income "leaks out" into savings at each round of expansion.

In later chapters we'll use the concept of the multiplier to analyze the effects of fiscal and monetary policies.

> > > > > > > > > > > > > > > > > > > > > >

**1.** Explain why a decline in investment spending, caused by a change in business expectations, would also lead to a fall in consumer spending.

*Solution appears at back of book.*

# The *AS–AD* Model

From 1929 to 1933, the U.S. economy moved down the short-run aggregate supply curve as the aggregate price level fell. In contrast, from 1979 to 1980 the U.S. economy moved up the aggregate demand curve as the aggregate price level rose. In each case, the cause of the movement along the curve was a shift of the other curve. In 1929–1933, it was a leftward shift of the aggregate demand curve—a major fall in consumer spending. In 1979–1980, it was a leftward shift of the short-run aggregate supply curve—a dramatic fall in short-run aggregate supply caused by the oil price shock.

So to understand the behavior of the economy, we must put the aggregate supply curve and the aggregate demand curve together. The result is the **AS–AD model,** the basic model we use to understand economic fluctuations.

## Short-Run Macroeconomic Equilibrium

We'll begin our analysis by focusing on the short run. Figure 16-11 shows the aggregate demand curve and the short-run aggregate supply curve on the same diagram. The point at which the *AD* and *SRAS* curves intersect, $E_{SR}$, is the **short-run macroeconomic equilibrium:** the point at which the quantity of aggregate output supplied is equal to the quantity demanded by domestic households, businesses, the

In the **AS–AD model,** the aggregate supply curve and the aggregate demand curve are used together to analyze economic fluctuations.

The economy is in **short-run macroeconomic equilibrium** when the quantity of aggregate output supplied is equal to the quantity demanded.

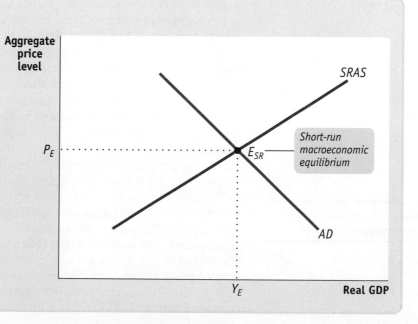

**Figure 16-11**

**The *AS–AD* Model**

The *AS–AD* model combines the short-run aggregate supply curve and the aggregate demand curve. Their point of intersection, $E_{SR}$, is the point of short-run macroeconomic equilibrium where the quantity of aggregate output demanded is equal to the quantity of aggregate output supplied. $P_E$ is the short-run equilibrium aggregate price level, and $Y_E$ is the short-run equilibrium level of aggregate output. **>web...**

government, and the rest of the world. The aggregate price level at $E_{SR}$, $P_E$, is the **short-run equilibrium aggregate price level.** The level of aggregate output at $E_{SR}$, $Y_E$, is the **short-run equilibrium aggregate output.**

In the supply and demand model of Chapter 3 we saw that a shortage of any individual good causes its market price to rise but a surplus of the good causes its market price to fall. These forces ensure that the market reaches equilibrium. The same logic applies to short-run macroeconomic equilibrium. If the aggregate price level is above its equilibrium level, the quantity of aggregate output supplied exceeds the quantity demanded. This leads to a fall in the aggregate price level and pushes it toward its equilibrium level. If the aggregate price level is below its equilibrium level, the quantity of aggregate output supplied is less than the quantity demanded. This leads to a rise in the aggregate price level, again pushing it toward its equilibrium level. In the discussion that follows, we'll assume that the economy is always in short-run macroeconomic equilibrium.

We'll also make another important simplification based on the observation that in reality there is a long-term upward trend in both aggregate output and the aggregate price level. We'll assume that a fall in either variable really means a fall compared to the long-run trend. For example, if the aggregate price level normally rises 4% per year, a year in which the aggregate price level rises only 3% would count, for our purposes, as a 1% decline. In fact, since the Great Depression there have been very few years in which the aggregate price level of any major nation actually declined—Japan's deflation after about 1995 is one of the few exceptions. There have, however, been many cases in which the aggregate price level fell relative to the long-run trend.

Short-run equilibrium aggregate output and the short-run equilibrium aggregate price level can change either because of shifts of the *SRAS* curve or because of shifts of the *AD* curve. Let's look at each case in turn.

## Shifts of the *SRAS* Curve

An event that shifts the short-run aggregate supply curve, such as a change in commodity prices, nominal wages, or productivity, is known as a **supply shock.** A *negative* supply shock raises production costs and reduces the quantity producers are willing to supply at any given aggregate price level, leading to a leftward shift of the short-run aggregate supply curve. The U.S. economy experienced severe negative supply shocks following disruptions to world oil supplies in 1973 and 1979. In contrast, a *positive* supply shock reduces production costs and increases the quantity supplied at any given aggregate price level, leading to a rightward shift of the short-run aggregate supply curve. The United States experienced a positive supply shock between 1995 and 2000, when the increasing use of the Internet and other information technologies caused productivity growth to surge.

The effects of a negative supply shock are shown in panel (a) of Figure 16-12. The initial equilibrium is at $E_1$, with aggregate price level $P_1$ and aggregate output $Y_1$. The disruption in the oil supply causes the short-run aggregate supply curve to shift to the left, from $SRAS_1$ to $SRAS_2$. As a consequence, aggregate output falls and the aggregate price level rises, a movement up along the $AD$ curve. At the new equilibrium, $E_2$, the equilibrium aggregate price level, $P_2$, is higher, and the equilibrium aggregate output level, $Y_2$, is lower than before.

The combination of inflation and falling aggregate output shown in panel (a) has a special name: **stagflation,** for "stagnation plus inflation." When an economy experiences stagflation, it's very unpleasant: falling aggregate output leads to rising unemployment, and people feel that their purchasing power is squeezed by rising prices. Stagflation in the 1970s led to a mood of national pessimism. It also, as we'll see shortly, poses a dilemma for policy makers.

A positive supply shock, shown in panel (b), has exactly the opposite effects. A rightward shift of the *SRAS* curve from $SRAS_1$ to $SRAS_2$ results in a rise in aggregate

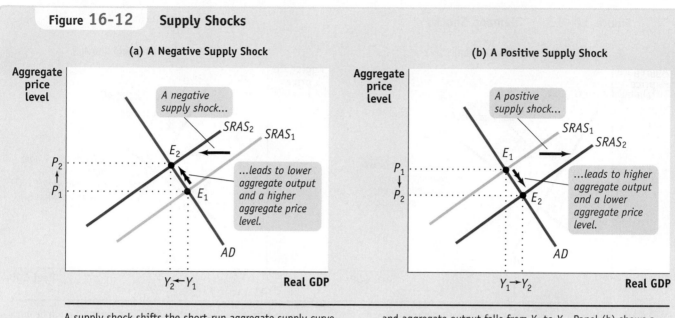

**Figure 16-12    Supply Shocks**

A supply shock shifts the short-run aggregate supply curve, moving the aggregate price level and aggregate output in opposite directions. Panel (a) shows a negative supply shock, which shifts the short-run aggregate supply curve leftward and causes stagflation—lower aggregate output and a higher aggregate price level. Here the short-run aggregate supply curve shifts from $SRAS_1$ to $SRAS_2$, and the economy moves from $E_1$ to $E_2$. The aggregate price level rises from $P_1$ to $P_2$, and aggregate output falls from $Y_1$ to $Y_2$. Panel (b) shows a positive supply shock, which shifts the short-run aggregate supply curve rightward, generating higher aggregate output and a lower aggregate price level. The short-run aggregate supply curve shifts from $SRAS_1$ to $SRAS_2$, and the economy moves from $E_1$ to $E_2$. The aggregate price level falls from $P_1$ to $P_2$, and aggregate output rises from $Y_1$ to $Y_2$.

output and a fall in the aggregate price level, a movement down along the $AD$ curve. The favorable supply shocks of the late 1990s led to a combination of full employment and declining inflation. That is, the aggregate price level fell compared with the long-run trend. This combination produced, for a time, a great wave of national optimism.

The distinctive feature of supply shocks, both negative and positive, is that they cause the aggregate price level and aggregate output to move in *opposite* directions.

## Shifts of Aggregate Demand: Short-Run Effects

An event that shifts the aggregate demand curve, such as a change in expectations, wealth, the stock of physical capital, or the use of fiscal or monetary policy, is known as a **demand shock.** The Great Depression was caused by a negative demand shock, the collapse of wealth and of business and consumer confidence that followed the stock market crash of 1929 and the banking crisis of 1930–1931. The Depression was ended by a positive demand shock—the huge increase in government purchases during World War II. In 2001 the U.S. economy experienced another significant negative demand shock as the stock market boom of the 1990s turned into a bust and nervous businesses drastically scaled back their investment spending.

Figure 16-13 on page 416 shows the short-run effects of negative and positive demand shocks. A negative demand shock shifts the aggregate demand curve, $AD$, to the left, from $AD_1$ to $AD_2$, as shown in panel (a). The economy moves down along the $SRAS$ curve from $E_1$ to $E_2$, leading to lower equilibrium aggregate output and a lower equilibrium aggregate price level. A positive demand shock shifts the aggregate demand curve, $AD$, to the right, as shown in panel (b). Here, the economy

An event that shifts the aggregate demand curve is a **demand shock.**

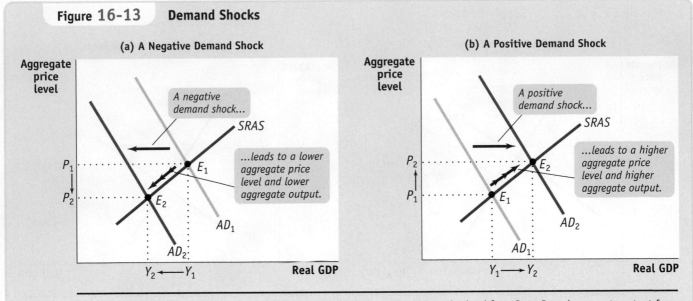

**Figure 16-13** **Demand Shocks**

**(a) A Negative Demand Shock**

*A negative demand shock...*

SRAS

*...leads to a lower aggregate price level and lower aggregate output.*

$E_1$

$P_1$

$P_2$

$E_2$

$AD_1$

$AD_2$

$Y_2 \longleftarrow Y_1$

Real GDP

Aggregate price level

**(b) A Positive Demand Shock**

*A positive demand shock...*

SRAS

*...leads to a higher aggregate price level and higher aggregate output.*

$E_2$

$P_2$

$P_1$

$E_1$

$AD_2$

$AD_1$

$Y_1 \longrightarrow Y_2$

Real GDP

Aggregate price level

A demand shock shifts the aggregate demand curve, moving the aggregate price level and aggregate output in the same direction. In panel (a) a negative demand shock shifts the aggregate demand curve leftward from $AD_1$ to $AD_2$, reducing the aggregate price level from $P_1$ to $P_2$ and aggregate output from $Y_1$ to $Y_2$. In panel (b) a positive demand shock shifts the aggregate demand curve rightward, increasing the aggregate price level from $P_1$ to $P_2$ and aggregate output from $Y_1$ to $Y_2$.

moves up along the *SRAS* curve, from $E_1$ to $E_2$. This leads to higher equilibrium aggregate output and a higher equilibrium aggregate price level. In contrast to supply shocks, demand shocks cause aggregate output and the aggregate price level to move in the *same* direction.

There's another important contrast between supply shocks and demand shocks. As we've seen, monetary policy and fiscal policy enable the government to shift the *AD* curve, meaning that governments are in a position to create the kinds of shocks shown in Figure 16-13. Are there good policy reasons to do this? We'll turn to that question soon. First, however, let's look at the difference between short-run macroeconomic equilibrium and long-run macroeconomic equilibrium.

## Long-Run Macroeconomic Equilibrium

Figure 16-14 combines the aggregate demand curve with both the short-run and long-run aggregate supply curves. The aggregate demand curve, *AD,* crosses the short-run aggregate supply curve, *SRAS,* at $E_{LR}$. Here we assume that enough time has elapsed that the economy is also on the long-run aggregate supply curve, *LRAS*. As a result, $E_{LR}$ is at the intersection of all three curves, *SRAS, LRAS,* and *AD*. So short-run equilibrium aggregate output is equal to potential output, $Y_P$. Such a situation, in which the point of short-run macroeconomic equilibrium is on the long-run aggregate supply curve, is known as **long-run macroeconomic equilibrium.**

To see the significance of long-run macroeconomic equilibrium, let's consider what happens if a demand shock moves the economy away from long-run macroeconomic equilibrium. In Figure 16-15, we assume that the initial aggregate demand curve is $AD_1$ and the initial short-run aggregate supply curve is $SRAS_1$. So the initial macroeconomic equilibrium is at $E_1$, which lies on the long-run aggregate supply curve, *LRAS*. The economy, then, starts from a point of short-run and long-run macroeconomic equilibrium, and short-run equilibrium aggregate output equals potential output at $Y_1$.

The economy is in **long-run macroeconomic equilibrium** when the point of short-run macroeconomic equilibrium is on the long-run aggregate supply curve.

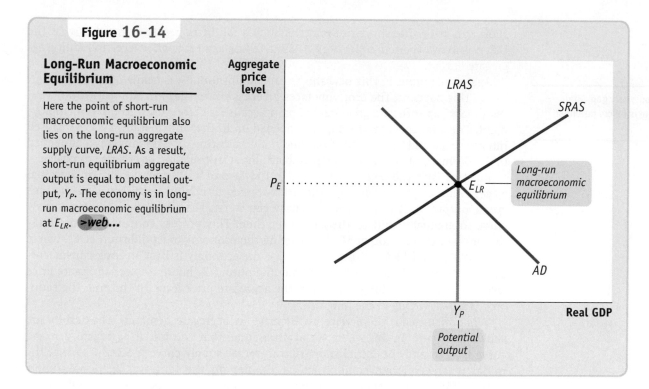

**Figure 16-14**

**Long-Run Macroeconomic Equilibrium**

Here the point of short-run macroeconomic equilibrium also lies on the long-run aggregate supply curve, *LRAS*. As a result, short-run equilibrium aggregate output is equal to potential output, $Y_P$. The economy is in long-run macroeconomic equilibrium at $E_{LR}$.  **>web...**

Now suppose that for some reason—such as a sudden worsening of business and consumer expectations—aggregate demand falls and the aggregate demand curve shifts leftward to $AD_2$. This results in a lower equilibrium aggregate price level at $P_2$ and a lower equilibrium aggregate output level at $Y_2$ as the economy settles in the

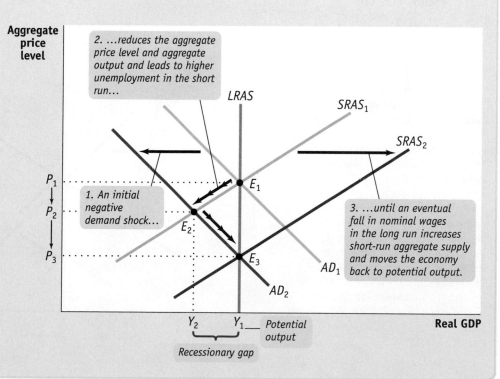

**Figure 16-15**

**Short-Run versus Long-Run Effects of a Negative Demand Shock**

In the long run the economy is self-correcting: demand shocks have only a short-run effect on aggregate output. Starting at $E_1$, a negative demand shock shifts $AD_1$ leftward to $AD_2$. In the short run the economy moves to $E_2$ and a recessionary gap arises: the aggregate price level declines from $P_1$ to $P_2$, aggregate output declines from $Y_1$ to $Y_2$, and unemployment rises. But in the long run nominal wages fall in response to high unemployment at $Y_2$, and $SRAS_1$ shifts rightward to $SRAS_2$. Aggregate output rises from $Y_2$ to $Y_1$, and the aggregate price level declines again, from $P_2$ to $P_3$. Long-run macroeconomic equilibrium is eventually restored at $E_3$.

There is a **recessionary gap** when aggregate output is below potential output.

short run at $E_2$. The short-run effect of such a fall in aggregate demand is what the U.S. economy experienced in 1929–1933: a falling aggregate price level and falling aggregate output.

Aggregate output in this new short-run equilibrium, $E_2$, is below potential output. When this happens, the economy faces a **recessionary gap.** In the real world, a recessionary gap inflicts a great deal of pain because it corresponds to high unemployment. The large recessionary gap that opened up in the United States by 1933 caused intense social and political turmoil. And the devastating recessionary gap that opened up in Germany at the same time played an important role in Hitler's rise to power.

But this isn't the end of the story. In the face of high unemployment, nominal wages eventually fall, as do any other sticky prices, ultimately leading producers to increase output. As a result, a recessionary gap causes the short-run aggregate supply curve to gradually shift to the right over time. This process continues until $SRAS_1$ reaches its new position at $SRAS_2$, bringing the economy to equilibrium at $E_3$, where $AD_2$, $SRAS_2$, and $LRAS$ all intersect. At $E_3$, the economy is back in long-run macroeconomic equilibrium; it is back at potential output $Y_1$ but at a lower aggregate price level, $P_3$, reflecting a long-run fall in the aggregate price level. In the end, the economy is *self-correcting* in the long run.

What if, instead, there were an increase in aggregate demand? The results are shown in Figure 16-16, where we again assume that the initial aggregate demand curve is $AD_1$, and the initial short-run aggregate supply curve is $SRAS_1$, so that the initial macroeconomic equilibrium, at $E_1$, lies on the long-run aggregate supply curve, $LRAS$. Initially, then, the economy is in long-run macroeconomic equilibrium.

Now suppose that aggregate demand rises, and the $AD$ curve shifts rightward to $AD_2$. This results in a higher aggregate price level, at $P_2$, and a higher aggregate output level, at $Y_2$, as the economy settles in the short run at $E_2$. Aggregate output in this new short-run equilibrium is above potential output, and unemployment is low in order to produce this higher level of aggregate output. When this happens, the economy

**Figure 16-16**

**Short-Run versus Long-Run Effects of a Positive Demand Shock**

Starting at $E_1$ a positive demand shock shifts $AD_1$ rightward to $AD_2$, and the economy moves to $E_2$ in the short run. This results in an inflationary gap as aggregate output rises from $Y_1$ to $Y_2$, the aggregate price level rises from $P_1$ to $P_2$, and unemployment falls to a low level. In the long run, $SRAS_1$ shifts leftward to $SRAS_2$ as nominal wages rise in response to low unemployment at $Y_2$. Aggregate output falls back to $Y_1$, the aggregate price level rises again to $P_3$, and the economy self-corrects as it returns to long-run macro-economic equilibrium at $E_3$.

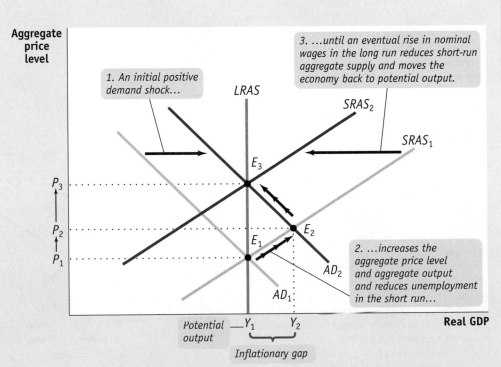

experiences an **inflationary gap.** As in the case of a recessionary gap, this isn't the end of the story. In the face of low unemployment, nominal wages will rise, as will other sticky prices. An inflationary gap causes the short-run aggregate supply curve to shift gradually to the left as producers reduce output in the face of rising nominal wages. This process continues until $SRAS_1$ reaches its new position at $SRAS_2$, bringing the economy to equilibrium at $E_3$, where $AD_2$, $SRAS_2$, and $LRAS$ all intersect. At $E_3$, the economy is back in long-run macroeconomic equilibrium. It is back at potential output, but at a higher price level, $P_3$, reflecting a long-run rise in the aggregate price level. Again, the economy is self-correcting in the long run.

There is an important lesson about the macroeconomy to be learned from this analysis. When there is a recessionary gap, nominal wages eventually fall, moving the economy back to potential output. And when there is an inflationary gap, nominal wages eventually rise, also moving the economy back to potential output. So in the long run the economy is **self-correcting:** shocks to aggregate demand affect aggregate output in the short run but not in the long run.

> There is an **inflationary gap** when aggregate output is above potential output.

> In the long run the economy is **self-correcting:** shocks to aggregate demand affect aggregate output in the short run but not the long run.

# *economics in action*

## Supply Shocks Versus Demand Shocks in Practice

How often do supply shocks and demand shocks, respectively, cause recessions? The verdict of most, though not all, macroeconomists is that recessions are mainly caused by demand shocks. But when a negative supply shock does happen, the resulting recession tends to be particularly nasty.

Let's get specific. Officially there have been ten recessions in the United States since World War II. However, two of these, in 1979–1980 and 1981–1982, are often treated as a single "double-dip" recession, bringing the total number down to nine. Of these nine recessions, only two—the recession of 1973–1975 and the double-dip recession of 1979–1982—showed the distinctive combination of falling aggregate output and a surge in the price level that we call stagflation. In each case, the cause of the supply shock was political turmoil in the Middle East—the Arab–Israeli war of 1973 and the Iranian revolution of 1979—that disrupted world oil supplies and sent oil prices skyrocketing. In fact, economists sometimes refer to the two slumps as "OPEC I" and "OPEC II," after the Organization of Petroleum Exporting Countries, the world oil cartel.

So seven of nine postwar recessions were the result of demand shocks, not supply shocks. The two supply-shock recessions, however, were the two worst as measured by the unemployment rate. Figure 16-17 shows the U.S. unemployment rate since 1948, with the dates of the 1973 Arab–Israeli war and the 1979 Iranian revolution marked on the graph. The two highest unemployment rates since World War II came after these two big negative supply shocks.

There's a reason the aftermath of a supply shock is particularly nasty: macroeconomic policy has a much harder time dealing with supply shocks than with demand shocks. We'll see why in a minute.

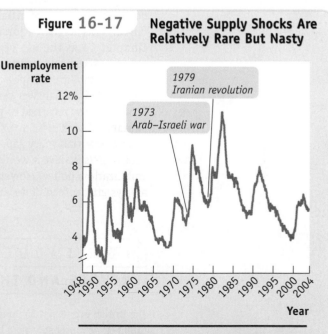

**Figure 16-17    Negative Supply Shocks Are Relatively Rare But Nasty**

Only two of nine postwar recessions seem to fit the profile of a recession caused by a negative supply shock: the recession that followed the increase in oil prices after the 1973 Arab–Israeli war and the recession that followed another surge in oil prices after the Iranian revolution. These two recessions were, however, the worst in terms of unemployment.

## >> CHECK YOUR UNDERSTANDING 16-4

1. Describe the short-run effects of each of the following shocks on the aggregate price level and on aggregate output.
   a. The government sharply increases the minimum wage, raising the wages of many workers.
   b. Solar energy firms launch a major program of investment spending.
   c. Congress raises taxes and cuts spending.
   d. Severe weather destroys crops around the world.

2. A rise in productivity increases potential output, but some worry that demand for the additional output will be insufficient even in the long run. How would you respond?

*Solutions appear at back of book.*

# Macroeconomic Policy

We've just seen that the economy is self-correcting in the long run: it will eventually trend back to potential output. Most macroeconomists believe, however, that the process of self-correction takes several years—typically a decade or more. In particular, if aggregate output is below potential output, the economy can suffer an extended period of depressed aggregate output and high unemployment before it returns to normal.

This belief is the background to one of the most famous quotations in economics: John Maynard Keynes's declaration, "In the long run we are all dead." We explain the context in which he made this remark in For Inquiring Minds below.

Economists usually interpret Keynes as having recommended that governments not wait for the economy to correct itself. Instead, it is argued by many economists, but not all, that the government should use monetary and fiscal policy to get the economy back to potential output in the aftermath of a shift of the aggregate demand curve. This is the rationale for an active stabilization policy, which we defined in Chapter 14 as the use of government policy to reduce the severity of recessions and rein in excessively strong expansions.

Can stabilization policy improve the economy's performance? If we reexamine Figure 16-4, the answer certainly appears to be yes. Under active stabilization policy, the U.S. economy returned to potential output in 1996 after an approximately six-year recessionary gap. Likewise, in 2001 it also returned to potential output after an approximately four-year inflationary gap. These periods are much shorter than the decade or more that economists believe it would take for the economy to self-correct in the absence of active stabilization policy. However, the ability to improve the economy's performance is not always guaranteed. It depends on the kinds of shocks the economy faces.

> ## FOR INQUIRING MINDS
> ### KEYNES AND THE LONG RUN

The British economist Sir John Maynard Keynes (1883–1946), probably more than any other single economist, created the modern field of macroeconomics. In 1923 Keynes published *A Tract on Monetary Reform,* a small book on the economic problems of Europe after World War I. In it he decried the tendency of many of his colleagues to focus on how things work out in the long run—as in the long-run macroeconomic equilibrium we have just analyzed—while ignoring the often very painful and possibly disastrous things that can happen along the way. Here's a fuller version of the quote:

> This *long run* is a misleading guide to current affairs. *In the long run* we are all dead. Economists set themselves too easy, too useless a task if in tempestuous seasons they can only tell us that when the storm is long past the sea is flat again.

## Policy in the Face of Demand Shocks

Imagine that the economy experiences a negative demand shock, like the one shown in Figure 16-15. If policy makers react quickly to the fall in aggregate demand, they can use monetary or fiscal policy to shift the aggregate demand curve back to the right. And if policy were able to perfectly anticipate shifts of the aggregate demand curve, it could short-circuit the whole process shown in Figure 16-15. Instead of going through a period of low aggregate output and falling prices, the government could manage the economy so that it would stay at $E_1$.

Why might a policy that short-circuits the adjustment shown in Figure 16-15, and maintains the economy at its original equilibrium, be desirable? For two reasons. First, the temporary fall in aggregate output that would happen without policy intervention is a bad thing, particularly because such a decline is associated with high unemployment. Second, *price stability* is generally regarded as a desirable goal. So preventing deflation—a fall in the aggregate price level—is a good thing.

Does this mean that policy makers should always act to offset declines in aggregate demand? Not necessarily. Some policy measures to increase aggregate demand, especially those that increase budget deficits, may have long-term costs in terms of lower long-run growth. Furthermore, in the real world policy makers aren't perfectly informed, and the effects of their policies aren't perfectly predictable. This creates the danger that stabilization policy will do more harm than good; that is, that attempts to stabilize the economy may end up creating more instability. Despite these qualifications, most economists believe that a good case can be made for using macroeconomic policy to offset major negative shocks to the *AD* curve.

Should policy makers also try to offset positive shocks to aggregate demand? It may not seem obvious that they should. After all, even though inflation may be a bad thing, aren't more output and lower unemployment a good thing? Not necessarily. Policy makers today usually try to offset positive as well as negative demand shocks. We can see evidence of this in panel (a) of Figure 16-4. Attempts to eliminate recessionary gaps and inflationary gaps usually rely on monetary rather than fiscal policy. During the recessionary gap of the early 1990s the Federal Reserve cut interest rates to stimulate consumer and investment spending. And it raised interest rates during the inflationary gap of the late 1990s to generate the opposite effect.

But how should macroeconomic policy respond to supply shocks?

## Responding to Supply Shocks

We've now come full circle to the story that began this chapter. We can now explain why the stagflationary recessions of the 1970s posed such a policy puzzle.

Back in panel (a) of Figure 16-12 we showed the effects of a negative supply shock: in the short run such a shock leads to lower aggregate output but a higher aggregate price level. As we've noted, policy makers can respond to a negative *demand* shock by using monetary and fiscal policy to return aggregate demand to its original level. But what can or should they do about a negative *supply* shock?

In contrast to the aggregate demand curve, there are no easy policies that shift the short-run aggregate supply curve. That is, there is no government policy that can easily affect producers' profitability and so compensate for shifts of the short-run aggregate supply curve. So the policy response to a negative supply shock cannot be simply to try to push the curve that shifted back to its original position.

And if you consider using monetary or fiscal policy to shift the aggregate demand curve in response to a supply shock, the right response isn't obvious. Two bad things are happening simultaneously: a fall in aggregate output *and* a rise in the aggregate price level. Any policy that shifts the aggregate demand curve helps one problem only by making the other worse. If the government acts to increase aggregate demand, it reduces the decline in output but causes more inflation. If it acts to reduce aggregate demand, it curbs inflation but causes a further decline in output.

It's a nasty trade-off. In the end, the United States and other economically advanced nations suffering from the supply shocks of the 1970s chose to stabilize prices. But being an economic policy maker in the 1970s meant facing even harder choices than usual.

# *economics in action*

## The End of the Great Depression

In 1939, a full decade after the 1929 stock market crash, the U.S. economy remained deeply depressed, with 17% of the labor force unemployed. But then the economy began a rapid recovery, growing an amazing 12% per year until 1944. By 1943 the unemployment rate had fallen below 2%.

What caused this turnaround? The answer, without question, was the huge increase in aggregate demand caused by World War II.

Although World War II began in September 1939, the United States didn't become a combatant until the attack on Pearl Harbor in December 1941. But the war boosted aggregate demand before the United States became involved in the fighting. A U.S. military buildup began as soon as the risk of war was apparent. In addition, Britain began buying large amounts of U.S. military equipment and other goods during 1940, boosting U.S. exports. And once the United States was directly involved, government spending on arms increased at a spectacular rate.

Did the behavior of prices match the predictions of the *AS–AD* model? Yes. At the height of the war, many goods were subject to price controls and rationing. Still, the aggregate price level as measured by the GDP deflator rose 30% during the war years and shot up further after the war as controls were removed. ∎

A spectacular rise in government spending on arms during World War II spurred women to enter the workforce in droves and was the catalyst that ended the Great Depression.

< < < < < < < < < < < < < < <

**>>CHECK YOUR UNDERSTANDING 16-5**

1. Suppose someone says, "Expansionary monetary or fiscal policy does nothing but temporarily overstimulate the economy—you get a brief high, but then you have the pain of inflation."
   a. Explain what this means in terms of the *AS–AD* model.
   b. Is this a valid argument against stabilization policy? Why or why not?

Solutions appear at back of book.

> **QUICK REVIEW**

> Stabilization policy is the use of fiscal or monetary policy to offset demand shocks. There can be drawbacks, however. Such policies may lead to a long-term rise in the budget deficit. And, due to incorrect predictions, a misguided policy can increase economic instability.

> Negative supply shocks pose a policy dilemma because fighting the slump in aggregate output worsens inflation and fighting inflation worsens the slump.

> The role of World War II in ending the Great Depression is the classic example of how fiscal policy can increase aggregate demand and thereby increase aggregate output.

**• A LOOK AHEAD •**

The *AS–AD* model is a powerful tool for understanding both economic fluctuations and the ways economic policy can sometimes fight adverse shocks. Now we're ready to look at the role of government and government policy.

We begin by introducing taxes, transfers, and government purchases into our model. As we'll see, putting the government in leads us immediately to one of the key insights of macroeconomics: sometimes the government can do something about the business cycle. We'll explore the potential benefits and the difficulties of *fiscal policy*—changes in taxes, transfers, and government purchases designed to affect macroeconomic outcomes—in Chapter 17. Then in Chapter 18 we'll turn to an even more important tool in the government's hands, *monetary policy*.

# SUMMARY

1. The **aggregate supply curve** shows the relationship between the aggregate price level and the quantity of aggregate output supplied.

2. The **short-run aggregate supply curve** is upward-sloping because **nominal wages** are sticky in the short run: a higher aggregate price level leads to higher profit per unit output and increased aggregate output in the short run. Changes in commodity prices, nominal wages, and productivity lead to changes in producers' profits and shift the short-run aggregate supply curve.

3. In the long run, all prices, including nominal wages, are flexible and the economy produces at its **potential output.** If actual aggregate output exceeds potential output, nominal wages will eventually rise in response to low unemployment and aggregate output will fall. If potential output exceeds actual aggregate output, nominal wages will eventually fall in response to high unemployment and aggregate output will rise. So the **long-run aggregate supply curve** is vertical at potential output.

4. The **aggregate demand curve** shows the relationship between the aggregate price level and the quantity of aggregate output demanded. It is downward-sloping for two reasons. The first is the **wealth effect of a change in the aggregate price level**—a higher aggregate price level reduces the purchasing power of households' wealth and reduces consumer spending. The second is the **interest rate effect of a change in the aggregate price level**—a higher aggregate price level reduces the purchasing power of households' and firms' money holdings, leading to a rise in interest rates and a fall in investment spending and consumer spending. The aggregate demand curve shifts because of changes in expectations, changes in wealth not due to changes in the aggregate price level, and changes in the stock of physical capital. Policy makers can use fiscal policy and monetary policy to shift the aggregate demand curve.

5. An **autonomous change in aggregate spending** leads to a chain reaction in which the total change in real GDP is equal to the **multiplier** times the initial change in aggregate spending. The size of the multiplier, $1/(1 - MPC)$, depends on the **marginal propensity to consume,** $MPC$, the fraction of an additional dollar of disposable income spent on consumption. The larger the $MPC$, the larger the multiplier and the larger the change in real GDP for any given autonomous change in aggregate spending. The **marginal propensity to save,** $MPS$, is equal to $1 - MPC$.

6. In the **AS–AD model,** the intersection of the short-run aggregate supply curve and the aggregate demand curve is the point of **short-run macroeconomic equilibrium.** It determines the **short-run equilibrium aggregate price level** and the level of **short-run equilibrium aggregate output.**

7. Economic fluctuations occur because of a shift of the short-run aggregate supply curve (a *supply shock*) or the aggregate demand curve (a *demand shock*). A **supply shock** causes the aggregate price level and aggregate output to move in opposite directions as the economy moves along the aggregate demand curve . A particularly nasty occurrence is **stagflation**—inflation and falling aggregate output—which is caused by a negative supply shock. A **demand shock** causes them to move in the same direction as the economy moves along the short-run aggregate supply curve.

8. Demand shocks have only short-run effects on aggregate output because the economy is **self-correcting** in the long run. In a **recessionary gap,** an eventual fall in nominal wages moves the economy to **long-run macroeconomic equilibrium,** where aggregate output is equal to potential output. In an **inflationary gap,** an eventual rise in nominal wages moves the economy to long-run macroeconomic equilibrium.

9. The high cost—in terms of unemployment—of a recessionary gap and the future adverse consequences of an inflationary gap lead many economists to advocate active stabilization policy: using fiscal or monetary policy to offset demand shocks. Fiscal policy affects aggregate demand directly through government purchases and indirectly through changes in taxes or government transfers that affect consumer spending. Monetary policy affects aggregate demand indirectly through changes in the interest rate that affect consumer and investment spending. There can be drawbacks, however, because such policies may contribute to a long-term rise in the budget deficit that may lead to lower long-run growth. Also, erroneous predictions can increase economic instability.

10. Negative supply shocks pose a policy dilemma: a policy that counteracts the fall in aggregate output by increasing aggregate demand will lead to higher inflation, but a policy that counteracts inflation by reducing aggregate demand will deepen the output slump.

## KEY TERMS

Aggregate supply curve, p. 395
Nominal wage, p. 396
Short-run aggregate supply curve,
   p. 396
Long-run aggregate supply curve, p. 400
Potential output, p. 401
Aggregate demand curve, p. 404
Wealth effect of a change in the aggregate
   price level, p. 405
Interest rate, p. 406
Interest rate effect of a change in the
   aggregate price level, p. 406

Marginal propensity to consume (MPC),
   p. 409
Marginal propensity to save (MPS), p. 410
Autonomous change in aggregate spending,
   p. 412
Multiplier, p. 412
AS–AD model, p. 413
Short-run macroeconomic equilibrium,
   p. 413
Short-run equilibrium aggregate price level,
   p. 414

Short-run equilibrium aggregate output,
   p. 414
Supply shock, p. 414
Stagflation, p. 414
Demand shock, p. 415
Long-run macroeconomic equilibrium,
   p. 416
Recessionary gap, p. 418
Inflationary gap, p. 419
Self-correcting, p. 419

## PROBLEMS

1. Your study partner is confused by the upward-sloping short-run aggregate supply curve and the vertical long-run aggregate supply curve. How would you explain why these slopes differ?

2. Suppose that in Wageland all workers sign annual wage contracts each year on January 1. No matter what happens to prices of final goods and services during the year, all workers earn the wage specified in their annual contract. This year, prices of final goods and services fall unexpectedly after the contracts are signed. Answer the following questions using a diagram and assume that the economy starts at potential output.

   **a.** In the short run, how will the quantity of aggregate output supplied respond to the fall in prices?

   **b.** What will happen when firms and workers renegotiate their wages?

3. In each of the following cases, in the short run, determine whether the events cause a shift of a curve or a movement along a curve. Determine which curve is involved and the direction of the change.

   **a.** As a result of an increase in the value of the dollar in relation to other currencies, American producers now pay less in dollar terms for foreign steel, a major commodity used in production.

   **b.** An increase in the quantity of money by the Federal Reserve increases the quantity of money that people and firms wish to lend, lowering interest rates.

   **c.** Greater union activity leads to higher nominal wages.

   **d.** A fall in the aggregate price level increases the purchasing power of households' money holdings. As a result, they borrow less and lend more.

4. A fall in the value of the dollar against other currencies makes U.S. final goods and services cheaper to foreigners even though the U.S. aggregate price level stays the same. As a result, foreigners demand more American aggregate output. Your study partner says that this represents a movement down

the aggregate demand curve because foreigners are demanding more in response to a lower price. You, however, insist that this represents a rightward shift of the aggregate demand curve. Who is right? Explain.

5. Suppose that local, state, and federal governments were obliged to cut government purchases whenever consumer spending falls. Then suppose that consumer spending falls due to a fall in the stock market. Draw a diagram and explain the full effect of the fall in the stock market on the aggregate demand curve and on the economy. How is this similar to the experience of stagflation in the 1970s?

6. Due to an increase in consumer wealth, there is a $40 billion autonomous increase in consumer spending in the economies of Westlandia and Eastlandia. Assuming that the aggregate price level is constant, the interest rate is fixed in both countries, and there are no taxes and no foreign trade, complete the accompanying tables to show the various rounds of increased spending that will occur in both economies if the marginal propensity to consume is 0.5 in Westlandia and 0.75 in Eastlandia. What do your results indicate about the relationship between the size of the marginal propensity to consume and the multiplier?

### Westlandia

| Rounds | Incremental change in GDP | Total change in GDP |
|---|---|---|
| 1 | $\Delta C = \$40$ billion | ? |
| 2 | $MPC \times \Delta C =$            ? | ? |
| 3 | $MPC \times MPC \times \Delta C =$            ? | ? |
| 4 | $MPC \times MPC \times MPC \times \Delta C =$            ? | ? |
| . . . | . . . | . . . |
| **Total change in GDP** | $(1/(1 - MPC)) \times \Delta C =$            ? | |

**Eastlandia**

| Rounds | Incremental change in GDP | | Total change in GDP |
|--------|---------------------------|---|----------------------|
| 1 | $\Delta C = \$40$ billion | | ? |
| 2 | $MPC \times \Delta C =$ | ? | ? |
| 3 | $MPC \times MPC \times \Delta C =$ | ? | ? |
| 4 | $MPC \times MPC \times MPC \times \Delta C =$ | ? | ? |
| . . . | . . . . . . | | |
| Total change in GDP | $(1/(1 - MPC)) \times \Delta C =$ | | ? |

7. Assuming that the aggregate price level is constant, the interest rate is fixed, and there are no taxes and no foreign trade, how much will the aggregate demand curve shift and in what direction if the following events occur?

   a. An autonomous increase in consumer spending of $25 billion; the marginal propensity to consume is 2/3.

   b. Firms reduce investment spending by $40 billion; the marginal propensity to consume is 0.8.

   c. The government increases its purchases of military equipment by $60 billion; the marginal propensity to consume is 0.6.

8. The economy is at point A in the accompanying diagram. Suppose that the aggregate price level rises from $P_1$ to $P_2$. How will aggregate supply adjust in the short run and in the long run to the increase in the aggregate price level?

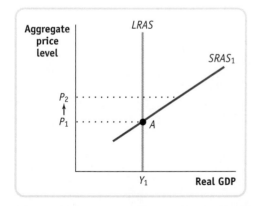

9. Suppose that all households hold all their wealth in assets that automatically rise in value when the aggregate price level rises (an example of this is what is called an "inflation-indexed bond"—a bond whose interest rate, among other things, changes one-for-one with the inflation rate). What happens to the wealth effect of a change in the aggregate price level as a result of this allocation of assets? What happens to the slope of the aggregate demand curve? Will it still slope downward? Explain.

10. Suppose that the economy is currently at potential output. Also suppose that you are an economic policy maker and that a college economics student asks you to rank, if possible, your most preferred to least preferred type of shock: positive demand shock, negative demand shock, positive supply shock, negative supply shock. How would you rank them and why?

11. Explain whether the following government policies affect the aggregate demand curve or the short-run aggregate supply curve and how.

    a. The government reduces the minimum nominal wage.

    b. The government increases Temporary Assistance to Needy Families (TANF) payments, government transfers to families with dependent children.

    c. To reduce the budget deficit, the government announces that households will pay much higher taxes beginning next year.

    d. The government reduces military spending.

12. In Wageland, all workers sign an annual wage contract each year on January 1. In late January, a new computer operating system is introduced that increases labor productivity dramatically. Explain how Wageland will move from one short-run macroeconomic equilibrium to another. Illustrate with a diagram.

13. Using aggregate demand, short-run aggregate supply, and long-run aggregate supply curves, explain the process by which each of the following economic events will move the economy from one long-run macroeconomic equilibrium to another. Illustrate with diagrams. In each case, what are the short-run and long-run effects on the aggregate price level and aggregate output?

    a. There is a decrease in households' wealth due to a decline in the stock market.

    b. The government lowers taxes, leaving households with more disposable income, with no corresponding reduction in government purchases.

14. Using aggregate demand, short-run aggregate supply, and long-run aggregate supply curves, explain the process by which each of the following government policies will move the economy from one long-run macroeconomic equilibrium to another. Illustrate with diagrams. In each case, what are the short-run and long-run effects on the aggregate price level and aggregate output?

    a. There is an increase in taxes on households.

    b. There is an increase in the quantity of money.

    c. There is an increase in government purchases.

15. The economy is in short-run macroeconomic equilibrium at point $E_1$ in the accompanying diagram.

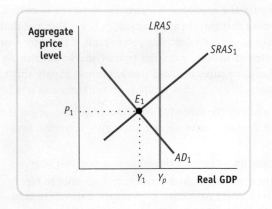

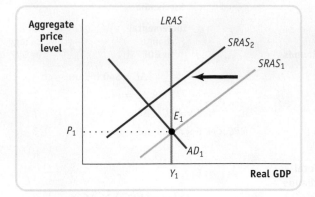

a. Is the economy facing an inflationary or a recessionary gap?

b. What policies can the government implement that might bring the economy back to long-run macroeconomic equilibrium? Illustrate with a diagram.

c. If the government did not intervene to close this gap, would the economy return to long-run macroeconomic equilibrium? Explain and illustrate with a diagram.

d. What are the advantages and disadvantages of the government's implementing policies to close the gap?

16. In the accompanying diagram, the economy is in long-run macroeconomic equilibrium at point $E_1$ when an oil shock shifts the short-run aggregate supply curve to $SRAS_2$.

a. How do the aggregate price level and aggregate output change in the short run as a result of the oil shock? What is this phenomenon known as?

b. What fiscal or monetary policies can the government use to address the effects of the negative supply shock? Use a diagram that shows the effect of policies chosen to address the change in real GDP. Use another diagram to show the effect of policies chosen to address the change in the aggregate price level.

c. Why do negative supply shocks present a dilemma for government policy makers?

17. The late 1990s in the United States were characterized by substantial economic growth with low inflation; that is, real GDP increased with little, if any, increase in the aggregate price level. Explain this experience using aggregate demand and aggregate supply curves. Illustrate with a diagram.

---

**>web...**   To continue your study and review of concepts in this chapter, please visit the Krugman/Wells/Olney website for quizzes, animated graph tutorials, web links to helpful resources, and more.

**www.worthpublishers.com/krugmanwellsolney**

# >>Fiscal Policy

## A BRIDGE TO PROSPERITY?

IN 1998 THE JAPANESE GOVERNMENT completed the longest suspension bridge in the world. The 6,500-foot span linking Awaji Island to the city of Kobe cost $7.3 billion to build. Yet as skeptics had predicted, it currently carries very little traffic—about 4,000 cars a day. By comparison, America's longest suspension bridge, the Verrazano Bridge that links New York City's Staten Island to the borough of Brooklyn, carries more than 300,000 cars a day.

In Japan, stories like this are common. During the 1990s the Japanese government spent around $1.4 trillion on infrastructure that included many construction projects of questionable usefulness. But the main purpose of construction spending in Japan wasn't to provide useful infrastructure. It was to prop up aggregate demand.

During the 1990s, the Japanese government built bridges, roads, dams, breakwaters, and even parking garages in an effort to combat persistent shortfalls in aggregate demand. Japan's use of government construction spending to stimulate its economy is an example of *discretionary fiscal policy*—the deliberate use of government spending or taxation to manage aggregate demand. The U.S. government has also tried to spend its way out of economic slumps, though on a smaller scale. Indeed, many countries attempt to manage aggregate demand by using discretionary fiscal policy. Governments also adjust taxes in an attempt to manage aggregate demand. They may reduce taxes to try to stimulate the economy or raise taxes when they believe that aggregate demand is too high.

In this chapter, we will learn how discretionary fiscal policy fits into the model of short-run fluctuations we developed in Chapter 16. We'll see how deliberate changes in government spending and tax policy affect real GDP. We'll also see how changes in tax revenue caused by short-run

The Akashi Kaikyo Bridge was built by the Japanese government in the 1990s to prop up aggregate demand.

*AFP Getty Images*

fluctuations in GDP—an automatic response that occurs without deliberate changes in policy—help stabilize the economy. Finally, we'll examine the long-run consequences of government debt and budget deficits.

## What you will learn in this chapter:

➤ What fiscal policy is and why it is an important tool in managing economic fluctuations

➤ Which policies constitute an **expansionary fiscal policy** and which constitute a **contractionary fiscal policy**

➤ Why fiscal policy has a multiplier effect and how this effect is influenced by **automatic stabilizers**

➤ Why governments calculate the **cyclically adjusted budget balance**

➤ Why a large **public debt** may be a cause for concern

➤ Why **implicit liabilities** of the government are also a cause for concern

# Fiscal Policy: The Basics

Let's begin with the obvious: modern governments spend a great deal of money and collect a lot in taxes. Figure 17-1 shows government spending and tax revenue as percentages of GDP for a selection of high-income countries in 2003. As you can see, the Swedish government sector is relatively large, representing nearly 60% of the Swedish

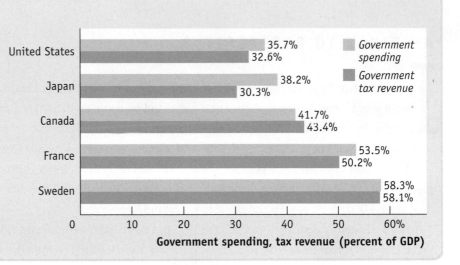

**Figure 17-1**

## Government Spending and Tax Revenue for Some High-Income Countries in 2003

Government spending and tax revenue are represented as a percentage of GDP. Sweden has a particularly large government sector, representing nearly 60% of its GDP. The U.S. government sector, although sizable, is smaller than those of Canada and most European countries.

*Source:* Organization for Economic Cooperation and Development.

economy. The government of the United States plays a smaller role in the economy than those of Canada or most European countries. But that role is still sizable, meaning that the government plays a major role in the U.S. economy. Changes in the federal budget—changes in government spending or in taxation—can potentially have large effects on the American economy.

To analyze these effects, we begin by showing how taxes and government spending affect the economy's flow of income. Then we can see how changes in spending and tax policy affect aggregate demand.

## Taxes, Purchases of Goods and Services, Government Transfers, and Borrowing

In Figure 15-1 we showed the circular flow of income and spending in the economy as a whole. One of the sectors represented in that figure was the government. Funds flow *into* the government in the form of taxes and government borrowing; funds flow *out* in the form of government purchases of goods and services and government transfers to households.

What kinds of taxes do Americans pay, and where does the money go? Figure 17-2 shows the composition of U.S. tax revenue in 2004. Taxes, of course, are required payments to the government. In the United States, taxes are collected at the national level by the federal government; at the state level by each state government; and at the local levels by counties, cities, and towns. At the federal level, the main taxes are income taxes on both personal income and corporate profits as well as *social insurance* taxes, which we'll explain shortly. At the state and local levels, the picture is more complex: these governments rely on a mix of sales taxes,

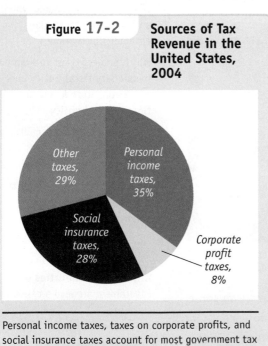

**Figure 17-2**   **Sources of Tax Revenue in the United States, 2004**

Personal income taxes, taxes on corporate profits, and social insurance taxes account for most government tax revenue. The rest is a mix of property taxes, sales taxes, and other sources of revenue.

*Source:* Bureau of Economic Analysis.

property taxes, income taxes, and fees of various kinds. Overall, taxes on personal income and corporate profits accounted for 43% of total government revenue in 2004; social insurance taxes accounted for 28%; and a variety of other taxes, collected mainly at the state and local level, accounted for the rest.

Figure 17-3 shows the composition of total U.S. government spending in 2004, which takes two forms. One form is purchases of goods and services. This includes everything from ammunition for the army to the salaries of public schoolteachers (who are treated in the national accounts as providers of a service—education). The big items here are national defense and education. The large category labeled "other goods and services" consists mainly of state and local spending on a variety of services, from police and firefighters to highway construction and maintenance.

The other form of government spending is government transfers, which are payments by the government to households for which no good or service is provided in return. In the modern United States, as well as in Canada and Europe, government transfers represent a very large proportion of the budget. Most U.S. government spending on transfer payments is accounted for by three big programs:

- Social Security, which provides guaranteed income to older Americans, disabled Americans, and the surviving spouses and dependent children of deceased beneficiaries

- Medicare, which covers much of the cost of health care for Americans over 65

- Medicaid, which covers much of the cost of health care for Americans with low incomes

The term **social insurance** is used to describe government programs that are intended to protect families against economic hardship. These include Social Security, Medicare, and Medicaid, as well as smaller programs such as unemployment insurance and food stamps. In the United States, social insurance programs are largely paid for with special, dedicated taxes on wages—the social insurance taxes we mentioned earlier.

But how do tax policy and government spending affect the economy? The answer is that taxation and government spending have a strong effect on total aggregate spending in the economy.

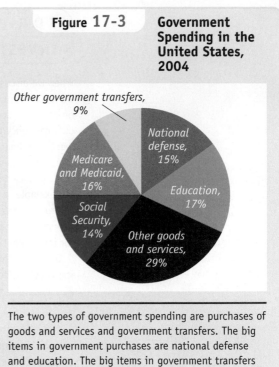

**Figure 17-3** **Government Spending in the United States, 2004**

The two types of government spending are purchases of goods and services and government transfers. The big items in government purchases are national defense and education. The big items in government transfers are Social Security and the Medicare and Medicaid health care programs.

*Source:* Office of Management and Budget.

**Social insurance** programs are government programs intended to protect families against economic hardship.

## The Government Budget and Total Spending

Let's recall the basic equation of national income accounting:

**(17-1)** $GDP = C + I + G + X - IM$

The left-hand side of this equation is GDP, the value of all final goods and services produced in the economy. The right-hand side is aggregate spending, total spending on final goods and services produced in the economy. It is the sum of consumer spending ($C$), investment spending ($I$), government purchases of goods and services ($G$), and the value of exports ($X$) minus the value of imports ($IM$). It includes all the sources of aggregate demand.

The government directly controls only one of the variables on the right-hand side of Equation 17-1: government purchases of goods and services ($G$). But that's not the only effect fiscal policy has on aggregate spending in the economy. Through changes in taxes and transfers, it also influences consumer spending ($C$) and, in some cases, investment spending ($I$).

When we discuss changes in taxes in this chapter, we focus mainly on the effects of these changes on consumer spending. However, there is one tool of fiscal policy that is designed to affect investment spending—*investment tax credits*.

An investment tax credit is a tax break given to firms based on their investment spending. For example, a firm might be allowed to deduct $1 from its tax bill for every $10 it spends on investment goods. This increases the incentive for investment spending.

One more thing about investment tax credits: they're often temporary, applying only to

investment spending within a specific period. For example, Congress introduced an investment tax credit in 2002 that only applied to investment spending over the next two years. Like department store sales that encourage shoppers to spend a lot while the sale is on, temporary investment tax credits tend to generate a lot of investment spending when they're in effect. Even if a firm doesn't think it will need a new server or lathe for another year or so, it may make sense to buy it while the tax credit is available, rather than wait.

To see why the budget affects consumer spending, recall from Chapter 14 that *disposable income*, the total income households have available to spend, is equal to the total income they receive from wages, dividends, interest, and rent, *minus* taxes, *plus* government transfers. So either an increase in taxes or a decrease in government transfers *reduces* disposable income. And a fall in disposable income, other things equal, leads to a fall in consumer spending. Conversely, either a decrease in taxes or an increase in government transfers *increases* disposable income. And a rise in disposable income, other things equal, leads to a rise in consumer spending.

The government's ability to affect investment spending is a more complex story, which we won't discuss in detail (but see For Inquiring Minds above). The important point is that the government taxes profits, and changes in the rules that determine how much a business owes can increase or reduce the incentive to spend on investment goods.

Because the government itself is one source of aggregate demand in the economy, and because taxes and transfers can affect spending by consumers and firms, the government can use changes in taxes or government spending to *shift the aggregate demand curve*. And as we saw in Chapter 16, there are sometimes good reasons to shift the aggregate demand curve. For example, the Japanese government has spent trillions of dollars in an effort to increase aggregate demand. Japan's use of massive government construction spending to prop up its economy in the 1990s is a classic example of *fiscal policy:* the use of taxes, government transfers, or government purchases of goods and services to stabilize the economy by shifting the aggregate demand curve.

## Expansionary and Contractionary Fiscal Policy

Why would the government want to shift the aggregate demand curve? Because it wants to close either a recessionary gap, created when aggregate output falls below potential output, or an inflationary gap, created when aggregate output exceeds potential output.

Figure 17-4 shows the case of an economy facing a recessionary gap. *SRAS* is the short-run aggregate supply curve, *LRAS* is the long-run aggregate supply curve, and $AD_1$ is the initial aggregate demand curve. At the initial short-run macroeconomic equilibrium, $E_1$, aggregate output is $Y_1$, below potential output, $Y_P$. What the government would like to do is increase aggregate demand, shifting the aggregate demand curve rightward to $AD_2$. This would increase aggregate output, making it equal to potential output. Fiscal policy that increases aggregate demand, called **expansionary fiscal policy,** normally takes one of three forms:

**Expansionary fiscal policy** increases aggregate demand.

- An increase in government purchases of goods and services, such as the Japanese government's decision to launch a massive construction program

## Figure 17-4

### Expansionary Fiscal Policy Can Close a Recessionary Gap

At $E_1$ the economy is in short-run macroeconomic equilibrium where the aggregate demand curve $AD_1$ intersects the $SRAS$ curve. At $E_1$, there is a recessionary gap of $Y_P - Y_1$. An expansionary fiscal policy—an increase in government purchases, a reduction in taxes, or an increase in government transfers—shifts the aggregate demand curve rightward. It can close the recessionary gap by shifting $AD_1$ to $AD_2$, moving the economy to a new short-run macroeconomic equilibrium, $E_2$, which is also a long-run macroeconomic equilibrium. **>web...**

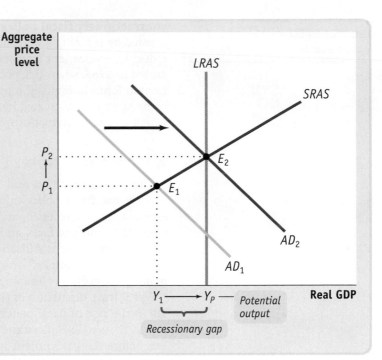

- A cut in taxes, such as the one the United States implemented in 2001
- An increase in government transfers, such as unemployment benefits

Figure 17-5 shows the opposite case—an economy facing an inflationary gap. Again, $SRAS$ is the short-run aggregate supply curve, $LRAS$ is the long-run aggregate supply curve, and $AD_1$ is the initial aggregate demand curve. At the initial equilibrium, $E_1$, aggregate output is $Y_1$, above potential output, $Y_P$. Policy makers often try to head off inflation by eliminating inflationary gaps. To eliminate the inflationary gap shown in Figure 17-5, fiscal policy must reduce aggregate demand and shift the aggregate demand curve leftward to $AD_2$. This reduces aggregate output and makes it equal to potential output. Fiscal policy that reduces aggregate demand, called

## Figure 17-5

### Contractionary Fiscal Policy Can Close an Inflationary Gap

At $E_1$ the economy is in short-run macroeconomic equilibrium where the aggregate demand curve $AD_1$ intersects the $SRAS$ curve. At $E_1$, there is an inflationary gap of $Y_1 - Y_P$. A contractionary fiscal policy—reduced government purchases, an increase in taxes, or a reduction in government transfers—shifts the aggregate demand curve leftward. It can close the inflationary gap by shifting $AD_1$ to $AD_2$, moving the economy to a new short-run macroeconomic equilibrium, $E_2$, which is also a long-run macroeconomic equilibrium. **>web...**

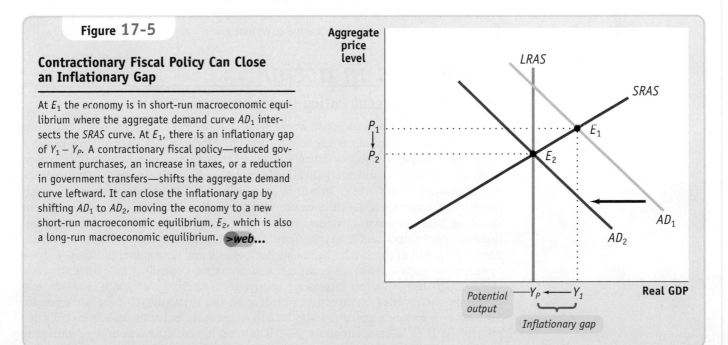

**Contractionary fiscal policy** reduces aggregate demand.

**contractionary fiscal policy,** is the opposite of expansionary fiscal policy. It is implemented by reducing government purchases of goods and services, increasing taxes, or reducing government transfers. A classic example of contractionary fiscal policy occurred in 1968, when U.S. policy makers grew worried about rising inflation. President Lyndon Johnson imposed a temporary 10% surcharge on income taxes—everyone's income taxes were increased by 10%. He also tried to scale back government purchases, which had risen dramatically because of the cost of the Vietnam War.

### A Cautionary Note: Lags in Fiscal Policy

Looking at Figures 17-4 and 17-5, it may seem obvious that the government should actively use fiscal policy—always adopting an expansionary fiscal policy when the economy faces a recessionary gap and always adopting a contractionary fiscal policy when the economy faces an inflationary gap. But many economists caution against an extremely active stabilization policy, arguing that a government that tries too hard to stabilize the economy—through either fiscal policy or monetary policy—can end up making the economy less stable.

We'll leave discussion of the warnings associated with monetary policy to Chapter 18. In the case of fiscal policy, the reason for caution is that there are important *time lags* in its use. To understand the nature of these lags, think about what has to happen before the government increases spending to fight a recessionary gap. First, the government has to realize that the recessionary gap exists: economic data take time to collect and analyze, and recessions are often recognized only months after they have begun. Second, the government has to develop a spending plan, which can itself take months, particularly if politicians take time debating how the money should be spent and passing legislation. Finally, it takes time to spend money. For example, a road construction project begins with activities such as surveying that don't involve spending large sums. It may be quite some time before the big spending begins.

Because of these lags, an attempt to increase spending to fight a recessionary gap may take so long to get going that the recessionary gap may have turned into an inflationary gap by the time the fiscal policy takes effect. In that case, the fiscal policy will make things worse instead of better.

This doesn't mean that fiscal policy should never be actively used. After all, time lags didn't pose a problem for Japanese fiscal policy in the 1990s, which was attempting to fight a recessionary gap that lasted for many years. But the problem of lags makes the actual use of both fiscal and monetary policy harder than you might think from a simple analysis like the one we have just given.

## *economics in action*

### Expansionary Fiscal Policy in Japan

"In what may be the biggest public works bonanza since the pharaohs, Japan has spent something like $1.4 trillion trying to pave and build its way back to economic health," began one newspaper report on Japan's efforts to prop up its economy with fiscal policy.

Japan turned to expansionary fiscal policy in the early 1990s. In the 1980s the country's economy boomed, driven in part by soaring values of stocks and real estate, which boosted consumer spending through the wealth effect and also encouraged investment spending. Japanese economists now refer to this period as the "bubble economy," because the rise in stock and land values could not be justified in terms of rational calculations. At the end of the 1980s the bubble burst—stock and land values plunged, and the economy slid into recession as consumer and investment spending fell. Since the early 1990s Japan has relied on large-scale government purchases of goods and services, mainly in the form of construction spending on infrastructure, to prop up aggregate demand. This spending has been scaled back in recent years, but at its peak it was truly impressive. In 1996 Japan spent about $300 billion on infrastructure, compared with only

$180 billion spent in the United States, even though Japan has less than half America's population and considerably less than half its GDP. Superb roads run through sparsely populated regions, ferries to small islands have been replaced by bridges, and many of the country's riverbeds have been paved, so that they resemble concrete aqueducts.

Has this policy been a success? Yes and no. Many economists believe that without all that government spending the Japanese economy would have slid into a 1930s-type depression after the bubble in stock and land values burst. Instead, the economy suffered a slowdown but not a severe slump: growth has been sluggish and unemployment has risen, but there has been no depression.

Furthermore, alternative policies weren't readily available. The alternative to using fiscal policy to prop up a slumping economy is using monetary policy, in which the central bank expands the money supply and drives down interest rates. Japan has done that, too; since 1998 short-term interest rates have been approximately zero! Since interest rates can't go below zero, there was no room for further interest rate cuts, yet the economy remained sluggish. So expansionary fiscal policy was the only obvious way to increase aggregate demand.

However, expansionary fiscal policy has not yet produced a full recovery in Japan. And the years of deficit spending have led to a rising government debt–GDP ratio that worries many financial experts. ■

> > > > > > > > > > > > > > > > > > > > > >

## >>CHECK YOUR UNDERSTANDING 17-1

1. In each of the following cases, determine whether the policy is an expansionary or contractionary fiscal policy.
   a. Several military bases around the country, which together employ tens of thousands of people, are closed.
   b. The number of weeks an unemployed person is eligible for unemployment benefits is increased.
   c. The federal tax on gasoline is increased.

2. Explain why federal disaster relief, which should quickly disburse funds to victims of natural disasters such as hurricanes, floods, and large-scale crop failures, will stabilize the economy more effectively than relief that must be legislated.

*Solutions appear at back of book.*

# Fiscal Policy and the Multiplier

An expansionary fiscal policy, like Japan's program of public works, pushes the aggregate demand curve to the right. A contractionary fiscal policy, like Lyndon Johnson's tax surcharge, pushes the aggregate demand curve to the left. For policy makers, however, knowing the direction of the shift isn't enough: they need estimates of *how much* the aggregate demand curve is shifted by a given policy. To get these estimates, they use the concept of the multiplier, which we introduced in Chapter 16.

## Multiplier Effects of an Increase in Government Purchases of Goods and Services

Suppose that a government decides to spend $50 billion building bridges and roads. The government's purchases of goods and services will directly increase total spending on final goods and services by $50 billion. But as we learned in Chapter 16, there will also be an indirect effect because the government's purchases will start a chain reaction throughout the economy. The firms producing the goods and services purchased by the government will earn revenues that flow to households in the form of wages, profit, interest, and rent. This increase in disposable income will lead to a rise in consumer spending. The rise in consumer spending, in turn, will induce firms to increase output, leading to a further rise in disposable income, which will lead to another round of consumer spending increases, and so on.

In Chapter 16 we introduced the concept of the *multiplier:* the ratio of the change in real GDP caused by an autonomous change in aggregate spending to the size of that autonomous change. We saw there that in the simplest case (where there are no taxes or international trade, so that any change in real GDP accrues entirely to households, and the aggregate price level and the interest rate are fixed) the multiplier is $1/(1 - MPC)$. Recall that $MPC$ is the *marginal propensity to consume,* the fraction of an additional dollar in disposable income that is spent. For example, if the marginal propensity to consume is 0.6, the multiplier is $1/(1 - 0.6) = 1/0.4 = 2.5$.

An increase in government purchases of goods and services is an example of an autonomous increase in aggregate spending. Its effect is illustrated in Figure 17-6. Given a multiplier of 2.5, a $50 billion increase in government purchases of goods and services will shift the $AD$ curve rightward from $AD_1$ to $AD_2$, a distance representing an increase in real GDP of $125 billion at a given aggregate price level, $P^*$. Of that $125 billion, $50 billion is the initial effect from the increase in G, and the remaining $75 billion is the subsequent effect arising from the increase in consumer spending.

What happens if government purchases of goods and services are instead reduced? The math is exactly the same, except that there's a minus sign in front: if government purchases fall by $50 billion and the marginal propensity to consume is 0.6, the $AD$ curve shifts leftward by $125 billion.

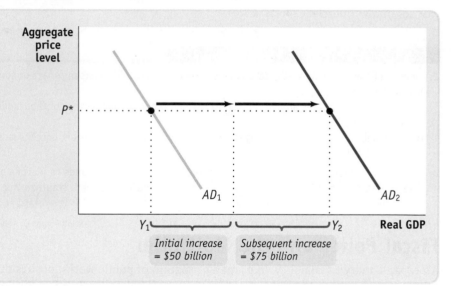

### Figure 17-6

#### The Multiplier Effect of an Increase in Government Purchases of Goods and Services

A $50 billion increase in government purchases of goods and services has the direct effect of shifting the aggregate demand curve to the right by $50 billion. However, this is not the end of the story. The rise in real GDP causes a rise in disposable income, which leads to an increase in consumer spending, which leads to a further rise in real GDP, which leads to a further rise in consumer spending, and so on. The eventual shift, from $AD_1$ to $AD_2$, is a *multiple* of the increase in government purchases.

## Multiplier Effects of Changes in Government Transfers and Taxes

Expansionary or contractionary fiscal policy need not take the form of changes in government purchases of goods and services. Governments can also change transfer payments or taxes. In general, however, a change in government transfers or taxes shifts the aggregate demand curve by *less* than an equal-sized change in government purchases.

To see why, imagine that instead of spending $50 billion on building bridges, the government simply hands out $50 billion in the form of government transfers. In this case, there is no direct effect on aggregate demand as there was with government purchases of goods and services. Real GDP goes up only because households spend some of that $50 billion. How much will they spend? Because the $50 billion transfer payment increases disposable income, households will engage in a first-round increase in consumer spending of $MPC \times$ $50 billion. For example, if $MPC = 0.6$, the first-round increase in consumer spending will be $30 billion ($0.6 \times$ $50 billion = $30 billion). Like an increase in government purchases, this initial rise in consumer spending will lead to a series of subsequent rounds in which real GDP, disposable income, and consumer spending rise further. In this example, although the transfer costs the government the same amount as the increase in spending on goods and services, the

## WORK IT OUT

### FISCAL POLICY MULTIPLIER

Suppose the government has a goal of increasing aggregate demand by $500 billion per year. The marginal propensity to consume is 0.5.

**Multiplier:** How big is the multiplier for a change in government purchases?

SOLUTION: The multiplier is $1 / (1 - MPC)$. So in this case, the multiplier is $1 / (1 - 0.5) = 2$.

**Effect of multiplier:** If the government wants to achieve its goal by increasing government purchases of goods and services $G$, by how much should it increase $G$? If instead the government wants to achieve its goal by increasing transfer payments $TR$, by how much should it increase $TR$?

SOLUTION: The goal is to increase aggregate demand by $500 billion per year. The multiplier is 2. So the government should increase G by $500 billion per year / 2 = $250 billion per year. If, instead, the government increases TR, the relevant multiplier is $MPC / (1 - MPC) = 1$. So the government should increase TR by $500 billion per year / 1 = $500 billion per year.

**Effect of change in MPC:** Suppose instead that the MPC is 0.8. The goal remains the same. Now how big is the multiplier? Now, if the government wants to achieve its goal by increasing $G$, by how much should it increase $G$? If, instead, the government wants to achieve its goal by increasing $TR$, by how much should it increase $TR$?

SOLUTION: With an MPC of 0.8, the multiplier is $1 / (1 - 0.8) = 5$. So to increase aggregate demand by $500 billion per year, the government should increase G by $500 billion per year / 5 = $100 billion per year. If instead the government wants to achieve its goal by increasing TR, the relevant multiplier is $0.8 / (1 - 0.8) = 4$. So the government should increase TR by $125 billion per year.

**Policy choice:** Suppose the government can identify two groups: one with an MPC of 0.5 and one with an MPC of 0.8. If the government wants to achieve its goal with the smallest change in government spending, which group should it target?

SOLUTION: The group with the MPC of 0.8 will spend more of every dollar of disposable income than will the group with the MPC of 0.5. So each government dollar will have a larger impact if the government targets its spending toward the group with an MPC of 0.8.

autonomous increase in aggregate spending from the transfer ($30 billion) is smaller than the autonomous increase in aggregate spending from government spending ($50 billion), and the overall effect on real GDP will also be smaller. In general, $1 of transfer payments will increase GDP by $MPC/(1 - MPC)$, less than the effect of the multiplier for increases in government purchases, which is $1/(1 - MPC)$. For example, if the marginal propensity to consume is 0.6, $1 of transfer payments raises real GDP by only $0.6/(1 - 0.6) = $1.50, while a $1 increase in government purchases of goods and services raises real GDP by $1/(1 - 0.6) = $2.50.

A tax cut has an effect similar to the effect of a transfer. It increases disposable income, leading to a series of increases in consumer spending. But the overall effect is smaller than that of an equal-size increase in government purchases: the autonomous increase in aggregate spending is smaller because households save part of the amount of the tax cut.

In practice, economists often argue that it also matters *who* among the population gets tax cuts or increases in government transfers. For example, compare the effects of an increase in unemployment benefits with a cut in taxes on profits distributed to shareholders as dividends. Consumer surveys indicate that the average unemployed worker will spend a higher share of any increase in his or her disposable income than would the average recipient of dividend income. That is, people who are unemployed tend to have a higher *MPC* than people who own a lot of stocks because the latter tend to be wealthier and to save more of any increase in disposable income. If that's true, a dollar spent on unemployment benefits increases aggregate demand more than a dollar's worth of dividend tax cuts. As the Economics in Action that follows this section explains, such arguments played an important role in recent policy debates.

## How Taxes Affect the Multiplier

The type of tax we just analyzed is called a **lump-sum tax,** a tax in which the amount of tax a household owes is independent of its income. But few taxes in the real world are lump-sum taxes. Instead, the great majority of tax revenue is raised via

A **lump-sum tax** does not change when real GDP changes.

A **proportional tax** increases when real GDP increases and decreases when real GDP decreases.

**proportional taxes,** taxes that depend positively on the level of real GDP. When real GDP increases, the tax bill rises. When real GDP decreases, the tax bill falls. And taxes that depend positively on real GDP change the size of the multiplier.

When we introduced the analysis of the multiplier in Chapter 16, we simplified matters by assuming that a $1 increase in real GDP raises disposable income by $1. In fact, however, government taxes capture some part of the increase in real GDP that occurs in each round of the multiplier process since most government taxes depend positively on real GDP. As a result, disposable income increases by considerably less than $1 once we include proportional taxes in the model.

The increase in government tax revenue when real GDP rises isn't the result of a deliberate decision or action by the government. It's a consequence of the way the tax laws are written. Most taxes are proportional taxes, not lump-sum taxes, so most sources of government revenue increase *automatically* when real GDP goes up. For example, income tax receipts increase when real GDP rises because the amount each individual owes in taxes depends positively on his or her income, and households' disposable income rises when real GDP rises. Sales tax receipts increase when real GDP rises because people with more income spend more on goods and services. And corporate profit tax receipts increase when real GDP rises because profits increase when the economy expands.

The effect of these automatic increases in tax revenue is to reduce the size of the multiplier. Remember, the multiplier is the result of a chain reaction in which higher GDP leads to higher disposable income, which leads to higher consumer spending, which leads to further increases in real GDP. The fact that the government siphons off some of any increase in real GDP means that at each stage of this process the increase in consumer spending is smaller than it would be if taxes weren't part of the picture. The result is to reduce the multiplier.

Many macroeconomists believe it's a good thing that in real life taxes reduce the multiplier. In Chapter 16 we argued that most, though not all, recessions are the result of negative *demand shocks*. The same mechanism that causes tax revenue to increase when the economy expands causes it to decrease when the economy contracts. Since tax receipts decrease when real GDP falls, the effects of these negative demand shocks are smaller than they would be if there were no taxes. The decrease in tax revenue reduces the adverse effect of the initial fall in aggregate demand. By cutting the amount of taxes households pay, the automatic decrease in government tax revenue generated by a fall in real GDP acts like an automatic expansionary fiscal policy implemented in the face of a recession. Similarly, when the economy expands, the government finds itself automatically pursuing a contractionary fiscal policy—a tax increase. Government spending and taxation rules that cause fiscal policy to be expansionary when the economy contracts and contractionary when the economy expands, without requiring any deliberate action by policy makers, are called **automatic stabilizers.**

The rules that govern tax collection aren't the only automatic stabilizers, although they are the most important ones. Some types of government transfers also play a stabilizing role. For example, more people receive unemployment insurance when the economy is depressed than when it is booming. The same is true of Medicaid and food stamps. So transfer payments tend to rise when the economy is contracting and fall when the economy is expanding. Like changes in tax revenue, these changes in transfers tend to reduce the size of the multiplier because the total change in disposable income that results from a given rise or fall in real GDP is smaller.

As in the case of government tax revenue, many macroeconomists believe that it's a good thing that government transfers reduce the multiplier. More generally, expansionary and contractionary fiscal policies that are the result of automatic stabilizers are widely considered helpful to macroeconomic stabilization.

**Automatic stabilizers** are government spending and taxation rules that cause fiscal policy to be expansionary when the economy contracts and contractionary when the economy expands.

An example of a discretionary fiscal policy was the Works Progress Administration (WPA), a relief measure established during the Great Depression. The unemployed were put to work on public works projects, building bridges, roads, buildings, and parks.

What do we call fiscal policy that *isn't* the result of automatic stabilizers? **Discretionary fiscal policy** is fiscal policy that is the direct result of deliberate actions by policy makers rather than automatic adjustment. For example, during a recession, the government may pass legislation that cuts taxes and purposely increases government spending in order to stimulate the economy.

> **Discretionary fiscal policy** is fiscal policy that is the result of deliberate actions by policy makers rather than rules.

## *economics in action*

### How Much Bang for the Buck?

In 2001 the U.S. economy experienced a recession, followed by a 2002–2003 "jobless recovery" in which real GDP grew but overall employment didn't. There was widespread agreement among economists that the country needed an expansionary fiscal policy to stimulate aggregate demand. And the government did, in fact, pursue an expansionary fiscal policy: tax cuts combined with increased government spending undoubtedly helped increase aggregate demand and output.

But was the expansionary fiscal policy carried out in the right way? Critics argued that a different mix of policies would have yielded more "bang for the buck"—they would have done more to increase aggregate demand, but led to a smaller rise in the budget deficit.

A particularly clear (and nonpartisan) example of this criticism was an analysis by Mark Zandi, the chief economist of economy.com, a consulting firm. Zandi estimated the multiplier effects of a number of alternative fiscal policies, shown in Table 17-1. He argued that many of the tax cuts enacted between 2001 and 2003 had smaller effects on

**TABLE 17-1**

### Differences in the Effect of Expansionary Fiscal Policies

| Policy | Estimated increase in real GDP per dollar of fiscal policy | Explanation of policy |
|---|---|---|
| Extend emergency federal unemployment insurance benefits | $1.73 | Extends the period for unemployment benefits, increasing transfers to the unemployed |
| 10% personal income tax bracket | 1.34 | Reduces tax rate on some income from 15% to 10%, mainly benefiting middle-income families |
| State government aid | 1.24 | Provides financial aid to state governments during recessions so states do not have to raise taxes or cut spending |
| Child tax credit rebate | 1.04 | Increases the income tax reduction for each child, mainly benefiting middle- and lower-income families |
| Marriage tax penalty | 0.74 | Reduces the "marriage penalty," an increase in combined taxes that can occur when two working people marry |
| Alternative minimum tax adjustments | 0.67 | Revises the alternative minimum tax, designed to prevent wealthy people with many deductions from paying too little tax, to exclude those not considered sufficiently wealthy |
| Personal marginal tax rate reductions | 0.59 | Reduces tax rates for people in higher income brackets |
| Business investment writeoff | 0.24 | Temporarily allows companies to deduct some investment spending from taxable profits |
| Dividend–capital gain tax reduction | 0.09 | Reduces taxes on dividends and capital gains |
| Estate tax reduction | 0.00 | Reduces the tax paid on the value of assets passed to heirs upon a person's death |

Source: economy.com

The **budget balance** is the difference between tax revenue and government spending.

The **budget surplus** is the difference between tax revenue and government spending when tax revenue exceeds government spending.

The **budget deficit** is the difference between tax revenue and government spending when government spending exceeds tax revenue.

aggregate demand compared to other types of tax cuts because they went to people who probably wouldn't spend much of the increase in their disposable income. He was particularly critical of tax cuts on dividend income and on the value of inherited estates, arguing that they did very little to raise consumer spending. According to his analysis, an alternative set of fiscal policies that put more disposable income into the hands of unemployed workers, lower-income taxpayers, and cash-strapped state and local governments would have created a larger increase in spending at the same cost. This would have led to both lower budget deficits and a larger increase in real GDP—and so to lower unemployment. This view was shared by many economists, though certainly not by all.

Despite the criticisms, there was widespread agreement that the tax cuts of 2001–2003 helped generate an economic expansion. As Richard Berner, an economist at the investment firm Morgan Stanley, put it, the tax cuts might not have generated a lot of bang per buck, but they were still effective because they involved a lot of bucks. ■

< < < < < < < < < < < < < < < < < <

>>CHECK YOUR UNDERSTANDING 17-2

1. Explain why a $500 million increase in government purchases of goods and services will generate a larger shift in the aggregate demand curve than a $500 million increase in government transfers.

2. Explain why a $500 million reduction in government purchases of goods and services will generate a larger shift in the aggregate demand curve than a $500 million reduction in government transfers.

*Solutions appear at back of book.*

## The Budget Balance

Headlines about the government's budget tend to focus on just one point: whether the government is running a surplus or a deficit and, in either case, how big. People usually think of surpluses as good: when the federal government ran a record surplus in 2000, many people regarded it as a cause for celebration. Conversely, people usually think of deficits as bad: when the federal government ran a record deficit in 2004, many people regarded it as a cause for concern, and the White House promised to bring the deficit down over time.

How do surpluses and deficits fit into the analysis of fiscal policy? Are deficits ever a good thing and surpluses a bad thing? Let's look at the causes and consequences of surpluses and deficits.

### The Budget Balance as a Measure of Fiscal Policy

What do we mean by surpluses and deficits? The budget balance is the difference between the government's income, in the form of tax revenue, and its spending, both on goods and services and on government transfers, in a given year. That is, the **budget balance** is equal to

(17-2)     Budget Balance $= T - G - TR$

where $T$ is the value of tax revenues, $G$ is government purchases, and $TR$ is the value of government transfers. A **budget surplus** is a positive budget balance and a **budget deficit** is a negative budget balance.

Other things equal, expansionary fiscal policies—increased government purchases of goods and services, higher government transfers, or lower taxes—reduce the budget balance for that year. That is, expansionary fiscal policies make a budget surplus smaller or a budget deficit bigger. Conversely, contractionary fiscal policies—reduced govern-

OH... SOMEONE MUST HAVE BALANCED THE BUDGET.

Patrick O'Conncr

ment purchases of goods and services, lower government transfers, or higher taxes—increase the budget balance for that year, making a budget surplus bigger or a budget deficit smaller.

You might think this means that changes in the budget balance can be used to measure fiscal policy. In fact, economists often do just that: they use changes in the budget balance as a "quick-and-dirty" way to assess whether current fiscal policy is expansionary or contractionary. But they always keep in mind two reasons this quick-and-dirty approach is sometimes misleading:

- Two different changes in fiscal policy that have equal effects on the budget balance may have quite unequal effects on aggregate demand. As we have already seen, changes in government purchases have a larger effect on aggregate demand than equal-size changes in taxes and government transfers.

- Often, changes in the budget balance are themselves the result, not the cause, of fluctuations in the economy.

To understand the second point, we need to examine the effects of the business cycle on the budget.

## The Business Cycle and the Cyclically Adjusted Budget Balance

Historically there has been a strong relationship between the federal government's budget balance and the business cycle. The budget tends to move into deficit when the economy experiences a recession, but deficits tend to get smaller or even turn into surpluses when the economy is expanding. Figure 17-7 shows the federal budget deficit as a percentage of GDP since 1970. Shaded areas indicate recessions; unshaded areas indicate expansions. As you can see, the federal budget deficit increased around the time of each recession and usually declined during expansions. In fact, in the late stages of the long expansion from 1991 to 2000 the deficit actually became negative—the budget deficit became a budget surplus.

The relationship between the business cycle and the budget balance is even clearer if we compare the budget deficit as a percentage of GDP with the unemployment rate, as we do in Figure 17-8 on page 440. The budget deficit almost always rises when the unemployment rate rises and falls when the unemployment rate falls.

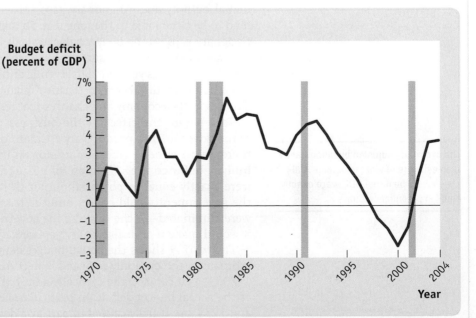

**Figure 17-7**

**The U.S. Federal Budget Deficit and the Business Cycle**

The budget deficit as a percentage of GDP tends to rise during recessions (indicated by shaded areas) and fall during expansions.

*Source:* Congressional Budget Office, National Bureau of Economic Research.

### Figure 17-8

**The U.S. Federal Budget Deficit and the Unemployment Rate**

There is a close relationship between the budget balance and the business cycle: a recession moves the budget balance toward deficit, but an expansion moves it toward surplus. Here, the unemployment rate serves as an indicator of the business cycle, and we should expect to see a higher unemployment rate associated with a higher budget deficit. This is confirmed by the figure: the budget deficit as a percentage of GDP moves closely in tandem with the unemployment rate. **>web...**

*Source:* Congressional Budget Office, Bureau of Labor Statistics.

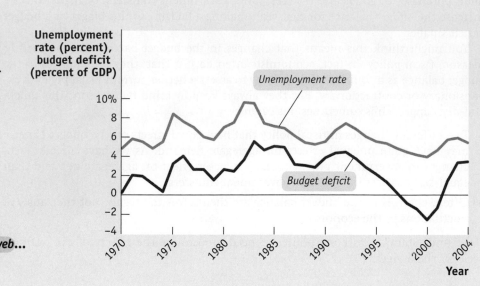

Is this relationship between the business cycle and the budget balance evidence that policy makers engage in discretionary fiscal policy, using expansionary fiscal policy during recessions and contractionary fiscal policy during expansions? Not necessarily. To a large extent the relationship in Figure 17-8 reflects automatic stabilizers at work. As we learned in the discussion of automatic stabilizers, government tax revenue tends to rise and some government transfers, like unemployment benefit payments, tend to fall when the economy expands. Conversely, government tax revenue tends to fall and some government transfers tend to rise when the economy contracts. So the budget tends to move toward deficit during recessions and toward surplus during expansions even without any deliberate action on the part of policy makers.

In assessing budget policy, it's often useful to separate changes in the budget balance due to the business cycle from changes due to deliberate policy changes. The former are affected by automatic stabilizers and the latter, by deliberate changes in government purchases, government transfers, or taxes. For one thing, business-cycle effects on the budget balance are temporary: both recessionary gaps (in which real GDP is below potential output) and inflationary gaps (in which real GDP is above potential output) tend to be eliminated in the long run. So taking out the effects of recessionary and inflationary gaps on the budget balance sheds light on whether the government's taxing and spending policies are sustainable in the long run. In other words, do the government's tax policies yield enough revenue to fund its spending in the long run? Also, it's useful to distinguish between "passive" changes in the budget balance that result from changes in the economy and changes that result from actions by policy makers.

To separate the effect of the business cycle from the effects of other factors, many governments produce an estimate of what the budget balance would be if there were neither a recessionary nor an inflationary gap. The **cyclically adjusted budget balance** is an estimate of what the budget balance would be if real GDP were exactly equal to potential output. It takes into account the extra tax revenue the government would collect and the transfers it would save if a recessionary gap were eliminated—or the revenue the government would lose and the extra transfers it would make if an inflationary gap were eliminated.

Figure 17-9 shows the actual budget deficit and the Congressional Budget Office estimate of the cyclically adjusted budget deficit, both as a percentage of GDP, since 1970. As you can see, the cyclically adjusted budget deficit doesn't fluctuate as much as the actual budget deficit. In particular, large actual deficits, such as those of 1975 and 1983, are usually caused in part by a depressed economy.

The **cyclically adjusted budget balance** is an estimate of what the budget balance would be if real GDP were exactly equal to potential output.

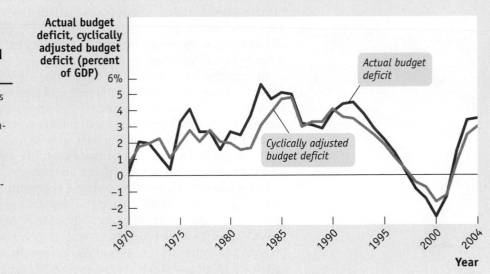

**Figure 17-9**

**The Actual Budget Deficit Versus the Cyclically Adjusted Budget Deficit**

The cyclically adjusted budget deficit is an estimate of what the budget deficit would be if the economy were at potential output. It fluctuates less than the actual budget deficit, because years of large budget deficits also tend to be years when the economy has a large recessionary gap.

*Source:* Congressional Budget Office.

## Should the Budget Be Balanced?

Persistent budget deficits can cause problems for both the government and the economy. Yet politicians are always tempted to run deficits because this allows them to cater to voters by cutting taxes without cutting spending or by increasing spending without increasing taxes. As a result, there are occasional attempts by policy makers to force fiscal discipline by introducing legislation—even a constitutional amendment—forbidding the government from running budget deficits. This is usually stated as a requirement that the budget be "balanced"—that revenues at least equal spending each fiscal year. Would it be a good idea to require a balanced budget annually?

Most economists don't think so. They believe that the government should only balance its budget on average—that it should be allowed to run deficits in bad years, offset by surpluses in good years. They don't believe the government should be forced to run a balanced budget *every year* because this would undermine the role of taxes and transfers as automatic stabilizers. The tendency of tax revenue to fall and transfers to rise when the economy contracts helps to limit the size of recessions. But falling tax revenue and rising transfer payments push the budget toward deficit. If constrained by a balanced-budget rule, the government would have to respond to this deficit with contractionary fiscal policies that would tend to deepen the recession.

Yet policy makers concerned about excessive deficits sometimes feel that rigid rules prohibiting—or at least setting an upper limit on—deficits are necessary. As Economics in Action explains, Europe has had a lot of trouble reconciling rules to enforce fiscal responsibility with the problems of short-run fiscal policy.

## *economics in action*

### Stability Pact—or Stupidity Pact?

In 1999 a group of European nations took a momentous step when they adopted a common currency, the euro, to replace their national currencies, such as French francs, German marks, and Italian lira. Along with the introduction of the euro came the creation of the European Central Bank, which sets monetary policy for the whole region.

As part of the agreement creating the new currency, governments of member countries signed on to the European "stability pact." This agreement required each government to keep its budget deficit—its actual deficit, not a cyclically adjusted number—below 3% of the country's GDP or face fines. The pact was intended to prevent irresponsible deficit spending arising from political pressure that might eventually undermine the new currency. The stability pact, however, had a serious downside: it limited a country's ability to use fiscal policy.

In fact, the stability pact quickly became a problem for the two largest economies in the euro zone. In 2002 both France and Germany were experiencing rising unemployment and also running budget deficits in excess of 3% of GDP. Moreover, it seemed likely that both countries' deficits would go up in 2003, which they did. Under the rules of the stability pact, France and Germany were supposed to lower their budget deficits by raising taxes or cutting spending. Yet contractionary fiscal policy would have led to even higher unemployment.

In October 2002, reacting to these economic problems, one top European official described the stability pact as "stupid." Journalists promptly had a field day, renaming it the "stupidity pact." In fact, when push came to shove, the pact proved unenforceable. Germany and France both had enough political clout to prevent the imposition of penalties. Indeed, in March 2005 the stability pact was rewritten to allow "small and temporary" breaches of the 3% limit, with a special clause allowing Germany to describe aid to the former East Germany as a temporary expense.

Before patting themselves on the back over the superiority of their own fiscal rules, Americans should note that the United States has its own version of the stupidity pact. The federal government's budget acts as an automatic stabilizer, but 49 of the 50 states are required by their state constitutions to balance their budgets every year. When recession struck in 2001, most states were forced to—guess what?—slash spending and raise taxes in the face of a recession, exactly the wrong thing from a macroeconomic point of view. Not surprisingly, some states, like some European countries, found ways to cheat. ∎

‹ ‹ ‹ ‹ ‹ ‹ ‹ ‹ ‹ ‹ ‹ ‹ ‹ ‹ ‹ ‹ ‹ ‹ ‹

>> **CHECK YOUR UNDERSTANDING 17-3**

1. When your work–study earnings are low, your parents help you out with expenses. When your earnings are high, they expect you to contribute toward your tuition bill. Explain how this arrangement acts like an automatic stabilizer for your economic activity.

2. Explain why states required by their constitutions to balance their budgets are likely to experience more severe economic fluctuations than states not held to that requirement.

*Solutions appear at back of book.*

# Long-Run Implications of Fiscal Policy

The Japanese government built the bridge to Awaji Island as part of a fiscal policy aimed at increasing aggregate demand. As we've seen, that policy was partly successful: although Japan's economy was sluggish during the 1990s, it avoided a severe slump comparable to what happened to many countries in the 1930s. Yet the fact that Japan was running large deficits year after year made many observers uneasy. By 2000 there was a debate among economists about whether Japan's debt was starting to reach alarming levels.

No discussion of fiscal policy is complete if it doesn't take into account the long-run implications of government budget surpluses and deficits. We now turn to those long-run implications.

## Deficits, Surpluses, and Debt

When a family spends more than it earns over the course of a year, it has to raise the extra funds either by selling assets or by borrowing. And if a family borrows year after year, it will end up with a lot of debt.

The same is true for governments. With a few exceptions, governments don't raise large sums by selling assets such as national parkland. Instead, when a government spends more than the tax revenue it receives—when it runs a budget deficit—it almost always borrows the extra funds. And governments that run persistent budget deficits end up with substantial debts.

To interpret the numbers that follow, you need to know a slightly peculiar feature of federal government accounting. For historical reasons, the U.S. government does not keep books for calendar years. Instead, budget totals are kept for **fiscal years,** which run from October 1 to September 30 and are named by the calendar year in which they end. For example, fiscal 2004 began on October 1, 2003, and ended on September 30, 2004.

At the end of fiscal 2004, the U.S. federal government had total debt equal to almost $7.4 trillion. However, part of that debt represented special accounting rules specifying that the federal government as a whole owes funds to certain government programs, especially Social Security. We'll explain those rules shortly. For now, however, let's focus on **public debt:** government debt held by individuals and institutions outside the government. At the end of fiscal 2004, the federal government's public debt was "only" $4.3 trillion, or 37% of GDP. If we include the debts of state and local governments, total government public debt was approximately 44% of GDP. Figure 17-10 compares the U.S. public debt–GDP ratio with the public debt–GDP ratios of other wealthy countries in 2003. As of 2003, the U.S. debt level was more or less typical.

U.S. federal government public debt at the end of fiscal 2004 was larger than it was at the end of fiscal 2003, because the federal government ran a budget deficit during fiscal 2004. A government that runs persistent budget deficits will experience a rising level of public debt. But why is this a problem?

**Fiscal years** run from October 1 to September 30 and are named by the calendar year in which they end.

**Public debt** is government debt held by individuals and institutions outside the government.

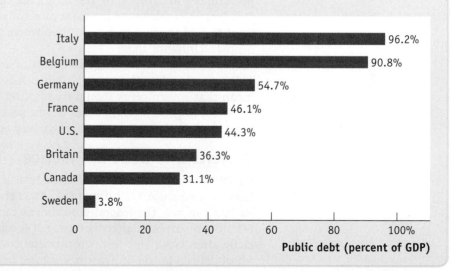

### Figure 17-10

**Public Debt as a Percentage of GDP, 2003**

Public debt as a percentage of GDP is a widely used measure of how deeply in debt a government is. The United States lies in the middle range among wealthy countries. Governments of countries with high public debt–GDP ratios, like Italy and Belgium, pay large sums in interest each year to service their debt.

*Source:* OECD.

| Country | Public debt (percent of GDP) |
| --- | --- |
| Italy | 96.2% |
| Belgium | 90.8% |
| Germany | 54.7% |
| France | 46.1% |
| U.S. | 44.3% |
| Britain | 36.3% |
| Canada | 31.1% |
| Sweden | 3.8% |

## Problems Posed by Rising Government Debt

There are two reasons to be concerned when a government runs persistent budget deficits. When the government borrows funds in the financial markets, it is competing with firms that plan to borrow funds for investment spending. As a result, the interest rate rises. Because of the higher interest rate, however, businesses will engage in less investment spending than they otherwise would have. This negative effect of

**Crowding out** is the negative effect of budget deficits on private investment.

budget deficits on private investment spending is called *crowding out*. When a budget deficit causes **crowding out,** the economy adds less private physical capital each year than it would if the budget were balanced or in surplus.

But there's also a second reason: today's deficits, by increasing the government's debt, place financial pressure on future budgets. The impact of current deficits on future budgets is straightforward. Like individuals, governments must pay their bills—including interest payments on their accumulated debt. When a government is deeply in debt, those interest payments can be substantial. In fiscal 2004, the U.S. federal government paid 1.4% of GDP—$160 billion—in interest on its debt. The two most heavily indebted governments shown in Figure 17-10, Italy and Belgium, each paid interest of more than 5% of GDP in 2004.

Other things equal, a government paying large sums in interest must raise more revenue from taxes or spend less than it would otherwise be able to afford—or it must borrow even more to cover the gap. But a government that borrows to pay interest on its outstanding debt pushes itself even deeper into debt. This process can eventually push a government to the point where lenders question its ability to repay. Like a consumer who has maxed out his or her credit cards, it will find that lenders are unwilling to lend any more funds. The result can be that the government defaults on its debt—it stops paying what it owes. Default is often followed by financial and economic turmoil.

The idea of a government defaulting sounds far-fetched, but it is not impossible. In the 1990s Argentina, a relatively high-income developing country, was widely praised for its economic policies—and it was able to borrow large sums from foreign lenders. By 2002, however, Argentina's interest payments were spiraling out of control, and the country stopped paying the sums that were due. We describe that default in the Economics in Action that follows this section.

Default creates havoc in a country's financial markets and badly shakes public confidence in both the government and the economy. Argentina's debt default was accompanied by a crisis in the country's banking systems and a very severe recession. And even if a highly indebted government avoids default, a heavy debt burden typically forces it to slash spending or raise taxes, politically unpopular measures that can also damage the economy.

One question some people ask is, can't a government that has trouble borrowing just print money to pay its bills? Yes, it can, but this leads to another problem: inflation. In fact, budget problems are the main cause of very severe inflation. Governments do not want to find themselves in a position where the choice is between defaulting on their debts and inflating those debts away.

Concerns about the long-run effects of deficits need not rule out the use of fiscal policy to stimulate the economy when it is depressed. However, these concerns do mean that governments should try to offset budget deficits in bad years with budget surpluses in good years. In other words, governments should run a budget that is approximately balanced over time. Have they actually done so?

## Deficits and Debt in Practice

Figure 17-11 shows how the U.S. federal government's budget deficit and its debt have evolved since 1939. Panel (a) shows the federal deficit as a percentage of GDP. As you can see, the federal government ran huge deficits during World War II. It briefly ran surpluses after the war, but it has normally run deficits ever since, especially after 1980. This seems inconsistent with the advice that governments should offset deficits in bad times with surpluses in good times.

The **debt–GDP ratio** is government debt as a percentage of GDP.

However, panel (b) shows that these deficits have not led to runaway debt. To assess the ability of governments to pay their debt, we often use the **debt–GDP ratio,** government debt as a percentage of GDP. We use this measure, rather than simply looking at the size of the debt, because GDP, which measures the size of the economy as a whole, is a good indicator of the potential taxes the government can collect. If the government's debt grows more slowly than GDP, the burden of paying that debt is actually falling compared with the government's potential tax revenue.

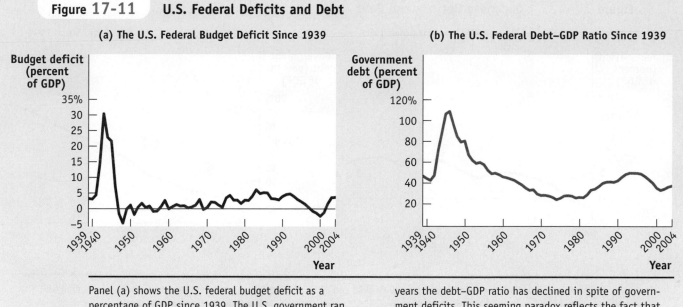

**Figure 17-11     U.S. Federal Deficits and Debt**

**(a) The U.S. Federal Budget Deficit Since 1939**

**(b) The U.S. Federal Debt–GDP Ratio Since 1939**

Panel (a) shows the U.S. federal budget deficit as a percentage of GDP since 1939. The U.S. government ran huge deficits during World War II and has usually run smaller deficits ever since. Panel (b) shows the U.S. debt–GDP ratio. Comparing panels (a) and (b), you can see that in many years the debt–GDP ratio has declined in spite of government deficits. This seeming paradox reflects the fact that the debt–GDP ratio can fall, even when debt is rising, as long as GDP grows faster than debt.

*Source:* Economic Report of the President (2005).

What we see from panel (b) is that although the federal debt has grown in almost every year, the debt–GDP ratio fell for 30 years after the end of World War II. This shows that the debt–GDP ratio can fall, even when debt is rising, as long as GDP grows faster than debt. For Inquiring Minds below, which focuses on the large debt the U.S. government ran up during World War II, explains how growth and inflation sometimes allow a government that runs persistent budget deficits to nevertheless have a declining debt–GDP ratio.

Still, a government that runs persistent *large* deficits will have a rising debt–GDP ratio when debt grows faster than GDP. Panel (a) of Figure 17-12 on page 446 shows Japan's budget deficit as a percentage of GDP and panel (b) shows Japan's debt–GDP ratio, both since 1991. As we have already mentioned, Japan began running large

## FOR INQUIRING MINDS

### WHAT HAPPENED TO THE DEBT FROM WORLD WAR II?

As you can see from Figure 17-11, the U.S. government paid for World War II by borrowing on a huge scale. By the war's end, the public debt was more than 100% of GDP, and many people worried about how it could ever be paid off.

The truth is that it never was paid off. In 1946 public debt was $270 billion; that number dipped slightly in the next few years, as the United States ran postwar budget surpluses, but the government budget went back into deficit in 1950 with the start of the Korean War. By 1956 the debt was back up to $270 billion.

But by that time nobody was worried about the fiscal health of the U.S. government because the debt–GDP ratio had fallen almost by half. The reason? Vigorous economic growth, plus mild inflation, had led to a rapid rise in GDP. The experience was a clear lesson in the peculiar fact that modern governments can run deficits forever, as long as they aren't too large.

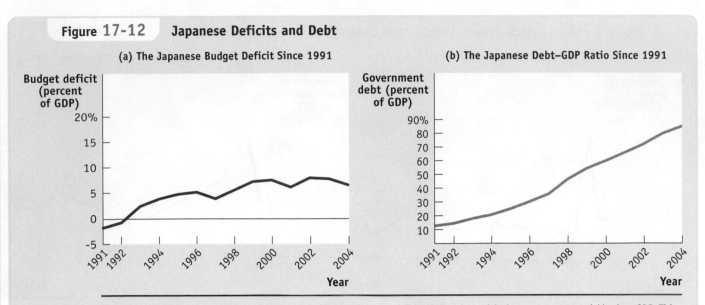

**Figure 17-12    Japanese Deficits and Debt**

(a) The Japanese Budget Deficit Since 1991

(b) The Japanese Debt–GDP Ratio Since 1991

Panel (a) shows the budget deficit of Japan since 1991 and panel (b) shows its debt–GDP ratio, both expressed as percentages of GDP. The large deficits that the Japanese government began running in the early 1990s have led to a rapid rise in its debt–GDP ratio as debt has grown more quickly than GDP. This has led some analysts to express concern about the long-run fiscal health of the Japanese economy.

*Source:* OECD.

deficits in the early 1990s, a by-product of its effort to prop up aggregate demand with government spending. This has led to a rapid rise in the debt–GDP ratio. For this reason, some economic analysts have begun to express concern about the long-run fiscal health of the Japanese government.

## Implicit Liabilities

Looking at Figure 17-11, you might be tempted to conclude that the U.S. federal budget is in fairly decent shape: the return to budget deficits after 2001 caused the debt–GDP ratio to rise a bit, but that ratio is still low compared with both historical experience and some other wealthy countries. In fact, however, experts on long-run budget issues view the situation of the United States (and other countries such as Japan and Italy) with alarm. The reason is the problem of *implicit liabilities*. **Implicit liabilities** are spending promises made by governments that are effectively a debt despite the fact that they are not included in the usual debt statistics.

The largest implicit liabilities of the U.S. government arise from two transfer programs that principally benefit older Americans: Social Security and Medicare. The third-largest implicit liability, Medicaid, benefits low-income families. In each of these cases the government has promised to provide transfer payments to future as well as current beneficiaries. So these programs represent a future debt that must be honored, even though the debt does not currently show up in the usual statistics. Together, these three programs currently account for about 40% of federal spending.

The implicit liabilities created by these transfer programs worry fiscal experts. Figure 17-13 shows why. It shows current spending on Social Security, and on Medicare and Medicaid as percentages of GDP, together with Congressional Budget Office projections of spending in 2010, 2030, and 2050. According to these projections, spending on Social Security will rise substantially over the next few decades and spending on the two health care programs will soar. Why?

In the case of Social Security, the answer is demography. Social Security is a "pay-as-you-go" system: current workers pay payroll taxes that fund the benefits of current retirees. So demography—specifically, the ratio of the number of workers paying into

**Implicit liabilities** are spending promises made by governments that are effectively a debt despite the fact that they are not included in the usual debt statistics.

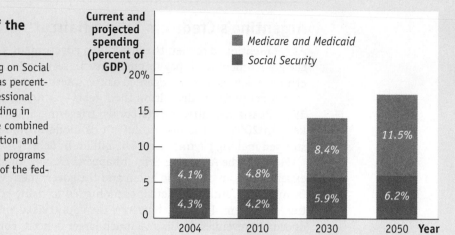

### Figure 17-13

**The Implicit Liabilities of the U.S. Government**

This figure shows current spending on Social Security, Medicare, and Medicaid as percentages of GDP, together with Congressional Budget Office projections of spending in 2010, 2030, and 2050. Due to the combined effects of the aging of the population and rising health care spending, these programs represent large implicit liabilities of the federal government.

*Source:* Congressional Budget Office.

Social Security to the number of retirees drawing benefits—is an important measure for managing Social Security's finances. There was a huge surge in the U.S. birth rate between 1946 and 1964, the years of the baby boom. Baby boomers are currently of working age—which means they are paying taxes, not collecting benefits. As the baby boomers retire, they will stop earning income that is taxed and start collecting benefits. As a result, the ratio of retirees receiving benefits to workers paying into the Social Security system will rise. In 2004 there were 30 retirees receiving benefits for every 100 workers paying into the system. By 2030, according to the Social Security Administration, that number will rise to 46; by 2050 it will rise to 50. This will raise benefit payments relative to the size of the economy.

The aging of the baby boomers, by itself, poses only a moderately sized long-run fiscal problem. The projected rise in Medicare and Medicaid spending is a much more serious concern. The main story behind projections of higher Medicare and Medicaid spending is the long-run tendency of health care spending to rise faster than overall spending, both for government-funded and for privately funded health care.

To some extent, the implicit liabilities of the U.S. government are already reflected in debt statistics. We mentioned earlier that the government had a total debt of $7.4 trillion at the end of 2004, but that only $4.3 trillion of that total was owed to the public. The main explanation for that discrepancy is that both Social Security and part of Medicare (the hospital insurance program) are supported by *dedicated taxes:* their expenses are paid out of special taxes on wages. At times, these dedicated taxes yield more revenue than is needed to pay current benefits. In particular, since the mid-1980s the Social Security system has been taking in more revenue than it currently needs in order to prepare for the retirement of the baby boomers. This surplus in the Social Security system has been used to accumulate a Social Security *trust fund,* which was $1.7 trillion at the end of 2004.

The $1.7 trillion in the trust fund is held in the form of U.S. government bonds, which are included in the $7.4 trillion in total debt. You could say that there's something funny about counting bonds in the Social Security trust fund as part of government debt. After all, they're owed by one part of the government (the government outside the Social Security system) to another part of the government (the Social Security system itself). But the debt corresponds to a real, if implicit, liability: promises by the government to pay future retirement benefits. So many economists argue that the gross debt of $7.4 trillion, the sum of public debt and government debt held by Social Security and other trust funds, is a more accurate indication of the government's fiscal health than the smaller amount owed to the public alone.

# *economics in action*

## Argentina's Creditors Take a Haircut

As we mentioned earlier, the idea that a government's debt can reach a level at which the government can't pay its creditors can seem far-fetched. In the United States, government debt is usually regarded as the safest asset there is.

But countries *do* default on their debts—fail to repay the money they borrowed. In 1998 Russia defaulted on its bonds, triggering a worldwide panic in financial markets. In 2001, in the biggest default of modern times, the government of Argentina stopped making payments on $81 billion in debt.

How did the Argentine default happen? During much of the 1990s, the country was experiencing an economic boom and the government was easily able to borrow money from abroad. Although deficit spending led to rising government debt, few considered this a problem. In 1998, however, the country slid into an economic slump that reduced tax revenues, leading to much larger deficits. Foreign lenders, increasingly nervous about the country's ability to repay, became unwilling to lend money except at very high interest rates. By 2001 the country was in a vicious circle: to cover its deficits and pay off old loans as they came due, it was forced to borrow at much higher interest rates, and the escalating interest rates on new borrowing made the deficits even bigger.

Argentine officials tried to reassure lenders by raising taxes and cutting government spending. But they were never able to balance the budget due to the continuing recession and the negative multiplier impact of their contractionary fiscal policies. These strongly contractionary fiscal policies drove the country deeper into recession. Late in 2001, facing popular protests, the Argentine government collapsed, and the country defaulted on its debt.

Creditors can take individuals who fail to pay debts to court. The court, in turn, can seize the debtors' assets and force them to pay part of future earnings to their creditors. But when a country defaults, it's different. Its creditors can't send in the police to seize the country's assets. They must negotiate a deal with the country for partial repayment. The only leverage creditors have in these negotiations is the defaulting government's fear that if it fails to reach a settlement, its reputation will suffer and it will be unable to borrow in the future. (A report by Reuters, the news agency, on Argentina's debt negotiations was headlined "Argentina to unhappy bondholders: so sue.")

It took three years for Argentina to reach an agreement with its creditors because the new Argentine government was determined to strike a hard bargain. And it did. Here's how Reuters described the settlement reached in March 2005: "The deal, which exchanged new paper valued at around 32 cents for every dollar in default, was the biggest 'haircut,' or loss on principal, for investors of any sovereign bond restructuring in modern times." Let's put this into English: Argentina forced its creditors to trade their "sovereign bonds"—debts of a sovereign nation, that is, Argentina—for new bonds worth only 32% as much. Such a reduction in the value of debt is known as a "haircut."

It's important to avoid two misconceptions about this "haircut." First, you might be tempted to think that because Argentina ended up paying only a fraction of the sums it owed, it paid little price for default. In fact, Argentina's default accompanied one of the worst economic slumps of modern times, a period of mass unemployment, soaring poverty, and widespread unrest. Second, it's tempting to dismiss the Argentine story as being of little relevance to countries like the United States. After all, aren't we more responsible than that? But Argentina wouldn't have been able to borrow so much in the first place if its government hadn't been well regarded by international lenders. In fact, as late as 1998 Argentina was widely admired for its economic management. What Argentina's slide into default shows is that concerns about the long-run effects of budget deficits are not at all academic. Due to its large and growing debt–GDP ratio, one recession pushed Argentina over the edge into economic collapse. ■

< < < < < < < < < < < < < < < < < < <

---

**>> QUICK REVIEW**

- Persistent budget deficits lead to increases in *public debt*.
- Rising public debt can lead to government default. In less extreme cases, it can *crowd out* investment spending, reducing long-run growth. This suggests that budget deficits in bad *fiscal years* should be offset with budget surpluses in good fiscal years.
- A widely used indicator of fiscal health is the *debt–GDP ratio*. A country with rising GDP can have a stable debt–GDP ratio even if it runs budget deficits if GDP is growing faster than the debt.
- In addition to their official debt, modern governments have *implicit liabilities*. The U.S. government has large implicit liabilities in the form of Social Security, Medicare, and Medicaid.

## >>CHECK YOUR UNDERSTANDING 17-4

1. Explain how each of the following events would affect the public debt or implicit liabilities of the U.S. government, other things equal. Would the public debt or implicit liabilities be greater or smaller?
   a. An increase in real GDP
   b. Retirees live longer
   c. A decrease in tax revenue
   d. Government borrowing to pay interest on its current public debt

*Solutions appear at back of book.*

### • A LOOK AHEAD •

Fiscal policy isn't the only way governments can stimulate aggregate demand when the economy is slumping or reduce aggregate demand when it is too high. In fact, although most economists believe that automatic stabilizers play a useful role, many are skeptical about the usefulness of discretionary fiscal policy due to the time lags in its formulation and implementation.

But there's an important alternative: monetary policy. In the next chapter we'll learn about monetary institutions and see how monetary policy works.

## SUMMARY

1. The government plays a large role in the economy, collecting a large share of GDP in taxes and spending a large share both to purchase goods and services and to make transfer payments, largely for **social insurance.** *Fiscal policy* is the use of taxes, government transfers, or government purchases of goods and services to shift the aggregate demand curve. But many economists caution that a very active fiscal policy may in fact make the economy less stable due to time lags in policy formulation and implementation.

2. Government purchases of goods and services directly affect aggregate demand, and changes in taxes and government transfers affect aggregate demand indirectly by changing households' disposable income. **Expansionary fiscal policies** shift the aggregate demand curve rightward, while **contractionary fiscal policies** shift the aggregate demand curve leftward.

3. Fiscal policy has a multiplier effect on the economy. Expansionary fiscal policy leads to an increase in real GDP larger than the initial rise in aggregate spending caused by the policy. Conversely, contractionary fiscal policy leads to a fall in real GDP larger than the initial reduction in aggregate spending caused by the policy. The size of the shift of the aggregate demand curve depends on the type of fiscal policy. The multiplier on changes in government purchases, $1/(1 - MPC)$, is larger than the multiplier on changes in **lump-sum taxes** or transfers, $MPC/(1 - MPC)$, because part of any change in taxes or transfers is absorbed by savings in the first round of spending. So changes in government purchases have a more powerful effect on the economy than equal-size changes in lump-sum taxes or transfers.

4. With **proportional taxes,** the government's tax revenue changes when real GDP changes. Proportional taxes and some transfers act as **automatic stabilizers,** reducing the size of the multiplier and automatically reducing the size of fluctuations in the business cycle. In contrast, **discretionary fiscal policy** arises from deliberate actions by policy makers rather than from the business cycle.

5. Some of the fluctuations in the **budget balance** are due to the effects of the business cycle. An increase in real GDP increases taxes and reduces transfers, making **budget deficits** smaller and **budget surpluses** larger. In order to separate the effects of the business cycle from the effects of discretionary fiscal policy, governments estimate the **cyclically adjusted budget balance,** an estimate of the budget balance if the economy were at potential output.

6. U.S. government budget accounting is calculated on the basis of **fiscal years.** Persistent budget deficits have long-run consequences because they lead to an increase in **public debt.** This can be a problem for two reasons. Public debt may **crowd out** investment spending, which reduces long-run economic growth. And in extreme cases, rising debt may lead to government default, resulting in economic and financial turmoil.

7. A widely used measure of fiscal health is the **debt–GDP ratio.** This number can remain stable or fall even in the face of moderate budget deficits if GDP rises over time. However, a stable debt–GDP ratio may give a misleading impression that all is well because modern governments often have large **implicit liabilities.** The largest implicit liabilities of the U.S. government come from Social Security, Medicare, and Medicaid, the costs of which are increasing due to the aging of the population and rising medical costs.

## KEY TERMS

Social insurance, p. 429
Expansionary fiscal policy, p. 430
Contractionary fiscal policy, p. 432
Lump-sum tax, p. 435
Proportional tax, p. 436
Automatic stabilizers, p. 436

Discretionary fiscal policy, p. 437
Budget balance, p. 438
Budget surplus, p. 438
Budget deficit, p. 438
Cyclically adjusted budget balance, p. 440
Fiscal years, p. 443

Public debt, p. 443
Crowding out, p. 444
Debt–GDP ratio, p. 444
Implicit liabilities, p. 446

## PROBLEMS

1. The accompanying diagram shows the current macroeconomic situation for the economy of Albernia. You have been hired as an economic consultant to help the economy move to potential output, $Y_P$.

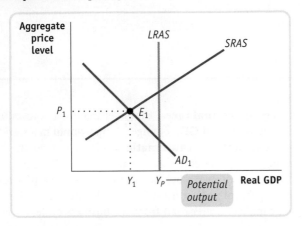

a. Is Albernia facing a recessionary or inflationary gap?

b. Which type of fiscal policy—expansionary or contractionary—would move the economy of Albernia to potential output, $Y_E$? What are some examples of such policies?

c. Illustrate the macroeconomic situation in Albernia with a diagram after the successful fiscal policy has been implemented.

2. The accompanying diagram shows the current macroeconomic situation for the economy of Brittania; real GDP is $Y_1$ and the aggregate price level is $P_1$. You have been hired as an economic consultant to help the economy move to potential output, $Y_P$.

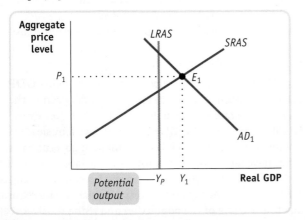

a. Is Brittania facing a recessionary or inflationary gap?

b. Which type of fiscal policy—expansionary or contractionary—would move the economy of Brittania to potential output, $Y_P$? What are some examples of such policies?

c. Illustrate the macroeconomic situation in Brittania with a diagram after the successful fiscal policy has been implemented.

3. An economy is in long-run macroeconomic equilibrium when each of the following aggregate demand shocks occurs. What kind of gap—inflationary or recessionary—will the economy face after the shock, and what type of fiscal policies would help move the economy back to potential output?

a. A stock market boom increases the value of stocks held by households.

b. Firms come to believe that a recession in the near future is likely.

c. Anticipating the possibility of war, the government increases its purchases of military equipment.

d. Interest rates increase.

4. Show why a $10 billion decrease in government purchases will have a larger effect on real GDP than a $10 billion reduction in government transfers by completing the table at the top of page 451 for an economy with a marginal propensity to consume (MPC) of 0.6. The first and second rows of the table are filled in for you: in the first row, the $10 billion decrease in government purchases decreases real GDP and disposable income, YD, by $10 billion, leading to a decrease in consumer spending of $6 billion (MPC × change in disposable income) in row 2. However, the $10 billion reduction in transfers has no effect on real GDP in round 1 but does lower YD by $10 billion, resulting in a decrease in consumer spending of $6 billion in round 2.

| Rounds | Decrease in *G* = −$10 billion Billions of dollars | | | Decrease in *TR* = −$10 billion Billions of dollars | | |
|---|---|---|---|---|---|---|
| | Change in *G* | Change in real GDP | Change in *YD* | Change in *TR* | Change in real GDP | Change in *YD* |
| 1 | Δ*G* = −$10.00 | −$10.00 | −$10.00 | Δ*TR* = −$10.00 | $0.00 | −$10.00 |
| 2 | Δ*C* = 6.00 | −6.00 | −6.00 | Δ*C* = −6.00 | −6.00 | −6.00 |
| 3 | Δ*C* = ? | ? | ? | Δ*C* = ? | ? | ? |
| 4 | Δ*C* = ? | ? | ? | Δ*C* = ? | ? | ? |
| 5 | Δ*C* = ? | ? | ? | Δ*C* = ? | ? | ? |
| 6 | Δ*C* = ? | ? | ? | Δ*C* = ? | ? | ? |
| 7 | Δ*C* = ? | ? | ? | Δ*C* = ? | ? | ? |
| 8 | Δ*C* = ? | ? | ? | Δ*C* = ? | ? | ? |
| 9 | Δ*C* = ? | ? | ? | Δ*C* = ? | ? | ? |
| 10 | Δ*C* = ? | ? | ? | Δ*C* = ? | ? | ? |

**a.** When government purchases decrease by $10 billion, what is the sum of the changes in real GDP after the 10 rounds?

**b.** When the government reduces government transfers by $10 billion, what is the sum of the changes in real GDP after the 10 rounds?

**c.** Using the formula for the multiplier for changes in government purchases and for changes in transfers, calculate the total change in real GDP due to the $10 billion decrease in government purchases and the $10 billion reduction in government transfers. What explains the difference?

**5.** In each of the following cases, either a recessionary or inflationary gap exists. Assume that the short-run aggregate supply curve is horizontal so that the change in real GDP arising from a shift of the aggregate demand curve equals the size of the shift of the curve. Calculate both the change in government purchases of goods and services and the change in government transfers necessary to close the gap.

**a.** Real GDP equals $100 billion, potential output equals $160 billion, and the marginal propensity to consume is 0.75.

**b.** Real GDP equals $250 billion, potential output equals $200 billion, and the marginal propensity to consume is 0.5.

**c.** Real GDP equals $180 billion, potential output equals $100 billion, and the marginal propensity to consume is 0.8.

**6.** Most macroeconomists believe it is a good thing that taxes act as automatic stabilizers and lower the size of the multiplier. However, a smaller multiplier means that the change in government purchases of goods and services, government transfers, or taxes necessary to close an inflationary or recessionary gap is larger. How can you explain this apparent inconsistency?

**7.** The accompanying table shows how consumers' marginal propensities to consume in a particular economy are related to their level of income:

| Income range | Marginal propensity to consume |
|---|---|
| $0–$20,000 | 0.9 |
| $20,001–$40,000 | 0.8 |
| $40,001–$60,000 | 0.7 |
| $60,001–$80,000 | 0.6 |
| Above $80,000 | 0.5 |

**a.** What is the "bang for the buck" in terms of the increase in real GDP for an additional $1 of income for consumers in each income range?

**b.** If the government needed to close a recessionary or inflationary gap, what types of fiscal policies would you recommend to close the gap with the smallest change in either government purchases of goods and services or taxes?

**8.** The government's budget surplus in Macroland has risen consistently over the past five years. Two government policy makers disagree as to why this has happened. One argues that a rising budget surplus indicates a growing economy; the other argues that it shows that the government is using contractionary fiscal policy. Can you determine which policy maker is correct? If not, why not?

**9.** Figure 17-9 shows the actual budget deficit and the cyclically adjusted budget deficit as a percentage of real GDP in the United States since 1970. Assuming that potential output was unchanged, use this figure to determine in which years since 1992 the government used discretionary expansionary fiscal policy and in which years it used discretionary contractionary fiscal policy.

**10.** You are an economic adviser to a candidate for national office. She asks you for a summary of the economic consequences of a balanced-budget rule for the federal government and for your recommendation on whether she should support such a rule. How do you respond?

11. In 2005, the policy makers of the economy of Eastlandia projected the debt–GDP ratio and the deficit–GDP ratio for the economy for the next 10 years under different scenarios for growth in the government's deficit. Real GDP is currently $1,000 billion per year and is expected to grow by 3% per year, the public debt is $300 billion at the beginning of the year, and the deficit is $30 billion in 2005.

| Year | Real GDP (billions of dollars) | Debt (billions of dollars) | Budget deficit (billions of dollars) | Debt (percent of real GDP) | Budget deficit (percent of real GDP) |
|---|---|---|---|---|---|
| 2005 | $1,000 | $300 | $30 | ? | ? |
| 2006 | 1,030 | ? | ? | ? | ? |
| 2007 | 1,061 | ? | ? | ? | ? |
| 2008 | 1,093 | ? | ? | ? | ? |
| 2009 | 1,126 | ? | ? | ? | ? |
| 2010 | 1,159 | ? | ? | ? | ? |
| 2011 | 1,194 | ? | ? | ? | ? |
| 2012 | 1,230 | ? | ? | ? | ? |
| 2013 | 1,267 | ? | ? | ? | ? |
| 2014 | 1,305 | ? | ? | ? | ? |
| 2015 | 1,344 | ? | ? | ? | ? |

a. Complete the accompanying table to show the debt–GDP ratio and the deficit–GDP ratio for the economy if the government's budget deficit remains constant at $30 billion over the next 10 years. (Remember that the government's debt will grow by the previous year's deficit.)

b. Redo the table to show the debt–GDP ratio and the deficit–GDP ratio for the economy if the government's budget deficit grows by 3% per year over the next 10 years.

c. Redo the table again to show the debt–GDP ratio and the deficit–GDP ratio for the economy if the government's budget deficit grows by 20% per year over the next 10 years.

d. What happens to the debt–GDP ratio and the deficit–GDP ratio for the economy over time under the three different scenarios?

12. Your study partner argues that the distinction between the government's budget deficit and debt is similar to the distinction between consumer savings and wealth. He also argues that if you have large budget deficits, you must have a large debt. In what ways is your study partner correct and in what ways is he incorrect?

13. In which of the following cases does the size of the government's debt and the size of the budget deficit indicate potential problems for the economy?

a. The government's debt is relatively low, but the government is running a large budget deficit as it builds a high-speed rail system to connect the major cities of the nation.

b. The government's debt is relatively high due to a recently ended deficit-financed war, but the government is now running only a small budget deficit.

c. The government's debt is relatively low, but the government is running a budget deficit to finance the interest payments on the debt.

14. How did or would the following affect the current public debt and implicit liabilities of the U.S. government?

a. In 2003, Congress passed and President Bush signed the Medicare Modernization Act, which provides seniors and individuals with disabilities with a prescription drug benefit. Some of the benefits under this law took effect immediately, but others will not begin until sometime in the future.

b. The age at which retired persons can receive full Social Security benefits is raised to age 70 for future retirees.

c. For future retirees, Social Security benefits are limited to those with low incomes.

d. Because the cost of health care is increasing faster than the overall inflation rate, annual increases in Social Security benefits are increased by the annual increase in health care costs rather than the overall inflation rate.

---

> **web...** To continue your study and review of concepts in this chapter, please visit the Krugman/Wells/Olney website for quizzes, animated graph tutorials, web links to helpful resources, and more.
> ### www.worthpublishers.com/krugmanwellsolney

# >>Money, the Federal Reserve System, and Monetary Policy

## EIGHT TIMES A YEAR

WHEN THE FOMC TALKS, PEOPLE listen.

Eight times a year, economists and investors around the world wait anxiously for word from the dozen men and women who make up the Federal Open Market Committee (FOMC) of the Federal Reserve. The FOMC controls the federal funds rate, the interest rate charged on reserves that banks lend each other to meet reserve requirements. What the world wants to know is the FOMC's decision—whether it has decided to increase the federal funds rate, reduce it, or leave it unchanged. Financial market analysts also carefully read the committee's accompanying statement and wait anxiously for the official minutes of the meeting, released three weeks later.

Why such a high degree of scrutiny? Because the statements of the FOMC, although usually written in jargon, offer clues to the future stance of monetary policy. A careful reading of FOMC statements, where seemingly minor changes in wording can be highly significant, can help predict whether monetary policy will be relatively expansionary (or loose), leading to a fall in interest rates, or relatively contractionary (or tight), leading to a rise in interest rates.

For example, the FOMC statement in December 2003 said, as it had after the past several meetings, that "policy accommodation can be maintained for a considerable period." The phrase "policy accommodation" means "keeping interest rates low." But in January 2004 these words were replaced with slightly different wording: "The Committee believes that it can be patient in removing its policy accommodation." The new wording suggested that the FOMC would soon begin raising the federal funds rate, and stocks and bonds plunged at this news.

## What you will learn in this chapter:

➤ The various roles **money** plays and the many forms it takes in the economy

➤ How the actions of private banks and the Federal Reserve determine the **money supply**

➤ How the Federal Reserve uses **open-market operations** to change interest rates

➤ How monetary policy affects aggregate output in the short run

The FOMC's decision about interest rates is anxiously watched by traders like these, and by investors around the world.

In this chapter we will learn about the structure of the Federal Reserve system and about how its open-market operations affect the money supply and interest rates.

Then we'll look at how monetary policy works—how actions by the FOMC can turn recession into expansion, and vice versa.

# The Meaning of Money

In everyday conversation, people often use the word *money* to mean "wealth." If you ask, "How much money does Bill Gates have?" the answer will be something like, "Oh, $40 billion or so, but who's counting?" That is, the number will include the value of the stocks, bonds, real estate, and other assets he owns.

But the economist's definition of money doesn't include all forms of **wealth.** The dollar bills in your wallet are money; other forms of wealth—such as cars, houses, and stock certificates—aren't money. What, according to economists, distinguishes money from other forms of wealth?

## What Is Money?

Money is defined in terms of what it does: **money** is any asset that can easily be used to purchase goods and services. An asset is **liquid** if it can easily be converted into cash. Money consists either of cash itself, which is liquid by definition, or of other assets that are highly liquid.

You can see the distinction between money and other assets by asking yourself how you pay for groceries. The person at the cash register will accept dollar bills in return for milk and frozen pizza—but not stock certificates or a collection of vintage baseball cards. If you want to convert stock certificates into groceries, you have to sell them—trade them for money—and then use the money to buy groceries.

Of course, many stores allow you to write a check on your bank account in payment for goods (or to pay with a debit card that is linked to your bank account). Does that make your bank account money, even if you haven't converted it into cash? Yes. **Currency in circulation**—actual cash in the hands of the public—is considered money. So are **checkable bank deposits**—bank accounts on which people can write checks.

Are currency and checkable bank deposits the only assets that are considered money? It depends. As we'll see later, there are several widely used definitions of the **money supply,** the total value of financial assets in the economy that are considered money. The narrowest definition is the most liquid because it contains only currency in circulation, traveler's checks, and checkable bank deposits. Broader definitions include other assets that are "almost" checkable, such as savings account deposits that can be transferred into a checking account with a phone call. All definitions of the money supply, however, make a distinction between assets that can easily be used to purchase goods and services, and those that can't.

Money plays a crucial role in generating *gains from trade,* because it makes indirect exchange possible. Think of what happens when a cardiac surgeon buys a new refrigerator. The surgeon has valuable services to offer—namely, heart operations. The owner of the store has valuable goods to offer: refrigerators and other appliances. It would be extremely difficult for both parties if, instead of using money, they had to directly barter the goods and services they sell. In a barter system, a cardiac surgeon and an appliance store owner could trade only if the store owner happened to want a heart operation *and* the surgeon happened to want a new refrigerator. This is known as the problem of finding a "double

---

A household's **wealth** is the value of its accumulated savings.

**Money** is any asset that can easily be used to purchase goods and services.

An asset is **liquid** if it can be quickly converted into cash without much loss of value.

**Currency in circulation** is cash held by the public.

**Checkable bank deposits** are bank accounts on which people can write checks.

The **money supply** is the total value of financial assets in the economy that are considered money.

---

## PITFALLS

### PLASTIC AND THE MONEY SUPPLY

In twenty-first-century America, many purchases are made with neither cash nor a check, but with cards. These cards come in two varieties. *Debit cards,* like bank ATM cards that can also be used at the supermarket, automatically transfer funds from the buyer's bank account. So debit cards allow you to access your bank account balance, which is part of the money supply.

But what about credit cards? *Credit cards* in effect allow you to borrow money to buy things at the store. Shouldn't these be counted as part of the money supply? The answer is no—the money supply is the value of *financial assets,* and credit cards are not assets. Credit cards access funds you can borrow—a liability, not an asset. Your credit card balance is what you currently owe. Your available credit is the maximum amount you can borrow. Since your credit card balance and your available credit are both liabilities, not assets, neither is part of the money supply.

Both debit and credit cards make it easier for individuals to make purchases. But they don't affect measures of the money supply.

coincidence of wants": in a barter system, two parties can trade only when each wants what the other has to offer. Money solves this problem: individuals can trade what they have to offer for money and trade money for what they want.

Because money makes it easier to achieve gains from trade, it increases welfare, even though it does not directly produce anything. As Adam Smith put it, money "may very properly be compared to a highway, which, while it circulates and carries to market all the grass and corn of the country, produces itself not a single pile of either."

Let's take a closer look at the roles money plays in the economy.

## Roles of Money

Money plays three main roles in any modern economy: it is a *medium of exchange,* a *store of value,* and a *unit of account.*

**Medium of Exchange**  Our cardiac surgeon–refrigerator example illustrates the role of money as a **medium of exchange**—an asset that individuals use to trade for goods and services rather than for consumption. People can't eat dollar bills; rather, they use dollar bills to trade for edible goods and their accompanying services.

> A **medium of exchange** is an asset that individuals acquire for the purpose of trading rather than for their own consumption.

In normal times, the official money of a given country—the dollar in the United States, the peso in Mexico, and so on—is also the medium of exchange in virtually all transactions in that country. During troubled economic times, however, other goods or assets often play that role. For example, during economic turmoil other countries' moneys frequently become the medium of exchange: U.S. dollars have played this role in Latin American countries, and euros have done so in Eastern Europe. In a famous example, cigarettes functioned as the medium of exchange in World War II prisoner-of-war camps. Even nonsmokers traded goods and services for cigarettes, because the cigarettes could in turn be easily traded for other items. During the extreme German inflation of 1923, goods such as eggs and lumps of coal became, briefly, mediums of exchange.

**Store of Value**  In order to act as a medium of exchange, money must also be a **store of value**—a means of holding purchasing power over time. To see why this is necessary, imagine trying to operate an economy in which ice-cream cones were the medium of exchange. Such an economy would quickly suffer from, well, monetary meltdown: your medium of exchange would often turn into a sticky puddle before you could use it to buy something else. Of course, money is by no means the only store of value. Any asset that holds its purchasing power over time is a store of value. So the store-of-value role is necessary but not distinctive.

> A **store of value** is a means of holding purchasing power over time.

**Unit of Account**  Finally, money normally serves as a **unit of account**—a measure individuals use to set prices and make economic calculations. A new CD costs about five times as much as a Big Mac, but Amazon.com lists the price of a CD as $14, not five Big Macs.

> A **unit of account** is a measure used to set prices and make economic calculations.

## Types of Money

In some form or another, money has been in use for thousands of years. For most of that period, people used **commodity money:** the medium of exchange was a good, normally gold or silver, that had other uses. These other uses gave commodity money value independent of its role as a medium of exchange. For example, cigarettes, which served as money in World War II POW camps, were also valuable because many prisoners smoked. Gold was valuable because it was used for jewelry and ornamentation, aside from the fact that it was minted into coins.

> **Commodity money** is a good used as a medium of exchange that has other uses.

In the United States during the 18th and first sixty years of the 19th centuries, most money consisted of paper notes rather than gold or silver coins. Unlike modern dollar bills, however, those notes were issued by private banks, which promised to exchange their notes for gold or silver coins on demand. That is, the paper currency was a **commodity-backed money,** a medium of exchange with no intrinsic value whose

> A **commodity-backed money** is a medium of exchange with no intrinsic value whose ultimate value is guaranteed by a promise that it can be converted into valuable goods.

ultimate value was guaranteed by a promise that it could always be converted into valuable goods.

The big advantage of commodity-backed money over gold and silver coins is that it ties up fewer valuable resources. A country in which gold and silver coins have been replaced by paper money can normally rely on the fact that on any given day holders of only a fraction of its paper notes will demand to have them converted into gold or silver coins. So the note-issuing bank needs to keep only a portion of the total value of its notes in circulation in the form of gold and silver in its vaults. It can lend out the remaining gold and silver to those who wish to use it. This allows society to use that gold and silver for other purposes, all with no loss in the ability to achieve gains from trade.

At this point you may ask, why make any use at all of gold and silver as a medium of exchange in the monetary system? In fact, today's monetary system goes even further. A U.S. dollar bill isn't commodity money, and it isn't even commodity-backed. Its value arises entirely from the fact that it is generally accepted as a means of payment, a role that is ultimately decreed by the U.S. government. Money whose value derives entirely from its official status as a means of exchange is known as **fiat money** because it exists by government *fiat*, a historical term for a policy declared by a ruler.

**Fiat money** is a medium of exchange whose value derives entirely from its official status as a means of payment.

## Measuring the Money Supply

The Federal Reserve (an institution we'll talk about shortly) calculates three **monetary aggregates,** overall measures of the money supply, which differ in how strictly money is defined. The three aggregates are known, rather cryptically, as M1, M2, and M3. M1, the narrowest definition, contains only currency in circulation (also known as cash), traveler's checks, and checkable bank deposits. M2 adds several other kinds of assets, often referred to as **near-moneys**—financial assets that aren't directly usable as a medium of exchange but can be readily converted into cash or checkable bank deposits, such as savings accounts. Examples are deposits that aren't checkable but can be withdrawn at any time with little or no penalty. Most monetary analyses focus on either M1 or M2. There is, however, a third aggregate, M3, which adds yet another group of somewhat more "distant" near-moneys—assets that are somewhat harder to convert into cash or checkable bank deposits, such as deposits that come with larger penalties for early withdrawal. M1 is therefore the most liquid measure of money because currency and checkable deposits are directly usable as a medium of exchange.

A **monetary aggregate** is an overall measure of the money supply.

**Near-moneys** are financial assets that can't be directly used as a medium of exchange but can be readily converted into cash or checkable bank deposits.

Figure 18-1 shows the makeup of M1 and M2 in June 2005, in billions of dollars. M1, valued at $1,368.4 billion, consisted roughly of half currency in circulation and

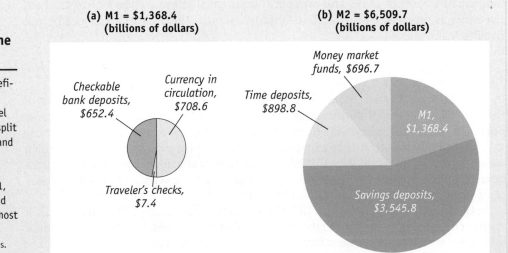

### Figure 18-1

**Monetary Aggregates, June 2005**

The Federal Reserve uses three definitions of the money supply: M1, M2, and M3 (not shown). As panel (a) shows, M1 is almost equally split between currency in circulation and checkable bank deposits. M2, as panel (b) shows, has a much broader definition: it includes M1, plus a range of other deposits and deposit-like assets, making it almost five times as large.

*Source:* Federal Reserve Bank of St. Louis.

(a) M1 = $1,368.4
(billions of dollars)

Checkable bank deposits, $652.4
Currency in circulation, $708.6
Traveler's checks, $7.4

(b) M2 = $6,509.7
(billions of dollars)

Money market funds, $696.7
Time deposits, $898.8
M1, $1,368.4
Savings deposits, $3,545.8

half checkable bank deposits, with a tiny slice of traveler's checks. In turn, M1 made up slightly less than 25% of M2, valued at $6,509.7 billion. The rest of M2 consisted of two types of bank deposits, known as savings deposits and time deposits, which both are considered noncheckable, plus money market funds, which are mutual funds that invest only in liquid assets and bear a close resemblance to bank deposits.

## *economics in action*

### The History of the Dollar

U.S. dollar bills are pure fiat money: they have no intrinsic value, and they are not backed by anything that does. But money in America wasn't always like that. In the early days of European settlement, the colonies that would become the United States used commodity money, consisting in part of gold and silver coins. But such coins were scarce on this side of the Atlantic, so the colonists relied on a variety of other forms of commodity money. For example, settlers in Virginia used tobacco as money and settlers in the Northeast used "wampum," a type of clamshell.

Later in American history, commodity-backed paper money came into widespread use. But this wasn't paper money as we now know it, issued by the government and bearing the signature of the Secretary of the Treasury. Before the Civil War, the U.S. government didn't issue paper money at all. Dollar bills were issued by private banks, which promised holders that these bills could be redeemed for silver coins on demand. These promises weren't always credible because sometimes banks failed. People were reluctant to accept currency from banks suspected of being in financial trouble. In other words, some dollars were less valuable than others.

Counting money 1870s style: Iroquois chiefs from the Six Nations Reserve read wampum belts.

Electric Studio/Library and Archives Canada

A curious legacy of that time was notes issued by the Citizens' Bank of Louisiana, based in New Orleans, that became among the most widely used bank notes in the southern states. These notes were printed in English on one side and French on the other. (At the time, many people in New Orleans, originally a colony of France, spoke French.) Thus, the $10 bill read *Ten* on one side and *Dix*, the French word for "ten," on the other. These $10 bills became known as "dixies," probably the source of the nickname of the U.S. South.

The U.S. government began issuing official paper money, called "greenbacks," during the Civil War. At first greenbacks had no fixed value in terms of commodities. After 1873 the U.S. government guaranteed the value of a dollar in terms of gold, effectively turning dollars into commodity-backed money.

In 1933, when President Franklin D. Roosevelt broke the link between dollars and gold, his own federal budget director declared ominously, "This will be the end of Western civilization." It wasn't. The link between the dollar and gold was restored a few years later, then dropped again—seemingly for good—in August 1971. Despite the warnings of doom, the U.S. dollar is still the world's most widely used currency. ■

< < < < < < < < < < < < < < < <

**>> CHECK YOUR UNDERSTANDING 18-1**

1. Suppose you hold a gift certificate, good for certain products at participating stores. Is this gift certificate money? Why or why not?

2. Although most bank accounts pay some interest, depositors can get a higher interest rate by buying a certificate of deposit, or CD. The difference between a CD and a checking account is that the depositor pays a penalty for withdrawing the money before the CD comes due—a period of months or even years. Small CDs are counted in M2, but not in M1. Explain why they are not part of M1.

Solutions appear at back of book.

# The Monetary Role of Banks

About half of M1, the narrowest definition of the money supply, consists of currency in circulation—$1 bills, $5 bills, and so on. It's obvious where currency comes from: it's printed by the U.S. Treasury. But the other half consists of bank deposits, and deposits account for the great bulk of M2 and M3, the broader definitions of the money supply. Bank deposits, then, are a major component of the money supply. And this fact brings us to our next topic: the monetary role of banks.

## What Banks Do

A **bank** is a **financial intermediary** that uses liquid assets in the form of **bank deposits** to finance the illiquid investments of borrowers. Banks can create liquidity because it isn't necessary for a bank to keep all of the funds deposited with it in the form of highly liquid assets. Except in the case of a *bank run*—which we'll get to shortly—all of a bank's depositors won't want to withdraw his or her funds at the same time. So a bank can provide its depositors with liquid assets yet still invest much of the depositors' funds in illiquid assets, such as mortgages and business loans.

Banks don't, however, lend out all the funds placed in their hands by depositors because they do have to satisfy any depositor who wants to withdraw his or her funds. In order to meet these demands, banks keep substantial quantities of liquid assets on hand. In the modern U.S. banking system, these assets take the form either of currency in the banks' vaults or deposits held in the bank's own account at the Federal Reserve. In this sense, the Federal Reserve acts as a bank's bank. Federal Reserve deposits can be converted into currency more or less instantly. The currency and Federal Reserve deposits held by banks are called **bank reserves.** Because bank reserves are held by banks and the Federal Reserve, and not by the public, they are not considered part of currency in circulation.

**Figure 18-2**

**Assets and Liabilities of First Street Bank**

A T-account summarizes a bank's financial position. The bank's assets, $900,000 in outstanding loans to borrowers and reserves of $100,000, are entered on the left side. Its liabilities, $1,000,000 in bank deposits held for depositors, are entered on the right side. **>web...**

| Assets | | Liabilities | |
|--------|--------|--------|--------|
| Loans | $900,000 | Deposits | $1,000,000 |
| Reserves | $100,000 | | |

To understand the basic role of banks in determining the money supply, let's consider a hypothetical example. Figure 18-2 shows the financial position of First Street Bank, which is the repository of $1 million in bank deposits. The bank's financial position is described by the *T-account,* a type of financial spreadsheet, as shown in the figure. On the left side are First Street's **assets**—claims on individuals and businesses, consisting of the value of its outstanding loans—and its reserves. On the right side are the bank's **liabilities**—claims held by individuals and firms against the bank, consisting of the value of bank deposits.

In this example, First Street Bank holds reserves equal to 10% of its bank deposits. The fraction of bank deposits that a bank holds as reserves is its **reserve ratio.** In the modern American system the Federal Reserve—which, among other things, regulates banks—sets a minimum required reserve ratio that banks are required to maintain. To understand why banks are regulated, we need to look at a problem banks can face: *bank runs.*

An **asset** is a claim that provides income in the future.

A **liability** is a requirement to pay in the future.

The **reserve ratio** is the fraction of bank deposits that a bank holds as reserves.

## The Problem of Bank Runs

Banks can lend out most of the funds deposited in their care because all depositors normally won't want to withdraw all their funds at the same time. But what would happen to a bank if, for some reason, all or at least a large fraction of its depositors *did* try to withdraw all their funds during a short period of time, such as a couple of days?

The answer is that the bank wouldn't have enough cash and reserves at the Federal Reserve to meet its depositors' demands for immediate cash withdrawals. The bank would have a hard time coming up with the cash, even if it had invested depositors' funds wisely, because bank loans are relatively illiquid. Bank loans can't easily be converted into cash on short notice. To see why, imagine that First Street Bank has lent $100,000 to Drive-A-Peach Used Cars, a local dealership. To raise cash, First Street can sell its loan to Drive-A-Peach to someone else—another bank or an individual investor. But if First Street tries to sell the loan quickly, potential buyers will be wary: they will suspect that First Street wants to sell the loan because there is something wrong and the loan might not be repaid. As a result, First Street Bank can sell the loan quickly only by offering it for sale at a deep discount, say a discount of 50%, or $50,000.

The upshot is that if First Street's depositors all suddenly decide to withdraw their funds, any effort to raise the necessary cash forces the bank to sell off its assets very cheaply. Inevitably, it will not be able to pay off its depositors in full.

What might start this whole process? That is, what might lead First Street's depositors to rush to pull their money out? A plausible answer is a spreading rumor that the bank is in financial trouble. Even if they aren't sure the rumor is true, depositors are likely to play it safe and get their money out while they still can. And it gets worse: a depositor who simply thinks that *other* depositors are going to panic and try to get their money out will realize that this could "break the bank." So he or she joins the rush. In other words, fear about a bank's financial condition can be a self-fulfilling prophecy: depositors who believe that other depositors will rush for the exit will rush for the exit themselves.

A **bank run** is a phenomenon in which many of a bank's depositors try to withdraw their funds due to fears of a bank failure. Moreover, bank runs aren't bad only for the bank in question and its depositors. Historically, they have often proved contagious, with a run on one bank leading to a loss of faith in other banks, causing additional bank runs. The Economics in Action on the following page describes just such a contagion, the wave of bank runs that swept the United States in the early 1930s. In response to that experience and similar experiences in other countries, the United States and most other modern governments have established a system of bank regulations that protect depositors and prevent bank runs.

A **bank run** is a phenomenon in which many of a bank's depositors try to withdraw their funds due to fears of a bank failure.

## Bank Regulation

Should you worry about losing money in the United States because of a bank run? No. After the banking crises of the 1930s, the United States and most other countries put into place a system designed to protect depositors and the economy as a whole against bank runs. This system has three main features: *deposit insurance, capital requirements,* and *reserve requirements*.

**Deposit Insurance** Almost all banks in the United States advertise themselves as a "member of the FDIC"—the Federal Deposit Insurance Corporation. It provides **deposit insurance,** a guarantee by the federal government that depositors will be paid even if the bank can't come up with the funds, up to a maximum amount per account. The FDIC currently guarantees the first $100,000 of each account.

**Deposit insurance** guarantees that a bank's depositors will be paid even if the bank can't come up with the funds, up to a maximum amount per account.

It's important to realize that deposit insurance doesn't just protect depositors if a bank actually fails. The insurance also eliminates the main reason for bank runs: since depositors know their funds are safe even if a bank fails, they have no incentive to rush to pull them out because of a rumor that the bank is in trouble.

> ## FOR INQUIRING MINDS
>
> ### IS BANKING A CON?
>
> Banks make it possible for any individual depositor to withdraw funds whenever he or she wants. Yet the cash in a bank's vault, and its deposits at the Federal Reserve, wouldn't be enough to satisfy all or even most depositors if they all tried to withdraw funds at the same time. Does this mean that there is something fundamentally dishonest about the banking business?
>
> Many people have thought so; every once in a while a prominent critic of the banking industry demands regulations that would stop banks from making illiquid loans. But an analogy may help explain what banks do and why it's productive.
>
> Think about car-rental agencies. Because of
>
> these agencies, someone who travels, say, from Atlanta to Cincinnati can normally count on having a car when he or she needs one. Yet there are many more potential travelers to Cincinnati than there are cars available to rent; the rent-a-car business depends on the fact that only a fraction of those potential visitors show up in any given week. There's no trickery involved. Travelers believe they can almost always get a car when needed, even though the number of cars actually available is limited— and they are right. Banks do the same thing. Depositors believe they can almost always get cash when they need it, even though the amount of cash actually available is limited— and they are right too.

**Capital Requirements** Deposit insurance, although it protects the banking system against bank runs, creates a well-known incentive problem. Because depositors are protected from loss, they have no incentive to monitor their bank's financial health. Meanwhile, the owners of banks have an incentive to engage in overly risky investment behavior, such as making risky loans at high interest. If all goes well, the owners profit; and if things go badly, the government covers the losses through federal deposit insurance.

To reduce the incentive for excessive risk taking, regulators require that the owners of banks hold substantially more assets than the value of bank deposits. That way, the bank will still have assets larger than its deposits even if some of its loans go bad, and losses will accrue against the bank owners' assets, not the government. The excess of a bank's assets over its bank deposits and other liabilities is called the bank's capital. In practice, banks' capital is equal to 7% or more of their assets.

**Reserve Requirements** Another way to reduce the risk of bank runs is to require banks to maintain a higher reserve ratio than they otherwise would. **Reserve requirements** are rules set by the Federal Reserve that determine a bank's minimum reserve ratio. For example, in the United States, the minimum reserve ratio for checkable bank deposits is 10%.

> **Reserve requirements** are rules set by the Federal Reserve that determine the minimum reserve ratio for a bank.

## How Banks Create Money

If banks didn't exist, the quantity of currency in circulation would equal the money supply. And since all U.S. currency in circulation—coins, $1 bills, $5 bills, and so on—is issued by the government, the money supply would be determined directly by whoever controls the minting and printing presses. But banks do exist, and they affect the money supply in two ways. First, they take some currency out of circulation: dollar bills that are sitting in bank vaults, as opposed to sitting in people's wallets, aren't considered part of the money supply. Second, and much more important, is that banks, by offering deposits, create money, allowing the money supply to be larger than the quantity of currency in circulation.

Suppose you deposit $1,000 in currency into a checkable account at your local bank. The bank is subject to a rule that sets a minimum required reserve ratio. Currently in the United States, banks are required to hold 10% of deposits in reserves. Banks can lend out any of their **excess reserves,** reserves over and above required reserves.

> **Excess reserves** are a bank's reserves over and above its required reserves.

So you deposit $1,000 in cash into your checkable bank account—your checking account. At this point, there is no change in the money supply since both currency in circulation (which has just dropped by $1,000) and checking account balances (which have just risen by $1,000) are counted in the money supply. The bank keeps $100, which is 10% of your deposit, in its reserve account and lends out the other $900 to another student in town. This loan can be made in cash, or by increasing the borrower's checking account balance by $900. Either way, the money supply has just increased by $900. So who creates money? Banks do. Banks create money by making loans with their excess reserves. What limits the amount of money banks can create? The required reserve ratio. And who monitors banks' reserve holdings? We'll address that question in the next section.

# *economics in action*

## It's a Wonderful Banking System

Next Christmas time, it's a sure thing that at least one TV station in your home town will show the 1946 film *It's a Wonderful Life,* featuring Jimmy Stewart as George Bailey, a small-town banker whose life is saved by an angel. The movie's

Diego Guidice/AP Photo

Argentina's economic crisis led to massive bank runs, angry public protests, and despair as many middle- and working-class families lost jobs and savings and were plunged into poverty.

climactic scene is a run on Bailey's bank, as fearful depositors rush to take their funds out.

When the movie was made, such scenes were still fresh in Americans' memories. There was a wave of bank runs in late 1930, a second wave in the spring of 1931, and a third wave in early 1933. By the end, more than a third of the nation's banks had failed. To bring the panic to an end, on March 6, 1933, the newly inaugurated president, Franklin Delano Roosevelt, declared a national "bank holiday," closing all banks for a week.

Since then, regulation has protected the United States and other wealthy countries against bank runs. In fact, the scene in *It's a Wonderful Life* was already out of date when the movie was made. But the last decade has seen several waves of bank runs in developing countries. For example, bank runs played a role in an economic crisis that swept Southeast Asia in 1997–1998 and in the severe economic crisis in Argentina, which began in late 2001. ∎

< < < < < < < < < < < < < < < < < < <

## >>QUICK REVIEW

> - Banks are *financial intermediaries* that hold *bank reserves* of currency plus deposits at the Federal Reserve. The *reserve ratio* is the ratio of reserves, a bank *asset*, to *bank deposits*, a bank *liability*.
> - *Bank runs* were a serious problem in the past, but in the contemporary United States, banks and their depositors are protected by *deposit insurance*, capital requirements, and *reserve requirements*.
> - Banks create money: when currency is deposited into a bank, the bank can lend *excess reserves* out, which leads to new deposits in the banking system and an increase in the money supply.

## >>CHECK YOUR UNDERSTANDING 18-2

1. Suppose you are a depositor at First Street Bank. You hear a rumor that the bank has suffered serious losses on its loans. Every depositor knows that the rumor isn't true, but each thinks that most other depositors believe the rumor. Why, in the absence of deposit insurance, could this lead to a bank run? Why does deposit insurance change the situation?

2. A con man has a great idea: he'll open a bank without investing any capital and lend all the deposits at high interest rates to real estate developers. If the real estate market booms, the loans will be repaid and he'll make high profits. If the real estate market goes bust, the loans won't be repaid and the bank will fail—but he will not lose any of his own wealth. How would modern bank regulation frustrate his scheme?

Solutions appear at back of book.

# The Federal Reserve System

Who's in charge of ensuring that banks maintain enough reserves? Who conducts monetary policy? The answer, in the United States, is an institution known as the Federal Reserve (or, informally, as the "Fed").

## The Fed: America's Central Bank

A **central bank** is an institution that oversees and regulates the banking system and conducts monetary policy.

The Federal Reserve is a **central bank**—an institution that oversees and regulates the banking system, and conducts monetary policy. Other central banks include the Bank of England, the Bank of Japan, and the European Central Bank, or ECB. The ECB acts as a common central bank for 12 European countries: Austria, Belgium, Finland, France, Germany, Greece, Ireland, Italy, Luxembourg, the Netherlands, Portugal, and Spain. The world's oldest central bank, by the way, is Sweden's Sveriges Rijksbank, which awards the Nobel Prize in economics.

The legal status of the Fed, which was created in 1913, is unusual: it is not exactly part of the U.S. government, but it is not really a private institution either. Strictly speaking, the Federal Reserve system consists of two parts: the Board of Governors and the 12 regional Federal Reserve Banks.

The Board of Governors, which oversees the system from its offices in Washington, D.C., is set up like a government agency: its seven members are appointed by the president and must be approved by the Senate. However, they are appointed for 14-year terms, to insulate them from political pressure. The chairman is appointed on a more frequent basis, every 4 years, but it's traditional for chairmen to be reappointed and serve much longer terms. William McChesney Martin was chairman of the Fed from 1951 until 1970. Alan Greenspan served for over 18 years, beginning in 1987. Ben Bernanke, formerly an economics professor at Princeton University, was appointed Fed chairman in January 2006.

The 12 Federal Reserve Banks each serve a region of the country, providing various banking and supervisory services. For example, they audit the books of private-sector banks, to ensure that they are financially sound. Each regional bank is run by a board of directors chosen from the local banking and business community. The Federal Reserve Bank of New York has a special role: it carries out *open-market operations*, the main tool of monetary policy. Figure 18-3 shows the Federal Reserve districts and the city in which each regional Federal Reserve Bank is located.

Decisions about monetary policy are made by the Federal Open Market Committee, which consists of the Board of Governors plus five of the regional bank presidents. The president of the Federal Reserve Bank of New York is always on the committee, and the other four seats rotate among the 11 other regional bank presidents. The chairman of the Board of Governors normally also serves as the chairman of the Open Market Committee.

The effect of this complex structure is to create an institution that is ultimately accountable to the voting public, because the Board of Governors is chosen by the president and confirmed by the Senate, all of whom are themselves elected officials. But the long terms served by board members, as well as the indirectness of the process by which they are appointed, largely insulate them from short-term political pressures.

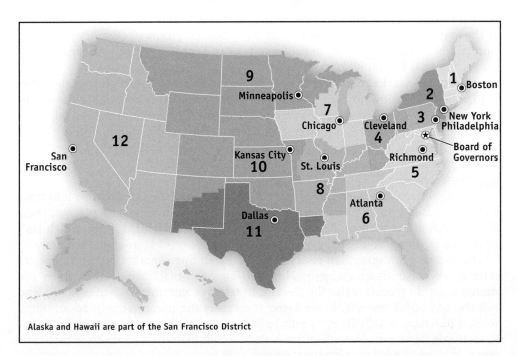

**Figure 18-3 The Federal Reserve System** The Federal Reserve system consists of the Board of Governors in Washington, D.C., plus regional Federal Reserve Banks, each serving its district. This map shows each of the 12 Federal Reserve districts. *Source:* Board of Governors of the Federal Reserve system.

## What the Fed Does: Reserve Requirements and the Discount Rate

The Fed has three main policy tools at its disposal: *reserve requirements, the discount rate,* and, most importantly, *open-market operations.*

In our discussion of bank runs, we noted that the Fed sets a minimum reserve ratio requirement, currently equal to 10% for checkable bank deposits. Banks that fail to maintain at least the required reserve ratio on average over a two-week period face penalties.

What does a bank do if it looks as if it has insufficient reserves to meet the Fed's reserve requirement? Normally, it borrows additional reserves from other banks. Banks lend money to each other in the **federal funds market,** a financial market that allows banks that fall short of the reserve requirement to borrow reserves—usually just overnight—from banks that hold excess reserves. The interest rate in this market is determined by supply and demand—but the supply and demand are both strongly affected by Federal Reserve actions. As we'll see momentarily, the **federal funds rate,** the interest rate determined in the federal funds market, plays a key role in modern monetary policy.

Alternatively, banks can borrow reserves from the Fed itself. The **discount rate** is the rate of interest the Fed charges on loans to banks. Currently, the discount rate is set 1 percentage point above the federal funds rate in order to discourage banks from turning to the Fed.

In practice, today's Fed doesn't use changes in either reserve requirements or the discount rate as an active policy tool. The last significant change in reserve requirements was in 1992. The discount rate, as we've noted, is set 1 percentage point above the federal funds rate. Monetary policy is, instead, conducted using the Fed's third policy tool: open-market operations.

> The **federal funds market** allows banks that fall short of the reserve requirement to borrow funds from banks with excess reserves.
>
> The **federal funds rate** is the interest rate determined in the federal funds market.
>
> The **discount rate** is the rate of interest the Fed charges on loans to banks.

## Open-Market Operations

Like the banks it oversees, the Federal Reserve has assets and liabilities. The Fed's assets consist of government debt it holds, mainly short-term U.S. government bonds with a maturity of less than one year, known as U.S. Treasury bills. Remember, the Fed isn't exactly part of the U.S. government, so those U.S. Treasury bills are a liability of the government but an asset of the Fed. Its liabilities consist of currency in circulation and bank reserves (either in bank vaults or in deposits that private banks maintain at regional Federal Reserve Banks).

In an **open-market operation** the Federal Reserve buys or sells some of the existing U.S. Treasury bills, normally through a transaction with *commercial banks*—banks that mainly make business loans, as opposed to home loans. When the Fed buys U.S. Treasury bills, it pays for them by crediting (increasing) the accounts of these banks with additional deposits, which increases the banks' reserves. When the Fed sells U.S. Treasury bills to commercial banks, it debits (decreases) the banks' accounts, reducing their reserves.

> An **open-market operation** is a purchase or sale of government debt by the Fed.

You might wonder where the Fed gets the funds to purchase U.S. Treasury bills from banks. The answer is that it simply creates them with a stroke of the pen (or, these days, a click of the mouse). Remember, the modern dollar is fiat money, which isn't backed by anything. So the Fed can create additional reserves at its own discretion.

The increase or decrease in reserves caused by an open-market operation doesn't directly affect the money supply. However, an open-market operation starts the money creation process. After the increase in reserves, commercial banks would lend out the additional reserves, immediately increasing the money supply. So an open-market purchase of U.S. Treasury bills leads to a rise in the money supply. An open-market sale has the reverse effect: bank reserves fall, requiring banks to reduce their loans, leading to a fall in the money supply.

The Federal Open Market Committee, as its name suggests, sets policy on open-market operations—that is, it gives instructions to the New York Fed to buy or sell U.S. Treasury bills. When the Fed buys Treasury bills, interest rates fall. When the Fed sells Treasury bills, interest rates rise. Interest rates fall when the Fed buys Treasury bills because the Fed has increased bank reserves, which allows banks to make more loans. This increase in funds available to lend—an increase in the supply of loanable funds—lowers the price of loans. And the price of a loan is just the interest rate.

So two things happen when the FOMC directs the New York Fed to buy Treasury bills: the money supply rises and interest rates fall. And two things happen when the Fed sells Treasury bills: the money supply falls and interest rates rise. The fact that both things happen—the change in the money supply and the change in interest rates—means that the FOMC can focus its policy efforts on either the money supply or the interest rate. Changing one will change the other. So what does the Fed focus on? We'll address that question in the next section.

## *economics in action*

### Building Europe's Fed

Until the last year of the twentieth century, the Federal Reserve was a giant among central banks. Because the U.S. economy was far larger than any other nation's, no other nation's central bank was remotely comparable in influence. But that all changed in January 1999, when 11 European nations adopted the euro as their common currency, placing their joint monetary policy in the hands of the new European Central Bank, generally referred to as the ECB.

Like the Fed, the ECB has a special status: it's not a private institution, but it's not exactly a government agency either. In fact, it can't be a government agency, because there is no pan-European government! Luckily for puzzled Americans, there are strong analogies between European central banking and the Federal Reserve system.

First of all, the ECB, which is located in the German city of Frankfurt, isn't really the counterpart of the whole Federal Reserve system: it's the equivalent of the Board of Governors in Washington. The European counterparts of regional Federal Reserve Banks are Europe's national central banks: the Bank of France, the Bank of Italy, and so on. Until 1999, each of these national banks was the equivalent of the Fed. For example, the Bank of France controlled the French monetary base. Today these national banks, like regional Feds, provide various financial services to local banks and businesses, and actually carry out open-market operations. That doesn't mean that they are small institutions: together, the national central banks employ more than 50,000 people, while the ECB employs fewer than 1,300.

Each country gets to choose who runs its own central bank. The ECB is run by an executive board that is the counterpart of the Fed's Board of Governors; its members are chosen by unanimous consent of the governments of countries that use the euro. The counterpart of the Federal Open Market Committee is the ECB's Governing Board. Just as the Fed's Open Market Committee consists of the Board of Governors plus a rotating group of regional Fed presidents, the ECB's Governing Board consists of the executive board plus a rotating group of national central bank heads. But there's a special twist: the frequency with which any country's central bank gets a seat at the table is determined by a formula that reflects the size of the country's economy. In other words, Germany, which had a GDP of $2.7 trillion in 2004, gets a seat on the board a lot more often than Greece, which had a GDP of only $205 billion.

In the end, the details probably don't matter much. Like the Fed, the ECB is ultimately answerable to voters but is highly insulated from short-term political pressures. ■

> > > > > > > > > > > > > > > > > > > > > > >

# Monetary Policy and Aggregate Demand

In Chapter 17 we saw how fiscal policy can be used to stabilize the economy. Now we will see how monetary policy—changes in the money supply or the interest rate, or both—can play the same role.

## Expansionary and Contractionary Monetary Policy

As we have just seen, the Fed moves the interest rate down or up by increasing or decreasing the money supply. In practice, at each meeting the FOMC decides on the interest rate to prevail for the next six weeks, until its next meeting. The Fed sets a **target federal funds rate,** a desired level for the federal funds rate. The Open Market Desk of the Federal Reserve Bank of New York adjusts the money supply through the purchase and sale of Treasury bills until the actual federal funds rate equals the target rate.

Changes in the interest rate, in turn, change aggregate demand. Other things equal, a fall in the interest rate leads to a rise in investment and consumer spending and therefore a rise in aggregate demand. And, other things equal, a rise in the interest rate leads to a fall in investment and consumer spending and therefore a fall in aggregate demand. As a result, monetary policy, like fiscal policy, can be used to close either a recessionary gap or an inflationary gap.

Figure 18-4 shows the case of an economy facing a recessionary gap, where aggregate output is below potential output. *SRAS* is the short-run aggregate supply

The **target federal funds rate** is the Federal Reserve's desired federal funds rate.

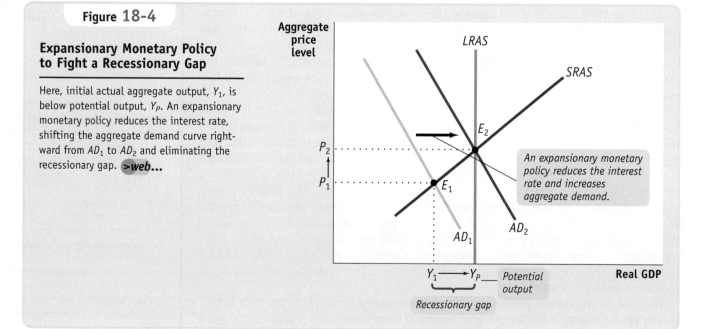

**Figure 18-4**

**Expansionary Monetary Policy to Fight a Recessionary Gap**

Here, initial actual aggregate output, $Y_1$, is below potential output, $Y_P$. An expansionary monetary policy reduces the interest rate, shifting the aggregate demand curve rightward from $AD_1$ to $AD_2$ and eliminating the recessionary gap. **>web...**

An expansionary monetary policy reduces the interest rate and increases aggregate demand.

curve, *LRAS* is the long-run aggregate supply curve, and $AD_1$ is the initial aggregate demand curve. At the initial short-run macroeconomic equilibrium, $E_1$, aggregate output is $Y_1$, below potential output, $Y_P$. Suppose the Fed would like to increase aggregate demand, shifting the aggregate demand curve rightward to $AD_2$. This would increase aggregate output to potential output. The Fed can accomplish that goal by decreasing interest rates and increasing the money supply. A lower interest rate leads to higher investment and consumer spending leading to a rise in aggregate demand. Monetary policy that increases aggregate demand is called **expansionary monetary policy.** Commentators often call an expansionary monetary policy a "loose" monetary policy because it is associated with a loosening of the money supply.

Figure 18-5 shows the opposite case—an economy facing an inflationary gap, where actual output is above potential output. *SRAS* is the short-run aggregate supply curve, *LRAS* is the long-run aggregate supply curve, and $AD_1$ is the initial aggregate demand curve. At the initial short-run macroeconomic equilibrium, aggregate output, $Y_1$, is above potential output, $Y_P$. As we've previously mentioned, policy makers often try to head off inflation by eliminating inflationary gaps. To eliminate the inflationary gap illustrated in Figure 18-5, aggregate demand must be reduced. By raising the interest rate, the Fed can cause a leftward shift of the aggregate demand curve, from $AD_1$ to $AD_2$, which reduces aggregate output to potential output. Monetary policy that reduces aggregate demand is called **contractionary monetary policy.** Commentators often refer to this as a "tight" monetary policy because it is associated with a restriction of the money supply.

Does monetary policy, like fiscal policy, have a multiplier effect on aggregate demand? Yes, although it's important to have a clear understanding of what is being multiplied.

*"I told you the Fed should have tightened."*

**Expansionary monetary policy** is monetary policy that increases aggregate demand.

**Contractionary monetary policy** is monetary policy that reduces aggregate demand.

---

### Figure 18-5

**Contractionary Monetary Policy to Fight an Inflationary Gap**

Here, initial actual aggregate output, $Y_1$, is above potential output, $Y_P$. A contractionary monetary policy raises the interest rate, shifting the aggregate demand curve leftward from $AD_1$ to $AD_2$ and eliminating the inflationary gap.

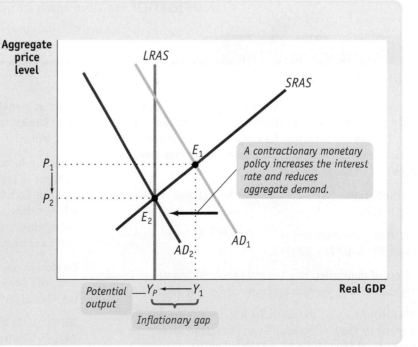

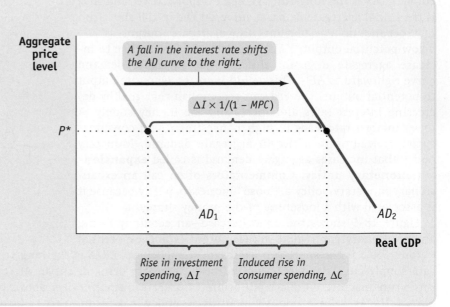

**Monetary Policy and the Multiplier**

An expansionary monetary policy drives down the interest rate, leading to an initial rise in investment spending, $\Delta I$. This raises disposable income, which causes a rise in consumer spending, which further raises disposable income, and so on. In the end, the $AD$ curve shifts rightward by a *multiple* of the initial rise in $I$.

## Monetary Policy and the Multiplier

Suppose the Fed drives down the interest rate, causing a rightward shift of the aggregate demand curve. How expansionary is this? That is, how much does the $AD$ curve shift to the right? We'll use the multiplier analysis of Chapter 16 to answer that question. In particular, we'll analyze how monetary policy, via a change in the interest rate, affects aggregate demand. (For the purposes of this analysis, we'll ignore the effect of taxes or foreign trade on the multiplier and hold the aggregate price level constant.)

Figure 18-6 shows the aggregate demand curve shifted to the right due to a fall in the interest rate. As you can see, the quantity of aggregate output demanded at any given aggregate price level increases. To calculate how much the quantity of aggregate output demanded increases, we need to know how much a fall in the interest rate increases real GDP at a given aggregate price level, such as $P^*$.

### WORK IT OUT

### MONETARY POLICY

Suppose the Fed has a goal of increasing aggregate demand by $500 billion per year. The marginal propensity to consume is 0.5. The Fed estimates that for every ¼ percentage point (25 basis points) decrease in interest rates, investment spending rises by $50 billion per year.

**Multiplier:** How big is the multiplier for a change in investment spending?

SOLUTION: The multiplier is $1 / (1 - MPC)$. So in this case, the multiplier is $1 / (1 - 0.5) = 2$.

**Effect of multiplier:** How big of a change in investment spending is needed to increase aggregate demand by $500 billion?

SOLUTION: Because the multiplier is 2, to increase aggregate demand by $500 billion requires an increase in investment spending of $500 billion / 2 = $250 billion.

**Effect of monetary policy:** By how much will the Fed need to lower interest rates in order to increase aggregate demand by $500 billion?

SOLUTION: To increase aggregate demand by $500 billion with a multiplier of 2 requires an increase of $250 billion in investment spending. Each $50 billion increase in investment spending requires a ¼ percentage point drop in interest rates. So the Fed needs to decrease interest rates by $5 \times$ ¼ = 1.25 percentage points in order to raise investment spending by $5 \times$ $50 billion = $250 billion.

**Conduct of monetary policy:** Does the FOMC direct the New York Fed's Open Market Desk to sell U.S. Treasury bills or buy U.S. Treasury bills? Will the money supply increase or decrease?

SOLUTION: To lower interest rates, the Fed needs to buy U.S. Treasury bills from banks. When the Fed buys U.S. Treasury bills, banks have more reserves and the money supply increases.

Assume that the initial aggregate demand curve is $AD_1$, and that the decline in the interest rate increases investment spending at the aggregate price level $P^*$ by an amount $\Delta I$. This is an example of an autonomous rise in aggregate spending, a phenomenon we studied in Chapter 16. From this point on, the analysis is exactly the same as that of any autonomous change in aggregate spending. The initial increase in real GDP translates into an increase in disposable income. This causes a rise in consumer spending, $C$, and a second-round rise in real GDP. This second-round increase in real GDP leads to yet another rise in consumer spending, and so on. At each round, however, the increase in real GDP is smaller than in the previous round, because some of the increase in disposable income "leaks out" into savings due to the fact that the marginal propensity to save, $MPS$, is positive. In the end, the $AD$ curve shifts to a new position such as $AD_2$.

So a fall in the interest rate, $r$, leads to a rise in investment spending, $\Delta I$. This rise in investment spending leads, in turn, to a rightward shift of the $AD$ curve that reflects both the increase in investment spending, $\Delta I$, and an induced rise in consumer spending, $\Delta C$. As we saw in Chapter 16, the total rise in real GDP, assuming a fixed aggregate price level and no taxes or foreign trade, is a multiple of the initial rise in investment spending:

$$(18\text{-}6) \quad \Delta Y = \Delta I \times \frac{1}{1 - MPC}$$

where $MPC$ is the marginal propensity to consume—the increase in consumer spending if disposable income rises by $1.

## economics in action

### The Fed and the Output Gap, 1985–2004

In Figures 18-4 and 18-5 we showed how monetary policy can play a useful role: expansionary monetary policy can close recessionary gaps, and contractionary monetary policy can close inflationary gaps. A look back at U.S. monetary policy between 1985 and 2004 shows that the Federal Reserve did indeed tend to cut interest rates when the economy had a recessionary gap and raise interest rates when the economy had an inflationary gap.

The vertical axis on the left of Figure 18-7 shows the federal funds rate; the line labeled "federal funds rate" shows the average yearly value of that rate between 1985

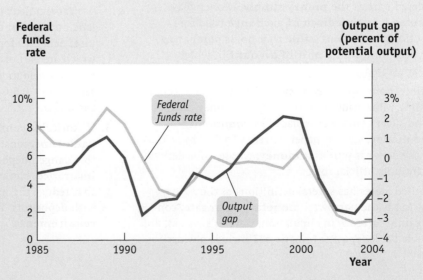

**Figure 18-7**

**Federal Reserve Policy and the Business Cycle**

The left vertical axis measures the federal funds rate. The right vertical axis measures the output gap, calculated as the difference between actual and potential output as a percentage of potential output. Over the past 20 years, the Fed has pursued a contractionary monetary policy when the economy was operating above potential output—that is, raising the federal funds rate when there was an inflationary gap. It has pursued an expansionary monetary policy when the economy was operating below potential output—that is, reducing the federal funds rate when there was a recessionary gap.

and 2004. The vertical axis on the right shows the Congressional Budget Office estimate of the output gap, measured as a percentage of potential output. This number is positive when there is an inflationary gap, as in 1999 and 2000, and negative when there is a recessionary gap, as in 2001 through 2004.

As you can see, there's a positive association between the federal funds rate and the output gap: the Fed tended to raise interest rates when aggregate output was moving above potential output and to reduce them when aggregate output was moving below potential output. In other words, the Fed was following pretty much the policy illustrated in Figures 18-4 and 18-5.

The two lines aren't perfectly synchronized. As you can see, the Fed did not raise interest rates in 1998 and 1999, even though the economy had developed a substantial inflationary gap. The main reason was that the Federal Reserve wasn't sure at the time that there was an output gap. Some economists believe that the Fed *should* have raised rates during that period.

The important lesson, however, is that over the past two decades the Fed's actual policy has largely followed our basic analysis of how monetary policy should work. ∎

< < < < < < < < < < < < < < < < < <

**▶▶CHECK YOUR UNDERSTANDING 18-4**

1. Suppose the economy is currently suffering from a recessionary gap and the Federal Reserve uses an expansionary monetary policy to close that gap. Describe the short-run effect of this policy on the following:
   a. The interest rate
   b. Investment spending
   c. Consumer spending
   d. Aggregate output
   e. The aggregate price level

*Solutions appear at back of book.*

## SUMMARY

1. **Money** is the most **liquid** way in which individuals hold their **wealth.** Money is any asset that can easily be used to purchase goods and services. **Currency in circulation** and **checkable bank deposits** are both considered part of the **money supply.** Money plays three roles: it is a **medium of exchange** used for transactions, a **store of value** that holds purchasing power over time, and a **unit of account** in which prices are stated.

2. Over time, **commodity money,** which consists of goods possessing value aside from their role as money, such as gold and silver coins, was replaced by **commodity-backed money,** such as paper currency backed by gold. Today the dollar is pure **fiat money,** whose value derives solely from its official role.

3. The United States has several definitions of the money supply. M1 is the narrowest **monetary aggregate,** containing only currency in circulation, traveler's checks, and checkable bank deposits. M2 and M3 include a wider

range of assets called **near-moneys,** mainly other forms of bank deposits, that can easily be converted into checkable bank deposits.

4. **Banks,** one type of **financial intermediary,** allow depositors immediate access to their funds, but they also lend out most of the funds deposited in their care. To meet demands for cash, they maintain **bank reserves,** which are part of the bank's **assets,** composed of both currency held in vaults and deposits at the Federal Reserve. Bank deposits are a bank's **liabilities.** The **reserve ratio** is the ratio of bank reserves to bank deposits.

5. Historically, banks have sometimes been subject to **bank runs,** most notably in the early 1930s. To avert this danger, depositors are now protected by **deposit insurance,** bank owners face capital requirements that reduce the incentive to make overly risky loans with depositors' funds, and banks must satisfy **reserve requirements.**

6. When currency is deposited in a bank, it starts a process in which banks lend out **excess reserves,** leading to an increase in the money supply—so banks create money.

7. The Federal Reserve is the **central bank** of the United States. The Federal Reserve system combines some aspects of a government agency with some aspects of a private institution. The Fed sets reserve requirements. To meet those requirements, banks borrow and lend reserves in the **federal funds market** at the **federal funds rate.** Banks can also borrow from the Fed at the **discount rate.**

8. **Open-market operations** by the Fed are the principal tool of monetary policy: the Fed can increase the money supply and decrease interest rates by buying U.S. Treasury bills from banks. The Fed can decrease the money supply and increase interest rates by selling U.S. Treasury bills to banks.

9. In practice, the Fed uses open-market operations to achieve a **target federal funds rate. Expansionary monetary policy,** which reduces the interest rate and increases aggregate demand while increasing the money supply, is used to close recessionary gaps. **Contractionary monetary policy,** which increases the interest rate and reduces aggregate demand while decreasing the money supply, is used to close inflationary gaps.

10. Like fiscal policy, monetary policy has a multiplier effect, because changes in the interest rate lead to changes in consumer spending as well as investment spending. In the short run, a change in the interest rate results in a change in real GDP through the multiplier effect.

## KEY TERMS

Wealth, p. 454
Money, p. 454
Liquid, p. 454
Currency in circulation, p. 454
Checkable bank deposits, p. 454
Money supply, p. 454
Medium of exchange, p. 455
Store of value, p. 455
Unit of account, p. 455
Commodity money, p. 455
Commodity-backed money, p. 455

Fiat money, p. 456
Monetary aggregate, p. 456
Near-moneys, p. 456
Bank, p. 458
Financial intermediary, p. 458
Bank deposit, p. 458
Bank reserves, p. 458
Asset, p. 459
Liability, p. 459
Reserve ratio, p. 459
Bank run, p. 460

Deposit insurance, p. 460
Reserve requirements, p. 461
Excess reserves, p. 461
Central bank, p. 462
Federal funds market, p. 464
Federal funds rate, p. 464
Discount rate, p. 464
Open-market operation, p. 464
Target federal funds rate, p. 466
Expansionary monetary policy, p. 467
Contractionary monetary policy, p. 467

## PROBLEMS

1. For each of the following transactions, what is the effect (increase or decrease) on M1? On M2?

   a. You sell a few shares of stock and put the proceeds into your savings account.

   b. You sell a few shares of stock and put the proceeds into your checking account.

   c. You transfer money from your savings account to your checking account.

   d. You discover $0.25 under the floor mat in your car and deposit it in your checking account.

   e. You discover $0.25 under the floor mat in your car and deposit it in your savings account.

2. There are three types of money: commodity money, commodity-backed money, and fiat money. Which type of money is used in each of the following situations?

   a. Mother-of-pearl seashells were used to pay for goods in ancient China.

   b. Salt was used in many European countries as a medium of exchange.

   c. For a brief time, Germany used paper money (the "Rye Mark") that could be redeemed for a certain amount of grain rye.

   d. The town of Ithaca, New York, prints its own currency, the Ithaca HOURS, which can be used to purchase local goods and services.

| Year | Currency in circulation | Traveler's checks | Checkable bank deposits | Money market funds | Time deposits smaller than $100,000 | Savings deposits | M1 | M2 | Currency in circulation as a percentage of M1 | Currency in circulation as a percentage of M2 |
|------|------|------|------|------|------|------|------|------|------|------|
| 1995 | $372.1 | $9.1 | $745.9 | $448.8 | $931.4 | $1,134.0 | ? | ? | ? | ? |
| 1996 | 394.1 | 8.8 | 676.5 | 517.4 | 946.8 | 1,273.1 | ? | ? | ? | ? |
| 1997 | 424.6 | 8.5 | 639.5 | 592.2 | 967.9 | 1,399.1 | ? | ? | ? | ? |
| 1998 | 459.9 | 8.5 | 627.7 | 732.7 | 951.5 | 1,603.6 | ? | ? | ? | ? |
| 1999 | 517.7 | 8.6 | 597.7 | 832.5 | 954.0 | 1,738.2 | ? | ? | ? | ? |
| 2000 | 531.6 | 8.3 | 548.1 | 924.2 | 1,044.2 | 1,876.2 | ? | ? | ? | ? |
| 2001 | 582.0 | 8.0 | 589.3 | 987.2 | 972.8 | 2,308.9 | ? | ? | ? | ? |
| 2002 | 627.4 | 7.8 | 582.0 | 915.5 | 892.1 | 2,769.5 | ? | ? | ? | ? |
| 2003 | 663.9 | 7.7 | 621.8 | 801.1 | 809.4 | 3,158.5 | ? | ? | ? | ? |
| 2004 | 699.3 | 7.6 | 656.2 | 714.7 | 814.0 | 3,505.9 | ? | ? | ? | ? |

3. The table above shows the components of M1 and M2 in billions of dollars for the month of December in the years 1995 to 2004 as published in the *2005 Economic Report of the President*. Complete the table by calculating M1, M2, currency in circulation as a percentage of M1, and currency in circulation as a percentage of M2. What trends or patterns about M1, M2, currency in circulation as a percentage of M1, and currency in circulation as a percentage of M2 do you see? What might account for these trends?

4. Indicate whether each of the following is part of M1, M2, or neither:
   a. $95 on your campus meal card
   b. $0.55 in the change cup of your car
   c. $1,663 in your savings account
   d. $459 in your checking account
   e. 100 shares of stock worth $4,000
   f. A $1,000 line of credit on your Sears credit card

5. The government of Eastlandia uses measures of monetary aggregates similar to those used by the United States, and the central bank of Eastlandia imposes a required reserve ratio of 10%. Given the following information, answer the questions below.

   Bank deposits at the central bank = $200 million
   Currency held by public = $150 million
   Currency in bank vaults = $100 million
   Checkable bank deposits = $500 million
   Traveler's checks = $10 million

   a. What is M1?
   b. Are the commercial banks holding excess reserves?
   c. Can the commercial banks increase checkable bank deposits?

6. Using Figure 18-3, find the Federal Reserve district in which you live. Go to http://www.federalreserve.gov/bios/pres.htm and identify the president of that Federal Reserve Bank. Go to http://www.federalreserve.gov/fomc/and determine if the president of the Fed is currently a voting member of the Federal Open Market Committee (FOMC).

7. Go to the FOMC page of the Federal Reserve Board's website (http://www.federalreserve.gov/FOMC/) to find the statement issued after the most recent FOMC meeting. (Go to the bottom of the web page and click on the most recent statement listed in the calendar.)
   a. What is the target federal funds rate?
   b. Is the target federal funds rate different from the target federal funds rate from the previous FOMC statement? If yes, by how much does it differ?
   c. Does the statement comment on macroeconomic conditions in the United States? How does it describe the U.S. economy?

8. An economy is facing the recessionary gap shown in the accompanying diagram. To eliminate the gap, should the central bank use expansionary or contractionary monetary policy? How will the interest rate, investment spending, consumer spending, real GDP, and the aggregate price level change as the monetary policy closes the recessionary gap?

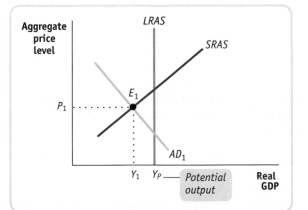

9. An economy is facing the inflationary gap shown in the accompanying diagram. To eliminate the gap, should the central bank use expansionary or contractionary monetary policy? How will the interest rate, investment spending, consumer spending, real GDP, and aggregate price level change as the monetary policy closes the inflationary gap?

10. During the Great Depression, businesspeople in the United States were very pessimistic about the future of economic growth and reluctant to increase investment spending even when interest rates fell. How did this limit the potential for monetary policy to help alleviate the Depression?

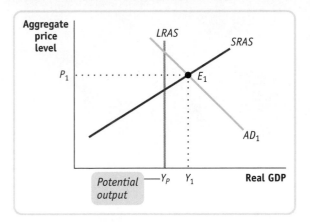

>**web**... To continue your study and review of concepts in this chapter, please visit the Krugman/Wells/Olney website for quizzes, animated graph tutorials, web links to helpful resources, and more.

**www.worthpublishers.com/krugmanwellsolney**

# >> Solutions to "Check Your Understanding" Questions

This section offers suggested answers to the "Check Your Understanding" questions found within chapters.

## Chapter One

### 1-1

1. **a.** This illustrates the concept of opportunity cost. Given that a person can only eat so much at one sitting, having an additional slice of chocolate cake requires that you forgo eating something else, such as a slice of the coconut cream pie.
   **b.** This illustrates the concept that resources are scarce. Even if there were more resources in the world, the total amount of those resources would be limited. As a result, scarcity would still arise. For there to be no scarcity, there would have to be unlimited amounts of everything (including unlimited time in a human life), which is clearly impossible.
   **c.** This illustrates the concept that people usually exploit opportunities to make themselves better off. Students will seek to make themselves better off by signing up for the tutorials of teaching assistants with good reputations and avoiding those teaching assistants with poor reputations. It also illustrates the concept that resources are scarce. If there were unlimited spaces in tutorials with good teaching assistants, they would not fill up.
   **d.** This illustrates the concept of marginal analysis. Your decision about allocating your time is a "how much" decision: how much time spent exercising versus how much time spent studying. You make your decision by comparing the benefit of an additional hour of exercising to its cost, the effect on your grades of one less hour spent studying.

2. **a.** Yes. The increased time spent commuting is a cost you will incur if you accept the new job. That additional time spent commuting—or equivalently, the benefit you would get from spending that time doing something else—is an opportunity cost of the new job.
   **b.** Yes. One of the benefits of the new job is that you will be making $50,000. But if you take the new job, you will have to give up your current job; that is, you have to give up your current salary of $45,000. So $45,000 is one of the opportunity costs of taking the new job.
   **c.** No. A more spacious office is an additional benefit of your new job and does not involve forgoing something else. So, it is not an opportunity cost.

### 1-2

1. **a.** This illustrates the concept that markets usually lead to efficiency. Any seller who wants to sell a book for at least $X does indeed sell to someone who is willing to buy a book for $X. As a result, there is no way to change how used textbooks are distributed among buyers and sellers in a way that would make one person better off without making someone else worse off.
   **b.** This illustrates the concept that there are gains from trade. Students trade tutoring services based on their different abilities in academic subjects.
   **c.** This illustrates the concept that when markets don't achieve efficiency, government intervention can improve society's welfare. In this case the market, left alone, will permit bars and nightclubs to impose costs on their neighbors in the form of loud music, costs that the bars and nightclubs have no incentive to take into account. This is an inefficient outcome because society as a whole can be made better off if bars and nightclubs are induced to reduce their noise.
   **d.** This illustrates the concept that resources should be used as efficiently as possible to achieve society's goals. By closing neighborhood clinics and shifting funds to the main hospital, better health care can be provided at a lower cost.
   **e.** This illustrates the concept that markets move toward equilibrium. Here, because books with the same amount of wear and tear sell for about the same price, no buyer or seller can be made better off by engaging in a different trade than he or she undertook. This means that the market for used textbooks has moved to an equilibrium.

2. **a.** This does not describe an equilibrium situation. Many students should want to change their behavior and switch to eating at the restaurants. Therefore, the situation described is not an equilibrium. An equilibrium will be established when students are equally as well off eating at the restaurants as eating at the dining hall—which would happen if, say, prices at the restaurants were higher than at the dining hall.
   **b.** This does describe an equilibrium situation. By changing your behavior and riding the bus, you would not be made better off. Therefore, you have no incentive to change your behavior.

## Chapter Two

### Check Your Understanding
### 2-1

1. **a.** False. An increase in the resources available to Tom for use in producing coconuts and fish changes his production possibility frontier by shifting it outward. This is because he can now produce more fish and coconuts than before. In the accompanying figure, the line labeled Tom's original *PPF* represents Tom's original production possibility frontier, and the line labeled Tom's new *PPF* represents the new production possibility frontier that results from an increase in resources available to Tom.

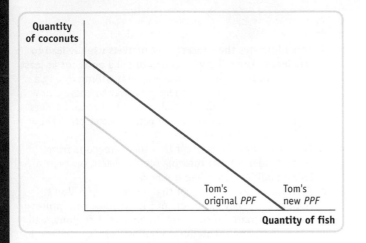

**b.** True. A technological change that allows Tom to catch more fish for any amount of coconuts gathered results in a change in his production possibility frontier. This is illustrated in the accompanying figure: the new production possibility frontier is represented by the line labeled Tom's new *PPF*, and the original production frontier is represented by the line labeled Tom's original *PPF*. Since the maximum quantity of coconuts that Tom can gather is the same as before, the new production possibility frontier intersects the vertical axis at the same point as the old frontier. But since the maximum possible quantity of fish is now greater than before, the new frontier intersects the horizontal axis to the right of the old frontier.

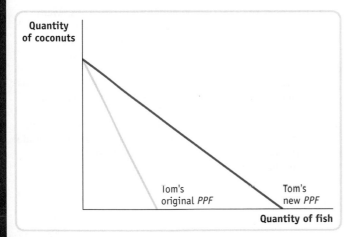

**c.** False. The production possibility frontier illustrates how much of one good an economy must give up to get more of another good only when resources are used efficiently. If an economy is producing inefficiently—that is, inside the frontier—then it does not have to give up a unit of one good in order to get another unit of the other good. Instead, by becoming more efficient, this economy can have more of both goods.

2. **a.** The United States has an absolute advantage in automobile production because it takes fewer Americans (6) to produce a car in one day than Italians (8). The United States also has an absolute advantage in washing machine production because it takes fewer Americans (2) to produce a washing machine in one day than Italians (3).

**b.** In Italy the opportunity cost of a washing machine in terms of an automobile is $\frac{3}{8}$: $\frac{3}{8}$ of a car can be produced with the same number of workers and in the same time it takes to produce 1 washing machine. In the United States the opportunity cost of a washing machine in terms of an automobile is $\frac{2}{6} = \frac{1}{3}$: $\frac{1}{3}$ of a car can be produced with the same number of workers and in the same time it takes to produce 1 washing machine. Since $\frac{1}{3} < \frac{3}{8}$, the United States has a comparative advantage in the production of washing machines: to produce a washing machine, only $\frac{1}{3}$ of a car must be given up in the United States but $\frac{3}{8}$ of a car must be given up in Italy. This means that Italy has a comparative advantage in automobiles. This can be checked as follows. The opportunity cost of an automobile in terms of a washing machine in Italy is $\frac{8}{3}$, equal to $2\frac{2}{3}$: $2\frac{2}{3}$ washing machines can be produced in the time it takes to produce 1 car in Italy. And the opportunity cost of an automobile in terms of a washing machine in the United States is $\frac{6}{2}$, equal to 3: 3 washing machines can be produced in the time it takes to produce 1 car in the United States.

**c.** The greatest gains are realized when each country specializes in producing the good for which it has a comparative advantage. Therefore the United States should specialize in washing machines and Italy should specialize in automobiles.

3. An increase in the amount of money spent by households results in an increase in the flow of goods to households. This, in turn, generates an increase in demand for factors of production by firms. Therefore there is an increase in the number of jobs in the economy.

### Check Your Understanding
### 2-2

1. **a.** This is a normative statement because it stipulates what should be done. In addition, it may have no "right" answer. That is, should people be prevented from all dangerous personal behavior if they enjoy that behavior—like skydiving? Your answer will depend on your point of view.

**b.** This is a positive statement because it is a description of fact.

2. **a.** True. Economists often have different value judgments about the desirability of a particular social goal. But despite those differences in value judgments, they will tend to agree that society, once it has decided to pursue a

given social goal, should adopt the most efficient policy to achieve that goal. Therefore economists are likely to agree on adopting policy choice B.

b. False. Disagreements between economists are more likely to arise because they base their conclusions on different models or because they have different value judgments about the desirability of the policy.

c. False. Deciding which goals a society should try to achieve is a matter of value judgments, not a question of economic analysis.

# Chapter Three

## Check Your Understanding

### 3-1

1. a. The quantity of umbrellas demanded is higher at any given price on a rainy day than on a dry day. This is a rightward *shift of* the demand curve, since at any given price the quantity demanded rises. This implies that any specific quantity can now be sold at a higher price.

b. The quantity of weekend calls demanded rises in response to a price reduction. This is a *movement along* the demand curve for weekend calls.

c. The demand for roses increases the week of Valentine's Day. This is a rightward *shift of* the demand curve.

d. The quantity of gasoline demanded falls in response to a rise in price. This is a *movement along* the demand curve.

## Check Your Understanding

### 3-2

1. a. The quantity of houses supplied rises as a result of an increase in prices. This is a *movement along* the supply curve.

b. The quantity of strawberries supplied is higher at any given price. This is a rightward *shift of* the supply curve.

c. The quantity of labor supplied is lower at any given wage. This is a leftward *shift of* the supply curve compared to the supply curve during the school vacation. So, in order to attract workers, fast-food chains have to offer higher wages.

d. The quantity of labor supplied rises in response to a rise in wages. This is a *movement along* the supply curve.

e. The quantity of cabins supplied is higher at any given price. This is a rightward *shift of* the supply curve.

## Check Your Understanding

### 3-3

1. a. The supply curve shifts rightward. At the original equilibrium price of the year before, the quantity of grapes supplied exceeds the quantity demanded. This is a case of surplus. The price of grapes will fall.

b. The demand curve shifts leftward. At the original equilibrium price, the quantity of hotel rooms supplied exceeds the quantity demanded. This is a case of surplus. The rates for hotel rooms will fall.

c. The demand curve for secondhand snowblowers shifts rightward. At the original equilibrium price, the quantity of secondhand snowblowers demanded exceeds the quantity supplied. This is a case of shortage. The equilibrium price of secondhand snowblowers will rise.

## Check Your Understanding

### 3-4

1. a. The market for large cars: this is a rightward shift in demand caused by a decrease in the price of a complement, gasoline. As a result of the shift, the equilibrium price of large cars will rise and the equilibrium quantity of large cars bought and sold will also rise.

b. The market for fresh paper made from recycled stock: this is a rightward shift in supply due to a technological innovation. As a result of this shift, the equilibrium price of fresh paper made from recycled stock will fall and the equilibrium quantity bought and sold will rise.

c. The market for movies at a local movie theater: this is a leftward shift in demand caused by a fall in the price of a substitute, pay-per-view movies. As a result of this shift, the equilibrium price of movie tickets will fall and the equilibrium number of people who go to the movies will also fall.

2. Upon the announcement of the new chip, the demand curve for computers using the earlier chip shifts leftward, as demand decreases, and the supply curve for these computers shifts rightward, as supply increases.

a. If demand decreases relatively more than supply increases, then the equilibrium quantity falls, as shown here:

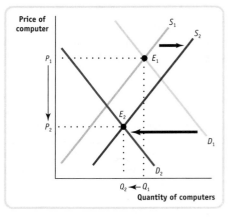

b. If supply increases relatively more than demand decreases, then the equilibrium quantity rises, as shown here:

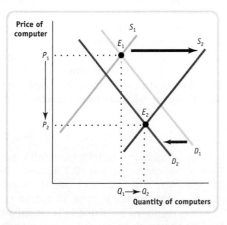

In both cases, the equilibrium price falls.

# Chapter Four

## Check Your Understanding

### 4-1

**1.** **a.** Fewer homeowners are willing to rent out their driveways because the price ceiling has caused a decrease in the payment they receive. This reflects the concept that the quantity supplied decreases as the price decreases. It is shown in the following diagram by the movement from point E to point A along the supply curve, a reduction in quantity of 400 parking spaces.

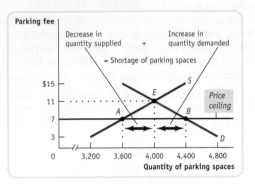

**b.** The quantity demanded increases by 400 spaces as the price decreases. At a lower price, more fans are willing to drive and rent a parking space. It is shown in the diagram by the movement from point E to point B along the demand curve.

**c.** Under a price ceiling, the quantity demanded exceeds the quantity supplied; as a result, shortages arise. In this case, there will be a shortage of 800 parking spaces. It is shown by the horizontal distance between points A and B.

**d.** Price ceilings result in wasted resources. The additional time fans spend to guarantee a parking space is wasted time.

**e.** Price ceilings lead to inefficient allocation of a good—here, the parking spaces—to consumers.

**f.** Price ceilings lead to black markets.

**2.** **a.** False. By lowering the price that producers receive, price ceilings lead to a decrease in the quantity supplied.

**b.** True. Price ceilings lead to a lower quantity supplied than in a free market. As a result, some people who would have been willing to pay the market price, and therefore would have gotten the good in a free market, are unable to obtain it when a price ceiling is imposed.

**c.** True. Those producers who still sell the product now receive less for it and are therefore worse off. Other producers will no longer find it worthwhile to sell the product at all and therefore will also be made worse off.

## Check Your Understanding

### 4-2

**1.** **a.** Some gas station owners will benefit from getting a higher price. Point A indicates the sales (0.7 million gallons) made by these owners. But some will lose; there are those who made sales at the market price of $2 but do not make sales at the regulated price of $4. These missed sales are indicated on the graph by the fall in the quantity demanded along the demand curve, from point E to point A. Overall, the effect on station owners is ambiguous.

**b.** Those who buy gas at the higher price of $4 probably will receive better service; this is an example of *inefficiently high quality* caused by a price floor as gas station owners compete on quality rather than price. But opponents are correct to claim that consumers are generally worse off—those who buy at $4 would have been happy to buy at $2, and many who were willing to buy at a price between $2 and $4 are now unwilling to buy. This is indicated on the graph by the fall in the quantity demanded along the demand curve, from point E to point A.

**c.** Proponents are wrong because consumers and some gas station owners are hurt by the price floor, which creates "missed opportunities"—desirable transactions between consumers and station owners that never take place. Moreover, the inefficiency of wasted resources arises as consumers spend time and money driving to other states. The price floor tempts people to engage in black market activity. With the price floor of $4, only 0.7 million gallons are sold. But at prices between $2 and $4, there are drivers who cumulatively want to buy more than 0.7 million gallons and owners who are willing to sell to them, a situation likely to lead to illegal activity.

## Check Your Understanding

### 4-3

**1.** **a.** The price of a ride is $7 since the quantity demanded at this price is 6 million: $7 is the *demand price* of 6 million rides. This is represented by point A in the following figure.

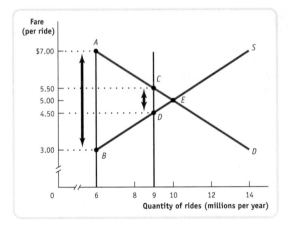

**b.** At 6 million rides, the supply price is $3, represented by point B in the figure. The wedge between the demand price of $7 and the supply price of $3 is the quota rent per ride, $4. This is represented in the figure above by the vertical distance between points A and B.

**c.** At 9 million rides, the demand price is $5.50, indicated by point C on the figure, and the supply price is $4.50, indicated by point D. The quota rent is the difference between the demand price and the supply price: $1.

**2.** The figure shows how a decrease in demand by 4 million rides, represented by a leftward shift of the demand curve from $D_1$ to $D_2$: at any given price, the quantity demanded falls by 4 million rides. This eliminates the effect of a quota limit of 8 million rides. At point $E_2$, the new market equilibrium, the equilibrium quantity is equal to the quota limit; as a result, the quota has no effect on the market.

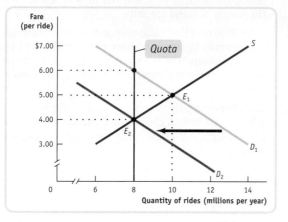

## Check Your Understanding

# 4-4

**1. a.** It doesn't matter who sends the money to the government. You can shift the demand curve, or the supply curve—your answer will be the same. But don't shift both! Either shift the demand curve down by the $1 tax as in panel (a), or shift the supply curve up by the $1 tax as in panel (b).

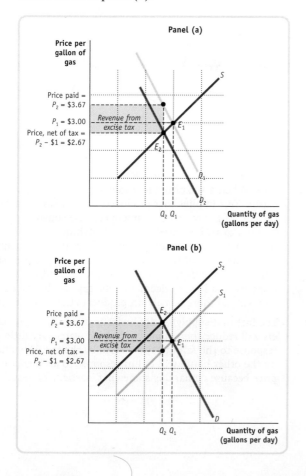

**b.** The new price paid by consumers is $3.67 per gallon. After the $1 excise tax is paid, the sellers receive $2.67 per gallon.

**c.** The buyers bear ⅔ of the burden of the $1 tax: the price they pay rises by ⅔ of the tax, 67 cents. The sellers bear ⅓ of the burden: the price they receive, net of the tax, falls by ⅓ of the tax, 33 cents.

# Chapter Five

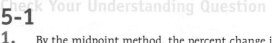

## Check Your Understanding Question

# 5-1

**1.** By the midpoint method, the percent change in the price of strawberries is

$$\frac{\$1.50 - \$1.00}{(\$1.50 + \$1.00)/2} \times 100 = \frac{\$0.50}{\$1.25} \times 100 = 40\%$$

Similarly, the percent change in the quantity of strawberries demanded is

$$\frac{200,000 - 100,000}{(100,000 + 200,000)/2} \times 100 = \frac{100,000}{150,000} \times 100 = 67\%$$

Therefore the price elasticity of demand using the midpoint method is $67\%/40\% = 1.7$.

**2.** By the midpoint method, the percent change in the quantity of movie tickets demanded in going from 4,000 tickets to 5,000 tickets is

$$\frac{5,000 - 4,000}{(4,000 + 5,000)/2} \times 100 = \frac{1,000}{4,500} \times 100 = 22\%$$

Since the price elasticity of demand is 1 at the current consumption level, it will take a 22% drop in the price of movie tickets to generate a 22% increase in quantity demanded.

**3.** Since price rises, we know that quantity demanded must fall. Given the current price of $0.50, a $0.05 increase in price represents a 10% change, using the method in Equation 5-2. This implies that

$$\frac{\% \text{ change in quantity demanded}}{10\%} = 1.2$$

so that the percent change in quantity demanded is 12%. A 12% decrease in quantity demanded represents 100,000 × 0.12, or 12,000 sandwiches.

## Check Your Understanding Question

# 5-2

**1. a.** Elastic demand. Consumers are highly responsive to changes in price. For a rise in price, the quantity effect (which tends to reduce total revenue) outweighs the price effect (which tends to increase total revenue). Overall, this leads to a fall in total revenue.

**b.** Unit-elastic demand. Here the revenue lost to the fall in price is exactly equal to the revenue gained from higher sales. The quantity effect exactly offsets the price effect.

**c.** Inelastic demand. Consumers are relatively unresponsive to changes in price. For consumers to purchase a given percent increase in output, the price must fall by an even greater percent. The price effect of a fall in price (which tends to reduce total revenue) outweighs the quantity effect (which tends to increase total revenue). As a result, total revenue decreases.

d. Inelastic demand. Consumers are relatively unresponsive to price, so a given percent fall in output is accompanied by an even greater percent rise in price. The price effect of a rise in price (which tends to increase total revenue) outweighs the quantity effect (which tends to reduce total revenue). As a result, total revenue increases.

2. a. Once bitten by a venomous snake, the victim's demand for an antidote is very likely to be perfectly inelastic because there is no substitute and it is necessary for survival. The demand curve will be vertical, at a quantity equal to the needed dose.

   b. Students' demand for green erasers is likely to be perfectly elastic because there are easily available substitutes: non-green erasers. The demand curve will be horizontal, at a price equal to that of nongreen erasers.

## Check Your Understanding Question 5-3

1. By the midpoint method, the percent increase in Chelsea's income is

$$\frac{\$18,000 - \$12,000}{(\$12,000 + \$18,000)/2} \times 100 = \frac{\$6,000}{\$15,000} \times 100 = 40\%$$

Similarly, the percent increase in her consumption of CDs is

$$\frac{40 - 10}{(10 + 40)/2} \times 100 = \frac{30}{25} \times 100 = 120\%$$

Chelsea's income elasticity of demand for CDs is therefore 120%/40% = 3.

2. Sanjay's consumption of expensive restaurant meals will fall more than 10% because a given percent change in income (10% here) induces a larger percent change in consumption of an income-elastic good.

3. The cross-price elasticity of demand is 5%/20% = 0.25. Since the cross-price elasticity of demand is positive, the two goods are substitutes.

## Check Your Understanding Question 5-4

1. By the midpoint method, the percent change in the number of hours of web-design services contracted is

$$\frac{500,000 - 300,000}{(300,000 + 500,000)/2} \times 100 = \frac{200,000}{400,000} \times 100 = 50\%$$

Similarly, the percent change in the price of web-design services is:

$$\frac{\$150 - \$100}{(\$100 + \$150)/2} \times 100 = \frac{\$50}{\$125} \times 100 = 40\%$$

The price elasticity of supply is 50%/40% = 1.25; hence supply is elastic.

2. True. An increase in demand raises price. If the price elasticity of supply of milk is low, then relatively little additional supply will be forthcoming as the price rises. As a result, the price of milk will rise substantially to satisfy the increased demand for milk. If the price elasticity

of supply is high, then a relatively large amount of additional supply will be produced as the price rises. As a result, the price of milk will rise only by a little to satisfy the higher demand for milk.

3. False. It is true that long-run price elasticities of supply are generally larger than short-run elasticities of supply. But this means that the short-run supply curves are generally steeper, not flatter, than the long-run supply curves.

4. True. When supply is perfectly elastic, the supply curve is a horizontal line. A change in demand therefore has no effect on price; it affects only the quantity bought and sold.

## Check Your Understanding Question 5-5

1. The fact that demand is very inelastic means that consumers will reduce their demand for textbooks very little in response to an increase in the price caused by the tax. The fact that supply is somewhat elastic means that suppliers will respond to the fall in the price by reducing supply. As a result, the incidence of the tax will fall heavily on consumers of economics textbooks and very little on publishers as shown in the accompanying figure.

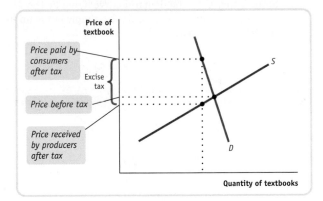

2. True. When a substitute is readily available, demand is elastic. This implies that producers cannot easily pass on the cost of the tax to consumers because consumers will respond to an increased price by switching to the substitute. Furthermore, when producers have difficulty adjusting the amount of the good produced, supply is inelastic. That is, producers cannot easily reduce output in response to a lower price net of the tax. So the tax burden will fall more heavily on producers than consumers.

3. The fact that supply is very inelastic means that producers will reduce their supply of bottled water very little in response to the fall in price caused by the tax. Demand, on the other hand, will fall in response to an increase in price because demand is somewhat elastic. As a result,

the incidence of the tax will fall heavily on producers of bottled spring water and very little on consumers as shown in the accompanying figure.

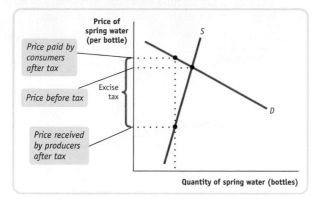

4. True. The lower the elasticity of supply, the more the burden of a tax will fall on producers rather than consumers, other things equal.

## Chapter Six

### Check Your Understanding 6-1

1. A consumer buys each pepper if the price is less than (or just equal to) the consumer's willingness to pay for that pepper. The demand schedule is constructed by asking how many peppers will be demanded at any price. The accompanying table illustrates the demand schedule.

| Price of pepper | Quantity of peppers demanded | Quantity of peppers demanded by Casey | Quantity of peppers demanded by Josie |
|---|---|---|---|
| $0.90 | 1 | 1 | 0 |
| 0.80 | 2 | 1 | 1 |
| 0.70 | 3 | 2 | 1 |
| 0.60 | 4 | 2 | 2 |
| 0.50 | 5 | 3 | 2 |
| 0.40 | 6 | 3 | 3 |
| 0.30 | 8 | 4 | 4 |
| 0.20 | 8 | 4 | 4 |
| 0.10 | 8 | 4 | 4 |
| 0.00 | 8 | 4 | 4 |

When the price is $0.40, Casey's consumer surplus from the first pepper is $0.50, from his second pepper $0.30, from his third pepper $0.10, and he does not buy any more peppers. Casey's individual consumer surplus is therefore $0.90. Josie's consumer surplus from her first pepper is $0.40, from her second pepper $0.20, from her third pepper $0.00 (she is just indifferent between buying it and not buying it, so let's assume she does buy it), and she does not buy any more peppers. Josie's individual consumer surplus is therefore $0.60. Total consumer surplus at a price of $0.40 is therefore $0.90 + $0.60 = $1.50.

### Check Your Understanding 6-2

1. A producer supplies each pepper if the price is greater than (or just equal to) the producer's cost of producing that pepper. The supply schedule is constructed by asking how many peppers will be supplied at any price. The accompanying table illustrates the supply schedule.

| Price of pepper | Quantity of peppers supplied | Quantity of peppers supplied by Cara | Quantity of peppers supplied by Jamie |
|---|---|---|---|
| $0.90 | 8 | 4 | 4 |
| 0.80 | 7 | 4 | 3 |
| 0.70 | 7 | 4 | 3 |
| 0.60 | 6 | 4 | 2 |
| 0.50 | 5 | 3 | 2 |
| 0.40 | 4 | 3 | 1 |
| 0.30 | 3 | 2 | 1 |
| 0.20 | 2 | 2 | 0 |
| 0.10 | 2 | 2 | 0 |
| 0.00 | 0 | 0 | 0 |

When the price is $0.70, Cara's producer surplus from the first pepper is $0.60, from her second pepper $0.60, from her third pepper $0.30, from her fourth pepper $0.10, and she does not supply any more peppers. Cara's individual producer surplus is therefore $1.60. Jamie's producer surplus from his first pepper is $0.40, from his second pepper $0.20, from his third pepper $0.00 (he is just indifferent between supplying it and not supplying it, so let's assume he does supply it), and he does not supply any more peppers. Jamie's individual producer surplus is therefore $0.60. Total producer surplus at a price of $0.70 is therefore $1.60 + $0.60 = $2.20.

### Check Your Understanding 6-3

1. The quantity demanded equals the quantity supplied at a price of $0.50, the equilibrium price. At that price, a total quantity of five peppers will be bought and sold. Casey will buy three peppers and receive consumer surplus of $0.40 on his first, $0.20 on his second, and $0.00 on his third pepper. Josie will buy two peppers and receive consumer surplus of $0.30 on her first and $0.10 on her second pepper. Total consumer surplus is therefore $1.00. Cara will supply three peppers and receive producer surplus of $0.40 on her first, $0.40 on her second, and $0.10 on her third pepper. Jamie will supply two peppers and receive producer surplus of $0.20 on his first and $0.00 on his second pepper. Total producer surplus is therefore $1.10. Total surplus in this market is therefore $1.00 + $1.10 = $2.10.

2. a. If Josie consumes one less pepper, she loses $0.60 (her willingness to pay for her second pepper); if Casey consumes one more pepper, he gains $0.30 (his willingness to pay for his fourth pepper). This results in an overall loss of consumer surplus of $0.60 − $0.30 = $0.30.

**b.** Cara's cost of the last pepper she supplied (the third pepper) is $0.40, and Jamie's cost of producing one more (his third pepper) is $0.70. Total producer surplus therefore falls by $0.70 – $0.40 = $0.30.

**c.** Josie's willingness to pay for her second pepper is $0.60; this is what she would lose if she were to consume one less pepper. And Cara's cost of producing her third pepper is $0.40; this is what she would save if she were to produce one less pepper. If we therefore reduced quantity by one pepper, we would lose $0.60 – $0.40 = $0.20 of total surplus.

## Check Your Understanding
### 6-4

**1. a.** At a price paid by consumers of $0.70, Casey's consumer surplus is $0.20 from his first pepper (he loses $0.20 compared to the market equilibrium), $0.00 from his second pepper (he loses $0.20), and he no longer buys the third pepper. Josie's consumer surplus is $0.10 from her first pepper (she loses $0.20), and she no longer buys the second pepper (she loses $0.10 of consumer surplus that she previously got from that second pepper). So the loss in consumer surplus is $0.70.

**b.** At a price received by producers of $0.30, Cara's producer surplus is $0.20 from her first pepper (she loses $0.20), $0.20 from her second pepper (she loses $0.20), and she no longer produces the third pepper (she loses $0.10 that she previously got from that third pepper). Jamie's producer surplus is $0.00 from his first pepper (he loses $0.20), and he no longer produces his second pepper. So the loss in producer surplus is $0.70.

**c.** Since three peppers are now sold and the tax on each is $0.40, the government tax revenue is 3 × $0.40 = $1.20.

**d.** Introduction of the tax resulted in a loss of total surplus of $0.70 + $0.70 = $1.40. Of that amount, $1.20 went to the government in the form of tax revenue. But $0.20 is lost: that is the amount of deadweight loss from this tax.

**2. a.** The demand for gasoline is inelastic because there is no close substitute for gasoline itself, and it is difficult for drivers to arrange substitutes for driving, such as taking public transportation. As a result, the deadweight loss from a tax on gasoline would be relatively small, as shown in the accompanying diagram.

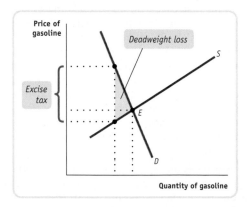

**b.** The demand for milk chocolate bars is elastic because there are close substitutes: dark chocolate bars, milk chocolate kisses, and so on. As a result, the deadweight loss from a tax on milk chocolate bars would be relatively large, as shown in the accompanying diagram.

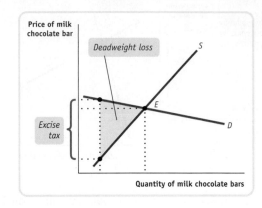

## Chapter Seven

## Check Your Understanding
### 7-1

**1. a.** The fixed input is the 10-ton machine, and the variable input is electricity.

**b.** As you can see from the declining numbers in the third column of the accompanying table, electricity does indeed exhibit diminishing returns: the marginal product of each additional kilowatt of electricity is less than that of the previous kilowatt.

| Quantity of electricity (kilowatts) | Quantity of ice (pounds) | Marginal product of electricity (pounds per kilowatt) |
|---|---|---|
| 0 | 0 | |
| | | 1,000 |
| 1 | 1,000 | |
| | | 800 |
| 2 | 1,800 | |
| | | 600 |
| 3 | 2,400 | |
| | | 400 |
| 4 | 2,800 | |

**c.** A 50% increase in the size of the fixed input means that Bernie now has a 15-ton machine. So the fixed input is now the 15-ton machine. Since it generates a 100% increase in output for any given amount of electricity, the quantity of output and marginal product are now as shown in the accompanying table.

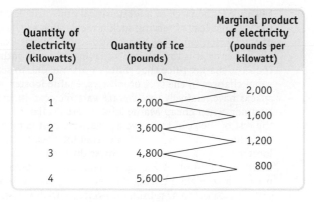

| Quantity of electricity (kilowatts) | Quantity of ice (pounds) | Marginal product of electricity (pounds per kilowatt) |
|---|---|---|
| 0 | 0 | |
| | | 2,000 |
| 1 | 2,000 | |
| | | 1,600 |
| 2 | 3,600 | |
| | | 1,200 |
| 3 | 4,800 | |
| | | 800 |
| 4 | 5,600 | |

**2.** **a.** Supplies are an explicit cost because they require an outlay of money.
   **b.** If the basement can be used in some other way that generates money, such as renting it to a student, then the implicit cost is that money forgone. Otherwise, the implicit cost is zero.
   **c.** Wages are an explicit cost.
   **d.** By using the van for their business, Karma and Don forgo the money they could have gained by selling it. So use of the van is an implicit cost.
   **e.** Karma's forgone wages from her job are an implicit cost.

## Check Your Understanding 7-2

**1.** **a.** As shown in the accompanying table, the marginal cost for each pie is found by multiplying the marginal cost of the previous pie by 1.5. Variable cost for each output level is found by summing the marginal cost for all the pies produced to reach that output level. So, for example, the variable cost of three pies is $1.00 + $1.50 + $2.25 = $4.75. Average fixed cost for Q pies is calculated as $9.00/Q since fixed cost is $9.00. Average variable cost for Q pies is equal to variable cost for the Q pies divided by Q; for example, the average variable cost of five pies is $13.19/5, or approximately $2.64. Finally, average total cost can be calculated in two equivalent ways: as TC/Q or as AVC + AFC.

| Quantity of pies | Marginal cost of pie | Variable cost | Average fixed cost of pie | Average variable cost of pie | Average total cost of pie |
|---|---|---|---|---|---|
| 0 | | $0.00 | — | — | — |
| | $1.00 | | | | |
| 1 | | 1.00 | $9.00 | $1.00 | $10.00 |
| | 1.50 | | | | |
| 2 | | 2.50 | 4.50 | 1.25 | 5.75 |
| | 2.25 | | | | |
| 3 | | 4.75 | 3.00 | 1.58 | 4.58 |
| | 3.38 | | | | |
| 4 | | 8.13 | 2.25 | 2.03 | 4.28 |
| | 5.06 | | | | |
| 5 | | 13.19 | 1.80 | 2.64 | 4.44 |
| | 7.59 | | | | |
| 6 | | 20.78 | 1.50 | 3.46 | 4.96 |

   **b.** The spreading effect dominates the diminishing returns effect when average total cost is falling: the fall in AFC dominates the rise in AVC for pies 1 to 4. The diminishing returns effect dominates when average total cost is rising: the rise in AVC dominates the fall in AFC for pies 5 and 6.

   **c.** Alicia's minimum-cost output is 4 pies; this generates the lowest average total cost, $4.28. When output is less than 4, the marginal cost of a pie is less than the average total cost of the pies already produced. So making an additional pie lowers average total cost. For example, the marginal cost of pie 3 is $2.25, whereas the average total cost of pies 1 and 2 is $5.75. So making pie 3 lowers average total cost to $4.58, equal to (2 × $5.75 + $2.25)/3. When output is more than 4, the marginal cost of a pie is greater than the average total cost of the pies already produced. Consequently, making an additional pie raises average total cost. So, although the marginal cost of pie 6 is $7.59, the average total cost of pies 1 through 5 is $4.44. Making pie 6 raises average total cost to $4.96, equal to (5 × $4.44 + $7.59)/6.

## Check Your Understanding 7-3

**1.** **a.** The accompanying table shows the average total cost of producing 12,000, 22,000, and 30,000 units for each of the three choices of fixed cost. For example, if the firm makes choice 1, the total cost of producing 12,000 units of output is $8,000 + 12,000 × $1.00 = $20,000. The average total cost of producing 12,000 units of output is therefore $20,000/12,000 = $1.67. The other average total costs are calculated similarly.

| | 12,000 units | 22,000 units | 30,000 units |
|---|---|---|---|
| Average total cost from choice 1 | $1.67 | $1.36 | $1.27 |
| Average total cost from choice 2 | 1.75 | 1.30 | 1.15 |
| Average total cost from choice 3 | 2.25 | 1.34 | 1.05 |

Therefore, if the firm wanted to produce 12,000 units, it would make choice 1 because this gives it the lowest average total cost. If it wanted to produce 22,000 units, it would make choice 2. If it wanted to produce 30,000 units, it would make choice 3.

   **b.** Having historically produced 12,000 units, the firm would have adopted choice 1. When producing 12,000 units, the firm would have had an average total cost of $1.67. When output jumps to 22,000 units, the firm cannot alter its choice of fixed cost in the short run, so its average total cost in the short run will be $1.36. In the long run, however, it will adopt choice 2, making its average total cost fall to $1.30.

   **c.** If the firm believes that the increase in demand is temporary, it should not alter its fixed cost from choice 1 because choice 2 generates higher average total cost as soon as output falls back to its original quantity of 12,000 units: $1.75 versus $1.67.

**2.** **a.** This firm is likely to experience constant returns to scale. To increase output, the firm must hire more workers, purchase more computers, and pay additional telephone charges. Because these inputs are easily available, their long-run average total cost is unlikely to change as output increases.

**b.** This firm is likely to experience diseconomies of scale. As the firm takes on more projects, the costs of communication and coordination required to implement the expertise of the firm's owner are likely to increase.

**c.** This firm is likely to experience economies of scale. Because diamond mining requires a large initial set-up cost for excavation equipment, long-run average total cost will fall as output increases.

# Chapter Eight

## Check Your Understanding
## 8-1

**1. a.** With only two producers in the world, each producer will represent a sizable share of the market. So the industry will not be perfectly competitive.

**b.** Because each producer of gas from the North Sea has only a small market share of total world supply of natural gas, and since natural gas is a standardized product, the natural gas industry will be perfectly competitive.

**c.** Because each designer has a distinctive style, high-fashion clothes are not a standardized product. So the industry will not be perfectly competitive.

**d.** The market described here is the market in each city for tickets to baseball games. Since there are only one or two teams in each major city, each team will represent a sizable share of the market. So the industry will not be perfectly competitive.

## Check Your Understanding
## 8-2

**1. a.** The firm should shut down immediately when price is less than minimum average variable cost, the shut-down price. In the accompanying diagram, this is optimal for prices in the range 0 to $P_1$.

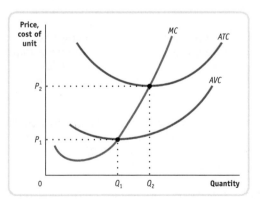

**b.** When price is greater than minimum average variable cost (the shut-down price) but less than minimum average total cost (the break-even price), the firm should continue to operate in the short run even though it is making a loss. This is optimal for prices in the range $P_1$ to $P_2$ and quantities $Q_1$ to $Q_2$.

**c.** When price exceeds minimum average total cost (the break-even price), the firm makes a profit. This happens for prices in excess of $P_2$ and results in quantities greater than $Q_2$.

**2.** This is an example of a temporary shut-down by a firm when the market price lies below the shut-down price, the minimum average variable cost. In this case, the mar-

ket price is the price of a lobster meal and variable cost is the variable cost of serving such a meal, such as the cost of the lobster, employee wages, and so on. In this example, however, it is the average variable cost curve rather than the market price that shifts over time, due to seasonal changes in the cost of lobsters. Maine lobster shacks have relatively low average variable cost during the summer, when cheap Maine lobsters are available; during the rest of the year, their average variable cost is relatively high due to the high cost of imported lobsters. So the lobster shacks are open for business during the summer, when their minimum average variable cost lies below price; but they close during the rest of the year, when price lies below their minimum average variable cost.

## Check Your Understanding
## 8-3

**1. a.** A fall in the fixed cost of production generates a fall in the average total cost of production and, in the short run, an increase in each firm's profit at the current output level. So in the long run new firms will enter the industry. The increase in supply drives down price and profits. Once profits are driven back to zero, entry will cease.

**b.** An increase in wages generates an increase in the average total cost of production at every output level. In the short run, firms incur losses at the current output level, and so in the long run some firms will exit the industry. As firms exit, supply decreases, price rises, and losses are reduced. Exit will cease once losses return to zero.

**c.** Price will rise as a result of the increased demand, leading to a short-run increase in profits at the current output level. In the long run, firms will enter the industry, generating an increase in supply, a fall in price, and a fall in profits. Once profits are driven back to zero, entry will cease.

**d.** The shortage of a key input causes that input's price to increase, resulting in an increase in average total costs for producers. Firms incur losses in the short run, and some firms will exit the industry in the long run. The fall in supply generates an increase in price and decreased losses. Exit will cease when losses have returned to zero.

**2.** In the accompanying diagram, point $X_{MKT}$ in panel (b), the intersection of $S_1$ and $D_1$, represents the long-run industry equilibrium before the change in consumer tastes. When tastes change, demand falls and the industry moves in the short run to point $Y_{MKT}$ in panel (b), at the intersection of the new demand curve $D_2$ and $S_1$, the short-run supply curve representing the same number of egg producers as in the original equilibrium at point $X_{MKT}$. As the market price falls, an individual firm reacts by producing less—as shown in panel (a)—as long as the market price remains above the minimum average variable cost. If market price falls below average variable cost, the firm would shut down immediately. At point $Y_{MKT}$ the price of eggs is below minimum average total cost, creating losses for producers. This leads some firms to exit, which shifts the short-run industry supply curve leftward to $S_2$. A new long-run equilibrium is established at point $Z_{MKT}$. As this occurs, the market price rises again, and, as shown in panel (c), each remaining producer reacts by increasing output (here, from point Y to point Z). All remaining producers again make zero profits. The decrease in the quantity of eggs supplied in the industry comes entirely from the exit of some producers from the industry. The long-run industry supply curve is the curve labeled *LRS* in panel (b).

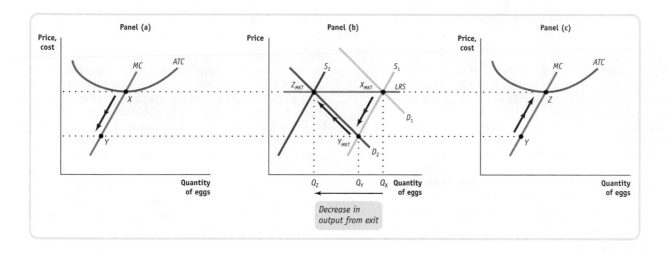

## Chapter Nine

### Check Your Understanding

## 9-1

1. Many college professors will depart for other lines of work if the government imposes a wage that is lower than the market wage. Fewer professors will result in fewer courses taught and therefore fewer college degrees produced. It will adversely affect sectors of the economy that depend directly on colleges, such as the local shopkeepers who sell goods and services to students and faculty, college textbook publishers, and so on. It will also adversely affect firms that use the "output" produced by colleges: new college graduates. Firms that need to hire new employees with college degrees will be hurt as a smaller supply results in a higher market wage for college graduates. Ultimately, the reduced supply of college-educated workers will result in a lower level of human capital in the entire economy relative to what it would have been without the policy. And this will hurt all sectors of the economy that depend on human capital. The sectors of the economy that might benefit are firms that compete with colleges in the hiring of would-be college professors. For example, accounting firms will find it easier to hire people who would otherwise have been professors of accounting, and publishers will find it easier to hire people who would otherwise have been professors of English (easier in the sense that the firms can recruit would-be professors with a lower wage than before). In addition, workers who already have college degrees will benefit; they will command higher wages as the supply of college-educated workers falls.

### Check Your Understanding

## 9-2

1. **a.** As the demand for services increases, the price of services will rise. And as the price of the output produced by the industries increases, this shifts the *VMPL* curve upward—that is, the demand for labor rises. This results in an increase in both the equilibrium wage rate and the quantity of labor employed.

   **b.** The fall in the catch per day means that the marginal product of labor in the industry declines. The *VMPL* curve shifts downward, generating a fall in the equilibrium wage rate and the equilibrium quantity of labor employed.

2. When firms from different industries compete for the same workers, then each worker in the various industries will be paid the same equilibrium wage, *W*. And since, by the marginal productivity theory of income distribution, $VMPL = P \times MPL = W$ for the last worker hired in equilibrium, the last worker hired in each of these different industries will have the same value of the marginal product of labor.

### Check Your Understanding

## 9-3

1. **a.** False. Income disparities associated with gender, race, or ethnicity can be explained by the marginal productivity theory of income distribution provided that differences in marginal productivity across people are correlated with gender, race, or ethnicity. One possible source for such correlation is past discrimination. Such discrimination can lower individuals' marginal productivity by, for example, preventing them from acquiring the human capital that would raise their productivity. Another possible source of the correlation is differences in work experience that are associated with gender, race, or ethnicity. For example, in jobs where work experience or length of tenure is important, women may earn lower wages because on average more women than men take childcare-related absences from work.

   **b.** True. Companies that discriminate when their competitors do not are likely to hire less able workers because they discriminate against more able workers who are considered of the wrong gender, race, or ethnicity. And with less able workers, such companies are likely to earn lower profits than their competitors who don't discriminate.

   **c.** Ambiguous. In general, workers who are paid less because they have less experience may or may not be the victims of discrimination. The answer depends on the reason for the lack of experience. If workers have less experience because they are young or have chosen to do something else rather than gain experience, then they are not victims of discrimination if they are paid less. But if workers lack experience because previous job discrimination prevented them from gaining experience, then they are indeed victims of discrimination when they are paid less.

## 9-4

**1. a.** Clive is made worse off if, before the new law, he had preferred to work more than 35 hours per week. As a result of the law, he can no longer choose his preferred time allocation; he now consumes fewer goods and more leisure than he would like.

   **b.** Clive's utility is unaffected by the law if, before the law, he had preferred to work 35 or fewer hours per week. The law has not changed his preferred time allocation.

   **c.** Clive can never be made better off by a law that restricts the number of hours he can work. He can only be made worse off (case a) or equally as well off (case b).

**2.** The substitution effect would induce Clive to work fewer hours and consume more leisure after his wage falls—the fall in wage means the price of an hour of leisure falls, leading Clive to consume more leisure. But a fall in his wage also generates a fall in Clive's income. The income effect of this is to induce Clive to consume less leisure and therefore work more hours, since he is now poorer and leisure is a normal good. If the income effect dominates the substitution effect, Clive will in the end work more hours than before.

## Chapter Ten

## 10-1

**1. a.** Before the change in preferences, the Bountifullian labor market is in equilibrium, defined by the condition $VMPL_C$ = wage rate = $VMPL_S$. After preferences change, a greater demand for breakfast cereal will induce an increase in the price of cereal, $P_C$. $VMPL_C = P_C \times MPL_C$ will therefore rise, with the result that $VMPL_C$ > wage rate. A lower demand for sausage will induce a decrease in the price of sausage, $P_S$. $VMPL_S = P_S \times MPL_S$ will fall, with the result that $VMPL_S$ < wage rate. Sausage producers will let some of their workers go; these workers will move to cereal producers, who are hiring additional workers. As labor moves from the sausage to the cereal industry, $MPL_C$ and $VMPL_C$ fall, but $MPL_S$ and $VMPL_S$ rise.

   **b.** You will know that the economy has fully adjusted when the labor market has reattained equilibrium: when $VMPL_C$ = wage rate = $VMPL_S$ again. Because all consumers face the same price for cereal, $P_C$, and the same price for sausage, $P_S$, there will be *efficiency in consumption:* every consumer who consumes a good has a higher willingness to pay for it than someone who does not. Next, because cereal producers and sausage producers compete for workers in a perfectly competitive labor market, there will be no surplus of labor and all labor will be fully employed. So there will be *efficiency in production:* there is no way to produce more of one good without producing less of the other. Finally, there will be *efficiency in output levels:* any other mix of cereal and sausage reduces welfare. Because $VMPL_C$ = wage rate = $VMPL_S$ in equilibrium, the allocation of labor to the two industries, and therefore the mix of outputs of the two goods, fully reflects consumers' valuations of the two goods.

## 10-2

**1.** There is an objective way to determine whether an economy is efficient: determine whether there is another allocation of production and/or consumption that makes some people better off without making others worse off. If not, it is efficient; if yes, it is inefficient. It is much harder to determine whether an economy is fair because there is no objective measure of determining this. What a person deems is fair typically depends upon his or her viewpoint.

**2. a.** The problem with this statement is that what one "should contribute" or "should receive" is subject to interpretation. Suppose one person has worked extremely hard to become wealthy but another is born wealthy and has never worked. Should each person be required to contribute the same to society? Some would say yes (those who think the amount of money a person has is the only criterion) but others would say no (those who think that people should be rewarded for working hard relative to those who don't)—it depends upon the person's viewpoint. Similarly, suppose one person needs an operation to be able to see, another person needs an operation to be able to walk, and society doesn't have the resources to perform both operations. Whose need is more important? Again, the answer is unclear because society has no way of measuring whether one person's needs are more compelling than another's.

   **b.** This statement is also subject to very different interpretations. First, how do we define "work hard"? Do people who spend years working on something they enjoy, such as writing a classical sonata, "work harder" than those who do less intense but very unappealing work? Also, this statement implies that people who cannot work hard for reasons outside their control—say, due to illness—should be rewarded less. Whether or not this is fair is again subject to a person's viewpoint.

## 10-3

**1.** The London congestion charge acts like a Pigouvian tax on driving in central London. If the marginal external cost in terms of pollution and congestion of an additional car driven in central London is indeed £5, then the scheme is an optimal policy.

**2. a.** Planting trees imposes an external benefit: the marginal social benefit of planting trees is higher than the marginal benefit to individual tree planters, since many people (not just those who plant the trees) can benefit from the increased air quality and lower summer temperatures. The difference between the marginal social benefit and the marginal benefit to individual tree planters is the marginal external benefit. A Pigouvian subsidy could be placed on each tree planted in urban areas in order to increase the marginal benefit to individual tree planters to the same level as the marginal social benefit.

b. Water-saving toilets impose an external benefit: the marginal benefit to individual homeowners from replacing a traditional toilet with a water-saving toilet is zero, since water is virtually costless. But the marginal social benefit is large, since fewer rivers and aquifers need to be pumped. The difference between the marginal social benefit and the marginal benefit to individual homeowners is the marginal external benefit. A Pigouvian subsidy on installing water-saving toilets could bring the marginal benefit to individual homeowners in line with the marginal social benefit.

c. Disposing of old computer monitors imposes an external cost: the marginal cost to those disposing of old computer monitors is lower than the marginal social cost, since environmental pollution is borne by people other than the person disposing of the monitor. The difference between the marginal social cost and the marginal cost to those disposing of old computer monitors is the marginal external cost. A Pigouvian tax on disposing of computer monitors, or a system of tradable permits for their disposal, could raise the marginal cost to those disposing of old computer monitors sufficiently to make it equal to the marginal social cost.

## Check Your Understanding

## 10-4

**1. a.** With 10 Homebodies and 6 Revelers, the marginal social benefit schedule of money spent on the party is as shown in the accompanying table.

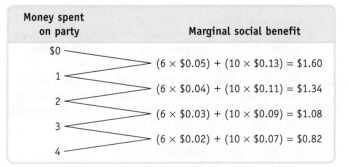

| Money spent on party | Marginal social benefit |
|---|---|
| $0 | |
| | $(10 \times \$0.05) + (6 \times \$0.13) = \$1.28$ |
| 1 | |
| | $(10 \times \$0.04) + (6 \times \$0.11) = \$1.06$ |
| 2 | |
| | $(10 \times \$0.03) + (6 \times \$0.09) = \$0.84$ |
| 3 | |
| | $(10 \times \$0.02) + (6 \times \$0.07) = \$0.62$ |
| 4 | |

The efficient spending level is $2, the highest level for which the marginal social benefit is greater than the marginal cost ($1).

**b.** With 6 Homebodies and 10 Revelers, the marginal social benefit schedule of money spent on the party is as shown in the accompanying table.

| Money spent on party | Marginal social benefit |
|---|---|
| $0 | |
| | $(6 \times \$0.05) + (10 \times \$0.13) = \$1.60$ |
| 1 | |
| | $(6 \times \$0.04) + (10 \times \$0.11) = \$1.34$ |
| 2 | |
| | $(6 \times \$0.03) + (10 \times \$0.09) = \$1.08$ |
| 3 | |
| | $(6 \times \$0.02) + (10 \times \$0.07) = \$0.82$ |
| 4 | |

The efficient spending level is now $3, the highest level for which the marginal social benefit is greater than the marginal cost ($1). The efficient level of spending has increased from that in part a because with relatively more Revelers than Homebodies, an additional dollar spent on the party generates a higher level of social benefit compared to when there are relatively more Homebodies than Revelers.

**c.** When the numbers of Homebodies and Revelers are unknown but residents are asked their preferences, then Homebodies will pretend to be Revelers to induce a higher level of spending on the public party. That's because a Homebody still receives a positive individual marginal benefit from an additional $1 spent, despite the fact that his or her individual marginal benefit is lower than that of a Reveler for every additional $1. In this case the "reported" marginal social benefit schedule of money spent on the party will be as shown in the accompanying table.

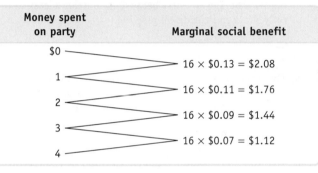

| Money spent on party | Marginal social benefit |
|---|---|
| $0 | |
| | $16 \times \$0.13 = \$2.08$ |
| 1 | |
| | $16 \times \$0.11 = \$1.76$ |
| 2 | |
| | $16 \times \$0.09 = \$1.44$ |
| 3 | |
| | $16 \times \$0.07 = \$1.12$ |
| 4 | |

As a result, $4 will be spent on the party, the highest level for which the "reported" marginal social benefit is greater than the marginal cost ($1). Regardless of whether there are 10 Homebodies and 6 Revelers (part a) or 6 Homebodies and 10 Revelers (part b), spending $4 in total on the party is clearly inefficient because marginal cost exceeds marginal social benefit at this spending level.

As a further exercise, consider how much Homebodies gain by this misrepresentation. In part a, the efficient level of spending is $2. So by misrepresenting their preferences, the 10 Homebodies gain, in total, $10 \times (\$0.03 + \$0.02) = \$0.50$—that is, they gain the marginal individual benefit in going from a spending level of $2 to $4. The 6 Revelers also gain from the misrepresentations of the Homebodies; they gain $6 \times (\$0.09 + \$0.07) = \$0.96$ in total. This outcome is clearly inefficient—when $4 in total is spent, the marginal cost is $1 but the marginal social benefit is only $0.62, indicating that too much money is being spent on the party.

In part b, the efficient level of spending is actually $3. The misrepresentation by the 6 Homebodies gains them, in total, $6 \times \$0.02 = \$0.12$, but the 10 Revelers gain $10 \times \$0.07 = \$0.70$ in total. This outcome is also clearly inefficient—when $4 is spent, marginal social benefit is only $0.12 + $0.70 = $0.82 but marginal cost is $1.

# Chapter Eleven

## Check Your Understanding

## 11-1

**1. a.** This does not support the conclusion. Texas Tea has a limited amount of oil, and the price has risen in order to equalize supply and demand.

**b.** This supports the conclusion because the market for home heating oil has become monopolized, and a monopolist will reduce the quantity supplied and raise price to generate profit.

**c.** This does not support the conclusion. Texas Tea has raised its price to consumers because the price of its input, home heating oil, has increased.

**d.** This supports the conclusion. The fact that other firms have begun to supply heating oil at a lower price implies that Texas Tea must have earned profits—profits that attracted the other firms to Frigid.

**e.** This supports the conclusion. It indicates that Texas Tea enjoys a barrier to entry because it controls access to the only Alaskan heating oil pipeline.

## Check Your Understanding

## 11-2

**1. a.** The price at each output level is found by dividing the total revenue by the number of emeralds produced; for example, the price when 3 emeralds are produced is $252/3 = $84. The price at the various output levels is then used to construct the demand schedule in the accompanying table.

**b.** The marginal revenue schedule is found by calculating the change in total revenue as output increases by one unit. For example, the marginal revenue generated by increasing output from 2 to 3 emeralds is ($252 − $186) = $66.

**c.** The quantity effect component of marginal revenue is the additional revenue generated by selling one more unit of the good at the market price. For example, as shown in the accompanying table, at 3 emeralds, the market price is $84; so, when going from 2 to 3 emeralds the quantity effect is equal to $84.

**d.** The price effect component of marginal revenue is the decline in total revenue caused by the fall in price when one more unit is sold. For example, as shown in the table, when only 2 emeralds are sold, each emerald sells at a price of $186/2 = $93. However, when Emerald, Inc. sells an additional emerald, the price must fall by $9 to $84. So the price effect component in going from 2 to 3 emeralds is (−$9) × 2 = −$18. That's because 2 emeralds

can only be sold at a price of $84 when 3 emeralds in total are sold, although they could have been sold at a price of $93 when only 2 in total were sold.

| Quantity of emerald demanded | Price of emerald | Marginal revenue | Quantity effect component | Price effect component |
|---|---|---|---|---|
| 1 | $100 | | | |
| | | $86 | $93 | −$7 |
| 2 | 93 | | | |
| | | 66 | 84 | −18 |
| 3 | 84 | | | |
| | | 28 | 70 | −42 |
| 4 | 70 | | | |
| | | −30 | 50 | −80 |
| 5 | 50 | | | |

**e.** In order to determine Emerald, Inc.'s profit-maximizing output level, you must know its marginal cost at each output level. Its profit-maximizing output level is the one at which marginal revenue is equal to marginal cost.

**2.** As the accompanying diagram shows, the marginal cost curve shifts upward to $400. The profit-maximizing quantity falls, and so does profit, from $3,200 to $300 × 6 = $1,800. Competitive industry profits, though, are unchanged at zero.

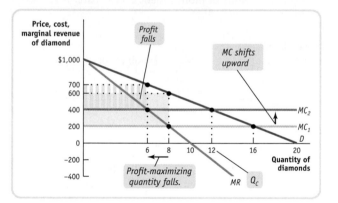

## Check Your Understanding

## 11-3

**1. a.** Cable Internet service is a natural monopoly. So the government should intervene only if it believes that price exceeds average total cost, where average total cost is based on the cost of laying the cable. In this case it should impose a price ceiling equal to average total cost. Otherwise, it should do nothing.

**b.** The government should approve the merger only if it fosters competition by transferring some of the company's landing slots to another, competing airline.

**2. a.** False. As can be see from Figure 11-8, panel (b), the inefficiency arises from the fact that some of the consumer surplus is transformed into deadweight loss (the orange area), not that it is transformed into profit (the green area).

**b.** True. If a monopolist sold to all customers who have a valuation greater than or equal to marginal cost, all mutually beneficial transactions would occur and there would be no deadweight loss.

**3.** As shown in the accompanying diagram, a monopolist produces $Q_M$, the output level at which $MR = MC$. A monopolist who mistakenly believes that $P = MR$ produces the output level at which $P = MC$ (when, in fact, $P > MR$, and at the true profit-maximizing level of output, $P > MR = MC$). This misguided monopolist will produce the output level $Q_C$, where the demand curve crosses the marginal cost curve—the same output level produced if the industry were perfectly competitive. It will charge the price $P_C$, which is equal to marginal cost, and make zero profit. The entire shaded area is equal to the consumer surplus, which is also equal to total surplus in this case (since the monopolist receives zero producer surplus). There is no deadweight loss since every consumer who is willing to pay as much as or more than marginal cost gets the good. A smart monopolist, however, will produce the output level $Q_M$, and charge the price $P_M$. Profit equals the green area, consumer surplus corresponds to the blue area, and total surplus is equal to the sum of the green and blue areas. The orange area is the deadweight loss generated by the monopolist.

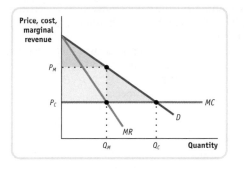

Check Your Understanding

# 11-4

**1. a.** False. A price-discriminating monopolist will sell to some customers that a single-price monopolist will refuse to—namely, customers with a high price elasticity of demand who are willing to pay only a relatively low price for the good.
**b.** False. Although a price-discriminating monopolist does indeed capture more of the consumer surplus, inefficiency is lower: more mutually beneficial transactions occur because the monopolist makes more sales to customers with a low willingness to pay for the good.
**c.** True. Under price discrimination consumers are charged prices that depend on their price elasticity of demand. A consumer with highly elastic demand will pay a lower price than a consumer with inelastic demand.

**2. a.** This is not a case of price discrimination because all consumers, regardless of their price elasticities of demand, value the damaged merchandise less than undamaged merchandise. So the price must be lowered to sell the merchandise.

**b.** This is a case of price discrimination. Senior citizens have a higher price elasticity of demand for restaurant meals (their demand for restaurant meals is more responsive to price changes) than other patrons. Restaurants lower the price to high-elasticity consumers (senior citizens). Consumers with low price elasticity of demand will pay the full price.
**c.** This is a case of price discrimination. Consumers with a high price elasticity of demand will pay a lower price by collecting and using discount coupons. Consumers with a low price elasticity of demand will not use coupons.
**d.** This is not a case of price discrimination; it is simply a case of supply and demand.

# Chapter Twelve

Check Your Understanding

# 12-1

**1. a.** The world oil industry is an oligopoly because a few countries control a necessary resource for production, oil reserves.
**b.** The microprocessor industry is an oligopoly because two firms possess superior technology and so dominate industry production.
**c.** The wide-bodied passenger jet industry is an oligopoly because there are economies of scale in production.

**2.** When Margaret builds a missile, Nikita's payoff from building a missile as well is −10; it is −20 if he does not. The same set of payoffs holds for Margaret when Nikita builds a missile: her payoff is −10 if she builds one as well, −20 if she does not. So it is a Nash (or noncooperative) equilibrium for both Margaret and Nikita to build missiles, and their total payoff is (−10) + (−10) = −20. But their total payoff is greatest when neither builds a missile: their total payoff is 0 + 0 = 0. But this outcome—the cooperative outcome—is unlikely. If Margaret builds a missile but Nikita does not, Margaret gets a payoff of +8, rather than the 0 she gets if she doesn't build a missile. So Margaret is better off if she builds a missile but Nikita doesn't. Similarly, Nikita is better off if he builds a missile but Margaret does not: he gets a payoff of +8, rather than the 0 he gets if he doesn't build a missile. So both players have an incentive to build a missile. Both will build a missile, and each gets a payoff of −10. So unless Nikita and Margaret are able to communicate in some way to enforce cooperation, they will act in their own individual interests and each will build a missile.

**3. a.** Future entry by several new firms will increase competition and drive down industry profits. As a result, there is less future profit to protect by behaving cooperatively today. So each oligopolist is more likely to behave noncooperatively today.
**b.** When it is very difficult for a firm to detect if another firm has raised output, then it is very difficult to enforce cooperation by playing "tit for tat." So it is more likely that a firm will behave noncooperatively.
**c.** When firms have coexisted while maintaining high prices for a long time, each expects cooperation to continue. So the value of behaving cooperatively today is high and it is likely that firms will engage in tacit collusion.

## Check Your Understanding 12-2

**1. a.** This is likely to be interpreted as evidence of tacit collusion. Firms in the industry are able to tacitly collude by setting their prices according to the published "suggested" price of the largest firm in the industry. This is a form of price leadership.

**b.** This is not likely to be interpreted as evidence of tacit collusion. Considerable variation in market share indicates that firms have been competing to capture each others' business.

**c.** This is not likely to be interpreted as evidence of tacit collusion. These features make it more unlikely that consumers will switch products in response to lower prices. So this is a way for firms to avoid any temptation to gain market share by lowering price. This is a form of product differentiation used to avoid direct competition.

**d.** This is likely to be interpreted as evidence of tacit collusion. In the guise of discussing sales targets, firms can create a cartel by designating quantities to be produced by each firm.

**e.** This is likely to be interpreted as evidence of tacit collusion. By raising prices together, each firm in the industry is refusing to undercut its rivals by leaving its price unchanged or lowering it. Because it could gain market share by doing so, refusing to do it is evidence of tacit collusion.

## Check Your Understanding 12-3

**1. a.** Perfectly competitive industries and monopolistically competitive industries both have many sellers. So it may be hard to distinguish between them solely in terms of number of firms. And in both market structures, there is free entry into and exit from the industry in the long run. But in a perfectly competitive industry, one standardized product is sold, while in a monopolistically competitive industry, products are differentiated. So you should ask whether products are differentiated in the industry.

**b.** In a monopoly there is only one firm, but a monopolistically competitive industry contains many firms. So you should ask whether or not there is a single firm in the industry.

**2. a.** An increase in fixed cost raises average total cost and shifts the average total cost curve upward. In the short run firms incur losses, and some will exit the industry. In the long run, this results in a rightward shift of the demand curves for those firms that remain in the industry, since each one now serves a larger share of the market. Long-run equilibrium is reestablished when the demand curve for each remaining firm has shifted rightward to the point where it is tangent to the firm's new, higher average total cost curve. At this point each firm's price just equals its average total cost, and each firm makes zero profit.

**b.** A decrease in marginal cost lowers average total cost and shifts the average total cost curve and the marginal cost curve downward. Because firms make profits, in the long run new entrants are attracted into the industry. In the long run, this results in a leftward shift of each firm's demand curve since each firm now has a smaller share of the market. Long-run equilibrium is reestablished when each firm's demand curve has shifted leftward to the point where it is tangent to the new, lower average total cost curve. At this point each firm's price just equals average total cost, and each firm makes zero profit.

**3.** If all the existing firms in the industry joined together to create a monopoly, they would achieve monopoly profits. But this would induce new firms to create new, differentiated products and then enter the industry and capture some of the monopoly profits. So in the long run it would be impossible to maintain a monopoly. The problem arises from the fact that because new firms can create new products, there is no barrier to entry that can maintain a monopoly.

## Check Your Understanding 12-4

**1. a.** This is economically useful because such advertisements are likely to focus on the medical benefits of aspirin.

**b.** This is economically wasteful because such advertisements are likely to focus on promoting Bayer aspirin versus a rival's aspirin product. The two products are medically indistinguishable.

**c.** This is economically useful because such advertisements are likely to focus on the health and enjoyment benefits of orange juice.

**d.** This is economically wasteful because such advertisements are likely to focus on promoting Tropicana orange juice versus a rival's product. The two are likely to be indistinguishable by consumers.

**e.** This is economically useful because the longevity of a business gives a potential customer information about its quality.

**2.** A successful brand name indicates a desirable attribute, such as quality, to a potential buyer. So, other things equal—such as price—a firm with a successful brand name will achieve higher sales than a rival with a comparable product but without a successful brand name. This is likely to deter new firms from entering an industry in which an existing firm has a successful brand name.

# Chapter Thirteen

## Check Your Understanding 13-1

**1. a.** According to the Heckscher–Ohlin model, this pattern of trade occurs because the United States has a relatively larger endowment of factors of production, such as human capital and physical capital, that are suited to the production of movies, but France has a relatively larger endowment of factors of production suited to wine-making, such as vineyards and the human capital of vintners.

**b.** According to the Heckscher–Ohlin model, this pattern of trade occurs because the United States has a relatively larger endowment of factors of production, such as human and physical capital, that are suited to making machinery, but Brazil has a relatively larger endowment of factors of production suited to shoe-making, such as labor and leather.

Check Your Understanding
# 13-2

**1.** In the accompanying diagram, $P_A$ is the price of U.S. grapes in autarky and $P_W$ is the world price of grapes under international trade. With trade, U.S. consumers pay a price of $P_W$ for grapes and consume quantity $C_T$, U.S. grape producers produce quantity $Q_T$, and the difference, $C_T - Q_T$, represents imports of Mexican grapes. As a consequence of the strike by truckers, imports are halted, the price paid by American consumers rises to the autarky price, $P_A$, and U.S. consumption falls to the autarky quantity $Q_A$.

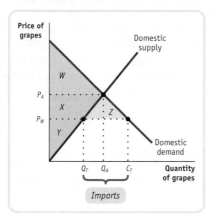

**a.** Before the strike, U.S. consumers enjoy consumer surplus equal to the area $W + X + Z$. After the strike, their consumer surplus shrinks to the area $W$. So consumers are worse off, losing consumer surplus represented by the area $X + Z$.

**b.** Before the strike, U.S. producers have producer surplus equal to the area $Y$. After the strike, their producer surplus increases to the area $Y + X$. So U.S. producers are better off, gaining producer surplus represented by the area $X$.

**c.** U.S. total surplus falls as a result of the strike by an amount represented by the area $Z$, the loss in consumer surplus that does not accrue to producers.

**2.** Mexican grape producers are worse off because they lose sales in the amount of $C_T - Q_T$, and Mexican grape pickers are worse off because they lose the wages that were associated with the lost sales. The lower demand for Mexican grapes caused by the strike implies that the price that Mexican consumers pay for grapes falls, making them better off. American grape pickers are better off because their wages increase as a result of the increase of $Q_A - Q_T$ in U.S. sales.

Check Your Understanding
# 13-3

**1. a.** If the tariff is $0.50, the price paid by domestic consumers for a pound of imported butter is $0.50 + $0.50 = $1.00, the same price as a pound of domestic butter. Imported butter will no longer have a price advantage over domestic butter, imports will cease, and domestic producers will capture all the feasible sales to domestic consumers, selling amount $Q_A$ in the accompanying figure. But if the tar-

iff is less than $0.50—say only $0.25—the price paid by domestic consumers for a pound of imported butter is $0.50 + $0.25 = $0.75, $0.25 cheaper than a pound of domestic butter. American butter producers will gain sales in the amount of $Q_2 - Q_1$ as a result of the $0.25 tariff. But this is smaller than the amount they would have gained under the $0.50 tariff, the amount $Q_A - Q_1$.

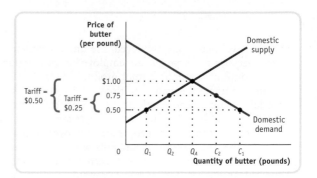

**b.** As long as the tariff is at least $0.50, increasing it more has no effect. At a tariff of $0.50, all imports are effectively blocked.

**2.** All imports are effectively blocked at a tariff of $0.50. So such a tariff corresponds to an import quota of 0.

Check Your Understanding
# 13-4

**1.** There are many fewer businesses that use steel as an input than there are consumers who buy sugar or clothing. So it will be easier for such businesses to communicate and coordinate among themselves to lobby against tariffs than it will be for consumers. In addition, each business will perceive that the cost of a steel tariff is quite costly to its profits, but an individual consumer is either unaware of or perceives little loss from tariffs on sugar or clothing.

**2.** Countries are often tempted to protect domestic industries by claiming that an import poses a quality, health, or environmental danger to domestic consumers. A WTO official should examine whether domestic producers are subject to the same stringency in the application of quality, health, or environmental regulations as foreign producers. If they are, then it is more likely that the regulations are for legitimate, non–trade protection purposes; if they are not, then it is more likely that the regulations are intended as trade protection measures.

# Chapter Fourteen

Check Your Understanding
# 14-1

**1. a.** This is a microeconomic question because it considers the economic circumstances facing an individual firm.

**b.** This is a macroeconomic question because it considers how the overall level of an activity changes as the whole economy changes.

**c.** This is a microeconomic question because it addresses the economic decision-making of a single individual.

**2.** There is typically less scope for government intervention in microeconomics because government intervention in markets reduces society's welfare except in certain well-defined cases. There is more scope for government intervention in macroeconomics because society's welfare is enhanced when the government can reduce the severity of economic fluctuations.

## Check Your Understanding 14-2

**1.** When fewer people are employed, the unemployment rate rises. Because fewer people are employed in production, the amount of aggregate output produced falls. As a result, the unemployment rate rises when aggregate output falls. When more people are employed, the unemployment rate falls. The amount of aggregate output produced rises because more people are employed in production. So the unemployment rate falls when aggregate output rises. Putting all these facts together means that the unemployment rate and aggregate output move in opposite directions over the business cycle.

**2.** A high unemployment rate results in lost wages for people who would like to be employed but aren't. It results in lost output for firms, output of goods and services that consumers could have enjoyed. It can also result in political instability.

**3.** An economy with a successful stabilization policy experiences relatively few and shallow recessions. Equivalently, the economy experiences a low unemployment rate over time. It also experiences few overly robust expansions and therefore fewer inflationary pressures.

## Check Your Understanding 14-3

**1. a.** You are better off because your wages have risen 5 percentage points more than prices (10% increase in wages − 5% increase in prices = 5%).

**b.** You are worse off because your wages have risen 5 percentage points less than prices (10% increase in wages − 15% increase in prices = − 5%).

**c.** You are better off because your wages have risen 12 percentage points more than prices (10% increase in wages + 2% fall in prices = 12%).

## Chapter Fifteen

## Check Your Understanding 15-1

**1.** Let's start by considering the relationship between the total value added of all domestically produced final goods and services and aggregate spending on domestically produced final goods and services. These two quantities are equal because every final good and service produced in the economy is either purchased by someone or added to inventories. And additions to inventories are counted as spending by firms. Next, consider the relationship between aggregate spending on domestically produced final goods and services and total factor income. These two quantities are equal because all spending that is channeled to firms to pay for purchases of domestically

produced final goods and services is revenue for firms. Those revenues must be paid out by firms to their factors of production in the form of wages, profit, interest, and rent. Taken together, this means that all three methods of calculating GDP are equivalent.

**2.** Firms make sales to other firms, households, the government, and the rest of the world. Households are linked to firms through the sale of factors of production to firms, through purchases from firms of final goods and services, and through lending funds to firms in the financial markets. Households are linked to the government through their payment of taxes, their receipt of transfers, and their lending of funds to the government to finance government borrowing via the financial markets. Finally, households are linked to the rest of the world through their purchases of imports and transactions with foreigners in financial markets.

**3.** You would be counting the value of the steel twice—once as it was sold by American Steel to American Motors and once as part of the car sold by American Motors.

## Check Your Understanding 15-2

**1. a.** In 2004 nominal GDP was (1,000,000 × $0.40) + (800,000 × $0.60) = $400,000 + $480,000 = $880,000. A 25% rise in the price of french fries from 2004 to 2005 means that the 2005 price of french fries was 1.25 × $0.40 = $0.50. A 10% fall in servings means that 1,000,000 × 0.9 = 900,000 servings were sold in 2005. As a result, the total value of sales of french fries in 2005 was 900,000 × $0.50 = $450,000. A 15% fall in the price of onion rings from 2004 to 2005 means that the 2005 price of onion rings was 0.85 × $0.60 = $0.51. A 5% rise in servings sold means that 800,000 × 1.05 = 840,000 servings were sold in 2005. As a result, the total value of sales of onion rings in 2005 was 840,000 × $0.51 = $428,400. Nominal GDP in 2005 was $450,000 + $428,400 = $878,400. To find real GDP in 2005, we must calculate the value of sales in 2005 using 2004 prices: (900,000 french fries × $0.40) + (840,000 onion rings × $0.60) = $360,000 + $504,000 = $864,000.

**b.** A comparison of nominal GDP in 2004 to nominal GDP in 2005 shows a decline of (($880,000 − $878,400) / $880,000) × 100 = 0.18%. But a comparison using real GDP shows a decline of (($880,000 − $864,000) / $880,000) × 100 = 1.8%. That is, a calculation based on real GDP shows a drop 10 times larger (1.8%) than a calculation based on nominal GDP (0.18%): in this case, the calculation based on nominal GDP underestimates the true magnitude of the change.

**2.** A price index based on 1990 prices will contain a relatively high price of electronics and a relatively low price of housing compared to a price index based on 2000 prices. This means that a 1990 price index used to calculate real GDP in 2005 will magnify the value of electronics production in the economy, but a 2000 price index will magnify the value of housing production in the economy.

## Check Your Understanding 15-3

1. The advent of websites that enable job-seekers to find jobs more quickly will reduce the unemployment rate over time. However, websites that induce discouraged workers to begin actively looking for work again will lead to an increase in the unemployment rate over time.

2. Both parts a and b are consistent with the relationship between growth in real GDP and changes in the unemployment rate that is illustrated in Figure 15-6: during years of above-average growth, the unemployment rate fell, and vice versa. They are consistent with this relationship because they both entail either a fall in the unemployment rate during a recovery or a rise in the unemployment rate during a recession. However, part c is not consistent: it implies that a recession is associated with a fall in the unemployment rate.

## Check Your Understanding 15-4

1. This market basket costs, pre-frost, $(100 \times \$0.20) + (50 \times \$0.60) + (200 \times \$0.25) = \$20 + \$30 + \$50 = \$100$. The same market basket, post-frost, costs $(100 \times \$0.40) + (50 \times \$1.00) + (200 \times \$0.45) = \$40 + \$50 + \$90 = \$180$. So the price index is $(\$100/\$100) \times 100 = 100$ before the frost and $(\$180/\$100) \times 100 = 180$ after the frost, implying a rise in the price index of 80%. This increase in the price index is less than the 84.2% increase calculated in the text. The reason for this difference is that the new market basket of 100 oranges, 50 grapefruit, and 200 lemons contains proportionately more of the items that have experienced relatively lower price increases (the lemons, whose price has increased by 80%) and proportionately fewer of the items that have experienced relatively large price increases (the oranges, whose price has increased by 100%). This shows that the price index can be very sensitive to the composition of the market basket. If the market basket contains a large proportion of goods whose prices have risen faster than the prices of other goods, it will lead to a higher estimate of the increase in the price level. If it contains a large proportion of goods whose prices have risen more slowly than the prices of other goods, it will lead to a lower estimate of the increase in the price level.

2. **a.** A market basket determined 10 years ago will contain fewer cars than at present. Given that the average price of a car has grown faster than the average prices of other goods, this basket will underestimate the true increase in the price level because it contains relatively too few cars.

   **b.** A market basket determined 10 years ago will not contain broadband Internet access. So, it cannot track the fall in prices of Internet access over the past few years. As a result, it will overestimate the true increase in the price level.

3. Using Equation 15-3, the inflation rate from 2003 to 2004 is $(188.9 - 184.0)/184.0 \times 100 = 2.7\%$.

## Chapter Sixteen

## Check Your Understanding 16-1

1. **a.** This represents a movement along the *SRAS* curve because the CPI—like the GDP deflator—is a measure of the aggregate price level, the overall price level of final goods and services in the economy.

   **b.** This represents a shift of the *SRAS* curve because oil is a commodity. The *SRAS* will shift to the right because production costs are now lower, leading to a higher quantity of aggregate output supplied at any given aggregate price level.

   **c.** This represents a shift of the *SRAS* curve because it involves a change in nominal wages. An increase in legally mandated benefits to workers is equivalent to an increase in nominal wages. As a result, the *SRAS* curve will shift leftward because production costs are now higher, leading to a lower quantity of aggregate output supplied at any given aggregate price level.

2. You would need to know what happened to the aggregate price level. If the increase in the quantity of aggregate output supplied was due to a movement along the *SRAS* curve, the aggregate price level would increase at the same time as the quantity of aggregate output supplied increases. If the increase in the quantity of aggregate output supplied was due to a rightward shift of the *LRAS* curve, the aggregate price level might not rise. Alternatively, you could make the determination by observing what happened to aggregate output in the long run. If it falls back to its initial level in the long run, then the temporary increase in aggregate output was due to a movement along the *SRAS* curve. If it stays at the higher level in the long run, the increase in aggregate output was due to a rightward shift of the *LRAS* curve.

## Check Your Understanding 16-2

1. **a.** This is a shift of the aggregate demand curve. A decrease in the quantity of money raises the interest rate, since people now want to borrow more and lend less. A higher interest rate reduces investment and consumer spending at any given aggregate price level, so the aggregate demand curve shifts to the left.

   **b.** This is a movement up along the aggregate demand curve. As the aggregate price level rises, the real value of money holdings falls. This is the interest rate effect of a change in the aggregate price level: as the value of money falls, people want to hold more money. They do so by borrowing more and lending less. This leads to a rise in the interest rate and a reduction in consumer and investment spending. So it is a movement along the aggregate demand curve.

   **c.** This is a shift of the aggregate demand curve. Expectations of a poor job market, and so lower average disposable incomes, will reduce people's consumer spending today at any given aggregate price level. So the aggregate demand curve shifts to the left.

   **d.** This is a shift of the aggregate demand curve. A fall in tax rates raises people's disposable income. At any given aggregate price level, consumer spending is now higher, so the aggregate demand curve shifts to the right.

e. This is a movement down along the aggregate demand curve. As the aggregate price level falls, the real value of assets rises. This is the wealth effect of a change in the aggregate price level: as the value of assets rises, people will increase their consumption plans. This leads to higher consumer spending, so it is a movement along the aggregate demand curve.

f. This is a shift of the aggregate demand curve. A rise in the real value of assets in the economy due to a surge in real estate values raises consumer spending at any given aggregate price level. So the aggregate demand curve shifts to the right.

## Check Your Understanding
## 16-3

1. A decline in investment spending, like a rise in investment spending, has a multiplier effect on real GDP—the only difference in this case is that real GDP falls instead of rises. The fall in *I* leads to an initial fall in real GDP, which leads to a fall in disposable income, which leads to lower consumer spending, which leads to another fall in real GDP, and so on. So consumer spending falls as an indirect result of the fall in investment spending.

## Check Your Understanding
## 16-4

1. a. An increase in the minimum wage raises the nominal wage and, as a result, shifts the short-run aggregate supply curve to the left. As a result of this negative supply shock, the aggregate price level rises, and aggregate output falls.

   b. Increased investment spending shifts the aggregate demand curve to the right. As a result of this positive demand shock, both the aggregate price level and aggregate output rise.

   c. An increase in taxes and a reduction in government spending both result in negative demand shocks, shifting the aggregate demand curve to the left. As a result, both the aggregate price level and aggregate output fall.

   d. This is a negative supply shock, shifting the short-run aggregate supply curve to the left. As a result, the aggregate price level rises and aggregate output falls.

2. As long-run growth increases potential output, the long-run aggregate supply curve shifts to the right. If, in the short run, there is now a recessionary gap (aggregate output is less than potential output), nominal wages will fall, shifting the short-run aggregate supply curve to the right. This results in a falling aggregate price level and a rise in aggregate output. As prices fall, we move along the aggregate demand curve due to the wealth and interest rate effects of a change in the aggregate price level. Eventually, as long-run macroeconomic equilibrium is reestablished, aggregate output will rise to be equal to potential output.

## Check Your Understanding
## 16-5

1. a. An economy is overstimulated when an inflationary gap is present. This will arise if an expansionary monetary or fiscal policy is implemented when the economy is currently in long-run macroeconomic equilibrium. This shifts the aggregate demand curve to the right, in the short run rais-

ing the aggregate price level and aggregate output and creating an inflationary gap. Eventually nominal wages will rise and shift the short-run aggregate supply curve to the left, and aggregate output will fall back to potential output. This is the scenario envisaged by the speaker.

   b. No, this is not a valid argument. When the economy is not currently in long-run macroeconomic equilibrium, an expansionary monetary or fiscal policy does not lead to the outcome described above. Suppose a negative demand shock has shifted the aggregate demand curve to the left, resulting in a recessionary gap. An expansionary monetary or fiscal policy can shift the aggregate demand curve back to its original position in long-run macroeconomic equilibrium. In this way, the short-run fall in aggregate output and deflation caused by the original negative demand shock can be avoided. So, if used in response to demand shocks, fiscal or monetary policy is a an effective policy tool.

# Chapter Seventeen

## Check Your Understanding
## 17-1

1. a. This is a contractionary fiscal policy because it is a reduction in government purchases of goods and services.

   b. This is an expansionary fiscal policy because it is an increase in government transfers that will increase disposable income.

   c. This is a contractionary fiscal policy because it is an increase in taxes that will reduce disposable income.

2. Federal disaster relief that is quickly disbursed is more effective than legislated aid because there is very little time lag between the time of the disaster and the time it is received by victims. Hence, it will stabilize the economy after a disaster. In contrast, legislated aid is likely to entail a time lag in its disbursement, leading to potential destabilization of the economy.

## Check Your Understanding
## 17-2

1. A $500 million increase in government purchases of goods and services directly increases aggregate spending by $500 million, which then starts the multiplier in motion. It will increase real GDP by $500 million × $1/(1 - MPC)$. A $500 million increase in government transfers increases aggregate spending only to the extent that it leads to an increase in consumer spending. Consumer spending rises by $MPC for every $1 increase in disposable income, where *MPC* is less than 1. Thus, a $500 million increase in government transfers shifts the aggregate demand curve only *MPC* times as much as a $500 million increase in government purchases of goods and services. It will increase real GDP by $500 million × $MPC/(1 - MPC)$.

2. This is the same issue as in problem 1, but in reverse. If government purchases of goods and services fall by $500 million, the initial fall in aggregate spending is $500 million. If there is a $500 million reduction in government transfers, the initial fall in aggregate spending is $MPC ×$ $500 million, which is less than $500 million.

## Check Your Understanding 17-3

**1.** When your work–study earnings are low, your parents help softens the impact on your disposable income: your disposable income (and so your consumer spending) does not fall by as much as it otherwise would. But when your earnings are high, the requirement that you contribute to your tuition bill dampens the increase in your disposable income: your disposable income (and so your consumer spending) does not rise by as much as it otherwise would. As a result, the arrangement reduces the size of the fluctuations of your disposable income: it acts like the automatic stabilizing effect of the government's budget.

**2.** In recessions, real GDP falls. This implies that consumers' incomes, consumer spending, and producers' profits also fall. So in recessions, states' tax revenue (which depends in large part on consumers' incomes, consumer spending, and producers' profits) falls. In order to balance the state budget, states have to cut spending or raise taxes. But that implies deepening the recession. Without a balanced-budget requirement, states could use expansionary fiscal policy during a recession to lessen the fall in real GDP. The same is true during an expansion but with contractionary fiscal policy instead of expansionary fiscal policy. As real GDP rises, government revenue also rises. To balance the budget, states have to increase spending or cut taxes, further boosting real GDP and leading to an even greater expansion. Without a balanced-budget requirement, states could use contractionary fiscal policy during expansions to dampen the rise in real GDP.

## Check Your Understanding 17-4

**1. a.** An increase in real GDP implies that tax revenue will increase. If government spending remains constant and the government runs a budget surplus, the size of the public debt will be less than it would otherwise have been.
  **b.** If retirees live longer, the average age of the population increases. As a result, the implicit liabilities of the government increase because spending on programs for older Americans, such as Social Security and Medicare, will rise.
  **c.** A decrease in tax revenue without offsetting reductions in government spending will cause the budget balance to decrease. If the government runs a budget deficit, the public debt will increase.
  **d.** If the government runs a budget deficit, public debt will increase as a result of government borrowing to pay interest on its current public debt.

## Chapter Eighteen

## Check Your Understanding 18-1

**1.** The defining characteristic of money is its liquidity: how easily it can be used to purchase goods and services. Although a gift certificate can easily be used to purchase a very defined set of goods or services (the goods or services available at the store issuing the gift certificate), it cannot be used to purchase any other goods and services. A gift certificate is therefore not money, since it cannot easily be used to purchase all goods or services.

**2.** Again, the important characteristic of money is its liquidity: how easily it can be used to purchase goods and services. M1, the narrowest definition of the money supply, contains only currency in circulation, traveler's checks, and checkable bank deposits. CDs aren't checkable—and they can't be made checkable without incurring a cost because there's a penalty for early withdrawal. This makes them less liquid than the assets counted in M1.

## Check Your Understanding 18-2

**1.** Even though you know that the rumor about the bank is not true, you are concerned about other depositors pulling their money out of the bank. And you know that if enough other depositors pull their money out, the bank will fail. In that case, it is rational for you to pull your money out before the bank fails. All depositors will think like this, so even if they all know that the rumor is false, they may still rationally pull their money out, leading to a bank run. Deposit insurance leads depositors to worry less about the possibility of a bank run. Even if a bank fails, the FDIC will pay each depositor up to $100,000 per account. This will make you much less likely to pull your money out in response to a rumor. Since other depositors will think the same, there will be no bank run.

**2.** The aspects of modern bank regulation that would frustrate this scheme are *capital requirements* and *reserve requirements*. Capital requirements mean that a bank has to have a certain amount of capital—the difference between its assets (loans plus reserves) and its liabilities (deposits). So the con man could not open a bank without putting any of his own wealth in because the bank needs a certain amount of capital—that is, it needs to hold more assets (loans plus reserves) than deposits. So the con man would be at risk of losing his own wealth if his loans turn out badly.

## Check Your Understanding 18-3

**1.** If the Fed wants to lower interest rates, it should buy Treasury bills. When the Fed buys Treasury bills, banks receive additional reserves, which they can use to make loans, creating money. The money supply increases.

**2.** If the Fed decides it wants to lower the money supply, it should sell Treasury bills. When the Fed sells Treasury bills, interest rates rise.

## Check Your Understanding 18-4

**1. a.** The interest rate falls.
  **b.** Investment spending rises, due to the fall in the interest rate.
  **c.** Consumer spending rises, due to the multiplier process.
  **d.** Aggregate output rises because of the rightward shift in the aggregate demand curve.
  **e.** The aggregate price level rises because the economy moves up the short-run aggregate supply curve.

# Glossary

**absolute advantage:** the advantage conferred by the ability to produce a good more efficiently—at lower cost of *resources*—than other producers.

**absolute value:** the value of a number without regard to a plus or minus sign.

**accounting profit:** revenue minus *explicit costs* and depreciation.

**aggregate demand curve:** a graphical representation of the relationship between the aggregate price level and the quantity of aggregate output demanded by households, businesses, the government, and the rest of the world. The aggregate demand curve has a negative slope due to the *wealth effect of a change in the aggregate price level* and the *interest rate effect of a change in the aggregate price level*.

**aggregate output:** the economy's total production of final goods and services for a given time period, usually a year. Real GDP is the numerical measure of aggregate output typically used by economists.

**aggregate price level:** the overall price level for final goods and services in the economy.

**aggregate spending:** the sum of consumer spending, investment spending, government purchases, and exports minus imports. It is the total spending on domestically produced final goods and services in the economy.

**aggregate supply curve:** a graphical representation of the relationship between the aggregate price level and the quantity of aggregate output supplied.

**antitrust policy:** legislative and regulatory efforts of the government to prevent industries from becoming or behaving like *monopolies*.

**AS–AD model:** the basic model used to understand fluctuations in aggregate output and the aggregate price level. It uses the *aggregate supply curve* and the *aggregate demand curve* together to analyze the behavior of the economy in response to shocks or government policy.

**asset:** a claim that provides income in the future.

**autarky:** occurs when a country cannot trade with other countries.

**automatic stabilizers:** government spending and taxation rules that cause fiscal policy to be expansionary when the economy contracts and contractionary when the economy expands. Taxes that depend on disposable income are the most important example of automatic stabilizers.

**autonomous change in aggregate spending:** a change in the desired level of spending by firms, households, or government at a constant level of GDP.

**average cost:** an alternative term for *average total cost*; the *total cost* divided by the total quantity of output.

**average fixed cost:** the *fixed cost* per unit of output.

**average total cost:** *total cost* divided by the total quantity of output.

**average variable cost:** the *variable cost* per unit of output.

**bank:** a *financial intermediary* that provides *liquid* assets in the form of *bank deposits* to lenders and uses those funds to finance the illiquid investments or investment spending needs of borrowers.

**bank deposit:** a claim on a *bank* that obliges the bank to give the depositor his or her cash when demanded.

**bank reserves:** currency held by banks in their vaults plus their deposits at the Federal Reserve.

**bank run:** a phenomenon in which many of a bank's depositors try to withdraw their funds due to fears of a bank failure.

**bar graph:** a graph that uses bars of varying height or length to show the comparative sizes of different observations of a variable.

**barrier to entry:** something that prevents other firms from entering an industry. Crucial in protecting the profits of a *monopolist*. There are four types of barriers to entry: control over scarce resources or inputs, *economies of scale*, technological superiority, and government-created barriers such as *licenses*.

**barter:** the direct exchange of goods or services without the use of money.

**black market:** a market in which goods or services are bought and sold illegally, either because it is illegal to sell them at all or because the prices charged are legally prohibited by a *price ceiling*.

**bond:** a legal document issued by a corporation or government promising the repayment of a loan, usually with interest.

**brand name:** a name owned by a particular firm that distinguishes its products from those of other firms.

**break-even price:** the market price at which a firm earns zero profits.

**budget balance:** the difference between net tax revenue and government spending. A positive budget balance is referred to as a *budget surplus*; a negative budget balance is referred to as a *budget deficit*.

**budget deficit:** the difference between net tax revenue and government spending when government spending exceeds tax revenue; dissaving by the government in the form of a budget deficit is a negative contribution to national savings.

**budget surplus:** the difference between net tax revenue and government spending when tax revenue exceeds government spending; saving by the government in the form of a budget surplus is a positive contribution to national savings.

**business cycle:** the short-run alternation between economic downturns, known as *recessions*, and economic upturns, known as *expansions*.

**capital:** the combined value of assets; includes equipment, buildings, tools, inventory, and financial assets.

**cartel:** an agreement among several producers setting production quotas for each, thereby leading to oligopoly profits.

**causal relationship:** the relationship between two variables in which the value taken by one variable directly influences or determines the value taken by the other variable.

**central bank:** an institution that oversees and regulates the banking system and conducts monetary policy.

**checkable bank deposits:** bank accounts on which people can write checks.

**circular-flow diagram:** a model that represents the transactions in an *economy* by two kinds of flows around a circle: a flow of physical things such as goods or labor and the flow of money to pay for these physical things.

**Coase theorem:** the proposition that even in the presence of *externalities* an *economy* can always reach an *efficient* solution as long as transaction costs are sufficiently low.

**collusion:** cooperation among producers to limit production and raise prices so as to raise one another's profits.

**commodity:** output of different producers regarded by consumers as all the same good; also referred to as a *standardized product.*

**commodity money:** a good that is used as a medium of exchange but also has intrinsic worth because it has other uses. Gold or silver coins are commodity money.

**commodity-backed money:** a medium of exchange that has no intrinsic value but is guaranteed by a promise that it can be converted into valuable goods. Paper money that can be exchanged freely for gold or silver coins is commodity-backed money.

**comparative advantage:** the advantage conferred on an individual or nation if it can produce a good at a lower *opportunity cost* than another producer.

**compensating differentials:** wage differences across jobs that reflect the fact that some jobs are less pleasant or more dangerous than others.

**competitive market economy:** an *economy* in which all markets, for goods and for factors, are perfectly competitive. All market participants are price-takers.

**competitive market:** a market in which all market participants are price-takers.

**complements:** pairs of goods for which a fall in the price of one good results in greater demand for the other.

**constant returns to scale:** a range of production in which *long-run average total cost* is constant as output increases.

**consumer price index (CPI):** a measure of the cost of a market basket intended to represent the consumption of a typical urban American family of four. It is the most commonly used measure of prices in the United States.

**consumer spending:** household spending on goods and services produced by domestic and foreign firms.

**consumer surplus:** a term often used to refer both to *individual consumer surplus* and to *total consumer surplus.*

**contractionary fiscal policy:** *fiscal policy* that reduces aggregate demand by increasing taxes, decreasing transfers, or decreasing government purchases.

**contractionary monetary policy:** *monetary policy* that, through the raising of the interest rate, reduces aggregate demand and therefore output.

**cost** (of potential seller): the lowest price at which a seller is willing to sell a good.

**cost-benefit analysis:** an estimate of the costs and benefits of providing a good. When governments use cost-benefit analysis, they estimate the social costs and social benefits of providing a public good.

**cross-price elasticity of demand:** the ratio of the percent change in the *quantity demanded* of one good to the percent change in the price of another good; a measure of the effect of the change in the price of one good on the quantity demanded of the other.

**crowding out:** the negative effect of budget deficits on private investment, which occurs because government borrowing drives up interest rates.

**currency in circulation:** cash, in either paper or coin form, held by the public.

**curve:** a line on a graph, which may be curved or straight, that depicts a relationship between two variables.

**cyclically adjusted budget balance:** an estimate of what the *budget balance* would be if real GDP were exactly equal to potential output.

**deadweight loss** (from a tax): the extra cost in the form of inefficiency that results because a tax discourages mutually beneficial transactions; also referred to as *excess burden.*

**debt–GDP ratio:** government debt as a percentage of GDP, frequently used as a measure of a government's ability to pay its debts.

**deflation:** a falling *aggregate price level.*

**demand curve:** a graphical representation of the *demand schedule,* showing how much of a good or service consumers would buy at a given price.

**demand price:** the price of a given quantity at which consumers will demand that quantity.

**demand schedule:** a list or table showing the relationship between price and the quantity of a good consumers would buy.

**demand shock:** any event that shifts the *aggregate demand curve.* A positive demand shock is associated with higher demand for aggregate output at any price level and shifts the curve to the right. A negative demand shock is associated with lower demand for aggregate output at any price level and shifts the curve to the left.

**dependent variable:** the determined variable in a causal relationship.

**deposit insurance:** a guarantee that a bank's depositors will be paid even if the bank can't come up with the funds, up to a maximum amount per account.

**depression:** a very deep and prolonged downturn.

**diminishing returns to an input:** the effect observed when an increase in the quantity of an *input,* while holding the levels of all other inputs fixed, leads to a decline in the *marginal product* of that input.

**discount rate:** the rate of interest the Federal Reserve charges on loans to banks that fall short of *reserve requirements.*

**discouraged workers:** nonworking people who are capable of working but have given up looking for a job because they believe no jobs are available.

**discretionary fiscal policy:** *fiscal policy* that is the result of deliberate actions by policy makers rather than rules.

**diseconomies of scale:** a range of production in which *long-run average total cost* increases as output increases.

**disposable income:** income plus *government transfers* minus taxes; the total amount of household income available to use for consumption and saving.

**domestic demand curve:** a *demand curve* for domestic consumers.

**domestic supply curve:** a *supply curve* for domestic producers.

**dominant strategy:** in *game theory,* an action that is a player's best action regardless of the action taken by the other player.

**duopolist:** one of the two firms in a *duopoly.*

**duopoly:** an *oligopoly* consisting of only two firms.

**economic aggregate:** an economic measure that summarizes data across different markets for goods, services, workers, and assets.

**economic growth:** a *long-run* trend toward the production of more goods and services.

**economic profit:** revenue minus the *opportunity cost* of *resources;* often less than *accounting profit.*

**economic signal:** any piece of information that helps people make better economic decisions.

**economics:** the study of *economies,* at the level of individuals and of society as a whole.

**economies of scale:** a range of production in which *long-run average total cost* declines as output increases.

**economy:** a system for coordinating a society's productive activities.

**efficiency-wage model:** a model in which some employers pay an above-equilibrium wage as an *incentive* to better performance.

**efficient allocation of resources:** the case in which there is no way for an economy to reallocate *factors of production* among producers to produce more of some goods without producing less of others.

**efficient in consumption:** description of an *economy* in which there is no way to redistribute goods that makes some consumers better off without making others worse off.

**efficient in output levels:** description of an *economy* in which no different mix of output would make some consumers better off without making others worse off.

**efficient in production:** description of an *economy* in which there is no way to produce more of some goods without producing less of others.

**efficient:** description of a market or *economy* that uses its resources in such a way as to exploit all opportunities to make some individuals better off without making others worse off.

**elastic demand:** when the *price elasticity of demand* is greater than 1. A percentage increase in price will cause a correspondingly greater percentage decrease in quantity demanded, and vice versa.

**employment:** the number of people currently employed for pay in the economy.

**equilibrium:** an economic balance in which no individual would be better off doing something different; an equality of supply and demand.

**equilibrium price:** the price at which the market is in *equilibrium,* that is, the quantity of a good demanded equals the quantity supplied; also referred to as the *market-clearing price.*

**equilibrium quantity:** the quantity of a good bought and sold at the *equilibrium* (or *market-clearing) price.*

**equilibrium value of the marginal product:** the additional value produced by the last unit of a factor employed in the *factor market* as a whole.

**equity:** fairness; because individuals can disagree about what is "fair," equity is not as well defined a concept as efficiency.

**excess burden** (from a tax): the extra cost in the form of inefficiency that results because a tax discourages mutually beneficial transactions; also referred to as *deadweight loss.*

**excess reserves:** a *bank's reserves* over and above the reserves required by law or regulation.

**excise tax:** a tax on the consumption of a given good or service.

**excludable:** referring to a good, describes the case in which the supplier can prevent those who do not pay from consuming the good.

**expansion:** a period when output and employment are rising; also referred to as a recovery.

**expansionary fiscal policy:** *fiscal policy* that increases aggregate demand by decreasing taxes, increasing transfers, or increasing government purchases.

**expansionary monetary policy:** monetary policy that, through the lowering of the interest rate, increases aggregate demand and therefore output.

**explicit cost:** a cost that requires an outlay of money.

**exporting industries:** industries that produce goods or services for sale abroad.

**exports:** goods and services sold to residents of other countries.

**external benefit:** an uncompensated benefit that an individual or firm confers on others; also known as *positive externalities.*

**external cost:** an uncompensated cost that an individual or firm imposes on others; also known as *negative externalities.*

**externalities:** *external benefits* and *external costs.*

**factor distribution of income:** the division of total income among labor, land, and *capital.*

**factor intensity:** the difference in the ratio of factors used to produce a good in various industries. For example, oil refining is capital-intensive compared to clothing manufacture because oil refiners use a higher ratio of capital to labor than do clothing producers.

**factor markets:** markets in which *firms buy factors of production.*

**factors of production:** the *resources* needed to produce goods or services. Labor and capital are examples of factors.

**federal funds market:** the market in which banks that fall short of *reserve requirements* can borrow funds from banks with *excess reserves.*

**federal funds rate:** the interest rate at which banks short of reserves can borrow from other banks with *excess reserves.* It is determined in the *federal funds market.*

**fiat money:** a medium of exchange that derives its value entirely from its official status as a means of payment. The U.S. dollar is fiat money.

**final goods and services:** goods and services sold to the final, or end, user.

**financial intermediary:** an institution, such as a *mutual fund, pension fund, life insurance company,* or *bank,* that trans-

forms the funds it gathers from many individuals into financial assets.

**financial markets:** the banking, stock, and bond markets, which channel private savings and foreign lending into investment spending, government borrowing, and foreign borrowing.

**firm:** an organization that produces goods or services for sale.

**fiscal policy:** a type of stabilization policy that involves the use of changes in taxation, government transfers, or government purchases of goods and services.

**fiscal year:** the time period used for much of government accounting, running from October 1 to September 30. Fiscal years are named by the calendar year in which they end.

**fixed cost:** a cost that does not depend on the quantity of output produced; the cost of a *fixed input.*

**fixed input:** an *input* whose quantity is fixed and cannot be varied (for example, land).

**forecast:** a simple prediction of the future under current assumptions.

**free entry and exit:** describes an industry that potential producers can easily enter or current producers can leave.

**free trade:** *trade* that is unregulated by government *tariffs* or other artificial barriers; the levels of *exports* and *imports* occur naturally, as a result of supply and demand.

**free-rider problem:** when individuals have no *incentive* to pay for their own consumption of a good, they will take a "free ride" on anyone who does pay; a problem with goods that are *nonexcludable.*

**gains from trade:** the benefit that each party receives from a trade, which, because of *specialization,* is greater than if each attempted to be self-sufficient.

**game theory:** the study of behavior in situations of *interdependence.* Used to explain the behavior of an *oligopoly.*

**GDP deflator:** for a given year, 100 times the ratio of *nominal GDP* to *real GDP* in that year.

**GDP per capita:** GDP divided by the size of the population; equivalent to the average GDP per person.

**general equilibrium:** an economic balance in which the *quantity supplied* is equal to the *quantity demanded* in all markets in an economy.

**government borrowing:** funds borrowed by the government in financial markets.

**government purchases of goods and services:** government expenditures on goods and services.

**government transfers:** payments by the government to individuals for which no good or service is provided in return.

**gross domestic product (GDP):** the total value of all final goods and services produced in the economy during a given year.

**Heckscher–Olin model:** a *model* of international trade that shows how a country's *comparative advantage* can be determined by its supply of *factors of production.*

**horizontal axis:** the horizontal number line of a graph along which values of the *x*-variable are measured; also referred to as the *x-axis.*

**horizontal intercept:** the point at which a curve intersects the horizontal axis, showing the value of the *x*-variable when the value of the *y*-variable is zero.

**household:** a group of people that share a dwelling and their income (a household may also consist of one person).

**human capital:** the improvement in labor created by the education and knowledge embodied in the workforce.

**imperfect competition:** a market structure in which no firm is a *monopolist,* but producers nonetheless have *market power* they can use to affect market prices.

**implicit cost:** a cost that does not require the outlay of money; it is measured by the value, in dollar terms, of forgone benefits.

**implicit cost of capital:** the *opportunity cost* of the capital used; that is, the income that could have been realized had the capital been used in the next best alternative way.

**implicit liabilities:** spending promises made by governments that are like a debt although they are not included in the usual debt statistics. In the United States, the largest implicit lia-

bilities arise from Social Security and Medicare, which promise transfer payments to current and future retirees (Social Security) and to the elderly (Medicare).

**import quota:** a legal limit on the quantity of a good that can be imported.

**import-competing industries:** industries that produce goods or services that are also imported.

**imports:** goods and services purchased from residents of other countries.

**incentive:** a reward offered to people who change their behavior.

**incidence** (of a tax)**:** a measure of who actually bears the burden of a tax.

**income effect:** the change in the quantity of a good consumed that results from the change in a consumer's purchasing power due to the change in the price of the good.

**income elasticity of demand:** the ratio of the percentage change in *quantity demanded* of a good or service to the percentage change in a consumer's income.

**income-elastic demand:** when the *income elasticity of demand* is greater than 1. Occurs when the demand for certain goods (such as luxury goods) rises faster than the increase in income.

**income-inelastic demand:** when the *income elasticity of demand* is positive but less than 1. Occurs when the demand for certain goods (such as food and clothing) rises but more slowly than the increase in income.

**increasing marginal cost:** *marginal cost* that becomes greater with each additional unit of the activity.

**independent variable:** the determining variable in a causal relationship.

**individual choice:** the decision by an individual of what to do, which necessarily involves a decision of what not to do.

**individual consumer surplus:** the net gain to an individual buyer from the purchase of a good; equal to the difference between the buyer's *willingness to pay* and the price paid.

**individual labor supply curve:** a graphical representation of the relationship between the wage rate and the number of hours supplied by an individual worker.

**individual producer surplus:** the net gain to an individual seller from selling a good; equal to the difference between the price received and the seller's *cost*.

**industrial policy:** a policy that supports industries believed to yield *positive externalities*.

**industry supply curve:** a graphical representation that shows the relationship between the price of a good and the total output of the industry for that good.

**inefficient allocation of sales among sellers:** a form of inefficiency in which sellers who are willing to sell a good at a lower price are not always those who actually manage to sell it; often the result of a *price floor*.

**inefficient allocation to consumers:** a form of inefficiency in which consumers who are willing to pay a high price for a good do not get it, and those willing to pay only a low price do; often a result of a *price ceiling*.

**inefficient:** describes a market or *economy* in which there are missed opportunities for making some individuals better off without making others worse off.

**inefficiently high quality:** a form of inefficiency in which sellers offer high-quality goods at a high price even though buyers would prefer a lower quality at a lower price; often the result of a *price floor*.

**inefficiently low quality:** a form of inefficiency in which sellers offer low-quality goods at a low price even though buyers would prefer a higher quality at a higher price; often a result of a *price ceiling*.

**inelastic demand:** when the *price elasticity of demand* is less than 1. A percentage increase in price will cause a correspondingly lesser percentage decrease in quantity demanded, and vice versa.

**inferior good:** a good for which a rise in income decreases the demand for the good.

**inflation:** a rising *aggregate price level*.

**inflation rate:** the percent change per year in a price index—typically the *consumer price index*. The inflation rate is positive when the aggregate price level is rising (*inflation*) and negative

when the aggregate price level is falling (*deflation*).

**inflationary gap:** occurs when aggregate output is above *potential output*.

**input:** a good used to produce another good.

**interaction** (of choices): the mutual influence of the choices of various parties (the results are often quite different from what was intended).

**interdependence:** the relationship among firms when their decisions significantly affect one another's profits; characteristic of oligopolies.

**interest rate:** the price, calculated as a percentage of the amount borrowed, charged by lenders to borrowers for the use of their savings for one year.

**interest rate effect of a change in the aggregate price level:** the effect on consumer and investment spending caused by a change in the purchasing power of consumers' money holdings when the aggregate price level changes. A rise (fall) in the aggregate price level decreases (increases) the purchasing power of consumers' money holdings. In response, consumers try to increase (decrease) their money holdings, which drives up (down) interest rates, thereby decreasing (increasing) consumption and investment.

**intermediate goods and services:** goods and services, bought from one firm by another firm, that are inputs for production of final goods and services.

**internalize the externality:** take into account *external costs* and *external benefits*.

**international trade agreements:** treaties by which countries agree to lower *trade protections* against one another.

**investment spending:** spending on productive physical capital, such as machinery and construction of structures, and on changes to inventories.

**invisible hand:** a phrase used by Adam Smith to describe the way in which an individual's pursuit of self-interest can lead, without the individual intending it, to good results for society as a whole.

**labor force:** the number of people who are either actively employed for

pay or unemployed and actively looking for work; the sum of *employment* and *unemployment*.

**law of demand:** a higher price charged for a good, other things equal, leads to a smaller quantity of the good demanded.

**leisure:** the time available for purposes other than earning money to buy marketed goods.

**liability:** a requirement to pay income in the future.

**license:** the right, conferred by the government or an owner, to supply some good or perform some activity, often in exchange for a fee.

**linear relationship:** the relationship between two variables in which the *slope* is constant and therefore is depicted on a graph by a *curve* that is a straight line.

**liquid:** refers to an asset that can be quickly converted into cash without much loss of value.

**long run:** the time period in which all *inputs* can be varied.

**long-run aggregate supply curve:** a graphical representation of the relationship between the aggregate price level and the quantity of aggregate output supplied if all prices, including nominal wages, were fully flexible. The long-run aggregate supply curve is vertical because the aggregate price level has no effect on aggregate output in the long run; in the long run, aggregate output is determined by the economy's *potential output*.

**long-run average total cost curve:** a graphical representation showing the relationship between output and *average total cost* when *fixed cost* has been chosen to minimize *total cost* for each level of output.

**long-run industry supply curve:** a graphical representation that shows how *quantity supplied* responds to price once producers have had time to enter or exit the industry.

**long-run macroeconomic equilibrium:** a situation in which *short-run macroeconomic equilibrium* is also on the *long-run aggregate supply curve*; so *short-run equilibrium aggregate output* is equal to *potential output*.

**long-run market equilibrium:** an economic balance in which, given

sufficient time for producers to enter or exit an industry, the *quantity supplied* equals the *quantity demanded.*

**lump-sum tax:** a tax that is the same for everyone, regardless of any actions individuals take.

**macroeconomics:** the branch of *economics* concerned with the overall ups and downs in the *economy.*

**marginal analysis:** the study of *marginal decisions,* those resulting from small changes in an activity.

**marginal benefit:** the additional benefit derived by performing one more unit of an activity.

**marginal cost:** the additional cost incurred by performing one more unit of an activity.

**marginal cost curve:** a graphical representation showing how the cost of undertaking one more unit of an activity depends on the quantity of that activity that has already been done.

**marginal decision:** a decision made at the "margin" of an activity to do a little more or a little less.

**marginal product:** the additional quantity of output produced by using one more unit of a given *input.*

**marginal productivity theory of income distribution:** the proposition that every *factor of production* is paid its *equilibrium value of the marginal product.*

**marginal propensity to consume, or MPC:** the increase in consumer spending when income rises by $1. Because consumers normally spend part but not all of an additional dollar of disposable income, *MPC* is between zero and one.

**marginal propensity to save, or MPS:** the increase in household savings when disposable income rises by $1.

**marginal revenue:** the change in *total revenue* generated by an additional unit of output.

**marginal revenue curve:** a graphical representation showing how *marginal revenue* varies as output varies.

**marginal social benefit of a good or activity:** the *marginal benefit* that accrues to consumers plus the marginal *external benefit.*

**marginal social cost of a good or activity:** the *marginal cost* of produc-

tion plus the marginal *external cost* to society of that production.

**market basket:** a hypothetical set of consumer purchases of goods and services, used to measure changes in the overall price level.

**market economy:** an *economy* in which decisions about production and consumption are made by individual producers and consumers.

**market failure:** occurs when a market fails to be efficient.

**market power:** the ability of a producer to raise prices.

**market share:** the fraction of the total industry output represented by a given producer's output.

**market-clearing price:** the price at which the market is in *equilibrium,* that is, the quantity of a good demanded equals the quantity supplied; also referred to as the *equilibrium price.*

**markets for goods and services:** markets in which households buy goods and services from *firms.*

**maximum:** the highest point on a *nonlinear curve,* where the *slope* changes from positive to negative.

**medium of exchange:** an asset that individuals acquire for the purpose of trading rather than for their own consumption. One of *money*'s main roles in the economy is to serve as the primary medium of exchange.

**microeconomics:** the branch of *economics* that studies how individuals make decisions and how those decisions interact.

**midpoint method:** a technique for calculating the percent change in which changes in a variable are compared with the average, or midpoint, of the starting and final values.

**minimum:** the lowest point on a *nonlinear curve,* where the *slope* changes from negative to positive.

**minimum wage:** a legal floor on the wage rate. The wage rate is the market price of labor.

**minimum-cost output:** the quantity of output at which the *average total cost* is lowest—the bottom of the U-shaped average total cost curve.

**model:** a simplified representation of a real-life situation that uses data and

assumptions to make predictions about that situation and understand it better.

**monetary aggregate:** an overall measure of the money supply. The most common monetary aggregates in the United States are M1, which includes *currency in circulation,* traveler's checks, and *checkable bank deposits,* and M2, which includes M1 as well as *near-moneys.*

**monetary policy:** a type of *stabilization policy* that involves changes in the quantity of money in circulation or in the interest rate, or both.

**money**: any asset that can easily be used to purchase goods and services.

**money supply:** the total value of financial assets in the economy that are considered money. There are several different measures of the money supply, called *monetary aggregates.*

**monopolist:** a firm that is the only producer of a good that has no close substitutes.

**monopolistic competition:** a market structure in which there are many competing producers in an industry, each producer sells a differentiated product, and there is *free entry and exit* into and from the industry in the *long run.*

**monopoly:** an industry controlled by a *monopolist.*

**movement along the demand curve:** a change in the *quantity demanded* of a good that results from a change in the price of that good.

**movement along the supply curve:** a change in the *quantity supplied* of a good that results from a change in the price of that good.

**multiplier:** the ratio of the eventual change in GDP caused by an autonomous change in aggregate spending to the size of that autonomous change.

**Nash equilibrium:** in *game theory,* the *equilibrium* that results when all players choose their optimal action given the actions of other players, ignoring the effect of that action on the *payoffs* of other players; also known as *noncooperative equilibrium.*

**national income and product accounts:** an accounting of *consumer spending,* sales of producers, business *investment spending,* and other flows

of money between different sectors of the economy; also referred to as national accounts. Calculated by the Bureau of Economic Analysis.

**natural monopoly:** a *monopoly* that arises because *economies of scale* over the range of output of an industry provide a large cost advantage to having all output produced by a single firm.

**near-money:** a financial asset that can't be directly used as a medium of exchange but can be readily converted into cash or checkable bank deposits.

**negative externalities:** *external costs.*

**negative relationship:** a relationship between two variables in which an increase in the value of one variable is associated with a decrease in the value of the other variable. It is described by a *curve* that slopes downward from left to right.

**net exports:** the difference between the value of *exports* and the value of *imports.* A positive value for net exports indicates that a country is a net exporter of goods and services; a negative value indicates that a country is a net importer of goods and services.

**nominal:** refers to a measure or quantity that has not been adjusted for changes in prices over time.

**nominal GDP:** the value of all final goods and services produced in the economy during the year, calculated using the prices current in the year in which the output is produced.

**nominal wage:** the dollar amount of the wage paid.

**noncooperative equilibrium:** in *game theory,* the *equilibrium* that results when all players choose their optimal action given the actions of other players, ignoring the effect of that action on the *payoffs* of other players; also known as *Nash equilibrium.*

**nonexcludable:** referring to a good, describes the case in which the supplier cannot prevent those who do not pay from consuming the good.

**nonlinear curve:** a curve whose *slope* is not constant.

**nonlinear relationship:** the relationship between two variables in which the *slope* is not constant and therefore is depicted on a graph by a *curve* that is not a straight line.

**nonrival in consumption:** referring to a good, describes the case in which the same unit can be consumed by more than one person at the same time.

**normal good:** a good for which a rise in income increases the demand for that good—the "normal" case.

**normative economics:** the branch of economic analysis that makes prescriptive statements about how the *economy* should work.

**oligopolist:** a firm in an industry with only a small number of producers.

**oligopoly:** an industry with only a small number of producers.

**omitted variable:** an unobserved *variable* that, through its influence on other variables, creates the erroneous appearance of a direct *causal relationship* among those variables.

**open-market operation:** a purchase or sale of U.S. Treasury bills by the Federal Reserve, undertaken to change the *money supply* and interest rates.

**opportunity cost:** the real cost of an item, including what must be given up to obtain it.

**optimal output rule:** profit is maximized by producing the quantity of output at which the *marginal cost* of the last unit produced is equal to its *marginal revenue.*

**origin:** the point where the axes of a two-variable graph meet.

**other things equal assumption:** in the development of a model, the assumption that all relevant factors except the one under study remain unchanged.

**payoff:** in *game theory,* the reward received by a player (for example, the profit earned by an *oligopolist*).

**payoff matrix:** in *game theory,* a diagram that shows how the *payoffs* to each of the participants in a two-player game depend on the actions of both; a tool in analyzing *interdependence.*

**perfect price discrimination:** charging each consumer the maximum that consumer is willing to pay.

**perfectly competitive industry:** an industry in which all producers are price-takers.

**perfectly competitive market:** a market in which all participants are price-takers.

**perfectly elastic demand:** the case in which any price increase causes the *quantity demanded* to fall to zero; the *demand curve* is a horizontal line.

**perfectly elastic supply:** the case in which even small changes in price lead to large changes in the *quantity supplied,* so the *price elasticity of supply* is infinite; the *supply curve* is a horizontal line.

**perfectly inelastic demand:** the case in which the *quantity demanded* does not respond to price; the *demand curve* is a vertical line.

**perfectly inelastic supply:** the case in which the *price elasticity of supply* is zero, so changes in price have no effect on the *quantity supplied;* the *supply curve* is a vertical line.

**physical capital:** human-made physical resources, such as buildings and machines, that are used in production.

**pie chart:** a circular graph that shows how some total is divided among its components; the proportions are indicated by the sizes of the "wedges."

**Pigouvian subsidy:** a payment designed to encourage activities that yield *external benefits.*

**Pigouvian taxes:** taxes designed to reduce *external costs.*

**positive economics:** the branch of economic analysis that describes the way the *economy* actually works.

**positive externalities:** *external benefits.*

**positive relationship:** a relationship between two variables in which an increase in the value of one variable is associated with an increase in the value of the other variable. It is described by a *curve* that slopes upward from left to right.

**potential output:** the level of real GDP the economy would produce if all prices, including nominal wages, were fully flexible. Although an economy's actual output is rarely exactly at potential output, potential output defines the trend around which actual output fluctuates from year to year.

**price ceiling:** a government-set maximum price that sellers are allowed to charge for a good; a form of *price control.*

**price controls:** legal restrictions on how high or low a market price may go.

**price discrimination:** charging different prices to different consumers for the same good.

**price elasticity of demand:** the ratio of the percent change in the *quantity demanded* to the percent change in price at a given point on the *demand curve*.

**price elasticity of supply:** the ratio of the percent change in the *quantity supplied* to the percent change in price at a given point on the *supply curve*.

**price floor:** a government-set minimum price that buyers are required to pay for a good; a form of price control.

**price index:** a measure of the overall price level; it measures the cost of purchasing a given market basket in a given year, where that cost is normalized so that it is equal to 100 in the selected base year.

**price regulation:** a limitation by the government on the price a *monopolist* is allowed to charge.

**price stability:** a low but positive rate of inflation targeted by most central banks.

**price war:** a collapse of prices when *tacit collusion* breaks down.

**price-taking consumer:** a consumer whose actions have no effect on the market price of the good bought.

**price-taking firm's optimal output rule:** the profit of a price-taking firm is maximized by producing the quantity of output at which the *marginal cost* of the last unit produced is equal to the market price.

**price-taking producer:** a producer whose actions have no effect on the market price of the good sold.

**principle of marginal analysis:** the proposition that the optimal quantity of an activity is that at which *marginal benefit* is equal to *marginal cost*.

**prisoner's dilemma:** a game for two players in which the pursuit of self-interest rather than cooperation, if followed by both players, makes both worse off.

**private good:** a good that is both *excludable* and *rival in consumption*.

**private savings:** *disposable income* minus *consumer spending*; disposable income that is not spent on consumption.

**producer price index (PPI):** a measure of the cost of a typical basket of goods and services purchased by producers. Because these commodity prices respond quickly to changes in demand, the PPI is often regarded as a leading indicator of changes in the inflation rate.

**producer surplus:** a term often used to refer both to *individual producer surplus* and to *total producer surplus*.

**product differentiation:** the effort by firms to convince buyers that their products are different from those of other firms in the industry. If firms can so convince buyers, they can charge a higher price.

**production function:** the relationship between the quantity of *inputs* used and the quantity of output produced.

**production possibility frontier:** illustrates the trade-offs facing an economy that produces only two goods. It shows the maximum quantity of one good that can be produced for any given production of the other.

**proportional tax:** a tax that increases when real GDP increases and decreases when real GDP decreases.

**protection:** an alternative term for *trade protection;* policies that limit *imports.*

**public debt:** government debt held by individuals and institutions outside the government.

**public good:** a good that is both *nonexcludable* and *nonrival in consumption.*

**public ownership:** control of an industry by a public agency of the government to provide a good and protect the interests of the consumer; a response to *natural monopoly.*

**quantity control:** an upper limit, set by the government, on the quantity of some good that can be bought or sold; also referred to as a *quota.*

**quantity demanded:** the actual amount of a good or service consumers are willing to buy at some specific price.

**quantity supplied:** the actual amount of a good or service sellers are willing to sell at some specific price.

**quota:** an upper limit, set by the government, on the quantity of some good that can be bought or sold; also referred to as a *quantity control.*

**quota limit:** the total amount of a good under a *quota* or *quantity control* that can be legally transacted.

**quota rent:** the difference between the *demand price* and the *supply price* at the *quota limit;* this difference, the earnings that accrue to the license-holder, is equal to the market price of the *license* when the license is traded.

**real:** refers to a measure or quantity that has been adjusted for changes in prices over time.

**real GDP:** the value of all final goods and services produced in the economy during the year, calculated using the prices of a selected base year.

**recession:** a period when output and employment are falling.

**recessionary gap:** occurs when aggregate output is below *potential output.*

**rental rate:** the cost, implicit or explicit, of using a unit of land or capital for a given period of time.

**reserve ratio:** the fraction of deposits that a bank holds as reserves. In the United States, the minimum required reserve ratio is set by the Federal Reserve.

**reserve requirements:** rules set by the Federal Reserve that determine the minimum reserve ratio for a bank. For checkable bank deposits in the United States, the minimum reserve ratio is set at 10%.

**resource:** anything, such as land, labor, and capital, that can be used to produce something else; includes natural resources (from the physical environment) and human resources (labor, skill, intelligence).

**reverse causality:** the error committed when the true direction between *variables* is reversed, and the *independent variable* and the *dependent variable* are incorrectly identified.

**Ricardian model of international trade:** a model that analyzes international *trade* under the assumption that *production possibility frontiers* are straight lines.

**rival in consumption:** referring to a good, describes the case in which one unit cannot be consumed by more than one person at the same time.

**scarce:** in short supply; a *resource* is scarce when the quantity available is

insufficient to satisfy all productive uses.

**scatter diagram:** a graph that displays points that correspond to actual observations of the *x*- and *y*-variables; a curve is usually fitted to the scatter of points to indicate the trend in the data.

**self-correcting:** refers to the fact that in the long run, shocks to aggregate demand affect aggregate output in the short run, but not the long run.

**shift of the demand curve:** a change in the *quantity demanded* at any given price, represented graphically by the movement of the original *demand curve* to a new position.

**shift of the supply curve:** a change in the *quantity supplied* at any given price, represented graphically by the movement of the original *supply curve* to a new position.

**short run:** the time period in which at least one *input* is fixed.

**short-run aggregate supply curve:** a graphical representation of the relationship between the aggregate price level and the quantity of aggregate output supplied that exists in the short run, the time period when many production costs can be taken as fixed. The short-run aggregate supply curve has a positive slope because a rise in the aggregate price level leads to a rise in profits, and therefore output, when production costs are fixed

**short-run equilibrium aggregate output:** the quantity of aggregate output produced in *short-run macroeconomic equilibrium.*

**short-run equilibrium aggregate price level:** the aggregate price level in *short-run macroeconomic equilibrium.*

**short-run individual supply curve:** a graphical representation showing how an individual producer's optimal output quantity depends on the market price, taking *fixed cost* as given.

**short-run industry supply curve:** a graphical representation that shows how the quantity supplied by an industry depends on the market price, given a fixed number of producers.

**short-run macroeconomic equilibrium:** a situation in which the quantity of aggregate output supplied is equal to the quantity demanded.

**short-run market equilibrium:** an economic balance that results when the *quantity supplied* equals the *quantity demanded,* taking the number of producers as given.

**shortage:** the insufficiency of a good when the quantity supplied is less than the quantity demanded; shortages occur when the price is below the *equilibrium price.*

**shut-down price:** the price at which a firm ceases production in the short run because the market price has fallen below the minimum *average variable cost.*

**single-price monopolist:** a *monopolist* that charges all consumers the same price.

**slope:** the ratio of the "rise" (the change between two points on the *y*-axis) to the "run" (the difference between the same two points on the *x*-axis); a measure of the steepness of a curve.

**social insurance:** government programs—like Social Security, Medicare, unemployment insurance, and food stamps—intended to protect families against economic hardship.

**specialization:** occurs when each person concentrates on the task that he or she is good at performing; generally leads to improved quality or to increase in output.

**stabilization policy:** policy efforts undertaken to reduce the severity of recessions and to rein in excessively strong expansions. There are two main tools of stabilization policy: *monetary policy* and *fiscal policy.*

**stagflation:** the combination of rising inflation and falling aggregate output.

**standardized product:** output of different producers regarded by consumers as all the same good; also referred to as a *commodity.*

**stock:** a share in the ownership of a company held by a shareholder.

**store of value:** an asset that is a means of holding purchasing power over time. In a well-functioning economy, *money* is one of the assets that plays this role.

**strategic behavior:** actions taken by a firm that attempt to influence the behavior of other firms.

**substitutes:** pairs of goods for which a fall in the price of one results in less demand for the other.

**substitution effect:** the change in the quantity consumed when a consumer substitutes a good that has become relatively cheaper in place of one that has become relatively more expensive.

**sunk cost:** a cost that has already been incurred and is not recoverable.

**supply and demand model:** a model that describes how a *competitive market* works.

**supply curve:** a graphical representation of the *supply schedule,* showing how much of a good or service would be supplied at a given price.

**supply price:** the price of a given quantity at which producers will supply that quantity.

**supply schedule:** a list or table showing the relationship between price and the quantity of a good or service that would be supplied to consumers.

**supply shock:** any event that shifts the *short-run aggregate supply curve.* A negative supply shock raises production costs and reduces the quantity supplied at any aggregate price level, shifting the curve leftward. A positive supply shock decreases production costs and increases the quantity supplied at any aggregate price level, shifting the curve rightward.

**surplus:** the excess of a good that occurs when the quantity supplied is greater than the quantity demanded; surpluses occur when the price is above the *equilibrium price.*

**tacit collusion:** cooperation among producers, without a formal agreement, to limit production and raise prices so as to raise one anothers' profits.

**target federal funds rate:** the Federal Reserve's desired *federal funds rate.* The Federal Reserve adjusts the money supply through the purchase and sale of Treasury bills until the actual rate equals the desired rate.

**tariff:** a tax levied on *imports.*

**technology spillover:** an *external benefit* that is conferred when knowledge spreads among individuals and firms.

**time allocation:** the decision about how many hours to expend on different activities, which leads to a decision about how much labor to supply.

**time-series graph:** a two-variable graph in which the values on the *horizontal axis* are dates and those on the *vertical axis* are values of a variable that occurred on those dates.

**tit for tat:** in *game theory,* a strategy in which players begin cooperatively, then each repeats the other player's action in the previous round.

**total consumer surplus:** the sum of the *individual consumer surpluses* of all the buyers of a good.

**total cost:** the sum of the *fixed cost* and the *variable cost* of producing a given quantity of output.

**total cost curve:** a graphical representation of the *total cost,* showing how total cost depends on the quantity of output.

**total producer surplus:** the sum of the *individual producer surpluses* of all the sellers of a good.

**total product curve:** a graphical representation of the *production function,* showing how the quantity of output depends on the quantity of the *variable input* for a given amount of *fixed input.*

**total revenue:** the total value of sales of a good (the price of the good multiplied by the quantity sold).

**total surplus:** the total net gain to consumers and producers from trading in a market; the sum of the *consumer surplus* and the *producer surplus.*

**trade:** the exchange of goods or services for other goods or services.

**trade protection:** policies that limit *imports.*

**trade-off:** a comparison of costs and benefits; the amount of a good that must be sacrificed to obtain another good.

**transaction costs:** the expenses of negotiating and executing a deal.

**transfer payment:** money received by an individual from the government for which no good or service is returned to the government.

**truncated:** cut; in a truncated axis, some of the range of values are omitted, usually to save space.

**U-shaped average total cost curve:** a distinctive graphical representation of the relationship between output and *average total cost;* the average

total cost curve at first falls when output is low and then rises as output increases.

**underemployment:** the number of people who work during a *recession* but receive lower wages than they would during an *expansion* due to fewer number of hours worked, lower-paying jobs, or both.

**unemployment:** the number of people who are actively looking for work but aren't currently employed.

**unemployment rate:** the percentage of the total number of people in the *labor force* who are unemployed. It is calculated as: unemployment rate = *unemployment / (unemployment + employment).*

**unions:** organizations of workers that engage in collective bargaining to raise wages and improve working conditions for their members.

**unit of account:** a measure used to set prices and make economic calculations.

**unit-elastic demand:** the case in which the *price elasticity of demand* is a specific percentage increase in price leads to an equal percentage decrease in quantity demanded, and vice versa.

**utility** (of a consumer): a measure of the satisfaction derived from consumption of goods and services.

**utility possibility frontier:** on a graph plotting the total *utility* of two individuals or groups, the curve that shows how well off one individual or group could be for each given total utility level of the other.

**value added** (of a producer): the value of sales minus the value of input purchases.

**value of the marginal product curve:** a graphical representation showing how the *value of the marginal product* of a factor depends on the quantity of the factor employed.

**value of the marginal product:** the value of the additional output generated by employing one more unit of a given factor, such as labor.

**variable:** a quantity that can take on more than one value.

**variable cost:** a cost that depends on the quantity of output produced; the cost of a *variable input.*

**variable input:** an *input* whose quantity can be varied (for example, labor).

**vertical axis:** the vertical number line of a graph along which values of the *y*-variable are measured; also referred to as the *y-axis.*

**vertical intercept:** the point at which a curve intersects the vertical axis, showing the value of the *y*-variable when the value of the *x*-variable is zero.

**wasted resources:** a form of inefficiency; consumers waste resources when they must spend money and expend effort to deal with shortages caused by a *price ceiling.*

**wealth** (of a household): the value of accumulated savings.

**wealth effect of a change in the aggregate price level:** the effect on consumer spending caused by the change in the purchasing power of consumers' assets when the aggregate price level changes. A rise in the aggregate price level decreases the purchasing power of consumers' assets, so they decrease their consumption; a fall in the aggregate price level increases the purchasing power of consumers' assets, so they increase their consumption.

**wedge:** the difference between the *demand price* of the quantity transacted and the *supply price* of the quantity transacted for a good when the supply of the good is legally restricted. Often created by a quota or a tax.

**willingness to pay:** the maximum price a consumer is prepared to pay for a good.

**World Trade Organization:** an international organization of member countries that oversees *international trade agreements* and rules on *trade* disputes.

**world price:** the price at which a good can be bought or sold abroad.

**x-axis:** the horizontal number line of a graph along which values of the *x*-variable are measured; also referred to as the *horizontal axis.*

**y-axis:** the vertical number line of a graph along which values of the *y*-variable are measured; also referred to as the *vertical axis.*

**zero-profit equilibrium:** an economic balance in which each firm makes zero profit at its profit-maximizing output level.

# Index

## A

**Absolute advantage, 28**
**Absolute value, 46**
**Accounting profit, 193**
AD. *See* Aggregate demand
Advanced Micro Devices
    (AMD), 276
Advertising
    indirect signals, 323
    role, 323–324
AFC. *See* Average fixed cost
African-American workers,
    unemployment rates,
    382
Aggregate demand (AD),
    404–409
    change, 412
    shifts, 415–416
**Aggregate demand (AD)**
    **curve, 404**, 404–410
**Aggregate output, 359**, 360
    **Aggregate price level, 362,**
      400, 406
**Aggregate spending, 371**
Aggregate supply (AS), 395–404
    Relationship with aggregate
      demand, 394
**Aggregate supply (AS) curve,**
    **395**
Airlines
    competition, 313
    decisions, 291–292
    prices, differences, 293
Ajinomoto, 301, 303, 306
Amazon.com, 455
AMD. *See* Advanced Micro
    Devices
American Economic
    Association, 5
**Antitrust policy, 310**
Apartheid, 229–230
Archer Daniels Midland
    (ADM), 301, 303, 306,
    308, 311–312
Argentina, 444, 448–449
AS. *See* Aggregate supply
***AS-AD* model, 413**
    development, 389
    predictions, 422
    usage, 413–420
**Asset, 459**
ATC. *See* Average total cost
**Autarky, 336**
**Automatic stabilizers, 436**
**Autonomous change in**
    **aggregate spending,**
    **412**
**Average cost, 171**, 173. *See*
    *also* Average total cost
    concept, 168–175
    curve, 173

**Average fixed cost (AFC), 172**
**Average total cost (ATC),**
    **171,** 178
**Average variable cost (AVC),**
    **172,** 173

## B

Bangladesh, 33, 333
**Bank, 458.** *See also* Central
    bank
    capital requirements, 461
    deposits, 454, 456–457
    function, 458–459
    monetary role, 458–462
    regulation, 460–461
    reserve requirements, 461
**Bank deposit, 458**
**Bank reserves, 458**
**Bank run, 460**
**Bar graph, 48,** 50
**Barrier to entry, 275**
**Barter, 30**
Belgium, ECB member, 462
Bentham, Jeremy, 240
Bertrand, Marianne, 229
**Black market, 88**
Board of Governors, 463
**Bond, 369**
**Brand name, 324**
**Break-even price, 197,** 199
British Telecom, 288
Brooks, Jr., Frederick P., 167
**Budget balance, 438,** 441
    usage, 438–442. *See also*
      Fiscal policy
**Budget deficit, 438**
**Budget surplus, 438**
**Business cycle, 357**
    budget balance, relationship,
      439

## C

Cable service, monopolistic
    characteristics, 290
Canada
    government transfers, 429
    production possibility fron-
      tier, 29
**Capital, 193.** *See also* Human
    capital; Implicit cost of
    capital; Physical capital
**Cartel, 303**
**Causal relationship, 42–43**
CBO. *See* Congressional Budget
    Office
**Central bank, 462**
**Checkable bank deposits,**
    **454,** 456–457
China, inefficiency, 246
**Circular-flow diagram, 30,**
    244–245, 368–371

Climate, differences, 332
Clothing production, 333
Coase, Ronald, 254
**Coase theorem, 254**
COLAs. *See* Cost-of-living
    allowances
Cold War, 306
Collective bargaining, 227
College degree, value, 213
**Collusion, 303**
**Commodity, 188**
**Commodity-backed money,**
    **455,** 456
**Commodity money, 455**
**Comparative advantage, 27,**
    28. *See also* International
      trade; Trade
    international trade, relation-
      ship, 331–335
    sources, 332–334
**Compensating differentials,**
    **226**
Competition, problems,
    189–190
**Competitive market, 57,**
    78–79, 84
**Competitive market econo-**
    **my, 239**
**Complements, 61**
Congressional Budget Office
    (CBO), 401
**Constant returns to scale,**
    **180**
**Consumer price index (CPI),**
    362, **386**
    1913–2004, 387
    bias, 387
    increase, 364
    indexing, 388–389
    makeup in 2004, 386
Consumers
    inefficient allocation, 87. *See*
      *also* Inefficient alloca-
      tion to consumers
    price-takers, 187
**Consumer spending, 368,**
    375
    budget, impact, 430
    increase, 410
**Consumer surplus,** 135, **138,**
    336. *See also* Individual
      consumer surplus
    application, 151–155
    decrease, 148
    demand curve, relationship,
      136–142
    imports, impact, 337
    price change, impact,
      139–141
Consumption
    efficiency, 239–241
    nonexcludable, 259

nonrival, 259
**Contractionary fiscal policy,**
    **432,** 436
    impact, 431
    multiplier, 448
**Contractionary monetary**
    **policy,** 466–468, **467.**
    *See also* Inflationary gap
**Cost, 143**
    explicit, 165
    external, 251
    fixed, 165
    implicit, 165, 222
    marginal, 168–175
    producer surplus and,
      142–145
    total, 166
    transaction, 254
    variable, 165, 166
**Cost-benefit analysis, 263,**
    264
Cost-of-living allowances
    (COLAs), 389
Council of Economic Advisers,
    37
CPI. *See* Consumer price index
Credit cards, 454
**Critically adjusted budget**
    **balance, 440**
**Cross-price elasticity of**
    **demand, 120,** 126
**Crowding out, 444**
Currency
    In circulation, 461
    location, 457
**Currency in circulation, 454**
**Curve, 43**
    graphing, 43
    slope, 44–48
Cyclically adjusted budget bal-
    ance, 440

## D

**Deadweight loss, 151,**
    153–155
    calculation, 155–156,
      343–344
    example, 155
    triangle, 155
Death tax, 250
De Beers monopoly, 273,
    276–279, 281–282
Debit cards, 454
Debt
    impact, 442–443
    problems. *See* Government
**Debt-GDP ratio, 444**
Deficit. *See* Budget deficit
**Deflation, 362**
    impact, 363
    since 1929, 364

Demand. *See* Aggregate demand, Cross-price elasticity of demand; Income elasticity of demand; Price elasticity of demand
decrease, 60–61, 75
elasticities, 120–122
increase, 59, 75
law of, 59, 111
shift, 61
**Demand curve, 58**
equilibrium with supply, 73
movement/shift, contrast, 60
shifts, 59–61
impact, 72–73
understanding, 60–62
simultaneous shift, 74–75
usage, 57–62
**Demand price, 97**
**Demand schedule, 58**
**Demand shock, 415,** 416
policy, impact, 422
**Dependent variable, 43**
**Deposit insurance, 460**
**Depression, 357**
Derived demand, 214
Diamond monopolies, control, 276–277
Diminishing returns
effect, 172–173
idea/concept, 165, 167–168
**Diminishing returns to an input, 163**
**Discount rate, 464**
**Discouraged workers, 359**
**Discretionary fiscal policy,** 427, **437**
Discrimination, 228–229
Disease prevention, public good, 259
**Diseconomies of scale,** 179, **180**
**Disposable income, 370**
Diversity, value, 322
Dividend-capital gain tax reduction, 437
Dollar, history, 457–458
**Domestic demand curve, 336**
**Domestic supply curve, 336**
**Dominant strategy, 305**
**Duopolist, 303**
**Duopoly, 303**

**E**

eBay, efficiency, 151
ECB. *See* European Central Bank
Eckaus, Richard, 367
**Economic aggregates, 355**
Economic analysis, usage, 228–229
**Economic growth, 4**

impact, 25
**Economic profit, 193,** 201
**Economics, 2**
**Economic signal, 240**
*Economics of Welfare, The* (Pigou), 253
**Economies of scale,** 179, **180,** 275–276
impact, 275
Economists
agreement, timing, 36
disagreements, reasons, 35
**Economy, 2**
factors of production, 214–216
production, capability, 12
Education and earnings, 226
Efficiency, 89, 238–246
and equity, 247–250
concept, 23
wages, 227, 228
**Efficiency-wage model, 228**
**Efficient, 14**
**Efficient allocation of resources, 241**
**Efficient in consumption, 240**
**Efficient in output levels, 242**
**Efficient in production, 241**
**Elastic demand, 114, 115, 118, 154**
Elasticity, 114, 153–155
calculation, midpoint method (usage), 111–113
defining/measuring, 110–113
estimation, 113
total revenue, relationship, 116–118
usage, 127–129
**Employment,** 357, **359**
Environmental policy, 253–254
**Equilibrium, 13**
**Equilibrium price, 68,** 77–78, 205
changes, 72–74
**Equilibrium quantity, 68,** 77–78
changes, 72–74
**Equilibrium value of marginal product, 223**
**Equity, 15,** 238
Estate tax reduction, 437
European Central Bank (ECB), 462, 465–466
European Union
price floors, 125
product sale, loss, 93
**Excess burden, 151**
**Excess reserves, 461**
**Excise tax, 101**
concept, 151

consumer payment, 127
description, 127
impact, 152, 343
producer payment, 128
revenue, generation, 103
who pays, 102–103
**Excludable, 259**
**Expansion, 357**
**Expansionary fiscal policy,** **430,** 430–432, 437–438
**Expansionary monetary policy,** 466–468, **467**
Expectations, changes, 61–62, 66–67, 407
**Explicit cost, 165**
**Exporting industries, 339**
**Exports, 331,** 370. *See also* Net exports
domestic market, relationship, 338
impact, 338–341
**External benefit, 251,** 255
**External cost, 251**
**Externalities, 251.** *See also* Negative externalities; Positive externalities
impact, 250–257
optimal Pigouvian tax, relationship, 256
private solutions, 254–255
Exxon, 287, 310

**F**

Factor demand
curve, shifts, 220–221
**Factor distribution of income, 214**
Factor incomes, 214–215
**Factor intensity, 333**
**Factor markets, 30,** 213
**Factor of production, 30,** 213–216
Factor prices, importance, 214
Fairness, 247–248, 250
FC. *See* Fixed cost
FDIC. *See* Federal Deposit Insurance Corporation
Federal Deposit Insurance Corporation (FDIC), 460
**Federal funds market, 464**
**Federal funds rate, 464,** 469. *See also* Target federal funds rate
Federal Insurance Contributions Act (FICA), 104, 129
Federal Open Market Committee (FOMC), 453, 463–464
Federal Reserve Bank of New York, 463, 466
Federal Reserve System (Fed), 453, 462–466
function, 464
money policy, 408

output gap, relationship, 469–470
policy, business cycle (relationship), 469
role, 458
**Fiat money, 456**
FICA. *See* Federal Insurance Contributions Act
**Final goods and services, 359, 371**
production value, GDP measurement, 372–373
**Financial intermediary, 458**
**Financial markets, 370**
**Firm, 30**
factor income earned, GDP measurement, 374–375
price-takers, 192, 195
profit-maximizing output quantity, 317
short-run supply curve, 199
**Fiscal policy,** 355, **361,** 408, 427
lags, 432
long-run implications, 442–49
measure, budget balance (usage), 438–439
multiplier, 433–438
**Fixed cost (FC), 165**
change, 200–201
level, selection, 177
**Fixed input, 161,** 164
FOMC. *See* Federal Open Market Committee
Ford, Henry, 325
**Forecast, 34**
France, 442, 462
**Free entry and exit, 189**
**Free-rider problem, 259**
**Free trade, 341–342**

**G**

**Gains from trade, 12,** 28
**Game theory, 303**
Gasoline
pretax market, 104
price floor, 95
Gates, Bill, 454
GDP. *See* Gross domestic product
**GDP deflator,** 362, **388,** 400
**GDP per capita, 379**
**General equilibrium, 239**
General Motors, 325
*General Theory of Employment, Interest, and Money, The* (Keynes), 357, 377
Generic drugs, 189
Germany, 442, 462
Goods

consumers, 256
demand, 118, 245
production, 334
supply, 245
trade, 332
Government
budget, 429–430
debt, 443–444
economists, impact, 36–37
funds, flow, 428
intervention, 16
revenue, 342
tax revenue, 440
transfers, multiplier effects,
433–435
**Government borrowing, 370**
**Government purchases of
goods and services,
370,** 374
**Government transfers, 370,**
428–429
Graphs, 89
curves, usage, 43–44
function, explanation,
41–44
interpretation, 52
scale, impact, 52
Great Depression, 355
aggregate output, 356
deflation, 388, 394
impact, 356–357
negative demand shock,
impact, 415
nominal wages, decrease,
397
prices/output, 403–404
unemployment rate, 356
Greenspan, Alan, 463
**Gross domestic product
(GDP), 371.** *See also*
Nominal GDP; Real
GDP
calculation, 371–376
components, 375
numbers, usage, 376
per capita, 49–50
usage, 371–377
**Gross domestic product
(GDP) deflator,** 362,
**388,** 400
**Gross domestic product
(GDP) per capita,
379**

## H

**Heckscher-Ohlin model,** 332,
**333**
**Horizontal axis (x-axis), 42**
Horizontal curve, slope, 45–46
**Horizontal intercept, 44**
**Household, 30**
Houthakker, Henrik S., 113
**Human capital, 214,** 226

differences, unfairness, 227
*Human Development Report*
(United Nations),
379–380

## I

Illiquid assets, 458
IMF. *See* International
Monetary Fund
**Imperfect competition, 302**
**Implicit cost, 165,** 222
**Implicit cost of capital, 194**
**Implicit liabilities, 446,**
446–447
**Import-competing indus-
tries, 339**
**Import quota, 344**
**Imports, 331, 370**
domestic market, 336
impact, 335–338
spending (IM), 374
total surplus, 340
**Incentive, 9**
**Incidence of a tax, 103**
Income
changes, 61, 62
distribution, 213, 214
expenditure, BLS survey,
122–123
**Income effect, 231**
**Income-elastic, 122**
**Income elasticity of demand,**
120, **121,** 126
**Increasing marginal cost,
170**
**Independent variable, 43**
**Individual choice, 6,** 6–10
interaction, principles, 12
**Individual consumer surplus,
138**
**Individual labor supply
curve, 232**
**Individual producer surplus,
143**
**Industrial policy, 257**
Industrial Revolution, 215
Industry
free entry/exit, 314–315
set-up costs, 180
**Industry supply curve,** 186,
**202,** 202–208
Inefficiency, 238
monopoly, impact, 286
price ceiling, impact, 86–88
price floor, impact, 93–94
problem, 99
**Inefficient, 86**
**Inefficient allocation of sales
among sellers, 93**
**Inefficient allocation to con-
sumers, 87**
**Inefficiently high quality,**
93

**Inefficiently low quality, 87**
Inefficient policies, problems,
249–250
**Inelastic, 114**
Inelastic demand, 111, 115,
118, 154
Inelastic supply, 154
Infant industry argument, 345
**Inferior good, 61**
**Inflation, 362,** 362–364
acceleration, 388
**Inflationary gap, 419,** 440,
466
contractionary fiscal policy,
431
contractionary monetary pol-
icy, 467
**Inflation rate, 363, 386**
Inheritance tax, 250
**Input, 66,** 161–164
Intel, computer chip maker,
77
**Interaction, 11,** 11–16
**Interdependence, 303,** 304
**Interest rate, 406**
effect, 405, 406
Fed cut, 421
**Interest rate effect of a
change in the aggre-
gate price level, 406**
**Intermediate goods and serv-
ices, 371**
**Internalize the externality,
254**
International Monetary Fund
(IMF), 37
International trade, 330
agreements, WTO, 346–347
comparative advantage,
28–29
gains, 337
impact, 340
**International trade agree-
ments, 347**
**Investment spending,** 355,
**371**
government impact, 430
Investment tax credits, 430
**Invisible hand, 3**
Ireland, 375, 462
Italy, 95, 462
ECB member, 462
labor regulations, 95

## J

Japan
bank of, 462
budget deficit, 446
deficit/debt, 446
expansionary fiscal policy,
432–433
high real GDP per capita,
380

infrastructure, expenses,
432–433
Job creation, 345
Jobless recoveries, 384
Johnson, Lyndon, 432

## K

Keynes, Sir John Maynard, 357,
377, 420
Kuznets, Simon, 377

## L

Labor
marginal product of, 162
market equilibrium, 223
**Labor force, 359**
**Law of demand, 59,** 111
**Leisure, 231,** 231–232
Leontief, Wassily, 334
**Liability, 459**
**License, 96**
Linear curve, slope, 44–45
**Linear relationship, 43**
**Liquid asset, 454**
**Long run, 161**
**Long-run aggregate supply
(LRAS) curve, 400,**
401, 402–403
**Long-run average total cost
curve (LRATC), 178**
**Long-run industry supply
curve,** 200, **206,**
206–207
**Long-run macroeconomic
equilibrium, 416,**
416–419
**Long-run market equilibri-
um, 205**

## M

M1, 456–457
M2, 456–457
Macroeconomic policy,
420–422
**Macroeconomics, 4,** 353,
354–355
concept, 354–355
policy, 355
usage, 352
Malthus, Thomas, 165, 167
**Marginal analysis, 9**
**Marginal benefit, 218,** 262
**Marginal cost (MC), 169,**
168–175, 192
increase, 170
usage, 169–171
**Marginal cost curve (MC),
170,** 173
**Marginal decisions, 9**
**Marginal product, 162,** 164
Marginal productivity, 216–224
wage inequality, 226–227

**Marginal productivity theory of income distribution,** 213, **223,** 224
reality/truth, 225–230
Marginal product of labor (MPL), 163
**Marginal propensity to consume (MPC), 409,** 410, 435
**Marginal propensity to save (MPS), 410,** 411
**Marginal revenue (MR), 191,** 277
**Marginal revenue (MR) curve, 192**
**Marginal social benefit of a good or activity, 256**
**Marginal social cost of a good or activity, 252**
**Market basket, 385**
cost, 388
calculation, 385
price indexes, relationship, 385–386
**Market-clearing price, 68**
**Market economy, 2**
**Market failure, 3, 251**
intervention, 258–264
review, 257
**Market power,** 227–228, **274,** 280, 314
Market price, 70–71
Markets
efficiency, 15, 16, 148–150
equilibrium, 13–14, 69
structure, 271–273
**Markets for goods and services, 30**
**Market share, 188**
Marshall, Alfred, 1, 4
Martin, William McChesney, 463
**Maximum point, 48**
MC. *See* Marginal cost
McDonald's
location, 122
opening, 364
value, 324
Medicare/Medicaid
GDP percentages, 446
spending, 447
**Medium of exchange, 455**
**Microeconomics, 3**
macroeconomics, contrast, 353–357
Microsoft, monopolistic characteristics, 276
**Midpoint method, 112**
**Minimum-cost output, 174**
**Minimum point, 48**
**Minimum wage, 91**
as price floor, 94–95
Mississippi River, course change (impact), 264

Mobil, 310
**Model, 21,** 34–36
**Monetary aggregate, 456**
**Monetary policy,** 355, **361,** 408, 453
aggregate demand, relationship, 466–470
**Money,** 453, **454**
creation by banks, 461
flow, 369
models, 21
roles, 454, 455
types, 455–456
**Money supply, 454**
measurement, 456–457
**Monopolist, 273**
**Monopolistic competition,** 272–273, 302, **314**
**Monopoly,** 271, **273**
control, 290
perfect competition, contrast, 282
prevention, 287
price, discovery, 282
public policy, relationship, 285–291
welfare effects, 286–287, 289
**Movement along the demand curve, 60**
**Movement along the supply curve, 65**
MPC. *See* Marginal propensity to consume
MPL. *See* Marginal product of labor
MPS. *See* Marginal propensity to save
MR. *See* Marginal revenue
MSB. *See* Marginal social benefit
Mullainathan, Sendhil, 229
**Multiplier,** 409–413, **412,** 433
Mutually beneficial trades, prevention, 16
*Mythical Man-Month, The* (Brooks, Jr.), 167

**N**

NAFTA. *See* North American Free Trade Agreement
**Nash equilibrium, 306**
**National accounts, 368**
creation, 377
usage, 368–377
National Bureau of Economic Research (NBER), 358
National defense, public good, 259
**National income and product accounts, 368**
National security, 345

**Natural monopoly, 275**
interaction, 287–290
regulation, 288–289
NBER. *See* National Bureau of Economic Research
**Near-moneys, 456**
**Negative externalities, 251,** 252
**Negative relationship, 44**
**Net exports, 376**
**Nominal, 362**
**Nominal GDP, 378**
real GDP, contrast, 379–381
**Nominal wage, 396,** 399, 403
**Noncooperative equilibrium, 306**
**Nonexcludable, 259**
**Nonlinear curve, 46,** 47
**Nonlinear relationship, 43**
**Nonrival in consumption, 259**
**Normal good, 62**
**Normative economics, 34**
North American Free Trade Agreement (NAFTA), 347

**O**

Oil
cartel, ups/downs, 309
exporting countries, embargo (1973), 84–85
prices, increase, 116
production, 113
revenues, increase, 130
shortages (1970s), 90–91
world demand, 110
**Oligopolist, 302**
**Oligopoly,** 301–310, **302**
focus, 301
legal framework, 310–311
practice, 310–312
understanding, 303
**Omitted variable, 52**
OPEC. *See* Organization of Petroleum Exporting Countries
**Open-market operation,** 463–465, **464**
**Opportunity cost, 7,** 7–8, 23–24, 87
**Optimal output rule, 191**
Organization of Petroleum Exporting Countries (OPEC)
nonmember producers, 123, 308–309, 419
**Other things equal assumption, 21,** 59, 164
Output, 161–164
costs, unit, 171

levels, efficiency, 239, 242–246
profit-maximizing level, 201, 277, 283–284

**P**

Paradox of Thrift, 354
Pauper labor, fallacy, 332
**Payoff, 303**
**Payoff matrix, 303**
Perfect competition, 187–190, 272
comparison, 284
conditions, 187–188
supply curve, relationship, 186
**Perfectly competitive industry, 187**
**Perfectly competitive market, 187**
**Perfectly elastic, 114**
**Perfectly elastic supply, 124**
**Perfectly inelastic, 114**
**Perfectly inelastic supply, 124**
**Perfect price discrimination, 293,** 293–295
Perfect substitutes, 321
Personal income tax bracket, 437
**Physical capital, 214,** 226, 355
stock, changes, 407
**Pie chart, 48, 50**
Pigou, A.C., 253
**Pigouvian subsidy, 256**
**Pigouvian taxes, 253**
Pollution, elimination, 251
Population, changes, 233
Portugal
ECB member, 462
economic crisis, 367–368
**Positive economics, 34**
**Positive externalities, 251**
**Positive relationship, 44**
**Potential output, 401**
PPI. *See* Producer price index
Premium, earning, 228
**Price ceiling, 84,** 84–89
display, 89
effect, 86
existence, reasons, 88–89
modeling, 85–86
**Price controls, 84**
**Price discrimination, 291,** 291–296
elasticity, relationship, 292–293
logic, 291–292
prices, change, 294
**Price elasticity of demand,** 109, **111,** 126, 283
determination, factors, 116

equation, 111
estimation, amounts, 113
extreme cases, 114
impact, 119
interpretation, 113–118
levels, 114, 128
total revenue, relationship, 118
**Price elasticity of supply, 123,** 123–126
determination, factors, 124–125
extreme cases, 124
levels, 128
measurement, 123–124
**Price floor, 84,** 89, 91–93
effects, 92
**Price index, 385**
aggregate price level, relationship, 384–389
**Price regulation, 288**
Prices
changes, 385
data, interpretation, 389
decrease, 400
effect, 117, 279
equilibrium level, impact, 70, 71
government control, reasons, 84
**Price stability, 363,** 421
**Price-taking consumer, 187**
**Price-taking firm's optimal output rule, 192**
**Price-taking producer, 187**
**Price war, 312**
**Principle of marginal analysis, 191**
**Prisoners' dilemma, 304,** 304–308
**Private goods, 259**
**Private savings, 370**
**Producer price index (PPI), 387**
Producers
price-takers, 202, 277
profit, maximization, 217
**Producer surplus, 135, 144**
application, 151–155
decrease, 149, 152
gain, 144
imports, impact, 337
supply curve, relationship, 142–146
**Product differentiation, 272,** 302, 314, **320**
location differentiation, 321–322
quality differentiation, 322
style/type differentiation, 320–321
Production
economies of scale, 272
efficiency, 239, 241–242

profitability, 194–197
**Production function, 161,** 161–168
**Production possibility frontier, 22,** 241
trade-offs, 22–24
**Profit, 190**
amount, 319
equation, 196
maximization, 316
**Proportional tax, 436**
**Protection, 342**
**Public good, 258–264, 259**
providing, 259–260
**Public ownership, 288**

**Q**

**Quantity control, 96,** 96–100
cost, 99–100
**Quantity demanded, 58,** 112
**Quantity supplied, 63**
**Quota, 96**
taxes, comparison, 100–105
**Quota limit, 96**
**Quota, rent, 98**

**R**

**Real GDP,** 357, **378**
aggregate output, relationship, 378–381
calculation. *See* Simple economy
nominal GDP, contrast, 379–381
unemployment, relationship, 383
**Real measure, 362**
**Recession, 4, 357**
1973–1975, 395
1979–1982, 395
defining, 358
since 1948, 358
**Recessionary gap, 418,** 466
expansionary monetary policy and, 466
impact, 418, 430
Recoveries, 357
Regulation, 288–290. *See also* **Price regulation**
**Rental rate, 222**
Rent-controlled apartments, 88
**Reserve ratio, 459**
**Reserve requirements, 461**
**Resource, 6.** *See also* Inefficient allocation of resources; Wasted resources
scarcity, 6–7, 10
usage/efficiency, 14–15
**Reverse causality, 53**
Rhodes, Cecil, 273
Ricardo, David, 341–342

**Rival in consumption, 259**
Rockefeller, John D., 287, 310
Roosevelt, Franklin D., 458, 462

**S**

**Scarce, 6, 275**
**Scatter diagram,** 48, **50**
Scientific research, public good, 259
**Self-correcting, 419**
Sherman Antitrust Act of 1890, 310
**Shift of the demand curve, 60**
**Shift of the supply curve, 64**
**Shortage, 70,** 89
creation, 71
**Short run, 161**
**Short-run aggregate supply (SRAS) curve, 396**
example, 397
leftward shift, 398, 402
rightward shift, 398, 402
shifts, 398–399, 402–403, 414–415
usage, 395–397
**Short-run equilibrium aggregate output, 414,** 416
**Short-run equilibrium aggregate price level, 414**
**Short-run individual supply curve, 198, 199**
long-run industry supply curves, contrast, 207
**Short-run industry supply curve, 200, 203**
**Short-run macroeconomic equilibrium, 413**
usage, 413–414
**Short-run market equilibrium, 203,** 204–205
**Shut-down price, 199**
**Single-price monopolist, 291**
Sloan, Alfred P., 325
**Slope, 44**
calculation, 45
equation, 46–47
Smith, Adam, 3, 12, 357, 455
Smoot-Hawley tariff, 347
**Social insurance, 429**
taxes, 428
Social norms, changes, 233
Social Security, 446
finances, 447
South Africa, apartheid, 229–230
**Specialization, 12,** 28
Spreading effect, 172–173
SRAS. *See* Short-run aggregate supply
**Stabilization policy, 361**
**Stagflation, 414**
**Standardized product, 188**
Standard Oil, 287, 310
Starbucks, differentiation, 321

**Stock, 369**
**Store of value, 455**
**Strategic behavior, 306**
**Substitutes, 61**
**Substitution effect, 231**
**Sunk cost, 199**
Supply
decrease, 65, 75
increase, 75
**Supply and demand model, 57**
**Supply curve, 64,** 160
equilibrium, 74
existence. *See* Monopoly
movement/shift, contrast, 65
shifts, 64–66
impact, 73–74
understanding, 66–67
simultaneous shift, 74–75
usage, 63–67
**Supply price, 97**
**Supply schedule, 63**
supply curve, interaction, 63–64
**Supply shock, 414,** 415
demand shock, contrast, 419–420
response, 421–422
**Surplus, 70,** 89
change, 340
creation, 70
exports, impact, 339
impact, 442–443
imports, impact, 337

**T**

**T-account, 459**
**Tacit collusion, 308.** *See also* Prisoners' dilemma
achievement, difficulty, 312
price wars, relationship, 311–312
**Target federal funds rate, 466**
Tariffs
decrease, 347–348
impact, 342–344
international negotiation, 345
quota, 344
Taxes
changes, multiplier effects, 434–435
comparison. *See* Quota
deadweight loss, 154
efficiency costs, 151–155
impact, 428–429
incidence, 127
revenue
automatic increases, impact, 436
decrease, tendency, 441
role, 409
wedge, 153

Taylor, Lester D., 113
TC. *See* Total cost
Technology
    change, 66, 67, 221
    differences, 332–334
**Technology spillover, 255**
*Theory of Justice, A* (Rawls), 247
Thrift. *See* Paradox of Thrift
**Time allocation, 230**
**Time-series graph, 48, 49**
**Tit for tat, 306,** 307
**Total consumer surplus, 138**
**Total cost (TC), 166.** *See also*
    Average total cost
    increase, 170
**Total cost (TC) curve, 166.**
    *See also* Farms
Total factor income, 372
Total industry-wide marginal
    cost, 252
**Total producer (TP) surplus,
    144**
**Total product (TP) curve,
    161,** 164
    flattening, 170–171
**Total revenue, 116**
    calculation, 116
    elasticity and, 116–118
    price increase, impact, 117
**Total surplus, 147**
    calculation, 155
    decrease, 150
    example, 155
    maximization, market equi-
        librium (impact), 150
    monopoly, inclusion, 286
    perfect competition, inclu-
        sion, 286
    relationship. *See* Imports
    tariff, impact, 343
TP. *See* Total product
*Tract on Monetary Reform, A*
    (Keynes), 420
**Trade, 12,** 20. *See also*
    International trade
    comparative advantage, 25–29
    gains, 12–13, 25–29, 330. *See*
        *also* Gains from trade
    Heckscher-Ohlin model, 339

protection, 345–346
**Trade-off, 8,** 20
**Trade protection, 342**
    arguments, 345–346
    impact, 341–345
    political economy, 345–348
Traffic
    reduction, 62–63
    sides, selection, 13
**Transaction costs, 254**
**Truncated, 51**
Two-part tariffs, 295

## U

**Underemployment, 359**
**Unemployment, 359**
**Unemployment rate, 356, 359**
    2002, 51–52
    analysis, 382
    equation, 359
    measurement, 382
    1900-present, 361
    1948-present, 258
    understanding, 381–383
**Unions, 227**
United States
    Army Corps of Engineers,
        impact, 264
    central bank, 462–463
    comparative advantage,
        334–335
    currency in circulation, 461
    debt, 445
    economic growth, 32
    factor distribution of income,
        215–216
    federal budget deficit, 445
    federal debt-GDP ratio, 445
    gasoline prices, 111–112
    GDP, 376
        government bonds, 447
        government implicit liabil-
            ities, 447
        government spending, 429
        government transfers, 429
        imports/exports, 1960-
            2003, 331
        labor force, growth, 233

negative supply shocks, 414
production possibility fron-
    tier, 29
tax revenue source, 428
trade protection, 344–345
unemployment rate, 361
**Unit-elastic, 114**
Unit-elastic demand, 115, 118
**Unit of account, 455**
U.S. Postal Service, 288
**U-shaped average total cost
    curve, 171**
**Utility, 231**
**Utility possibility frontier,
    249**
    usage, 248–250

## V

**Value added, 373**
Value-added tax, 35–36
**Value of the marginal prod-
    uct, 218**
    factor demand, relationship,
        218–220
    usage, 216–218
**Value of the marginal prod-
    uct curve, 218,** 219
    examination, 220
    shift, 221
**Variable, 41**
**Variable cost (VC), 165**
    equation, 166
**Variable input, 161**
VC. *See* Variable cost
**Vertical axis (*y*-axis), 42**
Vertical curve, slope, 45–46
**Vertical intercept, 44**
Volume discounts, 295
Voting, public good, 263

## W

Wages
    disparities, usage, 225–226
    inequality. *See* Marginal pro-
        ductivity
    inflation adjustment, 232
    labor supply, relationship,
        231–232

nineteenth century levels, 341
rates, 232
Wal-Mart
    entry, 6
    store number, increase, 399
**Wasted resources, 87,** 93
**Wealth, 454**
    changes, 234, 407
    effect, 405
**Wealth effect of a change in
    the aggregate price
    level, 405,** 407
*Wealth of Nations* (Smith), 3,
    12, 357
**Wedge, 98**
Wholesaler price index, 387
**Willingness to pay, 136**
Women, work, 10–11
**World price, 336**
**World Trade Organization
    (WTO), 347**
World War II, 419
    debt, 445
    global trade negotiations, 347
    government purchases,
        increase, 415
    government spending, 408
    POW camps, 455
    prices, government-imposed
        ceilings, 84
    prison camps, exchange sys-
        tem, 21

## X

**X-axis, 42**
    confusion, 42
X-variable, 42
    value, 44

## Y

Yacht tax (1990), 156
**Y-axis, 42**
Y-variable, 42
    change, 44

## Z

**Zero-profit equilibrium, 317**

# Visit the Krugman/Wells/Olney website

## www.worthpublishers.com/krugmanwellsolney

On the website, key graphs from the textbook have been animated in a Flash format, allowing students to manipulate curves and plot data points when appropriate. Every interactive graph has accompanying questions that quiz students on key concepts from the textbook and provide feedback on student progress. Student responses and interactions are tracked and stored in an online database that can be accessed by the instructor. The following list indicates the graphs that are available:

## LIST OF ANIMATED FIGURES

### Chapter 2
2-1: The production possibility frontier, 23
2-2: Increasing opportunity cost, 24
2-4: Production possibilities for two castaways, 26
2-6: Comparative advantage and international trade, 29
2A-1: Plotting points on a two-variable graph, 42
2A-2: Drawing curves, 43
2A-3: Calculating the slope, 45
2A-4: Nonlinear curves, 46

### Chapter 3
3-2: An increase in demand, 59
3-6: A decrease in supply, 65
3-9: Market equilibrium, 69
3-10: Price above its equilibrium level creates a surplus, 70
3-11: Price below its equilibrium level creates a shortage, 71
3-12: Equilibrium and shifts of the demand curve, 73
3-13: Equilibrium and shifts of the supply curve, 74

### Chapter 4
4-1: The market for apartments in the absence of government controls, 85
4-3: The market for butter in the absence of government controls, 91
4-4: The effects of a price floor, 92
4-6: Effect of a quota on the market for taxi rides, 98

### Chapter 5
5-3: Unit-elastic demand, inelastic demand, and elastic demand, 115
5-4: Total revenue, 117
5-7: An excise tax paid mainly by producers, 128

### Chapter 6
6-3: Consumer surplus, 139
6-5: A fall in the price increases consumer surplus, 141
6-8: Producer surplus, 145
6-9: A rise in the price increases producer surplus, 146
6-10: Total surplus, 147
6-11: Reallocating consumption lowers consumer surplus, 148
6-12: Reallocating sales lowers producer surplus, 149
6-14: A tax reduces consumer and producer surplus, 152
6-15: The deadweight loss of a tax, 153

### Chapter 7
7-2: Marginal product of labor curve for George and Martha's farm, 163
7-6: Total cost and marginal cost curves for Ben's Boots, 170
7-7: Average total cost curve for Ben's Boots, 172
7-8: Marginal cost and average cost curves for Ben's Boots, 173
7-10: More realistic cost curves, 175

### Chapter 8
8-2: Costs and production in the short run, 195
8-3: Profitability and the market price, 196
8-5: The short-run market equilibrium, 203
8-8: Comparing the short-run and long-run industry supply curves, 207

### Chapter 9
9-2: The production function for George and Martha's farm, 217
9-3: The value of the marginal product curve, 219
9-4: Shifts in the value of the marginal product curve, 221
9-6: Equilibrium in the labor market, 223
9-9: The individual labor supply curve, 232

### Chapter 10
10-1: The production possibility frontier and efficiency in production, 241
10-3: How an economy achieves efficiency in output levels, 244
10-5: The utility possibility frontier, 248
10-7: Negative externalities and production, 252
10-8: Positive externalities and production, 255
10-9: A public good, 262

### Chapter 11
11-2: What a monopolist does, 274
11-3: Economies of scale create natural monopoly, 275
11-5: A monopolist's demand, total revenue, and marginal revenue curves, 280
11-7: The monopolist's profit, 283
11-8: Monopoly causes inefficiency, 286
11-10: Two types of airline customers, 292